The Encyclopedia of
Superheroes on Film
and Television

ALSO BY JOHN KENNETH MUIR
AND FROM McFARLAND

Eaten Alive at a Chainsaw Massacre:
The Films of Tobe Hooper (2002)

Horror Films of the 1970s (2002)

An Analytical Guide to Television's
One Step Beyond, *1959–1961* (2001)

Terror Television: American Series, 1970–1999 (2001)

The Films of John Carpenter (2000)

A History and Critical Analysis of Blake's 7,
the 1978–1981 British Television Space Adventure (2000)

A Critical History of Doctor Who *on Television* (1999)

An Analytical Guide to Television's Battlestar Galactica (1999)

Wes Craven: The Art of Horror (1998)

Exploring Space: 1999: *An Episode Guide and Complete History*
of the Mid–1970s Science Fiction Television Series (1997)

OTHER WORKS BY JOHN KENNETH MUIR

Space: 1999 — The Forsaken (Ponys, 2003)

An Askew View: The Films of Kevin Smith (Applause, 2002)

The Encyclopedia of Superheroes on Film and Television

JOHN KENNETH MUIR

McFarland & Company, Inc., Publishers

Jefferson, North Carolina, and London

Library of Congress Cataloguing-in-Publication Data

Muir, John Kenneth, 1969–
The encyclopedia of superheroes on film and television / John Kenneth Muir.
p.   cm.
Includes bibliographical references and index.

ISBN 0-7864-1723-4 (illustrated case binding : 50# alkaline paper)

1. Superhero films — United States — Encyclopedias.
2. Superhero television programs — United States — Encyclopedias.   I. Title.

PN1995.9.S76M85   2004   791.43'652 — dc22   2003025048

British Library cataloguing data are available

Cover art: ©2003 Digital Vision

Manufactured in the United States of America

McFarland & Company, Inc., Publishers
Box 611, Jefferson, North Carolina 28640
www.mcfarlandpub.com

To Kathryn,
the superhero of my life.
And to my late grandfather, Bob Muir,
who passed away while this book was in production.
Thank you, Grandfather, for the silver dollars,
and the love you showed Kathryn, Lulu and me.

ACKNOWLEDGMENTS

Warmest thanks to all the people and supporters whose ideas and comments helped to forge this book. My greatest gratitude goes to genre author William Latham and *Destinies: The Voice of Science Fiction* host Howard Margolin. Their assistance, knowledge and expertise of the field proved critical in the formation of this text.

As always, special gratitude goes to my wife Kathryn, who endured umpteen hours of the best and worst superhero productions of the last fifty years.

TABLE OF CONTENTS

PART III: CONCLUSION

PART IV: THE APPENDICES

"Thank God You're Here!"
An Introduction

People have always adored their super-heroes, those larger-than-life figures who rescue the weak, preserve the species, and fight evil in all its forms. Our ongoing delight with superheroes is evident even in the earliest recorded works. After all, what is the great Greek hero Hercules, son of Olympian Zeus and the mortal woman Alcmena, but a "super man," half human and half divine? His great strength and power, granted by his demigod heritage, no doubt makes Hercules one of the earliest known and oft-imitated representatives of the genre.

However, going out on something of a limb, one might say that the superhero really came into his (or her) own in the United States of America of the twentieth century, which gave birth to Superman, Captain America, Spider-Man, Batman, Buffy the Vampire Slayer, the X-Men, Daredevil, the Incredible Hulk and many more. Perhaps it is not difficult to understand how or why the superhero evolved in this manner. Scarcely over two hundred years old, the United States of America remains a young country in the scheme of world history, and because of that youth lacks a coherent and comforting "old world" mythology such as those of Ancient Greece or the Roman Empire.

A melting pot of immigrants from all the planet's nations, the United States represents a synthesis of peoples, religions and legends. Still, many common ideals, notably those of freedom and opportunity, are shared among new arrivals to American shores, and those common ideals must be championed in a new and relevant mythology. What could be more appropriate than the mythology of the justice-seeking superhero? Thus Batman and the other contemporary representatives of the genre replace the mostly irrelevant, old or classical myths, like England's Robin Hood, France's Three Musketeers or Greece's pantheon of heroes (such as Hercules, Theseus, and Perseus).

Notably, Jerry Siegel and Joe Shuster's long-lived creation, Superman, "the man of tomorrow," is actually a child of yesterday, representing the late nineteenth and early twentieth century immigrant experience. Kal-El is a child of foreign origin, from the planet Krypton, adopted by American parents (much as America adopts all immigrants) and given a solid, American sounding name of rock-hard strength: Clark Kent. He matures in the safety and security of the corn-fed American heartland of Kansas, is raised to respect traditional family values, and then moves to the big city, Metropolis, where he lives out the American dream. He pursues a sacred American right, freedom

The ultimate superhero: Christopher Reeve is the Man of Steel in Richard Donner's master-piece, *Superman: The Movie* (1978).

of speech, through his job as an investigative reporter. And, as the heroic Superman, Clark pursues the nation's enduring values of truth, justice, democracy and the American way. How? By locking up criminals, righting wrongs, and protecting the innocent. As Kevin Smith has aptly written about the Man of Steel:

> Superman is the Ultimate Immigrant.... He works hard, pays his bills and still finds time to stop Brainiac from enslaving Earth.... Wrapped in the flag, he's come to stand for the American dream....[1]

Another popular superhero, Batman, is a succinct updating of the popular Zorro character. But, like Superman, the dark knight is effectively an orphan, and it is the American culture that becomes his *ad hoc* parents. Just as Superman carries his alien heritage (super powers) and uses it to the advantage of America in general and Metropolis specifically, Batman uses his heritage — money and social standing — to fight

crime. A child of deceased upper class parents (part of an American aristocracy?), Batman utilizes money and social position (as millionaire philanthropist Bruce Wayne) to protect the citizenry from harm.

As Hercules was always connected to his proud city of Thebes, so is Batman the product of dark, grimy Gotham; Superman inhabits the clean brightness of Metropolis. Superheroes, like the heroes of Greek mythology, have their own particular stomping grounds.

But Batman represents something else too: a streak of anti-authoritarianism in the American people. Americans champion privacy, personal liberty and other freedoms of the individual, and often suspect local and federal bureaucracies of corruption and malfeasance. Batman is a vigilante, a man who has suffered implicitly because of governmental and societal failures (criminals killed his folks; the villains should have been in jail). Nursing this wound, he has elected to take matters into his own hands, using his own resources.

Marvel's X-Men, a team of heroic if angst-ridden mutants, are also uniquely American, representing an underclass disdained by mainstream America. Storm, Cyclops and Professor Xavier are not a traditional minority group in terms of skin color, but these characters are "mutants," and, let's face it, not everybody wants mutants dating their daughters, riding the public bus, or visiting for dinner. Once more, the superhero experience feels uniquely American, in this case a reflection of the 1960s Civil Rights movement. The X-Men may be disenfranchised and disdained, but like all good Americans, they nonetheless believe in their country and act in its best interest, even when some people are too bigoted to accept them. The X-Men represent not just immigrants making good (like Superman), but American generations backing ideas of social justice in a society that began in the quagmire of racism, slavery and sexism.

They represent any underclass striving to overcome ingrained bigotry and discrimination.

Many other superheroes also speak to universal human truths in uniquely American settings. Joss Whedon's Buffy the Vampire Slayer — the Chosen One — is not only a powerful superhero who combats demons, she is a teenage girl who must survive adolescence and, worst of all, the terrors of a high school education. "Coming of age" may be a universal rite of passage, but Buffy-speak, that delightful and witty Valley-girl manner of twisting a phrase, is all–American, a reminder that in free Western society heroism can spring from even the most unlikely source. One need not be rich like Bruce Wayne or invulnerable like Clark Kent, or even counter-culture like the X-Men. Sometimes a child can be our savior.

Peter Parker, Stan Lee's Spider-Man, is another solid American symbol, that of the blue collar "every man." He is a meat-and-potatoes, lower-middle-class kid who financially supports his old aunt, maintains a bad, low-paying job as a newspaper photographer, and yet still finds time to fight psychotic bad guys like Doctor Octopus or Green Goblin, both of whom boast superior resources (read: money). What could be more American and more twentieth century than a character who carves out his "hero time" amidst a hundred competing daily problems?

The list of superheroes reflecting America's new mythology could go on and on, right down to the most obscure. Glen Larson's holographic Automan, a character seen on TV for only a few months in 1983, represents an acceptance of the 1980s home computer revolution and a belief that technology could be beneficial, our friend. Marvel's Incredible Hulk, as a TV and comic book character, symbolizes an acknowledgment of our inner demons, national fears of atomic testing, and so forth.

No matter who the hero, the fact remains that it is in America, home of the brave and land of the free, that superheroes have found their greatest voice, especially since the 1950s with the advent of that technological marvel, the television. As a medium of communication, television reaches far more people than does even the most popular comic book. For a myth to thrive, develop, evolve and last in today's culture, it must be carried via a mass-media format. In the early days of mankind, stories were perpetuated through oral recitations and retellings; later ages brought the theater and books. Film and television are simply the most modern ways of spreading stories, bringing America's myths into our local neighborhood theaters and into our very living rooms.

With Americans having so much leisure time and so many choices in entertainment, the superhero myth has thrived. For example, DC Comics' Clark Kent character has been seen no less than four times in live action TV series: *The Adventures of Superman* (1952–1958), *Superboy* (1988–1992), *Lois and Clark: The New Adventures of Superman* (1993–1997) and *Smallville* (2001–). The character has also appeared in four movies, with more to come if director Bret Ratner's successor has his way, and innumerable cartoons to boot. Americans, it seems, can't get enough of this guy — or of Batman, or Blade, or Buffy.

Why is it that superheroes like Superman remain so enduring, so popular in the American culture of today? George Slosser, curator of the Science Fiction and Fantasy Collection at the University of California, Riverside, offers one idea:

> They're the embodiment of the American myth of the lone, rugged individual who comes into society and cleans it up. We all want to do it, but we don't know how to do it. We live our everyday lives that don't allow for this kind of simplistic vision. So we cheer for it.[2]

One might argue effectively, like Slosser, that the cowboy, a western hero of times past, is

Old Chums: Batman (Adam West) and Robin (Bruce Ward) race from the batmobile to challenge a new foe in the campy 1960s TV series, *Batman*.

actually still with us. He's merely been re-tooled. The Lone Ranger has morphed into Batman. The loner, the cowboy, has transformed into the modern American superhero. They are both individuals with superior senses of justice, unique garb, and mostly lame sidekicks. And they are both separated from society even as they defend it.

But make no mistake: despite the colorful costumes, outrageous villains and high-tech gadgetry, this newfangled American cowboy is no mere kid stuff, either thematically or for the multi-million dollar corporations that own these "franchise" characters. These heroes are so popular that major toy companies like Mattel license character toys (of DC characters) at prices estimated at half a billion dollars,[3] hardly chump change.

In 2002, the three hundred top comic book titles (superhero titles) saw sales in excess of 300 million dollars, and big conventions drew as many as 60,000 fans apiece.[4] In the summer of '02, Sam Raimi's *Spider-Man* grossed 114 million dollars on its opening weekend, the biggest debut in film history. And the second season premiere of *Smallville* in September of the same year actually drew the WB Network's highest ratings ever. These demographics make the point: everybody, not just children, loves the superhero.

Looking at all these facts, at least economically speaking, there has never been a more appropriate time to examine the superheroes that have appeared on our TV and movie screens for half a century. Following the terror attacks on New York City and Washington, D.C., on September 11, 2001, the form of escapism offered by this entertainment is no doubt more necessary and cathartic than ever before. We all want desperately to believe that good can defeat evil, and, perhaps more to the point, that there is a clear line differentiating these opposing philosophies. Perhaps America cannot stop George W. Bush's "Axis of Evil," a modern-day Legion of Doom, in the real world. But in the universe of superheroes, defenders like the Flash, Green Lantern, Wonder Woman, Daredevil, and the X-Men show us how we would like the world to be.

Also, as superhero creator and comic book icon Stan Lee succinctly noted recently, special effects technology has reached the point where movies finally can do justice visually to the amazing super heroics of a Spidey or a Supes.[5] The advent of C.G.I. (Computer Generated Imagery) represents a full-scale revolution in film technology and a turning point in the history of the superhero. Now it is easy for Spider-Man to swing from a web through Manhattan's urban jungle, or for Superman to fly high above the streets of Metropolis, and no heroic deed is beyond the purview of the special effects man. If it can be imagined on the comic book page, it can be represented now on the movie stage or inside a computer screen.

This book's quest is twofold. Its first mission is to survey more than a half-century of superheroes on film and television, including some very general, basic information on many animated series. The text is structured with character-by-character entries to provide easy reference to TV series, individual episodes, casts and credits, and movie franchises. But at the same time, this volume seeks to note how America's greatest heroes, these fantastic new myths, have thrived and remained vital by changing with the times. "Batman went from dark avenger to campy TV star back to dark avenger," because "every generation needs to remake its screen superheroes in its own image," noted journalist James Poniewozik in *Time Magazine*.[6]

Part of the fun in gazing at this popular sub-genre is documenting the consistency — and surprising lack thereof — in many prominent franchises as they stretch across the years. Some Hollywood producers don't understand that each superhero has a unique history and lore (or myth, as it were) that should be respected. Walt Flanagan, the "Fan Boy" of Kevin Smith's Askewniverse and owner of the comic book store Jay & Silent Bob's Secret Stash in Red Bank, New Jersey, laments:

> I think Hollywood tries to make films for everybody, and when you try to make things for a wide audience, you take a risk of watering them down; changing the aspect that appeal to certain people in the first place. If you're really in love with a character and want to do a movie, I don't understand why Hollywood wants to change it.[7]

Flanagan makes a good point. Many of the productions surveyed in this book are not well loved by the fans of the comic book characters that form the source material. Why? Because in many cases the adaptations show no respect for the comics. And frankly, critics don't have much love for this genre either, and have even noted that these costumed heroes "appear in our cinemas every few years, like a new strain of hepatitis" and that these films are "almost universally dreadful."[8]

Where appropriate, this book notes how superheroes appearing on television and in films differ from their four-color origins. Art imitates life, and likewise our favorite superheroes have often adapted to fit the times. In the 1960s, these characters were parodies of authority figures, representing the counter culture. In the 1980s, superheroes went dark, reflecting societal fears about out-of-control crime. Post–September 11th, superheroes have become comforting and safe, like creamy vanilla ice cream, reflecting pure values and innocence.

The last matter to consider before beginning this study is the definition of the word "superhero" itself. For purposes of this book, a superhero is a character of extraordinary capabilities or powers who has a propensity to fight evil in all its forms, whether criminal, terrorist or demonic. For the most part, superheroes also wear unique or recognizable costumes that separate them from "normal" heroes, but even that distinction is not always the case, as demonstrated by *Buffy, Angel, The Six Million Dollar Man* and the like.

Although Superman is included in this text, it seems evident that not all extra-terrestrials are superheroes merely by point of origin. *Star Trek*'s (1966–1969) Mr. Spock, the Time Lord of *Doctor Who* (1963–1989) and the kids of *Roswell* (1999–2002) are aliens with unusual and super-human abilities, but few would argue that they are superheroes. James Bond, XXX, Sidney Bristow of *Alias* (2001–), *24*'s (2001–) Jack Bauer and other secret agents may seem to have "super luck" during their many globe-hopping adventures, but they are not seen as superheroes, at least as defined here.

Mighty Mouse, Dyno-Mutt, Batfink, Captain Caveman and other distinctly non-human kiddie heroes are also held out of this mix. For the most part, this book seeks to focus on the human and the superhuman, not the *über*-canine and its anthropomorphic ilk.

And, finally, just to put a little finer point on it, not all comic book characters are necessarily superheroes. Flash Gordon and Buck Rogers, for instance, are special because of their humanity in seemingly inhuman realms, not for powers above and beyond those of mortal man. Ditto for Dick Tracy. Characters from sword-and-sorcery dramas and out-and-out fantasy worlds (like those of *Beast Master, Highlander* and Kevin Sorbo's *Hercules*) have also been excluded, mostly because of other books devoted to such fantastic realms. The line just had to be drawn somewhere … but even if there's room for debate, we all know a superhero when we see one, don't we?

With those thoughts in mind, this looks like a job for Superman. Up, up and away!

Part I

A HISTORY OF FILM AND TELEVISION SUPERHEROES

In the Beginning: Superheroes with Straight Faces (1938–1957)

Although this book is specifically designed to examine the modern age of superheroes, from 1951 to 2003, many great comic book icons actually came into being well before that period, in the 1940s, the decade of world war and film noir. Considering this past, it is appropriate to begin with a brief reflection on and summary of that earlier era, and the humble, often low-budget cinematic beginnings of popular "super" characters, before leaping whole hog into the later, better known productions.

Perhaps it is no surprise that between the years of 1938 and 1945, some of the most famous American superheroes were born, both on the comic book page and on the burgeoning silver screen: Superman, Batman, Wonder Woman, Captain Marvel, the Phantom, the Shadow, and Captain America among them. After all, these were the terrifying years when fascism tightened its grip on Germany in the form of the Nazi Party. In the end, Hitler nearly devoured all of Europe in a conflagration of destruction; heroes were not merely desired, they were required because America was facing the greatest threat it yet knew. A juggernaut of conquest swept a subcontinent, and armies fell before it.

Then, mid-way through that seven-year period, in 1941, America became the next victim of fascist imperialism during a surprise attack by the Japanese at Pearl Harbor. In response to the ambush, the United States went to war to defeat twin regimes, Germany and Japan. In part because of carefully orchestrated government propaganda, these enemy countries were viewed by U.S. citizens not in terms of moral relativism, cultural differences, or even competing economic policies, but in the starkest terms of good and evil. Not surprisingly then, the superheroes born of that time were depicted as heroic and sterling through-and-through, with no derogatory humor or lampooning elements to lighten the mood of action, adventure, nobility and patriotism.

Movie audiences hungered to see good triumph over villainy, and that is precisely the menu served in the movie era of the time—via low-budget chapter plays or serials, usually produced by Columbia or Republic Studios. These efforts brought villains, often Far Eastern in origin, low while simultaneously championing American values of justice and individual freedom.

"There was an enormous desire to see social justice," DC Comics president Paul

Tom Tyler strikes a heroic pose as Captain Marvel in the serial *The Adventures of Captain Marvel.*

Levitz noted of this epoch when interviewed by *Time Magazine* in 2002. "Superman was a fulfillment of a pent-up passion for the heroic solutions."[1] Thus the first superheroes came to the silver screen in the 1940s, not surprisingly, to "defend democracy"[2] in the global war against totalitarianism.

Today, these early productions appear rather primitive for two reasons. Firstly, they were low-budget, black-and-white ventures intended purely as "escapist" entertainment that would appeal to children while instilling the right values. And secondly, they contained little subtext beyond the obvious Nazi or Jap-baiting. Instead, these serials were straight-faced adventures about good, solid American crime-fighters. A powerful punch to the kisser could often solve the most complex of problems. Villains were evil spies or mad scientists whose motivations for crime were rarely explored beyond their allegiance to corrupt foreign regimes. They were simply bad, and, like rabid dogs, had to be put down before they could harm America.

First out of the gate in this protean format was likely *The Adventures of Captain Marvel*, a 12-chapter serial. It pitted the cape-garbed hero (replete with lightning bolt logo on his torso) against a villain called Scorpion that was seeking, like the James Bond film villains of the future 1960s, world domination. Actor Tom Tyler played the heroic captain whose transformation into super-strong gent Captain Marvel was accomplished by speaking the word "Shazam!" Tyler later donned a different superhero suit to play Lee Falk's character *The Phantom* in a 1943 Columbia serial.

Even more on the nose for a wartime entertainment was the original 1943 *Batman* serial. It pitted the soon-to-be-famous Caped Crusader not against the Joker, Riddler, Catwoman, Penguin or any common villain of comic history, but rather a devious Nazi scientist, Dr. Daka (J. Carrol Naish). Daka's plot: to steal valuable resources from the United States to buttress his beloved Axis regime.

In 1944, *Captain America* (played by Dick Purcell) brought the war home when the red-white-and-blue-costumed U.S. defender fought a villain called Scarab, another foreigner. Again, the approach was completely straight-faced and morally simplistic. Evil had to be smashed and America defended, and these costumed patriots raised hardly an eyebrow as they fought for American values.

World War II ended in 1945, but the same approach to comic heroes continued through the end of the decade. *Superman* (1948) starred the lithe Kirk Alyn and in-

troduced the movie-going world to the Man of Steel's amazing exploits. In his first feature, the hero who fought for "truth, justice and the American way" combated the evil Spider Woman. In the 1950 sequel *Atom Man vs. Superman*, he dealt more explicitly with a bugaboo of the post-war period: atomic power and its dangerous ramifications.

It was at this point, perhaps, that one can make the claim that the modern age of superheroes really commenced. After a low-budget feature entitled *Superman and the Mole People* (1951), starring George Reeves as Superman, the franchise and its new star moved to the new art form called television. A syndicated black-and-white series, consisting of more than a hundred half-hour episodes, ran for six seasons, until 1958.

A low-budget production featuring spare set decorations, few costume changes and rudimentary plots, *The Adventures of Superman*, despite budgetary shortcomings, set the tone for no less than five decades of superhero programming on the tube. Because it lasted so many episodes (over a hundred), it eventually featured every story and superhero formula known to Hollywood, ideas that would one day become cliché. These included the origin tale ("Superman on Earth"), evil twins or doubles ("The Face and the Voice"), time travel ("Through the Time Barrier") and amnesia ("Panic in the Sky").

The series also set the character archetypes for generations. Clark Kent was the "mild-mannered" secret identity of a more distinguished, virtually invincible hero named (of course) Superman. Lois Lane, played by Noel Neill and then Phyllis Coates, was the feisty damsel in distress, smart enough to work as a prize-winning journalist yet oblivious enough not to realize the truth about her co-worker Clark. Jimmy Olsen (Jack Larson) was the young, inexperienced and prone-to-trouble sidekick, always in need of a timely rescue. Perhaps the most oft-imitated character was Perry White himself, the gruff boss with a heart of gold and curmudgeonly, difficult-to-approach exterior.

In his long escapades flying over Metropolis, Superman and star Reeves became the prototypical superhero to a generation of TV watchers. Even after the actor's untimely and mysterious death in 1958, his famous TV series inspired a long run of similar shows.

The Adventures of Superman did not highlight crazed super villains, as later series and films in the genre so often would, but furthered the straight-faced ethos of its serial predecessors. Today many viewers consider these adventurous half-hours corny or tongue-in-cheek, but in fact they are just painfully earnest representations of a hero that is considered rather "square." There is some situationally appropriate (and sometimes dated) humor in the series too, but in virtually all respects *The Adventures of Superman* remains wholesome, clean, straightforward fun. It is a representation of its context, the 1950s. Although the Cold War was hot, America had defeated evil before, during World War II, and was undergoing a period of prosperity and growth. Accordingly, the villains were more often of the domestic variety (jewel thieves, mobsters and other small-time crooks) than terrorists or spies.

Then There Was Camp: The Age of Batman (1966–1975)

With the advent of the 1960s came a counter-culture revolution in America, and the stirrings of the women's liberation movement. The television set was no longer a simple curiosity, a device existing only in a select number of lucky homes. Now it was everywhere, and color television arrived in the middle of the decade to spur the tech-nology's popularity to even more incredible heights. As a result, pop culture influences had a new and surprisingly powerful platform from which to reach millions. In particular, the youth culture rallied to the entertainment of the period on the radio, TV and at theaters, including such phenomena as the Beatles and the James Bond films.

More importantly, the 1960s were a highly turbulent decade politically, a period when a foreign war was waged in Vietnam and the race-related, Civil Rights battles were fought on the domestic front. A United States president had been assassinated in 1963, and many Americans suspected a cover-up, spurring dissatisfaction among the electorate and paving the way for more distrust of government for decades to come. Basically, the 1960s were a far more complicated time than the conforming but optimistic fifties, which had witnessed the popularity of Reeves' noble and pure-hearted, pro-establishment Superman.

After *The Adventures of Superman* went off the air in the late 1950s, a new and different style of superhero did not emerge in the nation until 1966. And boy was he a different breed! His name was Batman, and in this incarnation he reflected his times to an incredibly high — and some might insist, alarming — degree. To wit, he was a self-parody. Just as the James Bond films sported a self-mocking nature, and as authoritarian figures like policemen and politicians fell out of favor, so was the new champion of the establishment, the superhero, to take a hit.

In January of 1966, *Batman* premiered on ABC television, and it was unlike anything the world had seen before. With colorful sets, outrageous villains and the most square, incorruptible hero imaginable (in the person of actor Adam West), *Batman* became an overnight sensation, a phenomenon to rival Beatlemania. The rub, especially for comic book fans, was that Gotham

City's Caped Crusader was played for "camp," i.e. tongue in cheek. In other words, Batman was as square as could be (more square even than Superman), but his pronouncements and beliefs were so stolid, so earnest, that he became laughable, a figure for audiences to poke fun at.

The policemen on the series, especially Commissioner Gordon (Neil Hamilton) and Chief O'Hara (Stafford Repp), were portrayed as brown-nosing incompetents that could not solve a crime even if their lives depended on it. And Robin, Batman's sidekick, as played by Burt Ward, had none of the angst, anger or sexual longings so much on display in the adolescents of the age. The purpose of the 1960s superhero, it seemed, was to mock the innocence of the 1950s.

In the 1960s, Gotham City had Batman to protect it from the likes of the weirdest super villains imaginable. Joker (Cesar Romero), Riddler (Frank Gorshin), Penguin (Burgess Meredith), Catwoman (Julie Newmar and later Eartha Kitt), Egghead (Vincent Price), King Tut (Victor Buono), the Bookworm (Roddy McDowall), Mr. Freeze (George Sanders, Otto Preminger and Eli Wallach), Minerva (Zsa Zsa Gabor), the Puzzler (Maurice Evans), Chandell (Liberace) and Louie the Lilac (Milton Berle) stood up to be counted as the most evil of bad dudes. Importantly, these villains never had very realistic plots or aims. Instead, they had crazy plots to kill the Caped Crusader or take over the world, and rarely, if ever, used guns to fight Batman and his sidekick.

Yet despite the absurdities of the series, in essence a sitcom such as *Bewitched* [1964–1972] or *I Dream of Jeannie* [1965–1970], *Batman* immediately resonated with American audiences. It was gorgeous, amusing entertainment, and children, at least, did not detect the camp aspects. They were thus able to enjoy the show as their parents and grandparents had enjoyed the straight-faced

serials of the 1940s. Only those who were faithful to the Batman comic books complained about the silly approach, which saw an obsessive-compulsive Batman label virtually every object in his Bat Cave Headquarters, and saw him equipped with the most ridiculous gadgets imaginable in his impossibly crowded utility belt.

Though it was rewarding to see fantastic guest stars like Tallulah Bankhead (as the Black Widow), Michael Rennie (as Sandman), and Art Carney (as the Archer) menace West's stolid hero, the superhero was clearly being lampooned in order to fit in with the anti-establishment trend of the time. As entertaining as the *Batman* series was, it was also poking fun at the protagonist (as later Bond films poked fun at that unflappable icon).

Still, the series proved incredibly popular, and the competing TV networks (CBS and NBC) attempted in 1967 to out-*Batman* the Caped Crusader with their own camp-inspired superhero creations. Along came Buck Henry's creation *Captain Nice* (portrayed by William Daniels) and the generally horrible *Mr. Terrific*. Neither of these series lasted even a full season. In a strange bit of historical irony, both shows premiered on the same night and finished their abbreviated runs on the same night too. That was the problem — few viewers could tell the undistinguished, copycat series apart.

The proliferation of "jokey" superhero programs only proved that to America in the 1960s, crime fighting was a laughing matter, and superheroes, if part of the establishment, had to be played as jokes. When in 1967 William Dozier (the creator of the TV *Batman*) produced a serious, straight-faced superhero adventure, *The Green Hornet*, its ratings were generally terrible. Audiences now expected to be amused rather than thrilled, and to many the "straight" adventures of the crime-bashing, seething Green Hornet (Van Williams) and

Quick, to the Bat Cave! Robin (Burt Ward) and Batman (Adam West) puzzle over a new clue in the movie version of the camp 1960s series *Batman*. Note the carefully labeled Chemo-Electric Secret Writing Detector.

sidekick Kato (Bruce Lee) lacked the element that made *Batman* such a hoot: humor. The series folded after twenty-six episodes and never reached *Batman*'s level of success, despite a bevy of gadgetry that included a tricked-up car called the Black Beauty.

As for *Batman*, it emerged as the most influential TV series in superhero history, but it was a distinctly double-edged success. Adults enjoyed the humor, the children the

adventure, and everybody could appreciate the fine comedic performances and wonderful sets. But soon TV audiences tired of the overly repetitive *Batman* formula. During its first two seasons, the series aired twice a week, and the same formula was always utilized, right down to the ludicrous cliffhanger at the end of the first episode and the final battle with the villain at the end of the second. The latter always featured animated titles like "ZONK" and "CRASSSH!" and "ZAP!" over the fisticuffs.

A 1966 *Batman* movie was produced after the first season of the series, but the film, directed by Leslie Martinson, only contributed to a growing sense of "Bat Fatigue," and the "bat" phenomena died out quickly. In the third season of the TV series, in an attempt to boost sagging ratings, actress Yvonne Craig was added to the mix as the athletic and sexy Batgirl, but even that inspired casting stunt could not save the programming from faltering ratings and its own utter predictability. The series was cancelled in 1968, after two-and-a-half seasons on the air.

The wounds inflicted by the TV version of *Batman* are difficult to assess objectively. Anybody who grew up watching the series nurtures a real affection for it. For many, it is their first encounter with the superhero milieu, and thus carries the glow of nostalgia with it. It has played exceedingly well in reruns over the last generation or two, in part because it is very well done and quite amusing. And yet, who among the Batman faithful would argue that the series did not damage or belittle their favorite hero and the genre he represented?

"Unfortunately, the lasting impact of the show was probably detrimental to the way superheroes and comic books are viewed," opined Howard Margolin, host of the New York–based genre radio program *Destinies: The Voice of Science Fiction* and expert on superheroes. Describing the fallout, Margolin observed: "Thirty years later, every time someone does an article about superheroes or comic books, it is always accompanied with the line *POW! ZAM! ZAP!— Superheroes aren't just for kids!* *Batman* colored the impression of what superhero comics and TV should look like for everybody who wasn't a reader of comics. And if people dislike the series, I think that's why. Despite the efforts of many credible people to change that perception, it is still

hard to shake. Think about it this way: tens of millions of people have watched *Batman* on TV, and only a couple hundred thousand people read the comics."

As funny, charming and well-produced as it most certainly was, the 1960s *Batman* cast a pall over superhero TV series that was difficult to overcome. That established, Adam West, to many, remains the ultimate Batman, even after Michael Keaton, Val Kilmer and George Clooney assumed the role in bigger-budgeted, more recent productions.

The practical fallout after *Batman* failed in 1968 was easy to chart. Network executives became terribly gun shy about new superhero productions. *Captain Nice*, *Mr. Terrific*, *Green Hornet* and eventually *Batman* fell before lackluster ratings, and even the longest-lived of the bunch (*Batman*) did not make it through three full seasons. One thing was for certain, if superheroes were to return to the cathode ray galaxy again any time soon, they would look very different than they had on the camp-ridden *Batman* series.

One historical note: the last gasps of "camp" superheroes actually came on the tube in the mid–1970s. A 1975 TV production of the 1960s musical *It's a Bird! It's a Plane! It's Superman!* interpreted the Man of Steel mythos with a similarly satirical slant ... and was a terrible, low-budget production that has been all but forgotten. Finally, Adam West and Burt Ward resumed their Dynamic Duo roles in a short-lived 1977 series called *Legend of the Superheroes*. It ran for two episodes.

The Age of Americana: Nostalgia Reigns Supreme (1973–1985)

If the 1960s were rough, the 1970s were downright scary. President Nixon was ousted from office following a terrible scandal in 1974. America lost the Vietnam War and retreated with dishonor. And, on top of that, there was double-digit inflation (Whip Inflation Now!), an energy crisis, and U.S. hostages in Iran to contend with. America, a country that had once seemed invulnerable, appeared to be failing morally, politically, in battle, and even economically. The result, at least in terms of superhero productions, was a generation of entertainment that looked backward rather than forward.

This trend began in the early 1970s with the advent of the wholesome "bionic" shows. To wit, there were two TV series (*The Six Million Dollar Man* [1973–1978] and *The Bionic Woman* [1976–78]) that concerned super-strong secret agent/cyborgs laboring for our country in a secret branch of the government called the O.S.I. (Office of Scientific Investigation). This trend of wholesome, innocent entertainment accelerated with the release of the George Lucas film *Star Wars* in May of 1977. Without putting too fine a point on the comparison, the impressive space opera was essentially a latter day 1930s serial, like *Flash Gordon*. The tale of farm boy Luke Skywalker "coming of age" in a universe of robots, fireworks-like laser beams and whooshing spaceships was innocent, straight-faced, good humored, and, most of all, clean fun with clearly defined good guys dressed in white and bad guys in black. The nation ate it up.

The age of nostalgia was upon the United States, and not surprisingly that meant a renaissance in superhero productions. First up was a TV series based on the DC Comics character Wonder Woman. Starring the beautiful Lynda Carter, bedecked in a brass brassiere and a red, white and blue leotard, this heroine's adventures were set in the last age of innocence and moral constants, the 1940s. In the first season of the series, Wonder Woman and her beau, Steve Trevor (Lyle Waggoner), fought the Nazis during World War II. Later sea-

sons brought Wonder Woman into the more controversial seventies, generally to lesser effect. The show petered out in 1979 after several seasons on the air.

Then came *The Incredible Hulk* in 1978. In the comic book version of this legend (from Marvel Comics), scientist Bruce Banner was affected by terrible gamma rays when a new and deadly H-bomb was test detonated by the military. That may have been too controversial an origin for the wholesome age of Americana, so in the TV series Dr. David Banner (Bill Bixby) conducted a scientific test on himself in a laboratory, becoming, basically, a guinea pig in a test that could benefit others. Naturally, the experiment had unforeseen effects, turning him into a giant, hulking monster played by body-builder and Mr. Universe Lou Ferrigno.

The explicit metaphor of *The Incredible Hulk* TV series was anger management. The generation of the 1970s understood that rage, uncontrolled, could literally turn people into monsters. The fear over government bomb building, it seemed, was no longer so current.

Like *Wonder Woman*, *The Incredible Hulk* (1978–1982) gazed longingly backward — though not to previous historical periods, but to old television formats instead. Each week David Banner crossed the country in search of a cure for his condition, and was hounded by a relentless pursuer (a busybody reporter named McGee, played by Jack Colvin). All the while, the caring Banner helped those unfortunate people he met, like abused children, exploited senior citizens, or the homeless. *The Incredible Hulk* was actually a not-so-subtle variation on the popular 1960s TV series *The Fugitive* (1963–1967), only this time with a green tint.

The Amazing Spider-Man (1977–78) also debuted in the late 1970s, but unlike his comic book counterpart, Peter Parker, series star Nicholas Hammond was a respectable-looking establishment figure in his twenties, a full-fledged photographer at *The Daily Bugle.* He fought solidly on the side of the establishment and had little of the comic book Spidey's sense of humor or irony about his situation. It was a safe, mainstream and bland adaptation of a distinctly anti-authority, individual comic book character, and one that neither lasted nor resonated.

Ditto Reb Brown's *Captain America* (1979), who appeared in two unfortunate TV movies in the age of nostalgia. In this situation, Steve Rogers was not a patriot going off to fight a "good" war and defeat master villains like Red Skull, but a "groovy" and mellow hippie artist that just wanted to help people and "check out." He was part and parcel of the freewheeling, post–Vietnam, leftist '70s, and a real slap in the face to long-standing Cap fans. Where was the character's sense of patriotism? Selflessness? In the comics, Steve Rogers sacrificed family ties, security and emotional connections to become a top-secret super-soldier and fight for his country! But that, it seems, was too hokey for the 1970s.

Doctor Strange, another TV movie of the late 1970s, re-cast its comic book title character (another Marvel property) as a Luke Skywalker wannabe, an apprentice learning from an old Obi Wan Kenobi–type mystical master. There were laser zaps, dimensional flights, and other signs of *Star Wars'* ubiquitous influence, but few viewers tuned in to watch.

As the seventies faded and the "bionic" trend showed signs of diminishing, the ultimate nostalgia movie arrived in theaters. In 1978, director Richard Donner (*The Omen* [1976]) introduced the world to *Superman: The Movie,* a big budget, lavish origin story for the popular Man of Steel. The original script by Mario Puzo (*The Godfather* [1972]), Robert Benton, and Leslie and David Newman was prepped by director Guy Hamilton (*Goldfinger* [1963]) for a 1975 release, but would have been a camp

movie in the style of the '60s *Batman.* Telly Savalas was slated to appear in a cameo as Kojak, replete with his ever-present lollipop.

However, Donner, a comic fan since childhood, wisely jettisoned the jokey approach to the icon and instead prepared *Superman* as a top-of-the-line, A-list motion picture. Superstar Marlon Brando was cast — at a cost of one million dollars — as Jor-El, Superman's father. Gene Hackman joined up as the villainous Lex Luthor, while Margot Kidder played Lois Lane; but it was charismatic and charming Christopher Reeve, a young unknown, that made the biggest impression in the film as a compassionate, tender, but very strong Superman.

Tagged with an ad-line that simultaneously promised sincerity, belief and special effects aplomb ("you'll believe a man can fly"), *Superman: The Movie* boasted brilliant flight sequences and visuals, plus a rousing orchestral score by *Star Wars* composer John Williams. The picture also featured a thoroughly impressive three-part structure. The first, harking back to *Star Wars,* showcased the destruction of the alien world Krypton — a special effects showstopper.

The second segment depicted young Clark Kent's life in Smallville, Kansas. With picturesque views of 1950s farmhouses, wheat fields, and natural vistas, this section of the film capitalized on the trend towards nostalgia, remembering a simpler time in American history.

The third segment, Superman's battle against madman Lex Luthor in modern-day Metropolis, proved just as charming and interesting with Kidder proving to be a delightfully modern and sexy Lois Lane.

The nostalgic approach to the middle portion of the film, connected to the fast-moving "city life" 1970s final portion of the effort, reminded viewers of a link to the past.

Let's do the twist. Superman (Christopher Reeve) takes General Zod (Terence Stamp) out for a spin in Richard Lester's 1981 sequel, *Superman II.*

That link, in no small part, was the honesty, sincerity, and traditional values of Superman. He was a fish out of water in the post–Watergate America, but also an explicit reminder that the values we grew up with are still relevant, and can be made relevant again, in the contemporary world.

Superman: the Movie became one of the biggest hits of 1978 and quickly spawned a well-regarded sequel, *Superman II* (1981). Reeve, Hackman and Kidder returned for the encore, this time facing off against a trio of Kryptonian revolutionaries that escaped imprisonment in the mirror-like Phantom Zone. Directed by Richard Lester, *Superman II* conquered the box office along with another paean to cinematic glories of old, Steven Spielberg's 1930s serial pastiche *Raiders of the Lost Ark.*

The success of the second *Superman* film promptly led to a series of "super" sequels from producers Ilya and Alexander Salkind. Alas, these films eventually watered down the appeal of the hero. 1983's *Superman III* starred comedian Richard Pryor, and pitted Superman against a tycoon (Robert Vaughn) and his super-computer. 1984's *Supergirl*, starring Helen Slater, was a harmless (and toothless) fantasy that lacked much in the way of menace and urgency despite the presence of Faye Dunaway as the villainess, a witch named Selena. 1987's low-tech and rather embarrassing *Superman IV: The Quest for Peace*, with a story penned by Christopher Reeve, saw Superman disarming the world of nuclear missiles, only to face a new threat from Luthor (Hackman)—a twisted Superman clone called Nuclear Man (Mark Pillow).

By the final Superman movie, the appeal of nostalgia and Americana was fading fast, and a new template for contemporary superheroes was desperately required.

On television in the mid–1980s, producer Glen Larson envisioned the future with *Automan* (1983), a TV series about a walking and talking "superhero" hologram. With special effects inspired by the movie *Tron* (1982), and a good sense of humor to boot, one might have thought that the technological *uber man* was the next big, exploitable fad. Alas, *Automan*, along with Larson's other superhero of the same vintage, the metamorphic *Manimal* (1983), promptly tanked in the ratings.

Much more popular was *The Greatest American Hero* (1981–1983), a series with a catchy theme song and a terrific cast. This effort concerned an "average Joe" (William Katt) that became a superhero overnight when visiting aliens left him a red costume endowed with super powers (including flight and invisibility). Teamed with a sardonic F.B.I. agent (Robert Culp) and a lovely girlfriend (Connie Sellecca), Katt's character saved the world on a regular basis, usually with a great deal of kvetching. The series was wholesome fun, and far more character-driven than the previous generation of superhero embodied by *Wonder Woman*, *The Amazing Spider-Man* and *The Incredible Hulk*. As audiences demanded ever more realism in their entertainment—in gritty cop shows like *Hill Street Blues*, gritty hospital shows like *St. Elsewhere* and gritty law shows like *L.A. Law*—*The Greatest American Hero* was also on the vanguard of the movement. It began to ask the practical questions that *The Adventures of Superman* and *Batman* had not. If you were a superhero, how would it impact your personal life? Your professional life? How would it be irritating? What responsibilities would come with it? In asking and answering these questions in humorous fashion, *The Greatest American Hero* represented a giant step forward in the genre.

When *The Greatest American Hero* was cancelled after three seasons, the future for superheroes looked uncertain. If nostalgia and Americana had run its course, what was to be the next trend?

Who could save us now?

The Dark Age (1985–1998)

The 1980s promised another shift in America's ideals. With the election to the presidency of the avuncular conservative Ronald Reagan, new vistas, philosophies and notions came into being. Strong and resolute on national defense, Reagan's eight-year tenure in the Oval Office witnessed massive increases in Federal spending but fewer opportunities for many in the poorer classes. While the 1980s heralded the arrival of the "yuppies," an upwardly mobile middle class with money to burn, Reagan's policy of deficit spending and "trickle down" economics saw to it that the rich grew richer only as the poor grew poorer. Corporate criminals, like the one played by Michael Douglas in *Wall Street* (1989), became millionaires by outmaneuvering the system via insider trading. A divide between classes grew in America for the first time in a generation.

As a result of these new inequities, violent crime, poverty, and homelessness multiplied. Even racial tensions worsened. In fact, racial views were a central issue of the first Bush Administration, which surged to electoral victory in 1988 by exploiting the white middle class fear of black intruders with a widely broadcast TV advertisement about a violent offender named Willie Horton. Put a "liberal" in office, Bush warned, and a black man will break into your home to rape your wife and kill you. Republicans (and superheroes) were needed.

By the beginning of the 1990s, America plunged into economic recession, and the popular music of the age (grunge and alternative) expressed the dissatisfaction of a generation. One role model for the young generation dubbed "X" was Kurt Cobain of the band Nirvana. He committed suicide, exposing the despondency of the generation. Independent films like *Slacker* (1991) and Kevin Smith's *Clerks* (1994) further symbolized the ennui of a disaffected youth culture.

How could superheroes fit into such a world?

This future of the superhero came from an unexpected source in 1986. Seemingly from out of nowhere, Frank Miller (with Klaus Janson and Lynn Varley) penned a revolutionary and highly influential graphic novel miniseries, *The Dark Knight Returns*. It was a thoroughly unconventional Batman story that cast the old hero in a totally new light. The story's setting was a crime-ridden future of scandal, immorality and chaos. Joker was a celebrity, Batman a vigilante and the Batmobile, in essence, an armored troop transport.

Most noticeably, Batman was not a squarer-than-square hero, but a full-fledged creature of the night, a black avenger in the dark, a bitter, tortured, twisted hero. Frankly, he had as much in common with Clint Eastwood's neo-fascist cop Dirty Harry Callahan as he did with Adam West's clean-cut Caped Crusader of the 1960s.

But this Batman reflected the age. While the rich denizens of Gotham City lived in lavish penthouses, their riches had not "trickled down" to the poor citizens on the streets far below. Corruption reigned high above, while gangsters, rapists, murderers and poverty ruled far below.

The response to the Miller comic was incredibly enthusiastic. At last fans had a new template, a new direction, and were taking Batman seriously again. The "camp" past was buried by this re-do, which seemed more like a post-apocalyptic *Mad Max* world than the Gotham City imagined by our fathers. Simultaneously, other comic book artists moved in the same direction, incorporating the dark approach with much success. *The Killing Joke*, by Alan (*Watchmen*) Moore, and artists Brian Bollard and John Higgins, came in 1988 and featured the crippling of Batgirl, courtesy of the Joker's bullet.

It did not take filmmakers long to seize on the new approach, and a *Batman* film went into production for release in 1989. Interestingly, however, a few other "dark" superheroes actually pre-dated *Batman* on the big screen. In 1982, Wes Craven, a horror film director, presented a low-budget version of the popular and dark DC Comic character Swamp Thing.

Forever transformed into a plant creature (by an accident in his lab), this character could never again be anything but an outsider to the human race. Isolated and alone, and uncertain of what he was (a human transformed into a plant, or a plant with the "absorbed" memories of a human), Swamp Thing had no chance for a happy ending. Perhaps because of the source material, perhaps because of the director's horror film experiences, Craven's film was an early step to the dark side (and surely a prototype for Todd McFarlane's Spawn).

Then, in 1987, director Paul Verhoeven's (*Starship Troopers* [1997]) R-rated *RoboCop* played in theaters and became a huge hit. Set in a cynical world of corporate scandal and crime run amok, one very reminiscent of Miller's *Dark Knight* comic, *RoboCop* concerned an Irish-Catholic policeman named Murphy (Peter Weller) murdered by heavily-armed, brutal gangsters. But portions of his brain and corpse were then utilized as "spare parts" in the making of a law enforcement cyborg called RoboCop. Murphy's consciousness and conscience survived the transfer to the clanking, metal body, as did his crime-fighting skills, and the story was a dark one about rediscovering humanity, even when you are no longer human.

The film was especially notable for graphic, bloody violence (especially in Murphy's sadistic, brutal death scene), and tongue-in-cheek "breaks" between scenes (commercials from the capitalistic, corporate-run "futuristic" society). Kurtwood Smith played Clarence Boddecker, a cold-blooded villain always accompanied by a gang of cackling, vicious thugs; and in

A deadly duel of the monsters in Wes Craven's *Swamp Thing* (1982), one of the early "dark" superhero movies.

some manner *RoboCop* pointed to the direction of Tim Burton's *Batman* two years later.

When *Batman* finally landed on movie screens in the summer of 1989, there had been so much studio hype that the film obliterated all competition even before critics could adjudge its quality. The film starred the diminutive Michael Keaton as Bruce Wayne/Batman, a social misfit (though millionaire) with more angst than any previous incarnation of the superhero.

Bitter over the death of his parents, this Batman prowled the night fighting criminals and going head-to-head with a psychotic monster called the Joker (Jack Nicholson). Quirky, odd, claustrophobic and virtually without coherent plot, *Batman* set the pace for all future superhero pictures. It took its subject matter seriously, and portrayed the hero as "flawed" and "dark," a bizarre reflection of his evil, twisted opponent.

When *Batman* grossed over 200 million dollars at the box office, the Dark Age

commenced in earnest, and soon every superhero film and TV series seemed like a knock-off of Burton's picture. *The Flash* came to television briefly in 1990, featuring a bombastic Danny Elfman score (like *Batman*), extensive night shooting, and a vengeance-hungry hero out to avenge the death of his brother. It even stole *Batman*'s oft-quoted line to Joker: "I made you? You made me!"

A more original production was Sam Raimi's rousing and appropriately named *Darkman* (1990), a stylish virtuoso effort that showcased a burned hero (Liam Neeson) as much *Phantom of the Opera*–style monster as savior of the people. When Dr. Peyton Westlake (Neeson) was burned beyond recognition in a laboratory fire, his nerve endings were severed, making him impervious to pain. Lacking a face, the brilliant Westlake made use of a flesh substitute that could survive in the sun for an hour-and-a-half. A master of disguise, he could imitate his opponents with the fake flesh, leading them to grisly demises in delicious set pieces. One daredevil helicopter

Dark Knight in Black Rubber: The new look of Batman (Michael Keaton) in Tim Burton's 1989 blockbuster. Notice the sculpted muscle, dearth of color and long, pointed bat ears, all of which distinguish this caped crusader from his TV predecessor.

assault sequence, with Darkman hanging on by a rope, was alone worth the price of admission.

As *RoboCop*, *Darkman* and *Batman* sequels populated American theaters, matters grew even darker. In 1994, director Alex Proyas' adaptation of the James O'Barr comic book *The Crow* arrived amidst a flood of controversy. Its star, Brandon Lee, had died on the set in a terrible gun accident while the film was still in principal photography, and the movie had to be completed with special effects trickery and body dou-

bles for Lee. The concept of the movie was as grim as the incident that claimed the life of its star: a man is brutally murdered by thugs in a city of rampant crime, along with his girlfriend. A crow brings him back to Earth to right those wrongs and kill those who hurt him.

The Crow represented eye-for-an-eye vengeance all the way, a story told in impenetrable nights, under incessant rain, and in a haze of hatred and gloom. The film was a look at the worst of human ugliness with the most horrible, brutal villains this side of a *Death Wish* movie. And there was no hope to be grasped, because audiences realized throughout the crusade that the Crow's avenger, Eric Draven (Eric the Raven) would eventually return to the land of the dead. He was back on Earth only to kill, only for revenge. You don't get much darker than that.

Actually, scratch that last sentence.

In 1997, the movie version of the popular *Spawn* comic book, created by Todd McFarlane, was released. This New Line film, one that made the nihilistic *Crow* look like a trip to Disneyland, concerned a righteous man, a warrior for the American government, that was betrayed by his superior (Martin Sheen) and cast down to Hell. There he was forced to lead Satan's (er, Malebolgia's) armies in a war against Heaven. To do so, he was transformed into a burned, scarred, pitiable creature with hellish body armor, hence the moniker Spawn. Once on Earth again, however, Spawn began to see things differently and never really served the Devil; but his scarred visage separated him from humanity and the loved ones he left behind, a wife and child.

Actor John Leguizamo (*Carlito's Way* [1993]) added to *Spawn*'s disgust factor by playing the film's villain, a drooling, obese clown/demon with a penchant for eating maggot-ridden garbage. And Spawn was a superhero?! Well, yes. In an effort to distance themselves from the righteous,

Battle Royale: A Phantom of the Opera–like Dr. Peyton Westlake (Liam Neeson) is pursued by helicopter during the action-packed finale of Sam Raimi's *Darkman* (1990).

square, costumed heroes of the past (particularly the satirical 1960s), franchises such as *Spawn* traveled far in the opposite direction, becoming so dark and depressing that one could not help but take them very, very seriously. It was overcompensation, no doubt, but much revamping was deemed necessary to erase the popular image of TV's *Batman*.

While the Dark Age reigned supreme, there was an interesting counter movement in superhero films that failed to take hold. In particular, it was 1930s-style movie serial nostalgia that informed *The Rocketeer* (1991), *The Shadow* (1994) and *The Phantom* (1996), all reflections of a more innocent era. Without exception, audiences rejected these productions, squashing the counter movement and assuring that the "dark" template represented the future of superhero productions.

As the 1990s wore on, the Dark Age eventually ended in something akin to disgrace. *Batman Returns* (1992), a darker sequel

to the original *Batman*, featured a black-blooded, deformed Penguin (Danny DeVito) that ate raw fish and joked about eating pussy with Michelle Pfeiffer's Catwoman. This villain scared children out of the theater, and didn't exactly sell Happy Meals.

The updated version of *The Shadow* in 1994 (starring Alec Baldwin) drew almost no audience with its mind-clouding avenger and look back to the 1930s, and both *The Crow* and *RoboCop* sequels saw quality diminish significantly. Eventually, both of the latter franchises ended up on television, gutted, simplified and blanderized to the point of anonymity.

Finally, even the *Batman* franchise ushered out the trend Frank Miller had begun a decade earlier in graphic novel form. The last two *Batman* films, *Batman Forever* (1995) and the terrible *Batman and Robin* (1997) welcomed back the absurd, camp-style humor of the *Batman* TV series, but this time with little or no charm. The fact that three different actors played Batman in four films (Keaton, Val Kilmer and George Clooney) did not build empathy for the franchise, which eventually became a freak show featuring state-of-the-art, but gaudy, special effects and a surfeit of gay jokes.

There was one shining star among the latter-day "dark" heroes, however. In 1998, Wesley Snipes portrayed a comic character called Blade, another gloom'n'doom superhero. Isolated, alone, combating an addiction (to blood), Blade (a Marvel property from an obscure 1970s comic called *Tomb of Dracula*) fought not criminals, but the undead, a secret society living just out of view in contemporary Los Angeles.

A film filled with martial arts thrills and great action sequences, *Blade* represented a new dawn at the end of a very long, dark tunnel. The dark approach was still valid, still powerful, but now superheroes were fighting their own "demons" (literally) rather than the scum of human society.

In 2003, *Daredevil*, starring Ben Affleck, promised to resume the "dark city" trend exemplified by the late 1980s and early 1990s "age of darkness" superhero franchises. An appropriate selection since a Bush was in the White House again, and for the first time in nearly a decade the stock market was tanking and deficit spending was again the order of the day. With over two million jobs lost in America in two years, and the worst economic performance since Herbert Hoover, the new President Bush's policies heralded a return to gloom and doom in the world of film and TV superheroes. Dark nostalgia or Americana — you make the call.

The Dawn of Woman:
The Ascent of Buffy
(1997–2002)

With the Batman movies all but killing off the "dark knight" trend in 1997, superhero fans began to look for new heroes and ideas, especially with a 20 percent dip in comic book sales since 1993.[3] Again they found the future of the genre in the most unusual and unexpected place. In this case, it was a low-budget TV series airing on the WB network, one that was based on, of all things, a failed horror movie from the early 1990s, *Buffy the Vampire Slayer* (1992).

Created by Joss Whedon (*Toy Story* [1995], *Alien Resurrection* [1997]) and starring the delightful Sarah Michelle Gellar as Buffy, an ordinary California teenager chosen to slay vampires and demons, *Buffy* was a revelation. The TV series was smart, funny, and touching. It was also exciting and packed wall-to-wall with rousing fight sequences. The feminist *Xena: Warrior Princess* (1995–2001) had premiered earlier with great impact, a spin-off of *Hercules: The Legendary Journeys* (1994–2000), but this sword and sorcery epic did not explicitly focus on super-heroism, but rather action-adventure. It helped to prime audiences for *Buffy*, but it was *The Vampire Slayer* that forecast the dominance of the woman in superhero productions.

Buffy very quickly became required TV viewing, as each season the Slayer butted heads against characters the series termed "the Big Bad," a new and ever more interesting series of villains. In the first season, Buffy fought a Nosferatu-like master vampire (Mark Metcalf). In the second, her vampire ex-boyfriend, Angel (David Boreanaz), threatened to suck the world into Hell. In the third, Buffy fought a demonic politico, the mayor of Sunnydale, Richard Wilkins (Harry Groener). In the fourth she battled a demon-robot hybrid named Adam, and in the fifth a brain-sucking god called "Glory" (Clare Kramer).

With a team of sidekicks called the Scooby Gang, Buffy moved from the WB to the UPN network for a further two seasons before Gellar and company called it quits. It was a highly influential production for a number of reasons. First and foremost, it effortlessly reflected the peace and prosperity of the Clinton Era in American history. Crime rates had dropped to their lowest since those statistics were recorded in the late '60s and early '70s. With no inflation to speak of, more available jobs, a technology boom (thanks to the Internet) and very low interest rates, there was a shift in the population's outlook about crime and violence. The old criminal standbys — robbers, rapists, murderers, thieves and other thugs — no longer carried the resonance they had in the crime-ridden and "dark" 80s. The gang-banging villains inhabiting the poverty-struck, garbage-bedecked city streets of *RoboCop*, *The Crow* and even *Batman* were now passe, out of step with the times.

So *Buffy the Vampire Slayer* pulled a brilliant switch, one emulated by many other TV series. Instead of fighting traditional criminals, Buffy's enemies were all of the supernatural variety: demons, vampires, poltergeists and the like.

Perhaps more importantly, *Buffy the Vampire Slayer* set the tone for future productions, both in the roles of women as heroes, and in superhero "language." Before Buffy, even positive female role models like Wonder Woman were weighed down by baggage, as somehow being less "worthy" heroes than men. In the 1970s version of Wonder Woman, her theme song had noted that the Amazonian warrior fought for "our rights" wearing her "satin tights." That was a patronizing attitude. The same problem plagued other female heroes in the comics, as Trina Robbins, author of *The Great Women Super Heroes*, articulated:

> Sue Storm, the Invisible Girl, serves coffee, goes to fashion shows and faints.... Unlike the insecurities and self doubt that afflicted male heroes and which encouraged identification and evoked admiration when the heroes overcame them, Sue Storm's power and flaws were almost a caricature of Victorian notions of the feminine, an invisible woman who faints when she tries to exert herself.[4]

But Buffy was determinedly different. She could kick any man's ass, and did so on a regular basis. There were no excuses made, and she always fought to the bitter end, through emotional and physical injuries.

Buffy liked to deliver one-liners and puns while staking vamps, and her lingo was one part teenage girl, one part ribald wit. The program's dialogue — this "Buffy Speak" — has been oft-imitated (*Charmed*, *Dark Angel*, *Birds of Prey* to name just three) but never equaled.

Buffy the Vampire Slayer was also uncanny in its superhero references, noting how one sidekick (Xander Harris) had no special powers and was thus "the Jimmy Olsen" of the bunch. In all, *Buffy the Vampire Slayer* was a delightful series, and, along with *The Adventures of Superman* and *Batman* of the 1960s, one of the three most influential TV series in history.

Almost immediately, *Buffy* inspired a gaggle of women superhero shows, including *Black Scorpion* (1999) on the Sci-Fi Channel, *Dark Angel* (2000–2002) on Fox, *Sheena* (2000–2002) in syndication, and the dreadful *Birds of Prey* on the WB, *Buffy*'s former network.

Probably the best of the post–*Buffy* pack was *Witchblade*, a TNT original production that ran for two seasons and featured actress Yancy Butler as a cop "chosen" to wield a mystical weapon known as the Witchblade. All of these series proved that women could be as effective as men in fighting bad guys, and in many cases, more fun to watch.

"Men like seeing women in black leather," *Destinies* host Margolin notes of the female superheroes. "People like to hear women talk about sex and make jokes while they kick ass. There's undeniably an appeal to that. But these shows have succeeded, I think, because of more realistic dialogue. They've sort of imprinted the *Sex and the City* mentality on the superhero show."

Buffy the Vampire Slayer was one of the

longest running superhero shows ever, and with good reason. The title character is one part of the past (her name, like Jaime in the '70s, is *Summers*) and one part of the future. But she is all fun, and innately heroic. Her constant battle to maintain a normal life and normal relationships in an abnormal profession makes her the most interesting TV superhero character since *Batman* first appeared on the scene.

Renaissance and "Re-imagination"— Superheroes Triumphant (1999–2003)

As the millennium changed, superhero fans again began searching for the future, for the next relevant permutation of the popular superhero myth. The old heroes (like Superman and Batman) were still quite popular, but many of these characters needed facelifts after nearly three-quarters of a century fighting criminals. The "dawn of the woman" faded to twilight with the almost simultaneous cancellations of *Dark Angel, Sheena* and *Witchblade,* and so the era of "re-imagination" and renaissance officially began.

The term "re-imagination" probably first entered the pop culture lexicon in 2001 as Tim Burton promoted his big summer release *Planet of the Apes.* His version was not a remake of the popular 1968 *Apes* film starring Charlton Heston, the director insisted, nor a new adaptation of the classic Pierre Boulle novel. Instead, it was a "re-imagining" of the *Planet of the Apes* concept in general, picking and choosing elements from various previous installments in novel, movie and TV form.

As one might expect, "re-imagination" very shortly became the buzz word *du jour* in Hollywood, a euphemism used when a contemporary artist imposed his/her "unique" views/ideas on a new version of an older, well established or classic production. Very

soon, there was a re-imagination of the early days of *Star Trek,* called *Enterprise* (2001–). Then writer Ron Moore began work on a "re-imagination" of *Battlestar Galactica* (1978) for the Sci-Fi Channel. In it, Captain Apollo hated his father and was renamed Lee(?), Starbuck was a girl, Cylons were humanoid, and the central metaphor was not Pearl Harbor but September 11.

In the world of superheroes, *Alias* creator J.J. Abrams wrote a screenplay "re-imagining" the mythos of Superman for a new Man of Steel origin movie. Abrams' script, once scheduled to be directed by Brett Ratner (*Red Dragon* [2002]) was allegedly to feature a Kryptonian Lex Luthor, *Matrix*-style fight scenes, a gay Jimmy Olsen and the survival of the planet Krypton after Kal-El's sudden departure. If produced as written, this "re-imagination" of Superman would toss out seventy years of precedent and established character lore. In other words, it is a slap in the face to the faithful fans (as was the *Galactica* work).

What began this trend? Likely it was a 1999 release entitled *The Matrix.* The story of a black-leather garbed human messiah, Neo (Keanu Reeves), fighting a virtual reality society and its mechanical custodians, *The Matrix* was revolutionary, a "re-imagination," if you will, of movie visuals in general. "But for *Matrix,* I don't think there would have been an *X-Men. Matrix* helped make comic-book superheroes hip. The breakthrough there was that they showed you don't need the spandex," says *Batman* movie producer Michael Uslan.[5]

For years, people had heard the phrase that Superman was faster than a speeding bullet. *The Matrix,* for the first time in film history, effectively dramatized what this phrase could mean. Neo, by breaking free of the confines of his virtual reality prison, was able to dodge bullets. Slow motion, computer graphics, and animated bullet trails (like mini-tornado corkscrews), were used in a new way to show audiences something

Adaptation X-tasy. From left to right: Wolverine (Hugh Jackman), Cyclops (James Marsden), Professor Xavier (Patrick Stewart), Storm (Halle Berry) and Jane Grey (Famke Janssen) form a dramatic team in Bryan Singer's serious-minded *X-Men* (2000).

they'd never seen before: believable-seeming superpowers. Neo could not fly, at least until the film's climax, but he could jump, hover in mid-air, wrangle helicopters and perform other incredible deeds in jaw-dropping fashion. The special effects advances of *The Matrix* meant that Superman, Spider-Man and other super-powered folk could suddenly appear more real than ever, and the floodgates opened.

Some re-imaginations seemed less harmful or radical than others. Bryan Singer's *X-Men* (2000) would indeed probably qualify as an early and mild re-imagination, even if nobody used that term in regards to it. Importantly, it suited the mutant team in *Matrix*-like black leather, rather than in the yellow spandex of the comic.

M. Night Shyamalan's *Unbreakable* (2000) re-imagined the whole superhero movie into a more kitchen-sink, dramatic style, offering plausible and innovative rationales behind the existence of superheroes in contemporary society.

The most successful "re-imagination" of a long-standing mythos arrived in the fall of 2001, entitled *Smallville*. This was a WB Network series about Clark Kent as a youth, a.k.a. Superboy, but with a very different focus than previous *Superboy* efforts. Here Clark never donned a costume or tights, could not fly, and did not even wear eyeglasses to conceal his identity. When his spaceship crashed in Smallville, it also brought along a storm of Kryptonite meteors (or "meteor rocks" as they were known on the program). These rocks granted many Smallville denizens super powers too, thus granting the *Superboy* legend a ready-made cadre of freaks and villains for Clark and his high school buddies to investigate.

These misbehaving mutants, rejects from *The X-Files* (1993–2002), could control insects, suck the youth out of unsuspecting victims, or even spontaneously start fires. Following *Buffy the Vampire Slayer*'s lead, the new Clark Kent was concerned not with gangsters, crooks, jewel thieves or even megalomaniacs, but with super-powered creatures beyond human pale.

Perhaps more interestingly, *Smallville*, a prequel to Superman's adventures in Metropolis, posited a close and trusting friendship between Clark and Lex Luthor (Michael Rosenbaum), a character some day destined to represent pure evil. These changes were all drastic, and yet in the case of *Smallville* the "re-imagination" seemed to work just fine, in no small part because the Superboy mythos has often been contradictory. Did Clark reside on Earth alone, or with a super dog named Krypto? When did he meet Lex? How did Lex lose his hair? Was he born bald, or did Clark cause a chemical accident in the lab that rendered him hairless? These questions were issues before *Smallville* premiered, so many enthusiasts of the character welcomed the series as canon.

Other series have not been so lucky. *Birds of Prey* (2002–03) re-cast Batman as a dead-beat Dad that abandoned his own daughter, Helena Kyle (Ashley Scott). Worse, it dismissed his entire crime-fighting career as an urban legend that most people either did not remember or knew nothing about. Again, there were no "common" criminals to combat, just super-powered "meta-humans," another variation on demons (*Buffy*), meteor freaks (*Smallville*) and mutants (*Dark Angel*). These drastic and ill-considered changes were simply too insulting a "re-imagination," and the series lost viewers faster than a speeding bullet.

On the horizon, more radical "re-imaginations" loom. The USA Network hopes to revive Jaime Sommers, *The Bionic Woman*, in the new centruy, this time without Steve Austin. She will no longer be a tennis pro, but a TV news producer.

Early glimpses of Ang Lee's *The Hulk* feature film indicated a new origin for that character. Ironically, Marvel's comic book origin has yet to be used in live-action film

or television, despite a popular series and the new movie.

Despite frequently lackluster re-inventions of old heroes, the new millennium also promises something positive: Superheroes Triumphant. *Spider-Man* (2002) rocked the box office, and *Daredevil* (2003), *The Hulk* (2003) and *The League of Extraordinary Gentleman* (2003) were all promised in fast succession, with a slew of other properties, including *The Fantastic Four*, Guillermo Del Toro's *Hellboy*, and *Spider-Man 2: The Amazing Spider-Man*, following in close pursuit.

In the wake of the terrible attacks of September 11, 2001, superheroes — with their fantastic worlds and sterling morals — helped soothe a mourning nation at war, much as those serials did in the 1940s. Perhaps America has come full circle.

"Fireman and policeman are heroes without costumes, no question about it," Margolin reflects on the terror attacks and the way they changed perceptions of superheroes. "Uniforms certainly, but not costumes. So you take that idea to an extreme and you have a guy that looks like us, in a plaid shirt and jeans, but he can see through walls, or run really fast, or lift a car. It makes the superhero more relatable than a guy ready to fight for 'truth, justice and the American way.'"

So we go back to the past in one sense, facing a global war. But in another sense, the world of superheroes moves forward, becoming more realistic while retaining the fantastic qualities that enabled so many of DC's and Marvel's characters to survive for so long.

In a dangerous and uncertain world, America can always count on Superman, Batman, Buffy the Vampire Slayer, Spider-Man, and other strange visitors from the world of comics, TV and film to walk beside us — at least in our entertainment and fondest wishes. In 2003, as one source reported, more than 200 superhero projects

The Boy of Steel reimagined: Clark Kent (Tom Welling) rescues the town jock, Whitney (Eric Johnson), in an episode from the WB's *Smallville*.

were waiting in the wings,[6] just gearing up to fly.

Looking at the history of superheroes in broad strokes, it is interesting to note the overall shape of their evolution. Superheroes went from being iconic, ideal-bearing national heroes (the 1940s and 1950s) to clowns (the 1960s). Then they became reflections of a simpler age (1970s), at least until morphing into dark, angst-ridden, revenge-hungry vigilantes (the 1980s). Next they transformed into demon-baiting women (1990s) before becoming ultra-realistic, almost inconspicuous "regular joes" (with the advent of *Unbreakable, Smallville, Spider-Man* and other 21st century productions). Does this trend mean that patriotic standard bearers are relics, and that our future superheroes will be more flawed, more human, more like us than ever before?

Only time will tell.

A Cartoon (and Kid-Vid) Nation

It is appropriate to end this thumbnail history of the superhero mythology on television and film with a brief notation on animated productions and Saturday morning children's programming. Unlike most live-action productions, animated series have almost universally, at least before the early 1990s, been targeted at children. This means that even as superheroes transformed into angst-ridden vigilantes in the 1980s, superheroes in animation remained positive and upbeat, maintaining their position as role models.

The 1960s brought adaptations of Superman, Batman, Aquaman, and The Fantastic Four, usually from Filmation Studios or Hanna Barbera. In the 1970s, Saturday morning TV was considered an important revenue source for networks, and became, for children, prime Superhero time. The 1970s introduced an animated legend to the world, *The Super Friends* (from Hanna Barbera), a "team" featuring popular DC heroes working in tandem from the Hall of Justice to fight evil, personified in later years by Lex Luthor's Legion of Doom.

The Super Friends were teachers too, providing lessons for the less experienced among their number, Marvin and Wendy, and later the shape-shifting Wonder Twins. The 1970s were also the heyday of two companies that produced exemplary, live-action Saturday morning programs. Sid and Marty Krofft, creators of *Land of the Lost* (1974–1976), introduced the world to *ElectraWoman and DynaGirl* in 1976–77, two super-powered lasses that were the female equivalent of Batman and Robin.

Lou Scheimer and Norm Prescott, shepherding Filmation, brought the world a live-action version of Captain Marvel in *Shazam* (1974–77), and then introduced his female counterpart, Isis, in 1975. All these characters taught children valuable moral lessons. If anything, in brief half-hour form and with simplistic plotting, these shows evoked memories of the 1940s superhero serials.

In the 1980s and 1990s, even the darkest of characters came to animation, and saw their edges blunted. In live action, *RoboCop* was a very violent franchise. In 1988, before the sequel even arrived in theaters, the cyborg became a cartoon superhero starring in his own animated series. Likewise, in 1990 Fox aired a brief animated mini-series version of Swamp Thing, another "adult" character re-imagined and softened for the eyes of children.

But everything changed in the world of animation in 1992, when *Batman: The Animated Series* premiered on the Fox Network. Voiced by A-list stars, written by comic book writers of the highest caliber, the series was conceived as an adult rendering of the character. There was no camp here, thank you. Instead, the visuals resembled the popular Max Fleischer Superman cartoons of the 1940s, and each half-hour tale included some interesting psychological evolution for the Dark Knight.

Fans and casual TV watchers loved the series, which spawned a renaissance in superhero animation, including a similarly mature *Superman* (1996), an updating of the Batman legend called *Batman Beyond* (1999), and an adult version of the Super Friends called *The Justice League of America* (2001). HBO's award-winning *Spawn* (1998) animated series, aired at night on the premium cable station, was aimed squarely at adults, with the sex and violence quotient raised considerably.

This new generation of animated series proved that cartoons need not be aimed at children, and that adult audiences would stay tuned if the writing was good enough. For the most part, the writing has been more than good enough (thanks to scribes like Bruce Timm, Rich Fogel and Larry Brody), and no doubt further productions of this caliber will arrive in years to come.

Part II
THE ENCYCLOPEDIA

The encyclopedia entries are arranged alphabetically. Each entry begins with a superhero's name (or, in a few cases, the name of the film or television show in which the character appeared). Next comes a detailed history of the character that discusses comic book origins (if applicable) and the context which gave rise to the pertinent production, with a brief discussion of the merits of the production. If there are multiple representations of the character in film, on television and in animation, these are all discussed within the primary text/entry, paragraph by paragraph. Some matters that are also discussed in the entries include a tallying of super powers, a look at villains, and notable episodes or franchise entries.

Following the text section, there is a more specific breakdown of detailed production information, notes from critics, information on cast and crew, episode guides or lists for TV series, and synopses for films. Following this information is a cast and credits list for animated programs if they exist for that character.

The Amazing Spider-Man

In the year 2002, Peter Parker's arachnid alter ego reigned as king of all superheroes and the box office, thanks in no small part to director Sam Raimi's high-grossing summer blockbuster, *Spider-Man*. But that dominance hasn't always been the case for this particular champion. In fact, Marvel's *Spider-Man* property struggled to reach the silver screen for years, with various directors attached and then unceremoniously detached from the project. *Texas Chain Saw Massacre* cult figure Tobe Hooper (for Cannon and Golan and Globus in the late '80s), King of the World James Cameron, and master of darkness David Fincher were all assigned (or nearly assigned) to helm a film adaptation during the last two decades.

Few fans remember that before all the movie talk and the hype surrounding production on the Raimi picture there was a short-lived, and rather bland, live-action TV series in the 1970s.

The legend of Spider-Man goes all the way back to the year 1962 and creators Stan Lee, Steve Ditko and Jack Kirby. This brain trust introduced the world to young Peter Parker, your typical American teenager who unexpectedly developed "spider powers" when bitten by a radioactive arachnid in *Amazing Fantasy Magazine*, issue 15. This unusual accident granted Peter "tingling" spider-senses, the ability to detect danger nearby. Developing the traits of a spider, Peter could also climb walls and dangle high above the city from his (synthetic) webs.

Within a year of the first issue, young

Peter Parker had his own Marvel title, *The Amazing Spider-Man*, and has been living comfortably there ever since, for forty years. The main factor differentiating Spider-Man from more established heroes like Batman or Superman was immediately obvious to the youth culture: *age*. "Superman and Batman were father-figure types, so much so they had teenage sidekicks. Spider-Man was a peer," explained the editor-in-chief at Marvel, Joe Quesada.[1] And that means one thing: teenage problems.

Another difference was professional. Parker was too young and inexperienced to be a full-fledged, confident professional like ace reporter Clark Kent. Despite his brilliant, inventive mind, he was also ensconced in the lower-middle class, which meant not much money on hand to fund his crime-fighting ventures, unlike millionaire Bruce Wayne. In fact, Parker lived with his Aunt May and Uncle Ben in a modest home, and learned about responsibility the hard way when Ben — a kindly, old father figure — was violently murdered. With Ben gone, Parker not only had to care for himself but the elderly (and often hospitalized) Aunt May.

In other startling departures from traditional comic book lore, Peter dealt with a universe of shifting relationships. His nemesis, the Green Goblin (a character introduced in 1964, in the fourteenth issue of the comic), killed Peter's first true love, the tragic Gwen Stacy. Worse, Peter felt to blame for her death.

There were other dramatic reversals of fate too. Peter's friend, Harry Osborn (misguided son of the first Green Goblin), became a junkie and switched allegiances, becoming a new Green Goblin to threaten Spidey. On his job at *The Daily Bugle* (as a freelance photographer), Parker learned that heroes don't always receive universal acclaim. The editor of the paper, J. Jonah Jameson, was no fawning Perry White. He vehemently hated Spider-Man and saw him as a menace to society. He was actually the flip side of the old, kindly (if curmudgeonly) Perry White character, a comic book archetype. Here, the unsolicited help of a superhero was anything but welcome.

In other words, life was neither static nor predictable in the *Spider-Man* universe. Friends and loved ones died, characters changed allegiances, and even Spider-Man himself changed over the years — donning a special new black spider suit for a time (later revealed as an extraterrestrial parasite…) before returning to his familiar blue, red and black uniform.

There was another character inversion too, as author and comic book fan William Latham (*Mary's Monster, Space: 1999 Resurrection*) relates: "The Spider-Man/Peter Parker characterization is classically compared to the Bruce Wayne/Batman and Clark Kent/Superman persona, where the hero is the real self, the secret identity the 'character' portrayed for the world. Here, Peter Parker is the real deal and Spider-Man the 'character.' As a message to young kids on how to live, Spider-Man offers a unique perspective — when you use your powers, other sides of yourself can emerge."

Popular from the get-go, the Spider-Man property first came to television in 1967 in a very cheap and limited cartoon format. Grantray Lawrence Animation, with Stan Lee working as a story and art consultant, produced *The Amazing Spider-Man*. This half-hour foray into adventure featured Peter Parker and the lovely Betty Brand of *The Daily Bugle* (just two "typical teenagers," according to Jameson) as they constantly ran into trouble while on assignment for the newspaper. They clashed with a variety of villains, including Doctor Octopus, Sub-Zero, Green Goblin, the Rhino, the Sandman and Mysterio, in episodes like "The Power of Dr. Octopus" and "Sub-Zero for Spidey." Sometimes the heroes battled more than one nemesis per show, making Spidey's life especially tough.

The cartoon featured a jazzy musical score, was faithful in design to the beloved comic, and boasted a catchy theme song, courtesy of composer Bob Harris and lyricist Paul Francis Webster, that no one could avoid humming or whistling for days after a viewing.

Then Spider-Man appeared in an even stranger venue. *The Electric Company* was an educational program that aired on PBS stations across America from 1971 to 1976. It was like *Sesame Street* for older children, intended to help kids develop their reading skills. From 1974 to 1976, Spider-Man appeared on *The Electric Company* in a series of five-minute sketches entitled *The Adventures of Spidey*. Actor Danny Segren portrayed the costumed hero, a character who never spoke but whose thoughts were given life in cartoon "balloons" right out of the comics. The character was never seen out of costume, in his real identity of Peter Parker, but then, at such brief running time, there was little chance for character depth.

Featuring another great theme song, this one written by Gary William Friedman ("*Spider-Man, where are you coming from....*"), *The Adventures of Spidey* very soon became the most popular and memorable of *The Electric Company* skits. During these adventures, Spider-Man would often clash with villains such as Morgan Freeman's Count Dracula, and learn a moral, grammatical and spelling "lesson" that had something to do with *The Electric Company*'s theme of the episode.

Then, a full ten years after the premiere of the *Spider-Man* cartoon, the costumed hero was resurrected for a short-lived, live-action, primetime TV series. Airing on CBS Wednesday nights at 8:00 P.M. (which pitted it against the ABC powerhouse family drama *Eight Is Enough*), *The Amazing Spider-Man* featured Nicholas Hammond as Peter Parker, Robert F. Simon as grouchy J. Jonah Jameson, and Irene Tedrow as kindly old Aunt May. The series diverged from comic book lore in both concept and design, and featured no amazing super-villains whatsoever.

Instead, it was part of the 1970s backlash against the campy 1960s *Batman* series. Suddenly, common villains were burglars and thieves ("The Con Caper," "Photo Finish," "The Chinese Web"), spies ("A Matter of State"), kidnappers ("Escort to Danger"), evil scientists ("Spider-Man," "Night of the Clones," "Wolfpack") or terrorists ("The Deadly Dust," "The Captive Tower"), and they wore no spectacular costumes or get-ups. Not one of the bunch seemed a real match for the web-slinging, wall-climbing Spider-Man.

The Spider-Man costume also underwent substantial change for the TV series. The hero was given a boxy and unwieldy metallic belt (like Batman's utility belt) and a wrist bracelet. In general, the bracelet and the belt took away from the sleek look of the classic, streamlined costume, and the costume's "eyes" seemed a little inappropriate too, as though reflective, oversized ski goggles had been inserted inside the costume. All of these touches bulked up a costume that should have appeared light and form fitting, an homage to the athletic male form.

Ratings for the series were generally weak after erratic scheduling of the first season. CBS cancelled the *Spider-Man* TV series quickly, and released into syndication seven so-called *Spider-Man* "movies"—actually no more than compilations of the televised episodes. By the late 1970s, many Marvel characters, like Spider-Man, had failed to find an audience, including Captain America and Doctor Strange, with only *The Incredible Hulk* surviving until the 1980s.

Spider-Man returned to television in cartoon format in 1982 in *Spider-Man and His Amazing Friends*. Operating out of an apartment that could turn into a headquarters/office (and which featured a poster of the Incredible Hulk on the wall), Spider-Man fought crime with two new heroes,

A publicity shot from the 1978 TV series *The Amazing Spider-Man*. Up front is Nicholas Hammond, the young Peter Parker. Flanking him, from left to right are Ellen Bry as Julie Mason, Robert F. Simon as J. Jonah Jameson and Chip Fields as Rita Conway. The web-slinger himself (replete with clunky belt) climbs the web.

Iceman and the female Fire-Star. Some episodes of the series ("A Fire-Star Is Born") featured crossovers with the X-Men, including Cyclops, Storm and Wolverine.

A third *Spider-Man* cartoon series fol-

lowed in 1992, this one executive produced by Avi Arad and Stan Lee. It was more faithful to the comic than previous ventures, with multi-track, multi-episode story arcs, again including crossovers with other Marvel characters, such as the X-Men. Finally, a fourth animated series was announced following the success of Sam Raimi's motion picture in 2002. It aired on MTV in 2003.

From approximately 1985 onward, Marvel hoped to shepherd their itsy-bitsy spider hero to the silver screen. After many false starts, different drafts, and contradictory announcements about directing assignments, the *Spider-Man* movie went into production in 2000 with *Evil Dead* (1982) and *Darkman* (2002) director Sam Raimi at the helm. Raimi selected young Tobey Maguire, an outstanding dramatic and serious young actor seen in *Deconstructing Harry* (1997), *The Ice Storm* (1997) and *The Cider House Rules* (1999), to play diffident Peter Parker.

Twenty-six years old, Maguire brought home a paycheck of four million dollars[2] and exercised six days a week to get in shape for the role.[3] The effort was worth it: he was physically convincing as the muscle-bound but very human Parker.

Cast opposite Maguire was Kirsten Dunst (*The Crow: Salvation* [1999]) as Mary Jane Watson, the girl of Spidey's dreams. And, emoting from inside a rigid green suit of armor, a revisionist get-up not based on comic book lore, was Willem Dafoe as the film's villain, the Green Goblin.

With *Spider-Man* in production, fans began to anticipate the arrival of the big-budget movie. Even before the film was released in 2002, some fans complained about it on the Internet. One major bone of contention was Raimi's decision to leave in a detail from a previous screenplay draft written by James Cameron. His Spider-Man boasted organic web spinners, while in the comic book series the webs were generated from a device that Parker created. Raimi reportedly felt that it was better to make the webs part of Parker's unusual powers than explain that an average teenager had come up with a miraculous invention that no one in the world could duplicate.

"Having webs come out of your body makes the character more like you and me," opined genre expert Howard Margolin. "It makes the movie more mainstream. After all, if he [Parker] could invent that web shooter, why was he so poor?" Why not just sell the adhesive to the police or 3M? If the web is produced out of Peter's own body, that question of believability is eliminated. If you look at this from a cinematic and logical point of view, the decision probably represented an improvement over the comic."

But, as strange as it sounds, this change was the subject of a major controversy, with many fans complaining that Raimi was not honoring the legacy of the character. This debate proved just how much enthusiasm and interest there was for a *Spider-Man* movie, if done right, and when the film was released on May 3, 2002, it boasted the biggest opening weekend of all time, generating more than 114 million dollars at the box office. The film was successful (for the most part) with critics as well, though some (including Roger Ebert) found the computer generated imagery used to depict Spidey's flights through New York City somewhat wanting.

By and large, however, fans adored the film, and it was announced that Raimi, Maguire and Dunst were all signed to a sequel, scheduled for release in summer 2004. The villain of that piece: Otto Octavius, Doctor Octopus (a character first seen in the comics in 1963). The title: *The Amazing Spider-Man!*

Looking at *Spider-Man* some half-a-year after its release, beyond the hype and criticism, it is not hard to discern that director Sam Raimi has contributed one of the best efforts in the genre since 1978's *Superman: The Movie*. Like that classic Donner picture, *Spider-Man* focuses squarely on its hero, telling the story of a boy that changes from callow, self-obsessed youth to responsible adult. A metaphor for adolescence and the impact of puberty, which changes one's body (not unlike a radioactive spider-bite), the film is probably better remembered for its notation that with "great power comes great responsibility."

Still, what makes *Spider-Man* special is its personal touch: the heartfelt romance between Peter and Mary Jane, the bittersweet Ben and Peter relationship, and even the father-son "triangle" involving Harry, Norman and Peter. These distinctly human touches make the more unbelievable moments (like Spidey's jaunts above the city) much more believable because the audience is deeply invested in the character.

So often in superhero films, over-the-top villains steal center stage, sucking all the air out of the theater and leaving no room for the hero. This has been the case in virtually every *Batman* film yet produced. Other superhero films have suffered by appearing too crowded, from introducing too many characters (*Batman Returns* and *X-Men* both leap to mind). For such an enormous blockbuster, *Spider-Man* is refreshingly modest in its narrative aspirations. It tells the story of a kid, his girlfriend, and his "maturation" into a responsible member of the community. This is one genre movie that puts the "hero" back in the superhero, and eschews the schizophrenia, sadism and fetishism of "the Dark Age."

The Amazing Spider-Man (1967)
ANIMATED SERIES

"The cartoon series had very effective music, from its bold opening song to its regular use of jazzy accompaniments and rock music backgrounds. A lot of the classic Spidey villains visited the cartoon series, from Electro to Doctor Octopus to the Green Goblin, with some classic appearances by the Lizard, the Rhino, the Sandman, and the Scorpion. Mysterio really seemed a natural for the cartoon series and those were particularly memorable episodes, even though Mysterio wasn't horribly exciting in the comic."
— William Latham, author of *Mary's Monster, Space: 1999 Resurrection.*

VOICE TALENTS: Bernard Cowan, Paul Kligman, Paul Soles, Peg Dixon.

CREDITS: *Produced by:* Grantray Lawrence Animation. *Executive Producer:* Robert L. Lawrence. *Producer:* Ray Patterson. *Series Direction:* Grant Simmons, Clyde Geronimi, Sid Marcus. *Story Supervisor:* June Patterson. *Writers:* Bill Danch, Al Bertino, Dick Robbins, Dic Cassarino, Phil Babet. *Spider-Man Theme Music:* Bob Harris. *Lyrics:* Paul Francis Webster. *Musical Score:* Ray Ellis. *Animation:* Hal Ambro, Bob Bentley, Dan Bassie, George Cannata, Herman Cohen, Howard Ellis, Bill Hous, Tom McDonald, Chic Otterstrom, Don Schloat, Ralph Summerville, Reuben Timmins, Harvey Toombs, Kay Wright. *Background:* Curt Parkins, Dick Thomas, Bill Butler, Mike Kawaguchi. *Layout:* Ray Aragon, Joe Asturino, Herb Hazelton, Jim Mueller, C.L. Hartman, John Ewing, Joel Sibel. *Production Supervisor:* Robert "Tiger" West. *Unit Production Manager:* Gene Meyers. *Editors:* Hank Gotzenberg, Bryce Corso. *Story and Art Consultants:* Smilin' Stan Lee, Jazzy John Romita. A Krantz Films Release.

The Amazing Spider-Man (1977–1979)
LIVE-ACTION SERIES

"Hammond was a little too grown-up for the part, a little too much the good looking actor one would expect in a 1970s television series. The special effects were almost painful, the costume didn't quite work, and the lack of any of the classic rogues gallery of villains all combined to pretty much make this series dead on arrival. If you think about it, however, given the technology of the time, TV and movies themselves weren't quite ready for Spider-Man and it's a

probably a good thing the character was left alone."
— William Latham, author of *Mary's Monster* and *Space: 1999 — Resurrection*.

"Hammond's performance was no more than adequate, and while his costume looked authentic, the neuroses which made him a believable and sympathetic character in the comics were glossed over with hypochondriac mumbo-jumbo, ho-hum plots, and lots of irrelevant action. The walking-up-wall special effects were nicely done, but the webbing which Spider-Man shoots from his gloves was awful."
— Douglas Menville and R. Reginald. *Futurevisions: The New Golden Age of the Science Fiction Film*. A Greenbriar Book, New Castle Publishing Company, 1985, pages 43–45.

"In place of the neurosis that lay at the center of the comic-book character, Swackhamer and writer Boretz have substituted the simple problem of Peter Parker/Spider-Man being, like so many superheroes of the past, sought after by the police as a suspicious character."
— Phil Hardy, *The Film Encyclopedia: Science Fiction*. William and Morrow Company, Inc., 1984, page 336.

CAST: Nicholas Hammond (Peter Parker/ Spider-Man); Robert F. Simon (J. Jonah Jameson); Chip Fields (Rita); Irene Tedrow (Aunt May). FIRST SEASON ONLY: Michael Pataki (Captain Barbera). SECOND SEASON ONLY: Ellen Bry (Julie Masters).

CREW: *Based on a Character Created by:* Stan Lee. *Executive Producer:* Charles Fries. *Producer:* Edward J. Montagne. *Music:* Stu Phillips (Season One), Dana Kaproff (Season Two); *Produced by:* Lionel E. Siegal, Arnold F. Turner, Robert Jones and Ron Satloff. *Script Consultant:* Stan Lee. *Art Director:* James Hulsey. *Theme Music:* Johnnie Spence.

1. "Spider-Man" (Series pilot, aired as TV movie, 90 minutes) Written by: Alvin Boretz. Directed by: E.W. Swackhamer. Airdate: April 19, 1977.

Working in a laboratory, a young and unassuming fellow named Peter Parker undergoes a transformation after being bitten by a radioactive spider. He is imbued with new powers (like the ability to climb walls) and senses (spider senses, which alert him to danger). While Parker uses these newfound powers to get a job as a photographer at a big city newspaper, a strange new criminal also surfaces in the city, demanding $50 million. Peter becomes a costumed crime-fighter called Spider-Man to stop the criminal, a scientist that has developed a form of brain washing/mind-control that causes innocent people to commit suicide. Before the final battle is waged, Peter himself comes under the spell of the villain, with danger all around...

GUEST CAST: David White (J. Jonah Jameson); Thayer David (Edward Byron); Robert Hastings (Monahan); Mary Ann Kasica (Aunt May); Lisa Eilbacher (Judy Tyler); Ivor Francis (Professor Tyler); Hilly Hicks, Barry Cutler, Len Lesser, Jim Storm, Ivan Bonnar, Norman Rice, Harry Cesar, George Cooper, Roy West, James E. Brodhead, Carmelita Pope, Kathryn Reynolds, Robert Snively, Ron Gilbert, Larry Anderson.

SEASON ONE (SPRING 1978)

2. "Deadly Dust" (two hours) Written by: Robert Janes. Directed by: Ron Satloff. Airdates: April 5 and 12, 1978.

Spider-Man has become a local celebrity, and Peter Parker is the only photographer who has managed to take photographs of the hero (for *The Daily Bugle* and grouchy editor J. Jonah Jameson). A beautiful reporter from Florida comes to the city to team up with Peter to get the "scoop" on the costumed crime-fighter, but Peter has bigger problems to contend with. At his university, a deadly material that could be used in an atomic bomb has been brought on campus by an arrogant professor. In protest, Peter's buddies at school plan to steal the deadly material and build a bomb, just to make a point, totally unaware that there is a villain in the area who would be very interested in getting his hands on an atomic bomb...

GUEST CAST: Joanna Cameron (Gale); Robert Alda (White); Randy Powell (Gregg); Simon Scott (Dr. Baylor); Anne Bloom (Carla);

Steven A. Anderson (Ted); Herbert S. Braha, Emil Farkas, Richard Kyker, Sid Clute, Leigh Kavanaugh, Ron Hajek, David Somerville, Gail Jensen, Walt Davis, Barbara Sanders, Jerry Martin.

3. "The Curse of Rava" Written by: Dick Nelson, Robert Janes. Directed by: Michael Caffey. Airdate: April 19, 1978.

Peter Parker takes photographs of a statue of Rava, an ancient South American God, at a local museum for an exhibit financed by J. Jonah Jameson. Unfortunately, many people believe that the god Rava is a dangerous one that can kill all those who look upon him. While true believers complain about the display, non-believers are struck down by the statue —*which seems to come to life*— for their desecration of the God. Before long, it's up to Spider-Man to ferret out the truth of this odd situation.

GUEST CAST: Theodore Bikel (Mandak); Adrienne LaRussa (Trina); Byron Webster, David Ralphe.

4. "Night of the Clones" Written by: John W. Bloch. Directed by: Fernando Lamas. Airdate: April 26, 1978.

A disgruntled scientist, angry at being overlooked for a prestigious award several years running, uses his super-fast, advanced cloning process to duplicate himself. Unfortunately, his vicious clone sets out to kill all the judges on the selection committee, and arranges a series of accidents. Before long, an unsuspecting Peter Parker is also cloned by this dangerous new process, resulting in a clash between friendly neighborhood spider-men.

GUEST CAST: Morgan Fairchild (Lisa Benson); Lloyd Bochner (Dr. Moon); Rick Traeger (Dr. Reichman).

5. "Escort to Danger" Written by: Duke Sandefur. Directed by: Dennis Donnelly. Airdate: May 3, 1978.

Peter is assigned to take pictures of visiting dignitaries, President Calderone and his lovely daughter Maria. Unfortunately, a kidnapper is after Maria, hoping to use her as a political tool against her father in their home country, and Spider-Man must save the day.

GUEST CAST: Alejandro Rey (President Calderone); Barbara Luna (Lisa Alverez); Madeline Stowe (Maria Calderone); Harold Sakata (Matsu); Michael Marsellos, Lachelle Price, Bob Minor.

SECOND SEASON (1978-1979)

6. "The Captive Tower" Written by: Gregory S. Dinallo. Story by: Bruce Kalish and Philip John Taylor. Directed by: Cliff Bole. Airdate: September 5, 1978.

Peter finds himself attracted to a competing journalist, Julie Masters, and they are both on hand for the dedication of a new skyscraper in the city. Unfortunately, terrorists are moving behind the scenes to take over the building and hold the dedication guests hostage. Taken captive, Peter realizes that Spider-Man is the only person who can save Julie and the others from the violent terrorists.

GUEST CAST: David Sheiner (Forster); Todd Susman (Farnum); Fred Lerner, Barry Cutler, Warren Vanders, Ed Sancho-Bonet.

7. "A Matter of State" Written by: Howard Dimsdale. Directed by: Larry Stewart. Airdate: September 12, 1978.

A Federal employee carrying classified documents is attacked at the city airport, necessitating a lock-down of the facility, cloaked as a "quarantine." Before long, rivals Julie and Peter are on the scene to get photographs, but Julie's curiosity leads to danger: she has inadvertently snapped photos of the bad guy, an FBI agent! Spider-Man must not only recover the stolen papers, but rescue Julie before she is "eliminated."

GUEST CAST: Nicholas Coster (Andre); John Crawford (Evans); Michael Santiago (Carl); James Victor (Martin), Erik Stern.

8. "The Con Caper" Written by: Gregory S. Dinallo. Story by: Brian McKay. Directed by: Tom Blank. Airdate: November 25, 1978.

A politician named Colbert, who served time for corruption, ends his prison sentence and comes out of jail as a "reformer," hoping to serve the good people of the city again by righting some of the wrongs in the municipal prison system. Peter, Julie and even Jameson are all impressed with the politician's efforts, unaware he has staged a riot in one prison so as to cloak his real plan: a multi-million-dollar robbery of a nearby vault!

GUEST CAST: William Smithers (James Colbert); Ramon Bieri (Cates); Andrew Robinson (Mcteague); Fred Downs.

9. "The Kirkwood Haunting" Written by: Michael Michaelian. Directed by: Don McDougall. Airdate: December 30, 1978.

Jameson asks Peter to look into the recent accidental death of an old-time buddy, and his wife's claims that the dead man is haunting their fabulous house (which she plans to sell, to escape the ghost). Peter heads to the Kirkwood home and learns that there is also a psychic researcher on the scene, looking into the possibility of the haunting, but the truth is not what it seems...

GUEST CAST: Marilyn Mason (Lisa Kirkwood); Peter MacLean (Dr. Polarsky); Paul Carr (Ganz); Peggy McCay, Del Monroe.

10. "Photo Finish" Written by: Howard Dimsdale. Directed by: Tony Ganz. Airdate: February 7, 1979.

Jameson embroils Peter Parker in a police investigation after assigning the young photographer to a case involving a rare and valuable coin collection. The collection is stolen, and one of Peter's photographs may finger the culprit, but Parker is uncertain about the photo, and even more uncertain what it represents, a hesitancy that puts him in direct opposition with the police.

GUEST CAST: Jennifer Billingsley (Mrs. Gray); Charles Haid (Lieutenant); Geoffrey Lewis (Gray); Milt Kogan.

11. "Wolfpack" Written by: Stephen Kandel. Directed by: Joseph Manduke. Airdate: February 21, 1979.

A friend of Peter's is developing a top-secret mind-control drug for a large chemical company, and an accident in the lab proves its efficacy at making men slaves to the will of others. The chemical company, upon learning of the drug's unexpected success, plans to use it for nefarious ends, resulting in an intervention by Spider-Man!

GUEST CAST: Gavan O'Herlihy (David); Wil Selzer (Art); Allan Arbus (Goerge Hansen).

12. "The Chinese Web" (2 hours) Written by: Lionel E. Siegel. Directed by: Don McDougal. Airdate: July 6, 1979.

A Chinese official faces charges of espionage from his own country, and goes to Jameson seeking help in clearing his name. Jameson assigns Peter to the case, unaware that assassins are already on the way to knock off this man, Min Lo Chan. Worse, an American businessman also wants Lo Chan dead because the Chinese official could cost him billions by scuttling a valuable business project.

GUEST CAST: Benson Fong (Min Lo Chan); Rosalind Chao (Emily); Hagan Beggs (Evans); Richard Erdman, Myron Healey, John Milford, Anthony Charnotta, George Cheung, Tony Clark, Ted Danson, Robert Mayo, Suzanne Vale, Zara Brierley, Joel Laykin, Hudson Leung, Michael Chang.

Spider-Man and His Amazing Friends (1982)
ANIMATED SERIES

VOICE TALENTS: Hans Conried, Walker Edmiston, Keye Luke, Annie Lockhart, Jerry Dexter, George Dicenzo, Alan Dinehart, Michael Evans, Al Pann, June Faray, Kathy Garver, Dan Gilvezan, John Haymer, Sally Julian, Dennis Marks, Alan Melvin, Shepard Menkin, John Stephenson, Janet Waldo, Frank Welker, William Woodson, Alan Young.

CREDITS: *Animation Directors:* Gerry Chiniquy, Steve Clark, John Gibbs, Sid Marcus, Bob Richardson, Nelson Shin, Arthur Vitello. *Voice Director:* Alan Dinehart. *Layout:* Bruce Bennett, Norman Cobral, Don Faucett, Neil Galloway, Greg Garcia, Gary Graham, Karl Hepworth, Stuart Heimdall, Elaine Haltrgen, Boyd Kirkland, Debra Pugh, Dave Sharp, Roy Smith, Tom Tholen, Grant Wilson, Roy Wilson, Bob Foster. *Storyboard:* Jan Green, Rick Hoberg, Cullen Houghtaling, Larry Houston, Sherman Labby, Will Meagniot, Dick Sebastian, Bob Schaffer, Don Shepard, Hank Tucker, Warren Tufts. *Music composed and conducted by:* John Douglas. *Supervising Editor:* Robert T. Gillis. *Music Editor:* Joe Siracusa. *Effect Editor:* Jim Blodgett, Richard Gannon. *Production Manager:* Kathy Condon. *Created for TV by:* Stan Lee. *Supervising Director:* Donald L. Jurwich. *Producer:* Dennis Marks. *Executive Producer:* Lee Gunther. Marvel Productions Ltd., a Cadence Company.

Spider-Man (1992)
ANIMATED TV SERIES

CREDITS: *Executive Producers:* Avi Arad and Stan Lee. *Supervising Producer:* Bob Richardson. *Producer and Story Editor:* John Semper. *Voice Director:* Tony Pastor. *Theme Music written and performed by:* Joe Perry. *Art Director:* Dennis Venzelos. *Production Designer:* Vladimir Spaso-jevic. *Character Design:* Dell Barras. *Storyboard Supervisor:* Hank Tucker. *Supervising Director:* Bob Shellhorn. *Supervising Editor:* Richard Allen. *Music Editor:* Mark Ryan. *Writing coordinator:* Virginia Roth. *Producer:* Stanley Liu. Marvel Productions.

Spider-Man (2002)
LIVE-ACTION FILM

"Tobey Maguire is pitch-perfect as the socially retarded Peter Parker, but when he becomes Spider-Man, the film turns to action sequences that zip along like perfunctory cartoons. Not even during Spidey's first experimental outings do we feel that flesh and blood are contending with gravity.... [H]e's as convincing as Mighty Mouse."
— Roger Ebert, *The Chicago Sun-Times*, May 3, 2002, page 1 of 3.

"...[It] may look like an action comic come to life, but its best feature is its romance.... It's that rare cartoon movie in which the villain is less involving than the love story."
— Kenneth Turan, *The Los Angeles Times:* "The Spider and the Fly Girl," May 3, 2002, page 1 of 3.

"With Sam Raimi's selection of Tobey Maguire to play Peter Parker in the 2002 film *Spider-Man*, things started falling into place. The technology was at least ready to make you "believe a man can swing" and the fundamentals of the character, particularly the "with great power comes great responsibility" message were all present in Raimi's film. If there's a complaint to be had with the film, it's a complaint against Hollywood and its own realities. The Gwen Stacy story line was flirted with and incorporated with Mary Jane Watson, and Spidey gets to save the girl this time around. That's just the nature of the box office, and Gwen's death in the comic was a serious downer, even if it added much to the mythos of Spider-Man. It probably would have killed the film, and I suspect only the purists out there would be offended."
— William Latham, author, *Mary's Monster* and *Space: 1999 Resurrection*.

CAST: Tobey Maguire (Spider-Man/Peter Parker); Willem Dafoe (Green Goblin/Norman

Osborn); Kirsten Dunst (Mary Jane); James Franco (Harry Osborn); Cliff Robertson (Ben Parker); Rosemary Harris (May Parker); J.K. Simmons (J. Jonah Jameson); Joe Manganiello (Flash Thompson); Gerry Becker (Maximillian); Bill Nunn (Joseph Robertson); Jack Betts (Henry); Stanley Anderson (General Slocum); Michael Papajohn (Carjacker); Bruce Campbell (Ring Announcer); Tim de Zarn (Phillip).

CREW: Columbia Pictures presents a Marvel Enterprises/Laura Ziskin Production of *Spider-Man. Directed by:* Sam Raimi. *Written by:* David Koepp. *Based on the Marvel Comic by:* Stan Lee and Steve Ditko. *Casting:* Francine Maisler and Lynn Kressler. *Co-Producer:* Grant Curtis. *Music:* Danny Elfman. *Costumes Designed by:* James Acheson. *Visual Effects Design by:* John Dykstra. *Film Editors:* Bob Murawski and Arthur Coburn. *Production Designer:* Neil Spisak. *Director of Photography:* Don Burgess. *Executive Producers:* Avi Arad and Stan Lee. *Produced by:* Laura Ziskin and Ian Bryce. *M.P.A.A. Rating:* PG-13. *Running time:* 121 minutes.

Nerdy high school outcast Peter Parker is bitten by a genetically engineered spider while on a field trip to the Columbia University Science Department. This accident endows Peter, who lives with his elderly Uncle Ben and Aunt May, with new agility, heightened "spider senses" and the ability to spin webbing from his wrist. Undergoing this change, Peter is as interested in courting the love of his life, Mary Jane Watson, and buying a new car as he is in using his gift for the betterment of mankind.

Elsewhere, Norman Osborn, the head of Oscorp, is on the line with the United States government for a failed experiment to develop a new weapons system, a flying suit and "performance enhancing" chemical compound for soldiers. So as not to lose the grant money, Norman tests the formula on himself and becomes the psychotic "Green Goblin." This change is a secret even to Norman, who develops schizophrenia, and his son Harry, Peter's best friend.

When Uncle Ben is killed by a carjacker that Peter could have stopped had he bothered, Parker realizes that with great power comes great responsibility, and so becomes a costumed superhero called Spider-Man. Looking for a job after graduation, Peter becomes a freelance photographer for *The Daily Bugle*, a paper run by the Spider-Man-hating J. Jonah Jameson.

At the same time that Spider-Man becomes a pop culture hero in Manhattan, the board of Oscorp sells out to its competitor, and an angry Norman kills the board members during the World Unity Festival. Spider-Man is on the scene to stop the glider-riding Green Goblin, but must rescue Mary Jane from a dangerous perch rather than follow Green Goblin, who swears they will meet again.

On Thanksgiving, Norman learns that his new nemesis, Spider-Man, is in fact young Peter Parker, and sets out to hurt all of Parker's loved ones after Spidey refuses to join him in his evil ways. The Green Goblin puts Aunt May in the hospital and kidnaps Mary Jane, forcing Spider-Man to take action.

High over New York City, the final confrontation between Green Goblin and Spider-Man results in the death of a family friend and the birth of a mature, responsible superhero, who will never forget the lessons he has learned about the consequences of power.

The Ambiguously Gay Duo

Hmmm. Did TV's do-gooders, Batman and Robin, share more than a *friendly* relationship? Well, they certainly spent a great deal of time in each other's company, and Robin's name was Dick. Humorously, one of the great mysteries involving superheroes over the ages is this very one, and the actors on the 1960s *Batman* series have admitted playing up the "gay" angle of their characters for purposes of humor.

Going further back, Dr. Frederic Wertham's 1954 book *The Seduction of the Innocent* proposed just what Adam West and Burt Ward were so cavalier about a decade later, that tights-wearing Batman and Robin, living together as mentor and ward, were actually a homosexual couple. Oh, and for good measure, Wertham suggested Wonder Woman was a lesbian dominatrix.

Considering this tradition of presumed (or suspected) homosexuality in superherodom, as well as the desire to be complete in coverage, it seems necessary (or at least interesting) to include *The Ambiguously Gay Duo*, an animated superhero team, in this encyclopedia of the superhero ethos in film and TV.

Ace and Gary, *The Ambiguously Gay Duo*, were superheroes that looked as though they would have been at home on the Hanna Barbera 1970s *Super Friends* cartoon. These two were fabulously fit in an Alex Toth kind of way, donned small black eye masks not unlike Robin's, bore late 1970s–style haircuts and even offered unimpressed children safety tips at opportune times, the latter another facet of the educational *Super Friends*.

But there was something a little ... *dif-ferent* about these heroes. They worked out together, were hopelessly square, and well ... could they be ... *gay?*

A spoof of 1960s and 1970s superhero animation programs, *The Ambiguously Gay Duo* was the brainchild of Robert Smigel. His animated shorts appeared between live-action skits on the popular NBC series *Saturday Night Live* from 1996 to 2000 as a gag called *TV Funhouse* (which later moved to Comedy Central).

Ace and Gary drove a phallus-shaped car, fought villains with names like "the Big Head" and "the Queen," and wrestled their opponents in the most suggestive poses, mimicking homosexual bedroom behavior. "They're extremely close in an ambiguous way," the theme song reminded viewers.

The Ambiguously Gay Duo appeared in nine three-minute shorts during their career on *SNL*. The titles of these installments were the stuff of gay innuendo: "It Takes Two to Tango" (September 28, 1996), "Queen of Terror" (November 2, 1996), "Don We Now or Never" (December 14, 1996), "Safety Tips" (April 19, 1997), "Blow Hot, Blow Cold" (November 15, 1997), "A Hard One to Swallow" (May 9, 1998), "Ace and Gary's Fan Club" (November 21, 1998), "AmbiguoBoys" (May 8, 1999) and "Trouble Coming Twice" (May 13, 2000).

Angel

In Joss Whedon's prime-time sequel to the popular *Buffy the Vampire Slayer*, Angel, the 244-year-old vampire with a soul played by David Boreanaz, opened up his own detective agency in seedy, nighttime Los Angeles. His mission: to aid lost souls in the war against evil forces, to "help the helpless," and to finally find his own redemption in the process. "I see *Angel* as the second half of *Buffy*," Joss Whedon noted in an interview with *Cinescape*. "He's sort of a reformed drunk [so-to-speak] fighting his way back to something resembling humanity and helping others do the same."[1]

In *Angel's* 1999 opener on the WB Network, entitled "City of," it also became abundantly clear that Angel, like the Slayer, was nothing less than a postmodern superhero. After dispatching a squad of evil vampires in the pre-title sequence, the hero was depicted walking sullenly down a dark city alleyway, filmed from a menacing low angle. Naturally, he was garbed in a flapping black trench coat (*a cape?*).

Clearly a dark avenger, one that critics have noted is endowed with "Batman-like wryness,"[2] Angel the "lost vampire" embodied all the angst and self-hatred of any self-respecting (or, rather, self-loathing) dark knight. And, in the first season of the series, Angel even operated out of an underground base that had a "real Bat Cave feel," according to his first sidekick, Doyle (Glenn Quinn). "Bats" were a good joke for the series, since vampires have long been associated with the nocturnal predators (and bats also formed the heart of the *Batman* legend). In other episodes, such as "The Ring," Angel was pointedly compared to other superheroes, such as Captain America.

Perhaps more importantly, there was the feeling on the series that Angel, searching for redemption through heroism, could easily make mistakes. He was destined to play a role in a prophesied apocalypse, but as the episode "Blood Money" acknowledged, whether that role was for good or bad was something of a gray area. Like Batman, Angel's dark side could pose a real problem, no matter what his heroic intent. He is of the "flawed" superhero school, not at all the perfect embodiment of goodness and light. In this sense he was a late addition to the "Dark Age" of superhero productions, even though he was, technically, a spin-off from *Buffy the Vampire Slayer*.

In his quest to help the helpless, Angel was aided first and foremost by the unemployed actress Cordelia Chase (Charisma Carpenter), a vain girl from Sunnydale (and *Buffy the Vampire Slayer*). Although she started out on the series as a bitchy, caustic character utilized primarily for comedic relief, by the fourth season Carpenter's Cordelia was a full-fledged superhero too. Mysteriously imbued with the power of prophetic visions, her human DNA was grafted onto demon DNA in the third season, and the result was a kind of "Saint Cordy," *X-Men*–like mutant figure of white light, awesome power, and endless patience (at least in dealing with the emotionally detached Angel).

In the third season finale, called "Tomorrow," the powerful Cordelia, on the verge of declaring her love for Angel, ascended to Heaven only to be trapped there as Season Four commenced in 2002. When she returned, she complicated matters by making love to Angel's rebellious son, Connor, and apparently engineering a sun-squelching apocalypse.

Other sidekicks came and went on *Angel* with alarming frequency, a facet of Joss Whedon's daring, tradition-breaking programs. The sensitive Doyle (the late Glenn Quinn), a half-demon with prophetic visions and a direct line to the deities called the "Powers That Be," died in an early first season episode entitled "Hero," passing on his "vision" legacy to the aforementioned Cordelia.

In the first two seasons, Angel also frequently crossed paths with Kate Lochley (Elizabeth Rohm), a tough-as-nails L.A.P.D. detective that found herself attracted to Angel, but later learned his dark secret. After attempting to commit suicide near the end of the second season, Kate has been M.I.A. on the series, in part because the actress moved to a starring role on NBC's *Law and Order*.

After Doyle's death, another recurring character from *Buffy the Vampire Slayer*'s third season, Wesley Price (Alexis Denisof), joined the Angel Investigations team, only to become an outcast toward the end of the third season when he abducted Angel's newborn son. On *Buffy*, Wesley was a bit of a nerd, but very soon on *Angel* he became a grim-faced fighter, an oracle of wisdom and knowledge.

J. August Richards portrayed the black-skinned vampire killer Gunn from the second season onward. Gunn was a street-smart fighter, one that could challenge Angel's strength in battle. He was a quipping and amusing young character with a chip on his shoulder, but with a soft side too. Gunn even got a girlfriend out of the skinny, brainy Fred (Amy Acker) in the third season. Fred was *Angel*'s resident genius and a character that had been trapped in an alternate dimension for five years.

Lorne, the Host (Andy Hallett), was another sidekick, the green-skinned, horned demon with a heart of gold (and nice singing voice) that eventually teamed up with the squad after his nightclub, Caritas, was destroyed. And, in the third season, Angel's infant son Connor (Vincent Kartheiser) spent time in a Hell dimension, returning as a rebellious teenager just months after his birth! He became a series regular in the fourth season and promised endless grief for the vampire with a soul.

As one would expect of any supernatural superhero program, the villains on *Angel* turned out to be quite fantastic, horrific and memorable. First and foremost among these was the Satanic law firm of Wolfram and Hart, Angel's constant nemesis. Different "faces" of Wolfram and Hart were seen over the years, including Holland Manners, and Lindsey and Gavin Park, but one remained constant and quite welcome throughout: that of actress Stephanie Romanov as the treacherous, endlessly evil Lilah Morgan, a human being more evil than the most demonic of demons. She arranged the torture of Cordelia ("That Vision Thing") attempted repeatedly to steal Angel's son when he was an infant, and regularly hired assassins to kill Angel ("Five by Five"). In one episode, "Carpe Noctem," she revealed a sexier side and nearly let Angel (possessed by another spirit) seduce her.

In the fourth season, Lilah became involved sexually with Wesley, and rumors were that the character was destined for an unpleasant demise before the end of the year.

On *Angel* there were also some crossovers from *Buffy the Vampire Slayer* in the villain department, including the rogue slayer Faith (Eliza Dushku) appearing in a first-season two-part drama, "Five by Five" and "Sanctuary." Even the charming Spike (James Marsters) dropped by to make trouble for Angel for a spell.

A vampiric Bonnie and Clyde couple ("Hearthrob"), a body-hopping senior citizen ("Carpe Noctem"), zombie cops ("The Thin Dead Line"), the vampire hunter Holtz (Keith Szarabajka), Gwen Raiden ("Ground State"), a psycho with a hatred of women ("Billy"), Angel's vampire lover Darla (Julie Benz), and Skilosh demons (creatures that laid the eggs of their young inside human skulls in "Epiphany") counted as the most memorable of the series' rogues.

During *Angel*'s second season, the vampire with a soul (alternately known as a "hunk of hero sandwich" by the Host and "the demon with the face of an angel" by the Watcher Diaries) relocated from an office building basement (his bat cave) to the Hyperion, a grand 1930s-style hotel. Unfortunately, the edifice required an immediate exorcism. Cordelia, meanwhile, lived in an apartment inhabited by a friendly ghost named Dennis.

As a series, *Angel* often dealt with "the aloneness" of the superhero. Angel was slow to emotionally integrate with his team, and for a time during the second season he fired his sidekicks and worked alone to bring down the villainous Darla. He had superstrength, but Angel remained socially inept and impulsive, a fact that often led to problems, as on the occasion he accidentally killed another champion of good in the second season opener, "Judgment."

Angel's only weakness (and a recurring one) was that he had been cursed by gypsies. If he ever experienced one moment of happiness, of true bliss, his soul would disappear and he would revert to his true demonic state as the merciless and monstrous Angelus. Often on the show, "bliss" meant "orgasm," so Angel was unable to engage in

The gang at Angel Investigations in Los Angeles—left to right: the genius Fred (Amy Acker); the "rogue demon hunter," Wesley Pryce (Alexis Denisof); a "hunk of hero sandwich," Angel (David Boreanaz); the girl with the visions, Cordelia Chase (Charisma Carpenter); and the "muscle," Gunn (J. August Richards).

sexual relations with Kate, Buffy, Cordelia, Gwen or any of the other lovelies that frequented the long-lived series. Worse than Kryptonite? You bet.

After a first season that involved mostly stand-alone stories, *Angel* developed a deep and twisted mythology and multiple story arcs in succeeding seasons. In the second season, Angel sought to redeem the woman that had made him a vampire (or, rather, "sired" him), the resurrected Darla. When that attempt failed rather dramatically, Angel went "dark" and set out to kill her.

In the third season, Darla returned to Los Angeles with news that she was pregnant with Angel's son. The season's episodes followed her pregnancy and the return of a nemesis named Holtz, a vampire hunter with a grudge against Angel from the 1700s. Holtz then stole Angel's boy, Connor, and turned him against his real father.

The fourth season, as of this writing, looked like it would concern Wesley's mental disintegration and flirtation with evil, as well as Cordelia's unusual plight, trapped in Heaven. Once she escaped, she found herself caught in a love triangle with father (Angel) and son (Connor). In fighting a terrible villain called "the Beast," Angel would have to willingly give up his soul and revert to demonic, psychotic form, as the powerful and cunning Angelus.

For its first two seasons on the air, the hour-long *Angel* ran on the WB Network on Tuesday nights at 9:00, following *Buffy the Vampire Slayer*. During its second year, many in the industry speculated *Angel* would fall before the heavily hyped James Cameron superhero series starring Jessica Alba called *Dark Angel*, but things did not turn out that way. *Angel* survived, and it was Fox's *Dark Angel* that tucked tail and switched time slots, moving to Friday nights instead. But *Angel* faced a new crisis at the end of its second season.

In a highly publicized move, *Buffy the Vampire Slayer* shifted networks and moved to UPN. This effectively meant that the Whedon spin-off had to stand completely on its own, not as the second half of an established classic, yet stand it did. *Angel* moved to Monday nights at 9:00 following the white-bread family drama *Seventh Heaven*. The ratings remained good, and the third season of *Angel* was the most enjoyable and surprising yet, at least from a creative standpoint.

For its fourth season, *Angel* moved to Sunday nights at 9:00 and went head-to-head with *Alias*, another popular "she hero" series on ABC. When the WB cancelled *Birds of Prey* at the end of 2002, *Angel* made another time switch, moving to Wednesday nights at 9:00 P.M. It was rumored that before the end of the fourth season, stars from *Buffy the Vampire Slayer*, including Alyson Hannigan, would again be allowed to guest star on *Angel*, despite the fact the two series aired on different networks.

Looking at *Angel* in terms of the history of superhero productions, it is interesting to note that Angel offers the most dramatic example yet of a split personality. Angel has a secret identity, like Batman, Superman, Wonder Woman, Spider-Man and the rest. He is do-gooder seeking to make amends but, after just a single mistake, his true nature as a vampire; could emerge, turning him into a soulless, manipulative monster called Angelus. Because of this, Angel is a Jekyll-Hyde figure, like Bruce Banner's Hulk. It would take very little to turn this hero into a really scary villain. The addict metaphor also works. When Angel is on the wagon (no sex; no slurping of human blood), he is a kind, decent being hoping to clear up his past. But when back on the juice, and lacking a soul, he is hell on wheels, capable of anything.

Coming at the end of the "Dark Age" in superhero history, Angel is different in at least one sense from the Crow, Daredevil or his other brethren because he has something they do not: hope. He believes he can reach his goal of becoming human, of becoming "good" and putting his bloody past behind him. It is this need to make amends that drives Angel to be a champion, not the need for vengeance over some personal "loss" in his history.

Unfortunately, the alcoholic metaphor and the redemption angle of *Angel* has taken a backseat in the last few seasons as the vampire's sidekicks have proliferated. At times the program is actually difficult to sit through because some of the characters have changed so much from their original personalities. Cordelia is a prime example of this unfortunate change. On *Buffy*, and in the first two years of *Angel*, she was a smart-mouthed, vapid, self-obsessed beauty; and the new characterization, as a suffering, Mother Theresa–type, has never fit. The addition of Fred has not helped matters, as she seems a poor imitation of Alyson Hannigan's wonderful Willow character on *Buffy*. At times, Gunn is far too glib.

And the addition of Connor, a teenage son for Angel from out of nowhere, mimics (badly) Buffy's "addition" of a younger sister, Dawn, in the fifth season of *Buffy the Vampire Slayer*. Overall, *Angel* has always had promise, and often delivered on it; but in the end, it is no *Buffy*.

Angel (1999–)
LIVE ACTION SERIES

"...[R]iskier ... more audacious from the norm ... an atmosphere entirely different from *Buffy*'s ... fully satisfying across a whole range of emotions."
— Ken Tucker, *Entertainment Weekly*, December 3, 1999.

"Besides its hulking, gloomy lead and self-absorbed-as-ever foil Cordelia, *Angel* also borrows *Buffy*'s stylish thrills and its flashes of humor, sharp and surprising as teeth on your neck in a dark alley."
— James Poniewozik, *Time Magazine:* "Angel," October 11, 1999, page 91.

"The help for hire angle is a dicey set-up that's a little too *A-Team* for such an edgy show, not to mention the disastrous results the same scenario produced for last season's human-based but creepier *Vengeance Unlimited*."
— Laura Fries, *Variety*, October 4, 1999, page 62.

CAST: David Boreanaz (Angel); Charisma Carpenter (Cordelia Chase); Alexis Denisof (Wesley Wyndham Pryce); FIRST SEASON ONLY: Glenn Quinn (Doyle); SECOND SEASON—FOURTH SEASON: J. August Richards (Gunn); THIRD SEASON—FOURTH SEASON: Amy Acker (Fred); FOURTH SEASON: Vincent Kartheiser (Connor).

CREW: *Created by:* Joss Whedon and David Greenwalt. *Consulting Producer:* Marti Noxon. *Producers:* Tim Minear and Kelly Manners. *Co-Producers:* James A. Contner, Skip Schoolnik. *Executive Producers:* Sandy Gallin, Gail Berman, Fran Rubel Kuzui, Kaz Kuzui, Joss Whedon, David Greenwalt. *Consulting Producer:* Howard Gordon. *Associate Producer:* R.D. Price. *Director of Photography:* Herbert Davis. *Production Designer:* Stuart Blatt. *Editor:* Mark Goldman.

SEASON ONE (1999-2000)

1. **"City of"** Written by: Joss Whedon and David Greenwalt. Directed by: Joss Whedon. Airdate: October 5, 1999.

Angel, the vampire with a soul, has relocated to Los Angeles where deities known as "the Powers That Be" send a half-human demon named Doyle to assist him in his quest to help the helpless and find redemption. Doyle receives prophetic visions of people in danger and tells Angel to seek out a girl named Tina, who needs help. While assisting the hopeful actress wannabe deal with a problem named Russell Winters, Angel runs into Cordelia Chase, a former Sunnydale High student destined to become his assistant in his new Angel Investigations Detective Agency. When Russell, a rich and powerful vampire, kills Tina, Angel goes after him and his lawyers, the nefarious and Satanic organization called Wolfram and Hart.

GUEST CAST: Vyto Ruginis; Christian Kane (Lindsey); Jon Ingrassia (Stacy); Renee Ridgeley (Marco); Sam Pancake (Manager); Josh Holloway (Good Looking Guy); Gina McCleain (Janice).

2. **"Lonely Hearts"** Written by: David Fury. Directed by: James A. Contner. Airdate: October 12, 1999.

Doyle receives a strange vision of somebody in danger at a popular singles nightclub. Angel, Cordy and Doyle canvas the club, handing out the company's new business cards, and Angel teams with a beautiful cop, Kate Lochley, unaware they all seek a monstrous, parasitic creature that can transfer from host to host during the sex act. The creature has found a perfect stomping ground in a town of casual sex and few personal connections; but to stop it, Angel will have to get in Kate's — and the law's — way.

Guest Cast: Elizabeth Rohm (Kate Lochley); Lillian Birdsell, Obi Ndefo; Derek Hughes (Neil); Johnny Messner (Kevin); Jennifer Tung, Tracey Stone, David Nisic, Ken Rush, Connor Kelley.

3. "In the Dark" Written by: Douglas Petrie. Directed by: Bruce Seth Green. Airdate: October 19, 1999.

Oz, Sunnydale's resident werewolf, travels to Los Angeles on a mission for Buffy Summers, the vampire slayer. He presents to Angel the relic known as the Gem of Amara, which makes vampires indestructible, and therefore able to walk in sunlight. Alas, another vampire — Spike — also wants the gem very badly and ends up in L.A. to make trouble for Angel. When Angel is kidnapped by another vampire, Spike tells Cordelia and Doyle he'll free Angel in exchange for the Gem of Amara.

Guest Cast: Seth Green (Oz); James Marsters (Spike); Kevin West (Marcus); Malia Mathis; Michael Yavnieli (Lenny); Ric Sarabia (Vendor); Tom Rosales (Manny the Pig); Gil Combs (Bouncer); Buck McDancer (Dealer); Jenni Blong (Young Woman).

4. "I Fall to Pieces" Written by: David Greenwalt. Directed by: Vern Gillum. Airdate: October 26, 1999.

Another of Doyle's all-too-enigmatic visions sends Angel to help a woman who is having trouble with a very unusual stalker: a man that can disassemble and re-assemble his own body parts at will. The recipient of "psychic surgery," this doctor of the bizarre challenges Angel to stop a menace whose every limb is a danger in and of itself.

Guest Cast: Elizabeth Rohm (Kate Lochley); Tushka Bergen (Melissa); Andy Umberger (Dr. Meltzer); Carlos Carrasco; Brent Sexton (Beat Cop); Garikayi Mutambirwa (Intern); Kent David (John); Ian Bartlett (Penny).

5. "Room w/a Vu" Written by: Jane Espenson. Directed by: Scott McGinnis. Airdate: November 2, 1999.

A demon hunts Doyle over an unpaid debt. Meanwhile, Cordelia looks for an apartment and ends up at a place that is almost too good to be true. Actually, it *is* too good to be true, and Cordelia learns her new apartment is inhabited by a very active ghost who seeks vengeance for a murder that occurred some fifty-five years earlier.

Guest Cast: Elizabeth Rohm (Kate Lochley); Beth Grant; Marcus Redmond (Griff); Denney Pierce (Vic); Greg Collins (Keith); Corey Klemow (Young Man); Lara McGrath (Manager); B.J. Porter (Dennis).

6. "Sense and Sensitivity" Written by: Tim Minear. Directed by: James A. Contner. Airdate: November 9, 1999.

Angel assists Kate (estranged from her tough-as-nails cop father), while tempers flare at Angel Investigations over Angel's management style. A demon working for Wolfram and Hart puts the "whammy" on Kate's police precinct, making all the police overly sensitive (and ineffectual).

Guest Cast: Elizabeth Rohm (Kate Lochley); John Capodice (Little Tony); John Mahon; Ron Marasco; Alex Skuby (Harlan); Kevin Will (Heath); Thomas Burr (Lee Mercer); Ken Abraham (Spivey); Jimmy Shubert (Johnny Red); Ken Grantham (Lieutenant); Adam Donshik (Uniform Cop #1); Kevin E. West (Uniform Cop #2); Wilson Bell (Uniform Cop #3); Colin Patrick Lynch (Beat Cop); Steve Shirripa (Henchman); Christopher Paul Hart (Traffic Cop).

7. "The Bachelor Party" Written by: Tracey Stern. Directed by: David Straiton. Airdate: November 16, 1999.

Doyle's heretofore unseen wife calls upon the hapless half-demon to sign divorce papers after many years of separation, and both Angel and Doyle are suspicious of her new demon betrothed. These worries prove well founded when Doyle attends the bachelor party and learns that his brain is to be the main course at the unusual event.

GUEST CAST: Kristin Dattilo (Harry); Carlos Jacott; Ted Kairys (Ben); Chris Tallman (Rick); Brad Blaisdell (Uncle John); Robert Hillis (Pierce); Lauri Johnson (Aunt Martha); Kristen Lowman (Mother Rachel); David Polcyn (Ross).

8. "I Will Remember You" Written by: David Greenwalt and Jeannine Renshaw. Directed by: David Grossman. Airdate: November 23, 1999.

Buffy Summers, the vampire slayer and great love of Angel's life, visits him in L.A., angry because he didn't see her in Sunnydale on a recent trip there. A strange "Mora" demon interrupts their reunion and its blood spills on Angel, turning him fully human. Angel revels in his humanity with Buffy for a time, until he learns that she will die in combat fighting an apocalypse. At Angel's behest, the powerful Oracles — a link to the Powers That Be — turn back time so Angel can be their champion once more. Unfortunately, by overwriting time, Angel will also lose his humanity and become a vampire once more.

GUEST CAST: Sarah Michelle Gellar (Buffy Summers); Care Cannon; Randall Slavin; David Wald (Mora Demon #1); Chris Durands (Mora Demon #2).

9. "Hero" Written by: Howard Gordon and Tim Minear. Directed by: Tucker Gates. Airdate: November 30, 1999.

Doyle sacrifices his life to save homeless demons from a fascist, demonic army and their doomsday weapon. Before he dies, Doyle shares a passionate kiss with Cordelia, transferring his psychic, prophetic powers to the surprised human.

GUEST CAST: Tony Denman (Rieff); Anthony Cistaro; Michelle Horn; Lee Arenberg; Sean Gunn; James Henriksen (Elder Lister Demon); David Bickford (Cargo Inspector); Christopher Comes, Paul O'Brien, Ashley Taylor.

10. "Parting Gifts" Written by: David Fury and Jeannine Renshaw. Directed by: James A. Contner. Airdate: December 14, 1999.

Cordelia and Angel cope with Doyle's death and face a new wrinkle: Cordelia has inherited Doyle's ability to experience prophetic visions. Meanwhile, Buffy's one-time watcher, Wesley Pryce, arrives in Los Angeles hunting an empathy demon named Barney, who is simultaneously being stalked by a horned Kungai Demon. But Angel and Wesley have everything backwards and learn that Barney is a collector of valuable occult gifts who hopes to steal Cordelia's power of vision ... by cutting her eyes out!

GUEST CAST: Maury Sterling; Carey Cannon; Randall Slavin; Alexis Denisof (Wesley); Jayson Creek (Producer #1); Sean Smith (Producer #2); Sara Devlin (Producer #3); Jason Kim (Goon); Brett Gilbert (Reptilian Demon); Henry King (Kungai Demon); Lawrence Turner (Hank); Cheyenne Wilder (Concierge); Dominique Jennings (Mac); Kotoko Kawamura (Ancient Korean Woman).

11. "Somnambulist" Written by: Tim Minear. Directed by: Winrich Kolbe. Airdate: January 18, 2000.

A deadly vampire psycho killer is on the loose in Los Angeles, leaving bloody cuts — crosses — on the faces of his young victims. Angel recognizes the devilish calling card from his own long history as Angelus and fears that he is sleep walking or in some other fashion unconsciously committing the murders. It turns out that he is wrong — it is actually an old friend doing the killing — but to expose the vampire would be to expose Angel's true nature to Kate.

GUEST CAST: Elizabeth Rohm (Kate Lochley); Jeremy Renner (Penn); Nick McCallum (Skateboard Kid); Kimberleigh Arn (Precinct Clerk); Paul Webster, Brian Dirito.

12. "Expecting" Written by: Howard Gordon. Directed by: David Semel. Airdate: January 25, 2000.

Cordelia has a new boyfriend named Wilson and spends the night with him. The fruit of their love bears terrible results, however: Cordelia is very, very pregnant. A concerned Angel is sure the lustful beau is a demon who impregnates human women, and that this isn't his first such encounter. For Cordelia, it is a race against time as she and other pregnant women prepare to give birth to a demonic brood...

GUEST CAST: Daphnee Duplaix (Serena); Ken Marino (Wilson Christopher); Josh Randall, Louisette Geiss, Stephen Roy, Julie Quinn, Maggie Connolly.

13. "She" Written by: David Greenwalt and Marti Noxon. Directed by: David Greenwalt. Airdate: February 8, 2000.

Angel helps a beautiful warrior from another universe as she frees her own kind from male subjugation on a transdimensional underground railroad. Jera, like others of her kind, is resisting a surgical operation that deprives women of their drive, spirit and independence. Not surprisingly, Angel develops a respect for this warrior and joins her cause, even though it means tangling with some very nasty demons.

GUEST CAST: Bai Ling (Jera); Colby French; Heather Stephens; Sean Gunn; Tracey Costello (Laura); Andre L. Roberson (Diego); P.J. Marino (Peter Wilkers); Honor Bliss (Girl); Chris Durand (Demon Henchman); Alison Simpson (Demon Girl #2); Lucas Dudley (Security Guard).

14. "I've Got You Under My Skin" Written by: Jeannine Renshaw. Directed by: R.D. Price. Airdate: February 15, 2000.

Angel, Wesley and Cordelia struggle to save an evil boy who seems to be possessed by a dark demon. In this case, however, the true evil resides not in inhumanity, but in the pit of human psychology...

GUEST CAST: Elisabeth Rohm (Kate Lochley); Will Kempe (Seth Anderson); Katy Boyer (Paige Anderson); Anthony Cistaro; Jesse James; Ashley Hiner (Stephanie Anderson); Patience Cleveland (Nan); Jerry Lambert (Rick the Clerk).

15. "The Prodigal" Written by: Tim Minear. Directed by: Bruce Seth Green. Airdate: February 22, 2000.

Angel runs afoul of Kate's father, triggering memories of his own father in the past. When Mr. Lochley dies, Kate blames Angel for his death, causing a rift between the two friends.

GUEST CAST: Elisabeth Rohm (Kate Lochley); Julie Benz (Darla); John Mahon (Lochley); J. Kenneth Campbell; Henri Lubatti; Frank Potter (Uniformed Delivery); Eliza Szonert (Chamber Maid); Bob Fimiani (Grounds Keeper); Christina Hendricks (Bar Maid); John Maynard (Uniformed Worker); Glenda Morgan Brown (Angel's Mother); Mark Ginther (Head Demon Guy); John Patrick Clerkin (Black Robed Priest); Mike Vendrell (Suit #2).

16. "The Ring" Written by: Howard Gordon. Directed by: Nick Marck. Airdate: February 29, 2000.

A beat-up fellow, Darren McNamara, hires Angel Investigations to save his brother Jack, a gambler who has been kidnapped by demons. Angel tracks Jack back to his bookie, then his "sale" by two howler demons to an underground gladiatorial show. But it is all a set-up: Jack and Darren are the game handlers that want Angel to be their newest champion. Forced to fight in competition with other demons, and imprisoned by cuffs that disintegrate disobedient fighters, Angel organizes resistance against the blood sport. While Wesley and Cordelia work to free him from enslavement, Wolfram and Hart associate Lilah Morgan offers Angel a deal for his release.

GUEST CAST: Stephanie Romanov (Lilah Morgan); Douglas Roberts, Scott Williams Winters.

17. "Eternity" Written by: Tracey Stern. Directed by: Regis B. Kimble. Airdate: April 4, 2000.

Angel protects a wealthy and beautiful celebrity named Rebecca from a stalker, but finds that the woman has become attracted to him — or, more appropriately, attracted to the risk and romance she perceives to be part and parcel of a vampire's existence. Rebecca drugs Angel, bringing forth the evil Angelus, in hopes that he will transform her into a vampire. Before long, it is Wes and Cordelia to the rescue...

GUEST CAST: Tamara Gorski (Rebecca); Michael Mantell, Robin Meyers.

18. "Five by Five" Written by: Jim Kouf. Directed by: James A. Contner. Airdate: April 25, 2000.

Faith, the rogue vampire slayer, arrives in Los Angeles and is quickly recruited by Wolfram and Hart to assassinate the troublesome Angel. When Angel tries to help Faith, she assaults Cordelia and tortures Wesley. Angel rushes to Wesley's rescue and confronts Faith in a knockdown, drag-out fight. Afterwards, Faith seeks Angel's help in finding redemption.

GUEST CAST: Eliza Dushku (Faith); Julie Benz (Darla); Christian Kane (Lindsey); Stephanie Romanov (Lila); Thomas Burr, Tyler Christopher.

19. "Sanctuary" Written by: Tim Minear and Joss Whedon. Directed by: Michael Lange. Airdate: May 2, 2000.

Wesley and Cordelia are angry with Angel over his attempts to rehabilitate the violent slayer Faith. Wolfram and Hart are upset too, because Angel has turned their assassin into a friend. They hire another assassin to kill their first assassin. Meanwhile, the Watchers Council and Buffy herself also arrive in L.A., hunting Faith and making

Angel's efforts to redeem her all the more difficult.

GUEST CAST: Sarah Michelle Gellar (Buffy Summers); Eliza Dushku (Faith); Elisabeth Rohm (Kate); Christiane Kane (Lindsey); Stephanie Romanov (Lilah); Thomas Burr; Alastair Duncan; Jeff Ricketts (Weatherby); Kevin Owers (Smith); Adam Vernier (Detective Kendrick).

20. "War Zone" Written by: Garry Campbell. Directed by: David Straiton. Airdate: May 9, 2000.

A resilient young African-American man, Gunn, is the protector of the streets, saving the homeless poor and innocents of L.A. from the vampire hordes. When Gunn loses his beloved sister to a vampire, he becomes more dangerous than ever, but Angel sees the courageous warrior not as an adversary, but as a would-be ally. Convincing Gunn that Angel — a vampire — can be trusted, however, is more difficult than one might imagine.

GUEST CAST: J. August Richards (Gunn); Michele Kelly (Alona); Maurice Compter (Chain); Mick Murray; Joe Basile; David Herman; Sean Parhm (Bobby); Sven Holmberg (Ty); Rebecca Klinger (Madame Dorion); Kimberly James (Lila); Ricky Luna (James).

21. "Blind Date" Written by: Jeannine Renshaw. Directed by: Thomas J. Wright. Airdate: May 16, 2000.

In court, Wolfram and Hart represents a new force on the streets, a strangely powerful blind girl named Vanessa. Lindsey has second thoughts about helping get this killer off the hook and goes to Angel for help, though the vampire has a tough time trusting his foe. While breaking into the Wolfram and Hart offices (with the help of Gunn), in hopes of learning more about the blind assassin, Angel steals an ancient scroll that will play an important part in his future.

GUEST CAST: Christian Kane (Lindsey); Stephanie Romanov (Lilah); Sam Anderson (Holland); J. August Richards (Gunn); Thomas

Burr (Lee); Jennifer Badger Martin (Vanessa); Keilana Smith (Mind Reader #1); Dawn Suggs (Mind Reader #2); Charles Constant (Security Center Guard); Scott Berman (Vendor); Derek Anthony (Dying Black Man); Rishi Kurmur (Blind Child #1); Karen Lu (Blind Child #2); Alex Buck (Blind Child #3).

22. "To Shanshu in L.A." Written and directed by: David Greenwalt. Airdate: May 23, 2000.

The scroll stolen from Wolfram and Hart reveals that Angel will some day become human and play a crucial role in the coming apocalypse. But even as he celebrates this revelation, Wolfram and Hart resurrects a deadly opponent: Darla. During a battle, Angel chops off Lindsey's hand...

GUEST CAST: Elisabeth Rohm (Kate Lochley); Christian Kane (Lindsey); Stephanie Romanov (Lilah); Sam Anderson (Holland); Todd Stashwick; Carey Cannon; Randall Slavin; David Herman; J. August Richards (Gunn); Julie Benz (Darla); Louise Claps (Homeless Woman); Darren Rice (Uniform #1); Jon Ecklund (Uniform #2); Lisa Johnson (Vendor); Robyn Cohen (Nurse); Susan Savage (Doctor); John Eddins (Monk #1); Gerald O'Donnell (Monk #2); Brahman Turner (Young Tough Guy).

SEASON TWO (2000–2001)

23. "Judgment" Written by: David Greenwalt. Story by: Joss Whedon and David Greenwalt. Directed by: Michael Lange. Airdate: September 26, 2000.

Cordelia has a frightening vision about a Priomoto demon, a creature bred to maim and massacre. Angel, Wesley and Cordelia attempt to locate the offending demon by contacting Wesley's stoolie, Merl, at a demon karaoke bar called Caritas. The club's host, a green, horned demon named Lorne, can read people's futures when he hears them sing. Though Angel refuses to sing, he nonetheless tracks down the Priomoto demon and kills him — a mistake, since the demon was protecting a pregnant woman and her unborn child from demon hordes.

Angel becomes the woman's champion, appearing before a mysterious tribunal.

GUEST CAST: Christian Kane (Lindsey); Stephanie Romanov (Lilah); Andy Hallett (The Host); Eliza Dushku (Faith); Julie Benz (Darla); Justina Machado; Rob Boltin (Johnny Fontaine); Iris Fields (Acting Teacher); Keith Campbell (Club Manager); Jason Frasca (White Guy); Andy Kreiss (Lizard Demon); Matthew James (Merl Demon); Glenn David Calloway (Judge); EJ Gage (Mordar the Bentback).

24. "Are You Now or Have You Ever Been?" Written by: Tim Minear. Directed by: David Semel. Airdate: October 3, 2000.

While he mulls over the idea of moving Angel Investigations into the abandoned Hyperion Hotel, Angel recalls his stay there during the conformist 1950s. The establishment was a hotbed of paranoia, murder and prejudice, but the culprit behind all the terrible crimes was really a paranoia demon playing on human insecurities. Now Angel and his friends must raise the demon in the flesh and kill him in order to free an old friend, a woman who, out of fear, once betrayed Angel to a mob.

GUEST CAST: Melissa Marsala (Judy); John Kapelos (Meeks); Tommy Hinckley; Brett Rickaby; Scott Thompson Baker; J.P. Manoux; Terrence Beasor (Old Man); David Kagen (Salesman); Julie Araskog (Over the Hill Whore); Tom Beyer (Blacklisted Writer); Eve Sigall (Old Judy).

25. "First Impressions" Written by: Shawn Ryan. Directed by: James A. Contner. Airdate: October 10, 2000.

While Gunn tries to fit in with Angel's crew, the vampire himself seems oddly detached, distracted and sleepy of late. It turns out that his old lover — and nemesis — Darla is infiltrating his dream world, leading Angel further and further from the light.

GUEST CAST: David Herman; Andy Hallett (The Host); Chris Babers; Cedrick Terrell; Julie Benz (Darla); Edwin Hodge (Keenan); Kucas Babin (Joey); Alan Shaw (Deevak); Angel Parker (Veronica); Ray Campbell (Desmond);

Sarah Brooke (Nurse); Janet Song (Dr. Thomas); Kelli Kirkland (Young Black Woman).

26. "Untouched" Written by: Mere Smith. Directed by: Joss Whedon. Airdate: October 17, 2000.

Angel and Wolfram and Hart (particularly Lilah) vie for the heart and mind of a powerful new L.A. player: a woman called Bethany that exhibits extraordinary telekinetic abilities. Even as Darla continues to visit Angel in his dreams, Angel grapples with the powerful Bethany, whose stress level and anger seem to enhance her destructive potential.

GUEST CAST: Stephanie Romanov (Lilah); Sam Anderson (Holland); Daisy McCrackin; Gareth Williams; Julie Benz (Darla); David J. Miller (Man #1); Drew Wicks (Uniform Officer); Michael Harte (Detective); Madison Eginton (Young Bethany).

27. "Dear Boy" Written and directed by: David Greenwalt. Airdate: October 24, 2000.

Darla continues to haunt Angel's dreamscape, and before long appears in the flesh, taunting the troubled vampire with a soul. Soon Darla — a pawn for Wolfram and Hart — is popping up everywhere, even on cases, and Angel confides in his team about her return and the impact it has had on his psyche. Interestingly, Wolfram and Hart has resurrected Darla as a human being…

GUEST CAST: Elisabeth Rohm (Kate Lochley); Christian Kane (Lindsey); Andy Hallett (The Host); Juliet Landau (Drusilla); Julie Benz (Darla); Stewart Skelton (Harold Jeakins); Sal Rendino (Man); Cheryl White (Claire); Matt North (Stephen); Derek Anthony (Hotel Security Guy); Darren Kennedy (Cop #1); Rich Hutchman (Detective Carlson).

28. "Guise Will Be Guise" Written by: Jane Espenson. Directed by: Krishna Rao. Airdate: November 7, 2000.

Unable to cope with Darla's return from the grave, Angel needs spiritual guidance. The Host (at Caritas) sends him to a healing master that can repair his psyche, unaware that the master has been killed and replaced by a demonic assassin sent by Wolfram and Hart to kill Angel. Meanwhile, Wesley impersonates Angel on an important case involving wealthy clients and a beautiful girl in jeopardy named Virginia. Wes learns that Virginia is to be sacrificed by her father, and gets to play the hero…

GUEST CAST: Andy Hallett (The Host); Art Le Fleur; Brigid Brannah (Virginia Bryce); Patrick Kilpatrick (Paul Lanier); Todd Susman; Danica Sheridan (Yeska); Saul Stein (Bennie); Frabkie Jay Allison (Thug #1); Michael Yama (Japanese Man #1); Eiji Inoue (Japanese Man #2); Ed Trotta (Man).

29. "Darla" Written and directed by: Tim Minear. Airdate: November 14, 2000.

Darla attempts to commit suicide because she is plagued by a soul. Among her painful remembrances: her death and rebirth at the Master's hand in the Virginia Colony in 1609, and Angel's introduction to the head vampire in 1760. In the present, Angel tracks down Darla after she escapes from Wolfram and Hart, assisted by Lindsey, who has fallen in love with her.

GUEST CAST: Mark Metcalf (The Master); Christian Kane (Lindsey); Sam Anderson (Holland); Julie Benz (Darla); Juliet Landau (Drusilla); James Marsters (Spike); Zitto Kazanin (Gypsy Man); Bart Petty (Security Guard).

30. "The Shroud of Rahmon" Written by: Jim Kouf. Directed by: David Grossman. Airdate: November 21, 2000.

Incarcerated and interrogated by the L.A.P.D., Wesley recounts the story of a job gone terribly wrong, one involving Angel and Gunn's secret infiltration of a gang planning to heist a relic from a museum. The demons planned to steal the Shroud of Rahmon, a mystical item worth two million dollars on the black market, but terribly dangerous because exposure to it drives those in close proximity to insane violence.

After stolen by Angel and the others, the shroud began to work its insidious magic, resulting in danger for Kate, who attempted to stop the theft in progress.

GUEST CAST: Elisabeth Rohm (Kate Lochley); W. Earl Brown, Dwayne L. Barnes, R. Emery Bright, Tom Kiesche, Tony Todd.

31. "The Trial" Written by: Douglas Petrie and Tim Minear. Story by: David Greenwalt. Directed by: Bruce Seth Green. Airdate: November 28, 2000.

Angel tracks down Darla with Gunn's assistance, but Wolfram and Hart has found her first. When Angel catches up with Darla he learns that she is dying of syphilis, with only two months to live, and therefore desperate to become an immortal vampire again. Instead of turning her into a vampire and taking her soul, Angel travels to a nether realm to face three deadly trials that, if he survives, promise to make Darla whole again. Angel survives the tests, but Darla can't be saved. Wolfram and Hart attacks Darla, using Drusilla to turn Darla once more into a soulless creature of the night.

GUEST CAST: Christian Kane (Lindsey); Andy Hallett (The Host); Julie Benz (Darla); Juliet Landau (Drusilla); Sam Anderson (Holland), Jim Piddock.

32. "Reunion" Written by: Tim Minear and Shawn Ryan. Directed by: James A. Contner. Airdate: December 19, 2000.

Darla re-awakens as a vampire (thanks to Drusilla), despite Angel's best efforts to help her find redemption. An obsessed Angel flies out of control, ignoring visions from the Powers That Be, as well as advice from his friends, and sets out to fight the two vampire women. But Darla and Drusilla are already making mischief: they kill a team of Wolfram and Hart lawyers (including Holland), leaving Lilah and Lindsay the only survivors. Worse, Angel permits the atrocity, and, to top off his unstable behavior, fires Gunn, Cordelia and Wesley.

GUEST CAST: Elisabeth Rohm (Kate Lochley); Christian Kane (Lindsey); Stephanie Romanov (Lilah); Sam Anderson (Holland); Julie Benz (Darla); Juliet Landau (Drusilla); Stephanie Manglaras (Landlord); Karen Tucker (Female Shopper); Erik Liberman (Erik); Katherine Ann McGregor (Catherine); Michael Rotondi (Burly Guy).

33. "Redefinition" Written by: Mere Smith. Directed by: Michael Grossman. Airdate: January 16, 2001.

Knowing he must confront the dangerous duo of Drusilla and Darla on his own terms, Angel has fired his staff and commenced training for the inevitable fight. Meanwhile, Lilah and Lindsey worry that they will be executed following Drusilla and Darla's massacre of Wolfram and Hart's executives in Holland Manners' wine cellar. Surprised, they discover instead that the vampires want their help in forming a demon posse to run L.A. Angel retaliates by setting Drusilla and Darla on fire.

GUEST CAST: Christian Kane (Lindsey); Stephanie Romanov (Lilah Morgan); Andy Hallett (The Host); Brigid Brannagh (Virginia Bryce); Julie Benz (Darla); Juliet Landau (Drusilla); Nicolas Surovy.

34. "Blood Money" Written by: Shawn Ryan and Mere Smith. Directed by: R.D. Price. Airdate: January 23, 2001.

Angel has been tracking down a girl, Anne, who works at a teen home for runaways supported by Wolfram and Hart. He learns that the organization is planning a charity ball for the shelter and suspects something terrible — and corrupt — is destined to occur there. At the same time, an old demon nemesis bearing a grudge against Angel arrives in town to finish him off, allying himself with Lilah and Lindsey. On the night of the charity ball, however, alliances change.

GUEST CAST: Christian Kane (Lindsey); Stephanie Romanov (Lilah Morgan); Sam Anderson (Holland Manners); Julia Lee (Anne

Steele); Matthew James (Merl); Gerry Becker, Mark Rolston.

35. "Happy Anniversary" Written by: David Greenwalt. Story by: Joss Whedon and David Greenwalt. Directed by: Bill Norton. Airdate: February 6, 2001.

Still separated from his friends and former employees at Angel Investigations, Angel finds himself becoming increasingly dark. The Host distracts the vampire from his brooding with the shocking announcement that the world is going to end in 24 hours. A grad student has been working on an experiment that can freeze time, an experiment secretly augmented by demons who wish to rid the world of the human "pestilence." When the student, Gene, learns that his girlfriend plans to dump him on their anniversary, he plans to make their love last forever — an experiment that will destroy time and space ... and the world!

GUEST CAST: Andy Hallett (The Host); Brigid Brannah (Virginia Bryce); Matt Champagne (Gene); Darby Stanchfield, Mike Hagerty.

36. "The Thin Dead Line" Written by: Jim Kouf and Shawn Ryan. Directed by: Scott McGinnis. Airdate: February 13, 2001.

Gunn, Wesley and Cordelia attempt to help Anne, whose runaway wards at the shelter have complained about crooked cops roughing them up. Angel investigates the matter and is accosted by a super-strong police officer, actually a zombie! While Angel recruits Kate to work the case, Wesley and Gunn take to the streets, and one of the zombie cops shoots Wesley in the stomach. With Gunn, Cordy and the injured Wesley under siege with Anne in the shelter, Angel confronts the captain of the zombie squad, a raiser of the dead.

GUEST CAST: Elisabeth Rohm (Kate Lochley); Julia Lee (Anne Steele); Mushond Lee, Jarrod Crawford.

37. "Reprise" Written by: Tim Minear. Directed by: James Whitmore, Jr. Airdate: February 20, 2001.

Lindsey and Lilah prepare for Wolfram and Hart's all-important "review," which occurs every 75 years. Meanwhile, Lindsay gives Darla sanctuary in his apartment and helps her recover from burn wounds. At the same time, Angel tries to foul Wolfram and Hart's review by the "senior partner" at the "home office," and ends up taking a tour of evil's domain. Following a discussion with Holland Manners (deceased), a despairing Angel willingly gives up everything to make love to the evil Darla.

GUEST CAST: Elisabeth Rohm (Kate Lochley); Christian Kane (Lindsey McDonald); Andy Hallett (The Host); Stephanie Romanov (Lilah Morgan); Sam Anderson (Holland Manners); Brigid Brannagh (Virginia Bryce); Julia Benz (Darla); Gerry Becker, Thomas Kopache.

38. "Epiphany" Written by: Tim Minear. Directed by: Thomas J. Wright. Airdate: February 27, 2001.

Angel has made love to Darla, but didn't lose his soul because he never experienced a moment of true happiness. Realizing he has hit bottom, Angel has an epiphany and tries to put the pieces of his life back together. His first task in that regard is to save Cordelia from a three-eyed Skilosh demon that has implanted its spawn in her skull. But winning over the still-resentful Wesley and Gunn is no picnic, nor is facing down an angry Lindsey, who is jealous over Angel's tryst with Darla.

GUEST CAST: Elisabeth Rohm (Kate); Christian Kane (Lindsey); Andy Hallett (The Host); Julia Benz (Darla); Marie Chambers (Mother); Kevin Fry (Skilosh Demon).

39. "Disharmony" Written by: David Fury. Directed by: Fred Keller. Airdate: April 17, 2001.

Angel Investigations is back together, and Cordelia's old high school friend, Harmony, now a vampire, pays a visit. At the same time, the agency investigates a vampire cult that has been recruiting aggressively in L.A. to fuel its occult pyramid scheme. Looking for her place in the world after being jilted by Spike, Harmony betrays Cordelia, Angel and the others to the cult.

GUEST CAST: Andy Hallett (The Host); Mercedes McNab (Harmony); Pat Healy; Alyson Hannigan (Willow); Adam Weiner (Caged Guy); Rebecca Avery (Caged Girl).

39. "Dead End" Written by: David Greenwalt. Directed by: James A. Contner. Airdate: April 24, 2001.

Cordelia has a vision of a suburban father stabbing himself in the eye with a butcher's knife, an incident related to Wolfram and Hart because Lindsey has received another transplant, a new hand, recently. Angel and his crew trace the deadly transplants back to a demonic clinic and a former Wolfram and Hart employee charged with embezzlement, Bradley Scott. The experience changes Lindsey, who leaves town and sees Lilah promoted.

GUEST CAST: Christian Kane (Lindsey); Stephanie Romanov (Lilah Morgan); Andy Hallett (The Host); Gerry Becker, Michael Dempsy, Mik Scriba.

40. "Belonging" Written by: Shawn Ryan. Directed by: Turi Meyer. Airdate: May 1, 2001.

While Cordelia grapples with a nasty director on a titillating commercial shoot, a portal opens in the Host's karaoke bar and in spills trouble: a terrible warrior demon from the Host's joyless, song-less dimension, Pylea. A vision helps the Angel Investigation team track down the demon, and Cordelia believes that a meek librarian, a beautiful girl named Fred, was once sucked into Pylea. Worse, in stopping the demon and sending him back to his own hell dimension, Cordelia is also sent to merciless Pylea.

GUEST CAST: Andy Hallett (The Host); Amy Acker (Fred); Jarrod Crawford; Darris

Love; Brody Hutzler; Kevin Otto (Seth); Maureen Grier (Woman); Lynne MacLean (Claire).

42. "Over the Rainbow" Written by: Mere Smith. Directed by: Fred Keller. Airdate: May 8, 2001.

Cordelia has been sucked into the demon dimension called Pylea, the homeland of the Host, where she is captured and enslaved. Angel and Wesley attempt to reopen the portal to the world where humans are considered "cows," but need help from the Host and Gunn. In Pylea, another lost human, a brilliant but shy girl named Fred, befriends Cordelia. Cordy's enslavement ends when the natives learn she has prophetic visions and promote her to Queen.

GUEST CAST: Andy Hallett (The Host); Amy Ackert (Fred); Daniel Dae Kim (Gavin Park); Susan Blommaert, Persia White, Michael Phenicie.

43. "Through the Looking Glass" Written and directed by: Tim Minear. Airdate: May 15, 2001.

Cordelia, now the ruler of Pylea, surprises Angel, Wes, Gunn and Lorne when they are brought to her throne room to be executed. In truth, the manipulative priests of the land believe Cordelia is part of a prophecy that will eventually grant them power, and are using her to mate with a hero known as "the Groosulag." Meanwhile, Angel befriends Fred, who has been hunted and alone for five years, since the portal sucked her to Pylea from L.A. Angel's demon side manifests itself in this strange world, and he is ashamed to show his face and true nature, but Fred proves to be a friend.

GUEST CAST: Andy Hallett (Lorne, the Host); Amy Acker (Fred); Brody Hutzler; Mark Lutz (Groosulag); Michael Phenicie, Brian Tahas, Andrew Parks.

44. "There's No Place Like Plrtz Glrb" Written and directed by: David Greenwalt. Airdate: May 22, 2001.

The politics of Pylea continue to create havoc for Angel and his gang, and, worse, Lorne has (seemingly) been executed. Angel realizes that Fred holds the key to sending them all back home, but first he must defeat the Groosulag in combat, who is no horrible monster, but a sensitive warrior who has fallen hard for Queen Cordelia. Now it is just a matter of unseating the evil priests and opening the portal back to L.A.— where bad news is waiting for Angel.

GUEST CAST: Andy Hallett (The Host, Lorne); Amy Acker (Fred); Alyson Hannigan (Willow); Brody Hutzler; Mark Lutz (Groo); Tom McLeister, Lee Reherman, Jamie McShane, Adoni Maropis, Danan Pere, Alex Nesic, Andrew Parks, Whitney Dylan.

SEASON THREE (2001–2002)

45. "Hearthrob" Written and directed by: David Greenwalt. Airdate: September 24, 2001.

Angel returns from a spiritual retreat in Sri Lanka following news of Buffy Summers' death in Sunnydale (battling the evil goddess Glory). Meanwhile, Fred is still adjusting to Los Angeles after years as a slave in Pylea. One of Cordelia's powerful visions leads Angel to kill Elizabeth, a vampire he and Darla ran with in the 1760s. Her mate, James, goes gunning for him after a special treatment from a demon doctor that grants him temporary invincibility. Elsewhere, a very pregnant Darla tries desperately to rid herself of Angel's unborn child.

GUEST CAST: Julie Benz (Darla); Andy Hallett (The Host); Ron Melendez (James); Kate Norby (Elizabeth); Keith Szarbajka (Holtz); Matthew James (Merl); Kaji Katoaka (Pilgrim); Sam Littlefield (Young Man Hostage); Dalila Brown Geiger (Sandy); Christian Hastings (Vamp #1); Bob Fimiani (Codger Demon); Robert Madrid (Rough Man); Bob Morrisey (Dr. Gregson).

46. "That Vision Thing" Written by: Jeffrey Bell. Directed by: Bill Norton. Airdate: October 1, 2001.

Cordelia's visions have grown increasingly painful and are taking grotesque physical manifestations, scarring, scratching and even burning her. Lilah is using a medium to send painful messages to Cordy to blackmail Angel into performing a task for Wolfram and Hart. Desperate to help Cordelia, Angel undertakes the mission and frees Lilah's client, a psycho boy named Billy Bloom, from Hell in exchange for a cure.

GUEST CAST: Andy Hallett (The Host); Stephanie Romanov (Lilah Morgan); Daniel Dae Kim (Gavin Park); Julie Benz (Darla); Frank "Sotonoma" Salsedo; David Denman; Justin Shilton (Young Man); Ken Takemoto (Old Chinese Man); Alice Lo (Old Chinese Woman); Mitchell Gibney (Innocuous Man); Bob Sattler (Masked Man); Kal Penn (Young Man in Fez).

47. "That Old Gang of Mine" Written by: Tim Minear. Directed by: Fred Keller. Airdate: October 8, 2001.

There's a gang of raging demon murderers on the loose, and the latest victim is Merl the stoolie. Gunn learns that his old street buddies are behind the rampage and has a hard time morally justifying Angel and Wesley's feelings about "harmless" demons. When Gunn's trigger-happy gang attacks Caritas, taking the Host hostage and murdering demons, Gunn must decide where his priorities are. Unable to fight in the demon sanctuary because of a spell, Angel sends Cordelia to visit three lovely furies that might be able to help.

GUEST CAST: Andy Hallett (The Host); Jarrod Crawford; Khalil Kain; Matthew James (Merl); Giancarlo Carmona (Gang Kid); Steve Niel (Huge and Horrible); Josh Kayne (Cowering Demon); Sam Ayers (Tough Guy Demon); Heidi Markhout (Fury #1); An Le (Fury #2); Madison Gray (Fury #3).

48. "Carpe Noctem" Written by: Scott Murphy. Directed by: James A. Contner. Airdate: October 15, 2001.

An old man at the Monserrat Home has been using occult spells to transfer himself into the bodies of virile, athletic young men. But when he is done with the hot bods, they are burned up, killing the original owners. Angel investigates the case, but the old man, Marcus, steals his body and traps the vampire in his own infirm body, wreaking havoc with the women of Angel's life, including Lilah, Fred and Cordelia. Realizing he is forever young, Marcus sets out to destroy his real body, still occupied by Angel.

GUEST CAST: Stephanie Romanov (Lilah); Daniel Dae Kim (Gavin Park); Rance Howard; Paul Benjamin; Misty Louwagie (Christina); Marc Brett (Health Club Guy); Paul Logan (Woody); Lauren Reina (Escort #1); Magdalena Zielinska (Escort #2); Steven W. Bailey (Ryan).

49. "Fredless" Written by: Mere Smith. Directed by: Marita Grabiak. Airdate: October 22, 2001.

Fred's trouble adjusting to her so-called normal life after five years in Pylea is exacerbated when her parents arrive unexpectedly in L.A. in hopes of bringing her home. When Fred disappears, Angel knows there is more going on than meets the eye.

GUEST CAST: Andy Hallett (Lorne); Gary Grubbs (Roger); Jennifer Griffin (Trish).

50. "Billy" Written by: Tim Minear and Jeffrey Bell. Directed by: David Grossman. Airdate: October 29, 2001.

Billy, the boy that Angel freed from his own private room in Hell to save Cordelia from physically debilitating prophecies, is on the loose again, transmitting his total hatred of women to any and all male passersby. Angel and his crew track Billy, but the psychotic puts the whammy on Wesley. Infused with "primordial misogyny," Wesley stalks Fred in the hotel, while Cordelia takes matters into her own hands to rid the world of Billy's brand of evil.

GUEST CAST: Stephanie Romanov (Lilah Morgan); Daniel Dae Kim (Gavin Park); Justin Shilton (Billy); Richard Livingston (Congress-

man); Jennifer Brooke (Clerk); Cheri Rae Russell (Female Officer); Gwen McGee (Detective); Kristoffer Polaha (Dylan); Ray Gallegos (Ramirez); Charles Parker (Guy); Joy Long (Amber); Timothy McNeil (Cab Driver).

51. "Offspring" Written by David Greenwalt. Directed by: Turi Meyer. Airdate: November 5, 2001.

Darla returns to confront Angel about their unborn child, while Wesley deciphers an ancient scroll revealing Angel's role in an upcoming apocalypse. Darla escapes from Angel's custody, but Angel catches up with her at an arcade and learns that their unborn child has a heartbeat ... and a soul. Meanwhile, a vengeful demon called Sahjhan resurrects the vampire hunter Daniel Holtz to hunt down Darla and Angel and show them "no mercy."

GUEST CAST: Julie Benz (Darla); Andy Hallett (The Host); Keith Szarabajka (Holtz); Jack Conley Sahjhan; Steve Tom; Heidi Markhout (Fury #1); An Le (Fury #2); Madison Gray (Fury #3); Robert Peters (Arney); Sergio Permol (Monsignor); Van Epperson (Bus Driver); Peyton and Christian Miller (Johnny); Kathleen McMartin (Mom); Theresa Arrison (Johnny's Mom).

52. "Quickening" Written by: Jeffrey Bell. Directed by: Skip Schoolnik. Airdate: November 12, 2001.

Darla's labor contractions have begun, and everyone at Wolfram and Hart is in a panic to capture the vampire child of Angel. At the hospital, however, Angel and his crew are attacked by a vampire cult hoping to worship the baby ... and eviscerate the parents. The group escapes and returns with Darla to the hotel to fetch the prophetic scrolls, but Holtz is waiting there for Angel, as is a commando team from Wolfram and Hart.

GUEST CAST: Julie Benz (Darla); Stephanie Romanov (Lilah Morgan); Daniel Dae Kim (Gavin Park); Keith Szarabajka (Daniel Holtz); John Rubinstein (Linwood); Jack Conley (Sahjhan); Jose Yenque; Matt Casper (Cyril); Bronwen Bonner-Davies (Caroline); Michael Robert

Branden (Psychic); William Ostrander (Commander); Kasha Kropinski (Sarah); John Durbun (Dr. Fetvanyich); Angel Surmelis (Tough Guy).

53. "Lullaby" Written and directed by: Tim Minear. Airdate: November 19, 2001.

Holtz holds Angel captive in the Hyperion as Darla's delivery nears. Angel escapes, but so does a guilt-wracked Darla. Angel tracks her and learns that her baby is letting her experience the feelings of a human soul. When push comes to shove and Holtz attacks again, destroying Caritas, Darla gives up her life to save Angel's child, Connor.

GUEST CAST: Andy Hallett (The Host); Julie Benz (Darla); Stephanie Romanov (Lilah Morgan); Daniel Dae Kim (Gavin Park); Keith Szarabajka (Holtz); John Rubinstein (Linwood), Jack Conley (Sahjhan); Jim Ortleib; Robert Peters (Armey); Bronwen Donnr-Davies (Caroline); Kasha Kropinski (Sarah).

54. "Dad" Written by: David Goodman. Directed by: Fred Keller. Airdate: December 10, 2001.

Everyone and everything, undead and alive, is after Angel's newborn son. Angel has difficulty caring for the always-crying human infant, even as Holtz and Wolfram and Hart separately mobilize to steal the child. With the hotel under constant siege, Angel leaves his friends behind and flees L.A. with his son. The gambit is a ploy, however, designed to thin out the pursuing demon throng. But one demon in particular, the wrathful Sahjhan, is busy making deadly plans…

GUEST CAST: John Rubinstein (Linwood); Andy Hallett (Lorne); Stephanie Romanov (Lilah Morgan); Daniel Dae Kim (Gavin); Jack Conley (Sahjhan); Laurel Holloman (Justine); Keith Szarabajka (Daniel Holtz); Kira Tiramacco (Doctor); Stephanie Courtney (Gwen).

55. "Birthday" Written by: Mere Smith. Directed by: Michael Grossman. Airdate: January 14, 2002.

On Cordelia's birthday she goes into a coma while experiencing an especially strong vision. While her body is unconscious, Cordelia visits the astral plane and encounters a demon named Skip who gives her a choice: die from her next vision or see time overwritten and never meet or work with Angel in the first place. When she learns that Angel thinks she is weak, Cordelia chooses an alternate life in which she is a popular TV star … until events draw her back to Angel's world.

GUEST CAST: Andy Hallett (The Host); Patrick Breen; Max Baker; David Denman; Heather Weeks (Tammy); Aimee Garcia (Cynthia).

56. "Provider" Written by: Scott Murphy. Directed by: Bill Norton. Airdate: January 21, 2002.

With its new web site and advertising, Angel Investigation's business goes through the roof. Angel attempts to clear out a vampire nest, Fred tries to solve a strange demon puzzle, and Wesley and Gunn work to cope with a young woman's zombie stalker boyfriend. In all cases, these well-paying clients turn out to be harboring troublesome and deadly secrets.

GUEST CAST: Andy Hallett (The Host); Jeffrey Dean Morgan (Sam Ryan); Keith Szarabajka (Holtz); Laurel Hollomon (Justine); Eric Bruskotter; Sonny Mabrey; Tony Pasqualini; Alan Henry Brown (Lead Manora); David Ramirez (Pizza Chef); Brett Wagner (Manoran Prince); Benjamin Benitez (Vamp #2).

57. "Waiting in the Wings" Written and directed by: Joss Whedon. Airdate: February 4, 2002.

Angel and his crew step out to see a world-renowned ballet. At the show, Angel realizes the dancers are the same ones he saw in 1890, but they haven't aged a day! An evil count is keeping a dancer in a temporal loop and enslaving her there because he can't bear the thought that she loves another man. The power of that age-old love affair possesses

Cordelia and Angel, and Wesley is hurt when Fred and Gunn begin a romantic relationship.

GUEST CAST: Andy Hallett (The Host); Mark Harelik; Mark Lutz (Groo); Summer Glau (Prima Ballerina); Thomas Crawford (Manager); Don Tiffany (Security Guard).

58. "Couplet" Written by Tim Minear and Jeffrey Bell. Directed by Tim Minear: Airdate: February 18, 2002.

Angel is just admitting his feelings of love for Cordelia when the warrior Groosulag, from Pylea, hops dimensions to win her heart. Wishing Cordelia the best, Angel sends Groo and Cordy on vacation, unaware his life is about to take a dramatic turn.

GUEST CAST: Andy Hallett (Lorne); Mark Lutz (Groo); Bernard K. Addison, Steven Hack, Fanshen Cox, Marissa Matarazzo.

59. "Loyalty" Written by: Mere Smith. Directed by: James A. Contner. Airdate: February 25, 2002.

Wesley translates a passage in a sacred ancient scroll and realizes with horror that Angel appears destined to kill his own son. When three portents signaling this unpleasant fate come to pass, including an earthquake, Wesley contemplates a shocking betrayal.

GUEST CAST: Stephanie Romanov (Lilah); Jack Conley (Sahjhan); Laurel Holloman (Justine); Keith Szarabajka (Holtz).

60. "Sleep Tight" Written by: David Greenwalt. Directed by: Terrence O'Hara. Airdate: March 4, 2002.

Sahjhan's plot for revenge comes to pass as Wesley kidnaps Connor, fearful Angel will kill the baby. On his way out of Los Angeles, Holtz's student, Justine, slits Wesley's throat and steals the baby, giving him to Angel's arch nemesis. With Angel in hot pursuit, Sahjhan opens a portal to the most grim of all Hell dimensions, and Holtz jumps through the gateway and disappears with Connor.

GUEST CAST: Andy Hallett (Lorne); Keith Szarbajka (Holtz); Stephanie Romanov (Lilah); Jack Conley (Sahjhan); Laurel Holloman (Justine).

61. "Forgiving" Written by: Jeffrey Bell. Directed by: Turi Meyer. Airdate: April 15, 2002.

Wesley recovers at the hospital while Angel desperately seeks to get his missing son back. The bad news is that there are no portals to this particular hell dimension, which means baby Connor and villainous Holtz are trapped there permanently. Hoping to find a different answer, Angel uses the darkest of all magic (courtesy of Wolfram and Hart) to make Sahjhan "flesh," and a confrontation ensues. Later, at the hospital, Angel attempts to kill Wesley for his betrayal.

GUEST CAST: John Rubinstein (Linwood); Andy Hallett (Lorne); Stephanie Romanov (Lilah); Kay Panabaker (Girl); Kenneth Dolin (Bum); Trip Pickell (Holtzian); Sean Makon (Truck Driver).

62. "Double or Nothing" Written by: David H. Goodman. Directed by: David Grossman. Airdate: April 22, 2002.

Cordelia and Groo return from their vacation to learn that Connor has been taken and Wesley injured. Meanwhile, a demon from Las Vegas arrives at the hotel looking to collect on an old debt and claim Gunn's soul as payment. Knowing he has only a matter of hours to "pay his bill," Gunn breaks up with Fred so she won't miss him. Angel is roused from his mourning over Connor to rescue Gunn from Jenoff, the soul-sucking demon.

GUEST CAST: Andy Hallett (The Host); Mark Lutz (Groo); Nigel D. Gibbs (Doctor); Jason Carter, Patrick St. Esprit, John David Conti.

63. "The Price" Written by: David Fury. Directed by: Marita Grabiak. Airdate: April 29, 2002.

The cost of summoning dark forces to make Sahjan real "flesh" is an infestation in Angel's hotel. The unwanted visitors are slug parasites that gestate inside living human hosts. Soon the hotel is overrun with the critters, and one of them jumps inside a helpless Fred. Gunn calls on Wesley, still an outcast from the group, to save his ailing girl.

GUEST CAST: Andy Hallett (Lorne, the Host); Stephanie Romanov (Lilah); Daniel Dae Kim (Gavin); Mark Lutz (Groo); Vincent Kartheiser (Connor/Steven); Wayne Ford (Road); Waleed Moursi (Manager); John Short.

64. "A New World" Written by Jeffrey Bell. Directed by: Tim Minear. Airdate: May 6, 2002.

Connor returns to Earth as a teenage warrior bent on murdering Angel. Meanwhile, Lilah offers Wesley a job at Wolfram and Hart while Connor escapes into seedy L.A. Soon, Connor meets up with the man he considers his real father: an aged Holtz.

GUEST CAST: Vincent Kartheiser (Connor); Andy Hallett (Lorne); Stephanie Romanov (Lilah); Mark Lutz (Groo); Keith Szarbajka (Holtz); Erika Thormalen, Anthony Stark, Deborah Zoe.

65. "Benediction" Written and directed by: Tim Minear. Airdate: May 13, 2002.

Holtz suggests Connor "walk" in Angel's world, and the boy visits the Hyperion. Later, Wesley, Lilah, Connor, Justine and Angel end up at a disco club with a gang of vampires. Holtz spies Connor and Angel fighting side by side and tells Connor to go to Angel permanently. But the plan backfires and Connor attempts to kill Cordelia.

GUEST CAST: Vincent Kartheiser (Connor/Steven); Laurel Holloman (Justine); Mark Lutz (Groo); Andy Hallett (Lorne); Stephanie Romanov (Lilah); Keith Szarbajka (Holtz).

66. "Tomorrow" Written and directed by: David Greenwalt. Airdate: May 20, 2002.

Believing Angel is responsible for the death of Holtz, Connor plans revenge against the vampire with a soul. Lilah continues to attempt to recruit Wesley, going so far as to bed him. Meanwhile, Wolfram and Hart stages an attack on Angel and Connor at a drive-in movie theater. Later, relationships change as Cordelia breaks up with Groo, Lorne plans to move out of town, and Connor executes his final revenge: locking Angel in a crate and dumping him at the bottom of the ocean. Cordelia is unable to save her true love because the demon world calls for her to ascend to another plane of existence.

GUEST CAST: John Rubinstein (Linwood); Vincent Kartheiser (Connor); Laurel Holloman (Justine); Mark Lutz (Groo); Andy Hallett (Lorne); Stephanie Romanov (Lilah); Daniel Dae Kim (Gavin); Keith Szarabajka (Holtz); David Denman (Skip).

SEASON FOUR (2002-2003)

67. "Deep Down" Written by: Steven S. DeKnight. Directed by: Terrence O'Hara. Airdate: October 6, 2002.

Angel is trapped in a coffin at the bottom of the sea, a trap sprung by Connor, where he undergoes starvation and hallucinations. Three months have elapsed, and a worried Fred and Gunn have been working with the duplicitous Connor to locate Angel and the missing Cordelia. The other players in Los Angeles, including Lilah at Wolfram and Hart and the lonely Wesley, also scour the land for the missing vamp. With the help of the traitorous Justine, Wesley locates and rescues Angel, whose first job is to cast out the son who victimized him. Meanwhile, Lilah stages a *coup d'etat* at her firm.

GUEST CAST: Andy Hallett (Lorne); John Rubinstein (Linwood); Laurel Holloman (Justine); Stephanie Romanov (Lilah); Daniel Dae Kim (Gavin Park); Noel Guglielmi (Driver Vamp); Rod Tate (Bruiser); Ingrid Sonray (Marissa).

68. "Ground State" Written by: Mere Smith. Directed by: Michael Grossman. Airdate: October 13, 2002.

Angel continues the search for the missing Cordelia, visiting a demi-goddess named Dinza for information on her whereabouts. She tells him to search for the Axis of Pythia, an ancient power talisman that can bridge all dimensions. Unfortunately, someone else is after the Axis too: Gwen Raiden, aka "Electro Girl," a freak mutant selling her electricity-based powers to the highest bidder — in this case, a client of Wolfram and Hart. Gwen and Angel lock horns over the Axis on first meeting, but soon team up to stop the evil client and use the Axis to locate Cordelia, now an angelic — but bored — higher being.

GUEST CAST: Stephanie Romanov (Lilah); Alexa Davalos (Gwen); Rena Owen; Tom Irwin (Elliott); Belinda Waymouth (Lydia Thorpe); Heidi Fecht (Mrs. Raiden); Michael Medico (Mr. Raiden); Jessica M. Kiper (Nick); Easton Gage (Young Boy); Megan Corletto (Young Gwen).

69. "Bloodlust" Written by: David Fury. Directed by: Marita Grabiak. Airdate: October 20, 2002.

Angel, Fred and Gunn go on a "retreat" to Las Vegas to see Lorne perform at the Tropicana. They learn that a corrupt casino owner is holding Lorne and forcing him to read the futures of valuable guests so he can steal those destinies and sell them to the highest bidder on the black market. Angel loses his future to the house, and only Cordelia, still trapped in a higher plane, can save him. Upon returning home to the hotel, Angel and the others are surprised to see an amnesiac Cordelia wandering the lobby.

GUEST CAST: Andy Hallett (Lorne); Clayton Rohner (Lee DiMarco); Maroceo Omari (Spencer); Jennifer Autry (Lornette #2); Matt Bushell (Security Guard #1); Tom Schind (Well-Dressed Man); Sven Holmberg (Delivery Boy); Brittany Ishibashi (Vivian); Diana Saunders (Be-jeweled Woman); John Colella (Croupier); Rod Tate (Bruiser).

70. "Slouching Toward Bethlehem" Written by: Jeffrey Bell. Directed by: Skip Schoolnik. Airdate: October 27, 2002.

Cordelia recalls nothing of her former life at Angel Investigations and is fearful Angel and the others are spies trying to deceive her. Worse, her return apparently heralds the approach of something evil and powerful, something that Lilah at Wolfram and Hart wants to know more about. Fearing he is the only one she can trust, Cordy runs off with Connor.

GUEST CAST: Andy Hallett (Lorne); Stephanie Romanov (Lilah).

71. "Supersymmetry" Written by: Elizabeth Craft and Sarah Fain. Directed by: Bill Norton. Airdate: November 3, 2002.

Fred writes an impressive article about string theory for a physics magazine and then gives a lecture on the subject at a local symposium. A dimensional rift opens while she is at the lectern, and a tentacled demon tries to snag her. Fred's old professor, Dr. Seidel, is orchestrating the attacks and is the man who sent Fred to Pylea in the first place. When Fred attempts to exact vengeance for the act, Angel, Gunn and Wesley rush — separately — to prevent her from making a mistake that she could regret forever.

GUEST CAST: Andy Hallett (Lorne); Stephanie Romanov (Lilah); Randy Oglesby; Jerry Trainor (Jared); Jennifer Hipp (Laurie).

72. "Spin the Bottle" Written and directed by: Joss Whedon. Airdate: November 10, 2002.

Lorne attempts a memory restoration spell to cure Cordelia's amnesia, but needs the help of Angel, Wesley, Fred and Gunn. The spell goes terribly wrong, turning everybody into amnesiacs that remember only their adolescence. Hostilities and revelations fracture the group, and Angel learns a deadly apocalypse is coming. Cordelia's memory is restored, but now she wishes she couldn't remember the evil that is coming...

GUEST CAST: Andy Hallett (Lorne); Vladimir Kulich; Sven Holmberg (Delivery Guy); Kam Heskin (Lola).

73. "Apocalypse, Nowish" Written by: Steven S. DeKnight. Directed by: Vern Gillum. Airdate: November 17, 2002.

Nature runs amok in Los Angeles, a harbinger of the soon-arriving apocalypse foretold by Cordelia and Lorne. Hoping to learn why she has been returned from a higher realm, Cordelia takes Connor to investigate and witnesses the arrival of a terrifying demon. Angel, Wesley, Gunn and Lorne fight the creature and lose ... spurring a citywide rain of fire and heralding apocalypse. Fearing the world is at an end, Cordelia succumbs to Connor's advances and becomes intimate with him.

GUEST CAST: Andy Hallett (Lorne); Stephanie Romanov (Lilah); Daniel Dae Kim (Gavin Park); Vladimir Kulich; Tina Moresco (Mrs. Pritchard); Molly Weber (Waitress).

Note: Series continuing. In the fifth season, Cordelia is in a coma, Spike has joined Angel Investigation, and Angel's team now runs Wolfram and Hart!

Aquaman

There may be no better example of the gradual superhero transformation from wholesome crusader to dark avenger than the individual case of Aquaman, King of the Seven Seas, a popular DC Comics character for many decades (since his appearance in 1959 in *Adventure Comics*).

In the 1960s and 1970s, Aquaman was a family man, a balanced, pro-establishment figure of the deep blue sea, often accompanied by aquatic figures of fun from the undersea kingdom with names like "Tusky" or "Imp." He had a son in Aqualad and a faithful woman in the beautiful Mera. Created by Mort Weisinger, Aquaman was a combination Tarzan and Superman, only wetter. Like the King of the Jungle, the King of the Seven Seas could communicate with animals, only this time it was sea animals, and the power was explicitly telepathic. Like Superman, Aquaman wore a colorful costume, fought criminals, and had a secret human identity, Arthur Curry.

In this wholesome incarnation, Aquaman wore green tights and gauntlets, fin-adorned boots, and an orange "scaly" shirt. He had the exact same hair as Superman, down to the curl, except it was golden blond, in essence making him a "golden boy."

It was this incarnation that most TV fans over the age of thirty remember. He appeared on *The Superman-Aquaman Hour of Adventure* in 1966, a Filmation production that was later rebroadcast as *The Adventures of Aquaman* in 1968. The series aired on CBS and featured a variety of five-minute adventures with titles like "Mephisto's Marine Marauders" and "Goliaths of the Deep Sea Gorge." In these tales villains, including Black Manta and the Reptile Men, often imperiled Mera. Superman and Aquaman were joined on these Filmation series by other superheroes, notably Green Lantern.

Perhaps more memorably, however, the wholesome, Superman-like Aquaman later starred in the 1970s powerhouse Saturday morning series *The Super Friends*, and all variations thereof, protecting the sea from villains. Aquaman's presence was especially helpful in the Wendy and Marvin years of *The Super Friends* because the threats were often of an environmental nature, leading to disasters in the ocean that required rectifying.

But soon things were changed for Aquaman. In the early 1990s, with input from writer Peter David, Aquaman was updated to a different, more contemporary (read: dark) breed of superhero. The Prince of the Sea, an Atlantean, suddenly became an overly buff, bare-chested, arrogant, long-haired, psychologically unstable superhero. His left hand was lost in battle (with Charybdis) and replaced by a hook.

In this version of reality, Aquaman still had the secret identity of Arthur Curry, a name acquired from a kindly fisherman who helped him. But as a child Aquaman was raised by dolphins (in further shades of the Tarzan legend) after being abandoned by his real mother, the Queen of Atlantis, on a reef. Aquaman returned from exile to rule Atlantis, freeing it from an oppressive regime. He married Mera, an alien queen, but saw his first son murdered by the Black Manta, no longer a man in advanced wetsuit, but an evil man-fish hybrid.

When a new *Justice League of America* animated TV series came about in 2001, Aquaman was discarded from the team, to the disappointment of many fans that remembered the old, more wholesome Aquaman. The new Aquaman, with his rage, instability and angst, closely resembles another superhero: Marvel's Sub-Mariner.

The Superman/Aquaman Hour of Adventure
(a.k.a. *The Adventures of Aquaman*) (1966–1968)
ANIMATED SERIES

VOICE TALENTS: Ted Knight (Aquaman); Jerry Dexter (Aqualad); Dianna Maddox (Mera).

CREW: A Filmation Production. *Produced by:* Lou Scheimer and Norm Prescott.

Series Director: Hal Sutherland. *Series Writers:* Robert Haney and Dennis Marks.

See also *The Justice League of America*

Automan

In the summer of 1982, a Disney genre film entitled *Tron* took moviegoers inside a fantastic computer landscape populated by "users," "programs" and other technical-sounding computer-related names. The adventure film starred Jeff Bridges, Bruce Boxleitner (as the titular *Tron*) and David Warner as the villain Sark. More importantly, the Steve Lisberger–directed flick featured a gaggle of revolutionary special effects: computer-generated racing, "light cycles," bright neon suits for the actors playing denizens of *Tron*'s world, and so forth. *Tron* premiered just as the early 1980s video game and home computer boom began, but disappointingly didn't earn the money Disney expected.

Nonetheless, *Tron*'s producer, Donald Kushner, gave the same technology and concept a second spin in 1983, this time with a different partner, creator/producer Glen Larson (*Battlestar Galactica* [1978–79], *Galactica 1980* [1980], and *Manimal* [1983]). The result was a short-lived ABC series, an hour-long dramatic superhero adventure called *Automan*.

The series starred Desi Arnaz, Jr., as Walter Nebicher, a nerdy tech guy and computer expert working for the Los Angeles Police Department. Nebicher dreamed of action, adventure and romance on the job, but his cranky superior, Captain Boyd (Gerald S. O'Loughlin), had other ideas and wanted the computer genius to stay at his desk in the Computer Room. In desperation, Walter spent his free time creating a heroic alter ego, Automan (Chuck Wagner), a hologram that looked, sounded, and felt real, the world's first "truly automatic man," hence the handle Automan. So special was Auto that he considered himself perfect. "On a scale of one to 10, think of me as an 11," he boasted in one episode.

Automan didn't wear a costume — he *was* the costume, and his torso glowed bright blue with powerful holographic energy. A new kind of superhero, Automan had a frequent sidekick, a buzzing computerized pal (an optical effect) called Cursor. A helpful friend, Cursor was a hologram generator that, in the lingo of the program, could "rezz up" just about anything needed to pursue bad guys, including customized transportation. He provided Automan with a zippy Autocar, an Autocopter and even, in one episode ("Renegade Run"), an Automotorcycle!

Interestingly, Automan also had one other defensive capability in his crime-fighting arsenal. In times of extreme danger, he and Walter could merge into a single entity ("The Great Pretender") to avoid death or catastrophic injury. But Automan was a successful detective for another reason: like R2-D2 before him, he could interface with computers and mechanical devices, including slot machines ("Staying Alive While Running a High Flashdance Fever"), thereby permitting him access to a whole new kind of "street" informant. On one occasion ("Zippers"), Auto even seduced a female super computer, scandalously boasting that he would "penetrate" her memory core, one way or another. A bit of a braggart, Automan was also prone to spontaneous (and not overly helpful) declarations such as, "I suddenly sense the presence of a microchip!"

Like all superheroes, the powerful Automan had an Achilles heel. His weakness came from the fact that his complex program required a great deal of power. Sometimes (especially in the first few episodes) he was unable to operate during the daytime, when demands on the California power grid were especially high. Luckily, Auto could re-charge himself via proximity to electrical outlets, sucking nourishing power through his fingers ("The Biggest Game in Town").

Automan's other major weakness was a more interesting one, a psychological foible based on his personality. Like the android Lieutenant Data on *Star Trek: The Next Generation* (1987–94), this artificial life form was something of a literal thinker. Although he fancied himself the "finest deductive reasoner on the planet," he did not understand people or human nature. Or, as executive producer and series writer Larry Brody explained:

> As a newcomer to this dimension, Automan is immensely curious. While it's his job to periodically save his friend Walter from villains, Walter has to save Automan from his own curiosity. He is a classically naïve hero. Our world is totally new to him.[1]

In other words, Automan was of the same archetype as Superman: a fish out of water, a stranger in a strange land. Our human customs seemed strange to him, and the curiosity Brody describes played out throughout the series' thirteen episodes in some unusual and entertaining ways. Very soon after the show commenced, a pattern emerged. In order to solve the crime of the week, Automan would first receive pertinent input (often "downloads" of movies and TV series) about human nature, and then he would mimic that behavior to catch the bad guys.

In "The Great Pretender," Automan absorbed data on gangster movies (such as *The Godfather* [1972]) and out-gangstered the bad guys as a new mob chief, "Otto." In "Staying Alive While Running a High Flashdance Fever," he viewed *Saturday*

The Man in the Blue Static Suit: Glen Larson's 1980s character Automan (Chuck Wagner) gets rezzed up for action.

Night Fever (1977) and *Flashdance* (1983), and these productions provided him with great moves on the dance floor. In "Renegade Run," Automan watched motorcycle movies and became a rider in the "Automaniacs," a gang he invented, which helped him rally other gang members against a corrupt law enforcement regime in Arizona.

In "Murder MTV," Automan donned a cheesy tuxedo, played guitar in the band called "Sweet Kicks" (with guest star Laura Branigan!), and "wanted to get down and boogie." His disguise helped him uncover a would-be assassin. In "Murder Take One," the hologram learned to become an actor to solve a mystery related to a film called *The Silver Dawn*. In "Death by Design," it was exposure to Dirty Harry movies and Clint Eastwood that transformed Automan into a tough-talking vigilante. Yet another episode, "Unreasonable Facsimile," guest starred Delta Burke and saw Automan fall in love after becoming obsessed with soap operas.

In superhero lingo, *Automan* was clearly a reflection of the Superman template, with a few interesting twists. In this case, Clark Kent and Superman were clearly split into two separate characters: meek and mild-mannered Nebicher, and confident Automan. The other series characters could also fit the same mold. Captain Boyd was the curmudgeonly Perry White character, gruff but generally clueless about the exis-

tence of the superhero in their midst. Heather McNair played Roxanne Caldwell, a lovely but hard-nosed detective not far away in concept from the feisty Lois Lane. Robert Lansing, essaying the role of Detective Jack Curtis, wasn't exactly a sidekick like Jimmy Olsen (being far more cynical — and mature — than that character), but he performed the same function as Jimmy in most series plots: he found trouble and always required a quick rescue by Automan and Walter.

The villains on *Automan* were of the most routine variety imaginable. No costumed super-freaks (like those on the Adam West *Batman*) were in evidence. In fact, Automan himself (and sidekick Cursor) were the only fantasy elements of the series; the bad guys tended to be run-of-the-mill "crooks" for the police to catch. In "The Biggest Game in Town" there was a trio of gamers conducting high-tech extortion; in "Renegade Run," a corrupt sheriff (played, as always, by Richard Lynch) threatened Walter; in "Flashes and Ashes" it was a corrupt Internal Affairs officer; and so forth. Never was there anybody fantastic or particularly memorable. Oddly, the underwhelming villains tended not to damage the show much, because so much time was spent developing the Automan character as he sought to learn more about human nature.

And, to its credit, *Automan* often demonstrated a keenly developed sense of humor, such as the occasion ("Club Ten") when Walter informed Automan that he could "trace his family tree back to Pong." In moments like that and others, the series played lightly with its *dramatis personae* and cast a pleasing, if lightweight, spell.

Although it was far more entertaining than *Manimal* (Glen Larson's other superhero series of the same vintage), *Automan* did not fare well in the Nielsen ratings in America. It aired for one month (December) in 1983 on Thursday nights from 8:00 to

9:00 and was crushed by the competition, *Magnum P.I.* on CBS and the Nell Carter comedy *Gimme a Break* on NBC. Then it was shuffled off the ABC schedule until March of 1984, where it lasted barely another month on Monday nights at 8:00, this time competing against Dick Clark's *Bloopers and Practical Jokes* (NBC) and *Scarecrow and Mrs. King* (CBS).

The final *Automan* episode, "Club Ten," did not air during the initial network run, and finally appeared on TV screens when the series surfaced on the Sci-Fi Channel ten years after *Automan*'s cancellation. Despite the abbreviated run, *Automan* remains fairly influential. Recent *Star Trek* series have explored in-depth the notion of a hologram as a sentient, developing life form (particularly *Voyager* [1995–2001]), a concept pioneered and examined rather thoroughly on the humorous Glen Larson series.

Also, in some ways, Automan was the right superhero at the right time. In the early 1980s, home computer PCs were beginning to supplant the Atari 2600 as the technological gadget of choice in American dens, and the hologram Automan, the friendly face of technology as it were, seemed designed to prove that high-tech gadgetry was not dangerous, but rather helpful. Unlike the Terminator, Automan showed that mankind could control his tools and harness them for beneficial purposes.

These days, *Automan* is amusing mainly because it feels so aged, being a product of the long-ago 1980s. Michael Jackson's "Beat It" plays in the background of "Staying Alive While Running a High Flashdance Fever," an episode set totally in a disco. And there is a lot of cheesy 1980s synthesizer music in evidence too. Stylistically, each story ends in a humorous "freeze frame," a television tradition that has often been lampooned. The series also lacks the mythos, the arc, that has become part and parcel of superhero series such as *Buffy the Vampire Slayer* (1997–2003) and *Smallville* (2001–). Making it all the more amusing, *Automan*'s understanding of computer science is, like *Tron*'s, generally archaic.

Automan (1983-84)
LIVE-ACTION SERIES

"*Automan* was an entertaining, tongue-in-cheek show that featured all the typical plots from 1980s television, to a ludicrous extent in some cases. There was very little in the way of variety of plot, but there was actually a (small) degree of character development as Auto became more independent. But basically, all you can say about *Automan* was that it was fun."

— Howard Margolin, Host of *Destinies: The Voice of Science Fiction.*

CAST: Desi Arnaz, Jr. (Walter Nebicher); Chuck Wagner (Automan); Heather McNair (Roxanne Caldwell); Gerald S. O'Loughlin (Captain Boyd); Robert Lansing (Lieutenant Jack Curtis); Cursor (as himself).

CREW: *Created by:* Glen Larson. *Supervising Producer:* Sam Egan. *Co-Producer:* Harker Wade. *Producers:* Peter Locke and Donald Kushner. *Executive Producer:* Glen A. Larson. *Co-Executive Producer:* Larry Brody. *Special Effects Conceived by:* Donald Kushner. *Executive Story Consultant:* Jack Sowards. *Associate Producers:* Gill Bettman, Randall Torno. *Director of Photography:* Frank Thackery. *Art Director:* Russell Forest. *Set Decorator:* Richard S. Wineholt. *Film Editor:* Irving Rosenblum. *Post-Production Supervisor:* Dann Cahn. *Executive Production Manager:* Mark Evans. *Unit Production Manager:* Sam Freedle. *First Assistant Director:* R. John Slosser. *Music:* Morton Stevens. *Music Supervisor:* Lionel Newman. *Automan Theme:* Billy Hinsche, Stu Phillips. *Supervisor of Visual Effects:* David Garber. *Special Effects Editor:* Steven Ramirez. *Technical Consultant, Automan's Vehicles:* Michael Scheffe. *Cursor Language:* Paul Fox. *Costume Design:* Jean-Pierre Dorleac. Computer Equipment Courtesy of Computer Engineers. *Casting:* Rachelle Farberman, Michael O. Hanks. From the Kushner-Locke Company. A Glen Larson Production.

1. "Automan" Written by: Glen A. Larson. Directed by: Lee H. Katzin. Airdate: December 15, 1983.

Tired of being left behind at a desk, L.A. cop and computer programmer Walter Nebicher creates the ultimate crime-fighting tool: a handsome and brilliant hologram called Automan. Armed with a sidekick named Cursor that can "rezz up" a car, a helicopter and other useful tools, Automan is the perfect cop Walter only wishes he could be. Together they solve Automan's first case, this one involving a string of missing persons.

GUEST CAST: Doug McClure, Patrick Macnee, Robert Hogan, Steven Keats, Jim Antonio, Robert Dunlap, Don Galloway, Mickey Jones.

2. "Staying Alive While Running a High Flashdance Fever" Written by: Glen A. Larson. Directed by: Winrich Kolbe. Airdate: December 22, 1983.

A meeting with an informant goes badly for Det. Jack Curtis, and Walter summons Automan to pursue a mob car. The chase leads to the home of Judge Alexander Farnsworth, but there is no sign of the informant there. In hopes of helping Automan better understand human interaction, Walter feeds Automan a diet of "young people" films, including *Saturday Night Fever, Staying Alive* and *Flashdance*, and the films lead the hologram to the informant, Farnsworth's secretary, in Las Vegas. But Farnsworth hasn't been corrupted as Walter and Automan suspect, he's been set up by his secretary and the mob.

GUEST CAST: Mary Crosby (Ellen Fowler); Dan Gordon (Mr. Martin); Robert F. Lyons (Jason); William Windom (Judge Alexander Farnsworth); Angela Aames; Jack Perkins (The Drunk); Jorge Cervera, Jr. (Jackson); Jim Storm (The Driver); Bud Davis (Sieger); Gary Epper (Brandt).

3. "The Great Pretender" Written by: Sam Egan. Directed by: Kim Manners. Airdate: December 29, 1983.

A shipment of government paper used to print money is hijacked, and Wally helps to solve the case — which leads to evidence of mob involvement and a notorious gangster named Brock. Hoping to help out, Automan absorbs data on gangster movies, then masquerades as a mobster himself: Mr. Otto. Automan takes the war to Brock, ruining his illegal operation and converting Brock's disloyal people to his new cause. Before long, Brock puts a hit out on his new competitor and Curtis is captured, exposing Walter as a cop.

GUEST CAST: Clu Gulager (Rudolph Brock); Michael Callan; Andrea Howard; Ed Griffith; James Andronica; Cliff Emmich; Paul Lambert; Fil Formicola, Todd Martin; William Long, Jr. (Russo); Ken Sansom (The Minister); K.C. Winkler (The Blonde); Richard Derr (Robinson); Barry Berman (Tate); Talbot Simone (Taxi Driver).

4. "Ships in the Night" Written by: Park Perine. Directed by: Bob Claver. Airdate: January 5, 1984.

A businessman working on new construction in the islands is drawn into a cocaine deal to finance his latest project. The deal goes badly, however, when the businessman is thrown from the plane in fight. Before long, the L.A. cops are off to San Cristobal to solve the riddle of the Americans being lured there and killed. Automan and Walter attempt to crush the crime ring led by a thug named Norris and the local police. But first they must spring detective Curtis from jail...

GUEST CAST: Scott Marlow; France Nuyen (LeAnne); Steve Hanks; Frank Aletter; Abraham Alvarez; Cesare Danova; Javier Grajeda (Desk Clerk); Branscombe Richmond (Johnson); Melanie Vince (Beautiful Girl); Bridget Sienna (The Croupier); Rick Garcia (Bank Guard).

5. "Unreasonable Facsimile" Written by: Sam Egan. Directed by: Winrich Kolbe. Airdate: January 12, 1984.

A whistle-blower named Innes is killed

by his unscrupulous corporate partners when he threatens to reveal before a big business deal that there are malfunctioning, sub-par parts on Vel Air 860 helicopters. Walter and Automan investigate the case, and the trail leads to an incriminating computer disk mailed to the dead man's daughter, Rachel. But, hooked on soap operas, Automan falls in love with Rachel and starts to feel that he's "out of phase." Automan poses as a wealthy businessman to draw out the murderers, and rescues Rachel from danger when she's abducted.

GUEST CAST: Robert Sampson; Glen Corbett (Jarrett); Gerald Gordon; Delta Burke (Rachel Innes); Lina Raymond; David S. Sheiner (Norman); Conroy Gedeon (Bartender); Walter Brooke (Mr. Behrens); Ruth Warshawsky (Mrs. Behrens); Tawny Schneider (Herself); Toni Nero (Francine); Dennis Scott; Tammy Alverson (Lisa).

6. "Flashes and Ashes" Written by: Doug Heyes, Jr. Directed by: Kim Manners. Airdate: January 19, 1984.

Corrupt police officers are running assault weapons illegally, leaving a path of destruction and killing a good cop named Cooney in the process. Curtis takes the case of the crooked cops, even as an Internal Affairs officer, Whittaker, gets involved. Walter's dead friend Cooney is implicated in the crimes, and Walter tries to clear his name posthumously, unaware that Whittaker is the true culprit. Automan exposes agent Whittaker — a candidate for district attorney — over a $25,000 game of tennis and a well-timed "psychic" manifestation in a night club act.

GUEST CAST: Jeff Pomerantz; Hari Rhodes; Anita Dangler; Danil Torppe; Ron Harvey; Roscoe Tanner (The Tennis Pro); Michael Horsley (Coe); James Emery (Springer); Tammy Brewer (Tisha); Tami Barber (Laurie); Africanus Roscius (Street Guy).

7. "The Biggest Game in Town" Written by: Larry Brody. Story by: Larry Brody and Shel Willen. Directed by: Winrich Kolbe. Airdate: January 26, 1984.

A triumvirate of crooks shut off the power in Los Angeles as part of the "biggest computer game ever played." Walter is at a gaming convention when the black-out occurs, and Automan recalls him to the police station to help. The villainous gamers soon demand ten million dollars to restore power, and then "play" with municipal computers (like flood control at a local dam). Then they threaten to mess with L.A.'s Air Traffic Control Computer System, endangering flights and passengers...

GUEST CAST: Kristen Meadows, Felton Perry, Rick Lenz, Timothy Blake, Stefan Zema, Michael Holden, Robert Gribner.

8. "Renegade Run" Written by: Larry Brody and Doug Heyes, Jr. Story by: Larry Brody. Directed by: Allen Baron. Airdate: March 5, 1984.

The corrupt sheriff of Bishop County, Arizona, Clay Horton, illegally apprehends a young biker named Chico and holds him, forcing him to sign important legal documents. Chico's sister is an old friend of Walter's, and she informs him of the situation and the manner in which the sheriff is forcing her and Chico to sell their parents' valuable land. Wally heads to Bishop County to settle the matter, but faces a new problem. Horton plants dope in Wally's car and then arrests him on drug charges that carry a mandatory ten-year sentence. Curtis and Automan race to Bishop County to rescue Walter and take down the corrupt Horton, who has been spending most of his county appropriations on his own avaricious needs. Meanwhile, to help Walter, Automan goes undercover as a motorcycle biker, recruiting Chico's angry gang, the Renegades, for a prison breakout.

GUEST CAST: Richard Lynch (Sheriff Clay Horton); Billy Drago (Carlos "Chico" Fernando); Terry Kiser (Stone); Richard Anderson (Carl Donovan); Greta Blackburn; Gina Gallego; Michael McRae (J.R. Crazy); Carol Webster (Miss Lucy); Bobby C. Green (Travis).

9. "Murder MTV" Written by: Guerdon Trueblood and Doug Heyes, Jr. Directed by: Bruce Seth Green. Airdate: March 12, 1984.

Walter gets assigned to guard "Sweet Kicks," a lovely rock-n-roll threesome, after all three singers are almost killed in a bomb scare. Fascinated by rock culture, Automan rescues the lead singer, the beautiful Jesse, from a deadly hit and run. Jesse's dad, the group's manager, reveals his secret: he accidentally killed a corrupt cop on the take and is being blackmailed by an unknown party. While Auto and Walter ferret out the culprit, Automan takes up guitar and plays in Sweet Kicks with the girls.

GUEST CAST: Michael McGuire; Laura Branigan (Jesse); Sander Johnson (Sam Clementine); Gerald Berne (Led Shane); Paul Haber (Delivery Boy); Miguel Nunez, Jr. (Parking Attendant).

10. "Murder Take One" Written by: Sam Egan. Directed by: Kim Manners. Airdate: March 19, 1984.

Hollywood gossip columnist Keith Gillette is murdered, and temperamental Hollywood star Veronica Everly — who he repeatedly dissed — is the prime suspect. Curtis asks Wally to help in the investigation and Automan learns that Gillette knew of a drug deal, one that financed production of the movie "The Silver Dawn." Digging deeper, Automan goes to the studio and is recruited to appear in the film's love scene. When Curtis is captured, Automan must stall production on the film while Walter tries to put all the pieces together.

GUEST CAST: Ed Lauter; Winnie Gardner; Tim Rossovitch; Bart Braverman; Peter Marshall (Keith Gillette), Greg Mullavey; Michelle Phillips (Veronica Everly); Hilary Thompson (Sheila); Floyd Levine (Seymour Grodkin); Mark Wheeler (Roland Green).

11. "Zippers" Written by: David Garber and Bruce E. Kalish. Directed by: Alan Crosland. Airdate: March 26, 1984.

A string of jewelry thefts lead back to a male strip club called Zippers, where only women are allowed on the premises. After Walter updates Automan's program to include data on "the birds and the bees," the hologram goes deep undercover as an erotic dancer — Otto, the "highly charged" electrician. Soon Walter and Auto learn that the robberies were organized from the back of the club, with wealthy customers as victims. Behind the burglaries, however, is a much deeper criminal plot involving the shadowy B.E.K. Corporation and the Federal witness protection program.

GUEST CAST: John Vernon (Rainer); James Morrison; Erik Stern; Billy Ray Sharkey; James Callahan; Jo Anne Astrow; Tom Everett (Stanley); Reginald T. Dorsey (Freddie); Don Mirault (Robin Hood); Nancy Jeris (Mrs. Stanton); Gertrude Marx (Woman); Cliff Carnell, Eric Lawson.

12. "Death by Design" Written by: Sam Egan. Directed by: Gil Bettman. Airdate: April 2, 1984.

A brutal hit goes down at the Sylvana Fashion Company, and an old friend of Curtis from his police academy days is shot during the stake-out. Hellbent on justice, Curtis investigates the murders with a vengeance, even though a cop-hating reporter is nosing around the station. Automan and Walter seek a syndicate hit man named LeBlanc, who may have been the shooter. Meanwhile, Curtis interrogates Sylvan's business partner, Tracy Mogan, who reveals that underworld kingpin Simon Rafferty may be the one who ordered the hit.

GUEST CAST: John Erickson; Anne Lockhart (Tracy Morgan); Luke Askew, Lance LeGault, Eric Server, David Spielberg, Michael Gazzo.

13. "Club Ten" Written by: Michael S. Baser and Kim Weiskopf. Directed by: Kim Manners. Airdate: Unaired.

Walter and Automan attempt to help Laura Ferguson, a travel writer and friend of Roxanne's. Laura disappeared at a wealthy resort club called Club Ten in which only "perfect 10s" in looks and wealth can recreate. Walter infiltrates Club Ten as Automan's valet, and together they discover her diary and set about retracing her last steps.

Before long, they learn about a cache of very rare and valuable diamonds — and "bluff" their way into a con, hoping it will lead them to the captured Laura.

GUEST CAST: Dennis Cole; Marshall Teague; Bruce Bauer; Brett Halsey; Robin Eisenman; Barbra Horan (Geri); Don Knight; John Alderson (Rummy); Abraham Gordon.

Batman

The long-lived Batman remains one of the two most famous and beloved superheroes in American history (Superman being the other). Ironically, the great Caped Crusader began as a deliberate homage to another popular comic/pulp character of the early 20th century. As many historians have noted, Batman creators Bob Kane and Bill Finger modeled their costumed crime fighter, at least partially, after Johnston McCulley's masked hero Zorro, a swashbuckling character that first appeared in 1919.

Like Zorro, Batman represented a kind of "split identity," a heroic avenger and righter-of-wrongs, as well as (when out of uniform) a handsome, resourceful and respected member of his community — in this case, Gotham City. The only substantive difference between legends is that Zorro looked romantically to the past, while Batman was more hard-edged and high-tech, and appealed to more contemporary and futuristic notions. Zorro rode a horse and fought with a sword in a western-style setting, while Batman drove a specially outfitted car, hunted in an urban jungle, and deployed a variety of modern accoutrements to get the job done.

Batman's "secret identity" throughout his history has been that of millionaire playboy Bruce Wayne, a philanthropist and prominent Gotham citizen. A traumatized Wayne became Batman in the first place to avenge the murder of his parents by Gotham's criminal element. He assumed the appearance of a bat because he believed it would strike dread into the hearts of criminals.

His inherited wealth provided Wayne the opportunity to outfit himself with all the high-tech tools that an underfunded, overstressed metro police force could not afford. In essence then, Batman was a Republican-style superhero, a "volunteer," a good citizen that used his own resources (rather than the government's) to do good deeds. Of course, there was another element of danger too: Batman could be arrested since he was operating outside the law. As creator Bob Kane described the situation:

> I always thought it would be more exciting for Batman to work outside the law rather than inside it. I guess growing up in the Bronx, we used to be vigilantes to survive.[1]

To achieve his ends, Batman had a secret headquarters (called the Bat Cave) teeming with equipment, and incredible transportation (the famous Batmobile, as well as, over the years, Batplanes, Batcopters, and Batboats). He had a means for Gotham's finest to contact him when his services were required (a Bat Signal), plus a dazzling array of law enforcement gadgets on his all-purpose utility belt (batarangs, batscopes, bat-cuffs, etc.).

Though technically Batman was considered a vigilante operating outside the precepts of American law, Gotham's Commissioner Gordon, a regular character in the comics, certainly seemed to appreciate the

Caped Crusader's interference in police matters. And how could he not? Batman fought the most dazzling and dangerous array of costumed freaks ever assembled, including the Joker — "the Clown Prince of Crime," the Catwoman, the Penguin, the Riddler, Two Face, Poison Ivy, Harley Quinn, Bane and many, many more.

The character Batman appeared for the first time in the issue of *Detective Comics* that hit comic stands in May of 1939, and has fascinated the world ever since. Like Hamlet, Dracula and James Bond, Batman's mythos has been constantly updated and tweaked to represent the changing times. For instance, the lantern-jawed, costumed hero was depicted as a Zorro-like crusader and patriotic hero in early movie serials. Lewis Wilson played Batman, and Douglas Croft was Robin, in Columbia's cheap programmer *Batman* (1943). Robert Lowery and Johnny Duncan assumed the roles in 1949's *Batman and Robin*.

Then, in the 1960s, Batman, as portrayed by the likable and very witty Adam West, became nothing less than a pop art masterpiece, a hip icon that lampooned superheroics and Batman's squarer-than-square attitude in a turbulent, anti-establishment decade. In the 1970s, Batman was made even more toothless, reduced to a child-friendly role model, a protective father figure in Saturday morning animated series such as *The Super Friends*.

However, all that changed with director Tim Burton's big-budget films of the late 1980s and early nineties. In this radical departure (a result of a graphic novel called *The Dark Knight Returns*, by Frank Miller), the mainstream, law-worshiping Batman was transformed into a tortured, psychologically wounded, even schizophrenic vigilante. He was on the side of the angels all right, but his methods hardly separated him from menaces like the Joker or Penguin.

Heck, over the generations some people have even seen Batman as a gay icon!

This notion is part and parcel of the strange, leather-clad and fetishistic vision imposed by director Joel Schumacher in *Batman Forever* (1995) and *Batman and Robin* (1997), at this writing, the final two films of the big-screen franchise.

Despite so many variations and changes in tone, the vast majority of elements in the Batman story have remained relatively stable since the 1940s. Kindly old Alfred has always been Wayne's helpful manservant, and perpetually youthful Dick Grayson, Robin the Boy Wonder, was introduced to the comic book goings-on in 1940. For over sixty years since, Batman has nearly always had a similar partner/sidekick. After Dick Grayson became an independent crime fighter known as Nightwing in the 1980s, DC introduced his successor as Robin, Jason Todd, then another, Tim Drake, and finally even a girl named Carrie Kelly.

Ironically, especially considering Schumacher's turn-of-the-millennium interpretations of the character, the idea of two men (garbed in tights no less) working closely and living together was considered too suggestive for some readers as far back as the 1950s. Thus, a whole Bat family was added to the comic book to downplay the so-called gay aspects of the mythos. Bathound first appeared in 1955, Batwoman the following year and Bat-Mite in 1959.

No doubt the most popular of the proliferating brood was Batgirl, Commissioner Gordon's daughter Barbara, who was introduced in 1968. These "bat"-additions silenced the critics like Frederic Wertham, whose *Seduction of the Innocent* suggested the Dynamic Duo shared a homosexual relationship.[2]

In the 1960s, producer William Dozier set out to produce a TV series based on the adventures of Charlie Chan, but the project fell through. ABC television offered him an alternate property: Batman. Dozier was not a comics book fan, nor did he necessarily understand the appeal of Batman, though it should be remembered that by the sixties, the DC Batman comics had already gone the route of self-mockery and ludicrous plots, pitting Batman against supernatural and extraterrestrial menaces on a regular basis. In any event, Dozier suspected that the only way to produce a successful TV series based on a comic book was to play the world of Batman for colorful laughs.

Dozier's version of Batman was played so straight that viewers just had to crack a smile watching him in action. This tongue-in-cheek approach, known in most corners as *camp*, would dominate the series. As much as fans of a "serious" Batman denigrated this approach, one cannot deny that it was revolutionary, and, perhaps more importantly, quite different from anything else on TV. As Dozier related to *The Saturday Evening Post* in the spring of 1966:

> I've always hated the so-called "serious" dramatic shows. They're nothing but semi-truths and evasions. We started out to do a pop-art thing and we're doing it.[3]

Helping producer Dozier envision this "camp" world of costumed superheroes and hissable villains was screenwriter Lorenzo Semple, Jr., a writer later derided for his "re-imaginings" of a number of other genre icons, including *King Kong* (1976) and *Flash Gordon* (1980). In the 1980s, Semple explained to *Starlog* reporter Steve Swires the idea of camp as he saw it: "It was a certain type of outrageously deadpan theater-of-the-absurd humor."[4]

With the concept cemented, actor Adam West was cast as Bruce Wayne/Batman, with young and agile newcomer Burt Ward essaying the role of Batman's physically fit and highly enthusiastic sidekick, Dick Grayson/Robin. Supporting cast members included Alan Napier as Alfred and Neil Hamilton as the hapless and helpless but oh-so-stolid Commissioner Gordon. Two new characters were also seen on the series: Madge Blake as Wayne's clueless Aunt Harriet, who had no idea Wayne and

Ward were Gotham's Caped Crusaders; and Stafford Repp as Police Chief O'Hara, a cop that relied heavily on the help of the "lawfully deputized" Dynamic Duo.

Batman's costume underwent something of a change for television. In the comics, Batman had, literally, spiked "bat" ears resembling long, ponted horns. On television, Batman's ears were clipped and rounded, becoming soft-tipped fabric stitch-ons to the sides of his mask. In the comics, the eyepieces of the Batman mask were often seen in black, but this too was changed on the series, with the entire mask becoming more of a sky-blue color.

The high-budgeted TV series featured elaborate and vibrant sets (often filmed from a cockeyed angle to represent the "crooked" haunts of the bad guys) and brought to life a vivid splash of comic book color and spectacle. The pilot film for the series, "Hi Diddle Riddle," drew some of the worst scores in the history of TV pilot testing when it was screened for an audience. Despite this, ABC backed the series to the hilt. Skywriters emblazoned the legend "BATMAN IS COMING" above the Rose Bowl in early 1966,[5] and the Hollywood hype machine went into overdrive.

The first episode of *Batman* premiered in January of 1966 and, unexpectedly, sparked a fan craze across America. "Batmania," not unlike Beatlemania, swept the nation, particularly the youth culture. In Detroit, a hairdresser invented the "Batcut," a hip new hairdo. At a nightclub called Wayne Manor, youths danced the Batusi with the Joker as their Maitre'd, while Wonder Woman served drinks. The Federal Communications Commission Chairman E. William Henry even got into the "bat"-act, donning a Batman costume to attend a Washington benefit. Series-related merchandise sales totaled 75–80 million dollars in 1966 alone.[6] And because *Batman* aired twice a week, on Wednesday and Thursday nights at 8:00 on ABC, it became the "first

Out of costume: Dick Grayson (Burt Ward) and millionaire philanthropist Bruce Wayne (Adam West) confer with Commissioner Gordon (Neil Hamilton) during a crisis. From the *Batman* TV series.

show to hold two spots on the season-end Nielson top ten".[7]

Batman became such an important cult phenomenon that celebrities quickly lined up for appearances on the TV show. The gorgeous Julie Newmar, decked out in Lurex/spandex, played Catwoman, "the Princess of Plunder." Latin lover Cesar Romero, replete with his famous moustache, became the green-haired Joker, the so-called "Jesting Jack Straw." Burgess Meredith appeared as Penguin, known also as "Pengy Baby." Malachi Throne was False Face, David Wayne was the Mad Hatter and Frank Gorshin was the Riddler. Every week, West and Ward were menaced by these primping, colorful villains, but the heroes always came out on top in ridiculous fight scenes. The fisticuffs were famously punctuated by comic book balloon titles superimposed over the action that read "ZZWAP,"

"ZONK," "SWOOWH," "WHAPT" and the ever-popular "AIEEEE."

For these and other unique flourishes, the series won legions of fans and influenced programming executives. A competing series, Irwin Allen's *Lost in Space* (1965–68), ditched its serious first-season format for a more campy and colorful, *Batman*-inspired second season. Only a few voices opposed the comedic aspects of the Dozier series, but they were cries in the wilderness. In particular, loyal Batman comic fans complained that the TV series turned their hero into a joke. Adam West, for one, disagreed:

> We didn't ruin Batman. To the contrary, we rescued the Caped Crusader from one foe he couldn't overcome: dismal sales. According to Bob Kane, in 1965 the Batman comic was on the verge of being cancelled after over a quarter century.[8]

Four campy arch-villains from *Batman: The Movie* (1966). Left to right: Penguin (Burgess Meredith), Riddler (Frank Gorshin), Catwoman (Lee Meriwether), and Joker (Cesar Romero).

With all of this success, plans were made for a *Batman* feature film, even as the first season wound down. Filmed during the hiatus between the first and second season of the program, the feature pitted West's Batman against his four greatest foes: Joker (Romero), Riddler (Gorshin), Penguin (Meredith) and Catwoman (Lee Meriwether, since Newmar was not available). Directed by Leslie H. Martinson, the film introduced a bevy of new gadgets and vehicles, including a Batcopter and a Batboat.

Like the TV series, the movie was silly to the point of absurdity. In one scene, Batman and Robin were saved from a speeding torpedo when a selfless porpoise(?) threw itself in front of the deadly device to save the Dynamic Duo. Another action sequence ended when the Batcopter dropped precipitously from the sky. It landed in the middle of a foam rubber convention (and an oversized demonstration mattress), softening the anticipated hard landing.

What made the film a nice change of pace from the TV series was that Adam West had more time to develop the Bruce Wayne character. And, say what one will about the "camp" *Batman*, at least this early film seemed to get some genuine jollies out of all the bat toys and technology, something that could never be said of Tim Burton's pictures. This 1966 *Batman* movie featured beautiful, revealing angles of the Caped Crusader's many colorful vehicles and gadgets, and that was enough to merit a recommendation from many Bat-fans.

Unfortunately, the *Batman* film signaled the beginning of cultural "Bat Fatigue." The movie under-performed at the box office, and the second season of the series, despite appearances from villains like Archer (Art Carney), King Tut (Victor

Buono) and Egghead (Vincent Price), evidenced a massive ratings decline. The series was renewed for a third season only because the crafty producers had another inspiration: they introduced the fetching Yvonne Craig as Barbara Gordon/Batgirl. Extremely athletic and sexy in her purple spandex suit, this costumed crime fighter made the weekly adventures a bit hotter than before. Unfortunately, the budget was also severely reduced in the third season, and the series was finally cancelled after only two-and-half seasons on the air.

Despite a relatively short run on prime-time television, the Adam West *Batman* series was highly influential to generations of superhero TV programming and even franchise films. Though some comic fans might complain that the negative ramifications of this "camp" Batman are still being felt decades after the series ran, others can see that the series was a daring and often funny initiative. It was one "interpretation" of Batman, and a very interesting — if controversial — one.

The 1960s *Batman* series included a number of running gags that are worth mentioning. For one thing, the series was absolutely obsessed with labels. Never in history has a TV series been more amusingly obsessive and compulsive. This meant that every single item in Batman's Bat Cave, no matter how obscure, is clearly labeled. "Lighted Lucite Map of Gotham City" ("Holy Rat Race") is one example, but there are more. The Bat Analyzer, Trap Door, Bat Poles, and Bat Tape Reader are seen throughout the series. This is pretty funny because Batman and Robin ostensibly deal with their equipment every day, and would not need labels to know what the devices are called.

Oddly, this joke is not exactly unfaithful to the Batman mythos. The cover art for *Batman* #65, for instance, showed the Dynamic Duo in front of two assiduously labeled file cabinets: "Rogue's Gallery" and "Undercover Police Agents." The same was true of the comic book Bat Cave. It was merely that the TV show took the notion to comedic extremes.

Another running gag involved the nature of Batman's technology. The hero always had *exactly* the right item to get him out of a sticky situation, and these devices were frequently ridiculous. An all-purpose Bat Fly Swatter and Bat Tweezers appeared in "The Penguin's Clean Sweep." Anti-Thermal Bat T-shirts appeared in "The Joker's Flying Saucer" to protect the Dynamic Duo from rocket engine blow-back. Bat Gas and its antidote Bat Wake were non-lethal means of taking down criminals in "Death in Slow Motion." Then there were "Anti-Mesmerizing Bat Reflectors" in "The Thirteenth Hat," Bat Springs in Bat Shoes in "Shoot a Crooked Arrow," and so forth. With all of these important items, one had to wonder where Batman found all the room in his utility belt.

Other running gags involved the total lack of hipness evidenced by Batman and Robin. "I never gamble," Batman deadpanned in "Ring of Wax," horrified by the thought. "Good City Government is its own reward," he reminded the Boy Wonder in "The Egg Foes in Gotham."

And in the episode "The Riddler's False Notion," Robin was saved from certain death by holding onto the dangling Bat Rope with his teeth. "Holy Molars," he exclaimed, glad to survive. Batman's response to the incident? "True. You owe your life to good dental hygiene." Played totally straight, these remarks generated real laughter.

The cliffhangers seen on the TV series were also highly inventive, if utterly preposterous. A gigantic reversing bellows menaced Batman in "Fine Finny Fiends." The Terrific Trio (Batman, Robin and Batgirl) was bound together into a giant "Siamese Human Knot" in "Nora Clavicle and the Ladies' Crime Club." The Joker attempted to transform Batman and Robin into human surfboards(?) after paralyzing them with poisonous sea urchin spines in "Surf's Up! Joker's Under!" Later, Batman and Robin faced certain death in a giant pressure cooker in "Minerva, Mayhem and Millionaires."

In the first two seasons, the initial episode of every two-parter ended with a cliffhanger, and producer William Dozier served as the breathless narrator, pleading with viewers to return for the conclusion at "the same Bat time, same Bat channel." A generation of kids grew up with Dozier's wordplay — and that particular phrase.

The villains seen on the 1960s series were all of a certain type. They had names that suggested the sum of their characteristics and criminal plots. For instance, Vincent Price was Egghead, a bald scientist that always wore white, so he looked like a giant egg. His dialogue consisted of endless "egg" references: "He's a tough egg," "eggspletives will get you nowhere," and so on.

Also, the *Batman* villains were always referred to with crazy but creative alliteration. The Archer, for instance, was called a "rapacious rapscallion" and a "malfeasant marksman." Interestingly, the villains rarely offered much motivation for their evil ways, let alone their obsessions with eggs (Egghead), Egypt (King Tut), umbrellas (Penguin), Cats (Catwoman), music (the Siren; Chantel) and so on. Even the Riddler acknowledged that for him the fun of crime was his crazy insistence on giving Batman clues to his crimes. "A crime is no fun without riddles. I'll have you know that's why I took up crime," he reported in "The Ring of Wax."

Stylish and funny, if patently absurd, *Batman* the TV series introduced many fans to the world of superheroes. And, frankly, children that watched the show did not necessarily understand that the comic book was being lampooned. Because of the straight performances, kids took the camp as "straight" action. "We were doing a live-action comic book," West has stated on many occasions, putting the matter succinctly. "And it was made where kids could enjoy it as an adventure show, while adults could laugh at its comic tone".[9]

In fact, many children (now adults) of the 1960s and 1970s still consider Adam West the greatest Batman of all, despite the fact that his version of the material is campy. The enthusiasm many feel for the 1960s *Batman* can also be seen in the fact that the show has never been off the air for long. Most recently, the series aired in prime time on TV Land, a cable network, and West noted that the series "keeps going in and going out, and never goes away."[10]

More interestingly, a CBS TV movie was developed to reunite Adam West and Burt Ward as their alter egos and tell the story behind the making of the classic series.[11] The movie, *Return to the Batcave: The Misadventures of Adam and Burt* aired March 9, 2003, and featured appearances from two Catwomen, Julie Newmar and Lee Meriweather, as well as Frank Gorshin. Playing young Adam West was Jack Brewer, and portraying young Burt Ward was Jason Marsden. The story of the film involved the sudden theft of the Batmobile, and West and Burt's efforts to get it back. "It's an homage to the past, but it's also about two guys who have come up with their own unique comedy team," West reported to *TV Guide*.[12]

Back in the 1970s, with nostalgia for the series not yet in vogue, Adam West and Burt Ward found themselves typecast by their gung-ho performances as the square-jawed superheroes, and even appeared as Batman and Robin again in a short-lived (two-episode) 1977 series called *Legend of the Superheroes*. In this effort (in which they faced off against Frank Gorshin's Riddler), the mode was again high camp. As for the character of Batman, he was mainstreamed even more thoroughly in the Saturday morning adventures of *The Super Friends*.

Through the years, he also headlined in a variety of relatively undistinguished animated series, including Filmation's *The Batman/Superman Hour* (1968–1969). Batman also appeared in the same studio's *The New Adventures of Batman and Robin* in the mid–1970s, adventures that were recirculated in *The Batman/Tarzan Adventure Hour* and *Batman and the Super Seven* for the remainder of the disco decade.

In 1980, producers Benjamin Melniker and Michael Uslan attempted to revive Batman as a movie franchise, hoping to follow up on the success of *Superman: The Movie* (1978). The intent at that point was to *not* cast Adam West and Burt Ward, and to treat Batman "seriously." As Melniker told *Starlog*:

> They [fans and producers] don't want a travesty, a satire, or a spoof. It's going to be an up-to-the-minute type of treatment, with Batman portrayed as incredibly intelligent and still have all the other attributes that make him stand out.[13]

This was a commendable attitude, and one that was appreciated by the stalwart comic fans that wanted Batman to be more a genuine hero and less a figure of fun. Fortunately for Melnicker and franchise producers, they soon had a "new" version of Batman on which they could model the film series.

In 1987, writer Frank Miller, who had spiced up Marvel's *Daredevil* title with increased sex and violence in the early 1980s, penned the four-part comic book miniseries called *The Dark Knight Returns*, a thorough, original, and incredibly imaginative update of the Batman mythos. Miller's mission was a "redefining" of a character "who had become laughably irrelevant."[14] More specifically, Miller turned the universe of Gotham City upside down. As noted by superhero authority Richard Reynolds, Miller's restructuring of Batman took "all the familiar and received ingredients of the Batman continuity — Robin, the Batmobile, Commissioner Gordon," and situated them

in a text that radically restructured "their meaning."[15] To wit, in Miller's brave new bat world:

> Robin becomes a thirteen-year-old Girl and Batman is accused of child endangerment; the Batmobile is transformed into a massive armoured personnel carrier; Commissioner Gordon is displaced by a much younger policewoman who proceeds to put out a warrant for Batman's arrest.[16]

Miller's new interpretation of the Batman legend commenced ten years after Wayne's retirement as a crime fighter, when a Mutant Gang runs rampant through the city and crime is spiraling out of control. Traditional values are dying and crime must be met with an eye-for-an-eye ferocity, which the older Batman seemed perfectly willing to mete. In other words:

> It [*The Dark Knight Returns*] presented a darker, more brutal Batman, an aging Batman who returns from retirement to face a world filled with ineffectual politicians, murderous teen gangs, twisted villains from his past and a new police commissioner opposed to his style of vigilantism.[17]

Author and genre critic William Latham (*Mary's Monster*) was interviewed for this book, and still remembers the impact that *The Dark Knight Returns* had on him as a reader and longtime fan of Batman. "It came out of nowhere to really hammer people's perceptions of the Batman character, and the subsequent film series and animated series have a direct lineage to Miller's graphic novel. *Dark Knight* showed Batman as an obsessed character, the personification of rage, grown to mythic proportions. This Batman genuinely enjoys doling out punishment, which is something we'd never seen before, even in the comic series itself. There was no camp here, with Miller portraying an almost gay Joker as Batman's partner in a kind of dance between the forces of order and chaos in the universe."

It was this new, bold, and rather harsh version of Batman that was to provide the template for the film series that began in 1989. At first, fans were disturbed (but aren't they always?) when it was learned that director Tim Burton had retained comedian Michael Keaton to fill the shoes of the Caped Crusader in the 32-million dollar extravaganza, perhaps because they feared another campy incarnation of their icon.

When the film premiered in the summer of 1989 and squashed the competition, including *Star Trek V: The Final Frontier, Licence to Kill* and *Indiana Jones and the Temple of Doom*, few fans had any reservations left. Or, at least they no longer voiced them.

Tim Burton's *Batman*, though a bit less radical than Miller's *Dark Knight*, was a movie that occurred almost totally at night, in shadows, putting the "dark" back into the legend of the Dark Knight. It depicted a Gotham City that had become "synonymous with crime," a giant, gothic, industrial disaster area that seemed like a hybrid of 1970s urban blight and 1930s/40s art deco architecture. The dangerous elements of the city were dramatized in the film's first scene, which saw a family terrorized by crooks that appeared emaciated and disease-ridden. In rather magnificent form, the first view of the modern Batman came early: a black-suited, pointy-eared creature of the night, a spectral avenger that could literally frighten people to death. In this version of *Batman,* the advent of *superhero noir,* the police of Gotham knew nothing of the vigilante, only that a "giant, menacing, supernatural bat" was terrorizing the city.

All but lost in the foam rubber muscle suit, Keaton nonetheless made quite the impression as Bruce Wayne. His version of the millionaire was one in keeping with Tim Burton's favored view of heroes as "outsiders." Keaton's Wayne was a misfit that did not know (or at least did not observe) the social graces, despite his wealth. He could hand out monetary grants without a thought in one scene, then deplore the ostentatious nature of his mansion's dining room in another.

"Some if it is very much me," he remarked of the vast and isolating Wayne Manor, and "some of it is not." This schizophrenic approach, making note of Wayne's two personalities, worked well. Keaton's Wayne was neither urbane nor refined, but he had an absent-minded charm and more than enough determination to fight the real star of the show, Jack Nicholson's Joker.

Of Nicholson's performance, one might note that psychosis has seldom been played so compellingly. After ghoulish back-alley plastic surgery leaves him scarred, Nicholson emerges in the last half of the movie as a vision of hell — a green-haired, devil-eyed, pasty-skinned monster. He is not at all a figure of fun or light humor, but a genuine nightmare brought to life. With his toxic "Smiley" nerve gas, acid-spewing flowers and electric shock buzzers, this Joker embodies all the menace one would hope for in a serious superhero myth. In fact, Nicholson's Joker is so powerful a force that the other characters in the film (including a dopey reporter played by Robert Wuhl and a blander-than-bland Kim Basinger as Wayne's love interest, Vicki Vale) suffer by comparison.

Today, many elements of Tim Burton's *Batman* do not hold up well to critical scrutiny. Many of the miniature effects seem dated, and too much of the movie occurs on a single stretch of backlot, where both the Cathedral and Monarch Theater are seen repeatedly. Like Burton's 2001 *Planet of the Apes* remake, the film feels claustrophobic, overcrowded and busy when it should be epic, sweeping and magnificent. And the story seriously meanders. There is no plot to speak of, and humor is scattershot at best. Worse, the action scenes are badly mishandled, particularly the climax in which the heavily armed and armored Bat Plane is

Top: Bruce Wayne (Michael Keaton), sans rubber suit, confers with his butler, Alfred (Michael Gough), in *Batman* (1989). *Bottom:* "I Made You? You Made Me!" Batman (Michael Keaton) and the Joker (Jack Nicholson) get close in Tim Burton's dark movie, *Batman* (1989).

taken out with a single well-placed bullet from Joker's pistol.

Yet even with these drawbacks, the atmospheric, *Blade Runner*–like qualities of Burton's film carry the day and make viewing the movie a memorable experience, even a decade later. There is one marvelous scene mid-way through the film in which Batman escorts Vicki Vale to the Bat Cave in the Batmobile. It is night, and the shadowy black car races along a wooded road in darkness as fallen leaves blow haphazardly across the screen in its wake. With Danny Elfman's expressionist, pounding score roaring on the soundtrack, this scene, like many others, casts a moody spell that is perfect for the material.

Batman fans and general audiences cheered the Burton film to the tune of some 251 million dollars at the box office, immediately paving the way for a sequel. Interestingly, Burton was given a free hand to go even further with his vision of Batman than in the first movie. He even went so far as to report that of all the films he had made, *Batman* was the one he liked the least — that he felt it got away from the total vision he wanted.[18]

In 1992, the world saw precisely what Burton had in mind for the Batman universe when *Batman Returns* arrived in movie theaters. Michael Keaton was back (reportedly with a ten-million-dollar paycheck) for the sequel, this time facing a troika of villains that included Danny DeVito as the Penguin, Michelle Pfeiffer as Catwoman and Christopher Walken as the villainous businessman Max Schreck.

There was even less of a coherent plot this time around, but the film's remarkable and atmospheric texture was positively Dickensian. The setting was Christmas time in urban Gotham, as tons of snow fell on the city, and a strange outsider named Oswald Cobblepot (the Penguin) sought vengeance on the Gothamite aristocracy that had discarded him because of his physical defor-

mities. At the same time, another misfit, Selina Kyle, sought revenge for her bad lot and directed it mostly at men, by becoming the seductive but fierce Catwoman. With a mayoral race on the line, Batman had to stop the villains from destroying the city.

The sequel went through five drafts, with the character of Robin being dropped from the story at the very last minute. Interestingly, the character had already been cast, with Marlon Wayons, an African-American, assuming the role. The *Batman Returns* script had many issues to lick, at least according to screenwriter Dan Waters, who was eventually rewritten by Wesley Strick at literally the last moment:

> I was going to be the first screenwriter to give Tim Burton a great story — three acts, bam-bam-bam. But after the first couple of weeks with Tim, you realize it's not going to happen. He just doesn't work that way. He operates on this abstract, associative level.[19]

The final film may have featured a confusing script, but it also included some of the most startling images ever to emerge from superhero cinema, including an army of penguins with missiles strapped to their backs marching on Gotham City. The funeral of the Penguin, dragged beneath the surface of an icy green pond by his fishy friends, was another fantastic moment, evocative of early expressionist horror cinema. The birth of Catwoman, heralded by a neon sign that read "Hell Here" (a corruption of the more cheerful "Hello There!") was also weird and haunting. The Christmas motif and ubiquitous snow also gave the film an incredibly unified look and moody feel. The viewer practically shivers while watching it.

Unfortunately, *Batman Returns* also earned the ire of many parents, who felt they would not have brought their children to see the film had they known it was going to feature a surfeit of disturbing imagery. Despite a strong start (a $45 million opening weekend), *Batman Returns* was shunned by many and earned significantly less than *Batman*, its final grosses coming in somewhere in the neighborhood of $162.8 million.[20]

And that, probably, is where the *Batman* movie saga should have ended. Michael Keaton and Tim Burton had labored with Jack Nicholson, Michelle Pfeiffer and Danny DeVito to bring the Dark Knight to life in two very serious-minded superhero flicks. They succeeded in that effort, for the most part. But instead of moving on, Warner Brothers wanted to continue the film series. A new director, Joel Schumacher, inherited the reins of the franchise and, complying with executives' wishes, lightened up the movies.

Feeling that he had been all but forgotten amidst so many villains in *Batman Returns*, Michael Keaton opted to leave the role of a lifetime. His departure made room for a new Batman, portrayed by the younger, more sarcastic Val Kilmer (*Tombstone* [1993], *The Saint* [1996]). With the conventionally handsome but sardonic Kilmer in the lead role, Chris O'Donnell was also introduced in *Batman Forever* as Robin, the Boy Wonder. The villains for this third spin were Tommy Lee Jones as Two-Face, a retread of Nicholson's insane Joker, and Jim Carrey as the manic Riddler.

The first frames of *Batman Forever* announced that a drastic change had occurred in the world of Batman since the final frames of *Batman Returns*. Gotham City became more exaggerated, more neon and colorful, less *noir*, with giant deco statues dotting the computer-generated landscape. Instead of shadow and light, blacks and whites, the film was filled with garish red, bright greens and other stereotypical, so-called "comic book" flourishes.

Kilmer was good as a more physically imposing, more macho Batman (replete with nipples on his Batsuit), but Jim Carrey went way over the top as a hyper-kinetic Riddler, and Tommy Lee Jones was not very memorable as the predictable, schizophrenic psycho Two-Face. Even a brand new Batmobile that could climb walls, and the presence of sexy Nicole Kidman as psychologist Meridan Chase, Wayne's new love interest, could not hide the fact that the *Batman* franchise was inching slowly back towards camp after conquering it so thoroughly in the last two films.

Despite the shift back to a jokier, more mainstream approach, *Batman Forever* emerged as a dramatic box-office champion, meriting the biggest opening weekend gross in history up to that point, an impressive 52.8 million dollars.

Two years later, *Batman and Robin*, the fourth entry in the series, was already in production, with Joel Schumacher at the helm once more. Val Kilmer elected not to return to the role of Batman, and George Clooney became the third actor in four movies to play the part. The multiple switches in lead actors had by now become dizzying, and for some the *Batman* franchise never regained momentum. It was genuinely difficult to appreciate and empathize with a character when he was switching appearances and personality every time out. At this point, the stalwart Adam West, who had stuck with the role through thick and thin, kept looking better.

Clooney and O'Donnell were joined in *Batman and Robin* by Arnold Schwarzenneger (Mr. Freeze), Uma Thurman (Poison Ivy) and Alicia Silverstone as Batgirl. Alas, even this diverse and creative cast could do nothing with a horrendous script, which rehashed point-for-point the action scenes and plot devices of *Batman Forever*, including a Gotham City gala turned confrontation. Worse, the series was back to out-and-out camp, with all the cast members indulging in cringe-inducing one-liners. In one groaner of a scene, *Batman* even flashed a credit card (Name: Batman; Expiration Date: Forever) from his overstocked utility belt. The film's gaudy lighting scheme, all icy blues (for Freeze) and hot red (for Ivy) made the film look cheaper than a Louisiana red light district.

Not surprisingly, audiences felt disappointed. After a strong opening weekend gross of $43 million, *Batman and Robin*'s second week gross dropped by some 63 percent to 15.7 million.[21] George Clooney, who did just fine as Batman but suffered because of the shallow script, was among the first to note the film's flaws. "The story got confused along the way. To say the least," he noted.[22] Clooney would end up giving great performances in non–*Batman* films such as *Out of Sight* (1998), *Three Kings* (2000) and *Solaris* (2002), so it is probably a safe bet he will not return to the franchise in a proposed — but much delayed — fifth installment, once to be titled *Batman Triumphant.*

As the long-lived *Batman* franchise soured on the big screen, and *Batman and Robin* became notorious for killing the movie series, fans were grateful that there was another venue in which Batman could prosper — namely, television animation. In 1992, *Batman: The Animated Series* began to air with great fanfare on Fox Network's Saturday morning line-up. Nominated for two Emmy Awards (and winning one for Outstanding Program in '93), the series even aired in prime time for a spell.

The series was animated in the style of the old Max Fleischer *Superman* cartoons of the 1940s, and seemed to be the perfect mix of Batman dark and Batman light. One episode even played lightly with the idea of the character's diverse mythos. In Robert Goodman's "Legends of the Dark Knight," three children prowled the streets of Gotham, discussing varying reports of the mysterious Batman and his incredible equipment. There was an "Old Chum," camped-up interpretation (*Batman* of the 1960s), replete with a ridiculous fight scene involving the Joker and a giant metronome. Then there was a Dark Knight–style, post-apocalyptic interpretation, with an older, more menacing Batman, mutant bad guys, the Batmobile as a heavy, tank-like vehicle, and a female Robin. Finally, the three children (two boys and a girl) met the real Batman, a grim opponent of crime, one who existed somewhere between camp joke and hard-bitten vigilante.

Other episodes included villains such as Bane (voiced by Henry Silva) and the Riddler (John Glover), and successfully evoked a very 1940s look and feel. It was a quality production with well-told stories, atmospheric animation and melodramatic music. This take on Batman was so well accepted that two animated features (*Batman: Mask of the Phantasm* [1993] and *Batman: Sub-Zero* [1998]), and even a video game for the Nintendo GameCube (2001's *Batman: Vengeance*), were based on its look and feel. Particularly well received was *Phantasm*, which made a tidy profit at the box office. Produced by Benjamin Melniker and Michael Uslan, and written by Alan Burnett, Paul Dini and Martin Pasko, the animated film saw Batman trying to clear his name when he's framed for murder. Stacy Keach, Jr., voiced the villain, the Phantasm, while Dana Delany and Mark Hamill (as the Joker) also contributed excellent work. *Sub-Zero* went right to home video but was similarly well drawn.

In the series' third season it changed titles and became known as *The Adventures of Batman and Robin,* but quality stayed constant. Fans remain almost universally in favor of this interpretation of the Dark Knight, and as anybody that knows the fans realizes, such satisfaction is not easy to come by.

In 1999 yet another new chapter was written in the Batman mythos. *Batman Beyond,* an animated series that ran on the WB Network, time-warped the character forty years into the future after *Batman: The Animated Series.* In this high-tech, futuristic world, Bruce Wayne has been retired from

Animated Action: Batman faces down the Phantasm and the Joker in the animated movie *Batman and the Mask of the Phantasm* (1993).

the crime-fighting business for two decades (following a heart attack). But he still thirsts to see justice meted, especially in a world where young teenagers join gangs based on the persona of a cult figure—a monster— called the Joker. Then one day a young teenager named Terry McGinnis stumbles upon the Bat Cave and learns the truth about Batman's secret identity. Like Bruce, McGinnis has an axe to grind. His father had been murdered by someone associated with Bruce Wayne, and he thirsts for vengeance. Seeing something of his younger self in the teen, Bruce becomes McGinnis's mentor and role model as the boy takes on the mantle of Batman, wearing a high-tech black suit with big, pointed ears and no cape.

The series, with episodes penned by Paul Dini, Rich Fogel, the late Hilary Bader and Bruce Timm, was an interesting and well-written production that appealed to as many adults as it did kids.

Some episodes of *Batman Beyond* even looked at the world outside Gotham City. In "The Call," for instance (written by Rich Fogel and directed by Butch Lukic), McGinnis was recruited into the Justice League of America in Metropolis. The episode featured a meeting between the elderly, crusty Wayne and the gray-haired but still-young-appearing Man of Steel, Superman. It was young McGinnis's job to expose a spy in the JLA, and he teamed with a group of interesting heroes, including a new Green Lantern (apparently an infant), Aqua Girl and Warhawk. These and other episodes offered intriguing mystery and adventure aspects, and rumor was for a time that if the Batman saga

is picked up again on the big screen, it would be in the format of *Batman Beyond*. If that happens, let all long-time Batman fans hope that Adam West is recruited to play the wise elder, Bruce Wayne.

In early 2003, it looked like there might be yet another twist to the *Batman* film saga. Director Christopher Nolan (*Memento* [2001], *Insomnia* [2002]) was tapped to take Batman back to basics — as a detective of sorts — in a film noir re-imagination called *Batman: The Frightening*. Guy Pearce (*Memento* [2001], *The Time Machine* [2002]) became the favorite to assume the mantle of Bruce Wayne/Batman. However, by late summer 2003, Bat-matters took another turn. British actor Christian Bale (*Little Women* [1994], *American Psycho* [1999], accepted the role of a youthful and tortured Bruce Wayne/Dark Knight, confronting difficulties during his first year of crimefighting. The project, a sort of "Young Batman," switched titles to *Batman: Intimidation*, and director Nolan was still at the helm, with a screenplay by *Blade* scribe David Goyer. Michael Caine was retained to play Alfred, and word soon came that Viggo Mortenson and Katie Holmes might join the cast.

Batman (1966–68)
LIVE-ACTION SERIES

"…[A] significant breakthrough in television as 'camp' art, in that it has living actors playing comic-strip roles with the utter simplicity of thought and speech of the printed characters…. Fishing in the backwaters of popular culture, it [TV] has achieved its first indigenous artistic triumph — it has upgraded the comics. Historians of culture in the future may well say that television's early attempts at art were smaller-than-life dramas of Chayefsky, Nash, Mosel and Foote, but that the medium attained full stature as an art form with the larger-than-life comic, *Batman*."
— Robert Lewis Shayon, *Saturday Review*: "All the Way to the bank," February 12, 1966, page 46.

"…[It is] a zippy program — sure-footed, full of nifty gadgets and ridiculous costumes, and with at least a couple of lines that could pass for wit on a foggy night."
— M.J. Ailer, *The New Yorker*, November 12, 1966, page 197.

"…[It is] an overnight hit … one of the most successful series ever to reach television. Kids went wild over Batman (Adam West) and Robin (Burt Ward), and the cartoon descriptions that accompanied the otherwise lackluster (though very athletic) fight sequences influenced a generation of children. The color coordination of the art director was fun, keeping with Dozier's idea of creating a pop art television form. *Batman*, though catering to low tastes … still offered an interesting example of cultural awareness."

— James Delson, Fantastic Films,
Volume 2, Number 2: "Science Fiction
on Television," June 1979, page 19.

"The 1960s TV series brought out the camp aspect of Batman, and in some ways, the character has never recovered. Everything about the series was over the top, from the fight scenes to the characterizations to the costumes. That doesn't make the series worthless by any means — for what it is, the series is a lot of fun, is great to watch as a kid, is funny to watch as an adult, and very much exemplifies "pop culture" — it was built as something to appeal to everyone. As pop culture, it doesn't get much better than *Batman*. Unfortunately, the camp character became ingrained in our sensibilities about the character, and came back to haunt the film series."

— William Latham, author of Mary's
Monster and Space: 1999 Resurrection

CAST: Adam West (Batman/Bruce Wayne); Burt Ward (Robin/Dick Grayson); Alan Napier (Alfred); Neil Hamilton (Commissioner Gordon); Stafford Repp (Chief O'Hara); SEASON ONE AND TWO: Madge Blake (Aunt Harriet Cooper); SEASON THREE: Yvonne Craig (Barbara Gordon/Batgirl).

CREW: A Greenway Production in association with 20th Century–Fox. *Executive Producer:* William Dozier. *Producer:* Howie Horwitz. *Executive Script Consultant:* Lorenzo Semple, Jr. *Associate Producer:* William P. D'Angelo. *Music:* Nelson Riddle. *Music Supervisor:* Lionel Newman. *Batman Theme:* Neal Hefti. *Production Supervisor:* Jack Sonntag. *Unit Production Manager:* Sam Strangis. *First Production Supervisor:* James Blakeley. *Director of Photography:* Howard Schwartz. *Art Directors:* Jack Martin Smith, Jack Collis. *Film Editor:* Harry Coswick. *Assistant Director:* Mark Sandrich. *Post-Production Coordinator:* Robert Mintz. *Set Decorators:* Walter N. Scott, Warren Welch. *Supervising Music Editor:* Leonard A. Engel. *Music Editor:* Sam Horta. *Supervising Sound Effects Editor:* Ralph B. Hickey. *Sound Effects Editor:* Harold Wooley. *Make-up Supervisor:* Ben Nye. *Hairstyling Supervision:* Margaret Donovan. *Batgirl Theme Music by:* Billy May, *and lyrics by:* Willy Mack. Based upon the characters created by Bob Kane appearing in *Batman* and *Detective Comics* magazines, published by National Periodical Publications, Inc. *Color:* De Luxe. William Self in Charge of Production for 20th Century–Fox.

SEASON ONE
(WINTER–SPRING 1966)

1A. "Hi Diddle Riddle" Written by: Lorenzo Semple, Jr. Directed by: Robert Butler. Airdate: January 12, 1966.

In metropolitan Gotham City, stern Commissioner Gordon calls millionaire and philanthropist Bruce Wayne and his young ward, Dick Grayson — Batman and Robin — into service to combat a master criminal known as the Riddler, who leaves behind clues for the authorities as to his diabolical schemes. This time the Riddler leads Batman and Robin to falsely arrest him so that he can vex them with a lawsuit.

GUEST CAST: Jill St. John (Molly); Frank Gorshin (The Riddler); Michael Fox, Allen Jaffe, Jack Barry.

1B. "Smack in the Middle" Written by: Lorenzo Semple, Jr. Directed by: Robert Butler. Airdate: January 13, 1966.

Robin has been captured by that "prince of puzzlers," the Riddler, and his girl Molly, but when Batman tries to rescue the Boy Wonder, a switch is made and Batman takes Molly, posing as Robin, back to the Bat Cave. After Molly falls to her death in the Bat Cave's atomic pile, Batman tracks the Riddler to his hideout under the Gotham City subway system, near Coolidge Square.

GUEST CAST: Jill St. John (Molly); Frank Gorshin (The Riddler); Michael Fox, Allen Jaffe, Jack Barry.

2A. "Fine Feathered Finks" Written by: Lorenzo Semple, Jr. Directed by: Robert Butler. Airdate: January 19, 1966.

The Penguin, a sinister, rascally criminal, has been released from prison and has opened K.G. Bird Umbrella Factory in Gotham City. On the lookout for crimes involving umbrellas, Batman and Robin fall into the clutches of the nefarious Penguin, and Bruce Wayne is nearly cast into an umbrella-forging furnace.

GUEST CAST: Burgess Meredith (The Penguin); David Lewis (Warden Crichton); Walter Burke (Snoop); Lewis Charles (Hawkeye).

NOTE: Commissioner Gordon explains the origin of the Bat Costume in this episode, noting that nothing strikes fear into the criminal mind like the shadow of a giant bat over them.

2B. "The Penguin's a Jinx" Written by: Lorenzo Semple, Jr. Directed by: Robert Butler. Airdate: January 20, 1966.

Bruce Wayne has fallen into a hot spot, but escapes. Meanwhile, Penguin captures a movie starlet — Dawn Robbins — shooting on location in Gotham City.

GUEST CAST: Burgess Meredith (The Penguin); Leslie Parrish (Dawn Robbins); David Lewis (Warden Crichton); Lewis Charles (Hawkeye).

3A. "The Joker Is Wild" Written by: Robert Dozier. Directed by: Don Weis. Airdate: January 26, 1966.

The Joker, the nefarious "clown prince of crime," escapes from Gotham Penitentiary seeking revenge against those who failed to nominate him as one of the great comedians of all time. He loots Gotham's Art Museum and the Comedian's Exhibit, but meets his old nemeses: Batman and Robin.

GUEST CAST: Cesar Romero (The Joker); Nancy Kovack (Queenie); David Lewis (Warden Crichton); Jerry Dunphy (Fred); Al Wyatt, Angelo DeMeo.

3B. "Batman Is Riled" Written by: Robert Dozier. Directed by: Don Weis. Airdate: January 27, 1966.

Countering Batman and Robin, the Joker develops his own tricks of the trade, a utility belt for crime! Then, making matters worse, he plots to unmask Batman and Robin on television.

GUEST CAST: Cesar Romero (The Joker); Nancy Kovack (Queenie); Al Wyatt, Angelo DeMeo.

4A. "Instant Freeze" Written by: Max Hodge. Directed by: Robert Butler. Airdate: February 2, 1966.

Mr. Freeze, the nefarious criminal who lives on "ice," so to speak, because of a battle with Batman, is back in Gotham City thirsting for vengeance. After Freeze steals a diamond, Batman and Robin get the lowdown on their foe, but fall victim to his paralyzing freeze ray.

GUEST CAST: George Sanders (Mr. Freeze); Selby Grant, Troy Melton, Guy Way, Roy Sickner, Robert Hogan, William O'Connell, Teri Garr.

4B. "Rats Like Cheese" Written by: Max Hodge. Directed by: Robert Butler. Airdate: February 3, 1966.

After being de-thawed, the Caped Crusaders must stop Mr. Freeze for good, and they think they know just how to do it, considering his need for diamonds...

GUEST CAST: George Sanders (Mr. Freeze); Selby Grant, Guy Way.

5A. "Zelda the Great" Written by: Lorenzo Semple, Jr. Directed by: Norman Foster. Airdate: February 9, 1966.

Zelda the Great has stolen a fortune on April 1, her yearly "robbery" date. Batman claims that the money was counterfeit, hoping he can lure the criminal into the open, but the plot backfires when Zelda kidnaps Aunt Harriet!

GUEST CAST: Anne Baxter (Zelda); Jack Kuschen (Evil); Barbara Heller, Frankie Darrow.

5B. "A Death Worse Than Fate" Written by: Lorenzo Semple, Jr. Directed by: Norman Foster. Airdate: February 10, 1966.

Batman and Robin must save an endangered Aunt Harriet from the fiendish clutches of Zelda, who is holding the kindly old woman for a king's (or Bruce Wayne's) fortune.

GUEST CAST: Anne Baxter (Zelda); Jack Kuschen (Evil); Barbara Heller, Frankie Darrow.

6A. "A Riddle a Day Keeps the Riddler Away" Written by: Fred De Gorter. Directed by: Tom Gries. Airdate: February 16, 1966.

Visiting King Boris is vexed by the mad criminal the Riddler, even as he plans to donate a statue of friendship to Gotham City. Batman and Robin race to defend Boris, but are captured by the Riddler and pinned to large spinning gears...

GUEST CAST: Frank Gorshin (The Riddler); Susan Silo (Mousey); Tim Herbert (Whiskers); Reginald Denny (King Boris).

6B. "When the Rat's Away, the Mice Will Play" Written by: Fred De Gorter. Directed by: Tom Gries. Airdate: February 17, 1966.

With the Riddler threatening to destroy King Boris's gift (a monument to freedom and liberty), unless he receives a million dollars, Batman and Robin must extricate themselves from the criminal's trap. They do so, only to find that the Riddler may be down, but he isn't out...

GUEST CAST: Frank Gorshin (The Riddler); Susan Silo (Mousey); Tim Herbert (Whiskers); Reginald Denny (King Boris).

7A. "The Thirteenth Hat" Written by: Charles Hoffman. Directed by: Norman Foster. Airdate: February 23, 1966.

Jervis Tetch, a.k.a. the Mad Hatter, is paroled from prison but immediately sets about stealing the hats of the twelve jury deliberators who convicted him. Aware that Batman's cowl would be the Hatter's prized possession, Batman and Robin trace the criminal to the studio of a sculptor, Octave Marbot, but Hatter springs a trap and buries Batman in "Super Fast Hardening Plaster."

GUEST CAST: David Wayne (The Mad Hatter); Roland La Starza (Cappy); Diane McBain (Lisa); Gil Perkins (Dicer); Sandra Wells (Babette); Alberto Morin (Octave Marbot); Monique Le Maire (Madame Magda); Ralph Montgomery (Silver Shop Manager); Bob Legionnaire (Sporting Goods Manager).

7B. "Batman Stands Pat" Written by: Charles Hoffman. Directed by: Norman Foster. Airdate: February 24, 1966.

The Mad Hatter continues his plan to possess Batman's cowl, even as the Caped Crusader escapes from his plaster tomb. The Mad Hatter steals the bowler of the last jury member, Turkey Bowinkle, but Batman uses a homing beacon (planted by Alfred) to find the criminal's hideout in the Hat Factory.

GUEST CAST: David Wayne (The Mad Hatter); Roland La Starza (Cappy); Diane McBain (Lisa); Gil Perkins (Dicer); Alberto Morin (Octave Marbot); Monique Le Maire (Madame Magda); George Conrad (Turkey Bowinkle).

8A. "The Joker Goes to School" Written by: Lorenzo Semple, Jr. Directed by: Murray Golden. Airdate: March 2, 1966.

The Joker has been out of jail just a week, and has purchased the controlling share of the One Arm Bandit Novelty Company, which produces vending machines. The Joker's first strike is at Dick Grayson's high school, Woodrow Roosevelt, where the vending machines start to go crazy, encouraging the students to live an "easy" life of crime. Unknown to Batman, one of Dick's classmates, a cheerleader named Sweet Susie, is in league with Joker and sets up a trap for the dynamic duo.

GUEST CAST: Cesar Romero (The Joker); Kip King (Nick); Greg Benedict (Two Bits); Bryan O'Byrne (Principal Schoefield); Tim O'Kelly (Pete); Glen Allan (Herbie); Sydney Smith (Mr. Vanderbilt); Donna Loren (Susie).

8B. "He Meets His Match, the Grisly Ghoul" Written by: Lorenzo Semple, Jr.

Directed by: Murray Golden. Airdate: March 3, 1966.

Batman and Robin are saved from electrocution by a fortunate power failure throughout Gotham City, and the Joker escapes. Dick Grayson goes undercover as a juvenile delinquent to join Joker's gang, but Nick, one of the henchmen, recognizes him as a phony, giving Batman one more opportunity to top the Joker before he destroys the school spirit of Woodrow Roosevelt High.

GUEST CAST: Cesar Romero (The Joker); Kip King (Nick); Greg Benedict (Two Bits); Donna Loren (Susie); Jim Menaghan (Fulton); Dick Bellis (Joe); Cherie Foster (Cheerleader # 1); Linda Harrison (Cheerleader #2).

9A. "True or False Face" Written by: Stephen Kandel. Directed by: William Graham. Airdate: March 9, 1966.

False Face challenges Batman and Robin to prove that the masked criminal, who always does the opposite of what he says, has actually committed any crime. The Dynamic Duo are too late to stop him from carrying off an armored car heist, and Batman and Robin learn that he plans to steal paper from the Official Bank Note Printing Company for a counterfeiting scheme.

GUEST CAST: Malachi Throne (False Face); Myrna Fahey (Blaze); Billy Curtis (Midget); Joe Brooks (Fat Man); Chuck Fox, S. John Launer, Patrick White.

9B. "Holy Rat Race" Written by: Stephen Kandel. Directed by: William Graham. Airdate: March 10, 1966.

With Alfred's assistance, Batman and Robin escape a trap (in which they're tied to the subway tracks) set by False Face. Meanwhile, False Face plots to get his counterfeit money into the bank, unaware that his first lieutenant, the beautiful Blaze, is secretly in love with Batman.

GUEST CAST: Malachi Throne (False Face); Myrna Fahey (Blaze); Billy Curtis (Midget); Joe Brooks (Fat Man); Mike Rogers.

10A. "The Purr-fect Crime" Written by: Stanley Ralph Ross and Lee Orgel. Directed by: James Sheldon. Airdate: March 16, 1966.

The Catwoman returns to Gotham in search of ancient, lost treasure. Two cat statues hold the key to the treasure's location, but in stealing one, the Catwoman runs afoul of the determined Dynamic Duo.

GUEST CAST: Julie Newmar (Catwoman); Jock Mahoney (Leon); Ralph Manza (Felix).

10B. "Better Luck Next Time" Written by: Stanley Ralph Ross and Lee Orgel. Directed by: James Sheldon. Airdate: March 17, 1966.

Catwoman has set a trap for Batman and Robin involving a very hungry tiger and a pit. Batman and Robin escape the jaws of death and must prevent Catwoman from finding the secret treasure she so desperately seeks.

GUEST CAST: Julie Newmar (Catwoman); Jock Mahoney (Leon); Ralph Manza (Felix).

11A. "The Penguin Goes Straight" Written by: Lorenzo Semple, Jr., and John Cardwell. Directed by: Leslie H. Martinson. Airdate: March 23, 1966.

Batman is suspicious when the Penguin seemingly gives up life as a crook to become a crime fighter. Batman's suspicions are confirmed when Penguin begins framing the Dynamic Duo for crimes.

GUEST CAST: Burgess Meredith (The Penguin), Kathleen Crowley, Harvey Lembeck.

11B. "Not Yet He Ain't" Written by: Lorenzo Semple, Jr., and John Cardwell. Directed by: Leslie H. Martinson. Airdate: March 24, 1966.

The Penguin has captured Batman and Robin and made them targets at a shooting gallery. Batman and Robin escape, even as Commissioner Gordon and Chief O'Hara unknowingly take aim at them; but then it's off in pursuit of the Penguin, who has plans to marry a celebrity and rob the wealthy guests at the wedding reception.

GUEST CAST: Burgess Meredith (The Penguin), Kathleen Crowley, Harvey Lembeck.

12A. "The Ring of Wax" Written by: Jack Paritz and Bob Rodgers. Directed by: James B. Clark. Airdate: March 30, 1966.

Just two weeks out of jail, the Riddler is back to his old lawbreaking ways, secretly operating out of a candle-making factory. His first target is a library vault where, with the help of his powerful new "universal wax solvent," he manages to break in and steal a text about the lost treasures of the Incas. Batman and Robin chase the Riddler down to Madame Soleil's Wax Museum, but the nefarious criminal turns the tables on the Dynamic Duo and strings them up over a boiling cauldron of wax...

GUEST CAST: Frank Gorshin (The Riddler); Linda Scott (Moth); Michael Greene (Matches); Elizabeth Harrower (Miss Prentiss); Al McGrahany (The Mayor), Joey Tata.

12B. "Give 'Em the Axe" Written by: Jack Paritz and Bob Rodgers. Directed by: James B. Clark. Airdate: March 31, 1966.

Batman and Robin escape their grim fate as "human candles" while the Riddler goes in search of lost Incan treasure at the Gotham City Museum and its display featuring the Sacrophagus of Hualpo Cuisi, an ancient Incan Emperor. When Robin is captured and stretched out on the rack, it's up to Batman — and the Batmobile's Bat Ram — to save the day.

GUEST CAST: Frank Gorshin (The Riddler); Linda Scott (Moth); Michael Greene (Matches); Joey Tata.

13A. "The Joker Trumps an Ace" Written by: Francis and Marian Cockrell. Directed by: Richard C. Sarafian. Airdate: April 6, 1966.

The Joker sets his sights on a visiting dignitary, the Maharajah, hoping to steal his wealth and win an ample ransom. When Batman and Robin pursue, the Joker traps them in a poison-filled chimney.

GUEST CAST: Cesar Romero (The Joker); Dan Seymour (Maharajah); Tol Avery; Angela Greene; Byron Keith (Mayor Linseed).

13B. "Batman Sets the Pace" Written by: Francis and Marian Cockrell. Directed by: Richard C. Sarafian. Airdate: April 7, 1966.

Escaping the Joker's deadly chimney trap, Batman and Robin must save the visiting Maharajah before the Joker succeeds in his quest to ransom him.

GUEST CAST: Cesar Romero (The Joker); Dan Seymour (Maharajah); Tol Avery; Angela Greene; Byron Keith (Mayor Linseed).

14A. "The Curse of Tut" Written by: Robert C. Dennis and Earl Barret. Directed by: Charles Rondeau. Airdate: April 13, 1966.

An Egyptology professor is struck on the head and becomes the new living embodiment of crime in Gotham City — the decadent King Tut. Tut sets about transforming the city into a new Egypt, sparking a confrontation with Batman and Robin.

GUEST CAST: Victor Buono (King Tut); Ziva Rodann (Queen Nefertiti); Frank Cristi, Olan Soule.

14B. "The Pharaoh's in a Rut" Written by: Robert C. Dennis and Earl Barret. Directed by Charles Rondeau. Airdate: April 14, 1966.

Bruce Wayne has been captured by the nefarious King Tut, and nearly meets his death when he is strapped to a gurney and thrown from the open doors of a speeding ambulance. Surviving the incident, Batman plots his next encounter with Tut.

GUEST CAST: Victor Buono (King Tut); Ziva Rodann (Queen Nefertiti); Frank Cristi, Olan Soule.

15A. "The Bookworm Turns" Written by: Rick Vollaerts. Directed by: Larry Peerce. Airdate: April 20, 1966.

A new, well-read criminal called "the Bookworm" menaces Gotham City, basing a crime spree on a series of literary plots from the classics. Threatening Commissioner Gordon and a city bridge, the Bookworm turns his scholarly eye to Batman and Robin, and plans to "ring" Robin's bell — permanently.

GUEST CAST: Roddy McDowall (The Bookworm); Francine York; John Crawford; Byron Keith (Mayor Linseed).

15B. "While Gotham City Burns" Written by: Rik Vollaerts. Directed by: Larry Peerce. Airdate: April 21, 1966.

Batman saves the Boy Wonder from Bookworm's trap: a fatal bell-ringing. Now Batman and Robin must use the Bookworm's own *modus operandi* (a love of books) against the master criminal before it's too late to stop his next crime.

GUEST CAST: Roddy McDowall (The Bookworm); Francine York; John Crawford; Byron Keith (Mayor Linseed).

16A. "Death in Slow Motion" Written by: Dick Carr. Directed by: Charles Rondeau. Airdate: April 27, 1966.

Dressed as Charlie Chaplin's Tramp, the Riddler robs Gotham City's Silent Film Festival. Batman tracks the Riddler to Mother Gotham's Bakery and learns that the Riddler is producing his own silent film. Meanwhile, the Riddler spikes the lemonade at a society party, causing tempers to flare, then captures the Boy Wonder and plots to saw him in half.

GUEST CAST: Frank Gorshin (The Riddler); Sherry Jackson (Pauline); Francis Bushman (Mr. Van Jones); Richard Bakalvan (CB); Burt Brandon (Wolf); Walker King (Theater Manager); Judy Page (Theater Cashier); Theo Marcuse.

16B. "The Riddler's False Notion" Written by: Dick Carr. Directed by: Charles Rondeau. Airdate: April 28, 1966.

Batman races to Gotham City Lumberyard to rescue Robin from the buzz saw, but the Riddler has replaced the Boy Wonder with a mannequin. Hoping to find the Boy Wonder, Batman interrogates Riddler's squeeze, Pauline, at the Bat Cave. He learns that the Riddler plans to film the spectacular climax of his silent movie soon — a scene that features Robin falling from the highest ledge of the Crossman Building!

GUEST CAST: Frank Gorshin (The Riddler); Sherry Jackson (Pauline); Francis Bushman (Mr. Van Jones); Richard Bakalvan (CB); Burt Brandon (Wolf).

17A. "Fine Finny Fiends" Written by: Sheldon Stark. Directed by: Tom Gries. Airdate: May 4, 1966.

The Penguin kidnaps Alfred on the eve of Bruce Wayne's Millionaire Charity Dinner to learn the secret location of the high-dollar function. Penguin brainwashes Alfred into revealing the information, while Batman and Robin trace the "waddling pirate of plunder" back to his hideout at Gotham's waterfront.

GUEST CAST: Burgess Meredith (The Penguin); Victor Lundin (Octopus); Bill Williams (Multi-millionaire); Pal Jenkins (Shark); Howard Wendell (Millionaire).

17B. "Batman Makes the Scenes" Written by: Sheldon Stark. Directed by: Tom Gries. Airdate: May 5, 1966,

Batman and Robin survive the Penguin's nefarious vacuum chamber and set their own trap for the arch-villain at the Millionaire Charity Dinner. A brainwashed Alfred sabotages Batman's trap, permitting the Penguin to steal the charity donations, but Batman and Robin aren't down for the count yet, and they stage a surprise for the Penguin in his own money vault.

GUEST CAST: Burgess Meredith (The Penguin); Victor Lundin (Octopus); Bill William

(Multi-millionaire); Pal Jenkins (Shark); Lisa Mitchell (Miss Natural Resources); Charles La Torre (Manager).

SEASON TWO (1966-1967)

18A. "Shoot a Crooked Arrow" Written by: Stanley Ralph Ross. Directed by: Sherman Marks. Airdate: September 7, 1966.

The Archer, "that rapacious rapscallion," robs stately Wayne Manor, then attacks police headquarters, temporarily blinding Batman, Robin, Chief O'Hara and Commissioner Gordon. Fancying himself a latter-day Robin Hood, the "malfeasant marksman" plans to steal from Gotham's rich and give to the poor, thereby winning the favor and popularity of the poverty-stricken.

GUEST CAST: Art Carney (The Archer); Dick Clark (Himself); Barbara Nichols (Maid Marilyn); Robert Cornthwaite (Alan A. Dale); Doodles Weaver (Crier Tuck); Loren Ewing (Big John); Archie Moore (Everett Bannister); Robert Adler (First Poor Person); Heidi Jensen (Second Poor Person); Kitty Kelly.

18B. "Walk the Straight and Narrow" Written by: Stanley Ralph Ross. Directed by: Sherman Marks. Airdate: September 8, 1966.

Batman and Robin use the Bat Springs in their boots to bounce out of harm's way as the Archer attempts to skewer them with jousting lances. The Wayne Foundation's financial advisor, Alan A. Dale, turns out to be a turncoat, bent on helping the Archer steal millions of dollars meant for the poor; but thanks to Alfred in disguise (as Batman), Bruce Wayne and Batman appear together to stop the criminal.

GUEST CAST: Art Carney (The Archer); Barbara Nichols (Maid Marilyn); Robert Cornthwaite (Alan A. Dale); Doodles Weaver (Crier Tuck); Loren Ewing (Big John); Vinton Hayworth (Marshall Roland); Steve Pendleton (The Armored Car Driver); Lee Dlano (Second Armored Car Driver); James O'Hara (Policeman); Sam Jaffe (Zoltan Zorba).

19A. "Hot Off the Griddle" Written by: Stanley Ralph Ross. Directed by: Don Weis. Airdate: September 14, 1966.

Catwoman is after two priceless violins, and has opened a school for cat burglars to attract the attention of the Dynamic Duo. The ploy works, and Catwoman orchestrates her greatest trap yet: she straps Batman and Robin under giant magnifying glasses and waits for them to be burned to a crisp!

GUEST CAST: Julie Newmar (Catwoman); Jack Kelly, James Brolin, Charles Horvath, George Barrows.

19B. "The Cat and the Fiddle" Written by: Stanley Ralph Ross. Directed by: Don Weis. Airdate: September 15, 1966.

Batman and Robin escape Catwoman's plan to burn them alive, and then pursue her as she seeks to get her hands on the violins.

GUEST CAST: Julie Newmar (Catwoman); Jack Kelly, James Brolin, Charles Horvath, George Barrows.

20A. "The Minstrel's Shakedown" Written by: Francis and Marian Cockrell. Directed by: Murray Golden. Airdate: September 21, 1966.

A singing electronics genius called the Minstrel blackmails the Gotham City Stock Exchange, causing Commissioner Gordon to bring Batman in on the case. The Caped Crusaders use a flying Bat Drone to locate Minstrel's secret broadcasting studio, but the villain sets a trap for Batman and Robin … binding them to the spit of a giant barbecue grill!

GUEST CAST: Van Johnson (The Minstrel); Leslie Perkins (Octavia/Amanda); Remo Pisani (Bass); Norman Grabowski (Treble); Del Moore (TV News Anchor); Phyllis Diller (Cleaning Woman); Army Archerd (Putnam); John Gallaudet (Courtland); Eddie Garrett (First Banker); Herbert Moss (Second Banker); Stu Wilson (Third Banker); James O'Hara (Policeman).

NOTE: This episode of *Batman* features an homage to the James Bond films. "Account number 007" at the Broccoli Bank is mentioned. Albert Broccoli, of course, was one of the producers (along with Harry Saltzman) of the Bond films during the 1960s.

20B. "Barbecued Batman?" Written by: Francis and Marian Cockrell. Directed by: Murray Golden. Airdate: September 22, 1966.

Batman and Robin barely escape the Minstrel's oversized radar grill, and use Octavia, Minstrel's squeeze, to track the criminal to his headquarters. An angry Minstrel plans to activate "Plan High C," which could bring Gotham City to its knees with artificially generated earthquakes.

GUEST CAST: Van Johnson (The Minstrel); Leslie Perkins (Octavia/Amanda); Remo Pisani (Bass); Norman Grabowski (Treble); Del Moore (TV News Anchor); Army Archerd (Putnam); John Gallaudet (Courtland); Eddie Garrett (First Banker); Herbert Moss (Second Banker); Stu Wilson (Third Banker); James O'Hara (Policeman).

21A. "The Spell of Tut" Written by: Robert C. Dennis, Earl Barret. Directed by: Larry Peerce. Airdate: September 28, 1966.

When King Tut relapses into his crooked ways and steals expensive amber beads, Batman and Robin track the Mad Monarch down to the Apex Apothecary in the Pyramid Building. There they tangle with Tut's minions and learn that he has extracted an extinct species of scarab from the amber so as to develop a "brainwashing" elixir. Robin is captured by Tut, and left dangling over the Mad Monarch's crocodile pit.

GUEST CAST: Victor Buono (King Tut); Marianna Hill (Cleo Patrick); Sid Haig (Royal Apothecary); Michael Pataki (Amonphic Tewfik); Rene Paull (Man of Distinction); Peter Mamakos (Royal Lapidary); Boyd Santell.

NOTE: This episode features a guest appearance by characters from the other Dozier superhero series, *The Green Hornet*. Batman and Robin, while climbing a wall, meet Kato (Bruce Lee) and the Green Hornet (Van Williams).

21B. "Tut's Case Is Shut" Written by: Robert C. Dennis and Earl Barret. Directed by: Larry Peerce. Airdate: September 29, 1966.

Batman saves Robin from the crocodile pit even as Tut and his goons, including Commissioner Gordon's replacement secretary, brainwash Gordon and Chief O'Hara with Tut's magic elixir. Next, Tut plans to dump his brainwashing potion into Gotham's water supply, turning the city's population into his loyal subjects, but Batman thinks he's devised an antidote to the elixir.

GUEST CAST: Victor Buono (King Tut); Marianna Hill (Cleo Patrick); Sid Haig (Royal Apothecary); Michael Pataki (Amonphic Twofik); Peter Mamakos (Royal Lapidary), Boyd Santell.

22A. "The Greatest Mother of Them All" Written by: Henry Slesar. Directed by: Oscar Rudolph. Airdate: October 5, 1966.

A gangster family, led by matriarch Ma Parker, attacks the Ladies Club in Gotham City, forcing Batman to contend with a new crisis. The Caped Crusader sets about capturing the "greatest mother of them all" before it's too late, unaware that the maternal Ma Parker has planted a bomb in the Batmobile!

GUEST CAST: Shelley Winters (Ma Parker); Tisha Sterling (Legs); Mike Vendever; James Griffith; David Lewis (Warden Crichton); Milton Berle (Lefty); Julie Newmar (Catwoman).

22B. "Ma Parker" Written by: Henry Slesar. Directed by: Oscar Rudolph. Airdate: October 6, 1966.

Batman and Robin survive the deadly bomb placed in the Batmobile, and return Ma Parker to prison, unaware she has taken over the penitentiary.

GUEST CAST: Shelley Winters (Ma Parker); Tisha Sterling (Legs); Mike Vendever; James Griffith; David Lewis (Warden Crichton).

23A. "The Clock King's Crazy Crimes" Written by: Bill Finger and Charles Sinclair. Directed by: James Nielson. Airdate: October 12, 1966.

A time-conscious criminal called Clock King invades Gotham with a vengeance, triggering a timely response from Batman and Robin. Hoping to rid himself of the pesky duo, Clock King buries them alive in giant hourglasses.

GUEST CAST: Walter Slezak (The Clock King); Eileen O'Neil (Millie Second); Herb Anderson, Sammy Davis, Jr., Michael Pate.

23B. "The King Gets Crowned" Written by: Bill Finger and Charles Sinclair. Directed by: James Nielson. Airdate: October 13, 1966.

Time is on their side when Batman and Robin escape an eternity buried alive in giant hourglasses, but how can they stop the nefarious Clock King before his next crime?

GUEST CAST: Walter Slezak (The Clock King); Eileen O'Neil (Millie Second); Herb Anderson, Michael Pate.

24A. "An Egg Grows in Gotham" Written by: Stanley Ralph Ross. Story by: Ed Self. Directed by: George Waggner. Airdate: October 19, 1966.

Criminal mastermind Egghead steals Gotham City's charter on the anniversary of the city's founding in hopes of seeing the land revert to its original owners, the Mohicans (represented by Chief Screaming Chicken). Then Egghead captures Bruce Wayne and two other Gotham millionaires in hopes of proving (with the help of his electro-thought transferer) that one of the tycoons is actually Batman.

GUEST CAST: Vincent Price (Egghead); Edward Everett Horton (Chief Screaming Chicken); Gail Hire (Ms. Bacon); Gene Dynarski (Benedict); Ben Welden (Foo Young); Steve Dunne (Tim Tyler); Albert Carrier (Pete Savage); Grant Woods (Guido).

24B. "The Yegg Foes in Gotham" Written by Stanley Ralph Ross. Story by: Ed Self. Directed by: George Waggner. Airdate: October 20, 1966.

Dick Grayson short circuits Egghead's brain sucker before Bruce can be exposed as Batman. When the lease on Gotham City expires, Chief Screaming Chicken puts Egghead in charge of the metropolis as provisional mayor ... and Batam and Robin must stop a citywide crime wave.

GUEST CAST: Vincent Price (Egghead); Edward Everett Horton (Chief Screaming Chicken); Gail Hire (Ms. Bacon); Gene Dynarski (Benedict); Ben Welden (Foo Young); Steve Dunne (Tim Tyler); Albert Carrier (Pete Savage); Byron Keith (Mayor Linseed); George Fennaman (Newsman); Burt Mastin (Old MacDonald); Jonathan Hole (Jewelry Store Owner); Mae Clarke (Lady).

25A. "The Devil's Fingers" Written by: Lorenzo Semple, Jr. Directed by: Larry Peerce. Airdate: October 26, 1966.

While Bruce and Dick are away from Gotham on a camping trip, Commissioner Gordon is hard-pressed to solve a crime involving famous pianist Chandell, who is wooing an unsuspecting Aunt Harriet. When they return to the city as the Caped Crusaders, Bruce and Dick are nearly transformed into giant music rolls at Chandell's now-defunct music factory.

GUEST CAST: Liberace (Chandell/Harry); Marilyn Hanold (Doe); Edy Williams (Rae); Sivi Aberg (Mimi); Diane Farrell, Jack Perkins.

25B. "The Dead Ringers" Written by: Lorenzo Semple, Jr. Directed by: Larry Peerce. Airdate: October 27, 1966.

Chandell and his mob twin, Harry, along with three kilt-wearing henchwomen, continue their reign of terror in Gotham, manipulating Aunt Harriet and nearly killing Batman and Robin.

GUEST CAST: Liberace (Chandell/Harry); Marilyn Hanold (Doe); Edy Williams (Rae); Sivi Aberg (Mimi); Diane Farrell, Jack Perkins.

26A. "Hizzoner the Penguin" Written by: Stanford Sherman. Directed by: Oscar Rudolph. Airdate: November 2, 1966.

Politics makes for strange bedfellows, and Batman is flabbergasted when Penguin renounces his life of crime to run for Mayor of Gotham City. Knowing a Penguin administration would be detrimental to Gotham, Batman tosses his hat into the ring and becomes a candidate for office as well.

GUEST CAST: Burgess Meredith (The Penguin); Cindy Malone (Lulu); Woodrow Parfrey; Allen Ludden; Byron Keith (Mayor Linseed).

26B. "Dizzoner the Penguin" Written by: Stanford Sherman. Directed by: Oscar Rudolph. Airdate: November 3, 1966.

Worried that his political opponent, Batman, may garner more votes in the race for Mayor, Penguin has plotted to drop his nemesis into a vat of acid. Batman escapes the trap and the race to become Mayor is on.

GUEST CAST: Burgess Meredith (The Penguin); Cindy Malone (Lulu); Woodrow Parfrey; Allen Ludden; Byron Keith (Mayor Linseed).

27A. "Green Ice" Written by: Max Hodge. Directed by: George Waggner. Airdate: November 9, 1966.

Mr. Freeze, the man with ice water in his veins, escapes from prison (in an ice cream truck) and plans to steal one of Gotham's beauties (Miss Iceland) to be his bride. Batman and Robin race to intervene but are turned into giant ice pops by the malevolent Mr. Freeze's ice ray gun.

GUEST CAST: Otto Preminger (Mr. Freeze); Marie Windsor (Nellie); Dee Hartford; Byron Keith (Mayor Linseed); Charles O'Donnell, Robert Wiensko.

27B. "Deep Freeze" Written by: Max Hodge. Directed by: George Waggner. Airdate: November 10, 1966.

Batman and Robin are de-thawed from Mr. Freeze's cold-hearted trap, where they were frozen as giant ice pops. Red hot with anger, the Dynamic Duo — humiliated by Freeze's caped imposters — sets out to stop Freeze's latest criminal plot.

GUEST CAST: Otto Preminger (Mr. Freeze); Marie Windsor (Nellie); Dee Hartford; Byron Keith (Mayor Linseed); Charles O'Donnell, Robert Wiensko.

28A. "The Impractical Joker" Written by: Jay Thompson and Charles Hoffman. Directed by: James B. Clark. Airdate: November 16, 1966.

Has the Joker developed a time machine? Batman doesn't think so, and soon he proves that the Joker has been hypnotizing victims, not traveling through time, to commit crimes. But still, how can he stop the Clown Prince of Crime?

GUEST CAST: Cesar Romero (The Joker); Kathy Kersh, Christopher Gary, Louis Quinn, Howard Duff.

29B. "The Joker's Provokers" Written by: Jay Thompson and Charles Hoffman. Directed by: James B. Clark. Airdate: November 17, 1966.

Batman is nearly pressed into a giant key-making machine in the Joker's lair, but its only the prologue to a new battle between Gotham's enemies.

GUEST CAST: Cesar Romero (The Joker); Kathy Kersh, Christopher Gary, Louis Quinn, Howard Duff.

30A. "Marsha, Queen of Diamonds" Written by: Stanford Sherman. Directed by: James B. Clark. Airdate: November 23, 1966.

The gorgeous Marsha, Queen of Diamonds, has all of Gotham under her spell — literally! She shoots Chief O'Hara, Commissioner Gordon and even Batman with "love darts" that places all of them under her spell — a perfect plan to steal her favorite new diamond, one which is crucial to powering the Bat Cave!

GUEST CAST: Carolyn Jones (Marsha, Queen of Diamonds); Woody Strode, Estelle Winwood.

30B. "Marsha's Scheme with Diamonds" Written by: Stanford Sherman. Directed by: James B. Clark. Airdate: November 24, 1966.

Batman has been seduced by Marsha, Queen of Diamonds, thanks to her special love potion darts, and she is still after the Batjewel running the Batcomputer. Though Batman is able to overcome the effects of the intoxicating chemical, Marsha has a back-up plan: she will kill Robin unless Batman meets her at the altar!

GUEST CAST: Carolyn Jones (Marsha, Queen of Diamonds); Woody Strode, Estelle Winwood.

31A. "Come Back, Shame" Written by: Stanley Ralph Ross. Directed by: Oscar Rudolph. Airdate: November 30, 1966.

A cowboy crook named Shame is on the lam in Gotham, and desperate to create a getaway vehicle that can outdistance the useful Batmobile. Batman sets a trap for him, but the tables are turned when Shame runs the Dynamic Duo into a stampede of cattle!

GUEST CAST: Cliff Robertson (Shame); Joan Staley (Okie Annie); Jack Carter; Timothy Scott; Werner Klemperer (Colonel Klink).

31B. "It's the Way You Play the Game" Written by: Stanley Ralph Ross. Directed by: Oscar Rudolph. Airdate: December 1, 1966.

Batman and Robin escape Shame's stampeding herd and set out to lasso the cowboy villain before he steals any more hot rods.

GUEST CAST: Cliff Robertson (Shame); Joan Staley (Okie Annie); Jack Carter; Timothy Scott; Werner Klemperer (Colonel Klink).

32A. "The Penguin's Nest" Written by: Lorenzo Semple, Jr. Directed by: Murray Golden. Airdate: December 7, 1966.

The Penguin opens up a chi-chi restaurant in Gotham with the express purpose of copying the signatures of wealthy patrons. Now he just needs to get arrested so he can return to prison and team up with a forgery expert who can help him execute his scheme.

GUEST CAST: Burgess Meredith (Penguin); Grace Gaynor (Chickadee); Lane Bradford; David Lewis (Warden Crichton); Ted Cassidy (Lurch).

32B. "The Bird's Last Jest" Written by: Lorenzo Semple, Jr. Directed by: Murray Golden. Airdate: December 8, 1966.

Batman and Robin save Chief O'Hara, kidnapped by the Penguin, and learn of his scheme to forge the names of wealthy Gothamites. Before long, Penguin is bounced back to prison, along with his plot to write bad checks.

GUEST CAST: Burgess Meredith (Penguin); Grace Gaynor (Chickadee); Lane Bradford; David Lewis (Warden Crichton).

33A. "The Cat's Meow" Written by: Stanley Ralph Ross. Directed by: James B. Clark. Airdate: December 14, 1966.

Catwoman is back, and this time she's developed a device that can steal the voices of innocent people. She's eager to test the machine out on British rock sensation Chad and Jeremy, guests at Wayne Manor, but ends up getting more than she bargained for when she runs afoul of Batman and Robin.

GUEST CAST: Julie Newmar (Catwoman); Chuck Henderson, Joe Flynn, Chad Stuart, Jeremy Clyde, Jay Sebring, Peter Leeds.

33B. "The Bats Kow Tow" Written by: Stanley Ralph Ross. Directed by: James B. Clark. Airdate: December 15, 1966.

Catwoman has apprehended Batman and Robin with tranquilizer claws and subjected them to the equivalent of Chinese Water Torture, but they escape her trap and set about bringing the furious feline to justice before she can collect a ransom for the stolen voices of rock singers Chad and Jeremy.

GUEST CAST: Julie Newmar (Catwoman); Chuck Henderson, Joe Flynn, Chad Stuart, Jeremy Clyde, Jay Sebring, Peter Leeds.

34A. "The Puzzles Are Coming" Written by Fred De Gorter. Directed by: Jeffrey Hayden. Airdate: December 21, 1966.

Batman and Robin match wits with the Puzzler, a new criminal on the loose in Gotham, this one bent on robbing a party of wealthy Gotham socialites. When Batman and Robin intervene, they are trapped in a hot air balloon set to explode high above the city.

GUEST CAST: Maurice Evans (The Puzzler); Barbara Stuart, Paul Smith, Robert Miller Driscoll.

34B. "The Duo Is Slumming" Written by: Fred De Gorter. Directed by: Jeffrey Hayden. Airdate: December 22, 1966.

Escaping the airborne trap set for them by the Puzzler, Batman and Robin get their feet on the ground and "puzzle" a way to defeat their new opponent.

GUEST CAST: Maurice Evans (The Puzzler); Barbara Stuart, Paul Smith, Robert Miller Driscoll.

35A. "The Sandman Cometh" Story by: Ellis St. Joseph. Written by: Ellis St. Joseph and Charles Hoffman. Directed by: George Waggner. Airdate: December 28, 1966.

Though she has promised to forsake her life of crime, Catwoman finds herself in cahoots with the European criminal called Sandman. Bruce and Dick must return home from a camping trip to face the criminals, determining that they are after the fortune of noodle magnate J. Pauline Spaghetti. Sandman brainwashes Robin and forces the Boy Wonder to stitch Batman to a mattress.

GUEST CAST: Julie Newmar (Catwoman); Michael Rennie (The Sandman/Dr. Somnambula); Richard Peel (Snooze); Tony Ballen (Nap); Valeri Kairys (Kitty); Pat Becker (Cattio); Jeanie Moore (Catarina); Spring Byington (J. Pauline Spaghetti).

35B. "The Catwoman Goeth" Story by: Ellis St. Joseph. Written by: Ellis St. Joseph, Charles Hoffman. Directed by: George Waggner. Airdate: December 29, 1966.

Batman escapes from Sandman's deadly quilt-stitching machine as Catwoman sets Robin adrift in a dangerous "Amazing Cat Maze" in her cat-a-combs. When Sandman double-crosses Catwoman and plans to marry millionaire J. Pauline Spaghetti, Catwoman helps Batman and Robin catch the criminal.

GUEST CAST: Julie Newmar (Catwoman); Michael Rennie (The Sandman/Dr. Somnambula); Richard Peel (Snooze); Tony Ballen (Nap); Valeri Kairys (Kitty); Pat Becker (Cattio); Jeanie Moore (Catarina); Spring Byington (J. Pauline Spaghetti); James Brolin (Reggie); Ray Montgomery (Dan); Lindsay Workman (Tuthill).

36A. "The Contaminated Cowl" Written by: Charles Hoffman. Directed by: Oscar Rudolph. Airdate: January 5, 1967.

The Mad Hatter returns to Gotham City, this time in hopes of stealing a valuable ruby. But when Batman intercepts the crazed hat aficionado, the Caped Crusader is sprayed with a radioactive compound, changing his cowl to a mauve color.

GUEST CAST: David Wayne (Jervis Tetch/The Mad Hatter); Jean Hale (Polly); Barbara Morrison (Hattie).

37B. "The Mad Hatter Runs a Foul" Written by: Charles Hoffman. Directed by: Oscar Rudolph. Airdate: January 6, 1967.

Batman and Robin escape from the Mad Hatter's monstrous X-Ray machine, and set out to capture the crazed criminal before more crimes are committed.

GUEST CAST: David Wayne (Jervis Tetch/ The Mad Hatter); Jean Hale (Polly); Barbara Morrison (Hattie).

38A. "The Zodiac Crimes" Written by: Stanford Sherman. Story by: Stephen Kandel. Directed by: Oscar Rudolph. Airdate: January 11, 1967.

In a terrifying conjunction of events, the Joker and the Penguin join forces, and Joker commits a crime spree related to the 12 astronomical signs of the Zodiac. Batman intervenes to stop the dastardly duo, but he and Robin are nearly crushed by a trap at Gotham Museum: a falling meteorite exhibit!

GUEST CAST: Burgess Meredith (The Penguin); Cesar Romero (The Joker); Terry Moore (Venus); Joe Di Reda (Mars); Hal Baylor (Mercury); Dick Crockett (Neptune); Charles Picerni (Uranus); Eddie Saenz (Saturn); Rob Reiner.

38B. "The Joker's Hard Times" Written by: Stanford Sherman. Story by: Stephen Kandel. Directed by: Oscar Rudolph. Airdate: January 12, 1967.

Batman and Robin continue to follow the criminal spree of Penguin and Joker, and nearly end up the dinner of a giant man-eating clam! As the crimes continue, Penguin and Joker plot to learn the true identities of their bat-nemeses.

GUEST CAST: Burgess Meredith (The Penguin); Cesar Romero (The Joker); Terry Moore (Venus); Joe Di Reda (Mars); Hal Baylor (Mercury); Dick Crockett (Neptune); Charles Picerni (Uranus); Eddie Saenz (Saturn); Rob Reiner.

38C. "The Penguin Declines" Written by: Stanford Sherman. Story by: Stephen Kandel. Directed by: Oscar Rudolph. Airdate: January 18, 1967.

Batman and Robin escape from the maw of a man-eating mussel. After a marathon of criminal ventures, the Penguin and Joker finally meet their Waterloo, their attempt to reveal the secret identities of Batman and Robin a total failure.

GUEST CAST: Burgess Meredith (The Penguin); Cesar Romero (The Joker); Terry Moore (Venus); Joe Di Reda (Mars); Hal Baylor (Mercury); Dick Crockett (Neptune); Charles Picerni (Uranus); Eddie Saenz (Saturn); Rob Reiner.

39A. "That Darn Catwoman" Written by: Stanley Ralph Ross. Directed by: Oscar Rudolph. Airdate: January 19, 1967.

The Catwoman captures and brainwashes the Boy Wonder, turning Robin into a super criminal and new nemesis for Batman. Hoping to return his partner to the right side of the law, Batman is lured into a trap involving a giant mousetrap.

GUEST CAST: Julie Newmar (Catwoman); Leslie Gore (Pussycat); Pat O'Malley (Pat Pending); Jock Gaynor, George Sawaya, Tony Epper.

39B. "Scat, Darn Catwoman" Written by: Stanley Ralph Ross. Directed by: Oscar Rudolph. Airdate: January 25, 1967.

Things are looking grim for Batman: A brainwashed Robin has stolen a fortune from Wayne Manor, Catwoman is on the loose, and Batman is pinned to an oversized mousetrap! But Batman escapes the Catwoman's treacherous trap, and sets about saving Robin and apprehending the criminal kitty cat.

GUEST CAST: Julie Newmar (Catwoman); Leslie Gore (Pussycat); Pat O'Malley (Pat Pending); Jock Gaynor, George Sawaya, Tony Epper.

40A. "The Penguin Is a Girl's Best Friend" Written by: Stanford Sherman. Directed by: James B. Clark. Airdate: January 26, 1967.

The Penguin and Marsha, Queen of Diamonds, lure Batman into a trap and threaten legal action if he doesn't appear in a movie they are producing. After shooting incriminating footage of the Caped Crusader, intimately linked with Marsha, the Penguin plots a nefarious criminal scheme.

GUEST CAST: Burgess Meredith (The Penguin); Carolyn Jones (Marsha, Queen of Diamonds); Estelle Winwood (Aunt Hilda); Frank Baron, Frank Conte.

40B. "Penguin Sets a Trend" Written by: Stanford Sherman. Directed by: James B. Clark. Airdate: February 1, 1967.

After shooting incriminating footage of Batman for his silver screen opus, the Penguin plans to use a giant catapult to kill the Dynamic Duo.

GUEST CAST: Burgess Meredith (The Penguin); Carolyn Jones (Marsha, Queen of Diamonds); Estelle Winwood (Aunt Hilda); Frank Baron, Frank Conte.

40C. "Penguin's Disastrous End" Written by: Stanford Sherman. Directed by: James B. Clark. Airdate: February 2, 1967.

Using their "production" as a cover, the Penguin and Marsha, Queen of Diamonds, plot a crime spree. But Batman and Robin escape the giant catapult and arrive in time to make sure that the Penguin's movie is a "wrap."

GUEST CAST: Burgess Meredith (The Penguin); Carolyn Jones (Marsha, Queen of Diamonds); Estelle Winwood (Aunt Hilda); Frank Baron, Frank Conte.

41A. "Batman's Anniversary" Written by: William P. D'Angelo. Directed by: James B. Clark. Airdate: February 8, 1967.

Commissioner Gordon orchestrates a surprise "anniversary" party for Batman to commemorate the date he first began working with Gotham City's finest, but the Riddler crashes the party and tricks the Dynamic Duo into a giant party cake composed of quicksand!

GUEST CAST: John Astin (The Riddler); Deanna Lund (Anna Gram); Ken Scott (Down); Jim Lefebvre (Across); Bryon Keith (Mayor Linseed).

42B. "A Riddling Controversy" Written by: William P. D'Angelo. Directed by: James B. Clark: Airdate: February 9, 1967.

Batman and Robin escape the Riddler's quicksand cake and follow clues to track down the villain. Unfortunately, the Riddler gets his hands on a deadly weapon that can destroy Gotham City Police Headquarters, and plans to use it to have amnesty declared for all criminals.

GUEST CAST: John Astin (The Riddler); Deanna Lund (Anna Gram); Ken Scott (Down); Jim Lefebvre (Across); Bryon Keith (Mayor Linseed).

43A. "The Joker's Last Laugh" Written by: Lorenzo Semple, Jr. Directed by: Oscar Rudolph. Airdate: February 15, 1967.

Bruce Wayne has unwittingly become romantically involved with the Joker's hench-woman, just as the clown prince of crime returns to Gotham to wreak havoc, this time from a comic book plant. Following clues to his hideout, Robin is nearly crushed in the Joker's comic book printing press.

GUEST CAST: Cesar Romero (The Joker); Phyllis Douglas (Josephine); Lawrence Montaigne (Mr. Glee); Edward McKinley (Mr. Flamm).

43B. "The Joker's Epitaph" Written by: Lorenzo Semple, Jr. Directed by: Oscar Rudolph. Airdate: February 16, 1967.

Robin escapes from the Joker's "crushing" printing press, but Bruce Wayne has a nasty surprise in store, regarding his new girlfriend. Will Batman be cowed by the clown prince of crime and led into a deadly trap?

GUEST CAST: Cesar Romero (The Joker); Phyllis Douglas (Josephine); Lawrence Montaigne (Mr. Glee); Edward McKinley (Mr. Flamm).

44A. "Catwoman Goes to College" Written by: Stanley Ralph Ross. Directed by: Robert Sparr. Airdate: February 22, 1967.

Paroled from Gotham Penitentiary, Catwoman signs up for a college course in criminology to avoid being captured by Batman again! But the feline felon is up to her old tricks, and this time her game is to frame the Caped Crusader for a robbery he didn't commit.

GUEST CAST: Julie Newmar (Catwoman); Paul Mantee, Sheldon Allman, Jacques Bergerac, David Lewis.

44B. "Batman Displays His Knowledge" Written by: Stanley Ralph Ross. Directed by: Robert Sparr. Airdate: February 23, 1967.

Catwoman plots to steal rare opals, and has successfully destroyed Batman's reputation. Batman and Robin escape from her bizarre trap (a giant coffee cup below a pot of acid!), and set about restoring Batman's honor and tracking down the cat burglar.

GUEST CAST: Julie Newmar (Catwoman); Paul Mantee, Sheldon Allman, Jacques Bergerac, David Lewis.

45A. "A Piece of the Action" Written by: Charles Hoffman. Directed by: Oscar Rudolph. Airdate: March 1, 1967.

Holy crossovers! Batman and Robin collide with another crime-fighting duo, the Green Hornet and Kato, as they track down a nasty criminal called Colonel Gumm. But even four superheroes aren't enough to stop this villain, who plans to turn the dynamic foursome into human postage!

GUEST CAST: Van Williams (The Green Hornet); Bruce Lee (Kato); Roger C. Carmel (Colonel Gumm); Seymour Cassel (Cancelled); Harry Frazier (Mr. Stample).

45B. "Batman's Satisfaction" Written by: Charles Hoffman. Directed by: Oscar Rudolph. Airdate: March 2, 1967.

Batman and Robin, the Green Hornet and Kato survive Colonel Gumm's nasty human postage–maker and team up against Colonel Gumm. Marshalling their resources, the super foursome defeats the villain handily, and a friendship of sorts is forged.

GUEST CAST: Van Williams (The Green Hornet); Bruce Lee (Kato); Roger C. Carmel

(Colonel Gumm); Seymour Cassel (Cancelled); Harry Frazier (Mr. Stample).

46A. "King Tut's Coup" Written by: Stanley Ralph Ross. Story by: Leo and Pauline Townsend. Directed by: James B. Clark. Airdate: March 8, 1967.

King Tut returns to Gotham, this time bent on capturing a wealthy Gothamite that bears a resemblance to Cleopatra. When Batman intervenes, he is captured and threatened with a fate worse than death: immersion in boiling oil!

GUEST CAST: Victor Buono (King Tut); Grace Lee Whitney (Neila); Lee Meriwether (Lisa); Richard Bakalyan, Lloyd Haines.

46B. "Batman's Waterloo" Written by: Stanley Ralph Ross. Story by: Leo and Pauline Townsend. Directed by: James B. Clark. Airdate: March 9, 1967.

Batman escapes a grim fate in King Tut's lair, breaking out of the casket that could immerse him in boiling oil. King Tut's nefarious plan to wed the daughter of a wealthy millionaire is hampered by Batman and Robin when they turn the tables on the deluded professor of Egyptology.

GUEST CAST: Victor Buono (King Tut); Grace Lee Whitney (Neila); Lee Meriwether (Lisa); Richard Bakalyan, Lloyd Haines.

47A. "Black Widow Strikes Again" Written by: Robert Mintz. Directed by: Oscar Rudolph. Airdate: March 15, 1967.

Black Widow returns to Gotham City and uses a "cerebrum short-circuiter" on a bank teller, Irving Cash, to steal money. Batman and Robin feed all their data on Black Widow into the Batcomputer to no avail, and finally realize she is robbing Gotham's banks in alphabetical order. They chase her to her underground lair, and she traps them in a giant spider's web with two female black widows.

GUEST CAST: Miss Tallulah Bankhead (Black Widow); Donald Barry (Tarantula); Al

Ferrara (Trap Door); Michael Lane (Daddy Longlegs); George Chandler (Grampa); Grady Sutton (Irving Cash); Pitt Herbert (Irving Leghorn); Walker Edmiston (Teller); Meg Wyllie (Grandma).

48B. "Caught in the Spider's Den" Written by: Robert Mintz. Directed by: Oscar Rudolph. Airdate: March 16, 1967.

Batman manages to electrocute the attacking spiders with his utility belt minicharge, and frees himself and Robin from the giant spider's web. But Black Widow uses her short-circuiter to brainwash Batman into becoming her accomplice. Disguised as Robin, Black Widow employs the Batmobile in the next bank robbery. The real Boy Wonder frees Batman from the Widow's clutches and springs a trap for her, even as Commissioner Gordon and Chief O'Hara put out an APB on the dynamic duo.

GUEST CAST: Miss Tallulah Bankhead (Black Widow); Donald Barry (Tarantula); Al Ferrara (Trap Door); Michael Lane (Daddy Longlegs); Richard Krisher (Policeman); George Chandler (Grampa); Don Biggs (Irving Irving).

NOTE: For some reason, all the bank tellers in this episode are named Irving. There is even one named Irving Irving...

49A. "Pop Goes the Joker" Written by: Stanford Sherman. Directed by: George Waggner. Airdate: March 22, 1967.

The Joker defaces Gotham City's precious art treasures, but because tastes are what they are, his destruction is itself heralded as "artistic." Suddenly popular for his "talent," the Joker opens an art school for millionaires, secretly a bid to hold them for ransom.

GUEST CAST: Cesar Romero (The Joker); Diana Ivarson (Baby Jane); Reginald Gardiner (Bernie Parks); Jerry Catron, Jack Perkins.

49B. "Flop Goes the Joker" Written by: Stanford Sherman. Directed by: George Waggner. Airdate: March 23, 1967.

In the Joker's art school for millionaires, Bruce Wayne and other Gotham elite are held captive by the clown prince of crime, and Robin barely survives a deadly trap involving knives. Once separated but now reunited, the Dynamic Duo take down the Joker.

GUEST CAST: Cesar Romero (The Joker); Diana Ivarson (Baby Jane); Reginald Gardiner (Bernie Parks); Jerry Catron, Jack Perkins.

50A. "Ice Spy" Written by: Charles Hoffman. Directed by: Oscar Rudolph. Airdate: March 29, 1967.

Mr. Freeze is back with a deadly scheme to create "instant ice," but first he must kidnap Dr. Isaacson, a scientist that has developed the formula for the miraculous "quick freeze." After a daring abduction aboard the Gotham Queen, an ocean liner, Freeze captures Batman and Robin and traps them in a sub-zero "freezer."

GUEST CAST: Eli Wallach (Mr. Freeze); Leslie Parish (Glacia Galze); Elisha Cook, Jr. (Professor Isaacson); H.M. Wyant (Frosty).

50B. "The Duo Defy" Written by: Charles Hoffman. Directed by: Oscar Rudolph. Airdate: March 30, 1967.

Batman and Robin escape Mr. Freeze's deadly trap at an ice skating rink, and a series of clues lead them to his hideout. Now they must rescue Dr. Isaacson and stop the deployment of "instant ice" before it's too late for Gotham City!

GUEST CAST: Eli Wallach (Mr. Freeze); Leslie Parish (Glacia Galze); Elisha Cook, Jr. (Professor Isaacson); H.M. Wyant (Frosty).

SEASON THREE (1967-68)

51. "Enter Batgirl, Exit the Penguin" Written by: Stanford Sherman. Directed by: Oscar Rudolph. Airdate: September 14, 1967.

The Penguin abducts Barbara Gordon, Police Commissioner Gordon's daughter, and plans to make her his wife. But what the Penguin doesn't know is that Barbara has a secret identity: she is the motorcycle-riding, newest addition to the "bat family": Batgirl!

GUEST CAST: Burgess Meredith (The Penguin); Elizabeth Harrower (Drusilla); Jonathan Troy (Reverend Hazlitt); John Walter.

52. "Ring Around the Riddler" Written by: Charles Hoffman. Directed by: Sam Strangis. Airdate: September 21, 1967.

The Riddler is back in town, planning to control professional boxing. He teams up with a lovely and alluring villainess, the Siren, and then meets his nemesis, Batman, in the ring.

GUEST CAST: Frank Gorshin (The Riddler); Joan Collins (Siren); James Brolin, Peggy Ann Garner, Gil Perkins.

53. "The Wail of the Siren" Written by: Stanley Ralph Ross. Directed by: George Waggner. Airdate: September 28, 1967.

The seductive criminal called the Siren brainwashes Commissioner Gordon into revealing the secret location of the Batcave. The Siren's seven-octave vocal range then hypnotizes Bruce Wayne too, allowing Siren to steal the Wayne Foundation riches. She then attempts to make the millionaire commit suicide!

GUEST CAST: Joan Collins (The Siren); Cliff Osmond (Andante); Mike Mazurk (Allegro).

54. "The Sport of Penguins" Written by Charles Hoffman. Directed by: Sam Strangis. Airdate: October 5, 1967.

The Penguin is back to wreak havoc, this time leaving deadly umbrella bombs at the site of his most recent crime. Soon he has teamed up with another criminal named Lola Lasagne, and raised the ire of Batman and Robin.

GUEST CAST: Burgess Meredith (The Penguin); Ethel Merman (Lola Lasagne); Horace McMahon, Lewis Charels, Constance Davis.

55. "A Horse of Another Color" Written by Charles Hoffman. Directed by: Sam Strangis. Airdate: October 12, 1967.

The Penguin and Lola Lasagne plan to "fix" a horse racing event sponsored by the Wayne Foundation, with all proceeds going to charity. But if Penguin and Lola win, they'll be millionaires!

GUEST CAST: Burgess Meredith (The Penguin); Ethel Merman (Lola Lasagne); Horace McMahon, Lewis Charels, Constance Davis.

56. "The Unkindest Tut of All" Written by: Stanley Ralph Ross. Directed by: Sam Strangis. Airdate: October 19, 1967.

A supposedly reformed King Tut returns to Gotham City, this time endowed with the ability to foresee future crimes — actually crimes that he has orchestrated himself! Tut tracks the Batmobile and learns the secret identities of Batman and Robin, but how can the Dynamic Duo prove that they aren't who they really are?

GUEST CAST: Victor Buono (King Tut); Patti Gilbert, James Gammon, Cathleen Cordell.

57. "Louie, the Lilac" Written by: Dwight Taylor. Directed by: George Waggner. Airdate: October 26, 1967.

Louie the Lilac has cornered the flower market in Gotham City to co-opt the hippie flower children to his nefarious criminal causes. When Batman and Robin are incapacitated by poison flowers and man-eating lilacs at Lila's Flower Shop, it's up to Batgirl to come to their rescue.

GUEST CAST: Milton Berle (Louie the Lilac); Lisa Seagram (Lila); Richard Bakalyan (Arbutis); Karl Lukas (Acacia); Jimmy Boyd (Dogwood).

58. "The Ogg and I" Written by: Stanford Sherman. Directed by: Oscar Rudolph. Airdate: November 2, 1967.

That cunning fiend, Egghead, and his lovely but merciless companion Olga, kidnap Commissioner Gordon and use crying gas to paralyze Batman, Robin and Batgirl. Now they intend to ransom Gotham City for the safe return of Gordon.

GUEST CAST: Vincent Price (Egghead); Anne Baxter (Olga, Queen of Cossacks); Alfred Dennis (Orloff); Alan Hale, Jr. (Gilligan); Violet Carlson, Billy Corcoran, James O'Hara.

59. "How to Hatch a Dinosaur" Written by: Stanford Sherman. Directed by: Oscar Rudolph. Airdate: November 9, 1967.

Egghead and Olga plan further havoc for Gotham City, intending to hatch a prehistoric dinosaur egg. They plan to raise the beast and terrorize the inhabitants of the city with a living, breathing monstrosity from another age!

GUEST CAST: Vincent Price (Egghead); Anne Baxter (Olga, Queen of Cossacks); Alfred Dennis (Orloff); Alan Hale, Jr., Violet Carlson, Billy Corcoran, James O'Hara.

60. "Surf"s Up! Joker's Under" Written by: Charles Hoffman. Directed by: Oscar Rudolph. Airdate: November 16, 1967.

Joker kidnaps surfing champion Skip Parker at Gotham Point and uses his experimental "Surfing Experience and Ability Transferometer" to steal the boy's knowledge of the sport. Before long, Batman, Robin and Batgirl are on the case with Commissioner Gordon and Chief O'Hara (dressed as beach bums...). Now Batman competes against the Joker in a surfing contest, lest Joker win the admiration of Gotham's youth.

GUEST CAST: Cesar Romero (The Joker); Sivi Aberg (Undine); Ronnie Knox (Skip Parker); John Mitchum (Hot Dog Harrigan); Skip Ward (Riptide); Johnny Green and the Green Men.

61A. "The Londinium Larcenies" Written by: Elkan Allan and Charles Hoffman. Directed by: Oscar Rudolph. Airdate: November 23, 1967.

Batman, Robin and Batgirl are called in to solve a baffling crime in Londinium, and face a criminal mastermind unlike any they've faced before: Lord Phogg. Worse, the criminal is expecting them and sets a deadly trap involving the Batmobile.

GUEST CAST: Rudy Valley (Lord Phogg); Glynis Johns (Lady Penelope Peasoup); Lyn Peters (Prudence); Lynley Lawrence (Kit); Stacy Maxwell, Aleta Rotell, Maurice Dallimore, Larry Anthony, Monty Landis, Harvey Jason, Gil Stuart.

61B. "The Foggiest Notion" Written by: Elkan Allan and Charles Hoffman. Directed by: Oscar Rudolph. Airdate: November 30, 1967.

Still in Londinium, operating out of a European Bat Cave of sorts, Batman, Robin and Batgirl clash with Lord Phogg and Lady Penelope Peasoup. Phogg has developed a form of fog to cloak his crime: the theft of the crown jewels!

GUEST CAST: Rudy Valley (Lord Phogg); Glynis Johns (Lady Penelope Peasoup); Lyn Peters (Prudence); Lynley Lawrence (Kit); Stacy Maxwell, Aleta Rotell, Maurice Dallimore, Larry Anthony, Monty Landis, Harvey Jason, Gil Stuart.

61C. "The Bloody Tower" Written by: Elkan Allan and Charles Hoffman. Directed by: Oscar Rudolph. Airdate: December 7, 1967.

In Londinium, the Terrific Trio gets the upper hand in their battle of wills and cunning with Lord Phogg and Penelope Peasoup.

GUEST CAST: Rudy Valley (Lord Phogg); Glynis Johns (Lady Penelope Peasoup); Lyn Peters (Prudence); Lynley Lawrence (Kit); Stacy Maxwell, Aleta Rotell, Maurice Dallimore, Larry Anthony, Monty Landis, Harvey Jason, Gil Stuart.

62. "Catwoman's Dressed to Kill" Written by: Stanley Ralph Ross. Directed by: Sam Strangis. Airdate: December 14, 1967.

The Catwoman objects when Rudi Gernreich awards a fashion medal to Batgirl, and then she detonates a hair-raising bomb. Her real plan is to steal the golden fleece, a priceless garment owned by Belgravia's Queen Bess, and then kidnap Batgirl.

GUEST CAST: Eartha Kitt (Catwoman); James Griffith (Manx); Karen Huston (Queen Bess); Rudi Gernreich (Himself).

63. "The Ogg Couple" Written by: Stanford Sherman. Directed by: Oscar Rudolph. Airdate: December 21, 1967.

Egghead and Olga make a nasty return to Gotham City, robbing the metropolitan museum and a bank before Batman can stop them. Batgirl, meanwhile, hopes to persuade Egghead to give up his life of crime and betray Olga, but Egghead is leading her on, planning to end her life in a giant vat of caviar!

GUEST CAST: Vincent Price (Egghead); Anne Baxter (Olga, Queen of the Cossacks); Violet Carson (Old Woman); Billy Corcoran, Donald Elson, Ed Ling.

64A. "The Funny Feline Felonies" Written by: Stanley Ralph Ross. Directed by: Oscar Rudolph. Airdate: December 28, 1967.

The Joker is released from Gotham prison and teams up with Catwoman for a deadly criminal scheme: the robbery of a Federal Bank Depository. Batman, Robin and Batgirl race to the scene to stop the deadly duo, but Catwoman's evil trap could squeeze the life out of Batgirl if the dynamic duo doesn't save her in time...

GUEST CAST: Earth Kitt (Catwoman); Cesar Romero (The Joker); Kick Kallman (Little Louie Kallman); Ronald Long (Karnaby Katz); Sandy Kevin (The Giggler); Bobby Hall (Laughter); David Lewis (Warden Crichton).

64B. "The Joke's on Catwoman" Written by: Stanley Ralph Ross. Directed by: Oscar Rudolph. Airdate: January 4, 1968.

The Joker and Catwoman are apprehended, put on trial, and represented by the scoundrel Lucky Pierre, but it's a sham to buy them time as they make preparations (through thievery) to rob the Federal Bank Depository. As usual, Batman sees through the masterminds' criminal scheme and takes steps with his caped cohorts to seize the day for justice.

GUEST CAST: Earth Kitt (Catwoman); Cesar Romero (The Joker); Kick Kallman (Little Louie Kallman); Ronald Long (Karnaby Katz); Sandy Kevin (The Giggler); Bobby Hall (Laughter); Pierre Salinger (Lucky Pierre); Louis Quinn (Mr. Keeper); Christine Nelson (Mrs. Keeper).

65. "Louie's Lethal Lilac Time" Written by: Charles Hoffman. Directed by: Sam Strangis. Airdate: January 11, 1968.

The flower-loving, power-mad Louie the Lilac captures Bruce Wayne and Dick Grayson in hopes of getting their money to bankroll his latest financial plan, but Commissioner Gordon is at a loss to save them without Batman and Robin. A desperate Alfred seeks the help of Batgirl in rescuing the millionaire and his ward, but Louie has a nasty trap waiting for the distaff bat hero.

GUEST CAST: Milton Berle (Louie the Lilac); Nobu McCarthy (Lotus); Percy Helton (Gus); Ronald Knight (Sassafras); John Dennis (Saffron).

66. "Nora Clavicle and the Ladies Crime Club" Written by: Stanford Sherman. Directed by: Oscar Rudolph. Airdate: January 18, 1968.

At the behest of his feminist wife, Mayor Linseed discharges Commissioner Gordon and appoints the woman's lib crusader Nora Clavicle in his position. Her first act in office is to fire all the male police officers of Gotham City and give Batman and Robin an "extended vacation." While planning to destroy Gotham City to collect the insurance money, Clavicle and her fiendish minions tie Batman, Robin and Batgirl into a human knot!

GUEST CAST: Barbara Rush (Nora Clavicle); Jean Byron (Mrs. Linseed); June Wilkinson (Evelina); Inga Neilson (Angelina); Byron Keith (Mayor Linseed); Ginny Gan (Police Woman); Larry Gelman (Bank Manager); Elizabeth Bauk (Fourth Policewoman).

NOTE: A bank manager actually says, "Thank goodness you're here, Batman," in this episode. That line has become the standard introductory line of the "superhero" game on the sketch show hosted by Drew Carey, *Whose Line Is It Anyway?* In this game, a person runs in and says, "Thank goodness you're here..." and then names a new superhero, which another performer must pretend to be. This author's favorite improvisation is Colin Mochrie's character Captain Blood Loss.

67. "Penguin's Clean Sweep" Written by: Stanford Sherman. Directed by: Oscar Rudolph. Airdate: January 25, 1968.

The Penguin breaks into Gotham City's mint, and Batman and Robin intercept him there, only to learn he hasn't yet stolen anything! The terrific trio soon discovers that Penguin has laced Gotham's money with a bacteria that causes "sleeping sickness." The villain has immunized himself and his gang against the Ligerian disease, and plans to collect Gotham's contaminated cash.

GUEST CAST: Burgess Meredith (The Penguin); Monique Van Vooren (Miss Clean); Abel Fernandez (Thug #1); Angela Posito (Thug #2); Len Folder (Policeman); William Phillips (Mint Supervisor).

68A. "The Great Escape" Written by: Stanley Ralph Ross. Directed by: Oscar Rudolph. Airdate: February 1, 1968.

Calamity Jan uses a stolen tank to break her lover, cowboy criminal Shame, out of Gotham Penitentiary. Shame plans to steal a valuable diamond and a roll of cash from two performers in the Gotham City Opera — until the Terrific Trio put a crimp in his plans.

GUEST CAST: Cliff Robertson (Shame); Dina Merrill (Calamity Jan); Hermione Baddeley (Frontier Fanny); Ted Bensinger (Prisoner); Barry Dennen (Fred); Victor Lundin (Chief Standing Pat).

68B. "The Great Train Robbery" Written by: Stanley Ralph Ross. Directed by: Oscar Rudolph. Airdate: February 8, 1968.

After paralyzing Batman, Robin and Batgirl with "Fear Gas," cowpoke Shame plots his next crime: the great train robbery. Batman and Robin are forced to exchange Frontier Fanny (Calamity Jan's Mom) for Batgirl, who has been abducted by Shame's gang. In the end, Batman and Shame agree to an old-fashioned duel on a condemned street ... but can Shame be trusted to abide by the rules of the game?

GUEST CAST: Cliff Robertson (Shame); Dina Merrill (Calamity Jan); Hermione Baddeley (Frontier Fanny); Barry Dennen (Fred); Victor Lundin (Chief Standing Pat); Robert Casper (Train Clerk); James Jeter (Train Guard).

69. "I'll Be a Mummy's Uncle" Written by: Stanley Ralph Ross. Directed by: Sam Strangis. Airdate: February 22, 1968.

King Tut escapes during one of his psychotherapy sessions and goes in search of a vein of rare metal located directly beneath stately Wayne Manor. Unfortunately, King Tut's impromptu mining operation will expose the Bat Cave and the connection between Bruce Wayne and Batman unless Batman and Robin can stop the nefarious criminal and keep Batgirl and Commissioner Gordon occupied.

GUEST CAST: Victor Buono (King Tut); Angela Dorian (Florence of Arabia); Henry Youngman (Manny); Joet Tata (Suleiman); Kathleeen Freeman (Rosetta Stone); Tony Epper (tutling); Jock Mahone (H.L. Hunter).

70. "The Joker's Flying Saucer" Written by: Charles Hoffman. Directed by: Sam Strangis. Airdate: February 29, 1968.

The Joker causes panic in Gotham City when he plants the rumor that Martians are on the loose and planning to invade the planet! Meanwhile, the Joker builds a flying saucer and demands that everyone on Earth surrender to him, planning to eliminate Batman with a time bomb hidden in the Batmobile.

GUEST CAST: Cesar Romero (The Joker); Corinne Calvet (Emerald); Richard Bakalyan (Verdigre); Ellen Cordy (Mrs. Green); Jeff Burton (Shamrock); Tony Gardner (Chartreuse); Byron Keith (Mayor Linseed); Fritz Feld (Professor Greenleigh).

71. "The Entrancing Dr. Cassandra" Written by: Stanley Ralph Ross. Directed by: Sam Strangis. Airdate: March 7, 1968.

A villain called Dr. Cassandra is on the loose in Gotham City, apparently armed with the power to make her henchmen invisible. Batman and Robin deduce that the next robbery will occur in a jewelry store where a certain diamond is Cassandra's quarry, but they are "flattened" by the crook's terrible new weapon.

GUEST CAST: Ida Lupino (Cassandra); Howard Duff (Caballa); David Lewis (Warden Crichton); Bill Zuckert (Prison Captain).

72. "Minerva, Mayhem and Millionaires" Written by Charles Hoffman. Directed by: Oscar Rudolph. Airdate: March 14, 1968.

The villainous spa owner Minerva uses her "Deepest Secret Extractor" to rob millionaire customers of their fortunes. When she learns of a stash of diamonds in the Wayne estate vault, she plans to brainwash Bruce and learn the combination to the safe. While Minerva steals the diamonds, her henchmen plot to pressure-cook Batman and Robin.

GUEST CAST: Zsa Zsa Gabor (Minerva); Bill Smith (Adonis); Mark Bailey (Apollo); Al Ferrara (Atlas); Yvonne Arnett (Aphrodite); Jacques Bergerec (Freddie the Fence); George Neise (Mr. Shubert).

Batman: The Movie (1966)
LIVE-ACTION FILM

"...West and Ward, both reprising their TV roles, indulge in as much verbal buffoonery as fisticuffs with their quartet of villains.... Similarly Martinson, who had been at the helm of several of the television episodes, repeats the flat look and garish colors for which the series had become noted. As a result, the film, though initially very successful...soon palls."
— Phil Hardy, *The Film Encyclopeida, Volume 2: Science Fiction.* William Morrow and Company, 1984, page 248.

"Screenwriter Lorenzo Semple, Jr. unfolds this superhero tale in the zany tradition of TV and there's not much more to say about it. Director Leslie H. Martinson treats it like just another quickie TV episode."
— John Stanley, *Creature Features Movie Guide Strikes Again,* Creatures at Large Press, 1994, page 34.

"The first *Batman* film with Adam West and Burt Ward pales in comparison to the television show — it was missing some of the zing. It has some wonderful moments, however, particularly Adam West running around a dockside holding a classic Hollywood cannonball bomb with its fuse sputtering smoke, announcing "Some days, you just can't get rid of a bomb." The Batcopter and the Batboat were introduced thanks to this film, and those props were always fun to see in the series, but the film is a little stale."
— William Latham, author of *Mary's Monster* and *Space:1999 Resurrection.*

CAST: Adam West (Bruce Wayne/Batman); Burt Ward (Dick Grayson/Robin); Lee Meriwether (Catwoman); Cesar Romero (The Joker); Burgess Meredith (The Penguin); Frank Gorshin (The Riddler); Alan Napier (Alfred); Neil Hamilton (Commissioner Gordon); Stafford Repp (Chief O'Hara); Madge Blake (Aunt Harriet); Reginald Denny (Commodore Schmidlapp); Milton Frome (Vice Admiral Fangschi-ester); Gil Perkins (Bluebeard); Dick Crockett (Morgan); George Sawaya (Quetch).

CREW: 20th Century–Fox presents A William Dozier Production, *Batman: The Movie. Written by:* Lorenzo Semple, Jr. *Produced by:* William Dozier. *Directed by:* Leslie H. Martinson. *Music:* Nelson Riddle. *Batman Theme:* Neal Hefti. *Orchestration:* Gil Grau. *Associate Producer:* Charles B. Fitzsimons. *Director of Photography:* Howard Schwartz. *Art Directors:* Jack Martin Smith, Serge Krizman. *Set Decorators:* Walter M. Scott, Chester L. Bayhi. *Unit Production Manager:* Sam Strangis. *Assistant Director:* William Derwin. *Film Editor:* Harry Gerstad. *Special Photographic Effects:* L.B. Abbott. *Sound:* Roy Meadows, Harry M. Leonard. *Makeup:* Ben Nye. *Hair Styles Supervised by:* Margaret Donovan. *Second Unit Director:* Ray Kellogg. *Second Unit Photography:* Jack Marta. *Aerial Photography:* Nelson Tyler. *Batboat:* Glastron. *Main Title:* Richard Kuhn and National Screen Services. *M.P.A.A. Rating:* G. *Running time:* 105 minutes.

Gotham City's saviors, Batman and Robin, are called to action to rescue those aboard a yacht carrying a new and revolutionary invention, Commodore Schmid-lapp's dehydrator. The Caped Crusaders race (via Batcopter) to the ocean, but the yacht vanishes before their eyes — it was nothing but a projection. Then a shark attacks Batman and is dispatched by his Shark Repellant Bat Spray.

At Police Headquarters, Commissioner Gordon and Chief O'Hara are baffled by the crime until they learn that four super-criminals are on the loose: the Catwoman, the Riddler, the Penguin and the Joker. Batman and Robin determine the crooks are working together and have already kidnapped Schmidlapp. The Caped Crusaders escape further peril (this time in the Bat Boat) when Penguin's submarine destroys the "image" projecter that had been used to trick the Dynamic Duo. Later, Batman comes to believe that the super-villains mean to harm Kitka, a beautiful Russian reporter. He romances her as Bruce Wayne, unaware that Kitka is actually Catwoman!

Meanwhile, the criminals plot to snatch the World Security Council at the United World Building. They succeed by using the dehydrator to turn the Council into piles of dust. Even as Penguin and his goons invade the Bat Cave, Batman and Robin learn of the nefarious plan that threatens world peace. The criminals demand one billion dollars (cash) per country for the safe return of each delegate, but Batman and Robin chase the villains at sea. The crooks are defeated, and Batman is horrified to learn that Catwoman is his beloved Kitka!

As the world watches with baited breath, Batman and Robin assiduously rehydrate the World Security Council and dispatch the four super-criminals to jail.

Batman (1989)
LIVE-ACTION FILM

"...[T]he picture has a haunting tone that sets it aside from most of its action-packed cousins.... Jack Nicholson provides the most memorable villain to seize the screen in ages."
— David Sterritt, *The Christian Science Monitor*, June 29, 1989, page 10.

"*Batman* is — if not a work of genius — a work of brilliance."
— Ken Hanke, *Films in Review*, October 1989, page 480.

"...[A] monumental pop edifice...[in which] some of the elements are already dated....But the movie is energetic and focused, rushing viewers down its mock–Wagnerian hallways with urgency."
— Ty Burr. *Entertainment Weekly*: "Comic Book Art," October 23, 1993, page 66.

"Tim Burton's *Batman* tried valiantly to capture much of the dark spirit of Frank Miller's work, and to some degree, succeeded. Although the film should really be called *The Joker*, it showed Batman as someone not quite normal, and gave us a very relaxed, but somewhat off-center Bruce Wayne in Michael Keaton, who brought much to the film. Keaton's Batman is every bit as "damaged" as is Jack Nicholson's Joker — they are both playing on the outer fringes of human psychology. The film's opening, with Batman portrayed as a kind of urban hunter, showed great promise for the film series, but as always, the car (and in this case, the love interest) shows that Hollywood can't leave the character where he belongs, as an isolated, obsessed, endlessly driven man fighting to create order in an insanely chaotic universe. Bruce Wayne and love are always difficult to put together, but Hollywood continues to try."

— William Latham, author of *Mary's Monster* and *Space:1999 Resurrection*.

CAST: Jack Nicholson (Jack Napier/The Joker); Michael Keaton (Bruce Wayne/Batman); Kim Basinger (Vicky Vale); Robert Wuhl (Alexander Knox); Pat Hingle (Commissioner Gordon); Billy Dee Williams (Harvey Dent); Michael Gough (Alfred); Jack Palance (Grissom); Jerry Hall (Alicia); Tracey Walter (Bob the Goon); Lee Wallace (Mayor Borg); William Hootkins (Detective Eckhardt); Richard Strange, Carl Chas, Mac MacDonald, George Lane Cooper, Terence Plummer, Philip Tan (Goons).

CREW: Warner Brothers presents a Guber-Peters Company Productions of a Tim Burton Film. Based upon characters appearing in magazines pubished by DC Comics Inc. *Casting:* Marion Dougherty. *Costume Design:* Bob Ringwood. *Ms. Basinger's Costumes:* Linda Henriksen. *Music:* Danny Elfman. *Songs written and performed by:* Prince. *Film Editor:* Ray Lovejoy. *Production Designer:* Anton Furst. *Director of Photography:* Roger Pratt. *Based upon Batman characters created by:* Bob Kane. *Executive Producers:* Benjmanin Melniker, Michael E. Uslan. *Co-Producer:* Chris Kenny. *Screenplay:* Sam

Hamm, Warren Skaaren. *Story:* Sam Hamm. *Produced by:* Jon Peters and Peter Guber. *Directed by:* Tim Burton. Filmed at Pinewood Studios. *M.P.A.A. Rating:* PG-13. *Running time:* 126 minutes.

The criminals of seedy Gotham City are fearful of a mythic creature called "the Bat" that frequents the night. Actually, the creature is Batman, a caped crusader in black costume by night, the millionaire misfit Bruce Wayne by day. The costumed crime fighter has gained the attention of a nosy reporter named Knox, now teamed with the lovely photo journalist Vicki Vale to get the story.

Meanwhile, Batman clashes with Jack Napier, henchman of crime boss Carl Grissom, at the old Axis Chemicals Plant. Jack falls into a vat of toxic chemicals and, after some bad plastic surgery, emerges as the twisted, green-haired, white-faced villain called the Joker. He goes on a terror spree, killing Boss Grissom (who set up him) and then lacing commercial products throughout Gotham City with a nerve gas that leaves its victims with a smile on their dead faces.

As the 200th anniversary of Gotham City nears, the battle between Joker and Batman intensifies. Vicki and Bruce became close romantically, and she learns of his dual nature (the orphaned Wayne and the hero Batman). Unfortunately, Joker also develops a fondness for Vale and kidnaps her. With a giant parade as the backdrop, Batman and Joker have a final clash at Gotham Cathedral.

Batman Returns (1992)
LIVE-ACTION FILM

"Tim Burton's exhaustingly inventive sequel offers many jolts of pleasure, but it's also a mess — a gilded sketchbook of a movie that keeps falling open to random pages."

— Owen Glieberman, *Entertainment Weekly*, July 31, 1992, page 42.

"*Batman Returns* is not as good a film as Burton's original, but it has its good moments. Michelle Pfeiffer's Catwoman is dead-on, the best character in the film. Christopher Walken's Max Schreck, created for the film as part of Burton's excessive nodding to German expressionist films, is a plot contrivance that adds little to the surroundings. Keaton's Batman/Bruce Wayne character is really only interesting in his relationship with Selina Kyle/Catwoman. And while Danny DeVito brought great things to the character of the Penguin, the character was not particularly well-imagined. This time around, Tim Burton put Tim Burton first, Batman second, and what we end up with is a hodgepodge of not particularly inspired action scenes and attempts at creating a kind of universe for these characters to inhabit. The only really memorable image in the film is the last-second reappearance of Catwoman. The rest of the film is just kind of bland, from Elfman's toned-down musical score to the badly written plot that just never seems to generate any real sense of threat."

— William Latham, author of *Mary's Monster* and *Space: 1999 Resurrection*.

"I find it the most adventurous and imaginative American film I've seen this year — and also the weirdest."

— David Sterritt, *The Christian Science Monitor*, June 23, 1992.

"As scripted by Daniel Waters, the movie seems like a long run-on sentence, full of sound and furiously overloaded action that doesn't make much sense."

— Barbara Cramer, *Films in Review*, October 1992, page 337.

"It is dark and playful and sick — all to the good — but undercut by a juvenile script and no really great moments to match the grandeur of its overarching sets and dread-inducing Danny Elfman score."

— Jami Bernard, *The New York Post*, June 19, 1992, page 25.

"It is a funny, gorgeous, mid-summer night's Christmas story about ... well, dating actually.... Accept no prequels."

— Richard Corliss, *Time*, June 22, 1992, page 69.

"I loved the scenes with Bruce and Selina. The scenes with Catwoman were great, and the chemistry between Keaton and Pfeiffer was terrific. Also, the interaction between Bruce and Alfred was extremely good. But I wasn't crazy about the Penguin. He was too disgusting, too weird. I remember watching it and thinking I wanted more Catwoman."

— Howard Margolin, host of *Destinies: The Voice of Science Fiction*.

CAST: Michael Keaton (Bruce Wayne/Batman); Danny DeVito (Oswald Cobblepot/The Penguin); Michelle Pfeiffer (Selina Kyle/Catwoman); Christopher Walken (Maximillian Shreck); Michael Gough (Alfred); Pat Hingle (Commissioner Gordon); Michael Murphy (Mayor); Vincent Schiavelli (Organ Grinder); Andrew Bryniarski (Chip); Cristi Conaway (Ice Princess); Steve Witting (Josh); Jan Hooks (Jen); John Strong (Sword Swallower); Rick Zumwalt (Tattooed Stranger); Branscombe Richmond (Terrifying Clown); Paul Reubens (Penguin's Father); Sean M. Whalen (Paperboy).

CREW: Warner Brothers Presents a Tim Burton Film, *Batman Returns*. Based upon characters appearing in magazines published by DC Comics, Inc. *Casting:* Marion Dougherty. *Special Penguin Make-up and Effects produced by:* Stan Winston. *Costume Designers:* Bob Ringwood, Mary Vogt. *Music composed and conducted by:* Danny Elfman. *Film Editor:* Chris Lebenzon. *Production Designer:* Bo Welch. *Director of Photography:* Stefan Czapsky. *Co-Producer:* Larry Franco. *Executive Producers:* Jon Peters, Peter Guber, Benjamin Melniker, Michael E. Uslan. *Based on Batman characters created by:* Bob Kane. *Screenplay:* Daniel Waters. *Story by:* Daniel Waters, Sam Hamm. *Produced by:* Denise Di Novi and Tim Burton. *Directed by:* Tim Burton. *M.P.A.A. rating:* PG-13. *Running time:* 126 minutes.

At Christmas time, a strange penguin-like creature that apparently lives in the sewers terrorizes Gotham City. Above ground, business tycoon Max Shreck wants to build a power plant, but his secretary, Selina Kyle, learns that his proposed new construction would actually suck power out of the city. When she confronts him with this information, he pushes her out of his office building and she plummets to her death. Only she doesn't die ... she survives, deranged, and becomes the female criminal/heroine avenger known as the Catwoman.

Meanwhile, the disfigured Oswald Cobblepot, a.k.a. the Penguin, becomes Gotham's favorite son when he rescues a child from a gang. Secretly allying himself with the corrupt Shreck, Cobblepot plans to run for mayor and unseat the honorable man that is preventing the construction of

Max's power plant. Cobblepot has further plans to blackmail the aristocracy of Gotham. He wants to kidnap their children, terrorizing the parents as revenge for his own parents' earlier abandonment of him.

Bruce Wayne and Selina date for a time, even as chaos engulfs the city. Batman is nearly done in by a bomb attached to the Batmobile. Later he clashes with Catwoman, falling hard for the lovely siren. Hoping to prevent Penguin's ascent to the mayorship, Bruce and his manservant Alfred use the Penguin's own words to discredit his campaign. But the Penguin's thirst for vengeance cannot be sated. He launches an attack on Gotham City from a defunct amusement park called Arctic World. He sends an army of penguins (with missiles strapped to their backs) against the populace. Batman intervenes to stop the deadly birds, even as Catwoman settles her personal score with Shreck. Amidst an apocalyptic battle, Catwoman and Batman acknowledge their feelings for one another, but it appears that only one of them will survive the battle with the Penguin.

Batman: The Animated Series
(a.k.a. *The Adventures of Batman and Robin*)
(1992–1998) ANIMATED SERIES

"It had some of the best writing I've ever seen on television. Not just for a cartoon. There are elements of that series that are just brilliantly scripted. I was never particularly thrilled with the design of character, but beyond that, the atmosphere and writing and darkness and intensity are all great."
— Howard Margolin, host,
Destinies: The Voice of Science Fiction.

"By far the most effective attempt by Hollywood to bring Batman to life has been *Batman: The Animated Series*. Nearly everything about this series, from the voices to the style to the writing is not only of surprisingly high quality, but faithful to its source. Batman is an urban hunter, the villains are true to their natures from the comics, and Batman seldom if ever has a love interest — and when he does, such as in *Mask of the Phantasm*, the full-length feature produced by the team behind the animated series, you just know it's not going to work out well."
—William Latham, author of *Mary's Monster* and *Space: 1999 Resurrection.*

VOICE TALENT: Kevin Conroy (Bruce Wayne/Batman); Loren Lester (Dick Grayson/Robin); Bob Hastings (Commissioner Gordon); Efrem Zimbalist, Jr. (Alfred Pennyworth).

CREW: *Produced by:* Alan Burnett, Paul Dini, Eric Radomski, Bruce W. Timm. *Theme Music:* Shirley Walker. *Supervising Composer:* Shirley Walker. *Music Composed by:* Michael McCuistion. *Casting and Voice Direction*: Andrea Romano. *Storyboards:* Brian Chin, Ronaldo De Carmen, Joe Denton, Butch Lukic. *Character Design:* Ronaldo Del Carmen, Michael Diederich, Glen Murakami, Dexter Smith. *Vehicle and Prop Design:* Christopher Dent, Shayne Poindexter, Jonathan Fisher. *Based on the DC Comics character created by:* Bob Kane. *Film Editors:* Joe Gail, Theresa Gilroy-Nielson. *Sound Services:* Monterey Post Services. *Sound Effects:* Russell Brower. *Animation Services:* Dong Yang Animation, Inc. *Layout and Animation Supervision:* Rich Machen. *Production Manager:* Haven Alexander. *Executive in Charge of Production:* Tim Sarnoff. *Executive Producers:* Jean MacCurdy, Tom Ruegger. From Warner Brothers.

Batman Forever (1995)
LIVE–ACTION FILM

"*Batman Forever* needs the radioactive Carrey: much of the film is heavy and clunky. Batman's hand-to-hand combats take place in muffling darkness; you can barely see the kung or the fu."

— Jack Kroll, *Newsweek,* June 26, 1995, page 54.

"*Batman Forever* gave us a new Batman, in Val Kilmer, and a lot of other pieces of Batman's world from the comics while signaling the beginning of the end of the film series. Kilmer is good as Batman and as Bruce Wayne. The rest of the film is fairly terrible. The camp aspects of the television series began to sneak into the franchise at this point, and the common perception that this is the beginning of a "gay" Batman series is not a perception that's easy to discredit. Director Joel Schumacher tries to camp up Gotham City into kind of the dark side of Oz, and the net result is something that wanders from the dark fantasy of Tim Burton into just plain fantasy. The villains are wasted — Jim Carrey spends the film trying to portray insanity, but not as presented by Jack Nicholson as the Joker, and the end result is someone who is more annoying than crazy. Tommy Lee Jones as "Harvey Two-Face" is not the character portrayed in the comics, and it's unfortunate that Billy Dee Williams wasn't carried over from Burton's first film as had been planned initially. Two-Face in the comics is every bit as obsessed as Batman, and in this film he's just something of a crackpot with a bad complexion. Once again, Batman must have a love interest, in the character of Chase Meridian, and there's little chemistry between the two. One wonders what Kilmer might have done with the character in a better film."

— William Latham, author of *Space: 1999 Resurrection* and *Mary's Monster*.

"Kilmer's evident discomfort both as the Caped Crusader and his alter ego, Bruce Wayne, only points out what a talented actor Michael Keaton really is. Or maybe the problem lies in the lack of a credible plot, the movie's flat one-liners or its two-dimensional villains. Jones is wasted as the cackling Two-Face, and Carrey's Riddler is merely irritating."

— Brian Bethune, *MacLeans*, June 26, 1995, page 58.

CAST: Val Kilmer (Bruce Wayne/Batman); Tommy Lee Jones (Harvey Dent/Two-Face); Jim Carrey (Edward Nygma/The Riddler); Nicole Kidman (Dr. Chase Meridian); Chris O'Donnell (Dick Grayson/Robin); Michael Gough (Alfred); Pat Hingle (Commissioner Gordon); Drew Barrymore (Sugar); Debi Mazar (Spice); Rene Auberjonois (Dr. Burton); Joe Grifasi (Bank Guard); Elizabeth Sanders (Gossip Gerty); Philip Moon (Newscaster); Jessica Tuck (Female Newscaster); Kimberly Scott (Margaret); Ramsey Ellis (Young Bruce Wayne); George Wallace (Mayor).

CREW: Warner Brothers Presents a Tim Burton Production of a Joel Schumacher Film, *Batman Forever*. *Casting:* Mali Finn. *Special Make-up Designed and Created by:* Rick Baker. *Visual Effects Supervisor:* John Dykstra. *Costume Designers:* Bob Ringwood, Ingrid Ferrin. *Music Composed and Conducted by:* Elliot Goldenthal. *Edited by:* Dennis Virkler. *Production Designer:* Barbara Ling. *Director of Photography:* Stephen Goldblatt. *Executive Producers:* Benjamin Melniker, Michael E. Uslan. *Based on Batman Characters Created by:* Bob Kane. *Story by:* Lee Batchelor, Janet Scott Batchelor. *Screenplay by:* Lee Batchelor, Janet Scott Batchelor and Akiva Goldsman. *Produced by:* Tim Burton and Peter MacGregor-Scott. *Directed by:* Joel Schumacher. *M.P.A.A. Rating:* PG-13. *Running time:* 122 minutes.

Batman matches wits with the schizophrenic Two-Face, once the respected district attorney of Gotham City, Harvey Dent. Before the battle, he meets Chase Meridian, the sexy psychologist and expert on men with "dual personalities," and she gives him advice on dealing with the criminal. Batman survives a trap set by Harvey, and Two-Face is believed killed in the action.

Sometime later, Bruce Wayne visits a Wayne Industries Research laboratory and meets the eccentric Edward Nygma, a man developing a powerful "brain wave manipulator." Bruce feels the project is too dangerous and cuts off funding to the project, inadvertently spurring Nygma's psychosis and causing the creation of a new super-villain, Nygma's mad-hatter psychotic, the Riddler.

While Bruce seeks Chase's help in grappling with the issues of his childhood, the forces of evil gather in Gotham. When the Riddler and Two-Face join forces to drain the minds of all Gothamites, they learn the secret of Batman. Now Wayne has little choice but to join up with Dick Grayson, a headstrong, rebellious teen athlete whose parents were killed trying to stop

Two-Face from detonating a bomb at the Gotham Circus. After Riddler and Two-Face destroy the Bat Cave, it is time for Batman and Grayson's new hero persona, the able Boy Wonder, Robin, to team up for the first time and stop the villains. The matter is especially urgent, as the lovely Chase Meridian has been kidnapped.

Batman and Robin (1997)
LIVE-ACTION FILM

"Trying to create a comedy of excess, Schumacher pushes every element of the production to a perverse extreme, from the production design to the oversexed costume. But what he achieves instead is kind of a meta-comedy, a parody of a parody in which the only thing funny about the movie is how unfunny it is....And George Clooney's Batman is swallowed up by the carnivalesque shenanigans he's dropped into."
— Michael Stewart, *Entertainment Weekly:* "Zeroes to Heroes: The Motley Crew of Mystery Men Save the Day, but Other Comical Caped Crusaders Don't Fly as High." January 14, 2000, page 80.

"*Batman and Robin* is a disaster on nearly all fronts. George Clooney's boyish charm is probably just wrong for the character. Schwarzenneger as Mr. Freeze and Uma Thurman as Poison Ivy are probably good casting decisions, but this film's script, its tone, and its end result are just a waste of material. The character of Bane, love him or hate him in the comics, offered one of the most challenging villains added to the Batman universe in decades, and in this film, he's a throwaway prop. Much like this film. Camp and Batman do not work together, and one would hope that Hollywood would just stop trying to make this happen. George Clooney is not what killed the Batman series, however. The introduction of Robin in the prior film already weakened a shaky franchise, and Batgirl was just too much for the series to bear."
— William Latham, author of *Mary's Monster* and *Space: 1999 Resurrection.*

"*Batman and Robin* is less a movie than a razzle-dazzle video game."
— David Sterritt, *The Christian Science Monitor*, August 1, 1997, page 20.

"...Clooney is the blandest Batman ever to don the cape-a-Batman without a dark side.... [T]he action unfolds as a garish melee of explosions, sparks and hectic effects. Cuisinart editing makes the fights impossible to follow. And suspending disbelief is a chore."
— Brian D. Johnson, *MacLeans*, July 1, 1997, page 10G.

CAST: Arnold Schwarzenneger (Victor Freeze/Mr. Freeze); George Clooney (Bruce Wayne/Batman); Chris O'Donnell (Dick Grayson/Robin); Uma Thurman (Dr. Pamela Isley/Poison Ivy); Alicia Silverstone (Barbara Wilson/Batgirl); Michael Gough (Alfred); Pat Hingle (Commissioner Gordon); Elle McPherson (Julie Madison); John Glover (Dr. Jason Woodrue); Vivica A. Fox (Miss B. Haven); Vendela K. Thommassen (Nora Fries); Elizabeth Sanders (Gossip Gerty); Jeep Swenson (Bane); John Fink (Aztec Museum Guard); Michael Reid MacKay (Antonio Diego); Jesse Ventura (Arkham Asylum Guard); Coolio (Banker); Nicky Katt (Spike).

CREW: Warner Brothers Presents a Joel Schumacher Film, *Batman and Robin*. Based on DC Comics. *Casting:* Mali Finn. *Co-Producer:* William M. Elvin. *Visual Effects:* John Dykstra. *Costume Designers:* Ingrid Ferrin, Robert Turtirice. *Music Supervisor:* Danny Bramson. *Music:* Elliot Goldenthal. *Edited by:* Dennis Virkler, Mark Stevens. *Production Designer:* Barbara Ling. *Director of Photography:* Stephen Goldblatt. *Executive Producers*: Benjamin Melniker, Michael Uslan. *Based on characters created by:* Bob Kane. *Written by:* Akiva Goldsman. *Producer*: Peter MacGregor-Scott. *Directed by:* Joel Schumacher. M.P.A.A. Rating: PG-13. Running Time: 125 minutes.

The newest villain in Gotham City, the icy Mr. Freeze, is stealing diamonds to power his sub-zero environmental suit. Batman and Robin, who are having trouble working as partners, fight a pitched battle in Gotham museum to stop the thief. Batman is particularly irritated when Freeze escapes after an elaborate chase that takes the Dynamic Duo from Earth's stratosphere to Gotham's underside.

Meanwhile, in a South American lab, an accident with chemicals transforms a scientist into the monstrous (and toxic) plant woman called Poison Ivy. She teams with a pumped-up, experimental super-soldier called Bane and returns to Gotham City to liberate the vegetation of the world.

At his headquarters, Freeze is trying to cure MacGregor's Disease, a sickness also affecting poor old Alfred. Freeze is desperate for a cure so he can awaken his wife, currently in suspended animation. Hoping to join with Freeze, Ivy kills his frozen wife and blames Batman for the crime. Now

Freeze's blood is chilled and his anger knows no bounds. He plans to use the Gotham Observatory as a base for his freeze ray, which could kill everybody in Gotham.

While disaster looms, Batman and Robin both find themselves falling for Poison Ivy, courtesy of her strange love potion. When they become angry competitors, it is up to Alfred's niece, Barbara, to help bring the team back together. She does so — as the new heroine Batgirl.

Before the day is over, heroism has a new female face, Batman and Robin reconcile, the villains are defeated, and Mr. Freeze agrees to provide Alfred with the cure that could save his life.

Batman Beyond (1999–2001)
ANIMATED SERIES

VOICE TALENTS: Will Fredle (Terry McGinnis/Batman); Kevin Conroy (Bruce Wayne); Stockard Channing (Commissioner Barbara Gordon); Rachael Lee Cook (Chelsea Cunningham).

CREW: Based on DC Comics Characters. *Theme/Music:* Kristopher Carter. *Supervising Composer:* Shirley Walker. *Voice Direction:* Andrea Romano. *Character Design:* Shane Glines, Steve Jones, Glen Murakami, Tommy Tijeda, Bruce Timm, Glen Wong. *Series Story Editors:* Stan Berkowitz, Alan Burnett, Paul Dini, Rich Fogel. *Series Writers:* Hilary J. Bader, Stan Berkowitz, Alan Burnett, Paul Dini, Rich Fogel, Roberg Goodman. *Series Directors:* Curt Geda, Butch Lukic, James Tucker. From Warner Brothers.

Return to the Batcave: The Misadventures of Adam and Burt (2003)
LIVE-ACTION TV MOVIE

CAST: Adam West (Himself); Burt Ward (Himself); Jack Brewer (Young Adam West); Jason Marsden (Young Burt Ward); Lee Meriwether, Frank Gorshin, Julie Newmar and Lyle Waggoner.

CREW: *Written by:* Duane Poole. *Directed by:* Paul A. Kaufman.

Former Caped Crusaders Adam West and Burt Ward, now past-their-prime actors, relive the glory days of the *Batman* TV series from the 1960s. But something terrible happens — the famous Batmobile is stolen. Now Adam and Burt must find the vehicle and get back in touch with their dynamic duo past, encountering friends and foes along the way.

The Bionic Woman

By America's bicentennial celebration in 1976, *The Six Million Dollar Man* (the story of a bionic man and secret agent named Steve Austin) was one of the most popular TV series of the era. Some of the highest rated episodes of the Lee Majors series involved his beautiful girlfriend, Jaime Sommers, played by actress Lindsay Wagner, and her subsequent introduction to the world of bionics. Like Col. Austin, Jaime was a victim of a terrible accident, this time skydiving, and the only way to save her life was immediate surgery to outfit her with mechanical limbs and replacements. Unlike Steve, who had his vision augmented by a bionic eye, Jaime was implanted with a bionic ear, significantly enhancing her ability to listen in on bad guys. She also had a bionic arm and two bionic legs, making her a virtual superwoman with incredible strength and speed.

In her last guest role as Jaime on *The Six Million-Dollar Man*, Wagner's character unexpectedly rejected her bionic implants and apparently died, leaving a grief-stricken Steve Austin to mourn her. But even death could not stand in the way of true love, superheroes, and the all-powerful possibility of good Nielsen ratings. Thus ABC resurrected Jaime Sommers in her own series, *The Bionic Woman*, which aired Wednesday nights from 8:00 to 9:00 P.M.

Almost immediately, the series ranked among the top fifteen shows on the tube (vanquishing *Good Times* on CBS). Twenty-six-year-old Wagner enjoyed a $500,000 salary per season and became a genre star, sometimes to her chagrin. "I'm a serious actress, and I'm trying like hell not to become Wonder Woman," she remarked at one point.[1] This was an especially ironic comment because *Wonder Woman* was another popular property of the 1970s that, after its contemporizing face-lift in the second season, was seen by many as attempting to compete with *The Bionic Woman*.

Like her male counterpart, the bionic woman worked as a secret agent for the O.S.I. (the Office of Scientific Investigation). Jaime took orders from Steve's boss, Oscar Goldman (Richard Anderson), and had her bionics tended to by Dr. Rudy Wells (Martin Brooks). Brooks and Anderson performed double duty for a spell, appearing on both bionic series simultaneously and providing a nice cross-series continuity.

In the 1977 season, after two years on ABC, turmoil came to the world of Jaime and Steve when *The Bionic Woman* moved to a new network, NBC (and aired opposite ABC's *Operation Petticoat*). Some believed this switch would signal the end to the crossovers that had occurred regularly between the two series, but, in fact, the cliffhangers continued. Sometimes an episode of *The Six Million-Dollar Man* on ABC would conclude with an episode of *The Bionic Woman* on NBC, or vice versa. In this manner, Steve and Jaime fought side-by-side and faced some of the same supervillains, including Steve's most famous nemesis, the Sasquatch (Ted Cassidy), a hairy bionic alien robot, and Jaime's superpowered foes, android robots called "Fembots" (built by guest star John Houseman).

Unlike Steve, who did not seem to mind working for the government, Jaime was a more independent-minded operative and sometimes disliked the jobs Oscar asked her to perform. She was a teacher on an airbase for a time, and was a much more colorful "human" character than her counterpart. Also, it would be hard to deny that Wagner, once considered for the role of Captain Janeway on *Star Trek: Voyager* (1995–2002), was a more charismatic performer than the strong but square Lee Majors.

Even though Wagner was game as the series lead, a role she allegedly did not always relish, the actress had little help from the plot lines on *The Bionic Woman*, which

Beast and the Beauty? The Sasquatch (Ted Cassidy) and bionic woman Jaime Sommers (Lindsay Wagner) face off.

very quickly became repetitive. One particular idea was re-hashed thoroughly: Jaime goes undercover in a colorful new job, and must defeat the bad guys without exposing her identity as an agent. She was a stewardess in "Fly Jaime," a nanny in "The Ghost Hunter," a wrestler in "In This Corner, Jaime Sommers," a nun in "Sister Jaime," a cop in "Jaime's Shield" and a bank robber in "Once a Thief." After a while, this bit grew tired and the formula sagged.

The third season attempted to inject new life into the series (perhaps in case Lindsay Wagner bolted) by introducing a new bionic character: a dog named Max. This helpful pup appeared at least three times before the end of the series, in "The Bionic Dog," "Max" and "Antidote." Some critics within the industry saw this as a desperation move, and as ratings sank, the series was cancelled. But *The Bionic Woman*,

like *The Six Million-Dollar Man*, very quickly rose to cult status. It is one of those bedrock staple shows of the 1970s, one that every kid from that era watched with nearly religious fervor. A line of toys, action figures, books, comic books and other paraphernalia sold well until the end of the decade.

In the late 1980s, Lindsay Wagner returned to the role that had made her a star (after suffering through failed series such as *Jesse* [1984]) in a trio of bionic TV movies, *Return of the Six Million Dollar Man and the Bionic Woman*, *Bionic Showdown* and *Bionic Ever After*. She re-teamed with Lee Majors in all three ventures, and the last of the trilogy concerned the long-awaited wedding of the bionic duo.

Since then, the world has not heard the last of *The Bionic Woman*. A rerun staple on the Sci Fi Channel, *The Bionic Woman* is the latest superhero series to go down the road of a proposed remake. In this case, the USA network is developing a re-imagination of the series, with the ex-tennis-pro-turned-teacher-turned-spy now serving as a news producer. The show will reportedly be "reinvented with intelligence, and a terrific sense of humor," according to the network.[2]

The Bionic Woman (1976–1978)
LIVE-ACTION SERIES

CAST: Lindsay Wagner (Jaime Sommers); Richard Anderson (Oscar Goldman); Martin E. Brooks (Dr. Rudy Wells).

CREW: *Based on the novel* Cyborg *by:* Martin Caidin. *Created by:* Kenneth Johnson. *Executive Producer:* Harve Bennett. *Producer:* Kenneth Johnson. *Theme Music:* Jerry Fielding.

SEASON ONE (1976)

1. "Welcome Home Jaime" (Parts I & II) Written by: Kenneth Johnson. Directed by: Alan Crosland. Airdates: January 14 and 21, 1976.

Newly outfitted with bionic legs, arm and a bionic ear, accident survivor Jaime Sommers begins her career as an O.S.I. secret agent. Her first job involves exposing a spy selling classified secrets to foreign governments, but Jaimie soon learns that there is a personal component to this kind of government work when she befriends the spy's son.

GUEST CAST: Lee Majors (Steve Austin); Kip Niven (Donald Harris); Dennis Patrick (Harris); Gordon Jump, Alycia Gardner, Nick Pellegrino.

2. "Angel of Mercy" Written by: James D. Parriott. Directed by: Alan J. Levi. Airdate: January 28, 1976.

Jaime must deal with discrimination and danger when she teams with a sexist helicopter pilot to rescue an American ambassador trapped in a South American country. Jaime's bionic skills become a necessity when the ambassador's wife is caught in a collapsing building.

GUEST CAST: Andy Griffith (Starkey); James Karen (Morehouse); Robbie Ris (Andrew); Jean Allyson (Judith Morehouse); Paul Berrones, Claudio Martinez.

3. "A Thing of the Past" Written by: Philip De Guere. Directed by: Alan Crosland. Airdate: February 18, 1976.

A man in the witness protection program is unexpectedly exposed on the air when he performs a heroic deed. Jaime and Steve Austin work together to help the man hold onto his life and escape detection by the mob criminals who would like to see him dead.

GUEST CAST: Lee Majors (Steve Austin); Donald O'Connor, Don Gordon, Robert Perry, Alycia Gardner, Brian Cutler, Robbie Walcott.

4. "Claws" Written by: Sue Milburn. Directed by: Phil Bondelli. Airdate: February 25, 1976.

An innocent lion becomes the focal point in a debate about nature versus nurture. The beast, a timid creature trained to respond to human kindness, has been targeted by angry ranchers as the beast that has been killing cattle. Jaime must help sort out the problem and find the real culprit, or an innocent animal will die.

GUEST CAST: Alicia Flee, Tippi Hedren, William Schallert, Jack Kelly, George Wallace, Robbie Rist.

5. "The Deadly Missiles" Written by: Wilton Denmark. Directed by: Alan J. Levi. Airdate: March 3, 1976.

Jaime must poke around the estate of a wealthy friend to learn if a deadly missile was launched from his property. Jaime is reluctant to finger a friend, but all evidence points to him ... or his henchman.

GUEST CAST: Lee Majors (Steve Austin); Forrest Tucker (Connors); Ben Piazza.

6. "Bionic Beauty" Written by: James D. Parriott. Directed by: Alan Crossland. Airdate: May 17, 1976.

Oscar has received a troubling communication that the Miss U.S.A. pageant is rigged and somehow tied in with a plan to sell American secrets. Hoping to learn more, he plants Jaimie in the beauty contest.

GUEST CAST: Bert Parks (Raymond); Gary Crosby, Helen Craig, Charlotte Moore, Henry Pollick.

7. "Jaime's Mother" Written by: Arthur Rowe. Story by: Worley Thorne. Directed by: Leo Penn. Airdate: March 24, 1976.

At the cemetery where Jaime's parents, once secret agents, are buried, a woman claiming to be Jaime's mother confronts her. Jaime wants to believe the stranger, but Oscar fears that a dangerous enemy is deceiving her.

GUEST CAST: Barbara Rush (Ann Sommers); Norma Connolly, Sam Chew, Joseph George, Dan Barton.

8. "Winning Is Everything" Written by: James D. Parriott. Directed by: Phil Bondelli. Airdate: April 7, 1976.

Jaime must navigate an international racing contest to help recover a stolen tape that contains American secrets.

GUEST CAST: John Elerick (Sanders); Alejandro Rey (Scappini); Nancy Jeris, Frank Cala, Stephen Colt.

9. "Canyon of Death" Written by: Stephen Kandel. Directed by: Jerry London. Airdate: April 14, 1976.

One of Jaime's students tells her that he has seen a flying man. Oscar and Jaime believe that what he actually saw was a stolen jetpack being tested.

GUEST CAST: Guillermo San Juan; Robbie Rist (Andrew); Gary Collins (Mallory); Paul Covonis, Don McGovern, Annette Cardona, Jack Stauffer, Dee Timberlake, Jim Ingersoll, Bill Conklin.

10. "Fly Jaime" Written by: Arthur Rowe. Story by: Mann Rubin. Directed by: Barry Crane. Airdate: May 5, 1976.

An assassin is after Dr. Wells, who is returning from a foreign convention with a scientific secret. Jaime poses as a stewardess to protect Wells on the airline, but a dangerous crash complicates her search for the hired killer.

GUEST CAST: Spencer Milligan (Reed); Jerry Douglas, Chris Stone, Arline Anderson, Jim Raymond.

11. "The Jailing of Jaime" Written by: Bruce Shelly. Directed by: Alan Crosland. Airdate: May 12, 1976.

Jaime gets caught in the middle of a spy ring when the information she delivered to the O.S.I. is discovered missing. Is the bionic woman really a spy selling American secrets?

GUEST CAST: Barry Sullivan (Hatch); Anne Schedeen (Cindy); Tom Bower, Ross Elliott, Skip Homeier, Ron Hayes.

12. "Mirror Image" Written by: James D. Parriott. Directed by: Alan J. Levi. Airdate: May 19, 1976.

A surgically altered woman, made to look identical to Jaime Sommers, infiltrates the OSI offices and imitates the agent. Meanwhile, Jamie — who is on vacation — is nearly silenced forever by assassins.

GUEST CAST: Don Porter, Herbert Jefferson, Jr., Terry Kiser, John Fink, Sam Chew, Jr.

13. "The Ghosthunter" Written by: Kenneth Johnson and Justin Edgerton. Directed by: Kenneth Johnson. Airdate: May 26, 1976.

Jaime goes undercover as the nanny of

a misbehaving child in order to get close to a parapsychologist who is investigating supernatural happenings. Jaime suspects there is more involved, including, perhaps, a plan to sell American secrets to foreign powers.

GUEST CAST: Paul Sehnar; Kristy McNichol (Amanda); Bo Brundin, Mary Loomis, Susan Fleming.

SEASON TWO (1976-77)

14. "The Return of Big Foot" Written by: Kenneth Johnson. Directed by: Barry Crane. Airdate: September 22, 1976.

Steve Austin is near death after fighting the extraterrestrial robot, Sasquatch, now controlled by alien revolutionaries. Jaime is called in to obtain a serum that could save Steve's life, but she too must fight the bionic beast.

GUEST CAST: Lee Majors (Steve Austin); Ted Cassidy (Big Foot); Severn Darden, John Saxon, Stephen Young, Sandy Duncan, Stefanie Powers, Charles Cyphers, Gavin James.

15. "In This Corner, Jaime Sommers" Written by: Robert L. McCullough and Kenneth Johnson. Directed by: Alan Crosland. Airdate: September 29, 1976.

To locate a missing OSI agent, Jaimi goes undercover as a female wrestler. She runs afoul of a plot to sell United States secrets to foreign powers.

GUEST CAST: Norman Fell (Bigelow); Marcia Lewis, Marj Dusay, Brett Dunham, Bill Keene, Bill Conklin, Sandy Parker.

16. "Assault on the Princess" Written by: Wilton Denmark. Directed by: Alan Crosland. Airdate: October 6, 1976.

A specially designed experimental fuel cell has been stolen, and Jaime goes undercover as a blackjack dealer in a floating casino to learn more about the theft. Oscar and the OSI fear that the casino owner may actually be a notorious double agent, Iceman.

GUEST CAST: Ed Nelson, John Durren, Vito Scotti, Dick Dinman.

17. "Road to Nashville" Written by: James D. Parriott. Directed by: Alan J. Levi. Airdate: October 20, 1976.

A country singer may be passing information to the enemy, so Jaime goes to Nashville to learn the truth about the plot.

GUEST CAST: Hoyt Axton (Buck); Ben Kramer, Scott Arthur Allen, Fionnula Flanagan, Robin Harlan, Dick Haynes.

18. "Kill Oscar" (Parts I and II) Written by: Arthur Rowe. Directed by Alan Crosland. Airdates: October 27 and November 3, 1976.

A disenfranchised scientist wants to rule the world using a revolutionary weather control device. To get the device, he uses his "fembots," bionic duplicates of OSI officials, and kidnaps Oscar. With the safety of the world hanging in the balance, Jaime and Steve team up to rescue Oscar and fight Dr. Franklin's fembots on his isolated island fortress.

GUEST CAST: Lee Majors (Steve Austin); John Houseman (Franklin); Janice Whitby, Jack Colvin, Jennifer Darling, Jack L. Ging.

19. "Black Magic" Written by: Arthur Rowe. Directed by: Barry Crane. Airdate: November 10, 1976.

A wealthy man died after inventing a unique formula. Now Jaime must recover the formula from the man's family in Louisiana, but even Jaime is unprepared for the strange dangers she finds in the bayou.

GUEST CAST: Vincent Price (Manfred); William Windom (Warfield); Julie Newmar (Claudette); Abe Vigoda (Barlow).

20. "Sister Jaime" Written by: Kenneth Johnson. Directed by: Alan J. Levi. Airdate: November 24, 1976.

Jaime goes undercover as a nun at a convent. She fears that nuns and priests are smuggling diamonds, but soon Jaime is invested in the convent's cause: keeping it open despite the efforts of a villainous priest.

GUEST CAST: Kathleen Nolan, Ellen Geer, Catherine Burns, Ron Hayes, Dran Hamilton, Al Hansen.

21. "The Vega Influence" Written by: Arthur Rowe. Directed by: Mel Damski. Airdate: December 1, 1976.

Jaime and a scientist make a stopover at an arctic base, only to find it abandoned. A strange meteor may be the cause, and Jaime must solve the mystery or suffer the same fate as the missing denizens of the base.

GUEST CAST: Rick Lenz; Philip Carey; Don Marshall (Colter); John Lawrence, Ray Poole.

22. "Jaime's Shield" (Parts I and II) Written by: James D. Parriott. Directed by: Alan Crosland. Airdates: December 15 and 22, 1976.

Jaime goes undercover as a police officer so she can be assigned to a detail protecting a foreign dignitary. She must uncover a deadly plot before the politician is assassinated.

GUEST CAST: George Maharis, Diane Civita, Rebecca Balding, Linden Chiles, Arch Johnson, James McEachin, Amy Joyce.

23. "Biofeedback" Written by: Dan Kibbie and Kenneth Johnson. Directed by: Alan J. Levi. Airdate: January 12, 1977.

A western scientist that has developed equipment to control minds defects to the communist bloc. With the scientist's brother in tow, Jaime travels overseas to stop the scientist from making a terrible mistake.

GUEST CAST: Granville Van Dusen, Peter Haskell, Lloyd Bochner.

24. "Doomsday Is Today" (Parts I and II) Written and directed by: Kenneth Johnson. Airdates: January 19 and 26, 1977.

A misguided scientist warns the world that his new supercomputer will destroy the planet should any country or power anywhere on the globe activate a nuclear device. Jaime goes with a team of scientists to examine the supercomputer and quickly learns that it could indeed destroy the Earth. Now she must defeat the computer and its security devices if Man is to control his own fate again.

GUEST CAST: Sam Chew, David Opatshu, Ken O'Brien, Lew Ayres, James Hong, Stack Pierce, Ned Wilson.

25. "Deadly Ringer" (Parts I and II) Written by: James D. Parriott. Directed by: Alan J. Levi. Airdates: February 2 and 9, 1977.

Jaime's surgically altered lookalike returns in another plot, this one designed to help her keep her ill-gotten identity forever. Meanwhile, a case of mistaken identity has Jaime on the run, unable to convince Oscar and others that she is the genuine article.

GUEST CAST: Don Porter, Warren Kemmerling, Katherine Helmond, John Zenda, Don Fenwick.

26. "Jaime and the King" Written by: Robert L. McCullough, C. Robert Brooks and Arthur Rowe. Directed by: Alan Crosland. Airdate: February 23, 1977.

In order to protect a Middle Eastern ruler, Oscar sends Jaime to teach the man's son, a young prince with very chauvinistic views about women. Jaime hopes to teach him a lesson or two, and save his father from certain death.

GUEST CAST: Robert Loggia, Lance Kerwin, Joseph Ruskin, Brioni Farrell.

27. "Beyond the Call" Written by: Dan Kibbie and Arthur Rowe. Directed by: Alan J. Levi. Airdate: March 9, 1977.

Jaime becomes embroiled in family politics and survival techniques when she involves herself in a secret plot to steal the secret of a new missile launching system offered on the black market.

GUEST CAST: Sam Groom, Sandy Ward, Madison Arnold.

28. "The Dejon Caper" Written by: Arthur Rowe. Directed by: Barry Crane. Airdate: March 16, 1977.

In France, Jaime infiltrates the art world to help capture a criminal who is putting forgeries on the market.

GUEST CAST: Rene Auberjonois (Lambert); Sydney Chaplin, Erik Holland, Bernard Behrens, Ben Wright.

29. "The Night Demon" Written by: Justin Edgerton. Directed by: Alan J. Levi. Airdate: March 23, 1977.

An archaeologist unearths a totem that supposedly resurrects an ancient demon. Jaime investigates the situation but finds there is no demon at all, only a plot to make one man sell his valuable land.

GUEST CAST: Jeff Corey (Bearclaw); Gary Lockwood (Cannon); John Quade (Hawkins); Jay Saunders.

30. "Iron Ships and Dead Men" Written by: James D. Parriott. Directed by: Mel Damski. Airdate: March 30, 1977.

Oscar has lived for years with a terrible shame. His brother was believed to have stolen money he was supposed to pass on to another sailor during the attack on Pearl Harbor. Now, decades later, the corpse of his brother has been found, and Oscar wants Jaime to help him discover the truth about what really happened all those years ago.

GUEST CAST: Ray Young, Stephen Elliott, Edward Walsh, Theodore Wilson.

31. "Once a Thief" Written by: Kenneth Johnson. Directed by: Alan J. Levi. Airdate: May 4, 1977.

Jaime goes undercover to stop a gang of bank robbers, but must participate in a crime to maintain her cover.

GUEST CAST: Elisha Cook, Ed Barth, Frank Cala.

SEASON THREE (1977–1978)

32. "The Bionic Dog" (Parts I & II) Written by: James D. Parriott. Story by: Harve Bennett and James. D. Parriott. Directed by: Barry Crane. Airdates: September 10 and 17, 1977.

Years before Steve Austin and Jaime Sommers, there was another bionic experiment, a dog named Max. Now, years later, Max may be rejecting his bionics, and has been scheduled for termination. Fearing she may someday face the same fate, Jaime frees Max from captivity and goes on the run with the friendly dog.

GUEST CAST: Taylor Lacher, Will Hare.

33. "Fembots in Las Vegas" (Parts I and II) Written by: Arthur Rowe. Directed by: Michael Preece. Airdates: September 24 and October 1, 1977.

The son of Fembot creator Dr. Franklin is creating new robots and plotting another attempt at world domination And he wouldn't mind destroying Jaime and Oscar, the people he deems responsible for the death of his father.

GUEST CAST: James Olson (Rod); Michael Burns, Jennifer Darling, Jeannie Wilson, Lorna Sands, Lisa Moore.

34. "Rodeo" Written by: Herman Groves and Kenneth Johnson. Directed by: Larry Stewart. Airdate: October 15, 1977.

A fellow named Cole is the only person that knows how to translate a secret code, but he also wants to be a riding champion at a nearby rodeo. When foreign agents triangulate on Cole, Jaime steps in to protect the rodeo rider.

GUEST CAST: Andrew Prine (Cole); Jason Evers (Raddick); Thomas Bellin, Don Gentry, John Crawford.

35. "African Connection" Written by: William Schwartz. Directed by: Alan J. Levi. Airdate: October 29, 1977.

Jaime travels to Africa to insure that an election is fairly administrated. A dastardly, power-hungry politician is planning to use a new microchip to alter the results, and Jaime must stop him; but she runs into the opposition first, and they suspect she is in on "the fix."

GUEST CAST: Dan O'Herlihy (Walker); Raymond St. Jacques (Azar); Don Pedro Colley, Joan Pringle.

36. "Motorcycle Boogie" Written by: James D. Parriott and Kenneth Johnson. Directed by: Ken Gilbert. Airdate: November 5, 1977.

Jaime is assigned to West Germany, where she must recover a stolen computer tape of national importance. She is aided in her mission by a motorcyclist daredevil ... Evel Knievel!

GUEST CAST: Spencer Milligan (Schmidt); Evel Knievel (Himself); Bernard Behrens (Petrov); Erik Holland.

37. "Brain Wash" Written by: James D. Parriott. Directed by: Michael Preece. Airdate: November 12, 1977.

A hair-styling salon is actually a front for a brainwashing scheme. Secrets are being sold to enemies through mind-controlled customers.

GUEST CAST: Jennifer Darling, Michael Callan, Sam Chew, David Watson.

38. "Escape to Love" Written by: Ellen Whitman and Lionel E. Siegal. Directed by: Alan J. Levi. Airdate: November 26, 1977.

Jamie helps two defectors cross over to the West. The rescue attempt goes badly and she must leave a young boy, one man's son, behind. She goes back to save him but that isn't the end of the story.

GUEST CAST: John Reilly, Peter Mark Richman, Phillip Abbott, Michael Richardson.

39. "Max" Written by: William Schwartz. Directed by: Don McDougall. Airdate: December 3, 1977.

The bionic dog, Max, returns, this time to guard an endangered scientist. With Jaime out of commission to have her bionics tested, it is up to the faithful dog to save the day.

GUEST CAST: Christopher Knight, Sam Chew, Jr., Bill Fletcher, Rudy Solari.

40. "The Over the Hill Spy" Written by: Joe Viola. Directed by: Ken Gilbert. Airdate: December 17, 1977.

A retired agent returns to active duty to fight an old nemesis. But he has his own agenda too, and sabotages his partner, Jaime Sommers.

GUEST CAST: Richard Erdman, Michael Toma, Jeff David, Rick Buckner, Alana Collins.

41. "All for One" Written by: James D. Parriott. Directed by: Larry Stewart. Airdate: January 7, 1978.

The OSI and enemy nations are both after a brilliant computer hacker who has been able to use computers to transfer funds from the OSI bank accounts. Jaime must get to the hacker before the enemy forces capture him.

GUEST CAST: Roger Perry (Tom); Franklin Ajae, Viola Stimpson, Garrett Pearson, Gary Burton.

42. "The Pyramid" Written by: Marget Armen, Alf Harris, Arthur Rowe and Lionel Siegel. Directed by: Barry Crane. Airdate: January 14, 1978.

While studying artifacts with her friend Chris, Jaime becomes trapped inside a strange pyramid, an extraterrestrial device belonging to a race that wishes to colonize the Earth. Jaime learns that an approaching spaceship will be destroyed in the atmosphere because of modern pollutants, and as a response the aliens will obliterate mankind. Now Jamie must escape the pyramid and warn the world of the danger to come from the skies.

GUEST CAST: Eduard Franz; Christopher Stone (Chris); Gavan O'Herilhy, June Barrett.

43. "The Antidote" Written by: Arthur Rowe, Tom and Helen August. Directed by: Don McDougall. Airdate: January 21, 1978.

When Jaime is unexpectedly poisoned on a job, it is up to Max, the bionic pooch, and her friend Chris, to get the antidote from a missing Dr. Wells.

GUEST CAST: Jennifer Darling; Christopher Stone (Williams); Brett Halsey (Hamilton); John Milford (Henderson).

44. "The Martians Are Coming, the Martians Are Coming" Written by: Robert A. Urso, Tom and Helen August. Directed by: Larry Stewart. Airdate: January 28, 1978.

Dr. Wells has been working on a secret project to track flying saucers. Unfortunately, Wells — in front of witnesses — is "beamed" aboard what appears to be a UFO. Now, Jaime must find a way to rescue him.

GUEST CAST: Jack Kelly, Frank Aletter, Frank Marth, Lynn Carlin.

45. "Sanctuary: Earth" Written by: Rudolph Borchert, Craig Schiller, and Tom and Helen August. Directed by: Ernest Pintoff. Airdate: February 11, 1978.

An outcast alien princess, Aura, requests sanctuary on Earth. Her planet is suffering the debilitating effects of a terrible war, and she can prevent it. Jaime is uncertain whether to believe this strange story of alien wars…

GUEST CAST: Christopher Stone (Chris); Helen Hunt (Aura).

46. "Deadly Music" Written by: Conner Everts and Lionel Siegel. Directed by: Tom Connors. Airdate: February 18, 1978.

Jaime must undertake an underwater mission to help rescue endangered submarines. Unfortunately, saboteurs have plotted a counter strike, exposing Jaime to an attack by killer sharks.

GUEST CAST: Frank Converse, Henry Darrow, Robert Ellenstein, Roger Cruz, Chip Lucia, Greg Barnett.

47. "Which One Is Jaime?" Written by: Jim Carlson and Terrence McDonnell. Directed by: Jack Arnold. Airdate: February 25, 1978.

Oscar's secretary and Max are captured by enemy agents, and will be released only for the bionic woman, Jaime Sommers.

GUEST CAST: Jennifer Darling, Sam Chew, Jr., James Sikking, Brock Peters.

48. "Out of Body" Written by: Steven E. De Souza and Deborah Blum. Directed by: Ernest Pintoff. Airdate: March 4, 1978.

A scientist electrocuted by his turncoat boss travels to the astral plane and, as a spirit, tries to help Jaime Sommers solve the case.

GUEST CAST: Nehemiah Persoff (Jennings); Richard Lynch (Denton).

49. "Long Live the King" Written by: Mel Goldbert, Dave Ketchum, Tony DiMarco, Tom and Helen August. Directed by: Gwen Arner. Airdate: March 25, 1978.

Oscar assigns Jaime to protect a foreign dignitary from assassins.

GUEST CAST: Carmen Argenziano, John Reilly, Charles Cioffi, Rachel Bard.

50. "Rancho Outcast" Written by: Arthur Rowe. Directed by: Ivan Nixon. Airdate: May 6, 1978.

Jaime travels to Central America to recover special monetary molds or plates. Unfortunately, she becomes embroiled in local politics.

GUEST CAST: Donald Calfa, Keenan Waynn, Diane Civita, David Cass, Robert Easton.

51. "On the Run" Written by: Steven E. De Souza. Directed by: Tom Blank. Airdate: May 13, 1978.

Tired of constant danger and little time for personal attachments, Jaime quits the OSI. Unfortunately, government agents refuse to let her resign, fearing she will be captured and examined by foreign powers. Now Jaime must find a way to live her life— and with her troublesome bionics.

GUEST CAST: Christopher Stone (Chris); Andrew Duggan, Skip Homeier, Juno Dawson, Johnny Timko.

The Return of the Six Million Dollar Man and the Bionic Woman (1987)
LIVE-ACTION TV MOVIE

Written by: Michael Sloan. Story by: Michael Sloan and Bruce Lansbury. Directed by: Ray Austin. Airdate: May 17, 1987.

A retired Steve Austin is called back to OSI duty by Oscar Goldman at the same time that he must deal with his headstrong, grown son. Worse, Jaime Sommers has recovered the memories of her pre-bionic years and is angry with Steve Austin that he never rekindled their romantic relationship. Jaime and Steve put their differences aside to fight a new enemy, a terrorist named Stenning. In the end, Steve's son, Michael, is badly injured in a fight, and the son of Austin becomes bionic too.

GUEST CAST: Martin Landau (Stenning); Gary Lockwood (Praiser); Bryan Cranston, Pamela Bryant.

Bionic Showdown: The Six Million Dollar Man and the Bionic Woman (1989)
LIVE-ACTION TV MOVIE

Written by: Michael Sloan and Ted Mann. Directed by: Alan J. Levi. Airdate: April 30, 1989.

The World Unity Games are threatened when an enemy agent with bionic powers injurs Oscar Goldman, the official responsible for security. Steve Austin, who has popped the question to Jaime Sommers, is among the suspects. Meanwhile, a young woman and friend of Jaime is also destined to become bionic.

GUEST CAST: Sandra Bullock (Katie); Jeff Yagher (Jimmy); Geraint Wyn Davies (Devlin); Robert Lansing, Jack Blum, Robert McClure.

Bionic Ever After? (1994)
LIVE-ACTION TV MOVIE

Written by: Michael Sloan and Norman Morrill. Story by: Michael Sloan. Directed by: Steven Stafford. Airdate: November 29, 1994.

The wedding of the six million-dollar man and bionic woman is stalled because of a threat to national security in the form of nuclear terrorism. Worse, Jaime shows signs, after all these years, of rejecting her bionics.

GUEST CAST: Anne Lockhart, Geordie Johnson, Michael Burgess, Ivan Sergei, Lee Majors II, Ann Pierce.

Birdman and the Galaxy Trio

A timely combination of *Star Trek* and *Batman*, two popular genre programs of the era, *Birdman and the Galaxy Trio* was a 1967 cartoon series that aired on Saturday mornings on NBC. Produced by Hanna-Barbera and designed by Alex Toth (*The Super Friends*), each installment of the series featured two Birdman adventures, and one adventure of an elite space police unit, the Galaxy Trio.

Birdman was actually Ray Randall (notice the superhero alliteration), a hero that developed the power of flight. As Birdman, he boasted vast Hawkman-like wings and a black eye mask with an upward sweep, suggesting flight. Because he drew his strength from the sun, his uniform was mustard-gold in coloring. In addition to his ability to fly, Birdman could shoot solar rays from his fists, a useful power in defeating bad guys

such as Mentor the Mind Taker, Morto, and the Metal Men. Birdman received assistance in his quest to fight evil from a sidekick called Bird Boy and a mascot, a noble eagle called Avenger.

The Galaxy Trio represented a more futuristic bunch than Birdman's nest of heroes, hence the *Star Trek* comparison. The Trio consisted of Vapor Man, who could turn into fog or mist, Galaxy Girl, who could fly, and Meteor Man, a hero of terrific strength. These three characters were the crew, as it were, of a starship called the Condor 1, which policed the galaxy and brought law and order to chaotic planets. Ted Cassidy, who guest-starred on *Star Trek* in the episode "What Are Little Girls Made Of," gave voice to Meteor Man, the pointy-eared character of the bunch.

Birdman and the Galaxy Trio (1967–68)
ANIMATED SERIES

VOICE TALENTS: Keith Andes (Ray Randall/Birdman); Don Messick (Falcon 7); Dick Beals (Birdboy); Don Messick (Vapor Man); Virginia Eiler (Galaxy Girl); Ted Cassidy (Meteor Man).

CREW: *Produced by*: William Hanna and Joseph Barbera. *Created and designed by:* Alex Toth. *Production Supervisor*: Howard Hanson. Hanna-Barbera Studios, 1967.

Birds of Prey

After *Smallville*'s successful freshman season during the 2001–2002 season, the WB network announced with great fanfare in 2002 the inauguration of another superhero TV series "re-imagining" called *Birds of Prey*. Just as *Smallville* tweaked the Superboy/Superman mythos of DC Comics, so was it intended that the heavily promoted

new program would reinvent the world of Batman and Gotham City. The WB called this initiative "the long awaited next chapter in the Batman legacy" and broadcast the series in high definition, letterbox format to give it the special aura of a feature film. More specifically, *Birds of Prey* posited a trio of superheroes, all women, that had "issues" with their past, but, like a Ya-Ya Sisterhood by way of the Justice League, would depend on one another emotionally when times were grim.

The TV series *Birds of Prey* was (very loosely) based on DC's comic book characters and a comic book of the same name. In the TV version, Huntress *(Dark Angel's* Ashley Scott) was the offspring of Batman and Selina Kyle, a.k.a. Catwoman. Interestingly, this unique lineage reflected the comic book version of the Huntress character seen in the 1950s through 1980s, a character killed during the *Crisis on Infinite Earths* mini-series in the mid–80s. This Huntress was Helena Kyle, a crossbow-wielding human with no super powers, only an expertise in the martial arts. When this Huntress, a lawyer, died during the *Infinite Earths* battle, her existence was erased from time. A new Huntress, Helena Bertinelli, consequently took her place.

This second Huntress had no relationship to Batman or Catwoman, and as the daugher of a former mob boss, was a rogue-like, cocksure character of frequently violent means. The TV version of the character retained the Helena Wayne origin, making Huntress the daughter of two comic icons, and one scarred by the death of her mother years before. But the rebellious attitude adopted by TV's Scott was all Bertilini's. Making matters even more confusing, this TV Huntress was a "meta-human" supercharged with cat DNA from her mother and a thirst for justice from her absentee father, Batman. In this sense, she more closely resembled *Dark Angel's* Max (Jessica Alba), a more-than-human fighting machine with animal-like reflexes. In the *Birds of Prey* pilot, cat "roaring" effects were heard as Huntress fought the bad guys. Also, like Alba's character in *Dark Angel*, Scott's Huntress frequently donned black leather and was involved in *Crouching Tiger, Hidden Dragon*-style fights on (usually) invisible wires.

The other characters seen on *Birds of Prey* were also variations of those depicted in *Birds of Prey* comics. Oracle, the brains of the team, was actually a paralyzed Batgirl, Barbara Gordon, played by Dina Meyer (*Starship Troopers* [1997], *Star Trek: Nemesis* [2002]). On the TV series, she had been shot and crippled by Joker ("Batgirl ... past tense") during a crime war that involved Batman some seven years earlier, an event dramatized in the Alan Moore Batman epic *The Killing Joke*. The paralyzed Batgirl, with her genius for crime fighting and computers, became a brilliant superhero team leader, Oracle. This character was first seen working with the "Suicide Squad" in 1989, a team comic penned by John Ostrander. During the *Birds of Prey* series pilot and other episodes ("Lady Shiva"), the wheelchair-bound Barbara, daughter of Commissioner Gordon, was seen to wear the famous Batgirl costume.

The third member of the *Birds of Prey* team on the TV series was a young psychic girl, Dinah Redmond (a.k.a. Dinah Lance), whose mother was the first superhero known as the Black Canary (played by Lori Loughlin in the episode "Sins of the Mother"). In the comics, Dinah became the second Black Canary, worked with the Justice Society of America, and eventually teamed with Oracle in the *Birds of Prey* comic book. On the TV series, this never quite happened, though it was clearly a "future" direction had the series survived. On the series, Dinah (Rachel Skarsten) was a Buffyesque teenager dealing with the daily vicissitudes of high school and issues of abandonment (her mother, the Black Canary, left her because she felt she would always be in danger from super-villains).

Though the characters Huntress (Barbara Joyce) and Black Canary (Danuta) had been seen in an obscure *Legend of the Superheroes* series in 1977, *Birds of Prey* probably represented the first time that casual TV viewers were introduced to these particular comic book characters. To help ease the transition (and explain the labyrinthine plot and character connections), Alfred (Ian Abercrombie), Batman's butler, was also seen on the series frequently, serving the trio of women in much the same capacity as he had served Bruce Wayne for so many years. Another familiar face was Mia Sara's Harley Quinn, the Joker's lover and a popular villainess from the comics. Batman even appeared in the pilot for *Birds of Prey*, as did the Joker (voiced by Mark Hamill).

Rounding out the *Birds of Prey* cast was the only alpha male around, hunky Shemar Moore. A winner of a daytime acting Emmy for *The Young and the Restless* and five consecutive NAACP Image Awards, Moore played Detective Jake Reese, a Gotham City cop that befriended Huntress and would solve many crimes with her help.[1] In "Sins of the Mother," Huntress gave Reese a "bat ring" so he could call her whenever he got into trouble.

The weekly format of *Birds of Prey* involved Helena, Barbara and Dinah learning to work together and put their traumatic pasts behind them in order to solve dangerous crimes in New Gotham City, a world of "freaks, myths and urban legends." Their emotional issues were post-traumatic stress (Barbara), abandonment (Helena) and more abandonment (Dinah). Their real-life opponents were strange meta-human supervillains. These bad fellas included Slick, an assassin that could turn into liquid (in "Slick"), and a meta-human-hating psychic psychopath (in "Prey for the Hunter"). Then there was a crime-family boss in "Sins of the Mother"; DarkStrike/Crawler, a Jekyll-Hyde act, in "Split"; and finally a vengeful martial arts thief, Lady Shiva, in "Lady Shiva."

At least some of these characters resembled those seen in DC Comics. For instance, Shiva, a martial arts expert, appeared in *Richard Dragon, Kung Fu Fighter* comics in the mid–1970s. The issue she faced in the comics was the same one noted on the TV

series — the unjust death of her younger sister. In the comics, Shiva, a mercenary named Sandra, was occasionally heroic, a transformation she didn't make on the TV series. Pulling the strings behind many of these villains was Mia Sara's Harley Quinn, who masqueraded as a psychiatrist named Dr. Harley Quinzel.

With an interesting cast, expensive special effects, a deep and layered story background and a great time slot (Wednesdays at 9:00 P.M.), hopes were high that *Birds of Prey* would, like *Smallville*, take flight. After the successes of *X-Men* in 2000, *Smallville* in 2001, and *Spider-Man* in 2002, superhero fans were beginning to believe that Hollywood had finally learned to give the genre some respect. When interviewed about the series, Dina Meyer picked up on the ideas that would make the show a successful venture:

> We're not just going to be fighting crime, we're going to be exploring relationships. When you think about it, look at comic books — they're all about relationships. We'll also have conflicts with each other.[2]

Alas, once the series actually began, it became obvious that these relationships were pat, and seemed piped in from other, more popular, series. Oracle, Huntress and Barbara all had issues, from physical paralysis and emotional abandonment to a distrust of men (after all, Batman was a derelict father...), but they also wore great clothes, seemed to want for nothing materially, and were gorgeous. When they began to wax pitiful about the men in their lives or their sad past, or their status as "freaks" in New Gotham City, different from human beings because of fun super powers, it was more than a little hard to swallow. It came off as whiny and insincere. When you're beautiful, every man lusts after you, and you wear black leather, how much of an outsider can you really be?

Another thing clipped *Birds of Prey*'s wings: a derivative tone. While fighting her

Meta-Yowza! Three Birds of Prey from the 2002 series of the same name. From left to right: Huntress (Ashley Scott), Oracle (Dina Meyer), and Black Canary (Rachael Skarsten). Do they look persecuted to you?

enemies, Huntress was prone to dishing out sassy one-liners: "I don't like it when the clothes get soiled," and so forth. Worse, the Huntress and Dinah mimicked "Buffy-speak," the distinctive voice of writer/creator Joss Whedon that, outside *Buffy* and *Angel*, just doesn't work. The dialogue patterns were so familiar (and copycat) that it was actually jarring to watch *Birds of Prey*.

From *Dark Angel* came the Huntress's

cat–DNA, a nighttime urban landscape, and the notion of a subculture operating just beneath the normal ebb and flow of human life. On *Dark Angel*, it was genetic freaks called TransGens or X5s. On *Birds of Prey* it was genetic freaks again, but this time labeled "meta-humans."

Also, just about every episode of *Birds of Prey* culminated with Huntress, Oracle and Dinah staring wistfully from their perch high above Gotham, outside their clock-tower headquarters. Viewers of *Dark Angel* may recall that most episodes of that series (especially in the first year) ended with Max staring wistfully from a tower in Seattle, looking over the third-world, post-apocalyptic landscape. And finally, Oracle's character seemed overly familiar to TV audiences. Where but *Dark Angel* (again) had viewers seen a paralyzed, wheelchair-bound computer expert before (Michael Weatherly's Logan Cale)?

The unholy love child of *Buffy the Vampire Slayer* and *Dark Angel*, *Birds of Prey* had one more, rather unfortunate, parent. When the three main characters began to hurl bitchy insults at each other in several episodes, such as the zinger, "there will be no use of super powers to settle domestic disputes" (in "Slick"), the series clearly evoked the WB series *Charmed*, about three (why is it always three?) witches. When writers miss the genuine wit of *Buffy the Vampire Slayer*, they invariably create instead a din of bitchy, pseudo-witty, sing-song dialogue that grates on the nerves. That was the tenor most *Birds of Prey* episodes achieved.

After heavy curiosity viewing (some seven million viewers for the premiere episode), the ratings of *Birds of Prey* went into steep decline. After only seven episodes aired, the WB announced it would not seek any episodes beyond the initial order for thirteen, in essence canceling the series. WB Entertainment President Jordan Levin discussed the reasons behind the show's failure:

> We think we can attribute the erosion of *Birds of Prey*, quite frankly, to a failure of execution. We think we had a very strong concept and just failed to execute it, and audiences abandoned the show as a result.[3]

Levin's explanation may or may not — like Slick, the liquid serial killer — hold water. The concept was not that good for a few reasons. One, few comic book fans were ready to "re-imagine" the heroic (if dark) Batman as a deadbeat dad. Two, *Birds of Prey* seemed to occur after all the good action had already taken place: Joker and Batman had fought a crime war almost a decade earlier, and that epoch seemed far more interesting. And three, as Bill Clinton might say, who could really "feel the pain" of those three lovely birds of prey? With their perfect hair, great costumes, picture-perfect make-up and seemingly comfy life (they even had a butler, for goodness sake!), most audiences were not inclined to weep over the fact that they felt like outsiders. Boo hoo.

On the other hand, Levin was correct that the series was poorly executed. The writing was generally horrible, or "meta-bad" as this author's wife remarked, and even on a technical level, the series was weak. New Gotham City was wholly computer generated, and looked more like *The Sims* than a real city; and the same gliding night and day shots were utilized over and over repetitiously, even in just eight episodes. Even the sound effects work on *Birds of Prey* was pretty terrible too. As noted above, in the pilot, Huntress made ridiculous-sounding "cat roars" whenever she moved and fought. Anybody who has ever owned a cat knows that felines do not make such ridiculous noises. Worse, the liquid serial killer Slick was accompanied, during his episode, by a sound that closely approximated the gurgle of a flushing toilet.

Probably about the worst thing about *Birds of Prey* was the lack of forward momentum. *Smallville* is a wholly enjoyable

TV series, one spiced with interesting references and hints of the future. When will Lex go bad? When will Clark learn to fly or put on the famous costume? Just about every show in the series plays lightly, or even darkly, with the mythos in a way that makes viewers want to come back the following week to learn more. Though *Birds of Prey* was clearly leading up to a confrontation with Harley Quinn, it had no other forward momentum. Batman clearly would not return, because the WB was not about to feature its movie franchise star on a weekly TV series. Dinah was destined to become the Black Canary, but that was not a very dramatic surprise. What could audiences look forward to, since the most interesting Batman characters were either missing (Batman), or dead (Commissioner Gordon, Catwoman and Joker) or crippled (Batgirl)?

Though there was the occasional mention of "Jason Todd, Tim Drake and Dick Grayson" (in "Slick"), it seemed *Birds of Prey* was not just a re-imagining of the Batman world, but a revision where all the good characters were ... elsewhere. Even sadder, their contributions to the universe did not seem to matter a lick. A weird quirk of *Birds of Prey* was that no one in the city knew of or remembered Batman and his crime-fighting campaign; he was merely an "urban legend." In other words, *Birds of Prey* occurred in a different universe than the Batman movie franchise, were Batman showed up at Gotham gala events on a regular basis (*Batman Forever, Batman and Robin*) and could not be written off as a myth.

No wonder viewers abandoned *Birds of Prey* (for ABC's *The Bachelor,* mostly). The series undid Batman's great legacy, turned him into a deadbeat absentee father, and left his territory, his beloved Gotham City, to the care of three beautiful but whiny — and ultimately empty-headed — punsters. "I think [Levin] was afraid of the Batman world being too dark for his air," series producer Brian Robbins noted in an interview for *Media Week.* He then added: "If I were running [the WB], I would have tried to figure out a way to survive until after *The Bachelor,* and then give it a chance."[4]

But no second chance came for *Birds of Prey,* and *Angel* replaced it on Wednesday nights beginning in mid–January 2003. A two-hour finale of *Birds of Prey* was produced, and it aired February 19, 2003, turning the tables and pre-empting *Angel.*

Birds of Prey (2002-2003)
LIVE-ACTION SERIES

"*Birds of Prey* featured too many arbitrary changes from the comic. Why does the Huntress have super powers? Neither of her parents (Catwoman and Batman) did! Why is she fighting crime with no mask? Both of her parents were smart enough to wear masks. In the comic, Black Canary and Oracle were very much equal in terms of experience; one was not a neophyte, the other a teacher. For some reason that was changed too, and the series made it a mother-daughter relationship rather than featuring the *Sex and the City*–style banter of the characters in the comic. Basically, the series was *Mutant X.* You've got Huntress and they turned her into a feral woman like Shalimar. Then you've got Dinah, who is inexplicably telepathic, like Emma. And they all wear leather jackets. That established, Dina Meyer was perfect for the part of Oracle and looked magnificent in the Batgirl costume."

— Howard Margolin, host of
Destinies: The Voice of Science Fiction.

"*Birds of Prey* is designed and packaged for the *Smallville* crowd. It is hip, foreboding and visually seductive in a metasexy kind of way.... Most of all, it doesn't take a campy approach to the superhero genre, meaning that if it connects with enough fans of the comic fable, it just might fly."

— Mark Washburn, *The Charlotte Observer:*
"*Birds of Prey.*" October 8, 2002.

"Meyer brings a good deal of balance as the seasoned veteran, but as a trio, the actors and characters are clunky. The power of three has been done before, and *Buffy the Vampire Slayer* has the lock on using the supernatural experience as an analogy for real life. Perhaps producers can learn from the demise of shows such as *Dark Angel* and realize that good looks and highly-stylized action aren't enough."

> — Laura Fries, *Daily Variety*: "*Birds of Prey.*" October 8, 2002, page 7.

"If you want some idea of just how difficult it is to make comic-book-style action dovetail with heartfelt emotionalism, tune in to *Birds of Prey*, a migraine-inducingly complex superhero saga.... *Birds* is certainly more fun than the soap opera of *Smallville* but ... the writers are trying too hard to incorporate Buffy-like pop self-consciousness."

> — Ken Tucker, *Entertainment Weekly*: "Wonder Women: The Dynamic Dames of Both *Alias* and *Birds of Prey* Deliver the Action, but Only One Packs an Emotional Punch." October 25, 2002, page 62.

"...[A]s visually sleek and occasionally funny as *Birds of Prey* starts out, the show will have to get out from under its tangled premise if it's to divert easily wandering attention. So far it's difficult to tell where the series might be headed..."

> — Manuel Mendoza, *The Dallas Morning News*: "*Birds of Prey* Premiering Wednesday on WB." October 8, 2002.

"It's hard to resist a supergirl series that has the gumption to kick off with more back story than the Forsyth Saga. It's fun, no-cal: a caprice that incongruously unfolds in the heavy shadows of New Gotham."

> — Tom Gilatto, Terry Kelleher, William Keck, *People Weekly*, November 4, 2002, page 33.

"...[F]lat performances and stock comic-book story lines keeps *Birds* grounded."

> — James Poniewozik, *Time*: "*Birds of Prey.*" October 14, 2002, page 86.

CAST: Dina Meyer (Barbara Gordon/The Oracle); Ashley Scott (Helena Kyle/The Huntress); Rachel Skarsten (Dinah Lance/The Black Canary); Shemar Moore (Detective Jake Reese); Ian Abercrombie (Alfred); Mia Sara (Harley Quinn).

CREW: *Co-Executive Producer:* Laeta Kalogridis. *Producer:* Peter Giuliano. *Developed for TV by:* Laeta Kalogridis. *Associate Producer:* Cathy M. Frank. *Directors of Photography (various episodes):* Chris Faloona, Clark Mathis. *Production Designer:* Jay Hinkle. *Film Editors (various episodes):* Robert A. Ferretti, Kevin Krasny, Michael S. Stern. *Music:* Mark Snow. *"Revolution" Performed by:* Aimee Allen. *Co-Executive Producers:* Hans Tobeason, Michael Katleman. *Executive Producers:* Ron Koslow, Mike Tollins, Joe Davola. *Associate Producer:* Hayli Halper. *Unit Production Manager:* Jeffrey Zeitlin. *First Assistant Director:* Arthur Anderson. *Second Assistant Director:* Susan Hellman. *Visual Effects Supervisor:* Jeffrey A. Okun. *Casting:* DeeDee Bradley, Elisabeth Rudolph. *Costumes:* Chris Karonides. *Set Decorator:* Donald Krafft. *Property Master:* Richard Hobaica. *Make-up:* Vicky Ogden. *Costumes:* Sara Markowitz Samuels. *Special Effects Coordinator:* John Gray. *Script Supervisor:* Pamela Alch. *Based on:* DC Comics Characters. A Tollins/Robbins Production for Warner Brothers Television.

SEASON ONE (2002-2003)

1. "Pilot" Written by: Laeta Kalogridis. Directed by: Brian Robbins. Airdate: October 9, 2002.

Seven years after the death of Catwoman and the disappearance of Batman, young Dinah Redmond travels to New Gotham City, spurred by disturbing psychic visions, to learn what became of Batgirl, Barbara Gordon, and Catwoman's daughter, Helena, after the Dark Knight's secret war with the Joker. She soon discovers that the two women are fighting crime together, as Gotham's new heroes: the paralyzed Barbara Gordon is Oracle, the brains of the operation, and the meta-human Helena is "the Huntress," the brawn. Dinah joins the crime-fighting team on their latest assignment, an investigation of several apparent suicides in New Gotham's business community. The trail leads to one businessman, an old friend of Helena's family, and an evil empire bent on resurrection.

GUEST CAST: Chris Ellis; Shawn Christian (Wade); Aaron Paul; Brent Sexton; Mark Hamill (The Voice of Joker); Amanda Michalka (Young Dinah); Maggie Baird (Mother); Maria Quiban (Newscaster); Joe Lala (Crowley).

2. "Slick" Written by: Laeta Kalogridis and Melissa Rosenberg. Directed by: Michael Katleman. Airdate: October 16, 2002.

Harley Quinn, a crime boss masquerading as a psychologist, retains the services of an unusual assassin, a man named "Slick" who can alter his molecular structure and become water, in order to hijack an armored truck filled with flamethrowers, surface-to-air missiles and plastic explosives. Meanwhile, Dinah prepares to go to New Gotham High School for the first time, and Barbara runs a background check on her only to find that she has no official records. The Birds of Prey work to stop Slick before he can kill handsome Detective Reese, who has been assigned to protect the armored car with two other now-deceased police officers. Huntress rescues Reese from the liquid-like "Slick," courtesy of a timely assist from Dinah.

GUEST CAST: Shawn Christian (Wade); Silas Weir Mitchell (Silas "Slick" Waters); Brian Tashi, Brent Sexton.

3. "Prey for the Hunter" Written by: Ed Kitsis and Adam Horowitz. Story by: Adam Armus. Directed by: Chris Long. Airdate: October 23, 2002.

A serial killer named Morton has an intense hatred for meta-humans and uses his position as a police officer to hunt them down and kill them. He partners with Agent Reese, who has his own doubts about meta-humans, and Huntress learns that Morton is a "meta" himself, a powerful man that can reflect back the powers of other meta-humans. Huntress goes to see Gibson, a meta-human that may have information about the killings, while Dinah adjusts to high school. Finally, Reese must choose which ally he trusts, Huntress or his new partner.

GUEST CAST: Joe Flanigan (Morton); Shawn Christian (Wade); Robert Patrick Benedict (Gibson); Callie De Fabry; Nathan Holland (Carl); Josh Waters (Frosty); Autumn Reese (Girlfriend); Charlene Hall (Kindly Teacher).

4. "Three Birds and a Baby" Written by: David Goodman and Julie Hess. Directed by: Craig Zisk. Airdate: October 30, 2002.

Huntress rescues a baby when the child's caretaker is murdered in a street fight with criminals. Harley Quinn wants the baby back, a "bio-engineered" assassin created to be the child she and Joker never had. Huntress, Oracle and Dinah take care of the baby, Guy, who grows up at an accelerated rate. Harley Quinn sends mercenaries after the fast developing Guy, just as Huntress teaches him the importance of preserving life ... but will her message mean anything to a life form destined to die in three days?

GUEST CAST: Riley Smith, Michael Welch, Bobby Edner, Kevin Rankin, Brody Hutzler, Matthew Josten.

5. "Sins of the Mother" Written by: Melissa Rosenberg. Story by: Melissa Rosenberg and Hans Tobeason. Directed by: Jeff Woolnough. Airdate: November 6, 2002.

Dinah's mother, the famous female superhero Black Canary, visits New Gotham hoping to re-claim the relationship with her estranged daughter. As relationships mend and Dinah learns that her mother left her with a foster family to protect her from criminals, Black Canary is kidnapped by an old enemy, the evil Hawk family. Dinah's first real mission is to save her mother, with a timely assist from Huntress and Reese. But there is a tragic end...

GUEST CAST: Lori Loughlin (Black Canary); Stephen McHattie (Al Hawk); Kristofer McNeeley; Robert Patrick Benedict (Gibson); Brent Sexton, Rainbow Borden.

6. "Primal Scream" Written by: Edward Kitsis and Adam Horowitz. Story by: Adam Armus, Kay Foster. Directed by: Jim Charleston. Airdate: November 13, 2002.

Reese brings in Huntress to infiltrate a masked gang of motorcycle-riding robbers. Meanwhile, Oracle's relationship with boyfriend Wade heats up when they become intimate. The further Helena goes undercover with the gang of thugs, the more she finds life outside the law appealing, at least until a disaster occurs that reminds her why she fights crime in the first place. With Reese and Helena at odds over their fledgling partnership, there is little opportunity to nail the boss behind the gang, the elusive Harley Quinn.

GUEST CAST: Shawn Christian (Wade Brixton); Shane Mikael Johnson, Brent Sexton, Sarah Joy Brown.

7. "Split" Written by: Adam Armus and Kay Foster. Story by: Edward Kitsis and Adam Horowitz. Directed by: James Marshall. Airdate: November 20, 2002.

A superhero named Dark Strike visits New Gotham on the trail of an abductor and murderer of women called Crawler, but Huntress sees Dark Strike's presence as a territorial challenge. Huntress is also having trouble in her relationship with Reese, so she is in no mood to work with Dark Strike, who possesses meta-human speed, strength, agility and hearing. Huntress also learns that Crawler and Dark Strike share a terrible connection, that Crawler killed Dark Strike's lover. Dinah uses her growing mental abilities to track Crawler after Huntress rescues his latest victim ... but there is a

twist in the tale, and Dark Strike, wracked with guilt, is one and the same with his nemesis.

GUEST CAST: Kristoffer Polaha (Dark Strike/John); Brian Thompson (Crawler); Annie Wersching (Lynne Syracuse); Samantha Streets (Ponytail Guy); Adam Russell (Boyfriend); Jonathan Fraser (Uniformed Police Officer).

8. "Lady Shiva" Written by: Adam Armus and Kay Foster. Story by: Edward Kitsis and Adam Horowitz. Directed by: John Kretchmer. Airdate: November 27, 2002.

Eight years ago, a rookie Batgirl vanquished a local villain called Lady Shiva, but now someone with her m.o. is back in New Gotham killing people. Reese believes the perpetrator is the legendary Batman, but Barbara and Huntress know better. At the same time, an old friend of Helena's returns to New Gotham after seven years, but she's really Shiva, looking for the opportunity to avenge herself on Batgirl, whose impulsive actions caused the death of Shiva's ten-year-old sister. Plagued by guilt, Barbara dons her Batgirl costume for a last time, and uses a special device to fight Lady Shiva on her own two feet.

GUEST CAST: Sung Hi Lee, Callie De Fabry, Ethan Brown, Michael Don Evans (Armed Guard).

Black Scorpion

Whatever its shortcomings in plotting or narrative, Tim Burton's 1989 blockbuster *Batman* permanently transformed the whole sub-genre of "the superhero," pushing formerly clean-cut icons (like Batman, the Flash and even Aquaman) into new and darker territory, one where angst, vigilantism and dirty fighting were the order of the day. Heroes now came equipped with complex psychological disorders, a schizophrenic dual nature, and even in some cases

(like Lamont Cranston, the Shadow) a lust for evil. From 1989 to 1997, virtually every new superhero project which came down the pike from Hollywood seemed guaranteed to feature an identical exchange between villains and heroes that went something like this: "I made you? You made me!" Yawn...

In other words, villains and heroes became intricately linked, viewed not as polar opposites (good vs. evil) but as two sides of the same twisted coin. TV's *The Flash* (1990), the Alec Baldwin vehicle *The Shadow* (1994), and *The Crow* franchise (1994–1999) all assumed this dark approach, one directly related to Burton's landmark film (and Frank Miller's groundbreaking book *The Dark Knight Returns*).

There was another superhero that came out of that "dark" Burton template, a sort of low-rent one. In 1995, co-creators Roger Corman and Craig J. Nevius imagined a dark female superhero called Black Scorpion. She was a cop named Darcy Walker by day, a superhero by night, a fetching *femme fatale* that could do "with a mask" what she "couldn't do with a badge." The lovely and fit Joan Severance (*Lake Consequence*) essayed the role in the first direct-to-video movie, *Black Scorpion*, which unexpectedly emerged as a huge hit on the home video rental market, not least because it smacked of soft porn. In one titillating scene, the kinky, leather-clad Black Scorpion came to her male partner, Michael Russo (a male Lois Lane–type, played by Bruce Abbott), by night and, after violently assaulting him, made love to him with her mask on and her shirt off.

Like Frank Miller and Bob Kane's "dark knight," Black Scorpion was envisioned as a hero who, because of a family tragedy (the death of her father, in this case), decided to fight crime outside the bounds of the law. Frustrated by all the rules involved in being a detective, lovely Darcy Walker thus fashioned herself a fetishist costume out of lingerie and other *Victoria's Secret*–like leather gear. Then she had a trusted friend, Argyle (Garrett Morris), a former crook gone straight and something of an automotive genius, develop a special vehicle for her: the Scorpion mobile.

A stingray that could "auto transform" or morph at her command (when she uttered the word "yo"), the Scorpion mobile featured a gaggle of helpful tools. 3-D maps, computer imaging, shields, and a scorpion icon emblazoned on the hood all helped Black Scorpion perform her crime-fighting duties. Protected by polarized and bulletproof glass, the vehicle was every bit the match of the Batmobile.

Still, there was at least one non sequitur involving the souped-up car: when shot at by pursuing bad guys, Russo and Darcy would often be seen to duck, despite the protective bulletproof glass. Perhaps that made the chase seem more dramatic.

Also like Batman, Black Scorpion's bag of tricks (i.e. gadgets) all related to her preferred choice of beasts: scorpions. Instead of Batarangs, bat-grapples and the like, it was always Scorpion-this, Scorpion-that. Adding insult to injury, some of the actual shots staged in the original *Black Scorpion* direct-to-video production also evoked (or, rather, mimicked) Burton's popular film. In one scene, Black Scorpion jumped down through a plate glass skylight in a museum to confront two female wrestlers, a reflection of Keaton's similar entrance in the art museum to rescue Kim Basinger from the clutches of Jack Nicholson's Joker.

Perhaps more notably, both *Black Scorpion* home video features ended on staging that this author labels "the gargoyle" shot. Seen in the *Batman* films, this shot features a uniformed icon looking down over his city, surrounded by the metal valley of skyscrapers. In *Batman*, it was the Caped Crusader whose flowing black cape fluttered over the night sky of Gotham, bat signal shining in the distance. In *Batman Returns*, it was Michelle Pfeiffer's Catwoman who poked up unexpectedly in the night, gazing at the urban jungle below. In both *Black Scorpions*, the heroine is also seen posing proudly, this time over Angel City, in a shot unrelated (and unconnected) to the story proper. It's a signature shot of superheroes, one made mandatory by the *Batman* films. It has since appeared, in one form or another, in *Spawn, Daredevil, Birds of Prey* and many, many more.

The second *Black Scorpion* direct-to-video feature pitted Darcy (Severance once more) against a female villain, After Shock, that could control earthquakes. Black Scorpion also fought Stoney Jackson's Gangster Prankster, a truly schizophrenic villain: he was cut down the middle, one-half street gangster, one-half Joker (er, clown...). Again the results were positive. The film (this time lacking the soft porn aspect) made a profit.

The surprising success of the *Black Scorpion* direct-to-video movies quickly led to interest in a weekly TV series, and in July of 2001 the Sci-Fi Channel acquired the exclusive rights to air the series, produced by Roger Corman's organization New Concorde.[1] Joan Severance was not re-hired as the titular character, and the former Miss Kansas and green belt holder in Tae Kwon Do, Michelle Lintel, was selected to replace her in a show billed as "*Batman* meets *Baywatch*," vaulting over some one hundred young actresses.[2] Twenty-two hour long episodes of the series were produced (shot in six days apiece for $400,000 each).[3] The show merited a great deal of publicity based on the fact it featured popular cult actors as villains (including Frank Gorshin, Lou Ferrigno and Adam West), and (perhaps more importantly) some seventeen *Playboy* playmates.[4]

The lithe Lintel represented a younger, more innocent-seeming Black Scorpion than her predecessor, though perhaps also a little less sultry. Still, the actress understood the character well: "Black Scorpion is a female Batman," she realized, "she's good during the day and bad at night."[5]

Joining Lintel on the series was former *Family Ties* star Scott Valentine as Rafferty, Darcy's new partner and love interest; and Guy Boyd took over the role of Captain Strickland, replacing Stephen Lee. Mechanical genius Argyle was also back, this time as portrayed by the younger and more hip-seeming "B.T."

The Scorpion mobile received a dramatic upgrade during the 22-episode run of the *Black Scorpion* series (which aired Friday nights on the Sci-Fi Channel). This time, it came equipped with "Stingers," little pointy scorpions that could drop from the car's underside and deflate the tires of chasing vehicles ("Armed and Dangerous"). In "Out of Thin Air," the car gained a "crystallizer," a weapon that could crystallize gasoline in the tank, thus immobilizing enemies. In "Blinded by the Light," Darcy utilized a remote communicator to drive the car from a distance and program it with specific instructions. The hand-held remote device, however, was actually a toy from Playmates: a *Star Trek: The Next Generation* Type One phaser. Hopefully not too many viewers noticed that.

Black Scorpion's villains were some of the strangest (and most famous) to appear on TV since *Batman* in the 1960s. The former Riddler, Frank Gorshin, played the time conscious Clockwise in "Crime Time," one of the more interesting episodes. Adam West portrayed (or rather gave voice to) the armored Breathtaker, a man lacking organic lungs, in several shows, including "Power Play" (directed by series star Valentine), "Out of Thin Air" and "Zodiac Attack."

Soupy Sales was Professor Prophet, a charlatan psychic who menaced Darcy in the two-part series finale, "Zodiac Attack." David L. Landers, Squiggy from *Laverne and Shirley* (1976–1983), played the plant-loving Green Thumb in "Roses Are Red ... You're Dead."

The second branch of villainy in the series came from those delectable *Playboy* playmates: beautiful, sexy young females who could vie with Lintel as eye candy. Lisa Boyle was the fetching Medusa in "No Stone Unturned," "Fire and Brimstone" and "Power Play." Athena Massey was a former environmentalist turned green-eyed villain because of toxic waste, the dangerous Hurricane in "Zodiac Attack" and "Wave Good-

Femme fatale: Black Scorpion (Michelle Lintel) patrols the streets in her Scorpionmobile.

bye." Renee Allman played a fitness guru gone wacky, named Aerobicide. And Shannon Whiri dramatized an evil rock singer called Vox Populi in "Face the Music."

Unfortunately, the tone of the TV series and its villains was pure camp, and most of the bad guy (or gal) roles simply involved spouting a bunch of really terrible character-related one-liners. It was like watching twenty-two hours of Arnold Schwarzenneger's pun-happy Mr. Freeze in *Batman and Robin*, nothing but bad joke after bad joke. Landers, for instance, really topped out with his vegetation-oriented jokes as

Green Thumb. "Let's make like a tree and leave." "Time to nip this chase in the bud." "Time to reap what you sow." "This bitter harvest isn't mine, it's yours." And so on, endlessly. That was the general level of wit.

Another problem with the series was the repetitive use of stock special effects, underlining its overall cheapness. Just about every episode of *Black Scorpion* commenced with a nighttime chase between the Scorpion mobile and the police. Fine, but the same car chase footage (and expensive explosions) were used and re-used constantly. The same car that blew up in "Blinded by the Light" did so again in "Armed and Dangerous," from the very same angle. During point-of-view chase footage, the same stretch of chain-link fences, road and warehouses was seen again and again. The same street corner showed up innumerable times. Worse, to make the chases seem dramatic, they were often pushed into fast-motion, a gimmick immediately detectable.

Formulaic plots also hampered the series. Just about every story was structured in the same simplistic way. A strange accident spawns a new super-villain; Darcy and Rafferty investigate; the criminal goes on a spree; and Black Scorpion defeats the new threat. Sometimes, the corrupt mayor (Richard Pine) would also be involved, but never get caught. But the villains (and their origins) seemed so simplistic that the series just became dull. *Batman* was able to survive and prosper on a similar premise, but it lasted only a half-hour. Stretched to an hour long, *Black Scorpion* felt slight, to put it mildly.

The reason for that feeling may very well be that the characters in the show were also poorly drawn. Rafferty and Darcy

sparred, but had little real spark. They began as clichés and never grew beyond their trite character descriptions. Rafferty was the "Lois Lane" character, pining for the uber-character (Black Scorpion) and failing to notice the meek but beautiful coworker (Darcy) in his midst, which hardly seemed likely considering she was a knockout. Captain Strickland was another variation of the Perry White prototype, in turns cantankerous, fatherly, irritable, and generally clueless. Perhaps most insultingly, Black Scorpion never really came off as a powerful woman or hero in her own right. That may have been excusable in years past, but in the age of women heroes like the ones on *Buffy the Vampire Slayer, Dark Angel, Witchblade* and *Alias*, the blatantly sexist overtones of the series disappointed. Yes, Black Scorpion (in both incarnations) was beautiful, endowed with a statuesque comic book figure (wide hips, ample breasts), but she was dimwitted instead of powerful, and that simply isn't sexy on a weekly basis.

Embarrassed by the show's general lack of quality, The Sci-Fi Channel very quickly relegated *Black Scorpion* to after-midnight showings, before dropping the series altogether. Though some episodes re-appeared on Superhero Land, a day-long block of superhero shows airing every Monday, the series has generally been forgotten.

Almost.

In August 2001, *Black Scorpion* rose like a phoenix from the ashes (or flies from a carcass). New Concorde announced that, hoping to squeeze more dollars out of the unsuspecting superhero fan, it would release episodes of the series on home video.[6] Let the buyer beware.

Black Scorpion (1995)
LIVE-ACTION FILM

CAST: Joan Severance (Darcy Walker/Black Scorpion); Rick Rossovich (Darcy's Father); Ashley Peldon (Little Darcy); Michael Wiseman (Hacksaw); Brad Tatum (Razor); Casey Semazko

(Dr. Goddard); Kimberly Roberts (Nurse); Kyle Fredericks (Orderly); Terri J. Vaughn (Tender Lovin'); Bruce Abbott (Michael Russo); Darryl M. Bell (E-Z Street); Garrett Morris (Argyle); Randy Ideish (Torg Leader); Stephen Lee (Captain Strickland); John Sanderford (Aldrdige); Steven Kravitz (Rookie #1); Shane Powers (Cop #2); Paula Tricky (Leslie Vance); Edmund Gilbert (Voice of Breathtaker); Heather O'Ryan (Teenage Runaway); Rick Tyler-Barns (Mugger); Vincent Chase (Accountant); Anita Hart (Scary Mary); Rosine Hatem (Connie the Crusher); Kurt Lott (Security Guard #1); Anthony Kramme (Security Guard #2); Rodman Flender (Hank); Matt Roe (Mayor); Rick Dean (Wino); Mike Elliott (Cop #1); Jonathan Winfrey (Bar Patron); Greg Brazzell (Guard in Store).

CREW: A New Horizons Production. *Casting:* Jan Glasser. *Supervising Production Designer:* NAVA. *Production Designer:* Eric Kahn. *Music:* Kevin Kiner. *Director of Photography:* Geoff George. *Scorpionmobile Effects and Computer Generated Imagery Supervised by:* Perry Harovas, Bob Farnham. *Special Digital Effects:* Digital Drama. *Special Make-up and Costumes:* Michael Burnett Productions. *Film Editors:* Tom Peterson, Gwyneth Gibby. *Executive Producers:* Roger Corman, Lance H. Robbins. *Written by:* Craig J. Nevius. *Produced by:* Mike Elliott. *Directed by:* Jonathan Winfrey. *Unit Production Manager:* Jud Crenna. *Music Supervisor:* Paul D. Franco. *Executive in Charge of Production:* Jan Kikumoto. *Stunt Coordinators:* Patrick Statham, Cole McCay. *Script Supervisors:* Kelly Akers, Jeffrey Orr. *Production Coordinator:* Nora Genelin. *Art Director:* Aaron Mays. *Set Design:* Kate Harrington. *Property Master:* Gregory B. Atkins. *Post Production Supervisor:* Mitchell Buroker. *Special Digital Effects:* Digital Drama. *Director of Digital Effects:* Perry Harevas. *Location Manager:* Alex Kirlen. *Running time:* 95 minutes.

In 1975, in Angel City, young Darcy Walker is devastated when her reckless cop father accidentally kills a doctor during a dangerous collar at a local hospital. Eighteen years later, Darcy is a cop on the job, posing as a streetwalker to bring in perpe-trators. When her bust goes bad, she talks to her drunk father, now a security guard, about her feelings of powerlessness.

Not long after their conversation, Angel City's district attorney kills Mr. Walker, apparently without motive. A disturbed Darcy threatens the incarcerated D.A. and is suspended for crossing the line of appropriate conduct. When a contact, Tender Lovin', is injured by her pimp, Darcy goes completely over the edge, fashioning a black costume and becoming a vigilante hero called "Black Scorpion."

Meanwhile, a villain called the Breathtaker uses asthma inhalers to control an army of asthmatics, making the wheezy warriors his slaves. When Darcy's car gets shot up on a mission to a museum, Darcy is forced to confide in Argyle, a friendly car thief and crook that can help her. While Darcy's relationship with her partner, Michael Russo, heats up, she faces unexpected competition from Black Scorpion! Michael is apparently in love with the superhero. Meanwhile, Argyle spices up Darcy's car, turning it into the gadget-laden Scorpion mobile.

After Darcy seduces Michael as Black Scorpion, she considers giving up her secret identity, but when Breathtaker threatens to poison the city, she resumes her crime-fighting duties. She learns that Breathtaker is actually Dr. Noah Goddard, the surgeon who was shot by her father all those years earlier. Now he's more man than machine and determined to take control of the city using a mind-control gas he used on the innocent district attorney. Black Scorpion confronts Breathtaker's minions at an atmosphere control tower. She defeats him, then uses his own gas to make him forget Darcy's secret identity.

Black Scorpion: After Shocks (1996)
LIVE-ACTION FILM

CAST: Joan Severance (Darcy Walker/Black Scorpion); Whip Hubley (Michael Russo); Stoney Jackson (Gangster Prankster); Sherrie Rose (Ursula Undershaft/Aftershock); Stephen Lee (Captain Strickland); Terri J. Vaughn (Tender Lovin'); Carl Banks (Grimace); David Harris (Heckler); Steven Kravitz (Slugger); Shane Powers (Specs); Linda Hoffman (Jane); Matt Roe (Mayor Worth); Laura Harring (Babette); Christina Solis (Bonita Bradley); Garrett Morris (Argyle); Gabrielle Bemford (Dispatch); Sean Gavigan (Yes Man #1); Kevin McLaughlin (Yes Man #2); Scott Valentine (Dick); Manny Fernandez (Bomb Squad Leader); Vincent Chase (Police Medic); Rick Rossovich (Construction Foreman); Jeffrey Scott Jensen (Truck Driver #1); Slade Barnett (Swastika Face); Mark Folger (Donkey Face); Jeannie Milar (Giggles); Diane Koskela (White Face); Kimberly Rowe (Divine); Jonathan Winfrey (Cop).

CREW: *Casting:* Jan Glaser. *Special Makeup and Costumes:* Robert Hall. *Music:* Kevin Kiner. *Production Design:* Trae King. *Co-Producer:* Joan Severance. *Editor:* Louis Cioffi. *Director of Photography:* Mark Kohl. *Executive Producer:* Lance H. Robbins. *Written by:* Craig Nevius. *Producer:* Roger Corman. *Directed by:* Jonathan Winfrey. *Associate Producer:* Darrin Spillman. *Executive in Charge of Production:* Cheryl Parnell. *Production Supervisor:* Marta M. Mobley. *Unit Production Manager:* Tim Andrews. *Post Production Supervisor:* Mitchell Buroker. *Stunt Coordinators:* Patrick Statham, Brett Davidson.

Angel City's finest, Darcy Walker (a.k.a. Black Scorpion), continues to fight injustice by ridding the streets of criminals, including a pair of maniacal jewel thieves.

One day, a criminal called the Gangster Prankster detonates a bomb in Darcy's precinct house and steals millions of dollars from the police vault. Darcy and her partner track him to his headquarters in a warehouse, but when Rick is apprehended by thugs, Black Scorpion is needed. An earthquake occurs and is fortuitously timed to help the superhero arrest the Gangster Prankster.

Meanwhile, the beautiful Dr. Ursula Undershaft of Angel Technologies has developed a device to stop earthquakes forever, but the corrupt Mayor of Angel City is unhappy because no earthquakes means no Federal relief money. He sends his identical-twin "yes men" to sabotage Undershaft's work, and she is fingered as the person responsible when the next earthquake strikes. Driven mad, Ursula becomes a sexy super-villain called Aftershock and steals a shipment of vibranium, a substance critical to the creation of earthquakes.

Aftershock frees Gangster Prankster from jail to steal the Scorpion mobile for her, and Prankster kidnaps Tender Lovin', Argyle's girlfriend, in order to coerce the mechanic into helping him.

With the powerful Scorpion mobile under his control, Gangster Prankster loots the ritzy Everly Heights, including the Mayor's Mansion. Black Scorpion is on the case quickly, going after the deadly duo before they can cause the biggest earthquake in Angel City's history...

Black Scorpion: The Series (2001)
LIVE-ACTION SERIES

"*Black Scorpion* was feces. It was the camp aspect of *Batman* with a dark sado-masochistic undertone and nothing much about it worked at all. It was badly acted. The lead actress [Lintel] was terrible and there was nothing naturalistic about her line delivery. It was like she was reading. Badly."

— Howard Margolin, host of *Destinies: The Voice of Science Fiction*.

CAST: Michelle Lintel (Darcy Walker/ Black Scorpion); Scott Valentine (Steve Rafferty); B.T. (Argyle); Enya Flack (Veronica/Tender Lovin'); Guy Boyd (Captain Strickland); Steven Kravitz, Shane Powers.

CREW: Roger Corman presents *Black Scorpion*. *Created by:* Roger Corman and Craig J. Nevius. *Casting:* Jan Glaser. *Music:* David Russell. *Film Editors (various episodes):* Brian J. Cavanaugh, Marcus Czyzewski, Beth Dewey, Barbara Kaplan, Anthony Miller, Eli Nilsen, Christine Rasmussen, Ruth Wald. *Production Designer:* Dave Blass. *Special Make-up and Black Scorpion Suit Created by:* Robert Hall/ALMOST HUMAN. *Directors of Photography (various episodes):* Todd Barron, Carlo Gonzalez, Michael Mickens. *Supervising Producer:* Craig J. Nevius. *Producer:* Marta M. Mobley. *Story Editor:* Frances Doel. *Associate Producer:* Siobhan McDevitt. *Executive Producers:* Roger Corman and Cheryl Parnell. *Costume Designer:* Jayme Bohn. *Unit Production Manager:* Kyle A. Clark. *Art Director:* Mark Harper. From New Concorde.

1. "Armed and Dangerous" Written by: Craig J. Nevius. Directed by: Gwyneth Gibby. Airdate: January 5, 2001.

Darcy Walker, a.k.a. the Black Scorpion, battles two villains: the heavily armored FireArm and a gun-happy general named Stryker. Argyle upgrades the Scorpion mobile to help Darcy stop the vengeance-mad FireArm.

GUEST CAST: Martin Kove (FireArm); Shae Marks (Babette); Ben McCain; David Groh (Lt. Walker); Elizabeth Huett (Young Darcy).

2. "Wave Goodbye" Written by: L.L. Shapira and Craig J. Nevius. Directed by: Robert Spera. Airdate: January 12, 2001.

During a high-speed police chase, Black Scorpion pursues a truck carrying massive amounts of toxic waste. The truck shakes loose the superhero, and criminals working for the Mayor dump the poison into Angel City Bay, where an environmentalist is exposed to toxins, becoming a green-eyed super-villainess called Hurricane. Rafferty and Walker stake out the beach and encounter Hurricane's henchmen, scientists turned ocean-life called "Squids." Meanwhile, Hurricane begins a life of crime, robbing banks and planning to destroy Angel City with her new invention: a hurricane magnifier.

GUEST CAST: Athena Massey (Hurricane); Robert Pine (Mayor); Soupy Sales (Sonny Dey); Shae Marks, Kevin West, Richard Tanner, Jerry Rector, Jeff Rector.

3. "Blinded by the Light" Written by: Craig J. Nevius. Directed by: Stanley Yung. Airdate: January 19, 2001.

Black Scorpion sends a car-jacker on a wild ride in the Scorpion mobile and is nearly arrested by Rafferty, all under the watchful eye of a nosy photographer named Allbright. Later, Allbright stages a crime in the hopes Black Scorpion will appear and he'll be able to photograph her sans mask. But Black Scorpion blinds the nosy photographer before he can learn her secret, and the vengeance-happy Allbright becomes a new villain: Flashpoint! His first crime is to rob an armored car, a ploy to finance an "ocular laser" that will blind everybody in Angel City.

GUEST CAST: Allen Scotti (Cameron Allbright/Flashpoint), Kimber West (Iris); Robert Pine (Mayor); Ben McCain; James Lew; Shae Marks; Paul Keith; Robby Robinson (Carjacker); Lola Stone (Mother); Abbot Alexander (Guard #1); Kevin Shaw (Guard #2); David Groh (Lt. Walker); Elizabeth Huett (Young Darcy).

4. "Home Sweet Homeless" Written by: Raly Radouloff. Directed by: Gwyneth Gibby. Airdate: January 26, 2001.

Ursula Undershaft, a.k.a. Aftershock, is back in Angel City even as the Mayor orders "Operation Clean Sweep," a crackdown on the homeless of the community. Aftershock develops an echo wave generator to menace the city, and steals "vibranium" to fuel her next deadly earthquake. She demands Angel City residents turn their homes over to the homeless, and then kidnaps the mayor.

GUEST CAST: Sherrie Rose (Aftershock); Robert Pine (Mayor Worth); Robert Hegyes; Ben McCaine; Rick Deane; James Lew; Joe Estevez; Shae Marks; Stan Yale (Squeegee Guy); Dave Kilde (Security Guard #1); Clint Lilley (Security Guard #2); David Groh (Lt. Walker); Elizabeth Huett (Young Darcy).

5. "Love Burns" Airdate: February 2, 2001.

Mayor Worth cuts back funds to the fire department, leaving a dedicated firefighter named Adam to do the job with only personal resources at his disposal. In pursuit of an arsonist, Adam is transformed into the fire-spewing villain called Inferno. Complicating matters are Darcy's romantic feelings for the handsome public servant.

GUEST CAST: Brent Huff (Adam/Inferno); Robert Pine (Mayor Worth); David Mustaine; David Groh (Lt. Walker); Elizabeth Huett (Young Darcy).

6. "Out of Thin Air" Written by: Heidi Gerrer and Nick Guthe. Directed by: Robert Spera. Airdate: February 9, 2001.

Dr. Phoenix, a mad but benevolent scientist, revives the evil Breathtaker in the Phoenix Institute in hopes of reforming him and making him a productive member of society. Remembering his clash with Lieutenant Walker and, years later, Darcy Walker, Breathtaker escapes from the lab, bent on revenge. He tests a nightmare-inducing chemical agent on the police and plans to unleash it in the atmosphere. Even Darcy is affected, hallucinating an adversarial, taunting relationship with Black Scorpion, her own alter ego.

GUEST CAST: Raye Birk (Dr. Phoenix); David Groh (Lt. Walker); Laura Harring (Ariana); Adam West (Breathtaker/Dr. Noah Goddard); Tony Pennello (Officer Franklin); Lucy Lin (Christine Callahan); David Kramer Rogers (Gason Filmore); John-Clay Scott (Ratface); George Fisher (Heavy); Andrew Craig(Thug #1); Duke Valenti (Thug #2); Amy Miller (Female Cop #1); Jill Murray (Female Cop #2); Elizabeth Huett (Young Darcy).

7. "No Stone Unturned" Written by: Craig J. Nevius. Directed by: Jeff Yonis. Airdate: February 16, 2001.

The villainous Medusa breaks into a posh restaurant with her oversized henchmen and turns a councilman into stone with a weapon called a "plaster blaster." She then goes after a TV anchorman, prompting an investigation by Darcy and Rafferty. Medusa, a girl named Minerva Stone who's been made beautiful by the minerals in her "river of rejuvenation," was once ugly and is now turning to stone all those men who rejected her … and putting these new statues in her rock garden. Medusa's real target, however, is Rafferty, and she wins a night with him at a police charity auction.

GUEST CAST: Lisa Boyle (Medusa); Ben McCain; Sylvester "Bear" Terkay; Brian McWhorter; Danica Sheridan (Bertha); David Ray Wagner (Waiter); Scott A. McPhail (Bruce); Jeff Winkless (Auctioneer); Melissa Braselle (Streetwalker #1); Monique Parent (Streetwalker #2); Cecile Krevey (Society Woman); Steven Meck (Councilman Blondell); David Groh (Lt. Walker); Elizabeth Huett (Young Darcy).

8. "Crime Time" Written by: Craig J. Nevius. Directed by: Tim Andrew. Airdate: February 23, 2001.

A very punctual and time-conscious villain called Clockwise is released from prison after serving twenty-five years, and he has a lot of catching up to do. After evading Black Scorpion by freezing time, Clockwise becomes interested in turning time forward—with the help of a special microchip created by Dr. Phoenix—in order to steal the futures of those people that imprisoned him. Darcy realizes Clockwise's next victim is his arresting officer from a quarter century ago—Captain Strickland!

GUEST CAST: Frank Gorshin (Clockwise); Victoria Silvstedt; Raye Birk (Dr. Phoenix); Lyman Ward; Ben McCain; Michael J. Anderson; Ted Rooney; Lucy Lee Flippin; Ralph Meyering, Jr.; John Phinney (Juror #1); David Groh (Lt. Walker); Elizabeth Huett (Young Darcy).

9. "No Sweat" Written by: Steve Gentile. Directed by: Rachel Samuels. Airdate: March 2, 2001.

Black Scorpion clashes with the fitness-crazed beauty Aerobicide, who has been robbing wealthy clientele (like Mayor Worth) at Angel City men's clubs. Darcy and Captain Strickland go undercover as new millionaires to prompt another robbery, but their cover is blown at Aerobicide's health club, where her alter ego is that of Suzie Payne, aerobics instructor. Black Scorpion and Aerobicide have a re-match as Captain Strickland is nearly exercise-cycled to death...

GUEST CAST: Renee Allman (Aerobicide/Suzie Payne); Faith Salie; Lyman Ward; Joseph Whipp; Lydia Cornell; Ava Fabian; Suzanne Turner; Shae Marks; Robert Pine (Mayor Worth); Nikki Schieler Ziering (Woman #1); David Groh (Lt. Walker); Young Darcy (Elizabeth Huett).

10. "An Officer and a Prankster" Written by: Elijah Aron. Directed by: Alex Cassini. Airdate: March 9, 2001.

Costumed freaks rob Argyle's Garage and assaults the mechanic to steal an urn containing the ashes of the nefarious criminal Gangster Prankster. Dr. Phoenix clones the villain but tries to reform his behavior with cranial shocks that kick in every time the super-villain experiences a criminal thought. Darcy and Rafferty arrest Gangster Prankster at a cop carnival (where police are costumed as clowns), but his mean, green cronies cause havoc. When Gangster Prankster saves the day by averting a bomb threat, the Mayor has him installed as a new police officer in Darcy's precinct!

GUEST CAST: Stoney Jackson (Gangster Prankster); Carl Banks; Raye Birk (Dr. Phoenix); Don Gibb; Ben McCain; Kelsey Mulrone; Greg Eagles; Jeannie Millar; Michael J. Pagan; John Michael Glover; Daniel Kamen; Pasha; David Groh (Lt. Walker); Elizabeth Huett (Young Darcy).

11. "Roses Are Red ... You're Dead" Written by: Malcolm Stephens. Directed by: Tim Andrews. Airdate: March 24, 2001.

The villain known as Green Thumb robs Angel City bank with his assistants African Violet and Tiger Lilly, incapacitating the workers with "poppy powder." Darcy arrives at the scene with Rafferty, where a bad cold makes her immune to the negative effects of Green Thumb's plants. After the criminal escapes during a chase (by hurling explosive potted plants at the Scorpion mobile), he plans to sell a plant called "gasperarius" that will rob the denizens of Angel City of air. Black Scorpion is on the case, which leads to the Mayor's office and one case of a (villain's) broken heart.

GUEST CAST: David L. Landers (Green Thumb); Gretchen Palmer; Ben McCain; Patricia Ford; Jody Howard; Tim Halderman; Shae Marks; Robert Pine (Mayor Worth); Cheryl Dent (Bank Teller #1); Steve Nevil (Bank Teller #2); Steve Hanks (Bank Guard); Brian Rosen (Delivery Man #1); Greg Marc Miller (Delivery Man #2); Jamie Logan (Waitress); Wes Hubbard (Waiter); Thomas C. Riley (Security Guard #1); Nicola Sworsky (Security Guard #2); Nina K. James (Carmen); David Groh (Lt. Walker); Elizabeth Huett (Young Darcy).

12. "Life's a Gas" Written by: Steve Gentile and Craig J. Nevius. Directed by: Gwyneth Gibby. Airdate: March 31, 2001.

A scientist who cares deeply about the environment and once studied under Noah Goddard (a.k.a. Breathtaker) is injured in a chemical spill and becomes the new scourge of Angel City. Taking up the handle "Pollutia," this scientist, Ariel, plots to cleanse the Earth of the plague that is humanity...

GUEST CAST: Adam West (Breathtaker); Julie McCullough (Ariel); Traci Bingham; Carrie Stevens; Steve Eastin; Howard George; David Groh (Lt. Walker); Elizabeth Huett (Young Darcy).

13. "Fire and Brimstone" Directed by: Robert Spera. Airdate: April 7, 2001.

Rafferty and Darcy go undercover as

sweethearts to nab the strange criminal called Cupid, who has kidnapped Argyle's girlfriend, Veronica. But, as fate would have it, former nemeses Medusa and Inferno have also returned to Angel City to wreak havoc, thanks to another misguided rehabilitation effort by Dr. Phoenix. Inferno visits Darcy, rekindling their romantic relationship, but Darcy doesn't bite and fights him as Black Scorpion. Meanwhile, Medusa goes after Rafferty again, the man who rejected her.

GUEST CAST: Lisa Boyle (Medusa); Brent Huff (Inferno); Raye Birk (Dr. Phoenix); Ben McCaine; Sylvester Terkay; Brian McWhorter; Arturo Gil; David Groh (Lt. Walker); Elizabeth Huett (Young Darcy).

14. "Virtual Vice" Written by: Craig J. Nevius. Directed by: Susan Tuan. Airdate: April 14, 2001.

A virtual reality researcher, Dr. Sarah Bellum, is transformed into a nasty villain called "Mindbender," and sets about controlling the minds of Angel City's unwitting populace. This new threat apprehends the Mayor, attempting to prove that reality isn't what it used to be...

GUEST CAST: Lana Clarkson (Mindbender/Dr. Sarah Bellum); Lou Ferrigno (Slave Master); Amy Miller; Lisa Alvarez; Ben McCain; Frank Kowal; Jacob Chambers; David Groh (Lt. Walker); Elizabeth Huett (Young Darcy).

15. "Bad Sport" Directed by: David Blass. Airdate: April 21, 2001.

Steve's buddy, a professional hockey player, is injured during a playoff game. Recuperating, he has a special suit made for him, one that turns him into the deadly new villain called Slap Shot. His first job: to go after those responsible for his accident. Steve is reluctant to collar his friend, or even believe he could be involved in the crimes...

GUEST CAST: Steven R. Schirrpa; Beckie Mullen; Gretchen Stockdale; Tom Likus; David Groh (Lt. Walker); Elizabeth Huett (Young Darcy).

16. "Kiss of Death" Written by: Mike Vitale and Craig J. Nevius. Directed by: Tim Andrew. Airdate: April 28, 2001.

A cop, Angela Archer, has broken the law, and Darcy does her duty by reporting her. Angela loses her badge over an issue of police brutality, and then, out of vengeance, transforms herself into a new villain, the Angel of Death. This avenging angel has it out for the police and Black Scorpion.

GUEST CAST: Nancy Valen (Angel of Death/Angela Archer); Patrick Bristow; David Groh (Lt. Walker); Elizabeth Huett (Young Darcy).

17. "He Who Laughs Last" Written by: Steve Gentile. Directed by: Michael Mickens. Airdate: May 5, 2001.

The Gangster Prankster plots to break out of prison to avenge himself on Charlie Chortle, the popular comedian who has been publicly roasting him. Worse, Argyle is framed for stealing the Mayor's limousine and is sent to prison. There Argyle engineers the Gangster Prankster's escape and is shattered when he (mistakenly) believes that Veronica has jilted him for another man. With Argyle's help, Prankster engineers a device called the "bust-a-gut," which could silence laughter in Angel City for all time.

GUEST CAST: Stoney Jackson (Gangster Prankster); Sung Hi Lee; Darl Banks; Greg Eagles; Ben McCain; Fred Travalena (Charlie Chortle); Elias McCabe (Military Guard); Tony Franchitto (Prison Guard); Krista Smith (Female Psychiatrist); David Groh (Lt. Walker); Elizabeth Huett (Young Darcy).

18. "Power Play" Written by: Steve Gentile and Craig J. Nevius. Directed by: Scott Valentine. Airdate: May 12, 2001.

Mayor Worth launches an anti-crime initiative from Pearl Gate Penitentiary, introducing the electric chair to Angel City. The chair malfunctions, transforming the deputy mayor into a new super-villain with electricity coursing through her veins: Stunner! Though crippled by the need to re-charge often, Stunner is a potent new threat who kidnaps the mayor and plans to succeed him in office as her alter ego, Edwina Watts. To keep Black Scorpion out of her hair, Stunner sees to it that the heroine faces new engagements with old foes Breathtaker, Medusa and Slap Shot.

GUEST CAST: Alison Armitage (Stunner); Adam West (Breathtaker); Lisa Boyle (Medusa); Greg Kean; Steve Eastin; Kevin Otto; Jamie Mc-Shane; Ben McCain; Shae Marks; Robert Pine (Mayor Worth); David Groh (Lt. Walker); Elizabeth Huett (Young Darcy).

19. "Photo Finish" Written by Craig. J. Nevius. Directed by: Tim Andrew. Airdate: May 19, 2001.

Flashpoint escapes from Pearl Gate Penitentiary with the assistance of his henchwoman "Vision." He plots to capture Black Scorpion on film and expose her secret identity to the world, a plot made more plausible by Flashpoint's camera device, which can dematerialize then re-materialize any subject it photographs. Darcy is captured, then unmasked, by Flashpoint. Her secret identity is revealed on TV and newspapers all over the city, and a betrayed Rafferty is assigned to bring the rogue Darcy in.

GUEST CAST: Allen Scott (Flashpoint); Raye Birk (Dr. Phoenix); Kimber West (Iris Lookingood/"Vision"); Ben McCain; Steve Eastin; Sam J. Jones (Space Case); John-Clay Scott (Newsstand Vendor); Timothy C. Riley (Security Guard #1); Nicole Zvorsky (Security Guard #2); David Groh (Lt. Walker); Elizabeth Huett (Young Darcy).

20. "Face the Music" Written by Craig J. Nevius. Directed by: Robert Spera. Airdate: June 16, 2001.

Untalented and crude (but sexy) rock singer Vox Populai and her evil band attack the audience at Club Edge when heckled. Meanwhile, Captain Strickland is ahead in the polls in his race to unseat the corrupt Mayor Worth. Desperate to hold onto power, Worth teams with Populi, allowing secret orders to be transmitted in her music (via the UltraSonic2000). These orders cause the youth of the city to become destructive looters and rebels. When Worth betrays Vox, she interrupts a debate with vengeance on her mind and a song in her heart.

GUEST CAST: Shannon Whirry (Vox Populi); Elan Carter; Angelica Bridges; Ben McCain; Steve Eastin; Jerry Rector (Yes Man); Jeff Rector (Yes Man); Shae Marks; Robert Pine (Mayor Worth); David Groh (Lt. Walker); Elizabeth Huett (Young Darcy).

21. "Zodiac Attack" Part One Written by: Craig J. Nevius. Directed by: Greg Aronowitz. Airdate: June 23, 2001.

A new villain, a TV fortune teller named Professor Prophet, forecasts the end of the world via a conjunction of elements: earth, air, fire and water. Threatened by his own personal apocalypse — low ratings and cancellation — Prophet frees four super-villains from the Phoenix Institute: Aftershock (earth), Breathtaker (air), Inferno (fire) and Hurricane (water). With Dr. Phoenix's crime inhibitor chips in the quartet's heads, Prophet controls the foursome and makes them do his bidding, according to his own broadcast prophecy. Working the graveyard shift, Rafferty and Darcy contemplate taking their relationship to a new romantic level, even as they confront the escaped criminals.

GUEST CAST: Soupy Sales (Professor Prophet); Brent Huff (Inferno); Athena Massey (Hurricane); Sherrie Rose (Aftershock); Raye Birk (Dr. Phoenix); Gerry Gibson; Carrie Stevens; Elizabeth Huett (Young Darcy); Adam West (Breathtaker); Max Daniels (Attacker); Meika Cooper (Waitress); Dave Kilde (Security Guard #1); Gary Wayton (Security Guard #2); May Boss (Old Woman); John-Clay Scott (Newsstand Vendor); Eddie "Doogie" Conna (Truck Driver); Bruce Paul Barbour (Sanitation Worker); Anthony Pennello (Storehouse Guy #1); Alex Daniels (Storhouse Guy #2); Jamies Thiel (Delivery Man #1); Jeffrey Thiel (Delivery Man #2).

22. "Zodiac Attack" Part Two Written by: Craig J. Nevius. Directed by: Greg Aronwitz. Airdate: June 30, 2001.

Black Scorpion is pounded during her explosive confrontation with Aftershock, Breathtaker, Hurricane and Inferno, but the police intervene in time to save her life. Defeated soundly by her opponents, Black Scorpion runs away from the battle, and Darcy consequently feels she is cowardly and afraid of death. She quits the police force to spend time with Rafferty and develop their romance, shocking her by-the-book partner. Trying to help, Argyle clones Darcy's dead father to convince her to return to the job. When Lt. Walker's life is put in jeopardy all over again, Darcy resurrects Black Scorpion.

GUEST CAST: Soupy Sales (Professor Prophet); Brent Huff (Inferno); Athena Massey (Hurricane); Sherrie Rose (Aftershock); Raye Birk (Dr. Phoenix); David Groh (Lt. Walker); Adam West (Breathtaker); Ben McCain; Gerry Gibson; Carrie Stevens; Elizabeth Huett (Young Darcy).

Blade

The African American vampire slayer named Blade first came to life in a Marvel comic book called *The Tomb of Dracula* (issue #10) in the year 1972. Adorned in a leather jacket and "cool" shades (sunglasses), the tough-talking character, like a 1970s-era blaxploitation movie star, even spoke a brand of "jive" talk, one that in the 21st century seems a bit archaic. Marv Wolfman penned the adventures of this unusual hero, a minor character in the *Dracula* comic, and Blade was drawn by artist Gene Colan.

As one might guess, *The Tomb of Dracula* involved the villainous exploits of Bram Stoker's legendary vampire, and the efforts of an assortment of heroes, including Quincy Harker, Rachel Van Helsing and, yes, Blade, to kill the long-lived Prince of Darkness. In the comic series, the knife-wielding Blade was immune to vampire bites because of his unusual and storied heritage: he was born after his mother became the meal of a white-haired, bearded vampire elder named Deacon Frost.

As an orphaned Blade grew up, he was raised by a vampire hunter named Jamal Afari and dedicated his life to destroying the creature of the night that killed his mother. In the comics, the bent-on-revenge Blade was occasionally teamed with other vampire killers, and was even something of a musician. A memorable and valuable combatant, the superhero soon appeared in a variety of Marvel comics, including *Dr. Strange* and *Nightstalkers,* in which he ran a detective agency with the half-vampire slayer named Hannibal King.

More than two decades after his birth on comic book pages, actor Wesley Snipes (*New Jack City* [1993], *Jungle Fever* [1995]), director Stephen Norrington and screenwriter David Goyer set about resurrecting the Blade character. Ironically, they chose to endow him with some of the characteristics of his once-partner, Hannibal King, notably King's half-vampire/half-human genetic make-up. This genetic gift gave the movie's Blade a variety of interesting strengths to use in combat — and an addiction to human blood to overcome. He boasted a vampire's super strength (and fangs), and was the only vampire able to walk in daylight (hence his legendary moniker of "the Daywalker").

In the $45 million film, Blade's birth in a Los Angeles hospital in the year 1967 was dramatized; but he was raised not by Afari, as in the comic, but by another heroic vampire slayer (also seen in the comics) named Whistler (played by Kris Kristofferson). Whistler, like Blade, had lost loved ones to vampires (his wife and daughter), and had dedicated his life to destroying the monsters by using his "genius" in creating weaponry and other gadgets.

The film's primary villain was Deacon Frost (Stephen Dorff), but he too had been re-interpreted for the movies. No longer a bearded, old, Gandalf/Obi-Wan Kenobi physical type, the new Deacon Frost was a sexy young hothead, a James Dean–type character. This villain created much trouble not only for Blade, but for the Council of the Vampire Nation as well, an underworld that did not want to be noticed (nor hunted) by mankind. Frost's goal in *Blade* was to sacrifice the "blue blood" vampire council to an ancient and malevolent blood god called La Magra. The film culminated with a ritual in which Frost became possessed by the monstrous and ancient blood demon, only to be vanquished by Blade and his damsel in distress, a lovely hematologist named Dr. Karen Jensen (N'Bushe Wright).

Unlike his comic book counterpart, the new Blade of the late 1990s was not much of a conversationalist, but rather a taciturn, gloomy, and very serious vampire killer. He still wore a leather jacket, but a black one instead of crimson, as well as body armor. In the film he used silver weaponry instead of wooden stakes, and his clothes were very tight and form fitting instead of long and flowing.

Thanks to Wesley Snipes, Blade's martial arts skills proved to be the most valuable vampire-fighting tool of all. The movie version of Blade was what the movie version of Batman should have been: a man who hunts "evil" by night, often without a sense of humor, often without significant human contact. Alone, isolated and embittered by his status as outsider, Blade is, in many ways, the ultimate dark knight, which may be why he has proven so appealing to moviegoers.

Creative ownership of Blade and his universe, like many superheroes, has been fiercely debated by fans and in courtroom litigation. Marv Wolfman claimed he created Blade while an independent "free lancer" working at Marvel. Marvel claimed that those who wrote for Marvel gave up the rights to their characters and stories. Regardless of its exact pedigree, the film version of *Blade* became a super-hit at the box office in August of 1998, raking in more than $70 million in general release (and outgrossing the other vampire hunter film of the year, *John Carpenter's Vampires*).

Wesley Snipes, who also hopes one day to play the superhero Black Panther, inhabited the role of the vampire slayer in a powerful manner, making Blade a dark, extremely physical hero that was one part Batman and one part Bruce Lee. And, in keeping with the trend of "dark," "angst"-ridden superheroes in films of the time, Blade was renowned not just for killing his enemies, but robbing them of valuables so that he could fund his operation against creatures of the night.

And, even more darkly, only one thing kept Blade from becoming a vampire himself: timely injections of an anti-viral agent that effectively suppressed his monstrous side for precious few hours at a time. Predictably, when greater ferocity was needed at the film's climax to defeat the blood demon La Magra, Blade let himself "vamp" out, embracing his internal darkness for the benefit of mankind.

Other villains in the initial film included "familiars"—vampire wannabes, humans that hoped to be bitten by the creatures of the night. Actor Udo Kier (*Andy Warhol's Dracula* [1974]) portrayed the aristocratic leader of the Vampire Nation, a character that experienced a charring demise in the film. But the scene that best encapsulated the Blade mythos was the movie's opening salvo, a scene set at a vampire rave party, replete with gorgeous women, techno/dance music, flashing strobe lights and a sprinkler system that doused reveling vampires in torrents of human blood.

Into this nightclub called "Bloodbath" came the glowering Blade — with an arsenal full of vampire-killing weapons. Like the pre-title sequences of the James Bond films, this scene set the tone of the saga with its martial arts stunts, eye-popping visual effects, spurting blood, adrenaline-pumping music, and gore to go.

Blade 2, released in early 2002, was an even better film than its predecessor. The sequel re-teamed Blade with a miraculously cured Whistler (who had died in the first film), but was notable primarily for director Guillermo Del Toro's (*The Devil's Backbone* [2001]) playing up of the franchise's horror aspects. If the first *Blade* was a terrific martial-arts action picture with horror elements, the second film was a full-fledged horror masterpiece as Blade faced off against a new and terrifying villain, a breed of uber-vampires called "reapers." The leader of this band of monsters was the Nosferatu-like man named Jared Nomack, and each of his carnivorous people were monstrous, vein-covered creations with slavering, ripping jaws that put the dental work of the creatures in *Predator* (1987) and *Alien* (1979) to shame.

When Blade realized that these reapers posed a significant threat to mankind, as well as the vampire nation, he reluctantly joined a team of vampires, lead by a beautiful and sexy undead woman, Nyssa (daughter of the new leader of the Vampire Nation, the ancient overlord Damaskinos). The film became an exercise in horror as Blade and his team (which included Ron Perlman as the disagreeable Reinhardt) scoured sewers, vampire nightclubs (one called the House of Pain) and even high-tech laboratories for the monstrous, contaminating reapers.

Equipped with ultra-violet flash bombs that could obliterate the bad guys in an instant, Blade took the war to the reapers, and Del Toro made one of the most stylish, effective, "dark" superhero movies in ages. The audience apparently felt the same way, and the film earned some 33 million dollars its first weekend of release. It went on to make more money than its highly regarded precursor, and later in the summer many critics even compared it favorably with the megahit *Spider-Man*.

As a result of *Blade 2*'s success with critics and audiences, *Blade 3* has been announced, with Snipes back in the lead role, as has production of a *Blade* TV series (to be produced by Snipes).

Blade (1998)
LIVE-ACTION FILM

"Snipes himself is the movie's biggest asset. He may snarl, hiss and twitch in ways that are often disorienting, but you can't take your eyes off of him."
— Gene Seymour, *The Los Angeles Times*, August 21, 1998, page 4.

"A surprisingly satisfying rock-em, sock 'em escapist romp through a techno-styled urban landscape."
— Rod Dreher, *The New York Post*, August 21, 1998, page 57.

"Blindingly overwrought hybrid of horror, action and Oedipal drama."

— Justine Elias, *The Village Voice*, September 1, 1998, page 114.

"As I watched it, I realized I'd seen it all before in *Mortal Kombat* and *Highlander*. Then there was some *Forever Knight* too, with a vampire trying to fight his destiny of becoming evil. *Blade* was just an amalgamation of everything that had come before."
— Howard Margolin, host of *Destinies: The Voice of Science Fiction*.

CAST: Wesley Snipes (Blade/Eric); Stephen Dorff (Deacon Frost); Kris Kristofferson (Abraham "Whistler"); N'Bushe Wright (Dr. Karen

Jenson); Donal Logue (Quinn); Udo Kier (Drag- onetti); Traci Lords (Racquel); Arly Jover (Mer- cury); Kevin Patrick Walls (Office Krieger); Jud- son Scott (Pallantine); Tim Guinee (Curtis Webb); Sanaa Lathan (Vanessa); Eric Edwards (Pearl); Donna Wong (Nurse); Carmen Thomas (Senior Resident); Kenneth Johnson (Heatseek- ing Dennis); Clint Curtis (Creepy Morgue Guy); Sidney Liufau (Japanese Doorman); Keith Leon Williams (Kam); Andray Johnson and Stephen R. Peluso (Paramedics); Marcus Aurelius (Prag- matic Policeman); John Enos III (Blood Club Bouncer); Eboni Adanis (Martial Arts Kid); Lycle Conway (Reichardt); Freeman White (Menacing Stud); D.V. De Vincents (Vampire Underling). Eril (Von Esper); Lennox Brow (Pleading Goon); Yvette Ocampo (Party Girl); Erence Stepa (Slavic Vampire); Jenya Lano (Rus- sian Woman); Levani (Russian Vampire).

CREW: New Line Cinema Presents an Amen Ra Films Production in association with Imaginary Forces, a Stephen Norrington Picture, *Blade*. *Written by:* David S. Goyer. *Directed by:* Stephen Norrington. *Casting:* Rachel Abroms, Jory Weitz. *Music Supervisor:* Dana Sand. *Make- up Special Effects:* Greg Cannom. *Co-Producers:* Andrew J. Horne, John Divens. *Costume Design:* Sanja Milkovic Mays. *Music:* Mark Isham. *Unit Production Manager:* Roee Sharon. *First Assistant Director:* Barry K. Thomas. *Second Assistant Di- rector:* Rebecca Strickland. *Film Editor:* Paul Rubell. *Production Designer:* Kirk M. Petrucelli. *Director of Photography:* Theo Van De Sande. *Executive Producer:* Lynn Harris. *Executive Pro- ducers:* Stan Lee, Avi Arad, Joseph Calamari. *Produced by:* Peter Frankfurt, Wesley Snipes, Robert Engelman. *Blade and Deacon Frost Char- acters Created for Marvel Comics by:* Marv Wolf- man, Gene Colan. *Stunt Coordinator:* Jeff Ward. *Martial Arts Choreography:* Jeff Ward, Wesley Snipes. *Executive in Charge of Production:* Carla Fry. *Post-Production Supervisor:* Sara Romilly. *Script Supervisor:* Nicole Cummins. *Art Director:* Barry Chusid. *Set Decorator:* Greg Grande. *Prop- erty Master:* Steven B. Melton. *Camera Operator:* Paul Edwards. *Sound Mixer:* Lee Orloff. *Visual Effects Producer:* Matthew Justice. *Visual Effects Supervisor:* Chuck Comisky. *M.P.A.A. Rating:* R. *Running time:* 120 minutes.

In 1967, a child is born to a woman bitten by a vampire. Thirty one years later, that boy is a man named Blade, a vampire- human hybrid dedicated to fighting the vampire scourge that infests Los Angeles.

One night, Blade interrupts a violent vampire rave called "Bloodbath." He burns Quinn, the assistant to vampire warlord Deacon Frost, but the vampire revives at the hospital and bites the attending physician, as well as a beautiful laboratory technician named Karen Jenson. Blade rescues Karen, but realizes she is infected by vampire blood. He takes her to his headquarters in an aban- doned factory, where she is treated by his friend, Whistler, with injections of garlic. Blade takes the injections himself, to keep his vampire characteristics strictly regulated and under control, but he is developing a re- sistance to it.

Meanwhile, Deacon Frost has defied the secret vampire nation and begun to translate ancient vampire scrolls in a com- puter archive. This disturbs Dragonetti, the head of the vampire council, but Frost tells the head vampire that he is obsolete. At the same time, Blade and Jenson team up to stop Deacon Frost, but first must learn what he's planning. They track his operation to a night club and find a secret passageway to the vampire archives. They confront the keeper of the records, an obese vampire named Pearl, and learn of a ritual to resur- rect an ancient vampire god called LaMagre. Captured by Deacon's goons, Blade and Karen are rescued by Whistler.

In his quest to resurrect LaMagre, Frost kills Dragonetti and then captures the rest of the vampire council. Then he kills Whistler and destroys Karen Jenson's lab, even as she labors to find a cure for Blade. Frost captures Karen as bait because he needs Blade for the ceremony, specifically the blood of the Chosen One, the "Day- walker." Since Blade is both man and vam- pire, able to withstand sunlight, Frost real- izes his nemesis is this mythical figure.

Armed with a serum that can infect the blood of vampires and destroy them, Blade goes after Karen and is promptly captured. Under Frost's care, he learns that his mother is a vampire minion of the villain. Worse, she shows little sympathy for her son, who is to be bled dry in the Temple of Eternal Night to resurrect LaMagra. The ceremony is completed, leaving Blade on the brink of death, but Karen lets him drink her blood so he can fight LaMagra. Revived, Blade battles Frost, now infused with the strength and restorative powers of the ancient vampire god. Blade is nearly defeated, but he uses Karen's serum to destroy the superpowered Frost. Weak, but still alive, Karen and Blade leave the site of the battle, realizing there is still a war to fight if humanity is to survive...

Blade II (2002)
LIVE-ACTION FILM

CAST: Wesley Snipes (Blade); Kris Kristofferson (Whistler); Ron Perlman (Reinhardt); Leonar Varela (Nyssa); Norman Reedus (Scud); Thomas Kretschmann (Overlord Eli Damaskinos); Luke Goss (Jared Nomak); Matthew Schulze (Chupa); Danny John Jules (Asad); Donnie Yen (Snowman); Karel Roden (Kounene); Marit Velle Kile (Verloune); Tony Curran (Priest); Daz Crawford (Lighthammer); Xuyen Tu Valdiria (Jigsaw); Marek Vasut (Golem); Santiago Segura (Rushi).

CREW: New Line Cinema Presents an Amen Ra Films Production in association with Imaginary Forces, a Guillermo Del Toro Film, *Blade II. Directed by:* Guillermo Del Toro. *Written by:* David S. Goyer. *Blade Character Created for Marvel Comics by*: Marv Wolfman and Gene Colan. *Producers:* Peter Frankfort, Wesley Snipes, Patrick Palmer. *Executive Producers:* Lynn Harris, Michael De Luca, David S. Goyer, Toby Emmerich, Stan Lee and Avi Arad. *Co-Producers:* Andrew J. Horne, Jon Divens. *Director of Photography*: Gabriel Beristain. *Production Design:* Carol Spier. *Film Editor:* Peter Amundson. *Music:* Marco Beltrami. *Additional Music:* Danny Saber. *Music Supervisor:* Happy Walters. *Visual Effects Supervisor:* Nicholas Brooks. *Costume Designer:* Wendy Partridge. *Casting:* Nancy Foy. *UK Casting:* Jeremy Zimmerman. *Stunt Coordinator:* Jeff Ward. *Fight Coordinators:* Jeff Ward, Wesley Snipes, Clay Fontenot. *Martial Arts Choreography:* Donnie Yen. *M.P.A.A. Rating:* R. *Running time:* 117 minutes.

Two years ago, Blade's partner and mentor, Whistler, was believed killed by the minions of vampire warlord Deacon Frost. In fact, the human was turned into a creature of the night and placed in stasis. Blade has been hunting him ever since and rescues him in Czechoslovakia, then uses an "accelerated retrovirus detox" to restore Whistler to human status.

As Whistler re-acquaints himself with Blade's operation — and his new assistant, the sarcastic young Scud — Blade faces a new challenge. A vampire commando team led by the beautiful Nyssa invades his headquarters. Under orders from her powerful father, Overlord Eli Damaskinos, Nyssa offers Blade a truce in their war. Something worse than the Daywalker has appeared on the streets: Reapers, a new breed of vampire organism bent on destroying man and vampire alike.

Though Whistler is skeptical of the alliance, Blade agrees to lead a crack team of vampire commandos called "the Blood Pact." His team includes the giant Littlehammer, the human-hating Chupa, the villainous Reinholdt, noble Asad and the martial arts expert, Snowman. The team's first assignment is to infiltrate a vampire night club called the House of Pain, where Blade has his first contact with the monstrous Reapers, who are immune to garlic, silver and bullets — only sunlight (or ultraviolet light) proves damaging to the mutants. The leader of the Reapers, Jared Nomak, survives a battle with Blade. After the battle, Nyssa conducts an autopsy on one of the creatures, learning that its heart is encased in bone — to prevent untimely stakings. The Reapers can survive only a short amount of time without feeding on new blood, so the real threat is the original Reaper who carries the disease: Nomak.

The Blood Pact searches out Reapers in the sewers, and much of the team is decimated. The vampires betray Blade and take the Daywalker and Whistler prisoner after hundreds of Reapers have been destroyed by sunlight. Blade is taken back to the Overlord's headquarters, where it is learned that Damaskinos genetically engineered Nomak in an attempt to breed out vampire weaknesses. Now he wants Blade's genes to engineer immunity to sunlight. Worse, Scud turns out to be a familiar, a human turncoat in the vampire war!

As Nomak invades the headquarters to destroy his hated "father," Damaskinos, Whistler rescues Blade from a "blood draining" machine. Damaskinos and the innocent Nyssa attempt to flee Nomak, but Nomak kills the Overlord and bites Nyssa, infecting her. Blade arrives for a final showdown with Nomak.

Blankman

Although it bombed financially and critically during its theatrical run, *Blankman,* created by *In Living Color*'s resident genius, Damon Wayans, is nonetheless a very funny movie, and a rare and lovely gift for those dedicated viewers that remember the 1960s *Batman* series with fondness. Indeed, it is a genuine love and admiration for that classic Adam West/Burt Ward–starring superhero program that seems to be the primary influence for this incredibly silly movie, a comedy superhero picture with a twist.

Even before the opening credits roll, the film dramatizes two black youngsters (Darryl and Kevin Walker) watching that old series on their TV set, manipulating the antenna and trying to get better reception as straight-arrows Batman and Robin fight the villains of the week in glorious ABC color. From that nostalgic beginning, the film's credits commence with a straight-faced redo of the West series' opening, down to an imitative animation style. Two very different cartoon superheroes (the raggedly garbed Blankman and his sidekick, the randomly named Other Guy) race at the screen, ready for a new adventure.

Even in its final battle, occurring ninety minutes later, *Blankman* remembers to reference the campy *Batman* series by inserting those colorful balloons with the words BAM and THUD over our heroes as they engage in fisticuffs with the bad guys. The film is an homage, pure and simple, and not at all an unpleasant one, despite its rather harsh critical reception.

Darryl Walker (Wayans), the slightly-not-right *Batman* fan that grows up to become Blankman, makes for an interesting character. If this were 1986 and Walker was on *Saturday Night Live*, William Shatner would no doubt admonish him to "get a life." Darryl spends all of his time dreaming of becoming a superhero and developing odd, Rube Goldberg–like inventions, searching for new raw materials to build further devices with his ambulatory robot, J5 — apparently an old washing machine adorned with a mop (as hair)!

Wearing yellow latex gloves and a rag around his head, the costumed Darryl becomes Blankman, defender of the community. He does so not for vengeance, not for hatred, not to become a vigilante, but because the community needs him. His neighborhood is going downhill, with crack houses, prostitution and gambling proliferating, and his dead grandmother, a dear woman that he worshipped, would want him to do something, *anything*, rather than let the bad guys take over.

Once upon a time, this was the job of the superhero — to preserve communities, to keep them together. But nowadays, such a preoccupation is considered hokey, and superheroes like Batman instead dwell on personal vendettas and interpersonal wars. Ironically, it seems that the African American community is the only one that remembers why superheroes became popular in America to begin with, offering us both *Blankman* and *The Meteor Man* within a span of a few years. Though both films are ostensibly comedies first and hero epics second, it is interesting that the message about community service comes through so sincerely.

It is unusual that a gross-out, over-the-top comedy like *Blankman* evidences such a heart. In worshipping and emulating *Batman* (and his deceased grandmother), Darryl's individual choice to fight crime successfully reminds the audience of the important of role models in a young person's life. For a change, this is a film that also shows how the influence of TV can sometimes (gasp!) be a positive force.

In his quest to become a superhero, Darryl has internalized the square-as-could-be (yet nonetheless valuable) lessons of the 1960s *Batman*: that one man can make a difference; that the law must be obeyed; that one man can fight for justice. Of course, Darryl's brother Kevin, who eventually becomes Blankman's sidekick "Other Guy," isn't so certain. After all, Batman had money; Darryl is just a kid from the hood.

That said, Darryl is extremely inventive (as is the *Blankman* screenplay) in developing the oddball crime-fighting devices this off-kilter character utilizes. There are stink bombs made from "concentrated flatulence," rocket-propelled roller blades, and this author's personal favorite, the "speculum of life"—perfect for prying open locked doors.

From an abandoned subway station, now the Blank Station, Blankman rides his Blank Wheel, a rail car, across the city, righting wrongs and rescuing nosy reporter Kimberly Jonz (Robin Givens) from the clutches of the film's mobster villain, Michael "the Suit" Minelli (Jon Polito).

Blankman's only weakness as a crime fighter is not Kryptonite, but the fact that he's a virgin. He is reduced to a quivering pile of jelly every time Jonz plants a kiss on him, and the film gets a lot of mileage out of that joke. Ditto the old-school comic book dialogue. "*Must ... get ... to Blank Belt ... now,*" Blankman groans during one particularly serious crisis, capturing perfectly the fun of this unique genre.

Almost as much fun is the moment when Darryl wants to change into his uniform in a phone booth, but only a smelly port-a-potty is available. His on-the-fly delivery of a baby (in a stuck elevator, no less) is another crazy set piece, one that gives the hero a name. "He's drawn a blank, ma'am," says Kevin, and thus the moniker "Blankman" is born (not exactly the studied choice of "Batman," hoping to strike fear into his enemies with the specter of a bat).

Blankman is no epic, no Donner *Superman*, Singer *X-Men*, Raimi *Spider-Man* or Burton *Batman*; nor does it try to be. However, it does remember the most important rule of superhero productions: it focuses on the hero, not the villain. And *Blankman* also pauses to remember something that those bigger productions don't always dramatize; that there are neighborhoods that need the efforts of one good man or woman to fight the tide of crime. Some of the big superhero productions have become so tied up in years of mythology, so obsessed with psychotic villains, that they seemingly forget that it is a superhero's job to help people. This fact was even more obvious in Robert Townsend's comedic superhero movie *The Meteor Man*, but in *Blankman* the concept is treated more lightly, less heavy-handed. It is never a "preachy" film.

Blankman is a silly lark; but for audiences that enjoy superhero movies, it pays homage to a classic of the genre (the 1960s *Batman*) and offers some nice points about community. It is also laugh-out-loud funny, despite a few slow moments early on.

Blankman (1994)
LIVE-ACTION FILM

"...[A] terrible little movie."
— Peter Rainer, *The Los Angeles Times*,
August 22, 1994, page 3.

"A dumb, clumsy comedy that only occasionally rises to the level of plodding mediocrity."
— Michael Medved, *The New York Post*,
August 22, 1994, page 27.

"Executive producer-co-writer-star Wayans and director Mike Binder can't seem to decide whether they're making a comedy with action digressions or an action film with comedy highlights, creating a film that is both unfunny and unexciting."
— Ralph Novak,
People Weekly: "Blankman,"
September 5, 1994, page 18.

"Wayans returned to his *In Living Color* roots to modify his physically challenged hero *Handi-Man* into *Blankman*. Where *Handi-Man: The Movie* could have at least offered a mix of high concept and low taste, *Blankman* is nothing more than a Jerry Lewis vehicle without the new blood necessary to pull it off."
— J.R. Taylor, *Entertainment Weekly:*
"Blankman," February 3, 1995, page 64.

CAST: Damon Wayans (Darryl Walker/Blankman); David Alan Grier (Kevin Walker/Other Guy); Robin Givens (Kimberly Jonz); Christopher Lawford (Mayor Harris); Lynne Thigpen (Grandma Walker); Jon Polito (Michael "The Suit" Minelli); Nicky Corello (Sammy the Blade); Jason Alexander (Mr. Stone); Harris Peet (Commissioner Gains); Joe Vassallo (Tony the Match); Michael Wayans (Young Darryl); Damon Wayans (Young Kevin); John Moschitta, Jr. (Mr. Crudd); Mike Binder (Dr. Norris); Arsenio Hall (Himself); Greg Kinnear (Talk Show Host); Tony Cox (Midget Man); Kevin West (Gay Man).

CREW: Columbia Pictures Presents a Wife 'n' Kids Production, a film by Mike Binder, *Blankman*. *Casting:* Aleta Chappelle. *Music Composed by*: Miles Goodman. *Executive Music Producer:* Happy Walters. *Costumes Designed by:* Michelle Cole. *Film Editor:* Adam Weiss. *Production Design:* James Spencer. *Director of Photography:* Tom Sigel. *Executive Producer:* Damon Wayans. *Art Director:* Keith Burns. *Co-Producer:*

Jack Binder. *Screenplay by:* Damon Wayans and J.F. Lawton. *Story by:* Damon Wayans. *Produced by:* Eric L. Gold and C.O. Erickson. *Directed by:* Mike Binder. *M.P.A.A. Rating:* PG-13. *Running time:* 96 minutes.

In the late 1960s, quarreling — but loving — brothers Darryl and Kevin Walker watch the Adam West *Batman* TV series with fascination. But when they've grown up, Darryl hasn't matured much, becoming a crazy but brilliant designer of odd superhero gadgets, like the robot companion J-5. Kevin, on the other hand, has accepted reality and has taken a job for a jerk named Stone at *Hard Edition*, a trashy tabloid series. There he secretly longs to get closer to a legitimate news anchor who works upstairs, the beautiful Kimberly Jonz.

A ruthless crime boss named Minelli rules Kevin and Darryl's neighborhood; and when a politician refuses to be bought, Minelli destroys his election headquarters and kills Darryl and Kevin's kindly grandmother. The politician, Harris, wins his race, but now he is in the pocket of Minelli. When the police threaten to strike, leaving the neighborhood undefended, Darryl becomes a superhero. Having developed an arsenal of homemade weapons (including stink bombs) and a solution that makes fabric impervious to bullets, Darryl makes a costume for himself (and one for a skeptical Kevin) and begins to fight crime in the neighborhood, at least until Kevin sends him to a shrink.

But then, dressed as this unusual superhero, Darryl saves a pregnant woman stranded in an elevator and delivers her baby, becoming a local hero. He spearheads a campaign as "Blankman" to clean up the city. He builds his Blank Station in an abandoned subway, and rides his crazy rail vehicle, the Blank Wheel, around the city.

Eventually, he falls in love with Kimberly Jonz.

Blankman interferes in an effort to rob the city bank, but Mayor Harris is killed, and Blankman becomes number one on Minelli's hit list. Minelli captures Kimberly, setting a trap for Blankman and his new partner, Kevin (er, Other Guy). Together, Blankman, Other Guy and J-5 race to save Kimberly from the clutches of a madman and defeat the villainous, murderous, diabolical fiend Minelli.

Bluntman and Chronic

In the late 1990s, independent filmmaker Kevin Smith jumped formats, going from movies to comic books, and became one of the most successful and admired writers in the field since Stan Lee and Jack Kirby. His efforts on the *Green Arrow* and *Daredevil* comics revitalized those superhero franchises and paved the way for Smith's work on the *Spider-Man* comic in the summer of 2002.

Yet, in his films from View Askew Productions, Kevin Smith also created an unlikely pairing of superheroes, Bluntman and Chronic. These gents were modeled after his favorite slacker characters, Jay and Silent Bob, who appeared in *Clerks* (1994), *Mallrats* (1995), *Chasing Amy* (1997), *Dogma* (1999) and *Jay and Silent Bob Strike Back* (2001). A Bluntman and Chronic comic book appeared in *Chasing Amy* (1997), co-authored by Holden McNeil (Ben Affleck) and Banky Edwards (Jason Lee), and was modeled on the adventures of Silent Bob and his hetero life-mate. In the last picture of the bunch, *Jay and Silent Bob Strike Back*, the stoners crashed the set of a "major" motion picture version of Bluntman and Chronic shot on the Miramax lot, in an effort to keep fan boy internet posters from writing unflattering remarks about them.

Who are Bluntman and Chronic? Quite simply, these heroes are Batman and Robin, only re-imagined as weed-smoking stoners. In *Batman*, there is a batmobile, a Bat Cave, a Batcomputer and so forth. In *Bluntman and Chronic*, this concept is tweaked to offer a Bluntmobile and a Blunt Cave. A blunt, for those who don't realize it, is slang for weed, or marijuana.

Bluntman (Kevin Smith) and Chronic (Jason Mewes) also arm themselves with "bong" sabers, and fight a villain called Cock Knocker. Cock Knocker is named after his most evil weapon, an oversized fist meant for … cock knocking.

Bluntman and Chronic are included in this encyclopedia because they have appeared in comic and "live" form in two films, and because they were envisioned in *Jay and Silent Bob Strike Back*, directed by Kevin Smith, as a tribute to the 1960s Adam West/Burt Ward *Batman* TV series. The Blunt Cave was a dead ringer for the Bat Cave, right down to the giant atomic pile in the background, behind the parked superhero car. Furthermore, the Bluntmobile was a nice approximation of the famous Batmobile, with marijuana-appropriate accouterments.

More significantly from a thematic standpoint, Kevin Smith pointed out in *Jay and Silent Bob Strike Back* that Hollywood has never been particularly faithful when translating superheroes from the medium of comics. "A 90 minute gay joke … just like *Batman and Robin* all over again," is how one of the characters in the film describes the final Bluntman and Chronic production, premiered at the film's finale.

Buffy the Vampire Slayer

In 1992, Joss Whedon wrote a screenplay entitled *Buffy the Vampire Slayer*. It was made into a forgettable film starring Kristy Swanson, Luke Perry, Donald Sutherland, Paul Reubens and Rutger Hauer. A comedy-horror film with little bite, the movie concerned a dim-witted, California valley girl, Buffy (Swanson), who learned she was actually the "Chosen One," a human being genetically designed to combat vampires.

On one hand, Buffy was a vapid, selfish mall-rat who loved the high school life; but on the other, Buffy was also the vampire slayer, scourge of monsters, with responsibilities and duties aplenty. The title of the piece exemplified the premise's central joke, but the film did not resonate with audiences or critics. As played by Swanson, Buffy was funny but not particularly sympathetic. The villains in the film were also less-than-inspiring: cape-donning, campy vampires lacking menace. A 1985 feature film, *Fright Night*, walked the same "vampire killer" steps before, and much more nimbly.

It was something of a surprise then, when the talented Whedon re-made *Buffy the Vampire Slayer* as a weekly TV series in late 1996, casting his horror property squarely into the realm of the superhero genre. As he noted of his re-invented creation:

> I invoke about five genres.... I love superheroes. I was a comic-book boy. I tend to create universes with the kind of sophomoric emotional bigness that really exists only in comic books and TV.... The show is about disenfranchisement, about the people nobody takes seriously.[1]

In the television re-do (which aired on the WB Network for its first five seasons, then on UPN for two more), Buffy (Sarah Michelle Gellar) became a much more honorable, compassionate character. She still spoke in sassy Buffy-speak, a quaint but witty Valley Girl–style, but she was also emotionally tortured, isolated, caring and a heroine to root for. Her destiny as the Slayer made her a fighter of demons not easily wounded in battle, a warrior of great strength and agility, but she was still, essentially, a child, a fragile soul learning all about the hardships of life and growing up.

"Called to service" by her fate, and policed by a callous council of watchers in England, the new Buffy had to live with much baggage, not the least of which was that most in her "profession" did not live past the tender age of 25. She was only one link in a long chain of young women that had been activated to fight evil, often losing their lives in the process.

Another interesting facet of the new series was Whedon's exemplary decision to give Buffy her very own Metropolis (or Gotham City) to safeguard. Only this time it was a happy little California 'burb called Sunnydale, a hamlet located above a mystical portal called the Hellmouth, where evil congregated.

In essence, Whedon re-imagined his own concept with a great deal more heart. He recast Buffy not as a popular homecoming queen/bitch, but as a resourceful and imaginative girl whose position as Slayer made her every bit as much an outcast as the geek (sidekick Xander Harris), the nerd (sidekick Willow) or anyone else. That Buffy's familial "origin" was in a broken home with a single parent made her more likable. That her watcher, Rupert Giles, developed into a surrogate father also added considerably to the human equation. And actress Sarah Michelle Gellar (*I Know What You Did Last Summer* [1997], *Scooby Doo* [2002]) brought a combination of deft virtues to her portrayal of this landmark and highly influential character. She combined strength, self-discipline and determination with healthy, athletic good looks. She meshed a rapier-like wit with a soft, vulnerable side. Most importantly, she transmitted a high level of humanity to the fine, allegorical stories, and made this unlikely superhero one that people could truly identify with.

On the hour-long series, which was midway through its seventh and final season as this was written, Buffy was aided in battle by a team of unusual sidekicks. Interestingly, much like Buffy herself, most of these secondary characters boasted a "double identity" and some element of super powers. The nerdy but very sweet Willow (Alyson Hannigan) became a powerful witch over the course of the series, able to draw power from the Earth to heal herself and exact wicked vengeance on those who crossed her. Rupert Giles (Anthony Stewart Head) was not just a librarian, mentor and teacher, he was "Ripper," an authority on the occult and a Watcher on the Watcher's Council. Taciturn Oz (Seth Green) was not only a mellow high-school musician with bad hair, but also a werewolf. Anya (Emma Caulfield) was not just an avaricious retailer (at an occult store called the Magic Box), but a former vengeance demon, still tuned in to the hellish dimensions (and in Season Seven she returned to her evil profession).

Even Buffy's sister, Dawn (Michelle Trachtenberg), who was added during the series' fifth season, had a secret identity of sorts. She wasn't really human at all, but a powerful "inter-dimensional key," a force of pure energy that was sought by evil forces. This meant that all of her memories were false, nothing more than conjured magic; and Dawn had to deal with the notion that she had been created only to serve evil.

Only stalwart Xander (Nicholas Brendon) lacked what people might commonly term super powers. Often referred to as the Jimmy Olsen of the group (in episodes like "The Zeppo"), Xander's primary quality was heart: no matter what went down, he was always loyal to Buffy. In another episode, he noted that he was the one who "saw" the others for what they really were, and lamented the difficulties of being the Not Chosen One.

Buffy had two other important allies in her fight against vampires, demons and other supernatural threats. The first was the vampire named Angel (David Boreanaz), a sullen, brooding but hunky character in search of redemption for his crimes for over a century as an unrepentant bloodsucker (please see the entry on *Angel*). Angel and Buffy found true love in the first few seasons of the series, but their relationship was complicated by the fact that gypsies had cursed Angel. If he ever experienced a moment of bliss (read: orgasm), he would lose his soul and become an evil monster known as Angelus. This, in fact, occurred during the second season of *Buffy the Vampire Slayer* in an episode entitled "Surprise," and Buffy was forced to kill her lover when he threatened to destroy the world in the two-part season finale, "Becoming." Angel eventually returned, soulful once more, in the third season of *Buffy*, and then went off to star in his own spin-off with another *Buffy* regular Cordelia (Charisma Carpenter).

Buffy's second vampire ally (and lover) was in many ways more interesting and original than Angel. Spike (James Marsters) was a 126-year-old, white-haired, British punk rocker vampire. He was introduced in the second season as a diabolical villain ("School Hard"), but quickly became an indispensable part of Buffy's team. He switched allegiances and helped Buffy combat Angel in the aforementioned "Becoming" two-parter. Then he was captured by a military/scientific organization called "the Initiative" in the fourth season. This government-sponsored group implanted an inhibitor chip in Spike's brain, causing him immense pain if he ever tried to injure a human. De-fanged, as it were, Spike inched closer to humanity and the side of good, but was never quite trusted.

The Slayer Sisters: Dawn (Michelle Trachtenberg, left) and Buffy (Sarah Michele Gellar), the Chosen One.

In Season Five, Spike realized to his horror that he was in love with Buffy, and proved a necessary and powerful ally when a nearly invincible villain called Glory sought to destroy Buffy's sister, Dawn. In Season Six, Spike finally became Buffy's lover and sought to regain his long-lost soul, an effort that met with success in the season finale. In Season Seven, Spike spent some time as a raving madman, unable to deal with his restored soul and feelings of guilt. For a spell he was captured by a villain called "the First Evil," but was eventually freed to fight side by side with Buffy once more. He even got to see his inhibitor chip removed.

Over the years, *Buffy the Vampire Slayer* introduced the world to a number of fascinating and intense comic-book-style villains. One of its greatest innovations was the introduction and development in each season of a new threat that would stretch across the span of twenty or so episodes, allowing for significant "growth" on the part of the Scooby Gang (as they jokingly labeled themselves) as they faced off against it.

Season One introduced the Master, a Nosferatu-like cult vampire leader. Season Two brought Buffy in conflict with the soulless Angel(us), a demented vampire seer named Drusilla (Juliet Landau) and Spike. Season Three introduced a psychotic rogue slayer named Faith (Eliza Dushku) and a demonic politician, the Mayor (Harry Groener), that spoke in the easy cadences of TV's Mr. Rogers.

Season Four brought the Initiative to Sunnydale, and introduced a Frankenstein Monster of sorts, the demon-robot hybrid Adam. Season Five introduced Buffy's "new" sister Dawn and the evil Goddess (Clare Kramer) Glory. Glory was so powerful and nasty a villain that Buffy died defending the world from her plans. When Glory attempted to open a rift to Hell, Buffy sealed the portal with her own blood, a brave effort that cost her her life.

Resurrected in Season Six, a revivified but emotionally drained Buffy faced off against a trio of tech-happy Nerds (Tom Lenk, Danny Strong, and Adam Busch), as well as her own wiccan friend Willow, turned evil over the murder of her lover, Tara (Amber Benson). Finally, in Season Seven, another evil was introduced, one older than time, called "the First Evil." It could shape shift into any of Buffy's previous nemeses, including Spike, and it deployed a monstrous uber-vamp to try and kill Buffy and all slayers-in-training, thus ending the line of "Chosen Ones."

In addition to these notable and memorable "Big Bads" (as the series termed its villains), there were many one-time beasts for the stalwart Slayer to put down. Among the more interesting were Dracula ("Buffy vs. Dracula"), demon bikers bent on raping and pillaging Sunnydale ("Bargaining"), and a flesh eater that preyed on fast food employees ("Doublemeat Palace").

Other villains included: a poltergeist released by repressed sexual desire ("Where the Wild Things Are"); Gachnar, a diminutive demon that fed on fear ("Fear, Itself"); an inter-dimensional demon "hitchhiker" ("After Life"); and a demon that could burn the humanity right out of people, called the Judge (Brian Thompson). And then, of course, there were a variety of nasty vampires. One recurring villain was Harmony (Mercedes McNab), a bitchy high school student that became a rather inept and hapless creature of the night.

The amazing thing about *Buffy*'s villains is that they all tended to be allegorical representations of some aspect of growing up. Angel's post-coital brush-off of Buffy in "Surprise" and "Innocence" was a clever nod to the fact that boyfriends sometimes change after they get sex. In "Go Fish," members of the Swim Team turned into fish monsters after taking performance-enhancing drugs, a thinly-veiled reference to steroid use in high school. In "Beauty and the Beasts," an abusive boyfriend was, literally, a monster, but his victimized girlfriend made excuses for his bad behavior, enabling the abuse to continue. Like the best comic book stories, *Buffy the Vampire Slayer*'s tales had real-life relevance, a lesson to be shared. And, delightfully, it wasn't in a pedantic or preachy way.

Historically, *Buffy the Vampire Slayer* became one of the most interesting superhero series of all time because it eschewed "the criminal element" as villains, at least for the most part (excluding the sixth season's Nerds of Doom). Common crime in the mid-to-late 1990s was at its lowest point in a generation, and the gang bangers, rapists, murderers and thieves of old-time TV series were no longer particularly relevant. And, since America seemed to have no foreign enemy to combat, spies were pretty much out of the picture as well. *Buffy the Vampire Slayer*'s creators took the next step forward in genre evolution by pitting their heroine against supernatural opponents, a factor in some comics (such as *Doctor Strange*), but one not necessarily very commonplace on TV.

This decision pointed the way for a new approach on several superhero programs. *Dark Angel* (2000–2002) pitted its heroine against genetically engineered "mutants" or "Transgens." *Birds of Prey* did likewise with "meta-humans." *Smallville* featured "Freaks of the week," people turned both evil and powerful by exposure to Kryptonite "meteor rocks." *Charmed* was essentially a bad version of *Buffy*, with three witches battling, again, more demons.

A positive role model for teens and just about everybody else, the heroine of *Buffy the Vampire Slayer* was important for other reasons. Buffy ushered in the historical period this author calls the "Dawn of the Woman," bringing to TV a gaggle of female superheroes, including *Black Scorpion*, Sara Pezzini on *Witchblade*, Max on *Dark Angel*, a new *Sheena*, the trio of crime fighters on *Birds of Prey,* and more. Though not technically a superhero, Sydney Bristow on *Alias* is a direct descendent of Buffy, trying to carve out a place for love in her "working" life as a spy.

Perhaps more importantly, *Buffy the Vampire Slayer* went deeper into the basic superhero psyche than any production in history. Buffy was fully developed as a character, and audiences witnessed not merely her romances and academic struggles, but her grieving over the death of her mother ("The Body"). She sacrificed her life at the end of the fifth season ("The Gift") and was not happy to be resurrected for the sixth. She would have rather remained in Heaven, her battle against evil finished. But brought back, she had to face depression, sadness, spiritual emptiness, and the feeling that she had been ripped out of Heaven.

The sixth season also examined Buffy's dark side, her attraction to evil, as she began an intense and erotic sexual relationship with Spike ("Wrecked," "Gone"). The same season explored the fact that superheroes don't get paid for their work and must therefore find jobs. To support Dawn and pay the bills, Buffy had to seek work at a variety of jobs, including construction in "Life Serial" and at a fast food restaurant in "Double Meat Palace."

In the seventh season, Buffy seemed to be coming out of her funk, finding work as a student counselor at Sunnydale High School, but she was still learning to accept the myriad responsibilities of adulthood. Then, all at once "the First" launched a vicious attack on the Watchers' Council and slayers-in-training around the world. Facing an apocalypse, Buffy became a general of sorts, inspiring and leading an army for Good.

In seven years, *Buffy the Vampire Slayer* developed its heroine from callow youth to mature, seasoned adult, and examined every important and relevant passage in her life. Audiences witnessed her go from the freedom of college (the fourth season), to sibling rivalry (the fifth season), to the death of a parent (fifth season), to depression and sexual passion (sixth season), to leadership (the seventh season) and beyond. There is no other superhero television program in history that has done so much to explore its central character, and that is why *Buffy*, along with *The Adventures of Superman* and *Batman*, is one of the most influential and important productions in the genre.

For superhero fans, *Buffy* is not only a series about a superhero called the Slayer, but actually a witty examination of the genre. Throughout the series there are references to superheroes such as Captain America, Superman, Batman and Spider-Man. In a clever bit of self-reflexive writing, the characters on the series are very aware of Buffy's status as a "real-life" superhero.

Most of the time, this reflexive dialogue comes from Xander, a natural choice, since he is a comic book geek in the series and can realistically put these adventures in context. In the sixth season, Buffy fought three such fan boys, devotees of comic books, superheroes, *Star Wars, Star Trek* and *Lord of the Rings*. These "arch nemeses" pointedly saw themselves in the context of a "Legion of Doom"–type outfit, and often compared themselves to Lex Luthor. They even developed weapons based on the long-standing clichés of comic books, including freeze rays, jet packs, and invisibility guns.

These episodes were not camp, but a successful recapitulation of old superhero conventions made fresh through post-modern, reflexive dialogue and unexpected narrative u-turns.

This intentional and witty referencing of the genre is an important element of *Buffy the Vampire Slayer*, analyzing the past of the superhero genre and re-imagining it for the future, taking the standard-bearers and icons and moving them forward into the next generation. Without *Buffy*, it seems fair to state, there would be no *Smallville,* which utilizes the same post-modern approach to tackle its comic-book-derived material.

Even when *Buffy* depended on gimmicks, like the death of its hero at the end of the fifth season, it did so by overturning clichés. As Joss Whedon remarked of this oft-used ploy:

> When you bring somebody back to life once they've been dead, you have a lot of disbelief on your hands from the audience. What's important is to always make the characters feel the way the audience does. You have to make it difficult, you have to earn it. You have to just get in there and make it very visceral and make everybody go through the experience....[2]

Not only did Whedon and his troupe of tal-

ented writers earn that plot, they carried it throughout the sixth season and presented the best season of the series. A particular highlight was a musical episode, "Once More with Feeling," that had Buffy express her spiritual woes in song and dance, most memorably. With lyrics and music by Whedon himself (also the creator of *Angel* and *Firefly* [2002]), this may have been the series' best episode ever, though there were other high water marks, including "Hush," an episode of the fourth season featuring no dialogue and truly gruesome villains called "the Gentleman." Another contender for best episode was "The Body," in which Buffy found the corpse of her mother in the family living room.

Buffy the Vampire Slayer aired on the WB at 8:00 P.M. as part of the New Tuesday line-up for several years. For a time, *Angel* followed it on the schedule at 9:00. At the end of the fifth season, however, *Buffy* moved to the United Paramount Network, where it was separated from its spin-off and hence unable to feature crossover episodes. The show continued to air on Tuesday nights at 8:00 P.M.

In 2002 it was followed by the short-lived horror series *Haunted*. As of this writing, the future of *Buffy the Vampire Slayer* on TV looked grim, as Sarah Michelle Gellar's contract was up. In late February of 2003, she decided to end the series while it was still at the top of its game, and Whedon promised a spin-off, perhaps to feature some of the other Scoobies. No matter where the Buffy-verse goes from here, it has proven influential. By ensuring constant quality, Joss Whedon has assured that *Buffy* will live for generations to come, and hopefully the franchise will continue in some form for years.

Already there are comic books and video games (*Chaos Bleeds*), based on the series, and much work was completed on an aborted animated series, taking the Scooby Gang back to high school.

Buffy the Vampire Slayer (1992)
LIVE-ACTION FILM

CAST: Kristy Swanson (Buffy); Donald Sutherland (Merrick); Rutger Hauer (Lothos); Luke Perry (Pike); David Arquette (Jacks); Paul Reubens (Vampire); Hilary Swank (Kimberly); Michelle Abrams, Andrew Lowery.

CREW: *Written by:* Joss Whedon. *Directed by:* Fran Rubel Kuzui. *Executive Producers:* Carol Baum, Sandy Gallin, Fran Rubel Kuzui. *Producers:* Kaz Kazui, Howard Rosenman. *Film Editor:* Jill Savitt. *Director of Photography:* Hames Hayman. *M.P.A.A. Rating:* PG-13. *Running time:* 90 minutes (approx.).

A vapid high school teenager named Buffy meets a stranger named Merrick, a "Watcher" that tells her she is actually a vampire slayer, the latest in a long line of "chosen ones" destined to fight evil forces. Buffy's own nightmares seem to reinforce this notion, as she dreams of the slayer line and historical encounters with a deadly vampire named Lothos. While the shallow Buffy trains and complains, Lothos visits town with his vampire lackeys and plans to kill the new slayer. Buffy gets assistance from a local guy named Pike, but finds that her heritage and destiny as a slayer makes her less popular among her high-school buddies. The final battle between Lothos and Buffy comes down to the prom...

Buffy the Vampire Slayer (1997–2003)
LIVE-ACTION SERIES

"Sarah Michelle Gellar plays the part ... with the right degree of put-upon resentment, and the cast—including Anthony Stewart Head as school librarian—is as smooth an ensemble as you could wish for in an hour long series."
— Tom Gliatto, *People Weekly*, March 31, 1997, page 17.

"It's Romeo and Juliet in black leather and mini skirts. Sarah Michelle Gellar as Buffy may have finally kicked asunder that tired cliché of the screaming maiden in distress. Here is a heroine who can be sexy without being trashy, tough without resorting to ... machismo, and funny without the forced goofiness prevalent in today's comedy."
— Frederick C. Szebin, *Cinefantastique*, October 1997, page 199.

"A ... post-feminist parable on the challenge of balancing one's personal and work life."
— *Time Magazine*, December 29, 1997, page 137.

"She's hyper-responsible about her ... chores, a sort of Bionic Woman with a superior work ethic. It sounds odd and goofy and off-putting.... But aside from the self-aware, brand-name-and-psychotherapy-rich patter, the show is the pretty traditional story of a girl in search of herself and the guy she loves."

— Barbara Lippert, *New York:* "Hey There, Warrior Girl," December 15, 1997, page 25.

"[A] literal scream and always a hoot. Better yet, it's smart, with unfailingly glib dialogue..."
— Matt Roush, *TV Guide*, January 2–8, 1999, page 23.

CAST: Sarah Michelle Gellar (Buffy Summers); Nicholas Brendon (Xander Harris); Alyson Hannigan (Willow Rosenberg). SEASONS 1–3: Charisma Carpenter (Cordelia Chase); David Boreanaz (Angel). SEASONS 4–7: Emma Caulfield (Anya "Anyanka"); James Marsters (Spike). SEASONS 1–5: Anthony Stewart Head (Rupert Giles). SEASONS 5–7: Michelle Trachtenberg (Dawn Summers).

CREW: *Created by:* Joss Whedon. *Executive Producer:* Joss Whedon. *Theme Song:* Nerf Herder. *Film Editors (various episodes):* Christopher Cooke, Regis B. Kimble, Geoffrey Rowland, Skip Schoolnik. *Production Designer:* Steve Hardie. *Musical Score:* Walter Murphie. *Executive Producers:* Sandy Gallin, Gail Berman, Fran Rubel Kuzui, Kaz Kazui. *Co-Executive Producers:* David Greenwalt. *Story Editors:* Matt Kiene, Joe Reinkemeyer, Robert Des Hotel, Dean Batali. *Special Make-up Effects:* John Vulich. *Main Title Design:* Montgomery/Coss. *Presented by:* Mutant Enemy, in association with Kuzui Enterprises, Sandollar Television, 20th Century–Fox Television.

SEASON ONE (1997)

1. "Welcome to the Hellmouth" (Part I) Written by: Joss Whedon; Directed by: Charles Martin Smith; Airdate: March 10, 1997.

Buffy, the Chosen One, arrives at Sunnydale High School, which sits on an evil mystical portal called the Hellmouth. There have been a rash of killings lately, and a student turns up dead in the school gym, a victim of a vampire attack. Buffy's new watcher, British librarian Rupert Giles, fears a major mystical upheaval will soon occur, but Buffy just wants to be a regular girl, not a vampire slayer. On her first night in town, Buffy meets a dark stranger named Angel who warns her about the Hellmouth and a frightening supernatural event called "the Harvest."

GUEST CAST: Mark Metcalf (The Master); Brian Thompson (Luke); Ken Lerner (Principal Flutie); Kristine Sutherland (Mrs. Summers); Julie Benz (Darla); J. Patrick Lawlor (Thomas); Eric Balfour (Jesse); Natalie Strauss (Teacher); Mercedes McNab (Harmony); Amy Chance, Tupelo Jereme, Persia White, Deborah Brown (Girls); Jeffrey Steven Smith (Guy in Computer Class); Teddy Lane, Jr. (Bouncer); Carmine D. Giovinazzo (Boy).

2. "Welcome to the Hellmouth" (Part II, a.k.a. "The Harvest") Written by: Joss Whedon. Directed by: John Kretchmer. Airdate: March 10, 1997.

Buffy teams up with geek Xander, computer expert and "brain" Willow, and librarian Rupert Giles to rescue their friend Jesse from the grasp of the Master, an ancient vampire/demon hoping to "ascend" to a position of power over the Hellmouth during the Harvest. In the underground tunnels beneath the school, Jesse is revealed to be a vampire, and Buffy and Xander seek escape. Later, the Master's vessel, Luke, and his minions attack partygoers at a nightclub called the Bronze in an effort to claim more souls for the Master and thereby open the door to the Hellmouth. Buffy and friends rush to a confrontation that could end in the subjugation and termination of the human race.

GUEST CAST: Mark Metcalf (The Master); Brian Thompson (Luke); Kristine Sutherland (Mrs. Summers); Julie Benz (Darla); Eric Balfour (Jesse).

3. "The Witch" Written by: Dana Reston. Directed by: Stephen Cragg. Airdate: March 17, 1997.

Giles is upset when Buffy tries out for the Sunnydale High Cheerleader Squad, fearing her attention will be diverted from slaying, but things take an ugly turn when a popular cheerleader almost spontaneously combusts during a rehearsal. While Buffy and the gang contemplate this bizarre incident, Buffy realizes that her relationship with her mother is not as close as that of friend Amy and her mother, a woman who was once a very popular cheerleader herself. When Amy fails to make the cheerleading squad, her mother retaliates with witchcraft and blinds Cordelia with a spell. Soon, cheerleaders are dropping like flies and Buffy is the next target.

GUEST CAST: Kristine Sutherland (Joyce Sommers); Elizabeth Anne Allen (Amy Madison); Robin Riker (Catherine "the Great" Madison); Jim Doughan (Mr. Pole); Nicole Prescott (Lishanne); Amanda Wilmshurst (Senior Cheerleader); William Monaghan (Dr. Gregory).

4. "Teacher's Pet" Written by: David Greenwalt. Directed by: Bruce Seth Green. Airdate: March 25, 1997.

Sunnydale's newest substitute (science) teacher is also Sunnydale's newest creature: a walking, talking praying mantis who murdered the regular biology teacher. Xander starts falling for Ms. French, even as another boy that was seen "after school" with her vanishes. Can Buffy save Xander before

Mrs. French mates with him, then kills him?

GUEST CAST: Ken Lerner (Principal Flutie); Musetta Vander (Ms. French); Jackson Price (Blayne); Jean Speeglle Howard (Old Ms. French); William Monaghan (Dr. Gregory); Jack Knight (Homeless Person); Michael Robb Verona (Teacher); Karim Oliver (Bud #1).

5. "Never Kill a Boy on the First Date" Written by: Rob Des Hotel and Dean Batali. Directed by: David Semel. Airdate: March 31, 1997.

The Master hatches another evil plan, this time by enlisting the services of a supernatural warrior called the Anointed One, who it is written can lead the Slayer to Hell. Meanwhile, Buffy goes out with Owen, an Emily Dickinson fan and high school hunk. As Buffy attempts to balance her job responsibilities as a slayer and the demands of her social life, the Order of Aurelius works to resurrect the Anointed One ... a resurrection which can only come about through the deaths of five innocent people. Ironically, the Anointed One is a helpless-seeming child.

GUEST CAST: Mark Metcalf (The Master); Christopher Wiehl (Owen Thurman); Geoff Meed (Man on Bus); Robert Mont (Van Driver); Andrew J. Ferchland (Boy/the Anointed One).

6. "The Pack" Written by: Matt Kiene & Joe Reinkmeyer. Directed by: Bruce Seth Green. Airdate: April 7, 1997.

A school field trip to the zoo goes badly for Buffy's class when a bunch of prankster students become possessed by wild animal (hyena) spirits. Even Xander is affected by the vicious "pack" mentality in Sunnydale, and it is up to Buffy to save her friend and stop the wilding spree in her high school. Among the victims of "the pack" are Principal Flutie and the school mascot.

GUEST CAST: Ken Lerner (Principal Flutie); Jeff Maynard (Lance); James Stephens (The Zookeeper); David Brisbin (Mr. Anderson); Bar-

bara K. Whinnery (Mrs. Anderson); Gregory White (Coach Herrold); Justin Jon Ross (Joey); Jeffrey Steven Smith (Adam); Paltrese Borem (Young Woman); Eion Bailey, Michael McRaine, Brian Gross, Jennifer Sky (The Pack).

7. "Angel" Written by: David Greenwalt. Directed by: Scott Brazil. Airdate: April 14, 1997.

The Anointed One is not really dead: He is a boy, a child, who is destined to lead an unknowing Buffy straight to Hell. Meanwhile, Buffy starts to develop an attraction to the mysterious Angel, especially after he saves her life from three warrior vampires of an ancient caste. As Angel starts to reciprocate Buffy's feelings, she learns that he is actually a 240-year-old vampire who has been cursed with a soul, which means that he feels remorse and regret for his evil actions. The Master sends vampire bitch Darla to kill Buffy's Mom, but Buffy becomes convinced that Angel, who was invited into her home, is actually the attacker.

GUEST CAST: Mark Metcalf (The Master); Kristine Sutherland (Joyce Summers); Julie Benz (Darla); Andrew J. Ferchland (Collin/The Anointed One); Charles Wesley (Meanest Vampire).

8. "I Robot — You Jane" Written by: Ashley Gable and Thomas A Swyden. Directed by: Stephen Posey. Airdate: April 28, 1997.

The naive Willow has made friends with a boyfriend over the Internet, but in this case, she has really accessed the chat room from Hell. A demonic creature called Moloch has been conjured up (read: scanned) from Giles' library book and is now in the Sunnydale High computer system, working towards murderous and deadly ends. In the end, Buffy is forced to put Willow's psychotic would-be love, a 7-foot-tall robot predator, on the scrap heap.

GUEST CAST: Robia La Morte (Jenny Calendar); Chad Lindberg (Dave); Jamison Ryan (Fritz); Pierrino Mascarino (Thelonius); Edith

Fields (School Nurse); Damon Sharp (Male Student); Mark Deakins (Moloch).

9. "The Puppet Show" Written by: Dean Batali and Rob DesHotel. Directed by: Ellen Pressman. Airdate: May 5, 1997.

Giles is forced to run the High School Talent(less) Show, much to the amusement of Buffy, Willow and Xander. New school principal Snyder has the last laugh, however, when he forces the trio to participate in the show as well. Little do these new "talents" realize that they will be sharing the stage with Sid, a very lively and quite terrifying ventriloquist's dummy that desires to be "Flesh." Worse, the dummy believes that by murdering Buffy, a girl of great strength and power, he can accomplish this goal.

GUEST CAST: Kristine Sutherland (Joyce Sommers); Richard Werner (Morgan); Burke Roberts (Marc); Armin Shimerman (Principal Snyder); Lenora May (Mrs. Jackson); Chasen Hampton (Elliot); Natasha Pearce (Lisa); Tom Wyner (Sid); Krissy Carlson (Emily/Dancer); Michelle Miracle (Locker Girl).

10. "Nightmares" Story by: Joss Whedon. Written by: David Greenwalt. Directed by: Bruce Seth Green. Airdate: May 12, 1997.

Sunnydale is going to hell, literally, when dreams and nightmares start to supplant everyday reality. A killer clown, a collection of nerds, a day without clothes, a fear of vampires, the death of loved ones, a fear of responsibility, parental rejection and, worst of all, spiders — these are the subconscious images manipulated for evil purposes by a hidden but powerful source. A youngster in a coma may be the key to this world gone crazy, but Buffy's own fears could jeopardize the entire town's future, especially when she imagines herself a vampire.

GUEST CAST: Mark Metcalf (The Master); Kristine Sutherland (Joyce Summers); Jeremy Foley (Billy Palmer); Andrew J. Ferchland (Collin); Dean Butler (Hank Summers); Justin

Urich (Wendell); J. Robin Miller (Laura); Terry Cain (Ms. Tishler); Scott Harlan (Aldo Gianfranco); Brian Pietro (Coach); Johnny Green (Way Cool Guy); Patty Ross (Cool Guy's Mom); Dom Magwili (Doctor); Sean Moran (Stage Manager).

11. "Out of Sight, Out of Mind" (a.k.a. **"Invisible Girl"**) Story by: Joss Whedon. Written by: Ashley Gable and Thomas A. Swyden. Directed by: Reza Badiyi. Airdate: May 19, 1997.

A lonely, unpopular girl at Sunnydale High becomes an unexpected menace when she recedes into the woodwork, becoming invisible to others. The popular crowd takes it on the chin from the invisible Marcie as she takes revenge for all the licks she has received in high school over the years. Buffy and friends must put their own wounds aside to help Cordelia's snobby clique before the battle between the popular and the transparent turns fatal — with the ultrasnooty Cordelia the target.

GUEST CAST: Clea Duvall (Marcie Ross); Armin Shimerman (Principal Snyder); Ryan Bittle (Mitch); Denise Dowse (Ms. Miller); John Knight (Bud #1); Mercedes McNab (Harmony); Mark Phelan (Agent Doyle); Skip Stellrecht (Agent Manetti); Julie Fulton (FBI Teacher).

12. "Prophecy Girl" Written and directed by: Joss Whedon; Airdate: June 2, 1997.

Giles comes across a disturbing prophecy in one of his texts: the Slayer is to be murdered by the villainous head vampire, the Master. Buffy learns of her unpleasant fate as Xander contemplates asking her to an important Spring dance. To the dismay of all her friends in school, the prophecy comes true as the Master drowns Buffy. But this is one Slayer that doesn't die easy, and when she returns from the afterlife, she vows to bring down the Master...

GUEST CAST: Mark Metcalf (The Master); Kristine Sutherland (Mrs. Joyce Summers); Robia La Morte (Jenny Calendar); Andrew J.

Ferchland (The Anointed One); Scott Gurney (Kevin).

SEASON TWO (1997-1998)

13."When She Was Bad" Written and directed by: Joss Whedon. Airdate: September 15, 1997.

After summer vacation, Buffy the Vampire Slayer of Sunnydale returns to high school with a sizable chip on her shoulder. At the same time, evil forces attempt to revive the dead Master for one more go-round with the Chosen One. If Buffy cannot get her act together in time, the evil she conquered once will return to rule the day. The ritual for reviving the Master includes assembling all the people that were near him at the time of his death — in this case, Willow, Cordelia and Giles!

GUEST CAST: Kristine Sutherland (Joyce Summers); Dean Butler (Hank Summers); Robia La Morte (Jenny Calendar); Andrew J. Ferchland (Collin); Tamra Braun (Tara); Armin Shimerman (Principal Snyder); Brent Jennings (Absalom).

14. "Some Assembly Required" Written by: Ty King. Directed by: Bruce Seth Green. Airdate: September 22, 1997.

Grave robbing is the activity of the week as a modern-day Frankenstein (and fellow high school student) starts to assemble a bride for his dead brother, who has also been brought back from the dead using spare parts. While Giles courts computer teacher Ms. Calendar, Buffy investigates the disappearance of several female body parts … and comes upon the deadly Frankenstein scenario. Can she stop the evil surgeon before the shapely Cordelia becomes part of the mix 'n' match Bride of a modern Frankenstein?

GUEST CAST: Robia La Morte (Jenny Calendar); Michael Bacall (Eric); Angelo Spizzirri (Chris); Ingo Neuhaus (Daryl); Melanie Mac-Queen (Mrs. Epps); Amanda Wilmshurst (Cheerleader).

15. "School Hard" Written by: David Greenwalt. Directed by: John Kretchmer. Airdate: September 29, 1997.

Two new vampires come to Sunnydale: the punk rocker Spike and his evil lover, the bizarre and sometimes psychic Drusilla. While Buffy works to bring off Parent-Teacher Night at school to raise her grade point average, the Anointed One joins forces with Spike and Drusilla to kill the Slayer that offed the Master. Before long, Spike and his minions have attacked the school on Parent-Teacher night and Buffy must not only save the day, but keep her secret identity as the Chosen One from her mother as well.

GUEST CAST: Kristine Sutherland (Joyce Summers); Robia La Morte (Jenny Calendar); Andrew J. Ferchland (The Anointed One); James Marsters (Spike); Juliet Landau (Drusilla); Alexandra Johnes (Sheila); Armin Shimerman (Principal Snyder); Alan Abelew (Brian Kirch); Keith MacKechnie (Parent); Joanie Pleasant (Helpless Girl).

16. "Inca Mummy Girl" Written by: Matt Kiene and Joe Reinkemeyer. Directed by: Ellen Pressman. Airdate: October 6, 1997.

Xander falls in love again, this time with Ampata, an ancient Peruvian mummy masquerading as an exchange student. The Mummy, once a "Chosen One" in her own culture, must kill to stay alive, and she commits her misdeeds with a deadly kiss. Now Buffy must save Xander from his own girlfriend, a girl that never had a chance in her own culture.

GUEST CAST: Kristine Sutherland (Joyce Summers); Ara Celi (Ampata/Mummy); Samuel Jacobs (Peruvian Boy); Kristen Winnicki (Gwen); Jason Hall (Devon); Gil Birmingham (Peru Man); Henrik Rosvall (Sven); Joey Crawford (Rodney); Danny Strong (Jonathan).

17. "Reptile Boy" Written and directed by: David Greenwalt. Airdate: October 13, 1997.

Cordelia is dating a fraternity boy with a dark secret: his brotherhood is sacrificing high school girls to a reptilian, subterranean demon called Makita. Buffy joins Cordelia at a frat party after she and Angel have a fight, and learns the unpleasant truth about this fraternity. Xander crashes the party and is mistaken for a new pledge at the same time Buffy is drugged by the boys of Delta Zeta Kappa and lined up to be sacrificed.

GUEST CAST: Todd Babcock (Tom Warner); Greg Vaughan (Richard); Jordana Spiro (Callie).

18. "Halloween" Written by: Carl Ellsworth. Directed by: Bruce Seth Green. Airdate: October 27, 1997.

Halloween is supposed to be a slow night for Buffy and Sunnydale because vampires tend to stay in, but this year turns out to be anything but quiet. An evil spell invokes the name of Janus, the two-faced Roman God, and changes the identities of trick-or-treaters to match the costumes they are wearing. Xander, in fatigues, becomes a macho soldier; Willow, as a ghost, becomes an apparition; and Buffy, in 1770s gown, becomes a shrinking violet. Normally, such a switch would be a nuisance but not fatal, yet on this Halloween Spike is on the prowl, and the services of a slayer are desperately required. An old "friend" of Giles from England, Ethan Rayne, is behind the Halloween fun.

GUEST CAST: James Marsters (Spike); Juliet Landau (Drusilla); Armin Shimerman (Principal Snyder); Robin Sachs (Ethan).

19. "Lie to Me" Written and directed by: Joss Whedon. Airdate: November 3, 1997.

An old flame of Buffy's named Billy "Ford" Fordham comes to Sunnydale to rekindle the affair, but in secret he is planning to give Buffy's life to Spike in exchange for the immortal life of a vampire. Angel and Willow suspect that something is not

right with "Ford," and attempt to convince Buffy that her old boyfriend has ulterior motives. As it turns out, Billy is dying of a terminal illness and he thinks that vampirism is his only chance to outlive the disease growing inside of him.

GUEST CAST: Robia La Morte (Jenny Calendar); James Marsters (Spike); Juliet Landau (Drusilla); Jason Behr (Billy Fordham); Jarrad Paul (Marvin Diego); Julia Lee (Chanterelle); Will Rothhaar (James).

20. "The Dark Age" Written by: Dean Batali and Rob DesHotel. Directed by: Bruce Seth Green. Airdate: November 10, 1997.

Giles' youthful indiscretions come back to haunt him when he learns that many of his friends in London, and one here in the U.S., are being killed. As it turns out, Giles experimented with demonic possession when he was an adolescent, and the same demon he once conjured is now jumping bodies and killing his friends ... while simultaneously framing him for the crimes. Before long, the demon has entered the body of Giles' lover, Ms. Calendar. Buffy and her friends must find a way to clear Giles of any suspicion and save Ms. Calendar before it is too late.

GUEST CAST: Robia La Morte (Jenny Calendar); Robin Sachs (Ethan Rayne); Wendy Way (Dierdre Page); Stuart McLean (Philip Henry); Michael Earl Reid (Custodian); Tony Sears (Morgue Attendant); Daniel Henry Murray (Creepy Cult Guy); John Bellucci (Man).

21. "What's My Line" (Part I) Written by: Marti Noxon and Howard Gordon. Directed by: David Solomon. Airdate: November 17, 1997.

Buffy is depressed during Career Week because her "job" has already been chosen without her consent: she is the Slayer, always and forever. Willow's future options look considerably brighter, but even that bit of good news cannot cure Buffy's blues, especially when Spike summons a group of bounty hunters to kill her. Just when things look like they can't get any worse, a new arrival in town changes the status quo: Kendra, a fellow vampire slayer, called when the Master drowned Buffy the previous year.

GUEST CAST: James Marsters (Spike); Juliet Landau (Drusilla); Armin Shimerman (Principal Snyder); Eric Saiet (Dalton); Bianca Lawson (Kendra); Norman Pfister (Kelly Connell); Michael Rothhaar (Suitman); P.B. Hutton (Mr. Kalish).

22. "What's My Line" (Part II) Written by: Marti Noxon. Directed by: David Semel. Airdate November 24, 1997.

Kendra, the vampire slayer, has come to Sunnydale to replace Buffy, who actually "died" during her confrontation with the Master some time back. Angel is captured by Drusilla, and Spike and is to be fodder in a ritual that will cure the sick Dru forever. Buffy feels useless, now that her skills are redundant, and even grows jealous as Giles and Kendra form a bond that seemingly threatens Buffy's own relationship with her watcher. Buffy must save Angel before she loses him forever.

GUEST CAST: James Marsters (Spike); Juliet Landau (Drusilla); Bianca Lawson (Kendra); Saverio Guerra (Willy); Danny Strong (Hostage Kid); Spice Williams (Patrice).

23. "Ted" Written by: David Greenwalt and Joss Whedon. Directed by: Bruce Seth Green. Airdate: December 8, 1997.

Buffy has trouble coping with her mother's smarmy new boyfriend, Ted. Making matters worse, everyone else seems to love the guy, a salesman and computer whiz. Ted shows his true colors to Buffy at a miniature golf game, proving to be an uptight, controlling disciplinarian ... but no one believes her. Ted and Buffy come to blows over their different approaches to domestic bliss, and Ted is believed dead until revealed to be a malfunctioning robot.

GUEST CAST: Kristine Sutherland (Joyce Summers); Robia La Morte (Jenny Calendar);

John Ritter (Ted Buchanan); James G. MacDonald (Detective Stein); Ken Thorley (Neal); Jeff Langton (Vampire).

24. "Bad Eggs" Written by: Marti Noxon. Directed by: David Greenwalt. Airdate: January 12, 1998.

As part of a health class assignment involving responsibility, Buffy and her classmates each take care of an offspring, an egg, and treat it like a human baby for a week. Unfortunately, these are no ordinary eggs, and each one contains a deadly parasitic life form that can control a human host through a process called "neural clamping." The parasites serve a larger, prehistoric mother organism that dwells beneath the school and is enslaving the human populace of Sunnydale.

GUEST CAST: Kristine Sutherland (Joyce Summers); Jeremy Ratchford (Lyle Gorch); James Parks (Tector Gorch); Rick Zeiff (Mr. Whitmore); Danny Strong (Jonathan).

25. "Surprise" Written by: Marti Noxon. Directed by: Michael Lange. Airdate: January 19, 1998.

As her birthday approaches, Buffy contemplates consummating her relationship with Angel, with all the angst that goes along with the decision to have sex. Meanwhile, Drusilla and Spike are up to their old tricks, planning once more to off the Slayer, this time with an invincible blue-skinned demon called "the Judge" that can burn the humanity right out of a person. Buffy and Angel finally sleep together, but something awful is borne of their union.

GUEST CAST: Kristine Sutherland (Joyce Summers); Robia La Morte (Jenny Calendar); Brian Thompson (The Judge); Vincent Schiavelli (Jenny's Uncle); James Marsters (Spike); Juliet Landau (Drusilla); Eric Saiet (Dalton).

26. "Innocence" Written and directed by: Joss Whedon. Airdate: January 20, 1998.

Angel loses his soul after a night of love

with Buffy, and one moment of pure happiness. This horrible event is a result of an ancient gypsy curse, but it bodes trouble for Sunnydale. Now Angel is a dark, evil vampire, far more dangerous than even Drusilla or Spike. Soon, Buffy realizes she will have to contemplate the impossible: killing the only man she has ever loved. When Angel teams with Spike, Dru and "the Judge," Buffy must bring out the big guns to stop the killers

GUEST CAST: Ryan Francis (Soldier); James Lurie (Teacher); Parry Shen (Student); Carla Madden (Woman).

27. "Phases" Written by: Rob Des Hotel and Dean Batali. Directed by: Bruce Seth Green. Airdate: January 27, 1998.

A werewolf is on the loose in Sunnydale, and it is up to Buffy and her friends to discover the identity of the offending monster. Xander thinks he knows the answer, but instead only "outs" a gay classmate named Larry. The werewolf in questions turns out to be none other than Oz, Willow's boyfriend and a cool member of the band Dingoes Ate My Baby.

GUEST CAST: Jack Conley (Cain); Camila Griggs (Gym Teacher); Larry Bagby III (Larry); Meghan Perry (Theresa Klusmeyer); Keith Campbell (Werewolf).

28. "Bewitched, Bothered and Bewildered" Written by: Marti Noxon. Directed by: James A. Contner. Airdate: February 10, 1998.

Xander is dumped at the Valentine's Day Dance by the fickle Cordelia, leaving him fuming with anger. Xander asks the local witch, Amy, for a potion which will make him irresistible to Cordelia. The spell goes wrong, leaving Cordelia still feeling indifferent over him. On the other hand, every other woman in Sunnydale, from Mrs. Summers to a bevy of vampires, find Xander absolutely irresistible…

GUEST CAST: Kristine Sutherland (Joyce Summers); Robia La Morte (Jenny Calendar);

Elizabeth Anne Allen (Amy); Mercedes McNab (Harmony); Jason Hall (Devon); Jennie Chester (Kate); Kristen Winnicki (Cordette); Scott Hamm (Jock); Tamara Braun (Frenzied Girl); James Marsters (Spike); Juliet Landau (Drusilla); Lorna Scott (Miss Beakman).

29. "Passion" Written by: Ty King. Directed by: Michael E. Gershman; Airdate: February 24, 1998.

The evil Angelus is bound and determined to kill Buffy, the woman he once loved. As Angel's torments become increasingly dangerous, threatening Buffy's friends and even her mother, Ms. Calendar, a gypsy herself, works desperately to undo the curse that has robbed Angel of his soul. In response to this act of kindness, Angel kills the beloved teacher, sending poor Giles into mourning.

GUEST CAST: Kristine Sutherland (Joyce Summers); Robia La Morte (Jenny Calendar); James Marsters (Spike); Juliet Landau (Drusilla).

30. "Killed by Death" Written by: Rob Des Hotel and Dean Batali. Directed by: Deran Sarafian. Airdate March 3, 1998.

Buffy is sick with the flu, but insists on challenging the demonic Angelus anyway. After Xander, Willow and Cordy save her life in battle, Buffy is sent to a hospital to recuperate. Buffy has always had a deep-seated fear of hospitals, ever since her cousin Celia died in one, and now Buffy learns why: sick children are being terrorized and murdered by an invisible personification of death that only the young can see. When a doctor attempting to save the children is slashed, killed and dragged away by Death, Buffy decides to remain in the hospital to protect the children and fight the demon.

GUEST CAST: Kristine Sutherland (Joyce Summers); Richard Herd (Dr. Stanley Backer); Willie Garson (Security Guard); Andrew Ducote (Ryan); Juanita Jennings (Dr. Wilkes); Robert Munic (Intern); Mimi Paley (Little Buffy); Denise Johnson (Celia); James Jude (Courtney).

31. "I Only Have Eyes for You" Written by: Marti Noxon. Directed by: James Whitmore, Jr. Airdate: April 28, 1998.

Sunnydale High is haunted on the eve of the Sadie Hawkins Dance by one, perhaps two, restless spirits. A dejected Giles suspects that Ms. Calendar is haunting the school, but the facts of the case bear out a different conclusion. In the mid–1950s a teacher and her student lover both died violently after a torrid love affair. Now Buffy and Angel are possessed by these spirits and find themselves acting out the moments leading up to the tragic deaths.

GUEST CAST: James Marsters (Spike); Juliet Landau (Drusilla); Armin Shimerman (Principal Snyder); Christopher Gorham (James Stanley); Meredith Salinger (Grace Newman); Miriam Flynn (Ms. Frank); John Hawkes (George); Sarah Bib, Brian Poth (Fighters); Anna Coman-Hidy and Vanessa Bodnar ('50s Girls); Brian Reddy (Policeman); James Lurie (Mr. Miller); Ryan Taszreak (Ben).

32. "Go Fish" Written by: David Fury and Elin Hampton. Directed by: David Semel. Airdate: May 5, 1998.

Sunnydale's winning swim team faces a new challenge when members start to die, seemingly devoured by green-scaled monster-humanoids from the sea. Buffy and friends look into the killings, and Xander goes undercover by joining the swim team. Buffy soon learns that the sea monsters are not devouring team members ... they *are* the team-members, transformed into beasts! The catalyst for this nefarious change is a Russian experimental steroid being administered by the team coach in the sauna.

GUEST CAST: Armin Shimerman (Principal Snyder); Charles Cyphers (Coach Marin); Conchata Ferrell (Nurse Greenleigh); Jeremy Garrett (Cameron Walker); Wentworth Miller (Gage Petronzi); Jake Patellis (Dodd McAlvy); Shane West (Sean); Danny Strong (Jonathan).

33. "Becoming" (Part I) Written and directed by: Joss Whedon. Airdate: May 12, 1998.

Even as final exams loom close, Buffy is worried about how and when to finish things with the murderous Angel once and for all. Meanwhile, Giles examines an ancient artifact recently unearthed near the Hellmouth, a statue that when activated properly via occult methods can open the doorway to Hell and suck all life on planet Earth into that nether region. While studying chemistry, Willow and Buffy find a spell belonging to the late Ms. Calendar that can restore Angel's lost soul. Kendra is killed in action while Willow tries to use the spell, Drusilla attacks the Scooby gang in the library, and Giles is kidnapped.

GUEST CAST: Kristine Sutherland (Joyce Summers); James Marsters (Spike); Juliet Landau (Drusilla); Armin Shimerman (Principal Snyder); Bianca Lawson (Kendra); Julie Benz (Darla); Jack McGee (Curator); Richard Riehle(Assistant); Shannon Wellese (Gypsy Woman); Zitto Kazaan (Gypsy Man); Ginger Williams (Girl); Nina Gervitz (Teacher).

34. "Becoming" (Part II) Written and directed by: Joss Whedon. Airdate: May 19, 1998.

Giles has been kidnapped, Kendra is dead, and Buffy is now a fugitive from the law. When the Slayer learns that Willow is in the hospital in a coma, she realizes it is time to end things with the soulless Angel. Buffy finds an unexpected ally in Spike, who is desperate to win Drusilla back from Angel. In a final gambit to rescue Giles and save the world, Buffy locks horns and swords with Angel, only to be faced with the most difficult and heart-wrenching task of her life.

GUEST CAST: Kristine Sutherland (Joyce Summers); Robia La Morte (Jenny Calendar); James Marsters (Spike); Juliet Landau (Drusilla); Armin Shimerman (Principal Snyder); James G. MacDonald; Susan Leslie and Thomas G. Waites (Cops).

SEASON THREE (1998-1999)

35. "Anne" Written and directed by: Joss Whedon. Airdate: September 29, 1998.

With Buffy out of town, despondent over her choice to send Angel to Hell, Xander, Willow and Oz try to fill her shoes as slayers in Sunnydale. Meanwhile, Buffy is in Los Angeles working at a greasy spoon under the name "Anne." She discovers there that teenage runaways are disappearing to a hellish underground where evil demons are using the humans as slave labor. Buffy descends to the underworld to save the captured teenagers, but she must act fast, lest she be prematurely aged in the bubble of "quick" time below the surface.

GUEST CAST: Kristine Sutherland (Joyce Summers); Julia Lee (Lilly); Carlos Jacott; Mary-Pat Green; Chad Todhunter; Larry Bagby III (Larry); Michael Leopard (Roughneck); Harley Zumbrum (Demon Guard); Barbara Pilavin (Old Woman); Harrison Young (Old Man); Alex Toma (Aaron); Dell Yount (Truck Guy).

36. "Dead Man's Party" Written by: Marti Noxon. Directed by: James Whitmore, Jr. Airdate: October 6, 1998.

Buffy returns home to Sunnydale to find that her friends have taken up slaying, and that her Mom has added an unusual decoration to the house: a strange Nigerian mask. When Buffy has a difficult time rebonding with her alienated friends and schoolmates, Buffy's Mom invites her friends over for a party. Willow and Xander's feelings of abandonment (by Buffy) come to the fore at the party, but soon Buffy must contend with the Nigerian mask, an evil artifact capable of re-animating the dead.

GUEST CAST: Kristine Sutherland (Joyce Summers); Nancy Lenehan (Pat); Armin Shimerman (Principal Snyder); Danny Strong (Jonathan); Jason Hall (Devon); Paul Morgan Stetler (Young Doctor); Chris Garnant (Stoner #1).

37. "Faith, Hope and Trick" Written by: David Greenwalt. Directed by: James A. Contner. Airdate: October 13, 1998.

While Buffy has recurring nightmares about Angel's death, a new vampire named Mr. Trick comes to town in the service of a vampire master called Coquistos, a beast so old his feet and hands are cloven. Another new arrival in town is the beautiful Faith, a second, and highly unorthodox, slayer called when Kendra was killed. Mr. Trick and his Master are out to kill Faith in revenge for a scar she branded Coquistos with, and now Buffy gets dragged into the conflict.

GUEST CAST: Kristine Sutherland (Mrs. Summers); K. Todd Freeman (Mr. Trick); Fab Filippo (Scott); Jeremy Roberts (Coquistos); Eliza Dushku (Faith); Armin Shimerman (Principal Snyder); John Ennis (Manager).

38. "Beauty and the Beasts" Written by: Marti Noxon. Directed by: James Whitmore, Jr. Airdate: October 20, 1998.

Someone or something is killing people by night in Sunnydale, and Buffy fears it is Angel (returned from Hell), and Willow fears the culprit is Oz (a werewolf during the full moon). While the girls worry about their respective men, the real answer lays with an experiment gone wrong. A high school kid named Pete is so insecure about his manhood that he has created a special formula to make him more macho … a formula which has also turned him into a monster and an abusive boyfriend.

GUEST CAST: Fab Filippo (Scott); John Patrick White (Mr. Platt); Danielle Weeks (Debbie); Phill Lewis (Pete); Eliza Dushku (Faith).

39. "Homecoming" Written and directed by: David Greenwalt. Airdate: November 3, 1998.

Boyfriend Scott dumps Buffy on the eve of the Homecoming Dance, and out of despair she decides to run for Homecoming Queen against Cordelia. At the same time, a slew of assassins arrive in town to off Buffy and Faith in what Mr. Trick calls "Slayerfest '98." On the way to the dance, Buffy and Cordelia are hijacked in their limo by the assassins, and the girls must stay alive while simultaneously settling their differences.

GUEST CAST: K. Todd Freeman (Mr. Trick); Fab Filippo (Scott); Ian Abercrombie (German); Harry Groener (Mayor Wilkins); Eliza Dushku (Faith); Jeremy Ratchford (Gorch); Jennifer Hetrick (Teacher); Danny Strong (Jonathan); Robert Treveiler (Gary); J.C. Quinn (Lone Customer).

40. "Band Candy" Written by: Jane Espenson. Directed by: Michael Lange. Airdate: November 10, 1998.

Principal Snyder orders Buffy and friends to sell candy to raise money for the Sunnydale High Marching Band. Unfortunately, the band candy has the unusual side effect of turning all of the adults in town, including Giles, Mrs. Summers and Snyder, into rampaging, rebellion-crazed adolescents. The contaminated candy is the latest evil plan sponsored by Mayor Wilkins and his new major domo, Mr. Trick. A teenage-acting Giles realizes his cultist former friend Ethan Rayne is also working on the contaminated candy.

GUEST CAST: K. Todd Freeman (Mr. Trick); Kristine Sutherland (Joyce Summers); Robin Sachs (Ethan); Harry Groener (Mayor Wilkins); Armin Shimerman (Principal Snyder); Jason Hall (Devon); Peg Stewart (Mrs. Barton).

41. "Revelations" Written by: Douglas Petrie. Directed by: James A. Contner. Airdate: November 17, 1998.

While Buffy continues to keep Angel's return to Sunnydale a secret, Faith's new watcher, Mrs. Gwendolyn Post, arrives in town. Post warns that a demon called Logos is seeking the all-powerful glove of Milligon, an occult object. Now Buffy and Faith must keep the artifact from falling into the wrong hands, but all is not as it seems on this particular hunt. Worse, Xander discovers that Angel is back in town, and, with the help of Willow, Oz, Giles and Cordelia, he stages an intervention for Buffy.

GUEST CAST: Serena Scott Thomas (Gwendolyn Post); Eliza Dushku (Faith).

42. "Lovers Walk" Written by: Dan Vebber. Directed by: David Semel. Airdate: November 24, 1998.

Buffy and the crew get their SAT scores, and Spike returns to Sunnydale, lovelorn and despairing for his estranged Drusilla. While Giles is away at a Druidic camp getaway, Buffy weighs her options for the future and wonders if she should leave town to go to college. Spike abducts Willow and forces her to conjure a love spell that he can use on Drusilla, who jilted him for a chaos demon. In rescuing Willow, Cordelia and Oz discover that Willow and Xander have become romantically entangled behind their backs.

GUEST CAST: Kristine Sutherland (Joyce Summers); Harry Groener (Mayor Wilkins); James Marsters (Spike); Jack Plotnick (Deputy Mayor); Marc Burnham (Lenny); Suzanne Krull (Clerk).

43. "The Wish" Written by: Marti Noxon. Directed by: David Greenwalt. Airdate: December 8, 1998.

An angry Cordelia, still smarting over Xander's infidelity with Willow, uses the powers of a magical "wish" necklace belonging to a student named Anya. Cordelia wishes that Buffy Summers had never come to Sunnydale, and reality suddenly alters drastically. Cordelia finds herself in a town overrun with vampires (including an undead Xander and Willow, and an "ascended" Master). Attacked by Xander, an injured Cordelia finds herself in the care of Giles, who is fighting vampires even in this dimension, and she warns him that this is not the way things are supposed to be.

GUEST CAST: Emma Caulfield (Anya/Anianka); Mark Metcalf (The Master); Mercedes McNab (Harmony); Nicole Bilderback (Cordette #1); Nathan Anderson (John Lee); Mariah O'Brien (Nancy); Gary Imhoff (Teacher); Robert Covarrubias (Caretaker).

44. "Amends" Written and directed by: Joss Whedon. Airdate: December 17, 1998.

As Christmas approaches, Angel is tortured by memories of victims he has taken throughout his long life, including his friends in 1838 Dublin. Meanwhile, Oz and Willow reconcile, and Buffy invites Faith to spend Christmas at her house. Angel seeks help with his plight from Giles, who simply cannot forgive Angel for the death of his true love, Jenny Calendar. As Angel's behavior grows more erratic, Buffy realizes that in order to save the angst-ridden vampire she will have to face down a monster beyond sin, beyond damnation: a creature of the darkness called "the First Evil."

GUEST CAST: Kristine Sutherland (Mrs. Summers); Eliza Dushku (Faith); Robia La Morte (Jenny Calendar); Shane Barach (Daniel); Saverio Guerra; Edward Edwards; Cornelia Hayes O'Herlihy; Mark Kriski (Weatherman); Tom Michael Bailey (Tree Seller Guy).

NOTE: This episode's villain "the First Evil," returns to haunt Buffy the seventh season.

45. "Gingerbread" Written by: Jane Espenson. Story by: Thania St. John and Jane Espenson. Directed by: James Whitmore, Jr. Airdate: January 12, 1999.

Buffy's mom joins Buffy for a night of slaying and is horrified by the brutal deaths of two young children in a playground. In response to this tragedy, Joyce organizes a group railing against occult-oriented violence, known as M.O.O. (Mothers Opposed to the Occult). This organization promptly confiscates inappropriate books from Giles' library and conducts searches of student lockers. Soon, witches in town (including Willow) are being bullied and turned into scapegoats, and Buffy must face down her Mom before Sunnydale becomes a fascist state bent on destroying all freedom and liberty.

GUEST CAST: Kristine Sutherland (Joyce Summers); Elizabeth Ann Allen (Amy); Harry Groener (Mayor Wilkins); Jordan Baker (Sheila Rosenberg); Armin Shimerman (Principal Snyder); Lindsay Taylor (Little Girl/Gretel); Shawn Pyfrom (Little Boy/Hansel); Blake Swendson

(Michael); Grant Garrison (Roy); Roger Morrissey (Demon); Daniel Tanim (Mooster).

46. "Helpless" Written by: David Fury. Directed by: James A. Contner. Airdate: January 19, 1999.

As Buffy turns 18, she faces two disappointments: her father cancels his visit to town, and she suddenly loses all of her slaying abilities. Giles proves unhelpful in solving the latter problem, and is, in fact, behind the inexplicably vanishing powers. At the behest of the Council of Watchers, Buffy is to be part of a slayer "rite of passage" in which she must kill a vampire while virtually defenseless and powerless. Locked in a tomb with a vicious vampire, Buffy must prove herself or die.

GUEST CAST: Kristine Sutherland (Joyce Summers); Jeff Kober (Zachary Craylag); Harris Yulin (Quentin Travers); Dominic Keating (Blair); David Haydn-Jones (Hobson); Nick Cornish (Guy); Don Dowe (Construction Worker).

47. "The Zeppo" Written by: Dan Vebber. Directed by: James Whitmore, Jr. Airdate: January 26, 1999.

Xander is tired of being the "zeppo," the useless part of the slaying group, and he buys a car to help distinguish himself from his friends. Unfortunately, notoriety is the last thing Xander needs when he hooks up with three undead gang boys who plot to detonate an explosive in the high school boiler room! While Xander contends with his problem, an apocalypse cult attempts to open the Hellmouth. Xander unexpectedly hooks up with the tempestuous Faith and proves his worth in more ways than one.

GUEST CAST: Saverio Guerra; Channon Roe (Jack O'Toole); Michael Cudlitz ("Big" Bob); Eliza Dushku (Faith); Darin Heames (Parker); Scott Torrence (Dickie); Whitney Dylan (Lysette); Vaughn Armstrong (Cop).

NOTE: An extraordinary episode, "The Zeppo" concerns Xander and his fear that, without powers, he is the "Jimmy Olsen" of the

Scooby gang. This episode proves that Xander, and thereby Jimmy, add value to their respective teams.

48. "Bad Girls" Written by: Douglas Petrie. Directed by: Michael Lange. Airdate: February 9, 1999.

A new watcher is in town to take over for Giles, but nobody likes the prissy, arrogant young Brit, Wesley. At the same time, a 15th century vampire cult serving an obese, fleshy demon called Balthazar also arrives in town to reclaim a powerful magic amulet. When Faith and Buffy go in search of the ancient vampire cult, Faith encourages a more loose, rebellious attitude in Buffy. This new tenor has deadly consequences for the Sunnydale Slayers when one of them accidentally kills a mortal, the town's deputy mayor, with a stake through the heart...

GUEST CAST: Kristine Sutherland (Joyce Summers); Harry Groener (Mayor Wilkins); K. Todd Freeman (Mr. Trick); Jack Plotnick (Deputy Mayor); Alexis Denisof (Wesley Windom Price); Christian Chlemenson; Eliza Dushku (Faith); Alex Skuby (Vincent); Wendy Clifford (Mrs. Taggart); Ron Rogge (Cop).

49. "Consequences" Written by: Marti Noxon. Directed by: Michael Gershman. Airdate: February 16, 1999.

Faith lies and tells Giles that Buffy murdered an innocent human while out slaying. This complicates things for Buffy, who has been assigned by Wesley to investigate the dead man's — the deputy mayor's — death. Soon, the police are involved and questioning Faith and Buffy about the unsolved murder. Matters go from bad to worse when Wesley kidnaps Faith from Angel's care and threatens to take her back to England to stand trial before the Watchers Council.

GUEST CAST: Kristine Sutherland (Joyce Summers); Harry Groener (Mayor Wilkins); K. Todd Freeman (Trick); Alexis Denisof (Wesley Windom Price); Eliza Dushku (Faith); Jack Plot-

nick (Deputy Mayor); James G. MacDonald; Amy Powell (TV News Reporter); Patricia Place (Woman).

50. "Doppelgangland" Written and directed by: Joss Whedon. Airdate: February 23, 1999.

Anianka, the vengeance demon that once granted Cordelia a devastating wish to change the fabric of creation, seeks to regain her power base, a lost amulet. Meanwhile, Buffy and Faith go through a rigorous physical and mental evaluation at the hands of the new watcher, and Willow is "asked" by Principal Snyder to tutor a flunking athlete. Anya masquerades as a normal high school student and enlists Willow's assistance in casting a spell that will return the wish amulet to her grasp. During the spell, the alternate Willow, a vampire from the other dimension, appears to confront the real Willow in this dimension.

GUEST CAST: Harry Groener (Mayor Wilkins); Alexis Denisof (Wesley Windom Price); Emma Caulfield (Anianka/Anya); Ethan Erickson (Percy); Eliza Dushku (Faith); Armin Shimerman (Principal Snyder); Jason Hall (Devon); Michael Hagy (Alfonse); Andy Umberger (O'Hoffryn); Megan Gray (Sandy); Norma Michaels (Older Woman); Corey Michael Blake (Waiter); Jennifer Nicole (Body Double Willow).

51. "Enemies" Written by: Douglas Petrie. Directed by: David Grossman. Airdate: March 16, 1999.

After Buffy and Angel see a movie together and confront the fact that they can never be together sexually without compromising Angel's immortal soul, Buffy and Faith meet with a demon who offers to sell them the "Books of Ascension" before Mayor Wilkins himself "ascends" on Graduation Day. Worried, the Mayor orders the double agent Faith to kill the demon before Buffy can get the books, and then Faith seeks solace from Angel for her wayward behavior. Buffy witnesses Faith and Angel in an embrace and mistakes his intentions, even as the Mayor determines it is time to rid Angel of his soul once more. Faith and a converted, evil, Angel kidnap Buffy and plot to torture her as the Mayor's big day approaches.

GUEST CAST: Kristine Sutherland (Joyce Summers); Harry Groener (Mayor Richard Wilkins III); Alexis Denisof (Wesley Windom Price); Eliza Dushku (Faith); Michael Mannasseri, Gary Bullock.

52. "Earshot" Written by: Jane Espenson. Directed by: Regis Kimble. Airdate: September 21, 1999.

Buffy vanquishes one of two new (mouthless) demons in town and then inherits one of the dead demon's "aspects"— specifically, his ability to read minds. Soon Buffy is hearing the thoughts of all her friends (excluding Angel, immune because he is a vampire) and starting to go crazy from the din. Then, in the cafeteria, Buffy hears the thoughts of a disaffected person who is planning to kill everybody in school the next day. The trail to the killer takes Buffy to the school newspaper editor, sad little Jonathan, and, finally, to a hulking cafeteria worker.

GUEST CAST: Kristine Sutherland (Joyce Summers); Alexis Denisof (Wesley Windom Price); Ethan Erickson; Danny Strong; Larry Bagby, III (Larry); Keram Malicki-Sanchez (Freddy Iverson); Justin Doran (Hogan); Lauren Roman (Nancy); Wendy Worthington (Lunch Lady); Robert Arce (Mr. Beach); Molly Bryant (Ms. Murray); Rich Muller (Student); Jay Michael Ferguson (Another Student).

NOTE: "Earshot" was scheduled to be aired on April 27, 1999, but it was shelved before airtime because of the tragic shootings at Columbine High School in Littleton, Colorado. The show was rescheduled for airing some five months later.

53. "Choices" Written by: David Fury. Directed by: James A. Contner. Airdate: May 4, 1999.

The Mayor sends Faith to the airport to retrieve a trunk that is crucial to his as-

cension. Meanwhile, Buffy's mother wants her to go away to college at Northwestern, and Buffy realizes she wants to go too ... which means stopping the Mayor's ascension before graduation. Buffy learns that the important crate is the Box of Gavrok, a container of more than 50 billion carnivorous hell-spiders. Buffy and friends stage a daring operation to steal the Box of Gavrok, but things go wrong when Faith captures Willow.

GUEST CAST: Kristine Sutherland (Joyce Summers); Harry Groener (Mayor Wilkins); Alexis Denisof (Wes); Eliza Dushku (Faith); Armin Shimerman (Principal Snyder).

54. "The Prom" Written by: Marti Noxon. Directed by: David Solomon. Airdate: May 11, 1999.

Anya, the wish demon trapped in teenage human form, asks Xander to the senior prom, and he accepts. Buffy's Mom goes to visit Angel because she is concerned that Buffy and Angel are from very different worlds. With the prom looming, Angel worries that he and Buffy cannot possibly share a future together, and he decides to leave Sunnydale for good. Meanwhile, three vicious hell-hounds try to crash the prom, and the jilted Buffy makes it her sacred duty to preserve the prom for her friends. At the prom, a surprised Buffy is named "class protector" for shepherding her class through the tumults of high school.

GUEST CAST: Kristine Sutherland (Joyce Summers); Alexis Denisof (Wes); Emma Caulfield (Anya); Brad Kane; Danny Strong (Jonathan); Bonita Friedericy (Mrs. Finkle); Andrea E. Taylor (Sales Girl); Mike Kimmel (Harry); Tove Kingsbury (The Boy); Michael Zlabinger (Student at Mic); Monica Serene Garnich (Pretty Girl); Joe Howard (Priest); Damien Eckhardt (Jack Mayhew); Stephanie Denise (Tux Girl).

55. "Graduation Day" (Part I) Written and directed by: Joss Whedon. Airdate: May 18, 1999.

Graduation Day and the Mayor's ascension of evil approach rapidly, and Xander fears his number is finally up. Meanwhile, Faith murders a professor, Lester Worth, that may have the knowledge to stop the ascension. Anya, the only Sunnydale resident, human or otherwise, to ever witness a demonic ascension, provides some pertinent information on the subject even as the Mayor prepares for his hellish commencement. Meanwhile, Faith shoots Angel with a poison arrow, and the only cure is the blood of a slayer.

GUEST CAST: Kristine Sutherland (Joyce Summers); Harry Groener (Mayor Wilkins); Alexis Denisof (Wesley Windom Price); Mercedes McNab (Harmony); Ethan Erickson (Percy); Emma Caufield (Anya); Eliza Dushku (Faith); Armin Shimerman (Principal Snyder); James Lurie (Mr. Miller); Hal Robinson (Lester); Adrian Neil (Vampire Lackey #1); John Rosenfield (Vampire Lackey #2).

56. "Graduation Day" (Part II) Written and directed by: Joss Whedon. Airdate: July 13, 1999.

Buffy fails to bring Faith home to Angel, who requires her blood, the blood of a slayer, to survive the poison. Buffy offers herself to Angel and, desperate, he accepts. Buffy ends up in the hospital just down the corridor from Faith and has a strange encounter with her on the dream plane. Soon, both the Mayor and Buffy are formulating strategies for their mutual commencements, ascension and graduation, the day when good and evil in Sunnydale will clash once and for all.

GUEST CAST: Harry Groener (Mayor Wilkins); Alexis Denisof (Wesley); Danny Strong (Jonathan); Mercedes McNab (Harmony); Ethan Erickson; Eliza Dushku (Faith); Armin Shimerman (Snyder); Paulo Andres (Dr. Powell); Susan Chuang (Nurse); Tom Bellin (Dr. Gold); Samuel Bliss Cooper (Vamp Lackey).

SEASON FOUR (1999-2000)

57. "The Freshman" Written and directed by: Joss Whedon. Airdate: October 5, 1999.

Buffy begins her college education at UC Sunnydale but is hazed by a nasty upperclassman vampire, Sunday. Buffy enrolls in Intro to Psychology with the hard-nosed Professor Walsh and her buff, kindly teaching assistant, Riley Finn. When a new friend, Eddie, is killed by Sunday and her clique of nasty vampires, Buffy re-teams with Xander and the Scoobies to fight back.

GUEST CAST: Kristine Sutherland (Joyce Summers); Marc Blucas (Riley Finn); Dagney Kerr (Kathy Newman); Katherine Towne (Sunday); Lindsay Crouse (Maggie Walsh); Pedro Balmaceda (Eddie); Mike Rad (Rookie); Shannon Hillary (Day); Mace Lombard (Tom); Robert Catrin (Professor Riegert); Scott Rinker (R.A.); Phina Cruchi (Olivia); Daniel J. Haley (Student Volunteer); Evie Peck (Angry Girl); Anil Raman (Earnest Fellow); Jason Christopher (Nonserious Guy); Jane Silvia (Conservative Woman); Mark Silverberg (Passing Student); Walt Borchert (New Vampire).

NOTE: "Avengers assemble," Xander jokes in this episode, referring to the famous Marvel superhero team, just another canny reference on the part of Whedon's team to the universe of comics and superheroes.

58. "Living Conditions" Written by: Marti Noxon. Directed by: David Grosman. Airdate: October 12, 1999.

A demon attacks Buffy's obnoxious roommate, Kathy, but the slayer holds him off and is consequently embroiled in a strange power struggle. Unbeknownst to Buffy, Kathy is a demon that is attending college without the permission of her clan, and so is attempting to steal Buffy's soul to prevent her family from locating her. As Buffy loses her soul a piece at a time, threatening to become a homicidal maniac and taking out her hostility on her Cher-loving roommate, her friends believe she's gone crazy, and stage an intervention. Meanwhile, a military unit operates in secret on the campus by night...

GUEST CAST: Dagney Kerr (Kathy Newman); Adam Kaufman (Parker Abrams); Clayton Barber (Demon #1); Walt Borchert (Demon #2);

Roger Morrissey (Tapparich); David Tuchman (Freshman).

59. "The Harsh Light of Day" Written by: Jane Espenson. Directed by: James A. Contner. Airdate: October 19, 1999.

After a night at the Bronze, Willow is attacked by Harmony, now a vampire. Meanwhile, smooth-talking lothario Parker Abrams makes a major play for Buffy at a party, while Anya, the former vengeance demon, returns to Sunnydale to pursue a relationship with Xander. Buffy learns that Spike and Harmony are seeking the Gem of Amara, a relic that allows vampires to walk in daylight, impervious to the rays of the sun. Now Buffy must stop Spike and deal with the fact that she has spent the night with womanizing Parker...

GUEST CAST: Emma Caufield (Anya); Adam Kaufman (Parker Abrams); Mercedes McNab (Harmony Kendall); James Marsters (Spike); Jason Hall (Devon); Melik (Brian).

60. "Fear, Itself" Written by: David Fury. Directed by: Tucker Gates. Airdate: October 26, 2000.

As Halloween approaches, Buffy is devastated by Parker's nasty treatment of her after their passionate night together. At the Alpha-Delta Fraternity house, plans are afoot for a Halloween party, and one of the brothers paints a dangerous mystical symbol in the attic, unaware of its power. At the party, Halloween horrors becoming frighteningly real, and Xander, Buffy, Oz and Willow become trapped inside, at the mercy of a demon called Gachnar that thrives on fear. The demon separates the Scooby gang, playing on each person's insecurities, but the monster turns out to be a smaller problem than Buffy or the others realize.

GUEST CAST: Kristine Sutherland (Joyce Summers); Marc Blucas (Riley Finn); Emma Caulfield (Anya); Adam Kaufman (Parker Abrams); Lindsay Crouse (Maggie Walsh).

61. "Beer Bad" Written by: Tracey Forbes. Directed by: David Solomon. Airdate: November 2, 1999.

Xander takes a job as a bartender, and Buffy drowns her sorrows over Parker in a strange brew called Black Forest. The beer makes Buffy's id lose control and reverts the slayer to a Neanderthal-like creature of pure instinct. When her three drinking partners also become cave dwellers, it's up to Buffy the cave slayer to rescue them — and Parker — from a deadly fire.

GUEST CAST: Marc Blucas (Riley Finn); Adam Kaufman (Parker Abrams); Paige Moss (Verruca); Eric Matheny; Stephen M. Porter; Lindsay Crouse (Maggie Walsh); Kai Penn (Hunt); Jake Phillips (Kip); Bryan Cuprill (Roy); Lisa Johnson (Paula); Joshua Wheeler (Driver); Patrick Helton (College Kid #1); Kaycee Shank (College Kid #2); Steven Jane (College Kid #3); Cameron Bender (Stoner); Kate Luhr (Young Woman).

62. "Wild at Heart" Written by: Marti Noxon. Directed by: David Grossman. Airdate: November 9, 1999.

Spike is captured by armed soldiers patrolling the campus of UC Sunnydale, while Oz begins to feel strangely drawn to a new singer at the Bronze, the mysterious and beautiful Verruca. On the night of the full moon, Oz transforms into a werewolf and learns that Verruca is a kindred lycanthrope whey awaken together nude in daylight! Professor Walsh reports being pursued by werewolves, and Buffy and Giles start to investigate. Willow learns of Oz's infidelity, spurring Oz's departure from campus, and Buffy gains further evidence of a covert military operation operating in Sunnydale.

GUEST CAST: James Marsters (Spike); Marc Blucas (Riley Finn); Paige Moss (Verruca); Lindsay Crouse (Maggie Walsh).

63. "The Initiative" Written by: Douglas Petrie. Directed by: James A. Contner. Airdate: November 16, 1999.

Spike is incarcerated in a high-tech

subterranean laboratory beneath Sunnydale. Meanwhile, Buffy challenges Professor Walsh for being cruel to Willow in her time of grief over Oz's departure. Spike escapes from his cell, but has been implanted with a chip that prevents him from biting or in any way harming human beings. A defanged Spike goes in search of the Slayer, whom he blames for his capture, while the military "Initiative," led by Professor Walsh and Riley Finn, hunt him down.

GUEST CAST: Marc Blucas (Riley Finn); Mercedes McNab (Harmony); Adam Kaufman (Parker Abrams); Lindsay Crouse (Maggie Walsh); Mace Lombard (Tom); Scott Becker (Lost Freshman); Bailey Chase, Leonard Roberts.

64. **"Pangs"** Written by: Jane Espenson. Directed by: Michael Lange. Airdate: November 23, 1999.

It's Thanksgiving in Sunnydale, and at the ceremonial ground-breaking of the new cultural center, Xander falls through a hole into an old buried Mission. There he unwittingly releases a vengeful Native American spirit whose people, the Shumas, were slaughtered by early American settlers. When Angel learns that the representative of the Shumash Tribe could endanger Buffy's life, he travels from L.A. to protect her. Xander's invasion of the sacred ground results in his suffering from a strange and deadly sickness, just one more dangerous factor impeding Buffy's plans for a perfect holiday.

GUEST CAST: David Boreanaz (Angel); Marc Blucas (Riley Finn); Mercedes McNab (Harmony); Emma Caulfield (Anya); Leonard Roberts (Forrest); Bailey Chase (Graham); Tod Thawley (Shumash Indian); Margaret Easley (Curator); William Vogt (Jamie); Mark Ankeny (Dean Guerrero).

65. **"Something Blue"** Written by: Tracey Forbes. Directed by: Nick Marck. Airdate: November 30, 1999.

Still smarting from Oz's sudden departure from Sunnydale, an angry and confused Willow resorts to magic to heal her pain and inadvertently wreaks havoc on her friends. Her angry words turn Xander into a "demon magnet," make Giles lose his vision, and cause arch-enemies Spike and Buffy to believe they're getting married and prepare for a big wedding. Impressed by Willow's magical screw-up, a powerful demon offers her a job as a vengeance demon.

GUEST CAST: Marc Blucas (Riley Finn); Emma Caulfield (Anya); Elizabeth Anne Allen (Amy).

66. **"Hush"** Written and directed by: Joss Whedon. Airdate: December 14, 1999.

Sunnydale is invaded by a cadre of floating ghouls called the Gentlemen that seek to steal the beating hearts of seven innocents. Making matters worse, the Gentlemen have "stolen" the collective voice of Sunnydale, making it a town of ghostly silence. Buffy and her friends set out to stop the Gentlemen before they gather their bloody hearts, and, in one confrontation, Riley and Buffy learn the secrets that they have been hiding from one another.

GUEST CAST: Doug Jones, Camden Troy, Don W. Lewis, Charlie Brumbly (Gentlemen); Elizabeth Truax (Little Girl).

67. **"Doomed"** Written by: Marti Noxon, David Fury and Jane Espenson. Directed by: James A. Contner. Airdate: January 18, 2000.

Buffy and Riley come clean about their mutual secret identities and find trust a little hard to come by. At the same time, an earthquake rocks Sunnydale and a cadre of demons attempt to open the Hellmouth in the old high school library. Meanwhile, Spike learns that the chip in his head does not prohibit him from fighting demons — a relief, since he's moved into Xander's basement and has been feeling impotent and suicidal.

GUEST CAST: Leonard Roberts (Forrest); Bailey Chase (Graham); Ethan Erickson (Percy); Anastasia Horne (Laurie); Anthony Anselm (Partier).

68. "The New Man" Written by: Jane Espenson. Directed by: Michael Gershman. Airdate: January 25, 2000.

It's Buffy's 19th birthday and Giles is feeling underappreciated because of Buffy's new friendship with Riley, Maggie Walsh and the Initiative. Ethan Rayne returns to Sunnydale, aggravating Rupert's concern, and uses magic to transform the former watcher into a demon. Nobody recognizes Giles as a demon except Spike, so they head out to catch Ethan, unaware that Buffy is hunting Giles because she believes that a demon (actually Giles...) murdered her beloved friend and mentor

GUEST CAST: Amber Benson (Tara); Emma Caulfield (Anya); Lindsay Crouse (Maggie Walsh); Elizabeth Penn Payne (Warren); Michelle Ferrara (Mother).

NOTE: In describing Buffy in this episode, Riley notes that she is "Spider-Man"–strong, just one superhero reference among many in the series.

69. "The I in Team" Written by: David Fury. Directed by: James A. Contner. Airdate: February 8, 2000.

Buffy is tested in combat by Maggie Walsh and her Initiative team, and Walsh is impressed with Buffy's slayer skills. As a result, Buffy is granted clearance and access to the Initiative's massive subterranean laboratory complex and given a tour by the dour Walsh. Meanwhile, Willow begins developing romantic feelings for her new friend and fellow Wiccan, Tara, and Spike is tracked by the Initiative. Afraid Riley is growing too close to Buffy, Dr. Walsh attempts to set a fatal trap for her. Buffy escapes, but Walsh is killed by Adam, her pet research project in Laboratory 314, an unholy amalgamation of technology, demon and human.

GUEST CAST: Emma Caulfield (Anya); Amber Benson (Tara); George Hertzberg (Adam); Leonard Roberts (Forrest); Bailey Chase (Graham); Lindsey Crouse (Maggie Walsh); Neil Daly (Mason); Jack Stehlin.

NOTE: Xander wears a Captain America sweatshirt in this episode.

70. "Goodbye, Iowa" Written by: Marti Noxon. Directed by: David Solomon. Airdate: February 15, 2000.

The late Dr. Walsh's masterwork of evil, Adam, has escaped from the Initiative, and Buffy attempts to convince the loyal Riley that the government organization is up to no good. Buffy and Xander infiltrate the Initiative and learn about their new enemy, while Riley, mysteriously ill, goes after them. At the Initiative, Buffy is confronted by Adam, a villain that wants to learn about himself and the world by dissecting other life forms. Buffy learns that Riley and all the Initiative soldiers have been taking meds that make them stronger, but since Maggie Walsh's death, they've been off the meds and getting sick.

GUEST CAST: Amber Benson (Tara); George Hertzberg (Adam); Leonard Roberts (Forrest); Bailey Chase (Graham); Jack Stehlin; J.B. Gaynor; Saverio Guerra; Emma Caulfield (Anya); Amy Powell (Reporter); Andy Marshall (Scientist #1); Paula Leighton (Rough Looking Woman); Karen Charnell (Shady Lady).

71. "This Year's Girl" Written by: Douglas Petrie. Directed by: Michael Gershman. Airdate: February 22, 2000.

Faith, the rogue slayer, awakens from her months-long coma, eager to settle scores with the Slayer for the defeat of the Mayor at his ascension. Riley leaves the hospital, recovered from his injuries, and reunites with Buffy. Faith switches bodies with Buffy by using a magical device left for her by the Mayor, and sets out to assume the Slayer's life...

GUEST CAST: Eliza Dushku (Faith); Kristine Sutherland (Joyce Summers); Amber Benson (Tara); Harry Groener (The Mayor); Leonard Roberts (Forrest); Bailey Chase (Graham); Chet Grissom, Alastair Duncan.

72. "Who Are You?" Written and directed by: Joss Whedon. Airdate: February 29, 2000.

The Watchers Council apprehends Buffy, trapped in Faith's body, in hopes of bringing the rogue slayer back to England for trial. Meanwhile, Faith impersonates Buffy, teasing Spike and making love to Riley. Buffy escapes from Council custody in time to help Faith dispatch Adam's cadre of vampires, holed up in a local church. After the battle, Buffy fights the rogue slayer to re-capture her own body.

GUEST CAST: Eliza Dushku (Faith); Kristine Sutherland (Joyce Summers); Amber Benson (Tara); Emma Caulfield (Anya); George Hertzberg (Adam); Leonard Roberts (Forrest); Chet Grissom; Alastair Duncan; Rick Stear (Boone); Jeff Ricketts (Weatherby); Kevin Owers (Smith); Amy Powell (Reporter); Rick Scarry (Sergeant); Jennifer S. Albright (Date).

73. "Superstar" Written by: Jane Espenson. Directed by: David Grossman. Airdate: April 4, 2000.

When the Slayer discovers a nest of vampires in a Sunnydale cemetery, she realizes only one person in the world is powerful enough to help: the great, the mighty ... Jonathan! This national hero is not only a movie star, friend of the Slayer, stalwart fighter and advisor to the Initiative, but the subject of a set of trading cards! When a demon attacks one of Jonathan's nubile fans and then Tara, Buffy starts to suspect there's something wrong with the universe. As it turns out, Jonathan has made a pact with the demon to be the most popular, successful and beloved man in the world, and now all his admirers, including the Scoobies, are having a hard time believing that their reality has been altered.

GUEST CAST: Amber Benson (Tara); Emma Caulfield (Anya); Danny Strong (Jonathan); Emma Caulfield (Anya); Leonard Roberts (Forrest); Bailey Chase (Graham), Robert Patrick Benedict (Vampire); John Saint Ryan; George Hertzberg (Adam); Erica Luttrell (Karen); Adam Clark (Cop); Inga (Chanie Costello); Ilsa (Julie Costello).

NOTE: Jonathan's only weakness in this episode is the demon that keeps reappearing, hence Xander's description of the monster as Jonathan's "kryptonite," yet another reference to Superman.

74. "Where the Wild Things Are" Written by: Tracey Forbes. Directed by: David Solomon. Airdate: April 25, 2000.

Adam has united the underworld, encouraging demons and vampires to fight side-by-side against Buffy and the rest of humanity. Meanwhile, strange events seem to be occurring at Riley's fraternity house in relation to Buffy and Finn's passionate couplings. Disembodied spirits, once the inhabitants of a repressive children's home on the premises, haunt a party and trap Riley and Buffy in their bedroom, drawing energy from them. A bickering Anya and Xander attempt to set the couple free, while Giles, Tara and Willow conduct a spell to quell the poltergeists.

GUEST CAST: Amber Benson (Tara); Emma Caulfield (Anya); Leonard Roberts (Forrest); Bailey Chase (Graham); Kathryn Joosten; Casey McCarthy (Julie); Neil Daley (Mason); Jeff Wilson (Evan); Bryan Cuprill (Roy); Jeffrey Sharmat (Drowning Boy); Jeri Austin (Running Girl); Danielle Pessis (Christy); David Engler (Initiative Guy); James Michael Conner (Scientist).

75. "New Moon Rising" Written by: Marti Noxon. Directed by: James A. Contner. Airdate: May 2, 2000.

Oz returns to Sunnydale, claiming that he has vanquished the werewolf within. Unfortunately, his return complicates matters for Tara and Willow, who are developing a romantic relationship. When Oz learns about Tara, he loses his temper and transforms into a werewolf, only to be captured by the Initiative. Buffy plans to break Oz out of containment with the help of Spike, but it is Riley — uncomfortable with demons and werewolves as friends — who saves the day, risking his own future in the military.

GUEST CAST: Amber Benson (Tara); Emma Caulfield (Anya); Seth Green (Oz); Leonard Roberts (Forrest); Bailey Chase (Graham); Robert Patrick Benedict (Vampire); Conor O'-Farrell (Colonel); George Hertzberg (Adam); James Michael Conner (Scientist); Mark Daneri (Scientist #2); Doron Keenan (Commando #2).

76. "The Yoko Factor" Written by: Doug Petrie. Directed by: David Grossman. Airdate: May 9, 2000.

Adam seeks help from Spike in defeating the Slayer and her friends. Buffy returns from a visit with Angel in L.A., and Riley is jealous. Meanwhile, Spike separates the Scoobies, relying on the "Yoko Factor" and playing upon their insecurities. When Angel follows Buffy to Sunnydale to apologize for fighting with her in L.A., Riley fights the vampire until Buffy steps in.

GUEST CAST: Amber Benson (Tara); Leonard Roberts (Forrest); Conor O'Farrell (Colonel); George Hertzberg (Adam); Emma Caulfield (Anya); David Boreanaz (Angel).

NOTE: In this episode, Xander jokes about hanging out at "the Bat Cave with Alfred."

77. "Primeval" Written by: David Fury. Directed by: James A. Contner. Airdate: May 16, 2000.

Adam has gained control of Riley through a behavior modification chip in his chest even as Buffy has been separated from her friends by Spike. Still smarting from the Spike-inflicted emotional wounds, the Scoobies re-team with great difficulty to save Riley and take down Adam, who is hoping to cause a war between humans and demons and then use the spare parts to build a new super-race of hybrid soldiers. While the Initiative and the incarcerated demons duke it out underground, Buffy and her friends conjure the spirit of the first slayer to enhance her ability to fight the nearly in-destructible Adam. In the final battle, a demonized Forrest, a zombified Maggie Walsh and Adam himself all bite the dust.

GUEST CAST: Leonard Roberts (Forrest); Amber Benson (Tara); Bailey Chase (Graham); Jack Stehlin; Conor O'Farrell (Colonel); George Hertzberg (Adam); Emma Caulfield (Anya); Lindsay Crouse (Maggie Walsh).

78. "Restless" Written and directed by: Joss Whedon. Airdate: May 23, 2000.

With Adam defeated, the Scoobies spend a quiet night at Buffy's house watching videos. Buffy, Giles, Xander and Willow each fall asleep during the night's viewing and are confronted in their dreams by a powerful and feral opponent: the spirit of the first slayer that they conjured to help defeat Adam. Xander, Willow and Giles all face enigmatic, frightening dreams about their female assailant, but only Buffy can defeat the beast.

GUEST CAST: Kristine Sutherland (Joyce Summers); Amber Benson (Tara); Mercedes McNab (Harmony); George Hertzberg (Adam); Emma Caulfield (Anya); Seth Green (Oz); Armin Shimerman (Principal Snyder); David Wells; Michael Harney; Sharon Ferguson (Primitive); Phina Oruche (Olivia); Rob Bollin (Soldier).

SEASON FIVE (2000–2001)

79. "Buffy vs. Dracula" Written by: Marti Noxon. Directed by: David Solomon. Airdate: September 26, 2000.

The Prince of Darkness, Dracula, arrives in Sunnydale to seduce and conquer the renowned Slayer. Riley becomes jealous when Buffy finds herself attracted to the master vampire, and Xander is transformed into a Renfield-like assistant by the devilish creature of the night. Buffy is bitten by Dracula when he visits her room one night, but musters the power to defeat the villain, at least temporarily.

GUEST CAST: Rudolph Martin (Dracula); Amber Benson (Tara); Kristine Sutherland

(Joyce Summers); E.J. Gage (Mover #1); Scott Berman (Mover #2); Marita Schaub, Leslie Jean Matta, Jennifer Simko (Vampire Girls).

80. "The Real Me" Written by: David Fury. Directed by: David Grossman. Airdate: October 3, 2000.

Buffy and her younger sister Dawn squabble over training, shopping and other matters. The Magic Shop owner is killed mysteriously, leading the Scoobies to investigate, even as Harmony returns to town to organize a posse of vampires to kill the Slayer. Harmony's minions capture Dawn, and it is Buffy to little sister's rescue.

GUEST CAST: Mercedes McNab (Harmony); Amber Benson (Tara); Kristine Sutherland (Joyce); Bob Morrissey; Brian Turk (Mort); Chaney Kley Minnis (Brad); Fait Abrahams (Peaches); Tom Lenk (Cyrus).

NOTE: Xander refers to Buffy's house as "The Fortress of Solitude" in this episode, a direct reference to the Superman mythos. Spike also weighs in on the lingo of the genre, telling Harmony the vampire to let him know how "the arch-villain" thing goes for her.

81. "The Replacement" Written by: Jane Espenson. Directed by: James A. Contner. Airdate: October 10, 2000.

Xander goes apartment hunting with the Scoobies, while Giles sets up his new business, a magic store called the Magic Box. A Toth Demon wants to kill the Slayer, and, during a pitched battle with the gang, splits Xander in two: one strong and confident, the other diffident and scattered. While the strong Xander ingratiates himself with his employers, Anya and his other friends, the wimpy Xander realizes he has nothing left and seeks Willow's help. Now Buffy must put Xander back together before the Toth Demon strikes again, splitting the Slayer into two parts. After the tussle, Riley reveals to Xander that he knows Buffy doesn't love him.

GUEST CAST: Michael Bailey Smith; Kristine Sutherland (Joyce); Kelly Donovan (Xander

Double); Cathy Cohen (Building Manager); David Reurs (Foreman); Fritz Greve (Construction Worker).

82. "Out of My Mind" Written by: Rebecca Rand Kirshner. Directed by: David Grossman. Airdate: October 17, 2000.

Spike and Riley keep getting in Buffy's way during vampire slaying patrols. At the Summers home, Buffy's mother falls mysteriously ill with some kind of neurological trauma and is rushed to the hospital, where Buffy meets a kindly young intern named Ben. At the same facility, Riley is diagnosed with a hyper pulse rate and is found to be in danger of experiencing a fatal heart attack, a leftover from his super-powered days as Dr. Walsh's lead soldier. Liking the feel of being a superhero, Riley refuses treatment for his condition, even as Spike realizes that the Initiative's doctor could be the key to removing the chip from his skull. After Riley is healed and Spike's plan is foiled, Spike is horrified to realize that he is in love with the Slayer.

GUEST CAST: Mercedes McNab (Harmony); Bailey Chase (Graham); Charlie Weber (Ben); Amber Benson (Tara); Kristine Sutherland (Joyce); Dierdre Holder (Hospital Doctor); Time Winters (Doctor).

NOTE: This episode is rife with references to superheroes and their specific set of problems. Harmony the vampire considers herself Buffy's "arch-nemesis." Riley is afraid of being "Joe Normal" when his girlfriend is a superhero, an insecurity made worse by Buffy's disparaging remark that he is not in "the super club."

83. "No Place Like Home" Written by: Douglas Petrie. Directed by: David Solomon. Airdate: October 24, 2000.

Under Giles' prissy proprietorship, the Magic Box opens, even as Buffy's mom must return to the hospital for further tests. Investigating a rash of mental illness in Sunnydale, Buffy runs up against a powerful new nemesis named Glory that is hell-bent on finding and retrieving a mystical key.

While attempting to learn the source of her mother's sickness and the origin of Glory, Buffy conducts a spell and learns that monks have hidden the all-important and mysterious key in human form ... as her sister Dawn! The powerful monks have manipulated reality to make everyone believe that there is a Summers sister, and Buffy realizes she must protect Dawn to save the world.

GUEST CAST: Clare Kramer (Glory); Charlie Weber (Ben); Ravil Isyanov (Monk); Kristine Sutherland (Joyce); James Wellington (Nightwatchman); Paul Hayes (Older Nightwatchman); Staci Lawrence (Customer); John Sarkisian (Old Monk).

NOTE: When confronting the powerful Slayer, the invincible goddess Glorificus makes note of her nemesis' identity as a superhero. "You have super powers! Can you fly?"

84. "Family" Written and directed by: Joss Whedon. Airdate: November 7, 2000.

Buffy has just learned that Dawn is not actually her kid sister, but a mystical "key" hidden in the Slayer's protective custody. Meanwhile, Willow's lady love, Tara, has her 20th birthday, an experience marred by a visit from her conservative father, cousin Beth and brother Danny, all of whom claim that she must return home with them or suffer the same fate as her mother and "turn evil." At the same time, Glory sends a gang of bone marrow–sucking demons to kill Buffy. Tara casts a spell so her friends can't see the demon within, but the spell blinds them to the presence of Glory's attackers.

GUEST CAST: Mercedes McNab (Harmony); Clare Kramer (Glory); Charlie Weber (Ben); Amber Benson (Tara); Amy Adams (Cousin Beth); Steve Ranking (Mr. McClay); Ezra Buzzington (Bartender); Peggy Goss (Crazy Person); Torry Pendergrass (Damon); Megan Gray (Sandy); Brian Tee (Intern); Kevin Rankin (Donny).

85. "Fool for Love" Written by: Douglas Petrie. Directed by: Nick Marck. Airdate: November 14, 2000.

Buffy is impaled on her own stake in a fight with a vampire, and the defeat rattles her, sending the Slayer to Spike — a two-time slayer killer — for advice about staying alive. Spike recounts his origin as a vampire, as well as his experiences with slayers in China in 1900 and in New York City in 1977. Meanwhile, Riley fills in for Buffy on patrol, with the help of hapless Xander, Anya and Willow.

GUEST CAST: David Boreanaz (Angel); Mercedes McNab (Harmony); Julie Benz (Darla); Juliet Landau (Drusilla); Kristine Sutherland (Joyce); Kali Rocha (Cecily Addams); Edward Fletcher (Male Partygoer); Katharine Leonard (Female Partygoer); Matthew Lang (Second Male Partygoer); Chris Daniels (Stabbing Vampire); Kenneth Feinberg (Chaos Demon); Steve Heinze (Vampire #1); Ming Lia (Chinese Slayer); April Wheedon-Washington (Subway Slayer).

NOTE: This episode presents the origin of a super-villain/superhero, Spike the vampire.

86. "Shadow" Written by: David Fury. Directed by: Daniel Attias. Airdate: November 21, 2000.

Buffy's mom undergoes more tests at Sunnydale Memorial Hospital, while Glory plans a spell that will conjure a creature that can locate her missing and all-important key. Buffy learns her mother has a shadow on her brain, a tumor, and surgery is scheduled. Glory's monster, a giant cobra, arises and seeks out Dawn, even as Riley struggles with his own feelings of uselessness by having a fling with a vampire junkie. After the snake identifies Dawn, Buffy must kill the creature before it reports to Glory that her little sister is the key.

GUEST CAST: Clare Kramer (Glory); Charlie Weber (Ben); Amber Benson (Tara); Kristine Sutherland (Joyce); Megan Gray (Sandy); Kevin Weisman, William Forward.

NOTE: Xander likens Riley to "Captain America" in this episode.

87. "Listening to Fear" Written by: Rebecca Rand Kirshner. Directed by: David Solomon. Airdate: November 28, 2000.

Riley doesn't show up for vampire patrol with Xander, Giles and Willow because he is still going to vampire safe houses and letting undead junkies feed on his blood. Meanwhile, a meteor crashes in Sunnydale, depositing a strange demon in the town, and Riley calls in the military to hunt the creature down. The demon infiltrates the hospital and follows the Summers women home, as the Scoobies learn it is a Queller demon, summoned to kill crazy people. In this case, the summoner is the medical intern Ben, who shares a mysterious relationship with Glory.

GUEST CAST: Charlie Weber (Ben); Amber Benson (Tara); Kristine Sutherland (Joyce); Bailey Chase (Graham Miller); Nick Chinlund; Kevin Weisman; Randy Thompson; Paul Hayes (Older Nightwatchman); Keith Allan (Skinny Mental Patient); Erin Leigh Pace (Vampire Chick); April Adams (Nurse Lampkin); Barbara C. Adside (Creature); Debbie Lee Carrington (Creature).

88. "Into the Woods" Written and directed by: Marti Noxon. Airdate: December 19, 2000.

Joyce's surgery is successful, but Riley's feelings of inadequacy grow as he continues to dally with vampire junkies. Spike learns what Riley is up to and takes Buffy to the vampire nest to see it for herself. A shattered Buffy and Riley have a falling out, and Riley contemplates rejoining his military unit for a dangerous mission in Central America. Buffy is prepared to let Riley go, until Xander reminds her of their love. Buffy races to stop Riley's departure, but is too late.

GUEST CAST: Bailey Chase (Graham); Nick Chinlund; Kristine Sutherland (Joyce); Randy Thompson (Dr. Kriegel); Rrand Ho Stout (Junkie Vampire Girl); Emmanuel Xuerer (Waif); Adam G. (Tough Vamp).

89. "Triangle" Written by: Jane Espenson. Directed by: Christopher Hibler. Airdate: January 9, 2001.

A bickering Anya and Willow inadvertently release a malevolent troll from captivity. With his powerful hammer, this troll — Anya's old boyfriend — trashes the Bronze in a fit. Xander stands up to the villain, but the Troll makes Xander choose who will survive his attack, either Anya or Willow.

GUEST CAST: Abraham Benrubi (Troll/Olaf); Kristine Sutherland (Joyce); Ranjani Brow (Nun).

90. "Checkpoint" Written by: Douglas Petrie and Jane Espenson. Directed by: Nick Marck. Airdate: January 23, 2001.

The Watchers Council arrives in Sunnydale, led by Quentin Travers, ostensibly to help Buffy understand her new foe, Glory. What they really want to do, however, is get Buffy back under their thumb. To that end, they begin questioning Buffy's friends about her skills, and run her through a series of tests. Buffy refuses to play their game, and learns that the Council desperately needs her, not vice versa. She learns from Travers that her new opponent, Glory, is no mere demon, but a god!

GUEST CAST: Clare Kramer (Glory); Charlie Weber (Ben); Cynthia LaMontagne; Oliver Muirhead; Kris Iyer; Kevin Weismen; Troy T. Blendell; Amber Benson (Tara); Harris Yulin (Travers); Kristine Sutherland (Joyce); Wesley Mask (Professor Roberts); Justin Corence (Orlando); Peter Husmann (Mailman); Jack Thomas; John O'Leary.

91. "Blood Ties" Written by: Steven S. De Knight. Directed by: Michael Gershman. Airdate: February 6, 2001.

Dawn is shattered to learn the secret that she is actually "the key" so desperately sought by Glory, not a "real" sister to Buffy. Terrified, Dawn runs away and is nearly killed by Glory after learning that Ben, the intern, and Glory share an identity. Buffy challenges Glory, and Willow helps out by transporting the Goddess away temporarily, leaving the slayer to explain that Dawn is made up of the same genetic material as she is — that they are, in a real sense, sisters.

GUEST CAST: Clare Kramer (Glory); Charlie Weber (Ben); Amber Benson (Tara); Kristine Sutherland (Joyce); Justin Corence (Orlando); Michael Emanuel (Burly Guard); Candice Nicole (Young Buffy); Elyssa D. Vito (Young Dawn).

92. "Crush" Written by: David Fury. Directed by: Daniel Attias. Airdate: February 13, 2001.

Dawn has a crush on Spike, and Spike has a crush on Buffy, a situation exacerbated by the return to Sunnydale of the evil vampire Drusilla. With the murderous Drusilla back to her old ways, the confused Spike must decide which woman best represents his future. He stages a confrontation between Drusilla and Buffy, but sees his plan foiled by Harmony, of all people.

GUEST CAST: Juliet Landau (Drusilla); Mercedes McNab (Harmony); Charlie Weber (Ben); Amber Benson (Tara); Kristine Sutherland (Joyce); Frederick Dawson (Porter); Greg Wayne (Student); Joseph Dia Giandomenico (Matt); Walter Borchert (Jeff); Asher Glaser (Boy in Bronze); Jennifer Bergman (Girl in Bronze); Nell Shanahan (Waitress).

93. "I Was Made to Love You" Written by: Jane Espenson. Directed by: James A Contner. Airdate: February 20, 2001.

A beautiful but strange girl arrives in Sunnydale in search of her boyfriend, but she's actually an anatomically-perfect robot programmed to please her creator, a geek named Warren Mears. After the robot throws Spike through a window for an inappropriate sexual suggestion, Buffy realizes she must stop the android and find her creator. After the robot's batteries die out during combat with Buffy, Spike goes to Warren and demands that the nerd build for him a perfect robot duplicate of the comely Slayer.

GUEST CAST: Clare Kramer (Glory); Charlie Weber (Ben); Shonda Farr (April); Adam Busch (Warren Mears); Amber Benson (Tara); Troy T. Blendell; Kristine Sutherland (Joyce); Amelinda Embry (Katrina); Paul Barringo (Driver); Gil Chrisenen (Resident); Kelly Felix (Teenager); Paul Walia (Friend).

94. "The Body" Written and directed by: Joss Whedon. Airdate: February 27, 2001.

Buffy arrives home to find that her mother, Joyce, has died suddenly of an aneurysm. A shell-shocked Buffy and her friends cope with the sudden, tragic and irreversible loss on a day none of them will ever forget. At the hospital, Dawn encounters a vampire in the morgue.

GUEST CAST: Kristine Sutherland (Joyce); Amber Benson (Tara); Randy Thompson, Kevin Cirstaldi, Stefan Umstead (Paramedics); John Michael Herndon (Vampire).

95. "Forever" Written and directed by: Marti Noxon. Airdate: April 17, 2001.

As Buffy mourns her mother, Dawn plans to use magic to resurrect Joyce. Though he thinks the effort ill advised, Spike assists and takes Dawn to a black magician named Doc who may be able to help. While Angel comforts Buffy after her mother's funeral, Spike and Dawn raid a demon nest looking for eggs to use in the resurrection spell. The spell works, but Buffy convinces Dawn to let their mother go.

GUEST CAST: David Boreanaz (Angel); Clare Kramer (Glory); Charlie Weber (Ben); Amber Benson (Tara); Joel Grey (Doc); Troy T. Blendell; Todd Duffey (Murk); Andrea Gall (Customer); Darius Dudley (Minister).

96. "Intervention" Written by: Jane Espenson. Directed by: Michael Gershman. Airdate: April 24, 2001.

While Buffy is away with Giles conferring with her spirit guide, the first Slayer, Spike has had the young genius named Warren build him a perfect robot duplicate of Buffy. At first, everybody is fooled by the replica, including Glory, who deduces that Spike is the "key" she so desperately seeks. Spike is tortured, but refuses to give up information about the key (i.e. Dawn). The real Buffy returns to Sunnydale spitting mad about Spike's sex-bot, but sees a flash of nobility in the vampire's refusal to surrender Dawn to the vengeful goddess.

GUEST CAST: Clare Kramer (Glory); Adam Busch (Warren); Amber Benson (Tara); Troy Blendell; Sharon Ferguson (Primitive); Todd Duffey (Murk).

97. "Tough Love" Written by: Rebecca Rand Kirshner. Directed by: David Grossman. Airdate: May 1, 2001.

Buffy drops out of college to care for Dawn even as Ben loses his job at the hospital. Meanwhile, Glory continues her search for the key by spying on Buffy's friends. Glory mistakenly deduces that Tara is her key and drains the girl's brain. A vengeful Willow uses dark magic to attack Glory, but the attempt fails, and a mentally devastated Tara inadvertently reveals that Dawn is actually Glory's key.

GUEST CAST: Clare Kramer (Glory); Charlie Weber (Ben); Tory T. Blendell; Anne Betancourt; Leland Crooke; Amber Benson (Tara); Tod Buffey (Murk); Alan Heitz (Stook).

98. "Spiral" Written by: Steven S. DeKnight. Directed by: James A. Contner. Airdate: May 8, 2001.

Now that Glory knows that Dawn is her key, Buffy realizes that the only way to survive is to retreat from town in hopes of evading the evil god. With Spike, Giles, Xander, Willow, Anya, Dawn and the handicapped Tara at her side, Buffy flees Sunnydale in an old RV. The Scoobies are attacked on the open road by a horde of knights that wish to destroy the key at all costs, and Giles is wounded in the confrontation. Buffy and her friends hide out in an abandoned gas station and call for Ben to tend to Giles, unaware that he is also Glory.

Giles is healed, but Glory makes an appearance and steals away with her key, Dawn!

GUEST CAST: Clare Kramer (Glory); Charlie Weber (Ben); Wade Andrew Williams; Karim Prince; Amber Benson (Tara); Justin Gorence (Orlando); Lily Knight (Gronx); Todd Duffey (Mary); Jack Donner (Cleric #1); Bob Morrisey (Crazy #1); Paul Bates (Crazy #2); Carl J. Johnson (Cleric #2); Mary Sheldon (Nurse).

NOTE: Continuing the use, sometimes in derogatory terms, of superhero lingo, Spike refers to Giles as "Captain Slow Poke" in this episode.

99. "The Weight of the World" Written by: Douglas Petrie. Directed by: David Solomon. Airdate: May 15, 2001.

Buffy slips into catatonia after losing Dawn to Glory, and Spike struggles to help the addled Scoobies realize that Glory and Ben are one in the same, since he's the only one who can see through the god's protective magic. Meanwhile, a concerned Willow uses magic to journey into Buffy's mindscape and help her find a way out of her self-imposed mental prison. At the same time, Glory begins to experience guilt and shame, emotions spilling over from Ben's human psyche. Willow helps Buffy overcome her own feelings of guilt about not being able to save Dawn, and there's a battle to fight.

GUEST CAST: Clare Kramer (Glory); Charlie Weber (Ben); Dean Butler (Mr. Summers); Kristine Sutherland (Joyce); Amber Benson (Tara); Joel Grey (Doc); Lily Knight (Gronx); Bob Morrisey.

100. "The Gift" Written and directed by: Joss Whedon. Airdate: May 22, 2001.

With Glory's ritual approaching, the deadly one that will kill Dawn and open the doorway to Hell, Buffy marshals her forces to defeat the god. The dagon sphere from the monks, Olaf's hammer and Spike's Buffybot are all recruited into service to prevent the ritual and save Dawn before her blood is spilled and dimensions blend. The battle is joined, but when the gate to Hell is opened, the Slayer must sacrifice her life to stop Glory and save the world.

GUEST CAST: Clare Kramer (Glory); Charlie Weber (Ben); Amber Benson (Tara); Joel Grey (Doc); Todd Duffey (Murk); Craig Zimmerman (Minion #1); Josh Jacobson (Tech); Tom Kiesche (Vampire).

SEASON 6 (2001–2002)

101. "Bargaining" (2 hours) Written by: Marti Noxon and David Fury. Directed by: David Grossman. Airdate: October 1, 2001.

Life goes on, after a fashion, in Sunnydale, after Buffy's death battling Glory and saving reality. The Buffybot, with help from Spike and the Scoobies, kills vampires and attends school conferences for Dawn, at least until one vampire learns that the Slayer is really deceased. Giles returns to England, and Willow, Xander, Anya and Tara plot to resurrect the real Buffy Summers utilizing a dangerous and powerful magic spell, even as demon bikers ride into Sunnydale and destroy the slayer-free town. On the night of the resurrection ritual, the evil road hellions loot the city and interrupt the ceremony, but Buffy returns. Before she can stop the demon bikers, however, she must dig free of her own grave.

GUEST CAST: Franc Ross; Amber Benson (Tara); Anthony Stewart Head (Giles); Geoff Meed (Nag); Mike Grief (Klyed); Paul Greenberg (Shempy Vamp); Joy De Michelle Moore (Ms. Lefcourt); Bru Muller (Teacher); Robert D. Vito (Cute Boy); Harry Johnson (Parent #1); Jelly Lynn Warren (Parent #2); Hila Levy (Pretty Girl); Richard Wharton (Homeowner).

102. "After Life" Written by: Jane Espenson. Directed by: David Solomon. Airdate: October 8, 2001.

Buffy is back from the dead, but not quite right, as the demon bikers flee Sunnydale. Unfortunately, a spirit from beyond the grave has returned with Buffy, a disembodied and evil wraith that can't come into full being until Buffy dies. When Willow makes the demon solid, Buffy decapitates it. Later, after the dust has settled, Buffy reveals to Spike that she was in Heaven — and yanked out of paradise by her friends.

GUEST CAST: Anthony Stewart Head (Giles); Amber Benson (Tara); Lisa Hoyle (Demon).

103. "Flooded" Written by: Douglas Petrie and Jane Espenson. Directed by: Douglas Petrie. Airdate: October 16, 2001.

The pipes in the Summers' basement explode, and that's just the beginning of Buffy's financial woes. Buffy applies for a loan, is rejected, and then seeks employment to help remedy the situation. Meanwhile, three Sunnydale geeks that fancy themselves super-villains, hire a demon to rob a bank, but the hell-beast just wants to murder the Slayer.

GUEST CAST: Anthony Stewart Head (Giles); Danny Strong (Jonathan); Adam Busch (Warren); Tom Lenk (Andrew); Amber Benson (Tara); Todd Stashwick; Michael Merton (Mr. Savitsky); John Jabalcy (Tito); Brian Kolb (Bank Guard).

NOTE: There is a reference to Spider-Man in this episode: "Action is his reward." Also, Xander calls himself "Captain Logic."

104. "Life Serial" Written by: David Fury and Jane Espenson. Directed by: Nick Marck. Airdate: October 22, 2001.

The nerdy trio, Warren, Jonathan and Andrew, tests the skill of their arch-nemesis, the Slayer. They saddle her with a variety of invasive devices, including one that alters time, and then cast a spell that puts her into a repeating time loop. Unfortunately, all of these distractions are occurring as she attempts to find a job to cure her financial woes.

GUEST CAST: Danny Strong (Jonathan); Adam Busch (Warren); Tom Lenk (Andrew); Amber Benson (Tara); Paul Gutrecht (Tony); Noel Albert Gugliemi (Vince); Jonathan Goldstein (Mike); Winsom Brown (Woman Customer).

105. "All the Way" Written by: Steven S. De Knight. Directed by: David Solomon. Airdate: October 30, 2001.

It's Halloween in Sunnydale again, which means more trouble for Buffy, especially when Dawn and a teenage friend end up on a double date with vampires. Meanwhile, Tara begins to feel troubled by Willow's excessive and inappropriate use of magic in everyday life. Xander announces to the Scoobies that he and Anya have become engaged, and Spike and Buffy start to form a closer friendship.

GUEST CAST: John O'Leary; Kavan Reece; Amber Tamblyn; Dave Power; Amber Benson (Tara); Charles Duckworth (Glenn); Dawn Worrell (Christy); Emily Kay (Maria); Adam Gordon (Carl); Steve Anthony Lawrence (Chunk Kid); Sabrina Speer (Girl); Chad Erikson (Guy); Dominic Rambaran (Paramedic #1); Anthony Sago (Paramedic #2); Lorin Becker (Witch Woman); Lily Jackson (Witchy Poo).

NOTE: "Who are you? Superman?" Dawn asks a powerful vamp in this episode.

106. "Once More, with Feeling" Written and directed by: Joss Whedon. Original Music and Lyrics by: Joss Whedon. Songs Produced and Arranged by: Jesse Tobias and Christophe Beck. Choreography: Adam Shankman. Score: Christophe Beck. Airdate: November 5, 2001.

Everyone in Sunnydale begins to sing and dance because a musical demon is in town, but all the production numbers have a terrible downside: the songs get so intense that people start to spontaneously combust! As they try to solve the riddle of the dancing, singing demon, Buffy and her friends succumb to revelatory songs. Buffy sings of her strange alienation after returning from the grave. Anya and Xander sing a duet about their fear of marriage. Spike serenades Buffy, revealing again his undying love for the Slayer. Even Giles sings a song, bemoaning the fact that his tutelage of Buffy has left her unprepared to stand on her own two feet. When Dawn is captured for sum-

moning the demon, Buffy must go it alone in a show-stopping production number...

GUEST CAST: Hinton Battle; Amber Benson (Tara); Anthony Stewart Head (Giles); David Fury (Mustard Man); Marti Noxon (Parking Ticket Woman); Daniel Weaver (Handsome Young Man); Icot Zeller (Henchman); Zachary Woodlee (Demon/Henchman); Timothy Anderson (Henchman); Alex Estronel (Henchman); Matt Jini (College Guy #1); Hunter Cochran (College Guy #2).

107. "Tabula Rosa" Written by: Rebecca Rand Kirshner. Directed by: David Grossman. Airdate: November 13, 2001.

The Scoobies are in chaos following their revelatory songs. Giles is bound and determined to return to England so Buffy can handle things on her own, and Tara is ready to split with Willow over her overuse of magic spells. Hoping to correct matters, Willow secretly uses Lethe's Bramble to help Buffy and Tara forget their respective hurts, but the spell goes wrong and causes all the Scoobies, including Spike, to lose their memories. The amnesia is especially poorly timed since a nasty loan shark is in Sunnydale looking to collect from Spike.

GUEST CAST: Anthony Stewart Head (Giles); Amber Benson (Tara); Raymon O'Connor; Geordie White (Vamp #1); Stephen Triplett (Vamp #2); David Franco (Vamp #3).

NOTE: Stricken with amnesia, Buffy uses her Slayer powers and notes, "I'm like a superhero or something!"

108. "Smashed" Written by: Drew Z. Greenberg. Directed by: Turi Meyer. Airdate: November 21, 2001.

Feeling abandoned and alone after Tara's departure, Willow conjures a way to turn Amy, a fellow witch that was transformed into a rat in high school, back into a human being. But Amy is a bad influence, and encourages Willow's use of magic. Meanwhile, Jonathan, Warren and Andrew — the self-proclaimed "Trio of Doom" — steal a diamond from a museum and use a freeze ray to immobilize a security guard. Spike helps Buffy investigate the case, and continues to get closer to the Slayer. When Spike learns that the chip in his head doesn't prevent him from fighting Buffy — who came back from the grave "less human" — the vampire uses the knowledge to seduce the Slayer.

GUEST CAST: Danny Strong (Jonathan); Adam Busch (Warren); Tom Lenk (Andrew); Elizabeth Anne Allen (Amy); Amber Benson (Tara); Patrice Walters (Woman); John Patrick Clerkin (Man); Jack Jozefson (Rusty); Rick Garcia (Reporter); Kelly Smith (Innocent Girl); Jordan Belfi (Ryan); Adam Weiner (Simon); Melanie Sirmons (Brie); Lauren Nissi (Girlfriend).

109. "Wrecked" Written by: Marti Noxon. Directed by: David Solomon. Airdate: November 27, 2001.

Buffy feels guilty after making love to Spike, and Willow continues to spiral out of control in her overuse of magic. Willow and Amy go to see a powerful warlock, Rack, who can grant them great powers, but at great cost. Soon Willow is addicted to Rack's magic, and she endangers Dawn's life. Spike and Buffy, still squabbling about their on-again-off-again sexual shenanigans, come to Dawn's rescue, and a strung-out Willow finally renounces magic.

GUEST CAST: Elizabeth Anne Allen (Amy); Jeff Kober (Rack); Amber Benson (Tara); Fleming Brooks (Mandraz); Mageina Tovah (Jonesing Girl); Michael Giordani (Jonesing Guy); Colin Malone (Creepy Guy).

110. "Gone" Written and directed by: David Fury. Airdate: January 8, 2002.

Willow goes cold turkey on magic and Buffy tries to steer clear of Spike. Meanwhile, the Trio of Doom develops an Invisibility Ray. Disturbed after a social worker puts her on probation for inadequate guardianship of Dawn, Buffy cuts her long hair. But coming home from the salon, she is accidentally rendered invisible by the nerds. Buffy has fun being invisible, torturing the officious social worker and playing sexual hide and seek games with Spike. But the condition could prove fatal if not corrected...

GUEST CAST: Danny Strong (Jonathan); Adam Busch (Warren); Tom Lenk (Andrew); Daniel Hagen; Susan Ruttan (Doris Kroger); Jessa French (Cleo); Kelly Parver (Girl in Park); Jeffrey Jacquin (Meter Man); Dwight Bacquie (Security Guard); Lyndon Smith (Little Boy); Melina Webberley (Little Girl); Elin Hampton (Co-Worker).

111. "Doublemeat Palace" Written by: Jane Espenson. Directed by: Nick Marck. Airdate: January 29, 2002.

Buffy gets a job at the fast food restaurant Doublemeat Palace and almost instantly suspects that the secret ingredient in their burgers may be human flesh. When she learns several employees have mysteriously vanished from the restaurant, her suspicions seem valid. Meanwhile, a demon friend of Anya's sows seeds of discontent in the ex–vengeance demon about her impending nuptials. Willow's witch friend and bad influence, Amy, drops by the house and throws Willow off the wagon.

GUEST CAST: Elizabeth Anne Allen (Amy); Pat Crawford Brown; Brent Hinkley; Kirsten Nelson; Kali Rocha; T. Ferguson (Gary); Marion Calvert (Gina); Douglas Bennett (Phillip); Andrew Reville (Timothy); Kevin C. Carter (Mr. Typical); John F. Kearney (Elderly Man); Sara La Wall (Housewife Type); Victor Z. Isaac (Pimply Teen).

112. "Dead Things" Written by: Steven S. De Knight. Directed by: James A. Contner. Airdate: February 5, 2002.

Warren, Jonathan and Andrew — the so-called Nerds of Doom — develop a cerebral dampener that turns women into their willing sex slaves. They test the machine on Katrina, Warren's former girlfriend, but when she learns what they've done she attempts to tell the authorities. Warren accidentally kills Katrina during the ensuing scuffle and, with the help of his cohorts and some strange demons, makes Buffy believe she murdered the innocent girl. Spike attempts to prevent Buffy from turning herself in to the police for the crime, but Buffy is convinced that her relationship with the seductive Spike is just another symptom that she came back from the grave wrong.

GUEST CAST: Danny Strong (Jonathan); Adam Busch (Warren); Tom Lenk (Andrew); Amelinda Embry (Katrina Silver); Amber Benson (Tara); Marion Calvert (Gina); Rock Reiser (Desk Sgt.); Bernard K. Addison (Cop #1); Eric Prescott (Cop #2).

113. "Older and Far Away" Written by: Drew Greenberg. Directed by: David Grossman. Airdate: February 11, 2002.

Anya's vengeance demon friend, Halfrek, masquerades as a school counselor and exploits Dawn's desire to be "closer" to all the important people in her life, including Buffy. Halfrek grants Dawn's wish, trapping Buffy, Spike, and the rest of the Scoobies in the Summers house for all eternity. Worse, they are trapped inside the home with a murderous demon.

GUEST CAST: Kali Rocha (Halfrek); Amber Benson (Tara); James C. Leary, Laura Roth, Ryan Browning.

114. "As You Were" Written and directed by: Douglas Petrie. Airdate: February 25, 2002.

Riley Finn returns to Sunnydale on a desperately important mission and recruits Buffy right from her shift at the Doublemeat Palace to help. Now a happily married man, Riley's still in the military and special ops, and is pursuing a dangerous demon, a breeder that has laid eggs in town. While hunting the beast and its lair, Buffy is introduced to Sam, Riley's gung-ho commando wife, and she experiences pangs of jealousy. Unfortunately, the trail of demons leads to a black market dealer called the Doctor ... Spike himself.

GUEST CAST: Marc Blucas (Riley Finn); Ivana Milicevic (Samantha Finn); Ryan Raddatz (Todd); Adam Paul (Skanky Vamp); Marilyn Brett (Lady); Alice Dinnean Vernon (Baby Demon Puppeteer).

115. "Hell's Bells" Written by: Rebecca Rand Kirshner. Directed by: David Solomon. Airdate: March 4, 2002.

Xander's family and Anya's demon relatives come together for the big wedding day, but a strange visitor — who claims to be Xander of the future — arrives to stop the festivities. He takes Xander aside before the ceremony and shows him a miserable future in which Buffy is dead and Anya and he are bitter old companions, abusive and angry. Fearful of hurting Anya, Xander leaves her at the altar. Betrayed, Anya is given a chance to become a vengeance demon once more.

GUEST CAST: Kali Rocha (Halfrek); Amber Benson (Tara); Casey Sander, Andy Umberger, Lee Garlington, Jan Hoga, George D. Wallace, Steven Gilborn.

116. "Normal Again" Written by: Diego Gutierrez. Directed by: Rick Rosenthal. Airdate: March 11, 2002.

Buffy searches for the three villainous nerds (Jonathan, Warren and Andrew), but when she gets close to their new rental property, the trio summons a strange demon to stop her. The demon stabs Buffy, injecting her with a serum that alters her sense of reality and makes her believe she is actually a sick girl in an insane asylum, merely imagining all these strange adventures. Meanwhile, Xander returns to Sunnydale to make reparations with Anya only to find her gone. Hoping to free herself of her super-heroic delusions, Buffy plots to kill Xander, Willow and Dawn.

GUEST CAST: Danny Strong (Jonathan); Adam Busch (Warren); Tom Lenk (Andrew); Dean Butler (Mr. Summers); Kristine Sutherland (Joyce Summers); Amber Benson (Tara); Michael Warren; Kirsten Nelson; Sarah Scivier (Nurse); Rodney Charles (Orderly); April Dion (Kissing Girl).

117. "Entropy" Written by: Drew Z. Greenberg. Directed by: James A. Contner. Airdate: April 29, 2002.

Spike continues to press Buffy to tell her friends about their relationship, even as Anya returns to Sunnydale as a demon herself, bent on wreaking bloody vengeance upon Xander for leaving her at the altar. Meanwhile, the Nerds of Doom plot to become invincible and steal a fortune. When Buffy learns that the trio has bugged the Doublemeat Palace, her home, the Bronze and other locales to keep an eye on her, Willow taps into the video feed and catches an intimate moment in the Magic Shop: a tryst between Spike and Anya.

GUEST CAST: Danny Strong (Jonathan); Adam Busch (Warren); Tom Lenk (Andrew); Kali Rocha (Halfrek); Amber Benson (Tara).

118. "Seeing Red" Written by: Steven S. De Knight. Directed by: Michael Gershman. Airdate: May 7, 2002.

Tara and Willow have reconciled, but Buffy is still hurting from Spike's fling with Anya. Buffy pursues the three nerds to their property, but they've set a deadly trap for her with buzz saws. They steal the ancient Orbs of Nezlakon to become invincible, until Buffy steals back their magic balls. Stripped of his magical powers, Warren shoots Buffy, and a stray bullet kills Tara.

GUEST CAST: Danny Strong (Jonathan); Adam Busch (Warren); Tom Lenk (Andrew); Amy Hathaway; Nichole Heltz; James Leary (Clem); Garrett Brawith (Frank); Tim Hager (Administrator); Stefan Marks (Guard #1); Christopher James (Guard #2); Kate Orsini (Girl at Bronze).

119. "Villains" Written by: Marti Noxon. Directed by: David Solomon. Airdate: May 14, 2002.

With Tara dead, Willow uses magic to pursue Warren, even as Buffy recovers from a gunshot wound in the hospital. Gone "dark" with terrible black magic, Willow is unstoppable in her wrath. Even flaying

Warren alive in the woods can't sate Willow's fury, so she decides to go after Jonathan and Andrew, now in jail. Meanwhile, Spike travels to Africa to face a challenge and be rewarded with a soul.

GUEST CAST: Danny Strong (Jonathan); Adam Busch (Warren); Tom Lenk (Andrew); Jeff Kober (Rack); Amelinda Embry; James C. Leary (Clem); Steven W. Bailey (Cave Demon); Tim Hodgin (Coroner); Michael Matthys (Paramedic); Julie Hermelin (Clerk); Alan Henry Brown (Demon Bartender); Maueen J. Ahmad (Doctor); Jane Cho (Nurse #1); Meredith Cross (Nurse #2); David Adefeso (Paramedic #2); Jeffrey Nicholas Brown (Vampire); Nelson Frederick (Villager).

120. "Two to Go" Written by: Douglas Petrie. Directed by: Bill Norton. Airdate: May 21, 2002.

Willow's pain over the loss of Tara is so immense that she pursues Jonathan and Andrew, even though they were not responsible for Tara's death. Buffy swears to protect the two nerds, not out of love, but to prevent Willow from crossing a moral line. The battle lines are drawn, however, when Willow finds Buffy and the nerds in the Magic Shop. Now it's Slayer versus Wicca — to the death.

GUEST CAST: Anthony Steward Head (Giles); Danny Strong (Jonathan); Tom Lenk (Andrew); Jeff Kober (Rack); Steven W. Bailey (Cave Demon); Jeff McCredie (Officer); Damian Mooney (Patrol Cop); Michael Young (Truck Driver); Brett Wanger (Trucker).

121. "Grave" Written by: David Fury. Directed by: James A. Contner. Airdate: May 21, 2002.

Willow and Buffy face off to the death in the Magic Box, but Giles teleports from England to intervene. Willow absorbs Giles new magical powers (given him by a powerful coven) and decides that the pain of the world is so immense that she must destroy it. As Willow plans to channel energy through a long-buried Satanic cathedral, Buffy and Dawn must battle underground demons, raised by their friend, in a cave beneath Sunnydale. Finally, in Africa, Spike survives several demonic challenges and is rewarded ... with a soul!

GUEST CAST: Anthony Stewart Head (Giles); Danny Strong (Jonathan); Tom Lenk (Andrew).

SEASON 7 (2002-2003)

122. "Lessons" Written by: Joss Whedon. Directed by: David Solomon. Airdate: September 24, 2002.

Willow recovers in Westbury, England, from her experience with the dark side, while back in Sunnydale Dawn begins to attend the new high school, rebuilt and reconstructed. Unfortunately, the new school is also built on the hellmouth and apparently haunted. Corporeal ghosts (raised by a talisman) attack Dawn in the bathroom and drag her down to the basement with two new friends, while Buffy runs into Spike, who has been driven crazy by his abruptly-returned soul. Buffy is offered a job as an outreach counselor by the new school principal, Mr. Wood.

GUEST CAST: Anthony Stewart Heard (Giles); Alex Breckenridge; Kali Rocha (Halfrek); D.B. Woodside (Principal Wood); Mark Metcalf (The Master); Juliet Landau (Drusilla); Harry Groener (Mayor Wilkins); George Hertzberg (Adam); Clare Kramer (Glory); Adam Busch (Warren); David Zepeda (Carlos); Jeremy Howard (Dead Nerd); Ken Strunk (Dead Janitor); Rachael Bella (Dead Girl); Ed F. Martin (Teacher); Simon Chernin (Student); Jeff Denton (Vampire).

123. "Beneath You" Written by: Douglas Petrie. Directed by: Nick Marck. Airdate: October 1, 2002.

Buffy dreams of a slayer's death in Frankfurt, Germany, and receives a vision that something from "beneath" will come to "devour" the living. At the same time, a monstrous worm attacks a new resident in Sunnydale, a girl named Nancy, and a repentant Spike helps Buffy track it down. Xander goes to Anya when he learns she turned Nancy's former boyfriend into the worm, but there is still bad blood between them. Buffy learns that Spike has a soul.

GUEST CAST: Anthony Stewart Head (Giles); Kaarina Au Franc (Nancy); D.B. Woodside (Principal Wood); Tess Hall (Punk Girl); Jack Sundmacher (Ronnie).

124. "Same Time, Same Place" Written by: Jane Espenson. Directed by: James A. Contner. Airdate: October 8, 2002.

After months in England being rehabilitated by Giles, Willow returns to Sunnydale only to realize she can't see her friends and they can't see her. Meanwhile, Buffy contends with Gnarl, a demon that paralyzes and then eats the skin of its victims. Willow also learns of Gnarl and sets out to kill him to redeem herself in the eyes of her friends. But Willow becomes trapped inside a cave with the demon, where it paralyzes her and begins to peel off strips of her skin.

GUEST CAST: Camden Toy (Gnarl); Anthony S. Johnson (Father); Matt Koruba (Teen Boy); Nicholette Dixon (Sister); Marshe Daniel (Brother).

125. "Help" Written by: Rebecca Rand Kushner. Directed by: Rick Rosenthal. Airdate: October 15, 2002.

Buffy deals with her first week as a counselor to the students at Sunnydale High, while Willow summons the strength to visit Tara's grave. Buffy meets an introspective but lively girl named Cassie who believes with all her heart that she is going to die within a week. Seeking out Spike's help to solve the mystery, Buffy finds a cult planning to sacrifice Cassie to a demon. But can Cassie's fate be changed, even with the intervention of the Slayer?

GUEST CAST: Azura Skye (Cassie Newton); Zachery Bryan; Glenn Morshower (Mr. Newton); Rick Gonzalez; D.B. Woodside (Principal Wood); J. Barton (Mike); Daniel Dehring (Red Robed #1); A.J. Wedding (Red Robed #2); Marcie Lynn Ross (Dead Woman).

126. "Anya" Written by: Drew Goddard. Directed by: David Solomon. Airdate: October 22, 2002.

As a vengeance demon, Anya executes a wish, resulting in a house full of dead fraternity brothers, their hearts torn out by a spider-like demon. After killing the demon, Buffy realizes she may have to kill Anya, and Xander objects. Buffy cannot be deterred, however, and faces down Anya, who has been dwelling on her long existence and history as a vengeance demon. Finally, Anya must pay a price for the deaths she has caused.

GUEST CAST: Abraham Benrubi (Olaf); Andy Umberger; Kali Rocha (Halfrek); Joyce Guy; Jennifer Schon; Taylor Sutherland (Villager #1); Marybeth Scherr (Villager #2); Alessandro Mastrobuono (Villager #3); Daniel Spanton (Viking #1); John Timmons (Viking #2).

127. "Him" Written by: Drew Z. Greenberg. Directed by: Michael Gershman. Airdate: November 5, 2002.

Spike moves out of the high school basement into Xander's apartment, while Dawn falls hard for a football quarterback. The crush makes Dawn act violently, and she pushes a competing athlete down the stairs. It turns out there is a love spell attached to the quarterback's letter jacket, one that affects not just Dawn but Buffy, Anya and even Willow. Now Spike and Xander must set things right before lust leads to murder.

GUEST CAST: Thad Luckinbill; Brandon Keener; W.B. Woodside (Professor Wood).

128. "Conversations with Dead People" Written by: Jane Espenson and Drew Goddard. Directed by: Nick Marck. Airdate: November 12, 2002.

The dead come calling in Sunnydale to warn of a coming apocalypse, including Joyce Summers, who pays Dawn a terrifying visit. Aware of encroaching evil, Andrew and Jonathan also return to Sunnydale to complete a secret task inside the high school basement, while Tara communicates from beyond the grave with Willow via an unusual proxy.

In a cemetery, Buffy fights a psychologically adroit vampire and former classmate.

GUEST CAST: Danny Strong (Jonathan); Adam Busch (Warren); Tom Lenk (Andrew); Kristine Sutherland (Joyce Summers); Azura Skye (Cassie); Jonathan Woodward.

129. "Sleeper" Written by: David Fury and Jane Espenson. Directed by: Alan J. Levi. Airdate: November 19, 2002.

Buffy is fearful that Spike has returned to his murderous ways, even though he denies it. Spike remembers his crimes — ten of them — and leads Buffy to the source, but it is a trap. A shape-shifting entity — a diabolical evil — is manipulating Spike to some dark end. Meanwhile, in England, Giles learns that the same dark evil has been murdering slayers-in-training.

GUEST CAST: Anthony Stewart Head (Rupert Giles); Robinne Lee, Rob Nagle.

130. "Never Leave Me" Written by: Drew Goddard. Directed by: David Soloman. Airdate: November 26, 2002.

Buffy realizes that to understand the evil threatening Sunnydale, she must stay close to Spike, who has been brainwashed. Meanwhile, Willow runs into Andrew, who is serving the same dark evil (this time appearing in the spectral form of the murdered Warren). In England, Quentin Travers and the Watchers Council desperately search for the missing Giles, and declare war on the evil threatening them, actually "the First," the most ancient of all terrors. In Sunnydale, the minions of "the First" use Spike in a ritual to resurrect a terrifying vampire.

GUEST CAST: Danny Strong (Jonathan); Adam Busch (Warren); Tom Lenk (Andrew); Cynthia LaMontagne; Oliver Muirhead; Kris Iyer; Harris Yulin (Quentin Travers); D.B. Woodside (Principal Wood); Donald Bishop (Butcher); Camden Toy (Ubervamp); Bobby Brewer (Hoffman); Roberto Santos (Grimes).

NOTE: Buffy's seventh season ended with a bang and included a visit from Faith. At least one Scooby died in the finale, and Spike completed his journey to redemption.

Captain America

Of all the superheroes that have made the leap to television and film, poor Captain America has been treated the most shabbily, relegated to two cheesy 1970s TV-movies starring Reb Brown and a low-budget direct-to-video clunker in the late 1980s. Created by Marvel's Joe Simon (who reportedly sold his rights to the character for a measly $3,750 in 1969) [1] and Jack Kirby, the Captain America mythos, as his name indicates, is a paean to patriotism, a particularly valuable commodity in the post–September 11, 2001, world.

Decked out in a costume of red, white and blue, this all–American hero first appeared in early 1941— well before the attack on Pearl Harbor — in Marvel's book *Captain America Comics*. On the cover of his first issue, the Captain was seen going *mano-a-mano* with none other than Adolf Hitler.

The story of Captain America was a rousing one. The hero began his life as Steve Rogers, an ordinary fellow not unlike Peter Parker, something of a scrawny featherweight, a kid that couldn't even fight in World War II because of his physical frailty. But Rogers' heart was pure and patriotic, and he was selected by Professor Reinstein and the U.S. government to take an experimental formula that would turn him into a physically superior super-soldier. "We shall call you Captain America … because like you, America shall gain the strength and the will to safeguard our shores," declared Reinstein upon Cap's creation in the lab after an injection of the formula.[2]

It couldn't have been said better, and America had a new hero. Unfortunately, Captain America was not only the first super-soldier created, but also the last, because Reinstein was murdered by a spy before any more could be forged. Nonetheless, Cap became a singular success in the war effort, battling against the Nazis with the help of an enthusiastic sidekick in the military named Bucky Barnes. Their primary enemy was the Red Skull, the psychotic Nazi agent with a bloated-looking scarlet skullcap.

With all of his flag-waving love of America, Captain America was a national hit, and in 1944 Republic released a 15-chapter serial based on his exploits. Starring Dick Purcell, and featuring Captain America in mortal combat with a villain called "Scarab," the film took great liberties with the character, restricting Captain America to U.S. soil, far from the European front, and tampering with his origin (making him, of all things, a lawyer).

World War II came to an end, with the U.S. victorious over the Axis powers, and *Captain America* comics, by necessity, changed with the times. Bucky left the series in the late 1940s, replaced by a woman sidekick named Betsy Ross. Despite the change, the comic series collapsed, only to be revived in the mid–1950s with a new Captain America (and Bucky too) returning to battle a new "Red" threat, this time Communism! The new anti–Soviet approach didn't necessarily take (and years later these stories were shunted aside as being the adventures of a *different* Captain America), and the hero disappeared once more — until another revival came along ten years later.

This time, Captain America (who had conveniently been frozen in Arctic ice for two decades) found himself alive and well in the 1960s, where he joined the Avengers (an association of heroes, including Giant-Man, Thor, Iron Man, Namor the Sub-Mariner and the Hulk). At that point, Captain America was especially upset about the death of his companion, Bucky, and uncertain of what a new Cold War future would entail for him. He shouldn't have worried—it only involved more successful comics, and Captain America has been going strong since his 1960s revival. He appeared in animated form in the mid–1960s TV series *The Marvel Superheroes*, along with his comic compatriots the Hulk, the Sub-Mariner, Iron Man and Thor.

His success established, one might think that Captain America would be the perfect source material for a contemporary motion picture or even a live-action TV series, but America's hero has had a particularly tough time in that regard. The 1940s serial *Captain America* was quickly forgotten, and in 1979 came the second take on the material, a TV movie that was equally unfaithful to the core concepts of the character created by Simon and Kirby.

This time around, beefy actor Reb Brown played Steve Rogers, the son of a great patriot and "super crime fighter" who had been disparagingly saddled with the name "Captain America" by his enemies. Before he died, Steve's father developed a steroid called F.L.A.G.—Full Latent Ability Gain. F.L.A.G. could allow a man (who usually only uses one-third of his capacities) to use 100 percent of his gifts. Steve Jr., naturally, was the only person in the world that could take F.L.A.G. and survive, becoming the super-soldier his dad was.

The only problem with this approach (besides the fact that it was set in the 1970s) was that the new Steve Rogers was envisioned as the opposite of his comic book namesake. He was not patriotic at all, and did not want to serve his country or government in a time of danger (facing off against a villain that had developed a neutron bomb for something called "Project Zeus").

In the comics, Captain America understood the importance of sacrifice, and, indeed, had given up family, friends and a normal life to defeat the Nazi evil. The 1970s Captain America was of the "me" gen-

eration. This is what he had to say about fighting evil, quoted directly from the show, penned by author Don Ingalls:

> I just want to get out on the road, look at the faces of America…. I don't want to report in or check out. I don't want to look forward to weekends…. I want every day to be the same. I just want to kick back and find out who I am.

For any other superhero, perhaps, this manifesto of self-discovery and "groovy" introspection might have been acceptable or even rather timely, but for stalwart Captain America? Not likely!

In addition to so radical a re-think of Captain America's mind-set, the two TV movies suffered from their selection of a leading actor. Reb Brown is a beefed-up muscle-head that exudes no intelligence or cunning whatsoever, a prerequisite for this particular hero, a dyed-in-the-wool Nazi smasher. "Who is mad at me?" he questions, empty-headed, at one critical juncture in the TV movie, and the character comes off as incredibly stupid and pathetic.

On top of all that, the producer of the TV movie (Allan Balter) even had the audacity to change Captain America's uniform. In the comics, he wore a form-fitting, soft, open-mouthed blue mask. In the TV movie, he wore a motorcycle helmet with goggles instead. Sure, he still had the red gloves, the blue cat suit and the letter "A" emblazoned on head gear, but the feel was entirely different—and inappropriate. Like the Nicholas Hammond Spider-Man costume of the 1970s, this new Captain America fashion was clunky and graceless, a far cry from the comics.

The second *Captain America* TV movie, *Death Too Soon*, was not particularly inspiring either. This time, Rogers (Reb Brown again) faced off against the villainous Christopher Lee as a terrorist named "Miguel." Described in the teleplay only as a "revolutionary," Miguel planned to blackmail American cities. If he wasn't paid a king's ransom, he would deploy a biological weapon, an instant aging chemical compound, on the unsuspecting populace.

The second *Captain America* TV movie featured a spectacular chase on a dam, filmed from a helicopter. During the action scene, Captain America, on his trademark motorcycle, went head to head with a squad of jeeps, and it proved rousing — considering the inaction of the remainder of the movie. During the climax, Cap's motorcycle turned into a hang-glider, which came in handy for catching Miguel (who was infected with his own aging compound at the climax).

Taken together, the two *Captain America* tele-films were a bit on the boring side; but, more importantly, they reinvented the character as a post–*Easy Rider* "artist" on a journey of self-discovery in his cool '70s van. Each TV movie featured too many shots of Rogers toolin' around the scenic West Coast in his van, helping those he would come across. Overall, the re-tool seemed pretty aimless.

A groovy kind of hero for the 1970s: Reb Brown as Captain America. Notice the updates in the character's uniform, including a transparent shield and a motorcycle helmet.

Captain America fans had high hopes that all that would change in the late 1980s. It was announced that Menahem Golan, in association with Marvel, would shepherd the famous hero to the big screen. In the age of superhero megahits like Tim Burton's *Batman*, it seemed a promising idea, but the movie, released in 1989, was so bad that it went straight to video and never played theaters.

At least the film boasted an interesting cast (Matt Salinger as Captain America, Ronny Cox as the President of the United States and Scott Paulin as Red Skull), and was relatively faithful to the Captain America ethos. Oddly, however, Red Skull was now an Italian, not a Nazi! In the end, however, the film proved to be another embarrassment, primarily because of its low budget and really horrendous special effects. Rear projection and inadequate miniatures rendered much of the action laughable.

In *Captain America* (1989), a young Steve Rogers joined "Project Rebirth" to become a World War II super-soldier for his government and oppose Red Skull, an Italian super-soldier created at Fortress Lorenzo for the Axis Powers. After becoming super-strong, and dealing with the assassination of his creator, Captain America undertook his first international mission: to prevent Red Skull from launching a deadly rocket attack on America. Strapped to the rocket by his nemesis, Captain America barely succeeded in saving the White House, and was then frozen for some 50 years — until 1990, when he had to take on the Red Skull again.

The problem with the material this

Back to basics: Matt Salinger is Steve Rogers in *Captain America* (1989). At least the costume was more authentic to the comic books this time.

and RFK assassinations. Thus America's great hero disappeared just when he was needed most!

It is also a disappointment that this film, directed by Albert Pyun, chose not to depict Bucky, but perhaps this energetic little character is today considered too clichéd. Though the movie does afford more emotional investment than the two 1970s TV movies, in part because it is about a man who has lost much of his life for fifty years, it is hampered by weak special effects and disappointing fisticuffs. The final battle between Red Skull and Captain America is barely noteworthy, let alone exciting.

September 11, 2001, re-ignited patriotism in America, and one can only hope that this will lead to the re-birth of a great hero that has not had much success at the movies. In recent years, there has been talk that Tom Cruise might step into the role, and he would seem to be a perfect choice to carry the Captain America mythos into the 21st century.

time was that Captain America was a disaster as a hero — he failed to stop the Red Skull, and, while Cap was unconscious, Red Skull continued to terrorize the world, claiming responsibility for the JFK, MLK

Captain America (1979)
LIVE–ACTION TV MOVIE

CAST: Reb Brown (Steve Rogers); Len Birman (Simon Mills); Heather Menzies (Wendy); Joseph Ruskin (Sandrini); Steve Forrest (Lou Brackett); Frank Marth; Lance LeGault; Chip Johnson; James Ingersoll (Lester Wiant); Jim B. Smith (F.B.I. Assistant); Jason Wingreen (Surgeon); June Dayton (Secretary); Diana Webster (Nurse); Dan Barton (Jeff Haden); Ken Chandler (First Doctor); Buster Jones (Anesthetist).

CREW: *Director of Photography:* Ronald W. Browne. *Executive Producer:* Allan Balter. *Teleplay:* Don Ingalls. *Story:* Don Ingalls, Chester Krumholz. *Directed by:* Rod Holcomb. *Associate Producer:* Martin Goldstein. *Music:* Mike Post and Pete Carpenter. *Art Director:* Lou Monte-jano. *Film Editor:* Michael S. Murphy. *Set Decorator:* Rich Reams. *Sound:* Bill Griffith. *Consultant:* Stan Lee. *Casting:* Joseph Z. Reich. *Unit Production Manager:* D. Jack Stubbs. *First Assistant Director:* Tom Connors III. *Second Assistant Director:* Mark Schilz. *Sound Effects Editor:* Bruce Bell. *Music Editor:* Ted Roberts. *Costume Design:* Charles Waldo. *Costume Supervisor:* Ron Archer. *Titles and Opticals:* Universal Title. *Running time:* 98 minutes.

Steve Rogers, son of a dead scientist, is called in to visit a secret government laboratory where he meets Simon Mills and Dr. Wendy Day, who want him to submit to tests of a super hormone, a steroid developed by his father called F.L.A.G. (Full Latent Ability Gain). He refuses to help until a friend, Jeff, is found murdered, killed as part of a conspiracy orchestrated by an oil tycoon named Brackett.

Steve learns that Brackett is developing a neutron bomb, and the criminal's men promptly set up a terrible motorbike accident to silence the interloper. Simon and Wendy give Steve the untested F.L.A.G. formula to save his life and heal his injuries. When Steve awakens, he still refuses to help; but when captured by Brackett's goons, Steve uses his newfound strength to overpower them at a meatpacking plant.

Recruited by Simon, and provided with a souped-up motorcycle and bulletproof shield, Steve again clashes with Brackett's men on a back-road training ground. He captures a helicopter with his super agility, increased hearing and superior vision.

Then, in his new guise as Captain America, Steve rushes to prevent Brackett from detonating his neutron bomb. He learns Brackett is planning to rob a gold repository in Phoenix, and Captain America intercepts Brackett's truck en route.

Captain America II: Death Too Soon (1980)
LIVE-ACTION TV MOVIE

CAST: Reb Brown (Steve Rogers/Captain America); Connie Sellecca (Dr. Day); Len Birman (Simon); Christopher Lee (Miguel); Katherine Justice (Helen Moore); Stanley Kamel (Kramer); Ken Swofford (Mr. Bliss); Lana Wood (Yolanda); Bill Lucking; Christopher Cary; Arthur Rosenberg (Doctor); Bill Mims (Dr. J. Brenner); Alex Hyde-White (Young Man); Lacheke Chamberlain (Young Girl); Susan French (Mrs. Shaw); Jahn Waldron (Peter Moore).

CREW: *Film Editor:* Michael S. Murphy. *Art Director:* David L. Snyder. *Director of Photography:* Vincent A. Martinelli. *Executive Producer:* Allan Balter. *Written by:* Wilton Schiller and Patricia Payne. *Directed by:* Ivan Nagy. *Second Unit Director:* Rod Holcomb. *Music Score:* Mike Post and Pete Carpenter. *Associate Producer:* Martin Goldstein. *Set Decorator:* Robert George Freer. *Sound:* Jerry E. Smith. *Consultant:* Stan Lee. *Casting:* Joe Reich. *Titles and Opticals:* Universal Title. *Unit Production Manager:* Ralph S. Singleton. *First Assistant Director:* Pat Duffy. *Second Assistant Directors:* Steven Saeta, Barry Wetherby. *Sound Effects Editor:* Bruce Bell. *Music Editor:* Ted Roberts. *Costume Designer:* Yvonne Wood. *Running time:* 88 minutes.

Steve Rogers continues to fight crime as Captain America, battling a gang preying on the elderly at a West Coast beach community. It isn't long, however, before the U.S. government needs Captain America again, this time to solve the mystery of a vanished immunologist that was working on a program to reverse the aging process. The prime suspect is a foreign revolutionary, a terrorist named Miguel.

Unbeknownst to Steve, Miguel is masquerading as a warden at a Federal penitentiary and forcing the abducted scientist to develop a drug that will spur rapid aging instead of slow it down. It is Miguel's plan to deploy the aging drug in a major American city unless his ransom demand, one billion dollars, is met by the government.

Steve tracks down a shipment of the immunologist's drugs to a small town where all the residents live in fear. After being attacked by five thugs with baseball bats, Steve befriends a single mom, Helen Moore, and her boy, who run a farm together. He learns that Miguel's forces are controlling the town, experimenting on livestock and threatening the populace. When the U.S. government refuses to negotiate with the terrorists, Miguel's men spray Portland with the rapid-aging gas.

Steve learns that the town of Belleville

lives in thrall to Miguel because it was the test site for his drug and all the people were exposed, then given just enough of the antidote to keep them under Miguel's thumb. Steve is able to track Miguel's operation back to the Waterford Penitentiary, with Helen's help.

Captain America battles Miguel, fending off contaminated laboratory dogs made crazy by the aging drug. He rescues the missing immunologist, but Miguel escapes the prison with vials of the drug. Captain America pursues on his motorcycle-turned-hang-glider, and in their final confrontation Miguel is splattered with a sample of the fast-aging agent and accelerated to death. With Miguel out of the way, Captain America sprays the antidote over Portland and saves the town of Belleville.

Captain America (1989)
LIVE-ACTION FILM

"The superhero movie takes another giant leap *backward*.... [It] degenerates into a meaningless collection of pitifully produced gun-and-fistfights that makes the 1979 Reb Brown made-for-television version look spectacular in comparison."

— S.C. Dacy, *Cinefantastique*, Volume 21, #2: "Film Ratings," September 1990, page 53.

"Held from release for two years before being dropped onto video shelves ... the movie isn't merely wrong for kids ... it's just all wrong. The shapeless blob of a plot pits Cap against his Marvel Comics foe, the Nazi Red Skull (Scott Paulin), now inexplicably Italian and mostly seen without a red skull..."

— Frank Lovece, *Entertainment Weekly*, July 31, 1992, page 74.

CAST: Matt Salinger (Steve Rogers/Captain America); Ronny Cox (President Tom Kimball); Ned Beatty (Sam Kalowitz); Darren McGavin (General Fleming); Michael Nouri (Colonel Lewis); Melinda Dillon (Mrs. Rogers); Francesca Neri (Valentina de Samalis); Bill Mumy (Young Fleming); Kim Gillingham (Bernice/Sharon); Scott Paulin (Red Skull); Carla Cassola (Dr. Maria Vaselli); Massimilio Massimi (Vodzio De Santis); Wayde Preston (Jack); Norbert Weisser (Alaskan Surveyor); Garette Ratliff (Young Tom Kimball); Bernarda Oman (Vadzio's Mother).

CREW: 21st Century Film Corp., in Association with Marvel Entertainment Group, Inc., presents a Menahem Golan Production of a film by Albert Pyun, *Captain America. Associate Producer:* Stephen Tolkin. *Line Producer:* Tom Karnowski. *Film Editor:* Jon Poll. *Production Design:* Douglas Leonard. *Music:* Barry Goldberg. *Director of Photography:* Philip Alan Waters. *Executive Producers:* Stan Lee, Joseph Calamari. *Based on Characters created by:* Joe Simon, Jack Kirby. *Screenplay by:* Stephen Tolkin. *Story by:* Stephen Tolkin, Lawrence J. Block. *Produced by:* Menahem Golan. *Directed by:* Albert Pyun. *Unit Production Manager:* Marc S. Fisher. *First Assistant Director:* Michael Katleman. *Special Visual Effects:* Fantasy II Film Effects. *Special Make-up Effects:* Greg Cannom. *Costume Design:* Heidi Lkaczenski. *Music Supervisors:* Evyen J. Klean, Paul Broucek. *Casting:* Ann Bell, Teri Blythe, Anna Dunn. *Production Supervisor:* Joel De Loache. *M.P.A.A. Rating:* PG. *Running time:* 103 minutes.

In 1936, the Axis Powers attempt to create super-soldiers, but their strange experiments result in the incredibly intelligent abomination called Red Skull — once a normal boy, now mutated and twisted by evil.

Several years later, an escaped scientist, Dr. Vaselli, helps the Americans perfect the dangerous "super-soldier" technique using a scrawny young man named Steve Rogers. The experiment is a success and Steve is code-named Captain America (as the living symbol of U.S. values). Though super strong, even Captain America is unable to prevent the assassination of Dr. Vaselli by an Axis spy.

Captain America's first mission takes him to Germany, where he must destroy a new rocket that can reach U.S. soil. Parachuting behind enemy lines in a fireproof uniform, and armed with a special shield, Captain America fights Red Skull but fails to stop him. Red Skull captures the stalwart Captain, straps the superhero to a rocket, and launches him towards the White House. Captain America manages to divert the rocket to Alaska, but in the process becomes frozen in the ice. An American boy, Tom Kimball, witnesses the heroic act and swears never to forget.

In the succeeding decades, Tom Kimball grows up and is eventually elected President of the United States in the 1980s. A new and controversial environmental protection plan rankles his advisers, including an evil general, putting the President on a collision course with Red Skull, who has only grown more evil since World War II. Fortunately, Captain America awakens and is rescued from an assassin by a reporter that shows him all he has missed in the decades he's been gone, including the deaths of leaders like JFK, RFK and MLK.

While adjusting to the 1980s, Captain America must deal with his lost past, and rescue a grateful President from the clutches of Red Skull.

Captain Nice

The campy 1960s *Batman* series cast a very long shadow across superhero productions in film and on television. It was so successful upon its premiere on ABC in the spring of 1966 that by the following January, both competing networks (NBC and CBS) had invented their own superhero shows to air Monday nights and challenge the supremacy of Adam West's Caped Crusader.

What remains so interesting about this historical convergence is that both networks sought to repeat *Batman*'s fame and fortune not by licensing well-known comic-book superheroes (with their own histories and fan base), but by creating totally new (and terribly lame) heroes instead.

Even more intriguing, both networks looked at *Batman* and apparently saw it only as comedy, a sitcom parody, and therefore made their two shows into situation comedies. Instead, they might have competed ably by producing a serious superhero show regarding the adventures of a hero like Green Lantern or the Flash. Indeed, that's how ABC (*Batman*'s network) counter-programmed against "camp" in 1967: with a serious adaptation of *The Green Hornet*.

The results of NBC and CBS's efforts were not pretty, and what emerged on TV in the winter of 1967 were two half-hour series that never managed to attain individual identities in the eyes of viewers: *Captain Nice* and *Mr. Terrific.*

Both shows lasted just one season. Even more ominously, both shows ended their primetime span (with reruns) on the same date: August 28, 1967. In fact, *Captain Nice* and *Mr. Terrific* both looked and sounded so much alike that they have forever been intermingled (and confused) in the minds of viewers (at least those who remember them at all)—an appropriate fate, perhaps, for enterprises designed to copy *Batman* so rigorously.

Of the two clone superhero series, NBC's *Captain Nice* had the better pedigree (and cast). It was created by *Get Smart* (1965–1970) genius Buck Henry, and starred William Daniels as the meek Carter Nash, a police scientist that developed a serum endowing him with super powers. Operating out of a city called Big Town, Nash had to contend not only with super powers, but with his adoration of a fellow officer, Sgt. Candy Kane (Ann Prentiss), and with an overbearing mother (Alice

Ghostley) who always thought she knew best.

Captain Nice's super powers included flight and great strength, and he was often seen wearing a baggy uniform that resembled jogging clothes. He had an oversized cape and wore glasses, and the name CAPTAIN NICE was emblazoned on his distinctly non-athletic torso.

The stories on *Captain Nice* involved typical (rather than "super") crimes and criminals. Carter had to protect a mob boss witness in "Who's Afraid of Amanda Woolf?," stop an art theft in "Beware of Hidden Prophets," deal with robbers in "Tastes Okay but Something's Missing," and so forth. Unlike *Mr. Terrific*, *Captain Nice* has actually been rerun in recent years, and seems to have developed a bit of a cult following (like Buck Henry's other genre farce: *Quark* [1978]).

Captain Nice (1967)
LIVE–ACTION TV SERIES

CAST: William Daniels (Carter Nash/Captain Nice); Ann Prentiss (Sgt. Candy Kane); Alice Ghostley (Mrs. Nash); Liam Dunn (Mayor Finney); William Zuckert (Police Chief Segal); Byron Foulger (Mr. Nash).

CREW: *Created by:* Buck Henry. *Theme Music written by:* Vic Mizzy. *Produced by:* Jay Sandrich. *Associate Producer:* Al Westen. *Executive Producer:* Buck Henry.

1. **"The Man Who Flies Like a Pigeon"** Written by: Buck Henry. Directed by: Jud Taylor. Airdate: January 9, 1967.

Carter Nash, a wimpy police scientist in Big Town, develops a serum that grants him superpowers. When thugs attack girlfriend and co-worker Candy Kane, Nash imbibes the formula and turns into a less-than-inspiring superhero called Captain Nice.

GUEST CAST: Kelton Garwood, Arthur Malet.

2. **"How Sheik Can You Get?"** Written by: Peter Myerson and Treva Silverman. Directed by: Gary Nelson. Airdate: January 16, 1967.

An assassin attempts to kill a visiting Middle East dignitary, but Big Town's hero, Captain Nice, saves the day. Unfortunately, the surviving sheik falls hard for Candy Kane and determines to add her to his harem at any cost.

GUEST CAST: Larry D. Mann, Fred Villani, Jan Arvan.

3. **"That Thing"** Written by: Peggy Elliott and Ed Scharlach. Directed by: Gary Nelson. Airdate: January 23, 1967.

A caterpillar drinks some of Carter's super formula and becomes a gigantic monster-sized threat to Big Town. It's Captain Nice to the rescue, with the help of a pet parakeet.

GUEST CAST: Johnny Haymer, Frank Maxwell, Ted Gehrin, Jason Wingreen.

4. **"That Was the Bridge That Was"** Written by: Al Gordon and Hal Goldman. Directed by: Gary Nelson. Airdate: February 6, 1967.

Big Town is scammed when its newest bridge nearly collapses following a dedication ceremony. Captain Nice saves the day, but his investigation leads him to a fly-by-night contractor's company and a plot to kidnap the mayor.

GUEST CAST: Edward Binns, Phil Roth, Sabrina Scharf.

5. **"The Man with Three Blue Eyes"** Written by: Treva Silverman and Peter Myerson. Directed by: Charles Rondeau. Airdate: February 20, 1967.

A mind reader, really a charlatan,

called the Great Medulla helps Carter (and Captain Nice) find the hidden loot of a crook named "Big Joe." But before long, in a case of mistaken identity, criminals mistake Carter for the prognosticator.

GUEST CAST: John Dehner, Ross Hagen, Ernest Sarracino, Daniel J. Travanti.

6. "Is Big Town Burning?" Written by: Buck Henry. Directed by: Gene Reynolds. Airdate: February 27, 1967.

Captain Nice's secret identity is jeopardized when a serial arsonist learns who he is following a terrible fire.

GUEST CAST: Vic Tayback, Marilyn Lowell, Tommy Ferrell.

7. "Don't Take Any Wooden Indians" Written by: Treva Silverman and Peter Meyerson. Directed by: Richard Kinon. Airdate: March 6, 1967.

An explorer from South America visits Big Town with murderous intentions against his financial backer. Captain Nice attempts to intervene, but is threatened by an Indian armed with a poison dart!

GUEST CAST: Joe Flynn, Joseph Perry, Ben Wright.

8. "That's What Mothers Are For" Written by: Martin Ragaway. Directed by: Gary Nelson. Airdate: March 13, 1967.

When Carter is let go from the department (due to the city's mounting money problems), along with many officers, his mother tries to prove their worth by unleashing a crime spree on the city. She succeeds, with the help of Carter's super potion, but soon becomes a hot commodity among Big Town's underworld denizens.

GUEST CAST: Felice Orlandi, Dennis Cross.

9. "Whatever Lola Wants" Written by: Arne Sulton. Directed by: Richard Kinon. Airdate: March 20, 1967.

Working late, Carter is drawn to a nearby bar, one filled with raucous sounds and patrons. There he is drugged and distracted, so as not to detect a very loud escape plan being orchestrated at the City Jail.

GUEST CAST: Barbara Stuart, Richard Wilson, Ron Foster, Julie Parrish.

10. "Who's Afraid of Amanda Woolf?" Written by: Mike Marmer and Stan Burns. Directed by: Hollingsworth Morse. Airdate: March 27, 1967.

Carter protects the sultry and aggressive wife of a mob boss who is willing to testify against her husband. Hoping to decipher a coded ledger featuring the names of prominent thugs, Carter takes the woman, Amanda Woolf, to his house, only to have to fend off her advances — and a murderous "hit" by her husband.

GUEST CAST: Madlyn Rhue, John Fiedler.

11. "The Week They Stole Payday" Written by: David Ketchum and Bruce Shelly. Directed by: Gary Nelson. Airdate: April 3, 1967.

A nefarious gang of counterfeiters steals the city payroll and replaces it with fake money. Carter knows the truth, but Candy Kane and his mother have been kidnapped, as insurance against him revealing the switch.

GUEST CAST: Pat Harrington, Victor French.

12. "Tastes OK, but Something's Missing" Written by: Peggy Elliott and Ed Scharlach. Directed by: Gary Nelson. Airdate: April 10, 1967.

Carter runs out of an ingredient for his super formula just when criminals are planning to rob a nearby post office. Carter tries to mix a new chemical, with unexpected and malodorous results.

GUEST CAST: Simon Oakland, Dick Curtis.

13. "May I Have the Last Dance?" Written by: David Ketchum and Bruce Shelly. Directed by: Charles Rondeau. Airdate: April 17, 1967.

Candy Kane helps Carter clear his name in a theft case, going undercover at a dance school. When Candy and Carter are discovered, however, they are faced with a trap that requires the appearance of Captain Nice, which will jeopardize Carter's secret identity.

GUEST CAST: Celeste Yarnall, Deanna Lund, Burt Mustin, Marilyn Mason.

14. "One Rotten Apple" Written by: Peter Meyerson and Treva Silverman. Directed by: Gary Nelson. Airdate: April 24, 1967.

Candy Kane goes undercover in a nightclub to help the owner, who believes he is the target of a murderer. Unfortunately, Carter's mom interferes with the investigation and jeopardizes everybody's safety.

GUEST CAST: Bob Newhart, John Milford, Jo Anne Worley, Charles Grodin.

15. "Beware of Hidden Prophets." Written by: Peter Meyerson and Treva Silverman. Directed by: Charles Rondeau. Airdate: May 1, 1967.

The Great Medulla is back, and in trouble once again, thanks to his involvement in an art theft. It's Captain Nice to the rescue.

GUEST CAST: John Dehner, Joseph Campanella.

Captain Planet and the Planeteers

During the late 1980s and early 1990s, a new awareness of "environment" suffused many aspects of mainstream American life. The Exxon-Valdez oil spill in the early 1990s hammered home the importance of caring for the planet's fragile ecosystem. Some scientists even began to propagate the theory that the Earth itself was a life form, an organism they named "Gaia." Other concerned scientists worried about global warming, a temperature shift that, if left unchecked, could change the agricultural and oceanic balance of the world for generations to come. Many people in and out of the scientific community scoffed at the theory, claiming it was not real science. Nonetheless, celebrities in Hollywood were among the vanguard of this new environmentalist movement, and they began to champion the cause, loudly in many cases, and usually at internationally televised award ceremonies.

In response, Ted Turner, the creator of the CNN and TBS networks (and the man behind the "colorization" process used on old black and white movies during the late 1980s), helped to launch an "environmental" superhero named Captain Planet. This animated character starred in his own series, *Captain Planet and the Planeteers* (1990–1995), for some four years, and Hollywood flocked to his moral cause. The series, which aired on TBS (and was produced for three seasons by DIC, one by Hanna-Barbera), was heavily didactic and aimed squarely at children. The battle was surely just: the protection of our priceless environment.

Stars such as Elizabeth Taylor, Ed Asner, Jeff Goldblum, Martin Sheen and Tim Curry quickly lined up to play guest-starring roles (usually as environmental polluters with names like Loot 'n' Plunder, Hoggish Greedly or Verminous Skum). These avaricious, exploiting, chemical dumping villains met their match in Captain Planet (David Coburn), a superhero that

He's here to save the Earth from litterbugs. A shot of the heroic Captain Planet from TBS's *Captain Planet and the Planeteers.*

defended Mother Nature, Gaia (Whoopi Goldberg).

Captain Planet had amazing powers (including enhanced strength), but also some very important help on his crusade — a team of five, representing nature's elements. There was Kwame (Earth), Linka (Air), Wheeler (Fire) and Gi (Water). Then there was the element of "love" or "heart," Ma-Ti.

The series was a half-hour in length, and was also known (during its final season) as *The New Adventures of Captain Planet.*

Captain Planet and the Planeteers (1990–1995)
ANIMATED SERIES

VOICE TALENTS: Captain Planet (David Coburn); Kwame (Levar Burton); Joey Dedio (Wheeler); Janice Kawayne (Gi); Kathy Soucie (Linka); Scot Menville (Ma-Ti); Whoopi Goldberg (Gaia).

CREDITS: *Created by:* Ted Turner. A DIC Entertainment/Hanna-Barbera Production. For TBS Networks.

Condorman

Back in the late 1970s and early 1980s, Walt Disney Studios was having a difficult time making the transition from animated kid films to more mature, live-action fare. *The Black Hole* (1979) and *Watcher in the Woods* (1980) were two high-profile failures in this department, big-budget productions that suffered from being a little too sophomoric for adults, a little too adult for the

kiddies. Critics disdained the films and audiences steered clear.

A third such failure was 1981's *Condorman,* a fairly obscure and rather strange superhero/secret agent film starring *Phantom of the Opera* star Michael Crawford as Woody Wilkins, a comic book writer who transformed (with the help of the C.I.A.) into his comic creation, the superhero called Condorman.

Condorman, as his name suggested, was a man dressed in yellow tights and a brown vest made to resemble condor feathers. He also wore a belt with the letter "C" on its buckle, and a bird-like helmet and goggles that formed a long yellow beak. Perhaps Condorman's most notable costume flourish was a glider that rested on his back and formed collapsible condor-like wings that, when unfurled, could lift the hero up, up and away into the air.

Not quite soaring to hilarious heights: Condorman (Michael Crawford) readies himself for a jump from the Eiffel Tower in 1981's *Condorman*.

An international production, *Condorman* was filmed in Paris, Monte Carlo, Switzerland, and at the famous Pinewood Studios in England. The behind-the-scenes personnel were top-notch. Academy Award winner Colin Chilvers, of *Superman* fame, worked on many of the special effects, while Dan Striepeke (make-up), Art Cruickshank (special effects) and Henry Mancini (music) were among the other notable behind-the-scenes contributors.

Disney even heralded the release of the film with a King Features comic strip that ran in 1981. Russ Heath, an acclaimed artist that had worked on strips such as *Arizona Kid, Kid Colt Outlaw, Terry and the Pirates* and *Flash Gordon*, drew the strip, which ran for some 20 weeks in 1981.[1]

All of the work was for naught, however. The finished film veered wildly in tone, mixing childish performances (especially from Crawford) with violent chases, gunfights and zippy special effects. A menacing, adult portrayal from the intense Oliver Reed clashed with the movie's juvenile atmosphere and the cringe-inducing double takes by the goofy Crawford.

The film's opening credits heralded the problems to come. An overly cute animated version of Condorman was seen schlepping around a live-action frame featuring picturesque views of Paris tourist attractions like the Eiffel Tower. As the little cartoon flew about the screen like an irritating gnat, "splatty" sound effects deposited the pulpy credits on the screen like so many pigeon droppings. All the while the soundtrack croaked, "Condor-maaaaan!"

The remainder of the movie strained believability, even for a child's film, as the not-very-resourceful C.I.A. depended on the civilian Wilkins (author of the comic strip called "Sponge Man") to rescue a Russian defector, the beautiful Barbara Carrera (*Never Say Never Again* [1983]) from Reed's KGB mastermind. In an effort to keep Wilkins happy, the C.I.A.— apparently in a matter of days — produced for him such expensive accoutrements as a Condorman sports car (that could become a hovercraft) and speedy Condorboat, as well as jet-pole rockets and a fully functioning set of designer glider wings. Nice to know taxpayer money was well spent...

The final scenes of *Condorman* laid the groundwork for a sequel that thankfully never came, and the overall tone of the film was one of patronizing condescension. Even the campy *Batman* of the 1960s was never this lame. Some of the improbable gadgets (including a walking cane/machine gun) were fun jokes, worthy of a lesser James Bond entry, but the story of a man that made himself into a superhero was riddled with plot holes and lacked any resemblance to reality. That established, Carrera made an especially fetching damsel-in-distress and doubled nicely as Wilkins' dream comic heroine, "The Laser Lady."

Condorman (1981)
LIVE-ACTION FILM

CAST: Michael Crawford (Woody Wilkins/Condorman); Oliver Reed (Sergei); Barbara Carrera (Natalia/"The Bear"); James Hampton (Harry Oslo); Jean-Pierre Kalfon (Morovich); Dana Elcar (Russ); Vernon Dobtcheff (Russian Agent); Robert Arden (C.I.A. Chief).

CREW: *Production Manager:* John Bloss. *Sound Supervisor:* Herb Taylor. *Sound Mixer:* Silliam Sivel. *Costumes:* Kent James and Jean Zay. *Make-up Supervisor:* Robert J. Schiffer. *Hair-Stylist:* Alex Archambault. *Sound Editor:* Ben F. Hendricks. *Music Editor:* Jack Wadsworth. *Make-up:* Dan Striepeke. *Second Unit Director:* Anthony Squire. *Script Supervisor:* Remy Julienne. *Special Effects Supervisor:* Colin Chilvers. *Special Photograph Effects:* Art Cruickshank. *Second Unit Camera:* Godrey Godar. *Title Animation:* Michael Cedeno. *Animation Effects Supervisor:* Jack Boyd. *Production Manager (France):* Philippe Moldave. *Assistant Directors:* Richard Larman, Denys Granier DeFerre, Paul Feyder. *Music:* Henry Mancini. *Production Designer:* Albert Withering. *Art Director (France):* Marc Frederix. *Director of Photography:* Charles F. Wheeler. *Executive Producer:* Ron Miller. *Screenplay by:* Marc Stirdivant. *Suggested by the Game of "X" created by:* Robert Sheckley. *Produced by:* Dan Williams. *Directed by:* Charles Jarrott. *M.P.A.A. Rating:* PG. *Running time:* 90 minutes.

Nebbish comic book author Woody Wilkins pens the *Condorman* superhero comic and wants it to be as authentic as possible. He travels to Paris to write an international tale of intrigue, and, while attempting to prove his book is true to life, nearly kills himself jumping off the Eiffel Tower in a homemade Condorman costume.

Woody is recruited by his friend in the intelligence community, Harry, to pass important secret papers to a civilian working for the Soviet Union. He meets the woman, Natalia, and claims to be a top level operative named Condorman. He rescues her from spies, bumbling successfully through a fight with several assassins. Natalia, in truth a high-ranking spy herself, reports back to her handler, the evil Sergei, who is disturbed by Condorman's success and fighting prowess.

When Natalia decides to defect to the West, the only agent she will work with is, of course, Condorman. In return for his help, Woody demands that the C.I.A. Fabrication Department construct an array of Condorman-style equipment to handle the transfer. Among these devices is a walking cane that turns into a machine gun.

In gypsy disguise, Condorman and

Natalia escape to Monte Carlo, pursued by the merciless, metal-eyed Soviet killer, Morovich. Woody eludes the Soviet assassins when his rickety old gypsy van transforms into a sporty yellow Condormobile, a heavily armed car decked with weaponry and doubling as a hovercraft.

When Sergei recaptures Natalia, Condorman and Harry go undercover as Arab sheiks to rescue her, bringing a freshly-uniformed Condorman (replete with wings) and a Condorboat to dramatic life.

The Crow

In the early 1980s, an artist named James O'Barr suffered a personal tragedy. He lost a loved one to the actions of a drunk driver. In working out his anger over that terrible twist of fate, O'Barr served as a U.S. marine and also began to draw a comic book/ graphic novel that would one day become *The Crow*. Hoping for catharsis, and inspired by literary and pop sources as diverse as George Batille, Antonin Artaud, Arthur Rimbaud, Iggy Pop, Lewis Carroll and Edgar Allan Poe,[1] O'Barr's first effort was published by Caliber Press in the year 1989.

Almost an instant hit with audiences, *The Crow* was not a traditional comic book or superhero story in any sense. Instead, it was a tragic tale about a man named Eric Draven (Eric — d — raven … get it?) that lost his beloved at the hands of rotten criminals, true scum-of-the-earth characters. But Eric's love for his beloved Shelly was so strong that he was able to survive even his own murder, at least in a sense. With a mission of vengeance on his mind, a spectral (i.e. "dead") Draven returned to the land of the living courtesy of the auspices of a crow, a talisman and vision guide of sorts.

In some sense, the story was certainly *Death Wish* (1974) with a twist. Eye-for-an-eye justice was championed, vengeance came from beyond the grave, and violence was the mode for revenge. The comic was a dark, bleak and very sad one. It was also rather touching in spots — especially for anyone who knows what it means to lose a loved one, or fears losing a loved one.

With Tim Burton's dark version of *Batman* a huge hit at the box office, it was not long before movie producers became interested in adapting *The Crow* to film. Alex Proyas, a talent that would later direct the brilliant future noir *Dark City* (1998), was hired to helm the movie, and Brandon Lee, the son of Bruce Lee (*The Green Hornet*) was cast in the lead role of Eric Draven. Shot in Wilmington, North Carolina, the low-budget production suffered its own tragedy when, near the end of the shoot, Brandon Lee was killed during a stunt involving simulated gunplay. A weapon had been erroneously loaded with a real bullet rather than a blank, and the strapping, powerfully charismatic Lee was fatally struck down on the set. No criminal charges were filed, and the shooting was declared an accident.

Rather than see Lee's contributions lost forever, *The Crow*'s production company utilized computer-generated effects and body doubles to complete Lee's role. A company in Simi Valley called Dream Quest employed a new technology called "image stabilization" to impose Lee's face over that of his double in certain unfinished sequences. Much of the picture occurred at night, in the rain, so disguising another actor as Lee was not difficult, given that he was wearing white-face and black painted tears as "the Crow" character, a holdover from the comics.

Much of the early press surrounding *The Crow* involved reports on Brandon Lee's tragic death, but audiences turned out in droves to see the film anyway. Rated R, the film seemed obsessed with death, a theme reinforced by viewer awareness that its star was speaking to them from the grave.

Unremittingly violent (it nearly received an NC-17 rating), *The Crow* was also a beautifully designed film. Set in a timeless world featuring 1940s architecture, 1980s-style crime, and band music on the radio, *The Crow*'s universe looked like a real glimpse of Hell, a peek at a rotting, over-run city on, appropriately, Devil's Night, the most violent night of the year. This city in flames, however, was more than background noise, it was the explicit backdrop for Shelly and Eric's tragic love story, and those aspects of the film were quite touching. Could love survive in a world where "there's no justice?" Perhaps not, but the upbeat ending saw spectral figures Shelly and Eric reunited. If their love could not survive here, then perhaps there was another realm, a better one.

Looking at the film as a whole, the moment that most distinctly put Eric into the category of superhero was one in which he left behind vengeance for an instant and set out to help a child, the girl Sarah (Rochelle Davis). Her mother had long ago become a drug addict, and with his powers of putting imagery into people's heads, the Crow dramatically reminded the mom that "morphine is bad," and that a mother should play a more loving role in her child's life. This shared moment between addict and avenger may not have been done with the gee-whiz attitude of *The Adventures of Superman* or the square-jawed solemnity of TV's *Batman*, but it was nonetheless an attempt on the part of a superhero to impose a moral directive on the immoral.

The box-office success of *The Crow* surprised a lot of industry insiders, who had assumed audiences would be too bummed out to see a superhero film in which the lead actor had died on the set. They were wrong, perhaps because the superhero genre was in

the midst of its gloomy "Dark Age." As sick and dirty as it may sound, the hubbub about Brandon Lee's death only seemed to play to the death-obsessed film's strengths. Art reflects life, one supposes. Regardless of the reasons for its success, plans were immediately drawn up for a sequel.

The Crow: City of Angels was released over Labor Day weekend in 1996 and promptly took the top box office spot, grossing over nine million dollars during its opening weekend.[2] Since franchise star Lee had died before the release of the first film, the makers of the second movie adopted a new strategy. Their sequel would involve the Crow bringing back to life another wronged man, another spirit to do battle with murderous criminals. This time, that man was potrayed by 32-year-old Vincent Perez, a Frenchman that had appeared in *Indochine* (1992) and *Queen Margot* (1994).

Perez played a character named Ashe that was drowned with his young son when they witnessed the crimes of a drug dealer named Judah (Richard Brooks). As in the previous film, this murder of a loved one led to death, violence and more pain.

The Crow had a helpful ally this time around in a lovely tattoo artist named Sarah (Mia Kirshner), a girl that had been a child in the first film and remembered the story of Eric Draven. Other than Sarah, there was no explicit connection to the first movie in terms of character or history. Different city, different Crow, different crime. The Crow, however, hadn't changed in terms of costume (black duds and white face-paint), logo (a fiery crow icon "ignited" at crime scenes in both films), or thirst for bloody vengeance.

In narrative terms, *Crow 2: City of Angels* was a dead duck. It was very much a re-hash of the first film's *Death Wish*–style formula. Like the original *Crow*, it featured a villain and his witch, a group of low-life lackeys that the Crow had to kill to get to the top man, and flashbacks of the terrible, tragic crime that instigated all the vengeance in the first place. The sequel substituted a Day of the Dead festival for the Devil's Night ritual, and even relied on the line popularized by *Batman* in 1989: "You made me what I am" (a variation of the "I made you/You made me" banter that has become *de rigueur* in the genre).

Perez was affecting as the wounded father, but somewhat less charismatic and awe-inspiring in the action scenes than his lithe predecessor. What truly made the film special was its strange autumnal atmosphere. Even the smog in the *City of Angels* has a golden touch. This place "where restless souls" wandered was beautifully realized, and the movie was luscious in its gritty attention to color, texture and detail. The pounding, heavy-metal soundtrack was a benefit too, enhancing the feel of a world (*sans* moon) where decadence and crime had taken over. Too often in Hollywood, style is championed over substance, but it must be declared that *City of the Angels* is a lovely, atmospheric film, even if its story is hackneyed.

In the end, *Crow 2* under-grossed the first film in the franchise by a substantial margin, and met with much negative criticism regarding its violence and lack of narrative innovation. A third entry in the film series was shunted directly to video, finally arriving in the summer of 2000. A terrible movie, *Crow: The Salvation* had the distinction of starring Kirsten Dunst shortly before she appeared in the much-more-successful superhero film *Spider-Man* (2002).

The story this time involved a man named Alex Corvis (Eric Mabius) that was framed for the murder of his girlfriend (Jodi Lynn O'Keefe) by corrupt police officers. After being executed in the electric chair, Corvis comes back as the Crow and sets out to right the wrongs of his life, a trail that eventually leads to his girlfriend's sado-masochistic police chief father, a rather bored looking Fred Ward (*Henry and June* [1988], *Tremors* [1989]).

With many scenes shot in a grungy green execution chamber, and others in glaring blue light, *Crow: Salvation* was a more ugly-looking film than either of its stylish predecessors and, as expected, it did not do much, from a narrative standpoint, to push the series into new territory. As always, the Crow was back to avenge a wrong, killing his enemies one at a time until he reached the top of the heap, but this time the cheapness of the enterprise (including some less-than-inspiring car chases) sunk the enterprise. Though a good actor, Mabius (*Resident Evil* [2002]) lacked the physical presence to pull off the heroic role, and his obsessive quest for the man with a scar (the man that killed him) reeked not of real drama but of *The Fugitive*'s search for the one-armed man. That Fred Ward was a "talking" James Bond–style villain that had explicit knowledge of the Crow legend (just enough to provide viewers with exposition) did not help the movie either.

While the third film entry in *The Crow* series languished unreleased, the franchise took an unexpected, sideways leap over to the boob tube. In 1998, Alliance Communications Corp (a Canadian company) and PolyGram television syndicated twenty-two episodes of a series entitled *The Crow: Stairway to Heaven*.

The series starred Mark Dacascos (*Brotherhood of the Wolf* [2001], *Cradle2Grave* [2003]) as the best incarnation of the Crow since Brandon Lee. And for once, the story was not obsessively focused on vengeance. Instead, it concerned, surprisingly, redemption. "I consider this 'Rocked by an Angel,'" Bob Sanitsky, president of Polygram noted. "Eric Draven is trying to earn his way back into heaven and be reunited with his love. We will strike a spiritual chord, but we'll be a real action hour too."[3]

In the first two episodes of *The Crow: Stairway to Heaven*, Eric Draven returned from the grave to avenge Shelly's death. In doing so, he learned that he becomes an

On the road to redemption is the Crow (Mark Dacascos), from the syndicated TV series *The Crow: Stairway to Heaven.*

alter ego, "the Crow" (no make-up required), at certain points of extreme rage, and the transformation is out of his control. It was almost as though he was the Hulk this time around, and it was a new wrinkle to the legend. After offing bad guy Top Dollar and punishing the thugs that had killed Shelly, Eric made another surprising discovery. As he told his friend Sarah (Katie Stuart) in the fourth episode, "Get a Life": "A returned spirit must not just have revenge, but find justice to balance the scales of justice." In other words, he had to help others in need, and it was here, at this point, that the Crow no doubt qualified one hundred percent as a superhero for perhaps the first time in his history.

The remainder of the syndicated series watched Draven attempt to "earn his wings," so to speak. He tooled around in the daytime on a motorcycle (a far cry from the nighttime, dark-hued feature films), and was aided in his quest by a cop named Albrecht (Marc Gomes), who eventually came

to accept him and his identity as the avenging Crow. Eric's dead lover, Shelly (Sabine Karsentias), was also a regular player on the show. She was often seen in a green, forest-like afterlife, or in "angel-style" manifestations on Earth. Naturally, her appearances prodded a lovelorn Eric to get his penance on Earth done faster, so he could join her in the great beyond (depicted, for some reason, as a suspension bridge over a jungle river).

The Crow: Stairway to Heaven successfully expanded the characters beyond the *Death Wish* template of the feature film series. Draven had to contend with his estranged brother in "Brother's Keeper," and a female Crow, the fetching Hannah (Bobbie Phillips), in "Birds of a Feather." In other stories he went up against a secret society called the Lazarus Group. The leader of this organization wanted to capture a Crow; and in the final episode, "Gathering Storm," the Lazarus Group succeeded in pitting Eric against his alter ego, the Crow.

One of the finest shows, "The People vs. Eric Draven," saw the law try Eric for the murder of Shelly — a real slap in the face to the character, considering his love for her. Impressively, bucking the superhero-on-trial trend in television history, Eric was found guilty and sent to jail, which is where he was to be found for the next few episodes. This was a nice continuing subplot, and one that showed that the TV series attempted to go, at least from a narrative standpoint, where the films had not dared.

Other elements of the series were not nearly so fun, and *The Crow: Stairway to Heaven* managed to hit quite a few of the genre clichés before vanishing from the airwaves after only one season. Eric fought gangbangers in "Like It's 1999"; rescued kidnap victims in "Dead to Rights"; and helped an abused, telepathic boy in the maudlin "Voices." Like Johnny Domino in *Nightman*'s "Amazing Grace" (and other series too), Eric even went on an *It's a Wonderful Life*–style tour of his life in an effort to change his past (in a story appropriately titled "It's a Wonderful Death").

Still, *The Crow: Stairway to Heaven* was frequently a very interesting show, and it was a shame it did not last beyond its first season, especially when terrible series like *Nightman, Charmed* and others droned on without end. The final episode of the series featured a cliffhanger ending that has never been resolved.

In all his incarnations, the Crow remained consistent in several respects. He has the power to "regenerate" or heal rapidly, making bullets and other weapons ineffective against him. Also, he is a sort of touch psychic — he can make people feel the emotional and physical pain of other people merely by touching them. And, finally, the crow itself, the black bird, is the character's equivalent of kryptonite. If it is injured or killed, the Crow hero becomes vulnerable and mortal.

In 2003, a new *Crow* film entitled *Wicked Prayer* was shot starring Edward Furlong as the next in the crow line. *Angels* David Borcanaz was cast as the film's villain.

The Crow (1994)
LIVE-ACTION FILM

"Relentlessly violent and darkly funny, it may repel some. But for the strong of stomach it offers an irresistible taste of hell."
— Joe Chidley, *MacLeans*,
May 16, 1994, page 60.

"...[A]lmost unremittingly grungy and overwrought...."
— Peter Rainer, *The Los Angeles Times*,
May 11, 1994.

"...[T]he pop-nihilist event of the season, a cinematic Black Mass combining stupendous music video–style visuals, perpetual violence, and a violently dead star playing a violently dead character."
— David Denby, *New York*,
May 23, 1994, page 72.

"The films comes from a comic book by James O'Barr and never rises above it. Cardboard characters strut through a post-apocalyptic setting. Director Alex Proyas revels in gratuitous, disgusting violence."
— Lawrence Toppman, *The Charlotte Observer*, May 10, 1994.

"The Crow has always been a kind of living dead Batman, in both the comic series and the first film, and surprisingly, it works. A very stylish film, *The Crow* plays with the same angst as does Batman, the glorification of anger as a positive motivation (in that it punishes evil). The nice twist, here, is that while Bruce Wayne longs for his parents, Eric Draven longs for a lost love. His desperation is somehow more severe, in that Bruce Wayne lost an idyllic past, while Eric loses an idyllic future with the death of his beloved. It's too bad the stylistic approach used in this film couldn't have been used in the *Batman* films, because Batman in the comics would inhabit these streets quite nicely."
— William Latham, author of *Mary's Monster* and *Space: 1999 Resurrection*.

CAST: Brandon Lee (Eric Draven); Ernie Hudson (Allbrecht); Rochelle Davis (Sarah); Michael Wincott (Top Dollar); Bai Ling (Myca); Sofia Salinas (Shelly); Anna Thomson (Darla); David Patrick Kelly (T-Bird); Ansel David (Shark); Laurence Masson (Tin Tin); Michael Massee (Funboy); Tony Todd; Jon Pilot (Gideon).

CREW: Miramax Presents, in association with Entertainment Media Corporation, an Edward Pressman Production in association with Jeff Most Productions, *The Crow. Directed by:* Alex Proyas. *Screenplay by:* David J. Schow, John Shirley. *Based on the comic book series and comic strip by:* James O'Barr. *Produced by:* Edward Pressman and Jeff Most. *Executive Producers:* Robert L. Rosen, Sherman L. Baldwin. *Co-Producers:* Caldecot Chubb, James A. Janowitz. *Director of Photography:* Darasz Wolski. *Production Designer:* Alex McDowell. *Film Editors:* Dov Hoenig, Scott Smith. *Music:* Graeme Revell. *Costume Design:* Arianne Phillips. *Casting:* Billy Hopkins, Suzanne Smith. *Associate Producer:*

Gregory A. Gale. *Unit Production Manager:* Grant Hill. *First Assistant Director:* Steve Andrews. *Second Assistant Director:* Randy LaFoulette. *Unit Production Manager (added scenes):* Ric Rondell. *Music Supervisor:* Jolene Cherry. *Visual Effects Supervisor:* Andrew Mason. *Art Director:* Simon Morton. *Set Designer:* William Barcley. *Wardrobe Supervisor:* Darryl Levine. *Make-up:* Sharon Ilson. *Special Effects:* J.B. Jones. *M.P.A.A. Rating:* R. *Running time:* 102 minutes.

On Devil's Night, 143 fires rage in a major, overpopulated city, and two lovers, musician Eric Draven and do-gooder Shelly Webster, are murdered in their apartment by four reprobates under the employ of local gang lord Top Dollar.

One year later, a black crow carries Draven's troubled soul back to the land of the living and resurrects the deceased musician to right the wrongs that sent his beloved to her grave. Disoriented at first, Draven comes to remember and experience the pain of the attack on Shelly as the thugs raped and murdered her. He also learns rather quickly that he is impervious to all wounds and able to regenerate rapidly. Garbed in black, his face coated in the white make-up of a harlequin, this new avenger sets out after those responsible for Shelly's death, including Gideon, a criminal pawn-broker, and a thug named Tin Tin.

Before long, Draven's quest takes him to bigger fish — namely, Top Dollar and his witch half-sister, Myca, who collects eye-balls. Draven learns Top Dollar wanted Shelly out of the way so he could exploit her neighborhood without complaints and interference.

Meanwhile, a kindly police officer, All-brecht, and a young waif named Sarah be-friend Eric and fill him in on the details of Shelly's lingering death in the hospital. Draven continues his quest for revenge, killing Top Dollar's thugs, T-Bird and Fun Boy. Now Top Dollar realizes he is facing a powerful opponent, and also that Draven's powers can be destroyed by killing the crow. A final confrontation at a dilapidated church wounds Draven, but Allbrecht shows up to help. In the final battle, Draven sends Myca and Top Dollar to their graves. His mission accomplished, Eric returns to the afterlife and is reunited with his beloved Shelly.

The Crow: City of Angels (1997)
LIVE-ACTION FILM

"*The Crow: City of Angels* offers the usual fragmentary 'visions' of apocalypse (Batman nightscapes, S&M revels, endless shots of ... crows), all mashed together into an occult junkyard that makes your typical horror-trash music video look like a model of coherence."
— Owen Gleiberman, *Entertainment Weekly:* "The Crow: City of Angels," September 13, 1996, page 112.

"Perverse violence, none of it interesting, and perverse sex, none of it sensual, fill this movie, as does the mumbo-jumbo mysticism that blighted the original."
— Ralph Novak, *People Weekly:* "The Crow: City of Angels," September 16, 1996, page 27.

CAST: Vincent Perez (Ashe/the Crow); Mia Kirshner (Sarah); Richard Brooks (Judah); Vin-cent Castellanos (Spider Monkey); Ian Dury (Noah); Tracey Ellis (Sybil); Thomas Jane (Nemo); Iggy Pop (Curve); Thuy Trang (Kali); Eric Acasta (Danny); Aaron Thell Smith (Tattoo Customer); Beverley Mitchell (Grace); Shelly Desai (Hindu); Alan Gelfant (Bassett); Kerry Russell (Zeke).

CREW: Miramax Films/Dimension Films Presents an Edward R. Pressman Production in association with Jeff Most Productions, *The Crow: City of Angels. Casting:* Lora Kennedy. *Musical score composed by:* Graeme Revell. *Costume Designer:* Kirsten Everberg. *Edited by:* Michael N. Knue, Anthony Redman. *Production Design:* Alex McDowell. *Director of Photography:* Jean Yves Esioffier. *Co-Producer:* Michael Flynn. *Executive Producers:* Bob Weinstein, Harvey Weinstein, Alessandro Camon. *Based on the comic book series and comic strip by:* James O'Barr. *Pro-*

ducers: Edward R. Pressman, Jeff Most. *Written by:* David S. Goyer. *Directed by:* Tim Pope. *M.P.A.A. Rating:* R. *Running time:* 86 minutes.

In the drug-infested City of Angels, young Sarah — who once witnessed the return of Eric Draven — is all grown up. This time, she experiences mysterious visions of another resurrection — of a man named Ashe, whose life was stolen by the stooges of a villainous drug dealer called Judah. Worse, the thugs killed his young son, Danny, and then threw both bodies into the river.

Ashe returns from the land of the dead, accompanied by a crow, to avenge the wrongs of his life. He travels up the criminal "food chain," killing Judah's villainous hangers-on and thugs. He sets one accomplice aflame in a factory, and then kills another, a sadistic voyeur, at a peep show. As the Day of the Dead festival approaches, Ashe's vengeance continues, and he goes after the worst of Judah's associates, the brutal Curve. But Judah learns that the crow is Ashe's link to the "next world" and sets out to destroy it.

Judah kidnaps Sarah to bring Ashe running, then captures and bloodies the crow, drinking its vital fluid. This act also steals away Ashe's supernatural powers, but a vision of his son during the festival spurs Ashe to fight back. And Sarah comes to the rescue, only to be stabbed by Judah. Finally, a flock of crows swoop down and stop Judah, carrying him to the land of the dead.

The Crow: Salvation (1999)
LIVE-ACTION FILM

"While nothing to crow about, *"The Crow: Salvation"* is a reasonably suspenseful, adequately made programmer true to the tradition of a lone avenger out to raise hell and clear his name."
— Lisa Nesselson, *Variety:* "The Crow: Salvation," June 26, 2000, page 22.

CAST: Kirsten Dunst (Erin Randal); Eric Mabius (Alex Corvis/the Crow); Jodi Lynn O'Keefe (Lauren Randall); William Atherton (Nathan Randall); Grant Shaud (Peter Walsh); Bruce McCarty (Madden); Dale Midkiff (Erlich); Tim De Kay (Toomey); Walton Goggins (Stan Roberts); Fred Ward (The Captain); Debbie Fan (Barbara Chen); Bill Mondy (Dutton).

CREW: Dimension Films Presents an Edward R. Pressman IMF Production, in association with Jeff Most Productions and Pacifica Film Distribution, *The Crow: Salvation.* A Bharat Nalluri Film. *Casting:* John Papsidera. *Visual Effects Supervisor:* Thomas C. Rainone. *Musical Supervisor:* Jeff Most. *Music:* Marco Beltrami. *Costume Design:* Marielos Pantelak, Chris M. Aysta. *Edited by:* Howard E. Smith. *Production Design:* Maia Javan. *Director of Photography:* Carolyn Chen. *Co-Producer:* Russ Markowitz. *Executive Producers:* Bob Weinstein, Harvey Weinstein, Christoph Sievernich, Moritz Borman, Alessandro Camon. *Based on the comic book series and comic strip by:* James O'Barr. *Producers:* Edward R. Pressman, Jeff Most. *Written by:* Chip Johannessen. *Directed by:* Bharat Nalluri. *M.P.A.A. Rating:* PG-13. *Running time:* 102 minutes.

A young man named Alex Corvis is slated for execution on his 21st birthday. His crime? The murder of his beautiful girlfriend, Lauren Randall. Alex maintains his innocence, and that a stranger with a scar on his arm actually committed the bloody murder, but nobody believes him. When Alex is put to death, he returns to the mortal coil as a supernatural avenger, the Crow.

He sets out to find Lauren's killer, tracking down police witnesses in the case. He visits Lauren's grave, confused by his status of not quite alive, not quite dead, and befriends Lauren's younger sister, Erin. He soon discovers that corrupt police officers were involved in a conspiracy to frame him for murder, and that they know the identity of "scar man."

Erin investigates too, and learns that her own father is a conspirator, involved with a company called D.E.R.T. and a secretive erotic club. When Mr. Randall is executed, the Crow pays the club a visit, unaware that the police captain—a depraved individual and the man with the scar—has set a trap that will steal the Crow's super-natural powers. When the captain kidnaps Erin (and sews her mouth shut), Alex must fight back even without the powers of the Crow.

The Crow: Stairway to Heaven (1998-1999)
LIVE-ACTION SERIES

"…[S]tarts out as a quasi-remake of the Brandon Lee film … then episode two kicks in, with a metaphysical mishmash involving a satanic tycoon and his demonic snake, turgidly setting the tone for future battles beyond the grave … C-"
— Michael Sauter, *Entertainment Weekly*, September 10, 1999, page 156.

CAST: Mark Dacascos (Eric Draven/the Crow); Marc Gomes (Detective Darryl Albrecht); Sabine Karsentias (Shelly Webster); Katie Stuart (Sara); Michael Crestejo (Crow Stunt Double).

CREW: *Based on the Comic Book Series by:* James O'Barr. *Developed for TV by:* Bryce Abel. *Directors of Photography (various episodes):* Attila Szalay. *Production Design:* Ian Thomas. *Film Editors (various episodes):* Havelock Gradidge, Elisabeth Pechlaner, Richard A. Schwadel, Ron Yoshida. *Music:* Peter Manning Robinson. *Supervising Producer:* Naomi Janzen. *Co-Executive Producer:* Brad Markowitz. *Producer:* Gordon Mark. *Executive Producers:* Bryce Zabel, Ed Pressman. *Production Manager:* Stewart Bethane. *First Assistant Director:* Peter Dashkewytch. *Second Assistant Director:* Glenn Bottomley. *Visual Effects Supervisor:* Jim Finn. *Visual Effects:* Rainmaker Digital. *Music Supervisor:* Janet York. Filmed entirely on location in Vancouver, British Columbia.

SEASON ONE (1998-1999)

1. "The Soul Can't Rest" Written by: Bryce Zabel. Directed by: Kari Skogland. Airdate: Week of September 21, 1998.

A year after the murder of Shelly Webster and musician Eric Draven, a crow carries Draven's soul back from the afterlife to avenge the terrible crime. Now it's Halloween again, and Draven—imbued with the ability to instantly regenerate himself after being wounded—begins his quest to find those who destroyed his life. While Detective Albrecht, still obsessed by the year-old murder case, narrows in on criminals Tin-Tin, T-Bird and Fun Boy, Eric makes contact with an old friend, a little girl named Sara. Draven, consumed by the dark character "the Crow," confronts his enemies, telepathically transmitting the pain of their victims back to them.

GUEST CAST: Lynda Boyd (Darla); Jon Cuthbert (Vincennes); John Pyper-Ferguson; Darcy Laurie (Tin-Tin); John Tench (T-Bird); Ty Olsson (Fun Boy); Marcus Hondro (Gideon); Elizabeth Orrea (Mexican Woman); Rik Kiviaho (Spanish Crow); Tom Heaton (Grave Digger); D. Neil Mark (Mitch); Jason Boychuk (Dancer); Julie Hill (Cynthia); Michael Crestejo (Stunt Double).

2. "Souled Out" Written by: Bryce Zabel. Directed by: Kari Skogland. Airdate: Week of September 28, 1998.

Eric Draven, returned from the grave, continues to adjust to his new life back on Earth and deal with his new, and more violent, alter ego, the white-faced Crow. Eric attempts to reconnect with his former life—and his band—but is treated as a freak. As Eric continues his quest for revenge, he faces a culprit that threatens to take him to an even darker place.

GUEST CAST: Lynda Boyd (Darla); Jon Cuthbert (Vincennes); Julie Dreyfus; John Pyper-Ferguson (Top Dollar); Mark Rolston; Michael Tiernan (Frank Voz); Jarred Blancard (Kenny Jeffers); Zak Alam (Curtis Bilbao); Luke Doucet (Egan); Terry Jang Barclay (Hawkins); Colleen Wheeler (Melissa Rampling); Karin Title (Receptionist); Marily Norry (Dr. Jocelyn Ross); Paul Magel (Crandall); Anuko Okuma (Pissaro); Jason Boychuck (Dancer).

3. "Voices" Written by: John Turman. Directed by: Steven Stern. Airdate: Week of October 5, 1998.

At a carnival, a boy struck by lightning — now a psychic — accurately predicts an old woman's murder. While Albrecht investigates the case, Eric takes Sara to the carnival to meet the boy, Jesse, with powers of prescience. When Jesse conveys a message from Shelly from beyond the grave, Eric thinks the boy may be his clue to explaining his renewed presence in "life." Eric and Albrecht learn that Jesse's exploitative guardian, Doc Connell, may be using the boy's abilities to rob those that Jesse "reads" at the carnival.

GUEST CAST: Jon Cuthbert (Vincennes); Sue Matthew (Cordelia); Brendan Fletcher; Gerard Plunkett; Wren Robertz (Beck Pryor); Anthony Ulc (Logan); Gillian Carfra (Marianne).

4. "Get a Life" Written by: Bryce Zabel and Brad Markowitz. Directed by: T.W. Peacocke. Airdate: Week of October 12, 1998.

A politician's daughter, Elise Franklin, is assassinated onstage during a press conference to announce funding for a new series of family crisis shelters, and her ex-boyfriend is framed for the attack. Back at the loft, Sara learns that a soul returned from the dead must not only seek vengeance, but actually right the scales of justice and help those in need. Accordingly, Shelly (in the afterlife) directs Eric to help in the case of Elise Franklin. Meanwhile, Eric is asked to pay rent for the loft by his disgruntled landlord, and gets a job at a club called "Black Out" ... even as he learns that Elise's murder was orchestrated by her own corrupt father.

GUEST CAST: Lynda Boyd (Darla); Julie Dreyfus; Jon Cuthbert (Vincennes); Sue Matthew (Cordelia); Peter Flemming; Donnelly Rhodes (Franklin); Ingrid Kavelaars (Elise Franklin); Mitch Kosterman (Kearny); Joe Maffei (Caleb Cowan); Ken Kirzinger (Koch); Chris Nelson Norris (Davies); Jason Griffith

(Hartley); Mike Dopud (Urbaniak); Merrett Green (Brent Carlton); Mecca Menard (Young Elise).

5. "Like It's 1999" Written by: Naomi Janzen. Directed by: Tony Westman. Airdate: Week of October 17, 1998.

A friend of Sara's named Kyle becomes involved with a roving gang of thugs that break their way into upper-class homes and occupy them for destructive parties. Kyle introduces Sara to the criminal "family," and she learns the group sees destruction as a patriotic act, in preparation for the Y2K crash. Since there is no way to leave this particular family alive, Eric is soon on his way to rescue Sara. Meanwhile, the gang uses Sara to break into another rich estate, and Eric must discredit the leader of the family, who plans an explosive denouement to this particular celebration.

GUEST CAST: Lynda Boyd (Darla); Jon Cuthbert (Vincennes); J.R. Bourne; Marya Delver; Davie Paetkau (Kyle); Gerry South (Jace); Scott Heindl (Damon); Ken Camroux (Kenneth); Joe Maffei (Caleb Cowan); Pamela Perry (Marcia); Gaetana Korbin (Shea Marino); Deanne Henry (Scared Housewife).

6. "Solitude's Revenge" Written by: Chad and Corey Hayes. Directed by: Scott Williams. Airdate: Week of October 24, 1998.

On a day he's scheduled to take a look at a new house with his live-in girlfriend, Detective Albrecht is kidnapped by the man who killed his partner and is now seeking revenge against Albrecht for sending him to jail. Eric comes to the rescue, but their opponent hunts them across an island. In one confrontation, Eric is shot up with a machine gun, and Albrecht is recaptured by the crook he sent away fourteen years earlier. Eric engineers a second rescue, after a brief vision of his beloved Shelly.

GUEST CAST: Lynda Boyd (Darla); Jon Cuthbert (Vincennes); Sue Mathew (Cordelia); Christopher Shyer; Dan Joffre (Marcus); Aaron

Pearl (Lee); Ken Roberts (Robert Thorton); Sadie Lawrence (Kim); Brian Anderson (Short and Bald Patient); Wendy Donaldson (Fairy Patient); Richard Side (Shadow Patient); Steve Oatway (Bernson).

7. "Double Take" Written by David Ransil. Directed by: T.W. Peacocke. Airdate: Week of November 2, 1998.

Eric is shocked to learn that, at least according to some sources, Shelly is apparently still alive. Investigating the mystery, Eric finds that a woman on the lam from the mob has taken over his lover's identity. And worse, law enforcement and criminals alike are chasing after her.

GUEST CAST: Lynda Boyd (Darla); Jon Cuthbert (Vincennes); Joy Tanner; Glenn Morshower; Harrison Coe (John Broughtman); Mark Acheson (Lot Attendant); Brian Jensen (Krasowski); Damon Gregory (Burns); Mark Gibbon (Scarangello); Gaetana Korbin (Shea); Kelly Fiddick (Anton); Douglas Newell (Grady); P. Adrian Dorval (Gun Store Robber).

8. "Give Me Death" Written by: Peter M. Lenkov. Directed by: Scott Williams. Airdate: Week of November 9, 1998.

Eric's nemesis, the man who ordered Shelly's death, is Top Dollar, and he has a terrible secret. He learns that if killed by the Crow in an act of revenge, he can also come back to life, but as a force of pure evil, powerful and virtually immortal. A strange African American cowboy figure of mystical powers wants Eric to abandon his mission of vengenace against Top Dollar or face the consequences.

GUEST CAST: Lynda Boyd (Darla); Julie Dreyfus; Kadeem Hardison (The Skull Cowboy); Jon Pyper-Ferguson (Top Dollar); Gaetana Korbin (Shea); Marilyn Norry (Dr. Ross); Simon Longmore (Moleman); Jason Griffith (Martinez).

9. "Before I Wake" Written by: Gregg Fienberg and Bryce Zabel. Directed by: Alan Simmonds. Airdate: Week of November 16, 1998.

Eric seeks help in contacting Shelly from his quirky friend Dr. Dorset. Dorset uses hypnotic regression to send Eric back to a former life in which he was an Indian named Blackfeather. There, Eric becomes enmeshed in the details and love of another life.

GUEST CAST: Don Most (Dr. Dorset); Jon Cuthbert (Vincennes); Christina Cox (Capshaw); Michelle Thrush; Jimmy Herman; Ty Olsson (Fun Boy); Joy Coghill (Laura Stansbury); Terence Kelly (Preacher Morgan); Shaun Johnston (Roy Jackson); Patrick Stevenson (McGee); Jim Thorburn (Skinner); Leonard George (Shaman); James Nicholas (Totem Carver).

10. "Death Wish" Written by: Jeff Androsky and Jackie Zabel. Directed by: James Head. Airdate: Week of December 12, 1998.

In his quest for redemption, Eric becomes embroiled in a strange case. The ghost of a young boy named Casey is trying to protect his living father from hit men, and Eric must help.

GUEST CAST: Jon Cuthbert (Vincennes); Christina Cox (Capshaw); John Hawkes; Jared Zabel; Jason Schombing; Bill Croft (Greg Doersch); Brad Kelly (Beresford); Jayme Knox (Eve Thompson); Marc Baur (Joey Rundle); Mark Schooley (Paramedic).

11. "Through a Dark Circle" Written by: John Turman. Directed by: Tibor Takacs. Airdate: Week of January 11, 1999.

Eric uses black magic to open the portal to the afterlife in hopes of bringing Shelly through to his reality, but succeeds only in resurrected something evil, a psychotic serial killer named Richard Lee Wilbanks. The madman attacks Eric and then abducts a woman named Karen Harris, who during his life testified against him and saw to it that he was sent to the electric chair. Next, "the Circle Killer," as he is known, pursues one of the witnesses at his execution, Albrecht's girlfriend, Cordelia. To rid the world of Wilbanks once and for all, Eric must take the killer back to the land of the damned, a dimension of darkness that could envelop the Crow.

GUEST CAST: Jon Cuthbert (Vincennes); Christina Cox (Capshaw); Sue Mathew (Cordelia); Lawrence S. Smilgys (Richard Lee Wilbanks); Alex Karzis (Nytmare); Sarah Deacons (Karen Harris); Andrew McIlroy (Dennis Dobbs).

12. "Disclosure" Written by: Bill Taub. Directed by: James Head. Airdate: Week of January 18, 1999.

Morgan Fine, an officer at internal affairs, investigates Albrecht's caseload, discovering that many of his cases include strange eyewitness testimony involving a ghost-like figure in black, the Crow! Meanwhile, the gangster husband, Frank Moran, of Eric's friend Louise purchases the Black Out. Draven goes to Albrecht for help in dealing with Moran, and Albrecht plans to have the Crow infiltrate Moran's criminal organization. Even as Fine closes in on Albrecht and Draven, Eric is given his first assignment by Moran — the murder of a City Council member. Later, Eric is arrested for the murder of Shelly Webster, even as Albrecht is suspended from duty.

GUEST CAST: Tim Kelleher (Morgan Fine); Lynda Boyd (Darla); Christine Cox (Capshaw); Jon Cuthbert (Vincennes); Gaetana Korbin; Kavan Smith; Dion Luther (Fairburn); Philip Maurice Hayes (Eddie); Zoran Vukelic (Sal); Bob Dawson (Sloman); Dario Delasco (Fairburn Guard).

13. "The People vs. Eric Draven" Written by: Edward Tirnan. Directed by: Tibor Tikacs. Airdate: Week of January 25, 1999.

Eric is in jail for the murder of Shelly Webster, and Sara begs Albrecht to get Cordelia, his estranged girlfriend (and a DA), to help him. The case goes to trial and the prosecutor claims that Eric Draven was a jealous lover who orchestrated Shelly's murder and faked his own death. His de-

fense attorney counters that Eric has been helpful to the police, and does not understand how he is back "alive" after his fall from the sixteenth story loft window. The jury's verdict: Draven is guilty, and remanded to the county lock-up until sentencing.

GUEST CAST: Jaimz Woolvett; Maria del Mar (Prosecutor); Lynda Boyd (Darla); Jon Cuthbert (Vincennes); Sue Mathew (Cordelia); Ty Olsson (Fun Boy); Zak Alam (Curtis Bilbao); Jerry Wasserman (Judge Morrison); B.J. Harrison (Jury Foreman); Bobby Stewart (Bailiff).

14. "It's a Wonderful Death" Written by: Andy Baker, Brent Friedman. Directed by: Gilbert Shilton. Airdate: Week of February 8, 1999.

The mysterious black man known as the "Skull Cowboy" materializes inside Draven's jail cell and grants him a wish, in this case to go back in time to the Devil's Night preceding Shelly's death. The wish comes true and Eric desperately attempts to prevent their double murders, recruiting Albrecht and Sara to help stop it. When Eric's trip to the past is a failure, he is permitted to go back in time again; this time he tries another plan, breaking up with Shelly and being ready when the bad guys arrive at his loft to kill him. Again, as before, events take a tragic turn.

GUEST CAST: Lynda Boyd (Darla); Jon Cuthbert (Vincennes); Kareem Hardison; John Tench (T-Bird); Darcy Laurie (Tin-Tin); Ty Olsson (Fun Boy); Zak Alam (Curtis Bilbao); Luke Doucet (Egan); Jarred Blancard (Jeffers); Curtis Bechdholt (Walsh).

15. "Birds of a Feather" Written by: Bryce Zabel. Directed by: Alan Simmonds. Airdate: Week of February 15, 1999.

After the judge in Eric's trial mysteriously releases him from prison, Eric encounters a female crow, "Talon," a short-haired beauty named Hannah Foster who has her own vendetta to pursue. Her daughter, Rebecca, was kidnapped and kept locked in an attic until she died. Now Hannah, a lost soul, wants to go on a killing spree as vengeance. Hoping to save her soul, the Crow makes one of the culprits confess and go to jail. Unfortunately, he is too late to stop Hannah from killing one of the perpetrators, who comes back from the dead as a force of evil.

GUEST CAST: Bobbie Phillips (Hannah Foster/Talon); Christina Cox (Capshaw); Jon Cuthbert (Vincennes); Mackenzie Gray; Gaetana Korbin; Sue Mathew (Cordelia); William MacDonald (Gordon Bedford); Jerry Wasserman (Judge Morrison); Greg Michaels (Desk Sergeant); Alisa Tortolano (Rebecca Foster); Christ Gibson (Ben Foster); Reese McBeth (Flash); Kmantray Smith (Trash); John MacLaren (Store Owner); Carla White (Party Girl).

16. **"Never Say Die"** Written by: David Ransil. Story by: Edward Tivnan. Directed by: Scott Summersgill. Airdate: Week of February 22, 1999.

The dangerous and terrifying spirit of Rasputin is resurrected by a mad Russian who needs the portal in Eric's loft to complete the task and protect himself from the evil.

GUEST CAST: Christina Cox (Capshaw); David Lovgren; David Palfrey (Father Peter); Stephen Dimopoulos (Father Andrew); Jed Rees (Nytmare); Vitaliy Kravechenko (Boris); Martin Novotny (Gregor); Alexander Kalugin (Krensky); Oleg Palme (Father Ivan).

17. **"Lazarus Rising"** Written by: Jonathan Vankin, John Whalen. Directed by: Scott Summersgill. Airdate: Week of April 13, 1999.

Dr. Dorset, Eric's friend, puts him in contact with the scientists at the Lazarus Group, a secret society that has existed for a thousand years and is interested in the amazing regenerative abilities of the Crow. Meanwhile, Albrecht sees an attorney about getting his badge back. Eric agrees to be tested by the secret society — on the condition that the group helps him contact Shelly. The Lazarus Society agrees, and Dr. Sachs uses a soul displacement device to transport Eric to the land of the dead, but all is not as it seems.

GUEST CAST: Don Most (Dr. Dorset); Christina Cox; Mavor Moore; Robert Wisden (Dr. Sachs); Terry David Mulligan (Steve Fentress); Jerry Wasserman (Judge Morrison); Lance Gibson (Batboy); Norman Sherry (Crossbow); Judy Racicot (Snake Eyes).

18. **"Closing Time"** Written by: Brad Markowitz and Edward Tivnan. Directed by: William Gereghty. Airdate: Week of April 20, 1999.

The Crow pays a visit to Fun Boy in prison to cleanse him and make him see the pain he caused Eric and Shelly. Unfortunately, Fun Boy has another guest too, an agent of evil for the deceased Top Dollar, who also claims to be a record agent pursuing a deal with Eric's former band. Meanwhile, Albrecht is made detective again, and a freed Fun Boy torments Darla and Sara. The plot of Top Dollar and his minion is to make Eric kill Fun Boy, a cleansed innocent, resulting in Eric becoming evil himself.

GUEST CAST: Gabriel Casseus; Lynda Boyd (Darla); Jon Cuthbert (Vincennes); John Pyper-Ferguson (Top Dollar); Gaetana Korbin; Sue Mathew (Cordelia); Ty Olsson (Fun Boy); Zoltan Buday (Shilling); Zak Alam (Bilbao); Jarred Blancard (Jeffers); Luke Doucet (Egan); Curtis Bechdholt (Jare Walsh).

19. **"The Road Not Taken"** Written by: Chad and Carey Hayes. Directed by: Brenton Spencer. Airdate: Week of April 26, 1999.

Hannah, the female Crow, receives a dire psychic message concerning a missing child and her tormented mother, and tries to help. The trail of baby Celia leads to a man named Phil Romano, but it turns out to be a set-up. Meanwhile, Eric is on a vision quest, reliving memories of Shelly, but finally comes to Hannah's aid and sets out with the reinstated Albrecht to rescue the baby. Once the baby is saved, however, Hannah isn't sure she can give it up...

GUEST CAST: Bobbie Phillips (Hannah Foster/Talon); Lynda Boyd (Darla); Jon Cuthbert (Vincennes); Christina Cox (Capshaw); Stellina Rusich; Garwin Sanford; Hailey and Jerry Clayford-Beckie (Baby Celia); Alisa Tortolano (Rebecca Foster); Peter Kent (Phil Romano); Meghan Ory (Alice); Ron Selmour (Bart Conklin); Rafe McDonald (Sarge); Ian Carter (Holcomb).

20. "Brother's Keeper" Written by: Chad Hayes and Carey Hayes. Directed by: Peter Dashkewytch. Airdate: Week of May 4, 1999.

A strange uniformed man leads Eric into a vision, telling him that his estranged brother, Chris, needs help. Eric's brother is in trouble for stealing money, and every time thugs beat Chris, Eric feels the pain of the blows. He has a troubled history of mistrust with Chris, but the brothers have always loved each other despite a father who apparently didn't want them in his life. As Eric tries to extricate Chris from trouble by going to Albrecht, a revelation from beyond the grave puts a new perspective on the Draven boys' long-missing father.

GUEST CAST: Corey Feldman (Chris Draven); Christina Cox (Capshaw); Colin Cunningham; Benz Antoine (Bouespa); Brad Loree (Slidell); Adam Harrington (Ghost Soldier); Simon Baker (Young Eric Draven); Lane Gates (Young Chris Draven); April Telek (Lily); Jan Bailey (Veronica); Jude Lee (Vietnamese Woman); Michael La Page (American Soldier).

21. "Dead to Rights" Written by: Brad Markowitz. Directed by: Alan Simmonds. Airdate: Week of May 11, 1999.

A cop killer is using kidnapped women as bait to lure police officers to their deaths, but Eric is hesitant to become involved because he's trying to keep the Crow out of his life. Another woman is kidnapped, Vincennes' wife, and Albrecht is on the case.

Vincennes seeks the killer, a former cop named Truax, but walks into a trap. Eric helps Albrecht bring down the murderous psychopath before more innocents die.

GUEST CAST: Anthony Michael Hall (Reid W. Truax); Lynda Boyd (Darla); Christina Cox (Capshaw); Jon Cuthbert (Vincennes); Patricia Haras; Alexander Pollock (Jason Vincennes); Lauren Zabel (Libby Vincennes); Eva De Viveiros (Beth); Keith Gordey (Rios); Bill Rowat (Melton); Marrett Green (Joe Ross); Barry Greene (Father Truax); Spencer Moen (Young Truax); Rodney De Croo (Scruggs); Tina Hildebrandt (Eleanor Truax); Mateya Langton (Reporter #1); James Tsirpoulous (Reporter #2).

22. "A Gathering Storm" Written by: Gregg Fienberg. Directed by: Brenton Spencer. Airdate: Week of May 18, 1999.

A desperate Judge Morrison, the man that freed Eric from prison, seeks police protection and immunity for his part in the secretive and dangerous Lazarus Group. The society's leader, Balsam, has secretly appropriated a young healthy body, succeeding in his quest for immortality; and now he is determined to raise the Crow of Eric Draven. The young Balsam is successful, an evil Crow is resurrected, and he promptly sets out to kill Fun Boy in jail. A worried Shelly returns from the land of the dead to help Eric face his twisted alter ego, who has been dispatched by Balsam to kill the judge. The Crow is no longer a part of Eric, and is separated from Eric's conscience — but he still wants and desires Shelly.

GUEST CAST: Michael Weatherly (Frederick Balsam); Lynda Boyd (Darla); Jon Cuthbert (Vincennes); Mavor Moore (Old Balsam); Myron Natwick; Jared Zabel (Casey Thompson); Ty Olsson (Fun Boy); Jerry Wasserman (Judge Paul Morrison); Marcus Hondro (Gideon); Joe Maffei (Caleb Cowen); Kirsten Williamson (Mako).

Daredevil

Known to criminals as "the Man Without Fear," Daredevil is a Marvel Comics hero that first appeared in 1964 during the so-called Silver Age of comic books. Like other Marvel heroes, Daredevil is a superhero who carries around much personal baggage. It isn't racial prejudice (as in the case of the X-Men), a dual nature (like the Incredible Hulk), or even a host of personal neuroses (like young Peter Parker). Instead, Daredevil's problem is a physical handicap: blindness. As a boy, young Matt Murdock was splashed with radioactive chemicals during an accident, an event that rendered him sightless.

Fortunately, the same spill had positive effects as well. Each of Matt's remaining four senses was dramatically enhanced by the incident, and he was even able to see, after a fashion, via a kind of sonar. Matt also developed newfound agility and balance, important physical skills for a superhero that crawled across rooftops by blackest night.

A child of Hell's Kitchen, Matt Murdock grew up to use his new sensory skills in the fight against criminals, putting the fear of God into the corrupt with his redhorned, devil-inspired costume. By day, Matt fought for justice too, but as a noble defense attorney. Essentially a vigilante, Daredevil believed that he could fix by night the wrongs that the American justice system couldn't take care of in the courtroom by day.

Daredevil is the creation of writer Stan Lee and artist Bill Everett, but other illustrators and writers soon made the Murdock mythos their own, including John Romita and Gene Colan. Before lending his talents to the Batman franchise with *The Dark Knight Returns* in the mid–1980s, Frank Miller took a crack at Daredevil, writing and illustrating the book starting in 1980. Even then, Miller was a superhero revolu-

tionary, and one of his most controversial efforts saw the brutal death of a character called Elektra, a beautiful warrior and romantic partner for Daredevil, in issue 181 of the title. Elektra not only died, she was virtually savaged by her opponent, the deadly assassin called Bullseye.

Independent film icon and director Kevin Smith has added his own unique voice to Daredevil comics (in the 1990s), improving slumping comic book sales considerably and even bringing his Irish-Catholic upbringing into the dazzling storytelling. But even if the character has been revitalized twice in the comics, his visibility has not been good in Hollywood, at least until 2003. The character's first appearance came in a forgettable TV-movie, a backdoor pilot for a prospective Daredevil series, called *Trial of the Incredible Hulk*.

In this story, based on the 1970s *Hulk* series, Dr. David Banner (Bill Bixby) went on trial for a murder he did not commit, and was defended by none other than Murdock, the sightless Daredevil, played by Rex Smith. The film (written by Gerald Di Pego and directed by Bill Bixby) aired on May 7, 1989, but the entertainment world hardly noticed.

One could not make the same accusation about the big-screen adaptation of *Daredevil*. Shot in June of 2002 by writer/director Mark Steven Johnson, the film's production followed hot on the heels of 2002's *Spider-Man* success, and 20th Century–Fox pumped some 100 million dollars into the high-profile effort.[1] Ben Affleck, *People* magazine's "Sexiest Man Alive" for 2002, was cast in the leading role of Matt Murdock, and was afforded incredible, big-name support in the persons of *Alias* star Jennifer Garner as Elektra, imposing Michael Clarke Duncan as Kingpin and Connor Farrell as Bullseye. Kevin Smith reportedly gave the script a polish, and even appeared in the movie as a coroner named

Daring to make a difference: The Incredible Hulk (Lou Ferrigno) and Daredevil (Rex Smith) dou-ble-team the bad guys in the TV-movie *The Trial of the Incredible Hulk* (1989).

"Kirby," along with Frank Miller (as another of Bullseye's targets).

No expense was spared to bring Daredevil's nighttime world to visceral life, and the film was filled with amazing stunt work and fight choreography. One especially riveting scene, set in a bar, dramatized how Daredevil could "see" those around him during a fight. Despite such thrilling moments and a stellar cast, many in the industry speculated the picture would be no good, citing as evidence its premiere date in mid–February (Valentine's Day)— hardly a prime season for promising films, and traditionally a dumping ground for unwanted movies. But proving the naysayers wrong, *Daredevil* effortlessly struck box office gold, boasting the second best opening in February history, beaten only by 2000's *Hannibal*. The early totals were impressive. *Daredevil* grossed some 43.5 million dollars its first weekend, and then followed that victory with a second week as America's box-office champ, grossing another 18.9 million dollars the weekend of February 21. The film successfully extended "the superheroes triumphant" trend at the box office, keeping audience attention riveted until a summer season that would include a second *X-Men* movie, Ang Lee's adaptation of *The Incredible Hulk* and Stephen Norrington's *LXG: League of Extraordinary Gentlemen*.

A success with audiences, *Daredevil* received especially nasty reviews on its release, most of them directed against Ben Affleck. In point of fact, Affleck did a creditable job in the motion picture, both as a blind man and as a superhero icon. He was targeted for such derision probably because he is so vastly popular and successful. Engaged to Jennifer Lopez, and saddled with that "sexiest man alive" moniker, he was something of an easy mark for jealous critics, and the hard-hearted reviews reflected that. Some reviews even mentioned Jennifer Lopez by name (and Ben's unofficial nickname, "Bennifer")— really a slap in the face to the fine

actor, and another indication that critics do not necessarily take superhero movies seriously. Affleck's girlfriend or status as "sexy" had little to do with *Daredevil* and its merits.

If anything, it was a solid, dramatic Ben Affleck that carried *Daredevil* with his winsome good humor and fine underplaying; and the film's primary failing was merely that the character seemed a second-string version of Batman, haunting the night and lamenting his violent past and the death of a parent. In point of fact, the Batman saga co-opted many of these elements from Daredevil comics in the first place, especially the Frank Miller era, so there was little *Daredevil* could do to overcome a sameness and triteness in its story.

Audiences had seen the "I made you? You made me!" scene before Daredevil and Kingpin play that confrontation again for the umpteenth time at the film's climax. Viewers have also previously met the investigative reporter out to prove the existence of a superhero. His name is Urich (Joe Pantoliano) in *Daredevil*, but it was Knox in Tim Burton's *Batman*.

The repeated story elements go on and on, to *Daredevil's* detriment. Audiences had seen their costumed superheroes perched impressively beside skyscraper gargoyles long before Murdock rests beside one in *Daredevil*. Audiences had mourned the death of a romantic companion in superhero films as diverse as *Superman: The Movie* (in which Lois was resurrected), *Batman Returns* (in which Catwoman was resurrected), *The Crow*, *RoboCop 3* and more. The only new wrinkle in that old cliché in *Daredevil* is that Elektra's resurrection has been saved, apparently, for the sequel.

On other fronts, Colin Farrell, a usually restrained performer, goes way over the top in his performance as Bullseye, lending the film an unwanted aspect of camp. Maybe it's the part, or maybe it's Farrell's choice to go bulge-eyed in the role, but it is hard to take seriously a character that commits murder with a peanut, as he does in one scene.

Any *Daredevil* film should concern itself with the "dual" philosophies of Matt Murdock. By day, he argues the law, obeying it and seeing it vindicated. By night, he takes the law into his own hands, usurping it. How would such a decent, honorable man feel about this contradiction? This film might have seemed smarter had it focused on this personal issue rather than boiling the whole notion down to Murdock's canned declaration that he is "not the bad guy." *Really*? He operates outside the law, acting as judge, jury, and, in one case, executioner. What is he going to do about it? How can he reconcile his behavior as Daredevil with his intellectual capacity to understand that the law, as flawed as it is, is the benchmark of civilization?

Filled with startling Catholic imagery and multiple scenes set inside a grand cathedral, the moral battle for Daredevil's very soul could have been the focal point of a tremendously affecting movie, one more like *Unbreakable* and less like *Black Scorpion*. How does Elektra's death and Kingpin's criminal scheming threaten the balance of Murdock's soul? Answering that question would have made for a more intelligent film, and lessened some of the similarities to the "avenger of the night" movies like *The Crow* and *Batman*.

These days it is not enough merely to pay lip service to the moral dilemmas of a superhero; successful productions must tackle them head on, and *Daredevil* just isn't daring enough. It plays things safe, relying on the conventions of the genre and, specifically, *Batman*, even while filling the screen with some enormously appealing performers that require better, more mature material.

Maybe the sequel will be better. In late '03, however, Affleck confessed in print that he had little interest in one.

Trial of the Incredible Hulk *see* The Incredible Hulk

Daredevil (2003)
LIVE-ACTION FILM

"A big man, Mr. Affleck is shriveled by the one-dimensional role.... The director, Mark Steven Johnson ... missteps in a way new to comic-book movies. Instead of telegraphing a patronizing attitude towards Daredevil, Mr. Johnson is too worshipful of the idiom's conventions. His affection for the character leaves overly sincere puddles every step of the way."
— Elvis Mitchell, *The New York Times*:
"Blind Lawyer as Hero in Red Leather."
February 14, 2003, page 1 of 2.

"Couldn't the writer ... have come up with a better story than the tired, old now-standard one about a son avenging his father's death and an over-the-top grinning crime boss? ... The entire movie looks like an assembly line production pieced together merely to give a movie star the biggest perk of all — a franchise."
— Victoria Alexander, *FilmsInReview.com*,
February 14, 2003.

"Like Affleck himself, the film is perfectly satisfying without being deeply satisfying."
— Michael O'Sullivan, *The Washington Post*:
"In *Daredevil*, Justice Is Blind."
February 14, 2003, page WE45.

"The dialogue is dreadful, a stale sort of hokum that wouldn't make the cut at Marvel Comics."
— John Anderson, *Newsday*,
February 14, 2003.

CAST: Ben Affleck (Matt Murdock/Daredevil); Jennifer Garner (Elektra Natchios); Michael Clarke Duncan (Wilson Fisk/the Kingpin); Colin Farrell (Bullseye); Jon Favreau (Franklin Nelson); Joe Pantoliano (Urich); David Keith (Jack "the Devil" Murdock); Scott Terra (Young Matt Murdock); Kevin Smith (Kirby the Coroner); Frank Miller (Victim); Derrick O'Conner (Father); Stan Lee (Pedestrian); Leland Orser, Robert Iler.

CREW: 20th Century–Fox and Regency Enterprises present *Daredevil*. *Written and Directed by:* Mark Steven Johnson. *Based on Marvel Characters Created by:* Stan Lee and Bill Everett. *Director of Photography:* Ericson Core. *Film Editors:* Dennis Virkler, Armen Minisian. *Music:* Graeme Revell. *Production Design:* Barry Chisud. *Produced by:* Avi Arad, Gary Foster, Aron Milchan. *M.P.A.A. Rating:* PG-13. *Running time:* 96 minutes.

In Hell's Kitchen, the red-leather-clad vigilante known as "Daredevil" falls in battle, taking refuge in a church sanctuary. Near death, Daredevil's life flashes before his eyes, and the story of a tortured hero is recounted…

As a boy, young Irish Catholic Matt Murdock worships his father, a small-time boxing champ nicknamed "the Devil." One day, while coming home from school, Matt learns that his washed-up father is working for a local criminal named Fallon. Shattered by the moral betrayal, Matt runs away, and is subsequently blinded in an accident involving toxic chemicals.

Recovering in the hospital, Matt quickly discovers that his remaining four senses have been heightened to incredible levels, permitting him to develop his balance, agility and fighting abilities. Later, when a shadowy assassin kills Matt's father for failing to throw an important fight for Fallon, Matt swears to defend the innocent people of Hell's Kitchen from the criminals. He grows up to become a crusading attorney by day, an avenging superhero by night. Unfortunately, he is riddled with self-doubt and anxiety, wondering if he has crossed the line from hero to "bad guy." He frequently spends time confessing his sins to an understanding Catholic priest.

Now an adult, the blind Murdock is hounded by a reporter named Urich from *The New York Post* that seeks the truth about Daredevil. Meanwhile, Matt also falls for Elektra Natchios, a beautiful woman with uncommon fighting abilities and the heart of a warrior. When the local crime boss, Wilson Fisk, a.k.a. the Kingpin, assassinates her rich father with the help of a crazed, bald assassin named Bullseye, Elektra believes that Daredevil is the actual murderer and sets out for vengeance.

Matt attempts to set his new lover straight, but Bullseye kills Elektra in battle on a rooftop. Wounded and dying, Matt battles Bullseye in the church and learns the secret identity of the Kingpin. During the final confrontation with the Kingpin, Daredevil learns that he is facing not just the man that ordered Elecktra's assassination, but his father's murderer.

Dark Angel

As the twentieth century came to a close, it appeared to some skeptics that the superhero mythos had become completely irrelevant to contemporary life in the United States. Crime rates were at the lowest percentage in more than thirty years, and thus there was no real need for extra-legal vigilantes like Batman or tough-talking, square-shooting *uber*-cops like Robocop. There was no substantial foreign enemy like Nazi Germany (the bane of Captain America) or the Soviet Union, and America's economy soared to new and previously undreamed of heights.

So peaceful and satisfied was the country, in fact, that the contested year 2000 presidential election was all about "peace and prosperity," and how best to spend a financial surplus the government had accrued during a time of great profits and few enemies.

During this era, the only successful superhero programs on TV were *Buffy the Vampire Slayer* and *Angel*, two series that pitted superheroes not against conventional criminals, but supernatural menaces. No spies, no Nazis, no crooks. Only demons and vampires, the very definition of evil, could be counted on as villains in this new and happy world at the turn of the millennium.

Director James Cameron, who had dazzled moviegoers with dark, frightening, and dystopic futures in such films as *The Terminator* (1984), *Aliens* (1986) and *Terminator 2* (1991), understood the nature of the problem. The superhero mythology had to take a different turn or face immediate irrelevance. When he created *Dark Angel* in the fall of 2000 with writing partner Charles Eglee, he realized that the present was just too good, too peaceful, to require superheroes. So what did he do?

Cleverly, he jumped ahead some twenty years to tell the story of a new generation of superhero, focusing on a genetically enhanced woman named Max (Jessica Alba) living in a post-electromagnetic-pulse-ravaged Seattle in the year 2020. And her world was a total dystopia, with the United States having become a third-world country, It was this notion to take America's "optimistic, runaway prosperity and just drop-kick it," as the director noted in the press, that informed much of this new venture.[1]

Terese Blythe, of *Sojourners,* described the economically ravaged world of the new Fox series in a different but equally disturbing way:

> The world presented in *Dark Angel* is violent, filthy, urban and young. Seattle looks like our worst ghetto nightmare, with open-air buildings used as squatter apartments, graffiti on the walls, homeless people camped out everywhere and swarms of 20-somethings hanging around with nothing to do.... Max is a post-modern Robin Hood, stealing from the rich so she can help her friends, all of whom are poor.[2]

In other words, since the present at the turn of the millennium offered little possibility

for crime, squalor and other societal problems, it was necessary for Cameron to "resurrect Depression-era America, when gangsters ruled the streets and the little guy didn't have much of a chance and needed some help."[3]

In *Dark Angel,* Seattle became a "military protectorate" patrolled by mechanical, Frisbee-like hover drones that watched the population at all times. The city's government was corrupt and dangerous. Medicine was scarce. America's arts and treasures, including the Statue of Liberty, had been shipped overseas because of the Depression ("Art Attack").

The message of *Dark Angel,* according to star Valarie Rae Miller, interviewed by this author in late 2000, was ultimately that bad times bring communities together. "It's an interesting show with a very positive message," she noted. "It's about people banding together when times are bad, and it says that money isn't everything. A lot of people who grew up during the Depression have been watching it because they can relate to it."

Appropriately, considering America's ethnic diversity, the characters on *Dark Angel* were diverse creations. Max was an X-5 soldier who had escaped from the genetic engineering program called Project Manticore with a dozen other "transgens" in 2009. She lost contact with the other "children," and now seeks to find them, while simultaneously attempting to blend in with normal "human" society.

Hunted by the mad and obsessive Lydecker (John Savage), Max came to trust Seattle's only living crusader, the heroic (but wheelchair-bound) Logan Cale, played by Michael Weatherly. Cale is a Bruce Wayne-type figure, wealthy and powerful and with good connections. He continually exposes the corrupt government on a "streaming video" transmission, "the only free voice left in the city," doing so under the secret identity of "Eyes Only."

A trio of *Dark Angel* stars: Up front is Jessica Alba as the genetically souped-up Max; to the right is "Eyes Only" Logan Cale (Michael Weatherly); to the left is the villainous Lydecker (John Savage).

The first season of *Dark Angel* featured a large supporting cast. Max worked as a bike courier at a company called Jam Pony with her friend, a lesbian named Original Cindy (Valarie Rae Miller). Also working there was the hapless Sketchy (Richard Gunn) and the barely comprehensible, thickly-accented Herbal (Alimi Ballard). Max's boss at Jam Pony was Normal (J.C. Mackenzie), a wrong-headed supervisor that Cindy described (in "Art Attack") as "a constipated, crusty ... rhythm-free Republican white man." Max was often called upon to help her friends when they got in trouble. All the while, she had to maintain her secret identity and evade detection by the evil Lydecker and his military squad.

Dark Angel launched with much fanfare in the fall of 2000. As Miller noted, a "large percentage of the [series] advertising is just pushing Jessica [Alba] as a beautiful girl. And there's so much more to her than that." Indeed, the attractive and lithe Alba was the show's initial major appeal. A dark beauty with piercing eyes, she worked out for over an hour every day and then often put in 15-hour days on the Vancouver set.[4] But it was the right ticket for success, at least in the era of the lovely Buffy the Vampire Slayer, Sydney Bristow and Yancy Butler. "Guys are easily stimulated," Alba noted. "All you have to do is dress up in a sexy outfit.... Guys are sort of stupid that way."[5] She was right, and for a time, Alba was the sci-fi superhero "It" girl.

The pilot for *Dark Angel* drew 17 million viewers to the tube on the Tuesday night it first premiered (competing against Joss Whedon's *Angel* on the WB) — a good number, considering the pilot alone had cost somewhere in the neighborhood of 12 million dollars. But before long, Fox seemed to lose interest in the show and began to pre-empt it, literally at almost every opportunity. "It's a running joke on the set," Miller told this author of the interruptions. "It's become a game for the cast members to see when we're actually going to be on the air. We've been pre-empted by the World Series, the Billboard Magazine Awards, Election 2000 coverage — you name it. I think the network likes the show, but they're also scared of it."

Fox renewed *Dark Angel* for a second season, but just barely. And, unfortunately, the powers-that-be behind the show decided it was time for a re-vamp. So, in the time-honored tradition of *Space: 1999* (1975–77) and *SeaQuest DSV* (1993–1996), *Dark Angel* underwent a second season dumbing down, with more overt science fiction concepts added. Although James Cameron promised to stay "very consistent with the themes and style" of the first season,[6] viewing individual episodes, it was difficult to see how that was the case. Savage's Lydecker character was written out of the series, replaced by a more testosterone-laden nemesis for Max named Ames White (played by Martin Cummins, from *Poltergeist: The Legacy* [1996–1999]).

Unfortunately, the series creators also added a host of "alien" creatures, all of them failed Manticore genetic creations. And so appeared lizard people, bat people, cat people, mermaids ("Gill Girl") and other far-fetched creations that seemed woefully out of place in the realistic world forged during the interesting first season of the series. Worst of all was the addition of a character named Joshua (Kevin Durand), a dog-boy that physically resembled Ron Perlman's Vincent from *Beauty and the Beast* (1988–1991) but acted more like Jar-Jar Binks. In one episode, he ate a tube of paint ("Medium Is the Message"), and in another prevented Logan and Max from consummating their relationship.

The show couldn't take the strain of this resident alien, who was probably there because the second season of the series had become overrun by *Star Trek* writers, including Kenneth Biller, Marjorie David and Rene Echevarria. Still, hopes were high as *Dark Angel* moved to Friday night, and Echevarria proclaimed "we think there's an opportunity to do what *The X-Files* did."[7]

Also added to the cast for the second season were two romantic foils for Max and Logan. In the first season, Logan had struggled to regain the ability to walk after a bullet wound had paralyzed him, and yet a real love affair was brewing between the pair. In the first episode of the second season, however, Logan was infected with a designer virus that would kill him if any physical contact occurred between him and Max. As if that weren't deterrent enough, along came Alec (Jensen Ackles), a hunky, roguish X-5 with a lust for Max, and sexy Asha (Ashley Scott of *Birds of Prey*), a resistance fighter pining away for the intellectual Logan.

"They are the love of each other's lives, but their relationship is going to be tested," writer-producer Echevarria noted of the new set-up involving Logan and Max.[8] Unfortunately, as a result of all these new characters, the Jam Pony characters were either axed (Herbal) or given short shrift (Original Cindy, Normal and Sketchy).

In fact, the second season of *Dark Angel* featured too many supporting characters, bug-eyed monsters, and new, poorly executed themes. Lydecker appeared, then disappeared. Manticore was revealed to be a front for an ancient cult, alternately known as "the Family" or the Conclave. The true creator of the X-5s was learned to be not Lydecker, but a mysterious "father figure" called "Sandaman." And Max was revealed to be "the Chosen One," a messiah foretold to prevent a coming apocalypse. It was a mishmash of ideas that were half-developed and in no way seemed related to the economically destroyed world of the first season.

Still, in its second year, *Dark Angel* did develop one valuable and interesting theme amidst the many plot strands. The transgens were treated as second-class citizens,

the targets of discrimination and bigotry by mainstream America. As racial profiling against Arabs commenced in the United States at the time (because of the terrorist attacks of September 11), this "fantastic" subplot mirrored reality almost as it happened, and reminded people that Americans can exist in any size, shape, sex or color. "We were made in America and we're staying here," one character declared in the finale, "Freak Nation," and *Dark Angel,* even amidst all of those silly second season monsters, had discovered a new relevance.

James Cameron directed "Freak Nation," the final episode of the second season, which aired May 3, 2002, the same day *Spider-Man* opened nationwide in theaters. The ratings were not what were expected, and the series was cancelled shortly thereafter. In this case, the expense of creating a series (1.3 million per show) was too much for a network to bear for such low ratings.

More importantly, the context of life in America had changed substantially since *Dark Angel*'s premiere a season earlier. The country had been the victim of terrorist attacks, and the Bush Administration had ushered in the worst economic period since the Hoover Administration. The surplus disappeared (thanks to a tax cut aimed at the rich), Enron collapsed (and took a lot of 401Ks with it), and, well, *Dark Angel*'s futuristic premise of recession in a Third World America did not look very farfetched any more. In fact, it became a depressing reminder that things could still get worse, and were headed down that road.

Still, Max remains an interesting superhero, one of a future era. Equipped with feline DNA (like Huntress in *Birds of Prey*), she has super-agility and strength, as well as a biannual urge to go into heat and mate. Also, the series put up a lot of interesting villains against this cunning, leatherclad warrior. There were super-powered assassins (high on chemicals emitted from a dangerous implant) called Reds in "Rising."

There were Steelheads, 1980s punk rockers with metal implants, in "Some Assembly Required"; and Max faced off against a transgen brother, Zack, rebuilt as a *Terminator*-style cybernetic organism, in the same episode.

These were interesting challenges, but it was a shame that so much time in each episode was spent on rescuing sidekicks and escaping bad guys. One week Max would require rescue. The next week it was Logan. The next week, Zack needed to be rescued, or Zack *and* Logan. Or Original Cindy. And so on. It got tiring, and the addition of the dog-man Joshua merely hastened the series' death.

Despite *Dark Angel*'s cancellation, Ballantine has released a series of original novels based on the program.[9] The series is currently available on DVD.

Dark Angel (2000–2002)
LIVE-ACTION SERIES

CAST: Jessica Alba (Max); Michael Weatherly (Logan Cale, "Eyes Only"); Valarie Rae Miller (Original Cindy); J.C. Mackenzie (Normal); Richard Gunn (Sketchy); FIRST SEASON ONLY: Alimi Ballard (Herbal); Jennifer Blanc (Kendra Maibum); John Savage (Lydecker). SECOND SEASON ONLY: Jensen Ackles (Alec); Kevin Durand (Joshua); Ashley Scott (Asha); Martin Cummins (White).

CREW: *Created by:* James Cameron, Charles H. Eglee. *Main Theme:* Chuck D, Gary G. Wiz. *Score:* Joel McNeely. *Directors of Photography (various episodes):* David Eddes, Brian Pearson, Steve Polivka. *Editors (various episodes):* John Refoua, James Wilcox. *Production Designer:* Jerry Wanek. *Producer:* Stephen Sassen. *Co-Producer:* Janace Tashjian. *Supervising Producer:* Patrick Harbinson. *Co-Executive Producers:* Joe Ann Fogle, Rae Sanchini, Rene Echevarria. *Executive Producer:* James Cameron. *Executive Story Editor:* Doris Egan. *Story Editors:* Moira Kirland Dekker, David Zabel. *Staff Writer:* Jose Molina. *Associate Producer:* Gina Lamar. *L.A. Casting:* Robert J. Ullrich, Eric Dawson, Carol Kritzer. *Canadian Casting:* Coreen Mayrs, Hake Brandstatton. *Co-Producer:* George Grieve. *First Assistant Director:* Morgan James Beggs. *Visual Effects Supervisors:* Elan Soltes, Randy Gerson. *Main Title Design:* Murder by Title. *Art Director:* John Macynuk. *Set Designer:* Tedd Kitchera. *Script Supervisor:* Nancy Eagles. *Location Manager:* Peter Stewart. *Gaffer:* Blair McDonald. *Special Effects Coordinator:* Andy Chamberlayne. *Stunt Coordinator:* Mike Mitchell. *Costume Designer:* Susan de Laval. *Head Make-up Artist:* Dana Michelle Hamel. *Camera Operator:* Brad Crassier. *Property Master:* Ken Hawryliw. *Directors of Photography, Second Unit:* Todd Elyzin.

SEASON ONE (2000–2001)

1. **"Dark Angel"** (two hours) Written by: James Cameron and Charles H. Eglee. Directed by: David Nutter. Airdate: October 3, 2000.

In the year 2019, America is a third-world country, the economy is in the sewer, and genetically engineered Max, an escapee from a military facility called Manticore, hides in plain sight at the parcel delivery company called Jam Pony. Hunted by the head of Manticore, Donald Lydecker, the powerful Max, an X-5, attempts to conceal her special nature while simultaneously searching for her "brothers and sisters" who escaped with her ten years earlier. Also in Seattle is Logan Cale, a wealthy crusader who runs the "streaming video" called "Eyes Only," which exposes the corruption of city officials in Seattle. At their first meeting, Logan and Max clash, but Max and Logan — the latter paralyzed in a hit — become fast friends and more.

GUEST CAST: Stanley Kamel; Kristin Bauer; Paul Popowich; Kim Hawthorne; Douglas O'Keeffe (Bruno Anselmo); Sarah Jane Redmond; Lauren Smith; Geneva Locke (Young Max); Chris Lazar (Young Zack); Kyley Statham (Young Jondy); Kent O'Connor (Struggling Child).

2. **"Heat"** Written by: Patrick Harbinson. Directed by: Michael Katleman. Airdate: October 10, 2000.

Max goes into heat, courtesy of her feline DNA. Meanwhile, as Lydecker searches for her and other Manticore escapees, Max goes in search of the kindly woman who picked her up on a stretch of road during her escape from captivity a decade earlier.

GUEST CAST: Peter Bryant; Eileen Pedde; Brand Williams; Stephen Lee; Vince Walker (Solinsky); Zinaid Memisevic (Captain); Carlene Furk (Lickety Split Girl); Geneva Locke (Young Max); Kyley Statham (Young Jondy).

3. **"Flushed"** Written by: Rene Echevarria and Charles H. Eglee. Directed by: Terrence O'Hara. Airdate: October 17, 2000.

To keep her delicate metabolism in balance, Max must regularly ingest Tryptophan, but her roommate and friends at Jam Pony fear she is using a controlled substance. When Max is arrested, Original Cindy follows her friend into jail to get her the medicine she needs, with Logan's help.

GUEST CAST: Abraham Benrubi, Peter Bryant, Kim Hawthorne, Byron Mann, Alan C. Peterson, Shannon Sutter, Stephen Lee, Michelle Goh, Geneva Locke (Young Max).

4. **"C.R.E.A.M."** Written by: David Zabel. Directed by: Chris Long. Airdate: October 31, 2000.

Logan recruits Max to help a desperate woman search for her missing father. Meanwhile, Sketchy runs afoul of the Seattle mob on one of his less-than-routine delivery runs for Jam Pony. Before long, Logan and Max realize that the person they are trying to help may have a secret agenda.

GUEST CAST: Peter Bryant; Byron Mann; Tony Perez; Lisa Rodriguez; Murray Lowry (Drunk); Geneva Locke (Yong Max); Chris Lazar (Young Zack); Ron Blecker (TAC Leader); Allesandro Juliani (Druid); Carlene Furk (Lickety Split Girl); Mike Mitchell (Guard #1); Duane Dickenson (Guard #2); Bruce Pinard (Guard #3); Maria Fabiana Dominguez (Rebecca); Michael Sunczyk (Rafe); Suleka Mathew (Reporter).

5. **"411 on the DL"** Written by: Doris Egan. Directed by: Joe Ann Fogle. Airdate: November 14, 2000.

Max becomes jealous when she learns that Logan was once married. His ex-wife returns to Seattle for help, in reality an attempt to steal money from him. At the same time, Max runs into her "brother" from her Manticore days, a fighter and leader named Zack that has more than a little romantic interest in Max. Max learns that Zack has been helping her fellow X-5 siblings find asylum.

GUEST CAST: Peter Bryant; Brenda James; William Gregory Lee (Zack); Rod Rowland; Stephen Lee; LeMark Cruise (Cop); Ralph Alderman (Impound Clerk); Allesandro Juliani (Druid); Alex Green (Security Guard); Fulvio Cecere (Sandoval).

6. **"Prodigy"** Written by: Patrick Harbinson. Story by: Charles H. Eglee and Rene Echevarria. Directed by: David Jackson. Airdate: November 21, 2000.

In hopes of learning more about her condition, Max attends a conference about genetic engineering at a local hotel, posing as a news reporter. Unfortunately, Lydecker is also a guest at the event, and takes a seat right beside Max, where he starts to hit on her. While evading Lydecker's obnoxious advances, Max must also contend with a new threat: terrorists overtake the event and police surround the building. Logan rushes to the scene, only to fall into jeopardy, requiring a dangerous, last minute rescue.

GUEST CAST: Peter Bryant; George Kee Cheung; Mark Houghton; Byron Mann; Troy Ruptash; Mike Weinberg; Biannca Gurniak (Girl); Geneva Locke (Young Max); Chris Lazar (Young Zack); Dylan Pearson (Young Manticore Boy); Shannon Powell (Terrorist); Wren Roberts (Terrorist); Chris Gora (Terrorist).

7. **"Cold Comfort"** Written by: Jose Molina. Directed by: Jeffery Levy. Airdate: November 28, 2000.

Max reluctantly re-teams with the headstrong X-5 resistance leader, Zack, this time to rescue one of their siblings, Brin, from the military. Unfortunately, Lydecker is also after Brin, resulting in an uneasy — and short-lived — alliance.

GUEST CAST: Nicole Bilderback; Peter Bryant; Robert Gossett; John Dennis Johnston; William Gregory Lee (Zack); Rick Dobran (Julio); Gustavo Febres (Fico); Darren Moore (AA Man); Josh Byer (Gate Soldier); Ron Selmour (Brig Guard #1); Chris Dugan (Brig Guard #2).

8. "Blah Blah Woof Woof" Written by: Moira Kirland Dekker. Directed by: Paul Shapiro. Airdate: December 12, 2000.

Lydecker goes to the police to help him track down Max, posting a $50,000 reward for her capture. Meanwhile, Logan must undergo a dangerous surgical procedure to remove the bullet fragment from his spine before it causes more internal damage. Lydecker's attack units try to pin down Max in the South Market Street Area, while Zack returns to town to help her; but in this case that means leaving Seattle and saying goodbye to Logan for good. When Logan becomes sick prior to his surgery, bleeding internally, Max risks a return to the city to provide him with a critical blood transfusion.

GUEST CAST: Joey Aresco (Captain Swanstorm); Peter Bryant (Bling); William Gregory Lee (Zack); Byron Mann (Detective Sung); Brian Markinson (Dr. Sam Carr); P.J. Johal (Technician); G. Michael Gray (Traidy); Bobby Stewart (Checkpoint Cop #1); D. Neil Mark (Checkpoint Cop #2); Marcus Sim (Teenager #1); Aaron Joseph (Teenager #2); Scantone Jones (Cop); Fulvio Cecere (Sandoval); Rydyr Morse (Thus); Leslie Spongberg (Girl); Russell Ferrier (Desk Cop); Donny Lucas (Paramedic); Lucia Walters (Nurse); Scott Bishop (Security Guard #1).

9. "Out" Written by: David Zabel. Directed by: Sarah Anderson. Airdate: January 9, 2001.

Captured by criminals, Logan is in dire need of rescuing by Max, but she's still ticked off at him because their relationship has remained undefined. Max pretends to be "Eyes Only" to save Logan, but will she be too late?

GUEST CAST: Peter Bryant, James Kidnie, Mack 10, Byron Mann, Kaare Anderson, Jose Vargas, Jessica Crockett.

10. "Red" Written by: Jose Molina and David Zabel. Story by: Rene Echevarria and Charles H. Eglee. Directed by: Michael Katleman. Airdate: January 16, 2001.

Logan asks Max to protect a thug — the man who shot and paralyzed him — because he is an important witness in an upcoming corruption case. Unfortunately, the witness, Anselmo, is an obnoxious jerk and can't get along with Max. Making matters worse, a troop of transgenics called "Reds," an early Manticore super-soldier experiment, are in hot pursuit. But are they after Max or Anselmo?

GUEST CAST: Peter Bryant; Patrick Kilpatrick; Douglas O'Keeffe; Alax Zahara; Mark Gibbon; David Livingstone (Max); Kendall Saunders (Britannica); Odessa Mounro (Ling Ling); Keir MacPherson (Concierge); Peter Scoular (Bellman); Christian Deans (Biker).

11. "Art Attack" Written by: Doris Egan. Directed by: James Contner. Airdate: February 6, 2001.

Logan invites Max to his cousin's wedding, even though it's an affair that promises to be snooty. Max steals a $6,000 dress for the event and helps Logan prepare his wedding toast. Meanwhile, Jam Pony delivers the wrong package to an art thief, and Normal seeks Original Cindy's help in correcting the error. Max is recruited to help recover Normal's lost item, a stolen painting, but at the same time she must keep Logan away from Daphne, a high-society ex-girlfriend.

GUEST CAST: Michael Benyaer (Onion Runyon); Susan Hogan (Aunt Margo); Master P

(Jean Baptiste Duvalier); Lawrence Pressman (Uncle Jonas); Ryan Robbins (Arnie); Samantha Smith (Daphne); Emily Holmes (Saleswoman); Michaschia Armstrong (Bodyguard #1); Bridget O'Sullivan (Matronly Woman); Michael Tiegen (Bennett); Lurene Music (Marianna); David Abbott (Minister); Antonio Cupo (Valet); Rob Bruner (Angilio Biondello); Gillian Carera (Woman); Michael Ann Conner (Woman at Boarding House); Carolyne Marghi (Tia); Rikha Sharma (Coroner); Carig Veroni (Airport Security).

12. "Rising" Written by: Moira Kirland Dekker and Doris Egan. Story: Jose Molina, David Zabel. Directed by: Duane Clark. Airdate: February 13, 2001.

Logan starts to feel sensations in his feet despite his spinal damage, and he thinks it is because he shared a blood transfusion with Max, and her Manticore transgen blood is filled with undifferentiated stem cells. Meanwhile, international super-assassins with dangerous implants still want to get their hands on Max and are trying to track her using her beeper. They track Max to Original Cindy's place, then to a bar where she escapes and kills one. Max saves Original Cindy from the Reds by taking the dangerous implant herself and fighting the bad guys, even though, at the end of the day, she must reveal her true identity to Original Cindy.

GUEST CAST: Peter Bryant (Bling); Patrick Kilpatrick (Red Five); Brian Markinson (Dr. Sam Carr); Alex Zahara (Johanssen); Taras Kostyuk (Red Seven); Shawn Reis (Red Eight); James Tsai (Neighbor); Julia Arkos (Tammy); Irene Chang (Sebastian's Nurse).

13. "The Kidz Are Alright" Written by: Rene Echevarria, Charles H. Eglee. Directed by: Jeff Woolnough. Airdate: February 20, 2001.

Zack has been apprehended, and Lydecker uses psychoactive drugs to make him reveal the locations of his people, including Max. In Seattle, Max and Logan plan a dinner date, but both are nervous now that the obstacle of Logan's wheelchair has been removed from their relationship. Their date is interrupted when Zack escapes from Manticore and calls Max for help. Unaware that he has a transmitter in his head, Max rescues Zack, who reveals the location of X5 transgens in San Francisco, L.A. and other locales.

GUEST CAST: Peter Bryant (Bling); Lisa Ann Cabasa (Tinga); Robert Gossett (James McGinnis); Rob Labelle (Manticore Doctor); William Gregory Lee (Zack); Rob Freeman (TAC Officer #1); Oscar Goncalves (Sector Cop #1); Geneva Locke (Young Max); Dean Aylesworth (Gas Station Attendant); Fulvio Cecere (Sandoval); Colin Lawrence (TAC Officer #2); Chris Gauthier (Mechanic); Glenn Ennis (TAC Officer #3).

14. "Female Trouble" Written by: Patrick Harbinson. Directed by: John Kretchmer. Airdate: March 13, 2001.

Logan's auto-immune system begins to reject the genetically enhanced stem cells that have enabled him to walk again, and he goes to see an expensive specialist about the situation. Suspicions about Logan's behavior lead Max to investigate the doctor's laboratory, and she saves Dr. Adriana Vertes from a female assassin, another Manticore soldier, Jace. Max learns that Dr. Vertes once worked for Manticore, and now the secret program is trying to kill her so she can't sell the technology to any foreign powers. Max promises to defend Vertes so Logan can continue his treatment, but the matter is complicated when Max captures Jace and learns that the assassin is pregnant.

GUEST CAST: Brenda Bakke (Dr. Adriana Vertes); Peter Bryant (Bling); Shireen Crutchfield (Jace); Bethoe Shirkoff (Mrs. Moreno); Geneva Locke (Young Max); Chris Lazar (Young Zack); Jonah Glasgow (Young Jace); Ron Blecker (Drill Sergeant); Fulvio Cecere (Sandoval).

15. "Haven" Written by: Jose Molina. Directed by: Michael Rhodes. Airdate: March 27, 2001.

Max and Logan travel to a small town on an "Eyes Only" mission, only to become embroiled in a local conspiracy. It seems certain townspeople have taken up vigilante justice, and there have been some innocent victims. Max and Logan delve into the mystery, but are endangered by their own weaknesses, Max's seizures, and Logan's handicap.

GUEST CAST: Ashley Crow; David Kaye; Byron Mann; Mark Rolston; Kurt Max Runte; Ian Tracey; James Ashcroft (Deputy Hallahan); Daniel Boileau (Benny); Paul Irani (Gilan); Tara Flynn (Emily).

16. "Shorties in Love" Written by: Adisa Iwa. Directed by: Paul Shapiro. Airdate: April 17, 2001.

Original Cindy's ex returns to town, but Max doesn't trust her. Her suspicions are confirmed when the woman, Diamond, proves to have a secret past and hidden agenda. Worse, she may be genetically re-engineered to carry a fatal biotoxin.

GUEST CAST: Alex Carter; Kim Hawthorne; Tangelia Rouse; Winnie Hung (Maid); Darrell Izzard (Bodyguard); Thomas B. DeSchutter (Lemkin); Danny Danado (Detective); Jason Diabloe (Mr. Scott); Jae C. Bell (Sebastian); Irene Chang (Nurse).

17. "Pollo Loco" Written by Doris Egan. Directed by: Thomas J. Wright. Airdate: April 24, 2001.

A transgenic is found dead in the woods, murdered by an incredibly powerful attacker, and Max seeks to learn more about her new enemy. The next day, another corpse turns up, one with an identical bar code on his neck, and Max starts to fear that her old friend from Manticore, Ben, is the violent assassin she seeks. Ben is killing in the name of the Virgin Mary, but Max is unable to stop him; so Logan contacts Lydecker for help in halting the psycho. Max confronts the deranged Ben after he abducts a Catholic priest, but now Lydecker is closing in on both of them.

GUEST CAST: Jensen Ackles (Ben); Peter Bryant (Bling); Robert Floyd (Father Destry); Nana Visitor (Elizabeth Renfro); Fulvio Cecere (Sandoval); James Kirk (Young Ben); Geneva Locke (Young Max); Jenn Forgie (Clerk at Coroner's Office); Chris Lazar (Young Zack); Glen Gould (Prisoner); Dylan Pearson (Young Jack).

18. "I and I Am a Camera" Written by: David Simkins. Directed by: Jeff Woolnough. Airdate: May 1, 2001.

Max and Logan run afoul of a strange character, a superhero with amazing powers. Max witnesses the superhero's abilities and learns that he has a special exoskeleton that makes him powerful — something that might also come in handy healing Logan's injuries. But the superhero isn't quite sane, and claims there is a police conspiracy to kill convicts recently released from prison. The plot leads back to a new villainess, the cold-blooded Madame X.

GUEST CAST: Rain Wilson; Peter Bryant (Bling); Kevin McNulty, Lawrence Pressman (Jonas); Madame X (Nana Visitor), Dexter Bell (Snuffy); Troy Turi (Thug); Sky Miles (Sky); Keith Dallas, Brad Mooney, Cindy Lou Powell.

19. "Hit a Sista Back" Written by: Moira Kirland Dekker. Directed by: James Whitmore, Jr. Airdate: May 8, 2001.

Lydecker is after Tinga, one of Max's X-5 sisters, and one with a family. Max and Logan try to help Tinga when her family is captured, unaware that another X-5, Brin, has teamed up with the nasty Madame X to capture Tinga for herself.

GUEST CAST: Nicole Bilderback (Brin); Lisa Ann Cabasa (Tinga); William Gregory Lee (Zack); Sebastian Spence (Charlie Smith); Nana Visitor (Madame X); Fulvio Cecere (Sandoval); Lorena Gale (Teacher); Jade C. Bell (Sebastian); Daniel Brown (Tech).

20. "Meow" Written by: David Zabel. Directed by: D.J. Caruso. Airdate: May 15, 2001.

Max is in heat again, a side effect of her feline genes, but she realizes that the man she loves is Logan, who has been repairing a mechanical exoskeleton in an effort to walk again. But the romance will have to wait: Zack has found that Lydecker is holding Tinga, and Max must free her sister. Unfortunately, Lydecker is waiting for Max…

GUEST CAST: Nicole Bilderback (Brin); R. Emery Bright; Lisa Ann Cabasa (Tinga); Fulvio Cecere (Sandoval); William Gregory Lee (Zack); Nana Visitor (Madame X); Jade C. Bell (Sebastian).

21. "…And Jesus Brought a Casserole" Written by: Rene Echevarria and Charles H. Eglee. Directed by: Joe Ann Fogle. Airdate: May 22, 2001.

Madame X at Manticore captures Max and Zack. They attempt to destroy the Manticore labs, but are wounded badly. Logan is forced to leave Max for dead, and Madame X explains that Max needs the heart of an X-5 to survive. Zack sacrifices himself to become a donor, but Max is still trapped in Madame X's clutches.

GUEST CAST: Joshua Alba; Nicki Aycox; Nicole Bilderback (Brin); Lisa A. Cabasa (Tinga); William Gregory Lee (Zack); Nana Visitor (Madame X); Sean Campbell (Special Op #1); Geneva Locke (Young Max); Chris Lazar (Young Zack).

SEASON TWO (2001-2002)

22. "Designate This" Written by: Moira Kirland Dekker. Directed by: Jeff Woolnough. Airdate: September 28, 2001.

Max has been given Zack's heart and been reintegrated into the Manticore program as X5 452, paired off with Ben's genetic twin, Alec (X5 494). At the same time, Logan "Eyes Only" makes it his personal mission to find the Manticore operation that he believes killed Max and shut it down. Max escapes the facility, run by the sadistic Elizabeth Renfro, with the help of a man/canine hybrid named Joshua, but unwittingly transmits a lethal retrovirus to Logan, one that could kill him if they have any fur-

ther intimate contact. Logan exposes Manticore to the world, and Renfro torches the facility, forcing Max to return and free all the children and failed genetic experiments, including Joshua.

GUEST CAST: Nana Visitor (Elizabeth Renfro); John Savage (Lydecker); Robert Gossett; Ashley Scott; Yee Jee Tso (Lanky Messenger); Antonio Cupo (Male X5); Ian Marsh (Drill Sergeant); Daniel Bacon (Control Room Technician #1); Norman Armour (Sleazy Clerk); Geneva Locke (Young Max); Paul J. Anderson (Manticore Guard); Grace Park (Female Breeding X5); Sean Bockhold (X7 Twin); Kevin Conway (Operative at Warehouse); David Cole (Forensics); Adam Henderson (Manticore Doctor); Brian Drummond (TAC Officer #1).

23. "Bag 'Em." Written by: Marjorie David. Directed by: Vern Gillum. Airdate: October 5, 2001.

Max returns home to Seattle, reuniting with Original Cindy and her friends at Jam Pony, while the escaped children of Manticore scrounge for food and face extinction at the hands of the U.S. government. Meanwhile, law enforcement tracks Alec, and the government blames the destruction of the Manticore labs on S1w, a progressive resistance group and ally to Logan. Max, re-teaming with Alec, rescues several Manticore children, but is captured by White, the new military man tracking down the transgen fugitives. Alec and the children rescue Max and send a message via satellite warning other Manticore survivors to flee the area.

GUEST CAST: John Savage (Lydecker); Ashley Scott; Jamie Bell; Nicki Clyne; Sarah Jane Morris; Jesse Moss; Jennifer Jasey (Shelly); Chris Kramer (Mike); Colin Cunningham (Transhuman [DAC]); Alana Husband (Female X5); Andrew Francis (Male X6); Catherine Lough Hagquist (Reporter); Steve Archer (Technician); Kyle Alisharon (Operative); Lisa Calder (Flo); Claude Duharel (Clerk); Cameron McDonald (Cop); Mark Lukyn (Lieutenant); Connor Widdows (Bugler); Sean Bockhold (X7); Craig Veroni (Soldier #1); Leanne Adachi (Computer Technician); Dallas Blake (Military Tech).

24. "Proof of Purchase" Written by: Tommy Thompson. Directed by: Thomas J. Wright. Airdate: October 12, 2001.

Alec is captured by White and recruited to track down and eliminate all Manticore transgenics, an explosive lodged in the back of his head to assure his loyalty. Meanwhile, Joshua has become a tabloid story, and Max and Logan go in search of him, fearing he is searching for his creator and the founder of Manticore, the mysterious Sandaman. While Alec continues to hunt down transgens, cutting off their bar codes as "proof of purchase," Max and Logan hire an ex–Manticore scientist to help cure the virus preventing them from having intimate contact. The scientist leaves Seattle with the job unfinished, but removes the explosive in Alec's neck, even as Joshua and Max find Sandaman's home.

GUEST CAST: John Savage (Lydecker); Ashley Scott; Ron Labelle (Manticore Scientist); Janet Wright; Shawn Stewart (Bloody Fighter #1); Ken Kirzinger (Bloody Fighter #2); John De Santis (The Mangler); Brendan Beiser (Blue Collar Husband); Jane Sowerby (Blue Collar Wife); Kyle Alisharan (Operative); John Hainsworth (Skinny Homeless Guy); Kimani Ray Smith (Bearded Homeless Guy); Deb Macatumpag (She-Beast); Vince Walker (Guy with Shotgun); Nick Harrison (Cop #1); Angela Uyeda (Cop #2); Ryan De Boer (X5-252); Stephen Aberle (Professor Lang); Brittany Cuelvas (Young Max, 6 Years Old); Norman Armour (Young Sandaman); Shakur Paleja (Trooper).

25. "Radar Love." Written by: Michael Angeli. Directed by: Jeff Woolnough. Airdate: October 26, 2001

A deformed transgen appears in Chinatown, and when citizens start to die, the authorities assume the transgen is somehow a contaminating factor. Meanwhile, Logan, Max and Joshua continue to search for Sandaman but divert their efforts when Asha must be rescued from police custody. The police kill the mutant transgen in a rundown motel, fearing he is dangerous, but it turns out he is clean of all pathogens. Logan

determines that someone is secretly testing a new bio-weapon that can distinguish between population groups.

GUEST CAST: Tyler Labine; Byron Mann; Kris Pope; Ashley Scott (Asha), Michael David Simms; Paul Jameson (Overcoat Man); David Libe (Vendor #1); Greg Chan (Vendor #2); Rick Tate (Proprietor); Jonross Fong (Henry); Zen Shane Lim (Young Chinese); Raugi Yu (Ticket Taker); Donald Fong (Dead Chinese #1); Laara Ong (Dead Chinese #2); Bob Wilde (Inspector); Winston Brown (Bartender); Rekha Sharval (Dr. Beverly Shankar); Paul Becker (Male X-5).

26. "Boo" Written by: Charles H. Eglee and Moira Kirland. Directed by: Les Landau. Airdate: November 2, 2001.

It's Halloween 2020, and Max invites Logan to a party at the Crash, but Joshua wants to go out because it is the one night of the year his appearance won't frighten the regular folk of Seattle. A transgenic assassin with the ability to flex his body in unusual ways, as well as separate from his own head(!), has an accident, and Max and Joshua try to help him, unaware that he is planning to kill a local religious leader. Also helping are Katarina, a feline transgen, and a lizard boy ... but it all turns out to be Max's nightmare.

GUEST CAST: Sarah Carter; C. Michael Earley; Kris Pope; Todd Stashwick; Travis Macdonald (Bum); Jillian Marie Hubert (Tonya); Deanne Henry (Serena); Leslie Jones (Waitress); Rob Deeluw (Man); Jana Ritter (Asha Look-a-like); Jaron Albertin (Logan Look-a-like); Angelina Baran (Pretty Redhead); French Tickner (Father McAllister); Brian Jensen (Cop at Venue).

27. "Two" Written by: Jose Molina. Directed by: Allan Kroeker. Airdate: November 10, 2001.

Alec botches Max's attempt to steal an expensive baseball in order to raise money for the cure to the bug separating her from Logan. Meanwhile, a savage transgen has gone on a killing spree, and Max fears that touchy Joshua could be the culprit. At the same time, Alec annoys Max by getting a job at Jam Pony and running a side business selling synthetic steroids. Evidence mounts, pinpointing Joshua as Seattle's newest serial killer, but in fact he has a homicidal twin named Isaac.

GUEST CAST: Micasha Armstrong; John Cassini; Fred Ewanuick; John Mann; David Parker (Officer Pearson); Stephonia Ciccone (Mr. La Pera); Ryan Nelson (Young Cop); Mike Dopud (Cop 3); Garfield Wilson (Gun-Happy Cop); Patrick Gallagher (Hispanic Cop); John Callander (Prisoner); Sonya Salomaa (Lux).

28. "Some Assembly Required" Written by: Robert Doherty. Directed by: Nick Marck. Airdate: November 16, 2001.

Zack is alive, but amnesiac and working for a gang of punk-like criminals called Steelheads. Max enlists Alec's help in finding the gang, which he had encountered the week before. The two X-5s find Zack and, with Logan's help, take him to a hospital. There the doctor reports that Zack has bio-synthetic organs and a cybernetic implant in his brain that allows his damaged temporal lobe to re-form. Memories of Zack's former life and relationship with Max resurface, but so does his Manticore "programming" to assassinate "Eyes Only."

GUEST CAST: William Gregory Lee (Zack); Micasha Armstrong; Fred Ewanuick; John Mann; Brian Markinson (Sam); Seth Rananveera (Shashi); Sony Salomaa (Lux); Todd Fenwick (Hulk); Winston Brown (Bartender); Fred Keating (Buddy Thompson).

29. "Gill Girl" Written by: Marjorie David. Directed by: Bryan Spicer. Airdate: December 7, 2001.

Logan enlists Max's help in taking care of his bratty young niece, Brittany, but has a close call with death when he contracts chicken pox from the child. At the same time, a fishing boat snags a gill girl, a so-called "mermaid," in the harbor. This unusual transgen girl becomes an attraction at a Seattle strip club, and Alec takes Max to

rescue her. The plan goes wrong, however, when Max and Alex inadvertently incapacitate a male water-breather, the mermaid's mate, and the villainous White gets his hands on the mermaid.

GUEST CAST: Scott Heindl; Darcy Laurie; Gus Lynch; Brian Markinson (Sam); Anita Brown (Gill Girl); Jese Hutch (Gill Guy); Jesica Amlee (Britanny); Kendall Cros (Bitsy); Angela Moore (Nurse Betty); Craig Veroni (Otto); Amanda Hardy (Veronica); Daryl Quon (Bouncer); Mark Lukyn (Tech).

30. "Medium Is the Message." Written by: Michael Angeli. Directed by: Jeff Woolnough. Airdate: December 15, 2001.

Max and Logan work independently to vanquish the virus preventing their intimacy. Realizing that Lydecker may hold the answer to solving their problem, Max and Logan search for the long-missing scientist. While Joshua strives to become a successful painter, Logan helps a desperate woman search for a missing child ... White's son! In recovering the boy for White's wife, Max runs up against two super-strong assassins — and discovers evidence that a precursor to Manticore has been around for over two thousand years ... and that White is a willing participant in the program.

GUEST CAST: Emily Holmes, Claudette Roche.

31. "Brainiac" Written by Chip Johannessen. Directed by Stephen Williams. Airdate: January 4, 2002.

Asha's rebel group, the S1W, has been betrayed, and Logan, Max and Alec attempt to free the revolutionaries from a prison bus. Alec and Max also encounter another Manticore x-series escapee, an I.T. "battle processor" that uses mathematics, probability and statistics to predict the future. One of his math-fueled visions reveals the death of Max in battle, and the I.T., who is in love with Max, decides he must intervene.

GUEST CAST: Noel Callahan (Vid Kid); Thom Millburn, Jr. (SWAT Cop #1); Simonee

Chichester (S1W1); Kuba (S1W3); Dean Redmons (S1W3); Dagmar Midcap (Newscaster); Simon Longmore (Arcade Cop); Sarah Greca (Young Woman); Tiffany Knight (TV Commercial); Darren Chod (SWAT cop #2).

32. "The Berrisford Agenda" Written by: Moira Kirland Dekker. Directed by: Thomas J. Wright. Airdate: January 11, 2002.

While working as a carrier at Jam Pony, Alec is haunted by memories of a dangerous covert mission he once undertook. The job involved a fancy house, a car bomb, and a beautiful woman he fell for. He soon learns that the past never dies, and that his deadly mission suffered much collateral damage, but not the way he once believed.

GUEST CAST: Fulvio Cecere, Michael Kopsa, Meghan Ory.

33. "Borrowed Time" Written by: Jose Molina. Directed by: David Straiton. Airdate: February 1, 2002.

Max needs $20,000 to pay for a new cure to the virus keeping her from intimate contact with Logan, so she steals the print of the unfinished *Star Wars Episode 7* from a vault at Fox, with Alec's help. Unfortunately, the cure proves to be temporary, leaving Logan and Max only one night together to consummate their relationship. The romantic evening is interrupted, however, when Joshua arrives at Logan's apartment and reports that a spitting, transgenic-hunting monster called a "gossamer" is on the loose. With time running out, Max and Logan, with Alec's help, seek the Gossamer in a nearby junkyard, only to become cocooned by the creature.

GUEST CAST: Scott Bellis; Tony Alcantar (Irving); Dee Jay Jackson (Gordie); Peter Williams (Hal); Fiona Hogan (Muriel); Sarah Cole-Burnett (Emma); Ryan Drescher (Tim).

34. "Harbor Lights" Written by: Robert Doherty. Directed by: Kenneth Biller. Airdate: February 8, 2002.

Waiting in line for gas, Max takes a bullet in the gut for an innocent child caught in the line of fire. Rushed to surgery at Harbor Lights hospital, Max is soon the subject of intense curiosity when the virus in her system is detected at the lab. The CDC races to the scene to examine this unusual specimen, and White isn't far behind. Logan attempts to get Max out of the hospital, even as White, masquerading as an FBI agent, closes in, along with a nurse-turned-assassin.

GUEST CAST: Brian Markinson (Sam Carr); Enuka Okuma; Sarah Strong; Jerry Wasserman; Tara Flynn (Mother at Gas Line-Up); Alexander Farquharson (Boy at Gas Line-Up); Ben Cotton (Biker at Gas Line-Up); Bobby Stewart (Sector Cop #1); Todd Talbot (Paramedic #1); Sharon Heath (Nurse); Alanis Pearl (Second Nurse); Kewsi Ameyaw (Lab Tech); Laara Sadiq (Attending Nurse); Craig Veroni (Cop); Ari Solomon (CDC Tech); Kaare Anderson (Sector Cop #2); Dagmar Midcap (Reporter); Mark Lukyn (White's Guy); Donovan Stinson (Bill); Oscar Gonzaels (Sector Cop #3); Robert Smith (Suited Man).

35. "Love in Vein" Written by: Michael Angeli. Directed by: David Grossman. Airdate: March 8, 2002.

Alec exploits the innocent Joshua, getting the dog-man to do his work for him at Jam Pony. On another front, Max faces a cult of genetically enhanced vampires, an army of mutants that feed on human blood. If she can't stop them, this army of bloodsuckers could destroy Seattle.

GUEST CAST: Keegan Connor Tracy; Sam Witwer; Matthew Currie Holmes; Camille Sullivan; Ian Marsh (Doorman); Juliet Dunn (Desk Nurse); Sky Miles (Sky); Carolyn Tweedle (Cat Woman); Zak Santiago, Eliza Murbach, Vishanti Moosai.

36. "Fuhgeddaboudit" Written by: Julie Hess. Directed by: Morgan James Beggs. Airdate: March 15, 2002.

Max and Logan are exposed by a transgenic hypnotist, and their real identities (as transgen and Eyes Only, respectively) could get them killed. Meanwhile, Alec looks to make a little money on the side by getting into boxing.

GUEST CAST: Frankie Jay Allison, David Gianopoulos, Byron Mann, Tracy Leah Ryan, Laurie Brunetti, John Juliani, Louis Chirllo, Peter Benson, Lee Jay Bamberry.

37. "Exposure" Written by: Moira Kirland Dekker. Directed by: Stephen Williams. Airdate: March 22, 2002.

Max and Logan learn the secret behind White's power. His son has been taken to a breeding cult, the Familiars, that has dire plans for transgens and the human race.

GUEST CAST: Callum Keith Rennie; Gabrielle Rose; Garwin Sanford; Malcolm Stewart; Emily Holmes; Aaron Douglas (Clerk); Mark Lukyn (Operative #1); Jose-Anthony Griffith (Operative #2); Craig Veroni (Otto); Mike Mitchel; Alex Rae.

38. "Hello, Goodbye" Written by: Cindi Grossenbacher and Jose Molina. Directed by: Jeff Woolnough. Airdate: April 5, 2002.

After another close call involving Logan and the virus that keeps them apart, Max puts the brakes on their romantic relationship. Meanwhile, Alec is fingered for one of the murders committed by his psychotic X-5 twin, Ben. The villainous White uses the murder as a propaganda tool, further endangering the persecuted transgenics in Seattle.

GUEST CAST: Kandyse McClure; Gabrielle Rose; Rehka Sharma; Noah Beggs (Det. Krakow); Gerry Durand (ND Cop); Jose-Anthony Griffith (Operative 2); Mike Mitchell (Mule); Craig Veroni (Otto); Evan Stewart (Anchorman).

39. "Dawg Day Afternoon" Written by: Robert Doherty. Directed by: Kenneth Biller. Airdate: April 12, 2002.

Joshua has fallen in love with a blind woman, but that doesn't make him immune to persecution, as he soon finds out in a deadly subterranean pursuit. Meanwhile, human anger and fear directed towards the transgenics reaches a fever pitch in Seattle, thanks to White's efforts to "publicize" the story to the press.

GUEST CAST: Kandyse McClure; Gabrielle Rose; Malcolm Stewart; Josh Byer; David Coles; Jorgito Vargas, Jr.; Evan Stewart (Anchorman); L. Harvey Gold (Lawyer); Mark Burgess (Reverend Caldwell); David Berner; Mitchell Kosterman; Bobby Stewart; Craig Veroni (Otto); Brad Loree.

40. "She Ain't Heavy" Written by: Michael Angeli and Robert Doherty. Directed by: Allan Kroeker. Airdate: April 19, 2002.

A clone of Max, #453, has been living a normal life in San Francisco, at least until her capture by White. The clone is used by White to hunt Max, with the price of loyalty being the safety of her husband and child. When Joshua plans to relocate to Terminal City — a sanctuary where diverse transgens live in peace — Max also contemplates a move. Before long, however, #453 tracks down #452, and White appears before a Congressional committee denouncing the transgens and declaring a war against them.

GUEST CAST: Brian Markinson (Sam Carr); Paul Perri; Malcolm Stewart; Fred Ewanuick; Brian Jensen; Darcy Laurie; Alessandro Juliani (David); Sky Miles (Sky); Cameron Crigger (Johnny); Jon Thorburn (Steve); Craig Veroni (Otto); Mark Lukyn (Operative); Jase-Anthony Griffith (Operative #2); Evan Stewart (Anchorman).

41. "Love Among the Runes" Written by: Moira Kirland Dekker and Jose Molina. Directed by: James Whitmore, Jr. Airdate: April 26, 2002.

Max, Joshua and Alec join a band of transgenic resistance fighters in Terminal City, as Logan seeks to re-establish "Eyes Only," recently shut down by the persistent

White. Meanwhile, Sandaman's son escapes from White's "Familiar" cult, and a row of Minoan tattoos — runes — appears mysteriously on Max's arm. She presses C.J. to learn the truth of the indecipherable tattoos, but it is White that reads them, identifying Max as the one person in the world who can threaten his cult's plan for world domination.

GUEST CAST: Henri Lubatti (C.J.); Paul Perri; Gabrielle Rose; Fred Ewanuick; Brian Jensen; Darcy Laurie; Michael Sbrizzi (Biggs); Dominika Wolski (Priestess); Craig Veroni (Otto); David Haysom (Checkpoint Captain); Peter Shinkoda (Albino X); Mark Lukyn (Operative); Jase-Anthony Griffith (Operative #2); Ron Selmour (Dan); Craig Lapthorne (Uniformed Cop); Bystander (Darren Moore).

42. "Freak Nation" Written by: Ira Steven Behr and Rene Echeverria. Story by: James Cameron and Charles H. Eglee. Directed by: James Cameron. Airdate: May 3, 2002.

The secret cult of Familiars, the "Conclave," calls on a highly-trained team of Phalanx warriors to take down Max in Terminal City, fearing she is the one person, prophesied in the runes, that can destroy

their plans for world domination. Meanwhile, Alec, Joshua and another transgen, a pregnant girl, are surrounded by the police in Jam Pony after a car accident. After negotiations with authorities fail, the Phalanx warriors move in, and Max comes to the rescue, defeating the team with the help of Logan. Later, Max takes a stand in Terminal City with the transgens, becoming the leader of a new "Freak Nation," with its own flag (painted by Joshua). The National Guard launches a siege against the transgens, even as their new flag flies over Terminal City.

GUEST CAST: Rick Worthy; Erin Karpluk; Gabrielle Rose; Fred Ewanuick; Brian Jensen; Darcy Laurie; Lita (Thula); Jeffrey Ballard (Dalton); Alison Matthews (Female Newscaster); Russell Ferrier (Sonny); Charlie Mayrs (Second Heckler); Lori Stewart, Steve McMichael, Simon Burnett, Chris Gordon (Phalanx Warriors); Lorin Heath (CeCe); Michael Sunczyk (Pick-up Truck Driver); Tahmon Pininkett (ND Cop); Ro Nielsen (ND Cop 1); Sky Miles (Sky); Liz Bakalar (Greta); Craig Veroni (Otto); Daren Moore (Man on the Streets); Christine Willes (Church Lady); Dion Luther (Bill Halley); Gardiner Millar (Man on the Street #2); Lance Gibson (Man on the Street #3).

Darkman

Michigan native Sam Raimi is one of the most inventive film directors working in Hollywood today. After his career began with a series of low-budget horror films (*Evil Dead* [1982], *Crimewave* [1985] and *Evil Dead II: Dead by Dawn* [1987]), he achieved mainstream success of a sort with his 1990 superhero film for Universal Studios entitled *Darkman*. Although years later, in 2002, Raimi would direct the mega-hit *Spider-Man*, in many ways *Darkman* remains the more stylish film. It also happens to be one of the best superhero movies ever created, recounting an origin story that expresses how it really feels to be an outsider.

Additionally, some frames of the film (such as the instantaneous transformation of Julie Hastings from horrified onlooker to graveside mourner) appear to have popped right out of some comic book's pages. As star Larry Drake, who played the villainous Robert G. Durant in *Darkman*, noted in a *Starlog* interview with Kyle Counts, Raimi's films boast "a poetic truth rather than a flat literal truth…. [H]e likes to push the limits of what's possible."[1] Indeed, Raimi's early film work (before *A Simple Plan* in 1998) is widely known for its crazy, expressive angles and take-no-prisoners energy. *Darkman* was a prime example of this approach, and reviewers have described it as a combination of *Phantom of the Opera* and *Batman*.

But *Darkman* was not an easy film to shoot. Its screenplay went through a dozen different drafts, and the shooting schedule lasted a hectic three months.[2] Budgeted at a tight eleven million dollars, the production did not have resources to spare, and much had to be accomplished with very little. Liam Neeson, not yet a star, played the film's title character, a scientist named Peyton Westlake who was trying to develop artificial skin for burn victims. Unfortunately, his work was cut short by a criminal enforcer, Durant (Drake), working for a more urbane corporate ganglord.

With Westlake's body burned beyond recognition, a surgeon (played by Jenny Agutter) severed Westlake's nerves, making him unable to feel pain and to become susceptible to surges of adrenaline (granting him, essentially, super strength). "When the body ceases to feel, the mind grows alienated; uncontrolled rage is not uncommon," the doctor noted, meaning that Westlake's humanity had been robbed from him. He could no longer feel love the way he did before; cut off from his feelings, he was given to bouts of incredible rage. Not only could Darkman feel nothing, but he was hideously ugly, the skin burned off three quarters of his face, his lips and hair gone completely. Like Spawn (who came along in 1992), and even Swamp Thing to a degree, Darkman was the epitome of the "ugly" superhero, one that had to remain in the dark not by affectation (like Batman) but because of his appearance. His mask was a swath of white bandages; his cape a cast-off long black jacket he found in an alley.

Darkman's physical ugliness is an important distinction, demonstrating how some rather shallow superhero series, such as *Birds of Prey*, like to play up the notion that the lead characters, such as Huntress (Ashley Scott), are "isolated" and "alone," reviled by society for their differences. Yet

A portrait of darkness: The scarred Darkman (Liam Neeson) sets his sights on revenge in the 1990 feature film *Darkman*.

just how hated can a gorgeous woman with perfect hair and expensive leather clothes really be? On that show, isolation is a forced and false issue, not very realistic because Huntress, Gibson, Dinah and the other meta-humans could "pass," as it were, for human. In *Darkman* the ugliness is essential to the main character's ethos, and dramatically motivated. In one crucial scene, the hero feared that he was a circus freak, an attraction at an outdoor carnival, and it was a gut-punching, visceral moment.

It is important to note that Darkman was also a real vigilante, not one working with organized law enforcement's tacit approval, or a wink and a nod. He desperately wanted revenge against those who had caused him the grievous loss of his humanity, and his deep love of Julie Hastings. Try as Darkman might to create new skin for himself, his scientific obsession would never return to normal, and it was his anger that propelled him.

The villains in the film, Durant and Colin Friels (Strack), were clearly cast in the normal (rather than outrageous) mode, and this worked to the film's advantage. Both men, a criminal enforcer and a corporate raider, had by default what Darkman could never attain, despite his intense desire and scientific acumen: the appearance of normality. They could hide their "evil" faces behind masks of normal-looking skin, hiding the darkness of their souls. Darkman, on the other hand, could not. His name said what he was, a man turned dark by his separation from humanity.

A dark story replete with spectacular action scenes, especially an over–L.A. helicopter assault that presaged a similar scene in *The Matrix* some nine years later, *Darkman* swept the box office, making a tidy profit for Universal in the process. The film was so popular, in fact, that it was envisioned as a new franchise. A *Darkman* TV show was planned, but aborted after a pilot was judged to be of poor quality. Finally, Darkman returned to screens in two low-budget, direct-to-video features in the mid–1990s.

Darkman II: The Return of Durant (1994), executive produced by Raimi and Renaissance Pictures partner Robert Tapert, was directed by cinematographer Bradford May. The new feature opened with clips from the first film, and noted how Darkman had chosen to live as a "creature of the night." Portrayed by Arnold Vosloo (*The Mummy* [1999], *The Mummy Returns* [2001]) instead of Liam Neeson, Westlake still sought the skin formula that he believed would restore his humanity. Unfortunately, he had to battle a resurrected Durant, who had been in a coma for 878 days after the climax of the original film. Since his factory headquarters was destroyed in the feature film, Darkman had relocated in the intervening years, and his headquarters, like those of Blankman, were now in an underground subway yard, a base he could reach via sewers and a specially designed rail car.

Darkman III: Die Darkman Die (1996) featured the same behind-the-scenes personnel and many of the same sets as its direct-to-video predecessor, with Vosloo resuming the role of Darkman. Though Larry Drake was missed as the villainous Durant,

the film took the franchise in a new direction. Darkman found himself longing for a normal life again, falling in love with a crime boss's (Jeff Fahey) wife (*Star Trek Voyager*'s B'Elanna Torres, Roxanne Dawson) and experiencing affection for their child, Jenny. In this case, Darkman used his artificial skin (which would only last 99 minutes) to imitate the husband and father, faking a normal life, as it were, and also reminding himself of the permanent relationships his life would never afford. The metaphor of *Beauty and the Beast* came to the fore when Jenny appeared in the story at a school play, and was certainly relevant to Westlake's situation.

The two direct-to-video features lacked the overt stylistics of Sam Raimi's inspired 1990 feature film, but were far better than most standard TV productions, and rather enjoyable overall. The only drawback is that the two video features appear to have been shot somewhat hurriedly, and in the same industrial park. Both films feature factories and warehouses as prominent settings. Also, *Darkman III* "borrowed" several scenes from *Darkman II*, particularly those involving Darkman working in his underground laboratory and developing the artificial skin.

Still, it was nice that some of the wit of the original film was maintained in these workman-like sequels. *Die Darkman Die*, for instance, offered a shot of a hat-rack in the lab, viewed as Darkman tosses his hat upon it. A second later, he tosses his artificial face on it too. Very clever, and a funny visual joke.

With a little money and attention, *Darkman* could easily become a continuing film franchise, but since Sam Raimi has moved on to develop the *Spider-Man* mythos, it is unlikely audiences will see a return to the dark and sad world of the vengeful Peyton Westlake.

Darkman (1990)
LIVE-ACTION FILM

"This is an uneasy film. Sam Raimi trying to appeal to a mainstream audience hot on the heels of success with *Evil Dead* shows some of his weaknesses as a director—when he's passionate, it's obvious, and when he's not, it's also obvious. *Darkman* had all the necessary components for a good superhero film and parts of the film work well. Liam Neeson is perhaps a little too over-the-top for this film, and its finest moment may be Bruce Campbell's cameo at the very end. This film tries hard, but doesn't really know what it wants to be, and suffers as a result."
— William Latham, author *Mary's Monster, Space: 1999 Resurrection*

"In the recent flurry of comics-derived movies, *Darkman* may not be the most popular. But, in some ways, it's the best: the only one that successfully captures the graphic look, rhythm and style of the superhero books."
— Michael Wilmington, *The Los Angeles Times*, August 24, 1990, page 10.

CAST: Liam Neeson (Peyton Westlake/Darkman); Frances McDormand (Julie Hastings); Colin Friels (Strack); Larry Drake (Robert G. Durant); Nelson Mashita (Lab Assistant); Jessie Lawrence Ferguson (Eddie Black); Rafael H. Rablado (Rudy Guzman); Danny Hicks (Skip); Theodore Raimi (Rick); Dan Bell (Smiley); Nicholas Worth (Pauly); Aaron Lustig (Martin Katz); Arsenio "Sonny" Trinidad (Hung Fat); Said Faraj (Convenience Store Clerk); Nathan Jung (Chinese Warrior); Bruce Campbell (Final Shemp).

CREW: Universal Studios and Renaissance Pictures Present *Darkman*. *Music:* Danny Elfman. *Make-up Effects:* Tony Gardner and Larry Hamlin. *Costume Design:* Grania Preston. *Supervising Editors:* Bud and Scott Smith. *Production Design:* Randy Ser. *Director of Photography:* Bill Pope. *Line Producer:* Daryl Kass. *Story by:* Sam Raimi *Screenplay by:* Chuck Pfarrer, Sam Raimi, Ivan Raimi, Daniel Goldin, Joshua Goldin. *Producer:* Robert Tapert. *Editor:* David Stiven. *Special Effects:* VCE/Peter Kuran. *Special Visual Effects:* Introvision Systems International, Inc. *Miniatures:* 4-Ward Productions. *Directed by:* Sam Raimi. *M.P.A.A. Rating:* R. *Running time:* 96 minutes.

Criminal gang leader Robert G. Durant has been pressuring businessmen all over the waterfront, getting them to sell their land to his secret employer. When he runs up against a stubborn underworld figure named Eddie Black who refuses to sell, Durant and his men muscle him.

Meanwhile, Dr. Peyton Westlake and his lab assistant continue to develop a new kind of synthetic skin. Unfortunately, they keep meeting with failure: after 99 minutes, the flesh decomposes. Then, one day, Westlake discovers that the artificial flesh can survive longer in the dark, and realizes that light plays a role. Unfortunately, Westlake's experiments have no further time to develop. His girlfriend, a lawyer named Julie Hastings, has inadvertently learned that her client, Mr. Strack, has bribed city officials to fund his waterfront revitalization project. She has a memo as evidence of the crime, and Strack sends his goon, Durant, to collect it. Unfortunately, Westlake has the memo in his possession, and Durant kills his lab assistant, maims Westlake and destroys the lab to get the incriminating document.

Westlake survives the destruction of his lab, with third-degree burns over most of his body. At a local hospital, a doctor has severed the nerves controlling and regulating pain, so that Westlake can escape total agony. A side effect is that his emotional impulses run out of control, and he is imbued with super-human strength. Scarred terribly and covered in bandages, Westlake escapes the hospital and sets out to recreate his lab in the industrial area of the city. There he works on a way to reconstruct his face and plots revenge against those who have harmed him.

After watching Durant's gang in secret, Westlake goes on the offensive, imitating the goons and even Durant in an attempt to screw up Strack's operation. Before long, Strack has learned that Westlake is alive and kidnaps Julie to bring him into the open. After dispatching Durant in a helicopter battle and killing the other members of his gang, Westlake — now a twisted avenger called Darkman — races to save Julie on the waterfront. There is a final battle between Strack and Darkman atop a half-constructed skyscraper, and Darkman must reveal his twisted, scarred face to his one-time lover.

Darkman II: The Return of Durant (1994)
LIVE-ACTION FILM

CAST: Larry Drake (Robert G. Durant); Kim Delaney (Jill Randall); Renee O'Connor (Laurie Brinkman); Lawrence Dane (Dr. Alfred Hathaway); Arnold Vosloo (Peyton Westlake/ Darkman); Jesse Collins (Dr. David L. Brinkman); David Feiry (Eddie); Rod Wilson (Ivan Druganov); Jack Langedijk (Latham); Sten Eirik (Whitey); Steve Mousseau (Roy); James Millington (Mr. Perkins).

CREW: Universal and MCA Home Entertainment Present a Renaissance Pictures Production, *Darkman II: The Return of Durant*. *Music:* Randy Miller. *Themes:* Danny Elfman. *Art Director:* Ian Brock. *Film Editor:* Daniel Cahn. *Director of Photography:* Bradford May. *Co-Producer:* David Eick. *Producer:* David Roessell. *Executive Producers:* Sam Raimi, Robert Tapert. *Screenplay:* Steven McKay. *Story:* Robert Eisele and Lawrence Hertzog. *Based on Characters Created by:* Sam Raimi. *Special Make-up Effects:* Kurtzman, Nicotero and Berger EFX Group. *Directed by:* Bradford May. *Running time:* 90 min (approximate).

Robert G. Durant awakens from a coma years after his confrontation with Darkman. He plans immediately to get back into the gun trade, manufacturing "new weapons for a new era."

Meanwhile, Darkman continues to work on his artificial liquid skin in the hopes of repairing his scarred face. The one man that can help him, Dr. David Brinkman, however, is living in a factory that Durant wants to appropriate for use in his gun manufacturing operation. Durant also springs the insane Dr. Hathaway from a hospital for the criminally insane to develop a powerful particle beam weapon. When Brinkman will not sell his property, which belonged to his father, Durant has him killed.

When Darkman learns Durant is back in the crime business, he plans to destroy his organization with the help of Jill Randall, a lovely reporter for *Street Copy*, and David Brinkman's sister, Laurie. Durant kills Jill for broadcasting information on Durant's return from the dead, and Darkman goes ballistic, wreaking final justice on his longtime nemesis.

Darkman III: Die Darkman Die (1996)
LIVE-ACTION FILM

CAST: Jeff Fahey (Peter Rooker); Darlanne Fluegel (Dr. Bridget Thorn); Roxann Biggs-Dawson (Mrs. Angela Rooker); Arnold Vosloo (Darkman/Peyton Westlake); Nigel Bennett (Nico); Alicia Panetta (Jenny Rooker); Rohn Sarosiak (Mack); Peter Graham (Joey); Shawn Doyle (Adam); Vieslav Krystyan (Ivan); Chris Adams (Whit).

CREW: Universal and MCA Home Entertainment Present a Renaissance Pictures Production. *Music:* Randy Miller. *Themes:* Danny Elfman. *Art Director:* Ian Brock. *Film Editor:* Daniel Cahn. *Director of Photography:* Bradford May. *Co-Producer:* David Eick. *Producer:* David Roessell. *Executive Producers:* Sam Raimi and Robert Tapert. *Written by:* Michael Colleary and Mike Webb. *Based Upon Characters Created by:* Sam Raimi. *Directed by:* Bradford May. *Running time:* 90 minutes (approximate).

Darkman interferes in the steroid selling operation of a local crime lord named

Peter Rooker. Darkman then uses the stolen money to develop a better grade of synthetic skin.

Meanwhile, Dr. Bridget Thorn contacts Darkman and promises to help him feel sensations again, reattaching his thalmic nerve. Darkman reluctantly teams with her, hoping to use her lab equipment to complete his work on synthetic skin. Unfortunately, Dr. Thorn turns out to be treacherous and hands Peyton over to Rooker, domesticating Darkman with a remote control device that activates his nerve impulses.

Thorn and Rooker want to use Peyton's blood to create a new super steroid that can amp up athletes.

Darkman yanks out the implant with a pair of rusty pliers and escapes from the lab. He then goes after Rooker, unexpectedly falling in love with Rooker's estranged wife, Angela, and coming to care deeply for his young daughter, Jenny. Masquerading as a family man, Darkman unexpectedly finds himself experiencing the life that he thought could never again be his. But the masquerade can't last forever...

Doctor Strange

The turbulent 1960s represented a decade of experimentation in American culture, and a decade of rebellion too. Comic book creators like Stan Lee understood that young people of that era were looking to comic books for inspiration and even new ways of thinking, hence Marvel titles such as *Doctor Strange*.

The character Steven Strange first appeared in *Strange Tales* in 1963, in an issue written by Lee and rendered by Steve Ditko. Strange was a prominent surgeon, a self-satisfied professional, a man that had bought completely into the notion of American enterprise, consumerism and wealth. At least, that is, until he was dealt a rough physical setback. Because of a car accident, he was no longer able to practice his surgical trade, a fact that led the embittered man on an odyssey of self-discovery in the Far East.

There Strange studied with a philosopher "master" called the Ancient One who dwelled in the Himalayas. But the Ancient One didn't merely mend Strange's hands, he allowed the narrow-minded American to learn and admire a whole other worldview, an Eastern, peaceful one. Thus the Steven Strange that returned to America was a changed man, one who understood that there was more to life than the material. He

became a noble white magician, a sorcerer, a "Master of the Mystic Arts," and began to defend humanity from evil wizards and demons with names like Baron Mordo.

And, unlike most conventional superheroes, Dr. Strange's adventures often conveniently carried him to dream planes and other realities, so the comic was, not unlike Kubrick's *2001: A Space Odyssey*, "the ultimate trip." These strange vistas and journeys were especially appealing to the drug culture of the late 1960s, as was the pro–Eastern (and pro-peace) philosophy.

Dr. Strange jumped around a great deal, moving to his own comic, *Dr. Strange*, in 1968. Then he appeared in *Marvel Premiere* for a short span, and was back in *Doctor Strange* in the mid–1970s. But no matter under which title the good doctor was found, he maintained a devoted cult (and occult) following. Then, in the 1970s, *The Six Million Dollar Man* and *The Bionic Woman* proved that superhero programs could work on TV again if they eschewed *Batman*-style camp, and every network began adapting popular comic properties. This was the era of Lynda Carter's *Wonder Woman*, Reb Brown's *Captain America* TV movies, *The Amazing Spider-Man*, Kenneth Johnson's melodramatic

Don't mess with his crystal balls. Peter Hooten is *Doctor Strange* (1978) in the TV movie.

adaptation of *The Incredible Hulk* and other such ventures.

Naturally, *Doctor Strange* was selected too. Rife with colorful costumes and optical special effects, the comic promised a whole new world of adventure for TV au-diences weaned on more traditional comic heroes like Superman or Batman.

Unfortunately, there had been another pop-culture influence in the 1970s as well, a little space fantasy called *Star Wars*. The immense success of that film dictated changes on an abundance of TV shows, and *Dr. Strange* was no exception. Before you could consult the Eye of Agamotto about the matter, changes in his origin were forged to play up the "dark side"–versus–"light side" spiritual battle that had been so popular in the opera of Skywalker.

In the TV movie produced by Phil DeGuere, Stephen Strange, played by Peter Hooten, was no longer a prominent surgeon, but a psychiatric resident. It was his parents who experienced a car accident (resulting in their deaths when he was eighteen). Instead of going on a journey of self-discovery to the East, it was simply his destiny, easily stumbled upon, to become a sorcerer, "a guardian of the light."

"You've been gifted with a clear mind and a love of humanity," an aging sorcerer revealed to Strange in the TV movie, thus discounting the entire moral and philosophical underpinning of the successful comic. The Ancient One, Strange's mentor and friend in the comics, changed rather dramatically too. No longer was he an Asian philosopher, but rather a WASP wizard that had more in common with Merlin, or perhaps Obi Wan Kenobi, than the mystical wise man of Lee's creation. His name on the TV show was Lindmer (John Mills), and he was dying. Thus he had to pick a successor before his life faded, an unfortunate thing because during that time of choosing a new evil also came to Earth: the Enchantress, the Dark Queen of Sorcerers, Morgana Le Fay (Jessica Walter). Lindmer had to train Strange and stop Morgana within the three-day time period it took him to expire.

As in the comic, the Dr. Strange of the TV movie had the assistance of a faithful servant named Wong (Clyde Kusatsu). The production also seemed to indicate that a woman named Clea would become the sorcerer's disciple, but otherwise things were quite different from the world Lee had forged in four colors. For one thing, TV's Strange didn't even believe in evil as a force, only the "human potentiality to do good."

In the TV movie, Strange had to rescue the damsel-in-distress, Clea, from the clutches of Morgana Le Fay, defeat the witch, and assume his rightful place as a sorcerer supreme. "In the name of Ryal, scourge of demons, I demand you go back," he frequently uttered as he flitted about (via astral projection) in a cheap-looking Hell dimension (which resembled nothing so much as a badly lit cave). The production values were weak, despite the fact that the film reportedly went over budget by as much as $100,000 and shot for five days over its intended schedule.[1] Though Walter (of *Play Misty for Me* [1971]) made a powerful villain (but not one from the comics), Peter Hooten was spectacularly miscast as Dr. Strange. He was too stolid and unimaginative, but then one can hardly fault him since Strange's interesting backstory and character arc had been removed. On another down note, the film featured sound effects that seemed to have come from George Pal's classic film *War of the Worlds* (1953), by then quite dated.

Despite a climax that left Morgana Le Fay alive and plotting further evil, *Dr. Strange* (like *Captain America*) never went to series form. In this case, one of the most interesting superhero properties of the 1960s had been watered down so much that it was unrecognizable, and without Stan Lee's powerful and timely themes and morality, the TV movie seemed merely ... *strange*. But not strange enough.

Doctor Strange (1978)
LIVE-ACTION TV MOVIE

"What made *Doctor Strange* work was its special effects and approach to the subject matter. The plot ... was handled in a perfectly straight manner — no tongue-in-cheek satire, no embarrassing self-indulgent feats of power, just a straightforward battle of the cosmos. Whereas the show was a bit padded to fit its two hour time slot, it used the time it had and the money it needed to produce an often stunning program."

— Mike Gold. *Fantastic Films #9*: "Why Superheroes Don't Work on TV," July 1979, page 51.

CAST: Peter Hooten (Dr. Stephen Strange); Jessica Walter (Morgana Le Fay); John Mills (Lindmer); Sarah Rush (Nurse); Clyde Kusatsu (Wong); Eddie Benton (Clea Lake), Philip Sterling (Dr. Taylor); June Barrett (Sara); Diana Webster (Head Nurse); Bob Delegall (Intern); Larry Anderson (Magician); Blake Marion (Dept. Chief); Lady Rowlands (Mrs. Sullivan); Inez Pedroza (Announcer); Michael Clark (Taxi Driver); Frank Catalano (Orderly).

CREW: Universal/MCA presents *Doctor Strange*. *Director of Photography:* Enzo A. Martinelli. *Produced by:* Alex Beaton. *Written and Directed by:* Philip DeGuere. *Executive Producer:* Philip DeGuere. *Associate Producer:* Gregory Hoblit. *Music:* Paul Chihara. *Art Director:* William H. Tuntle. *Film Editor:* Christopher Nelson. *Set Decorator:* Marc E. Meyer, Jr. *Sound:* Earl N. Crain, Jr. *Consultant:* Stan Lee. *Casting:* Joe Reich. *Unit Production Manager:* George Bisk. *First Assistant Director:* Leonard Blam. *Sound Effects Editor:* Roger A. Sword. *Music Editor:* Ted Roberts. *Costume Designer:* Yvonne Woods. *Special Effects:* Van der Veer Photographic Effects. *Visual Effects Consultant:* Thomas J. Wright. *Running time:* 105 minutes (approx.).

The Dark Lord summons long-exiled sorceress and villain Morgana Le Fay. He gives her three days to defeat the Earth's greatest sorcerer, Lindmer, and his apprentice, the new "chosen one." On Earth, Lindmer becomes aware of the plot against him and prepares to make contact with his new apprentice, the unsuspecting young resident psychiatrist Stephen Strange.

Morgana possesses the body of a beautiful young woman, Clea Lake, in an attempt to turn her into Lindmer's assassin. When Clea ends up on the psychiatric ward at Strange's hospital, Strange nurses her back to health, and Lindmer informs him that the only thing that can save Clea from Morgana's grasp is a mystical journey into the astral plane, a realm of magic. A rational man of science, Strange is slow to believe Lindmer, but is so caring a man that he will try anything to save his patient. With Lindmer's help, Strange summons "the fundamental power of the universe," rescues Clea from a coma, and casts into the nether regions one of Le Fay's demon minions.

The Dark One is angry with Morgana for botching a murder attempt against Strange (utilizing a city bus), and Le Fay admits she is attracted to the handsome young man. She is given one more chance to kill Lindmer and convert Strange to the ways of evil. With Clea safe, Strange abandons his new powers as a sorcerer and thanks Lindmer for his help. Unfortunately, Le Fay steals into the old sorcerer's house (in the form of a cat) and defeats the old man. She then transports Strange to a Hell dimension and tempts him with the secrets of the universe and supreme knowledge. Strange sees old Lindmer being tortured and resists the seduction, defeating Le Fay.

As the Devil punishes Morgana for her failure — robbing her of her youth and beauty — Strange embarks on a strange new life as Lindmer's apprentice. He renounces the pleasures of life, including offspring and "an easy death," and becomes the new master sorcerer.

Even as this transition of power occurs, Morgana Le Fay returns to Earth with a new plot to corrupt the minds of the young.

ElectraWoman and DynaGirl

In 1976, producers Sid and Marty Krofft were the undisputed kings of Saturday morning live-action TV, having created the very popular dinosaur epic *Land of the Lost* (1974–76). In the year of the bicentennial celebration they presented a new ABC Saturday morning program called *The Krofft Supershow*. It featured a number of different live-action series (including *Wonderbug*) under that title umbrella, and one of the weekly entries was a campy superhero series called *ElectraWoman and DynaGirl.*

Each episode of the series ran approximately fifteen minutes and featured the adventures of ElectraWoman and her sidekick DynaGirl as they faced off against costumed villains of the craziest variety. Among the nemeses: the Sorcerer (Michael Constantine), Ali Baba (Malachi Throne), the Pharaoh (Peter Mark Richman), and the Spider Lady (Tiffany Bolling). These villains were not only evil, but rather snippy. "Have your little Electra Fun!" or "Please ElectraWoman, I have no time for idle chitchat!" were the *bon mots* of choice.

ElectraWoman and DynaGirl had a two-part episode structure. The first fifteen-minute drama was the set-up for a dangerous cliffhanger (just like the Adam West *Batman* series), and the last fifteen-minute segment was the resolution of the story. And what cliffhangers the series featured too: DynaGirl and ElectraWoman trapped in an alternate dimension by Merlin's Mirror ("The Sorcerer"), or the duo squeezed between closing walls (like the famous trash compactor sequence in *Star Wars*) in "Glitter Rock." The way they escaped the latter crisis was by deploying the Electra Vibe, a device that could pulverize boulders and destroy brick walls. Good thing they had it with them.

Overall, the series' premise was quite simple, and also quite derivative of the *Bat-man* TV series mythos. From deep inside their underground ElectraBase, ElectraWoman and DynaGirl searched out crime on their Crime Scope (in "search alert mode"). They located criminals with their boat-like ElectraCar (or ElectraPlane), and then defeated them with their high-tech portable devices known as "ElectraComps"— very large, very 1970s lunky wristwatch-like mechanisms that could shoot "Electra-Beams" (an electromagnetic power that reverses the movement of any object). On other occasions, they would save the day by operating such items as the "ElectraGravitator." The overall gimmick, naturally, was electricity.

Young DynaGirl was also given to "holy!"-style declarations like her antecedent, Robin, including "Electra-cool!" "Electra-Easy!" "Electra-Fantastic," and so on.[1] What may have been most noticeable about the super-duo, however, were the incredibly tight and form-fitting spandex super-suits they could miraculously don simply by shouting "ElectraChange!"

By day, ElectraWoman (actress Deirdre Hall) was *Newsmaker* Magazine reporter Lori, and her crime-fighting partner was her assistant, Judy (Judy Strangis). The only person that knew their secret identities as superheroes was a friend named Frank. Oddly, ElectraWoman and DynaGirl looked the same in and out of uniform ... they made no effort to disguise themselves or otherwise cloak their identities! They didn't even wear glasses, let alone don masks.

Although *ElectraWoman and DynaGirl* ran for only eight episodes, it nonetheless accumulated a huge fan following among the youthful Saturday TV watchers, thanks to a campy and over-the-top tone and sexy costuming. As Sid Krofft recollected:

> When we show *ElectraWoman and Dyna-Girl* at a screening, the audience just goes

Electra-Fantastic! Seventies super-sirens DynaGirl (Judy Strangis) and ElectraWoman (Diedre Hall) strike a dramatic pose.

crazy ... screaming, because it's so way out, so whacked-out.... When you say *Electra Woman and DynaGirl*, only eight episodes, but everybody knows what you're talking about.[2]

The following remains so devout, in fact, that in the year 2000, producers Sid and Marty Krofft talked to this author about reviving the series for a new generation. "We're remaking it for the WB as a prime-time series," Marty Krofft noted at the time. "We're pulling the series together right now, and it's the same concept as before: two women superheroes fighting evil." The difference this time was that the series would be an adult re-imagining of the old concept, rather than one designed for Saturday mornings.

Since 2000, the updated *ElectraWoman* *and DynaGirl* has failed to materialize, and likely will not any time soon, considering that the WB Network has poured time and expense into airing another female superhero "partner" series: *Birds of Prey.* With the surprise failure of that series, it is unlikely that another female superhero team will be given a shot in prime time any time soon.

It's an Electra-Shame.

ElectraWoman and DynaGirl (1976-77)
LIVE-ACTION SERIES

"The series took all the worst elements of *Batman* without incorporating the good ones. I loved the show when I was thirteen years old. But they took all the camp elements and stylish filmmaking elements of *Batman*, right down to the scene changes with a spinning logo, but without incorporating any subtlety. Basically, ElectraWoman and DynaGirl fought crazy super-villains, and the shorter sidekick always used a catchphrase but it was "Electra-Wow" or something, instead of Robin's familiar "holy!" declaration. There's no subtext in *ElectraWoman and DynaGirl*, and maybe that's not surprising since it was a kids' show on Saturday morning, but it certainly wasn't very multi-layered."

— Howard Margolin, host of *Destinies:*
The Voice of Science Fiction.

CAST: Deidre Hall (Lori/ElectraWoman); Judy Strangis (Judy/DynaGirl); Norman Alden (Frank Heflin); Marvin Miller (Narrator).

CREW: *Created by:* Joe Ruby and Ken Spears. *Executive Producers:* Sid and Marty Krofft. *Produced by:* Walter C. Miller. *Developed for TV by:* Dick Robbins and Duane Pool. *Music by:* Jimmy Haskell. *Story Editors:* Dick Robbins and Duane Poole. From Krofft Entertainment.

1. "The Sorcerer" Written by: Dick Robbins and Duane Poole. Directed by: Walter C. Miller.

A villain called the Sorcerer has been on a stealing spree throughout the ages of man, thanks to a magical mirror that lets him travel through time and various dimensions. When ElectraWoman and DynaGirl try to stop the villain, he traps them in a weird nether-reality.

GUEST CAST: Michael Constantine (The Sorcerer); Susan Lanier (Dazzle); Billy Beck (da Vinci).

2. "Glitter Rock" Written by: Dick Robbins and Duane Poole. Directed by: Chuck Liotta.

A rock 'n' roll star-turned-super-villain, "Glitter Rock," hopes to steal a priceless jewel that will allow him to transmit his music world-wide. ElectraWoman and DynaGirl try to stop him, but find themselves in a tight squeeze as they fall into his trap.

GUEST CAST: John Mark Robison (Glitter Rock); Jeff David, Michael Blodgett.

3. "Empress of Evil" Written by: Dick Robbins and Duane Poole. Directed by: Walter C. Miller.

A new villainess, the Empress of Power, immobilizes ElectraWoman and DynaGirl by rendering all of their Electra devices powerless.

GUEST CAST: Claudette Nevins (Empress of Evil); Jacqueline Hyde, Jean Sarah Frost.

4. "Ali Baba" Written by: Dick Robbins and Duane Poole. Directed by: Walter C. Miller.

The evil Ali Baba uses a Russian scientist's strange personality-altering formula to turn DynaGirl into an unrepentant villain! ElectraWoman and Frank must act fast to save their friend, but they learn she is already trying to take down her former colleagues.

GUEST CAST: Malachi Throne (Ali Baba); Sid Haig (Genie); Ian Martin.

5. "Return of the Sorcerer" Written by: Dick Robbins and Duane Poole. Directed by: Walter C. Miller.

The Sorcerer is back, and this time he hopes to steal all the gold out of Fort Knox!

GUEST CAST: Michael Constantine (The Sorcerer); Susan Lanier (Dazzle).

6. "The Pharaoh" Written by: Greg Strangis. Directed by: Jack Regas.

The villain Pharaoh and his love Cleopatra match wits with ElectraWoman and DynaGirl over a powerful device known as "the Coptic Eye."

GUEST CAST: Peter Mark Richman (The Pharaoh); Jane Elliott (Cleopatra).

7. "Spider Lady" Written by: Gerry Gay and Bethel Leslie. Directed by: Walter C. Miller.

The nefarious Spider Lady doubles as ElectraWoman in hopes of stealing a priceless relic, a gold spider statue.

GUEST CAST: Tiffany Bolling (The Spider Lady).

NOTE: It's a bit of casting irony that Tiffany Bolling plays a character named the Spider Lady. In 1977 she co-starred with William Shatner in *Kingdom of the Spiders*, a film about tarantulas menacing a southwestern town. Bolling was one of the menaced.

8. "Return of the Pharaoh" Written by: Greg Strangis. Directed by: Jack Regas.

The Pharaoh and Cleopatra return to hold the city for ransom.

GUEST CAST: Peter Mark Richman (The Pharaoh); Jane Elliott (Cleopatra).

The Fantastic Four

Other than Captain America, few Marvel Comics characters have been treated as shabbily by Hollywood as Jack Kirby and Stan Lee's popular quartet the Fantastic Four. This fabulous foursome, a team created to rival the Justice League of America at DC, premiered in late 1961 and quickly became an ultra-successful comic title.

On an important space mission, Professor Reed Richards, wife Sue Storm, her brother Johnny, and friend Benjamin Grimm became exposed to weird "cosmic rays" that affected them in rather drastic ways. Richards became Mr. Fantastic, a man that could stretch his plastic body in unbelievable ways. Sue became the Invisible Girl, able to disappear at will. Short-tempered, impulsive Johnny was able to generate flames around his body, transforming into a hero called the Human Torch. Benjamin Grimm's transformation was perhaps the strangest of all: he became a giant, orange,

rock-like monster called the Thing. Together this comic book team challenged the whole array of Marvel villains, including Dr. Doom, Magneto, Galactus, Mole Man and Diablo.

The Fantastic Four would seem a natural as either a feature film or a TV series, but the history of *Fantastic Four* adaptations is not particularly good. In 1967 Hanna Barbera created a very dated version (Sue Storm looks like a blond Jackie Kennedy) that ran for 26 half-hour episodes. Despite its age and limited animation style, it remains the finest adaptation of the comic seen thus far.

In 1978 *The New Fantastic Four* premiered on NBC Saturday morning TV, and the team lost one of its key members, Johnny Storm, because of rights issues. The Human Torch was replaced in the foursome by a floating white robot that resembled a hovering R2-D2 (alas, *Star Wars* was pop-

The Fantastic Four? Wait a minute, where's the Human Torch? Alas, he's been replaced in this animated series (titled *The New Fantastic Four*) by a high-flying robot sidekick named H.E.R.B.I.E.

ular at the time). The robot was named H.E.R.B.I.E. (Humanoid Electronic Robot B-Model) and had a love/hate relationship with the Thing. In this version of the series, the team was also seen to fly in a Fantasticar as they battled Magneto and other villains.[1]

By 1994, one might think that anima-

tors would get things right, but the third version of the series, *The Fantastic Four*, was pretty underwhelming too. This *Fantastic Four* cartoon featured the vocal talents of guests Mark Hamill (Triton), Michael Dorn (Gorgon), Keith David (T'Challa), Richard Grieco (Ghost Rider), Ron Perlman (The

The Forgotten Four. The stars of Roger Corman's low-budget, unreleased *Fantastic Four* feature. From left to right: The Thing (Carl Ciarfalio), Sue Storm/Invisible Girl (Rebecca Staab), Reed Richards/ Mr. Fantastic (Alex Hyde-White) and Johnny Storm/the Human Torch (Jay Underwood).

Incredible Hulk) and John Rhys-Davies (Thor), but some animation gaffes marred the apparently-rushed production. Among the villains: Puppet Master, the Skrull and Galactus.

Also in 1994, Roger Corman produced a live-action version of *The Fantastic Four*— one that has never seen the light of day except in bootleg copies sold at conventions and over the Internet. Shot in four weeks and made for four million dollars, *The Fantastic Four* feature film was directed by Oley Sassone and starred a group of unknowns.[2] Some sources insist the quality of the movie was so bad that it was considered unreleasable, even on video. Other sources indicate the producer of the film, Bernd Eichin-

ger, purchased the film from Corman, choosing not to release it and marking time until he could produce a bigger-budgeted version of the material.[3]

Despite the efforts of fine special effects artists like John Vulich (*Buffy the Vampire Slayer, Angel*), the budget was so low that *The Fantastic Four* looked more like the *Embarrassing Four*. The script (by *Black Scorpion* writer Craig J. Nevius) did not help matters, and this movie has become a sort of "Holy Grail" of bad superhero movies, one much sought after by completists.

It has been announced that *The Fantastic Four* will finally have their day in a big-budget, A-list feature film due for release in 2005. We'll see.

The Fantastic Four (1967)
ANIMATED SERIES

VOICE TALENT: Gerald Mohr (Reed Richards/Mr. Fantastic); Jo Ann Pflug (Sue Storm/the Invisible Girl); Jack Flanders (Johnny Storm/the Human Torch); Paul Frees (Ben Grimm/the Thing).

CREW: A Hanna-Barbera Production. *Series Writers:* Philip Hahn, Jack Hanrahan. *Series Directors:* Joseph Barbera and William Hanna.

The New Fantastic Four (1978)
ANIMATED SERIES

VOICE TALENT: Mike Road (Reed Richards/Mr. Fantastic); Ted Cassidy (Ben Grimm/the Thing); Ginny Tyler (Sue Storm/the Invisible Girl); Frank Welker (H.E.R.B.I.E.).

CREW: A De Patrie–Freleng Enterprises Production. NBC.

The Fantastic Four (1994)
UNRELEASED LIVE-ACTION FILM

CAST: Alex Hyde-White (Professor Reed Richards/Mr. Fantastic); Jay Underwood (Johnny Storm/the Human Torch); Rebecca Staab (Sue Storm/the Invisible Girl); Michael Bailey Smith (Ben Grimm); Ian Trigger (The Jeweler); Joseph Culp (Victor von Doom/Dr. Doom); George Gaynes (Professor); Michele Brown (Alicia); Mercedes McNab (Young Sue Storm); Philip Van Dyke (Young Johnny Storm); Carl Ciarfalio (The Thing).

CREW: Concord–New Horizons Corporation Presents a film by Oley Sassone, *The Fantastic Four. Produced by:* Roger Corman and Steve Rabiner. *Screenplay by:* Craig J. Nevius and Kevin Rock. *Special Make-up by:* John Vulich, Everett Burrell. *Optical Special Effects:* Scott Phillips. *Directed by:* Oley Sassone. *Running time:* 90 minutes (approx.). *M.P.A.A. Rating:* NA, Unreleased.

After exposure to cosmic rays, a team of superheroes called the Fantastic Four is forged. They must do battle with a powerful masked madman called Dr. Doom.

The Fantastic Four (1994)
ANIMATED SERIES

VOICE TALENT: Beau Weaver (Reed Richards/Mr. Fantastic); Lori Allen (Sue Storm/the Invisible Girl); Chuck McCann (Ben Grimm/the Thing); Quinton Flynn (Johnny Storm/the Human Torch); Simon Templeton (Dr. Doom).

CREW: *Series Director:* Tom Tataranowicz.

The Flash

The fastest man alive, the Flash, began his superhero life in the comics in the 1940s as a fellow named Jay Garrick. Known as the "golden age" Flash, this character developed the ability to run at incredible speeds courtesy of a scientific experiment gone wrong. He also wore a funny and cumbersome World War I–style bowl helmet with wings on the sides.

But the Flash did not really catch on

with fans until the dawn of the comic book silver age, approximately October 1956, when writer Julius Schwartz reinvented the character with a new origin and a sleeker, scarlet costume with headgear that more closely resembled Captain America. Now Barry Allen was the Flash, and he developed his powers of super speed when a "flash" of lightning struck a cabinet full of chemicals and he was doused in a variety of formulae.

Barry Allen first appeared in *Showcase #4* in 1956, and the "whirlwind adventures of the fastest man alive" commenced in earnest. By 1959, the Flash was the star of his own title once more, picking up on DC's issue numbering from the 1940s. In his second incarnation, Barry was able to move so fast that his molecules would actually vibrate, allowing him to pass through solid objects. He was also known to give Superman a run for his money in the speed category, and, on some occasions, could use his velocity to travel back and forward through time.

Unfortunately, Barry Allen died in the mid–1980s, a victim of *Crisis on Infinite Earths* (issue #8). This left his protégé, Kid Flash, to take over. Wally West became the new Flash, and in an interesting twist it was Bart Allen, grandson of Barry, that became the second Kid Flash, now known as Impulse to avoid confusion. Got that? If so, here's another twist: Barry Allen didn't really die during the *Crisis on Infinite Earths* story line, he merely lost corporeality and traveled back in time to his accident, this time becoming the very lightning that endowed him with powers in the first place. Or, at least that is one theory…

Despite his popularity in the comics, no version of the Flash — Golden Age, Silver Age, Kid or Impulse — successfully made the trip to a series of live-action movies or TV shows until 1990 (following the success of Tim Burton's *Batman* in theaters). Though the character of Flash had made a half-dozen appearance in a cartoon called

The Superman-Aquaman Hour in 1967, and was a charter member of the Justice League of America in the 1970s version of *The Super Friends*, he just did not have much luck with his own franchise. The only live-action Flash seen before the TV series arrived came in two 1977 specials entitled *Legend of the Superheroes*, which featured Rod Haase as the fastest man alive.

The wait for a proper Flash franchise may have been the result of the Flash's particular subset of super powers. Running fast was not nearly as dramatic or "super" as flight, x-ray vision, or the like. On the other hand, incredible speed was not as farfetched as those capabilities either. Regardless of the reasons for the long delay, CBS finally optioned the property following the Burton *Batman*; and the Flash, like Batman before him, became a night-roaming avenger, one that wore a crimson spandex and foam latex suit.

The Flash suit (reportedly a $20,000 expense) was explained in the series as being a Soviet prototype for a deep-sea diving suit. It molded to Barry's body with a layer of "reactive insulation" and could withstand high velocities by regulating body temperatures — a must, since the Flash on the TV series could run 400 miles an hour.

In the pilot for the series, produced by Paul De Meo and Danny Bilson, police scientist Barry Allen (*Dawson Creek*'s John Wesley Shipp) experienced his hero-making accident in the lab, a faithful translation of the "chemical" spill origin from the comics. He also faced down a villainous motorcycle gang led by a guy named Pike (Michael Nader) that had killed his detective brother (Tim Thomerson). But to stop this villain, the revenge-minded Allen had to learn to develop and harness his out-of-control powers, and the series did not shy away from dramatizing his trials and errors in developing his abilities, not unlike *The Greatest American Hero*.

Allen was eventually helped in this re-

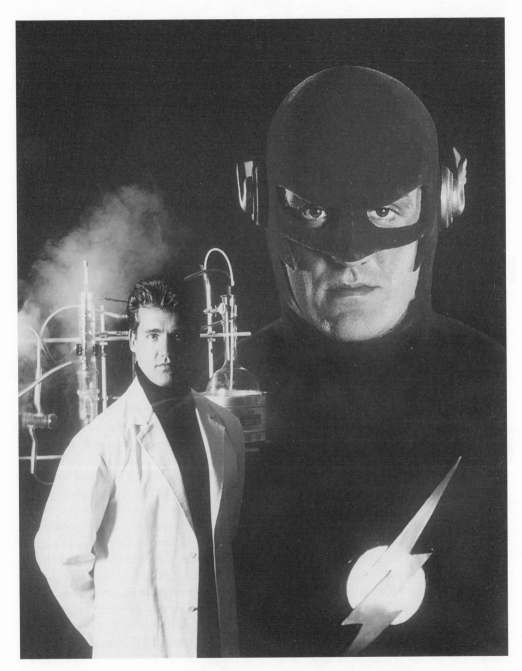

Two views of the Fastest Man Alive. John Wesley Shipp is *The Flash*.

gard by Dr. Christina McGee (Amanda Pays), a scientist and sidekick who worked for the mysterious Star Labs, a mainstay of DC Comics depicted also in *Lois & Clark: The New Adventures of Superman*.

Like most good superheroes, the Flash had an Achilles heel. He required a great deal of energy to maintain his accelerated metabolism, and, when weakened, would black out and faint from low blood sugar levels. This meant that he had to eat a lot, and the TV show had great fun dramatizing Shipp's Allen gulping pizzas and other meals literally "on the run."

Allen had to keep his secret identity from his family of cops, local authorities and the citizenry of Central City "a third rate Metropolis," as the Trickster called it. Later in the series, the Flash also developed a friendship with a sexy detective named Megan Lockhart (Joyce Hyser), and she came to know his secret.

One of the primary draws of *The Flash* TV series was the convincing special effects. The hyper-velocity of the hero was accomplished via a diverse array of TV illusions. There was fast-motion photography (with a still camera) used to show Barry racing around his apartment. When the Flash ran down a street, animated red streaks were optically added to the footage, making it seem as if the hero was running so fast that he could only be detected as a blur.

Then there was the third approach: actor John Wesley Shipp positioned in front of a blue screen, as super-fast footage was rear-projected behind him. Finally, point of view subjective shots (from the front of a racing vehicle) gave the impression of immense speed. Together, these techniques made the Flash's super speed seem believable.

The pilot of *The Flash* was quite exciting, though one had to cringe at some of the bald-faced "borrowings" from Tim Burton's *Batman*. Most notable were the Elfman-like, bombastic musical score; the dominance of night shooting (with neon lights everywhere); and the contemporary production design that consciously and subtly evoked elements of the 1940s (police uniforms, cars, and so forth). Worst of all was that wincer of a line, "I made you? You made me!" that has seemingly become *de rigueur* for all superhero films and TV shows post–Burton *Batman*.

Still, *The Flash* became a very good superhero show, and some fans consider it to be the best superhero series ever produced for television. This is because the show's writers (including Howard Chaykin, late of *Mutant X*) took the premise and characters seriously, and did not let the series lean towards camp or over-the-top humor. When *The Flash* began, there was a special effort to ground the series in reality. The villains were of the "kitchen sink," normal TV variety, which includes mad scientists ("Out of Control" and "Double Vision"), murderers ("Sins of the Father"), cult leaders ("Child's Play") and their like.

As the series continued, other superheroes were introduced, including Nightshade ("Ghost in the Machine," "Deadly Nightshade"). Following that appearance, along came the outrageous villains, most notably Mark Hamill's accurately costumed Trickster ("The Trickster" and "The Trial of the Trickster"), a mainstay of *The Flash* comics and a kind of Joker/Riddler character. Other villains from the comic book included Captain Cold ("Captain Cold") and the Mirror Master ("Done with Mirrors,") the latter played by former teen-idol David Cassidy.

The Flash made for some relatively witty viewing at times, as on the occasion in which Barry's girlfriend, Iris — also from the comic — noted his super speed in the bedroom. "I can't believe it was over so quickly," she complained, lounging beside her topless beau, and the audience jumped with shock and laughter. Of course, she was talking about a pay-per-view boxing match they were watching on TV, not hyper-accelerated sex with the Flash, but it was a perfectly executed joke.

In another humorous moment, a Superman costume showed up at a costume ball (in "The Trickster"), acknowledging the larger DC universe with a sight gag.

Despite a faithful adaptation, a serious demeanor, an attractive cast, good stories and fine special effects, *The Flash* failed to capture an audience for CBS on Thursday nights. The hour-long drama was sand-wiched between *The Cosby Show* on NBC and *The Simpsons* on Fox, both of which were strong ratings draw. The first Gulf War also raged at the time, resulting in frequent preemptions. After one season of just twenty-two shows, *The Flash* was gone from the airwaves faster than a speeding bullet, even though fans would remember the se-ries as no flash in the pan.

The Flash (1990-1991)
LIVE-ACTION SERIES

"*The Flash* will try to get by on moderately in-teresting special effects, some ominous *Twin Peaks*–ish music, and lots of lazy writing. I'm sticking around for a month or so because of Amanda Pays."
— John Leonard, *New York*, October 1, 1990, pages 61–62.

"This is a series that really had potential. The Flash is not an obvious choice for a live action series, but they pulled it off nicely. Shirley Walker did some fine music for the series, and the overall look and feel of the series showed enormous potential. This one died an all-too-quick death."
— William Latham, author of *Mary's Monster, Space: 1999 Resurrection*.

"The series was inspired by *Batman* (1989), right down to the fact that the theme song was writ-ten by Danny Elfman and sounded suspiciously like the *Batman* theme. And, of course, the Flash wore a sculpted muscle suit. Still, it was a very cool show, at least from a visual standpoint. When they did the common stuff like the biker gang, the evil twin or the runaway kid, it was ba-sically your everyday action-adventure with the same plots as every other show. But when they did shows unique to the character, like the Trick-ster episodes, the series stood out. John Wesley Shipp was perfect as the Flash. He looked the part and had the right combination of sensitiv-ity and physical presence."
— Howard Margolin, host of *Destinies: The Voice of Science Fiction*.

CAST: John Wesley Shipp (Barry Allen/the Flash); Amanda Pays (Christina McGee); Alex Desert (Julio Mendez).

CREW: *Theme:* Danny Elfman. *Music:* Shirley Walker. *Film Editors:* Frank Jiminez, Bill Zabala. *Production Designer:* Dean Mitzner. *Di-rectors of Photography:* Francis Kenny, Greg Gar-diner, Sandy Sissel. *Producers:* Don Kurt, Gail Morgan Hickman. *Developed by:* Paul De Meo and Danny Bilson. *Executive Story Consultant:* Howard Chaykin. *Based on the DC Comics Char-acters. Co-Producers:* David L. Beanes, Michael Lacoe. *Second Unit Director:* Danny Bilson. *Cast-ing:* April Webster. *Production Manager:* Paul Cajero. *Art Directors:* Francis J. Pezza, Richard Fernandez. *First Assistant Director:* Marty Schwartz. *Second Assistant Director:* Steve Hirsch. *The Flash Suit Conceptual Designer:* Dave Stevens. *The Flash Suit Designed and Created by:* Robert Short. *Set Decorator:* Jeannie Gunn. *Cos-tume Supervisor:* Gilda Texter. *Property Master:* Michael Casey. *Make-up:* William Myer. *Hair-stylist:* Allen Payne. *Transportation Captain:* Robert Benjamin. *Mural Designs:* Erni Gil Inc. *Stunt Coordinator:* Billy Burton. *Special Effects Coordinator:* Bill Schirmer. *Second Unit Director of Photography:* Greg Gardiner. *Sound Mixer:* Jim LaRue. *Sound Editor:* Sync-Pop, Inc. *Music Ed-itor:* Abby Treloggen. *Assistant Film Editor:* David Jimenez. *Visual Effects Supervisor:* David Stipes, Robert D. Bailey. *Visual Effects Editor:* Peter W. Moyer. *Computer Graphics:* Michael Okuda. *Visual Effects Coordinator:* Philip Bar-berio. *Special Visual Effects:* the Post Group. Pet Fly Productions, in Association with Warner Brothers Television.

SEASON ONE (1990-1991)

1. "**The Flash**" (two hours) Written by: Paul De Meo and Danny Bilson. Di-rected by: Robert Iscove. Airdate: Septem-ber 20, 1990.

Central City is under siege from a gang of heavily armed motorcyclists, and Barry Allen, a crime lab specialist, is determined to discover the identities of these "Dark Riders"— even as his brother Jay is put in charge of a task force assigned to stop the hoods. Working late in the laboratory one night, Barry is exposed to highly volatile and reactive chemicals when lightning strikes the building. Consequently, Barry suffers an unusual form of cell damage that speeds up his metabolism and enables him to move (and think) incredibly fast. Barry teams up with Dr. Christina McGee, a beautiful scientist at Star Labs, to help him develop his "accelerated" powers. While Barry tests the limits of his newfound abilities using a prototype Soviet deep-sea suit that molds to his muscles, Jay is killed by Pike, an ex-cop and leader of the Dark Riders. Bent on revenge, Barry modifies his suit and becomes a super-fast hero known as "the Flash." As the Flash, Allen terrorizes Pike's minions, defeats their plan to free Central City's convicts, and then goes for Pike himself...

GUEST CAST: Michael Nader (Nicholas Pike); Tim Thomerson (Jay Allen); Paula Marshall (Iris); Priscilla Pointer (Nora Allen); Lycia Naff (Lila); Richard Belzer (Joe Kline); Robert Hooks (Police Chief Arthur Cooper); M. Emmet Walsh (Henry Allen); Patrice Allen (Eve Allen); Biff Manard (Murphy); Vito D'Ambrosio (Bellows); Wayne Pere (Rick); Justin Burnette (Shawn Allen); Eric Dare (Tyrone); Ricky Dean Logan (Scott); Marcko Tse (Linda Park); Sam Vlahos (Dr. Lawrence); Josh Craze (Petrolli); David L. Crowley (SWAT Captain); Virginia Morris (Mother); Richard Hoyt-Miller (Young Father); Jan Stang (Young Mother); Brad "Cat" Sevy (Waiter).

2. "Out of Control" Written by: Gail Morgan Hickman. Directed by: Mario Azzopardi. Airdate: September 27, 1990.

The homeless people of Central City are dying, their bodies vanishing, and the police seem powerless to stop it. Dr. Tanner, Tina's old boyfriend, may hold the key to the disappearances: he's been playing Frankenstein, testing a new genetic drug on the hapless homeless. The Flash must come to the rescue, but Tina's feelings for the culprit complicate the matter.

GUEST CAST: Stan Ivar (Dr. Tanner); Jeff Perry (Charlie); John Toles-Bey (Father Michael); Robert Benedetti (Dr. Mortimer); Michael Earl Reid (Mickey); Mario Roccuzzo (Sam); Bill Dunnam (Jack); Macka Foley (Cop).

3. "Watching the Detectives" Written by: Howard Chaykin and John Francis Moore. Directed by: Gus Trikonis. Airdate: October 18, 1990.

The Flash meets Megan Lockhart, a flashy, impulsive and independent private "dick" that has been hired to learn his secret identity for the city's D.A. Unfortunately, the district attorney is corrupt and plans to use knowledge of the Flash's secret identity to enhance his position in the crime world.

GUEST CAST: Joyce Hyser (Megan Lockhart); Vincent F. Gustaferro (Thomas Castillo); Harris Laskawy (Arthur Simonson); Helen Martin (Sadie Grosso); Jordan Lund (Noble John Spanier); Hubert Braddock (Bartender); Pat Cupo (Lounge Lizard); Darrell Harris (Gillespie); Manual Perry (Gordo); Brenda Swanson (Slinky Dame); Frankie Thorn (Judith); Nicholas Trikonis (Pat).

4. "Honor Among Thieves" Written by: Milo Bachman, Danny Bilson and Paul De Meo. Story by: Howard Chaykin and John Francis Moore. Directed by: Aaron Lipstadt. Airdate: October 25, 1990.

Two people from Barry's past unexpectedly re-enter his life at the same time he is assigned to provide security for the priceless Mask of Rasputin at Central City's Museum. As Barry deals with his personal issues, a group of thugs plan to steal the death mask...

GUEST CAST: Ian Buchanan (Stan Kovac); Michael Greene (Mitch); Clarence Clemons (Hennings); Elizabeth Gracen (Celia Wayne); Paul Linke (Ted Preminger).

5. "Double Vision" Written by: Jim Trombetta. Directed by Gust Trikonis. Airdate: November 1, 1990.

After being rendered unconscious, the Flash is re-wired by a brain implant to serve the criminal causes of a crazy scientist. The strange doctor wants the Flash — with all his powers — to prevent the testimony of a witness in an important D.E.A. case.

GUEST CAST: Charles Hayward (Trachman); Karla Montana (Polama); Michael Fernandes (Calderone); Ricardo Gutierrez (Father Becerra).

6. "Sins of the Father" Written by: Stephen Hattman. Directed by: Jonathan Sanger. Airdate: November 8, 1990.

After eighteen years of incarceration, the violent criminal named Johnny Ray Hicks escapes from prison with a thirst for vengeance. In addition to collecting money left hidden for almost twenty years, he wants to murder the police officer that apprehended him, Allen's father!

GUEST CAST: Paul Koslo (Johnny Ray Hicks); Priscilla Pointer (Nora Allen); M. Emmett Walsh (Mr. Allen); Wes Studi (Roller); Robert Shaye (Reggie).

7. "Child's Play" Written by: Howard Chaykin and John Francis Moore. Story by: Stephen Hattman and Gail Morgan Hickman. Directed by: Danny Bilson. Airdate: November 15, 1990.

Two young teens on the streets of Central City encounter a 1960s-style cult led by an ex-hippie. The crazed cult leader is planning to inundate the metropolis with a new, highly addictive psychotropic drug he has developed, leading the teens to seek help from the Flash.

GUEST CAST: Jonathan Brandis (Terry); Perrey Reeves (Pepper); Mark Dacascos (Osako); Michele Lamar Richards (Sullivan); Jimie Skaggs (Beau Lesko).

8. "Shroud of Death" Written by: Michael Reaves. Story by: Howard Chaykin and John Francis Moore. Directed by: Mario Azzopardi. Airdate: November 29, 1990.

A woman out to avenge the death of her father sets her sights on Lt. Garfield. When Garfield's wife is injured in an attack, it is the lieutenant who now wants revenge, and the Flash who must enforce justice.

GUEST CAST: Lenore Kasdorf (Mavis); Walter Olkewicz (Callhan); Lora Zane (Angel); Don Hood (Frank De Joy); Fred Pinkard (Judge Foster); Marguerite Ray (Mrs. Foster).

9. "Ghost in the Machine" Written by: John Francis Moore and Howard Chaykin. Directed by Bruce Bilson. Airdate: December 13, 1990.

A retired superhero called "Nightshade" comes out of retirement when Central City is threatened by a super-villain that terrorized the city more than three decades earlier, a gadget-minded genius called "the Ghost." Nightshade and the Flash team up before the Ghost can disrupt Central City's main computer system.

GUEST CAST: Lois Nettleton (Belle); Ian Abercrombie (Skip); Anthony Starke (The Ghost); Jason Bernard (Dr. Powell/Nightshade).

10. "Sight Unseen" Written by: John Vorhaus. Story by: Gail Morgan Hickman and John Vorhaus. Directed by: Christopher Leitch. Airdate: January 10, 1991.

A man with the power to render himself invisible invades Star Labs and exposes Tina and her boss to a deadly virus. Unless a cure can be found they will die, but the Flash suspects the agent working the case is more interested in the virus than in saving Tina's life.

GUEST CAST: George Dickerson (Quinn); Deborah May (Ruth); Christopher Neame (Gideon); Francois Giroday (Cartwright); Robert Shayne (Reggie).

11. "Beat the Clock" Written by: Jim Trombetta. Directed by: Mario Azzopardi. Airdate: January 31, 1991.

A man has been falsely accused of the murder of his wife, and is scheduled for execution by the State at midnight. Barry is a friend of the suspect, a jazz musician, but time is running out to prove his innocence.

GUEST CAST: Thomas Mikal Ford (Elliott Catrell); Ken Foree (Whisper); Angela Bassett (Linda Lake); Jay Arlen Jones (Wayne Catrell).

12. "The Trickster" Written by: Howard Chaykin and John Francis Moore. Directed by: Danny Bilson. Airdate: February 7, 1991.

Barry receives an emergency message from Detective Megan Lockhart in Willowhaven and races to rescue her, unaware that she has been captured by a diabolical magician/serial killer named James Montgomery Jesse. After the Flash stops Jesse and saves Megan, the criminal escapes police custody and hides out in a prop warehouse where he turns himself into the dangerous new villain known as "the Trickster" — dedicated to defeating the Flash and winning the heart of Megan Lockhart. In Central City, the Flash escapes one of Trickster's dangerous traps and challenges the lunatic to a confrontation at the yearly Policeman's Costume Ball.

GUEST CAST: Mark Hamill (The Trickster); Joyce Hyser (Megan Lockhart).

13. "Tina, Is That You?" Written by: David L. Newman. Story by: Chad Hayes, Carey Hayes and David L. Newman. Directed by: William A. Fraker. Airdate: February 14, 1991.

An accident in the lab injures Tina, transforming her into a new super-villain. She joins a girl gang called "the Black Roses" and sets out to destroy the Flash.

GUEST CAST: Yvette Nipar (Lisa); John Santucci (Big Ed); Denise Dillard (Shann); Courtney Gebhart (Janie); William Forward (Dr. Whilwhite).

14. "Be My Baby" Written by: Jule Selbo. Directed by: Bruce Bilson. Airdate: February 21, 1991.

A woman is on the run from the mob with her young daughter and seeks Barry's help. Barry is left flabbergasted when the woman leaves him to take care of the infant by himself, but is in even more trouble when the villainous mobster "Moses" comes looking for his missing wife and child.

GUEST CAST: Priscilla Pointer (Nora Allen); Bryan Cranstone (Moses); Kimberly Neville (Stacy); Robert Z'Dar (Nuff); John Hostetter (Mills).

15. "Fast Forward" Written by: Gail Morgan Hickman. Directed by: Gus Trikonis. Airdate: February 27, 1991.

The Flash's first nemesis, motorcycle gang leader Pike, escapes from prison to destroy Central City's superhero. He shoots Barry with a powerful rocket, one that pushes the Flash a decade into the future when the city is in ruins and ruled by the iron grip of the nefarious Pike — now an elected official!

GUEST CAST: Michael Nader (Nicholas Pike); Robert O'Reilly (Kelso); Gloria Reuben (Sabrina); Justine Burnette (Shawn); Hank Stone (Cop).

16. "Deadly Nightshade" Written by: John Francis Moore and Howard Chaykin. Directed by: Bruce Bilson. Airdate: March 30, 1991.

A man claiming to be a new "Nightshade" appears in Central City and begins killing off criminals. The Flash must again ask the original Nightshade to come out of retirement to help him defeat this new terror.

GUEST CAST: Jason Bernard (Desmond Powell/Nightshade); Richard Burgi (Curtis); Denise Crosby (Frost); Will MacMillan (Keefe); Jeri Lynn Ryan (Felicia Kane).

17. "Captain Cold" Written by: Gail Morgan Hickman. Story by: Paul De Meo and Gail Morgan Hickman. Directed by: Gilbert Shilton. Airdate: April 6, 1991.

As her big break into the business, a reporter hopes to reveal the secret identity of the Flash. Meanwhile, a cold-powered assassin is hired to kill the superhero, utilizing an assortment of cryogenic and "freezing" weapons to do the job.

GUEST CAST: Michael Champion (Captain Cold); Lisa Darr (Terry); Jeffrey Combs (Swain); Francois Chau (Johnny); Jeffrey Anderson-Gunter (Nikolai).

18. "Twin Streaks" Written by: Stephen Hattman. Directed by: James A. Contner. Airdate: April 13, 1991.

Powers and all, Barry is cloned by an ambitious scientist. Unfortunately, Barry's clone is temperamental and irrational, sparking a confrontation.

GUEST CAST: Charley Lang (Ted Whitcomb); Lenny van Dohlen (Jason).

19. "Done with Mirrors" Written by: Howard Chaykin and John Francis Moore. Directed by: Danny Bilson. Airdate: April 27, 1991.

There's a new super-villain in Central City: the nefarious and cunning Mirror Master. This crook is known as a master of illusion and uses a variety of tools to get what he wants, including a very important item at Star Labs.

GUEST CAST: David Cassidy (Samuel Scudder); Signy Coleman (Master); Zack Norman (Talent); Carolyn Seymour (Weller); Gloria Reuben (Sabrina).

20. "Good Night, Central City" Written by: Jim Trombetta. Directed by: Mario Azzopardi. Airdate: May 4, 1991.

An ambitious Internal Affairs officer holds Barry responsible for a mishap at the morgue. Unfortunately, the investigation comes at a bad time: a gang of robbers plan to put Central City to sleep with a drug and then loot the entire metropolis!

GUEST CAST: Bill Mumy (Roger); Matt Landers (Milgrim); Pamela Gordon (Morgue Attendant).

21. "Alpha" Written by: Gail Morgan Hickman. Story by: Gail Morgan Hickman and Denise Skinner. Directed by: Bruce Bilson. Airdate: May 11, 1991.

Barry and Tina protect an android programmed to be an assassin when the female machine decides that murder is unethical. Unfortunately, Alpha's government developers want her back, and will resort to unethical behavior to get her.

GUEST CAST: Claire Stansfield (Alpha); Laura Robinson (Colonel Powers); Kenneth Tigar (Dr. Rossick); Sven-Ole Thorsen (Omega).

22. "The Trial of the Trickster" Written by: Howard Chaykin and John Francis Moore. Directed by: Danny Bilson. Airdate: May 18, 1991.

Three months after his capture at the hands of the Flash, the Trickster is on trial and Central City is abuzz with gossip about the case. Prank, Trickster's previously unknown sidekick, springs the criminal from court with a teddy bear filled with laughing gas. This accomplice turns out to be Zoey Clark, a toy store heiress who's into crime for the kicks. Soon Trickster is on the air threatening Megan Lockhart, but the Flash isn't able to save the day. Instead, the Trickster captures the Flash (with epoxy-based chewing gum) and brainwashes the superhero into conducting a crime wave with him. Now it's up to Tina and Megan to work together and save Barry—and the Flash's reputation—before it is too late.

GUEST CAST: Mark Hamill (The Trickster); Joyce Hyser (Megan Lockhart); Corinne Bohrer (Zoey); Richard Belzer (Joe Kline); Marsha Clark (Denise Cowan); Mike Genovese (Lt. Warren Garfield); Gloria Reuben (Sabrina); Tim Stack (Jim Kline); Parley Baer (Judge); Brad Sevy (Waiter); William Long, Jr. (Matthews); Christopher Murray (Williams).

The Gemini Man

Viewers who didn't tune in to *The Waltons* on CBS or *Welcome Back Kotter* on ABC in the fall of 1976 may well remember NBC's short-lived offering, *The Gemini Man*, a superhero TV series from the talents behind the smash-hit *The Six Million Dollar Man* (producers Harve Bennett and Leslie Stevens). As an interesting bit of TV trivia, the third executive producer of *The Gemini Man* was none other than Steve Bochco, the creator of *NYPD Blue* and other contemporary hit series.

Airing on Thursday nights, *The Gemini Man* followed the adventures of Sam Casey, a secret agent portrayed by Ben Murphy. Casey became a superhero unwittingly when an accident (shades of *Spider-Man*, *The Flash*, and others) radically changed and reordered his DNA. While attempting to recover a downed U.S. satellite, Casey was exposed to high levels of radiation and suddenly rendered invisible.

Scientists for the organization known as INTERSECT, Abby Lawrence (Katherine Crawford) and Dr. Leonard Driscoll (William Sylvester), devised a way to re-stabilize Casey's in-flux genetic structure, equipping him with a wristwatch device called "a DNA stabilizer" that could materialize and dematerialize the agent at a touch.

Unfortunately, the Gemini Man had a pesky Achilles heel. In this case, Casey could

What's his sign? Ben Murphy is mellow Sam Casey, the 1970s hero *The Gemini Man.*

remain invisible for only fifteen minutes in any twenty-four-hour period, or his DNA would become corrupted and he would die.

Despite some distinctively 1970s touches (like pseudo–O.S.I. settings and disco fashions), the series always acknowledged that it was based on source material from H.G. Wells, particularly his novel *The Invisible Man.*

Sam's unusual ability to become invisible at will — even briefly — made him the perfect agent for INTERSECT, and like the *Six Million Dollar Man* before him, Casey worked hard for the U.S. government and INTERSECT, trapping all variety of evil (though not super-powered) bad guys. He matched wits with the creator of a new fuel additive called "tripolidine" by posing as a trucker in the episode "Smithereens," and fought a mad scientist and his robot in "Minotaur."

He even exposed a spy, who was using a new weapon called "dutrium" against American jet fighters, in "Buffalo Bill Rides Again." Most of the time, conflicts were settled with fisticuffs, which became somewhat amusing because Casey was often invisible; thus, guest actors had to react as if struck by a fist, when in fact they were just air boxing.

Perhaps more impressively, Casey accomplished all of his myriad good deeds wearing tight bell-bottom jeans and maintaining a perfect grasp of 1970s "mellow" lingo (such as "hey, do you know who these turkeys were?"). More hip than Steve Austin, Sam also rode a motorcycle and was pretty laid back indeed, even when he was accused of murder ("Run Sam, Run") or facing an evil doppelganger ("Sam Casey, Sam Casey").

Once again, the well-established Superman character template seemed to be the foundation of a superhero show. Sam Casey never let people know he could become invisible, hiding his super power, as it were. Abby was the familiar Lois Lane figure, ever admiring her unique man, and finding new and inventive ways to get kidnapped. Dr. Driscoll was the cranky superior, another Perry White surrogate.

Like too much 1970s television, *The Gemini Man* was overlong at 50 minutes. Much of the hour-long show felt flat, like filler, and there was always some fetching eye-candy (damsels in distress) for Sam to rescue, including Pamela Susan Shoop, Kim Basinger, Laurette Spang, Pamela Franklin and Kate Woodville. That said, it also possessed innocent, quirky charm (despite the fact it was roasted on an episode of *Mystery Science Theater 3000*).

The Gemini Man was canceled after only half of its episodes aired, becoming an early casualty of the 1976 season. Eleven episodes were produced. Some episodes (such as "Smithereens" and "Buffalo Bill Rides Again") ended up in syndication as movies, with titles like "Riding with Death."

The Gemini Man (1976)
LIVE-ACTION SERIES

CAST: Ben Murphy (Sam Casey); Katherine Crawford (Abby); William Sylvester (Leonard Driscoll).

CREW: A Universal TV series. *Created for TV by:* Leslie Stevens, Harve Bennett, Steven Bochco. *Film Editors:* F. Earle Herdan, Robert F. Shugrue, Gene Ranney. *Art Directors:* David Marshall, Frank Grieco, Jr. *Director of Photography (various episodes):* Enzo A. Martinelli, Vincent A. Martinelli. *Producers:* Robert F. O'Neill, Frank Telford, Leslie Stevens. *Executive Producer:* Harve Bennett. *Story Editor:* Steven E. De Souza. *Associate Producer:* Richard L. Milton. *Music:* Lee Holdridge. *Unit Production Manager:* D. Jack Stubbs. *Based on the Novel by:* H.G. Wells. *Costume Design:* Charles Waldo. Produced in association with Harve Bennett Productions.

SEASON ONE (1976)

1. "The Gemini Man" (2 hours) Written by: Leslie Stevens. Directed by: Alan J. Levi. Airdate: May 10, 1976.

Sam Casey is injured on a salvage mission to recover a satellite, and his DNA is corrupted by radiation, rendering him invisible. Casey is rescued by INTERSECT, a top-secret branch of the government, and scientist Abbey Lawrence develops a method (a wristwatch control) by which he can modulate his invisibility for short periods of time. Casey's unique new powers make him a vital asset to the American government, and he reports to Leonard Driscoll as a secret agent on the side of good.

GUEST CAST: Richard Dysart (Driscoll); Dana Elcar, H.M. Wynant, Gregory Walcott.

2. "Smithereens" Written by: Frank K. Telford. Directed by: Alan J. Levi. Airdate: September 23, 1976.

Sam Casey is assigned to transport a scientist, Dr. Hale, along with a shipment of his efficient new fuel additive, tripolidine, in a trucker's rig. Unfortunately, Dr. Hale and his associate, Luthor Stark, have organized a double cross: they've stolen 10 million dollars from INTERSECT for the project and developed not a gas additive, but a highly flammable new explosive. Unbeknownst to Sam, Abby is trapped in the back of his rig with a jug of the explosives. Hale's men sabotage the rig to destroy the evidence, but a friendly trucker, Buffalo Bill, helps to save Casey's life on a particularly dangerous stretch of California highway.

GUEST CAST: Alan Oppenheimer (Dr. Hale); Jim Stafford (Buffalo Bill); Andrew Prine (Luthor Stark).

3. "Minotaur" Written by: Robert F. O'Neill and Frank Telford. Story by: Robert Bloch and Robert F. O'Neill. Airdate: September 30, 1976.

Interrupted during his off-duty time by the crisis, Sam must outsmart and defeat a mechanical menace called "Minotaur," a defense department robot built by Dr. Carl Victor and funded by INTERSECT. Victor has gone rogue, captured Driscoll, and is demanding a king's ransom to continue his research. If his demands are not met, he will use the Minotaur to destroy a city skyscraper, but Sam thinks a familial connection might help defuse the situation.

GUEST CAST: Ross Martin (Dr. Carl Victor); Deborah Winters (Nancy Victor); Cheryl Miller, William Boyett, Michael London, Dale Johnson.

4. "Sam Casey, Sam Casey" Written by: James D. Parriott. Directed by: Michael Caffey. Airdate: October 7, 1976.

An assassin is surgically altered to duplicate Sam Casey's facial features. The mission: the murder of Dr. Leonard Driscoll! Sam is abducted and replaced by the killer; can Sam stop his own villainous double before it is too late?

GUEST CAST: Pamela Susan Shoop (Barbie); Nancy Malone (Armstead); Jo An Pflug (Susie); Joan Crosby (Dora); Leslie Moonves.

5. "Night Train to Dallas" Written by: Steven E. De Souza. Directed by: Alan J. Levi. Airdate: October 14, 1976.

A student competing in a collegiate diving competition may hold the key to continuing the work of a dead scientist. The student has a photographic memory and may remember key details, but, unfortunately, she is uncooperative and unwilling to help Sam or INTERSECT. Sam tags along with the girl on a train trip, aware she is in danger and that foreign agents are closing in for the kill.

GUEST CAST: Kim Basinger (Sheila); Michael Fox (Conductor); Lane Bradbury (Amy); Ryan McDonald (Agent); Ann Shoemaker (Price).

6. "Run Sam, Run" Written by: Frank K. Telford. Directed by: Charles Rondeau. Airdate: October 28, 1976.

Sam awakens from a deep sleep with amnesia, uncertain who he is or where he is. His power of invisibility strikes a chord and he remembers INTERSECT ... but everybody at the agency, including Driscoll, seems bent on apprehending him. Even though Sam doesn't understand how, it seems he has murdered another agent and is on the run...

GUEST CAST: Laurette Spang (Maggie); Terry Kiser (Benton); Warren Berlinger (Harris); Michael Richardson (Bruce); Ted Hartley (Frank).

7. "Escape Hatch" Written by: Leslie Stevens. Directed by: Paul Stanley. Airdate: unaired.

Why is a wealthy American businesswoman, Ms. Carlyle, selling her considerable assets in a merchant ship company? Sam investigates the mystery, fearful that a foreign government may be pressuring her from behind the scenes. But he has a problem. How is he to reach Ms. Carlyle, who is already aboard a ship at sea, and being held against her will, pending the arrival of a foreign war ship?

GUEST CAST: Pamela Franklin (Daphne); Jane Wyatt (Ms. Carlyle); Bert Kramer, Morgan Jones, Barry Van Dyke, Polly Middleton, Walter Brooke.

8. "Targets" Written by: Jim Carlson and Terrence McDonnell. Directed by: Michael Caffey. Airdate: unaired.

Sam parachutes behind the Iron Curtain to help a lovely defector and her teenage daughter return to the West after a dozen years in the Eastern Bloc. The defector, a scientist, has developed a deadly nerve gas and antidote, and Driscoll wants the information, even though it means putting Sam at great risk during the mission. Worse, the defector is hostile, and makes things difficult for the Gemini Man.

GUEST CAST: Cesare Danova (Victor); Kate Woodville, Paul Mantee, Cynthia Eilbacher, George Ball, Cort Brackett.

9. "Eight — Nine — Ten, You're Dead" Written by: Frank K. Telford and Richard Fielder. Directed by: Andy Sidaris and Alan Crosland. Airdate: unaired.

A boxing legend sees his hopes for a comeback in the ring via a charity match (benefiting children) threatened by crooked promoters who want him to throw his big fight. Sam becomes involved to right the wrongs; but before the day is over, racketeering, kidnapping and all sorts of moral dilemmas arise.

GUEST CAST: Herbert Jefferson, Jr. (Kingston); Henry Darrow (Trent); Charles Lampkin, Delbert Reese, Derek Wells, Gene La Bell.

9. "Suspect Your Local Police" Story by: Rick Mittleman and Steven E. De Souza. Written by: Steven E. De Souza. Directed by: Paul Krasny. Airdate: unaired.

Officer Sam Casey? The Gemini Man goes deep undercover as a cop to snare a foreign-born police officer that may be involved in corruption. His target turns out to be an innocent man whose girlfriend has been kidnapped, and now the blackmailers want him to murder a foreign dignitary.

GUEST CAST: Richard Jaeckel (Nick Radinski); Bill Zuckett, Barbara George, Peggy Walton, Ben Hammer.

10. "Buffalo Bill Rides Again" Written by: Frank K. Telford. Directed by: Don McDougall. Airdate: unaired.

Casey searches for an elusive man named Robert Denby, a man that Driscoll suspects has been involved with every case of defense sabotage in the last five years. Casey finds Denby working on stock cars up north, and his old friend, the trucker Buffalo Bill, is there too. Denby sabotages a new fighter jet, the XJ-240, with "dutrium," a powerful new explosive, and Casey must save Buffalo Bill from driving a car that is also laced with the dangerous explosive.

GUEST CAST: Jim Stafford (Buffalo Bill); John Milford (Denby); Smith Evans (Cupcake); Don Galloway (Agent); Ed Nelson.

11. "Return of the Lion" Written by: Steven E. De Souza. Directed by: Alan J. Levi. Airdate: unaired.

When his homeland becomes embroiled in a bloody civil war, an exiled African leader must return home to bring peace. Making sure he accomplishes his mission is INTERSECT's finest agent, Sam Casey, reluctantly protecting the leader and flying him home by helicopter.

GUEST CAST: Raymond St. Jacques (Jamana); Quinn Redeker (Watson); Mills Watson, Don Maxwell.

Generation X

In the early 1990s, writer Scott Lobdell and artist Chris Bachalo introduced Marvel Comics' readers to the second string of *X-Men*. Their comic book, *Generation X*, premiered in 1994 (and ended after seventy-five issues, in the summer of 2001) and starred a team of maladjusted teenage mutants. Not teenage mutant *ninja turtles*, just teenage mutants.

These kids lived in the same universe as the popular *X-Men*, attended school at Xavier's School for Gifted Youngsters, worried about things like the bigoted Mutant Registration Act, and hoped to grow up and one day join the first string of Marvel superheroes. At the same time, they met with the prejudice of locals and had a hard time finding boyfriends and girlfriends. Again, as in Spider-Man and *Buffy the Vampire Slayer*, super powers and responsibilities were a metaphor for teen angst.

The student mutants of *Generation X* (with colorful names like Jubilation Lee, Mondo, and others) were instructed by two (more mature, if not always wise) adult mutants. The beautiful Emma Frost (also known as the White Queen) was a powerful telepath like her teacher, Professor Xavier, and served as Headmistress at the school. Sean Cassidy (no, not Shawn Cassidy!) was the other instructor, and his superhero name was Banshee.

In 1996, two years after the premiere of the comic, Fox TV produced a *Generation X* movie for its *Tuesday Night at the Movies* prime-time slot. Intended as a backdoor pilot for a series, the film starred *General Hospital*'s Finola Hughes as the beautiful Emma Frost, here a retired scientist that had once collaborated with the repressive government.

Max Headroom's Matt Frewer (playing so far over the top that he becomes a Jim Carrey imitator on steroids) appeared as a Riddleresque villain called Russell Tresh. It was his plan to access the dimension of dreams and terrorize people there, just like "Freddy Krueger." Ironically, the reference to the *Nightmare on Elm Street* bogeyman is the character's choice, not this author's, revealing something of the ludicrous nature of the TV movie.

Endangered by Tresh, who wants to absorb their powers in the dream world, the teens at Xavier School bonded, harnessed their individual abilities, learned to work together, and fought this evil madman.

In the TV movie of *Generation X*, a Cyclops-type character, "Refrax," was added to the mix, and the comic character of Husk was replaced with another character named Buff. As in the comic, Mondo could change his cellular specifications to any object he touched, a quality picked up by the similar character Jesse Kilmartin in the other *X-Men* pseudo-spin off, *Mutant X*.

"We're training you to be a superhero," Cassidy informed his wards in *Generation X*, using tools such as a cheesy-looking Cerebro to hone the group's crime-fighting abilities. Unfortunately, as game as the team was, the TV movie, shot in Vancouver, appeared terribly cheap and patched together, with ridiculous costumes and ludicrously cheap special effects. The final battle, set in the dreamscape, looked like something that would have been nixed from the 1960s *Batman* series. Still, Stan Lee told *TV Guide* he was "delighted with the results."[1] Not surprisingly, a *Generation X* TV series never emerged. With the comic book source material now defunct, it is not likely either.

The TV movie aired on February 20, 1996, and cost 4 million dollars to produce.

Generation X (1996)
LIVE ACTION TV MOVIE

"Think of it as Power Rangers on steroids…"— Susan Stewart, *TV Guide*, Febuary 17–23, 1996, page 49.

CAST: Matt Frewer (Russell Tresh); Finola Hughes (Emma Frost); Jeremy Ratchford (Banshee); Heather McComb (Jublilee); Agustin Rodriguez, Randall Slavin, Bumper Robinson, Suzanne Davis; Amarlis (Monet).

CREW: *Music:* J. Peter Robinson. *Director of Photography:* Bryan England. *Production Designer:* Douglas Higgins. *Film Editor:* Michael Schweitzer. *Executive Producers:* Avi Arad, Stan Lee. *Producer:* David Roessell. *Written by:* Eric Blakeney. *Based on the Marvel Comics Property "Generation X" Created by:* Scott Lobdell, Chris Bachald. *Directed by:* Jack Sholder. *Executive Producers:* Bruce Sallan, Erick Blakeney. *Stunt Coordinator:* Bill Ferguson. *Visual Effects:* Northwest Imaging and Special Effects. *Running time:* 90 minutes.

In the not-too-distant future, genetic mutants exist side-by-side with human beings in America, but with vastly reduced rights (due to the Mutant Registration Act). One girl, a fifteen-year-old mutant named Jubilation Lee, is arrested for being a mutant, but Emma Frost and Sean Cassidy, kindly mutant teachers at the Xavier School for the gifted, attempt to help her and refine her super abilities. They break her out of prison using Emma's telepathic abilities and bring her to the campus, where she meets another young mutant recruit, Espinoza, who can stretch and bend his skin to inhuman proportions.

Unfortunately, the gifted teens at the school don't immediately hit it off with the newcomers. They take classes together, learning the functions of the mutant detector Cerebro and enhancing their psychic abilities with Frost's help.

Elsewhere, a jealous former associate of Emma's named Russel Tresh has developed a machine that can access the dimension of dreams. He hopes to use the machine against Emma because she humiliated him professionally some years earlier. Now, with his method of controlling minds via dreams, Tresh threatens to become powerful.

Feeling left out at school, Jubilation and Espinoza gain access to Emma's dream machine and unwittingly connect with Tresh, who realizes mutants can help him attain domination of the dream domain. During contact with Espinoza, however, Tresh becomes separated from his body and lost on the dreamscape. He recruits Espinoza to help him reunite his body and mind. Espinoza does so, but Tresh captures him to use in his experiments.

Desperate, Espinoza telepathically calls on Jubilation to rescue him from fatal brain surgery. At school, Jubilation rounds up the other mutants, Emma and Sean to battle the nearly omnipotent Tresh.

The Greatest American Hero

In the year 1981, writer/producer Stephen J. Cannell (*The Rockford Files* [1974–80], *Tenspeed and Brown Shoe* [1980]) introduced the world to one of the most enjoyable and purely entertaining superhero TV programs to come down the pike in more than fifteen years: the humorous but emotionally resonant *The Greatest American Hero* (1981–1983). Cannell's unusual and amusing creation was the story of a man named Ralph Hinkley (William Katt). A pacifist schoolteacher and something of a schmuck, Ralph was unexpectedly given a great gift by extra-terrestrials: a flamboyant, red, alien "super-hero" suit (replete with cape) that granted him remarkable powers (including flight, invulnerability and super strength).

Ralph had a trusted mentor/sidekick in Bill Maxwell (the wonderful Robert Culp), a sarcastic, cynical F.B.I. agent with grand designs on the suit, all involving national security. Hinkley's adventures also included his beautiful girlfriend, an attorney named Pam Davidson (Connie Sellecca), a very strong, forthright character that had her own opinions on moral issues. For three seasons on ABC this unusual triumvirate fought evil terrorists, saboteurs, Russian spies and mobsters with an abundance of heart and perfect comedic timing.

A highly amusing series featuring Magicam special effects that in the twenty-first century appear rather dated because of a reliance on rear projection photography, *The Greatest American Hero* was a venture not appreciated by at least one important demographic — the legal department at DC Comics. They sued the creators of the show for copyright infringement. DC sought to stop the premiere of the show in 1981 be-

A terrific trio. Left to right: Pam (Connie Sellecca), Ralph (William Katt) and Bill (Robert Culp) in a publicity shot for *The Greatest American Hero*.

cause it felt the series' hero was a character patterned after their Superman property. DC even asked that "all infringing negatives, tapes, photographs and advertisements" related to the ABC program "be delivered to DC Comics for destruction."[1]

U.S. District Judge Constance Baker Motley considered the case and, after viewing various *Superman* productions and *The Greatest American Hero*, issued a ruling. The judge noted that "numerous differences" in the productions "undercut substantial similarities," and that *The Greatest American Hero* lead character was "an ordinary person who reluctantly takes on abnormal abilities ... and is comically inept," whereas Superman had super powers he wielded with "grace and confidence."[2]

Others in the entertainment industry felt, contrarily, that *The Greatest American Hero* had other antecedents — two 1960s

comic bombs called *Mr. Terrific* and *Captain Nice*, specifically. But there was a great difference. Though *The Greatest American Hero* boasted some wonderful character humor and pratfalls (whenever a clumsy Ralph took to the skies, or attempted to land without crashing into things), the action aspects of the series were strictly dramatic and top-notch. Whatever their relative strengths, *Captain Nice* and *Mr. Terrific* functioned basically as jokes by lampooning superheroes, whereas the characters in *The Greatest American Hero* took their situations seriously, and fought believably evil (if mostly non-super) villains. Series producer and frequent scribe Juanita Bartlett described the difference in approach and format:

> *The Greatest American Hero* is not a spoof. It's a show with comedy. In fact, the show is *really* the story of "everyman." The

humor comes from what would happen if *any* average guy got the suit. How would he behave? How would the suit affect his life?[3]

Series star Robert Culp, who went on to direct and write several episodes, felt that the program's formula featured another plus. Not only were the characters "real" and the humor genuine, but the show, like the best superhero productions, had a kind of mythic quality:

> Every mythology has an old geezer who has wisdom, essentially, and the callow youth, the kid who doesn't know anything but has the robust purity of innocence. And that's Ralph.... You take two really human, ordinary people, and you drop them into remarkable situations. There is no camp involved in this. It has to do with two real people trying to deal with the impossibility of the situation they've been dropped into.[4]

By highlighting dynamic actors, funny and involving stories, and a theme song ("Believe It or Not," written by Mike Post and sung by Joey Scarbury) that rocketed up the pop charts in the summer of 1981, the first season of *The Greatest American Hero* flew by at an entertaining pace. The series aired on Wednesday nights at 9:00 and easily flattened the competition, which included *Real People* on NBC, and *Mr. Merlin* and *WKRP in Cincinnati* on CBS.

When it came to Emmy time, the series was also recognized. Stephen J. Cannell was nominated for "Outstanding Writer in a Comedy Series" for his pilot episode script, and editor Craig Nelson was nominated for Outstanding Film Editing.[5]

With good ratings, *The Greatest American Hero* appeared to be primed for a long run, despite some weird oddities and hiccups. There was the disturbing DC lawsuit, and then the attempted Reagan assassination by a lunatic named Hinkley, John Hinkley. The "suits" (as Bill Maxwell would call them) at ABC panicked over the fact that their unlikely TV superhero had the same last name as the real-life Jodie Foster–obsessed assassin and briefly re-named him "Hanley."

Still, that weird desperation move was not nearly as damaging as the network's next initiative. Greatly overestimating its strength, they threw the series into the cutthroat 9:00 pm slot on Fridays for its second season, in head-to-head competition with the CBS powerhouse *Dallas* and the increasingly popular Glen Larson series *Knight Rider*. In this rougher environment, *The Greatest American Hero* did not prosper. It lasted there for only four weeks before shifting desperately to Thursday nights, where it could not recover its core audience. The series was pulled off the air during its third season, with the last six episodes never making it to broadcast TV.

Despite its relatively short life (some 40 episodes), *The Greatest American Hero* is one of the most memorable and beloved TV series of the 1980s, a show that absolutely everybody remembers. Perhaps more importantly, it humanized the superhero formula on television. It wasn't highly formulized camp like *Batman*. Nor was it so ridiculously square that it became boring (like *Wonder Woman* or *The Amazing Spider-Man*). Instead, it was the *Star Trek* of superhero shows, relying on a triumvirate of interesting, diverse and well-drawn characters in exciting, fun stories.

This was a series that, for once, examined what it really meant to be a superhero, to carry the responsibility and power. In "My Heroes Have Always Been Cowboys," Ralph was able to see himself and his role as champion in context with his own favorite hero, the Lone Ranger, a touching and interesting comparison. As for Bill, he suffered a mid-life crisis in "The Best Desk Scenario" and fell tragically in love in the Culp-written-and-directed episode "Lilacs, Mr. Maxwell."

It was also nice that the program creators allowed the characters to develop and grow as the series progressed. Ralph slowly became more proficient (and less wobbly) at flying, and he and Pam even got married in the third season episode "The Newlywed Game." So many superhero TV series are terminally static, with no change or maturity, offering only repetitive weekly battles with bad guys. *The Greatest American Hero* bucked that historical trend, and despite its focus on humor, seriously advanced the reputation of superhero programming on television.

Also refreshing was the fact that Ralph learned about different powers in various episodes, rather than becoming a great and accomplished superhero all at once. In "Here's Looking at You, Kid," he learned how to control the power of invisibility. In "Now You See It," he learned that the suit granted him precognitive abilities.

And then there were the running gags, which were a riot. Remember on *Star Trek* the infamous and colorful "Bones" McCoy/Mr. Spock feud? *The Greatest American Hero* had its own version of such dynamic character interaction, with Bill and Pam frequently butting heads over a variety of issues. More importantly, the show developed a series of memorable catchphrases (like *Star Trek's* "beam me up," "he's dead, Jim," and "fascinating") that became highly anticipated each week. In this case it was Bill's determination to develop a crime-fighting "scenario" (a favorite Maxwell word). And when he wanted to convince Ralph to don the suit, which Ralph was reluctant to wear, he would goad him with the assurance that, "this is the one the suit was meant for."

The program even took its own ridiculous premise into account, and one running gag featured the always-injured Bill getting in (ever escalating) trouble over the fact that he kept destroying company cars. If only *The A-Team* or *T.J. Hooker* had played so entertainingly with the repetitive elements and outrageous aspects of their respective formats. "The show had basically four types of plots," *Destinies* host Howard Margolin relates, "It was either a new power plot, a Bill case, something wrong with Ralph's students or helping Pam out. That's a lot more diversity than *Smallville*."

The weakest link on *The Greatest American Hero* was probably the run-of-the-mill villains that challenged the heroic threesome. The series brought up every superhero cliché in the book to threaten Ralph, Bill and Pam. There were the requisite nuclear terrorists ("Operation Spoilsport"), a previous owner of the suit turned evil ("Don't Mess Around with Him"), a motorcycle gang in "Hog Wild", neo-nazis in "Divorce, Venusian Style," saboteurs in "The Hand Painted Thai," and young computer hackers in "Space Ranger." Though there were no *Batman*-style costumed villains, *The Greatest American Hero* did occasionally look to the stars (and alien races) for villainy. On at least one occasion ("The Shock Will Kill You"), Ralph battled an evil extraterrestrial entity, in this case one that "sucked" energy.

By 1986, *The Greatest American Hero* was so well regarded that NBC network executive Brandon Tartikoff attempted to have it revived for a new prime-time berth. A 25-minute pilot was commissioned, called *The Greatest American Heroine*. This show saw Ralph passing on the red alien suit to a single mother (Mary Ellen Stewart), another left wing liberal, who also teamed with Robert Culp's conservative F.B.I. character, Bill Maxwell.[6]

The pilot did not go to series (though it was added to the syndication package); but it demonstrated that even after an untimely and ill-considered cancellation by ABC, there was still intense interest in the series, which championed the everyman in a very empowering way.

Currently, the series is due back in "the domestic marketplace" beginning in the autumn of 2002, according to *Daily Variety*.[7]

Even more encouragingly, the Sci-Fi Channel web site reported in summer '02 (shortly after the release of *Spider-Man*) that a movie remake of *The Greatest American Hero* is being prepped at Disney, to be written by Paul Hernandez.[8]

The Greatest American Hero (1981–83)
LIVE-ACTION SERIES

"The use of music in *The Greatest American Hero* was really phenomenal. Mike Post wrote a really great melody and his lyrics were strong. Joey Scarbury was a terrific vocalist who had a way around a song. What I loved most about the series was the character development. That was the strongest asset of the show. When Bill and Ralph first met, they hated each other, but as the show went on, over three years, they became best friends and the audience saw it happen in great character bits. Of course, the show was not terribly strong on continuity. The producers completely left out Ralph's son after the middle of season two. They forgot that his son ever existed. But the series had everything: good character development, intensity and humor."
— Howard Margolin, host of *Destinies: The Voice of Science Fiction.*

"The quality varied from exceptional to silly while the ratings remained average ... its inconsistencies have proven to be an annoyance."
— Robert Greenberger, *Starlog #60:* "Science Fiction Television in Review 1981–1982." July 1982, page 43.

"For every adolescent who loved Superman, this series was a natural. Anyone could put on this suit and be a hero. This was a guilty pleasure, however. The show itself wasn't nearly as compelling as its central conceit, and oh, how that theme song got tiresome."
— William Latham, author of *Space: 1999 Resurrection* and *Mary's Monster.*

CAST: William Katt (Ralph Hinkley/Hanley/Mr. H.); Robert Culp (Bill Maxwell); Connie Sellecca (Pam Davidson); Michael Pare (Tony); Faye Grant (Rhonda); Jesse D. Goins (Johnson); Don Cervantes (Rodriguez).

CREW: *Created and Produced by:* Stephen J. Cannell. *Executive Producers:* Stephen J. Cannell, Juanita Bartlett. *Co-Executive Producer:* Jo Swerling, Jr. *Supervising Producer:* Frank Lupo. *Art Director:* John Jeffries. *Directors of Photography:* Hector Figuera, Jacques Marquette. *Music:* Mike Post and Peter Carpenter. *Theme Song: ("Believe It or Not") by:* Mike Post and Stephen Geyer. *Sung by:* Joey Scarbury.

SEASON ONE (1981)

1. "The Greatest American Hero" Written by: Stephen J. Cannell. Directed by: Rod Holcomb. Airdate: March 18, 1981.

On a field trip to the desert with his class of underachievers, high-school teacher, Ralph Hinkley, runs into hard-nosed F.B.I. agent Bill Maxwell, working on a case involving the disappearance of another agent. Though they don't hit it off, Hinkley and Maxwell end up working together when a flying saucer appears, and strange aliens present a "suit" to the duo — a red suit that will endow its wearer with super-human powers. Though Ralph and Bill have trouble accepting what has happened, the skills of the suit are desperately required at the moment, as a power-hungry politician is killing F.B.I. agents in his quest to take over the country and attain the presidency. Ralph, a divorcee fighting for custody of his son, reluctantly accepts his charge to fight crime with the suit, but in a strange twist, he has misplaced the instruction manual and therefore has of trouble harnessing the extraterrestrial gift.

GUEST CAST: Richard Herd (Taft); Jeff MacKay, G.D. Spradlin, Bob Minor, Ned Wilson, Robbie Weaver, Edward Bell.

2. "The Hit Car" Written by: Stephen J. Cannell. Directed by: Rod Holcomb. Airdate: March 25, 1981.

Bill recruits Ralph and a reluctant attorney, Pam Davidson, Ralph's romantic interest, to help him on a case. For more than a dozen years, Bill has been trying to put away a crime boss named Damanti, and now there is a showgirl willing to testify against him. The only problem is that Damanti has employed a special "hit car" to kill agents and witnesses before, and the showgirl is afraid to fly. This means that Ralph, Pam and Bill must transport her by car from San Francisco to Los Angeles, and the road trip gives Damanti plenty of time to deploy the "hit car" one more time.

GUEST CAST: Gwen Humble (Scarlett); Gianni Russo (Damanti); Ken Holliday, Ernie Orsatti, William T. Zacha, Virginia Palmer.

3. "Here's Looking at You Kid" Written by: Juanita Bartlett. Directed by: Robert Thompson. Airdate: April 1, 1981.

A jet fighter testing a new targeting system unexpectedly disappears over the desert, and the U.S. government fears the technology has been stolen by a foreign power. Bill is assigned to the case, and recruits Ralph, who is already worried about an impending visit from Pam's parents. In search of the missing plane, Ralph develops the suit's latest power: invisibility! But will it be enough to track down the traitorous pilot and recover the stolen technology?

GUEST CAST: James Whitmore, Jr. (Gordon); June Lockhart (Mrs. Davidson); Bob Hastings (Mr. Davidson); Red West, Thomas W. Babson, Al Dunlop, Blake Clark.

4. "Saturday on Sunset Boulevard" Written by: Stephen J. Cannell. Directed by: Rod Holcomb. Airdate: April 8, 1981.

Bill's two-decade-long career in the Bureau is threatened when he fails a lie detector test, unable to answer truthfully about his relationship with Ralph and the alien suit. Put on suspension, Bill hopes that solving an important case involving a wealthy Russian couple will put him back in the good graces of his superiors. Meanwhile, Ralph re-examines his life choices after one of his students calls him a misfit.

GUEST CAST: Alexa Hamilton, Kai Wulff, David Tress, Richard Holley, Joseph Warren.

5. "Reseda Rose" Written by Juanita Bartlett. Directed by: Gabrielle Beaumont. Airdate: April 15, 1981.

Rhonda, one of Ralph's students, comes to Ralph for help on an already harried weekend. Her mother, an employee at a defense technology firm, didn't come home from work, and has disappeared. Though dealing with his ex-wife, Bill's "training" involving the suit, and a day trip with Pam and son Kevin, Ralph comes to the rescue, uncovering a secret plot involving the Russians and stolen documents.

GUEST CAST: E.J. Peaker, Simone Griffith, Peter White, Kurt Grayson, Al White, Nicholas Worth.

6. "My Heroes Have Always Been Cowboys" Written by: Stephen J. Cannell. Directed by: Arnold Laven. Airdate: April 29, 1981.

It is a time for reflection, as both Ralph and Bill face the difficulty of their lives as heroes and law enforcement officials. During one rescue, Ralph nearly becomes responsible for the death of innocent people, and only his love of the Lone Ranger reminds him of the need for heroes. Meanwhile, Bill becomes disillusioned when an old buddy plans to leave the force and turn to corruption, resorting to robbery and violence.

GUEST CAST: John Hart, Jack Ging, Ferdy Mayne, Frank McCarthy, Brandon Williams, Frank McCarthy, Bruce Tuthill, Glen Wilder, William Woodson.

7. "Fire Man" Written by: Lee Sheldon. Directed by: Gabrielle Beaumont. Airdate: May 6, 1981.

Another of Ralph's students gets into

trouble. This time it's rough-and-tumble Tony, who is accused of being an arsonist after a flame-thrower used in a violent crime is found in the trunk of a car he repossessed for his new employers. Tony goes on the run, and it is up to Ralph to clear his name. Bill is reluctant to help another of Ralph's troubled students, but comes through in the end, in no small part because of Ralph's threat to end their partnership if Bill refuses to help.

GUEST CAST: Sandy Ward, Timothy Carey, Raymond Singer, Scott Thompson, Danny Glover, Robert Weaver.

8. "The Best Desk Scenario" Written by: Juanita Bartlett and Stephen J. Cannell. Directed by: Arnold Laven. Airdate: May 13, 1981.

Bill feels the stirrings of a mid-life crisis after he is demoted to a desk job (following Ralph's inadvertent torching of his company car), while Ralph is promoted to vice principal at the school. As each man deals with the problems in their careers, Pam becomes embroiled in a dangerous situation when her new boss proves to be a criminal. Ralph and Bill leave their problems behind to help Pam out of trouble, and in the process, Bill finds some of his old purpose and drive again.

GUEST CAST: Duncan Regehr, Michael Ensign, Eric Server, Eugene Peterson, Rod Colbin.

SECOND SEASON (1981-1982)

9. "The Two-Hundred-Mile-an-Hour Fastball" Written by: Stephen J. Cannell. Directed by: George Stanford Brown. Airdate: November 4, 1981.

The Greatest American Hero meets the Great American Pastime when Ralph Hinkley goes undercover as a baseball pitcher to expose a crooked scheme involving gun runners and extortion. But will setting a new record for the world's fastest speedball

(thanks to the suit) give Hinkley a swelled head? And will he live long enough to enjoy his newfound fame?

GUEST CAST: Markie Post (Debbie); Michael London (Raymond); Carmen Argenziano, Ralph Maura, Hank Robinson, Charles McDaniels, Mike Douglas.

10. "Operation Spoilsport" Written by: Frank Lupo. Directed by: Rod Holcomb. Airdate: November 11, 1981.

A normal day goes from bad to worse when Ralph receives a message from the aliens warning that doomsday could be upon the Earth. Specifically, someone is manipulating the United States' nuclear missile arsenal and preparing to launch a devastating pre-emptive strike against the Soviet Union as part of something known as "Operation Spoilsport." Ralph and Bill must save the planet from nuclear annihilation before it's too late, but their only clue is a missing scientist.

GUEST CAST: John Anderson, Dudley Knight, Robin Riker, John De Fusco, Al White, James Burr Johnson, Russ Martin, Arnold Spivery, John Bristol.

11. "Don't Mess Around with Him" Written by: Stephen J. Cannell. Directed by: Robert Thompson. Airdate: November 18, 1981.

The death of a Howard Hughes–type billionaire, J.J. Beck, is actually a ruse designed to lure Ralph and Bill into his clutches. It seems that Ralph isn't the first "Greatest American Hero," and that Beck once wore a similar suit — until the aliens took it away because of his avarice and greed. Now Beck threatens to expose the truth about Ralph and Bill unless they help him recover his fortune.

GUEST CAST: Joseph Wiseman (Beck); Byron Morrow; Bernard Behrens (Dr. Springfield); Stan Lachow, William T. Zacha, Barry Cutler, Fred Lerner, Chuck Bowman, Sonny Shields, Carl Wickman.

12. "Hog Wild" Written by: Stephen J. Cannell. Directed by: Ivan Dixon. Airdate: November 25, 1981.

The socially inept Bill Maxwell makes enemies of a vicious motorcycle gang in the desert, and the bikers beat up Bill and Ralph. Bill swears vengeance, promising to arrest the bikers. The bikers, however, have other ideas when they learn of Ralph's super powers. The gang captures Bill and forces Ralph to help them exact revenge on a small town where they were once incarcerated. Ralph even loses the suit for a time before setting things right.

GUEST CAST: Gregory Sierria (Vargas); Dennis Burkley, Paul Koslo, Tony Burton, Dennis Fimple, Kerrie Cullen.

13. "Classical Gas" Written by: Frank Lupo. Directed by: Bruce Kessler. Airdate: December 2, 1981.

A villainous assassin called Hydra plans to hijack a shipment of deadly nerve gas and release it in the United States during a concert designed to protest the transportation of dangerous materials. Worse, Ralph's students will be at the concert, and the promoter of the event is romantically interested in Pam. Ralph and Bill must stop Hydra before thousands of innocent Americans are exposed to the deadly gas.

GUEST CAST: Edward Winter, George Loros, Garnett Smith, Christopher Thomas, Joe Horvath.

14. "The Beast in Black" Written by: Juanita Bartlett. Directed by: Arnold Laven. Airdate: December 9, 1981.

Ralph and Bill go through an old house that is due to be demolished and run face to face with the supernatural. A dead woman's spirit kills Bill and then possesses his body, seeking to return to the mortal coil. Ralph must save his friend by battling a monstrous spirit in its own evil dimension.

GUEST CAST: Christine Belford, Jeff Mac-Kay, Rae Allen, Jane Merrow, Vince Howard.

15. "The Lost Diablo" Written by: Juanita Bartlett. Directed by: Lawrence Doheny. Airdate: December 16, 1981.

Bill takes Ralph and his students on a strange quest: the search for the Diablo gold mine left to him by his first partner in the F.B.I., now deceased. Unfortunately, the mine is dangerously unstable, Bill and the students become consumed with greed for the gold, and a gang of unwashed mountain men set their villainous eyes on the group. It looks like a job for the Greatest American Hero...

GUEST CAST: Fred Downs, John Miranda, Joseph Whipp, Bill Quinn.

16. "Plague" Written by: Rudolph Borchert. Directed by: Arnold Laven. Airdate: January 6, 1982.

Ralph, Bill and Pam investigate the death of a mercenary by what appears to be a deadly new plague. As they dig deeper, they learn that a team of mercenaries plan to release the germ in the United States if their demands are not met.

GUEST CAST: Ed Grover (Bunker); Arthur Rosenberg, Jeff Cooper, Glenn Wilder, Melvin Allen, Robert Curtis.

17. "A Train of Thought" Written by: Frank Lupo. Directed by: Lawrence Doheny. Airdate: January 13, 1982.

Terrorists kidnap Bill and steal a train containing highly radioactive materials — a terrible weapon in the hands of America's enemies. In trying to rescue his friend, Ralph is injured and suffers amnesia, forgetting all about the suit and his status as a superhero. Pam is reluctant to tell Ralph the truth about his secret identity as a crime fighter, fearing it will destabilize his psyche, but Bill needs the suit — and Ralph — if the terrorist plan is to be averted.

GUEST CAST: Milt Kogan, James Lydon, Judd Omen, Nick Shields, Warren Munson, Perry Cook.

18. "Now You See It" Written by: Patrick Burke Hasburgh. Directed by: Robert Thompson. Airdate: January 20, 1982.

While testing new flight stabilizers (designed to help the airborne Ralph fly more steadily), Ralph crash lands and accidentally activates a new power of the suit: precognition. He has a disturbing vision of a plane crash, and by touch is able to share the phantasm with a shocked Maxwell. Worse, it seems that Pam is destined to die in that crash unless Ralph and Bill can change the future.

GUEST CAST: Christopher Lofton, Jon Cypher, Charles Bateman, Robert Covarrubias, Richard Beauchamp, Laurence Haddon, Patrick Cameron, Glenn Wilder, Gary Jensen.

19. "The Hand-Painted Thai" Written by: Frank Lupo, Stephen J. Cannell and Patrick Burke Hasburgh. Directed by: Bruce Kessler. Airdate: January 27, 1982.

It's "The Manchurian Candidate" all over again when Americans — once soldiers in Vietnam — are re-activated as saboteurs to destroy landmarks and kill important Americans. Hypnotized a dozen years earlier, these soldiers are unaware of their programming, but a wrong number and a cryptic phrase cue Ralph and Bill into the nefarious plan.

GUEST CAST: John Fujioka, Kurt Grayson, James Shigeta, Hilary Labow, Chris Hendry, James Saito, Lori Michaels.

20. "Just Another Three Ring Circus" Written by: Stephen J. Cannell. Directed by: Chuck Bowman. Airdate: February 3, 1982.

Bill's penchant for destroying company cars comes back to haunt him when his superior gives him the worst assignment possible: the recovery of a kidnapped clown. Ralph and Bill infiltrate a circus, and Ralph, in costume, takes a job as a human cannonball.

GUEST CAST: Catherine Campbell (Erica); Kai Wulff (Peter); Alex Rodine, Derek Thompson, Richard Doyle.

21. "The Shock Will Kill You" Written by: Stephen J. Cannell. Story by: Patrick Burke Hasburgh. Directed by: Rod Holcomb. Airdate: February 10, 1982.

An accident in space forces Ralph to journey to the final frontier, where he saves the space shuttle and returns it safely to Earth. Unfortunately, the crew is dead and the craft is inhabited by a hostile entity composed of pure energy. On the loose, the creature begins killing people and heads for Los Angeles, where it will drain the city's power. Worse, his encounter with the shuttle and entity has turned Ralph into a human magnet!

GUEST CAST: Don Starr (Crocker); Leonard Lightfoot, Doug Hale, Ned Bellamy, Randy Patrick.

22. "A Chicken in Every Plot" Written by: Danny Lee Cole and Jeff Ray. Directed by: Rod Holcomb. Airdate: February 17, 1982.

An F.B.I. friend of Bill's invites him to an island in the Caribbean. Bill accepts the invitation, along with Ralph, Pam and Ralph's class (including Rhonda and Tony). Unfortunately, they find that Bill's friend is dead, apparently the victim of voodoo. Worse, strange things start to happen to the group, and Pam is convinced that they have also become the target of voodoo warlords. But is there more going on behind the scenes on the island?

GUEST CAST: Ron O'Neal, Lincoln Kilpatrick, Thalmus Rasulala, Todd Armstrong, John Hancock.

23. "Between the Devil's Triangle and the Deep Blue Sea" Written by: Frank Lupo. Directed by: Sidney Hayers. Airdate: February 24, 1982.

While still on vacation, Ralph, Pam and the school kids become embroiled in a strange plot. Ralph rescues a girl in the ocean who claims her ship was attacked by a sea monster. Ralph calls Bill back to the island to investigate the story, but they find that it is a cover for piracy, and a conspiracy that may involve the police.

GUEST CAST: Jeremy Kemp (Deveraux); Glynn Turman (Le Clerc); Michael Halsey (Collins); Will Hare.

24. "It's All Downhill from Here" Written by: Patrick Burke Hasburgh. Directed by: Sidney Hayers. Airdate: March 3, 1982.

On vacation skiing, Ralph and Pam find trouble again. This time, they learn of a plot to murder the American contestant in a sporting competition, one being orchestrated by the Czechs. Ralph calls in Bill to help him, and they are surprised to learn that the C.I.A. may also be involved. Worse, Ralph's old girlfriend happens to be on the slopes, a fact that irritates Pam to no end.

GUEST CAST: Red West, Sandra Kearns, Michael Billington, Stefan Gierasch, Scott Templeton, Craig Schaeffer.

25. "Dreams" Written by: Stephen J. Cannell. Directed by: Bruce Kessler. Airdate: March 17, 1982.

A crook put behind bars by Ralph and Bill manages to beat the system and obtain his release. He immediately sets out to hunt down and kill the duo. Meanwhile, Ralph's advice to fellow teachers at school is putting him in hot water with his co-workers and superiors.

GUEST CAST: Elizabeth Hoffman, Robby Weaver, Nicholas Worth, Peter Trancher, Edward Bell, Nick Pellegrino.

26. "There's Just No Accounting" Written by: Frank Lupo. Directed by: Ivan Dixon. Airdate: March 24, 1982.

Bill becomes involved in the release of a kidnapped girl. Ralph helps him, but matters take a turn for the worse when the ransom money ends up at Ralph's place and is seen by an IRS agent conducting an audit of Hinkley. To the government, it appears that

Bill and Ralph were in cahoots to steal the ransom money!

GUEST CAST: James Whitmore, Jr. (Byron); Marc Alaimo (Donny); Jerry Douglas, Carol Mallory, Ted Gehring.

27. "The Good Samaritan" Written by: Rudolph Borchert. Directed by: Bruce Kessler. Airdate: March 31, 1982.

Ralph and Bill go after a pair of convicts that have already escaped one capture attempt. Meanwhile, Ralph wants to turn over a new leaf and use his alien suit for "good deeds" and acts of kindness. This gets under Bill's skin, as he prefers to smash notorious criminals and has little patience for Ralph's efforts to save a man from losing his home.

GUEST CAST: Keenan Wynn (Ira); Dennis Lipscomb, Carmen Argenziano, Harry Grant, Bill Quinn, Ron Thompson.

28. "Captain Bellybuster and the Speed Factory" Written by: Stephen J. Cannell and Frank Lupo. Directed by: Arnold Laven. Airdate: April 7, 1982.

The mascot for a fast food chain, "Hamburger Heaven," learns that the company is dealing illegal drugs. This "Captain Bellybuster" contacts Bill for help, but in the process of assisting the man, Bill and Ralph (in the suit) are exposed by an unscrupulous reporter. This leads to problems in the F.B.I. and a possible murder rap when the reporter is found dead.

GUEST CAST: Chuck McCann, Anthony Charnato, Stanley Grover, Danny Wells, Janet Winter, Jim Greenleaf.

29. "Who's Woo in America" Written by: Patrick Burk Hasburgh. Directed by: Bob Bender. Airdate: April 14, 1982.

Ralph's mother returns from Hawaii with a suspicious young fiancé who seems to have gotten himself in some trouble over a classified computer chip. Hunted by foreign agents, this fellow is more than a little trouble for Ralph and Bill, especially when there occurs a case of mistaken identity.

GUEST CAST: Barbara Hale (Mrs. Hinkley); Tom Hallick, Michael Prince, John Cedar, Don Maxwell, Gerald Jann, Brian Sheehan, Dinah Lindsey Smith.

30. "Lilacs, Mr. Maxwell" Written and directed by: Robert Culp. Airdate: April 28, 1982.

Bill Maxwell has had a spectacular success rate at the F.B.I. of late, and, of course, Ralph and the suit have a great deal to do with that. Unfortunately, a beautiful KGB agent infiltrates the F.B.I. to get close to Maxwell and learn the secret of his success. Bill falls for the lovely agent, unaware she has designs to kill him.

GUEST CAST: Ted Flicker, Adam Gregor, Arnold Turner, Dixie Carter, Gay Rowan, Craig Shreeve, Nick Shields, Stefanie Faulkner.

SEASON THREE (1982-83)

31. "Divorce, Venusian Style" Written by: Patrick Burk Hasburgh. Directed by: Ivan Dixon. Airdate: October 29, 1982.

Ralph and Bill have always held different world-views and philosophies, and have clashed over how best to use the suit. While on a stakeout, they finally have had enough of each other and part company, but Ralph is shot by neo–Nazis hoping to launch the Fourth Reich. The aliens return to heal Ralph, and they show the crime-fighting duo their own dead planet, in hopes that they will reconcile and cure the ills of planet Earth before it is too late for humanity too.

GUEST CAST: Jeremy Kemp (Franz); Dean Santoro, Kurt Grayson, Jason Bernard, Shane Dixon, Robert Gray.

32. "The Price Is Right" Written by: Stephen J. Cannell. Directed by: Ivan Dixon. Airdate: November 5, 1982.

An old high-school buddy of Ralph's is now a professional football player, one admired by millions of fans, including Bill

Maxwell. Bill meets the star, only to learn that he has fallen in with the wrong crowd and needs help to get out of trouble.

GUEST CAST: Stephen Shortridge (Price); Jack Andreozzi, Don Pulford, Patrick Collins, Chip Johnson, Dick Butkus, Doug France.

33. "This Is the One the Suit Was Made For" Written by: Babs Greyhosky. Directed by: Ivan Dixon. Airdate: November 12, 1982.

Since the suit came into his life, things have gotten complicated for Ralph. Not the least of his problems is Pam, who is tired of playing second fiddle to his superheroics. Ralph suggests a vacation to mend fences, but Bill's idea of a vacation spot is, in fact, the location where a fighter jet disappeared. Now Ralph must help recover the craft before the Russians get it, and also keep Pam out of the loop regarding his professional obligations.

GUEST CAST: Bo Brundin, Pepe Serna, Jay Varela, Dean Wein, Maurie Lauren.

34. "The Resurrection of Carlini" Written by: Frank Lupo. Directed by: Arnold Laven. Airdate: November 19, 1982.

A deceased magician has promised to come back from the dead and kill three other illusionists — and Bill. Bill investigates with Ralph and Pam, and finds that the reports of Carlini's death have been greatly exaggerated.

GUEST CAST: Andrew Robinson, Jack McGee, Randi Brooks, Sandy Martin, Timothy Carey, Troy Slater.

35. "The Newlywed Game" Written by: Babs Greyhosky. Directed by: Chuck Bowman. Airdate: January 6, 1983.

Ralph and Pam make preparations to wed, and Bill plans a bachelor party for his buddy. Unfortunately, the festivities are interrupted when Russian agents — claiming to be working for the President — arrive and conscript Ralph for top secret military work.

Ralph is unaware he is working for the enemy, but worried that he might miss his own wedding ceremony.

GUEST CAST: Hansford Rowe (Powell); Norman Alden (Davidson); Terrence McNally, Pamela Bowman, Dan Peterson, Alice Backes, Frank Wheaton, Cynthia Steele.

36. "Heaven Is in Your Genes" Written by: Patrick Burke Hasburgh. Directed by: Christian I. Nyby II. Airdate: January 13, 1983.

Pam and Ralph are distraught and saddened when Bill is killed in a road accident. Later, Ralph learns that Bill is still alive and has been captured by a fascist scientist. The Nazi believes that Bill is the perfect law enforcement official and plans to clone him.

GUEST CAST: William Price, Dennis Lipscomb, Andre the Giant, Carolyn Seymour, Ted Gehring.

37. "Live at Eleven" Written by: Babs Greyhosky. Directed by: Arnold Laven. Airdate: January 20, 1983.

A newsman running for president, and a plot to disable a nuclear reactor, are the ingredients in a mystery that Bill and Ralph must solve. Unfortunately, Ralph is exposed to a high level of radiation—which makes him glow!

GUEST CAST: William Windom (Williams); Alan Fudge (Cole); Miguel Fernandez (Canton); Eugene Peterson, Debra Mays, Woody Skaggs, Victoria Boyd, Mary York, Dudley Knight.

38. "Space Ranger" Written by: Rudolph Borchert. Directed by: Ivan Dixon. Airdate: January 27, 1983.

One of Ralph's more gifted students may be the hacker "Space Ranger" who has been stealing top secret information from Russian spy satellites and sending them to the C.I.A. Now the Russians and the Americans are after the kid.

GUEST CAST: Doug Warhit, Joe Santos, James Beach, Alex Rodine, Edward Bell.

39. "Thirty Seconds Over Little Tokyo" Written by: Danny Lee Cole and J. Duncan Ray. Directed by: Arnold Laven. Airdate: February 3, 1983.

Bill goes on a blind date with a friend of Pam's, with Ralph and Pam tagging along. The date is a disaster, but worse is the fact that a major crime goes down in the restaurant during dinner.

GUEST CAST: Soon-Teck Oh, Mako, Christine Belford, Peter Kowng, Dana Lee.

40. "Wizards and Warlocks" Written by: Shel Willens. Directed by: Bruce Kessler. Airdate: unaired.

A college role-playing game, "Wizards and Warlocks" becomes too real when one of the participants, a foreign prince, disappears while playing. Bill, Ralph and Pam investigate, and find a tangled web of "fantasy."

GUEST CAST: James Whitmore, Jr., Steve Peterman, Nick Minardos.

41. "It's Only Rock and Roll" Written by: Babs Greyhosky. Directed by: Christian I. Nyby II. Airdate: unaired.

Bill, Ralph and Pam must protect a rock star whose success was financed by a notorious biker gang.

GUEST CAST: Judson Scott, Anthony Charnato, Robert Dryer, Lesley Woods, Dennis Stewart, Sheila Frazer, Rick Dees.

42. "Desperado" Written by: Stephen J. Cannell and Frank Lupo. Directed by: Christopher Nelson. Airdate: unaired.

Pam and Ralph are horrified to learn that rustlers are abducting horses to use in a dog food factory. Ralph lures Bill to the scene to handle the situation, which gets worse by the moment. One horse, named Desperado, becomes the target of a rancher's vengeance.

GUEST CAST: John Vernon, James Hampton, Red West, Luke Askew, Rick Lenz, Linda Hoy.

43. "Vanity, Says the Preacher" Written and directed by: Robert Culp. Airdate: unaired.

Three decades ago, a young Bill Maxwell helped to cement democracy in a small foreign country. Now he has been named "Man of the Year" there for his efforts, but it is all a ruse to get him back into the country, where he is kidnapped. Later, Bill is critically wounded, precipitating a return of the aliens.

GUEST CAST: Isela Vega, Joseph Culp, Jason Culp, Luis Moreno, Julio Medina.

The Green Hornet

The Green Hornet began his long crime-fighting career as — and remains to this day — an urban variation of the western cowboy hero the Lone Ranger. In fact, the popular Green Hornet, a vigilante superhero, was first imagined by Lone Ranger originator George W. Trendle and writer Fran Striker in the late 1930s. First appearing in radio, Britt Reid's resemblance to the Lone Ranger was plain. Genealogically speaking, the Green Hornet, really *Daily Sentinel* owner and millionaire Britt Reid, was the grand-nephew of John Reid, the Lone Ranger.

More to the point, Britt modeled his life on his famous ancestor, right down to his life's mission, choice of sidekick and job-related gear. Instead of a Native American sidekick (Tonto), Britt Reid worked with another "ethnic" outsider, the Asian man-servant Kato. Instead of a great white steed named Silver, Britt chased down criminals in a rolling black arsenal called the Black Beauty. And both heroes fought criminals while wearing small eye-masks and hats (different makes, of course). The Green Hornet's main nemesis was the mob, rather than cattle rustlers or nefarious cowboys and Indians, but his dedication to fighting crime was the same as his grand-uncle's, no doubt about it. The setting had merely changed from the wild west to the mean streets of a contemporary city.

The Green Hornet successfully made the transition from a national radio program out of Michigan to movie theaters with two low-budget but popular multi-part serials in the early 1940s. Keye Luke played Kato and Gordon Jones was the heroic Britt Reid. *The Green Hornet* even made the leap to comics too. Over the years the character has appeared in comic books series from publishers Holyoke (1940s), Harvey (1940s), Dell (1950s) and, finally (to coincide with the 1960s TV series), Gold Key (for a very brief run).

Despite these various incarnations, the Green Hornet probably owes his continued popularity in the new millennium to the 1960s TV show created by *Batman* executive producer William Dozier. In the fall of 1966, all the major American networks were looking to repeat the success of the Adam West series, usually with other silly or campy superheroes like *Captain Nice* and *Mr. Terrific*. Dozier came up with the notion of adapting *The Green Hornet* for television, though he also had the rights to create TV projects from DC's Wonder Woman and Dick Tracy.

Dozier, who had so angered stalwart *Batman* fans by turning the Dark Knight into a camp joke, took a new and more thoughtful approach with Trendle's material. He played it all completely straight, with no comedy or condescension, as he describes in the passage below:

> This is a much straighter show. No exaggeration, no clichés. It's not a pop show. The only thing about *Batman* we want to imitate is its success.[1]

So far so good.

Even more encouragingly, Dozier cast the series well. Van Williams was an attractive hero — dashing and debonair as Britt Reid, and grim, grave and determined as his masked alter ego, the Green Hornet. Future star (and icon) Bruce Lee nicely filled Kato's shoes, proving to be a loyal companion and fierce fighter alongside his crime-fighting partner.

And though Lee would eventually garner most of the media attention as he became well-known, the real star of the Dozier show was a vehicle, one that could challenge the Batmobile: the Black Beauty. Dean Jeffries customized a 1966 black Chrysler Imperial to create an impressive and very imposing superhero car. The full-size vehicle came replete with green headlights, rocket launchers in the front and rear, and a gas gun that fired non-lethal Green Hornet gas. It also sported a pop-up scanner in the center of the truck, and even small brooms that could drop down and wipe away tire tracks to keep the vehicle's presence a secret.

Inside the car there were gadgets and oscilloscopes, and the vehicle could even go into "silent running mode" or "self-destruct mode." The Black Beauty reportedly cost some $50,000 to customize, but it was worth it. As stylish as the Batmobile, but with the appearance of a speeding tank, the Black Beauty was the crime-fighting centerpiece of Dozier's drama. On the series, the impressive vehicle was kept in a hidden garage on a rotating platform. One of the Green Hornet's most famous lines was, "Let's roll, Kato," a signal that the battle with evil was about to be joined.

In technique and approach, Britt Reid was a much tougher crime fighter than Dozier's goody-two-shoes Batman. The Green Hornet was ruthless in his fights with the mob, and guns actually figured into the confrontations, unlike in the Caped Crusader's TV adventures. The Green Hornet used green gas to incapacitate bad guys, and was also armed with a "stinger," a cattle

A study in grim determination: Van Williams plays the solemn and serious crimebuster *The Green Hornet.*

prod–like staff that could blow up locked doors, providing quite an entrance for the Green Hornet duo.

For the most part, criminals were not freaks who wore outrageous outfits, and their capers were realistic rather than bizarre and over-the-top. They were counterfeiters ("Programmed for Death") and bootleggers ("Eat, Drink and Be Dead"). They were art thieves ("The Ray Is for Killing"), racketeers ("The Preying Mantis"), corrupt politicians ("May the Best Man Lose"), drug runners ("The Secret of Sally Bell"), corrupt cops ("Bad Bet on a 459-Silent"), Green Hornet imposters ("Corpse of the Year"), arsonists ("The Hornet and the Firefly") and even saboteurs that pretended to be aliens ("Invasion from Outer Space").

The series also featured some authentic night shooting, which gave the program a grittier, more realistic feel than *Batman*, and seemed to have more expensive locations and production values. The fights were often brutal, the tension high, and when Bruce Lee leapt into kung-fu action, the series really took off.

Other than Britt and Kato, the characters on *The Green Hornet* were not very well defined. Wende Wagner played the much-imperiled secretary at the *Daily Sentinel*, Lenore "Casey" Case. She and Britt were clearly attracted to one another, though nothing romantic ever really developed. Lloyd Gough played Mike Axford, the series' version of Jimmy Olsen, a guy in the news business constantly getting into trouble.

Walter Brooke played D.A. Scanlon, a fine law enforcement official who had no idea Reid and the Green Hornet were one in the same person. In fact, the D.A. and all the police had no love of the Green Hornet and attempted to arrest him on many occasions. Britt treated this conflict like a game of chess, or a cat-and-mouse chase, and was good at evading the cops. Again, this was a far cry from *Batman*, wherein Commissioner Gordon and Chief O'Hara basically relied on Batman to police Gotham City.

The Green Hornet began its prime time run the day after *Star Trek* premiered in 1966, September 9. It ran on ABC at 7:30 P.M. on Friday nights, and each episode was a scant half-hour, just like *Batman*. Unfortunately, *The Green Hornet* had some rather stiff competition. On CBS was the fantastically inventive and popular *Wild Wild West* (1965–1970), and on NBC was the Ron Ely series *Tarzan* (1969). It was a night of three fantasy adventure series, and *The Green Hornet* got lost in the shuffle.

Also, there was a real problem with viewer expectations and the universe of superheroes. The audience knew that the creators of the *Batman* TV series were behind the adaptation, and they expected *The Green Hornet* to be funny and over-the-top. It was not, and many viewers felt disappointed. To some, the show even seemed a little boring, with its routine criminals and standard plots. Perhaps making it a period piece, setting it in the 1930s of the original radio dramas, would have solved this problem.

In an attempt to boost sagging ratings, executive producer Dozier arranged a crossover between the highly-rated *Batman* and the sinking-fast *The Green Hornet*. The superheroes met — and clashed — in a second season *Batman* episode entitled "A Piece of the Action," but the ensuing mish-mash only proved once and for all that the two series had diverse styles and belonged as far away from one another as possible.

As a result of low ratings, *The Green Hornet* was cancelled after just one season, and twenty-six, thirty-minute episodes. With that few episodes, it was rarely run in its original form in daily syndication.

Very shortly after *The Green Hornet*'s demise, Bruce Lee became a full-fledged star. After his death in 1974, he was still quite popular, and a compilation film consisting of *Green Hornet* episodes was released theatrically in the United States to great success. A second *Green Hornet* film, also culled from the series, entitled "Fury of the Dragon," played in theaters in 1976.[2]

In recent years there has been talk of a *Green Hornet* movie, to star Greg Kinnear (*Mystery Men*, *Blankman*) as Britt Reid, and Jason Lee Scott as Kato. But so far, these heroes haven't "rolled" back into action.

The Green Hornet (1966-67)
LIVE-ACTION SERIES

"*The Green Hornet* was something very special ... one of the few times a character was transferred faithfully from one medium to another and with exciting results."
— James Van Hise, *SFTV* #1:

"TV's Flip Side of Batman — The Green Hornet," December 1984, page 15.

"If *Batman* wasn't already a hit at the same time, this series might have had a lot of potential. Unfortunately, it smacked very much of a *Batman* knockoff, and never really had much of an opportunity to find its own identity. But you could certainly see the charisma of Bruce Lee. If the show had focused on Kato, it might have been a hit."

— William Latham, author *Space: 1999 Resurrection, Mary's Monster*.

CAST: Van Williams (Britt Reid/the Green Hornet); Bruce Lee (Kato); Wende Wagner (Lenore "Casey" Case); Lloyd Ghough (Mike Axford); Walter Brooke (D.A. Scanlon).

CREW: A Greenway Production, in Association with 20th Century–Fox. *Produced by:* Richard Bluel, Stan Shpetner. *Executive Producer:* William Dozier. *Based on the Popular Radio Dramas of:* The Green Hornet, Inc. *Created by:* George W. Trendle. *Associate Producer:* Jerry Thomas. *Assistant to Executive Producer:* Charles B. Fitzsimons. *Music:* Billy May. *Theme Played by:* Al Hirt. *Music Conducted by:* Lionel Newman. *Production Supervisor:* Jack Sonntag. *Unit Production Manager:* Mark Evans. *Assistant Directors:* Jack Martin Smith, Gibson Holley. *Film Editors:* Noel Scott, Fred Feitschans. *Post Production Supervisor:* James Blakeley. *Post Production Coordinator:* Robert Mintz. *Set Decorators:* Walter M. Scott, Robert de Vestel, Steve Potter. *Supervising Music Editor:* Leonard A. Engel. *Music Editor:* Ken Spears. *Supervising Sound Effects Editor:* Ralph B. Hickey. *Sound Effects Editor:* Harold Wooley. *Men's Wardrobe:* Andrew Pollack. *Make-up Supervisor:* Ben Nye. *Hair:* Margaret Donovan. *Special Photographic Effects:* L.B. Abbott.

SEASON ONE (1966-1967)

1. "The Silent Gun" Written by: Ken Pettus. Directed by: Leslie H. Martinson. Airdate: September 9, 1966.

The editor of the *Daily Sentinel* (and owner of a TV station too), Britt Reid, is secretly the vigilante hero the Green Hornet, wanted dead by criminals *and* the law. Assisted by his kung-fu fighting Asian manservant, Kato, Reid goes after an underworld figure that is using a very special weapon: a gun that produces no sound or noise when fired.

GUEST CAST: Charles Francisco (Trump); Lloyd Bochner (Carly); Henry Evans (Renner);

Kelly Jean Peters, Ed McGrealey, Max Kelvin, Bob Harvey.

2. "Give 'Em Enough Rope" Written by Gwen Bagni and Paul Dubov. Directed by: Seymour Robbie. Airdate: September 16, 1966.

The Green Hornet becomes embroiled in an insurance scam and cover-up, but cleaning it up could prove fatal to Reid's new girlfriend, an attorney representing a man supposedly injured in a phony accident.

GUEST CAST: Diana Hyland (Claudia); Mort Mills (Colony); Jerry Ayres, Joe Sirola, David Renard.

3. "Programmed for Death" Written by: Jerry Thomas and Lewis Reed. Directed by: Larry Peerce. Airdate: September 23, 1966.

One of Reid's top investigative reporters is killed by a leopard while on the trail of a deeper mystery. Searching the scene, Reid finds evidence of counterfeit diamonds and remembers a link to a case from the past.

GUEST CAST: Signe Hasso (Yolanda); Richard Cutting, Sheila Leighton, John Alvar, Don Eitner.

4. "Crime Wave" Written by: Sheldon Stark. Directed by: Larry Peerce. Airdate: September 30, 1966.

The Green Hornet is framed for a jewel heist aboard an airline. Worse, the crime was predicted by computer, and the same computer predicts that the nefarious Green Hornet will strike again. Reid finds himself in a bind, well aware that the culprit in these cases is not his alter ego.

GUEST CAST: Peter Haskell (Marcus); Sheila Wells (Spinner); Ron Burke (Joe); Denny Costello, Jennifer Stewart, Wayne Sutherland.

5. "The Frog Is a Deadly Weapon" Written by William L. Stuart. Directed by

Leslie H. Martinson. Airdate: October 7, 1966.

A private investigator claims he knows all about the return of a wanted underworld figure, but is soon murdered for that knowledge. The Green Hornet investigates and is disturbed to learn that Lenore Case, Reid's secretary, has also been abducted ... and possibly murdered.

GUEST CAST: Victor Jory (Charles); Thordis Brandt (Nedra); Barbara Babcock (Elaine); George Robotham.

6. "Eat, Drink and Be Dead" Written by Richard Landau. Directed by: Murray Golden. Airdate: October 14, 1966.

A group of thugs are trying to get their bootleg alcohol sold in the city taverns at all costs, even murder soon, the Green Hornet is soon on the case.

GUEST CAST:Jason Evers (Dirk); Harry Lauter (Brannigan); Harry Fleer (Evans); Eddie Ness, Shep Sanders, Jo Ann Milam.

7. "Beautiful Dreamer" (Part I) Written by: Ken Pettus and Lorenzo Semple, Jr. Directed by: Allen Reisner. Airdate: October 21, 1966.

The Green Hornet is tipped off that a college professor's life is in danger, but he arrives too late to save the man. Reid realizes that the only way to find the killer is to trace the warning call, a trail that leads him to the Vale of Eden Club.

GUEST CAST: Geoffrey Horne (Eden); Pamela Curran, Henry Hunter, Maurice Manson, Barbara Gates, Chuck Hicks, Sandy Kevin.

8. "Beautiful Dreamer (Part II) Written by: Ken Pettus and Lorenzo Semple, Jr. Directed by: Allen Reisner. Airdate: October 28, 1966.

The Green Hornet continues his investigation of the Vale of Eden Club, only to learn that the owners specialize in brainwashing. They have been using innocent clientele to kill and commit crimes, wiping their memory of the events afterward.

GUEST CAST: Geoffrey Horne (Eden); Pamela Curran, Henry Hunter, Maurice Manson, Barbara Gates, Chuck Hicks, Sandy Kevin

9. "The Ray Is for Killing" Written by: Lee Loeb. Directed by: William Beaudine. Airdate: November 11, 1966.

Thieves break into Reid's house and steal his expensive art collection. The criminals hold the priceless works of art for a million-dollar ransom, at least until the Green Hornet determines to return the art to its rightful owner.

GUEST CAST: Robert McQueeney (Richardson); Bill Baldwin (Bendix); Mike Mahoney, Grant Woods, Bob Gunner, Jim Raymond.

10. "The Preying Mantis" Written by Ken Pettus and Charles Hoffman. Directed by: Norman Foster. Airdate: November 18, 1966.

The Green Hornet and Kato learn that a nefarious protection racket is working in Chinatown, out of a small café. When the informant in the case is threatened, the Green Hornet and Kato put him under their special protection.

GUEST CAST: Mako, Tom Drake, Allen Jung, Al Huang, Lang Yung.

11. "The Hunters and the Hunted" Written by: Jerry Thomas. Directed by: William Beaudine. Airdate: November 25, 1966.

Someone is killing racketeers with unusual African weapons, and the trail of bodies leads to the city's Explorer Club, a hit list and a dead jockey. The crimes become personal when the Green Hornet learns that his name is also on the hit list. His nemesis is Quentin Crane, a wealthy socialite bent on taking over the city's underworld.

GUEST CAST: Robert Strauss (Bud); Charles Bateman (Quentin Crane); Douglas Evans (Stone); Bill Walker, Frank Gerstle, Dick Dial, Gene La Bell.

12. "Deadline for Death" Written by: Ken Pettus. Directed by: Seymour Robbie. Airdate: December 2, 1966.

Mike, a reporter for Reid's *Daily Sentinel*, is framed on a robbery charge because a series of burglaries oddly follow the details of his investigative story. The Green Hornet and Kato investigate, only to learn that it may not be the reporter, but the photographer — and an unsavory associate — who is guilty.

GUEST CAST: James Best (Burton); Lynda Day George (Ardis); Jacques Aubuchon, Kirby Brumfield, Glen Wilder, Roydon Clark.

13. "The Secret of Sally Bell" Written by: William Stuart. Directed by: Robert Friend. Airdate: December 9, 1966.

A cargo ship, the Sally Bell, is shipping drugs into the city, and the Green Hornet and Kato set out to stop the transaction. They capture a thug who knows where more than two million dollars of narcotics are stored, but there are other forces in the city wanting that information just as badly as the Green Hornet.

GUEST CAST: Warren Kemmerling (Sheldon); Beth Brickell, Greg Benedict, Ann Rexford, James Farley, Timothy Scott.

14. "Freeway to Death" Written by: Ken Pettus. Directed by: Allen Reisner. Airdate: December 16, 1966.

Reporter Mike Axford is in trouble again, this time over a story involving a construction company, and the Green Hornet is all that stands between the reporter and certain death. When Britt intervenes on Axford's behalf, the criminals plan to kill him too.

GUEST CAST: Jeffrey Hunter (Crown); Reggie Parton, John Hubbard, David Fresco, Harvey Parry.

15. "May the Best Man Lose" Written by: Judith and Robert Guy Barrows. Directed by: Allen Reisner. Airdate: December 23, 1966.

As he runs for re-election, district attorney Frank Scanlon is nearly assassinated. Behind the attempt is his competitor in the election, a corrupt fellow by the name of Ryland. The Green Hornet works to prove Ryland's guilt before Scanlon's life is endangered a second time.

GUEST CAST:Harold Gould (Ryland); Linden Chiles (Warren Ryland); Robert Hoy (Woody); Troy Melton.

16. "The Hornet and the Firefly" Written by: William L. Stuart. Directed by: Allen Reisner. Airdate: December 30, 1966.

An arsonist is loose in the city, destroying property and endangering lives. This villain, who calls himself "the Firefly," is actually a former employee of the city fire department, one that has an axe to grind over his dismissal from the job. It's the Green Hornet vs. the Firefly in a blazing battle of the bugs...

GUEST CAST: Gerald S. O'Loughlin (Wade); Russ Conway (Dolan).

17. "Seek, Stalk and Destroy" Written by Jerry Thomas. Directed by: George Waggner. Airdate: January 6, 1967.

A group of ex-soldiers steal a powerful tank from a military base in hopes of using it to break out a compatriot in prison awaiting his execution. With a dangerous tank on the streets, the only thing that stands in its way is the Green Hornet's own rolling arsenal, the magnificent Black Beauty.

GUEST CAST: Ralph Meeker (Evans); Raymond St. Jacques (Silver); Paul Carr (Carter); John Baer, E.J. Andre.

18. "Corpse of the Year" (Part I) Written by: Ken Pettus. Directed by: James Komack. Airdate: January 13, 1967.

A villainous double of the Green Hornet goes on the rampage, destroying property and endangering people all over the city. The real Green Hornet knows that the only way to lure his "double" into the open is to fake the superhero's death.

GUEST CAST:Joanna Dru (Sabrina); Celia Kaye (Melissa); Cesare Danova (Garth); Tom Simcox; Barbara Babcock (Elaine); Sally Mills, Angelique Pettyjohn.

19. "Corpse of the Year" (Part II) Written by: Ken Pettus. Directed by: James Komack. Airdate: January 20, 1967.

Having faked the death of the Green Hornet, Reid is able to track down his imposter and is surprised to find out that the *Daily Sentinel*'s biggest newspaper competitor may be involved the crimes.

GUEST CAST: Joanna Dru (Sabrina); Celia Kaye (Mellisa); Cesare Danova (Garth); Tom Simcox; Barbara Babcock (Elaine); Sally Mills, Angelique Pettyjohn.

20. "Ace in the Hole" Written by: J.E. Selby and Stanley H. Silverman. Directed by: William Beaudine. Airdate: February 3, 1967.

The Green Hornet contends with two warring crime families, and reporter Mike Axford gets in the way again. The Hornet must think quickly, or Mike will end up dead at the hands of the two crime rings.

GUEST CAST: Richard Anderson (Trager); Richard Slattery (Grant); Tonny Epper, Bill Hampton.

21. "Bad Bet on a 459-Silent" Written by: Judith and Robert Guy Barrows. Directed by: Seymour Robbie. Airdate: February 10, 1967.

Crooked cops are on the take during a jewelry store break-in, and the Green Hornet is framed for the crime. Worse, he is shot in the shoulder and badly injured — a fact that complicates Britt Reid's "normal" life.

GUEST CAST:Bert Freed (Clark); Jason Wingreen, Brian Avery, Nicholas Coser, Barry Ford, Dick Dial, Bud Perkins.

22. "Trouble for Prince Charming" Written by: Ken Pettus. Directed by: William Beaudine. Airdate: February 17, 1967.

A visiting dignitary is nearly assassinated, but the Green Hornet and Kato save him. Unfortunately, the prince's girlfriend is kidnapped, and the abductors demand that the Prince surrender rule of his country within two days or see his lover murdered.

GUEST CAST: Edmund Hashim, Susan Flannery, James Lanphier.

23. "Alias, the Scarf" Written by: William Stuart. Directed by: Allen Reisner. Airdate: February 24, 1967.

Two decades ago, a murderer called "the Scarf" went on a killing spree that terrorized the city. Now he's back and ready to confront the Green Hornet and Kato at a wax museum (where their lifelike wax duplicates look on).

GUEST CAST:John Carradine (Rancourt); Patricia Barry; Ian Wolfe (Wilman); Paul Gleason.

24. "Hornet, Save Thyself" Written by: Don Tait. Directed by: Seymour Robbie. Airdate: March 3, 1967.

A man that once attempted to wrest control of the *Sentinel* away from Reid is shot to death, apparently by Reid himself! Reid claims the gun went off in his hand, but the authorities feel differently, and Reid must run for his life to clear his name.

GUEST CAST: Michael Strong, Marvin Brody, Jack Perkins, Ken Strange.

25. "Invasion from Outer Space" **(Part I)** Written by: Arthur Weingarten. Directed by: Darrel Hallenbeck. Airdate: March 10, 1967.

Reid is shocked when a UFO crashes outside the city and aliens invade his office at the *Daily Sentinel*. They demand that he go on TV and announce to the police that a road be cleared for them so they can "return home." Then the aliens kidnap Lenore Case, forcing the Green Hornet and Kato to pursue.

GUEST CAST: Larry D. Mann (Dr. Eric Mabuse); Arthur Batanides; Linda Gaye Scott (Vama); Christopher Dark, Denny Dobbins, Joe Di Reda, Britt Kings, Lloyd Haynes, Troy Melton, Richard Poston.

26. "Invasion from Outer Space" (Part II) Written by: Arthur Weingarten. Directed by: Darrel Hallenbeck. Airdate: March 17, 1967.

In pursuit of men in silver jumpsuits who claim to be aliens, the Green Hornet learns that the threat is very terrestrial. The ringleader of the so-called aliens is a shunned scientist, Dr. Mabuse, who advocates preemptive nuclear war. Mabuse has had the roads cleared so he can intercept a military transport carrying a deadly H-bomb.

GUEST CAST: Larry D. Mann (Dr. Eric Mabuse); Arthur Batanides; Linda Gaye Scott (Vama); Christopher Dark, Denny Dobbins, Joe di Reda, Britt Kings, Lloyd Haynes, Troy Melton, Richard Poston.

Green Lantern

The Green Lantern was an interesting superhero, really gentleman Alan Scott, who first appeared in 1940 under the banner of *All-American Comics*. After escaping injury in an explosion, Scott carved a "power ring" out of a strange glowing (green) rock, one that had to be recharged periodically at a green lantern. This character, a stalwart crime-basher, was quite popular, but went dormant in the early 1950s.

In 1959, Green Lantern returned, "reimagined" by DC in a more science fiction/ fantasy vein. This time, the hero was a daring pilot named Hal Jordan, who had been "gifted" a power ring by an extraterrestrial being (a sort of intergalactic policeman and a member of the Green Lantern Corp.) who crash landed on Earth. The ring still had to be recharged at a green lantern every twenty-four hours; and among Green Lantern's nemeses were Solomon Grundy, Sinestro and the Harlequin. The ring gave Hal Jordan incredible powers, including flight (and space flight) and the ability to materialize useful items (like hammers and giant fists) out of green energy. On one occasion in the comics, a badly wounded Hal Jordan fell out of the sky in Metropolis, and passed the power ring to his friend, Clark Kent!

In film and television production, the Green Lantern has always been a kind of second string superhero, popular enough to appear in many "team" efforts, but apparently not enough to merit his own live-action TV series.

In the mid–1960s, Green Lantern shared the *Superman-Aquaman Hour of Adventure* with his DC cohorts. This animated Filmation production featured Hal Jordan/Green Lantern in episodes such as "Evil Is as Evil Does" and others.

In the 1970s, Hanna-Barbera included Green Lantern in many of the later incarnations of *The Super Friends*, including *Challenge of the Super Friends*, *The All-New Super Friends Hour* and *The Super Powers Team: Galactic Guardians*.

In 1977, Green Lantern, for the first time, became a live-action hero, played by actor Howard Murphy, appearing in the short-lived series *Legend of the Superheroes*. The character fared no better twenty years later, in 1997, when played by Matthew Settle in an unaired pilot version of the live-action *The Justice League of America*.

Finally, an African-American Green Lantern named Jon Stewart, not the long-lived Hal Jordan, became a critical member of the animated *Justice League of America* in 2001 on the Cartoon Network, continuing the Green Lantern legacy of team work (but not individual achievement) in film and television into the twenty-first century.

Green Lantern *see also* Aquaman;
The Justice League of America

The Incredible Hulk

Less than a year after the debut of their *Fantastic Four* comic, Marvel's Stan Lee and Jack Kirby were back with a vengeance, unveiling a new creation called the Incredible Hulk. In his inaugural comic in the late spring of 1962, the Hulk — a giant gray (er ... green) monster — appeared for the very first time.

Military scientist Dr. Bruce Banner, a latter day Dr. Jekyll, "birthed" the Hulk inadvertently when, during a test bomb detonation, he was exposed to gamma rays while trying to protect a young man named Rick Jones from the devastating side-effects. Like a movie werewolf, Bruce Banner was normal by day, but became a powerful, uncontrollable, heavily muscled monster by moonlight. Legendary Marvel artist, writer and creator Jack Kirby remembered in the *Comics Journal* the inspiration for the character:

> The Hulk I created when I saw a woman lift a car. Her baby was caught under the running board of this car.... She looked from the rear window of the car, and this woman in desperation lifted the rear end of the car. It suddenly came to me that in desperation we can all do that — we can knock down walls, we can go berserk...[1]

A metaphor for the monster within all human beings, Marvel's the Hulk survived only six issues in his own title, an unpopular failure. In 1963 he joined (if that is the right word for his surly membership), the Avengers in that team's book, and then reappeared in 1964 in the comic series *Tales to Astonish*.

Finally, in 1968, the Incredible Hulk was back in his own book and scored the popularity that had eluded Banner and his story the first time around. Grantray Lawrence Animation produced *The Marvel Superheroes* in the mid–1960s, an almost frame-by-frame, primitive animation of several popular characters, including the Incredible Hulk.

By the 1970s, the Incredible Hulk was a well-established member of the Marvel universe. Along with *The Amazing Spider-Man*, *The Man from Atlantis* (a pseudo–Sub Mariner), *Wonder Woman*, *Captain America*, and *Dr. Strange*, a TV version of the man-to-beast Hulk saga seemed a natural development. Kenneth Johnson, the writer /producer that had brought a human, three-dimensional aspect to the popular Lindsey Wagner series *The Bionic Woman*, was hired as *The Hulk* show creator, continuing his own long association with superheroes. (Later, in 1997, Johnson directed Shaquille O'Neal in *Steel*, another comic adaptation.) One of the first things that Johnson did for *The Hulk* TV series was cement a new, nonfantastic story template.

In Johnson's version, Bruce Banner, now David instead (actor Bill Bixby), became a research scientist no longer affiliated with the military (now out of vogue after the Vietnam War). His transformation into the Hulk was spurred not by a test bomb, but by an intentional bombardment of gamma rays in the lab after the death of his wife. David blamed himself for not having the strength to save his wife when she was trapped in a car during an accident, and believed that gamma rays could release that strength. It turned out to be a fateful experiment.

Instead of the Hulk speaking in monosyllabic grunts and sentences as in the comics, the creature (6'5", 270-pound Mr. Universe Lou Ferrigno) became mute for his TV stardom. Perhaps more dramatically, Johnson ditched the entire supporting cast, including the Hulk's companion Rick Jones, his female love interest in the comics, Betsy Ross, and General "Thunderbolt" Talbot. Super-villains were also removed from the equation, reflecting the further backlash against the campy *Batman*, meaning that Doctor Doom and other costumed threats were not welcome. The mantra was realistic drama, at least according to series producer Nick Corea:

> Any writer who comes in with clones or extraterrestrials, we steer in another direction. We don't want to hear about flying saucers or telekinesis or mad scientists out to take over the world.[2]

Instead of over-the-top battles with super-villains, Johnson saw to it that his concept of the Hulk was believable and emotionally resonant. *The Incredible Hulk* was true to the comics, however, in that it gazed deeply at the psychological impact of such a strange physical transformation. Instead of adopting the comic book "full moon" transformation shtick, the series saw Banner become the Hulk only when he couldn't control his temper, when he became angry. "Don't make me angry; you wouldn't like me when I'm angry," he warned during the episode credits every week ... and it was more than an idle threat!

Johnson explained the series premise in this way:

> What we tried to go for was a real *Jekyll and Hyde* sort of classic treatment to a real heavy-duty psychological problem, and not just do another comic book.[3]

Yet, without the comic book concepts, how would *The Incredible Hulk* stay interesting from week to week? In that regard, Johnson took a concept from the shelf of television history, not comic books. To wit: he remade

You won't like him when he's angry. Two views of the Incredible Hulk. Left: Lou Ferrigno as the muscular Hulk. Right: Bill Bixby as the more civilized Dr. David Banner.

The Incredible Hulk in the image of *The Fugitive* (1964–1967). In that famous series, Dr. Richard Kimble (David Jannsen) was framed for the murder of his wife and pursued by the dogged Lt. Gerard (Barry Morse). Each week Kimble would search for the One-Armed Man, the mysterious figure that really killed his wife, and in the process help out "guest stars" that were in trouble, always while on the run.

In *The Incredible Hulk*, David was pursued not by a policeman, but by another cliché of the superhero genre: the nosey reporter (as seen in *Superman*, Tim Burton's *Batman*, and *Daredevil*, to name just three). In this case, the fella was named McGee (Jack Colvin). And unlike Gerard on *The Fugitive*, Banner sought not a killer, but a cure to the ailment that transformed him into the Hulk and might some day turn him into a killer.

Each week on *The Incredible Hulk*, David and his alter ego would assist those in need. David and the Hulk helped a crippled girl in "A Death in the Family," a pregnant woman in "Life and Death," a retarded man in "Ricky," an abused child in "A Child in Need" and the mentally ill in "The Quiet Room." And so it went for several years.

In other words, there was very little Marvel-style character mythology or continuity in the series. Every week featured David in a new situation, undercover at a rodeo or as a boxer, or in a restaurant or in a disco, or in a laboratory or in a zoo, and so forth. The series formula was not only repetitive, it no doubt irked fans of the comics, who may have preferred a bolder, more fantastic, genuinely superheroic format. That established, *The Incredible Hulk* was a very well acted program, especially by the sensitive Bixby, a veteran of *My Favorite Martian* (1963–66) and *The Magician* (1973–74).

The show accomplished what Johnson set out to do in that it was a dramatic, often tragic series that proved highly entertaining, if rarely surprising, from week to week. In "Married," for instance, audiences wept as David remarried, then was just as promptly widowed when new wife Mariette Hartley died. In another episode, "Homecoming," David had to resolve family issues at Thanksgiving time, and so forth. These were tearjerker stories, and the sensitive piano score underlined the stories with a kind of quiet pain. The understated music was something of a masterstroke, totally human and touching, rather than pompous, heroic or overblown. The sensitivity of the music score contrasted with the great strength and power of the green behemoth.

The very best episode of *The Incredible Hulk* series might have been the pilot itself, which set up the premise of the series' five-season run in elegant fashion. Written and directed by Johnson, the pilot began with a look at Banner's "good life" in soft-focus. Audiences saw Banner and his wife play in their kitchen together, care for a kitten, warm themselves before a fireplace, sit together at a rowboat and prepare for a night out together. This montage, a typical "romantic" accumulation of scenes, may sound corny, but it established from frame that in losing his wife, David suffered the greatest loss imaginable in his life. It was this tremendous personal pain and feelings of guilt that led to Banner's obsession with gamma rays and tapping into the hidden strength within human beings.

It was also this loss that elevated David to the status of tragic hero. Like Victor Frankenstein, his obsession drove him to make mistakes and take risks that were far too great, in this case testing his gamma ray experiment on himself.

In directing the pilot, Johnson was wise to make the audience relive the terrible car accident with Banner and his wife. Flashbacks of the accident keep coming. And then, later, David hears the story of a woman that lifted a car to save a loved one, and the audience wonders, along with

David, why he was not able to tap into that well of power too, when the terrible moment came for him. And that question adds an element of guilt to Banner's obsession. *The Incredible Hulk* took these feelings of loss, obsession and shame, and spun them out in a surprisingly well-written story, which at times (during David's interview of test subjects, specifically) plays almost as a documentary. This is a story about the superhero within, and why some of us can tap into it and others can't.

But what remains so rewarding about the *Hulk* pilot and the series that followed is that Johnson clearly considered (and then explored) the themes of his series and found literary antecedents for David Banner's heroic journey. While the premise was part Jekyll and Hyde story (about the savage within), it was also pretty clearly an echo of James Whale's *Frankenstein* (1931). The pilot included a scene in which the Hulk approaches a little girl by a river, the visual allusion capturing the essence of this story perfectly. As fans of the horror film will remember, the Frankenstein Monster's encounter with a girl by the water was both touching and, ultimately, terrifying. The scene in *The Incredible Hulk* seems to remember that moment of ugliness meeting innocence, and takes it in new directions.

The Incredible Hulk also worked psychologically as a battle between science and emotion. The series reminded viewers that mankind is forever divided between rationality and emotion. We exist by controlling and harnessing our emotions, but in the Hulk those impulses break free. Today, psychologically inclined viewers would note that David Banner needed "anger management" courses, but back in the 1970s it was a matter of controlling the id, the beast inside that wanted to react to every challenge, fear and pain with raw emotion and brute force.

Not all episodes of *The Incredible Hulk* were as remarkable as the pilot, but the series was so successful, with its *Fugitive*-like formula, that soon other genre shows imitated it. *The Phoenix* (1982) saw New Age alien Judson Scott hunted by the government (in the person of Richard Lynch) as he roamed the country helping people. The same formula was revived in 1986 as *Starman*, starring Robert Hayes as a humanitarian alien. But the sensitivity and care Kenneth Johnson and Bill Bixby brought to *The Incredible Hulk* was missing from these later, more forgettable ventures.

Like its green namesake, *The Incredible Hulk* was a ratings powerhouse for CBS. In 1978 it ran at 9: 00 P.M. (right after *Wonder Woman*) and clocked the competition, including the *ABC Movie* and *The Rockford Files*. In 1978 it proved a significant challenge to *Fantasy Island* on ABC and *Shirley* on NBC. Ratings for the series did not slip until the later seasons, when the show's formula — which forever saw David going undercover and helping people in need — became overtly repetitive. After a few years, watching *The Incredible Hulk*, despite its expensive special effects and Hulk-out transformations, was not a very rewarding experience anymore. It was as rigidly formulaic as any Kabuki opera: David is in a new town working a new job, tangentially related to his search for a cure, and he meets somebody that needs help, somebody in trouble. Then the bad guy that is hounding that troubled person hurts David, spurring an appearance by the Hulk.

After *The Incredible Hulk* was cancelled in 1982, Lou Ferrigno appeared as the Hulk again on the Steven Spielberg NBC anthology *Amazing Stories* in an episode entitled "Remote Control." The same year, the Hulk joined *Spider-Man and His Amazing Friends* in a half-hour cartoon series narrated by Stan Lee. The Marvel production was known as *Spider Man and His Amazing Friends and the Incredible Hulk Hour.*

Even before the 1980s had ended, nostalgia arose for the early part of the decade, and Bill Bixby and Lou Ferrigno returned for three new *Incredible Hulk* TV movies. In the first (aired in 1988), entitled *The Incredible Hulk Returns*, David Banner encountered a friend who had discovered another popular Marvel Comics character, the arrogant Norse god called the Mighty Thor (Eric Kramer). Though the TV movie was intended as a back door pilot for a *Thor* TV series, nothing came of it.

In 1989 the same gambit was attempted a second time in *Trial of the Incredible Hulk*, with the embattled David Banner in court facing stiff penalties unless his defense attorney, the blind Matt Murdock (Rex Smith), could save him. Matt Murdock, of course, was the red-suited hero Daredevil, but no *Daredevil* series ever came to be, either. The 2003 *Daredevil* feature film was unrelated to this *Hulk* entry.

In 1990 *The Death of the Incredible Hulk* ended the saga of David Banner and his emerald alter ego once and for all, though rumors circulated of another TV movie, *The Rebirth of the Incredible Hulk*. When actor Bill Bixby died after a long battle with cancer in the early 1990s, it looked like the 1970s Kenneth Johnson version of the character was really and truly finished, representing the end of an era.

In 1996 a second *Incredible Hulk* cartoon ran for two seasons (twenty-one episodes) on UPN and featured Lou Ferrigno voicing the character he had made famous fifteen years earlier. Genie Francis and Luke Perry also contributed their vocal talents, and the series proved faithful to the comics, right down to visits from comic characters like She-Hulk and Grey Hulk.

However, without a doubt the most significant recent Hulk news has been the production of a major motion picture. With teasing previews airing before *Spider-Man* and *Daredevil*, the film was scheduled for release in June of 2003. Gale Anne Hurd (*The Terminator* [1984], *Tremors* [1989], *Ar-*

mageddon [1998]) was producer; Ang Lee, the director of *Crouching Tiger, Hidden Dragon*, directed, and young Eric Bana starred as Bruce Banner. Jennifer Connelly (*A Beautiful Mind* [2001]) played his love interest and Nick Nolte his psychotic father, a man with a secret. Eschewing painted musclemen, the new *Hulk* movie featured a completely computer generated Hulk! Perhaps more irritating for fans, it was a fairly unfaithful rendering of Stan Lee and Jack Kirby's long-lived juggernaut. This Hulk did not speak (except in one dream sequence) and was created not by military testing but by a bungle in the lab, much like the earlier television show.

Ads featured the tag line "Don't make him angry," harking right back to the 1970s TV show. Previews revealed that CGI work was totally inadequate in dramatizing the green behemoth. One preview shot showed the Hulk tossing a tank across the desert, looking like a blown-up cartoon, with no detail, depth or sense of reality. Fans could only hope that some last-minute tinkering would save the Jolly Green Giant from such embarrassment.

The Hulk premiered on June 20, 2003, and quickly took the box office by storm, but bad word-of-mouth sent the film's fortunes south. After a very busy summer, it had earned only slightly over $130 million at the box office, not enough to cover its massive budget and advertising costs. Critics and audiences split on the movie; some found it smart and ultimately worthwhile, while others wrote it off as boring. Though Ang Lee spiced up the proceedings with several split-screen compositions, visually alluding to frames in comic-books, the majority of the film was a washout, with Eric Bana barely registering as a likeable or human character. The first hour of the film seemed all laborious set-up and talk, with little by way of action or even subtext (unlike the TV series). And when the Hulk finally appeared on screen, he was incredible only in the breadth of the disappointment he produced, never once appearing to be anything more than a Roger Rabbit–style cartoon.

The filmmakers hedged their bets by concealing their first action scene, a ridiculous and murky sequence involving the Hulk and mutated poodles, in the dark of night. The special effects never improved, but one action scene involving the Hulk's surprise ride aboard the back of an American air force jet was genuinely exciting. At two hours and eighteen minutes, the film was overlong, and the final confrontation,

between father and son, lacked any punch whatsoever. In fact, the battle made little sense. Sam Elliott's General Ross simply let Banner *père* and *fils* go at it, setting the stage for massive destruction. The film's coda, a weak joke featuring the TV series' line "You wouldn't like me when I'm angry," only reminded audiences that the legend had seen much brighter days in the 1970s.

With *The Hulk* toys lining clearance racks in toy stores and the film's lackluster performance, the announced sequel appears pretty unlikely.

The Incredible Hulk (1978–1982)
LIVE-ACTION SERIES

"The Hulk, created by Stan Lee, was a neurotic Jekyll and Hyde figure whose rage couldn't be restrained in his human personality. In the hands of producer Johnson and his fellow writers, the Hulk is just another gimmicky hero (and indeed one who owes as much to the teleseries *Fugative* [sic] as to Marvel comics) encased in a glossy production."
> —Phil Hardy. *The Film Encyclopedia, Science Fiction*, William Morrow and Company, Inc., 1984, pages 341–342.

"The TV series ... had some good moments now and then ... largely due to the humanity and sympathy that Bixby was able to evoke in his *Fugitive*-like role of a man always on the run."
> —Douglas Menville and R. Reginald, with Mary A. Burgess. *Futurevisions— The New Golden Age of the Science Fiction Film*, a Green Briar Book, Newcastle Publishing Company, 1985, page 56.

"When Ken Johnson set about creating the format ... he totally abandoned the comic book–style superhero vs. super villain formula. Instead he turned to a more intelligent and dramatic approach of a man whose life is upset by the fact that he can become this uncontrollable creature."
> —Gary Gerani, *TV Episode Guides Volume*

II: "The Incredible Hulk," A Starlog Press Publication, 1982, page 64.

"This, in many ways, is the granddaddy of superhero television. It just worked. Bill Bixby made a fine David Banner (and would it have killed them to call him Bruce?), and Lou Ferrigno made the Hulk believable. The storylines were inevitably caught somewhere between *The Six Million Dollar Man* and *The Fugitive*, but it was just plain fun to watch someone, week after week, waiting to get upset and then go green."
> —William Latham, author of *Space: 1999 Resurrection, Mary's Monster*.

CAST: Bill Bixby (Dr. David Banner); Lou Ferrigno (The Incredible Hulk); Jack Colvin (Jack McGee).

CREW: *Created for Television by:* Kenneth Johnson. *Based on the Marvel Comic Created by:* Stan Lee. *Executive Producer:* Kenneth Johnson. *Producers:* Charles Bowman, Jeff Frelich, Karen Harris, Andrew Schneider, Robert Steinhauer, James D. Parriott. *Directors of Photography (various episodes):* John McPherson, Edward Rio Rotunno. *Film Editors (various episodes):* George O'Haniann, Jack Shoengarth. *Music:* Joe Harnell. *Associate Producers:* Alan Cassidy, Craig Schiller.

1. **"The Incredible Hulk"** (series pilot, aired as TV movie, 94 minutes); Written and directed by: Kenneth Johnson. Airdate: November 4, 1977.

Dr. David Bruce Banner is shattered when his wife Laura dies in a car accident and he is unable to save her. Eleven months later, the scientist is obsessed with research involving the strength potential of human beings. After conducting several interviews with his co-worker, Dr. Elaina Marks, Banner determines that extreme emotional attachment, anger, and an outside stimulus, gamma rays, can sometimes generate incredible strength in people. David subjects himself to a high concentration of gamma rays to imbue his own DNA with such strength, but the experiment goes wrong. Now when David grows angry, he transforms into a hulking green monster, a sub-human expression of his id. Elaina and David attempt to reverse the experiment that has resulted in Banner's periodic transformations, but a reporter from the *National Register* named McGee and the police are suspicious about this "incredible hulk" that has been seen in the woods nearby.

GUEST CAST: Susan Sullivan (Elaina Marks); Susan Batson (Mrs. Maier); Mario Gallo (Mr. Bram); Eric Server (Policeman); Charles Siebert (Ben); Terrence Locke (Young Man); June Whitley Taylor (Woman); George Brenlin (Man at Lake); Jake Mitchell (Jerry); William Larsen (Minister); Olivia Barash (Girl at Lake); Eric Deon (B.J.).

2. **"A Death in the Family"** (aired as TV movie, two hours) Written by: Kenneth Johnson. Directed by: Alan J. Levi. Airdate: November 28, 1977.

Working in anonymity, David Banner is shocked to learn that his new benefactor is poisoning his young stepdaughter, the heir to a fortune. Fearful that the kindly, crippled girl will be killed, Banner comes to the rescue as the Hulk, fending off assassins, mad dogs, and even a helicopter attack.

GUEST CAST: William Daniels, Gerald MacRaney, Laurie Prange, Dorothy Tristan.

SEASON ONE (1978)

3. **"The Final Round"** Written by: Kenneth Johnson. Directed by: Kenneth Gilbert. Airdate: March 10, 1978.

A down-on-his luck prizefighter saves David Banner from a pair of muggers, and becomes friendly with the scientist. As David learns more about his new pal — Rocky, he realizes that the naïve man has become involved in an illicit drug deal. Banner attempts to extricate Rocky from trouble, but the battle ends in the ring, and this time the Incredible Hulk is a contender!

GUEST CAST: Martin Kove (Rocky); Al Ruscio (Sariego); Johnny Witherspoon (Tom); Fran Myers (Mary).

4. **"The Beast Within"** Written by: Karen Harris and Jill Sherman. Directed by: Kenneth Gilbert. Airdate: March 17, 1978.

David Banner is now working in a zoo, but once again he runs into trouble, this time with a smuggling operation. At the same time, he grows close to a female scientist that is working on research pertinent to his metamorphosis. Before the day is done, the Hulk is out again, and this time he clashes with an adult gorilla!

GUEST CAST: Caroline McWilliams (Claudia); Dabbs Greer (Dr. Malone); Richard Kelton, Charles Lampkin, Bill Joan Beach.

5. **"Of Guilt, Models, and Murder"** Written by: James D. Parriott. Directed by: Larry Stewart. Airdate: March 24, 1978.

David Banner awakens after a transformation into the Hulk to find a corpse very close by. Now he must reconstruct the events that led to his metamorphosis, and discover if he is guilty of murder.

GUEST CAST: Loni Anderson (Sheila); Deanna Lund (Terry Ann); Ben Gerard, Jeremy Brett.

6. "Terror in Times Square" Written by: William Schwartz. Directed by: Alan J. Levi. Airdate: March 31, 1978.

Working in an arcade in New York City, Banner unexpectedly becomes embroiled in a murder plot. Before long, the Hulk makes an appearance.

GUEST CAST: Robert Alda (Jason); Pamela Susan Shoop (Carol); Arnie Freeman, Jack Kruschen.

7. "747" Written by: Thomas Szollosi and Richard Matheson. Directed by: Sigmund Neufeld. Airdate: April 7, 1978.

It's a flight into terror when a flight crew (really a band of criminals) abandons a plane in mid-air, leaving a rattled Banner attempting to land the plane. In such close quarters, Banner struggles to keep the Hulk at bay, holding in his anger as long as he can...

GUEST CAST: Brandon Cruz (Kevin); Edward Power, Sondra Currie, Shirley O'Hara.

8. "The Hulk Breaks Las Vegas" Written by: Justin Edgerton. Directed by: Larry Stewart. Airdate: April 21, 1978.

David gets a job at a casino in Las Vegas, and is drawn into helping a reporter uncover a story about gambling improprieties. Unfortunately, the reporter is partnered with McGee, the very man that has been pursuing Banner and the Hulk. While Banner attempts to duck McGee, he also faces the prospect of a transformation.

GUEST CAST: Don Marshall (Lee); Julie Gregg (Wanda); Dean Santoro, Simone Griffith, John Crawford, Paul Picerni.

9. "Never Give a Trucker an Even Break" Written by: Kenneth Johnson. Directed by: Kenneth Gilbert. Airdate: April 28, 1978.

On the road again, David becomes involved with a beautiful female trucker that is having problems on the highway with a stolen tanker truck. Before long it's a duel: the Hulk vs. a Mack truck.

GUEST CAST: Jennifer Darling, Frank Christi, John Calvin, Charles Alvin Bell.

10. "Life and Death" Written by: James D. Parriott. Directed by: Jeffrey Hayden. Airdate: May 12, 1978.

David seeks help at a nearby hospital conducting genetic experiments. On the way to find a cure, however, David runs across a pregnant woman in need of help from the Incredible Hulk!

GUEST CAST: Diane Civita (Carrie); Andrew Robinson (Dr. Rhodes); Carl Franklin (Crosby); John Williams, Julie Adams, Al Berry.

11. "Earthquakes Happen" Written by: Jim Tisdale. Directed by: Harvey Laidman. Airdate: May 19, 1978.

David poses as an inspector at a nuclear facility in hopes of gaining access to the gamma ray equipment there, equipment that could reverse his condition. But things go from bad to worse when David learns that the facility is built over an earthquake fault — and in danger of an imminent meltdown. Though David's ploy is discovered, it is only the Hulk that can avert a terrible catastrophe.

GUEST CAST: Sherry Jackson (Diane); Peter Brandon, Lynne Topping, John Alvin, Pamela Nelson.

12. "The Waterfront Story" Written by: Paul M. Belous and Walter Woltersoff. Directed by: Reza Badiyi. Airdate: May 31, 1978.

In the great state of Texas, David Banner becomes embroiled in a union war involving dock workers. The last president of the union died under mysterious circumstances, and now Banner fears his widow may face the same fate — unless, that is, the Hulk puts in an appearance.

GUEST CAST: James B. Sikking (McConnell); Sheila Larken (Josie); Jack Kelly, William Benedict.

Season Two (1978-79)

13. "Married" (two hours) Written and directed by: Kenneth Johnson. Airdate: September 22, 1978.

In Hawaii, David Banner works with Dr. Caroline Fields to reverse his condition. Before long, the two scientists have fallen deeply in love and set a wedding date. But disaster looms when Caroline's condition, not David's, threatens the holy union.

GUEST CAST: Mariette Hartley (Dr. Caroline Fields); Meeno Peluce, Brian Cutler, Duncan Gamble, Joseph Kim.

14. "The Antowuk Horror" Written by: Nicholas Corea. Directed by: Sigmund Neufeld. Airdate: September 29, 1978.

The Incredible Hulk is just the thing to bring life to a fading town's failing economy, but David is none-too-eager to see his alter ego play the part of tourist attraction. The town accommodates, generating its own fake monster to keep the tourists coming.

GUEST CAST: William Lucking; Lance Le Gault (Brad); Debbie Lytton, Dennis Patrick.

15. "Ricky" Written by: Jaron Summers. Directed by: Frank Orsatti. Airdate: October 6, 1978.

Ricky is the simple-minded brother of a driver in a New Mexico race. David ends up at the race and befriends the sensitive, retarded boy, but is drawn into danger when forced to drive an unsafe vehicle. Sensing the danger, the Hulk appears...

GUEST CAST: Mickey Jones (Rickey); Gerald McRaney (Sam); James Daughton, Eric Server.

16. "Rainbow's End" Written by: Karen Harris and Jill Sherman. Directed by: Kenneth Gilbert. Airdate: October 13, 1978.

David follows a lead for a cure to a horse track. There he learns that a scientist has developed a medicine that calms equine rage and nerves, and believes it might be beneficial in taming the Hulk. But David's attention is drawn to a particular horse that is being tormented by an angry track employee.

GUEST CAST: Craig Stevens, Ned Romero, Gene Evans, Warren Smith.

17. "A Child in Need" Written by: Frank Dandridge. Directed by: James D. Parriott. Airdate: October 20, 1978.

David is hired as a gardener at a local elementary school, where he befriends a sensitive child. As David grows close to the boy, he comes to suspect that the child's bruises have arisen not from accidents or mishaps, but from an abusive father at home. Only the Hulk can right the situation.

GUEST CAST: Sally Kirkland (Margaret); Dennis Dimster, Sandy McPeak, Rebecca York.

18. "Another Path" Written by: Nicholas Corea. Directed by: Joseph Pevney. Airdate: October 27, 1978.

Banner becomes the student of an Asian wise man, hoping he can use Oriental philosophy to tame the beast within. But when his mentor is jeopardized, Banner must release the Hulk to do battle with evil and injustice once more.

GUEST CAST: Mako, Tommy Lee Holland, Jane Chung, Joseph Kim.

19. "Alice in Disco Land" Written by: Karen Harris and Jill Sherman. Directed by: Sigmund Neufeld. Airdate: November 3, 1978.

David's latest job is at a wild disco, where he befriends a troubled, sensitive young dancer. David learns that the dancer is an alcoholic, spurred to drink by trauma in her life, and that the bar's owner is exploiting the girl. While David tries to help the dancer face her own inner traumas, it is the Hulk who must stop the unscrupulous owner.

GUEST CAST: Donna Wilkes (Alice); Jason Kincaid (Louie); Freeman King (D.J.); Marc Alaimo (Ernie).

20. "Killer Instinct" Written by: Joel Don Humpreys and William M. Whitehad. Directed by: Ray Danton. Airdate: November 10, 1978.

David signs on as an assistant coach at a high school in hopes of studying a physician's "anti-aggression" regimen. But David becomes involved with the team, and the Hulk is needed to rescue one team member from himself.

GUEST CAST: Denny Miller (Tobey); Barbara Leigh (June); Rudy Solari (Dr. Stewart); Wyatt Johnson.

21. "Stop the Presses" Written by: Susan Woolen. Directed by: Jeffrey Hayden. Airdate: November 24, 1978.

A tabloid magazine journalist photographs David while he works at a restaurant under investigation. When Banner realizes that McGee, among others, could recognize his picture, David must infiltrate the tabloid to destroy the incriminating evidence. The Hulk comes in handy in the effort.

GUEST CAST: Mary Frann (Karen); Julie Cobb (Jill); Art Metrano (Charlie); Pat Morita (Fred).

22. "Escape from Los Santos" Written by: Bruce Kalish and Philip John Taylor. Directed by: Chuck Bowman. Airdate: December 1, 1978.

David is arrested and incarcerated with a woman whose husband has been framed for murder. It's up to the Hulk to lead an escape from jail and confront the crooked authorities.

GUEST CAST: Shelly Fabares (Holly); Lee de Broux (Evans); Dana Elcar (Sheriff), W.K. Stratton.

23. "Wild Fire" Written by: Brian Rehak. Directed by: Frank Orsatti. Airdate: January 17, 1979.

David takes a job at an oil rig but finds danger when a saboteur sets a fire on the rig. The Hulk is needed not only to stop the fire but to confront the sneaky saboteur.

GUEST CAST: John Anderson, Billy Green Bush, Erni Orsatti, Christine Belford.

24. "A Solitary Place" Written by: Jim Tisdale and Midga Varak. Directed by: Jeffrey Hayden. Airdate: January 24, 1979.

Tired of dealing with the Hulk in public, David becomes a recluse and goes into hiding in the woods, living a simple life. Unfortunately, his idyll is interrupted by the arrival of a young woman, Gail, with her own secrets and problems. As David and Gail become friends, McGee tracks both of them down, threatening to end the quiet existence.

GUEST CAST: Kathryn Leigh Scott (Gail); Jerry Douglas (Frank); Bruce Wright (Richard).

25. "Like a Brother" Written by: Richard Christian Matheson and Thomas Szollosi. Directed by: Reza Badiyi. Airdate: January 31, 1979.

David gets a job at a car wash where he befriends a co-worker whose brother is dying. A crusading man of the cloth and a drug dealer complicate these matters, and the Hulk is once again the only solution to the problem.

GUEST CAST: Austin Stoker, Tony Burton, Stuart K. Roginson, Ernie Hudson (Lee).

26. "The Haunted" Written by: Karen Harris and Jill Sherman. Directed by: John McPherson. Airdate: February 7, 1979.

David helps a kindly woman return to her house of many years earlier, the estate where her twin sister "accidentally" drowned. David comes to learn that the same grim end awaits his new friend, and sets about to solve the mystery.

GUEST CAST: Carol Baxter (Renee); John O'Connell, Johnny Haymer, Jon Lormer.

27. "Mystery Man" (two hours) Written by: Nicholas Corea. Directed by: Frank Orsatti. Airdates: March 2 and 9, 1979.

David Banner has been in a terrible accident, and his face is wrapped in bandages. Vulnerable, he is found by McGee and transported via a plane to the authorities. Unfortunately, the plane crashes, trapping the reporter and the amnesiac Banner in a forest with one another. When a forest fire threatens to kill both men, McGee witnesses the transformation of Banner into the Incredible Hulk.

GUEST CAST: Victoria Carroll, Aileene Towne, Bonnie Johns, Don Marshall, Michael Payne.

28. "The Disciple" Written by: Nicholas Corea and James Hirsch. Directed by: Reza Badiyi. Airdate: March 16, 1979.

Banner returns to work with his Asian mentor, but is shocked to learn that the aging Oriental has had his faith shaken by a recent trauma. The mentor is trying to turn over control of his organization to a new leader, but David doesn't yet trust him.

GUEST CAST: Mako; Rick Springfield (Michael); Gerald McRaney (Colin); Stacy Keach, Sr. (Tim).

29. "No Escape" Written by: Ben Masselink. Directed by: Jeffrey Hayden. Airdate: March 30, 1979.

David is arrested again (this time as a vagrant), and he runs across two slightly mad people. When the Hulk emerges to free David from the prison van, the other detainees also escape.

GUEST CAST: James Wainwright; Sherman Hemsley (Robert); Thalmus Rasulala (Simon); Skip Homeier.

30. "Kindred Spirits" Written by: Karen Harris and Jill Sherman. Directed by Joseph Pevney. Airdate: April 6, 1979.

An archaeological dig has revealed that a creature like the Incredible Hulk may have lived in man's prehistory, and David rushes to the site, on an Indian burial ground, to learn more about this link to the past. Unfortunately, he is recognized, and McGee also arrives...

GUEST CAST: Whit Bissell (Professor Williams); Kim Cattrall (Dr. White); A Martinez (Ric Youngblood); Chief Dan George (Lone Wolf); Don Shanks.

31. "Confession" Written by: Deborah Dean Davis. Directed by: Barry Crane. Airdate: May 4, 1979.

McGee teams up with an inexperienced reporter from a tabloid to locate the Hulk. Oddly, an imposter claims to be the Hulk's alter ego.

GUEST CAST: Markie Post (Pamela); Richard Herd (Roberts); Barry Gordon (Harold); Elaine Joyce.

32. "The Quiet Room" Written by: Karen Harris and Jill Sherman. Directed by: Reza Badiyi. Airdate: May 11, 1979.

Banner is incarcerated in a mental institute where an ambitious doctor is using dangerous mind-control drugs on the inmates. Bound in a straitjacket, Banner is unable to help his fellow patients, at least until the Hulk leads a rebellion in the asylum.

GUEST CAST: Joanna Mills (Dr. Hill); Philip Abbott (Dr. Morrow); Robert F. Lyons (Sam).

33. "Vendetta Road" Written by: Justin Edgerton. Directed by: John McPherson. Airdate: May 25, 1979.

On the road, David runs across a pair of vigilantes that are systematically blowing up gas stations belonging to a competitor who bankrupted their family business. David attempts to help, evading the police, but with McGee on the scene there's little he can do to stop an appearance of the Hulk.

GUEST CAST: Ron Lombard, Christina Hart, Morgan Woodward, Chip Johnson.

SEASON THREE (1979-1980)

34. "Metamorphosis" Written by: Craig Buck. Directed by: Alan J. Levi. Airdate: September 21, 1979.

Banner has taken a job working for a New Wave band and its troubled rock star lead singer, Lisa. When the singer attempts suicide on stage during a concert, the Hulk risks exposure to save the show.

GUEST CAST: Mackenzie Phillips (Lisa); Gary Graham (Greg); Katherine Cannon.

35. "Blind Rage" Written by: Dan Ullman. Directed by: Jeffrey Hayden. Airdate: September 28, 1979.

David gets a job at a chemical warfare research and development plant, but regrets the assignment when he is blinded in a deadly accident, along with a friendly co-worker. Sightless, David attempts to find a cure to the exposure, but officials at the plant are already denying any accident occurred.

GUEST CAST: Lee Bryant, Nicholas Coster, Jack Rader, Don Dubbins, Michelle Stacy.

36. "Brain Child" Written by: Nicholas Corea. Directed by: Reza Badiyi. Airdate: October 5, 1979.

David crosses paths with a runaway genius in search of her mother. Unfortunately, both David and the prodigy are being hounded by the law.

GUEST CAST: June Allyson (Dr. Kate Lowell); Robin Deardon, Lynn Carlin, Taylor Homes, Fred Carnery.

37. "The Slam" Written and directed by: Nicholas Corea. Airdate: October 19, 1979.

Once more, David Banner is arrested and incarcerated. This time he is to serve out his sentence in a rough prison camp, where he promptly plays Cool Hand Luke to lead the inmates against their brutal oppressors. An appearance of the Hulk, however, brings McGee running.

GUEST CAST: Charles Napier (Blake); Marc Alaimo (Holt); Julius Harris (Aldin); Robert Davi (Radar); Charles Picerni (Harris).

38. "My Favorite Magician" Written by: Sam Egan. Directed by: Reza Badiyi. Airdate: October 26, 1979.

David befriends a kindly, aging magician and becomes his new assistant for a benefit performance. The greatest magic of all, however, will be explaining the appearance of the Incredible Hulk.

GUEST CAST: Ray Walston (Jasper); Anne Schedeen (Kimberly); Robert Altman (Giancarlo); Scatman Crothers (Edgar); Franklin Brown, Bob Hastings, Joan Leslie.

NOTE: This episode reunites Walston and Bixby, stars of the popular '60s sitcom *My Favorite Martian*.

39. "Jake" Written by: Chuck Bowman. Directed by: Frank Orsatti. Airdate: November 2, 1979.

Banner gets a job at a rodeo and befriends an aging cowboy, still trying to make a living, still holding onto his youth, despite a disease that could kill him. Meanwhile, the cowboy's brother has gotten involved with some cattle rustlers, and the Hulk battles a bull.

GUEST CAST: James Crittenden; L.Q. Jones (Jake); Sandra Kerns (Maggie); Jesse Vint (Terry).

40. "Behind the Wheel" Written by: Andrew Schneider. Directed by; Frank Orsatti. Airdate: November 9, 1979.

Banner's latest job is at a city taxi company run by a kindly older woman. She is disturbed because drug-runners are ruining her business, and it's up to the Hulk to save the day.

GUEST CAST: Esther Rolle (Colleen); Jon Cedar (Sam); Albert Popwell, Ed Reynolds.

41. "Homecoming" Written by Andrew Schneider. Directed by: John McPherson. Airdate: November 30, 1979.

Nostalgic, David returns home for Thanksgiving and runs into his sister, who informs him of trouble at the family farm. A plague is destroying the crops, and David thinks he can help, but first he must reconcile old differences with his stubborn father.

GUEST CAST: Diana Muldaur (Dr. Helen Banner); John Marley (D.W. Banner); Guy Boyd (Steve); Richard Armstrong.

42. "The Snare" Written by: Richard Christian Matheson and Thomas Szollosi. Directed by: Frank Orsatti. Airdate: December 7, 1979.

Stranded on an island, David becomes the prey of a wealthy hunter, and only the Hulk can make the hunter the hunted.

GUEST CAST: Bradford Dillman (Sutton); Bob Boyd (Pilot).

NOTE: This episode, based on *The Most Dangerous Game*, was only one of the many genre dramas in the 1970s to exploit that popular property. *Logan's Run* (1977) did it in an episode called "Capture," and so did *Space: 1999* (1975–77) in "Devil's Planet."

43. "Babaloa" Written by: Craig Buck. Directed by: Richard Milton. Airdate: December 14, 1979.

It's Mardi Gras time in New Orleans, and David Banner is there to help a local doctor allay the superstitious fears of her patients. Unfortunately, a witch doctor is also around, working at cross-purposes and prompting an appearance by the Hulk.

GUEST CAST: Louise Sorel (Dr. Renee Dubois); Bill Henderson (Antonio); Christine Avila, John D. Gowans.

44. "Captive Night" Written by: Sam Egan. Directed by: Frank Orsatti. Airdate: December 21, 1979.

Criminals take over the department store where David Banner is working as a stock clerk. They take employees hostage, and David knows only the Hulk can clean up the store before dawn.

GUEST CAST: Anne Lockhart (Karen); Paul Picerni (Jim); Stanley Kamel (Gary).

45. "Broken Image" Written by: Karen Harris and Jill Sherman. Directed by: John McPherson. Airdate: January 4, 1980.

David Banner learns that he has a doppelganger: a nefarious criminal that is all too willing to take advantage of their similar appearances. Police and McGee chase down Banner and his doppelganger in a case of mistaken identity, but only one of the men is the Incredible Hulk.

GUEST CAST: Karen Carlson, John Reilly, Jed Mills, George Caldwell.

46. "Proof Positive" Written by: Karen Harris and Jill Sherman. Directed by: Dick Harwood. Airdate: January 11, 1980.

A frustrated Jack McGee is taken off the trail of the Hulk when new owners take over his newspaper. McGee quits his job and sets out in earnest to prove once and for all that the Hulk isn't just a figment of his imagination.

GUEST CAST: Caroline Smith (Pat); Walter Brooke (Mark); Wayne Storm.

47. "Sideshow" Written by: Len Jenkins. Directed by: Nicholas Corea. Airdate: January 25, 1980.

Banner acquires a job as the manager of a traveling carnival with quite the reputation: death and destruction follow in its wake. David finds himself romancing one of the women carnies, Nancy, at the same time that he must protect the troupe from a vengeful madman.

GUEST CAST: Marie Windsor (Belle); Judith Chapman (Nancy); Bruce Wright (Jimmy); Terence Evans.

48. "Long Run Home" Written by: Alan Cole and Chris Bunch. Directed by: Frank Orsatti. Airdate: February 1, 1980.

Banner befriends the members of a motorcycle gang, and is mistaken for one of the group. Still, his presence proves helpful when an inter-gang problem threatens to step outside the bounds of the law.

GUEST CAST: Paul Koslo (Carl); Robert Tessier (Johnny); Mickey Jones (Doc); Albert Popwell, Pamela Bryant.

49. "Falling Angels" Written by: Eric Kaldor, Dee K. Krzemien & James Sanford Parker. Directed by: Barry Crane. Airdate: February 8, 1980.

David is working at an orphanage this week, and discovers that an adult Svengali is turning some of his new wards into little criminals. David moves to intervene, even as McGee arrives on the scene.

GUEST CAST: Annette Charles (Rita); Timothy O'Hagan (Peter); Cindy Fisher, Earl Billings, George Dickerson.

50. "The Lottery" Written by: Dan Ullman. Directed by: John McPherson. Airdate: February 15, 1980.

Of all things, David Banner unexpectedly wins the lottery. But, because of his situation, he can't claim the money. Instead, he sends a friend to get the dough, but the friend turns out to be a con artist who wants the money himself.

GUEST CAST: Robert Hogan (Harry); Peter Breck, David McKnight, Adam Thomas, Jimmy Hayes.

51. "The Psychic" Written by: Karen Harris and Jill Sherman. Story by: George Bloom. Directed by: Barry Crane. Airdate: February 22, 1980.

A psychic runs into David, who is being sought for murder, and learns of his secret identity as the Hulk. At the same time, she predicts the death of reporter McGee as a victim of the real murderer, who has killed a little boy.

GUEST CAST: Brenda Benet (Annie); Jason Ross, David Anthony.

52. "A Rock and a Hard Place" Written by: Andrew Schneider. Directed by:

Chuck Bowman. Airdate: February 29, 1980.

David is caught between a crooked gang and the F.B.I., and only the Hulk can extricate him from trouble.

GUEST CAST: Jeanette Nolan (Lucy Cash); Eric Server (Randolph); Robert Gray.

53. "Deathmask" Written by: Nicholas Corea. Directed by: John McPherson. Airdate: March 14, 1980.

David Banner rescues a girl from the clutches of a madman in a small town, but the girl names him, inadvertently, as her abductor. Now mob justice will have its way, unless Banner can escape the clutches of the real killer, a psychotic police officer.

GUEST CAST: Gerald McRaney (Frank Rhodes); Don Marshall, Frank Marth, Marla Pennington.

54. "Equinox" Written by: Andrew Schneider. Directed by: Patrick Boyrivan. Airdate: March 21, 1980.

A masquerade party on the island estate of a wealthy socialite is attended by both David Banner and his nemesis, McGee. The Hulk prevents a murder, but now McGee is alerted to the presence of his quarry.

GUEST CAST: Paul Carr (Alan); Mark McGee, Bob Yanetti, Joy Garrett, Christine De Lisle, Danny Dayton, Alexis Adams.

55. "Nine Hours" Written and directed by: Nicholas Corea. Airdate: April 4, 1980.

Working at a hospital, Banner must save the life of an endangered child, and he teams with an undependable, disgraced cop to do it.

GUEST CAST: Marc Alaimo (Joe); Sheila Larken (Rhonda); Frank De Kova (Sam); Dennis Haysbert (Guard).

56. "On the Line" Written by: Karen Harris and Jill Sherman. Directed by: L.Q. Jones. Airdate: April 11, 1980.

David escapes a terrible forest fire and then must help put the blaze out. Also on the scene: a female firefighter facing discrimination among her ranks, and McGee, who some believe started the fire.

GUEST CAST: Kathleen Lloyd (Randy); Don Reid (Eric); Peter Jason (Bennett).

SEASON FOUR (1980-1981)

57. "Prometheus" (two hours) Written and directed by: Kenneth Johnson. Airdates: November 7 and 14, 1980.

A falling meteorite has adverse effects on David Banner. To wit: he is trapped in a state of mid-transformation into the Hulk. The U.S. Army captures the hapless Banner in the belief that he is an extraterrestrial, and he is taken to a research lab for further study.

GUEST CAST: Laurie Prange (Katie); Monte Markham (Colonel); Whit Bissell (Dr. Zeterman); Carol Baxter (McGowan); John Vargas, Steve Bond.

58. "Free Fall" Written by: Chris Bunch and Allan Cole. Directed by: Reza Badiyi. Airdate: November 21, 1980.

David Banner reluctantly enters the world of sky diving and must resolve a dispute between a daredevil friend and a corrupt politician's son.

GUEST CAST: Sam Groom (Hank); Jared Martin (Jack); Sandy Ward (Max); Kelly Harmon (Jean); Erik Holland, John Zenda.

59. "Dark Side" Written by: Nicholas Corea. Directed by: John McPherson. Airdate: December 5, 1980.

David's latest attempt to suppress his transformations goes disastrously wrong. A new drug therapy only enhances the "evil" portions of David's psyche, and he is all too aware that this means the next metamorphosis into the Hulk could result in a brutal, murderous creature with little of his human goodness remaining.

GUEST CAST: Bill Lucking (Mike); Rosemary Forsyth (Ellen).

60. "Deep Shock" Written by: Ruel Fischmann. Directed by: Reza Badiyi. Airdate: December 12, 1980.

An electrical jolt renders David temporarily psychic. He develops precognitive abilities, but what he sees causes him no joy: a future in which a rampaging Hulk brings only death and destruction to the world. But can David change the future?

GUEST CAST: Sharon Acker (Dr. Olson); Edward Power (Frank); Saundra Sharp, Robert Alan Browne.

61. "Bring Me the Head of the Hulk" Written by: Allan Cole and Chris Bunch. Directed by: Bill Bixby. Airdate: January 9, 1981.

A determined bounty hunter sets his sights on a new — and dangerous — prey: the Incredible Hulk! But can David fight his new enemy, who is as unbalanced as he is unpredictable?

GUEST CAST: Jed Mills, Jane Merrow, Walter Brooke, Sandy McPeak, Laurence Haddon, Barbara Lynn Block.

62. "Fast Lane" Written by: Reuben Leder. Directed by: Frank Orsatti. Airdate: January 16, 1981.

David is hired to transport a car across country, but is also unknowingly transporting a suitcase filled with money. Before long, various parties are after David, and the Hulk's road rage is all that can help him.

GUEST CAST: Robert F. Lyons (Joe); Dick O'Neill (Callahan); Victoria Carroll (Nancy); Alex Rebar (Clyde); Lee de Broux (Leo).

63. "Goodbye, Eddie Cain" Written by: Nicholas Corea. Directed by: Jack Colvin. Airdate: January 23, 1981.

It's film noir when a private dick named Eddie Cain is on a case of murder, and runs into the Hulk.

GUEST CAST: Cameron Mitchell (Eddie Cain); Donna Marshall (Norma); Anthony Caruso (Dante); Jennifer Holmes (Victoria Lang); Ray Laska, Rosco Born, Virginia Hahn.

64. "King of the Beach" Written by: Karen Harris. Directed by: Barry Crane. Airdate: February 6, 1981.

An aspiring body builder (also played by Ferrigno) befriends David at his latest job working at a restaurant.

GUEST CAST: Lou Ferrigno (Carl); Leslie Ackerman (Mandy); Charlie Brill (Sol); George Caldwall, Angela Lee, Ken Waller.

65. "Wax Museum" Written by: Carol Baxter. Directed by: Dick Harwood. Airdate: February 13, 1981.

David becomes embroiled in new intrigue at his latest odd job, this time at a wax museum. He investigates a young woman in mourning over the death of her father. But did she start the fire that killed the man?

GUEST CAST: Christine Belford (Leigh); Ben Hammer (Kelleher); Natalie Masters, Michael Horsley.

66. "East Winds" Written by: Jill Sherman. Directed by: Jack Colvin. Airdate: February 20, 1981.

It's Chinatown intrigue for David when he befriends a slightly past-his-prime police detective and encounters an unusual mystery involving a very valuable bathtub.

GUEST CAST: William Windom (Jack Keeler); Richard Loo, Richard Narita, Tony Mumolo.

67. "The First" (two hours) Written by: Andrew Schneider. Directed by: Frank Orsatti. Airdate: March 6 and 13, 1981.

David is surprised to learn of a legendary Hulk creature in an isolated American town. He goes in search of the monster, hoping to find a link to his own terrible transformations.

GUEST CAST: Harry Townes (Dell); Lola Albright (Elizabeth); Jack Magee (Walt); Dick Durock (Creature); Julie Marine, Kari Michaelson.

68. "The Harder They Fall" Written by: Nancy Faulkner. Directed by: Michael Vejar. Airdate: March 27, 1981.

David is injured badly in a car accident — totally paralyzed, in fact. He comes to realize that by summoning the Hulk, he may have the power to regenerate the nerves and muscles that have been damaged. But is the cost of transformation into the dangerous creature too high?

GUEST CAST: Denny Miller (Paul); Peter Hobbs, Diane Shalet, Joe Dorsey.

69. "Interview with the Hulk" Written by: Alan Cassidy. Directed by: Patrick Boyrivan. Airdate: April 3, 1981.

A nosy reporter steals inside information from McGee and then sets out to make his reputation by being the first man ever to interview the Hulk. His plan doesn't go quite as intended.

GUEST CAST: Michael Conrad (Fletcher); Jan Sterling (Stella); Walter Brooke (Mark).

70. "Half Nelson" Written by: Andrew Schneider. Directed by: Barry Crane. Airdate: April 17, 1981.

The Big Green Guy meets a midget wrestler, as David befriends Buster, a man small in size but large in stature.

GUEST CAST: Tommy Madden (Buster); Elaine Joyce (Mitzi); David Himes, H.B. Haggerty.

71. "Danny" Written by: Diane Frolov. Directed by: Mark A. Burley. Airdate: May 15, 1981.

David gets a job on a farm and becomes mired in the competitive bickering of three crooked farm hands.

GUEST CAST: Don Stroud (Nat); Bruce Wright (Ben); Robin Dearden (Rachel).

72. "Patterns" Written by: Reuben Leder. Directed by: Nick Havinga. Airdate: May 22, 1981.

David gets a job in the garment industry this time, and is shaken down by loan sharks who believe he can settle a debt at his new job. The Hulk shakes them down instead.

GUEST CAST: Eddie Barth, Paul Marin, Robert O'Reilly, Joshua Shelly.

SEASON FIVE (1981)

73. "The Phenom" Written by: Reuben Leder. Directed by: Bernard McEveety. Airdate: October 2, 1981.

A rookie pitcher with great talent is the latest recipient of David Banner's help — and the Hulk's strength.

GUEST CAST: Anne Lockhart (Audrey); Robert Donner (Devlin); Brett Cullen, Ken Swofford.

74. "Two Godmothers" Written by: Reuben Leder. Directed by: Michael Vejar. Airdate: October 9, 1981.

Three female prison escapees capture David, all of them desperate because one of their number is with child.

GUEST CAST: Suzanne Charney, Penny Peyser, Sandra Kerns, Kathleen Nolan, John Steadman.

75. "Veteran" Written by Nicholas Corea and Reuben Leder. Story by: Nicholas Corea. Directed by: Michael Vejar. Airdate: October 16, 1981.

A Vietnam War veteran is unexpectedly targeted for assassination, a fact David becomes aware of; but to save the man means revealing his secret identity. Ultimately, the Hulk plays bodyguard to avert a murder.

GUEST CAST: Paul Koslo (Doug); Richard Yniguez (Frank); Bruce Gray (Cole).

76. "Sanctuary" Written by: Deborah Dean Davis. Directed by: Chuck Bowman. Airdate: November 6, 1981.

David seeks sanctuary by pretending to be a man of the cloth, but runs into a problem when he meets an immigrant in dire need of Heavenly help. Of course, help comes not from above, but from the Hulk!

GUEST CAST: Diana Muldaur (Sister Anita); Henry Darrow (Patrone); Edie McClurg (Sister).

77. "Triangle" Written by: Andrew Schneider. Directed by: Michael Vejar. Airdate: November 13, 1981.

David falls hard for a lovely woman named Gale, only to find that he has a competitor for her affections, a nasty lumber baron who will stop at nothing to get what he wants.

GUEST CAST: Andrea Marcovicci (Gale); Peter Mark Richman (Jordan); Mickey Jones (George); Charles Napier (Bert).

78. "Slaves" Written by: Jeri Taylor. Directed by: John Liberti. Airdate: May 5, 1982.

An angry, resentful black man makes David his slave. But no one can enslave the green-skinned Hulk.

GUEST CAST: Faye Grant (Christy); John Hancock (Isaac).

79. "A Minor Problem" Written by: Diane Frolov. Directed by: Michael Preece. Airdate: May 12, 1982.

A plague in heartland America begins to kill the locals, and David must find a cure.

GUEST CAST: Linden Chiles (Cunningham); Nancy Grahn (Patty); John Walter Davis (Mark).

The Incredible Hulk (1982–1984)
ANIMATED SERIES

VOICE TALENT: Michael Bell (Dr. Bruce Banner/The Incredible Hulk); Michael Horton (Rick Jones); Pat Fraley (Major Talbot); B.J. Ward (Betsy Ross); Robert Ridgely (General Ross); Stan Lee (Narrator).

CREW: A Marvel Production. *Based on Characters Created by:* Stan Lee and Jack Kirby.

The Incredible Hulk Returns (1998)
LIVE–ACTION TV MOVIE

Written and directed by: Nicholas Corea. Airdate: May 22, 1988.

After years of suffering transformations, the beleaguered David Banner is about to test a machine that could vanquish the Hulk forever. But just as he plans to use the device, an old friend hunts him down and tells him the strange news that he can now summon the ancient Viking god called Thor, ultimately resulting in a battle between the angry Norse god and the Hulk. This strange clash also brings about another unwelcome return, that of investigative reporter Jack McGee.

GUEST CAST: Steve Levitt (Donald); Tim Thomerson (Cole Le Beau); Eric Kramer (Thor); Lee Purcell (Maggie Shaw).

Trial of the Incredible Hulk (1989)
LIVE–ACTION TV MOVIE

Written by: Gerald Di Pego. Directed by: Bill Bixby. Airdate: May 7, 1989.

After helping a woman endangered by criminals in a subway station, David is unfairly arrested. His defense attorney turns out to be the blind Matt Murdock. Murdock is the superhero Daredevil, and he teams with Banner (and the Hulk) to stop another major crime from being committed. Their opponent, a crime boss called Kingpin.

GUEST CAST: Rex Smith (Matt Murdock/Daredevil); John Rhys-Davies (Wilson Fisk); Nancy Everhard (Christa Kleinn); Mitchell Kosterman, Ken Camroux.

Death of the Incredible Hulk (1990)
LIVE–ACTION TV MOVIE

Written by: Gerald Di Pego. Directed by: Bill Bixby. Airdate: February 18, 1990.

David Banner's day of reckoning comes as once again he attempts to find a scientific solution to his metamorphosis. After securing help from an understanding scientist, a complex web of events lead Banner and his alter ego to a day they thought would never come.

GUEST CAST: Elizabeth Gracen (Jasmine); Andreas Katsulas (Kasha); Carla Ferrigno, Dwight McFeen, Lindsay Bourne, Garwin Sanford, Judith Maxie, French Tickner, Anna Katerina, John Novak.

The Incredible Hulk (1996-1997)
ANIMATED SERIES

VOICE TALENT: Neal McDonough (Dr. Bruce Banner); Lou Ferrigno (The Incredible Hulk); Genie Francis (Betsy Ross); Luke Perry (Rick Jones); John Vernon (General Ross).

CREW: A Marvel Films/New World Production. For UPN.

The Hulk (2003)
LIVE-ACTION FILM

"Bruce and Betty have no chemistry. When the film begins, their relationship is already over, so we're left with a void between them. Also, there is no chemistry between Glenn Talbot and Betty. Glenn is such a bastard, you wonder why anyone would be interested in him. The movie suffers from Darth Vader/Batman/Daredevil Syndrome. The main villain is directly responsible for the hero's origin. And Nick Nolte literally chews the scenery…"
— Howard Margolin, host of *Destinies: The Voice of Science Fiction.*

"There's a fine line between darkness and glumness, one that *Spider-Man* bounced off buildings to avoid. *The Hulk* lumbers across it, despite tortured hero Bruce Banner's belated leaps in the desert…. By then, it's too little, too late, which may mean the movie's long-term box office won't be nearly as green as Bruce's new skin color."
— Mike Clark, *USA Today:* "Gloomy '*Hulk*' never mutates into something worthwhile." July 11, 2003, page 1 of 2, *www.usatoday.com*

"The more *The Hulk* strives for realism, the less it achieves it. When the characters get all 'Oprah' on us, yakking about repressed memory syndrome and the damage their daddies did to them, it doesn't fit with anything else in the movie. Especially since we're being asked to register the emotional pain of what is, essentially, a cartoon who, when he's not blabbing about finding his identity, spends most of his time playing leap-frog with Utah."
— Chris Hewitt, *The St. Paul Pioneer Press:* "Boring '*Hulk*' an unconvincing mess," June 20, 2003, page 1 of 2. *www.twincities.com*

CAST: Eric Bana (Dr. Bruce Banner/The Hulk); Jennifer Connelly (Betsy Ross); Nick Nolte (Dr. David Banner); Sam Elliott (General Ross); Josh Lucas (Glen Talbot); Paul Kersey (Young David Banner); Cara Buono (Edith Banner); Todd Tesen (Young General Ross); Mike Erwin (Teenage Bruce Banner); Lou Ferrigno (Security Guard); Stan Lee (Security Guard); Daniel Dae Kim (Aide).

CREW: *Produced by:* Gale Anne Hurd and Avi Arad. *Executive Producers:* Kevin Feige, Stan Lee. *Producers:* Larry J. Franco, Gale Anne Hurd, James Schamus. *Associate Producers:* David Womark, Cheryl Tkach. *Music by:* Danny Elfman. *Cinematography:* Frederick Elmes. *Film Editor:* Tim Squyres. *Make-up:* Rick Baker. *Character Created by:* Stan Lee and Jack Kirby for Marvel Comics. *Story by:* James Schamus. *Screenplay by:* John Turman, Michael France and James Schamus. *Directed by:* Ang Lee. *M.P.A.A. Rating:* PG-13. *Running time:* 138 minutes.

A quiet young scientist named Bruce Banner has grown up knowing little of his past, except that it was quite traumatic. He has memories of his mother, and of an eccentric father who did terrible things to him. Those repressed memories come to the surface and cause Bruce to bubble over with rage, an ill-timed emotional outburst since Bruce subsequently suffers a terrible accident in his laboratory, one involving gamma rays. Before long, Bruce's long-repressed emotions, and the experiments conducted on him by his father years earlier, cause the scientist to transform into a giant green monster. At first Bruce is protected by his ex-girlfriend, Betsy, but her father, General Ross, is concerned that Bruce may be a lunatic, just like his father. When Bruce's dad, Dr. David Banner, arrives on the scene to continue his experiments on Bruce, the matter goes from bad to worse.

Transformed into the Hulk, Bruce escapes from a subterranean military base in Utah and wreaks havoc with those sent to destroy him, including U.S. Army tanks, helicopters, and jets. He is finally captured but must now undergo a final confrontation with his father, also changed into a monster by gamma rays, if he is ever to quell the beast within.

The Invincible Iron Man

Iron Man is another Marvel Comics superhero that has not received his due in film or on television. The comic book character first appeared in 1962, the same year that brought the world Spider-Man, among others.

Iron Man was actually Tony Stark, a wealthy industrialist that owned the powerful and influential Stark Enterprises. Because of sabotage, he was forced to don an iron suit that granted him invulnerability and the power of flight. The orange and yellow suit made Stark appear like a robot, hence the title Iron Man.

In the mid–1960s, Grantray Lawrence Animation produced the low-budget *The Marvel Superheroes* program, a show that included multiple segments featuring the Hulk, Sub-Mariner, Captain America and Iron Man. In these very short, poorly rendered segments, Iron Man clashed with comic book foes that included Mandarin, Crimson Dynamo and Mole Man.

In 1994, Iron Man returned to television for another animated adventure, a two-season venture entitled, naturally, *Iron Man*. Actor Robert Hays gave voice to Stark, and Neil Dickson portrayed the villainous Dread Knight. The series' writer was Brooks Wachtel, the director, Tom Tataronwicz.

In early 2003 the Sci-Fi Channel announced on its news wire that the Iron Man property would at last be adapted to live-action film. New Line Cinema, Marvel Studios and Angry Films were joining forces for an Iron Man movie to be written by Alfred Gough and Miles Millar, of *Smallville* fame. Leonardo DiCaprio was the production's "dream choice" to play Tony Stark.

The film has been slated for a 2005 release, but of course that assumes that the "Superheroes Triumphant" stage of history continues for years to come at the box office. With the successful opening of *Daredevil*, that seems likely.

Isis

On one very special day, Andrea Thomas (Joanna Cameron), a schoolteacher at Larkspur High, saw her life change forever. On an archeological dig, she unearthed an ancient Egyptian amulet that had the power to transform her into Isis, a superhero with great agility, speed, strength and the incredible ability to communicate with animals. When activating the amulet, via an incantation to Isis (wife of the god

Osiris), Thomas would transform into the heroine — a white-gowned, jewelry bedecked knock-out with a cobra-shaped staff and an Egyptian-style headdress.

This was the premise of *Isis*, or *The Secrets of Isis*, a Filmation-produced, live action children's series that ran for two seasons on CBS on Saturday mornings. Isis was the sister program of Filmation's other then-popular live-action hit, *Shazam!*, the adventures of Captain Marvel and Billy Batson.

In many senses, the second series seemed to be a knock-off of *Shazam*'s format, with lovely Andrea becoming a superheroine magically through a recitation of special words. Like Superman, however, Isis had a double identity (teacher/crime fighter) and a Lois Lane-like sidekick, Rick Mason (Brian Cutler) that always pined for her alter ego and was in dire need of rescuing.

Despite the derivative format and overall lack of intensity and action (*Isis* was a kiddie show, remember), the series quickly became the highest rated program on Saturday morning TV, in no small part because of actress Joanna Cameron's charms as the attractive Thomas/Isis. Like Lynda Carter on *Wonder Woman*, or *Bionic Woman* Lindsay Wagner, Joanna Cameron carried herself with dignity and quite a bit of sex appeal, making her the favorite pin-up of every ten-year-old boy in America.

In its first season, *Isis* aired as part of *The Shazam/Isis Hour*, but in 1976 it became known separately as *The Secrets of Isis*. The series was so successful that it spawned a popular comic book all its own, and often

Saturday morning she goddess: Joanna Cameron starred as the deity Isis, seen here with her cobra staff.

featured crossovers with *Shazam!* Captain Marvel and Isis worked together in "The Funny Girl" and "Now You See It," a special two-part episode.

An animated version of Isis was seen as one of the installments in the 1978 TV series *Tarzan and the Super Seven*.[1]

The Secrets of Isis (1975-1976)
LIVE-ACTION SERIES

CAST: Joanna Cameron (Andrea Thomas/Isis); Brian Cutler (Rick Mason); Ronalda Douglas (Renee); Joanna Pang (Cindy Lee).

CREW: *Produced by*: Arthur H. Nadel. *Executive Producers*: Lou Scheimer, Norm Prescott, Richard M. Rosenbloom. *Music*: Yvette Blais, Jeff Michael. From Filmation.

SEASON ONE (1975)

1. **"Lights of Mystery Mountain"** Written by: Russell Bates. Directed by: Hollingsworth Morse. Airdate: September 6, 1975.

2. **"Only Fools"** Written by: David Dworski. Directed by: Hollingsworth Morse. Airdate: September 13, 1975.

3. **"Spots of the Leopard"** Written by: James Schmerer. Directed by: Arnold Laven. Airdate: September 20, 1975.

4. **"The Sound of Silence"** Written by: Sid Morse. Directed by: Arnold Laven. Airdate: September 27, 1975.

5. **"Rock Hounds Roost"** Written by: Robert F. Joseph. Directed by: Arnold Laven. Airdate: October 4, 1975.

6. "Lucky" Written by: Ann Udell. Directed by: Hollingsworth Morse. Airdate: October 11, 1975.

7. "Bigfoot" Written by: J. Michael Reaves. Directed by: Arthur H. Nadel. Airdate: October 18, 1975.

8. "How to Find a Friend" Written by: Henry Colman. Directed by: Hollingsworth Morse. Airdate: October 25, 1975.

9. "The Show Off" Written by: David Wise and Kathleen Barnes. Directed by: Arnold Laven. Airdate: November 1, 1975.

10. "The Outsider" Written by: David and Susan Dworski. Directed by: Hollingsworth Morse. Airdate: November 8, 1975.

11. "Drums and Trumpets" Written by: Arthur H. Nadel. Directed by: Hollingsworth Morse. Airdate: November 15, 1975.

12. "The Funny Girl" Written by: Sid Morse. Directed by: Hollingsworth Morse. Airdate: November 22, 1975.

13. "Girl Drivers" Written by: David Wise and Kathleen Burns. Directed by: Arnold Laven. Airdate: November 29, 1975.

14. "Scuba Duba Dooing" Written by: Sid Morse. Directed by: Arnold Laven. Airdate: December 6, 1975.

15. "Dreams of Flight" Written by: Brad and Susan Dworski. Directed by: Hollingsworth Morse. Airdate: December 13, 1975.

SEASON TWO (1976)

16. "The Seeing Eye Horse" Written by: Peter and Sarah Dixon. Directed by: Earl Bellamy. Airdate: September 11, 1976.

17. "Thumbs Out" Written by: Sid Morse. Directed by: Earl Bellamy. Airdate: September 18, 1976.

18. "Class Clown" Written by: Arthur H. Nadel and Norman Cameron. Directed by: Hollingsworth Morse. Airdate: September 25, 1976.

19. "The Desperate Cheerleader" Written by: Sid Morse. Directed by: Hollingsworth Morse. Airdate: October 2, 1976.

20. "Year of the Dragon" Written by: Ann Udell. Directed by: Hollingsworth Morse. Airdate: October 9, 1976.

21. "Now You See It" (Parts I & II) Written by: Len Janson and Chuck Menville. Story by: Arthur H. Nadel. Directed by: Arthur H. Nadel. Airdates: October 16 and 23, 1976.

The Justice League of America (a.k.a. The Super Friends)

DC Comics introduced the JLA (Justice League of America) to the world in 1960. Editor Julius Schwartz and writer Gardner Fox were behind the creation of this team, and it first appeared in *The Brave and the Bold*, before the superhero team got its own book scarcely six months later.[1] Included in the team: Aquaman, Martian

Manhunter, Green Lantern, the Flash, and Wonder Woman. Various other members came and went, including Batman, Black Canary, Superman, Captain Marvel, the Green Arrow and Captain Atom.

In 1973 the Justice League came to television on ABC in animated format. Along the way, however, the group became *The Super Friends*, a rather generic and harmless sounding handle for the diverse and powerful union of protagonists. The lesser-known members of the team, including Martian Manhunter, Black Canary, Captain Marvel, the Green Arrow, the Atom, and even Green Lantern and the Flash, were given their walking papers, and a new team was assembled, based mostly on mainstream popularity. In this first incarnation, *The Super Friends* consisted of Batman and Robin, Superman, Wonder Woman and Aquaman. This limited group was handed three apprentices to train: adolescents Wendy and Marvin, and their pet, Wonder Dog.

Oddly, none of the three students appeared to have super powers of any sort, or the drive to fight evil. Marvin's physique indicated that he had more in common with Scooby Doo's friend Shaggy than a genuine superhero. Designed by Alex Toth, the more mainstream, familiar superhero characters at least appeared patterned after the comic book, and occasionally would be joined by guest superheroes like Plastic Man, Green Arrow and the Flash. Together, these Super Friends worked from the glittering Hall of Justice Building and wore communicator rings that allowed them to keep in touch with one another, as well as with their headquarters.

Some thirty years later, the stories on *The Super Friends* appear rather generic and toothless, lacking the conflicts and strong confrontations usually associated with superheroes, no doubt because the show aired on Saturday mornings and was meant for the eyes of children.

In one episode, "Professor Goodfel-low's G.E.E.C.," for instance, the team of heroes went up against a computer programmed to handle manufacturing, transportation and business matters, thus sparing people the need to work. In addition to nicely forecasting the idea of C.G.I. actors, the show was meant to teach a valuable moral lesson about automation and the human need to strive for accomplishments. Without work, the team of Super Friends suggested, the "people [would] become vegetables." Originality and ambition would disappear from the human equation, and leisure would take over. "It's good for people to work, or they won't have a purpose," said the heroes, and that was the very clearly stated ideal. In the end, the G.E.E.C. (Goodfellow's Energy Eliminating Computer) was destroyed when a mouse got into the machinery, thereby proving that machines are not infallible.

This version of the *Super Friends*, so heavy on moral didacticism, ran for some sixteen episodes, until 1975. Then in 1977 the show was brought out of mothballs and given a new twist and slightly more adult format. Wendy, Marvin and the Wonder Dog were gone (thankfully!), replaced by new apprentices, these folks a bit more tolerable. Jayna and Zan were the Wonder Twins, and they had a little mascot, a space monkey called Gleek, working with them. Together, Jayna and Zan were powerful shape shifters, though, strangely, they had to announce what they planned to transform into before initiating their super powers. ("Wonder Twin Powers form of ... *an elephant*," and so forth).

Often finding themselves in trouble, the Wonder Twins required the help of the more experienced members of the Justice League, whose ranks had swelled since the Wendy and Marvin era. Hawkman and Hawkgirl joined the team, but so did a group of new heroes that has in many circles been derided as being somewhat politically correct. Black Vulcan was an African

You can count on them. A family portrait of the Hanna-Barbera *Super Friends*. At left and at right foreground are apprentices the Wonder Twins and monkey Gleek.

American superhero, Apache Chief (who could swell to gigantic proportions) was a Native American (right down to headdress and feather), and the Samurai was obviously Asian in origin. Though some critics may have sneered at these changes, they seemed to teach valuable lessons that children would benefit from. After fifteen episodes in this format, it was time for another change.

In 1977 *Star Wars* made a splash around the world, influencing hundreds of productions, for better or worse. *The Super Friends* was one of those efforts most seriously impacted by the innovative Lucasfilm, for when the animated heroes returned to the tube in 1978 in *The Challenge of the Super Friends*, it was a whole new ball game. This time, our heroes defended the world against the all-powerful Legion of Doom, who resided in a hall of injustice that was shaped very much like the black robotic head of one Darth Vader.

This floating black headquarters (Darth Vader's helmet, so to speak) was populated by a Rogue's gallery of great villains that added spice and serious conflict to the cartoon proceedings. The Legion was led by the evil genius Lex Luthor (wearing a pink shirt) and featured a dozen treacherous members. Black Manta was there to challenge Aquaman. Sinestro and Solomon Grundy arrived to challenge Green Lantern. Brainiac and Bizarro joined Lex Luthor in his attempts to destroy Superman. From Batman's Gotham City came the villainous Scarecrow and the Riddler. Toyman and others also took their shot at knocking the Hall of Justice from its perch as mankind's savior.

The Challenge of the Super Friends filled a 90-minute slot on Saturday mornings (three half-hour stories!), and remains to this day this author's favorite rendition of the white-bread *Super Friends*.

Over the next eight years, *The Super Friends* remained a powerful presence on Saturday morning television, appearing in *The World's Greatest Super Friends* (1980) and *Super Friends: The Legendary Super Powers Show* (1984), featuring a new villain called Darkseid (Darkside), and, finally, *The Super Powers Team: Galactic Guardians* in 1986.

The burgeoning popularity of superheroes in the 1970s, including the *Super Friends* on Saturday mornings, no doubt led to the creation of one of the strangest, most ill-advised and shortest-lived TV series of the genre. On September 2, 1977, and September 10, 1977, two episodes of a live-action production, *Legend of the Superheroes*, aired in primetime on NBC. "The Challenge" was the first episode, "The Roast" the second.

The series was basically a variation on the Justice League comic, but, for some reason, sans the famous title. Most noteworthy was the presence of three stars from the 1960s *Batman* series: Adam West as Batman, Burt Ward as Robin and Frank Gorshin as the Riddler. Though incredibly cheesy and cheap, and possessing a camp attitude to boot, this very short-lived effort featured some DC heroes that had not appeared in live action before. In particular, it offered the world a live-action Flash (Rod Haase), Hawkman (Bill Nuckals), Green Lantern (Howard Murphy), Captain Marvel (Garrett Craig), Huntress (Barbara Joyce), and Black Canary (Danuta).

On the side of the villains, assisting the Riddler were Red Cyclone, Sinestro and Solomon Grundy. The better of the two shows, "The Challenge" was a fairly straightforward episode involving clashing superheroes and villains. However, "The Roast" took on an overtly comedic tone in the format of a Friar's Roast, and involved a gathering of superheroes as they paid homage to a retiring member of their ranks. Naturally, the super-criminals arrived to make trouble.

It was a long time before the Justice League idea was attempted in live-action format again, but in 1997 a pilot was produced, entitled *The Justice League of America*. This time the group consisted primarily of DC's second-string players. Batman, Superman, Aquaman and Wonder Woman were nowhere to be found. Instead, the series featured Martian Manhunter (an embarrassed-looking David Ogden Stiers), Green Lantern, the Flash, the Atom, and two heroines, Fire and Ice. The villain was Miguel Ferrer, playing "the Weather Man." This pilot looked terribly cheap, with very poor costumes, and has never been presented on broadcast television. To this date it remains unaired, though bootleg copies are available at conventions.

Finally, in 2001, *The Justice League of America* received its due. No Wonder Dog. No Wonder Twins. No camp humor. Instead, the dedicated brain trust behind the 1990s animated versions of Batman and Superman, namely Rich Fogel and Bruce Timm, became involved with the JLA and opted to take the often lampooned material seriously. Though they acknowledged the "inherent goofiness to the DC Universe as a whole,"[2] and the clean-cut nature of the superheroic characters, they also took special pains to make the characters work:

> ...[W]e wanted to make sure that all the characters were unique unto themselves and working together interestingly as a team.... To put Batman and Superman together is conceptually such a great thing, but what we really feel, particularly as we go through the stories and the outlines, is that we're going to get great interest in the somewhat incidental characters.[3]

The result of these sincere efforts was, according to Rich Fogel, "the first time in 40 years — since *Johnny Quest* in the early 1960s — that anyone [had] tried action-adventure animation in prime time."[4] In the fall of 2001, the series began its scheduled run of 26 episodes, airing at 9:30 P.M. on Monday nights (against *Angel* on the WB).

The series began with "Secret Origins," an ambitious *Independence Day* (1996)/*War of the Worlds* (1951)–style science fiction adventure. When Earth was threatened by invading aliens, parasitic beings that fed on the psychic energies of their opponents, it was up to the stalwart Justice League to destroy the aliens and its supreme intelligence, the Imperium. On the side of good was Jon Stewart, the serious and grim Green Lantern; the wisecracking hot shot known as the Flash; Wonder Woman, an enthusiastic rookie with a warrior ethos; and Hawk Girl, the no-nonsense girl from Thanagar, a warlike world. Leading the team was the powerful Superman. On the periphery was the perpetual outsider, Batman. The first episode also introduced the shape-shifting Martian Manhunter, the last of his Martian kind.

"Secret Origin" went all out in the action category, depicting the destruction of Metropolis, a worldwide alien invasion, and even *Star Wars*–like dogfights between the Batplane and alien fighters. It also highlighted a now timely United Nations debate about weapons of mass destruction. In all, the well-produced pilot demonstrated how Bruce Timm and his group seemed bound and determined to bring feature film quality animation and storytelling to the small screen. Still, it was a hard act to follow.

Later episodes of *Justice League* simply could not compete with the grand opening. "In Blackest Night" was a routine "trial of a superhero" story with the Flash defending Green Lantern when Stewart is hauled before the Lantern Corps intergalactic court room. The show seemed like a rehash of old *Star Trek* episodes rather than a superhero program, replete with its hackneyed "trial" premise and swooping spaceships and Manhunters (robotic peace keepers and precursors to the current Lantern Corps).

Still, week in and week out, *The Justice League* has been a high-powered blast, the best and the most consistently entertaining adaptation of the comic yet put on the screen. Rife with celebrity guest voices, including Rene Auberjonois, Dennis Haysbert, James Marsden, Robert Englund, John Rhys Davies, Eric Roberts, and David Ogden Stiers, the show looks poised to repeat the multi-season success of *Batman: The Animated Series*. There's only one problem: no Aquaman (except as a guest star).

The Super Friends (1973–1986)
ANIMATED SERIES

"*The Super Friends* was never anything really remarkable. It was a very boring show in the Wendy and Marvin era because there were no villains. Everybody was doing something because they were concerned about the environment. They shrunk people because it would mean more room. They drew meteors down from space because the elements could be helpful. Everybody had an ulterior motive that would be fairly beneficial to the planet, but were misguided. Also, you were dealing with a network that did not allow violence, so nobody could throw a punch. That's not a great way to do television, especially a superhero show."
— Howard Margolin, host of *Destinies: The Voice of Science Fiction*.

VOICES: Sherry Alberoni, Danny Dark, Casey Kasem, Olan Soule, Norman Alden, Ted Knight, John Stephenson, Frank Welker.

CREW: *Executive Producers:* William Hanna, Joseph Barbera. *Series Director:* Charles A. Nichols. *Producer:* Iwao Takamoto. *Stories:* Fred Freiberger, Bernie Kahn, Ken Rotcop, Art Weiss, Willie Gilbert, Dick Robbins, Henry Sharp, Marshall Williams. *Story Direction:* Bernard Atkins, Clark Haas, George Singer, Chuck Couch, George Jorgensen, Irv Spector, Howard Swift. *Associate Producer:* Lew Marshall. *Titles:* Iraj Paran. *Dialogue Director:* Wally Burr. *Musical Direction:* Hoyt Curtin. *Music Supervisor:* Paul DeKorte. *Character Design:* Jerry Eisenberg, Alex Toth. *Supervising Film Editor:* Larry Cowan. *Music Editor:* Richard Allen. *Effects Editors:* Sam Gemette, Terry Moore. *Layout:* Robert Smitt, Monty Wedd. *Animation Supervisor:* Alex Toth. *Animation:* Jim Davis, Cam Ford, Sue Gilerist, Richard Jones, Ray Nowlan, Joe Shearer, Richard Dunn, Peter Gardiner, Gerry Grabner, Cynthia Leech, Vivian Ray, Stan Walker. *Background Styling:* F. Montealegre. *Backgrounds:* Graham Liney. *Sound Directors:* Richard Olson, Bill Getty. *Consultants:* Carmine Infantino, Nelson Bridwell, Julius Schwartz. A Hanna-Barbera Production. Produced at Eric Porter Studios.

Legend of the Superheroes: *Challenge of the Superheroes* (1977) and *The Superheroes Roast* (1977)
LIVE-ACTION SERIES

CAST: Adam West (Batman); Bruce Ward (Robin); Rod Haase (The Flash); Howard Murphy (Green Lantern); Garret Craig (Captain Marvel); Barbara Joyce (Huntress); Danuta (Black Canary); Frank Gorshin (The Riddler); Alfie Wise (The Atom); Mickey Morton (Solomon Grundy); Bill Nuckals (Hawkman); William Schallert (Rec Cyclone); Charlie Callas (Sinestro).

CREW: *Produced and directed by:* William Carruthers. *Associate Producer:* Joel Stein. *Costumes:* Warden Neils. *Stunts:* Buddy Joe Hooker. *Running time per episode:* 60 minutes (approximate).

Justice League of America (1997)
LIVE-ACTION UNAIRED SERIES PILOT

CAST: Matthew Settle (Green Lantern); Jon Kassir (The Atom); David Ogden Stiers (Martian Manhunter); Ken Johnston (The Flash); Kim Oja (Ice); Michelle Hurd (Fire); Miguel Ferrer (The Weather Man).

CREW: *Written by:* Scott Shepherd. *Directed by:* Felix Enriquez Alcala, Lewis Teague.

Music: John Debney. *Art Director:* Nicole Koenigsberger. *Produced by:* Lorne Cameron. *Running time:* approximately 65 minutes.

In New Metro City a terrible villain called the Weather Man threatens the safety of the citizenry. The Justice League, consisting of Green Lantern, the Flash, Martian Manhunter, the Atom, and Fire, bands together to stop him. Along the way, a new superhero, Ice, joins the team.

Justice League of America (2001–)
ANIMATED SERIES

"Old-school comic-book cool ... a cleverly wrought variation on *The Super Friends*.... The one *Justice League* drawback? The creaky series premiere storyline, a *War of the Worlds*–type tale of alien invasion, is a bite of rather musty, extraterrestrial trite.
— Mike Duffy, *Knight Ridder/Tribune News Service*, November 16, 2001.

"*Justice League* has the action, but it has a way to go on the stories and characters. I like the voice work, but I think some of the characterizations are limited. Hawkgirl is useless. The Flash is relatively one-dimensional, despite the fact he's voiced by Michael Rosenbaum."
— Howard Margolin, host of *Destinies: The Voice of Science Fiction*

VOICES: Kevin Conroy (Batman); Maria Canals (Hawkgirl); Susan Eisenberg (Wonder Woman); Phil La Marr (Green Lantern); Carl Lumbly (J'onn J'onzz/Martian Manhunter); George Newbern (Superman); Michael Rosenbaum (The Flash).

CREW: Based on DC Comics Characters. *Superman created by:* Jerry Siegel and Joe Shuster. *Batman Created by:* Bob Kane. *Wonder Woman Created by:* William Moulton Marston. *Producers:* Rich Fogel, Glen Murakami, Bruce Timm, James Tucker. *Associate Producer:* Sharon McLaughlin. *Series Story Editors:* Stan Berkowitz, Rich Fogel. *Series Directors:* Butch Lukic, Dan Riba. *Theme:* Lolita Ritmanis. *Music:* Kristopher Carter, Michael McCuiston, Lolita Ritmanis. *Voice Director:* Andrea Romano. *Casting Director:* Andrea Romano. *Executive Producers:* Jean MacCurdy, Sander Schwartz. From Warner Brothers.

The League of Extraordinary Gentlemen

Alan Moore, the beloved creator of such now-classic comics as *Watchmen*, *V for Vendetta*, *From Hell* and *Batman: The Killing Joke*, saw another of his popular if esoteric superhero properties adapted to the screen for release in the summer of 2003. His Jack the Ripper chronicle, *From Hell*, had been adapted to film in 2001 with great success, so a follow-up Moore movie was a certainty. Many in the comic industry hoped *Watchmen* would be next. Instead, they were surprised the less accessible *League of Extraordinary Gentlemen* was already in the making.

With art drawn by Kevin O'Neill, *The League of Extraordinary Gentlemen* comic book series is in essence a sort of Victorian era variation on *The Super Friends*, or rather, *The Justice League of America*. Described imprecisely, the premise holds that the most remarkable men and women of the late nineteenth century have teamed up with extraordinary abilities and minds to combat the forces of evil. Those on the team include Dracula's love, Mina Harker, adventurer Allan Quatermain, beautiful (but old) Dorian Gray, Jules Verne's Captain Nemo, the Invisible Man, and Dr. Jekyll/Mr. Hyde. In the first comic book published in 1999, evil came in the form of Sherlock Holmes' nemesis, Professor Moriarty.

The second issue (from 2002) featured invading Martians in a plot based on H.G. Wells' *War of the Worlds*, and added Dr. Moreau (as in *The Island of Dr. Moreau*) to the Victorian age crime-fighting ranks.

Stephen Norrington, director of 1998's successful Marvel property *Blade*, helmed an $80 million adaptation of Moore's comic in the summer of 2002 with principal photography set in the Prague and subsequently stalled because of terrible flooding and damaged sets.[1] Early buzz on the film was negative and reports in the press, particularly from *Entertainment Weekly*, alleged that star Sean Connery did not see eye-to-eye with Norrington during the seventeen-week shoot.

Additionally, there were changes made to Americanize Moore's complex, Brit-centric comic, particularly in the addition of a secret agent from the United States, one Tom Sawyer.

The film's plot involved the team's activation by Queen Victoria in 1898. The threat was a powerful new device created by a villain called The Fantom. *The League of Extraordinary Gentlemen* premiered on July 11, 2003, and failed to win its opening weekend at the box office, falling victim to the highly successful *Pirates of the Caribbean: Curse of the Black Pearl*. Reviews were generally very negative and the film earned only $60 million, a rather severe shortfall.

The League of Extraordinary Gentlemen (2003)
LIVE-ACTION FILM

"*LXG* was a disappointment. It lacked the subtlety of the comic, and was little more than a big action film with Victorian-era superheroes. The plot was weak, the villains unmemorable, and some of the concepts made little sense (e.g. Nemo builds a 1930s-style car that resembles a white movie Batmobile. Fine, I can accept that, considering he built the Nautilus. However, how is it that Tom Sawyer knows how to drive it expertly?) And how can Allan Quatermain (whose family name is spelled incorrectly on a grave early in the film) leap from a speeding car and 'stick' the landing like a gymnast? In short, as demonstrated by *From Hell*, the brilliance of Alan Moore remains difficult, if not impossible to translate to film."
— Howard Margolin, host of *Destinies: The Voice of Science Fiction*.

"It's all quite silly, really, but diverting enough as the movie devolves into increasingly outrageous set-pieces, pyrotechnics and so-called 'twists.'"
— Peter Debruge, *Premiere Magazine*, July 11, 2003. Page 1 of 1.
www.premiere.com

"There are nicely choreographed fights, bone-rattling explosions and...those chilling Jekyll/Hyde transformations. Not only is this film a sort of honorary sequel, but it succeeds in a way that the summer's other action sequels — and comic-book adaptations — don't.... *The League of Extraordinary Gentlemen* is more fun than any smart movie this summer and smarter than any fun movie out there."
— Jay Boyar, *The Orlando Sentinel*: "A super league of their own:

Extraordinary Gentlemen combines comic book fun with big-screen action."
July 11, 2003, page 1 of 3.
www.orlandosentinel.com

CAST: Sean Connery (Allan Quatermain); Stuart Townsend (Dorian Gray); Peta Wilson (Mina Harker); Shane West (Tom Sawyer); Jason Flemying (Dr. Jekyll/Mr. Hyde); Naseeruding Shah (Captain Nemo); Jason Isaacs (Bond); Rodney Skinner (The Invisible Man); Richard Roxburgh.

CREW: *Based on the Comic by*: Alan Moore and Kevin O'Neill. *Produced by*: Don Murphy, Trevor Albert and Jane Hamsher. *Music by*: Mark Isham. *Production Design*: Carol Spier. *Cinematography*: Dan Lautsen. *Screenplay by*: Alex Ayres and James Robinson. *Executive Producers*: Sean Connery and Mark Gordon. *Co-producer*: Michael Nelson. *Directed by*: Stephen Norrington. *M.P.A.A. Rating*: PG-13. *Running time*: 112 minutes.

In turn of the century Europe, a mysterious villain plans to wreck the peace by killing world leaders at a conference scheduled to convene in Venice. If the Fantom's plans come to fruition, the world could erupt into war, and the city of Venice could sink into the sea. A group of legendary — and highly individual heroes are called upon by Queen Victoria to work together and save the world. The group is led by the disillusioned hero Allan Quatermain. Others on the team include the Invisible Man, Dorian Gray, Mina Harker, Dr. Jekyll, and the inventor Captain Nemo. Also in the mix is a fresh-faced American secret agent, Tom Sawyer.

The Man from Atlantis

To this day, *The Man from Atlantis*, a mid–1970s superhero TV series, remains both beloved and despised. It is beloved by former children of the era, who watched the show religiously in 1977 and fell in love with the story of a web-handed survivor of Atlantis, Mark Harris (played by actor Patrick Duffy). Contrarily, the show is still hated by aficionados of Marvel Comics.

To explain further, Marvel already had its own well-established *Man from Atlantis*–style character before *The Man from Atlantis* came along on television: Bill Everett's Prince Namor, otherwise known as the Sub-Mariner.

Replete with an Adonis-like physique, a green bathing suit, and pointed ears and eyebrows, this arrogant grandson of King Thakorr was alternately known as "the Avenging Son of Atlantis" or the "Prince of Blood." In his long comic book history (which began in 1940), he often combated mankind — which he hated — and occasionally teamed with some allied countries, as when he fought Hitler and the Nazis as part of a superhero team called "the Invaders" in stories from the 1960s.

Arrogant Namor appeared on TV only in animated form before 1977, in the beloved 1966 series from Grantray Lawrence Animation Studios called *The Marvel Superheroes* (where his adventures were rotated with those of Captain America, the Mighty Thor, the Incredible Hulk and Iron Man). Thus, in the era when every property from Captain America to Doctor Strange to Wonder Woman was being translated to television, the Sub-Mariner seemed a natural selection for his own TV movie or series.

Unfortunately, the makers of *The Man from Atlantis* simply adopted a similar character concept (a water-breathing superhero from Atlantis) and created their own "original" series, thus avoiding any licensing fees owed to Marvel. Comic book fans were not impressed by the maneuver, to say the least. In the TV re-do, the Namor-type character lost every iota of attitude and pride, becoming the world's nicest, most even-tempered guy instead. He became a "groovy," New Age version of *Star Trek*'s Mr. Spock: a peaceful "alien" stranger that had many lessons to teach mankind. Patrick Duffy described his character, the Namor knock-off, in this way:

> I find him extremely, intelligently naïve. He's very quick. He's unencumbered by hang-ups.... He has a total lack of that kind of ego that stops us from taking a different direction because we hate to admit that the one we took in the first place was wrong. He's totally open to suggestion...[1]

Not exactly "the Prince of Blood" in concept. To comic book fans that wanted to see their prideful Namor, this idea of a "nice" Atlantean was nothing short of heresy. One of the prime components of the comic book was the timely notion that Namor hated man for polluting his home, the world's oceans. It was a great environmental conceit, and another idea jettisoned by the familiar sounding *Man from Atlantis*.

So in 1977, Mark Harris, *The Man from Atlantis*, washed ashore before American TV audiences. The last surviving denizen of the lost city of Atlantis, Harris had no memory of his background, boasted webbed feet and hands, and bore gills instead of lungs, which meant he could remain above water for only twelve hours at a stretch. Endowed with super-strength and senses, Harris could also swim incredibly fast, and in a unique dolphin-like motion as well.

On the TV series he worked with a nice, attractive scientist, the requisite damsel in distress, Dr. Elizabeth Merrill (Belinda Montgomery); and mid-way through the series he joined the crew of the *Cetacean*, an advanced U.S. government submarine not unlike the starship *Enterprise* (where, again, Harris was the resident alien). Harris's unofficial boss at the Foundation for Oceanic Research (the United Federation of Planets?) was C.W. Crawford (Alan Fudge).

Stories featured on *The Man from Atlantis* were the typical clichés of science fiction and superhero lore. Harris traveled to the Old West to take part in a shoot-out in the episode "Shoot Out at Land's End." He faced a genie (Pat Morita) who could revert people to their childhood in "Imp," and battled a Jekyll/Hyde chemical formula–created monster in "C.W. Hyde."

In one truly over-the-top outing, "The Naked Montague," Harris traveled into the past to prevent the bloody demises of Shakespeare's young lovers, Romeo and Juliet! Villains on the show ranged from a giant (Kareem Abdul-Jabbar) to a colossal jellyfish to the recurring "evil genius" Mr. Schubert (portrayed by Victor Buono). The tone of the series bordered on camp, and some of the episodes were hard to take seriously. Director Michael O'Herlihy went on record noting that it was this lack of a consistent (and serious) tone that hurt the show with viewers:

> I don't know if *Man from Atlantis* was science fiction or what the hell it was ... it could have been a remarkable show, but they turned it into some kind of underwater satire, which was a terrible shame.[2]

Mark Harris (Patrick Duffy) is a smooth-skinned visitor from the deep and *The Man from Atlantis*. Notice his webbed hands.

The first season of *The Man from Atlantis* ran sporadically on NBC as a series of two-hour movies on Thursday nights (competing against the popular *Hawaii Five-O* on CBS and *Barney Miller* on ABC). The second season settled down into a regular pattern, airing Tuesday nights in the fall of 1977 and spring of 1978 at 8:00 P.M., competing against the powerhouse combination of *Happy Days* and *Laverne and Shirley* on ABC. Despite good guest stars, including Pat Morita, Laurette Spang, Billy Barty, Ted Cassidy, James B. Sikking and John Shea (*Mutant X, Lois and Clark*), the show failed to draw a sizable enough audience for the network that had cancelled *Star Trek*, and *The Man from Atlantis* became lost at sea.

An interesting side note: *The Man from Atlantis* was the first American network program to be broadcast in mainland China, and it garnered a large fan-following there.

The Man from Atlantis (1977–78)
LIVE ACTION SERIES

"This seemed like a good idea when it started, and how many kids didn't emulate that swimming style in the pool at least once? The first few episodes showed promise, and then it got a little tired."
— William Latham, author of *Space: 1999 Resurrection, Mary's Monster.*

"It was supposed to be an adaptation of the Sub Mariner, a comic-book character who rules Atlantis, for television. But while the Sub Mariner was every bit as arrogant as you'd expect an undersea ruler to be, the Man from Atlantis was an even nicer guy than Bobby Ewing. He was too good to be true, too stupid to be entertaining, and too noble to be tolerated."
— David Bianculli, *The Best of Science Fiction TV*, Harmony Books, 1987.

"The series is so mindless it even makes one nostalgic for *Voyage to the Bottom of the Sea.*"
— John Brosnan, *Future Tense: The Cinema of Science Fiction*, 1978, page 304.

CAST: Patrick Duffy (Mark Harris/The Man from Atlantis); Belinda J. Montgomery (Dr. Elizabeth Merrill); Alan Fudge (C.W. Crawford); Victor Buono (Mr. Schubert). SEASON ONE: Kenneth Tigar (Dr. Simon). SEASON TWO: Robert Lussier (Brent); J. Victor Lopez (Chuey); Richard Laurence Williams (Jomo); Jean Marie Hon (Jane); Anson Downes (Allen).

CREW: *Executive Producer:* Herbert F. Solow. *Produced by:* Herman Miller. *Music:* Fred Karlin. *Special Effects:* Tom Fisher. *Swimming Advisor/Coach:* Paul Slater. *Shot at:* MGM.

SEASON ONE (1977)

1. "The Man from Atlantis" (two hours) Written by: Mayo Simon. Directed by: Lee H. Katzin. Airdate: March 4, 1977.

A strange water-breather, the last survivor of Atlantis, washes ashore in sunny California where he is resuscitated by the beautiful Dr. Elizabeth Merrill, a marine biologist who works for the Foundation for Oceanic Research. Though this stranger — renamed "Mark Harris" — has great strength and speed in his natural environment of the ocean, he has no memory of his true identity or place of origin. It turns out that Mark's great agility in the water could be a valuable weapon in vanquishing a psychotic, power-hungry scientist named Mr. Schubert. In accepting the mission, Harris joins forces with Merrill and the Foundation, all the while hoping to remember his past and learn the extent of his aquatic abilities.

GUEST CAST: Art Lund (Admiral Pierce); Larry Pressman (Roth); Dean Santoro (Ernie); Allan Cass, Joshua Bryant.

2. "Death Scouts" (two hours) Written by: Robert Lewin. Directed by: Marc Daniels. Airdate: May 7, 1977.

Working for the Foundation, Mark investigates the disappearance of three scuba divers. His search leads him to a couple of water-breathers, which raises the Man from Atlantis's hopes that he has found his own kind, but the evil duo turns out to be extraterrestrial in origin.

GUEST CAST: Tiffany Bolling, Burr De-Benning, Annette Cardona, Alan Mendell, Vincent Deadrick, Maurice Hill.

3. "Killer Spores" (two hours) Written by: John D.F. Black. Directed by: Lee H. Katzin. Airdate: May 17, 1977.

A space probe returns to Earth carrying deadly bacteria encased in spores. Mark is the only one who can deal with the spores, which are not only alive but actually sentient, and want to find a way home. Unfortunately, the spores kill humans and are being treated as a threat to the species.

GUEST CAST: James B. Sikking (Colonel Manzone); Vred Beir, Ivan Bonar.

4. "The Disappearances" (two hours) Written by: Luthor Murdoch. Story by: Jerry Sohl. Directed by: Charles Dubin. Airdate: June 20, 1977.

A demented female scientist, Dr. Smith, kidnaps Dr. Merrill and takes her to an island near South America for dastardly purposes. Hoping to rescue Elizabeth from grave danger, the Man from Atlantis pursues.

GUEST CAST: Darleen Carr (Dr. Smith); Pamela Peters Solow, Dennis Redfield, Ivor Francis, Fred Beir.

SEASON TWO (1977-1978)

5. "Melt Down" Written by: Tom Greene. Directed by: Virgil W. Vogel. Airdate: September 22, 1977.

Obsessed with the strange Man from Atlantis, the villainous scientist Mr. Schubert makes a deadly deal. He will save the world (from melting polar ice caps) if and only if Mark turns himself over to the villain for study — and possibly dissection.

GUEST CAST: Victor Buono; James E. Brodhead (Trubshaw).

6. "The Mudworm" Written by: Alan Caillou. Directed by: Don Weis. Airdate: October 13, 1977.

Mr. Schubert's latest invention, a robotic probe device designed to collect and study mineral samples under the sea, goes crazy and begins to murder marine life. Mark and Elizabeth, serving aboard the sub Cetacean, intervene to save the life at the bottom of the sea.

GUEST CAST: Victor Buono.

7. "Hawk of Mu" Written by David H. Balkan and Luthor Murdoch. Directed by: Harry Harris. Airdate: October 18, 1977.

The statue of a Hawk is a strange and valuable prize for Mr. Schubert, as it seems to possess the ability to interfere with electrical current and cause power shortages. Mark finds an unusual ally in fighting Mr. Schubert's latest plan for world domination: Schubert's daughter!

GUEST CAST: Vicky Huxtable (Juliette Schubert); Sydney Lassick (Smith); Carole Mallory (Vicky); Victor Buono.

8. "Giant" Written by: Michael Wagner. Directed by: Richard Benedict. Airdate: October 25 1977.

Mark is shocked to learn that a giant humanoid from another world is mining gold from the Earth's oceans. Worse, another human, named Muldoon, is trying to get the gold for himself.

GUEST CAST: Kareem Abdul-Jabbar (Thark); Ted Neeley (Muldoon).

9. "Man O'War" Written by: Larry Alexander. Directed by: Michael O'Herlihy. Airdate: November 1, 1977.

Mr. Schubert is back and raising more trouble. The cost of all his failed plans is bankruptcy, so he holds hostage a swimming competition by unleashing a giant jellyfish upon it.

GUEST CAST: Victor Buono; Harvey Jason (Dashki); Gary Owens (Announcer).

10. "Shoot Out at Land's End" Written by: Luthor Murdoch. Directed by: Barry Crane. Airdate: November 8, 1977.

In a strange quirk of fate, Mark Harris and his exact duplicate — a gunslinger from the Old West — change places. Now Mark is trapped in the domain of the cowboy, hunted by the law, and his doppelganger is aboard the Cetacean, stealing his very identity.

GUEST CAST: Pernell Roberts (Clint Hollister); Noble Willingham (Artemus Washburn); Jamie Smith Jackson, Bill Zuckert.

11. "Crystal Water, Sudden Death" Written by: Larry Alexander. Directed by: David Moessinger. Airdate: November 22, 1977.

Deep under the sea, a race of air-breathers dwell in relative peace, saved from the pressure of the ocean by a bubble-like force field around the city. This tranquility is threatened, however, when Schubert learns of the city and plots to steal the power crystals generating the protective barrier.

GUEST CAST: Rene Auberjonois, Tina Lennert, Flip Reade, Whitney Rydbeck.

12. "The Naked Montague" Written by: Stephen Kandel. Directed by: Robert Douglas. Airdate: December 6, 1977.

Mark is hurtled back through time by an explosion and becomes involved in the tragic romance of the not-so-fictional Romeo and Juliet. But can he change history ... or is the fate of the young lovers sealed?

GUEST CAST: Lisa Eilbacher (Juliet); John Shea (Romeo); Scott Porter (Mercutio).

13. "C.W. Hyde" Written by: Stephen Kandel. Directed by: Dan Cahn. Airdate: December 13, 1977.

The Foundation's C.W. Crawford ingests a mysterious fluid found at the bottom of the ocean. The strange chemical splits his personality in two: one good, one evil.

GUEST CAST: Val Avery (Calender); Pamela Peters Solow, Michele Carey.

14. "Scavenger Hunt" Written by: Peter Allan Fields. Directed by: David Moessinger. Airdate: April 18, 1978.

The search for missing (and deadly) gas containers leads Mark to an island paradise where that rogue Muldoon has been conning natives into sacrificing their young women to his ... cause. Mark intervenes and learns that Muldoon knows more about the missing gas containers than he is letting on.

GUEST CAST: Ted Neeley (Muldoon); Ted Cassidy (Conja); Yabo O'Brien, Eugenia Wright.

15. "Imp" Written by: Shimon Wincelberg. Directed by: Paul Krasny. Airdate: April 25, 1978.

A strange magical creature of diminutive proportions is imbued with the ability to turn grown men back into children, and his next target is the Man from Atlantis!

GUEST CAST: Pat Morita (Moby); Dick Gautier, Lyman Ward, Mel Scott.

16. "The Siren" Written by: Michael Wagner. Directed by: Ed Abroms. Airdate: May 2, 1978.

A mermaid with an alluring song is captured by pirates who believe that her power can help them get ahead. In this case, that means the capture of a scientist that holds top-secret government defense secrets.

GUEST CAST: Lisa Blake Richards (Jenny); Neville Brand; Laurette Spang (Amanda); Michael Strong (Hugh Trevanian); Timothy Scott.

17. "Deadly Carnival" Written by: Larry Alexander. Directed by: Dennis Donnelly. Airdate: June 6, 1978.

A government agent was last seen at a carnival before his unusual disappearance. Mark infiltrates the carnival and finds that a ring of thieves is bent on stealing an ancient Egyptian artifact.

GUEST CAST: Billy Barty (Moxie); Anthony James (Summersday); Sharon Farrell (Charlene).

Manimal

The same season producer Glen Larson gave the world *Automan,* he and producing partner and co-creator Donald Boyle also unleashed *Manimal,* one of the more absurd superhero TV series to come down the pike in a long time. The short-lived NBC series ran for eight hour-long episodes in the fall and winter of 1983, and chronicled the heroic exploits of one Dr. Jonathan Chase (Simon MacCorkindale).

Jonathan Chase was all things to all people. He was a bit of a rogue, a bit of a James Bond character, and even something of a messiah (witness his initials: J.C.). Most importantly, he was a man "with the brightest of futures, the darkest of pasts," as established by the weekly voice-over narration read by actor William Conrad. The dashing Chase was granted a special and unique legacy by his mysterious, well-traveled (and deceased) father, making Chase heir to and master of the secrets "that divide man from animal, animal from man."

In other words, long before the advent of morphing technology, Chase had the ability to change into animals, such as parrots, bulls, horses and a few other regulars (a black panther and a hawk). Thankfully, the special effects "transformations" were designed and executed by the amazing Stan Winston, who later worked on such landmark genre films as *Aliens* (1986), *Predator* (1986) and *Terminator 2* (1991). For their time, these man-to-beast (and beast-to-man) shifts were quite impressive, and even a little scary.

Where did the notion for *Manimal* come from? It is difficult to say, but the special effects transformations of two 1981 werewolf movies, *An American Werewolf in London* and *The Howling*, may have been part of the inspiration. Those productions proved that special effects technology, especially regarding man-to-beast metamorphosis, had come a long way from time-lapse photography and other antiquated techniques, and *Manimal* seemed designed to showcase the new effects. The only drawback in that regard was that such detailed, time-consuming transformations were also very expensive to orchestrate, and that meant that the series relied heavily on stock footage week after week.

In every episode of *Manimal*, Chase would turn into a panther and a hawk, and the same footage would be shown. The repeat footage was hard enough to accept, but *Manimal* really became absurd when it started inserting *inappropriate* stock footage into its transformation sequences. For example, in the episode entitled "Night of the Beast," Chase transformed into a panther while he was trapped inside a wooden crate. But as he "changed" into the beast, a jungle background was clearly in evidence behind him, so the footage didn't match the context of the scene at all.

In fact, most of Jonathan Chase's heroic feats were pretty ludicrous. In "High Stakes," Jonathan had to rescue a falling parachutist and turned into the hawk to do the deed. As the hawk, Chase pulled the appropriate parachute pin, so the chute would open just in the nick of time. In the same episode, as a panther this time, Chase opened and closed a desk drawer adroitly. The viewer saw a little dummy panther paw perform this stunt, and it looked pretty silly.

More to the point, these heroics raised questions about Chase's gift. As an animal, did he retain his human consciousness? A portion of it? A sense or feeling of it? Anything? The point was never even discussed, but one imagines that the precision needed to pull a parachute pin or open and close a desk drawer would be beyond most common animals. In *The Incredible Hulk*, for instance, it was established that the creature would not commit murder, because David Banner, his alter ego, was not capable of murder. It would have been rewarding had the creators of *Manimal* thought to describe the nature of these transformations a bit more clearly.

Another silly moment, in the episode "Illusion," saw Jonathan — as a hawk again — captured by a child's net in Central Park. It is pretty embarrassing for a superhero to get nabbed by a little kid in any regard, but one must wonder where this Achilles hero might have led the series. Had *Manimal* lasted longer, would Jonathan as a trout become hooked by a fisherman? As a white mouse, could he have stumbled into a mousetrap? Again, the nature of Jonathan's powers did not seem clear enough. He could pull a parachute pin as a hawk, but not remember enough to avoid a child's net?

Probably the height of absurdity in the series came with the episode "Breath of the Dragon," in which Chase reported that the study of martial arts actually began with animals — in observing how they attack and defend. In keeping with that bit of trivia, the episode culminated in a strange fight sequence in which series star MacCorkindale bounded absurdly about an opponent, adopting the movements and characteristics of a mountain gorilla. A man of refined British accent and dignified features, MacCorkindale looked utterly ridiculous imitating an ape.

The cheapness of *Manimal* was evident not just in its reliance on stock footage and all-too-silly plot gimmicks, but even in its depiction of locale. New York was the setting of the series, but the show was actually shot on a back lot in California. The answer to this dilemma? Not-so-clever special effects men matted the World Trade Centers over the studio back lot in episodes such as "Scrimshaw." It was a cheap fix, and immediately obvious to attentive viewers.

The characters in *Manimal* all came from the pile of superhero clichés that have littered the genre for years. Chase was a James Bond character, a one-liner type of guy prone to making really bad puns. After he turned into a horse, and his companion, Brooke MacKenzie mounted him in one episode ("High Stakes"), he noted, to groans everywhere, "She wasn't horsing around."

Chase's friend on the police force, Ty (Michael D. Roberts), was badly conceived as perhaps the hoariest of clichés: the sassy black cop with a "ghetto" sensibility and sense of humor. Oddly enough, this trite character has reappeared over the years (usually with a little more class) in series as di-

verse as *The Crow: Stairway to Heaven* (1998) and *John Doe* (2002–).

Melody Anderson played Chase's love interest, Brooke MacKenzie, but was often missing in action so that the handsome Chase could romance the attractive guest star of the week, including Tracy Scoggins ("High Stakes"), Lina Raymond ("Scrimsaw") and others. The police boss, Nick Rivera (Reni Santoni) was the same clueless curmudgeon, a Perry White clone, seen in a dozen other superhero dramas.

The villains dramatized on *Manimal*, like those seen on *Automan*, were the garden-variety criminals featured endlessly on so many cops and robbers dramas from the 1970s and 1980s. A foreign dignitary with diplomatic immunity (played by the ubiquitous Richard Lynch) vexed Jonathan in "Illusion." An unscrupulous businessman (Doug McClure) caused trouble in "Night of the Scorpion." An Asian gang threatened innocent shopkeepers in "Breath of the Dragon," and so forth.

Unlike *Automan*, however, *Manimal* had no overriding sense of humor or theme that could sustain it through the weak plotting and routine villains. Every week, Chase solved crimes by turning into animals, and that was about as deep as things went. Rarely was the origin or nature of his transformative gift addressed.

Critics hated *Manimal*, ranking it as one of the worst series of all time. It didn't stay on the air long, either, proving that audiences felt likewise. It ran on NBC Friday nights at 9:00 P.M. in the fall of 1983, but was mauled by *Dallas* on CBS. When it moved to Saturdays at 9:00 P.M., *The Love Boat* trounced it. Only eight episodes were made (and all were aired), but *Manimal* was quickly forgotten, except by lovers of really bad television.

In 1997, Simon MacCorkindale revived the character of Jonathan Chase on one episode of the Glen Larson syndicated superhero series *Nightman* (1997-1998). Entitled "Manimal," this second-season story revealed that Chase now had a fully-grown daughter who could also transform into an-

imals, and, oddly, also possessed the ability to time travel.

Manimal (1983)
LIVE-ACTION SERIES

"The developers of *Manimal* have ... given the show an unusual slant with the inclusion of Chase's powers. The actors are capable, attractive people that work well together but the show misses the mark because the focus is on the gimmick rather than the people...Give us more of the man and less of the animal in *Manimal.*"
— Cynthia Broadwater, *Daredevils* #4: Animal on the Loose: Tracking *Manimal,*" February 1984 page 27.

"...[A]n astonishingly silly, unintentionally hilarious crime series.... Able to transform into the beast of his choosing, Chase helped the NYPD battle bad guys even though he looked like an understudy from *Cats.*"
— *TV Guide*: "50 Worst Shows of All Time," July 20–26, 2002, page 22.

"Would you believe a crime-fighting professor with the superpowers that enable him to turn into a variety of animals? If you would, then this silly action series may be to your liking."
— *People Weekly*: "Manimal," October 3, 1983.

"The biggest problem was that the show made no sense. Fine, Jonathan Chase had the power to transform into animals. But when he would change, like Bill Bixby on *The Incredible Hulk*, his clothes would rip. Then, when he changed back, his clothes were miraculously restored. How did that happen? Besides that, Simon MacCorkindale was hardly the most personable lead and I recall the show being terribly boring."
— Howard Margolin, host of *Destinies: The Voice of Science Fiction.*

CAST: Simon MacCorkindale (Jonathan Chase); Melody Anderson (Brooke Mackenzie); Michael D. Roberts (Tyrone "Ty" Earl); Reni Santoni (Lt. Nick Rivera).

CREW: *Co-Executive Producer*: Paul Mason. *Supervising Producer*: Donald R. Boyle. *Produced by*: Paul Rudin, Michael Berk, Douglas Schwartz. *Created by*: Glen A. Larson and Donald R. Boyle. *Executive Producer*: Glen A. Larson. *Creative Consultant*: Robert Earll. *Associate Pro-*

ducers: Randall Torno, Keith Pierce. *Directors of Photography (various episodes)*: Chuck Arnold, Dennis Dalzell. *Art Director*: Fred Tuch. *Set Decorator*: Jim Hassinger. *Film Editors (various episodes)*: Neil MacDonald, Joe Morrisey. *Post-Production Supervisor*: Dann Cahn. *Executive Production Manager*: Mark Evans. *Music*: Alan Silvestri. *Music Supervisor*: Lionel Newman. *Manimal Theme by*: Paul Chihara. *Panther and Hawk Transformations Designed and Created by*: Stan Winston. *Second Unit Director*: David G. Phinney. *Costume Design*: Jean Pierre Dorleac. *Casting*: Rachelle Farberman. A Glen Larson Production.

SEASON ONE (1983)

1. "Manimal" (90 minutes) Written by: Glen A. Larson and Donald R. Boyle. Directed by: Russ Mayberry. Airdate: September 30, 1983.

The witty and urbane professor Jonathan Chase loves animals and the animal kingdom, and for good reason. He possesses the unusual ability, handed down to him by his mysterious father, to transform into all the beasts of the land, sea and air. Working with the New York Police Department and a gorgeous detective named Brooke MacKenzie, Chase tries to stop a gang of terrorists from making off with a cache of nerve gas that could kill hundreds of thousands of innocent people.

GUEST CAST: Ursula Andress, Lloyd Bochner, Glynn Turman, Floyd Levine.

2. "Illusion" Written by: Paul Mason. Directed by: Daniel Haller. Airdate: October 14, 1983.

A smuggler named Zoltan Gregory is apprehended by the police on a stakeout, but has diplomatic immunity and escapes prosecution. Jonathan sets out to catch the dangerous criminal before his next infraction, turning into a hawk to track his movements. The case leads to an illusionist act on stage and a mysterious murder blamed on an innocent tiger. Now Chase must catch Gregory red-handed or see the poor animal destroyed.

GUEST CAST: Christopher Stone; Jonathan Goldsmith; Peter Fox; David Hess; Richard Lynch (Zoltan Gregory); Christie Claridge (Jessica DeVere); Patrick Gorman (Billy's Father); Alan Koss (The Man); Maureen O'Connor (Secretary); Bob Jacoby (Billy); Talbot Simons (Cab Driver); Patrick Strong (Attendant); Michelle Rogers (Showgirl).

3. "Night of the Scorpion" Written by: Glen A. Larson. Directed by: Daniel Haller. Airdate: October 21, 1983.

A poisonous spider kills a man named Sloan on a cruise ship bound for New York, and Chase investigates the crime with the help of the dead man's daughter, Terri. The trail of the murderers leads to the Bahamas, where Jonathan and Terri run into a man named Sipes, Sloan's former business partner, who claims to be seeking money stolen by the dead man. The case takes an odd turn when Russian agents also go after the missing money. When Brooke joins Jonathan in the Bahamas, the investigators set up Sipes to discover the truth, and Chase transforms into a parrot to "overhear" Sipes' secret.

GUEST CAST: Doug McClure (Arnold Sipes); Mary-Margaret Humes (Terri Sloan); Robert O'Reilly; Albert Paulsen; Wolf Roth; Allen Williams; Glenn Corbett (Sloan); Floyd Levine (Murdock); Carl McKnight (Announcer); Darryl Milton (Waiter); Carol Carrington (Bank Manager); Rick Addison (Vendor).

4. "Female of the Species" Written by: Michael Berk and Douglas Schwartz. Directed by: George J. Fenady. Airdate: October 28, 1983.

The discovery and capture of a human girl raised by wild wolves in India fascinates Jonathan, but she escapes from custody when a saboteur intentionally sets a fire in her habitat. Jonathan pursues the wild girl across a busy city and transforms into a hawk to protect her from young thugs in a park. The wild girl escapes and makes for the zoo, where wolves attack until Chase, now a panther, saves her for a second time. Jonathan sets out to learn the secrets of the wolf girl's origins and the reason that somebody in New York City might want to kill her. That path leads to the discovery of a mysterious boating accident on the Ganges River in 1969 and a murderous plot enacted by Langley, the former business partner of the girl's father.

GUEST CAST: Rick Jason; Billy Ray Sharkey; Michael McGuire; Laura Cushing (Wolf Girl/Sarah Evers); Gloria Stuart (Bag Lady); Steve Burton (Reporter #1); Laura Levya (Reporter #2); Shashawnee Hall (Paramedic); Mindy Seeger (Harem Girl); Abraham Gordon (Photographer); Paul Haner (Gang Member #1); Ken Tebbel (Gang Member #2); Clyde R. Jones (Gang Member #3); Mark Harden (Gang Member #4).

5. "High Stakes" Written by: Michael Berk and Douglas Schwartz. Directed by: Sidney Hayers. Airdate: November 4, 1983.

A day at the horse races turns deadly when Chase must transform into a hawk to save a falling skydiver from certain death. Afterwards, Jonathan stumbles upon a cheating scheme involving a winning thoroughbred. The plot concerns a beautiful trainer named Cathy and an old case involving the kidnapping of a horse named Splendid Dancer —*and* an example of horse cosmetic surgery!

GUEST CAST: Peter Brown; Tracy Scoggins (Cathy); Thomas Babson; Gela Jacobsen; David Sheiner; Donald Bishop (Steward); Ed Gerrabrandt (Krebs); David K. Johnston (Assistant #2); James Ingersoll (Lyle Wittinton); Nick Konakas (Assistant #1); Fred S. Scott (Vet); Lew Horn (Harold Trout); Cynthia Frost (Woman).

6. "Scrimshaw" Written by: Michael Berk and Douglas Schwartz. Directed by: Chuck Bail. Airdate: December 3, 1983.

On a trip to the beach, Chase, Brooke and 12-year-old friend Corky free a seal trapped in a net. Unfortunately, they also discover a buried human skull with a boomerang imbedded in it, along with a priceless piece of scrimshaw. Corky's grandfather, Sea Dog Clancy, knows a secret about the carved ivory tusk: it's the map to the legendary treasure of Topaz Island. In disguise, Chase, Brooke, Ty and Corky infiltrate the Blue Fin restaurant/bar to learn more about the scrimshaw, but find only more trouble from thugs and a sexy woman named Miss Avery.

GUEST CAST: Bo Brundin; Charles H. Hyman; Lina Raymond (Lydia Avery); Robert W. Tessier; Meeno Peluce (Corky); Keenan Wynn (Clancy "Sea Dog" Morgan); Frank Annese (Sailor); Ann Ramsey (Referee); Ted Peterson (Bartender).

7. "Breath of the Dragon" Written by: Joseph Gunn. Directed by: Leslie Martinson. Airdate: December 10, 1983.

A gang in Chinatown has been forcing local merchants to pay tribute, leaving behind a threatening claw mark called the "mark of the dragon." Chase tries to help one family, whose young boy, Bobby, has become embroiled in a Chinese gang. Chase attempts to save Bobby by making a scene at a gang-owned casino, and only a timely transformation into a bull can save Chase and Ty from a deadly kung-fu fight. Chase challenges the gang leader, Kwan, to a battle before the local merchants, one which will settle the matter permanently.

GUEST CAST: George Kee Cheung; Marion Kodama Yue; Rummel Mor; James Hong (Mr. Tam); Peter Kwong (Moto); Lloyd Kino (Mr. Chang); Rana Ford (Girl); Edy Roberts (Girl); Deborah Bean (Mrs. Evans); Frank Moon (Mr. Evans); Richard Lee Sung (Pit Boss); John Mahon (Man); Nathan Jung (Tang); Lew Horn (Trout); Su-San Cheung (Dealer); Yung H. Sun (Merchant #1); Gerald Jann (Vendor).

8. "Night of the Beast" Written by: Sam Egan. Directed by: Russ Mayberry. Airdate: December 17, 1983.

In a stakeout, Brooke and Jonathan come to Ty's aid when their perp threatens to kill him. Successful, they all go camping in the supposedly quiet town of Birch Hollow, only to run afoul of a dangerous gangster organization controlling the 'burb with an iron grip of terror. Among the corrupt: the town sheriff, who locks up Ty and Brooke. Chase helps a beautiful woman named Maggie, who has been resisting the gangsters and whose brother has been kidnapped to "buy" her silence.

GUEST CAST: Jeff Corey (Zeke); Robert England [*sic*]; Dana Gladstone; Grainger Hines; Taylor Lacher; Fran Ran; Fred Sadoff; Hal England; Maggie Cooper (Maggie); Clayton Day (Powell); Wayne Heffley (Osmond); Alan Koss (The Man); Joe Stefano (Ray Garrett); Salvador Feliciano (Vendor); William Bumiler (Lyle).

NOTE: Though he is misidentified as Robert England, that's actually horror icon Robert Englund — Freddy Krueger himself — as one of the gangsters in this episode.

M.A.N.T.I.S.

From the minds of Sam Raimi, creator and director of *Darkman* (1990), and Sam Hamm, co-author of *Batman* (1989), emerged a one-season wonder entitled *M.A.N.T.I.S.*, a superhero story about a character named Miles Hawkins. A tall, handsome black man, Hawkins (Carl Lumbly of *Alias*) was a rich scientist and founder of the Hawkins Institute who had been paralyzed after taking a bullet in the spine.

In hopes of regaining the ability to walk, this genius developed a powerful exoskeleton suit, the Mechanically Augmented Neuro Transmitter Interception System, or M.A.N.T.I.S. But the special suit not only helped Hawkins walk again, it granted him

Something's bugging him. In full superhero regalia, Carl Lumbly is *M.A.N.T.I.S.*

super strength, which he was all too happy to utilize for the benefit of society. So no other souls would ever face the pain he had endured, Hawkins became M.A.N.T.I.S., a costumed superhero who fought crime with non-lethal measures like tranquilizer darts. Because of his personal fortune, he was, like Bruce Wayne, able to finance a high-tech and expensive crime-fighting organization. Hawkins' version of the popular Batmobile was a hovercraft called the Chrysalid, and he too boasted an underground bat cave, a headquarters deep beneath the city of Port Columbia. Few people suspected that the strong, mobile Mantis and the handicapped, wheelchair-bound Hawkins were one in the same, and Hawkins guarded his secret identity zealously.

The Fox Network purchased the *M.A.N.T.I.S.* concept based on the two-hour pilot directed by Eric Laneuville (*The Omega Man* [1971]) that aired in January of 1994 and received good ratings. In this early version of the series, M.A.N.T.I.S. toiled not in Port Columbia, but Ocean City, and all of his assistants/sidekicks were also African American citizens. A co-star of the pilot was the lovely and talented Gina Torres (also of *Alias*, and *Firefly*, and, just recently, Mrs. Laurence Fishburne).

Unfortunately, as the regular hour-long series was prepped for the fall of 1994, Fox ordered "a considerable lightening of tone" to homogenize the series, and the supporting black cast members were unceremoniously axed.[1] In the new version of the series, non-blacks assisted Dr. Hawkins: John Stonebrake (Roger Rees), an employee of Hawkins Technology and a good friend; and Taylor Savidge (Christopher Gartin), a young rebel without a cause, and a bike courier that knew the secret of M.A.N.T.I.S. and constantly sparred with Stonebrake. Sam Raimi and producer Rob Tapert were no longer associated with the series.

Despite the changing of the cast, no expense was spared to make *M.A.N.T.I.S.* a successful series, and each weekly installment cost 1.8 million dollars, making it not just expensive, but the most expensive prime time series on the air at the time.[2] Despite the production values, viewers were slow to warm to *M.A.N.T.I.S.* Fox afforded it a terrific time-slot, preceding the popular *X-Files* at 8:00 P.M. on Fridays. Still, it rated poorly and was yanked off the air by Fox in one year, despite a final cliffhanger. The network promised that it would re-evaluate the series for a "fall berth" the following season.[3] But *M.A.N.T.I.S.* never returned to the network's schedule, and was replaced on Friday nights at 8:00 by *VR.5*, another one-season wonder.

Like *The Flash* before it, *M.A.N.T.I.S.* began in a fairly realistic mode, but became more fantastic as it reached its final episode. The series commenced with "ordinary" villains who were nuclear terrorists ("Tango Blue"), assassins ("Cease Fire"), mad scientists ("Soldier of Misfortune") or arsonists ("Fire in the Heart"). By the end of the show, however, M.A.N.T.I.S. fought clones ("Progenitor"), aliens from another dimension ("Men in Black," "Spider in the Tower") and even a death-row convict who had returned from the dead in a new, electrical form ("Switches"). In one episode ("The Eyes of Beyond") Hawkins time traveled into the future to fight a Big Brother–like computer!

Carl Lumbly made for a great, powerful superhero (and has since given voice to J'onn J'Onzz, Martian Manhunter, on the Cartoon Channel's *Justice League of America*). In all, *M.A.N.T.I.S.* was a droll, entertaining hour that honored superhero tradition at the same time it tweaked it. With its fine pedigree, one would expect the networks would have let the series grow rather than cut it off in its youth, but networks will be networks.

M.A.N.T.I.S. (1994–95)
LIVE-ACTION SERIES

"*M.A.N.T.I.S.* lacks anything approaching a true pop sensibility to stake its claim on our attention. Indeed, even the schlock-pop affectation of *Mighty Morphin Power Rangers* is preferable to what is dropped on us here. In its commencement, *M.A.N.T.I.S.* fails to play it slyly or seductively enough to even score as a hokey comic-book-esque experience."

—Andrew Grossman, *The Hollywood Reporter*: "You Keep Praying *M.A.N.T.I.S.*, the Aborning Series on Fox, Will Suddenly Leap to Its Feet," August 26, 1994.

"Recently, there have been numerous efforts to create African American superheroes ... none, however, has been amusing as ... M.A.NT.I.S.... As directed by Eric Laneuville, M.A.N.T.I.S. has its spoofy aspects..."
— *Entertainment Weekly*, January 21, 1994, page 41.

"As was true of another superhero show of a few season ago, *The Flash*, *M.A.N.T.I.S.*'s costume is cool, but the plot and action scenes are lukewarm at best. *M.A.N.T.I.S.* should be praying for better scripts."
—David Hiltbrand, *People Weekly*: "*M.A.N.T.I.S.*" September 19, 1994, page 17.

CAST: Carl Lumbly (Dr. Miles Hawkins/M.A.N.T.I.S.); Roger Rees (John Stonebrake); Galyn Gorge (Lt. Maxwell); Christopher Russell Gartin (Taylor Savidge).

CREW: *Created by:* Sam Raimi and Sam Hamm. *Produced by:* Samm Hamm, Sam Raimi, Robert Tapert. *Executive Producers:* Coleman Luck, James McAdams. *Special Effects:* Jim Fisher. *Make-up:* Jo Ann Fowler. *M.A.N.T.I.S. Suit Created by:* Kurtzman, Nicotero and Berger EFX Group, Inc. *Coordinating Producer:* Dean Barnes. *Property Master:* Alex Kutschera. *Costume Designer:* Susan de Laval. *Co-executive Producer:* Bryce Zabel. *Developed for Television by:* Bryce Zabel. *Supervising Producer:* Mark Lisson. *Producer:* Paris Qualles. *Co-Producer:* Brad Markowitz. *Produced by:* David Roessell. *Music:* Christopher Franke. *Production Designer:* Lance King. *Film Editor:* George Appleby. *Director of Photography:* Rodney Charters. From Universal Television, Renaissance Pictures and Wilbur Force Productions.

SEASON ONE: (1994–1995)

1. "M.A.N.T.I.S." (two hours) Written by: Sam Hamm. Story by: Sam Hamm and Sam Raimi. Directed by: Eric Laneuville. Airdate: January 24, 1994.

Dr. Miles Hawkins, paralyzed after being shot, rises to defend his city from warring gangs as M.A.N.T.I.S., a costumed superhero with enhanced strength, thanks to a technological wonder, the Mechanically Augmented Neuro Transmitter Interception System (for which the hero is named). Investigating the gang war, M.A.N.T.I.S. realizes that a hidden force may have political motivations for increased crime in the city.

GUEST CAST: Billy Kane (DeCarlos); Philip Baker Hall, Bobby Hosea, Jeremiah Birkett, Yvonne Farrow, Dex Elliot, Alan Fudge, Obba Babatunde, Jerry Black, Laron Tate, Steve James, Francis McCarthy.

2. "First Steps" Written by: Bryce Zabel. Directed by: David Nutter. Airdate: August 26, 1994.

The M.A.N.T.I.S. must again take action in Port Columbia, this time over a problem he created. Years earlier he developed a virus, which though he thought he destroyed, is now killing people and could become a potent terrorist weapon.

GUEST CAST: Kenneth Mars (Reese); Cardelia Gonzels; Brion James (Solomon Box); Lorena Gale (Lynette); Jerry Wasserman (Det. Warren); Kevin McNulty (Saxon); Ric Reid (Hauck); Suki Kaiser; Martin Cummins (Dog Face); Robin Douglas, Harvey Thomison, Jason Lee.

3. "Tango Blue" Written by: Paris Qualles. Directed by: Joe Napolitano. Airdate: September 2, 1994.

A group of renegade Navy Seals are on the attack in Port Columbia, hoping to intercept a shipment of nuclear arms for their own nefarious purposes. The M.A.N.T.I.S. fights back...

GUEST CAST: Gregg Henry; Russell Curry; Hill Harper; Don S. Davis (Admiral); Roger R. Cross (Dixon); Jerry Wasserman (Det. Warren); David Kaye (Bill Murphy); Steve Bacic (Aquino).

4. "Days of Rage" Written by: Bryce Zabel and Brad Markowitz. Story by: Bryce Zabel and John B. Collins. Directed by: Les Landau. Airdate: September 9, 1994.

The FDA is just about to authorize the distribution of a new drug that is capable of raising the intellect of the taker. The M.A.N.T.I.S. learns that there are side effects to the drug, particularly extreme violence, when he looks into some test cases.

GUEST CAST: David Groh; Martin Cummins; Jennifer Copping; Robin Gammell; Akiko Morrison (Holloway); Barry Pepper (Jason Dirks); Byron Lucas (Cochran); Mitchell Kosterman (Policeman); Harvey Thomison (Dr. Zoom).

5. "Cease Fire" Written by: Mark Lisson. Directed by: Rob Bowman. Airdate: September 16, 1994.

Dr Hawkins' one great love, now the president of a nation in Africa, visits the United States for official purposes, but also plans to reconcile with the scientist. Unfortunately, assassins are targeting the diplomat for murder, and M.A.N.T.I.S. must defend her.

GUEST CAST: Boris Krutonog; Gay Thomas; Mari Morrow; Ken Foree; Ronald Guttman; Jerry Wasserman (Det. Warren); Nathanieal Deveaux, Andrew Kavadas, Dee Jay Jackson, Richard Leacock.

6. "Soldier of Misfortune" Written by: James Kramer. Story by: Jackie Zabel. Directed by: Kim Manners. Airdate: September 23, 1994.

The past comes back to haunt Hawkins in a most visceral way. A scientist that Hawkins snubbed, dismissing his robot soldier project from consideration before a committee in Congress, sends a monstrous opponent to kill the good doctor.

GUEST CAST: Gary Graham; Paul Guilfoyle; Deron McBee; Jan D'Arcy; Jerry Wasserman (Det. Warren); Lorena Gale (Lynette); Doug Abrahams (General Farley); Don MacKay, Paula Shaw, Douglas Stewart.

7. "Gloves Off" Written by: Bryce Zabel and Mark Lisson. Story by: Coleman Luck and Brad Markowitz. Directed by: Michael Caffey. Airdate: September 30, 1994.

The search for a woman's missing spouse leads Hawkins (and M.A.N.T.I.S.) to the discovery of an "underground" arena where gamblers watch people battle each other in the ring. Hawkins must rescue a man from enslavement in this mortal combat, but he won't do it without a fight.

GUEST CAST: Gary Graham; Sydney Walsh; Eric Allan Kramer; Barbara Tyson; Shashawnee Hall; Nils Allen Stewart (Mondo); Vladimir Kulich (Liakos); Bill Croft (Dolan); Paul McLean (Burkhardt).

8. "The Black Dragon" Written by: David Ransil. Story by: Nicholas Corea and David Ransil. Directed by: Mario Azzopardi. Airdate: October 7, 1994.

The Japanese mafia — the Yakuza — attempts to gain a foothold in Port Columbia. Their goal is to obtain illegal control of a new public sports facility. It is up to M.A.N.T.I.S. to stop them and their Samurai warriors.

GUEST CAST: Gary Graham; Michael Simms; Stephen M.D. Chang; Leonardo Cimino (Benny); Lorena Gale (Lynette); Hiro Kanagawa, David Bloom.

9. "To Prey in Darkness" Written by: Marc Scott Zicree. Story by Brad Markowitz and Marc Scott Zicree. Directed by: Cliff Bole. Airdate: October 14, 1994.

An agent of the Federal government is out to bring in M.A.N.T.I.S., a dark avenger that technically works "above the law." When video footage offers a clue to the superhero's true persona, M.A.N.T.I.S.'s secret identity is in jeopardy.

GUEST CAST: Gary Graham; John D'Aquino; Cylk Cozard; Blu Mankuma; Andrew Wheeler; Andrew Robinson (Solomon Box); Jo Bates.

10. "Fire in the Heart" Written by: Paris Quailles. Directed by: Rob Bowman. Airdate: October 21, 1994.

A young boy has the unusual ability to start fires psychically. He becomes the pawn of a ruthless land baron who believes the boy can make him wealthy by burning down properties, making them cheaper for him to purchase.

GUEST CAST: Patrick Malone; Lorraine Toussaint; George Touliatos; Eric King; Martin Cummins (Benton); Adrian Holmes (The Kid).

11. "Thou Shall Not Kill" Written by: Bryce Zabel and Brad Markowitz. Directed by: Michael Caffey. Airdate: November 4, 1994.

Framed for a crime he didn't commit, the M.A.N.T.I.S. is hunted by the Port Columbia police. Hoping to prove that he is no ordinary vigilante, Hawkins confides in Lt. Maxwell about his secret identity.

GUEST CAST: Gary Graham; Blu Mankuma; Jerry Wasserman (Det. Warren); Clabe Hartley; Robert Hooks (Mayor Mitchell); Andrew Robinson (Solomon Box); Jay Brazeau (Smith); Jeff Irvine, Ray Gordon.

12. "Revelation" Written by Bryce Zabel and Brad Markowitz: Directed by: David Grossman. Airdate: November 11, 1994.

Solomon Box, a cunning super-criminal, is behind the attempt to frame and discredit the M.A.N.T.I.S. But he seems to have the Port Columbia police wrapped around his finger, at least until Lt. Maxwell and Hawkins can prove who the real bad guy is.

GUEST CAST: Gary Graham; Blu Mankuma; Vicellous Shannon; Cyrus Farmer; Clabe Hartley; Robert Hooks (Mayor Mitchell); Andrew Robinson (Solomon Box); Jerry Wasserman (Det. Warren).

13. "Through the Dark Circle" Written by: Coleman Luck and Carel Gage Luck. Directed by: Kim Manners. Airdate: November 18, 1994.

Taylor and his current squeeze spend time in an old government facility, only to discover that it once housed a deadly device that opens portals to other worlds and dimensions. When the gate is opened, evil warriors from another reality spill into Port Columbia, bent on the conquest of Earth.

GUEST CAST: Jessica Collins, Philip Hayes, Andrew Kavadas, Harrison Coe, Barney O'Sullivan, Tom Heaton, Laura Harris.

14. "The Eyes Beyond" Written by: Coleman Luck and Carel Gage Luck. Directed by: Richard Compton. Airdate: December 9, 1994.

The M.A.N.T.I.S. unintentionally travels three decades into the future during an experiment on the Chrysalid. He is horrified to discover that Port Columbia is a totalitarian state run by a tyrannical computer.

GUEST CAST: Malachi Throne, Chris Barnes, Robert Bauer, A.J. Unger.

15. "Faces in the Mask" Written by: Coleman Luck. Story by: Scott Curtis and Coleman Luck. Directed by: Neill Fearnley. Airdate: December 16, 1994.

A cunning master of disguise is on the loose in Port Columbia and committing murders. Lt. Maxwell seeks the help of M.A.N.T.I.S. in tracking the killer and putting the wily, mysterious figure behind bars.

GUEST CAST: Peter Frechette, Morris Panych, Paul Hubbard, John Novak, Garry Chalk.

16. "The Sea Wasp" Written by: Paris Qualles. Directed by: John Nicolella. Airdate: January 6, 1995.

An obsessed female scientist hopes to improve the nature of man by making him capable of surviving underwater (and breathing in water environments). Unfortunately, she's interested in Hawkins for her experiments, and with pheromones attempts to seduce him into cooperating.

GUEST CAST: Cec Verrell, Alac Mapa, Derek Webster, Noah Heney, Judith Maxey.

17. "Progenitor" Written by: Bryce Zabel. Directed by: Mario Azzopardi. Airdate: January 20, 1995.

A renegade clone desperate to survive believes that Hawkins Industries may hold the key to prolonging life. Hawkins is abducted and cloned, and a switch is made; but will the truth be discovered before it is too late?

GUEST CAST: Malcolm Stewart, Spencer Garrett, Mark High, Vincent Schiavelli, Dean Wray.

18. "Switches" Written by: Coleman Luck and Carel Gage Luck. Directed by: Neill Fearnley. Airdate: January 27, 1995.

A convicted criminal is executed by the state in the electric chair; but only after his termination does the real reign of terror begin. Somehow, the killer's "aura" has been transferred into Port Columbia's complex electrical power grid, and the criminal is able to strike out at victims everywhere. When the criminal-turned-energy-form begins to pursue people involved with his arrest, the M.A.N.T.I.S. knows that Maxwell will be the next victim.

GUEST CAST: Stephen McHattie, Alex Hyde-White, James Gleason, Gary Graham, Benjamin Ratner, Gabrielle Miller, Tracy Waterhouse.

19. "The Delusionist" Written by: Coleman Luck, III. Directed by: Tucker Gates. Airdate: February 10, 1995.

The high school students of Port Columbia are targeted by a strange magician with psychological issues. Using hypnotic glasses, the magician is able to spark the dark, violent impulses in those who see him perform, and one of those unlucky kids happens to be Maxwell's sister.

GUEST CAST: Luca Bercovici, Samaria Graham, Garry Chalk, Frank Cassini, Jason Gray-Stanford, Christopher Bickford, Jackson Cole, Jude Lee.

20. "Fast Forward" Written by: David Kemper. Directed by: Cliff Bole. Airdate: February 17, 1995.

A criminal with a hyper-metabolism (rendering him invisible to the eye and incredibly fast) threatens Port Columbia. He wants revenge for the death of his wife, and M.A.N.T.I.S. must stop a madman who is quicker than the eye.

GUEST CAST: Curtis Armstrong; Raye Birk; Gary Graham; Terry David Mulligan (Police Chief); Michele Goodger (Rona).

21. "Spider in the Tower" Written by: Coleman Luck and Coleman Luck III. Directed by: Kim Manners. Airdate: March 3, 1995.

Those evil invaders from another dimension are back, and this time they take over Port Columbia. Their next mission: kill the fly in their ointment — M.A.N.T.I.S.!

GUEST CAST: Mark Sheppard; Duane Davis; Blu Mankuma; Garry Chalk; Philip Hayes; Andrew Kavadas; Harrison Coe; Hrothgar Mathews; Robert Hooks (Mayor Mitchell); Gary Graham.

22. "Ancestral Evil" Written by: Paris Qualles and Brad Markowitz. Directed by: Cliff Bole. Airdate: unaired.

The M.A.N.T.I.S. battles another deadly foe, this one from the past.

GUEST CAST: John Saint Ryan, Kathryn Cressida, Ron Suave, Gregory Smith, Susan Heynes.

23. "Ghosts of the Ice" Written by: David Kemper. Directed by: Kim Manners. Airdate: unaired.

The M.A.N.T.I.S. faces his last adventure in a life or death struggle with an unusual opponent.

GUEST CAST: M.C. Gainey.

Martian Manhunter

DC Comics introduced J'Onn J'Onzz in *Detective Comics* in the mid–1950s, an inscrutable Martian character who had been transported to Earth during a strange experiment. Unable to return home, the enigmatic J'Onn J'Onzz used his alien abilities (and logic) to solve crimes, becoming the powerful hero known as Martian Manhunter. In some ways, the character was a metaphor for the industrious foreigner making good in the United States while still maintaining an "individual" identity relative to his homeland and culture. He was, essentially, a Martian Charlie Chan.

J'Onn J'Onzz has appeared twice on television. Played by an embarrassed-looking David Ogden Stiers, Martian Manhunter appeared in an unaired live-action *Justice League of America* pilot in 1997. The character reappeared, more successfully, in the 2001 animated series *Justice League of America*, which aired on the Cartoon Network.

The character's origin was changed slightly for this updated re-do. Now J'Onn J'Onzz was a refugee from Mars, the last survivor from his planet, and his first mission was to protect Earth from the invading alien "hive" Imperium that had destroyed his culture of origin.

Martian Manhunter *see also* **The Justice League of America**

The Mask

"Smokin'!"

That was the catchphrase of choice for loser-turned-superhero Stanley Ipkiss (Jim Carrey) in the 1994 box office blockbuster from New Line Cinema, *The Mask*. The film's ad-line expressed the story just as well as Stanley's exclamation: "From Zero to Hero." Audiences grooved to this superhero adventure to the tune of $115 million at the box office, and Carrey (who had hit it big with *Ace Ventura: Pet Detective* [1993]) was reportedly contracted for a sequel and guaranteed a $20-million paycheck.

Based on a Dark Horse comic created by Randy Stradley and Mike Richard, the Mask (originally "the Masque") was a superhero with a difference. An ancient artifact — a mask, naturally — turned any wearer into a crazed, super-powerful, nearly invincible character. In the comics, the Mask was actually a rather dark, tumultuous character not always on the side of angels because (like the One Ring in *Lord of the Rings*) the mask could "corrupt" the owner after a time. The movie version of the mythos adopted a more Freudian approach: the ancient mask, a representation of Loki, God of Mischief, merely released the hidden urges and desires of its wearer, making for a Jekyll-and-Hyde-style transformation in its owner.

For wearer Ipkiss (Jim Carrey), who loved Tex Avery cartoons, this meant a descent into a cartoon-like existence in which his heart could literally beat out of his chest. Or his tongue would dart out of his mouth and roll to the floor like a carpet, and his arms could stretch to become rubbery extensions of himself. "We all wear masks, metaphorically," Ipkiss's psychiatrist informed him in the film, and for the meek loser that meant one thing: "With these powers ... I could be a superhero!"

The Mask remains an important superhero film because it represents the advent of C.G.I. (computer generated imagery) in film as a means of depicting heroes and their abilities. The computer technology was put to good use here, as Stanley's eyes bugged out of his head, machine guns (and long strands of over-sized ammo) extended from his arms, and other cartoonish accoutrements (like a giant mallet) sprang to life without having to look fully realistic or three-dimensional.

Other aspects of the film were impressive. Cameron Diaz made for a beautiful object-of-desire; Carrey's gung-ho performance proved highly entertaining, and Milo the Dog, an engaging canine sidekick, was the movie's real special effect. If there was any downside to the film it was that the villain, a small-time thug named Dorian (Peter Greene), hardly seemed a worthy opponent for the all-but-invincible Mask, who, in the picture's most entertaining scene, engaged a police squad in a ridiculous rumba.

Psychologically speaking, *The Mask* proved interesting for the manner in which it painted the dual nature of superheroes. Ipkiss was not merely mild-mannered in the tradition of Clark Kent, he was downright wimpy, a lame loser of a guy (but with a good heart). As the Mask, however, he was a walking, talking amalgamation of all of Stanley's inner dreams and pop culture fantasies. He could dance, fight, sing and crack a joke with the best of them. The Mask represented superhero as total wish fulfillment, and it was an intriguing take on the material.

The Mask was so successful that CBS produced an animated series based on the film in 1995. Created by Film Roman, Inc., who also produced *The Simpsons*, *Family Guy* and *The Critic*, the half-hour series ran for two seasons on Saturday mornings, lasting 24 episodes. The cartoon followed the same pattern as the film, but with Rob Paulsen, not Carrey, providing Stanley's voice. The villain was a mad scientist named Pretorious, voiced by *The Shadow*'s Tim Curry. Around the same time, New Line released a video game of *The Mask*, and just recently a sequel, *Son of the Mask* has been announced. Jamie Kennedy has been cast as Carrey's successor.

The Mask (1994)
LIVE-ACTION FILM

"I don't know what percentage of the film's 102 minutes is taken up by these cartoon sequences, but the moments are golden. Whether Stanley is eluding police, by putting a spell on them ... or taunting the mob with his plastic invulnerability, the screen is a colorful blur of happy surprises."
— Jack Mathews, *Newsday*,
July 29, 1994, page B2.

"This is probably still Jim Carrey's best film. It had some of the heart that *Roger Rabbit* tried to have — it would have been amazing to think of this film as directed by Joe Dante. When compared to something like DC Comics' Green Lantern character, where a foreign objects gives one special powers, the best thing about *The Mask* is it does more than give you powers — it changes your personality. The Jekyll and Hyde aspect of the character alone makes it interesting.
— William Latham, author of *Mary's Monster* and *Space: 1999 Resurrection*.

"This film is so much fun to watch."
— Arianna Pavia Rosati, *The Village Voice*,
August 9, 1994, page 48.

CAST: Jim Carrey (Stanley Ipkiss); Peter Riegert (Lt. Kellaway); Peter Greene (Dorian Tyrell); Amy Yasbeck (Peggy Brandt); Richard Jeni (Charlie); Orestes Mataceno (Niko); Tim Bagley (Irv); Nancy Fish (Ms. Peenman); Johnny Williams (Burt); Reginald E. Cathey (Freeze); Jim Doyghan (Dovie); Denis Forest (Sweet Eddie); Cameron Diaz (Tina Carlyle); Ben Stein (Dr. Arthur Newman); Max (Milo the Dog).

CREW: New Line Productions, in Association with Dark Horse Entertainment, Present a Charles Russell Film, *The Mask*. *Casting:* Fern Champion, Mark Paladini. *Music Supervisor:* Bonnie Greenberg. *Choreographer:* Jerry Evans. *Special Make-up Created by:* Greg Cannon. *Visual Effects Consultants:* Ken Ralston, Scott Squires, Steve "Spaz" Williams. *Costume De-*

signer: Ha Nguyen. *Music:* Randy Edelman. *Film Editor:* Arthur Coburn. *Production Designer:* Craig Stearns. *Director of Photography:* John R. Leonetti. *Associate Producer:* Carla Fry. *Executive Producers:* Mike Richardson, Charles Russell, Michael de Luca. *Story:* Michael Fallon, Mark Verheiden. *Screenplay:* Mike Werb. *Produced by:* Bob Engelman. *Directed by:* Charles Russell. *M.P.A.A. Rating:* PG-13. *Running time:* 101 minutes.

A loveable loser, Stanley Ipkiss, works at Edge City Bank and unwittingly becomes a pawn in a criminal plot to rob the establishment when he meets and falls for a lovely blond woman, Tina Carlyle. After a terrible night out club hopping, Stanley finds a strange mask that has floated up from the bottom of the sea. The mask, a fourth-century Scandinavian relic and representation of Loki, the Norse god of mischief, imbues him with incredible super powers. More to the point, it brings out his innermost desires, pulling from his psyche a superhero called "the Mask" that is based on his love of Tex Avery cartoons.

Imbued with confidence while wearing the mask, Stanley puts the fear of God into his evil landlady, then goes to a club,

Coco Bongo, to woo Tina, a singer there. Unfortunately, Tina is involved with Dorian Tyrell, a small-time crook whose gang plans to rob the bank. The Mask beats them to the punch, and Dorian attempts to kill the strange, cartoon-like hero. The police also close in on Stanley, certain that he robbed Edge City Bank.

When cornered by cops, the Mask dances an infectious rumba and flees the scene with reporter Peggy Brandt, only to learn she is working for Dorian. Tyrell steals the mask from Stanley, becoming a super-powered villain. The police, led by Lt. Kellaway, capture Stanley, but his highly intelligent dog, Milo, springs him. Together, Milo and Stanley attempt to regain possession of the mask at a charity ball that Dorian attacks.

Unfortunately, Dorian has captured Tina and is planning to destroy her, the Coco Bongo, and the mayor with a bomb. Before long, it's the Mask to the rescue, but not before the mask changes hands (and faces) several times. One of the wearers is even Milo, the dog.

The Mask: The Animated Series (1995–1997)
ANIMATED SERIES

VOICE TALENT: Rob Paulsen (Stanley Ipkiss); Jim Cummings (Doyle/Lars); Tim Curry (Pretorious); Tress MacNeille (Mrs. Peenan); Neil Ross (Lt. Kellaway); Hedi Shannon (Peggy Brandt); Charlie Schumacher (Mark Taylor); Frank Welker (Milo).

CREDITS: A Sunbow Entertainment Production with New Line Television and Film Roman, Inc. CBS.

The Meteor Man

African-American moviemaker Robert Townsend burst onto the film scene in 1987 with his self-financed, sharply satiric comedy concerning the black image in Tinsel Town, *Hollywood Shuffle*. The film was an unexpected hit, costing only $100,000 and earning more than twenty million at the box

office. In 1994 the 36-year-old actor/director brought the same sense of humor and razor-sharp wit to a much more expensive project: a 20-million-dollar superhero movie, a real labor of love called *The Meteor Man*.

A devoted fan of *Batman, Superman,*

Spiderman and *The Fantastic Four*, Townsend carefully created his own superhero myth, a comedic but good hearted one that stressed the importance of community activism.[1] He described his hero, meek and mild teacher Jefferson Reed in this way:

> He's a real hero who starts out as a regular guy who doesn't care. But once he makes the turn and sees all the little eyes watching: Whoa![2]

The Meteor Man is a genuine anomaly because, like Damon Wayan's *Blankman*, it was conceived when more mainstream (and high profile) superhero films were taking an opposite route, going for the dark and disturbing. Instead, the story of Reed, a man endowed with superpowers when a glowing green meteor strikes him, spotlighted and championed the good in human nature. "How can you complain when you do nothing?" one character asks pointedly in the film. And, in truth, Jefferson Reed becomes a real hero (not a super one) "after he has lost his super powers and looked inside himself," rallying the people in his community against villain Frank Gorshin (*Batman*'s the Riddler) and the nefarious gang called the Golden Lords.[3]

"There are more people in the community than there are gang members," Townsend commented in one interview, and his film becomes a powerful voice for activism, for standing up to crime — strength in numbers and struggling for a common goal.[4] In exploring these noble principles, *The Meteor Man* is quite successful. It may not be slick or epic, but it is, in its own funny way, quite touching. It's less blunt and sarcastic than *Blankman*, for instance, and a solid family film.

The Meteor Man, like *Captain Nice* or *The Greatest American Hero* before it, is about a regular Joe unexpectedly endowed

with great powers, but who uses them to comedic effect. For instance, Reed can absorb the full contents of any book simply by touching it, yet can't hold the knowledge for more than 30 seconds. At the end of the film, he flies through a Bookmobile — with amusing results, having absorbed knowledge about runway modeling, of all things.

Instead of Superman's X-ray vision, Reed develops the power to see through walls — and clothes (but, importantly, not underwear, thus carefully maintaining a family-friendly atmosphere).

The best joke in the film, however, involves the vaunted power of flight. Jefferson Reed is, you see, deathly afraid of heights. So when he flies patrol through the neighborhood, he does so at a height of about three feet. It's a great (and hilarious) image to see a costumed superhero hovering barely off the ground, looking down as he surveys his neighborhood (near Washington D.C.). At that height, he couldn't be seeing much other than asphalt.

All these jokes work well, and Robert Townsend assembled a great cast for the film, including Bill Cosby (as another "meteor man," who talks to animals), James Earl Jones, Robert Guillaume, Eddie Griffin, LaWanda Page, Marla Gibbs, Don Cheadle, and Sinbad. The only place the film falters is in an overlong, drawn-out climax.

Though *The Meteor Man* garnered raves from early preview screenings, it received only mediocre reviews on general release, and never found a substantial audience. That noted, it is a refreshingly funny movie that doesn't resort to camp for its humor. Like *Blankman*, there was genuine love of the superhero genre operating behind the scenes, and for those who enjoy the clichés and tropes of the genre, this will be a welcome, if mild, treat.

The Meteor Man (1993)
LIVE-ACTION FILM

"Despite its high-flown intentions, most of *The Meteor Man* comes across like a fairly clunky sitcom inflated with sequences of righteous do-goodism."
— Peter Rainer, *Los Angeles Times*, August 6, 1993, page 10.

"A clever spoof that shows the problems confronting a friendly, neighborhood superhero."
— Lawrence Cohn, *The New York Post*, August 6, 1993, page 27.

"A surprisingly funny movie ... [that] promotes individual responsibility, civic pride, and, well, a lot of other stuff."
— Regina Raiford, *The Village Voice*, August 24, 1993 page 64.

CAST: Robert Townsend (Jefferson Reed/ the Meteor Man); Marla Gibbs (Mrs. Reed); Eddie Griffin (Mike Anderson); Robert Guillaume (Mr. Reed); James Earl Jones (Mr. Moses); Roy Fegan (Simon); Cynthia Belgrave (Mrs. Harris); Marilyn Coleman (Mrs. Walker); Don Cheadle (Goldilocks); Bobby McGee (Uzi); Tiny Lister (Digit); Jenifer Lewis (Mrs. Williams); Stephanie Williams (Stacy); Frank Gorshin (Mr. Byers); Beverly Johnson (Woman Doctor); La Wanda Page (Old Nurse); Sinbad (Maliq/Bernard); Nancy Wilson (Ms. Laws); Luthor Vandross (Jamison); Bill Cosby (Marvin); Jonathan Witherspoon (Clarence James Carter III); Tommy R. Hicks (Officer Peterson); Sam Jackson (Dre). WITH SPECIAL APPEARANCES BY: Naughty by Nature, Cypress Hill, Biz Markle.

CREW: MGM Presents a Tinsel Townsend Production, a film by Robert Townsend, *The Meteor Man*. *Casting:* Eileen Mack Knight. *Costumes:* Ruth Carter. *Music:* Cliff Eidelman. *Film Editors:* Adam Bernardi, Richard Candib, Andrew London, Pam Wise. *Production Design:* Toby Corbett. *Director of Photography:* John A. Alonzo. *Produced by:* Loretha C. Jones. *Written and Directed by:* Robert Townsend. *Stunt Coordinator:* Jeff Ward. *M.P.A.A. Rating:* PG. *Running time:* 97 minutes.

In Washington, D.C., mild-mannered substitute teacher Jefferson Reed lives in the crime-plagued Castle Hills community, but is unwilling to take a stand against the ruling gang, "the Golden Lords." One night, after being chased by the Lords, Reed ends up in a dumpster and then an alley, where a falling meteor strikes him down. Knocked unconscious and taken to the hospital for burns, Reed is unaware that a homeless man in the neighborhood, Marvin, has also been affected by the green meteorite.

While recuperating in the hospital, Reed heals quickly and develops strange powers. He can see through clothes and even learn the entire text of a book just by touching it. When the Golden Lords attack his father, Reed develops super strengths and fights the villains, also demonstrating resilience to bullets and fisticuffs. Excited, his Mom works on a costume to make Reed into a superhero ... the Meteor Man! A meteor phone is installed in his apartment, though Reed is none too sure he wants to be a hero.

After crooks beat up an innocent old woman, Reed decides it is time to act, and accepts his role of superhero. He cleans up a crack house, brokers a peace between warring gangs and the police, and miraculously creates a park in the midst of the inner city community. Unfortunately, the crime lord behind the Golden Lords, Mr. Byers, wants Meteor Man dead for interfering in his business, and sends the villainous gang leader, Simon, to kill him. Worse, the Meteor Man is beginning to lose his powers.

With the Meteor Man off the streets, the Golden Lords run amuck, looting and defacing the community. Without his powers, Jefferson stands up to Simon, and the citizens (including the super-powered Marvin) rise to stand with him and kick the criminals out.

The Mighty Thor

The superheroes of the twentieth century are often reflections of old cultural myths or tales, but the Mighty Thor is different. Thor *is* actually a Norse/ Viking myth, but one updated for the comics by those geniuses at Marvel — Stan Lee, Jack Kirby and Larry Lieber. The Mighty Thor emerged in comic book form in 1962, but it was not until 1966 that the arrogant, god character was published under his own name, *The Mighty Thor*.

In the comics, a meek character named Donald Blake discovered the Hammer of Thor in Scandinavia, which transformed him into the powerful god-being. He grew long blond hair, wore a bullet-shaped helmet (with wings adorning both sides), and adopted a Middle English, painfully formal style of speech. In the comics, he battled the god of mischief, Loki, and other villains from Norse mythology.

Like many other Marvel superheroes before the "renaissance and superheroes triumphant" phase of the early twenty-first century, Thor has had little success in film and television. In 1967, *The Mighty Thor* was one segment of the popular but woefully low-budget *Marvel Super Heroes* syndicated series created by Grantray Lawrence Animation. This effort (which also featured the adventures of Sub-Mariner, the Incredible Hulk, and Captain America), was so cheap it looked as though frames of the comic books had actually been filmed, one at a time.

In the late 1980s, Thor became a live-action superhero for the first time. He appeared in the first of a series of reunion TV-movies for the 1970s Kenneth Johnson series *The Incredible Hulk*. The project was entitled *The Incredible Hulk Returns*, and was written and directed by Nicholas Corea.

The show aired in May of 1988 and featured actor Eric Kramer as Thor. The story involved David Banner (Bill Bixby) and his attempts to vanquish the Hulk, as well as his discovery that an old friend could summon the ancient and powerful Norse god, Thor. There was the inevitable clash between Thor and the Hulk, but the TV movie presented a ridiculous persona for the dignified, mighty Thor. On TV, he looked like a burly Fabio-esque body builder in a Halloween costume.

Though intended as a back-door pilot for a Thor TV show, *The Incredible Hulk Returns* did not sire a series for the Norse god, who has remained in superhero Valhalla ever since. Before settling on Spidey, director Sam Raimi once worked with Stan Lee on a proposed *Thor* feature but it did not come to pass.

The Mighty Thor *see also* The Incredible Hulk

Misfits of Science

Imagine *The Fantastic Four* doing shtick. Or *X-Men*, if they weren't persecuted by humans and oh-so-grim. Those may sound like unlikely possibilities, but in the fall of 1985, NBC Television, under the auspices of the late Brandon Tartikoff, brought to the airwaves a unique superhero series called *Misfits of Science*. It was a "team" superhero show (not unlike *Mutant X*), except that it was a lark and not to be taken seriously. "Our characters are much like the Fantastic Four — we're crime fighters, out to make what's weird right," noted series star Kevin Peter Hall of the unusual, quasi-serious format.[1]

Misfits of Science concerned a team of

three mutants, but they were not called mutants on the TV series. They were called "misfits," because they each possessed unusual powers and abilities that came about from a specific incident. Long before *Friends* (1995–2004) or the *Scream* trilogy (1996–1999), Courteney Cox starred in the program as one of these misfits, Gloria, a volatile young woman from the wrong side of the tracks that possessed ESP and telekinetic abilities. She was teamed with the very tall (seven feet, four inches) Kevin Peter Hall (*Predator* [1987], *Harry and the Hendersons* [1987]) as Dr. Elvin Lincoln, a giant of a man who could shrink down to the size of nine inches thanks to a special serum.

The last misfit of the bunch was actor Mark Thomas Miller as Johnny B., a rock-and-roller and all around troublemaker who could harness the power of electricity as a directed weapon, like Mulwray on *Mutant X*. He gained the power during an accident at a concert.

Together, these misfits honed their skills under the tutelage of an understanding "normal" human, Dr. Billy Hayes (the late Dean Paul Martin), at an organization called Humanidyne Research, run by *ALF*'s Max Wright.

Often times, the unusual group had to adopt a particular mission to protect an unwitting populace. During the course of the series, the group sought to prevent a museum robbery ("Sort of Looking for Gina"), discovered a long lost treasure ("Your Place or Mayan"), prevented international espionage ("Fumble on the One"), stopped the release of a deadly plague ("Grand Theft Bunny") and smashed a racketeering ring ("The Avenging Angel"). On one notable occasion, the team even went up against super-powered old folks ("Steer Crazy").

Though peppered with interesting guest spots, from the likes of Ray Walston, June Allyson, the ubiquitous Sid Haig, James Sloyan, John Schuck and others, *Misfits of Science* had a difficult time finding an audience on Friday nights at 9:00 P.M. The problem was the competition: the show went head-to-head with the CBS powerhouse soap opera *Dallas* and the ABC family-friendly sitcom *Webster*. Critics were also especially unkind, labeling *Misfits of Science* one of the worst shows of the season, if not TV history.

"It was one of those shows you either loved or hated; like *Manimal*," Courtney Cox noted in an interview with *Starlog* magazine. "It was a funny show with a lot of shtick…. There were many subtle adult things you could miss if you didn't look quickly."[2] Audience members generally disagreed with that assessment, and the series folded after airing fifteen of its sixteen hour-long episodes.

Interestingly, *Misfits of Science* is the first live-action superhero team series to make it to the airwaves. *Mutant X* did not arrive until 2001, *Birds of Prey* in 2002; and the unlucky *Fantastic Four* have never been lucky enough to merit their own series.

Misfits of Science (1985-86)
LIVE-ACTION SERIES

"Rank this one down there with *Manimal, Supertrain* and further failing examples of Jarvis' First Law: Even stupid shows should exhibit an IQ higher than the number of the channel on which they appear."
    — Jeff Jarvis, *People Weekly:* "Misfits of Science," October 21, 1985, page 7.

CAST: Dean Paul Martin (Dr. Billy Hayes); Kevin Peter Hall (Dr. Elvin Lincoln); Mark Thomas Miller (Johnny B.); Courteney Cox (Gloria Dinallo); Jennifer Holmes (Jane Miller); Max Wright (Stetmeyer); Diane Civita (Ms. Nance).

CREW: *Created by:* James D. Parriott. *Produced by:* Dean Zanetos. *Theme:* Basil Poledouris.

1. "Misfits of Science" (a.k.a. Deep Freeze; two hours) Written and directed by: James A. Parriott. Airdate: October 4, 1985.

At Humanidyne, Dr. Hayes and his associate, Dr. Lincoln, have been studying genetic mutants, or "misfits of science." Lincoln is one himself, able to shrink down to nine inches high. When a crisis arises needing the special abilities of mutants, Hayes and Lincoln recruit a team, including Johnny B, who can harness electricity and direct it out of his body, and Gloria, an incredibly powerful telekinetic.

GUEST CAST: Mickey Jones (The Iceman); Edward Winter (Dr. Strickland); Eric Christmas (Dr. Mamquist); Larry Linville (General Thiel); Kenneth Mars (Senator Donner); Bert Rosario (Gomez); Robert Starr (Stenker).

2. "Your Place or Mayan?" Written by: Donald Todd. Directed by: Alan J. Levi. Airdate: October 18, 1985.

When an archaeologist is killed, the Misfits of Science join forces with another oddity, a kid that can read and assimilate dead languages. This skill comes in handy when the Misfits go in search of a buried Mayan treasure, believed to be beneath Beverly Hills!

GUEST CAST: Dean Devlin (Angel); Nicholas Hormann (Stephen); Tony Acierto, Shane McCamey, Bob Larkin, Matthew Faison.

3. "Guess What's Coming to Dinner?" Written by: Morrie Ruvinsky. Directed by: Burt Brinkerhoff. Airdate: October 25, 1985.

A scientist believes that he has invented a device to help him communicate with aliens, and the Misfits investigate his claim. Unfortunately, the scientist has also been tagged by a skeptical Federal government.

GUEST CAST: James Sloyan (Harry); Gary Riley, Janice Kent, Tom Bower, Ashley McLean, John Zarchn, Michael Crabtree.

4. "Lost Link" Written by: Mark Jones. Directed by: Christopher Leitch. Airdate: November 1, 1985.

The Misfits come to the aid of a primitive island man who has traveled across the globe to attend the launching of a special rocket. It turns out he has something important — something personal — to contribute to the launch.

GUEST CAST: Jesse Dixon (Link); Allan Rich (Jomak); Stephanie Faulkner (Deanna); Billy Green Bush, Branscombe Richmond, Allan Graf, Leslie Morris.

5. "Sort of Looking for Gina" Written by: Michael Cassutt, James D. Parriott and Morrie Ruvinsky. Directed by: Jeffrrey Hayden. Airdate: November 8, 1985.

Johnny becomes enamored of a mysterious and elusive woman, leading the Misfits on a strange quest to find her. Unfortunately, the quest leads right to a crime: a museum robbery!

GUEST CAST: Rhonda Aldrich (Gina); Michael Halsey (Buckner); Gregory Martin, Christopher Murray.

6. "Sonar ... and Yet So Far" Written by: Donald Todd. Directed by: Burt Brinkerhoff. Airdate: November 15, 1985.

A slightly flaky scientist has gone Dr. Dolittle one better and claims he can talk to a dolphin. This makes the scientist a target for criminals who believe the dolphin can help them find sunken loot.

GUEST CAST: Gary Frank (Eddie); Sondra Currie, Robert Donavan, J. Michael Flynn, Jorge Cervera, Jr.

7. "Steer Crazy" Written by: James D. Parriott. Directed by: John Tracy. Airdate: November 29, 1985.

A radioactive meteor wreaks havoc when it affects cows, the primary ingredient in hamburgers, and the contaminated protein is ingested by a trio of disgruntled senior citizens. Endowed with super powers, the senior brigade plots mischief, at least until the Misfits arrive on the scene.

GUEST CAST: Ray Walston (Barney); June Allyson (Bessie); Dan Lauria, Dennis Stewart, David Selburg.

8. "Fumble on the One" Written by: Blaze Forrester. Directed by: Bob Sweeney. Airdate: December 6, 1985.

The Misfits meet up with a cyborg secret agent in France and become involved in his quest to regain possession of a top-secret briefcase that contains the triggering codes for the United States' nuclear warheads. But tracking the stolen item, and dealing with the part-artificial man, are no easy tasks.

GUEST CAST: Dale Robinette, Greta Blackburn, Sid Haig, Tige Andrews, Clement St. George.

9. "Twin Engines" Written by: Donald Todd and R. Timothy King. Directed by: Burt Brinkerhoff. Airdate: December 13, 1985.

Johnny's mechanic, Lonnie, experiences weird psychic flashes that involve a heretofore-unknown identical twin, and a plan to build a gas-efficient motorcycle engine.

GUEST CAST: Joel Polis; Joan Sweeney (Didi); Paul Koslo, Warren Munson, Roy Firestone, James Hornbeck, Joe Cala.

10. "Grand Theft Bunny" Written by: Pamela Norris. Directed by: Michael Switzer. Airdate: December 27, 1985.

Dr. Hayes and the Misfits take up what they think is a good cause when they attempt to free animals from an experimental lab. Unfortunately, some of the animals are carrying a designer plague that could wipe out mankind.

GUEST CAST: Robin Riker (Sarah); Robin Thomas (Vincent); Michael McGuire, Jordan Charney, Mark Hutter, Colin Hamilton.

11. "Grand Elusion" Written by: Morrie Ruvinsky. Directed by: Bernard McEveety. Airdate: January 10, 1986.

A Misfit magic show is the cover for a secret plot to help a Soviet agent defect to the United States and rejoin his daughter.

GUEST CAST: James Laurenson (Nikolai); Christy Houser; John Schuck (Gallinkov); Tom Dahlgren; Patricia Wilson; Andrew Divoff (Guard).

12. "Once Upon a Night" Written by: M.M. Shelby-Moore and Linda Campanelli. Directed by: Barbara Peters. Airdate: January 17, 1986.

A friend of Gloria's has gotten herself into deep trouble. She's stolen the royal jewels from a foreign kingdom, and agents are hot on her trail. Worse, Johnny has a crush on her.

GUEST CAST: Elaine Wilkes, Andrew Masset, Robert Alan Browne, Joseph Brutsman.

13. "Center of Attention" Written by: Sara Parriott. Directed by: Burt Brinckerhoff. Airdate: January 31, 1986.

Because of his status as a giant (who can shrink himself), Dr. Lincoln has always harbored the dream of being a professional basketball player. When he learns of a plot to fix games, Lincoln goes undercover in just such a capacity, with help from Gloria's formidable powers of telekinesis.

GUEST CAST: Wolfe Perry, Warren Berlinger, Barry Sattels, Liam Sullivan, Paul McCracken.

14. "Against All Oz" Written by: Morrie Ruvinsky. Directed by: Michael Switzer. Airdate: February 7, 1986.

Dr. Hayes experiences a weird phantasm while trying to set a world record for staying awake. But have the Misfits all really changed powers, jobs and character, or is he just sleep-deprived?

GUEST CAST: Patricia Wilson (Ms. Willis).

15. "The Avenging Angel" Written by: Daniel De Stefano. Directed by: Bernard McEveety. Airdate: February 21, 1986.

Gloria's powers of telekinesis again help a would-be athlete, but this time they give a wrestler the confidence he needs to fight criminals running a racket on him.

GUEST CAST: Vic Polizos, Jack Armstrong, Jimmy Lydon, Ivy Bethune, Dave Shelley, Wolf Muser, Patricia Wilson, Tim Patterson.

16. "Three Days of the Blender" Written by: Donald Todd. Directed by: Michael Switzer. Airdate: unaired.

Hayes is arrested and incarcerated by the United States government on charges of espionage, but it's all a big misunderstanding. Now the Misfits need to prove it.

GUEST CAST: Joe Dorsey, Douglas Warhit, Greg Lewis, Meg Wylie, Gordon Clark.

Mr. Terrific

What the heck is *Mr. Terrific*? That's a good question. The short answer is that it is the TV show most often mistaken for *Captain Nice*. This is the *other* show that was inspired by *Batman*. It premiered in the winter of 1967 and aired on the same night (Monday) as *Captain Nice*, but was quickly cancelled. *Mr. Terrific* was the one that starred Stephen Strimpell, not William Daniels. *Mr. Terrific* was the series *not* created by Buck Henry.

Mr. Terrific was the story of Stanley Beamish (Strimpell), a gas station attendant who worked for the government and the Bureau of Secret Projects. He could turn into a superhero simply by popping a "power pill" of unusual chemistry, but there was a drawback: The pill would only work for one hour before he returned to his mild-mannered self. Booster pills might give him an extra half-hour, but often that was not enough.

When endowed with super powers, Beamish (as Mr. Terrific) would flap his arms and fly all about in a silver costume adorned with curved wings. Unlike Captain Nice, Mr. Terrific wore a mask, one that very much resembled the Boy Wonder's.

Barton J. Reed (John McGiver)

was Beamish's contact at the Bureau, a man forever annoyed by the fact that Beamish seemingly had attention deficit disorder and would forget what time his powers ran out. Unfortunately for Reed (and often for Beamish), Stanley was the only person who could take the power pills without getting

It's a bird! It's a plane! It's a guy in a cheap silver suit! It's that pill-popping superhero, *Mr. Terrific* (Stephen Strimpell).

sick, which made him such a valuable commodity to the United States government. Hal Walters (Dick Gautier) was Beamish's clueless friend at the gas station.

Mr. Terrific is rarely, if ever, rerun, not merely because there are very few episodes for syndication, but because the series' odd premise came under scrutiny in the late '60s and early '70s. Essentially, this is a show about a guy who pops pills and can then do "miraculous" things like fly or beat people

up. In the era of LSD and rampant drug use, authorities were afraid some hippies might take *Mr. Terrific* all too literally and decide to pop some power pills of their own and go flying.

Essentially a lark (and a lame one at that), *Mr. Terrific* was, unlike most superheroes, considered a dangerous role model to emulate. It was an ignominious fate for a trifle of a series.

Mr. Terrific (1967)
LIVE-ACTION SERIES

CAST: Stephen Strimpell (Stanley Beamish/ Mr. Terrific); John McGiver (Barton J. Reed); Dick Gautier (Hal Walters); Paul Smith (Harley Trent).

CREW: *Producer:* David O'Connell. *Music:* Gerald Fried.

1. "Matchless" Airdate: January 9, 1967.
2. "Mr. Big Curtsies Out" Airdate: January 16, 1967.
3. "I Can't Fly" Airdate: January 23, 1967.
4. "Stanley the Safecracker" Airdate: January 30, 1967.
5. "The Formula Is Stolen" Airdate: February 6, 1967.
6. "Stanley, the Fighter" Airdate: February 27, 1967.
7. "My Partner, the Jailbreaker" Airdate: March 6, 1967.

8. "Fly, Ballerina, Fly" Airdate: March 13, 1967.
9. "Harley and the Killer" Airdate: March 20, 1967.
10. "Stanley and the Mountaineers" Airdate: March 27, 1967.
11. "Has Mr. Terrific Sold Out?" Airdate: April 3, 1967.
12. "Stanley Goes to the Dentist" Airdate: April 10, 1967.
13. "Stanley the Track Star" Airdate: April 17, 1967.
14. "Try This One On for Spies" Airdate: April 24, 1967.
15. "Stanley Joins the Circus" Airdate: May 1, 1967.
16. "The Sultan Has Five Wives" Airdate: May 8, 1967.

Mutant X

Young mutants join together under the tutelage of a wise leader to save the world from villains amongst their own people and the bigoted human race. They deploy their strange mutant abilities to fight for good and justice, often using an advanced jet to fly into battle and jeopardy.

Now, does that premise resemble *X-*

Men? Hopefully you think not, because it is actually the format for the syndicated action drama called *Mutant X*, a troubled series from the combined talents at Marvel and Tribune, and one that has seen its share of strife in its short history.

All the trouble began in the year 2000 when 20th Century–Fox's *X-Men* made more money at the box office than anyone expected. It became a blockbuster, easily cracking $100 million, and reignited interest in superhero film and TV projects. Apparently realizing the appeal of their property, Marvel subsequently set out to create a TV series based on the franchise concept: a team of diverse mutants fighting evil. And so *Mutant X* was born.

"It's got great marquee value, and certainly it is an established brand," said Rick Ungar, president of Marvel Characters Group, of the proposed new series. "It's a spin-off in a sense, but it kind of takes it to the next level."[1]

Others, including local programmers, quickly saw the value in an *X-Men*–style TV series, and *Mutant X* was promptly booked into 146 markets, representing some 93 percent of viewing audiences in the United States.[2] Better yet, the series seemed well cast. John Shea, Lex Luthor on the first season of *Lois and Clark: The New Adventures of Superman*, was recruited to star as Adam Xero (later renamed Kane). His mission was to rally a team of young, model-like actors of great physical beauty, among them the stunning Victoria Pratt as the "feral" mutant Shalimar.

Fans of superheroes were hopeful because Howard Chaykin, who had worked wonders on CBS's short-lived *The Flash* in 1990, was hired as head writer and executive consultant. His input promised the series would be neither campy nor derivative.

The only entity unhappy about the new mutant series was 20th Century–Fox. Back in 1993, Marvel had sold the rights to *X-Men* to Fox and agreed not to produce a live-action version of the show without Fox's permission.[3] Executives at Fox perceived that *Mutant X* was precisely what Ungar had claimed in the above-quoted interview, an extension of the *X-Men* "brand name," and a "spin-off." So Fox sought an injunction to prevent production of the series. Marvel quickly counter-sued, claiming

that *Mutant X* had no direct relationship to *X-Men*, and that all the characters and their histories differed from those in the *X-Men* canon (a true statement).

The intellectual property suit was presented in court, but a Federal judge was not convinced of Fox's case and elected not to stop the premiere of *Mutant X*.[4] Still, the last word on the series has not been said by any means. In early 2002, a Federal appeals court reinstated Fox's unfair competition claim over *Mutant X*, against Tribune and Marvel, but at least filed no injunction against the series, permitting it to debut a second season.[5]

Sordid history aside, *Mutant X* did look an awful lot like *X-Men*, at least at first glance. On the new series, "new mutants" (rather than merely "mutants") were considered a terrible danger, and even discriminated against — a long-standing tenet of *X-Men*. "Normal people don't want superpowered freaks living next door," a character noted in one episode of *Mutant X*, establishing the notion of prejudice among the masses. In another episode ("Russian Roulette"), the kindly Adam taught a bigoted boy a powerful lesson about the real nature of mutants.

Another similarity between the Marvel franchises was mode of transportation. The heroes of *Mutant X* often raced from their mountain sanctuary in a technologically advanced jet called the Double-Helix, much like Xavier's crew plane. Characters were a problem as well. Adam, the elder statesman and wise man of the group, could have subbed for Xavier any day, except he was neither handicapped nor bald.

Even the gorgeous young mutants themselves were fairly familiar characters. Emma (Lauren Lee Smith) could have been Jane Grey, a gorgeous "esper" with burgeoning telepathic powers. Brennan Mulwray (Victor Webster) could shoot electricity from his hands — a substitute for the lightning and weather control ability of a character like Storm, and the "directed beam" weaponry of Cyclops. The beautiful Shalimar was a "feral," an animalistic fighter with the heart and temper (if not adamantium claws) of the similarly animal-like Wolverine.

But *Mutant X* had other problems to contend with besides its rather blatant similarity to *X-Men*. For one thing, it was a terribly repetitive show. Tom McCamus played the regular villain, Mason Eckhart, in the first season, wearing a get-up that made him look like a dead ringer for Andy Warhol. McCamus appeared in every episode of the initial sortie, seeking to destroy Mutant X but failing.

Each week Eckhart had a new "guest" assistant, usually one with mutant powers, and he would lash out at them for failure all the time, killing them or imprisoning them. This repetitive character was Sonya in "Russian Roulette," Karen Bell in "Fool for Love," Kendra in "In the Presence of Mine Enemies," Charlotte Cook in "Altered Ego," a mutant with extraordinary hearing in "Blood Ties," and so on, endlessly.

The writers were also fairly lazy about how they began each story. Far too many episodes (including "Lazarus Syndrome" and "Blood Ties") commenced in a glitzy nightclub as the new mutants tried to pick up dates, characters that would never be seen again. This not only made Shalimar, Brennan and the rest seem rather shallow, but it became boring after a bit.

And, then, of course, in the first season every single character had to have his or her own love story, usually a tragic one. Brennan fell in love with the mutant of the week, Ashley, in "Lit Fuse," and was seduced by the scorpion-like Lorna Templeton in "Deadly Desire." Jesse acquired a girlfriend in "In the Presence of Mine Enemies." Emma fell for a dangerous vampire/mutant in "Lazarus Syndrome." Shalimar fell in love with another feral in "Fool for Love" and then had a fling with an old

boyfriend in "Ex Marks the Spot." Even Adam found a love interest in "Whiter Shade of Pale." The result, again, was boredom.

The basic problem with *Mutant X* was that it revolved around gorgeous people in gorgeous clothes who were not particularly good actors. The repetitive stories and situations were fairly two-dimensional, and the similarity to *X-Men* did not make the series any more likable. That noted, the series featured a rousing theme song and nice opening montage, and the show greatly improved during its sophomore season. The boring, over-utilized Eckhart was ditched as a regular villain, and the new nemesis, Michael Easton's Gabriel Ashlocke, was seen only intermittently, giving the series the opportunity to breathe, to branch out and look at other mutant-related issues and complexities. Time travel ("Past as Prologue") and mythological monsters ("Whose Woods Are These?") were added to the mix early in the second season, with pleasing results.

Historically, *Mutant X* may well be remembered for imitating the slow-motion wire-work action scenes popularized by recent movies such as *The Matrix* (1999) and *Crouching Tiger, Hidden Dragon* (2000). The syndicated series featured an abundance of fights on wires, with spinning cameras, zooms, slow-motion photography, and extreme high and low angles. On *Mutant X,* combatants did not merely fall down, they backflipped through mid-air (courtesy of harnesses) and were propelled literally dozens of feet during fight scenes. The only downside to this rock 'em, sock 'em approach was that on many occasions (including a fight in the episode "Whiter Shade of Pale") observant viewers could detect little "points" in the new mutant gear where the wire was attached to under-clothing harnesses. This tended to ruin the impact of the effects.

Mutant X (2001–)
LIVE-ACTION SERIES

"The series started out slow. In the beginning, the villain sent out operatives every week trying to capture Mutant X, and that plot device basically made it resemble the *Power Rangers*. You send out a monster to destroy the heroes every week, and fail. But the show has improved. The action is good and the character relationships have grown stronger. The team's powers are evolving and so they are not doing the same thing every week. John Shea is cool as Adam. Even though he does not have super powers, he can go head-to-head with any one on the team, or the villain of the week."

—Howard Margolin, *host of Destinies: The Voice of Science Fiction.*

CAST: Forbes March (Jesse Kilmartin); Victoria Pratt (Shalimar Fox); Lauren Lee Smith (Emma de Lauro); Victor Webster (Brennan Mulwray); John Shea (Adam Xero/Adam Kane).

CREW: *Executive Consultant:* Howard Chaykin. *Based on a Concept Created by:* Avi Arad. *Senior Supervising Consultant:* Mark Lisson. *Senior Consultant:* David L. Newman. *Story Consultant:* Elizabeth Keyishian. *Production Designer:* Rocco Matteo. *Director of Photography:* Jim Westenbrink. *Costume Designer:* Laurie Drew. *Film Editors:* Richard Wells. *Casting:* Forrest and Forrest Casting. *Theme:* Lou Natale. *Music:* Lou Natale Music, Inc. *Executive Producers:* Avi Arad, Rick Ungar. *Co-Executive Producer:* Tony Thatcher. *Produced by:* Jamie Paul Rock.

SEASON ONE (2001-2002)

1. "Shock of the New" Written by: Howard Chaykin. Directed by: T.J. Scott. Airdate: October 6, 2001.

Adam Kane, the former chief biogeneticist at Genomex, sets out to help one hundred of his genetically enhanced children, called "new mutants," and has been recruiting many of them for an underground team called "Mutant X." One night, Jesse Kilmartin, a mutant that can alter his molecular structure, and Shalimar, a woman with the feral strength of a tiger, rescue Emma, a new mutant telepath, from the thugs of powerful Genomex executive Mason Eckhart. When Emma refuses to believe that she is a mutant, she escapes from Adam's care and runs into another free mutant, Brennan Mulwray, an elemental who can shoot lightning bolts from his hands. At the end of the day, Brennan is captured by Mason, necessitating a rescue by Mutant X.

GUEST CAST: Cedric Smith; Tom McCamus (Mason Eckhart); Douglas O'Keeffe. Sean Bell (Michael); Matthew MacFadzean (Tony); Kevin Hicks (Carter); Chuck Byrn (Ruby); Ingrid Hart (Allison).

2. "I Scream the Body Electric" Written by: Howard Chaykin. Directed by: Jon Cassar. Airdate: October 13, 2001.

Brennan is forced to give up Mutant X, inhibited from using his electricity-based powers by Eckhart's "governing" device. Mutant X is jeopardized unless new recruit Emma can accept her nature and come to the rescue. Mutant X regroups after Brennan is forced to reveal the location of a safehouse, and a new team comes together for the first time.

GUEST CAST: Douglas O'Keeffe (Thorne); Chuck Byrn, Ingrad Hart, Lorne Hunchuck.

3. "Russian Roulette" Written by: Elizabeth Keyishian. Directed by: Jon Cassar. Airdate: October 20, 2001.

A beautiful Russian agent named Sonya shoots Brennan with a KGB weapon that can neutralize and kill new mutants. Now Adam and the others must recover the weapon and halt a destruct sequence so they can reverse the effects of the blast and save Brennan's life. Working for Eckhart, the beautiful Russian agent goes after a mutant, Tina, who has been hidden in a Mutant X safehouse with a friendly family. But the same family has been betrayed by the son, Daniel, and Adam teaches the boy, a developing mutant, a lesson about bigotry. Posing as Daniel, Jesse infiltrates the Russian gang to learn the secret of the weapon.

GUEST CAST: Dylan Bierk; Tom McCamus (Mason Eckhart); Ross Hull, Alexander Pervaokov, Alison MacLeod.

4. "Fool for Love" Written by: David L. Newman. Directed by: T.J. Scott. Airdate: October 27, 2001.

Shalimar attempts to recruit a seductive new mutant named Donna before Eckhart's Gestapo, the G.S.A., captures her. But Donna is no ordinary mutant — she is feral, animalistic and dangerous; and she is trying to become human, courtesy of a new serum. Searching for Donna, Shalimar meets the inventor of the serum, a feral man named Richard Saunders who is an associate researcher at Genomex. Shalimar and Richard fall in love, but soon learn that the serum is fatal when Donna turns up dead.

GUEST CAST: Yannick Bisson; Claudia Besso; Tom McCamus (Mason Eckhart); Monique Ganderton (Donna); Jake Simons (Jack); Lauran Jordan (Bartender); Desmond Campbell (Bouncer); Troy Blundell (Drunken Guy).

5. "Kiloherz" Written by: David L. Newman. Directed by: Andrew Potter. Airdate: November 3, 2001.

A terrorist called "Kilohertz" strikes, and bitter enemies Genomex and Mutant X suspect he is a new mutant in need of training and help. Eckhart sends a new recruit with dangerous "freezing" powers after Kilohertz. Mutant X tracks the dangerous character, who can intercept broadcasts and scramble communications links. When Kilohertz gets near Mutant X, he disrupts the Sanctuary's comm system, exposing the group to a new danger.

GUEST CAST: Jim Thornburn (Kilohertz); Adam MacDonald, Sandi Stahlbrand, John Friesen.

6. "The Meaning of Death" Written by: Brad Falchuk. Directed by: Graeme Campbell. Airdate: November 10, 2001.

A deadly plague is killing new mutants, and Adam's Mutant X team tries to help, teaming with the death-obsessed Charles Marlow, who happens to be invulnerable to all contagions. Soon Emma and Jesse succumb to the plague, and Marlowe's DNA — and Genomex Laboratories — are the only hope for a cure.

GUEST CAST: Anthony Lemke, Kevin Jubinville, Gina Sorell, Sherry Hilliard, Christopher David.

7. "Lit Fuse" Written by: Elizabeth Keyishian, David L. Newman. Story by: Tom Fudge. Directed by: John Bell. Airdate: November 17, 2001.

Everyone in the city, from Mutant X to Genomex, is after a developing new mutant, an elemental named Ashley who can drain power from electric power plants in a matter of seconds. Eckhart has hired a bounty hunter named Neil Cross to track her, and Brennan finds himself becoming attracted to Ashley because of their "shared mutantcy," an intense electromagnetic pull. Ashley enlists Brennan's help in rescuing her fiancé, Eric, who has actually betrayed her to Cross. Refusing to believe her boyfriend is in league with Cross, Ashley absorbs Brennan, stealing his powers and trapping his corporeal form.

GUEST CAST: Cordon Currie (Cross); Moya O'Connell (Ashley); Mark Lutz (Eric); Tom McCamus (Mason Eckhart); Reuben Thompson (Henshaw).

8. "In the Presence of Mine Enemies" Written by: Howard Chaykin. Directed by: John Bell. Airdate: November 24, 2001.

The Mutant X team runs simulations to breach Eckhart's tight security, but with disappointing results. Meanwhile, Eckhart is exposed on the news by cybercaster Proxy Blue. Angry, Eckhart sets out to subvert or destroy the "cartoon" news anchor, and control the news. At the same time, Jesse's new girlfriend, a hacker, is kidnapped to crack Proxy Blue's program for Eckhart, requiring the Mutant X team to use their training to infiltrate the Genomax facility.

GUEST CAST: Reagan Pasternak; Joy Tanner; Tom McCamus (Mason Eckhart); Greg Bryk.

9. "Crime of the New Century" Written by: Joe Johnson. Directed by: Graeme Campbell. Airdate: December 1, 2001.

The Mutant X team investigates when a boy with the power to mentally ignite fires is abducted for study by Eckhart. The young new mutant, Joshua, must develop his powerful and frightening abilities fast if he hopes to escape and return to his family. Fortunately, Shalimar and the others are determined to see the family reunited.

GUEST CAST: Tom McCamus (Eckhart); Jennifer Dale, Marc Donato, Paulino Nunes, Rod Wilson, Deborah O'Dell.

10. "Dark Star Rising" Written by: Philip LaZebnik. Directed by: Jon Cassar. Airdate: December 19, 2001.

Three people who seem to be "ferals" like Shalimar hail from Dark Star, an international anti-terror squad. They have learned that Eckhart subjected them to a Genomex experiment to transform them into new mutants, a concept they know nothing about. Only a special plant held at BioCorp can reverse the mutating process and restore their humanity, and Mutant X is poised to help.

GUEST CAST: Ralf Moeller, Anne Openshaw, Andrew Gillies, Anthony Tullo.

11. "Whiter Shade of Pale" Written by: Tony DiFranco. Directed by: Terry Ingram. Airdate: January 26, 2002.

A prototype stealth sequencer machine, one that renders people virtually invisible, is stolen from the Mutant X sanctuary by a stealth mutant whom Adam is familiar with, a woman he loved some six-

teen years earlier. He tracks the invisible woman, Danielle, but before long she has lost the sequencer to an agent from Genomex. Worse, it seems Eckhart and Adam are both in love with Danielle, whose DNA is breaking down because of her unusual new mutant stealth abilities. Further complicating matters, Danielle has a teenage daughter — also a new mutant — named Catherine, and her parentage is in question.

GUEST CAST: Guylaine St.-Onge; Christopher Bolton; Sarah Gadon; Tom McCamus (Eckhart); Xuan Fraser (Neil).

12. "Double Vision" Written by: Darrell Fetty. Directed by: Jon Cassar. Airdate: February 2, 2002.

Mulwray's old friend and partner in crime goes to work for Eckhart, and her newly "spliced" mutant powers alter Emma at a molecular level, splitting her into two individuals, one retreating and cowardly, the other rash and daring. The more aggressive Emma goes to work for Eckhart, while her double, something of a milquetoast, traps Adam and Brennan in lockdown in the Sanctuary because she does not want to rejoin with her more savage alternate self. The dark Emma plots final revenge against Genomex, threatening innocent lives, and Jesse and Shalimar are dispatched in the jet to stop her and return her to the Sanctuary to reverse the splitting process.

GUEST CAST: Joanne Vannicola; Andrew Gillies; Tom McCamus (Eckhart); Kedar (Axel).

13. "Blood Ties" Written by: Perry Dance. Directed by: John Fawcett. Airdate: February 9, 2002.

Jesse's secret agent father, Noah, shows up on the run, being tracked by Nexxogen, a corrupt cloning company and business partner to Eckhart's Genomex. Adam and Brennan uncover evidence that Jesse's father may have been attempting extortion, and that's the reason Nexxogen is after him. Eckhart dispatches a special field agent, a mutant with extraordinary hearing, to hunt him down. When Eckhart captures Noah, a desperate Jesse goes in search of his father, unable to believe Mutant X's claims that he is a criminal.

GUEST CAST: Art Hindle (Noah); Chick Reid (Nicole Carter); Tom McCamus (Mason Eckhart); Derwin Jordan (Calvin); James Binkley (Guard).

14. "Altered Ego" Written by: Elizabeth Keyishian. Directed by: Andrew Potter. Airdate: February 16, 2002.

A young mutant named Charlotte Cook bears a grudge against Adam because he sent her father to jail, and now she plots revenge: using her power to "manipulate moral polarity" and turn Adam from good guy to bad. Eckhart plots to get his hands on the powerful mutant even as she uses her abilities to temporarily affect Jesse and Shalimar, making them competitive and aggressive. When Charlotte touches Adam, she converts him into a power-mad psychotic out to destroy Mutant X. Adam goes to Eckhart with a disk of names and addresses of all new mutants, selling out the very people he has devoted his life to saving...

GUEST CAST: Emily Hampshire (Charlotte Cook); Joseph Scoren; Rob Sefaniuk; Tom McCamus (Mason Eckhart).

15. "Lazarus Syndrome" Written by: Mark Amato. Directed by: John Bell. Airdate: February 23, 2002.

A mutant vampire/serial killer named Caleb Matthias has been "draining" new mutants. He tries to kill Emma, but Brennan intervenes. When Caleb escapes, the Mutant X team hunts for the dangerous psychopath, and it is not long before the seemingly immortal Caleb is stalking Emma in the Sanctuary. When Caleb captures Emma, she is forced to team with one of Eckhart's mutants, an elemental who can raise and lower her body temperature.

GUEST CAST: Andrew Martin; Larissa Laskin; Andrew Gillies; Raven Dauda (Maria); Tom McCamus (Mason Eckhart).

16. "Interface" Written by: Mark Lisson. Directed by: Ken Girotti. Airdate: March 2, 2002.

An old friend of Emma's, a new mutant, is full of ambition to rise through the ranks of Genomex. Using her ability to rapidly interface with computers, she plans to sabotage Mutant X. Emma is betrayed by her friend when they meet to discuss their opposing viewpoints. Emma works on her friend's conscience, revealing Eckhart's genocidal plans for all new mutants. But whose side is the dangerous new mutant really on, and can she be trusted with the location of the Sanctuary?

GUEST CAST: Danielle Hampton (Michelle); Chris Owens, Jason Jones.

17. "Presumed Guilty" Written by: Darrell Fetty. Directed by: Ken Girotti. Airdate: March 30, 2002.

A villainous new mutant with the ability to absorb memories from others frames Adam for the murder of a new mutant. Confused and amnesiac, Adam rejoins Genomex, unaware of his betrayal.

GUEST CAST: Paul Popowich, Tiara Sorenson, Jocelyn Snowdon.

18. "Ex Marks the Spot" Written by: Howard Chaykin and David L. Newman and Mark Amato. Directed by: Jorge Montesi. Airdate: April 4, 2002.

The Mutant X team deals with Zack Lockhart, an old lover that made Shalimar's life miserable, even as Eckhart tries to get his hands on a valuable Fabergé egg. The rare treasure contains a secret data chip from the now-defunct communist equivalent of Genomex, a data chip that can control free will. Unfortunately, the slippery Zack's help is needed to break into a vault and replace the data chip with a dummy imitation.

GUEST CAST: Callum Keith Rennie (Zack Lockhart); Michael Anthony Rawlins; Tom McCamus (Mason Eckhart).

19. "Nothing to Fear" Written by: Elizabeth Keyishian. Directed by: T.J. Scott. Airdate: April 11, 2002.

A new mutant named Henry is a psionic agent working for Eckhart because he believes that the Mutant X team killed his beloved wife. After telepathically linking with Shalimar, Henry controls her subconscious and makes her worst fears come true. He mentally tortures her for Eckhart, hoping to learn the location of the Sanctuary. Next, he puts the whammy on Jesse, Brennan and Emma — exposing the Mutant X team to a dreamscape of terrible fears and nightmares.

GUEST CAST: Justin Louis (Henry Voight); Tom McCamus (Mason Eckhart).

20. "Deadly Desire" Written by: David L. Newman. Directed by: Brad Turner. Airdate: April 17, 2002.

Lorna Templeton, a new mutant with the sting of a scorpion and a seductive effect on men (thanks to a powerful pheromone), sets up a deadly criminal plot using her unique abilities. Meanwhile, Adam attempts to prevent Eckhart from getting his hands on "anamite," a technological virus that can bypass the security protections of any linked computer. Femme fatale Lorna seduces Brennan and recruits him into her gang of fanatic admirer/slaves. With Brennan's assistance, Lorna plans to sell Eckhart the anamite for five million dollars, but a kiss from Shalimar (via lipstick laced with scorpion anti-venom) brings Mulwray back to his senses just in time.

GUEST CAST: Krista Allen (Lorna Templeton); Matthew MacFadzean; Ted Whittal; Jim Codrington; Tom McCamus (Mason Eckhart); Clyde Whitham (Dr. Tork).

21. "Dancing on the Razor" Written by: Mark Amato. Directed by: Jorge Montesi. Airdate: May 1, 2002.

Proxy Blue transmits video imagery of a confrontation between Mutant X (Brennan and Jesse) and members of Eckhart's Genomex in an abandoned warehouse, threatening to expose members of both organizations to the public. The man with the video disk is ready to sell it to Proxy Blue, but the corrupt journalist betrays Shalimar to get closer to Mutant X. The risk of exposure brings Adam and his Mutant X team to a tense meeting with Eckhart.

GUEST CAST: Roman Podhura; James Gallanders; Tom McCamus (Eckhart).

22. "A Breed Apart" Written by: Howard Chaykin. Directed by: Brad Turner. Airdate: May 8, 2002.

The first child of Genomex, sociopath Gabriel Ashlock, is sprung from stasis, and with powers "off the meter," he is the most dangerous of all mutants. Ashlock becomes the new leader of a cult called "the Strand" that sees itself as an alternative to Mutant X and the underground. Meanwhile, in the Sanctuary, all of the Mutant X team members see their abilities kicked up a notch in what Adam terms a "new mutant growth spurt." When Ashlock abducts Shalimar, steals Adam's database, takes over Genomex and locks Mason Eckhart in his own stasis pods, these new abilities are the only thing that can stop Ashlock from taking over the world.

GUEST CAST: Michael Easton (Gabriel Ashlock); Tom McCamus (Mason Eckhart); Kim Schraner, Karen Le Blanc, Andrew Gillies.

SEASON TWO (2002-2003)

23. "Past as Prologue" Written by: Howard Chaykin. Directed by: T.J. Scott. Airdate: October 6, 2002.

Gabriel Ashlock has been on a killing spree, and on one mission he steals a valuable Egyptian urn, one that may hold the key to stabilizing his mutant DNA. Adam believes he can cure Ashlock, a course of action that enrages Shalimar, who is still holding a grudge against Gabriel for brainwashing her. Meanwhile, Ashlock is working on his cure, resurrecting an ancient and beautiful alchemist with the help of some stolen Egyptian artifacts.

GUEST CAST: Michael Easton (Gabriel Ashlock); Soo Garay.

24. "Power Play" Written by: Turi Meyer and Al Septien. Directed by: Milan Cheylov. Airdate: October 13, 2002.

The Mutant X team attempts to acquire a government laser defense shield, but it is stolen out from under their noses by a paramilitary organization. Meanwhile, exposure to nerve gas intermittently destabilizes Jesse's molecules, causing him to lose control of his powers. The shield has been stolen by Colonel Gaumont, a military officer ostensibly seeking revenge against the U.S. government for the abandonment of twelve of his men in the Middle East — but in fact trying to get his hands on a valuable form of radioactive material. Despite Jesse's condition, Adam orders the Mutant X team to stop the evil Colonel, unaware that Gaumont is counting on Jesse's unusual ability to alter his metabolism to help him get his hands on the radioactive loot.

GUEST CAST: Stephen McHattie (Colonel Eric Gaumont); Karen Holness.

25. "Time Squared" Written by: Elizabeth Keyishian. Directed by: John Bell. Airdate: October 20, 2002.

The Mutant X team pursues Ashlock as he abducts a new mutant, Diana Moller, hiding in a psychiatric ward. She holds the secret to cure Ashlock's fatal illness, and has the ability to send people back through time with her "molecular/psionic" genetic mix. Ashlock disappears through a time rift, a "gravitational dilation of time," with Shalimar and Brennan in hot pursuit, and they all end up on October 13, 1978, the day a young Adam was to begin his genetic experiments at Genomex. Ashlock sets out to change the past and prevent his own illness, even as Adam also travels back in time with Emma in hopes of preserving the time continuum.

GUEST CAST: Michael Easton (Gabriel Ashlock); Lindy Booth (Diana Moller).

26. "Whose Woods These Are" Written by: Darell Fetty. Directed by: Jorge Montesi. Airdate: October 27, 2002.

Brennan and Shalimar investigate a series of werewolf-like killings in the forest, fearing a new mutant connection. In battle with the strange creature, Shalimar is scratched and fears she could mutate into the animalistic beast. Meanwhile, Jesse and Emma learn that the creature — and another like it — are part of a secret government experiment to engineer special astronauts who can survive in alien environments. Adam works desperately to find a cure for Shalimar and the creature, even as Shalimar begins to sympathize more and more with the monster.

GUEST CAST: Jeff Wincott, Scott Hylands.

Mystery Men

"We're not your classic superheroes … we're the other guys, the ones nobody bets on," deadpans one character in the $70 million theatrical release, *Mystery Men* (1999), a superhero adventure that was more a comedy than a serious epic.

The team known as the Mystery Men originally emerged from the mind of writer/artist Bob Burden in the late 1970s, when he created a character named the Flaming Carrot for a comic line titled, appropriately, Flaming Carrot Comics. This unusual hero occasionally fought alongside a cadre of second-string, blue-collar heroes called Mystery Men. The team first appeared in a story entitled "I Cloned Hitler's Feet" (issue #16) and very soon became popular in its own right. Among the team were Captain Attack, Screwball, Red Rover, the Blue Rajah, and Jackpot.

Over the years, the Mystery Men were seen sporadically, and moved from comic line to comic line. In the 1980s they fought crime under the banner of Renegade Press, and in 1988 moved to Dark Horse. Today there have been more than thirty Mystery Men adventures published. The 1999 movie starred Ben Stiller (*Zoolander* [2001]) as Mr. Furious, Hank Azaria as Blue Rajah, William H. Macy as Shoveler, Janeane Garofalo as Bowler, Kei Mitchell as Invisible Boy and Paul Reubens as the Spleen.

The film premiered in the summer of 1999 with much ballyhoo, especially considering that many in the general audience had never heard of this particular team before. The goal of the film was to re-ignite the superhero craze, moribund after the disastrous *Batman and Robin*, with a fun template that twisted and poked at the edges of the genre. As producer Lloyd Levin described the approach:

> I love [superhero] movies, but people do seem burned out on them. The genre is at the same point as horror when *Scream* was released. The audience knows all the conventions. Our success hinges on making our characters as self-aware as the audience.[1]

This approach meant applying a healthy dose of reality to the superhero ethos. In other words, the popular Captain Amazing (Greg Kinnear), champion of Champion City, was a publicity-hungry celebrity. His suit was adorned with celebrity endorsements, and as the film opened, he was vexed because he had lost the Pepsi Cola account. In other words, "real" human nature — greed, avarice, selfishness — collided with the archetypal world of the perfect superhero, the crime fighter, the square-jawed goody-two-shoes.

More to the point perhaps, the superheroes of *Mystery Men* either had no powers to speak of, or very lame, questionable ones. Mr. Furious was just a very angry guy, a rage-aholic. The Blue Rajah could throw cutlery with so-so accuracy and faked a bad British accent, coming off as an effete. The Invisible Boy could only use his power (invisibility) when nobody was looking. Only the Bowler (who could toss a mean, ricocheting bowling ball and the Spleen (who could pass gas that was downright explosive) possessed abilities useful in a fight. And that was the point, one supposes. Captain Amazing possessed all the good looks, charm, resources, publicists, and popularity to ensure success, but was a dolt, and did not seem to care about anything beyond his own glorification. The other guys, Mr. Furious and the Shoveler in particular, had real heart, even if they didn't have real powers to go with it.

In other words, one might say that a superhero is forged in the heart, not the body, the car, the gadgetry or the costume. That message of self-empowerment was one worthy of sending. *Mystery Men* indicated that all of us can become superheroes, and it was a revelation how much fun it was seeing these unlikely heroes triumph over the evil of Casanova Frankenstein (Geoffrey Rush).

Anything but a by-the-numbers flick, *Mystery Men* was filled with wacky invention and jokes. The bad guys were one such example. One evil gang was called the Frat Boys. Their trademark? Lethal hazings. Then there was a bad guy's unique psychological weapon — called "a blame thrower."

Mystery Men, like *Unbreakable* in 2000, was a film more about the idea of superheroes than an adventure featuring superheroes, and, as such, it made audiences question assumptions. Could a superhero be a father and a dad? An unemployed guy? A diffident kid? Someone that lived at home with his mom? Perhaps, the film suggested, if those folks could overcome their personal issues and work together for the betterment of all mankind.

Fortunately, the look of *Mystery Men* was terrific. Champion City was Gotham City redux, half-way between Tim Burton's blighted metropolis and Schumacher's neon spectacular. The visual effects were dazzling, and even a little overpowering at times, but *Mystery Men*'s best feature was its in-the-know humor. At one critical juncture, for instance, the bionic sound effects from *The Six Million Dollar Man* were played on the soundtrack, a rousing homage to a program every 1970s kid grew up with.

Mystery Men (1999)
LIVE-ACTION FILM

"*Mystery Men*'s greatest asset is its cast. Stiller, Hank Azaria, and William H. Macy deftly showcase the comic potential of their wannabe superheroes as well as their underdog charm. By the end of the film they transcend all the tomfoolery to make you believe … that the idea of an honest person becoming a costumed crime fighter isn't quite so silly…"
— Michael Stewart, *Entertainment Weekly:* "Zeroes to Heroes," January 14, 2000, page 81.

"An amiable spoof of comic book heroes, *Mystery Men* may well contain more total yuks than the summer's other big pop send-up, the second *Austin Powers*, but it also spreads them over an ultimately tiresome two hours."
— Geoffrey Cheshire, *Variety:* "Mystery Men," August 2, 1999, page 32.

"As adapted by Neil Cuthbert from the *Mystery Men* comic book series, the film is a humorous deconstruction of the usual generic clichés, such as the notion that a superhero can create a convincing alter ego simply by putting on a pair of Clark Kent-ish eyeglasses. But this slight idea has been inflated until it achieves boredom."
— Robert W. Butler, *Knight-Ridder/ Tribune News Service:* "Mystery Men," August 3, 1999, page K6509.

"*Mystery Men* is a charming, witty farce, sometimes a little too broad but full of great touches."
— Paul Smith, *Computer Weekly:* Mystery Men DVD," June 29, 2000 page 65.

"[*Mystery Men*] misses the satiric bull's-eye for which it aimed…"
— Gary Frisch, *Video Business:* "No Mystery Here," January 17, 2000.

"Every other action picture is about the impossibly outsized Them; this one is about the just barely heroic US. It's about making the best of your small talents — about looking in the mirror and, despite all evidence to the contrary, smiling back."
— Richard Corliss, *Time:* "The Hero in the Mirror: In the Hip, Funny, *Mystery Men*, Saving the World Is Less Important Than Finding Yourself," August 9, 1999, page 66.

CAST: Hank Azaria (Blue Rajah); Janeane Garofalo (Bowler); William H. Macy (Shoveler); Kei Mitchell (Invisible Boy); Paul Reubens (Spleen); Ben Stiller (Mr. Furious/Roy); Wes Studi (Sphinx); Greg Kinnear (Captain Amazing/Lance Hunt); Geoffrey Rush (Casanova Frankenstein); Lena Olin (Dr. Leek); Eddie Izzard (Tony P.); Artie Lang (Big Red); Prakazrel Michel (Tony C); Claire Forlani (Monica); Tom Watts (Doc Heller); Louise Lasser (Violet); Ricky Jay (Vic Weems); Jennifer Lewis (Lucille); Ernie Lee Banks (Ted); Gerry Becker (Ranyon); Ned Bellamy (Funk); Corbin Bleu (Butch); Philip Bolden (Roland); Jake Cross (Thug); Kinka Usher (Moe); James Duke (Big Tobacco); Michael Bay (Frat Boy); Gabrielle Conferti (PMS Avenger); Dane Cook (Waffler); Oliver Clark (Reverse Psychologist); Jack Plotnick (Mr. Pups); Dana Gould (Squeegeeman).

CREW: Universal Pictures and Lawrence Gordon present a Golar/Lloyd Levin/Dark Horse Production, *Mystery Men. Directed by:* Kinka Usher. *Written by:* Neil Cuthbert. *Produced by:* Lawrence Gordon, Mike Richardson, Lloyd Levin. *Based on the Dark Horse Comic Created by:* Bob Burden. *Executive Producer:* Robert Engelman. *Director of Photography:* Stephen H.

Burum. *Production Designer:* Kirk M. Petruc-celli. *Film Editor:* Conrad Buff. *Casting:* Mindy Marin. *Music:* Stephen Warbeck. *Music Supervision:* Karyn Rachtman. *Costume Design:* Marilyn Vance. *Co-Producer:* Steven Gilder. *M.P.A.A. Rating:* PG-13. *Running time:* 122 minutes.

In Champion City, a second-rate superhero team (consisting of the Shoveler, Mr. Furious and Blue Rajah) fights a gang of red-haired thugs in a nursing home, but sees its thunder stolen by the popular and handsome Captain Amazing, the champion of Champion City. But Amazing is upset because he is losing product endorsements and facing a dearth of super-villains to keep him in the public eye. In secret, he plans to release his arch-nemesis, Casanova Frankenstein, from the insane asylum. But the freed villain very shortly turns the tables, blowing up the asylum and capturing Amazing.

With Captain Amazing missing in action, it is up to Mr. Furious, the Shoveler and Blue Rajah (who throws cutlery) to save the superhero and the endangered Champion City. When they fail to get past Casanova's henchmen — the Disco Boy gang — they start recruiting. They team up with the Invisible Boy (who can only become invisible when nobody is looking at him), the Spleen (who expels knockout flatulence)

and the Bowler, daughter of a famous murdered superhero. The Bowler keeps her father's skull in a bowling ball that can target villains with pinpoint accuracy. (Those who failed to make the grade for the team included Ballerina Man, PMS Avenger, and the Waffler.)

The first test of the new team involves a street chase with Casanova Frankenstein, but the confrontation ends in a draw. Their second test is less successful, resulting in the untimely demise of the captive Captain Amazing. Finally, the enigmatic Sphinx, a powerful, more experienced superhero joins the team and trains the group according to ancient tenets. Advocating teamwork, Sphinx becomes the impromptu leader of the gang, and Mr. Furious leaves in a fit of pique.

Before long, it is time to battle Casanova Frankenstein at his castle. A "nonlethal" weapons expert, Doc Heller, equips the team, but they must do battle with Frankenstein's ultimate weapon, a "psycho-fraculator," before it destroys the city at midnight. And worse, Mr. Furious's girlfriend, Monica, has been captured. Despite the cynicism of family and friends, Blue Rajah, the Shoveler, Mr. Furious, the Bowler, Invisible Boy, the Spleen and Sphinx rise to the occasion.

Nick Fury: Agent for S.H.I.E.L.D.

The Marvel Comics hero Nick Fury, like DC's Batman, possessed no real super powers to speak of, other than his consuming dedication to America and his thirst to preserve justice. In 1963 Nick Fury first appeared, courtesy of Stan Lee and Jack Kirby, in *Sgt. Fury and His Howling Commandos.* He was depicted as a vehement Nazi hater, and Fury's book was set during World War II.

But, hoping to compete with more timely franchises (and even the James Bond films), Marvel also introduced Nick Fury in another comic, one which saw him becom-

ing an agent for a fictional government organization called S.H.I.E.L.D. (Special Headquarters International Espionage Law Enforcement Division) after World War II.

In 1997 Fox television unveiled a TV movie (and backdoor pilot) entitled *Nick Fury: Agent of S.H.I.E.L.D.,* based on Fury's second life as a post–World War II hero. David Hasselhoff, of *Baywatch* and *Knight Rider* fame, portrayed this patriotic toughguy, replete with the comic character's ubiquitous cigar, eye patch and beard stubble.

The TV movie set the leather-clad

Fury and a team of greenhorns, including a Brit named Pierce and a psychic woman reminiscent of *Star Trek: The Next Generation*'s Counselor Troi, against the offspring of his old enemy, a fascist named Von Strucker. Unfortunately, the production was hampered by weak, two-dimensional performances that bordered on hysteria and camp. Viper Von Strucker's German accent, for instance, was the stuff of pulp comics, and that is not meant as a compliment.

Playing the ultimate Marvel bad ass, Hasselhoff had plenty of fun projecting a tough-guy attitude, but the no-nonsense, hard-as-nails Nick Fury persona did not fit with the image the affable actor had forged in his other programs. Hasselhoff just did not have the gravitas to pull off the role, which may be why no further Fury movies have appeared since this all-but-forgotten TV movie.

Nick Fury is a tad difficult to watch objectively today, as the finale featured two terrorist missiles aimed squarely at Manhattan's World Trade Center towers, an American icon that has taken on new meaning since September 11, 2001. Another flash-cut (an image in the mind of a Nazi named Dr. Zola), revealed more horrors: Manhattan struck by an atomic bomb. Of course, these are classic science fiction images, but, given the subsequent war on terrorism, they seem a little too powerful for so corny and cheesy a production. The ticking clock finale, as Nick Fury tries to prevent disaster, is notably lacking in suspense, especially as it includes an android duplicate of Fury, called an LMD (Life Model Decoy).

Some of the effects work is actually pretty interesting, particularly the floating fortress headquarters of S.H.I.E.L.D. which cleverly grafts the past (a World War II–era aircraft carrier) onto the future (giant hover units).

Nick Fury: Agent of S.H.I.E.L.D. (1997)
LIVE-ACTION TV MOVIE

CAST: David Hasselhoff (Colonel Nicholas "Nick" Fury); Lisa Rinna (Contessa Valentine, "Val"); Sandra Hess; Neil Roberts; Garry Chalk; Tracy Waterhouse; Tom McBeath; Ron Canada; Bill Croft; Roger R. Cross (S.H.I.E.L.D. Agent #1); Peter Haworth (Dr. Zola); Scott Heindl (Werner Von Strucker); Adrian Hughes (Quartermain); Campbell Lane (Baron Von Strucker); Terry David Mulligan (President of the United States); Rick Ravanello (Agent Vaughn).

CREW: *Music:* Kevin Kiner. *Film Editor:* Drake Sullivan. *Production Design:* Douglas Higgins. *Director of Photography:* James Bartle. *Executive Producers:* Avi Arad, Stan Lee, Tarquin Gotch, Bob Lemchen. *Producer:* David Roessell. *Written by:* David Goyer. *Directed by:* Rod Hardy. *Associate Producer:* Matthew Edelman. *Casting:* Fern Champion, Mark Paladini. *Canadian Casting:* Wendy O'Brien Livingstone. *Stunt Coordinator:* J.J. Makard. *Unit Production Manager:* Hugh Spencer Phillips. *First Assistant Director:* Brian Giddens. *Second Assistant Director:* Judy Slattery. *Visual Effects:* Gajdecki Visual Effects. *Make-up Effects:* Lindala Make-up Effects. *Costume Design:* Monique Prudhomme. *Location Manager:* Scott Harper. *Art Director:* Grant Van Der Slagt. *Set Decorator:* Mark Lane. *Script Supervisor:* Cristina Weigmann. *Running time:* 97 minutes (approx.)

At the top-secret Trinity Base, the body of the evil Baron Wolfgang Von Strucker is liberated from suspended animation by a team of armed commandos working for the terrorist organization called Hydra. The permanent multi-national strike force known as the Supreme Headquarters International Espionage Law Enforcement Division (S.H.I.E.L.D.) responds quickly, reactivating the retired, hard-nosed Colonel Nick Fury. Fury is embittered because he was put out to pasture five years earlier. When he learns that Strucker, an old enemy, is involved, Fury agrees to let bygones be bygones and join the mission.

Fury is escorted to S.H.I.E.L.D. HQ, a floating fortress in the sky, where he teams with a psychic, a rookie agent named Pierce, and his old girlfriend, Val. There he is updated with new equipment, including an LMD (a Life Model Decoy) and an electragun keyed only to his handprint I.D. He learns that Von Strucker's daughter, Viper, is rebuilding Hydra and has stolen her father's body to extract the Death's Head Virus from his DNA.

While questioning Dr. Zola, a Third Reich scientist, about the deadly disease, Fury is poisoned by a "kiss of death" from an in-disguise Viper. Only a blood sample from Viper can save Fury's life, so his mission becomes personal now. Meanwhile, Hydra plans to launch missiles (laced with the deadly virus) into Manhattan unless paid a huge ransom.

The agents for S.H.I.E.L.D., led by the authority-hating Fury, track down Hydra and the virus, with Nick's life and Manhattan's survival on the line.

Nightman

The superhero named Nightman is the creation of writer Steve Englehart. A character that first appeared in Malibu Comics and then was purchased for inclusion in the Marvel Universe, Nightman by day was actually a talented saxophone player named Johnny Domino (or Dominus). One day, Johnny was involved in a strange accident that granted many people incredible powers. On the outside periphery of the effect, Johnny merely developed the ability to sense "evil" thoughts, a helpful talent in ferreting out bad guys, but there was a trade-off. The accident also destroyed certain portions of Johnny's brain, making it impossible for him to sleep.

Trained in the martial arts since childhood, and imbued with a hero's need to protect others and foster justice (ingrained in him, perhaps, by his policeman father), Johnny became Nightman, a "superhero of the new millennium." In the comic book adventures, Johnny wore a black cape, boasted night vision, and sported long, flowing, Fabio-like hair. After another freak accident in which a duplicate was created, Nightman, or rather Nightman's clone, was able to shoot electricity out of his body, like the evil Emperor in *Return of the Jedi* (1983) or Brennan Mulwray in *Mutant X*.

In 1997, veteran TV producer Glen Larson, in association with Tribune Entertainment, brought *Nightman* to the TV screen, making the property his third attempt to create a successful superhero series (after the failures of *Automan* and *Manimal* in the early 1980s). Cleared for more than 60 percent of American households in syndication, and offering a mix of "sci-fi, action, adventure, mystery and more" (1), the new hour-long series also played fast and loose with much of the *Nightman* lore.

In the pilot, Johnny (stunt double turned actor Matt McColm) was struck by lightning while riding a cable car. This granted him the ability to sense "evil," a perceptual ability from mankind's distant future. Perhaps more importantly, he also got his hands on a stash of top-secret government weapons and equipment, including an anti-gravity bulletproof suit that allowed him to fly high above his native Bay City, a black mask with infra-red vision over one eye, a hologram generator, stealth equipment and more.

In the comics, Johnny was a pretty smart, adept guy, able to break into computers and such with aplomb, but in the TV series he was given an assistant in the person of Raleigh Jordan (actor Derek Webster

The Dark Knight? No, it's *Nightman* (Matt McColm)!

in the first season; Derwin Jordan in the second). Raleigh monitored Johnny's adventures from a laptop computer, and was his adviser on all things technical.

In the first season, Johnny also helped his cop father, played by Earl Holliman, solve crimes. His dad had no idea he was Nightman. Johnny also solved crimes in tandem with the cynical Lt. Dann (Michael Woods), another useless TV cop that couldn't put two and two together without the help of a superhero. Matters were spiced up a bit in the second season when Holliman and Woods departed from the production, and Jane Heitmeyer joined the cast as Johnny's sexier liaison to the Bay City police.

When not flying over the city, Johnny drove around town in his sleek Plymouth Prowler and played jazz at the House of Soul, a club owned by his friend Jesse (Felicia Bell). Because of his crime-fighting duties, he would often miss performing engagements there, and his hologram would perform his routine, with the audience unaware of the switcheroo. Like Woods and Holliman, Bell disappeared in Season Two as *Nightman* was revamped.

Unlike one-season-wonders *Automan* and *Manimal, Nightman* survived two seasons, and lived long enough to pit its muscle-bound, rubber-suited hero against a dazzling array of villains. Because *The X-Files* (1993–2002) was still quite popular during the time *Nightman* aired, many of the bad guys on the show were of supernatural, extraterrestrial or mystical origins. Invaders from space appeared in "Hitchhiker" and "It Came Out of the Sky." A monster from another dimension showed his hairy, rubbery face in "Still of the Night." A telepathic robber attacked in "Chrome II." A time-traveling Jack the Ripper challenged Nightman and Jonathan Chase (of *Manimal* fame) in the crossover episode "Manimal."

Other *Nightman* episodes, especially during the first season, proved more routine and dependent on the long-standing clichés

of the superhero genre. "I Left My Heart" recycled the plot of *Die Hard* (1987), but set it in a high-rise plastic surgeon's office. Johnny rescued a beautiful Russian woman from mobsters in "Lady in Red." In "Takin' it to the Streets" our hero had to stop a criminal from intimidating a high school athlete in a position to throw a big game. Most of the episodes were very predictable, and the special effects were ludicrously bad. When Nightman flew, he merely hovered, as very bad rear-projection footage unspooled behind him.

Johnny faced a recurring villain in the series' second season, a Bill Gates–type tycoon named Kieran Keyes (Kim Coates). This power-hungry free enterpriser invented a device called the "Ultraweb," a sort of demonic dimension accessed via computers. It was there that he recruited the Bogeyman to fight Nightman in "Fear City." In another episode, "The People's Choice," Keyes ran for Mayor of Bay City. He was always defeated at the last moment, but never with enough evidence to send him to jail. He always returned for one more round with his arch-nemesis.

Probably the worst episode of *Nightman* was "Amazing Grace," which recycled footage from previous installments to send Johnny on an *It's a Wonderful Life*–style tour of his filmed exploits (presumably from a very clichéd-looking, white-walled interpretation of Heaven). On the other hand, the best episode might have been the aforementioned *Manimal* crossover, which featured an interesting villain in Red Jack, the nostalgic return of an old '80s TV hero, and even the introduction of Chase's adult daughter (who had transformation powers of her own).

Nightman never earned high ratings or very good reviews, and was not seen in many parts of the United States, so cast and credit information on many of the episodes is scarce. WGN reran the show in the summer of 2001 before baseball games, but did not air the series in its entirety.

Nightman (1997–1999)
LIVE-ACTION TV SERIES

"The Cut-Rate Adventures of Cheap Man. If it had been a sitcom, it would have been a classic."
— *Cinescape:* "Voyage to the Bottom of the Barrel," September/October 1999, page 45.

"Routine plots and state-of-yesterdays-art special effects helped consign this show to the syndication market. Many fans of the comic have expressed disappointment."
— Roger Fulton and John Betancourt. *The Complete Sci-Fi Channel Encyclopedia of TV Science Fiction.* Warner Brothers Books, 1997, page 300.

"...[S]yndication's kookily quixotic new superhero show ... [is] loose and campy."
— Ken Tucker. *Entertainment Weekly:* "NightMan," July 17, 1998, page 38.

"*Nightman* was your typical Glen Larson show, and that means it is okay to watch, but will never make anybody's ten best list. It is your basic, average superhero show. I hated the stock footage, in that every week he [Johnny] would put on the costume and it would be the same footage, and the flying sequences were very poor, especially considering that it was 1999 when the show aired. On the other hand, *Nightman* mixed crime stories with supernatural stories and techno–science fiction stuff, and because it was about 'Nightman,' a mysterious character, they could get away with more. The variety of plot lines was entertaining and one of the few strengths of the series."
— Howard Margolin, host of *Destinies: The Voice of Science Fiction.*

CAST: Matt McColm (Johnny Domino); Derek Webster (Raleigh Jordan); Earl Holliman (Frank Dominus); Felicia Bell (Jessica "Jesse" Rodgers); Michael Woods (Lt. Charlie Dann). SECOND SEASON: Derwin Jordan (Raleigh); Jayne Heitmeyer (Briony Branca).

CREW: *Created by:* Glen A. Larson. *Based on:* the Marvel Comics comic book. *Casting:* Dan Shaner, Michael Testa, Mark Melville. *Director of Photography:* Mark Melville. *Production Design:* Bill Camden, Bill Parrett. *Costume Design:* Jerry Skeels. *Music:* Marc Bonilla. *Editors:* Howard Deane, David Howe. *Co-Producer:* Christopher Scott. *Producer:* J.C. Larson. *Line Producer:* Bob Simmonds. *Supervising Producer:* Michael Prescott. *Producer:* Scott Thomas. *Co-Executive Producers:* Glen A. Larson, Scott Mitchell Rosenberg, Gary Gittelsohn. *Executive for Tribune:* Karen Corbin. *Main Title Theme:* Glen A. Larson, Marc Bonilla. *First Assistant Director:* Daniel Carrey. *Key Make-up:* Georgia Dunn. *Stunt Coordinator:* Michael Justus. *Set Decorator:* Alison Howard. *Property Master:* Dan Clark. *Special Effects Costuming:* Radel DeBree. *Stunt Double:* Mike McColm. *Script Supervisor:* Nicole Finch. *Special Effects:* Paul Staples. *Location Manager:* Lynda Recht. *Script Coordinator:* Lynn Spraggins. *Nightman Suit Created by:* KNB EFX Group, Inc. *Visual Effects:* Stargate Films, Modern Videofilm, Laserpacific Media Corp, Engram Video, Flat Earth Productions.

SEASON ONE (1997-1998)

1. "Pilot" (two hours) Written by: Glen A. Larson. Directed by: Nick Daniel. Airdate: September 15, 1997.

Jazz saxophonist Johnny Domino tunes into the "frequency of evil" during a freak cable car accident in San Francisco, developing a telepathic skill hundreds of generations ahead of the rest of humanity. With the help of an engineer named Raleigh Jordan, and stolen government prototype technology (including a bullet-resistant suit, anti-gravity belt, holographic display unit and stealth gear), Johnny becomes the superhero known as Nightman. An international conglomerate of terrorists want to purchase the special technology from a rogue agent in the Justice Department, and the Chinese buyer abducts singer Carla Day, Johnny's sometime girlfriend, to use as leverage. Johnny and Raleigh track the weapons buyers back to a business called Strand Cybertech, but Raleigh and John's ex-policeman father, Frank, are kidnapped. Now Nightman must save them before they are killed in a demonstration of another new weapon, a powerful neutron gun.

GUEST CAST: Taylor Dane (Carla Day); Patrick Macnee; David Hasselhoff; Nicole

Nagel; Robert Kerbeck; Sal Lopez; Ric Young; Al Sapienza; Doug Crane (Agent Woodard); Eric Chen (Chinese Henchman).

2. "Whole Lotta Shakin'..." Story by: Bruce Kalish. Written by: Bruce Kalish and Stephen E. Miller. Directed by: Rex Piano. Airdate: October 6, 1997.

Seismology equipment is stolen from a Bay City laboratory by international terrorists, and Frank is injured attempting to save his seismologist friend, Meghan Farrell. Meanwhile, a strange fellow named Jubilee Jones accurately predicts an earthquake in town, but Johnny thinks the amusing scoundrel is just a patsy for a darker force. Then a mysterious figure appears on the TV and orders Bay City to pay him 100 million dollars or he will detonate a nuclear weapon and unleash a second round of deadly earthquakes. But the terrorists' real plan is to steal gold bullion from the largest private gold repository on the West Coast. At the same time, Frank uncovers a plot to sell organs on the black market when Meghan's daughter is denied a new kidney on the day of her operation.

GUEST CAST: Little Richard (Jubilee Jones); Michelle Clunie (Meghan Farrell); Brittany Alyse Smith (Madison Farrell); Michael E. Rodgers; Allan Miller; Kirk B.K. Woller; Sandra Phillips (Mayor Booker); Gary Simpson (Colonel Stratton); Hugh Holub (Dr. Carlson); Darlynne Reyes (Reporter).

3. "I Left My Heart" Written by: Stephen A. Miller. Directed by: Nick Daniel. Airdate: October 13, 1997.

Johnny plays sax at the gala celebration inaugurating the opening of a new high-rise plastic surgery center. Meanwhile, a crime boss who has contributed five million dollars to the new facility wants his face changed that very night, or Dr. Franklin's family will be murdered. When Columbian criminals seize the high-rise facility, a two-part operation commences: to perform plastic surgery on Jose Esquire, and to provide

the ailing thug with a new heart ... Johnny's heart! Johnny and Raleigh thwart the villains at every turn, and it's up to Nightman to save Frank Dominus, the replacement heart donor!

GUEST CAST: Eddie Velez (Mr. Cruz); Casey Biggs (Dr. Cameron Franklin); Henry Darrow (Jose Esquire); Cory Tyler (Buddy); Ramon Franco; Marco Rodriguez; Lobo Sebastian; Gil Birmingham (Vargas); Ron Harper (Elderly Man); Danielle Larson (Annette Franklin); James Howell (Dr. Chambers); Pat Hurley (Ambulance Driver).

4. "Still of the Night" Written by: D.G. Larson. Directed by: Clay Borris. Airdate: October 20, 1997.

Nightman saves a helpless young woman from an extra-dimensional monster roaming a city park, but is scratched by the beast during a scuffle. Bedford Consulting Foundation, a top-secret science/defense organization, has been trying to capture the creature, which Nightman felt possessed both "raw power" and "desperate need." The case reminds Nightman's dad, Frank, of a similar occurrence eight years earlier, when a boy named David Kelshaw died from exposure to a similar monster. A scientist on the project agrees to help Frank and Johnny face the monster, a male of its terrible species; but unless they can get a sample of its blood, Nightman will die from infection.

GUEST CAST: Martin Rayner (Parker); Robin Bliley (Elaine Barnes); J. Kenneth Campbell; Sarah Lancaster; Carlos Bernard; Rondi Reed; Michael Monks; Derk Cheetwood; Will Caceres (Security Guard); Stan Miller (Anchorman); Leona Tripp (Admitting Nurse); Sean A. Jones (Jake); Mike Ballew (Mike).

5. "Face to Face" Written by: Stephen A. Miller. Directed by: Robert Munic. Airdate: October 27, 1997.

A killer who can change his face (thanks to a new surgical technique) uses his ability to mimic the appearance of others to take revenge for his jail sentence.

GUEST CAST: Cyril O'Reilly; Brian Mc-Namara; Donald Trump (Himself).

6. "Chrome" Airdate: November 27, 1997.

A villainous telekinetic, Joran, can transform himself into a creature called "Chrome." Imbued with the same power as Johnny, Joran uses it for evil, hoping to absorb all the mystical energies (and abilities) of those he opposes. Nightman squares off against Chrome when a young woman — capable of teleporting — is attacked.

GUEST CAST: Patrick Macnee (Dr. Walton); Joran (Shane Brolik); Yasemine Bayton (Vanessa).

7. "Takin' It to the Streets" Written by: Stephen A. Miller. Directed by: Rex Piano. Airdate: November 10, 1997

Artemis Burton, a local crime lord who has united the three worst gangs in Bay City, attempts to convince a local basketball athlete, Kevin, to throw an important game. Johnny convinces the boy to do otherwise, and in revenge, Burton captures Raleigh, his girlfriend (a teacher named Tanya) and Frank, forcing Raleigh to fight in a gangland gladiatorial "pit." Nightman saves the day.

GUEST CAST: Evan Lionel, Jennifer Lee, Bo Brown, Mongo Brownlee.

8. "Lady in Red" Story by: Karl Bakke and Glen A. Larson. Written by: Karl Bakke. Directed by: Mark Andrew. Airdate: November 17, 1997.

Johnny rescues a Russian woman, Petra Medved, from a thug during an attack in a parking garage. The thug is a former Soviet KGB officer and member of the Russian Mafia, and Johnny senses that Petra may have once been involved in political assassination (though she claims to be a dispatcher). Her current mission: kill Johnny Domino and California's governor at a costume ball where Domino is scheduled to

play. Frank becomes disturbed when Johnny falls in love with Petra, and sets out to prove her complicity in the Russian underworld; but her loyalties are tested at the costume ball when the Russian mafia reveals that her innocent sister has been kidnapped.

GUEST CAST: Natasha Paylowki (Petra Medved); Valery Nikolaev; Levani; Boris Krutonos; Eliza Sroko; Greg Callahan (Chief Ludlow); Lee Grober (Drunk); Mark Gadbois (Spiderman); Randall Stanton (Elevator Drunk Man); David Montalbano (Police Marksman); J. Michael Ross (Skinney); Philip Munson (Sergi).

9. "That Ol' Gang of Mine" Airdate: November 24, 1997.

The illegitimate son of J. Edgar Hoover, a crazy inventor, resurrects a trio of deadly villains from America's past: Al Capone, Bonnie Parker and John Dillinger. The FBI recruits Johnny's alter ego to stop the gang of old-timers before they start a new crime spree in Bay City.

GUEST CAST: John Polito (Al Capone); Brian Fitzpatrick (Dillinger); Kiersten Warren (Bonnie Parker); Scott Kraft, Tim Maculan, Pat Crawford Brown, David Bowe.

10. "Bad Moon Rising" Airdate: January 11, 1998.

A university professor expecting a shipment of unusual plants from the Brazilian rain forest is unaware that drug smugglers are using the package as a cover for their heroin operation. Unfortunately, the South American plants have contaminated the heroin, making it fatal to customers. Now Johnny and Lt. Dann must bring down the drug dealers before people start dying

GUEST CAST: Ian Patrick Williams (Professor).

11. "Constant Craving" Airdate: January 18, 1998.

Frank Dominus gets more than he bargained for when he learns that his new employer is actually a vampire, and one hoping to become human. Trapped in a power struggle between two vampires, Frank learns that his blood holds the key to making one of the undead creatures a human being again.

GUEST CAST: Lysette Anthony (Erica Bolen); Francois Guery (Stanislaw Volker).

11. "You Are Too Beautiful" Airdate: January 25, 1998.

An ex-convict that bulked up in the joint could be the next wrestling superstar — or a pawn in an illicit scheme. When women begin dying in proximity to the wrestling tour, Johnny must go undercover as a wrestler.

GUEST CAST: Brian McGovern (Rod); Mick Murray (Paddy).

12. "Do You Believe in Magic?" Airdate: February 1, 1998.

The anniversary party for the House of Soul goes horribly wrong when the entertainment, a magician named Selene, turns out to be an evil sorceress. The evil woman makes everybody, including Johnny, experience their worst fears and nightmares. Only the kindly Dr. Walton can help break the spell.

GUEST CAST: Patrick Macnee (Dr. Walton); Jacinda Barrett (Selene).

13. "House of Soul" Airdate: February 8, 1998.

A century-old ghost with the power to generate Earthquakes is found to be dwelling beneath the House of Soul. Can Nightman confront this new danger and survive? Meanwhile, talk show host Jerry Springer visits Bay City.

GUEST CAST: Lily Liu (Bok Chan); Christopher Cousins; Francois Chau; Jerry Springer (Himself).

14. "Nightwoman" Airdate: February 15, 1998.

The origin of a superhero or super threat? A female cop's cover is blown and she is badly injured by the gangsters she was investigating. Now the cop takes on the identity of an avenging superhero to stop evil in Bay City, a fight that brings her face to face with Nightman. When she wounds Nightman, Lt. Dann, who knew the woman, must take action.

GUEST CAST: Jennifer Campbell (Laurie Davis); Brian Smlar.

15. "Chrome II" Written by: Stephen A. Miller and Glen Larson. Directed by: David Francis. Airdate: February 16, 1998.

Joran, the psychic vampire, teams up with Rachel Lang, a villain with the ability to telepathically impose her will on others. Meanwhile, Dann, Raleigh, Johnny, Frank and two reporters, Elaine and Jennifer, meet at the Rocky Mountain Jazz Festival for a fun weekend. Joran and Rachel set out to systematically destroy Johnny's friends, injuring Raleigh while he snowboards, exposing the reporters to a dangerous fire, and converting Johnny into a haughty, unpleasant boor. But Johnny's strange behavior is merely an act, and now he's ready to settle the score with Joran during a snow-sled chase up on Devil's Point.

GUEST CAST: Shane Brolik (Joran); Alexandra Hedison (Jennifer Parks); Fabiana Udenio (Rachel Lang); Robyn Bliley (Elaine Barnes); Darrow Igus; Mike Weston; David L. Prentiss (Announcer); Connie Cragel (Desk Clerk).

16. "Bad to the Bone" Airdate: March 1, 1998.

The survivor of a past clash with Nightman wants to unleash his vengeance upon Johnny. He plots to frame the jazz musician for a number of terrible murders. Then, when things can't get any worse, he manages to get his hands on a new prototype Nightman suit.

GUEST CAST: Cyril O'Reilly (Bridges); Patrick Macnee (Dr. Walton); Lyucinda Weist (Samantha).

17. "Hitchhiker" Written by: Glen A. Larson. Directed by: Nick Daniel. Airdate: April 20, 1998.

An alien spaceship crashes near San Francisco, and the U.S. Army sweeps in to silence the matter, transporting an alien corpse to a nearby base. But the alien is anything but dead, and can possess human beings—hitchhiking from body to body, as it were. Worse, it wants to send a message that Earth is a suitable site for invasion, leaving Raleigh and Johnny, on a night drive in the Prowler, to stop the alien before it signals its faraway brethren...

GUEST CAST: Tucker Smallwood (General Nordath); Will Jeffries; James Tillett; Ben Marley (Escort); Suzanne O'Donnell (Dr. Leslie); Will Hannah (M.P.); Ian Cassidy (Soldier); Dan Woren (Major Dunn); Adam Clark (M.P. #1).

18. "Devil in Disguise" Airdate: May 3, 1998.

Another old villain returns to menace Bay City, hoping to get at Nightman through Johnny. He abducts Johnny and drugs him into a dream state where he is forced to live a scenario involving the death of his father, Frank Dominus.

GUEST CAST: Ric Young (Chang); Patrick Macnee (Dr. Walton).

19. "Double Vision" Airdate: May 17, 1998.

Johnny is heartbroken when he believes that he accidentally killed a popular young athlete from the local university. However, when he sees the dead boy alive and well some time later, he discovers the existence of a sinister cloning plot, one that could lead to the creation of a race of super humans.

GUEST CAST: Donna Barnes (Dr. Hatcher); Roger Davis (Dr. Bowman); Michael Mahon (Wells); Jamie Pressley.

20. "Amazing Grace" Written by: D.G. Larson. Directed by: Nick Daniel. Airdate: May 11, 1998.

Johnny's saxophonist friend Buddy is killed by robbers leaving a gas station hold-up. A depressed Johnny quits his gig as Nightman, fearing that he is fighting a losing battle against evil. But after a car accident, Johnny is transported to Heaven to learn his place in God's creation. An angelic clerk named Simon realizes a terrible mistake has been made and tries to send Johnny back to Earth, showing the hero what the planet would be like without Nightman's services. Convinced by seeing many of his good deeds recounted, Johnny returns to Earth.

GUEST CAST: Cory Tyler (Buddy); Dan Martin (Simon); Cleo King (Buddy's Mom); Raymond Morris (Thug #1); Darron Johnson (Thug #2).

NOTE: This episode features footage from the pilot, "Whole Lotta Shakin'," "I Left My Heart," "Still of the Night," "Chrome," and "Chrome II," among others.

SEASON TWO (1998-1999)

21. "The Ultraweb" Airdate: October 5, 1998.

Johnny plays at a convention on internet technology while his father accepts a job working security for billionaire computer tycoon Mr. Keyes, a devilish soul and operator of Hot.com, a site he calls "Hell on the Web." Trying to save his dad from the grip of the madman, Nightman is teleported via Keyes' new technology, the Ultraweb, into a domain resembling Hell itself. There Johnny must learn Keyes' plan (involving the smearing of a popular U.S. senator) and rescue Frank, who has been "translated" digitally to the Ultraweb. There is a deadly confrontation, and Johnny's father does not survive the day.

GUEST CAST: Kim Coates (Keyes); Earl Holliman (Domino); Vanessa King; Jed Rees; Clay St. Thomas (Anchorman); Miriam Smith (Michelle's Mom); Richard Yee (Karate Instructor); P. Adrien Dorval (Long John); Cam Crown (Lazarus); Brent J.D. Sheppard (Millennium Announcer); B.J. Harrison (Executive Secretary); Kristina Matisic (TV Reporter); Ikkes Battle (Senate Guard); Tim Bissett (Clerk).

22. "The Black Knight" Airdate: October 12, 1998.

Johnny's car is stolen by a car-theft ring, and the search for the Prowler takes Briony and Johnny into conflict with an opponent called the Black Knight, a man capable of sucking energy out of all power sources. But, like Nightman himself, the Black Knight is secretly a force for good, using cast-off technology to combat crime.

GUEST CAST: Lynn Williams (The Black Knight).

23. "It Came from Out of the Sky" Written by: D.G. Larson. Directed by: Michael Kwan. Airdate: October 19, 1998.

Earth, the so-called "forbidden planet" is the battlefield for two warring alien factions, and Raleigh nearly kills a beautiful extraterrestrial bounty hunter when he strikes her with Johnny's Prowler. Meanwhile, three adolescent punks are possessed by her quarry: three escaped alien convicts in possession of a dangerous narcotic. Once again, it's Nightman to the rescue.

GUEST CAST: Brendan Fehr; Tyler Labine; Tara Spencer; A.J. Buckley; David Palffy (Captain); Brent Fidler (Co-pilot); Alonso Oyarzun (Street Kid); Rick Faraci (Bouncer); Jenn Griffin (Rhea); Cam Chai (Attendant); Darrell Izeard (Cop); Jonsye Jaud (Rhea's Voice).

24. "Book of the Dead" Airdate: October 26, 1998.

Johnny is disturbed to learn that a professor, Dr. Sutton, in mourning over the death of his wife, is planning to utilize a deadly grimoire that can raise the dead. Unfortunately, Nightman is unable to stop Sutton's ritual, and an evil lord of the dead called Barzon is resurrected. The dark lord calls forth the dead and buried, and Nightman must team with an unlikely ally to stop the forces of evil.

GUEST CAST: Claudette Mink (Trudy Thorp); David McNally (Dr. Sutton); Barzun (Mark Lindsay Chapman); Tom Heaton.

25. "Fear City" Written by: Steve Kriozere. Directed by: David Wilwing. Airdate: November 2, 1998.

A new game called "Fear City," invented by Keyes' Keyzar Group, premieres on Friday the 13th, but advance copies of the disk have been sucking hapless players (brilliant young computer science students) into a terrifying dimension inhabited by a floating bogeyman. When a girl named Shannon Stark is sucked into the mysterious level 13, Johnny investigates. An unsuspecting Raleigh gets pulled into the game, into Keyes' Ultraweb, and a wave of fear grips the citizenry of Bay City. The Bogeyman, powered by imagination, seeks to obtain a foothold in reality, at least until Nightman joins the fight.

GUEST CAST: Kim Coates (Keyes); Jason Schombing; Kiara Hunter; Robert C. Saunders; Heather Hanson (Singer); Adrienne Carter (Shannon Stark); Shane Kelly (Nance); Ingrid Tesch (Diane Stark); Britney Irvis (Elizabeth); Terry Howson (Cody); Kelly Dean Sereda (Joey); Chiara Zanni (Rebecca); Suzette Meyers (TV Newscaster); Brenda Critchlow (TV News Reporter); Christopher Gray (Teenage Boy).

26. "Manimal" Written by: Glen Larson. Directed by: Allan Eastman. Airdate: November 9, 1998.

Jonathan Chase, the professor with the unusual ability to transform into animals, has been hunting the murderous Jack the Ripper through time. He arrives in Bay City in the present, where his daughter and her pianist boyfriend, Trevor Stanfield, are endangered by the famous serial killer. It turns out Chase has been moving backward and forward through time (via a special crystal "tuned to the soul of the Earth") in hopes of "tipping the balance away from evil and towards good," but he ran afoul of the murderous Ripper. When Teresa is further threatened at a safehouse provided by Johnny, Chase hopes to encourage her to use her inherited ability to transform into beasts of nature, but it is Nightman who will prove to be a vital ally.

GUEST CAST: Simon MacCorkindale (Jonathan Chase); Gerard Plunkett (Jack the Ripper); Carly Pope (Teresa Chase); Shane Kelly (Nance); Beverley Stauton (Singer); Trevor Thompson (TV Announcer); Kyle Cassie (Trevor); Robin Driscoll (Bobby); Mark Holden (Doctor); Tristin Leffler (Waitress).

27. "Knight Life" Written by: Stephen A. Miller. Directed by: Mick McKay. Airdate: November 16, 1998.

A motorcycle-riding assassin named Slade kills a mob informant before Nightman can prevent the hit. Federal Inspector Grant comes to the Bay City to investigate, as does the superhero Black Knight. Slade has been killing other informants too, and he beats up the Black Knight during a confrontation — until Nightman steps in to help. Unfortunately, Slade may have an unexpected and highly placed ally in the Federal government.

GUEST CAST: L. Red Williams (The Black Knight); Blu Mankuma (Inspector Grant); Andrew Bryniarski (Slade); Enuka Okuma (Singer); Richard Leacock (Agent Harris); Edgar Davis (Mark Bugos); Gaston Howard (Agent Keller); James Bamford (Agent Aldrich).

28. "The People's Choice" Written by: Stephen A. Miller. Directed by: David Winning. Airdate: November 23, 1998.

Nightman rescues two amorous teens from a masked villain named Tricky Dick, even as the crook's associate, Keyes, announces his intention to run for the office of Mayor in Bay City. To that end, Keyes orchestrates a sex scandal for the incumbent Mayor Dodson and injures his legitimate challenger. Then he frames Johnny for an assassination attempt on him. With Raleigh's help, Johnny escapes police custody and pays a visit to the Ultraweb, where Bay City's future hangs in the balance.

GUEST CAST: Kim Coates (Kieran Keyes); Brendan Beiser (Tricky Dick); Kiara Hunter; BiF Naked; Shane Kelly (Nance); Sarah Richardson (Singer); Lesley Ewen (Marian Price); Allan Lysell (Mayor Dodson); Lisa Marie Caruk (Patricia); Aaron Smolinski (David); Pamela Martin (Newscaster).

29. "Ring of Fire" Airdate: January 10, 1999.

In China Town, gang members are being killed by a mysterious supernatural force, causing Nightman to face off against, of all things, a dragon.

30. "Sixty Minute Man" Airdate: January 17, 1999.

A new villain arrives in Bay City from the depths of space, the enigmatic Pentecost. This villain not only determines Johnny Domino's secret identity, but can apparently turn back the hands of time — an especially helpful ability (courtesy of a unique wristwatch) in criminal plots.

GUEST CAST: Christopher Shyer (Pentecost), Joely Collins, Tatina Henceroff, Shane Kelly, Larry Musser, Patrick Stevenson, Zoran Vukeliv, John Sampson, Clay St. Thomas, Micasha Armstrong.

31. "Blader" Written by: Jim Korris. Airdate: January 24, 1999.

Criminal roller-bladers are on the loose in Bay City, robbing and looting the town. The high-tech roller-skaters attack Raleigh one night, stealing his car. The design of the high-tech skates leads an injured Raleigh and Nightman to a wronged and financially destitute engineer who has turned to crime. Now it's time for Johnny to infiltrate the roller-blading gang.

GUEST CAST: William McDonald (Tom); Eric Johnson (Alec).

32. "Double Double" Airdate: January 31, 1999.

Arch-nemeses Kieran Keyes and Nightman face-off again, this time over

Keyes plot to combine virtual reality and good old-fashioned reality. Unfortunately, Raleigh and Briony are captured by Keyes, forcing Nightman to return to the Ultraweb.

GUEST CAST: Kim Coates (Keyes); Travis Woloshyn, Jared Van Snellenberg.

33. "Burning Love" Written by: Mark Onspaugh and Scott Thomas. Airdate: February 7, 1999.

Johnny crosses paths with a beautiful "fire elemental," a long-lived creature that has the power to make her enemies spontaneously combust. Johnny is strangely drawn to the beautiful woman, Aurora, but her powers make her a dangerous acquaintance, as Briony learns ... the hard way.

GUEST CAST: Sarah Wynter (Aurora); Adam Harrington (Burton); Alex Diakun (Dr. Thorn); Sean Campbell, Stuart O'Connell, Warren Takeuchi, Robert Weiss, Charles Payne, Fred Henderson.

34. "Scent of a Woman" Written by: D.G. Larson. Airdate: February 14, 1999.

Nightman must defend the future rulers of the distant planet Alastra, who plan to wed to stop a terrible galactic war. Unfortunately, dissidents have sent an assassin — a deadly alien vegetable — to Earth to kill the lovers.

GUEST CAST: Monika Schnarre (Zentare); Fiona Lowei (Lar); Larry Musser, Russell Ferrier.

35. "Dust" Airdate: February 21, 1999.

During a bungled robbery at a museum, Nightman inadvertently causes the resurrection of the evil Egyptian queen Neftalah. Attempting to stay young and beautiful, the vain — and murderous — Neftalah uses every weapon at her disposal, including laser beams and hypnosis. She brainwashes a hapless Raleigh, forcing him to serve her evil whims and help build a machine that will keep her forever young.

GUEST CAST: Saskia Garel (Neftalah).

36. "Spellbound" Airdate: February 28, 1999.

A young girl whose parents were killed is held in thrall by a malevolent priest, actually a deadly warlock. Nightman helps the adolescent, Lily, calling on her unusual heritage to help him defeat the evil Father Michael.

GUEST CAST: Garwin Sanford (Father Michael); Amber Rothwell (Lily); Jody Thompson, Jill Teed, Allan Gray, Saskia Garel.

37. "Love and Death" Written by: Stephen A. Miller. Airdate: March 7, 1999.

An old enemy of Briony's is out of prison and seeking revenge. This complicates a date with Johnny. Meanwhile, Raleigh has his own problem to contend with.

GUEST CAST: Douglas H. Arthurs (Kane); Yanna McIntosh.

38. "The Enemy Within" Airdate: April 25, 1999.

Raleigh experiences a terrible precognition, and learns that his efforts to hack into Kieran Keyes' network could have catastrophic effects on those he loves. Before long, Nightman is once again dealing with his most dangerous opponent.

GUEST CAST: Kim Coates (Keyes).

39. "Gore" Directed by: David Winning. Airdate: May 2, 1999.

The creators of the evil super-soldier Slade strike again with a new creation: the child-like "Gore." Nightman clashes with Gore, who hopes to find a "bride" for his master.

40. "Revelations" Airdate: May 9, 1999.

A family secret obsesses Johnny Domino, and he learns of a long-lost twin, abducted at birth.

41. "Nightwoman Returns" Airdate: May 16, 1999.

Nightman re-teams with Night-woman, this time to help settle political issues on San Marcos, an island where voodoo is the dominant faith. In this case, a young boy's lineage could change the island's destiny for all time, unseating a brutal dictator.

GUEST CAST: Deanna Milligan (Night-woman); Steve Bacic (Raul Marquez).

42. "Keyes to the Kingdom of Hell"
Airdate: May 23, 1999.

Nightman does battle with Keyes one more time, as the villain attempts to rebuild his nefarious Ultraweb. Unfortunately, Johnny is incarcerated after being framed for trying to kill Keyes.

GUEST CAST: Kim Coates (Keyes); Stacy Grant, Saskia Garel.

Now and Again

The rather generically named *Now and Again* is the inventive brainchild of producer Glenn Gordon Caron, who made his name on the TV series *Moonlighting*, a 1980s-era romantic comedy about bickering, sparring detectives (in the persons of Bruce Willis and Cybill Shepherd). Although some critics compared Caron's 1999-2000 series to *The Six Million Dollar Man* (because *Now and Again* concerned an artificial — but organic, not mechanical — man built by the United States government), the focus of the Caron series was completely different. In this program, humor and family drama were as important as the mission of the week, and the characters were more developed than Steve Austin or Oscar Goldman on the classic bionic series.

Now and Again began as forty-five-year-old Michael Wiseman (John Goodman) learned that he was being replaced on the job at Empire Insurance by a scheming and insufferable 27-year-old back-stabber (Chad Lowe). After a night out drinking with his buddy and co-worker Roger Bender (Gerrit Graham), Wiseman headed home from Manhattan to his house in the suburbs, only to fall victim to a terrible accident. He was accidentally pushed in front of a speeding subway car and killed instantly. Michael thus left behind a shattered family, including the beautiful but acerbic Lisa Wiseman (Margaret Colin), his wife, and troubled teenager Heather (Heather Matazzaro).

But Wiseman's death was just the beginning of this strange tale. In fact, Wiseman's brain was transplanted into an artificial body (Eric Close of *Dark Skies* [1996-97]) shortly after his demise. Working for the government, the stern and temperamental Dr. Theodore Morris (Dennis Haysbert, of *24*) had created the first "super-soldier," a warrior — or superhero, in perfect physical condition. Formerly overweight at 292 lbs., the resurrected Wiseman — now buff and healthy at 172 lbs.— was delighted to learn he had been granted a second chance at life. Delighted, that is, until he learned that there were some rules governing this new existence. The most important of these was that he could no longer have contact of any kind with his wife and daughter, on penalty of their deaths. For Michael, this was an intolerable situation. A family man through and through, he was still very much in love with Lisa, and he missed the close relationship he shared with Heather.

Also making matters with Dr. Morris uncomfortable, Michael still had the appetites of an overweight, middle-aged man, and his trim new body could not accommodate such toxins. Thus Michael was forced to exercise almost constantly, and not allowed to eat anything but green vegetables and a specially prepared "goop." His urine and fecal matter was even retained in a special toilet for study by diligent scientists.

Moonlighting as superheroes — the cast of *Now and Again* (1999-2000). From left to right: Lisa Wiseman (Margaret Colin), Michael Wiseman (Eric Close) and Dr. Theodore Morris (Dennis Haysbert).

Locked in a spartan apartment in Manhattan that he called a "terrarium" (in the episode "By the Light of the Moon"), Michael was often made to feel a prisoner — or, more appropriately, a laboratory rat. A loving man and free thinker, he had a difficult time adjusting to a so tightly regulated life, and Dr. Morris did not make it easy for him. "You're dead," he said to Michael in one story, "you're just going to have to live with that."

From a certain standpoint, Morris's attitude seemed rational. Unlike Colonel Steve Austin, after all, the new Michael Wiseman cost the government a fortune in millennial monetary terms. His pituitary alone cost $47 million, and his pancreas cost $19 million! Considering the expense, it was to Morris's advantage to help Michael cope with his new life. On one occasion ("By the Light of the Moon") he even threw a lovely female physical trainer at Wiseman, in hopes of making the family man forget his past, but it did not work.

The bulk of *Now and Again* concerned Michael's feelings of isolation from his wife and child, and their attempts to move on with their lives following the tragedy that claimed his life. The series was about a love affair that even death could not sever, and thus was romantic in a very tragic, very touching manner. Often Michael would escape from his apartment and attempt to see his family, or happen to run into them during the course of his mission ("Pulp Turkey"). At other times, Michael was sent on death-defying missions that did not intersect at all with his former life, and only his abilities as a man-made superman carried him through the day.

And what abilities those were! Michael could hold his breath for six minutes and eleven seconds ("Over Easy"), bend machine-gun barrels with his bare hands ("I've Grown Accustomed to His Face"), lift full-grown adults over his head with a single finger ("By the Light of the Moon") and perform other miraculous feats. His only weakness (like kryptonite) was a photosensitivity syndrome (revealed in "Deep in My Heart Is a Song"). He reacted adversely to lights flashing at a certain frequency and would slip into a coma. Naturally, this weakness occurred at the worst time, during a government review of Morris's project, and Michael's life was jeopardized.

Above all these genre elements, the thing that made this superhero so sympathetic and fun to watch was his emotionality, his humanity, and the difficulty of his predicament. "He's got a regular guy's brain, and I think that's what people are interested in," said Eric Close, the actor who played Michael throughout the short-lived series.[1]

Fortunately for fans, notorious for their impatience in such matters, *Now and Again* was not merely a family drama about loss, grief and moving on. It was also a full-blown superhero adventure featuring plenty of interesting villains and action. The terrorist known as the Eggman was the most notorious of the show's rogue's gallery. In "Origins," "On the Town," "Over Easy" and "The Eggman Cometh," this elderly Asian terrorist threatened to spread a terrible biological plague across Manhattan. He carried his specially designed, deadly agent in eggshells, and then, while wearing a protective gas mask, cracked the eggs in crowds and watched as helpless populations fell before his weapon of mass destruction, bleeding profusely from their eyes and noses.

Other villains included a corrupt government agent (Ed O'Ross in "One for the Money") and a greedy insurance salesman (played by Chad Lowe in "The Insurance Man Always Rings Twice"). There was also a dying millionaire who wanted a healthy new body and kidnapped Dr. Morris in "I've Grown Accustomed to Your Face," and even standard old bank robbers in "Film at Eleven." Bob Balaban played an organ harvester running a "chop shop" in "Lizzard's Tale," and there was a crazed environmentalist controlling an army of deadly insects in the two-part episode called "The Bugmeister." Naturally, young Heather had a crush on the bug guy, complicating matters.

Superhero fans could rejoice over other well-tuned elements in *Now and Again* as well. As in the oeuvre of Joss Whedon, there were many humorous references to superhero lore sprinkled throughout the show. "Can I fly, like Superman?" Michael asked in "Origins." "Thanks, Commissioner Gordon," he quipped to an official in "Wonder Boy," and so on. The point to these numerous references was that Michael found his situation as a "real" superhero patently absurd, and thus compared it to the stories he was familiar with — those of Batman, Superman and even Captain America (in "Film at Eleven"). It was a humanizing and funny touch.

Though it was never preachy or saccharine, *Now and Again* also presented a number of intriguing human topics. Michael dealt with jealousy in "On the Town" when Lisa began dating, and contemplated the morality of murder in "One for the Money." The very set-up and premise of the series, which saw a middle-aged man literally replaced by a younger man, concerned ageism, and it served as a recurring theme throughout the show. Could a middle-aged woman find love with the young Michael Wiseman, or rather his alias, Michael Newman?

Those very names spelled out the theme of the series. In exchanging an older, experienced body for that of a young man's, the wise man had become the new man. And, of course, "man" is the suffix of all good superheroes, isn't it? Spider-MAN. BatMAN. SuperMAN. *Now and Again* offered audiences the blending of WiseMAN and NewMAN, the heroic combination of wise mind and young body. It was an artistic conceit and one that served the series very well.

It would be a delight to report that

Now and Again had a long run on network television after its debut in late September 1999. But, of course, that did not happen. The series met with critical accolades, and *Entertainment Weekly*'s Bruce Fetts called it "funny, scary and surprisingly addictive." Accordingly, the show was highly rated at first, airing on Friday nights at 9:00 P.M. on CBS (against Chris Carter's *Harsh Realm* on Fox, and *Dateline* on NBC). The series tied for first place among 18 to 49 year olds, a key demographic, early in the season, but eventually slipped some 34 percent.[2] Why the drastic ratings slip? As usual, it had nothing to do with the series itself, but network interference.

In this case, CBS preempted *Now and Again* almost constantly, for specials such as the *Miss USA Pageant*, the NCAA Basketball Tournament, and even a *Candid Camera* special! Often times, if audiences were lucky, they might get to watch *Now and Again* twice a month.

If that was not bad enough, *Now and Again* in 2000 had to face a new and surprising ratings powerhouse, the ABC game show hosted by Regis Philbin called *Who Wants to Be a Millionaire*.

Then there was the matter of the series' title. *Now and Again* aired the same season as the ABC divorce drama *Once and Again* (starring *The Rocketeer*'s Billy Campbell) and the MSNBC news summary series hosted by Jane Pauley called *Time and Again*. Which show was which? Viewers didn't care to find out, and none of the three "again" series survived for long. Had *Now and Again* been called *The 50 Million Dollar Man*, it might have stayed on the air a lot longer.

Reruns of *Now and Again* began airing in primetime during the summer of 2001 on the Sci-Fi Channel, but were abruptly pulled off the air in favor of reruns of *The Outer Limits* remake. The show then moved to Sunday mornings at 10:00 A.M. for a spell in 2002 before disappearing from the schedule.

Now and Again (1999–2000)
LIVE–ACTION TV SERIES

"As the brains behind the year's most surprising romance/comedy/sci-fi drama, Glenn Gordon Caron obviously has learned a few things from his long TV absence since *Moonlighting* ... the wonders of network television never cease."
> — Ken Tucker. *Entertainment Weekly:* "The Best and Worst: Television." 1999 Year End Special, page 130.

"Caron uses sci-fi to delve into the depths of familial love and loss. That such diverse themes work so well together is a tribute to Caron's talents as a storyteller. But he also gets lots of help from his appealing cast...It makes for interesting, entertaining and ... touching television."
> —Allan Johnson, *Cinescape:* "Out of Body Experience." March/April 2000. *http://sundance.hispeed.com/ naa/magazines/misc/cine1.html*

"The strength of Now and Again was that it wasn't really a superhero show. Yes, it was a bionic man–type of situation, but the series concentrated just as much on Lisa's character as it did Michael's. It was as much human drama as it was action adventure. Probably more so. Had it been a straight action-adventure, it would have been The Six Million Dollar Man all over again. Instead, the missions came occasionally, sporadically, and I preferred that approach because it was more human. I just hate the fact that the series ended on a cliffhanger."
> — Howard Margolin, host of Destinies: The Voice of Science Fiction.

"It's quirky, it's mesmerizing, it's addictive.... It is so wildly original it defies conventional categorization."
> —Ray Richmond, *Variety*, September 20, 1999, page 40.

"...[S]tylish, clever and unpredictable."
> —*People*, November 1, 1999, page 31.

CAST: Eric Close (Michael Wiseman); Dennis Haysbert (Dr. Theodore Morris); Gerrit Graham (Roger Bender); Margaret Colin (Lisa Wiseman); Heather Matazzaro (Heather).

CREW: *Created by:* Glenn Gordon Caron. *Produced by:* Henry Bronchtien. *Coordinating Producer:* Jessie Ward. *Supervising Producer:* Rene Echevarria. *Associate Producers:* Marlane Meyer, Alysse Bezahler.

1. "Origins" Written and directed by: Glenn Gordon Caron. Airdate: September 24, 1999.

Overweight, middle-aged insurance salesman Michael Wiseman has a very bad day. First he is passed over for a promotion in favor of smarmy, 27-year-old Craig Spence, and then he is hit by a subway train and killed. The United States government, however, saves his brain and transplants it into a specially engineered young male body. Though Michael's new mentor, Dr. Theodore Morris, sets him up in a Manhattan apartment, he also warns Michael that under no circumstances would he be allowed to make contact with his beloved wife Lisa and their daughter, Heather, who are still mourning his death. Meanwhile, a mysterious terrorist, "the Eggman," kills innocent civilians with poison eggs.

GUEST CAST: John Goodman (Michael Wiseman); Chip Zien (Gerald Misenback); Chad Lowe (Craig Spence); Kim Chan (The Eggman).

2. "On the Town" Written by Glenn Gordon Caron. Directed by: Christopher Misiano. Airdate: October 1, 1999.

While testing the strength and agility of his new super body at a gym, Michael breaks free from his government bodyguards and attempts to reconnect with his former life, particular his old friend and co-worker Roger Bender. At the same time, Eggman continues his reign of terror from a cyber-latte bar. Back in Manhattan, Michael persuades Roger to take him to the Wiseman house, his old home in the suburbs. After catching his first glimpse of Lisa since his death, he realizes she is going out on a date with her attorney, Gerald. Before his recapture by Morris, Michael talks to Lisa—

without revealing his identity — and makes an impression on his former wife.

GUEST CAST: Chip Zien (Gerald); Kim Chan (Eggman).

3. "Over Easy" Written by: Glenn Gordon Caron. Directed by: Alan Taylor. Airdate: October 8, 1999.

The Eggman strikes accidentally, releasing a nerve gas egg and wiping out everyone on his floor at a New York City hotel. As the Eggman plots a second attack, Dr. Morris decides that his new superman, Michael Wiseman, will be the one to deliver the ransom payment to the terrorist at a meeting set up on a train. At the time of the transfer, Michael is startled to see Roger, Lisa and Heather also on the commuter train. He seeks Lisa's help in removing the poison egg from the subway before going after the Eggman and ending the villain's reign of terror.

GUEST CAST: Kim Chan (Eggman).

4. "One for the Money" Written by: Hans Tobeason. Directed by: Susan Seidelman. Airdate: October 15, 1999.

Dr. Morris and Michael meet with an operative for the government, an old friend of Theodore's named Murphy. Michael is assigned to accompany Murphy on a mission to assassinate a double agent in a foreign country, even though he's resistant to the idea of killing anybody. While Lisa attempts to get a job to support the Wiseman family, Murphy and Michael infiltrate the penthouse of their target ... and Murphy attempts to sell U.S. secrets to the mark. When offered a cut of the reward, Michael faces temptation...

GUEST CAST: Ed O'Ross (Murphy); Cynthia Harris, Robert Hogan, Patricia Maucery, Libby Larson, Kit Flanagan.

5. "The Insurance Man Always Rings Twice" Written by: Rene Echevar-

ria. Directed by: Vincent Misiano. Airdate: October 22, 1999.

When Michael learns that Grand Empire Insurance and his replacement, Craig Spence, have denied his family their rightful benefits from his death, he petitions Morris to intervene. Things have gotten so bad for Lisa that she will lose the family house if she doesn't get some money, but agendas align when Morris reveals that Spence is under investigation by the government. With Roger's assistance, Michael acquires a new job at Grand Empire as Spence's assistant in an effort to expose his illegitimate business ventures. On a high hotel ledge, Michael exacts some nasty revenge, forcing a terrified Spence to pay up and save Lisa's house.

GUEST CAST: Chad Lowe (Craig Spence); Al Roffe (Sanchez).

6. "Nothing to Fear but Nothing to Fear" Written by: Michael Angeli. Directed by: Tim Van Patten. Airdate: November 5, 1999.

A woman terrified of heights climbs a tower on Coney Island and allows herself to plunge to her death rather than be rescued by the police. While Lisa goes on a blind date, Michael researches the case, learning of a pharmacist who has developed a formula that helps people overcome fears and inhibitions. While Morris and Michael hunt Lomax, the developer of the drug that alters brain chemistry, Lisa plans a date with Michael Newman, Wiseman's alias. Unable to reestablish contact with his wife, Michael is forced to stand her up at the restaurant, a hurtful gesture he deeply regrets.

GUEST CAST: Chip Zien (Gerald Misenback); John DeVries, Bruce MacVittie, John Bedford Lloyd, Joyce Van Patten.

7. "A Girl's Life" Written by: Marlane Emily Gornard. Directed by: Bryan Spicer. Airdate: November 12, 1999.

Heather is struck by lightning while

watching a light show in the sky — which, in fact, happens to be Michael, working on Dr. Morris's latest anti-gravity experiment. Morris tells Michael that Heather is in a coma and permits him to visit the hospital. Because of the strange luminescent "superconductor" suit he is wearing, Heather mistakes Michael for an angel as she awakens. When she tells her story at school, the local press runs with it, and many people believe she is crazy.

GUEST CAST: Charlie Hofheimer, Mark Nelson.

8. "Pulp Turkey" Written by: Ted Humphrey. Directed by: Harry Winer. Airdate: November 19, 1999.

Thanksgiving Day arrives, and Lisa and Heather have trouble dealing with Michael's absence. And, since it is a Federal holiday, that means Michael must celebrate with Morris's family. Unfortunately, holiday plans are interrupted when Roger is drawn into a robbery of priceless Russian jewels, and thieves follow him to Lisa's house. When Theo's car breaks down close to Westchester, Michael has the opportunity to visit — and rescue — his family on Thanksgiving.

GUEST CAST: Brian Tarantina, Erik LaRay Harvey.

9. "By the Light of the Moon" Written by: Rene Echevarria. Directed by: Vincent Misiano. Airdate: November 26, 1999.

Dr. Morris seems perturbed when a physical trainer, a beautiful woman named Dr. Taylor, is brought in by the government to enhance Michael's fighting capabilities. Michael becomes attracted to Dr. Taylor, while, elsewhere, Lisa's attorney, Mr. Misenback, courts her affection. Independently of one another, Michael and Lisa both go on dates with their new significant others, but end up simply remembering their own, undying love.

GUEST CAST: Chip Zien (Gerald Misenback); Reiko Aylesworth (Dr. Taylor).

10. "I've Grown Accustomed to His Face" Written by: Rene Echeverria. Story by: Marlane Meyer. Directed by: David Jones. Airdate: December 17, 1999.

On a day he expects to participate in survival training, Michael is surprised when Dr. Morris fails to report in the morning. He finds Morris's front door open and sets off the security alarm, but there is no sign of his friend/captor ... only armed soldiers in biological suits. Michael escapes and seeks help from the police, but is pursued; while at the same time a strange man approaches Roger and Lisa separately, asking questions about Michael's whereabouts. Michael tracks the man down and finds a kidnapped Dr. Morris, who is being held against his will by a dying millionaire, a man who wants his brain transplanted into a healthy, young body.

GUEST CAST: Stephen Bogardus, Tom Aldredge, William Hill, Bruce Altman.

11. "Fire and Ice" Written by: Ted Humphrey. Directed by: Vincent Misiano. Airdate: January 7, 2000.

In New York, a seemingly normal woman spontaneously combusts, with her body reduced to ashes. Across town, in the lab, Theo exposes Michael's super body to extremes of cold and heat, and also falls in love with a doctor, Lauren, working there. Meanwhile, as the Wisemans' wedding anniversary draws near, Lisa is having trouble sleeping because of the memories. While Michael plays Cyrano for Dr. Morris, another spontaneous combustion occurs...

GUEST CAST: Ellen Bethea (Dr. Lauren Rivers); Peter McRobbie.

12. "Disco Inferno" Written by: Marlene Mayer. Directed by: Jace Alexander. Airdate: January 14, 2000.

A series of unexplained deaths, apparently spontaneous human combustion, continue to plague the New York area. Michael and Theo investigate the crimes, while in the suburbs, Roger attempts to teach Heather to drive.

GUEST CAST: Timothy Devlin.

13. "I Am the Greatest" Written by: Michael Angeli. Directed by: Vincent Misiano. Airdate: January 28, 2000.

Before Michael, the government attempted to create a perfect super-soldier once before, but that "version" disappeared without a trace. Now Theo and the government believe the first super-soldier may be hiding out as a boxer, and assign Michael to find out the truth. Meanwhile, Lisa's first buyer at the real estate firm is someone with more than a professional interest in her.

GUEST CAST: Jamey Sheridan.

14. "Film at Eleven" Written by: Debbie Sarjeant. Directed by: Ronald L. Schwary. Airdate: February 11, 2000.

While Lisa fends off the amorous advances of a married man, Michael is permitted to walk around Manhattan during Theo's visit with the President of the United States. Trying to buy flowers for Lisa for Valentine's Day, Michael gets caught in a bank robbery and is locked in a vault. When another prisoner in the vault has a heart attack, Michael breaks down the substantial metal door to help. Unfortunately, there is a camera in the vault, and Michael could be exposed as a superhero, even as Lisa learns that a secret admirer has sent her flowers.

GUEST CAST: Jamey Sheridan, Faith Prince, Adam LeFevre.

15. "Deep in My Heart Is a Song" Written by: Thomas Edward Bray. Directed by: Vincent Misiano. Airdate: February 18, 2000.

Theo and Michael are nervous as they await word on their project funding. On the morning of the meeting to discuss continuance of the project, Michael inexplicably falls into a coma, a problem that plagued him before his death. At the time, he went to a hospital for tests, and Lisa feared he might be having an affair. As it turns out, the problem is photosensitivity syndrome.

GUEST CAST: John Goodman (Michael Weisman); Michael Weaver (Young Doctor); James Rebhorn, Tim Hopper.

16. "Everybody Who's Anybody" Written by: Dan E. Fesman and Harry Victor. Directed by: Stephen Cragg. Airdate: February 25, 2000.

A special party for a politician becomes an opportunity for embarrassment when both Michael, on a mission, and Lisa, on a date, end up attending the soiree.

GUEST CAST: Jamey Sheridan, Chad Lowe.

17. "Boy Wonder" Written by: Ted Humphrey. Directed by: Vincent Misiano. Airdate: March 10, 2000.

A mentally retarded youngster named Jimmy fancies himself a superhero and is thrilled when he secretly witnesses Michael in action. He finds Michael's apartment and worshipfully contacts his new hero, but Theo and Michael try to discourage his fantasies. But Jimmy isn't so easily dissuaded, and his accidental knowledge of a foreign terrorist plot proves handy. Meanwhile, Roger dabbles — dangerously — in online trading, hoping to prove a point to the insulting Craig Spence.

GUEST CAST: Chad Lowe (Craig Spence); Maurice Dwyer.

18. "Lizzard's Tale" Written by: Deborah Sarjeant. Directed by: Bob Balaban. Airdate: March 31, 2000.

Michael is getting bored and tired of his new life, with no TV, no newspapers and no friends, so Theo takes him to the Human Construction Sciences Seminar, where Morris is presenting a paper. Meanwhile, Heather is seeing a new boyfriend, and Lisa is trying to make a go of her floundering career in real estate, with the unlikely support of Roger. At the conference, a biotech company owner, Freddie Lizzard, Theo's medical school roommate, attempts to recruit Theo to the private sector. Unfortunately, Lizzard is running a secret "chop shop" and stealing healthy organs to sell to the highest bidder; and when he learns Michael's secret, he thinks he's found the holy grail of organ replacement.

GUEST CAST: Bob Balaban (Freddie Lizzard).

19. "There Are No Words" Written by: Thomas Edward Bray. Directed by: Aaron Lipstadt. Airdate: April 14, 2000.

Michael wants a book to read, but Theo won't let him have any reading material. The next day Theo is horrified to learn that books in a nearby library are being drained of print, of all words! The phenomenon repeats at the Wiseman home, and Theo comes to fear that nano-bots in Michael's blood have become airborne and are devouring the printed word. As books become a valuable commodity, and the world changes forever, Theo is in store for another shock.

GUEST CAST: Doris Belack.

20. "The Bugmeister" Written by: Michael Angeli. Directed by: Sandy Smolan. Airdate: April 21, 2000.

Powerful men are being attacked and killed by disease-carrying insects. In fact, a young scientist at a New York museum — Heather's new crush — is utilizing insects to wreak vengeance on the wealthy establishment poisoning the Earth and injuring insects. He sends an army of red ants to kill the transgenic crop producer who finances his work, hiding his real plans from a curious Heather. At Theo's suggestion, Michael is deployed to capture one of the rampaging bugs.

GUEST CAST: Matt McGrath (Stanley Bing); David Wohl, Faith Prince, Michael Gaston.

21. "The Bugmeister Part II" Written by: Michael Angeli. Directed by: Vincent Misiano. Airdate: April 28, 2000.

After jumping off the roof of a building in the city to catch one of Bing's attacking insects, the homing device in Michael's nose is removed and placed inside the captured bee. Meanwhile, Lisa asks Roger to move out of the house — where he has been staying with the Wisemans during his separation of 17 days — and encourages him to reconcile with his wife, Ruth. The bugmeister plots to strike again, unaware that Heather has told Lisa about her suspicions regarding him. The tracking device leads Michael to Bing, and he rescues Heather from the bug man, even as he faces a swarm of a quarter-million bees carrying bubonic plague.

GUEST CAST: Matt McGrath (Dr. Bing).

22. "The Eggman Cometh" Written by: Rene Echevarria. Directed by: Ronald L. Schwary. Airdate: May 5, 2000.

For the first time since his rebirth, Michael has no tracking device inside his head, courtesy of his confrontation with "the bugmeister." At the Wiseman house, Lisa soon learns from an attorney that her husband didn't die on impact, that he survived the train accident, at least for a time. Even more disturbing, the terrorist known as "the Eggman" engineers an escape from prison with the help of his burly cellmate. Finally, when Michael learns that Lisa's life may be in jeopardy from Theo, he breaks out of custody, runs to the Wiseman house, and flees with Lisa and Heather.

GUEST CAST: Paul Guilfoyle (Ed Bernstadt); Kim Chan (The Eggman); Faith Prince, WWF Superstar Mick Foley.

Once a Hero (a.k.a. *Captain Justice*)

Nearly forgotten in the twenty-first century is this very short-lived ABC comedic TV series from 1987. It follows firmly in the amusing tradition of *Captain Nice, Mr. Terrific* and to some degree, *The Greatest American Hero.*

In short, *Once a Hero* is the tale of a confused superhero, Captain Justice, who must contend with a changing world, and often has trouble doing so. The problem is that the universe seems to have passed Captain Justice by. He lives in Pleasantville, a comic book town that looks vaguely two di-mensional. There he fights villains such as Destructo and Mr. Mayhem, but, basically, has some questions about his existence. Why is it that he has been fighting the same super-villains for thirty years? Why doesn't he just kill them? And what about that hot little number, Rachel Kirk? He's been in love with her for just as long, but has never tried to romance her. Why is that? And she can't ever seem to figure out his not-too-se-cret secret identity, either.

But none of these problems are as crucial as the one facing Pleasantville: with-out people in the real world (i.e. fans) to keep their universe alive, all of Captain Jus-tice's friends and enemies fading from exis-tence.

Optimistic that the riddle can be solved, Captain Justice believes that the an-swer to his questions may exist on the other side of "the Forbidden Zone"—on Earth—where his creator, an elderly comic book writer named Abner Davis, lives and writes. Justice crosses the zone to meet his maker, only to learn that his myriad powers (such as infrared vision) don't operate outside Pleasantville. Worse, his yellow collar, red costume and shoulder pads stand out like a sore thumb in the real world. Without his super powers, Captain Justice fears he is nothing but a coward.

That's the premise of *Once a Hero*, a cheap-looking but witty superhero series. Particularly entertaining are the many self-reflexive jokes about comic book super-heroes. Captain Justice is the property of Pizzazz Comics, an organization that has just cancelled his book because it is no longer appealing to children—and because Abner has resisted the temptation to add "uzis" and the "swift retribution" style of then-contemporary heroes like Rambo. Worse, Captain Justice is such a goody two-shoes that some neighborhood kids think he might be gay...

Once a Hero aired only three times (on Saturday nights) in 1987, and featured the ongoing misadventures of Captain Justice and his square alter ego, Brad Steele. Sur-rounded by friends, including a comic book gumshoe (played by Robert Forster), his real-life creator Abner (Milo O'Shea) and a sitcom family (the Greeleys) with the req-uisite Mom and smart-aleck child, Captain Justice learned a special lesson in each story. The show was a little sappy and saccharine, but not totally without merit because of its observations about the changing climate and character of superheroes; and it cham-pioned the view that people don't have to have super powers to make a difference in our world.

The fourth episode of the series fea-tured Adam West as the TV incarnation of Captain Justice, an embittered, out-of-work actor typecast in similar roles. Unfortu-nately, *Once a Hero* was cancelled after the third episode, and West's story never saw a wide audience. Other guest stars on the se-ries included Larry Drake (*Darkman* [1990]), Fran Drescher and Martine Beswicke.

Once a Hero (1987)
LIVE-ACTION SERIES

CAST: Jeff Lester (Captain Justice/Brad Steele); Robert Forster (Gumshoe); Caitlin Clarke (Emma Greely); Josh Blake (Woody Greely); David Wohl (Edward Kybo); Milo O'Shea (Abner Bevis).

CREW: *Music:* Dennis Dreith. *Art Directors:* Bob Fox, K.C. Fox. *Film Editors:* Stuart Bass, Michael Berman. *Director of Photography:* Joao Fernandes. *Producer:* Paul Pompian. *Executive Producer:* Dusty Kay. *Costume Designer:* Merril Greene. *Special Effects Coordinator:* Ron Trost. *Production Manager:* Scott Maitland. *First Assistant Director:* Richard Graves. *Associate Producer:* Peter Rich. *Stunt Coordinator:* Steve Kelson. *Property Master:* Christopher Amy. *Set Decorator:* Keith Barrett.

1. "Once a Hero" Written by: Dusty Kay. Directed by: Claudia Well and Kevin Inch. Airdate: September 19, 1987.

Abner Bevis, the creator of Captain Justice comic books, has been getting old, relegating the straight-arrow superhero to old-fashioned, rerun adventures. Unbeknownst to Abner, Captain Justice is alive and well in the dimension of fiction, and disturbed that he is losing popularity in the real world. Unless he can somehow restore his reputation in Abner's universe, he — and all his friends and foes alike — will fade into nothingness. Captain Justice crosses the Forbidden Zone, with a film noir gumshoe hot on his heels, to restore the world's faith in him, starting with a juvenile delinquent named Woody Greely, who believes he has outgrown the goody-goody Captain Justice.

GUEST CAST: William Griffis; Diana Kay; Harris Laskawy; Richard Biggs; Michael Currie; Ronalda Douglas; Carolyn Megini; Deborah Offner; Josh Richman; Michael Rider; Dana Short; Vince McKewn (Photographer); Sean Patrick (Irwen); Ian Pettrella (Eugene); Mescal Wasilewski (Punk #2); Jerry Corley (Technician); Dick Drumm (Shopkeeper); Alan David Gelman (Bernie Rosen); Stephan Anthony Henry (Shelly); Judy Kain (Barbara Lasker); Ron Karabatos (Mr. Avalon); Jeffrey Lambert (Mark Barnes); Fred Lerher (Thug); Dason Marin (Paperboy); Michael Masters (Henchman); Scott Menville (Cubby); Charlie Messenger (Well-Heeled Man); E. Danny Murphy (Crook #2).

2. "Triangle" Written by: Carolyn Shelby and Christopher Ames. Directed by: Win Phelps. Airdate: September 26, 1987.

Captain Justice's comic book damsel love, Rachel Kirk, follows him into the real world, but it is the comic hero's creator, Abner, who is most affected by her arrival. When creating the comic, he modeled Rachel after his real-life soul mate, his wife (now deceased), and Abner can't help loving her.

GUEST CAST: Dana Lee Gant, William Griffis, Trevor Henley.

3. "The Return of Lazarus" Written by: Ira Steven Behr. Directed by: Kevin Hooks. Airdate: October 3, 1987.

The evil Victor Lazarus, the archnemesis of Captain Justice, makes the journey to the real world to confront his longtime, but now missing, enemy. But what he really wants to know (from Abner) is why he was created a monster in the first place.

GUEST CAST: Dennis Fimple, William Griffis, Richard Lynch.

4. "Things Get Ugly" Written by: Dusty Kay. Directed by: Paul Schneider. Airdate: unaired.

Captain Justice meets another alterego, the actor who played him on a TV series and has been typecast in the role, much to his chagrin. Meanwhile, Gumshoe takes a trip back to Pleasantville.

GUEST CAST: Adam West, Martine Beswicke, Christopher Neame, David Fimple.

5. "Manos Arriba Mrs. Greely" Written by: Richard Manning and Hans Beimler. Directed by: Harry Hurwitz. Airdate: unaired.

Gumshoe investigates an incriminating roll of film in Central America.

GUEST CAST: Larry Drake, Fran Drescher, Mark Holton.

The Phantom

The Ghost Who Walks — or, as he is more famously known, the Phantom — first appeared in King Features comic strips in 1936. This was several years before the world became acquainted with Batman, Superman and other famous superheroes, making the Lee Falk (1911–1999) creation one of the earliest costumed crime fighters of the twentieth century. Falk had already created Mandrake the Magician (in 1934), but it was the Phantom (which he created at age 25) that was his most influential work of art, in many ways a prototype for the many heroes that would follow the Ghost's footsteps. He based the legend of his superhero on the literature he enjoyed most, including Greek mythology, Arthurian legend, Rudyard Kipling's *The Jungle Book,* Zorro and the Scarlet Pimpernel. The character was drawn by Ray Moore.

The Phantom, garbed in a purple (or gray) jumpsuit and small eye-mask (with no pupils), had a simple origin. The multi-generation story began in the sixteenth century with a shipwreck off the coast of Africa. A young boy named Walker saw his parents murdered before his very eyes by pirates of the Singh Brotherhood, and consequently swore vengeance. He thus donned a skull ring (which always left quite an impression on villains) and sleek costume to fight the pirates from a secret location in the African jungle, the Skull Cave. Although a local tribe of pygmies knew his secret, most people in the world believed that the Phantom was an immortal, a ghost, when in fact the mantle of superhero was simply passed on from father to son, generation to generation.

The most famous Phantom was the twenty-first, Kit (sometimes Kip) Walker, the one that fought in the years leading up to World War II. Accompanied by Devil, a faithful wolf companion, and Hero, a stallion (like the Lone Ranger's Silver), the Phantom fought pirates, Nazis and other standard villains of the 1930s while also leading his Jungle Patrol. Over the years, the Phantom's adventures appeared in King Feature strips, and in Harvey, Gold Key, Charlton and DC Comics. Like Batman, this hero possessed no super powers, only the will and resources to fight crime. Like Batman, he was incredibly buff and strong, and like Superman, he had a woman in his life, the athletic Diana Palmer, whom he eventually married in the 1980s comics, thus setting up the next generation of Phantom.

The Phantom originally appeared onscreen in a 1940s serial starring Tom Tyler as the Ghost Who Walks, but today it is the 1996 film that is remembered as the most interesting take on the Falk legend. Horror great Joe Dante (*Piranha* [1978], *The Howling* [1981]) was originally slated to direct the project, which filmed in Thailand and Australia, but it was Simon Wincer who eventually directed the 1990s movie. The film starred a very fit Billy Zane, who had trained vigorously for the part for over a year, as the dashing Kit Walker. He was paired with spunky Kristy Swanson, the screen's original *Buffy the Vampire Slayer*, playing Diana Palmer. The villain of the film was Drax (Treat Williams); and his henchwoman, Sala, was portrayed by a fetching future superstar, Catherine Zeta-Jones.

The big-screen *Phantom* opened in the summer of 1996 (June 7) in direct compe-

A hero in the shadows. *The Phantom* (Billy Zane) ponders the future in his creepy Skull Cave.

tition with the megahits *Independence Day* and *The Rock*, and the big-budgeted superhero film tanked at the box office. Advertised with the ad-line "Slam Evil," *The Phantom* generated only five million dollars its opening weekend, and a total of seventeen million before disappearing from theaters. And this was on an investment of some $50 million. Considering the box-office failure of other recent "retro" period superhero movies, such as *The Rocketeer* (1991) and *The Shadow* (1994), it was something of a miracle that *The Phantom* was produced at all.

Though audiences did not warm to the film, it was a remarkably faithful adaptation of the story of the twenty-first Phantom, set in 1930s art deco New York City. The first half of the picture played as an Indiana Jones–style action movie with an exciting set piece involving an upside-down truck snared on a dangerous suspension bridge.

Later, there was another great stunt: a daring jump from a plane (running out of fuel) onto horseback during a chase in the jungle. Regarding superhero lore, the film copied the obligatory "suiting up" scene featured prominently in *Batman Forever* (1995) and, later, *Batman and Robin* (1997), offering close-ups of Phantom gear (mask, belt, and hip holster).

The most likely reason *The Phantom* failed to connect with viewers was that the script relied on old-fashioned joys like great live-action stunts rather than gadgetry and technological wonders, and in some sense, audiences had outgrown these simple pleasures. There was no Batmobile; no super-powered, over-the-top villains; and no complex mythology. Also, the villain Drax seemed rather lame, as portrayed by the affable and non-menacing Williams.

And, most importantly, the final confrontation of the film occurred in a setting that looked too much like the Disney theme park attraction Pirates of the Caribbean.

Worse, the film evoked the memorable, metaphysical, spiritual ending of *Raiders of the Lost Ark* (1981) when a series of skull relics were joined to form a monstrous death ray. It was a weak and derivative ending to an otherwise lightweight and enjoyable film; and Billy Zane was a perfect Kit Walker, both physically and personality-wise. He had a way with tongue-in-cheek humor that made it all seem entirely appropriate and even charming.

A *Phantom* cartoon series appeared in the mid–1990s. *The Phantom 2040* was an updating of the Phantom story, involving the twenty-fourth Phantom as he fought evil forces in the twenty-first century. The syndicated cartoon ran for 33 episodes from 1994 to 1996 and featured a young Kit Walker (the voice of *Black Scorpion*'s Scott Valentine) battling a corporate villain, Maxwell Madison, in the future city of Metropia. The adventures took place after the unification of Africa and the death of the twenty-third Phantom in a terrible catastrophe.

Guest voices on the series included Mark Hamill (as Dr. Jak), Deborah Harry, Ron Perlman, Roscoe Lee Brown and Rob Paulsen. Though the series was not picked up for a third season, it eschewed the old, familiar 1930s touches of the serial and 1996 movie in favor of a futuristic, technological background.

On October 24, 2002, *Variety* reported that Crusader Entertainment and Hyde Park had teamed with screenwriter Steven De Souza to produce a new *Phantom* feature film, one with a more contemporary, futuristic vibe, putting Lee Falk's long-lived hero in the same category as recent hits *Spider-Man* and *The Matrix*. That version had not yet been produced at the time of this writing.

The Phantom (1996)
LIVE-ACTION FILM

"...[O]ne of the best-looking movies in any genre I have ever seen ... [it is] smashingly entertaining..."
— Roger Ebert, *The Chicago Sun Times*, June 7, 1996.

"It is characteristic of *The Phantom*'s aims that even its physical action is mostly human-scaled, involving not computer images, but tricky moves by flesh-and-blood stunt people. It's nice to see some things done the old way."
— Kenneth Turan, *The Los Angeles Times*, June 7, 1996, page 1.

"*The Phantom* is energetic, unpretentious, silly, simple-minded, summer-movie-fun — and a welcome relief from the gloomy intensity of the *Batman* series and its imitators."
— Michael Medved, *The New York Post*, June 7, 1996, page 41.

"What *The Phantom* has in spades is a wry sense of humor, fabulous sets, and some pretty good performances. Zane, all muscle and earnestness, is a perfect comic-strip hero."

— Jack Mathews, *Newsday*, June 7, 1996, page B2.

CAST: Billy Zane (The Phantom/Kit Walker); Kristy Swanson (Diana Palmer); Treat Williams (Xander Drax); Catherine Zeta-Jones (Sala); James Remar (Quill); Jon Tenney (Jimmy Wells); Cary-Hiroyuki Tagawa (Kabai Seng); Patrick McGoohan (The Phantom's Dad); Bill Smitrovich (David Palmer); Casey Siemaszko (Morgan); David Proval (Charlie Zephyr); Joseph Ragno (Ray Zephyrs); Samantha Eggar (Lilly Palmer); Al Rusci (Police Commissioner Farley); Leon Russom (Mayor); Bernard Kates (Fakmoore); John Capodice (The Cabby); Bob Kane (Mounted Cop); William Jones and John Prosky (Cycle Cop); Alan Zitner (Dr. Flemming); Dane Carson (Corporal Weeks); Chatpon "Jim" Petchlor (Zak); Dana Farwell (Breen); Jared Chandler (Styles); Radma-Agon Joo, William Zappa, Clint Lilley, Agoes Widjaya Soedjarwo, Jo Phillips, Austin Peters, Victor Modrana, Valerie Flueger, Rod Dailey.

CREW: Paramount Pictures Presents in Association with Robert Evans and the Ladd Company a Village Roadshow Pictures Production, a Simon Wincer Film, *The Phantom. Directed by:* Simon Wincer. *Written by:* Jeffrey Boam. *Based on the Phantom Characters Created by:* Lee Falk. *Produced by:* Robert Evans, Alan Ladd, Jr. *Executive Producers:* Dick Vane, Joe Dante, Graham Burke, Greg Coote, Peter Sjoquist, Bruce Sherlock. *Co-Producer:* Jeffrey Boam. *Director of Photography:* David Burr. *Production Design:* Paul Peters. *Editors:* Nicholas Brown, Bryan H. Carroll. *Costume Designer:* Marlene Stewart. *Music:* David Newman. *Casting:* Deborah Aquila, Jane Shannon Smith. *Associate Producer:* Bonnie Abounza. *Unit Production Manager:* Steven Felder. *First Assistant Director:* Robert J. Donaldson. *Second Assistant Director:* Simon Warnick. *Special Effects Coordinator:* Alan E. Lorimer. *M.P.A.A. Rating:* PG. *Running time:* 96 minutes (approximate).

In the Bengalla jungle in 1938, a fortune hunter named Quill seeks a legendary treasure in the land protected by "the Ghost Who Walks," a seemingly immortal superhero called the Phantom. On a mission for American millionaire Drax, Quill seeks to recover a sacred relic, a jeweled skull. Quill is also the man that killed an earlier incarnation of the Phantom, but on this day he escapes the hero's grasp.

The current incarnation of the four-hundred-year-old legend known as the Phantom is a young man named Kit Walker.

His research indicates that there are three skulls like the one stolen by Quill, and that when brought together they will give the bearer invincibility and other incredible powers. Kit's ex-girlfriend, Diana Palmer, is suspicious of Drax and is also seeking the skulls. When captured by Drax's beautiful but deadly femme fatale, Sala, things look grim for Diana, at least until the Phantom comes to her rescue.

Diana and Kit return to the United States to stop Drax's acquisition of the skulls and their supernatural powers. They learn the second skull, one made of jade, is stored in the Museum of World History, but Drax steals it right out from under them. In contact with one another for the first time, perhaps ever, the two skulls pinpoint the location of the third and last skull — inside the Devil's Vortex! Drax captures Diana Palmer and drags her to a hidden island in the Pacific, with the Phantom in hot pursuit. The villains find an underground cave protected by Singh Pirates, the pirate organization that owned the skulls in the first place.

Now the Phantom must rescue Diana, defeat the Singh Brotherhood, and stop the villainous Drax from assembling the skulls and building the ultimate weapon. In the end, there is a fourth skull — on the Phantom's own ring — which proves to be the key to averting doomsday.

The Phantom 2040 (1994–1996)
ANIMATED SERIES

VOICE TALENT: Scott Valentine (Kit Walker/the Phantom/the Ghost Who Walks); Margot Kidder (Rebecca Madison); J.D. Hall (Guran); Jeff Bennett (Maxwell Madison).

CREDITS: *Developed for Television by:* David J. Corbett. *Based on Characters Created by:* Lee Falk. *Story Editors:* Judith and Garfield Reeves-Stevens. *Line Producers:* Gwen Wetzler, Michael Lyman. *Voice Direction:* Stu Rosen. *Supervising Producer:* Mary Corbett. *Music:* Gerald O'Brien. *Executive Producers:* William E. Miller, David Corbett. *Created for TV by:* Hearst Entertainment Inc.

Plastic Man

The 1940s introduced the world to a whole generation of superheroes, many of which are still with us, in one form or another. In 1941, Police Comics presented one of the most bizarre such heroes: Eel O'Brian, a small-time crook who was doused with chemicals and forever affected by the experience. His body became incredibly flexible, and he could stretch into any form, like a rubber band. O'Brian switched sides to fight for goodness, donning a rubber costume and going by the moniker of Plastic Man, or "Plas."

Over the years, Plastic Man became a DC Comics character, and in the 1970s had something of a renaissance in popularity. He was a recurring guest "hero" on *The Super Friends*, lending his help to the folks at the Hall of Justice, and then starred in two Ruby-Spears produced, comedy-oriented Saturday morning programs. From 1979 to 1980 he appeared on ABC's *The Plastic Man Comedy Adventure Show*; and then from 1980 to 1981 the bendable hero became the patriarch of a family, starring in *The Plastic Man/Baby Plas Super Comedy*.[1] These ventures were particularly juvenile, and the latter one saw the Elastic Plastic Man dealing with his trouble-making, very powerful son.

RoboCop

In the late 1980s, American cities were tearing themselves apart for a variety of reasons. Because of the "trickle down" economic policies of the government, the poor had grown poorer during the balance of the decade, the rich grew richer, and the middle class was suffering too. Homelessness was at its worst rate in American history, and street crime was spiraling out of control. The bottom of society was ravaged by crime, and the yuppies at the top of society, the corporate millionaires, were corrupt, stealing millions through insider trading and other illegal perks. This was the era of "greed is good," as exemplified by the character Gordon Gekko in Oliver Stone's *Wall Street* (1989) and the portrayal of the homeless as outsiders (personified in films such as John Carpenter's *They Live* [1988]). Politicians cynically played on the average citizen's fear of crime to win office, notably the Willie Horton campaign advertisement, which made note of a criminal African-American robbing, raping and killing good, white citizens. The message of the era was plain: the ends justify the means.

In 1987 a new kind of superhero film gazed closely at these problems. The result was the creation of a popular character that has never left the pop culture landscape since, appearing over the years in films, TV series, animation, comic books, toy stores and the like. Described as "the future of law enforcement," RoboCop was the character's given name. He was a crime-fighting cyborg, a hero that could walk the savage streets of a city in chaos — in this case, Detroit — and clean up the board rooms where the decadent rich snorted cocaine, soaked the poor, and went unregulated by a winking government. Part Charles Bronson, part Batman and part Clint Eastwood, RoboCop was introduced in a 1987 film directed by 48-year-old Dutchman Paul Verhoeven (*Basic Instinct* [1991], *Starship Troopers* [1997]), and starring Peter Weller as the titular character.

Like Batman, RoboCop was a distinctly split personality. His programming, imposed by OCP (Omni Consumer Products), was that of a crime-smashing machine, a street avenger in silver metal. But he also carried within him the organic remains of an Irish-Catholic street cop, Murphy (Weller again). Murphy had been murdered on the job, and his human side formed the emotional and organic gestalt of the dedicated cyborg cop. RoboCop, again like Batman, was angst-ridden, but in this case it was because the cyborg actually remembered his life as a human being, a husband and father, an "emotional" creature that was more than circuits and gears. Once he was a man that loved, and RoboCop has "flashes" of those days.

RoboCop was shot in thirteen weeks during the late summer of 1986 on a budget of ten million dollars in Dallas and Pittsburgh, with remarkably little fanfare.[1] Verhoeven was attracted to the film, eventually rated R for violence, because of its comic-book type of "origin" story and texture. "I like comic books, in part because they're stylized," he noted during an interview with Starlog Magazine. "Although RoboCop is an action adventure, it has a very stylized feel that reminds me of a comic."[2]

Star Weller detected that RoboCop, with its board-room intrigue, funny news clips and other allegorical touches was actually a humorous indictment of the 1980s. "[It] plays funnier than it reads," he told Bill Warren, "it's a satire...."[3]

Part of the fun of that satire involved the fact that RoboCop accurately predicted both the corporatization of mainstream American culture and the coarsening of the media. Some of the more pertinent jokes in the screenplay, by Edward Neumeier and Michael Miner, involved a "Lee Iococca Elementary School" and a family game glorifying nuclear war called Nuke'Em. The latter was based on 1970s commercials for the game Battleship ("You sunk my battleship!"), remodeled to accommodate the nuclear age.

Even America's propensity to drive gas-guzzling, gigantic cars was satirized. Commercials depicted in RoboCop adver-tised a new vehicle, the 6000 SUX (not SUV, SUX), that offered a whopping 18 miles to the gallon. The film was also brutally funny in its depiction of corporate one-upmanship, with OCP businessmen not only vying for stock options and promotions, but actually killing one another left and right to gain an advantage. The competitive world of Wall Street literally became cutthroat, and this view of "big business" and other American institutions has prevailed in genre entertainment ever since, a world populated by cutthroat lawyers (Angel's Wolfram and Hart), corrupt politicians (Buffy's Mayor Wilkins), and so forth.

RoboCop also accurately predicted the right wing, GOP push towards the privatization of municipal and government programs, like George W. Bush's desire to privatize Social Security. Particularly, much of RoboCop involved OCP's funding and running of the Detroit Police Department as a business designed to make money. This was especially pertinent, since one often thinks that the police should be impartial representatives of the law, not people beholden to business — especially corrupt business.

In all, it was an unregulated world of business run amuck, and criminals and executives worked together to ruin the life of the average Joe. Ronny Cox played Richard Jones, the Bill Gates–like businessman who wants to push his pet project, an "urban pacification" droid program called the ED-209, into production, despite the fact that it is riddled with (murderous) glitches. Representing street crime was Kurtwood Smith as Clarence Boddecker, an old-fashioned gangster with his own wild bunch of cackling, despicable thugs at his side.

On the side of good with RoboCop/ Murphy was his new partner on the police force, Anne Lewis (Nancy Allen). She had known Murphy as a human being for one day, and felt responsible for his death at the hands of Boddecker's crew. Consequently, she became RoboCop's ally through thick

Murphy (Peter Weller) is a crime-fighting cyborg and the future of law enforcement in Paul Verhoeven's social satire, *RoboCop* (1997).

and thin. Together, RoboCop and Murphy took down Richard Jones and Boddecker in the first, very exciting, action-packed film, an enterprise that grossed more than 100 million dollars worldwide.

Critics raved about the movie, noting its social value as satire, as well as its numerous well-drawn action sequences. Some media watchdogs decried the amount of violence in the film, essentially a big-screen comic book, but even the blood and guts were relevant to Verhoeven's indictment of contemporary morals. Just two years earlier, *Rambo: First Blood Part II* (1985) depicted similar levels of horrific violence, but cloaked it with the fabric of the U.S. flag and patriotism, thereby escaping criticism. Those that condemned *RoboCop* for its gore missed an important point: its violence was actually meaningful, criticizing the level of violence acceptable in mainstream entertainment.

RoboCop was so popular that almost immediately the title character was translated to comic books and an animated TV series, created in association with Marvel television. Stan Lee served as executive story editor on the program, and the animated show appeared faithful in design and story to the feature film, only without the extreme and graphic violence that would have drawn the ire of watchdog groups. In *RoboCop: The Animated Series*, there was a great deal of weapons fire, but nobody ever died or was visibly bloodied. Officer Lewis was also noticeably less "butch" in cartoon form, and more emotionally friendly; but OCP was still around, trying to foist later models of the ED-209 (ED-260) on an unsuspecting public.

In "Crime Wave" by Rich Fogel and Mark Seidenberg, RoboCop had to stop the robbery of a blood bank, a rather typical plot for a cartoon series. In "Robot's Revenge," by John Shirley, the evil Dr. McNamara built the ED-260A to replace RoboCop, even as Murphy and Lewis protected Middle East diplomats from an assassination conspiracy. On the cartoon series, RoboCop was equipped with a flying car called the *Robo One*, which could fire missiles and perform other daring feats.

If the animated series softened the world of RoboCop to appeal to children, the second feature film, *RoboCop 2* (1990) went in the opposite direction. Director Irvin Kershner (*Eyes of Laura Mars* [1978],

The Empire Strikes Back [1980], *Never Say Never Again* [1983]) teamed with writer-artist Frank Miller (*The Dark Knight Returns*) to present a thoroughly nihilistic, cynical vision of a futuristic world where business and crime had spiraled out of control.

The satirical commercials were back, including one for a car-theft protection device that electrocuted car jackers, but the touch was not so light and deft as before. One of the main characters in the film was a ten-year-old crime lord (Gabriel Damon), a drug dealer and murderer totally lacking in conscience. The technological nemesis of the film was a second RoboCop cyborg, RoboCop 2, a gigantic robot addicted to drugs and powered by the maniacal brain of a serial killer named Cain (Tom Noonan).

The film also saw RoboCop drawn and quartered by the young crime lord in a warehouse, and lobotomized into being a "good citizen" by a slew of new programming directives. A reassembled RoboCop then committed metaphorical suicide, purging himself with an electrical jolt to remove this "evil" programming and return to his gun-toting, Clint Eastwood–like former self.

Critics hated the sequel, decrying its ugly, fascist tone, and audiences stayed away in droves, disappointed by an overly violent, even hateful entertainment. Actress Nancy Allen had a bad experience with the film, and explained some of the problems:

> The script kept changing, and it was the first time I didn't have a good relationship with the director I was working with.... I thought the second one [film] was heartless.[4]

RoboCop 2 was successful in Europe and Japan, even if despised in America, and the pendulum swung again, resulting in the production of a *RoboCop 3*, this one featuring less overt social satire and graphic violence. Frank Miller's ideas again formed the basis of the screenplay, Fred Dekker directed, and Nancy Allen returned for her final outing as Lewis. Peter Weller, all but invisible in the clunky metallic Robo-Cop suit, opted out of this sequel, handing the role to Robert Burke (*Dust Devil* [1992]).

Theatrically released after a long time on the shelf, the toothless *RoboCop 3* premiered to weak reviews and poor box office in 1993. In this second sequel, the stalwart cyborg tangled with a ninja, a motorcycle gang, and faced the death of his beloved partner, Lewis. He also came equipped with a jetpack that allowed him to fly over the streets of Detroit.

Considering the poor reception afforded the later *RoboCop* movie sequels, it was something of a surprise when *RoboCop* quickly moved to the realm of television in 1994. Airing in syndication and starring Richard Eden as RoboCop, the series (produced by franchise originators Edward Neumeier and Michael Minor) returned to its roots to feature more overt (and fun) satire. The series, according to producers, would "rely heavily on the three H's: humor, humanity and hormones."[5]

Various episodes saw RoboCop denounced as Satanic ("Prime Suspect"), dealing with government conspiracies ("Ghosts of War"), fighting a drug that caused people to lose their inhibitions ("Zone Five") and even facing the specter of reality TV ("Inside Crime"). Filmed in Canada on a low budget, the series teamed RoboCop with new partners in Detective Lisa Madigan (Yvette Nipar) and Sgt. Stanley Parks (Blu Mankuma).

Although it lasted only one season, *RoboCop: The TV Series* garnered generally high ratings and positive reviews when it aired in syndication on KCOP in Los Angeles, WWOR in New York and WGN in Chicago, among others.[6] The series was later rerun on the Sci-Fi Channel, the ultimate

destination also for the final RoboCop production (as of this writing): *RoboCop: Prime Directives* (2001).

Prime Directives was a package of four, two-hour tele-films, budgeted in total at 15 million dollars. Page Fletcher inherited the role of RoboCop (becoming the fourth actor to don the suit), and the series was set some twenty years after the first movie, seemingly ignoring the stories of the sequels and 1994 TV series. In "Dark Justice," the first of the four installments of the miniseries, RoboCop faced off against the Bone Machine, a criminal vigilante who somehow related to an old case involving a villain called "the Mangler."

In the second two-hour venture, "Meltdown," RoboCop went rogue and fought a former partner named Cable, also transformed into a crime-fighting cyborg. "Resurrection" and "Crash and Burn" charted the evolution of another OCP creation, the artificial intelligence "brain" called S.A.I.NT. (Sentient Artificial Intelligence Neural Net Turbulence). S.A.I.N.T. was designed to control all functions of Delta City, Detroit's successor and Robo-Cop's home.

Lacking overt satire, and starring a gaggle of second-string Canadian performers, *Prime Directives* was essentially eight long hours of hemming and hawing. It was filled with endless scenes of gunfire and bullet shells ricocheting off of RoboCop's invulnerable armor. Worse, RoboCop and RoboCable shared the same style of costume, and were nearly impossible to differentiate, resulting in many action sequences impossible to follow. Given that RoboCop has proven to be such a durable superhero for fifteen years, it was a shameful way to treat the character; and one hopes that Robo, once the future of law enforcement, will one day return to "A" budgeted and scripted material.

RoboCop (1987)
LIVE-ACTION FILM

"*RoboCop* was an absolutely cynical and thoroughly marvelous film. Its commercial parodies alone were worthy of the early days of *Saturday Night Live*. Its message about humanity's ultimate value might get lost in the shuffle, but there are so many good things about this film that one hardly notices. Seeing a corporation as the ultimate savior and the villain at the same time, where a man becomes a product, gave this film special meaning in the 1980s."

— William Latham, author of *Mary's Monster, Space: 1999 Resurrection*

"*RoboCop* is 102 minutes of ferocious, heavy-metal entertainment designed for the most jaded connoisseurs of hardened cinematic violence. It is also well-made, clever, witty, satirical and sometimes even touching."

— Michael Scheinfeld, *Films in Review*, October 1987, page 492.

"It's been assembled with ferocious, gleeful expertise, crammed with human cynicism and jolts of energy. In many ways it's the best action movie of the year."

— Michael Wilmington, *The Los Angeles Times*, July 17, 1987.

"Its pace is zappy, its script is witty and the political satire is acute."

— Judith Williamson, *New Statesman*, February 19, 1987, page 38.

"*RoboCop* is shrewdly enjoyable, more enjoyable *because* of its shrewdness, a film of comic-book violence that is also a parody of comic-book violence."

— Sean French, *Sight and Sound*, winter 1987/88, page 66.

CAST: Peter Weller (Murphy/Robocop); Nancy Allen (Ann Lewis); Ronny Cox (Richard Jones); Kurtwood Smith (Clarence Boddecker); Daniel O'Herlihy (The Old Man); Miguel Ferrer (Morton); Robert DoQui (Sgt. Reid); Ray Wise (Leon); Felton Perry (Johnson); Paul McCrane (Emil); Jesse Goins (Joe); Del Zamera (Kaplan); Calvin Jung (Minh); Rick Lieberman (Walker); Lee DeBroux (Sam); Mark Carlton (Miller); Edward Edwards (Manson); Michael Gregory (Lt. Heddecock); Fred Hice (Bobby); Neil Summers (Dougy); Gene Wolande (Prisoner); Ken Page (Kinney); Yolanda Williams (Ramirez), Leeza Gibbons.

CREW: An Orion Pictures Release, *RoboCop*. *Directed by:* Paul Verhoeven. *Written by:* Edward Neumeier, Michael Miner. *Executive Producer:* Jon Davison. *Produced by:* Arne Schmidt. *Film Editor:* Frank J. Urioste. *Director of Photography:* Jost Vacano. *Production Designer:* William Sandell. *Music:* Basil Poledouris. *Robocop Designed and Created by:* Rob Bottin. *Casting:* Sally Dennison, Julie Selzer. *Co-Producer:* Edward Neumeier. *Associate Producers:* Stephen Lim, Phil Tippett. *ED-209 Sequences:* Phil Tippett. *Special Photographic Effects:* Peter Kuran. *Matte Paintings:* Rocco Gioffre. *Optical Supervisor:* Robert Blalock, Praxis Film Works. *Costume Design:* Erica Edell Phillips. *Production Manager:* Charles Newirth. *Special Effects:* Dale Martin. *First Assistant Director:* Michele A. Panelli. *Script Supervisor:* Paula Squires Asaff. *Art Director:* Gayle Simon. *Set Decorator:* Robert Gould. *Set Designer:* James Tocci. *Property Master:* Bill MacSem. *Make-up:* Carla Palmer. *M.P.A.A. Rating:* R. *Running Time:* 103 minutes.

A young cop, Murphy, is transferred from Metro South to the war-torn and battle-weary Detroit Police Department, now funded and run by the mega-corporation called Omni Consumer Products. When Murphy is brutally murdered his first day on the job by Detroit's crime boss, Clarence Boddecker, he becomes a guinea pig in Omni's latest attempt to control crime in the city. He becomes RoboCop, a cyborg police officer of virtual invincibility.

RoboCop goes on duty in Detroit, teamed up with his former partner, Ann Lewis, who recognizes him as her ill-fated friend. In short order, the heroic RoboCop becomes a role model to the citizenry as he cleans up the streets of Detroit. Only one person is unhappy about the state of affairs: Richard Jones, OCP Vice President, who had been developing his own "urban pacification" robot called the ED-209, at least until RoboCop was developed by young hotshot Morton.

When Murphy's human memories of

his death and family life resurface, Robo-Cop pursues Boddecker's gang in a quest for vengeance. The cyborg arrests Bodecker, and the thug fingers Richard Jones as his boss! When RoboCop confronts Jones about this allegation, a secret fourth directive in his programming prevents him from harming Jones. RoboCop nearly shuts down, and is in no condition to fight when Jones sends his pet project after him, the massive battle droid, ED-209. RoboCop defeats the monster machine (on a staircase), but Jones has sabotaged Murphy, informing the Detroit police that he has gone rogue. Though reluctant to go after one of their own, the police attempt to kill RoboCop; badly injured, he is rescued by Lewis.

RoboCop and Lewis hide out in Detroit's industrial section, but Jones wants the cyborg dead because RoboCop has amassed evidence against him in, among other crimes, the brutal slaying of his competitor, Morton. Armed with state-of-the-art military hardware, Bodecker and his goons go after Robocop. Robo and Lewis defeat Bodecker's gang, and RoboCop presents evidence to the OCP President, "the Old Man," that Jones was complicit in criminal acts. The Old Man fires Jones, allowing RoboCop to overcome his fourth directive and kill the villain.

When asked his name, RoboCop responds that he is — and always will be — Murphy.

RoboCop: The Animated Series (1988)
ANIMATED SERIES

VOICE TALENTS: Robert Bockstael, Jan Hennessy, Barbara Budd, Ron James, Len Carlson, Gordon Maston, Alan Stewart Coates, Greg Morton, Rex Hagon, Susan Roman, Chris Ward.

CREW: *Based on Characters Created by:* Edward Neumeier, Michael Miner. *Story Editors:* Rich Fogel, Mark Seidenburg. *Executive Story Editor:* Stan Lee. *Produced by:* Boyd D. Kirkland, Bill Hutton, Tony Love. *Series Directors:* Bill Hutton, Tony Love. *Production Manager:* David Perry. *Animation Supervisor:* Armand Shaw. *Art Director:* Will Meugniot. *Voice Directors:* Stu Rosen. *Music:* Haim Saban, Shuki Levy. *Animation Film Editor:* Al Breitenbach. *Music Supervisor:* Andrew Dimitroff. *Executive in Charge of Production:* Jim Graziano. *Executive Producers:* Margaret Loesch Stimpson, Joseph M. Taritero. Produced in Association with Akom Productions, Ltd. Marvel Productions Ltd, 1988.

RoboCop 2 (1990)
LIVE-ACTION FILM

"Masquerading as social satire, the movie actually is a relentless indulgence in sadism with a child sadist/criminal as a central character."
— M.S. Mason, *The Christian Science Monitor*, August 13, 1990, page 11.

"*RoboCop 2* isn't a disgrace, but things are no longer in such dazzling balance and the movie spills over into sadism, meaningless jolts and the sort of giant monster fisticuffs the Japanese used to do more cheaply and entertainingly."
— David Edelstein, *The New York Post*, June 22, 1990, page 21.

"Practically everything in this brutish sequel, directed unobtrusively by Irvin Kershner, is a sick joke, as well as a dig at the flimsiness of civilization."
— Georgia Brown, *The Village Voice*, July 3, 1990, page 65.

"*RoboCop 2* was not as good a film as its predecessor, even with Frank Miller adding his two cents to the script (elements of which were also used in the follow-up, *RoboCop 3*). Where the first film had heart along with cynicism, *RoboCop 2* turns up the cynicism, and the uproar over an amoral child in the film actually garnered more discussion than the film itself. Peter Weller is given little to do with his character, and an element of message-overkill hurt this film."

　　　—William Latham, author of *Mary's Monster* and *Space: 1999 Resurrection*.

CAST: Peter Weller (Murphy/RoboCop); Nancy Allen (Anne Lewis); Tom Noonan (Cain); John Glover (Magnavolt Salesman); Mario Machado (Casey Wong); Leeza Gibbons (Jess Perkins); John Ingle (Surgeon General); Roger Aaron Brown (Whittaker); Mark Rolston (Stef); Tommy Rosales (Chet); Brandon Smith (Flint); Michael Medeiros (Caleb); Gabriel Damon (Hob); Galyn Gorg (Angie); Angie Bolling (Ellen Murphy); Jeff McCarthy (Holzgang); Willard Pugh (Mayor Kuzak); Daniel O'Herlihy (Old Man); Belinda Bauer (Juliette Fox); Robert Do'Qui (Sgt. Reed); Stephen Lee (Duffy); Wanda DeJesus (Estevez).

CREW: A Jon Davison Production of an Irvin Kershner Film, an Orion Pictures Release, *RoboCop 2. Directed by:* Irvin Kershner. *Screenplay:* Frank Miller and Walon Green. *Story by:* Frank Miller. *Produced by:* Jon Davison. *Executive Producer:* Patrick Crowley. *Casting:* Sally Dennison, Julie Selzer, Justine Jacoby. *Director of Photography:* Mark Irwin. *Production Designer:* Peter Jamison. *Supervising Film Editor:* William Anderson. *Music Conducted and Composed by:* Leonard Rosenman. *Unit Production Manager:* Patrick Crowley. *First Assistant Director:* Tom Daviews. *Second Assistant Director:* Thomas A. Irvine. *RoboCop 2 Animation Sequence by:* Phil Tippett. *RoboCop Designed and Created by:* Rob Bottin. *Special Effects:* Peter Kuran. *Film Editors:* Deborah Zeitman, Lee Smith, Armen Minasian.

Costume Design: Rosanna Norton. *Based on Characters Created by:* Edward Neumeier, Michael Miner. *Associate Producers:* Jane Bartelme, Phil Tippett. *M.P.A.A. Rating:* R. *Running time:* 105 minutes (approx).

　　Detroit's finest, RoboCop, is still struggling to understand the complexities of his identity. He is troubled by his memories of his wife and child, but OCP demands he stop "stalking" the Murphy family, and RoboCop issues an apology to his former loved ones, assuring them he is only a machine.

　　Meanwhile, Detroit is in chaos and OCP is still scheming to privatize the police force. While RoboCop and Murphy clash with a young drug dealer named Hob, they also face the impending threat of a police strike. OCP reprograms RoboCop to be more "user friendly" to the public, even as a scheming executive, Juliette Fox, plots to build a replacement cyborg. Unfortunately, she chooses a drug-addicted criminal named Cain as the "brain" at the center of her new law enforcement prototype, a mistake that threatens the safety of the city when it runs amuck at a dramatic public presentation. A re-calibrated RoboCop must stop his own successor before it is too late.

RoboCop 3 (1993)
LIVE-ACTION FILM

"RoboCop is no longer a movie character but a merchandising franchise which rakes in untold millions a year in licensed toys. Accordingly, *RoboCop 3* has been produced as little more than a poorly executed cartoon with dull characters and ridiculous plot twists..."

　　—Bill Hoffmann, *The New York Post*, November 5, 1993.

"Dark Knight comic scribe Frank Miller got it right this time by creating a delightful mayhem..."

　　—Henry Cabot Bell, *The Village Voice*, November 16, 1993, page 67.

"There's probably sufficient energy and violence in *RoboCop 3* to satisfy undemanding action fans, but it's as mechanical as its cyborg hero. RoboCop is headed for a TV series, but this by-the-numbers third installment makes us feel we're already there."

　　—Kevin Thomas, *The Los Angeles Times*, November 5, 1993.

"*RoboCop 3* lightened the mood a bit, and tried to hark back to some of the humanity of the first film. Peter Weller's absence is barely noticed. But like many film series, the concept was getting a little tired this time around, and it's always sad

to watch Hollywood struggling to keep something interesting by throwing props at the problem (a flying RoboCop?) rather than a more compelling story."
— William Latham, author of *Mary's Monster* and *Space: 1999 Resurrection*.

CAST: Robert Burke (Murphy/RoboCop); Nancy Allen (Lewis); Mario Machado (Casey Wong); Remy Ryan (Nikko); Rip Torn (CEO); CCH Pounder (Bertha); Robert DoQui (Sgt. Reed); Angie Bolling (Ellen Murphy); Randall Taylor (Starkweather); Shane Black (Donnelly).

CREW: An Orion Pictures Release, *Robo-Cop 3. Art Director:* Cate Bangs. *Film Editor:* Bert Lovitt. *Director of Photography:* Gary B. Kibbe. *Original Music:* Basil Poledouris. *Producer:* Patrick Crowley. *Associate Producer:* Andy Lamarca. *Production Designer:* Hilda Stark. *Based on Characters Created by:* Ed Neumeier and Michael Miner. *Screenplay by:* Frank Miller and Fred Dekker. *Story by:* Frank Miller. *RoboCop Design:* Rob Bottin. *Special Effects:* Jeff Jarvis. *Stunt Coordinators:* Dick Hancock and Conrad E. Palmisano. *Directed by:* Fred Dekker. *M.P.A.A. Rating:* PG-13. *Running time:* 105 minutes.

OCP is finally ready to execute its grandest scheme yet: the destruction of Old Detroit. The nefarious conglomerate plans to build its own metropolis, Delta City, in place of the old city, regardless of the impact on current residents. OCP execs plot a campaign of terror, hiring mercenaries to make life in Old Detroit miserable. When Robo-Cop intervenes to help the residents of the beleaguered city, OCP realizes it must destroy its own creation, and sends a Ninja robot to assassinate the popular RoboCop.

RoboCop teams with rebels to stop OCP, but his battle is complicated when his partner, Officer Lewis, is killed in action. Now RoboCop is angrier than ever and will use every tool at his disposal, including a jetpack, to keep Detroit intact for its people.

RoboCop: The TV Series (1994)
LIVE-ACTION SERIES

"For a cheesy-looking action show, *RoboCop* boasts scripts that are far more dense and allusive than most of the junk cluttering syndication."
— Ken Tucker, *Entertainment Weekly:* "RoboCop," April 22, 1994, page 44.

CAST: Richard Eden (Alex Murphy/Robo-Cop); Yvette Nipar (Det. Lisa Madigan); Blu Mankuma (Sgt. Stanley Parks); Andrew Roth (Diana Powers); David Gardner (OCP Chairman); Sarah Campbell (Gadget); Kevin Quinn (RoboCop Stunt Double).

CREW: *Created by:* Edward Neumeier and Michael Miner. *Produced by:* J. Miles Dale. *Executive Producers:* Kevin Gillis, Brian K. Ross. *Co-Producer:* John Sheppard. *Costume Design:* Linda Kemp.

1. "The Future of Law Enforcement" (two hours) Written by: Michael Miner & Edward Neumeier. Directed by: Paul Lynch. Airdate: Week of March 18, 1994.

Dr. Millardo wants to rule Delta City, and believes he has the tool to do it: a supercomputer run by the brain of a (dead) human being. RoboCop, the OCP cyborg that was once policeman and family man Alex J. Murphy, intervenes to stop the madman.

GUEST CAST: Cliff DeYoung (Dr. Cray Millardo); John Rubinstein (Chayken); Ed Sahely (Lippencott); Jennifer Griffin (Nancy Murphy); Peter Costigan; Dan Duran; Jennifer Dale; James Kidnie (Pudface Morgan); Chris Kennedy, Patrick McKenna, Chris Bondy.

2. "Prime Suspect" Written by: Lincoln Kibbee. Directed by: Paul Shapiro. Airdate: Week of March 25, 1994.

Is RoboCop the future of law enforcement or an agent of the Devil? That's a question the police of Delta City need answered after an evangelist who had denounced Robo is found murdered, and the cyborg is unable to provide a satisfactory alibi.

GUEST CAST: Richard Comar; Richard Paul; Ed Sahely (Lippencott); Jennifer Griffin (Nancy Murphy); Chris Wiggins, Dan Duran, Erica Ehm, Deborah McGrath, Christopher Bondy, Richard Waugh, Jordan Hughes.

3. "Trouble in Delta City" Written by: William Gray. Directed by: Paul Shapiro. Airdate: Week of April 1, 1994.

The crazed Dr. Millardo is cooking up trouble again, this time in the form of an addictive diet pill that causes those who ingest it to become insanely violent. Unfortunately, Madigan is on the drug herself...

GUEST CAST: Tony Rosato; Cliff De Young (Dr. Millardo); Ed Sahely (Lippencott); James Kidnie (Pudface Morgan); Dan Duran, Erica Ehm, Wayne Best, Graham Harley.

4. "Officer Missing" Written by: Robert Hopkins. Directed by: Paul Lynch. Airdate: Week of April 8, 1994.

It's desperation time when Robo-Cop — experiencing system malfunctions — and the greedy chair of OCP Corporation end up in the badlands of Old Detroit. While they confront a youth angry over OCP's budget cuts to the city's infrastructure, a violent gang plans to take more serious action.

GUEST CAST: Maurice Dean Wint; Ed Sahely (Lippencott); Jennifer Griffin (Nancy Murphy); Jason Blicker, Dan Duran, Erica Ehm, Patrick McKenna, Ted Dykstra.

5. "What Money Can't Buy" Written by: Aubrey Solomon. Directed by: Michael Vejar. Airdate: Week of April 15, 1994.

An innocent child is endangered when black marketeers intercept the pair of lungs he so desperately requires for transplant surgery. RoboCop is on the case, not just for justice, but to repay a personal debt.

GUEST CAST: Gregory Scott Cummins; Ann Turkel; Ed Sahely (Lippencott); Jennifer

Griffin (Nancy Murphy); Dan Duran, Erica Ehm, Jane Spidell, Ted Dykstra.

6. "Ghosts of War" Written by: John Sheppard. Directed by: Alan J. Levi. Airdate: Week of April 22, 1994.

A group of commandos infiltrate Delta City's power net in hopes of revealing the truth about their exposure to a deadly chemical weapon in a long-forgotten war.

GUEST CAST: Jon Cypher (Omar); Roger Earl Mosley; Ed Sahely (Lippencott); Dan Duran, Erica Ehm, John Bourgeois, Juan Chioran, Jackie Richardson.

7. "Zone Five" Written by: Ted Harris and Blazes Boylan. Directed by: Timothy Bond. Airdate: Week of April 29, 1994.

Another illicit drug is on the market. This one is called "FUN" because it removes all traces of inhibitions from its users; and, unfortunately, Murphy's son may be involved in peddling the dangerous substance.

GUEST CAST: Scott Colomby; Jennifer Griffin (Nancy Murphy); Peter Costigan, Dan Duran, Erica Ehm, Richard Waugh, Patrick McKenna, Greg Spottiswood, Don McKellar, Bruce Beaton.

8. "Provision 22" Written by: Robert W. Gilmer. Directed by: Alan J. Levi. Airdate: Week of May 7, 1994.

RoboCop's human wife, Nancy, protests a new OCP initiative to privatize an important social program that she has been enrolled in (against her will). RoboCop has a duty to stop the demonstration and incarcerate his wife ... but will his human memories interfere with his sworn duty as a police officer?

GUEST CAST: Sondra Currie; Geraint Wyn Davies (Martin); Jennifer Griffin (Nancy Murphy); Ed Sahely (Lippencott); Peter Costigan, Dan Duran, Erica Ehm, Jackie Richardson, Jack Langeduk, Aidan Devine, Christine Reeves.

9. "Faces of Eve" Written by: John Considine. Directed by: Paul Lynch. Airdate: Week of May 14, 1994.

The nefarious Pudface Morgan has a new toy with which to vex RoboCop: a device that can allow its wearer to change form, essentially becoming a shape shifter. His first task is to replace the Chairman of OCP.

GUEST CAST: David Hemblen; James Kidnie (Pudface Morgan); Jennifer Griffin (Nancy Murphy); Ed Sahely (Lippencott); Peter Costigan, Dan Duran, Erica Ehm, Wayne Robson, Jason Blicker, Peter Messaline, Garfield Andrews.

10. "When Justice Fails" Written by: Simon Muntner. Directed by: Michael Vejar. Airdate: Week of May 21, 1994.

RoboCop's latest assignment causes another moral dilemma. He must protect an ultra-capitalist whose dangerously unstable new rocket fuel could endanger men in space; but RoboCop has no love for the man, and being his bodyguard seems counterproductive.

GUEST CAST: Lori Hallier; Jeremy Ratchford; Ed Sahely (Lippencott); Dan Duran, Erica Ehm, Patrick McKenna, Graham McPherson, Tondy DeSantis, Michael Sampson.

11. "The Human Factor" Written by: John Considine. Directed by: Mario Azzopardi. Airdate: Week of May 28, 1994.

Two decades before the dawn of RoboCop, Officer Murphy — Alex's father — put away a crazed criminal. Now cyborg son and Irish cop father must team up to stop the lunatic one more time.

GUEST CAST: Martin Milner; Dan Duran; Erica Ehm; Robert Morelli; Nigel Bennett (Granger).

12. "Inside Crime" Written by: William Gray. Directed by: Michael Vejar. Airdate: Week of July 1, 1994.

Pudface Morgan is the latest American idol! A new reality show, "Inside Crime," follows criminals on the street, including Pudface. But RoboCop has the stuff to be the ultimate survivor, even when a simper-

ing TV producer proves to be the weakest link.

GUEST CAST: Marla Sucharetza; Ed Sahely (Lippencott); James Kidnie (Pudface Morgan); Dan Duran, Erica Ehm, Patrick McKenna, Jason Blicker, Wayne Robson, Ian D. Clark.

13. "RoboCop vs. Commander Cash" Written by: Pamela Hickey and Dennys McCoy. Directed by: Allan Eastman. Airdate: Week of July 8, 1994.

A renegade within OCP uses Commander Cash — a superhero corporate mascot — to push a new breakfast cereal laced with a deadly drug that controls minds.

GUEST CAST: Roddy Piper (Captain Cash); Barry Flatman; Lisa Howard; Ed Sahely (Lippencott); Dan Duran, Erica Ehm, Matt Cooke, Jordan Hughes.

14. "Illusions" Written by: Robert Hopkins. Directed by: Timothy Bond. Airdate: Week of July 15, 1994.

A notorious assassin, "the Magician," has selected his latest target: the Chairman of OCP. When Madigan also happens to fall in love with a man who is a magician by trade, RoboCop begins to suspect a dangerous connection to the ruthless killer.

GUEST CAST: Cali Timmins; Maurice Godin; Daniel Kash; Ed Sahely (Lippencott); Dan Duran, Erica Ehm, Richard Waugh, Neil Crone.

15. "The Tin Man" Written by: Pamela Hickey and Dennys McCoy. Directed by: Allan Eastman. Airdate: Week of July 22, 1994.

It's RoboCop Mark II! OCP develops a second cyborg, based on Alex Murphy's former partner, to go after a gambling ring in Delta City. Unfortunately, the RoboCops don't see eye to eye in how to seek justice.

GUEST CAST: Kim Coates (Malloy); Ron Lea; Daniel Kash; Ed Sahely (Lippencott); Dan Duran, Erica Ehm, Patrick McKenna.

16. "Sisters in Crime" Written by: Diane K. Shah. Story by: John Arcudi. Directed by: Mario Azzopardi. Airdate: Week of July 29, 1994.

OCP faces the possibility of a hostile takeover, and only the Chairman can prevent losing control of the organization to an even nastier regime. Unfortunately, the Chairman has been captured by a cadre of femi–Nazis who are angry over his denigrating remarks about women and their role in society. They force him to do housework...

GUEST CAST: John Rubinstein; Marla Sucharetz; Jennifer Griffin (Nancy Murphy); Ed Sahely (Lippencott); Dan Duran; Erica Ehm; Jason Blicker; Patrick McKenna; Colin Fox (Hammersmith).

17. "Heartbreakers" Written by: Alison Bingeman. Directed by: Michael Vejar. Airdate: Week of September 8, 1994.

A ruthless gunrunner discovers Robo-Cop's secret former human identity as Murphy. He uses this knowledge like a weapon, kidnapping Mrs. Murphy and forcing Robo-Cop to steal weapons or see his once-wife die horribly.

GUEST CAST: Stephen Shellen; Ed Sahely (Lippencott); Jennifer Griffin (Nancy Murphy); Dan Duran, Erica Ehm, Peter Costigan, Robert Hollinger.

18. "Mother's Day" Written by: Manny Coto. Directed by: Kari Skogland. Airdate: Week of September 15, 1994.

The department mascot, a young girl nicknamed "Gadget," becomes the focal point of a criminal plot when her natural mother shows up seeking custody. Unfortunately, she may be involved with the Russian mafia.

GUEST CAST: Camilla Scott; Rosemary Dunsmore; Jennifer Griffin (Nancy Murphy); Ed Sahely (Lippencott); Dan Duran, Erica Ehm, Peter Costigan, Wayne Robinson.

19. "Nano" Written by: Alan Templeton and Mary Crawford. Directed by: William Gereghty. Airdate: Week of September 22, 1994.

The development of miniature robots — nanotechnology — becomes a danger to Delta City when a scientist is forced to develop criminal varieties of the useful tools. At the same time, Madigan is in an accident.

GUEST CAST: Ed Sahely (Lippencott); Dan Duran, Erica Ehm, William Colgate.

20. "Corporate Raiders" Written by: Pamela Hicky and Dennys McCoy. Directed by: T.J. Scott. Airdate: Week of November 11, 1994.

Alex Murphy's father returns to seek RoboCop's help on another old case he was never able to solve. He thinks that an old suspect he failed to collar is responsible for a series of robberies at wealthy companies.

GUEST CAST: Martin Milner; Gwynyth Walsh (Stark); Peter Costigan, Dan Duran, Erica Ehm, Richard Chevolleau, Nonnie Griffin, Ron Gabriel.

21. "Midnight Minus One" Written by: Mary Crawford and Alan Templeton. Directed by: J. Miles Dale. Airdate: Week of November 18, 1994.

A criminal sentenced to die is innocent of the crime for which he was condemned. RoboCop and Madigan rush to find justice for the man before his time runs out.

GUEST CAST: David Orth; Chuck Shamata; Daniel Kash; Ed Sahely (Lippencott); Dan Duran, Erica Ehm, Patrick McKenna, Kathryn Miller, Sherry Miller, Lawrence Bayne.

22. "Public Enemies" Written by: William Gray. Directed by: Michael Vejar. Airdate: Week of November 25, 1994.

A trifecta of evil takes up residence in Delta City: Dr. Millardo, Chayken and Pudface Morgan. Their new mission: Kill the (female) President of the United States when she bestows upon the OCP Chairman a new honor.

GUEST CAST: Cliff DeYoung; John Rubinstein; Linda Sorenson; David Keeley; James Kidnie; Ed Sahely (Lippencott); Richard Waugh, Dan Duran, Erica Ehm, Wayne Robson, Donald Burda, Bruce Gray, Catherine Swing.

Robocop: Prime Directives (2001)
LIVE–ACTION SERIES

CAST: Page Fletcher (Alex J. Murphy/Robocop); Maurice Dean Wint (John Cable/RoboCable); Maria Del Mar (Sara Cable); Anthony Lemke (James Murphy); Kevin Jubinville (Damien Lowe); David Fraser (Ed Hobley).

CREW: Fireworks Entertainment Presents a Julian Grant Production, *RoboCop: Prime Directives. Casting:* Jon Comerford, Brian Levy. *Special Effects:* Brock Jolliffe. *Visual Effects:* Sundog Films Inc. *Robocop and RoboCable Designed and Created by:* Rob Bottin. *Music:* Norman Orenstein. *Executive Producers:* Jay Firestone and Adam Haight. *Based on Characters Created by:* Edward Neimeier and Michael Miner. *Produced by:* Julian Grant. *Creative Executive:* Debbie Firestone. *Production Supervisor:* Tony Thatcher. *Line Producer:* Paul Spike Lees. *Supervising Editor:* David Ransley. *Director of Photography:* Russ Goozee. *Production Designer:* Tim Boyd. *Costume Designer:* Judith England. *First Assistant Director:* Ian Robertson. *Stunt Coordinators:* John Stoneham, Jr., John Stoneham, Sr. *Robocop Stunts:* Patrick Mark. *RoboCable Stunts:* Lloyd Adams. *Location Manager:* Oliver Churchill. *Script Supervisor:* Danielle Depeyre. *Art Director:* Andrew Hull. *Picture Editors:* Chuck Kahn, Joycelyn Poon, Marlon Moskal, Bill Towgood. Produced in association with Chum Television.

1. "Dark Justice" (two hours) Written by: Brad Abraham and Joseph O'Brien. Directed by: Julian Grant. Airdate: July 16, 2001.

RoboCop celebrates his tenth year of operation in the Detroit/Delta City area, even as a terrorist named Bone Machine runs loose, interfering in a police bust of the gang called "De Bombs" at Chelsea Clinton Savings and Loan. OCP Corporation, on the verge of bankruptcy, deploys the brainchild of greedy executive Damien Lowe — a "thinking" machine called S.A.I.N.T. (Sentient Artificial Intelligent Neuralnet Terminus) designed to automate the city. Meanwhile, RoboCop learns that Bone Machine's weaponry was OCP-issued, and shares this information with his old partner, John Cable. At the same time, Murphy's son, James, who has been raised by OCP, joins a secret "Trust" in OCP headed by Sara Cable, John's scheming ex-wife. When John Cable gets too close to exposing OCP's involvement, Sara sabotages RoboCop and orders him to kill John. In the final battle, RoboCop kills John Cable and Bone Machine, but becomes aware that he has been manipulated.

GUEST CAST: Tedde Moore (The Old Woman); Meg Hobarth (Dr. Colleen Frost); Richard Fitzpatrick (The Bone Machine); Leslie Ann Coles (Ashley St. John-Smyth); Sara Sahr (P.J. Flinders).

2. "Meltdown" (two hours) Written by: Brad Abraham and Joseph O'Brien. Directed by: Julian Grant. Airdate: July 17, 2001.

A trio of beautiful tech thieves, led by Ann R. Key, break into OCP Headquarters to steal information on the rapidly developing S.A.I.N.T. project, and manage to elude RoboCop. At the same time, OCP "Trust" conspirator Sara Cable oversees the unauthorized creation of another Robocop cyborg, this one utilizing the brain and organic matter of her dead husband, John Cable. This new cyborg, RoboCable, attacks the Old Woman, the Head of OCP; but Murphy is blamed for the assault, and RoboCop is consequently recalled. RoboCop escapes a confrontation with OCP and the mechanical Cable, and goes into hiding in Detroit. In the poorest, most heavily populated region of Old Detroit, RoboCop befriends Ann's daughter, Jordan, and later teams up with her mother, Ann R. Key. When a crack assassin team from OCP threatens to kill RoboCop, Ann, Murphy and RoboCable join forces to fight back. Meanwhile, Damien Lowe is fired by the Old Woman, but the shifty executive strikes back against OCP, killing the Old Woman and the entire board of directors with S.A.I.N.T.'s powerful new environmental controls.

GUEST CAST: Leslie Hope (Ann R. Key); Francoise Yip (Lex); Tedde Moore (The Old Woman); Meg Hobarth (Dr. Colleen Frost); Leslie Ann Coles (Ashley St. John-Smyth); Sara Sahr (P.J. Flinders).

3. "Resurrection" (two hours) Written by: Brad Abraham and Joseph O'Brien. Directed by: Julian Grant. Airdate: July 18, 2001.

James Murphy learns that RoboCop is his father, even as Murphy and Cable — both cyborgs — team up to stop the assassination team on their trail in old Detroit. With the board of OCP all dead, Damien Lowe becomes president of the corporation and promises to ensure peace by putting more guns on the street with his new Plowshares Into Swords program. Ann R. Key and her tech thieves rescue a badly wounded RoboCop during a firefight and try to restore him to peak efficiency, even as Sara Cable orders James Murphy to execute all Robocops, no matter the cost. Dr. David Kaydick, an evil genius, captures RoboCable and programs him to assist him in a deadly plan of vengeance against OCP and the people of Delta City. Ann. R. Key and the tech thieves reactivate RoboCop's frontal lobe, restoring many of Alex Murphy's memories; while at the same time, Dr. Kaydick makes preparations to unleash a deadly plague called "Legion" that can destroy flesh and technology with equal precision. RoboCop and Ann R. Key team up with James Murphy to stop Kaydick before he and Cable succeed in creating "evolution by apocalypse."

GUEST CAST: Geraint Wyn Davies (Dr. David Kaydick); Leslie Hope (Ann R. Key); Rebecca Coles-Budrys (Jordan); Meg Hobarth (Dr. Frost); Mark Breslin (Archie Nemesis); Juliette Powell (Bunny); Brandi Marie Ward (Rikki); Jack Duffy (Dr. Hill); Trevor Owens (Todd); Francois Yip (Lex).

4. "Crash and Burn" (two hours) Written by: Brad Abraham and Joseph O'Brien. Directed by: Julian Grant. Airdate: July 19, 2001.

James Murphy, RoboCop and Ann R. Key chase Kaydick, Cable and the abducted Jordan (the secret carrier of the Legion plague) to OCP Headquarters as the city prepares for S.A.I.N.T. to go online and automate all of Delta City. However, there are glitches in the system, and S.A.I.N.T.'s programmer, Ed Hobley, worries that the machine is writing its own programming. RoboCop, Ann and James fight Kaydick and Cable as time runs out and loyalties are tested. Damien Lowe meets an unpleasant end when S.A.I.N.T. turns against him; and in the final battle, RoboCop and Cable meet their respective fates — and find their respective humanity.

GUEST CAST: Geraint Wyn Davies (Dr. David Kaydick); Leslie Hope (Ann R. Key); Rebecca Coles-Budrys (Jordan); Mark Breslin (Archie Nemesis); Leslie Ann Coles (Ashley St. John-Smyth); Sara Sahr (P.J. Flinders).

The Rocketeer

In the early 1950s, one hero of the cliffhanging movie serials was a dashing and courageous gent named Commando Cody. This hero often wore a leather flight suit, a bullet-shaped helmet, and a rocket pack. Via a small panel (with two switches) on the front of his zippered suit, Cody could activate the rocket pack and fly through the air, controlling speed and altitude with relative simplicity.

In *King of the Rocketmen* (1952), Tris Coffin played Cody, of Science Associates, and the stalwart character clashed with a villain named Mr. Vulcan in Republic's 12-part adventure. The flying hero (now played by George Wallace) returned in 1953's *Commando Cody* (a.k.a. *Radar Men of the Moon*). This time he tussled with an alien warlord named Retik (armed, naturally, with a death ray). *Zombies of the Stratosphere* (1954) was the last adventure featuring "Rocket Man" Cody and his high-flying gear. He was sort of a technologically endowed Superman, given his gift of flight by the rocket pack, rather than innate abilities.

In the early 1980s, writer and artist Dave Stevens imagined a very Commando Cody–like hero when he created a character called "the Rocketeer" for *Pacific Comics Presents*. The Rocketeer was actually a small-time pilot, an ace named Cliff Secord. He accidentally discovered the X-3, a rocket pack that ran on alcohol, and used it to combat the forces of evil in a pre–World War II world, regressing the Cody-style, fifties action and adventure to swinging Los Angeles in 1938.

Secord's friend, a mechanic and inventor named Peeve, developed a helmet for him (carved from an art deco radio), and Secord became an updated Commando Cody—except that his helmet was a tad more dashing. It boasted a long fin across the dorsal side, nicely evoking images of the

god Mercury. In the film version, the helmet was referred to jokingly as a "hood ornament."

In the 1980s, another 1930s-era hero, George Lucas and Steven Spielberg's Indiana Jones, hit it big in three blockbuster movies: *Raiders of the Lost Ark* (1981), *Indiana Jones and the Temple of Doom* (1984) and *Indiana Jones and the Last Crusade* (1989). At the same time, *Batman* was enormously popular, so it seemed an opportune time to translate *The Rocketeer* comic to the silver screen. After five years of development hell, two screenplays, six rewrites and a lawsuit from Marvel Comics over which company actually owned the rights to the character, that is finally what happened.[1] Disney/Touchstone prepped the film version for a summer release in 1991, with Joe Johnson (*Jurassic Park III*) in the director's chair.

Young Billy Campbell (*Once and Again*) was cast as Secord, Alan Arkin played his sidekick Peeve, and 2001 Academy Award–winner Jennifer Connelly provided the eye candy as the Betty Page–like beauty Jenny Blake. Starring as the villain—an Errol Flynn–type actor (and secret Nazi spy) named Neville Sinclair—was Timothy Dalton, fresh from his two-film stint as James Bond.

In another interesting homage to early movie tradition, Dalton's villainous and hulking assistant was designed (through extensive—and eerie—make-up) to resemble "the Creeper," a character played by actor Rondo Hatton in the films *Pearl of Death* (1944) *The Brute Man* (1946), and *House of Horrors* (1946). In real life, Hatton was something of a tragic figure, his face distorted by a disease called acromegaly after distinguished military service in World War I.[2] The deformed actor appeared as a menacing "ghoul" in more than 100 films of the period. In *The Rocketeer*, the Hatton-like character "Lothar" (Tiny Ron) performed the same role as Jaws in *The Spy Who Loved Me* or Oddjob in *Goldfinger*, providing the physical threat to the hero (being the "soldier villain," as it were).

Filmed in Los Angeles, *The Rocketeer* cost some 40 million dollars to produce and featured fantastic flying effects designed by George Lucas's Industrial Light and Magic. In this case, however, it was the actors who forged the magic of the tale, with Paul Sorvino (as gangster Eddie Valentine) and Terry O'Quinn (as Howard Hughes) offering wonderful support to the leads. This author remembers seeing the film in the Claridge Theater in Montclair, New Jersey, upon its release in 1991, and the wild audience enthusiasm and delight after Sorvino delivered a patriotic speech about being "an American," despite his ties to the mob. The target of his speech was Dalton's villainous Nazi, a screen stereotype that will probably never outlive its usefulness in pulp movies.

A fun movie, *The Rocketeer* looked terrific. From costuming to cars to the kitschy nighttime dance spot "The South Seas Club," the period design was perfectly realized. Like *The Shadow* and *The Phantom*, *The Rocketeer* was clearly a "retro" superhero film wherein detail for a bygone era was intended to substitute for tricked-out gadgetry, sadism and the extreme violence popularized by more mainstream, contemporary genre pictures.

One highlight of *The Rocketeer* was a short animated film, a bit of Nazi propaganda, detailing how rocket pack–sporting shock troopers intend to attack America. Animated in black and white, with Wagnerian music accompanying it, the jingoistic spirit of this little presentation film perfectly suited the story's time frame.

Another nice touch was cameo appearances by W.C. Fields and Clark Gable lookalikes. Perhaps more fun was the answer to the question of precisely how and why the word "LAND" fell off that great "HOLLYWOOD" sign on the hill. Also engaging were the numerous (and droll) references to the cutthroat world of moviemaking. Dalton's Neville Sinclair was declared the "number three" box-office draw in America, and plenty of amusement arose from this particular actor's ego and carousing.

Innocent and charming, action-packed and fun, *The Rocketeer* should have been a big box-office hit. Alas, it opened during the summer of *Terminator 2: Judgment Day*, Kevin Costner's *Robin Hood*, and the chickflick *Thelma and Louise*. *The Rocketeer* earned a modest return on its investment, but not nearly enough to encourage producers to forge a sequel or a franchise. *The Shadow* and *The Phantom* would, in a few short years, also attempt to revive interest in 1930s serial–type heroes, also with markedly little success.

The Rocketeer (1991)
LIVE-ACTION FILM

"The movie has a determinedly sweet, innocuous spirit, some nifty sets ... and action scenes that are mercifully more bouncy than bonecrunching. But the screenplay ... could use a bit more sophisticated sparkle."
— David Ansen, *Newsweek*, June 24, 1991, page 61.

"*The Rocketeer* showed great potential, but underutilized its strongest asset — that rocket pack. The film comes alive when the Rocketeer is in

flight, but all too often, he's on foot. Perhaps too much attention was paid trying to capture the period of the film and not enough on the heroics that this film offered, but then barely delivered."
— William Latham, author of *Mary's Monster, Space: 1999 Resurrection*.

"...Johnston's film is a visual feast, a treat for cinematic genrephiles and comic-book devotees alike."

— Mark Kermode, *Sight and Sound,*
August 1991, page 55.

"Like the rocket, *The Rocketeer* is compact, cuddly and streamlined, producing a low-grade, if mechanical, form of exhilaration."
— J. Hoberman, *The Village Voice,*
July 2, 1991, page 57.

CAST: Bill Campbell (Clifford Secord); Alan Arkin (Peeve); Jennifer Connelly (Jenny Blake); Paul Sorvino (Eddie Valentine); Terry O'Quinn (Howard Hughes); Ed Lauter (Fitch); Timothy Dalton (Neville St. Claire); James Handy (Woody); Tiny Ron (Lothar); Robert Gry Miranda (Spanish Johnny); John Lavachielli (Pasti); Jon Polito (Bigelow); Eddie Jones (Malcolm); William Sanderson (Skeets); Max Grodenchik (Wilmer); Clint Howard (Monk); Rick Overton (South Seas Patron); Clark Gable (Gene Daily).

CREW: Walt Disney Pictures Presents, in Association with Silver Screen Partners IV, a Gordon Company Production, a Joe Johnston Film, *The Rocketeer. Casting:* Nancy Foy. *Costume Designer:* Marilyn Vance-Straker. *Music Composer:* James Horner. *Co-Producer:* Dave Stevens. *Editor:* Arthur Schmidt. *Production Design:* Jim Bissell. *Director of Photography:* Hiro Narita. *Executive Producer:* Larry Franco. *Based on the Graphic Novel "The Rocketeer" Created by:* Dave Stevens. *Story:* Danny Bilson, Paul De Meo, William Dear. *Screenplay by:* Danny Bilson, Paul De Meo. *Produced by:* Lawrence Gordon, Charles Gordon, Lloyd Levin. *Directed by:* Joe Johnston. *Running Time:* 108 minutes *M.P.A.A. Rating:*PG.

Ambitious but hapless young pilot Cliff Secord steps into the middle of a car chase between Federal agents and gangsters, and accidentally gets his hands on a top-secret rocket pack, a new super-weapon developed by Howard Hughes called the X-3. Since Cliff and his mechanic Peeve's plane is destroyed during the chase, they find this new flying device especially interesting and begin testing it.

Meanwhile, the movie matinee idol (and number three box-office draw in America) Neville Sinclair retains the services of gangster Eddie Valentine to recover the rocket pack, though the thugs are unaware that Sinclair is secretly a Nazi spy. Uncertain of Valentine's loyalty, Sinclair also hires "muscle" in the form of Lothar, a giant deformed creep. Sinclair soon learns that Clifford has the X-3 engine and sets about courting the pilot's girl, fledgling actress Jennifer Blake.

At the airfield, Clifford dons the rocket pack and a special helmet to prevent an air show disaster, and members of the press at the event go wild at the debut appearance of the "Rocketman," or "Rocketeer." Secord's exploits become front-page news, and before long Lothar is after Secord and Peeve. When Cliff learns that Jenny is in danger, he races to the South Seas Club to save her from Sinclair; but he's too late, and she falls into the Fascist agent's hands.

Valentine orders Secord to bring the rocket pack to the Griffith Observatory in exchange for Jenny, but the Feds capture Cliff and take him to meet Howard Hughes. The inventor/millionaire shows Peeve and Cliff a film of German rocket troops and all is made clear: the rocket must not fall into the wrong hands. Cliff escapes to reach the rendezvous and tells Valentine — a patriot — that Sinclair is working for the Nazis. When Nazi troops arrive to back up the spy, it is the mob versus the Germans, and Sinclair escapes with Jenny aboard a Nazi dirigible touring the West Coast.

The Rocketeer goes into action one last time to fight a battle on the blimp in midair. Aware that the rocket is leaking gasoline, Cliff turns it over to the villainous Sinclair, and the Nazi is obliterated when he activates it trying to escape. Now Jenny and Cliff are stuck on an out-of-control blimp flying over Hollywood with precious few options for escape.

The Shadow

The Shadow is an interesting 1930s superhero character with a long and complex history. He began his pop-culture life in 1931 as a hero of gritty, action-laden pulp novels (not unlike *The Destroyer* or *Doc Savage*) penned by the prolific Maxwell Grant (really Walter B. Gibson). However, the Shadow was not truly a superhero in his earliest incarnation so much as a gangbuster, an avenger (lacking any fantastical attributes) who went after criminals for his own dark purposes. He formed a network of contacts and associates to enforce his personal sense of justice, including reporter Clyde Burke and taxi driver Moe Shrevnitz. As for the Shadow himself, readers were not originally certain who the disguised hero really was. As his name portends, he was a mystery.

In the mid–1930s, however, the Shadow landed on radio (on *The Detective Story Hour*), and some of his personal details were revealed (such as his real identity — playboy Lamont Cranston, a Bruce Wayne–like millionaire living in New York City). This time around, he fought supernatural foes as well as the more routine criminal opponents. And most importantly, he developed the helpful (and bizarre) knack of "clouding" the minds of evil men, thus making himself invisible to them. The Shadow also gained a Lois Lane–like girlfriend in Margo Lane, the only person who knew his secret identity.

Citizen Kane (1941) director Orson Welles gave voice to Cranston on the radio drama, while Agnes Moorhead played his beloved Margo. Of all his myriad agents, only Moe the taxi man survived the transition to the new medium.

By the 1940s the Shadow was an incredibly popular character, seen in his own comic book and even a movie serial (though in the comic book series he lost the talent to cloud men's minds and go "cloaked"). In the 1960s he reappeared in another comic and battled the evil villain named Shiwan Khan, heir to the Genghis Khan name, while at the same time regaining the "clouding minds" ability. Then, for DC Comics in the 1970s, the Shadow lost his most valuable super power again. And back and forth it has gone ever since, over the years, in more than three hundred written adventures.

A film version of the Shadow appeared in theaters in the summer of 1994 and adopted many different aspects of the Shadow character, blending them together in a fairly coherent and highly entertaining package. The movie retained the original era and setting of the first pulp stories — an art deco, pre–World War II New York City. From the 1960s comic came the picture's primary villain, Shiwan Khan. And the Shadow kept his 1970s identity as an almost inhuman–appearing character. He wore a large hat and scarf (covering his mouth), and bore a long and pointed witch's nose. He also came armed with two revolvers that seemingly never required reloading. Like the radio figure of Orson Welles, the movie version of the Shadow presented in the 1990s feature could cloud men's minds (thanks to training in Tibet), and the film's familiar ad-line echoed the radio series' famous refrain, "Who knows what evil lurks in the hearts of men?" Alec Baldwin, who starred as Lamont/the Shadow, even mimicked (rather nicely) the Shadow's trademark evil cackle.

Because it premiered in 1994, *The Shadow* followed a contemporary trend in superhero films. Capitalizing on the style of Tim Burton's *Batman*, *The Shadow* was rather dark, and its hero was an angst-ridden, no-nonsense fellow. Although the film was one of the "retro" superhero entries set in the late '30s or early '40s (along with *The*

Rocketeer and *The Phantom*), its mood was very much in the spirit of *Batman*. A prologue introduced Lamont as a troubled American ex-patriot in Tibet, the "butcher of Lhasa," before he was abducted and tamed, learning from a Master how to control his dark side. And most of the movie's action occurred at night, accompanied by a bombastic Jerry Goldsmith score, generating a "dark knight"–style atmosphere.

Just as Batman terrorized street vermin in the opening scenes of Burton's 1989 *Batman*, so did the menacing Shadow intimidate crooks into confessing their guilt in the early scenes of this film, scaring villains with his throaty voice and seeming invisibility. An early action set piece on the Brooklyn Bridge involving a criminal named "Duke" was a flat-out retread of *Batman*'s opening scene — with criminals shaking and quaking in horror at the appearance of an urban legend, a "mythical" and dark superhero. The screenplay by David Koepp (*Spider-Man, Panic Room*) was unremittingly sharp, clever and knowing, even with the *Batman* format firmly in place, and that helped make the movie very enjoyable.

What distinguished *The Shadow* (and ultimately made it a better film than *The Phantom*) was its fantastically well-depicted 1930s world, filled with glittering night clubs, deco skyscrapers and other vintage touches (such as an ad for Llama Cigarettes). The picture was also well served by a restrained sense of humor and knowledge of "future" history. "There's a new world order coming," one character explained, knowingly invoking a Bushian 1990s phrase for purposes of irony. "Psychically, I'm well-endowed," a grim Cranston revealed at another point, also rather humorously. These moments added some lightness to the film's dark atmosphere. Superhero fans will also enjoy seeing Ian McKellen, Magneto of *X-Men*, in the role of a rather hapless scientist who unknowingly creates the first atom bomb.

Character-wise, *The Shadow*, directed by Russell Mulcahy (*Highlander* [1984]), remained remarkably faithful to the origin (or origins) of the characters, perhaps because its Shadow legend had so much wiggle room due to its various incarnations over the decades. Moe Shrevnitz was still around, driving that cab, played by the delightful Peter Boyle. Margo Lane (Penelope Ann Miller) was the glamorous love interest; and in the tradition of the comics, she learned Cranston's secret, here through the power of low-grade telepathy. Shiwan Khan was also a good menace, developing an invisible fortress in the center of Manhattan and plotting the ruin of mankind with a spherical atomic device.

The best performance in *The Shadow*, however, belonged to Alec Baldwin, an imposing actor who at his then-age (and then-weight) would probably have been the ultimate screen Batman. He has a dark complexion, a personal charisma, and an aura of confidence and arrogance that is well-suited to the Caped Crusader and his alter ego Bruce Wayne. As the Shadow, Baldwin played a tortured soul with a morbid sense of humor and glint in his eye. Watching him play the part, one senses he really does know the evil that lurks in the hearts of men because of his own personal experience. It would have been nice to see him reprise the role in a sequel.

A thoroughly entertaining picture that resurrects the age of the Empire State Building in perfect detail and loving color, it is hard to imagine why *The Shadow* failed at the box office. But fail it did, and on a grand scale. When it opened on more than 1600 screens nationwide, America's mind seemed clouded to the film's visual appeal, and the movie grossed only about $30 million. This proved to be a disastrous showing, since it cost over 40 million to make, with some additional 30 million reportedly spent on advertising and merchandising.

The Shadow, like *The Rocketeer* before

it and *The Phantom* after it, supports an interesting thesis about superhero films and their audience. Apparently, viewers are completely apathetic to genre period pieces. They want their icons working in modern-day cities, armed with the best gadgetry and high-tech weaponry money can buy. All attempts at resurrecting the simpler and more gentle era and aura of the 1930s and '40s have failed rather magnificently — despite the fact that these three films from the 1990s all have their merits, including excellent production values, great casts, and entertaining, humorous stories.

The Shadow (1994)
LIVE-ACTION FILM

"...[It] has much to recommend it.... The sets are evocative, the effects dazzling, and the photography seductive. But unlike its two most obvious counterparts, *Batman* and *Indiana Jones and the Temple of Doom*, there's never much sense of urgency or identification with the title character..."
— James M. Faller. *Cinefantastique*, Volume 25, #6: "Reviews," September 1994, page 123.

"[It is] terrific ... a lot less pretentious than *Batman* and a whole lot of fun."
— Jeff Laffel, *Films in Review*, July 1994, page 58.

"Not bad. Not great. Alec Baldwin was good. This probably failed because we were getting tired of hero movies by the time it was released."
— William Latham, author of *Mary's Monster* and *Space: 1999 Resurrection*.

"...[It is] the most embarrassing big studio bomb of the summer."
— Michael Medved, *The New York Post*, July 1, 1994, page 42.

CAST: Alec Baldwin (Lamont Cranston/the Shadow); John Lone (Shiwan Khan); Penelope Ann Miller (Margo Lane); Ian McKellen (Reinhardt Lane); Peter Boyle (Moe Shrevnitz); Jonathan Winters (Barth); Tim Curry (Farley Claymore); Joseph Maher (Isaac Newboldt); John Kapelos (Duke Rollins); Max Wright (Berger); Sab Shimono (Dr. Tam); Brady Tsuratani (Tulku); Andre Gregory (Burbank); James Hong (L. Peng); Arsenio "Sonny" Trinidad (Wu); Aaron Lustig (Doctor); Ethan Phillips (Nelson); Sinoa (Singer); Rudolph Willrich and Verlon Edwards (Waiters); Wesley Mann (Bellboy); Joe d'Angerio (English Johnny); Larry Joshua (Maxi); Taxi Driver (Larry Hankin).

CREW: Universal Studios Presents a Bregman/Baer Film, a Film by Russell Mulcahy, *The Shadow*. *Casting:* Mary Calquhoun. *Costume Designer:* Bob Ringwood. *Music Composed and Conducted by:* Jerry Goldsmith. *Music Supervisor:* Jellybean Benitez. *Co-Executive Producer:* Stan Weston. *Film Editor:* Peter Honess. *Production Designer:* Joseph Nemec, III. *Director of Photography:* Stephen H. Burum. *Executive Producers:* Louis A. Stroller, Rolf Deyhle. *Production Manager:* Patricia Churchill. *First Assistant Director:* Louis Desposito. *Second Assistant Director:* Douglas S. Ornstein. *Based on:* Advance Magazine Publishers Inc.'s character *The Shadow*. *Written by:* David Koepp. *Produced by:* Martin Bregman, Willi Baer, Michael S. Bregman. *Directed by:* Russell Mulcahy. *M.P.A.A. Rating:* PG. *Running time:* 100 minutes (approx.).

In the opium fields of Tibet, an ex-patriot westerner, Lamont Cranston, struggles against his own "black heart," committing murder and running drugs. But the corrupt American is unexpectedly redeemed by a mysterious Tibetan teacher, one who instructs him in the ways of "clouding men's minds." Cranston becomes one of the Master's most valued and powerful servants.

Years later, Lamont Cranston has created an alter-ego — a hero named "the Shadow" who strikes fear into the hearts of scoundrels and criminals in New York City. He can successfully cloud the minds of lesser men, making himself visible to them (though there is just one part of himself he can't hide — his shadow — hence his name). From his underground sanctum, the Shadow protects innocent men from gangsters and thieves, and then recruits the grateful citizens into his heroic organization, creating a web of informants.

A rich playboy, Lamont falls in love with Margo Lane, daughter of a prominent scientist, and is drawn into a strange conflict. A new evil has awakened in the city. Arriving in a Tibetan sarcophagus is the warlord descendant of Genghis Khan, Shiwan Khan. Khan plans to rule the world, and he shares Cranston's dangerous ability to cloud minds. With the help of an opportunistic industrialist, Farley Claymore, and the unwitting help of an enslaved Dr. Lane, Khan plans to take over the world by wielding a deadly new weapon of mass destruction — a barillium sphere, or early atom bomb.

Soon, the Shadow is hot on the trail of Khan, but his mission is complicated when Margo — vaguely telepathic — learns that Lamont is, in fact, the Shadow.

After escaping a trap set by Claymore, the Shadow confronts Khan at his secret headquarters, the Hotel Monolith, which the warlord has rendered "invisible" to all New Yorkers. Lamont detects it and vanquishes Claymore, while a freed Dr. Lane and his daughter deactivate the atom bomb. Finally, the Shadow faces off against Khan.

Shazam! (a.k.a. *Captain Marvel*)

Captain Marvel was a superhero character created by artist C.C. Beck and writer Bill Parker for *Whiz Comics* in the winter of 1940. The character's mission: to compete with the ever-popular published adventures of Superman, then the mega-star of superhero comic books. Unlike the Man of Steel, however, Captain Marvel was no extraterrestrial, but the product of magical forces. On one day, diffident teenager Billy Batson encountered a sorcerer who revealed to him the secret of transforming into a full-blown, adult superhero called Captain Marvel. All the boy had to do was utter the strange (and now famous) word "Shazam!"

This nonsense term, now part of the popular culture lexicon, was actually a call to the gods to endow Batson with their particular powers. "Solomon" (wisdom), "Hercules" (physical strength), "Atlas" (endurance and constitution), "Zeus" (power), Achilles ("bravery") and Mercury ("speed").

Upon uttering the magic word, Batson transformed into a grown-up — a mature, physically robust hero wearing a red uniform and cape (not to mention a lightning bolt insignia). The character not only played upon the secret wish of every young person to become a great superhero, but, in more general terms, to become a handsome, powerful and respected adult.

The talents behind Captain Marvel (including another author, Otto Binder) did their job well, perhaps too well. Sales went through the roof, and a popular movie serial was produced starring the ubiquitous Tom Tyler as Captain Marvel in 1941. As a result of the title's success, comic book competitor DC sued Whiz Comics over the character. DC claimed that Captain Marvel too closely resembled Superman, given his strength, costume and ability to fly. Eventually, DC won the challenge; so it was not the frequenty-appearing mad scientist nemesis Dr. Sivana who defeated Captain Marvel, but the U.S. statutes on copyright infringement.

When Captain Marvel resurfaced in the comics in the early 1970s, it was under DC's banner. Then, in 1974, the successful animation studio called Filmation produced a live-action adaptation of the comic, airing it on Saturday mornings. Executives Lou Scheimer and Norm Prescott had shepherded Filmation through a particularly successful era with the adaptation of *Star*

Trek as a cartoon series in 1973 and 1974, and this effort was part of their progressive approach to children's programming. In the past, their animated TV adaptations had proved popular, but it was Filmation's shift into live-action children's fantasy television in the early 1970s that (along with the programming of Sid and Marty Krofft) ushered in a whole generation of fascinating programming, including *Shazam!* (1974–1976), another superhero series, *Isis,* and several futuristic adventures (*Ark II* [1976], *Space Academy* [1977] and *Jason of Star Command* [1977-1978]).

Shazam! was the earliest of these ventures. A half-hour series that ran for three years, *Shazam!* followed the adventures of a typical 1970s kid, Billy Batson (Michael Gray), who could transform into Captain Marvel (John Davey in the first two years; Jackson Bostwick in the third). The title *Captain Marvel* could not be used because Marvel Comics now owned that name and had another (different) superhero using that moniker.

In the TV series, Billy traveled around the United States in a Winnebago RV with a kindly adult named Mentor (Les Tremayne). Batson received sage life advice not only from Mentor but from a Greek chorus of sorts, the gods that granted him his powers, known as the Elders.

Because it aired on Saturday mornings and was intended for the eyes of children, *Shazam!* eschewed violence and intense action. Instead, it was a show about morality and civic responsibility, and each week Billy learned how to become a better person. He would often teach others the same lesson.

In "Thou Shall Not Kill," for instance, Batson worked with a young girl (Pamelyn Ferdin) who feared that her horse would be put to death by an angry rancher. Billy helped the girl stay within the bounds of the law and use the legal system to win the horse a stay of execution. Captain Marvel came into the picture to prevent the rancher from killing the horse; but understanding among all sides was forged, and every party learned a special lesson about truth, justice and the American way.

In its second and third seasons, *Shazam!* was seen as part of the CBS superhero block *The Shazam/Isis Hour.* There were several "crossover" adventures featuring both Captain Marvel and Isis. The series was rerun as late as 1980, even though only 28 episodes were produced.

After *Shazam!* was cancelled in 1976, the character of Captain Marvel reappeared in *The Kid Super Power Hour with Shazam!,* another venture between Filmation and DC Comics. The cartoon ran on NBC and featured the adventures of Billy Batson, along with other members of the DC "Marvel" family (including Captain Marvel Junior and Mary Marvel). The animated series offered classic comic book villains, including Dr. Sivana (voiced by Alan Oppenheimer).

Shazam (1974–76)
LIVE-ACTION SERIES

Cast: Michael Gray (Billy Batson); Les Tremayne (Mentor); FIRST SEASON–SECOND SEASON: John Davey (Captain Marvel); THIRD SEASON: Jackson Bostwick (Captain Marvel).

CREW: *Creative Consultant:* Carmine Infantino. *Producers:* Robert Chenault, Arthur H. Nadel. *Executive Producers:* Norm Prescott, Richard M. Rosenbloom, Lou Scheimer. *Music:* Yvette Blais, Jeff Michael. *Film Editor:* A Ray Williford. *Cinematography:* Robert Sparks. *Casting:* Meryl O'Louglin. *Costume Design:* Thalia Phillips. From Filmation.

SEASON ONE (1974)

1. "**The Joyriders**" Written by: Len Janson. Directed by: Chuck Menville. Airdate: September 7, 1974.

2. "**The Brothers**" Written by: Len Janson and Chuck Menville. Directed by: Hollingsworth Morse. Airdate: September 14, 1974.

3. "**Thou Shall Not Kill**" Written by: Marianne Mosner. Directed by: Arthur H. Nadel. Airdate: September 21, 1974.

4. "**The Lure of the Lost**" Written by: Jim Ryan and Bill Danch. Directed by: Arthur H. Nadel. Airdate: September 28, 1974.

5. "**The Road Back**" Written by: Jim Ryan and Bill Danch. Directed by: Arthur H. Nadel. Airdate: October 5, 1974.

6. "**The Athlete**" Written by: Bill Canning. Directed by: Hollingsworth Morse. Airdate: October 12, 1974.

7. "**The Treasure**" Written by: Bill Danch and Jim Ryan. Directed by: Robert Douglas. Airdate: October 19, 1974.

8. "**The Boy Who Said No**" Written by: Rik Vollaerts. Directed by: Hollingsworth Morse. Airdate: October 26, 1974.

9. "**The Doom Buggy**" Written by: Jack Mendelsohn and Jack Kaplan. Directed by: Robert Douglas. Airdate: November 2, 1974.

10. "**The Brain**" Written by: Donald F. Glut. Directed by: Hollingsworth Morse. Airdate: November 9, 1974.

11. "**Little Boy Lost**" Written and Directed by: Arthur H. Nadel. Airdate: November 16, 1974.

12. "**The Delinquent**" Written by: Marianne Mosner. Directed by: Robert Chenault. Airdate: November 23, 1974.

13. "**The Braggart**" Written by: Len Janson and Chuck Menville. Directed by: Arthur H. Nadel. Airdate: November 30, 1974.

14. "**The Past Is Not Forever**" Written by: Paolo Orsini. Directed by: Robert Douglas. Airdate: December 7, 1974.

15. "**The Gang's All Here**" Written by: Paolo Orsini. Directed by: Robert Douglas. Airdate: December 14, 1974.

SEASON TWO (1975)

16. "**On Winning**" Written by: Barry Greenfield and Frank Granville. Directed by: Hollingsworth Morse. Airdate: September 6, 1975.

17. "**Debbie**" Written by: Michael Pressman. Directed by: Hollingsworth Morse. Airdate: September 13, 1975.

18. "**Fool's Gold**" Written by: Olga Palsson Simms. Directed by: Hollingsworth Morse. Airdate: September 20, 1975.

19. "**Double Trouble**" Written by: Michael Sutton. Directed by: Arnold Laven. Airdate: September 27, 1975.

20. "**Pet Wolf**" Written by: Bill Danch and Jim Ryan. Directed by: Arnold Laven. Airdate: October 4, 1975.

21. "**Speak No Evil**" Written by: Arthur H. Nadel and Olga Palsson Simms. Directed by: Arnold Laven. Airdate: October 11, 1975.

22. "**The Odd Couple**" Written by: Sid Morse. Directed by: Hollingsworth Morse. Airdate: October 18, 1975.

SEASON THREE (1976)

23. "The Contest" Written by: J. Michael Reaves. Directed by: Hollingsworth Morse. Airdate: September 11, 1976.

24. "Bitter Herbs" Written by: Ray Gladstone. Directed by: John Peyser. Airdate: September 18, 1976.

25. "Ripcord" Written by: Arthur H. Nadel. Directed by: Henry J. Lange, Jr. Airdate: September 25, 1976.

26. "Finders Keepers" Written by: Susan Dworski. Directed by: Hollingsworth Morse. Airdate: October 2, 1976.

27. "The Sound of a Different Drummer" Written by: Len Janson. Directed by: John Peyser. Airdate: October 9, 1976.

28. "Out of Focus" Written by: Paolo Orsini. Directed by: Hollingsworth Morse. Airdate: October 16, 1976.

The Kid Super Power Hour with Shazam! (1982)
ANIMATED SERIES

VOICE TALENTS: Burr Middleton (Billy Batson/Captain Marvel); Dawn Jeffery (Mary Marvel); Barry Gordon (Captain Marvel, Jr.); Alan Oppenheimer (Dr. Sivana).

CREW: From Filmation for NBC. *Produced by:* Lou Scheimer and Norm Prescott. In Association with DC Comics. In color.

Sheena

The alluring Queen of the Jungle named Sheena, the creation of Jerry Iger and Will Eisner, first appeared in *Jumbo Comics* in 1938. Her adventures in the African jungle were seen in a weekly magazine drawn by Mort Meskin. Sheena's comic book ran from 1942 to 1952, and several artists (including Bob Powell, John Celardo, Dan Zolnerowich and Richard H. Webb) drew the wild girl, a kind of sexy pin-up and distaff version of Edgar Rice Burroughs' Tarzan legend. Then, in 1955, statuesque Irish McCalla portrayed Sheena in a syndicated black-and-white TV series of widespread popularity.

The character was revived on the screen in 1984. This time, Sheena was given the royal treatment, a $20-million motion picture filmed in Kenya and directed by John Guillermin. Tanya Roberts (*A View to a Kill* [1985]) made for a particularly vapid (if athletic) version of the jungle heroine,

who, like Tarzan, could communicate with animals when trouble came.

Through the years, Sheena has been cast as a fantasy figure, no doubt. However, this action/adventure–style star did not officially enter the realm of the superhero until the re-imagination that aired on TV from 2000 to 2002, during the "ascent of woman" period popularized by *Buffy the Vampire Slayer* (and, no doubt, the fantasy femme *Xena: Warrior Princess*). This time around, Sheena did not merely communicate with animals, she became a full-fledged shapeshifter, able to transform into wild beasts of the land, sea and air. Like Jonathan Chase on *Manimal*, she often took the form of a hawk.

Most interestingly, Sheena could also take the fighting form of a long-clawed, mud-soaked, snout-nosed humanoid creature called the Darak'na. It was in this terrifying form that the Queen of the Jungle would defend her African country, the La

A Jungle Queen and friend. Gena Lee Nolin stars as Sheena in the syndicated TV series.

Mistas, from meddling outsiders and other Westerners.

Former *Baywatch* star and model Gene Lee Nolin essayed the role of the orphaned jungle heroine for a season and a half on the new series. Her mentor and adopted mother was a local shaman named Kali (Margo Moorer), and Sheena's love interest was rough-and-tumble Matt Cutter (John Allen Nelson), an ex-patriot American and former C.I.A. agent who ran a tourist company called *Cutter Unlimited*. Cutter was an old-fashioned scoundrel with a heart of gold, and he and Sheena shared a sparring relationship of mutual attraction.

Mild comic relief was provided on the short-lived syndicated series by Mendelsohn (Kevin Quigley), Cutter's cowardly and quirky assistant. In the last episode of the series, "The World According to Mendelsohn," this character was abducted by natives and elevated to the status of king or wise man in the village, at least until Sheena and Cutter came to the rescue.

The twenty-first century *Sheena* was perhaps as much a romantic adventure and good-natured spoof as it was a serious action series, though it often featured rousing and fierce fight sequences. Many episodes simply sent Sheena and Cutter off into the jungle together to tantalize the audience with the notion that the attractive duo might finally get together. "Forbidden Fruit" saw Sheena and Cutter's inhibitions stripped away when affected by a strange unexplored place called the "closed valley."

Other episodes featured more pedestrian plots about the corrupt local government, and Sheena's regular nemesis was the exploitative President N'Gama (Jim Coleman). Fortunately, she also had a friend in the local constable, Rashid (Veryl Jones), thus providing a balanced view of the population. Most often, Sheena was seen rescuing Westerners from bad guys. She tangled with mercenaries in "Jewel," warring local clans in "Between a Rock and a Hard Place," the mob in "The Fool Monty," terrorists in "Still Hostage After All These Years," and slavers in "Unsafe Passage."

Evidencing a good sense of humor, the series lampooned the popular *Crocodile Hunter* nature series in "The Fool Monty." It re-tooled Alfred Hitchcock's *The Birds* in "Revenge of the Jirds," ribbed *The X-Files* in "The Maltaka Files," and even attempted a re-do of the classic Charlton Heston picture *The Naked Jungle* (1951) in "Marabunta," which concerned an army of killer ants stalking the La Mistas.

A great deal of humor also arose from Sheena's "outsider" perspective. She never really understood Western culture, and Cutter often attempted to "educate" her in its ways. Sheena was a literal thinker (like Automan or Lt. Data) and spent a great deal of time reading books from the West to gain a greater insight into the culture. She read *A Farewell to Arms* ("Sanctuary"), and in "The Lost Boy" quoted *All the President's Men.*

Although the fight scenes on *Sheena* were quite well done, all with half-naked beauties beating up men, many of the other special effects were weak. A C.G.I. Sheena seen climbing a mountain in "The Lost Boy" and (on other occasions) reeked of phoniness. Also, the series was filmed in Florida, and apparently all of the footage of Africa was stock footage. Stock ants appeared in "Marabunta" (alongside C.G.I. ants), and "Stranded in the Jungle" lifted a parachuting stunt right out of stock. These transitions from "real" Sheena footage to stock elephants, landscapes and action scenes were often jarring.

Before the series ended abruptly in the middle of its second season due to low ratings in syndication, *Sheena* offered an array of interesting guests. Ron Ely, TV's *Tarzan* (1966–69), appeared in "The Feral King," and Muhammad Ali's daughter, Laila, starred in "Meltdown in Maltaka." Horror make-up legend Tom Savini (*Dawn of the Dead* [1979]) headlined in "The Lost Boy," playing a duplicitous photographer. Veteran actor Carl Weathers (*Rocky* [1976], *Predator* [1987]) directed several *Sheena* episodes.

Sheena (2000–2002)
LIVE-ACTION SERIES

"…[Sheena] closely resembles a resident of the Playboy Mansion [and] … Gena Lee Nolin … plays the title role as if in a constant fog. The only question you'll have about her is where in the jungle she finds all that peroxide for her blond locks."
— John Maynard, *The Washington Post*, October 7, 2000, page C07.

"…[It] doesn't do a thing for the African jungle except perpetuate the Hollywood fantasy. It doesn't help women's rights. It's not good dramatically. What *Sheena* does offer is plenty of action and a lot of intentional and unintentional humor. It's bubble gum entertainment…"
— Kathie Huddleston, *Sci Fi Weekly*, On Screen: "Sheena — Queen of the TV Jungle," October 2000.

CAST: Gena Lee Nolin (Sheena); John Allen Nelson (Matt Cutter); Margo Moorer (Kali); Kevin Quigley (Mendelson).

CREW: *Developed by:* Steven L. Sears and Douglas Schwartz. *Music:* Sean Callery. *Co-Producer:* Mike Steven. *Consulting Producer:* Bill Taub. *Co-Executive Producer:* Babs Greyhosky. *Producer:* Boris Malden. *Executive Producers:* Douglas Schwartz and Steven L. Sears. *Director of Photography:* Ed Morey. *Production Design:* Orvis Rigsby. *Film Editor:* Pete Opotowsky. *Unit Production Manager:* Boris Malden. *First Assistant Director:* Frank Falvey. *Second Assistant Director:* Cheeba White. *Production Supervisor:* Bill Hill. *Florida Casting:* Pati Robinson. *L.A. Casting:* Beth Hymson-Ayer. *Costume Designer:* Beverly Nelon Safier. *Make-up:* Diane Maurno. *Hair Stylist:* Mary Lampert. *Special Effects Make-up/Prosthetics:* Lee Grimes. *Wardrobe Supervisor:* Jule Bubis.

SEASON ONE (2000-2001)

1. "Sheena" (Pilot) Written by: Steven L. Sears and Douglas Schwartz. Directed by: Jon Cassar. Airdate: October 7, 2000.

Sheena, a beautiful young female warrior, lives in deepest Africa, guided by her adopted mentor, Kali, after her parents were killed years earlier. Sheena has the ability to transform into the mythical beast called the Darak'na, a skill she uses to keep corrupt white civilization out of the La Mistas. Sheena meets Cutter, of *Cutter Unlimited*, an American ex–C.I.A. agent, now an entrepreneur in Africa. They work together for the first time to stop strip miners intending to exploit the nearby mountains for jewels and gold.

GUEST CAST: Peter J. Lucas (Norliss); Cullen Douglas; Jeff Moldovan; Jason Gray; Jay Amar; Dean Murray; Vickie Phillips (Sheena Stunt Double); Dale Cannon (Cutter Stunt Double); Don McLoud.

2. "Fallout" Written by: William Taub. Directed by: Jon Cassar. Airdate: October 14, 2000.

A top-secret American spy satellite crashes somewhere in the La Mistas, spurring a hunt for the important technology. Cutter and Sheena team up with Cutter's old rival, a man named Tyler, to locate the satellite before it becomes necessary for the United States military to destroy it — an act which means bombing the La Mistas!

GUEST CAST: Jim Coleman (President N'Gama); Peter Onorati; Russ Blackwell; Steven West; Vickie Phillips (Sheena Stunt Double); Don McCloud.

3. "Revenge of the Jirds" Written by: Babs Greyhosky. Directed by: Scott Paulin. Airdate: October 21, 2000.

Sheena and Cutter battle animal poachers after what should have been a routine coffee shipment to *Cutter Unlimited* turns out to be a crate filled with small, hairy, rat-like creatures called Jirds. Knowing that the animals need to be preserved and are worth millions on the world market, Sheena takes action.

GUEST CAST: Jennifer Hammon; Dave Corey; Isaac Singleton; Steve Zurk; Vickie Phillips (Sheena Stunt Double); Dale Cannon (Cutter Stunt Double).

4. "A Rite of Passage" Written by: Babs Greyhosky. Directed by: Walter Von Huene. Airdate: October 28, 2000.

Sheena's birthday celebration is interrupted when fierce gorillas attack the village and injure Kali. Sheena and Cutter learn that the wild animals may have once been human beings that mystically altered their form when they became disenchanted with humanity. Meanwhile, Sheena reflects on the past that left her an orphan in Africa.

GUEST CAST: Veryl Jones (Rashid); Paul Brodie.

5. "Tourist Trap" Written by: Keith Thompson. Directed by: Scott Paulin. Airdate: November 4, 2000.

Terrorists kidnap Cutter and plan to release the deadly Ebola virus on unsuspecting villagers. The sample of the virulent disease was stolen from N'Gama, but now Sheena has a decision to make. Can she use her powers of transformation to help save an infected girl's life?

GUEST CAST: Jim Coleman (President N'Gama); Veryl Jones (Rashid); Tony Armatrading; Kayla Campbell; Elizabeth Fendrick; Bob Lipka; Nancy Tait; Tyrone C. Wiggins; Vicki Phillips (Sheena Stunt Double); Dale Cannon (Cutter Stunt Double).

6. "Buried Secrets" Written by: Steven L. Sears and Babs Greyhosky. Directed by: Corey Eubanks. Airdate: November 11, 2000.

A nearby volcano erupts and causes earthquakes in the La Mistas. Sheena becomes trapped in a cave-in and finds evidence that leads her to believe her parents were not the victims of an accident, but murder. And the murderer may still be close by...

GUEST CAST: Veryl Reid (Rashid); Carol Grow (Amanda); David Horner (Roberts); Brittany Robertson (Young Sheena); Vicki Phillips (Sheena Stunt Double).

7. "The Lost Boy" Written by: Tony Blake and Paul Jackson. Directed by: Nelson McCormick. Airdate: November 18, 2000.

Cutter is nearly killed in an attack while accompanying investigative journalist Peter Reynold, spying on Phillip Coulter's Agmes Corporation doing survey work in the jungle. After Sheena saves the endangered duo from a jeep perched on the edge of a mountainside, she and Cutter attempt to determine why the peaceful Soman tribe has become violent and is waging war against the foreign corporation. When Peter is captured during a bombing on a Petroleum plant, Sheena and Cutter stage their own capture by purposefully blundering into a Soman booby trap. They promptly discover that the leader of the Soman is a young Western lad, a cadet from a Texas military academy. But will he lead them to victory or defeat at the hands of Agmes and President N'Gama? And what is the secret Peter Reynold is hiding?

GUEST CAST: Tom Savini (Peter Reynold/ Phillip Coulter); Yvonne Suhor; Jim Coleman; Steven West; Russ Bogart (David); Bill Cordell (Mamadou); Brian O. Ward (Getu); Vicki Phillips (Sheena Stunt Double).

8. "Wild Thing" Written by: Steven L. Sears. Directed by: Corey Eubanks. Airdate: November 25, 2000.

Sheena becomes trapped in animal form, and white hunters want to capture her as a trophy.

GUEST CAST: Veryl Jones (Rashid); Vickie Phillips (Wild Sheena); Hanke Stone; Andy Martin (Poacher); Thomas Stearns (Jimmy).

9. "Doing as the Romans" Written by: Craig Volk. Directed by: Jon Cassar. Airdate: January 13, 2001.

N'Gama abducts a would-be bride in Kali's village. Sheena must rescue the woman, but to do so means going undercover as a guest at the wedding. Cutter teaches Sheena the ways of civilization to complete her disguise, but Sheena finds the customs of his people most confusing.

GUEST CAST: Jim Coleman (President N'Gama); Erin LeShawn Wiley; Steven West; Jeffrey LaMar (Sekani); Maury Covington (Cardinal Rigetti); Jane Park (Sims); Vicki Phillips (Sheena Stunt Double).

10. "Children of the La Mistas" Written by: Tony Blake and Paul Jackson. Directed by: Scott Paulin. Airdate: January 20, 2001.

Sheena pursues the enemy that set her on the path of the warrior a decade ago, but, in an effort to act civilized, does not kill him. Consequently, she learns that he has been conducting DNA experiments on innocent local people, transforming them from human to animal.

GUEST CAST: Leland Crooke; Antoni Cornacchione; Neil Brown, Jr.; Timothy Washington; Cheryl Lewis; Vicki Phillips (Sheena Stunt Double).

11. "Prey" Written by: Jeffrey Vlaming. Directed by: Scott Paulin. Airdate: January 27, 2001.

The hunters become the hunted when Sheena and Cutter are pursued by big-game hunters they had been tracking.

GUEST CAST: Tom Nowicki; Emilio Plana; Darryl Van Lee; Marc Macaulay; Tim Goodwin (Mannix); Heather Avery Clyde (Tourist); Patrick Holland; Lawrence Benjamin; Vicki Phillips (Sheena Stunt Double).

12. "Divas of the Jungle" Written by: Jonathan Latt. Story by: Kevin Beggs and Jonathan Latt. Directed by: Scott Paulin. Airdate: February 3, 2001.

A photographer and his stable of gorgeous models hire Cutter to escort them to a wild African pasture for a bikini shoot, but the photography is to take place perilously close to a military prison. When a flat tire halts Cutter's truck near the jail, the supermodels wander off on their own, only to fall into quicksand and need rescuing, courtesy of Sheena. The photographer, Marcus, secures permission to shoot at the prison for an hour but he is actually planning a secret mission that only Sheena has detected: to free his uncle Umbutu, an honorable entrepreneur, from the prison of N'Gama. Sheena agrees to help Marcus in his quest and, with the aid of the seductive models, works to free the unjustly imprisoned hero.

GUEST CAST: Waren "Philadelphia" Plowden (Marcus); Amy Weber (Ruby); Dyan Handeland (Pearl); Tiffany Phillips (Jade); Anthony Hubert (Commandant); Lou Walker; Gary Alderman (Prisoner); Robert Carruth (Driver); Joe Reed (Umbutu); Kurt Smildson (Orvis McShain); Vicki Phillips (Sheena Stunt Double).

13. "Forbidden Fruit" Written by: Babs Greyhosky. Directed by: Gary Jones. Airdate: February 10, 2001.

Sheena and Cutter search by boat for two missing botanists. While navigating a treacherous patch of fog, they crash ashore on the inlet of Funga Bondee, the Bermuda Triangle of the La Mistas. Their boat is dissolved by acid, and Sheena and Cutter find the land inhospitable: trees with razor-sharp palms, and soil that burns when touched. After running through a malodorous forest, they come across the botanist's campsite and nearly make love when intoxicated by the scent of the unusual campfire. The next morning, Sheena and Cutter are inexplicably angry with one another and start to harbor homicidal urges — a result of the strange, dangerous berries they've been eating.

GUEST CAST: Veryl Jones; Vicki Phillips (Sheena Stunt Double).

14. "The Fool Monty" Written by: William Taub. Directed by: Gary Jones. Airdate: February 17, 2001.

The host of the cable TV series "Wylde's Animals," the obnoxious Monty Wylde, interrupts the peace between two tribes in the La Mistas, as brokered by Kali. Wylde's goal is to track down the legendary Darak'na, and, as Cutter finds out the hard way, there may be more than one. Secretly, Monty has hired a shady woman to play the Darak'na to boost his show's ratings, but his actions don't sit well with Sheena. When the imposter Darak'na attempts to kidnap Kali, it could be war in the La Mistas.

GUEST CAST: Nick Meaney (Monty Wylde); Joe Candelora (Mr. Dom Donald); Sophie Crawford (Camille); Rick Pearrow (Felix); Jimmy Rogers (Mitina); Vicki Phillips (Sheena Stunt Double).

15. "Sanctuary" Written by: Tony Blake, Paul Jackson. Directed by: Chuck Bowman. Airdate: February 24, 2001.

In search of refugees from a local civil war, Sheena and Cutter are attacked by armed guerillas in the service of the warlord Zenabu. They learn that a troop of U.N. soldiers and several refugees are trapped in a nearby animal sanctuary. Sheena and Cutter end up with the soldiers in an Alamo-like situation, surrounded by enemies on all sides.

GUEST CAST: John Beshara; Ralph Wilcox; James Bates (Meyer); Rick Kelly (Mishuma); Cynthia Calhoun (Fatouma); Karen Fraction (Miku); Jane Park (Sima); Vicki Phillips (Sheena Stunt Double).

16. "Jewel" Written by: Steven L. Sears. Story by: Steven L. Sears and Jon Valenti. Directed by: Chuck Bowman. Airdate: April 14, 2001.

The sacred Jewel of Kamata is supposed to be returned from America to its native owners in the La Mistas, but the precious stone is lost when tossed from a plane in flight. Sheena recruits a recalcitrant Cutter to chart the plane's flight path and track down the emerald-like jewel. They are followed through the jungle by high-paid mercenaries who have taken Mendelson hostage.

GUEST CAST: Paul Townsend; Tom Waite; Karen Fraction (Masuya); Jane Marilyn Taylor (Selma); Vicki Phillips (Sheena Stunt Double).

17. "Friendly Fire" Written by: Babs Greyhosky. Directed by: Terry Ingram. Airdate: April 21, 2001.

An old friend of Sheena's, now estranged after her departure years ago, returns to the La Mistas in search of a special plant with healing powers. Unfortunately, there are other, unscrupulous forces who also want to get their hands on the plant.

GUEST CAST: Veryl Jones (Rashid); Juliette Jeffers; Keith Hudson; Terry Allen Jones; Ashleey Pane; Vicki Phillips (Sheena Stunt Double).

18. "Between a Rock and a Hard Place" Written by: Babs Greyhosky. Directed by: Terry Ingram. Airdate: April 28, 2001.

The four tribes of the La Mistas (Aragai, Karugu, Kiptalami, and Manir) are at war over possession of a stone icon, a holy relic that has been seized by the power-hungry Kiptalami warlord Tuma. When Cutter and Sheena capture Tuma's son following a terrible massacre, they realize they've acquired a valuable bargaining chip in the explosive conflict. The power-mad Tuma kills his own son rather than negotiate for peace, and the treacherous N'Gama enters the fray by arming one tribe, the Manir, with powerful rifles. To save the people of the La Mistas from endless war, Sheena chooses to destroy the sacred stone that means so much to Kali.

Grand L. Bush (Tuma); James Coleman (N'Gama); Veryl Jones (Rashid); Steven West; Tony Major (Aragai Chief); Joe Reed (Karugu Chief); Dallas Davis (Kiptalami Warrior); Lamont Lofton (Manir Chief); Lawrence

Benjamin (Karugu Warrior); Martin Roberts (Manir Warrior); Denise Loden (Sheena Stunt Double).

19. "Tyler Returns" Written by: William Taub. Directed by: Carl Weathers. Airdate: May 5, 2001.

Cutter's rival, Tyler, returns to Africa on a mission to take out a terrorist bomber.

GUEST CAST: Peter Onarati (Tyler); Chet Anekwe; Cedric Pendleton; Jim Coleman (President N'Gama); Steven West; Brian Minyard (Jericho); Chi Von Peoples (Dalia); Brian Ward (General); Vicki Phillips (Sheena Stunt Double).

20. "Unsafe Passage" Written by: Steven L. Sears. Directed by: Carl Weathers. Airdate: May 12, 2001.

Kali and Sheena are captured by a slave ring operating out of Maltaka. Calling on his friends in the C.I.A., Cutter launches a rescue mission to save them. Once freed, Sheena and Kali attempt to save other locals destined for slavery.

GUEST CAST: L. Warren Young; Eric Hissom; Veryl Jones (Rashid); Neil Brown, Jr. (Taa); Andrew Clark (Harbormaster); Michael Hartson (Carl); Rahman Johnson (Gumada); Stacy Meadows (Man); Denise Loden (Sheena Stunt Double).

21. "Marabunta" Written by: Deborah Schwartz. Directed by: Christian I. Nyby, Jr. Airdate: May 19, 2001.

Near Thompson's Creek, two tourists are overcome by marabunta — man-eating ants! Investigating, Sheena and Cutter run afoul of the carnivorous ant army and hide in a shack as their opponent masses. Sheena develops an ant killer, using viper venom and sulfur; but Cutter has already been poisoned by ant bites, and has become dehydrated. With Cutter dying, Sheena orchestrates a dangerous escape plan to reach a nearby river, and safety.

GUEST CAST: Veryl Jones; Jeffrey William Evans (Sy); William Preston Ewen (The Pilot); Tom Hillman (Ben); Kent Lindsey (Mark);

Michael Macy (Fred); Vicki Phillips (Sheena Stunt Double).

22. "Cult of One" Written by: William Taub. Directed by: Nelson McCormick. Airdate: May 26, 2001.

Cutter attempts to rescue a missing American missionary. When Sheena becomes involved, the trail of misdeeds leads to the abducted girl and President N'Gama.

GUEST CAST: Jim Coleman (N'Gama); Veryl Jones (Rashid); James Black; Steven West; Joseph Bertot (Keeper of the Key); Jed Carpenter (Koro); Cindy Oliver (Elizabeth); Vicki Phillips (Sheena Stunt Double).

SEASON TWO (2001-2002)

23. "Rendezvous" Written by: Tony Blake and Paul Jackson. Directed by: Chuck Bowman. Airdate: October 6, 2001.

Sheena stands up Cutter for a dinner date when she runs into Cody, an undercover Interpol agent fleeing from a powerful international drug runner named Nicodemus. Sheena leads the injured Cody to his rendezvous point across the border even as the agent, a widower, finds himself growing increasingly attracted to her. Nicodemus hires a team of mercenaries, led by a villain named Steele, to kill Cody. Meanwhile, Cutter, with Mendohlson's help, searches for the missing duo. Over the course of their moonlit adventure, however, Sheena and Cody grow unexpectedly intimate.

GUEST CAST: Peter Reckell (Cody); Veryl Jones (Rashid); Quinn Duffy; Tom Schuster; Vicki Phillips (Sheena Stunt Double).

24. "The Feral King" Written by: Melissa Good. Story by: Christopher Mack. Directed by: Carl Weathers. Airdate: October 13, 2001.

Sheena and Cutter search for a jungle boy that may be the heir to a fortune in oil money. Jared, the "feral" boy, is rumored to have the powers of the Darak'na.

GUEST CAST: Ron Ely (Jonathan Bixby); Rick Perkins (Jared); Justine Eyre (Andrea); Peter Pendel; Robert Herrick; Edward Walker, Jr.; Denise Loden (Sheena Stunt Double).

25. "Mind Games" Written by: Tony Blake and Paul Jackson. Directed by: Walter Van Huene. Airdate: October 20, 2001.

A group of deranged natives attack a village, and Sheena suspects a villainous Shaman, the leader of another tribe, may be forcing locals to act strangely through the use of a powerful and forbidden "voodoo powder." Rashid suspects the Shaman is a man once banished by his father, still embittered; and Sheena and Cutter investigate, since Mendehlson is out in the bush with a tour group and therefore endangered.

GUEST CAST: Afemo Omilami; Veryl Jones (Rashid); Jermaine D'Aguiar (Michou); Peggy Sheffield (tourist); Todd Rogers; Denise Loden (Sheena Stunt Double).

26. "Collateral Damage" Written by: Rick Husky. Directed by: Chuck Bowman. Airdate: October 27, 2001.

A female assassin named Cassandra wounds Rashid in an intricately planned "hit." Sheena and Cutter immediately take different approaches to handling this assassin attempt, and Cutter calls his C.I.A. contacts to get the scoop on Cassandra. He learns that Rashid was not her target.

GUEST CAST: Veryl Jones (Rashid); Karen Kim; Christian Boeving; Andrew Stoddard; Vicki Phillips and Denise Loden (Sheena Stunt Doubles).

27. "Meltdown in Maltaka" Written by: Gene Miller and Karen Kavner. Directed by: Jon Cassar. Airdate: November 3, 2001.

A young female boxer would do anything to live up to the legacy of her successful father, also a world-renowned pugilist. Cutter and Mendelsohn help her become a contender, but there are others that want her to lose her big fight—and will do anything to see that happen.

GUEST CAST: Laila Ali, Jim Borda, Leesa Halstead, Johnny McClain, Tristen Spears.

28. "Treasure of Sienna Mende" Written by: Harry Dunn. Directed by: Goran Gajic. Airdate: November 10, 2001.

A hidden treasure may be the only thing to save a village suffering a terrible drought. Discovery of the treasure could mean money for supplies and more importantly, the development of an irrigation system that would benefit everybody. Unfortunately, a female thief wants the hidden treasure for herself.

GUEST CAST: Alexander Tydings, Mira Furlan, Thomas Merdis, Gregory Davis.

29. "The Darkness" Written by: Steven L. Sears. Directed by: Terry Ingram. Airdate: November 17, 2001.

A mythical monster called "the Darkness" is on the loose, committing crimes for the financial benefit of a hidden party. Meanwhile, Sheena and Cutter think about taking the next step in their romantic relationship.

GUEST CAST: Patricia Tallman; Veryl Jones (Rashid); John K. Brown, Dennis Neal, Simon Needham.

30. "Still Hostage After All These Years." Written by: Babs Greyhosky. Directed by: Walter Von Huene. Airdate: November 24, 2001.

In Kali's village, the people have contracted hepatitis from contaminated water, and the plane carrying the vaccine is hijacked by terrorists. As Rashid attempts to negotiate a peace settlement, Sheena works to steal the vaccine from the cargo hold, but fails as N'Gama's forces arrive and the incident turns volatile. With villagers dying, and the peace of Maltaka threatened, Cutter summons his ex-wife, an expert hostage negotiator, to intervene. Sheena grows jealous of Cutter's rapport with Amanda, but they are able to work together to defeat the terrorists.

GUEST CAST: Veryl Jones (Rashid); Yvette Nipar (Amanda Prentiss Cutter); Jim Coleman (President N'Gama); Steven West; Mel Johnson (Rabul); Ronald McCall (Qaba); LeRoy Mitchell (Bikolo).

31. "Return of the Native" Written by: Babs Greyhosky. Directed by: Goran Gajic. Airdate: January 26, 2002.

Cutter is jealous when he learns that Sheena had an intimate relationship with Mako, N'Gama's new education minister, now returned to Maltaka. Mako's mission to open a new education center, apparently with N'Gama's endorsement, is met with hostility by Mako's old tribal rival, Bantee. Sheena saves Mako from an assassin, but Bantee's next target is the education center's two new teachers. Sheena uses her skills of animal transformation to find the teachers and save the school.

GUEST CAST: Rick Worthy (Mako); Jim Coleman (N'Gama); Veryl Jones (Rashid); Chet Johnson (Bantee); Kelvin J. Payton (Aide); Mylo Thoroughgood (Rafika); Vicki Phillips (Sheena Stunt Double).

32. "The Maltaka Files" Written by: Tony Blake and Paul Jackson. Story by: Harold Apter. Directed by: Terry Ingram. Airdate: February 2, 2002.

Stories of alien abduction circulate around Maltaka, and Cutter believes he has found a tourist attraction to rival the Darak'na. While Sheena searches for answers to the riddle, Cutter seeks photos as evidence of the aliens' existence. The alien mystery involves a disappearing shepherd and cattle, and an eyewitness that claims he saw a light in the sky.

GUEST CAST: K. Danor Gerald; John Hostetter; Michelle Howard; Jim Helsinger; Margo Peace; Raleigh Stewart; Robert Carruth (Guard); Lucious Conway (Almos); James Zelly (Strohm); Denise Loden (Sheena Stunt Double).

33. "Stranded in the Jungle" Written by: Carla Wagner. Directed by: Carl Weathers. Airdate: February 9, 2002.

A group of tourists enter a survival contest in the jungle to win five million dollars, and one of the contestants is an author, Glen Pollett, who Sheena remembers from her childhood. Cutter is forced to parachute out of his plane with the vacationers when it strays into closed air space and is shot down. The tourists are hunted by armed soldiers involved in a regional civil war, and Sheena becomes desperate to rescue Pollett, who may be the key to understanding her past. Worse, there is a murderer among the game contestants.

GUEST CAST: Gary Graham (Glenn Pollett); Ryan Fafarnte; Brett Rice; Elena Wohl; Mark Daniel (Lieutenant); Mark Lainer (Kelstrom); Willie E. Teacher (Khumalo); Denise Loden (Sheena Stunt Double).

NOTE: This episode reveals Sheena's given name for the first time: Cheryl Hamilton.

34. "Coming to Africa" Written by: Robin Burger. Directed by: Terry Ingram. Airdate: February 16, 2002.

A local princess has been living in the United States and has become assimilated by the culture there, but now she is needed to wed a local villager if two tribes are to find peace. Could the wedding plans be sabotaged by the bride's embittered sister?

GUEST CAST: Magalyn Echukoniwoke; Martin Roberts; Lawrence Benjamin; Cynthia Calhoun; Vicki Phillips (Sheena Stunt Double).

35. "The World According to Mendehlson" Written by: Tom Blomquist. Directed by: Jon Cassar. Airdate; February 23, 2002.

Villagers who believe he is a legendary messianic figure kidnap Mendelsohn. Unfortunately, the mercenaries who murdered the village's previous king have similar plans for Mendelsohn, prompting involvement from Cutter and Sheena.

GUEST CAST: Stacy Meadows, Kevin O'Neil, Birdsong, Jennifer Bergeron, Harold Briscoe, Ray Fuller.

Silver Surfer

The Silver Surfer, the "Skyrider of the Spaceways," was a strange Marvel character created by Stan Lee, Jack Kirby and artist John Buscema that began his life as a guest star (and a villainous one) in *The Fantastic Four* comic of the mid–1950s. Originally, the Surfer was a servant of the popular Marvel villain called Galactus. An alien named Norrin Rad, the Surfer parted ways with the oversized bad guy and remained on Earth, where he developed into something of a philosopher.

The Silver Surfer was a humanoid being whose body had been encased (by his master, Galactus) in a white-silver suit of armor, and his mode of transport was basically a flying surfboard. A noble, introspective creature (and an extraterrestrial one to boot), the Silver Surfer was one of Marvel's most unusual and fascinating charac-ters, and one that finally received his own comic in the late 1960s (when aliens were all the rage, thanks to *Star Trek*'s Mr. Spock). In fact, the Silver Surfer was utilized in much the same way as Nimoy's Spock or Jonathan Frid's tortured vampire, Barnabas, on *Dark Shadows*. He was an outsider with a unique perspective of humanity, an important trait considering the tumult of the 1960s which included the Civil Rights Movement, the Vietnam War, the Hippie Movement and other cultural milestones. Lee and Kirby used the character as a mouthpiece to comment on this context specifically, and mankind in general.

In 1980, Lee Kramer, of L-K Productions, optioned the *Silver Surfer* property from Marvel, hoping to make a big movie that would star Olivia Newton John as the lead female character.[1] That version never happened, and it was not until 1998 that *The Silver Surfer* surfed onto the small screen for thirteen episodes of an animated series that aired on Fox Kids Network for three months (February to May of '98). The show was cancelled abruptly (on a cliffhanger, naturally) when differences reportedly arose between show creator Saban and character owner Marvel Studios.

Larry Brody, an experienced TV author who had worked on a variety of programs in his career, including HBO's *Spawn* (1997–99), *Star Trek: The Animated Series* (1973-74) and Glen Larson's *Automan* (1983-84), served as the head writer of the animated program. He reportedly prepped a full season of new stories for *The Silver Surfer*'s second year. Thus far, the second season has never materialized, but the first thirteen episodes have become a cult favorite among fans.

The Silver Surfer (1998)
ANIMATED SERIES

VOICE TALENTS: Paul Essiembre (The Silver Surfer); Camilla Scott (Shalla Bal); Colin Fox (The Watcher); James Blendick (Galactus); Gary Krawford (Thanos); David Hemblin (Supreme Intelligence); Norman Spencer (Drax).

CREW: *Based on Characters Created by:* Stan Lee for Marvel Comics. *Head Story Writer:* Larry Brody. *Producer/Animator:* Roy Allen Smith. *Executive Producer:* Sidney Iwanter. *Casting:* Karen Goora. *Art Director:* Dale Hendrickson. *Production Designer:* Geoff Kater and Shannon Denton. From Saban for Fox Kids Network.

The Six Million Dollar Man

In the mid–1970s, *The Six Million Dollar Man* was the favorite TV show of nearly every red-blooded six-year-old boy and girl living in the United States. And rightfully so, for the super-powered TV series turned out to be a great deal of fun, if not a terribly intellectual venture. Based on the novel *Cyborg* by Michael Caidin, the series was created by Kenneth Johnson (*The Bionic Woman* [1976–78], *The Incredible Hulk* [1978–82] and *Steel* [1997]). The producer was Harve Bennett, who later rose to even greater fame when he rescued the faltering *Star Trek* film franchise following the poorly received *Star Trek: The Motion Picture* (1979). Lee Majors, a stoic actor who had been seen on the western *The Big Valley* (1965–69), played the titular character.

The Six Million Dollar Man followed the adventures of a macho and athletic American astronaut, Colonel Steve Austin. Badly injured in a test flight for a new NASA craft, he underwent emergency surgery to save his life. He received fully functional "bionic" replacements (two legs and one arm) for his own crushed limbs. Also, he came equipped with a bionic eye that would allow him to see over vast distances.

Once he became a bionic man (at a price tag of six million dollars), Steve had some adjusting to do, but eventually joined Oscar Goldman (Richard Anderson) and the OSI (Office of Scientific Investigation) as a highly skilled secret agent. Dr. Rudy Wells (played by Alan Oppenheimer, then later by Martin Brooks), the inventor of bionics, tended to Steve's equipment, always making sure it wasn't over-taxed (which would result in rejection by Austin's biological systems).

Since special effects were still rudimentary at the time of the series (the pre–*Star Wars* era), slow-motion photography was utilized extensively during the action

Colonel Steve Austin (Lee Majors) takes his new bionic body out for a slow-motion spin. From *The Six Million Dollar Man.*

sequences on *The Six Million Dollar Man.* So when Steve was supposed to run at incredible speeds, he would actually be seen running very, very slowly, accompanied by the distinctive "*ch-ch-ch-ch-ch-ch*" sound effects that became a trademark of the bionic shows. This unique solution to visually dramatizing super speed resulted in a generation of children running in slow motion on playgrounds to emulate their hero.

At first, during a series of TV movies and in the early episodes, *The Six Million*

Dollar Man seemed rather dull. There was very little character building, and the audience rarely received insight into Steve's feelings — particularly about being part man, part machine. The villains he faced were initially pretty pedestrian too. They were the usual suspects, including assassins ("Survival of the Fittest"), snipers (Gary Lockwood in "Eyewitness to Murder" and "Steve Austin, Fugitive"), terrorists and mad scientists.

But then, perhaps a year into *The Six Million Dollar Man*'s run on ABC primetime, there was a shift in format to the more overtly fantastic (and romantic). The ratings soared.

Suddenly, Austin was meeting new and ultra-dangerous challenges that called on him to use his wits and smarts, as well as his facility with heavy lifting. William Shatner played a menacing fellow astronaut with strange powers in "Burning Bright," and Monte Markham appeared twice ("The Seven Million Dollar Man," "The Bionic Criminal") as the world's second bionic man, a dangerous psychotic. Unlike responsible Steve Austin, this bionic man became drunk with the power of bionic strength, and turned rogue in very destructive fashion.

Perhaps more famously, Steve Austin squared off against a brilliant new nemesis, the Sasquatch, in several episodes beginning in 1976. These episodes ("The Secret of Big Foot," "The Return of Big Foot," "Bigfoot V," et al.) revealed that the mythical beast once believed to roam the Pacific Northwest was actually the bionic, superstrong cyborg servant of a race of highly advanced, visiting aliens. Sometimes Big Foot (Ted Cassidy) was Steve's friend, sometimes an intractable foe. But whenever this beast fought Steve Austin in bionic-hand-to-bionic-hand combat, their slugfest drew the attention of America's six-year-old population.

Other popular episodes involved

Steve's encounter with android "Fembots" ("Kill Oscar") and a dangerous Russian space probe that returned to Earth and caused massive destruction in the American heartland ("Death Probe" and "Return of the Death Probe"). These plots may sound cheesy, but *The Six Million-Dollar Man* truly found its identity when Austin faced off against super-powered fantasy figures. As a spy, Steve was just so-so, but as a superhero he kicked ass.

Over the course of the series' five-season run, the bionic family swelled. In 1975 *The Six Million Dollar Man* introduced a character named Jaime Sommers (Lindsay Wagner), a beautiful former love interest of Steve's. Injured in a skydiving accident, Jaime was equipped with bionics, becoming the Bionic Woman. Unfortunately, at the end of the initial two-part special, "The Bionic Woman," her body rejected the bionic implants and the lovely woman died. Though devastated, Steve went on bravely, having lost the love of his life.

Stellar ratings, however, dictated that Jaime Sommers be resurrected. Star Richard Anderson (Oscar Goldman) explained the situation to *Filmfax* magazine:

> The first year, they decided they needed a lady — some romance; they brought in Lindsay ... to read and play that part. At the end of the two hours she died. The place went *crazy*! The world just loved her. So now, we gotta figure out a way to bring her back. So, they used cryogenics to bring her back. We froze her, defrosted her.[1]

Not only did Jaime Sommers (and Lindsay Wagner) return to *The Six Million Dollar Man*) in "Return of the Bionic Woman" and "Welcome Home, Jaime," she went off and starred in her own hit series, *The Bionic Woman*! Steve and Jaime often made crossover appearances, even when, after scheduling changes, their programs aired on opposing networks.

The same gambit was tried again later,

with less success. Vincent Van Patten played a bionic teenager in "The Bionic Boy," but never won his own series. On *The Bionic Woman*, Jaime took care of Max, a bionic dog, for a time; but the canine was, like Van Patten, denied a slot in primetime.

But if Steve loved Jaime, series star Lee Majors boasted his own romantic squeeze: wife Farrah Fawcett Majors. The *Charlie's Angels* (1976–81) star and sexy pin-up appeared several times on *The Six Million Dollar Man* (in three different roles), in "Rescue of Athena One" (written by genre veteran Dorothy Fontana), "The Peeping Blonde," "The Golden Pharaoh" and "Nightmare in the Sky." The Majors' marriage, however, quickly became a source of public scrutiny and controversy. *Cyborg* author Martin Caidin remembers that the specifics of that marriage may have resulted in the series' cancellation in 1978:

> Two things killed that show. One, I couldn't convince the producers to update the technology.... The other thing that killed it was the star ... Lee Majors' personal life was getting so public, it had a deleterious effect on the audience. I told the producers to kill him off and bring in Monte Markham, who had been our first choice for the part.[2]

The Six Million Dollar Man aired Friday nights on ABC from 1974 to 1975, but from1975 to 1978 it played Sunday nights at 8:00 P.M. When the ratings dipped, the show moved briefly (in the winter of '78) to Mondays at 8:00. However, by that time the bionic cycle was waning. *The Bionic Woman* was cancelled the same year.

As with *The Bionic Woman*, toys from *The Six Million Dollar Man* were mass-produced in the 1970s and are hot collector's items on eBay today. For a time, Charlton published the comic book adventures of both bionic heroes, resulting in a reversal of the usual superhero fortune. Instead of starting in comics and moving to TV, the bionic agents went the opposite route.

A series of reunion TV movies followed the cancelled series in the late-eighties and early 1990s, the final tele-film culminating with the marriage of Steve Austin and Jaime Sommers.

Watching the series today remains a pleasant nostalgia trip, and there has been persistent talk in Hollywood of a new *Six Million Dollar Man* feature film. Reportedly, because of inflation, it will be called *The Six Billion Dollar Man*. In the late 1990s, Kevin Smith wrote a treatment for a new movie, but just recently star and comedian Jim Carrey signed up for the remake, a virtual assurance the project would be little more than a joke.

The Six Million Dollar Man (1973–78)
LIVE-ACTION SERIES

"Basically an update of Superman, it is very much on a comic book level."
— John Brosnan, *Future Tense: The Cinema of Science Fiction*, 1978, page 301.

"When I was a child, I used to love *The Six Million Dollar Man*. As an adult, I found I had little interest in it because it was always the same thing. This week, Steve protects the Princess of Arabia. Next week, Steve must test pilot a new jet. There was very little concentration on the human aspect of the stories and as an adult I want to see characters more than I do plot."

— Howard Margolin, host of *Destinies: The Voice of Science Fiction*.

"Steve Austin is probably the best-loved hero from the small screen in the 1970s. We all dreamed of getting bionic everything at some point. We imagined we were running in slow motion, imagined that eerie sound as our bionic eyes focused on some impossibly distant object. When Jaime Summers died, part of us died with her. When she came back, we were glad, and then we were sad that she wasn't going to be hanging out more with Steve. When Ted Cassidy played Bigfoot, what kid of the age wasn't thinking this was the greatest thing ever? The secret strength of these shows was Oscar Goldman. The government guy you could trust. With everything happening in Watergate, it was nice to have someone on the government payroll that seemed interested in doing the right thing. What made Steve Austin special? Regular guy, just like us. Some special equipment made him a superman. In the 1970s, when consumerism was running rampant and the idea that you could buy happiness was actually believed, Steve Austin was practically built for the era — you can buy yourself into being a hero. The cost? Six million dollars."

— William Latham, author of *Mary's Monster* and *Space: 1999 Resurrection.*

CAST: Lee Majors (Colonel Steve Austin); Richard Anderson (Oscar Goldman); FIRST SEASON ONLY: Alan Oppenheimer (Dr. Rudy Wells); SECOND SEASON ONLY: Martin E. Brooks (Dr. Rudy Wells).

CREW: *Based on the Novel* Cyborg *by:* Martin Caidin. *Created by:* Kenneth Johnson. *Executive Producer:* Harve Bennett. *Producer:* Lionel E. Siegel. *Theme Music:* Oliver Nelson.

1. "The Six Million Dollar Man" (aired as TV movie, 90 min.) Story by: Martin Caidin. Written by: Henri Simoun. Directed by: Richard Irving. Airdate: March 7, 1973.

Astronaut Steve Austin is injured and near death after an experimental space flight goes terribly wrong. With his life hanging in the balance, Steve is revived using a technology called "bionics." His damaged arm and legs (and eye) are replaced with mechanical enhancements, making him the first successful human cyborg. OSI Chief Oscar Goldman recruits the super-strong, super-agile Colonel Austin as a secret agent to defend America from espionage.

GUEST CAST: Darren McGavin (Spencer); Barbara Anderson (Jean); Martin Balsam (Rudy Welles); Olan Soule, Robert Cornthwaite, George Wallace, Norma Storch.

2. "Wine, Women and War" (aired as TV movie, 90 min.) Written by: Glen A. Larson. Directed by: Rus Mayberry. Airdate: October 20, 1973.

Colonel Austin becomes entangled in a web of intrigue and deception as he deals with a plot to sell nuclear missiles on the black market. With foreign agents on his trail, beautiful damsels in distress all around him, and snipers trying to pick him off, Steve must decide who to trust.

GUEST CAST: Britt Ekland (Katrina); Eric Braeden, Earl Holliman, David McCallum, Lee Bergere, Dennis Rucker.

3. "Solid Gold Kidnapping" (aired as TV movie, 90 min.) Written by: Larry Alexander and Michael Gleason. Directed by: Russ Mayberry. Airdate: November 17, 1973.

An international kidnapping ring strikes, abducting an ambassador and then a high-ranking government official. The ransom — a billion dollars in gold — is stolen en route, and soon Steve Austin, the world's first bionic man, is on the case.

GUEST CAST: Leif Erickson (Cameron); Elizabeth Ashley, John Vernon, Lucianna Paluzzi, Maurice Evans, Terry Carter, David White, Polly Middleton.

SEASON ONE (1974)

4. "Population: Zero" Written by: Elroy Schwartz, Lionel E. Siegel and Harve Bennett. Directed by: Jeannot Szwarc. Airdate: January 18, 1974.

An entire town has been destroyed, its population decimated. Now a power-mad scientist threatens to bring the same terror to another populated hamlet — unless Steve Austin can stop him.

GUEST CAST: Don Porter, Penny Fuller, Paul Fix, Walter Brooks, Paul Carr, David Valentine.

5. "Survival of the Fittest" Written by: Mann Rubin, Lionel E. Siegel and Harve Bennett. Directed by: Leslie H. Martinson. Airdate: January 25, 1974.

On the eve of a conference to further cement peace between the U.S. and the U.S.S.R., Oscar's plane goes down and crashes on a remote island. Steve Austin is protecting him there, but one of the survivors of the plane crash is an assassin who will stop at nothing to prevent peace.

GUEST CAST: James McEachin, William Smith, Christine Belford, Randy Carver, Laurette Spang, JoAnne Worley, Reed Smith, Dale Johnsons.

6. "Operation Firefly" Written by: Ric Hardman, Sy Salkowitz and Lionel E. Siegel. Directed by: Reza Badiyi. Airdate: February 1, 1974.

A scientist who has developed a powerful new laser weapon is kidnapped by criminals. With the scientist's daughter, a psychic, helping, Steve scours the world for the missing professor and finds him in the Florida Everglades.

GUEST CAST: Pamela Franklin (Susan); Simon Scott, Jack Hogan, Joseph Ruskin, Erick Holland, Bill Conklin.

7. "Day of the Robot" Written by: Harold Livingston, Del Reisman and Lionel E. Siegel. Directed by: Leslie H. Martinson. Airdate: February 8, 1974.

An important U.S. military officer has been replaced by an identical robot and assigned to steal a top-secret anti-missile device. Steve Austin must fight the robot and keep the device from falling into enemy hands.

GUEST CAST: John Saxon (Sloan); Henry Jones, Lloyd Bochner, Charles Bateman, Noah Keen, Robert Rothwell, Michael Alaimo.

8. "Little Orphan Airplane" Written by: Elroy Schwartz. Directed by: Reza Badiyi. Airdate: February 22, 1974.

Steve races to rescue a downed pilot whose airplane equipment may have photographed evidence of international treaty violations. Unfortunately, those behind an illegal gun-running deal are aware of the pilot's proof and go after the pilot too, making a last minute repair job of the plane — downed in Africa — an absolute necessity.

GUEST CAST: Greg Morris (Perkins); Marge Redmond, Susan Powell, Arnold Turner, Dave Turner, Paul Bryar, Ji-Tu Cumbuka.

9. "Doomsday and Counting" Written by: Larry Brody and Jimmy Sangster. Directed by: Jerry Jameson. Airdate: March 1, 1974.

A Russian general wants detente with the United States, at least concerning a joint space program mission. Unfortunately, a disaster in the Arctic nearly destroys a Russian nuclear installation and traps the general's beloved under tons of rubble. Now only Steve Austin can rescue her and prevent a nuclear explosion.

GUEST CAST: Gary Collins (Zukov); William Smithers (Kosenko); Jane Merrow, Bruce Glover, Walker Edmiston, William Boyette, James Gavin.

10. "Eyewitness to Murder" Written by: William Driskill. Directed by: Alf Kjellin. Airdate: March 8, 1974.

A critical witness in a Federal mob trial is nearly assassinated by a well-known, highly successful sniper. Unfortunately, the shooter has an ironclad alibi, at least until Steve takes on the case and is able to more closely examine him.

GUEST CAST: Gary Lockwood (Hopper); William Schallert, Ivor Barry, Leonard Ston, Al Dunlap, Allen Joseph, Richard Webb.

11. "Rescue of Athena One" Written by: D.C. Fontana. Directed by: Lawrence Doheny. Airdate: March 15, 1974.

America's first female astronaut, beautiful Kelly Wood, is endangered in space aboard a U.S. capsule. This necessitates a fast rescue and a return to space for former astronaut Steve Austin.

GUEST CAST: Farrah Fawcett (Kelly Wood); Paul Kent, Dean Smith, Jules Bergman.

12. "Dr. Wells Is Missing" Written by: Bill Keenan, Krishna Shah, Elroy Schwartz and Lionel E. Siegel. Directed by: Virgil W. Vogel. Airdate: March 29, 1974.

The brilliant Dr. Wells, the man who invented bionics, is kidnapped while abroad at a conference and held captive by a criminal syndicate that wants the doctor to build them their own bionic man. Steve heads overseas to Austria to pick up the missing professor's trail, but will he be too late to save his friend?

GUEST CAST: Jim Shane, Michael Dante, Curt Lowens, Cynthia Lynn.

13. "The Last of the Fourth of Julys" Written by: Richard Landau. Directed by: Reza Badiyi. Airdate: April 5, 1974.

A powerful criminal mastermind has been retained by war-hungry power brokers to use a special space laser to destroy an international conference. When the OSI becomes aware of the plot, Steve is sent to the criminal's island fortress, but must evade a nest of high-tech defensive weaponry and other security measures to prevent the laser from being fired.

GUEST CAST: Steve Forrest, Arlene Martell, Tom Reese, Tom Hayden, Kevin Tighe, Ben Wright.

14. "Burning Bright" Written by: Del Reisman. Directed by: Jerry London. Airdate: April 12, 1974.

A fellow astronaut and friend of Steve's, Josh Lang, returns from a space mission strangely affected by an unknown electrical phenomenon in orbit. Emboldened by advanced mental powers and other strange telepathic abilities (including inter-species communication), Josh begins to break down, obsessed by an event in his own personal history. Hoping to help his friend before it is too late, Steve must confront the powerful fellow astronaut.

GUEST CAST: William Shatner (Lang); Warren Kemmerling (Dr. Haldane); Ann Schedeen (Tina).

15. "The Coward" Written by: Elroy Schwartz. Directed by: Reza Badiyi. Airdate: April 19, 1974.

A mystery from the past involving World War II and the loyalty of Steve Austin's father takes center stage as Steve investigates the reappearance of an old U.S. warplane that disappeared in the Himalayas decades earlier while carrying critical battle plans. But, as Steve soon discovers, there is more at stake than his father's legacy.

GUEST CAST: George Montgomery, Ron Soble, France Nuyen, George Takei, Martha Scott.

16. "Run, Steve, Run" Written by: Lionel E. Siegel. Directed by: Jerry Jameson. Airdate: April 26, 1974.

The robot-maker Steve confronted once before, Dr. Dolenz, plans to steal all the gold from Fort Knox with a criminal associate, but realizes that his nemesis, the six million dollar man, would stop the crime. He sets out to capture Steve, and if necessary dissect the bionic man, to find out just what makes his bionics tick.

GUEST CAST: Noah Berry, George Murdock, Henry Jones, Melissa Greene, Bill Conklin.

SEASON TWO (1974-1975)

17. "Nuclear Alert" Written by: William Driskill. Directed by: Jerry London. Airdate: September 13, 1974.

A homemade atom bomb comes up for sale on the black market, and a foreign power harboring hatred for the United States is interested in purchasing it. Steve and a lovely scientist attempt to infiltrate the gang that made the bomb, but the U.S. military has orders to shoot down the aircraft carrying all of them to the rendezvous point.

GUEST CAST: Carol Lawrence, Fred Beir, George Gaynes, Thomas Bellin, Stewart Moss, Irene Tedrow, Stuart Nisbet, Sid Haig.

18. "The Pioneers" Story by: Katey Barrett. Written by: Bill Svanoe. Directed by: Christian I. Nyby II. Airdate: September 20, 1974.

Steve must hunt down a renegade scientist who has developed abnormally strong mental powers after surviving an experiment in suspended animation

GUEST CAST: Mike Farrell (Tate); Joan Darling, Milt Kogan, Bill Sorrells, Robert Simon, Vince Howard.

19. "Pilot Error" Written by: Edward J. Lasko. Directed by: Jerry Jameson. Airdate: September 27, 1974.

A U.S. senator facing charges of corruption is involved in a plane crash that could prove damaging not only to himself, but to his passengers as well, including Steve Austin. Temporarily blinded, Steve must utilize his bionics to fix the damaged aircraft, but depend on the "eyes" of the other trapped people.

GUEST CAST: Pat Hingle (Senator Hill); Alfred Ryder, Stephen Nathan, Jill Denby, Hank Brandt, Dennis McCarthy.

20. "The Pal Mir Escort" Written by: Margaret Schneider and Paul Schneider. Directed by: Larry Dobkin. Airdate: October 4, 1974.

Peace talks stall when the leader of one foreign country suffers a devastating heart attack. Steve races to transport the prime minister to an operation to receive a bionic heart transplant, but there are those on both sides who would like to see the peace process die on the operating table with the patient.

GUEST CAST: Anne Revere, Leo Fuchs, Denny Miller, John Landis, Virginia Gregg, Robert Rothwell.

21. "The Seven Million Dollar Man" Written by: Peter Allan Fields. Directed by: Richard Moder. Airdate: November 1, 1974.

Again Steve is forced to do battle with a super-powered rogue created by his own government. This time, his opponent is Barney Miller, an unstable man who has become the world's second recipient of bionic implants and abilities.

GUEST CAST: Monte Markham (Barney Miller); Maggie Sullivan, Fred Lerner, Joan Van Ark.

22. "Straight on Till Morning" Written by: D.C. Fontana. Directed by: Lawrence Doheny. Airdate: November 8, 1974.

A family of peaceful alien explorers arrive on Earth, unaware that radioactive properties of their physiology are damaging to human tissue. Local police set out to kill the family, but Steve Austin intervenes to be certain that a just accommodation is reached and that the surviving alien can be returned to her spaceship in orbit.

GUEST CAST: Meg Foster, Cliff Osmond, Donald Billett, Robert Bruce Lang, Al Dunlap.

23. "The Midas Touch" Written by: Peter Allan Fields, Donald Gould, Lester Berke. Directed by: Bruce Bilson. Airdate: November 15, 1974.

Has Oscar been involved in a corrupt scheme to profit from his knowledge of a government gold mine? When Goldman disappears in Las Vegas, Steve must investigate his boss and the possibility that he has been making an ill-gotten fortune from his inside knowledge of certain government operations.

GUEST CAST: Farley Granger, Noam Pitlik, Dave Morick, Richard Hurst, Louise Elias, Marcus Smith.

24. "The Deadly Replay" Written by: Wilton Denmark. Directed by: Christian Nyby. Airdate: November 22, 1974.

The space vessel destroyed when Steve Austin crashed months earlier has been rebuilt and is due to be flight tested again, once more with Colonel Austin at the helm. Before long, Steve learns that the accident that nearly took his life (and resulted in his bionic implants) was no accident, but sabotage.

GUEST CAST: Clifton James, Robert Symonds, Jack Ging, Lara Parker, Andrea Collins, Jack Manning.

25. "Act of Piracy" Written by: Peter Allan Fields. Story by: Dave Ketchum. Directed by: Christian Nyby. Airdate: November 29, 1974.

Steve, out of the country on a mission, becomes embroiled in a political firestorm when a nearby nation severs relations with the United States. Working in the ocean on seismic scanners, Steve and his team of scientists are captured by the enemy.

GUEST CAST: Stephen McNally, Lenore Kasdorf, Frank Ramirez, Hagan Beggs.

26. "Stranger in Broken Fork" Written by: Bill Svanoe and Wilton Denmark. Story by: Bill Svanoe. Directed by: Christian Nyby. Airdate: December 13, 1974.

Steve is involved in a plane crash, and this time the injury is a mental one: he develops amnesia. Uncertain of who or where he is, Steve befriends a crusading woman, a scientist who becomes increasingly imperiled by residents of the nearby town.

GUEST CAST: Sharon Farrell (Angie); Arthur Franz (Carlton); Bill Henry, Eric Mason, Sally Yarnell.

27. "The Peeping Blonde" Written by: William T. Zacha and Wilton Denmark. Story by: William T. Zacha. Directed by: Herschel Daugherty. Airdate: December 20, 1974.

A beautiful blond reporter accidentally obtains footage of Steve Austin using his incredible bionic powers, constituting a serious breach of security. Certain she has uncovered the scoop of her career, the nosy journalist plots to learn more about Colonel Austin, unaware that her superior is just

as interested in the bionic man, but for reasons that have nothing to do with the news.

GUEST CAST: Farrah Fawcett (Vickie); Roger Perry (Colby); Hari Rhodes (Carl); Chris Nelson, Martin Speer.

28. "Cross Country Kidnap" Written by: Ray Brenner and Stephen Kandel. Directed by: Christian Nyby. Airdate: January 10, 1975.

Steve is assigned to protect a government worker, an expert in computer code. Unfortunately, she is also an accomplished equestrian, which means that Steve has a tough time keeping up with her, even with foreign saboteurs on the scene.

GUEST CAST: Donna Mills (Lisa); Tab Hunter (Blake); Frank Aletter, John Gabriel, Ben Wright.

29. "Lost Love" Written by: Richard Carr. Story by: Mel and Tom Levy. Directed by: Arnold Laven. Airdate: January 17, 1975.

Steve learns that a romantic interest from his past has recently become a widow and sets out to rekindle the old love. This happens at an opportune time, for Linda Marsh is nearly kidnapped, and Steve thwarts the effort. But then questions arise when he receives a phone call from her dead husband! Is it a trap, or has Mr. Marsh returned from the dead?

GUEST CAST: Jeff Corey, Joseph Ruskin.

30. "The Last Kamikaze" Written by: Judy Burns. Directed by: Richard Moder. Airdate: January 19, 1975.

An atomic bomb has gone down in the Pacific, on a nearly deserted island. Unfortunately, it has fallen into the hands of a paranoid Japanese soldier who is not aware that World War II ended many decades earlier. Now Steve must face off against a cunning foe who knows the territory and hope to convince him that they are no longer mortal enemies.

GUEST CAST: John Fujioka, Robert Ito, Jimmy Joyce, Edmund Gilbert, Paul Vaughn.

31. "Return of the Robot Maker" Written by: Mark Frost. Directed by: Phil Bondelli. Airdate: January 26, 1975.

Dr. Dolenz builds a robot duplicate of Oscar Goldman to fool Steve Austin and send him on a false mission.

GUEST CAST: Henry Jones, Ben Hammer, Troy Melton, Sarah Simmons, Jean Lee Brooks.

32. "Taneha" Written by: Margaret Armen and Lionel Segal. Directed by: Earl Bellamy. Airdate: February 2, 1975.

A beautiful cougar will soon be the last of its near-extinct species unless Steve can protect it from poachers and ranchers, many of whom bear a grudge against the animal they believe is a murderer of men.

GUEST CAST: James Griffith, Jess Walton, Bill Fletcher, Jim B. Smith, Trent Dolan.

33. "Look Alike" Written by: Richard Carr. Story by: Gustave Field. Directed by: Jerry London. Airdate: February 23, 1975.

Via plastic surgery, a saboteur is made to resemble Steve Austin, and he steals top-secret files from the OSI offices. Steve retaliates quickly, unaware that Oscar already has a man on the inside of the theft ring.

GUEST CAST: George Foreman, Robert Do Qui, Eddie Fontaine, Robert Salvio, Mary Rings, Jack Colvin, Arthur Space.

34. "The ESP Spy" Written by Lionel Siegel. Directed by: Jerry London. Airdate: March 2, 1975.

Are telepathic agents stealing OSI secrets concerning a new and top-secret laser weapon? The only way for Steve to find out is to team up with a man who possesses unusual powers of ESP.

GUEST CAST: Philip Bruns; Dick Van Patten (Harry); Alan Bergman, Robbie Lee, Bert Kramer.

35. "The Bionic Woman" (Parts I and II) Written by: Kenneth Johnson. Directed by: Richard Moder. Airdates: March 16 and 23, 1975.

Steve Austin returns to his hometown to find the love of his life, the beautiful Jaime Sommers. The two old friends hit it off and plan marriage, but tragedy intervenes. Jaime is nearly killed during a skydiving accident, and the only way to save her life is with bionics (legs, arm and an ear). Once Jaime recovers, Oscar wants to use her as an agent for OSI, but Steve has already risked losing Sommers once and is reluctant to see her endangered. Then Jaime's body begins to reject the bionics ... a process that will lead to her death.

GUEST CAST: Lindsay Wagner (Jaime Sommers); Malachi Throne, Martha Scott, Ford Rainey, Harry Hickox, Sidney Clute, Paul Carr.

36. "Outrage in Balinderry" Written by: Paul Schneider. Story by: Paul and Margaret Schneider. Directed by: Earl Bellamy. Airdate: April 20, 1975.

A U.S. ambassador's wife is captured and held hostage in the land of Balinderry, and Steve is assigned to rescue her. He must act fast, or the delicate peace process overseen by the ambassador will crumble.

GUEST CAST: Martine Beswick, Richard Erdman, Alan Caillou, Morgan Fairchild, William Sylvester, Richard O'Brien, Gavan O'Herlihy.

37. "Steve Austin, Fugitive" Written by: Mark Frost and Richard Carr. Directed by: Russ Mayberry. Airdate: April 27, 1975.

An old foe, a deadly sniper, plans to take revenge on Steve Austin, framing him for a murder he did not commit. Before long, Steve is on the run, trying to prove his innocence, but the authorities are already in close pursuit.

GUEST CAST: Gary Lockwood (Hopper); Andy Romano, Jennifer Darling Bernie Hamilton, Reb Brown, Marco Lopez.

Season Three (1975-1976)

38. "Return of the Bionic Woman" (Parts I and II) Written by: Kenneth Johnson. Directed by: Richard Moder. Airdate: September 14 and 21, 1975.

To his total surprise, Steve learns that the love of his life, Jaime Sommers, did not die. Instead, he was led to believe she had died, when in fact she was put into suspended animation. Now she is awake and the problems with her bionics have been resolved, but she is suffering from headaches and having trouble remembering the details of her life. Steve tries to nurse Jaime back to health, but they soon run afoul of a terrorist plot and their combined bionic skills are required.

Guest Cast: Lindsay Wagner (Jaime Sommers); Richard Lentz, Tony Giorgio, Al Ruscio, Ford Rainey, Virginia Gregg.

39. "Price of Liberty" Written by: Kenneth Johnson. Directed by: Richard Moder. Airdate: September 28, 1975.

A laid-off scientist is disgruntled with the government and plants a bomb on the Liberty Bell at a bicentennial celebration. Steve and Oscar recruit a convicted felon — a bomb expert — to help defuse the situation.

Guest Cast: Chuck Connors, Sandy Ward, Henry Beckman, Bill Quinn, Joe Brooks.

40. "The Song and Dance Spy" Written by: Jerry Divine. Directed by: Richard Moder. Airdate: October 5, 1975.

Is a famous entertainer really a spy for a foreign power? Oscar Goldman fears it is true, and assigns Steve, the entertainer's friend, to find out.

Guest Cast: Sonny Bono (John); Bruce Glover, Robin Clarke, Fred Holliday.

41. "The Wolf Boy" Written by: Judy Burns. Directed by: Jerry London. Airdate: October 12, 1975.

Steve teams up with the Japanese soldier he once fought on a Pacific island to help a boy raised by wolves adjust to life in the 1970s. Steve is sure the boy has a distinguished family legacy and wants to integrate him back into society.

Guest Cast: John Fujioka, Buddy Foster, Quinn Redeker, Bill Saito.

42. "The Deadly Test" Written by: James D. Parriott. Directed by: Christian Nyby. Airdate: October 19, 1975.

Steve is working at a flight training school for the U.S. Air Force and learns that some of his wards may be pawns in an effort by two nations to foment a bloody war.

Guest Cast: Tim O'Connor, Frank Marth, Martin Speer, Erik Estrada, Leigh Christian, Harry Pugh, Bill Scherer.

43. "Target in the Sky" Written by: Larry Alexander and Kenneth Johnson. Directed by: Jerry London. Airdate: October 26, 1975.

A serious threat to the President's cabinet causes Steve to search for a missing missile by going undercover as a lumberjack. If Steve doesn't find it fast, important officials could be shot down during a flyby over the forest.

Guest Cast: Rafer Johnson, Denny Miller, Ivor Francis, Hank Stohl.

44. "One of Our Running Backs Is Missing" Written by: Kenneth Johnson and Elroy Schwartz. Directed by: Lee Majors. Airdate: November 2, 1975.

A desperate athlete forced into retirement has bet his future on the next big game. To be certain he doesn't come up short, the athlete kidnaps an up and coming player, and Steve must rescue him.

Guest Cast: Larry Csonka, Pamela Csonka, Lee Josephson, Dick Butkus, Mike Henry, Eral Faison, Carl Weathers, Tom Mack.

45. "The Bionic Criminal" Written by: Richard Carr. Story by: Peter Allan Fields. Directed by: Leslie H. Martinson. Airdate: November 9, 1975.

The world's second bionic man, the unstable Barney Miller, returns to aggravate Steve Austin and the OSI, this time when activated for an important mission. Barney's powers run amok again as he is beset with guilt and goes crazy, resulting in another bionic confrontation.

GUEST CAST: Monte Markham (Barney); Maggie Sullivan, John Milford, Donald Moffatt.

46. "The Blue Flash" Written by: Sheridan Gibney and Sidney Field. Directed by: Cliff Bole. Airdate: November 16, 1975.

Steve poses as a longshoreman to expose a group of smugglers.

GUEST CAST: Rodney Allen Rippy, Janet MacLachlan, Michael Conrad, Jason Wingreen.

47. "The White Lightning War" Written by: Wilton Denmark. Directed by: Phil Bondelli. Airdate: November 23, 1975.

Steve ends up in a small southern town awash in corrupt politics; politics so corrupt, in fact, that they stretch all the way back to Washington, D.C. Steve befriends the wife of a dead friend, hoping to shatter the conspiracy and learn the reasons behind the murder.

GUEST CAST: Austin Stoker (Quinten); Benn Hammer, Robert Donner, Red West, Randy Kirby, Katherine Helmond.

48. "Divided Loyalty" Written by: Jim Carlson and Terrence McDonnell. Directed by: Alan Crosland. Airdate: November 30, 1975.

Steve goes behind the Iron Curtain to rescue a defector, but getting the defector's son to return to the West is no easy task. Worse, enemy agents are zeroing in and planning to cut off the only escape route.

GUEST CAST: Radames Pera, Michauel McGuire, Curt Lowens, Larry Levine, Rod Haase, Ralph Traeger, Ned Romero.

49. "Clark Templeton O'Flaherty" Written by: Frank Dandridge. Directed by: Ernest Pintoff. Airdate: December 14, 1975.

The unlikeliest of people, a janitor at OSI, is actually a spy. But—and this is the rub—he is working to expose the enemy, not hurt the United States. Now Steve must ally himself with the janitor to prove his innocence.

GUEST CAST: Lou Gossett (Clark); Ryan MacDonald, H.M. Wynant, Louise Latham, Lillian Randolph.

50. "The Winning Smile" Written by: Gustave Field and Richard Carr. Directed by: Arnold Laven. Airdate: December 21, 1975.

Oscar's secretary is accused of being a spy, and Steve must clear her name. He starts to suspect that her boyfriend, a dentist, may be the real culprit.

GUEST CAST: Jennifer Darling, Stewart Moss, Milton Selzer, Harry Lewis, Ben Andrews, James Ingersoll.

51. "Welcome Home, Jaime" Written by: Kenneth Johnson. Directed by: Alan Crosland. Airdate: January 11, 1976.

Breaking Steve's heart, Jaime still does not remember their previous romantic relationship. As she continues to recuperate, Oscar gets her a job as a teacher at a military base. At the same time, Jaime agrees to work as a secret agent for the OSI.

GUEST CAST: Lindsay Wagner (Jaime Sommers); Richard Lenz, Dennis Patrick, Roger Davis, Alicia Gardner.

52. "Hocus Pocus" Written by: Richard Carr. Directed by: Barry Crane. Airdate: January 18, 1976.

Important Navy codes have disappeared, along with an armored car filled with cash, and Steve fears the solution may be found in the world of illusion. Teaming with a friend possessing psychic abilities, Steve goes undercover as a magician.

GUEST CAST: Robbie Lee, Chris Nelson, Jack Colvin, Pernell Roberts, Mark Wilson.

53. "The Secret of Big Foot" (Parts I & II) Written by: Kenneth Johnson. Directed by: Alan Crosland. Airdates: February 1 and 4, 1976.

Investigating the disappearance of scientists in the Pacific Northwest, Steve comes to believe that Sasquatch, the legendary Big Foot, is involved. He soon confronts the hairy monster, actually a bionic robot created by visiting alien scientists. Steve befriends one of the scientists, the beautiful Shalon, but the Sasquatch remains a real threat, especially since the forest is seismically unstable and it may be necessary to take drastic steps to reverse the instability — a feat which could hurt Big Foot and the aliens.

GUEST CAST: Ted Cassidy (Bigfoot); Stefanie Powers (Shalon); Charles Cyphers, Chuck Bowman, Donna White.

54. "The Golden Pharoah" Written by: Margaret and Paul Schneider. Directed by: Cliff Bole. Airdate: February 8, 1976.

A foreign nation's prized statue has been replaced by a phony, and Steve thinks he knows where it has gone. Unfortunately, to get into the enemy headquarters he will need the help of an untrustworthy ally — a flim-flam girl, ex-girlfriend and compulsive gambler named Trish. Not surprisingly, she has a double cross on her mind, one that will end with the vital statue in her possession.

GUEST CAST: Farrah Fawcett Majors (Trish); Gordon Connell, Michael Lane, Joe Maross, Rudy Challenger, Gary Vinson.

55. "Love Song for Tanya" Written by: David H. Balkan and Alan Folsom. Directed by: Phil Bondelli. Airdate: February 15, 1976.

A Russian gymnastics star named Tanya develops a teenage crush on her American escort in the States, Steve Austin. Falling hard for the six million dollar man, she decides she wants to defect, a decision that could have international repercussions.

GUEST CAST: Cathy Rigby (Tanya); Terry Kiser (Alexi); Lindsay Wagner (Jaime Sommers); Walker Edmiston.

56. "The Bionic Badge" Written by: Wilton Denmark. Directed by: Cliff Bole. Airdate: February 22, 1976.

Steve goes undercover as a policeman to either expose or vindicate a cop who could be corrupt.

GUEST CAST: Noah Beery, Alan Bergmann, Thomas Bellin, Mike Santiago, Susan Powell.

57. "Big Brother" Written by: Kenneth Johnson and Richard Carr. Directed by: Lionel Siegel. Airdate: March 7, 1976.

Steve becomes a Big Brother to a troubled youth, but has a long way to go in proving his good intentions.

GUEST CAST: Lindsay Wagner (Jaime Sommers); Michael Salcido, Carl Crudup, Ralph Wilcox, Jorge Cervera.

SEASON FOUR (1976–1977)

58. "The Return of Big Foot" (Parts I and II) Written by: Kenneth Johnson. Directed by: Barry Crane. Airdate: September 19, 1976.

The aliens from space have returned with their powerful robot, Sasquatch. This time, however, they plan to steal many of the Earth's greatest treasures, a plan opposed by the peaceful Shalon. Steve must solve the riddle of several bionic thefts, save Shalon and stop the more powerful Sasquatch. To do so, he will need the help of Jaime Sommers, the bionic woman.

GUEST CAST: Lindsay Wagner (Jaime Sommers); Ted Cassidy (Bigfoot); John Saxon; Sandy Duncan; Stefanie Powers (Shalon); Severn Darden, Charles Cyphers.

59. "Nightmare in the Sky" Written by: Jim Carlson and Terrence McDonnell. Directed by: Alan Crosland. Airdate: September 27, 1976.

Kelly Wood, the first female astronaut in the United States, becomes embroiled in a strange plot while test piloting a new government plane. It seems a Japanese World War II–era fighter plane, a zero, shot her out of the skies! Though others find this explanation hard to swallow, especially since Kelly is confused about how it happened, Steve and Oscar believe her story and set out to learn the truth.

GUEST CAST: Farrah Fawcett Majors (Kelly Wood); Hank Stohl, Donald Moffatt, Dane Elcar.

60. "Double Trouble" Written by: Jerry Devine. Directed by: Phil Bondelli. Airdate: October 3, 1976.

A local comedian may be the pawn of a foreign government, thanks to a strange microchip embedded in his head. Oscar assigns Steve to accompany the comedian, who has a knack for getting into trouble.

GUEST CAST: Flip Wilson (Billy); Simon Scott, Rick Podell, Jerome Guardino.

61. "The Most Dangerous Enemy" Written by: Judy Burns. Directed by: Richard Moder. Airdate: October 17, 1976.

Rudy and Steve fly to a remote island to investigate a professor's project involving monkeys and a brain-and-strength-enhancing serum. When Rudy is bitten by one of the beasts that has taken the serum, he becomes a crazed wild man and a serious rival to the bionic man.

GUEST CAST: Ina Balin.

62. "H + 2 + 0 = Death" Written and directed by: John Meredyth Lucas. Airdate: October 24, 1976.

Spies are after a powerful new energy source that separates hydrogen and oxygen in water, and Steve must be sure that the villains don't get their hands on the top-secret formula or the beautiful scientist who created it, Ilsa.

GUEST CAST: Elke Sommer (Ilsa); Linden Chiles, Robert Hogan, Todd Martin, Frank Parker.

63. "Kill Oscar" Written by: Arthur Rowe, William T. Zacha and Wilton Schiller. Directed by: Barry Crane. Airdate: October 31, 1976.

A power-mad scientist named Franklin attempts to kill Oscar Goldman during his efforts to gain possession of a weather control device. Worse, he has been replacing high-placed government operatives with his powerful "fembot" robots. Steve joins Jaime Sommers on the case, racing to rescue Oscar from the grasp of Franklin on his remote island.

GUEST CAST: Lindsay Wagner (Jaime Sommers); John Houseman (Dr. Franklin); Jennifer Darling (Callahan); Jack Ging, Sam Jaffe, Byron Morrow, Howard K. Smith.

64. "The Bionic Boy" (Parts I and II) Written by: Tom Greene, Lionel Siegel, Wilton Schiller. Directed by: Phil Bondelli. Airdate: November 7, 1976.

A young man named Andy becomes the first bionic teenager after surviving an accident in which his legs are paralyzed. Steve monitors the boy as he develops his bionic abilities and seeks to go on a very personal mission that would clear the name of his disgraced father.

GUEST CAST: Vincent Van Patten (Andy); Joan Van Ark (Valerie); Carol Jones, Kerry Sherman, Richard Erdman, Greg Evigan, Dick Van Patten.

65. "Vulture of the Andes" Written by: Ben Masselink. Directed by: Cliff Bole. Airdate: November 21, 1976.

American jet fighters become the object of interest for an international terrorist hoping to overthrow the government of his foreign country. He plots nuclear blackmail to force America to comply with his demand.

GUEST CAST: Henry Darrow, Barbara Luna, Bernie Koppel.

66. "The Thunderbird Connection" (Parts I and II) Written by: Jim Carlson and Terrence McDonnell. Directed by: Christian Nyby. Airdate: November 28, 1976.

More foreign intrigue in the Middle East as Steve Austin goes undercover in an air show as a fighter pilot; his real mission: protect a young heir to the throne before elements of his government steal power away permanently.

GUEST CAST: Robert Loggia, Ned Romero, Jim McMullan, Barry Miller, Martine Beswick.

67. "A Bionic Christmas Carol" Written by: Wilton Schiller. Directed by: Gerald Mayer. Airdate: December 12, 1976.

This modern-day, bionic version of the Dickens classic has Steve bringing the Christmas spirit to a nasty, hard-hearted government Scrooge.

GUEST CAST: Ray Walston (Horton); Dick Sargent (Bob); Antoinette Bower (Nora); Howard McGillin, Natasha Rye, Adam Rich, Noah Keen.

68. "Task Force" Written by: Robert C. Dennis and Wilton Schiller. Directed by: Barry Crane. Airdate: December 19, 1976.

Steve infiltrates a gang planning a multi-million dollar U.S. missile theft. He cannot contact Oscar directly, or risk blowing his cover, so he must find other means to get information back to the OSI.

GUEST CAST: Jennifer Darling, Alex Cord, Taylor Lacher, Edmund Gilbert.

69. "The Ultimate Imposter" Written by: Lionel Siegel. Directed by: Paul Stanley. Airdate: January 2, 1977.

Rudy has invented a revolutionary process that allows memories and knowledge from one mind to be implanted into another. This could be a boon to secret agents going undercover or assuming false identities, but the test subject, Steve's buddy, undergoes an interesting transformation.

GUEST CAST: Stephen Macht, Pamela Hensley, David Sheiner, Kim Basinger, Morgan Fairchild, Harry Pugh.

70. "Death Probe" (Parts I and II) Written by: Steven E. De Souza. Directed by: Richard Moder. Airdates: January 9 and 16, 1977.

A Soviet space probe crash lands in the American heartland, but believes it has reached the inhospitable terrain of the planet Venus. The heavily armed and powerful probe sets out to destroy all life and obstacles it encounters, and the OSI must send Steve Austin, their strongest agent, to stop it.

GUEST CAST: Nehemiah Persoff, Jane Merrow, Beverly Garland, Walter Brooke, Don Dubbins, Ross Elliott, Austin Stoker.

71. "Danny's Inferno" Written by: Tom Greene. Directed by Cliff Bole. Airdate: January 23, 1977.

A child named Danny accidentally develops a super-powerful new chemical reaction that could be used as rocket fuel. Before long, both the OSI and a more unscrupulous company are vying to control the teen's discovery — with explosive results.

GUEST CAST: Lanny Horn, Frank Marth, David Opatshu, John Hoyt.

72. "The Fires of Hell" Written by: Orville Hampton. Directed by: Ed Abroms. Airdate: January 30, 1977.

A trio of conspirators has been hiding a uranium deposit beneath an oil well. When the OSI begins nosing around the site, the villains start a fire and blame it on an environmental organization. Steve goes undercover as an oil-field worker to determine the truth of the situation.

Guest Cast: Ken Swofford (Roy); Heather Menzies (Alison); Charles Aidman, Bruce Glover, Larry Watson.

73. "The Infiltrators" Written by: Sam Ross and Wilton Schiller. Directed by: Phil Bondelli. Airdate: February 6, 1977.

A group of international assassins have been targeting athletes. Steve goes undercover as a boxer to learn the identities of the villains, but is drugged and rendered unconscious before he can stop the next murder.

Guest Cast: Yvonne Craig, Harold Sylvester, Michael Conrad, Jerry Quarry.

74. "Carnival of Spies" Written by: Robert C. Dennis. Directed by: Richard Moder. Airdate: February 13, 1977.

The new B-1 bomber may be the intended target of a scientist who is secretly an enemy spy. Austin grows suspicious of the scientist after he simulates a heart attack, and tracks the scientist to a carnival, which may house many secrets underneath its big top tent.

Guest Cast: Lloyd Bochner, Cheryl Miller, Bob Minor, Michael Strong, H.M. Wynant.

75. "U-509" Written by: Michael Wagner. Directed by: Phil Bondelli. Airdate: February 20, 1977.

An English naval commander goes bad and, using a recovered German U-boat from World War II, plans to unleash deadly nerve gas upon an American city. Steve must race to the commander's headquarters, the submarine, and stop him from using the weapon of mass destruction; but getting so far underwater and surviving is a task that challenges Steve's bionic strength.

Guest Cast: Ian Abercrombie, Ted Hamilton, William Sylvester.

76. "Privacy of the Mind" Written by: Vanessa Boos and Wilton Schiller. Directed by: Jerry London. Airdate: February 27, 1977.

Steve goes undercover as a brilliant but absent-minded scientist to learn about a Russian plot to link human minds and computer brains, a ruse which he cannot maintain for long. As suspicions grow, Steve must find a way to disable the project and escape.

Guest Cast: Suzanne Charny, Curt Lowens, Roger Perry, Bob Neill, Leslie Moonves, Paul Mantee.

77. "To Catch the Eagle" Written by: Judy Burns and Peter R. Brooke. Directed by: Phil Bondelli. Airdate: March 6, 1977.

Steve is sent to Native American lands to rescue two OSI scientists who were checking a mountain on the reservation for radioactive ore. They have been captured by an Indian named Iron Fist. He will not free them unless Steve proves his worth to the medicine man in an ancient Native American ritual.

Guest Cast: Gerald MacRaney, Kathleen Beller.

78. "The Ghostly Teletype" Written and directed by: Wilton Schiller. Airdate: unconfirmed.

Steve is framed for espionage after secret information in his possession seems to vanish. Hoping to clear his name, Steve finds that the information, which concerns human longevity and immortality, has been stolen by telepathic twins whose accelerated growth process threatens their lives.

Guest Cast: Robert Harris, Christina Hart, Elizabeth Kerr.

FIFTH SEASON (1977–1978)

79. "Sharks!" (Parts I & II) Written by: Arthur Weingarten. Directed by: Alan J. Levi. Airdates: September 11 and 18, 1977.

Hoping to rescue a damaged submarine at sea, Steve navigates a school of fierce man-eating sharks. The deadly fish are controlled by a disgruntled Navy officer who is hoping to get his hands on the missiles aboard the damaged sub.

GUEST CAST: William Sylvester (Admiral Prescott); Stephen Elliott, Greg Walcott, Marc Alaimo, Cynthia Grayland, Pamela Hensley.

80. "Deadly Countdown" (Parts I and II) Written by: Gregory S. Dinallo and Lionel E. Siegel. Directed by: Cliff Bole. Airdates: September 25 and October 2, 1977.

Steve's latest mission puts him in mortal jeopardy when saboteurs hope to steal the high-tech computer brain of his space rocket and sell it to a foreign power. To get the computer, the villains must first assassinate the pilot...

GUEST CAST: Jenny Agutter (Dr. Russell); Phillip Abbott, Lloyd Bochner, Melissa Mc-Grath, Martin Caidin.

81. "Bigfoot V" Written by: Gregory S. Dinallo and Richard Landau. Directed by: Rod Holcomb. Airdate: October 9, 1977.

Steve is surprised when a photographer snaps a shot of Sasquatch, the bionic robot and tool of the aliens, whom he believed had returned to his home planet. Now Steve must contact the Sasquatch, who is behaving erratically, and keep him out of the public eye.

GUEST CAST: Ted Cassidy (Bigfoot); Geoffrey Lewis, Tony Young.

82. "Killer Wind" Written by: Gregory S. Dinallo and Richard Landau. Directed by Richard Moder. Airdate: October 16, 1977.

A fierce storm has trapped a group of children inside a tram high in the mountains. Steve races to the rescue, but runs afoul of a bank robber. Now Steve must race against time to save the kids as a tornado approaches.

GUEST CAST: Sylvia Walden, Adam Roarke, Sheila DeWindt, James McEachin.

83. "Rollback" Written by: Steven E. De Souza. Directed by: Don McDougall. Airdate: October 30, 1977.

Steve goes undercover in a roller derby in hopes of ferreting out the identity of a group of burglars that may in fact be saboteurs.

GUEST CAST: Robert Loggia, Paul D'Amato, Rick Springfield.

84. "Dark Side of the Moon" (Parts I and II) Written by: John Meredyth Lucas. Directed by: Cliff Bole. Airdates: November 6 and 13, 1977.

Steve Austin is ordered back to outer space when a lunar mining facility shifts the moon's orbit and causes a series of catastrophes on Earth. Steve must restore the natural satellite's correct orbit, even though the scientist on the moon claims he is mining for an energy source that would change life on Earth.

GUEST CAST: Jack Colvin, Skip Homeier, Simone Griffeth, Walter Brook.

85. "Target: Steve Austin" Written by: Donald L. Gold, Lester Burke and Richard Landau. Directed by Ed Abroms. Airdate: November 27, 1977.

Steve and a beautiful OSI agent go undercover as newlyweds on their honeymoon, but in fact protect a small and very powerful energy unit safeguarded by the OSI. A group of international saboteurs want the device and will kill to get it.

GUEST CAST: Quinn Redecker, Curt Lowens, Larry Levine, Ian Abercrombie, Tony Epper.

86. "The Cheshire Project" Written by: John Meredyth Lucas. Directed by: Richard Moder. Airdate: December 18, 1977.

Steve's girlfriend has disappeared while

flying a top-secret aircraft, and Steve must find her and the plane before she is killed and the military aircraft goes to the highest bidder.

GUEST CAST: Suzanne Sommers, John Larch, Robert Hogan, Stanley Waxman, Terry Leonard, Fred Lerner.

87. "Walk a Deadly Wing" Written by: Jim Carlson, Terrence McDonnell and Richard Landau. Directed by: Herb Wallerstein. Airdate: January 1, 1978.

Once again, Steve goes undercover, this time as a "wing walker" at an air show. He is searching for a scientist who has developed a new technology that he fears may be used as a weapon.

GUEST CAST: Eric Braeden, John Devlin, Steve Eastin, Eddie Fontaine.

88. "Just a Matter of Time" Written by: Neal J. Sperling and Gregory S. Dinallo. Directed by: Don McDougall. Airdate: January 8, 1978.

Steve is unexpectedly time-warped several years forward, and the future is not very rosy. He is believed to be a spy working for the Russians, and his life is on the line. Steve must prove his innocence and return to his own time.

GUEST CAST: Leigh Christian (Donna); Charles Cioffi, John Milford, Paul Carr.

89. "Return of the Death Probe" (Parts I and II) Written by: Howard Dimsdale. Directed by: Tom Connors. Airdates: January 22 and 29, 1978.

The destructive Russian space probe returns to wreak more havoc, controlled by a foreign government hoping to blackmail the United States, and only Steve Austin's bionic strength stands between the out-of-control machine and a city populated by thousands. Steve makes every attempt to stop the rampaging machine, but it is even more powerful than before.

GUEST CAST: Ken Swofford, Than Wyenn, David Sheiner.

90. "The Lost Island" (two hours) Written by: Mel Goldberg. Story by: Lou Shaw. Directed by Herb Wallerstein. Airdates: January 30, 1978.

Steve becomes embroiled in strange politics on a distant island inhabited by alien beings. They are being blackmailed by an evil leader, and face the prospect of a deadly disease if they leave their island.

GUEST CAST: Jared Martin, Robin Mattson, Anthony Geary, Alf Kjellin, Robert Symonds.

91. "The Madonna Caper" Written by: Gregory S. Dinallo. Directed by: Herb Wallerstein. Airdate: February 6, 1978.

Art thieves steal an important painting, and Steve inadvertently helps them do so. Unfortunately, the painting also possesses a microdot of important secrets, and Austin must find a way to get it back.

GUEST CAST: Bibi Besch, Len Berman, Frank Parker, Mike McManus, Rudy Challenger, Bruce Glover.

92. "Dead Ringer" Written by: Robert Holt. Story by: Charles Mitchell. Directed by: Arnold Laven. Airdate: February 13, 1978.

A black-garbed grim reaper figure begins to haunt Steve Austin. The normally very rational astronaut begins to fear that death, feeling cheated by his survival as a bionic man, is looking to right the cosmic scales.

GUEST CAST: Linda Dano, Mel Allen, Robert Karnes.

93. "Date with Danger" (Parts I and II) Written by: John Meredyth Lucas and Wilton Schiller. Directed by: Rod Holcomb. Airdates: February 20 and 27, 1978.

A psychotic but very powerful defense computer is intent on taking over the world and killing Steve Austin. The agent's first link to stopping the machine is a dating service...

GUEST CAST: Robert Walker, Jr., Elaine Giftos, Luke Askew, Hank Brandt, Eric Lawrence.

94. "The Moving Mountain" Written by: Stephen Kandell. Directed by: Don McDougall. Airdate: March 6, 1978.

A terrorist gets his hands on Soviet and American nuclear hardware, and plans to blackmail the world. It's Steve Austin to the rescue one more time.

GUEST CAST: John Colicos, Michael Ebert, Paul Coufos, George Clifton, Susan Fleming.

The Return of the Six Million Dollar Man and the Bionic Woman (1987)
LIVE-ACTION TV MOVIE

Written by: Michael Sloan. Story by: Michael Sloan and Bruce Lansbury. Directed by: Ray Austin. Airdate: May 17, 1987.

A retired Steve Austin is called back to OSI duty by Oscar Goldman at the same time that he must deal with his headstrong, grown son. Worse, Jaime Sommers has recovered her memory and is angry with Steve

Austin that he never rekindled their relationship. Jaime and Steve put their differences aside to fight a new enemy, a terrorist named Stenning. In the end, Steve's son, Michael, is badly injured in a flight, and the son of Austin becomes bionic too.

GUEST CAST: Martin Landau (Stenning); Gary Lockwood (Praiser); Bryan Cranston, Pamela Bryant.

Bionic Showdown: The Six Million Dollar Man and the Bionic Woman (1989)
LIVE-ACTION TV MOVIE

Written by: Michael Sloan and Ted Mann. Directed by: Alan J. Levi. Airdate: April 30, 1989.

The World Unity Games are threatened when the man responsible for security, Oscar Goldman, is injured by a person with bionic powers. Steve Austin, who has

popped the question to Jaime Sommers, is among the suspects. Meanwhile, a young woman and friend of Jaime is also destined to become bionic.

GUEST CAST: Sandra Bullock (Katie); Jeff Yagher (Jimmy); Geraint Wyn Davies (Devlin); Robert Lansing, Jack Blum, Robert McClure.

Bionic Ever After? (1994)
LIVE-ACTION TV MOVIE

Written by: Michael Sloan and Norman Morrill. Story by: Michael Sloan. Directed by: Steven Stafford. Airdate: November 29, 1994.

The wedding of the six million dollar man and bionic woman is stalled because of a threat to national security in the form of

nuclear terrorism. Worse, Jaime shows signs, after all these years, of rejecting her bionics.

GUEST CAST: Anne Lockhart, Geordie Johnson, Michael Urgess, Ivan Sergei, Lee Majors II, Ann Pierce.

Spawn

And you thought that Batman was dark!

Todd McFarlane's creation, Spawn, takes the notion of a dark, isolated superhero as far as the concept can possibly go. The central character, Al Simmons, is a dead soldier, a maggot-ridden corpse. He has been transformed into "a Hell spawn" to do the Devil's (Malebolgia) bidding on Earth, and every time someone is killed by Spawn, their souls go straight to Hell or Heaven, adding more soldiers to the apocalyptic battle between good and evil.

And Spawn is afforded little emotional comfort. His wife, Wanda, has remarried — to Al's best friend, Terry Fitzgerald — and even if she had not done so, she would be terrified by his hideous, scarred appearance. Not surprisingly, Spawn is a creature of anger ("anger is your weakness" his mentor, Cogliostro, reminds him); and eventually Spawn comes to a reckoning and decides he's "through doing Hell's dirty work," meaning that he is, essentially, a creature without a nation, without allegiances. He is alone in the universe, an unloved monster reengineered by Hell for one purpose: to kill.

This daring conceit of a dark-as-black superhero on the verge of an abyss comes from the brilliant Todd McFarlane, a Canadian artist who once worked on comics as diverse as *The Incredible Hulk, Batman: Year Two* and *The Amazing Spider-Man*. He eventually left his job penciling at Marvel Comics to form his own group, Image Comics, and it was under that banner that *Spawn* first appeared as a title in May of 1992. McFarlane, who later formed a very successful toy company, McFarlane Toys, was a *cause célèbre* in the comic industry, and the first issue of *Spawn* sold one-and-a-half million comics upon its release.

New Line Cinema purchased the rights to make a movie version of the Spawn mythos, and in August of 1997 the feature film, featuring hundreds of digital special effects from more than 20 different post-production houses, premiered in U.S. theaters.[1] It raked in more than 50 million dollars in three weekends. Reviews were generally positive, and the film was heralded far and wide for its revolutionary special effects.

In particular, the film did not back away from Spawn's (Michael Jai White) unusual abilities and "Hell" gear. Because of his "necroplasmic" body, Spawn could eject chains and grappling hooks from his very body. He could regenerate or even become invisible, depending on the requirements of the situation. More dramatically, Spawn bore a giant shroud, a massive scarlet cape that put the cowls of Batman and Superman to shame. The cape, a vast fluttering drape with a life of its own, could literally carry Spawn about, making him fly, it seemed.

The movie version of Spawn, like the comic that inspired it, was not very pretty or upbeat. It was dark and black, occurring mostly at night. And Spawn, the central character, was horribly ugly to behold — burned and scarred (courtesy of make-up by Robert Kurtzman, Gregory Nicotero and Howard Berger). His CGI transformations (by Industrial Light and Magic) looked terribly painful, but what else could one expect from the general of Hell's army?

Jai White made an interesting hero, another African American to stand tall in the genre beside Carl Lumbly's M.A.N.T.I.S. or Wesley Snipes' Blade. A martial artist for more than two decades, Jai White was physically convincing in the role. He saw his portrayal and character as one that "people will be able to identify because it's a universal thing. A hero is defined by what he does."[2]

Spawn's central nemesis, the obese Clown (John Leguizamo), was, perhaps, the nastiest villain ever to appear in a superhero film. A farting, belching, and really fat freak, Clown ate a maggot-covered pizza on-camera, turned into a cheerleader in mini-skirt with pom-poms (yuck, yuck, yuck), and was the living embodiment of a nightmare. Martin Sheen gave a fine performance as the villainous Jason Wynn, the man manipulating events behind the scenes, but the James Bond–like villain was overshadowed by an over-the-top and compelling Leguizamo.

Emotionally, the film version of *Spawn* was also bleak. The battle between darkness and light was seen to have many casualties, including the decent man Simmons, who did not deserve to go to Hell in the first place; and the film, directed by Mark A.Z. Dippe, was stunningly shot by director of photography Guillermo Navarro. *Spawn* took no prisoners and transported viewers into the pit of a fiery and miserable Hell. The idea of human ugliness was broached powerfully as the burned Spawn was derided by his fellow man and even his wife as a freak, a monster, and forced to live off garbage in an alley, finding comfort only among other outcasts, the homeless.

As it concerned horror and real evil in the world, *Spawn* was an unabashedly dark trip, and it was a good sign that the film did not soften Spawn's universe. The movie even carried the general, unspoken message of the Spawn comics: that it is better to be your own man, to control your anger and vengeance, than be led around on a leash by it. Simmons, as Spawn, could have given over to evil, bitter about his fate and that his wife moved on without him, but he did not surrender even after being transformed into a hell-spawn.

More to the point, he could never let his anger dominate him, because it was his emotional state that dictated the actions of the necroplasmic uniform. If out of control,

he could not be effective as a warrior; so discipline, or, rather, *self-discipline*, was the order of the day. Most comic book movies carry some kind of positive message, and in its own dark and perverted way, *Spawn* concerned the primacy of individuality and self-control.

If the film version could be faulted on any grounds, it was probably in the orchestration of the "big" action scenes that are so much a part of the genre. Like *X-Men* (2000), there is a claustrophobic, television feel to *Spawn*, a sense that its makers forgot they had a big screen to explore. A motorcycle chase through dark city streets, an escape up the wall of a skyscraper and even a battle of hell-beasts in a grimy city alleyway all seem terribly confining—small and close instead of grand or epic. The final battle, for instance, occurred in a family residence, a living room, and the scale was simply too tight and constrained to generate awe, or even much excitement.

As for Spawn himself, he is well depicted in the film, with his piercing green eyes and amazing red shroud, but sometimes the suit looks a little too thick and a bit on the foam rubbery side. Spawn should not appear fat or bloated, but sleek, and sometimes that distinction blurs.

In 1997 another version of Spawn came along, and, interestingly, it was one that most Spawn fans preferred to the New Line movie. HBO produced six episodes of *Spawn: The Animated Series*, which aired in May of that year, just before the movie bowed. Todd McFarlane was heavily involved in the series, which was even more faithful to the ethos of the comics than the motion picture, and writer John Leekley significantly deepened the world of Spawn by asking questions about what is good and what is evil. Spawn was not always certain which side he was fighting for, especially when tactics did not seem to differ.

A second season of six animated episodes followed in 1998, and then a third season came in May of 1999. The third season was the best received batch of episodes, and the animated series even won an Emmy Award for HBO. There has been persistent talk of a direct-to-video fourth season, but that has not yet emerged.

As of this writing, a sequel to the 1997 live-action film has been announced as a 2004–05 release for Columbia Pictures. Writer Hans Rodionoff has been hired to pen the screenplay.

Spawn (1997)
LIVE-ACTION FILM

"…[D]irector Mark A.Z. Dippe does a considerable job recreating the feel of McFarlane's books; the scenes in Hell are particularly ghoulish and otherworldly; the fire-scarred Simmons, who has metamorphosed into Spawn, takes the disquiet and self-loathing of the modern comic hero to new heights."
— John Anderson, *The Los Angeles Times*, August 1, 1997, page 20.

"With dazzling, nonstop special effects from Industrial Light and Magic and gross out humor, *Spawn* is perfectly pitched for teenage boys. For the rest of us, the live-action comic book burns out quickly. It's half-baked."
— Thelma Adams, *The New York Post*, August 1, 1997, page 43.

"[C]ooly effective, low-fuss summer moviemaking."
— Gary Dauphin, *The Village Voice*, August 12, 1997, page 74.

"*Spawn* is a moodily malevolent, anything-goes revenge fantasy that relies more upon special visual and digitally animated effects for its intended appeal than any comics-derived sci-fier to date. Based on Todd McFarlane's enormously successful comic books … this narratively knuckle headed, visually teeming film will appeal to the comics' abundant fan base."
— Todd McCarthy, *Variety*, August 4, 1997, page 34.

"Although there are some decent special effects the movie's story … is phantasmagoric gobbledygook that only the most ardent fans of the comic book will willingly endure."
— Leah Rozen, *People*, August 18, 1997, page 21.

CAST: John Leguizamo (Clown); Michael Jai White (Al Simmons/Spawn); Martin Sheen (Jason Wynn); Theresa Randle (Wanda); Melina Clarke (Jessica Priest); Miko Hughes (Boy); Sydni Boudoin (Cyan); Nicol Williamson (Cogliostro); D.B. Sweeney (Terrence Fitzgerald).

CREW: New Line Cinema Presents in Association with Todd McFarlane Entertainment, a Dippe, Goldman, Williams Production, *Spawn*. *Casting:* Mary Jo. Slater, Bruce H. Newberg. *Music:* Graeme Revell. *Special Make-up and Animal Creature Effects by:* Robert Kurtzman, Gregory Nicotero, Howard Berger. *Industrial Light and Magic Special Effects:* Christophe Henry, Habib Zargarpour, Christian Kabsch, Dennis Turner. *Associate Producer:* Terry Fitzgerald. *Special Effects Producer:* Tom C. Peitzman. *Visual Effects Supervisor:* Steve "Spaz" Williams. *Costume Designer:* Dan Lester. *Editor:* Michael N. Knue. *Production Design:* Philip Harrison. *Director of Photography:* Guillermo Navarro. *Based on the Comic Book by:* Todd McFarlane. *Co-Executive Producers:* Brian Witten, Adrianna AJ. Cohen. *Executive Producers:* Todd McFarlane, Alan C. Blomquist. *Screenplay:* Alan McElroy. *Screen story:* Alan McElroy, Mark A.Z. Dippe. *Produced by:* Clint Goldman. *Directed by:* Mark A.Z. Dippe. *M.P.A.A. Rating:* R. *Running time:* 97 minutes.

The power-hungry Jason Wynn tricks Al Simmons, a top-secret government agent, into undertaking a deadly mission in North Korea. It is a trap, and Simmons is killed in action, leaving behind a mourning wife, a daughter and a dog named Spaz.

Cast down to Hell to serve the Evil One, Malebolgia, Simmons faces an eternity of torment unless he serves the armies of the apocalypse forming there. But Simmons cannot let go of his life, or his love of Wanda, and Malebolgia obligingly returns him to Earth to settle matters, some five years after his death. He is now a horribly disfigured, burned and hideous creation called "Spawn." He finds that his family has moved on since the tragedy that claimed his life, and only Spaz remembers him.

A devilish and obese creature, Clown, contacts Spawn and reminds him that he struck a bargain with the Dark One to lead his army in exchange for seeing Wanda and also killing Wynn. But Spawn does not accept his fate and is visited by a man named Cogliostro, a mentor and friend. Cogliostro helps Spawn deal with his seemingly sentient cape/shroud, a giant red thing, as well as all the strange mechanisms of his baroque uniform.

Meanwhile, Wynn is plotting to release a deadly disease — for which only *he* holds the vaccine — throughout the globe. An angry Spawn challenges Wynn at a gala reception for Wynn's foreign partners, and puts Wynn's sexy agent, Priest, into the grave. Spawn flees the scene when the police arrive.

Working both sides, Clown suggests to Wynn that the power-hungry maniac connect his heart to the releasing device for the deadly plague, so that if his heart stops, the world dies. This is part of the Devil's strategy to destroy the world, but Spawn does not like his role in the upcoming apocalypse, and confronts the Clown, who turns into a giant hell-beast.

Wynn attacks Wanda, spurring Spawn's vengeance. But if Spawn kills Wynn, he will be killing all of the innocent people in the world.

Spawn (1997–1999)
ANIMATED SERIES

"HBO's animated series was much better than the feature film, following the original story lines from the comics much more closely (although John Leguizamo really brought the Clown character to life in the film). Spawn lives somewhere between Spider-Man, the Crow, and Batman, but with decided supernatural elements; and how interesting is it that he's basically working for the man downstairs, but we still like him?"

— William Latham, author of *Mary's Monster, Space: 1999 Resurrection*

VOICE TALENTS: Keith David (Spawn/Al Simmons); Dominique Jennings (Wanda); Richard Dysart (Cogliostro); John Rafter Lee (Jason Wynn); Michael Nicolasi (Clown); Kath Soucie (Cyan); Ronny Cox (Senator McMillan).

CREW: *Based on the Image Comic Created by:* Todd McFarlane. *Developed for Television by:* Alan McElroy. *Animation:* Sheen Productions. *Executive Producer:* John Leekley. *Animation Director:* Brad Rader. *Directors:* Thomas A. Nelson and Frank Paur. *Writers:* Rebekah Bradford, John Leekley. From HBO Animation.

A soldier named Al Simmons is selected by the Devil, Malebogia, to lead his Hellish army against the forces of God. Simmons agrees to serve, on the condition he can see his beloved wife Wanda one last time. Malebolgia honors the deal, after a fashion, and the dead Simmons is returned to Earth as a "hell-spawn," a rotting, decaying beast with unusual powers. But five years have passed since his death, and Wanda is remarried. Now Spawn must decide if he is going to fight, and for which side. During the course of his new "life" as the hideous, shrouded Spawn, Simmons battles an obese clown, the power-hungry Jason Wynn and even a cyborg called Overkill.

Steel

In the mid–1990s, the brain trust at DC Comics decided to shake up their familiar world of superheroes, going off in new and unpredictable directions. Batman was injured on the job, and Superman, at least for a time, was actually dead. The "retirement" of these two standard-bearers, DC's greatest legends, resulted in a whole slew of "next generation" replacements, new blood to reenergize a slumping comics market. One such notable replacement was Jon Bogdanove's and Louise Simonson's heroic new creation called the Man of Steel, or, simply, Steel.

In his origin issue in 1994, an African American weapons designer named John Henry Irons leaves behind his government career in Washington, D.C., and becomes a construction worker in the city of Metropolis. One day, he nearly dies on the job, but Superman saves his life by rescuing him from a dangerous fall. Later, when Superman dies, Irons feels inspired to take his place, to defend Superman's city from danger. To this end he designs and builds a suit of armor (made from steel, naturally), and takes up the Kryptonian's crime-fighting gig.

Armed with a giant sledgehammer, this African American hero kept the city safe, at least until it was time for Superman's (inevitable) resurrection. Then Steel moved back to Washington, D.C., to continue his fight there.

In 1996 the *Batman* movie series was still going strong at Warner Brothers, with the disastrous *Batman and Robin* just months from general release, and a *Steel* motion picture went into development with Kenneth Johnson, the creator of television's *The Incredible Hulk*, directing. Twenty-five-year-old Shaquille O'Neal — a basketball sensation standing over seven feet tall and weighing more than 300 lbs.— signed on as the imposing lead character. Richard Roundtree, of *Shaft* (1973) fame, played Steel's uncle, while Annabeth Gish (*The X-Files*) assayed the role of his attractive, wheelchairbound friend Sparky.

The Los Angeles Lakers star felt that Steel offered a chance to play a superhero without going over the top. "He's realistic," Shaq noted of the character. "He doesn't fly or do superhuman things. And he's a gentle guy like I am."[1]

The film version of *Steel* was adequately budgeted, with Quincy Jones coproducing, but the script by Johnson made radical changes to Steel's comic-book origin. In the film, there was no connection whatsoever to Superman (except that O'Neal bore a tattoo on one arm that read "Man of Steel" and featured the famous "S" emblem), and the locale was moved from Metropolis to a nighttime L.A. Therefore, the very reason for Steel's decision to fight crime (a debt of gratitude owed to Kal-El) was excised from the movie — replaced by a more generic "concern for the community."

Why remove the Superman link from Steel's story? Well, the *Superman* film franchise was moribund in the mid–1990s, awaiting resurrection, and it may have been considered a risk to go ahead with a movie that even tangentially featured the famous Man of Steel. At that point in the 1990s, *Clerks* director Kevin Smith was writing a *Superman Reborn* script, presumably to star Nicolas Cage, and Warner Brothers may not have wished to steal (or steel...) the thunder of that would-be blockbuster.

On another level, Kenneth Johnson is a talented producer who has always kept his productions, no matter how fantastic in concept, grounded in logic and human emotions. His version of *The Incredible Hulk* in the 1970s was very popular with many TV audiences, not so much so with comic book fans. It drastically reduced the "fantastic" elements of the comic series, making the Hulk a more realistic, psychological, and believable character. The same is true of Johnson's *Steel*. Having a man in tights flying to the rescue of star Shaquille O'Neal in the opening moments of the film would have violated any sense of dramatic realism. Without Supes present, there are very few things that are difficult for the average moviegoer, unfamiliar with the *Steel* comics, to grasp or believe during the film. The comic book origin might have changed that.

As a result, however, the movie version of *Steel* has no real link to its comic book context. It was nice that Johnson brought Irons' weapon of choice to life — a big metal hammer that housed a sonic gun in the handle, could fire tear gas, or emit a dog whistle — but in the end, *Steel* the movie just felt kind of generic. Judd Nelson made for an adequate villain, a guy whose motto was "accidents happen," but he lacked the physical menace to go up against an opponent as big as Shaquille O'Neal. In fact, there was

nobody in the film that could believably face the "tin man on steroids," and so the action, though mildly entertaining, never became terribly involving. Critics were particularly nasty about O'Neal's thesping, but he was fine in the film, with his big, amiable screen presence. If only the tiresome jokes about missing free throws had been avoided...

Though rated PG-13, *Steel* felt very family-oriented, with little swearing and just enough violence to carry out the scenario believably. O'Neal was a good role model for little kids — wholesome, courageous, inventive and lacking the "dark" character elements that made Tim Burton's *Batman* so controversial a figure. Yet, in the era of *Buffy the Vampire Slayer*, *Witchblade* and others, *Steel* was notably missing something, a sense of immediacy perhaps, and a willingness to go for the "fantastic" over the mundane. Maybe that is why the film felt ho-hum: The story of a man who built a new suit of armor and fought crime sounded almost plausible — too plausible for fans seeking new flights of fantasy.

Steel (1997)
LIVE-ACTION FILM

"Writer-director Kenneth Johnson provides a tinny story and a leaden pace for his tarnished titan. There's a coziness and simplicity to the production that would be better served on TV. Cinema-size, it comes off as corny, antiquated and slightly cheesy."
—Leonard Klady, *Variety*, August 18, 1997, page 33.

"As written and directed by Kenneth Johnson, it all comes off like a sub-par variation on *The Incredible Hulk*.... The mix of silly plot twists, ho-hum special effects and painfully weak humor seem all too familiar."
— Larry Worth, *The New York Post*, August 16, 1996, page 26.

CAST: Shaquille O'Neal (John Henry Irons/Steel); Annabeth Gish (Sparky); Judd Nelson (Lt. Nathaniel Burke); Richard Roundtree

(Uncle Joe); Irma P. Hall (Grandma Odessa); Ray J (Martin); Charles Napier (Colonel David); Kerrie Keane (Senator); Eric Pierpont (Major); Tembi Locke (Norma); Thom Barry (Senior Cop); Gary Graham (Detective); Eric Saiet (Young Cop); George Lemore (Cutter); Joseph Palmer (Holdecker); Steve Mattila (Big Willy); Tim de Zarn (Skinhead Leader); Claire Stansfield (Duvray).

CREW: Warner Brothers Presents a Quincy Jones, David Salzman Entertainment Production, *Steel*. *Casting:* Shana Landsburg, Laura Adler. *Stunt Coordinators:* M. James Arnett, John Epstein. *Costume Designer:* Catherine Adair. *Steel's Suit Created by:* Greg Cannom. *Music:* Mervyn Warren. *Co-Producer:* Mark Allan. *Film Editor:* John F. Link. *Production Designer:* Gary Wissner. *Director of Photography:* Mark Irwin. *Based Upon the Character Published by:* DC

Comics. *Steel Created by:* Louise Simons, Jon
Bagdonove. *Executive Producers:* Shaquille O'Neal,
Leonard Armato, Bruce Binkow. *Associate Producer:* Venita Ozols-Graham. *Art Director:* Ger-
shon Ginsburg. *Set Designer:* Adam Scher. *Camera Operator:* Andrew Rowlands. *Visual Effects
Supervisor:* Rainmaker Digital Pictures. *Written
and Directed by:* Kenneth Johnson. *M.P.A.A. Rating:* PG-13. *Running time:* 97 minutes.

A military weapons builder in the U.S.
Army named John Henry Irons is disillusioned when his new device, a sonic cannon, is misused by a fellow officer, Lt.
Nathaniel Burke, during a test. As a result,
a U.S. senator is killed and John's lovely
friend, Sparky, is crippled.

Irons quits the military and heads
home to Los Angeles, where he stays at his
grandmother's apartment with his little
brother, Martin. Meanwhile, Burke also
heads to L.A. to illegally develop Irons'
weaponry from specs on stolen discs. He
promptly uses the particle beam and sonic
weapons to commit a robbery. In the process, a cop friend of Irons' is injured.

When Colonel David and the military
won't get involved, Iron decides to take matters into his own hands. He breaks Sparky
out of a veterans hospital and brings the
wheelchair-bound technician to L.A. to
help him build counter-weapons. Along
with his Uncle Joe, Irons and Sparky forge
a steel armor suit for John, as well as a giant,
well-equipped sledgehammer. In no time,
John is fighting local crime as "the Man of
Steel," or simply "Steel."

After John intercedes in a gang war and
evades local police, the Steel Man draws the
interest of Burke. The villain robs the Federal Reserve, and the police apprehend Steel
at the scene, but none of the people Steel
saved from Burke will identify him in a line-
up as the superhero. Sparky springs Irons
from prison just in time to stop a gun auction being run by Burke. Steele, Sparky and
Uncle Joe take on Burke and his weapons,
with the military racing to the scene.

Superboy

If imaginative readers of the Superman
comic book ever wondered what it was like
to be a teenager with super powers, there
was an easy way to find out. In 1945, DC
Comics (using the names of Jerry Siegel and
Joe Shuster) introduced Superboy in *More
Fun Comics* #101. Superboy, as his name suggests, was a diminutive Superman, and the
comic told the story of Clark Kent (Kal-El
of Krypton) as a lad.

The comic was set in Smallville, Kansas (a reflection of Siegel and Shuster's home,
Glenville), and there were a number of new
characters added to the future Man of Steel's
mythos. Prime among these new additions
was Lana Lang, a beautiful teenage girl that,
like Lois Lane, often found trouble and required timely rescue. Pete Ross was Clark's

closest high school buddy, and Clark's parents, farmers Jonathan and Martha Kent,
were also on hand to offer sage advice.

In various stories, Clark arrived on Earth
as a baby, met up with Krypto, the super pup,
and even tangled with a young Lex Luthor,
thus setting the stage for future conflicts in
Metropolis during Kent's manhood. Fun and
breezy, the Superboy comics sometimes
seemed inconsistent with Man of Steel lore.
For instance, wouldn't feisty reporter Lois
Lane have tracked the appearance of a uniformed, super-powered hero from Metropolis back to Smallville in relatively short order?

More to the point, was Clark the only
arrival from Krypton (as some depictions of
the Superman origin noted), or did he actually have a friendly, super-powered pet, a

canine named Krypto? The mythos seemed inconsistent and in the early 1990s, DC even took the step of writing Superboy out of the Superman mythos, indicating that Clark's adventures in costume did not begin until his (adult) arrival in Metropolis. This was the approach taken by *Lois and Clark: The New Adventures of Superman*. The first episode of that series dramatized Mrs. Kent experimenting with costume designs for Clark at the beginning of his crime-fighting career.

Despite the contradictions in his backstory, the idea of a youthful Clark Kent growing up and fighting evil as an adolescent has held widespread appeal for Hollywood producers. When *The Adventures of Superman* closed shop in the late 1950s, producers were desperate to continue the popular program, even without its star George Reeves. Superboy was a powerful option to explore, and *The Adventures of Superboy*, a pilot starring John Rockwell as Clark, was produced in 1960. The pilot never went to series, and never aired, but has since become a popular collector's item for fans.

In 1967 an eight-minute section of the Superman animated series was given over to *The Adventures of Superboy*, with Bob Hasting providing the voice of young Clark Kent during the brief adventures. Lana and Krypto were also on hand.

In the 1980s, the Superboy property again became a powerful plan "B" for producers looking to cash in on the Superman phenomenon. Ilya and Alexander Salkind had sold the rights to Superman to Cannon after *Superman III* (1983), but maintained the rights to other characters in the Superman family, including Superboy. When *Superman IV: The Quest for Peace* (1987) tanked at the box office, and Christopher Reeve expressed no interest in resuming the part that had made him a superstar, the Salkinds took an alternate route: television.

At the time, first-run syndicated programming was taking off, especially in the

categories of science fiction and fantasy. *Star Trek: The Next Generation* (1987–1994) became the highest rated syndicated series of all time, but it was followed by many, many more genre efforts, including *Friday the 13th: The Series* (1987–1990), *Freddy's Nightmares* (1988–1990), *War of the Worlds* (1988–1990), *Dracula: The Series* (1990-1991) and others. In this environment, the Salkinds felt, a *Superboy* TV series might just become the next ratings buster.

The Salkinds set up shop at the Disney MGM studio in Florida, and with producer Fred Freiberger (*Star Trek, Space: 1999*) working as story editor, commenced casting the new superhero series. John Haymes Newton won the role of Superboy, Stuart Whitman played Pa Kent, and Salome Jens played Martha. The gorgeous Stacy Haiduk (*SeaQuest DSV* [1993–1995]) appeared as Lana Lang, and was one of the few performers to last throughout the program's full run.

The setting of the series was Shuster University, where Clark and Lana attended school together, along with T.J. White (Jim Calvert), son of *Daily Planet* editor Perry White. Together, this troika of young adults grappled with jewel thieves, mobsters and other common criminals, even while dealing with their cunning and treacherous fellow student, Lex Luthor (Scott Wells).

Airing in 175 markets, representing nearly 95 percent of the United States,[1] *Superboy* started off slow, plagued by weak acting and poor story lines. Special effects were bottom drawer, and many critics took note of the flaws. A new format and a vastly improved cast turned things around, however, for the second season. The production moved to Universal Studios in Orlando, and Gerard Christopher replaced lead Newton as Clark Kent, reportedly because the earlier star had requested a sizable raise and argued with the Salkinds over his interpretation of the character.

Lex Luthor also underwent a drastic

change. Scott Wells left the series, replaced by actor Sherman Howard, a veteran performer who was at least a decade older than Wells. This change was explained by Luthor's decision to undergo plastic surgery and alter his appearance, all in a plot to vex Superboy. T.J. was also ditched, replaced by another comic relief character, Andy McAlister (Ilan Mitchell-Smith). Only the Kents and Haiduk's Lana Lang provided some much-needed continuity.

Fortunately, special effects and stories also improved during the second season of *Superboy*, and Gerard Christopher made an excellent transition into the role, at times eerily mimicking Christopher Reeve's portrayal of Clark Kent. As the series developed, it began to call upon the rich heritage of the Superboy/Superman comics, introducing a number of popular comic book foes, including the defective Superboy clone in "Bizarro, the Thing of Steel," "Bride of Bizarro" and "To Be Human."

Other comic book villains included Metallo, who possessed a heart of Kryptonite ("Metallo," "Super Menace," and "The People vs. Metallo"), and the imp from another dimension, Mr. Mxyzptlk (Michael J. Pollard), in "Meet Mr. Mxyzptlk" and "Mr. and Mrs. Superboy."

After a breezy, engaging and much-improved second year, *Superboy* flew even higher in its third season. Clark and Lana experienced another change of venue. This time, the college juniors interned at the Bureau for Extra Normal Matters, a government agency that researched, for all intents and purposes, X-File–type stories. Peter J. Fernandez joined the cast as agent Matt Ritter, a co-worker, and Robert Levine played C. Dennis Jackson, the boss of the bureau.

The new "office" setting allowed Clark and Lana to officially investigate all sorts of villains, including werewolves ("The Werewolf") and Brian Thompson's menacing Golem ("The Golem"). These supernatural foes proved good additions to the series,

even as the Superman mythos was plumbed deeper. Lex Luthor, Metallo and Bizarro all continued to menace the Boy of Steel, and Gilbert Gottfried played a villainous inventor, Nick Knack, in two stories.

Jack Larson and Noell Neill, stars of the 1950s *Adventures of Superman*, appeared in one nostalgic episode, titled "Paranoia." Other stories sent Clark (and Superboy) to alternate dimensions to confront his life as it could have been in different circumstances. Unlike Superman in the film series, or in *Lois and Clark*, Superboy really never came to understand the full breadth of his Kryptonian heritage. In one story, aliens claiming to be his parents (George Lazenby and Britt Ekland) were actually just hoping to kidnap him and make him an attraction at an intergalactic zoo! Such diverse tales resulted in an enjoyable, fun series. At a half-hour in length, each episode of *Superboy* moved at an incredible, and often exciting, pace.

Superboy (or *The Adventures of Superboy*, as it was officially known after the third season) lasted an impressive four seasons, a real hit in syndication. However, after the fourth season, Warner Brothers, the copyright holder for Superman, claimed that the series infringed on their rights and sued the program right out of existence. To this day, the series has not been rerun in America, a fact that has cost the actors, producers and writers involved in the show millions of dollars in royalties. Because of this, *Superboy* is not well remembered by the general TV fan today. Those critics that do remember it mostly saw it during the weak first season and do not recall it with fondness. There remains, however, a dedicated cadre of fans (a force on the Internet) who watched the impressive series throughout its run and are still fighting for it today, ten years after its cancellation.

Immediately after the cancellation of *Superboy*, ABC aired the "approved" revamp of the Man of Tomorrow's mythos: *Lois and*

Smallville's alpha males. From left to right: Jonathan Kent (John Schneider), Lex Luthor (Michael Rosenbaum) and Clark Kent (Tom Welling).

Clark: The New Adventures of Superman (1993–1996).

In 2001, scarcely ten years after the cancellation of the Salkinds' *Adventures of Superboy*, a re-imagination of the Boy of Steel's mythos arrived on the WB. This time the series was called *Smallville* (think *Roswell*), and all of the comic book characters were close at hand. Clark Kent (chiseled Tom Welling) went to high school with beautiful Lana Lang (Kristin Kreuk) and buddy Pete Ross, an African American played by Sam Jones, III. He was friends with nosy cub reporter Chloe Sullivan (Allison Mack), the editor of the Smallville High newspaper, the *Torch*.

Also in town was a nasty jock, Whitney Ellsworth (Eric Johnson), a competitor for Lana's affection and a character who was killed off during the show's second season. Annette O'Toole (*Superman III*) and John Schneider portrayed Clark's white bread, farmer parents.

Most interesting of all, however, was Lex Luthor, played with stylish depth by Michael Rosenbaum. Anything but a typical villain, this charismatic character was an insecure, Machiavellian young adult who had learned to be suspicious and cynical from his nasty, cutthroat father, Lionel (John Glover). Despite this upbringing, Lex was a very human guy, someone hoping to hone good instincts and become a decent person, a venture constantly thwarted by his father's machinations and his own inability to trust others.

In this series, Clark and Lex were the best of friends, leading to the expectation that someday there would be an irreparable falling out. As Miles Millar, creator and executive producer of *Smallville*, noted of the premise:

> The interesting thing about the series is that you know how it's going to end. You know Lex and Clark will end up in Metropolis and be bitter enemies.... For us

it's how interesting and unexpected is that journey to Metropolis, because that's what the series is about. We are going to play with people's expectations and what they think Lex and Clark are about.[2]

In this sense, *Smallville* was a genuine prequel to the adventures of Superman, focusing on the dramatic relationships and the events that made Clark and Lex the men — and enemies — they would become.

More controversial than the prequel premise, however, was the fact that *Smallville* willfully and determinedly eschewed all "up front" elements of the Superman mythos. In other words, the character's colorful costume and some of his abilities, particularly the power of flight, were dropped. "We do not want to do Superboy," Alfred Gough, a writer and producer on the series commented. "To reinvent it, you have to shake it up. We're sort of respectful to the Superman legend without being slavish to it."[3]

One of the reinventions that helped facilitate the believability of the series was the producers' decision to have baby Clark arrive in Smallville along with a storm of meteors. This natural disaster was the catalyzing force in all of the characters' lives, the one thing that "changed" them forever. For Clark, it was his arrival on Earth. For the Kents, it was their chance to have a child — and the beginning of a long secret they needed to protect. For Lana, the meteors killed her parents, leaving her an orphan, forever in search of her heritage. For Chloe, the meteor storm proved an inspiration, and her journalistic obsession became the "Wall of Weird" — strange events occurring in Smallville since the day of the storm. Even a youthful Lex was in Smallville on the day of the meteor devastation, a phenomenon that robbed him of all his hair. In one way or another, all the major characters of Smallville owe their existence to the space rocks that heralded Clark's arrival on Earth, and that makes for an interesting and unifying premise worthy of exploration.

On the downside, early *Smallville* very closely resembled other WB–spawned series rather than establishing its own individual identity. Without his cape and tights and most-heralded power (flight), Clark Kent simply became another alien teenager hiding on Earth, hence the frequent comparison to *Roswell* (1999–2002), another series about adolescent alien beings going through high school.

Smallville at its worst could come off like a very poor copy of *Buffy the Vampire Slayer*. Clark was Buffy, the super-powered teen who had to hide his secret identity. Peter Ross was Xander, the loyal but powerless friend. Chloe was Willow, a long-time friend with a knack for computers and research. Whitney was a distaff Cordelia Chase, the nasty jock and foil for Clark. Even Lex seemed to fit in the *Buffy* mold as a kind of Spike/Angel nemesis/friend, a character of great charisma who could function either as villain or ally. And, since the meteor rocks spawned so many mutations and villains in Smallville, it was, in essence, another version of Sunnydale's Hellmouth, a "convergence" of evil forces.

With no costumes (a trademark of the Superman character) and no flying (a trademark power), *Smallville* was pretty hard-put to seem like an original venture, especially since it continued the *Buffy/Charmed/Roswell* tradition of featuring "hot" musical scores from current chart toppers. No Doubt was heard on the soundtrack during "Nocturne," Jewel in "Cool," John Mayer in "Obscura," NewGoundGlory in "Heat," P.O.D. in "Kinetic," and so on.

Other problems with the program's reinvented format became apparent only after several episodes. In the first season at least, *Smallville* fell into a narrative rut. Every story concerned Clark clashing with the meteor rock–spawned "freak of the week." He fought a "bug boy" in "Metamorphosis." He battled a rage-a-holic "firestarter" in "Hothead." Then there was a boy that sucked heat out of people's bodies in "Cool," a youth stealer in "Hour Glass," a spontaneous combuster in "Reaper," a body-hopper in "Leech," an invisible girl in "Shimmer," and a teen that eats people to stay thin in "Cravings."

All of these stories carried the same premise: a Smallville resident, usually a student, is turned into a monster by exposure to green meteor rocks (kryptonite), and must be stopped before hurting Clark's friends, usually Lana. During the final battle with the villain each week, Clark is always close enough to the meteor rocks to see his powers hampered. This mutant-of-the-week formula was reminiscent of some *X-Files* episodes, and though it did provide villains, it made the show more repetitive than *Friday the 13th: The Series*, in which the same plot was used every week for three years.

Despite a soft, WB–teen look, a repetitive formula and an uncomfortable resemblance to *Buffy the Vampire Slayer*, *Smallville* remains an intriguing and interesting series to watch. Like *Buffy*, it works hard to use super powers as a metaphor for adolescence. Young, awkward Clark goes weak in the knees whenever he gets too close to Lana — not because he is nervous, but because she wears a necklace of meteor rocks. In "Shimmer," a girl named Amy feels invisible because of her unrequited love for Lex. In "Heat," Clark becomes sexually aroused by a new science teacher, and when excited he shoots heat rays from his eyes, a premature ejaculation of sorts.

In "Leech," Clark longs to be normal, deriding his status as an outsider, though he might as well be crying because he is a nerd, a geek or some other unpopular "faction" of contemporary high school life. In "Heat," Clark is exposed to red kryptonite and becomes an insensitive, womanizing cretin, an affliction that many teenage boys, victims of their raging hormones, suffer from time to time. In the episode "Meta-

morphosis," Clark reveals that he has "nocturnal dreams" (read: nocturnal emissions) about flying and levitation. Thus puberty and super powers are equated rather nicely. Though imitative of *Buffy*'s ethos, it works and is often highly amusing.

Smallville's greatest strength, however, is its predilection for (often witty) foreshadowing. In the episode called "Dichotic," Clark forges an "S" emblem in Industrial Arts class, the future symbol of the Man of Steel. In "Hug," as he contemplates his career future, Clark notes that he "doesn't want to put on a suit and do a lot of flying," a nice reference to Superman's future duties. The producers and writers have, in fact, been remarkably clever about laying the groundwork for the birth of Superman.

In the episode called "Stray," for instance, a young psychic boy named Ryan meets Clark and tells him of his favorite comic book character, a superhero called Warrior Angel, a "strange visitor from another planet" who protects the weak. In a follow-up episode ("Ryan"), the same child discusses Warrior Angel again, this time with Lex, noting that issue number 66 is the most important because in it a friend of Warrior Angel becomes a deadly foe. This, of course, is the path Lex is destined to travel. "The road to darkness is a journey, not a light switch," Ryan warns the perplexed Lex.

Perhaps the most fascinating *Smallville* moment came early in the series, in an episode entitled "Hourglass." A blind seer named Cassandra was able to see the future of each character. Looking deeply at Lex, she saw a vision of the youthful Luthor in the West Wing of the White House as the President of the United States. That image of power quickly turned ugly, however, as Luthor stands in an empty field while crimson blood rains down on his immaculate white suit. His future is one of great promise and great terror, power and evil … a chilling prophecy that kills the elderly seer. "I'm not a criminal mastermind," Luthor jokes in "X-Ray," but the image conjured by Cassandra calls his assertion into question.

By contrast, Cassandra also sees Clark's future. "It's your destiny to help people," she explains, helping to write the legacy of a future hero.

In portentous moments like these, *Smallville* shows its worth, becoming a program with its own identity and dramatic purpose: the depiction of a superhero's first steps into adulthood. When these moments come together powerfully, as in the vision of Lex in the White House, *Smallville* is a genre treat. When it resorts to treacly stories about Lana's efforts to win over her newly discovered biological father (Patrick Cassidy), or Chloe's unrequited loved for Clark, the series lives down to its WB teen standards: *Dawson's Creek* meets *Roswell*.

Smallville premiered in the autumn of 2001, scarcely a month after the terrorist attacks that brought down the World Trade Center. America was deep in mourning and denial, and the colorful, cornfed and safe appeal of *Smallville* hit the spot. It was set in the heartland and featured sterling "traditional" values about honor, family and justice. The cast members were all perfect for their parts, too. Tom Welling offered an iron jaw line and the tough, penetrating stare of the best Supermen. Kreuk made for a winsome and lovely damsel in distress, and Rosenbaum was the best new TV villain to come down the pike in ages. To borrow a cliché, *Smallville* was as American as apple pie. Of course, that is perfectly appropriate: Superman has always been the most patriotic, most stereotypically American genre hero.

For all these reasons, *Smallville* took off. With eight-and-a-half million viewers tuning in, it made the biggest series debut in WB history.[4] After the premiere, it settled in as the second highest rated program on the network, right behind the Christian drama *7th Heaven*.[5] Renewed promptly for a second season, *Smallville* showed dramatic signs of narrative improvement. The second season, broadcast in high definition, dumped the "freak-of-the-week" format and plunged headlong into more character-oriented stories. Pete Ross learned Clark's secret; Lex had to contend with his father, blinded after an accident; and there was even strife in the Kent marriage as Martha went to work for Lionel Luthor to save the family farm.

After January 2003, it was announced that the former Superman, Christopher Reeve, was scheduled to make a guest appearance on the series, a good omen that the program was taking its legacy seriously and looking to honor the long tradition of Superboy and Superman on television.

Superboy (a.k.a. *The Adventures of Superboy*) (1988–1992)
LIVE-ACTION SERIES

"This syndicated series isn't half bad..."
— David Hiltbrand, *People Weekly:* "The Adventures of Superboy." November 11, 1991, page 15.

"Ok, it isn't great art. What it is is good entertainment, pure and simple, and superior to the vast majority of its made-for-syndication competitors."
—William E. Anchors, *Epi-Log Magazine*

#22: "The Adventures of Superboy." September, 1992, page 5.

CAST: Stacy Haiduk (Lana Lang); Stuart Whitman (Jonathan Kent); Salome Jens (Martha Kent). FIRST SEASON ONLY: John Haymes-Newton (Clark Kent/Superboy); Lex Luthor (Scott Wells); Michael Menno (Leo); Jim Calvert (T.J. White). SECOND THROUGH FOURTH SEASONS: Gerard Christopher (Clark Kent/

Superman); Lex Luthor (Sherman Howard); SECOND SEASON ONLY: Ilan Mitchell-Smith (Andy McAlister); THIRD AND FOURTH SEASONS: Peter J. Fernandez (Matt Ritter); Robert Levine (C. Dennis Jackson).

CREW: *Produced by:* Alexander and Ilya Salkind. *Executive Producer:* Ilya Salkind. *Story Consultant/Editor, First Season:* Fred Freiberger. *Executive Story Consultants:* Mark Jones and Cary Bates. *Original Series Casting:* Lynn Stalmaster. *Music:* Kevin Kiner. *Executive Producer (Third and Fourth Seasons):* Gerard Christopher. *Characters Created by:* Jerry Siegel and Joe Shuster. *Distributor:* Viacom.

SEASON ONE (1988-1989)

1. "The Jewel of Techacal" Written by: Fred Freiberger. Directed by: Reza Badiyi. Airdate: October 8, 1988.

Lana Lang's father, an archaeologist, visits Shuster University, bringing with him a cursed ancient artifact. Superboy is busy full-time helping Professor Lang avoid the dangers of the curse, and ruthless student Lex Luthor plans to get his hands on the priceless jewel, regardless of the danger.

GUEST CAST: Peter White (Professor Lang); Michael Manno, Todd Davis, Forest Neal, Bob Barnes.

2. "A Kind of Princess" Written by: Michael Morris. Story by: Howard Dimsdale. Directed by: Reza Badiyi. Airdate: October 15, 1988.

Sarah, a beautiful student at Shuster University, becomes a pawn between her gangster father and a rival mob boss. Clark develops feelings for Sarah and must intervene to rescue the girl.

GUEST CAST: Ed Winter (Danner); Julie McCullough (Sarah); Harry Cup, Steven Anthony, Dennis Underwood, Dennis Michael, Antoni Corone.

3. "Back to Oblivion" Written by: Fred Freiberger. Directed by: Colin Chilvers. Airdate: October 22, 1988.

An eccentric holocaust survivor, fearing a new Nazi takeover, has built a junkyard fortress, replete with scrap-built robots to defend his terrain. Lana shows the old man great kindness, but the delusional fellow mistakes her for his murdered daughter, forcing a confrontation with Superboy.

GUEST CAST: Abe Vigoda (Wagner); Dennis Michael.

4. "The Russian Exchange Student" Written by: Vida Spears and Sara V. Finney. Directed by: Reza Badiyi. Airdate: October 29, 1988.

A Russian exchange student is suspected of sabotage after a series of dangerous accidents occur at the University. Clark and Lana set out to clear her name and prove her innocence before she returns home to the Soviet Union.

GUEST CAST: Ray Walston (Professor Gordon); Heather Haase, Courtney Gaines, Tania Harley, Roger Pretto, Chase Randolph.

5. "Countdown to Nowhere" Written by: Fred Freiberger. Directed by: Colin Chilvers. Airdate: November 5, 1988.

While heading an on-campus protest against the development of a powerful new laser weapon, Lana is captured by a gang of criminals who plan to use the device against the space shuttle. Clark realizes Superboy must make his first public appearance if Lana is to be rescued in time.

GUEST CAST: Doug Barr (Williams); Durell Harris (Theodore); Noah Meeks, Fred Broderson, Jay Glick, Paul Darby.

6. "Bringing Down the House" Written by: Michael Morris. Story by: Howard Dimsdale. Directed by: Colin Chilvers. Airdate: November 12, 1988.

A rock star named Faust returns to Schuster campus, and Lana Lang falls hard for the romantic rocker. Unfortunately, the singer may be behind a rash of deadly accidents at theme parks around town, a possibility that only the jealous Clark is aware of.

GUEST CAST: Leif Garrett (Faust); Don Sheldon, Antonio Fabrizio, Dennis Michael.

7. "The Beast and Beauty" Written by: Bernard M. Kahn. Story: Toby Martin and Bernard M. Kahn. Directed by: Jackie Cooper. Airdate: November 19, 1988.

A Superboy imposter holds up a jewelry store in hopes of winning the affections of a cold beauty queen. Clark must clear Superboy's name, evade the police, and stop the deluded imposter before his crush on the girl turns deadly.

GUEST CAST: David Marciano, Lonnie Shaw, Roger Pretto, Jeff Moldovan, Dan Barber.

8. "The Fixer" Written by: Alden Schwimmer. Directed by: Colin Chilvers. Directed by: November 26, 1988.

Lex Luthor uses incriminating photographs to blackmail a popular basketball star in an effort to see Shuster University lose an important game. Clark and Lana try to help the beleaguered athlete, unaware that another player on the team may also be working for Lex.

GUEST CAST: Michael Landon, Jr. (Stretch); James Hampton, Curley Neal, Michael Manno, Ron Segall.

9. "The Alien Solution" Written by: Michael Carlin and Andrew Helfer. Directed by: Colin Chilvers. Airdate: December 3, 1988.

A monstrous alien life form, one lacking corporeal form, can control the bodies of others. It possesses Lana Lang in an effort to control and eventually possess Earth's most powerful warrior: Superboy!

GUEST CAST: Jeff Moldovon, Dennis Michael, Christine Page, Todd Seeley.

10. "Troubled Waters" Written by: Dick Robbins. Directed by: Reza Badiyi. Airdate: December 10, 1988.

Back in Smallville, Jonathan Kent wages a battle against a greedy land developer eager to buy up farm land at any cost. When Kent falls victim to an unexplained accident, Clark returns to his hometown to investigate and learns that an underground river is the developer's secret goal. He plans to buy the land and then sell the water off to the highest bidders.

GUEST CAST: Julie Donald, Peter Palmer, Norman Lund, Joe Tomko.

11. "The Invisible People" Written by: Mark Evanier. Directed by Jackie Cooper. Airdate: January 21, 1989.

Clark comes to the rescue of a homeless community when it is threatened by a greedy land developer.

GUEST CAST: Greg Morris (Damon); Cynthia Ann Rose, Bill Orsini, Jack Malone.

12. "Kryptonite Kills" Written by: Michael Carlin and Andrew Helfer. Directed by: Jackie Cooper. Airdate: January 28, 1989.

A geology professor at Schuster University comes into possession of a powerful chunk of green kryptonite, which he believes is a great power source. Clark is adversely affected by it, and Lex plots to steal it to use against the city during a massive crime spree.

GUEST CAST: Pamela Bach, Michael Manno, Cyndi Vance, Larry Francer.

13. "Revenge of the Alien" (Parts I and II) Written by: Andrew Helfer and Michael Carlin. Directed by David Grossman and Peter Kiwatt. Airdates: February 4 and 11, 1989.

Old problems resurface when the vanquished non-corporeal alien from another planet escapes captivity in the Shuster lab and possesses Clark's father, Jonathan Kent. The alien plans to kill Clark with the chunk of kryptonite recently sent to Shuster University, and his bait is, once again, Lana Lang.

GUEST CAST: Glenn Scherer, Roger Pretto, Jerry Eden, Mark Macaulay, Dean Lockhardt, Alan Jordan.

14. "Stand Up and Get Knocked Down" Written by: David Patrick Columbia and Toby Martin. Story by: Toby Martin. Directed by: David Grossman. Airdate: February 18, 1989.

T.J. begins an investigation of a local comedy club when a good friend is murdered after performing there. Unfortunately, the owner of the club learns of T.J.'s investigation and plans a second murder.

GUEST CAST: Gary Lockwood (Dexter Linton); Hayden Logston, Cindy Hamsey, Lester Bibbs, Joe Hess, Brett Rice.

15. "Meet Mr. Mxyzptlk" Written by: Dennis O'Neil. Directed by: Peter Kiwatt. Airdate: February 25, 1989.

A strange creature from another dimension, Mr. Mxyzptlk, escapes to Earth, planning to learn all of Superboy's secrets. He transforms into a double of Clark Kent to get close to Lana Lang, a deception that causes no end of problems.

GUEST CAST: Michael J. Pollard (Mr. Mxyzptlk); Russ Wheeler, Steve Dash, James Rios.

16. "The Birdman of the Swamps" Written by: Bernard M. Kahn. Directed by Reza Badiyi. Airdate: March 4, 1989.

When a nearby construction project designed to help the poverty-stricken suffers several inexplicable incidents of vandalism, Clark, T.J. and Lana investigate the situation. They find a Native American woman using magic to sabotage the project for personal reasons; but she is not the real cause of evil, as Clark soon discovers.

GUEST CAST: James Arthur (Hogan); Mike Walters, Ted Science, Jack Swanson, Kim Crow, Liz Vassey.

17. "Terror from the Blue" Written by: George Kirgo. Directed by: Peter Kiwatt. Airdate: March 11, 1989.

Corruption in the local police becomes an issue for Lana, who witnesses a terrible crime. A murdered police officer is just the first piece of the puzzle, but soon the corrupt officers go after Lana for knowing too much.

GUEST CAST: Cary-Hiroyuki Tagawa (Detective Slade); Roger Prett (Det. Harris); Chase Randolph, David Hauser, Michael Stark, Jim Howard.

18. "War of the Species" Written by: Steven L. Sears. Directed by: Peter Kiwatt. Airdate: March 18, 1989.

The death of a scientist at a local laboratory leads Clark, T.J. and Lana to uncover a plot with global repercussions. A race of deadly androids is planning to take over the planet and destroy the human race … at least until Superboy intervenes.

GUEST CAST: Kevyn Major Howard, John Matuzak, Rita Rehn, Byron Mace.

19. "Little Hercules" Written by: Wayne Rice. Directed by: David Grossman. Airdate: April 15, 1989.

A teenager accidentally triggers the computer codes that inform a U.S. submarine to begin the launch countdown on its nuclear missiles. Unless Superboy can stop the countdown, the submarine will initiate World War III.

GUEST CAST: Leaf Phoenix (Billy Hercules); Allen Hall (Lt. Redman); Elizabeth Marion, Dean Drapin, Robert Hollinger, Brian Solako, Jason Jacobs.

20. "Mutant" Written by: Michael Maurer. Directed by Andre Guffreund. Airdate: April 22, 1988.

Disfigured mutants from the twenty-fourth century travel back in time to twentieth century Earth to capture a nuclear scientist speaking at a convention. Clark and T.J. are covering the convention and learn that the visitors from the future need plutonium to continue their destructive future war.

GUEST CAST: Skye Aubrey (Val); Bill Christie, Jack Swanson, Edgar Allen Poe, IV.

21. "The Phantom of the Third Division" Written by: Bernard M. Kahn. Directed by: David Nutter. Airdate: April 29, 1989.

Jonathan Kent is kidnapped by an old enemy, "the Phantom," a veteran from the Korean War that blames Kent for his capture all those years ago. Visiting Smallville, Clark and Lana must find a way to rescue Kent's adoptive father.

GUEST CAST: Joe Campanella (The Phantom); Jay Glick, Bobby Brandt.

22. "Black Flamingo" Written by: Cary Bates. Directed by: Chuck Martinez. Airdate: May 6, 1989.

The youthful patrons at a local nightclub are being "triggered" as unwitting soldiers in political assassination plots. The villain is a hypnotizing guru named the Snakeman, and his next victim could be Superboy!

GUEST CAST: Fernando Allende, Ada Maris, Ron Russell, Scott Galin, Ron Knight.

23. "Hollywood" Written by: Fred Freiberger. Directed by: David Nutter. Airdate: May 13, 1989.

Superboy and an eccentric scientist are hurled back in time to the year 1939 by the scientist's malfunctioning time machine. Superboy ends up in Hollywood and falls in love with a famous movie star, the only person who can help him get back to his own time.

GUEST CAST: Doug McClure (Professor Zugo); Gail O'Grady (Victoria); Fred Buch, Nick Stannard Stephen Geng, Jeff Moldovan, Gene Tate, Arnie Cox, Emmet Fitzsimmons.

24. "Succubus" Written by: Cary Bates. Directed by: David Nutter. Airdate: May 20, 1989.

Pamela Dare, a youth-draining crea-

ture called a succubus, masquerades as a novelist promoting her new book at Shuster. Using Lana and T.J. as bait, she hopes to steal Superboy's powers, feeding her hunger for generations to come.

GUEST CAST: Sybil Danning (Succubus); Rita Rehn, T.J. Kelly, Lee Stevens.

25. "Luthor Unleashed" Written by: Stephen Lord. Directed by: David Nutter. Airdate: May 27, 1989.

Luthor's latest criminal plot goes wrong, and Superboy comes to the rescue in the lab. Unfortunately, Superboy's aid has a side effect, making Luthor permanently bald — and quite angry with his super nemesis.

GUEST CAST: Curly Neal, Michael Manno.

SEASON TWO (1989–1990)

26. "With This Ring, I Thee Kill" Written by Fred Freiberger. Directed by David Nutter. Airdate: October 7, 1989.

Lex Luthor returns to vex Superboy after changing his appearance. He wounds Superboy and captures Lana Lang, leading to another confrontation.

GUEST CAST: Michael Manno, Douglas Brush, Kevin Corrigan, Linda Perry, Jim Greene.

27. "Lex Luthor: Sentenced to Die!" Written by: Fred Freiberger. Directed by: David Grossman. Airdate: October 14, 1989.

A wounded Superboy fights back against Lex Luthor. After his defeat by the Boy of Steel, Lex manages to escape from custody, paving the way for future battles.

GUEST CAST: Michael Manno, Douglas Brush, Kevin Corrigan, Linda Perry, Jim Greene. Tracy Roberts, Richard Lake

28. "Metallo" Written by: Michael Carlin and Andrew Helfer. Directed by: David Grossman. Airdate: October 21, 1989.

During a confrontation with Superboy, an armored car robber named Corben suffers a terrible heart attack. After escaping from the hospital, Corben is transformed into a super-villain by a mad scientist. His new heart is made of kryptonite, a substance that makes him highly dangerous to Superboy.

GUEST CAST: Michael Callan (Metallo); Paul Brown, Dave Fennel.

29. "Young Dracula" Written by: Cary Bates. Story by: Ilya Salkind and Cary Bates. Directed by: David Nutter. Airdate: October 28, 1989.

A tortured young doctor, Byron Shelly, is actually a bloodthirsty vampire. The man is desperate to lift his curse and seeks a cure, unaware that another, ancient vampire has a vested interest in him, and wants to keep him "undead."

GUEST CAST: Kevin Bernhardt (Dr. Shelley); Lloyd Bochner, Dennis Neal.

30. "Nightmare Island" Written by: Mark Jones. Directed by: David Nutter. Airdate: November 4, 1989.

A boating trip goes wrong when Clark, Lana and Andy end up stranded on a mysterious island. There they encounter a dangerous alien creature.

GUEST CAST: Phil Fondacaro.

31. "Bizarro ... The Thing of Steel" Written by: Mark Jones. Directed by: Kenneth Bowser. Airdate: November 11, 1989.

An experiment in cloning goes terribly wrong, creating a twisted, evil version of Superboy called Bizarro. When Bizarro sets his deadly sights on Lana, Clark realizes he must stop his warped duplicate; he plans to use kryptonite, which hurts him but has no effect on Bizarro.

GUEST CAST: Barry Meyers (Bizarro); Valerie Grant, Billy Flanigan, Chris Lombardi.

32. "The Battle with Bizarro" Written by: Mark Jones. Directed by: David Nutter. Airdate: November 18, 1989.

Superboy survives his encounter with kryptonite and realizes he must battle Bizarro again. Unfortunately, Bizarro is already battling the police and facing a natural end, courtesy of his defective genetic nature.

GUEST CAST: Barry Meyers (Bizzaro); Tom Norwicki, Larry Lee, John McLoughlin.

33. "Mr. and Mrs. Superboy" Written by: Dennis O'Neil. Directed by: Peter Kiwatt. Airdate November 25, 1989.

The impish creature from another dimension, Mr. Mxyzptlk, returns to Earth, seeking Superboy's help. It seems he is being pursued by a vengeful leviathan and wants to be adopted by Superboy and Lana!

GUEST CAST: Michael J. Pollard (Mr. Mxyzptlk); Richard Kiel.

34. "Programmed for Death" Written by: Cary Bates. Directed by: David Nutter. Airdate: December 2, 1989.

Andy's trouble-making father gets in deep when he becomes involved with a deadly robot called Dreadbot. Now Superboy must stop the terrifying machine before it can absorb all the city's power and become an invincible opponent.

GUEST CAST: George Maharis, Bryce Ward, Eric Whitmore.

35. "Superboy's Deadly Touch" Written by: Cary Bates. Story by: Cary Bates and Mark Jones. Directed by: Kenneth Bowser. Airdate: December 9, 1989.

Superboy falls into a trap planned by Lex Luthor. Luthor captures the Boy of Steel and augments his otherworldly powers to the point where he can no longer control them and is a danger to himself and others.

GUEST CAST: Tracy Roberts, Ken Grant, Barry Cutler.

36. "The Power of Evil" Written by: Michael Prescott. Directed by: Danny Irom. Airdate: December 24, 1989.

A formless evil from a faraway land hunts Superboy. Hiding in the body of a karate instructor, it uses the boastful and hapless Andy to get to Clark.

GUEST CAST: Keye Luke (Sensei); Michael Champlin, Bret Cipes, Jim Becke, Michael Marzello.

37. "Superboy ... Rest in Peace" Written by: Michael Maurer. Directed by: Danny Irom. Airdate: January 7, 1990.

From the distant future arrive two strange visitors with plans for Superboy. One of the travelers hopes to destroy the future Man of Steel, but the other hopes to rescue him, causing no end of confusion and trouble for Clark, Andy and Lana.

GUEST CAST: Betsy Russell, Andreas Wisniewski, Alison Dietz, John Swindells, Lamont Lofton.

38. "Super Menace!" Written by: Michael Maurer. Directed by: Richard J. Lewis. Airdate: January 14, 1990.

Superboy is adversely affected by red kryptonite, which affects his mind. The Army recruits Metallo to stop Superboy, but Metallo plots to team with the new super-villain and commit a deadly crime spree.

GUEST CAST: Michael Callan (Metallo); Jim McDonald.

39. "Yellow Peri's Spell of Doom" Written by: Mark Jones and Cary Bates. Directed by: Peter Kiwatt. Airdate: January 21, 1990.

A homely girl uses magic to raise a demon. The demon transforms her into Yellow Peri, a new super-villain, and she casts a love spell on Superboy. Realizing Lana can break the spell over the Boy of Steel, Peri plots the untimely demise of Lang.

GUEST CAST: Elizabeth Keifer, George Sattles, John Glenn Harding.

40. "Microboy" Written by: Cary Bates. Directed by: Richard J. Lewis. Airdate: January 28, 1990.

A strange new superhero called Microboy has eyes for Lana. Unfortunately, his self-made powers yield unintended side effects, and he becomes a danger to everybody around him.

GUEST CAST: Frank Military (Microboy); Tony Fabozzi, Larry Francer, Tim Powell.

41. "Run, Dracula, Run" Written by: Ilya Salkind and Cary Bates. Directed by: Richard J. Lewis. Airdate: February 4, 1990.

Dr. Shelley, a vampire, returns, still trying to conquer his vampirism. Unfortunately, his anti-serum, which prevents his evil transformation, has been stolen. Shelley turns Lana to the dark side, and she becomes a monstrous vampire.

GUEST CAST: Kevin Bernhardt (Dr. Shelley); Louise Crume, Ivan Greene, Leslie Lacey.

42. "Brimstone" Written by: Mark Carlin and Andrew Helfer. Directed by: Andrew Guttfreund. Airdate: February 11, 1990.

Superboy confronts a mysterious and evil sorcerer called Brimstone who can raise zombies and control the dead.

GUEST CAST: Philip Michael Thomas (Brimstone); Carlos Gestero, Antoni Carone, Michael Leopard.

43. "Abandon Earth" Written by: Cary Bates and Mark Jones. Directed by: Richard J. Lewis. Airdate: February 18, 1990.

Two aliens arrive on Earth, claiming to be Jor-El and Lara, Superboy's biological parents from Krypton. They hope their son will leave his adopted family and world and return with them to the stars. Clark makes an agonizing decision to leave Earth...

GUEST CAST: Britt Ekland (Lara); George Lazenby (Jor-El); Ken Grant, Emily Lester, Eric Whitmore, Bob Wells.

44. "Escape to Earth" Written by: Cary Bates and Mark Jones. Directed by: Andre Guttfreund. Airdate: February 25, 1990.

Superboy's biological parents turn out to be alien con men with villainous designs on the Boy of Steel and his friends. Unfortunately, Superboy has already left Earth behind, and now the planet is threatened by the evil aliens.

GUEST CAST: Britt Ekland (Lara); George Lazenby (Jor-El).

45. "Superstar" Written by: Toby Martin. Directed by: Ken Bowser. Airdate: March 11, 1990.

A beautiful rock star with a strange secret is nearly assassinated during a concert. Clark investigates and learns that the young woman, bent on romancing him, is actually a front for a disfigured star from years past who still wants to see her songs performed.

GUEST CAST: Ami Dolenz (Jessica James); Kimberly Bronson, Kevin Quigley, Joe Candelora, Deborah DeFrancisco.

46. "Nick Knack" Written by: Mark Jones. Directed by: David Nutter. Airdate: April 9, 1990.

A villainous inventor has devised a way to steal Superboy's powers from the Boy of Steel. He has created a mechanical suit to absorb Clark's abilities, and it looks like his plot might just work.

GUEST CAST: Gilbert Gottfried (Nick Knack); David Hauser, Andrew Clark, Donna Lee Betz.

47. "The Haunting of Andy McAlister" Written by: Andrew Helfer and Michael Carlin. Directed by: David Nutter. Airdate: April 16, 1990.

A visit to the McAlister family mansion goes horribly wrong when mystical forces materialize Billy the Kid in the present. The outlaw threatens to kill Lana and Andy, and only Clark can stop the villain before he traps Andy in another dimension.

GUEST CAST: Thomas Shuster (Billy the Kid); Dan Kamin, Fred Ornstein, Ricard Rogers, Sandy Huelsman.

48. "Revenge from the Deep" Written by: Toby Martin. Directed by: Andre Guttfreund. Airdate: April 23, 1990.

Two creatures from Atlantis carry on a war of vengeance and use Lana as a pawn in their never-ending battle. Superboy intervenes to save Lana's life, but he has not accounted for the undying hatred of the two Atlantis-dwellers.

GUEST CAST: Donatella, Michael Shaner, Steve Latshaw, Connie Adams, Steve Zurk.

49. "The Secrets of Superboy" Written by: Toby Martin and Mark Jones. Directed by: Joe Ravitz. Airdate: April 30, 1990.

Armed with a powerful brain-reading device, the crazy inventor Nick Knack plans to learn all of Superboy's secrets. He captures Lana and Andy to orchestrate his plan, but if he uses the device on them, they could die.

GUEST CAST: Gilbert Gottfried (Nick Knack); Donna Lee Betz.

50. "Johnny Casanova and the Case of Secret Serum" Written by: Ilya Salkind and Mark Jones. Directed by: David Nutter. Airdate: May 7, 1990.

A not-very-likable fellow with a crush on Lana is surprised when his crook brother gives him a serum that makes him absolutely irresistible to women. The serum works on Lana, who is unaware that its original owner wants it back.

GUEST CAST: Mark Holton (Casanova); Glenn Maska, Robert Reynolds, Steve Dash, Gregory Ashburn.

51. "The Woman Called Tiger Eye" Written by: Michael Maurer. Directed by: Andre Guttfreund. Airdate: Mary 14, 1990.

An evil sorceress named Tiger Eye believes that Superboy can help her achieve invincibility by using his powers to fuse together five powerful ancient crystals. She captures Lana and, using the young woman as bait, plans to make Superboy her slave forever.

GUEST CAST: Skye Aubrey (Tiger Eye); Erik Freeman Erik Lindshield, Tony DiMartino, Ilse Earl.

SEASON THREE (1990-1991)

52. "The Bride of Bizarro" (Parts I & II) Written by: Michael Carlin and Andrew Helfer. Directed by: David Grossman. Airdates: October 7 and October 14, 1990.

Lex Luthor revives the confused duplicate of Superboy called Bizarro and promises the lonely monster a bride: a twisted Bizarro version of Lana Lang. When his plan goes awry, Luthor plots to create a Bizarro army, with himself as the model.

GUEST CAST: Barry Meyers (Bizarro); Tracy Roberts, Shanna Tears.

53. "The Lair" Written by: Stan Berkowitz. Directed by: David Grossman. Airdate: October 21, 1990.

When Matt Ritter disappears, Superboy investigates the existence of a legendary monster near a local nuclear plant. He finds the pitiable creature and sympathizes with it, unaware that others are planning to kill the monster and show it off as a trophy.

GUEST CAST: Jordan Williams, Michael Pniewski, Antoni Corone, Tom Nowicki.

54. "Neila" Written by: Stan Berkowitz. Directed by: Mark Vargo. Airdate: October 28, 1990.

An alien queen named Neila seeks the perfect mate, believing she has found it on Earth in Superboy. Unfortunately, Superboy's heart belongs to Lana Lang, and Neila must take extraordinary steps to beat the competition and win the affection of the Boy of Steel.

GUEST CAST: Christine Moore, James Van Harper, Arnie Cox.

55. "Roads Not Taken" (Parts I & II) Written by: John Francis Moore and Stan Berkowitz. Directed by: Richard J. Lewis. Airdates: November 4 and 11, 1990.

A new device opens gateways to alternate dimensions. Superboy and Lex Luthor are both tantalized by looking at the roads they didn't take. In one case, Superboy must face off against an alternate self who has become Earth's ruthless dictator. For Lex, he realizes there is a world which he can rule...

GUEST CAST: Kenneth Shippy, Tracy Roberts, Robert Reynolds, Robert Floyd, Brian Grant, Maureen Collins, Tim Powell.

56. "The Sons of Icarus" Written by: Paul Stubenrauch. Directed by: Richard J. Lewis. Airdate: November 18, 1990.

The unexpected discovery of another man who can fly leads Clark, Lana and Matt into an investigation of an ancient cult. Were Matt's ancestors once able to fly, and, if so, what has prevented their descendents from using that gift? The answer is a terrifying one...

GUEST CAST: Brent Jennings (Teo); Lou Walker (Joseph); Alice McGill, Rob Morris, Annelle Johnson, Wayne Brady.

57. "Carnival" Written by: Toby Martin. Directed by: David Grossman. Airdate: November 25, 1990.

Something wicked this way comes. A Satanic carnival has been operating for centuries, abducting and destroying unsuspecting strangers. The carnival is run by Deville, a Satanic figure who wants Lana with him so he can destroy Superboy.

GUEST CAST: Gregg Allman, Christopher Neame, Claudia Miller, John Edward Allen, Janice Shea.

58. "Test of Time" Written by: David Gerrold. Directed by: David Hartwell. Airdate: December 2, 1990.

Evil aliens intending to conquer Earth begin experimenting on Clark, unaware that his super powers are unique to him. They warp time, making it appear to stand still, but Superboy fights back.

GUEST CAST: Eric Conger, Bryce Word, Danny Haneman.

59. "Mindscape" Written by: Michael Carlin and Andrew Helfer. Directed by: David Nutter. Airdate: December 9, 1990.

Superboy is attacked by a strange parasitic organism. It threatens his life, feeding off his biological processes and adrenaline, and all looks lost as Superboy heads for the afterlife.

GUEST CAST: Lex Luger (Superboy Mark II); Judy Clayton, Sonya Mattox, Rod Ball, Kathy Polling.

60. "Superboy ... Lost" Written by: Michael Maurer. Directed by: Richard J. Lewis. Airdate: December 16, 1990.

Struck by amnesia after his collision with an asteroid on a direct course for Earth, Superboy wanders about Florida. He befriends a woman and her son, regular folks who are being victimized by a satanic cult.

GUEST CAST: Sara Essex, Kevin Quigley, Kevin Corrigan.

61. "Special Effects" Written by: Elliott Anderson. Directed by: David Grossman. Airdate: January 5, 1991.

In a very strange case, Clark and Lana investigate the murder of a film director ... apparently by a screen monster. But is the special effects creator of the monster the real culprit of the crime?

GUEST CAST: Richard Marcus, Barry Meyers, Denise Locca, Jim Cardes, Rob Burman, Caria Kneeland, Andrea Lively, Candice Miller.

62. "Neila and the Beast" Written by: Lawrence Klavan. Directed by: Jeff Kibbee. Airdate: January 13, 1991.

The alien queen, Neila, returns for one more round with Superboy, but this time she wants his assistance. It seems her royal subjects have tired of her rule and wish her dead.

GUEST CAST: Christine Moore (Neila); Terence Jenkins, Chris McCarty, Judy Clayton, Danny Dyer.

63. "The Golem" Written by: Paul Stubenruach. Directed by: Robert Weimer. Airdate: January 20, 1991.

An old Jewish man raises a supernatural avenger — a Golem — against a group of neo–Nazis. Unfortunately, the Golem runs out of control and begins a terrible murder spree.

GUEST CAST: Paul Coufos; Brian Thompson (Golem); Chris Vance, Kristopher Kazmarek.

64. "A Day in the Double Life" Written by: Stan Berkowitz and Paul Stubenruach. Directed by: David Nutter. Airdate: January 27, 1991.

The story follows a day in the life of Clark Kent, as recorded in his journal, with a few modifications to explain his frequent transformations into the hero Superboy.

GUEST CAST: Allyce Beasly, Tom Kouchalakos, Jeff Moldovan, Billy Gillespie, Barry Cutler.

65. "Body Swap" Written by: Paul Schiffer. Directed by: David Grossman. Airdate: February 3, 1991.

Luthor and Superboy switch bodies, thanks to an experimental machine. But will Lana know the difference between hero and villain when they come calling for help?

GUEST CAST: Nathan Adler, Ken Grant, Valerie Grant, Ryan Porter, Bob Barnes, Ann Morsello.

66. "Rebirth" (Parts I & II) Written by: Paul Diamond. Directed by: Richard J. Lewis. Airdates: February 10 and 17, 1991.

A deadly accident just may be Superboy's fault, and he retreats from public life in a fit of shame and guilt. Actually, the accident was really a set-up to shake his confidence; and now, with Superboy out of the way, a gang of crooks plans a crime wave.

GUEST CAST: Gregory Millar, Michael Owens, Kevin Benton.

67. "Werewolf" Written by: Toby Martin. Directed by: Bryan Spicer. Airdate: February 24, 1991.

A woman comes to Clark with fuzzy videotape of a werewolf. Clark believes her claims of seeing the beast, and ends up fighting a lycanthrope. Unfortunately, there is more than one werewolf on the prowl…

GUEST CAST: Jay Glick, Barry Cutler, Ray Russell.

68. "People vs. Metallo" Written by: Andrew Helfer and Michael Carlin. Directed by: Richard J. Lewis. Airdate: April 8, 1991.

Metallo is on trial for his life following his evil crimes, but uses a chunk of kryptonite to turn the tables on Superboy, putting him on trial, as it were. Lana is appointed Superboy's defender in court, but who will the jury believe — Metallo or Superboy?

GUEST CAST: Michael Callan (Metallo); Janis Benson, Tim Powell, Paul Brown.

69. "Jackson and Hyde" Written by: Toby Martin. Directed by: John Huneck. Airdate: April 21, 1991.

In this modern-day case of Jekyll and Hyde, a strange elixir turns Dennis Jackson into a villainous character.

GUEST CAST: Heather Ehlers (Gail); Juice Newton, Kelly Mullis.

70. "Mine Games" Written by: Sherman Howard. Directed by: Hugh Martin. Airdate: April 28, 1991.

Superboy and Lex Luthor are trapped together in a collapsed mineshaft. Can they work together to stay alive, or will the mortal enemies end up killing one another, especially since Luthor has kryptonite at his disposal?

GUEST CAST: None.

71. "Wish for Armageddon" Written by: Gerard Christopher. Directed by: Robert Weimer. Airdate: May 5, 1991.

A Satanic agent is using an unwitting Clark as the vehicle for Armageddon, trying to foment a war between the United States and Russia. Superboy dreams of terrible deeds, and he must solve the puzzle before mankind is destroyed in a nuclear conflagration.

GUEST CAST: Robert Miano, Marc Macaula, Peter Palmer, Rebecca Staples, Louise Crume, Angie Harper.

72. "Standoff" Written by: Joseph Gunn. Directed by: John Huneck. Airdate: May 12, 1991.

While at a party at a bar with other Bureau employees, Clark is taken hostage by an armed gunman. Unfortunately, he can't get away to turn into Superboy, and the hostage situation escalates.

GUEST CAST: Tom Schuster, Philip J. Celia, Barry Cutler, Alan Landers, Ralph Wilcox, Lou Bedford.

73. "The Road to Hell" (Parts I & II) Written by: Stan Berkowitz. Directed by: David Nutter. Airdates: May 19 and 26, 1991.

Superboy arrives in an alternate dimension where he was never adopted by the Kents and never knew Lana Lang. He learns his counterpart could become the pawn of Lex Luthor if he doesn't intervene to change the timeline.

GUEST CAST: Ron Ely (Superman); Joel Carlson, Kenneth Shippy, Carla Capps, Justina Vail.

SEASON FOUR (1991-1992)

74. "A Change of Heart" (Parts I & II) Written by: Paul Stubenrauch. Directed by: David Nutter. Airdates: October 13 and 16, 1991.

Lana's new boyfriend is a terrible criminal intending to destroy Superboy. His first nefarious act is to kill Lana Lang and frame Superboy for her death.

GUEST CAST: Bill Mumy (Puck); Michael Des Barres (Verrell); Carla Copps, Frank Matthews, Bill Cordell.

75. "The Kryptonite Kid" Written by: Michael Carlin and Andrew Helfer. Directed by: Thierry Notz. Airdate: October 20, 1991.

A boy becomes a super-powered menace, "the Kryptonite Kid," when exposed to a chunk of the green rock. Now Superboy must use a double, a convict, to fight the villain and avoid the dangers of the space meteor.

GUEST CAST: Jay Underwood, David Carr, Dawn McClendon.

76. "The Basement" Written by: Toby Martin. Directed by: Hugh Martin. Airdate: October 27, 1991.

Investigating a haunted house and basement, Lana is unexpectedly possessed by an alien life form.

GUEST CAST: Cassandra Leigh Abel.

77. "Darla Goes Ballistic" Written by: Sherman Howard. Directed by: John Huneck. Airdate: November 3, 1991.

Lex's girlfriend, Darla, interferes with his latest scheme and is unexpectedly turned into a super-smart, psychic super-villain.

GUEST CAST: Tracy Roberts, Ronald Knight.

78. "Paranoia" Written by: Paul Stubenrauch. Directed by: David Nutter. Airdate: November 10, 1991.

People at the Bureau begin to react unusually to pressure, becoming paranoid and crazed. At the same time, reports of a UFO come pouring in.

GUEST CAST: Jack Larson (Lou Lamont); Noel Neill (Alexis Andrews); Jordan Williams, Kevin Corrigan, Elizabeth Fendrick, Max Brown.

79. "Know Thine Enemy" (Parts I & II) Written by: J.M. DeMatteis. Directed by: Bryan Spicer. Airdates: November 17 and 24, 1991.

Tired of pain and defeat, Lex Luthor plots to destroy the world. Superboy enters Luthor's memories to stop the villain, and he learns that Luthor was the victim of an abusive father. The only light in Luthor's life was a beloved sister ... a sister who recently died.

GUEST CAST: Jennifer Hawkins, Denise Gossett, Kathy Gustafson-Hilton, Edgar Allen Poe IV, Ryan Porter.

80. "Hell Breaks Loose" Written by: James Ponti. Directed by: Robert Weimer. Airdate: December 1, 1991.

Is the Bureau building haunted? That is Lana's conclusion when a series of supernatural events occur inside. It turns out that a long-dead musician still has a bone to pick — and a story to tell to the living.

GUEST CAST: Bever-Leigh Banfield, James Michael Detmar.

81. "Into the Mystery" Written by: J.M. DeMatteis. Directed by: John Huneck. Airdate: December 8, 1991.

Superboy is caught between two supernatural foes, his aunt Cassandra and a spirit of destruction called Azrael.

GUEST CAST: Frances Peach, Peggy O'Neal.

82. "To Be Human" (Parts I & II) Written by: J.M. DeMatteis. Directed by: John Huneck. Airdates: January 19 and 26, 1992.

Bizarro is dying and Superboy comes to his aid. He transfers some of his normal brainwaves to the abnormal clone, unaware of the consequences to himself. Soon, Superboy is weakened just as the world needs him to stop a new villain called Chaos.

GUEST CAST: Paul McCrane; Patricia Helwick; Barry Meyers (Bizarro); Leith Audrey, Russ Blackwell, Michael Monroe.

83. "West of Alpha Centauri" Written by: Mark Jones. Directed by: Jeff Kibbee. Airdate: February 2, 1992.

Superboy and Lana are transported to a prison ship where the jailed inhabitants have been awaiting liberation at the hands of a messiah just like Superboy. Superboy and Lana help the crew of the ship stop the dictatorial authorities on the vessel.

GUEST CAST: Gregory Boyd, Andrew Clark, Kevin Quigley, Darren Dollar, Angie Harper, Michael Monroe.

84. "Threesome" (Parts I & II) Written by: Stan Berkowitz. Directed by: David Nutter. Airdate: February 9 and 16, 1992.

A prison psychiatrist once rejected by Superboy plots his demise. She releases two deadly foes, Metallo and Luthor, to destroy the Boy of Steel. The villains plot to decimate Smallville by turning the peaceful town into a crime-ridden gambling haven for crooks.

GUEST CAST: Justina Vail, Michael Callan (Metallo); David Hess, Bob Barnes.

85. "Out of Luck" Written by: Sandy Fries and Richard R. Willitson. Directed by: Robert Weimer. Airdate: February 23, 1992.

Superboy unexpectedly sees a reversal of fortune, becoming a harbinger of disaster — a jinx — when affected by the curse of an ancient coin.

GUEST CAST: Pat Cupo, Jack Swanson, Sam Ayers.

86. "Where Is Superboy" Written by: Stan Berkowitz. Directed by: Robert Weimer. Airdate: March 1, 1992.

A new computer could prove the key to the ultimate mystery: who is Superboy? Obsessed with the answer to that question, Lana seeks the truth.

GUEST CAST: Brett Rice; Joe Candlora; Bob Barnes; Barry Meyers (Bizarro); Gregory Miller, Christine Moore.

87. "Cat and Mouse" Written by: Gerard Christopher. Directed by: Peter Kiwatt. Airdate: April 19, 1992.

Clark is delighted when he receives a promotion at the Bureau. Unfortunately, his new position requires a psychological evaluation, and a nosy doctor becomes convinced that Kent is hiding a big secret — which, of course, he is: the identity of Superboy.

GUEST CAST: Erin Gray (Dr. Meyers); Michael Owens; Michael Ballin; Kevin Benton; Christine Moore; Michael Des Barres (Adam).

88. "Obituary for a Superhero" Written by: Stan Berkowitz. Directed by: John Huneck. Airdate: April 26, 1992.

Superboy is dead. At least that is what the denizens of Earth believe when a video transmission captures his last moments before being destroyed by a kryptonite bomb. Luthor steps up to take responsibility for the Boy of Steel's murder, but all is not as it seems.

GUEST CAST: Bill Mumy (Puck); Barry Meyers (Bizarro); Michael Callan (Metallo); George Sarris, Jim Grimshaw.

89. "Metamorphosis" Written by: Paul Coyle. Directed by: Robert Weimer. Airdate: May 3, 1992.

The mysterious owner of a youth club uses a special potion to steal the youth of his patrons. Lana is his latest victim.

GUEST CAST: Roddy Piper (Temple); Robin O'Neil (Sasha); Stacy Black, Roger Floyd, Joe Bradley.

90. "Rites of Passage" (Parts I & II)
Written by: Michael Carlin and Andrew Helfer. Directed by: David Grossman. Airdates: May 10 and 17, 1992.

As his birthday approaches, Clark begins to lose control of his powers. He must complete a Kryptonian ritual or else risk losing his powers forever. Unfortunately, he must return to Smallville to do so, and risk exposing himself when Lana and Jackson head an investigation of the crash that brought him to Earth 20 years ago.

GUEST CAST: Richard Casey, Bob Richards.

Smallville (2001–)
LIVE-ACTION SERIES

"…[It] essentially turns Superman into just another spooked and spooky kid from *Roswell*, except *Roswell*'s obviously called Smallville here…. [T]his entire personification of Superman is so whiny and self-pitying that it's really an insult to the comic book mythology…. Executive producers Alfred Gough and Miles Millar are so busy pandering to the WB's adolescent audience that they have robbed Superman of the qualities that made him super…. *Lois & Clark* had fun with the Superman character, but *Smallville* just flattens and trashes it."
— Tom Shales, *The Washington Post*: "*Smallville*: Superman's Tiresome Teen Years," October 16, 2001, page C01.

"For what it is — one more semi–soap opera about beautiful teens with self-esteem troubles — *Smallville* is well produced, and boasts some impressive special effects in its pilot episode. Ultimately, though, the familiarity of the story might work against the show."
— Steven Oxman, *Variety*: "*Smallville*," October 15, 2001, page 46,

"…[It] might turn out to be more than just another tale of tormented teens…"
— Doug Nye, "*Knight-Ridder/Tribune News Service*: "*Smallville* Premiering Tuesday Night on WB," October 12, 2001, page K7132.

"I like the actors. Rosenbaum is fantastic. What he brings to Lex Luthor is amazing, revealing the character as he grows darker. It's like the Anakin Skywalker story but better, because Rosenbaum can act. At first, the series was so formulaic that it was actually difficult to watch, but as *Smallville* develops and does more character-based shows, it improves. I would love to see Welling in a Superman suit, just to see how he plays it. He looks more like Superman than anybody since Christopher Reeve."

— Howard Margolin, host of *Destinies: The Voice of Science Fiction.*

CAST: Tom Welling (Clark Kent); Kristin Kreuk (Lana Lang); Michael Rosenbaum (Lex Luthor); Annette O'Toole (Martha Kent); John Schneider (Jonathan Kent); Sam Jones, III (Pete Ross); Allison Mack (Chloe Sullivan). FIRST SEASON ONLY: Eric Johnson (Whitney Ellsworth). SECOND SEASON ONLY: John Glover (Lionel Luthor).

CREW: *Producer:* Tim Iaocafano. *Executive Producers:* David Nutter, Alfred Gough, Miles Millar, Mike Tollin, Brian Robbins, Joe Davola. *Superman Created by:* Jerry Siegel and Joe Shuster. *Developed for Television by:* Alfred Gough, Miles Millar. *Associate Producer:* Tim Scanlan. *Directors of Photography (various episodes):* Attila Szalay, Peter Wunstorf. *Production Designer:* Bernard Hides. *Editors (various episodes):* David Ekstrom, Stephen Mark, Ron Spang. *Music:* Mark Snow. *First Assistant Director:* Jack Hardy. *Second Assistant Director:* Roger Russell. *Visual Effects Supervisor:* Elan Soltes. *Executive in Charge of Casting:* Barbara Miller. *Set Decorator:* Andrea French. *Property Master:* Wayne McGlaughlin. *Costume Designer:* Jenni Gullet. *Costume Supervisor:* L. Shane Deschamps. *Make-up Artist:* Lisa Love. *Hairstylist:* Anji Bemben. *Post-production Supervisor:* Tom Flores. *Post-production Coordinator:* Erika L. Johnson. *Sound Mixer:* Patrick Ramsey. *Re-Recording Mixers:* Dan Hiland, Gary D. Rogers. *Music Editor:* Chris McGeary. *Supervising Sound Mixer:* Mike Lawrence. *Based on DC Comics Characters. Color by:* Rainmaker Laboratory. For Warner Brothers Television.

SEASON ONE (2001-2002)

1. "Smallville" (70 minutes) Written by: Alfred Gough and Miles Millar. Directed by: David Nutter. Airdate: October 16, 2001.

In October of 1989, an alien spacecraft and a slew of meteors strike the tiny town of Smallville, Kansas, killing the parents of three-year-old Lana Lang and frying the red crop of hair right off of young millionaire Lex Luthor. Farmers Martha and Jonathan Kent meet and adopt the spacecraft's lone occupant, a humanoid boy. In 2001, that boy, Clark Kent, is an angst-ridden teenager with a crush on Lana and a desire to play on the high school football team. One day, Clark survives a car wreck with Lex Luthor, pulling the rich boy from his sinking automobile, and becomes aware that he has super powers unlike any human being on Earth. Meanwhile, a boy named Jeremy Creek, who was strung up like a scarecrow in a cornfield twelve years ago, comes out of a coma and kills those who humiliated him, utilizing his own super, electrically-based powers. When Clark becomes aware of his special powers, his father reveals Clark's alien origin and shows him his recovered spaceship, hidden in the Kent farm storm cellar. Lex saves Clark from becoming the football team's newest scarecrow, and Clark races to confront Jeremy before he kills everyone, including Lana, at the homecoming dance.

GUEST CAST: John Glover (Mr. Luthor); Sarah Jane Redmond (Lana Lang's aunt); Adrian McMorran, Jade Unterman, Malkolm Albuquerque, Matthew Munn, Dee Jay Jackson, Alvin Sanders, Steve Bacic, Justin Chatwin, Wendy Chmelaus Kas, Dan Odberg, Jay Kirby, Amy Esterle.

2. "Metamorphosis" Written by: Alfred Gough and Miles Millar. Directed by: Michael Watkins and Philip Sgriccia. Airdate: October 23, 2001.

A bug-loving teenager named Greg has become obsessed with Lana Lang, even videotaping her on prom night. Late one night, his kryptonite-irradiated insect collection breaks out of its cage and swarms around him, transforming him into Smallville's latest super villain. This "Bug Boy" orchestrates a car accident for Lana's boyfriend, Whitney, but Clark rescues him prior to his car's fiery explosion. When Luthor gives Kent Lana's necklace, Clark begins to recognize his unusual allergy to the meteor rocks (kryptonite). Meanwhile, Greg eats his mother and tries to mate with Lana, but Clark battles Bug Boy at the Creekside Foundry.

GUEST CAST: Chad E Donella (Greg); Gabrielle Rose (Greg's Mother).

3. "Hothead" Written by: Greg Walker. Directed by: Greg Beeman. Airdate: October 30, 2001.

Coach Walt of Smallville High has been anticipating the two-hundredth football win of his team, the Smallville Crows, and celebrating his legacy by taking saunas with kryptonite-laced rocks, a habit that has given him the power to telepathically generate fires. Coach Walt recruits Clark for the team, even though his father is dead set against it, fearing someone could be hurt by Clark's super powers. When the school principal threatens to suspend Coach Walt for helping the team cheat on exams, the coach tries to burn him up. After saving the principal, Clark must rescue Chloe when the coach strikes back at her for reporting on the cheating scandal in the school newspaper, the *Smallville Torch*.

GUEST CAST: John Glover (Mr. Luthor); Dan Lauria (Coach Walt Arnold); Sarah-Jane Redmond (Aunt Nell); Hiro Kanawaga (Principal Kwan); Jason Connery, David Paetkau, Allan Franz, Jada Stark.

4. "X-Ray" Written by: Mark Verheiden. Directed by: James Frawley. Airdate: November 6, 2001.

A dangerous shape-shifter is on the loose in Smallville just as Clark begins to experience painful flashes of x-ray vision.

The shape shifter is Tina Grier, a friend of Lana's who is jealous of Lana's life and so impersonates such people as Lex Luthor and Clark Kent. After killing her mother, Tina plots to replace Lana and lead her "perfect" life with money stolen from Smallville's bank. Tina locks Lana in a crypt, then dukes it out with Clark; until finally the young Kent must focus his x-ray vision to save the love of his life.

GUEST CAST: Sarah-Jane Redmond (Aunt Nell); Annabel Kershaw, Mark McConchie, Brian Jensen, Mitch Kosterman.

5. "Cool" Written by: Michael Green. Directed by: Jim Contner. Airdate: November 13, 2001.

Football star Sean Kelvin emerges from an accident at Crater Lake with the urge to suck the heat out of objects and people. Meanwhile, Lex challenges Clark to ask Lana to a Radiohead concert, and she accepts the invitation. But on the way to the show, Clark learns that Sean Kelvin, desperate to stay warm, has set his sights on Chloe. Clark rescues his friend and tracks the iceman to Lex's expansive estate, as the young millionaire offers Clark's parents a way to save their ailing farm.

GUEST CAST: Michael Coristine (Sean Kelvin); Tania Saulnier, Elizabeth McLaughlin, Ted Garcia.

6. "Hourglass" Written by: Doris Egan. Directed by: Chris Long. Airdate: November 20, 2001.

Clark, Lana and Pete Ross elect to spend their required 30 hours of community service at the Smallville Nursing Home. There Clark reads to a blind old seer named Cassandra while Lana tends to Mr. Volk, a nasty old man with a strange history. When Volk falls into a kryptonite-laden lake, he miraculously reverts in age to become a young man, and picks up his old hobby as a murderer. Volk sets out to kill the descendents of those who ended his career as a pi-

anist 60 years earlier, and Clark must intercept him, even if it means placing his own family in peril. Meanwhile, old Cassandra has a terrifying vision of Lex Luthor's future.

GUEST CAST: George Murdock (Mr. Harry Volk); Eric Christian Olsen (Young Harry Volk); Jackie Burroughs (Cassandra Carver); Lisa Calder, Alf Humphreys, Mitchell Kosterman, Reg Tupper, Lois Dellar.

7. "Cravings" Written by: Michael Green. Directed by: Philip Sgricca. Airdate: December 4, 2001.

As Lana's elaborate birthday party at the Luthor estate nears, Chloe's overweight friend, Jody, downs a kryptonite shake and drops her unwanted pounds overnight. She and Pete Ross plan to go the party together, but Jody's new weight-loss program causes her to binge uncontrollably. Jody's hunger pangs grow until soon she's devouring road kill and fellow students to feed her strange metabolism. On the night of the big party, Jody's hunger pangs strike again, forcing her to view Pete as her next meal, and Clark to miss his big night as Lana's escort.

GUEST CAST: Amy Adams (Jody Melville); Sarah-Jane Redmond (Aunt Nell); Joe Morton (Dr. Steve Hamilton); Malcolm Stewart.

8. "Jitters" Written by: Cherie Bennett, Jeff Gottesfeld. Directed by: Michael Watkins. Airdate: December 11, 2001.

Earl, a former worker at Luthor Corp. in Smallville, returns to Metropolis but suffers terrible spasms of pain. Meanwhile, the Kents go out to Metropolis to celebrate their anniversary, and Clark throws a party at the house. Earl, an old friend of the Kents, seeks Clark's help in dealing with his condition, a trail that leads back to the mysterious Level 3 of Luthor Corp.'s Smallville fertilizer plant. Earl holds a group of Clark's peers hostage until Luthor Corp. reveals the existence of the secret wing.

GUEST CAST: Tony Todd (Earl Jenkins); John Glover (Lionel Luthor); Robert Wisden (Gabe Sullivan).

9. "Rogue" Written by: Mark Verheiden. Directed by: David Carson. Airdate: January 15, 2002.

On a visit to the Metropolis Museum, Clark is spotted stopping a city bus from killing a hapless hobo. Unfortunately, the witness to his act is a crooked cop named Sam Phalen, a blackmailer who wants Clark to do a job for him in exchange for keeping Clark's secret. When Clark double crosses Phalen, the cop retaliates by framing Kent for murder and forcing Clark to steal a priceless armor vest worn by Alexander the Great. Meanwhile, in Smallville, an old flame, Victoria Hardwick, visits Lex, and Chloe is fired from the *Torch* and replaced by Lana Lang!

GUEST CAST: Kelly Brook (Victoria Hardwick); Cameron Dye (Sam Phalen); Hiro Kanawaga (Principal Kwan); Mitchell Kosterman, Dann Wattley, Costa Spangs, J.B. Bivens.

10. "Shimmer" Written by: Michael Green and Mark Verheiden. Directed by: D.J. Caruso. Airdate: January 31, 2002.

Amy, the daughter of Luthor's housekeeper, has developed a crush on Lex, as well as a hatred of his girlfriend, Victoria. As a result of exposure to kryptonite, an assailant can become invisible and is using the power to attack Victoria, who has been secretly sabotaging Lex's company files. But the assailant isn't the lovestruck Amy, it's her unbalanced brother, Jeff!

GUEST CAST: John Glover (Mr. Luthor); Kelly Brook (Victoria Hardwick); Sarah-Jane Redmond (Aunt Nell); Jesse Hutch, Kett Turton, Glynis Davies, Azura Skye, Brenda M. Crichlow.

11. "Hug" Written by: Doris Egan. Directed by: Chris Long. Airdate: February 5, 2002.

Two denizens of Smallville have been exposed to the meteor rocks, granting them the power to hypnotize others. One man, bearing a grudge against Lex, tries to buy the Kent farm from Jonathan, using his powers. Then he hypnotizes Lex into wanting to kill Clark. Ultimately, the other man with the same powers may be the only one who can stop the reign of terror.

GUEST CAST: Kelly Brook (Victoria); Rick Peters, Gregory Sporleder.

12. "Leech" Written by: Tim Schlattmann. Directed by: Greg Beeman. Airdate: February 12, 2002.

Clark loses his powers to a nerdy boy named Eric during a lightning storm. As Clark adjusts to nosebleeds, fatigue, cramps, and other facets of normal life, Eric utilizes his newfound strength to fight back against an abusive science teacher. When Eric stops a purse snatcher, he becomes known in town as "Superboy," making Clark wonder if he should have revealed his powers to the world when he had them. Meanwhile, Victoria betrays Lex in an attempt to bring down his father's company. Hoping to get his powers back, Clark realizes that the only thing that can stop Eric is the weakness that once vexed him: meteor rocks.

GUEST CAST: Kelly Brook (Victoria); Tom O'Brien (Nixon); Sarah-Jane Redmond (Aunt Nell); Shawn Ashmore (Eric Sommers); William Samples, Will Sanderson, Ashley Presidente, Julian Christopher, Mitchell Kosterman.

13. "Kinetic" Written by: Philip Levens. Directed by: Robert Singer. Airdate: February 26, 2002.

Three young crooks who can pass through walls (thanks to a metabolism sped up by meteor rock tattoos) rob the Luthor estate. In the execution of the heist, Chloe, there to interview Luthor, is injured when she falls from a high window. Clark blames himself for not being able to save her in time, and investigates the crime. The young thugs learn from a stolen disk that Luthor is skimming from his Dad to finance a special project in Smallville involving a particle accelerator, and they blackmail him to keep it quiet. Meanwhile, a despondent

Whitney, who has lost his football scholarship, is recruited unwittingly into the gang and initiated with a kryptonite tattoo of his own.

GUEST CAST: David Lovgren, Kavan Smith, David Coles, Kwesi Ameyaw.

14. "Zero" Written by: Mark Verheiden. Directed by: Michael Katleman. Airdate: March 12, 2002.

Years ago, something terrible went down at the ritzy Metropolis club called Club Zero involving a young and reckless Lex Luthor. Now someone seeking vengeance for that act is resurrecting the past to complicate matters for Luthor. Meanwhile, Chloe learns that Clark's adoption by the Kents was not exactly by the book, and begins to dig deeper.

GUEST CAST: Cameron Dye, Corin Nemec, Judy Tyler.

15. "Nicodemus" Written by: Michael Green. Directed by: James Marshall. Airdate: March 19, 2002.

After an accident on the road with a paranoid man, Jonathan Kent is exposed to a strange plant that alters his behavior. Soon Lana is also sprayed by the flower, and the mist changes her into a more lusty, aggressive character, just like Clark's sick dad. Lex learns that Dr. Hamilton, under his employ, has resurrected a "nicodemus" plant — which once reared its head in the 1870s and nearly destroyed the town.

GUEST CAST: Hiro Kanagawa (Principal Kwan); Joe Morton (Dr. Hamilton); Bill Monday, Julian Christopher.

NOTE: As Jonathan Kent is run off the road in his pick-up truck in the opening shots of this episode, his radio plays the theme from *Dukes of Hazzard*. Of course, John Schneider (Kent) was one of the leads on that series, twenty years before *Smallville*.

16. "Stray" Written by: Philip Levens. Directed by: Paul Shapiro. Airdate: April 16, 2002.

While driving home at night, Mrs. Kent accidentally strikes a young boy on the road as he flees from two robbers who have committed a murder. After learning that the boy, Ryan, has amnesia, the Kents invite him to stay at their farm. Meanwhile, Lex is offered a position at his dad's side in Metropolis. Later, the robbers/murderers track Ryan, who seems to have telepathic abilities, to Smallville.

GUEST CAST: John Glover (Mr. Luthor); Ryan Kelley (Ryan); Jim Shield (Stepfather); Brandy Ledford, Rekha Sharma, Bill Finck, Joe Maffei, Courtney Kramer, Jayme Knox, Shelley Adam.

17. "Reaper" Written by: Cameron Litvack. Directed by: Terrence O'Hara. Airdate: April 23, 2002.

Dominic Senatori, an employee of Lex Corp., arrives in Smallville to investigate Lex's activities, including his spending on a project profiling Clark and the Kent family. At the same time, another visitor in town, Tyler Randall, uses his meteor rock–spawned ability to kill people with a touch that turns people to ashes. Meanwhile, Whitley's dad has a devastating heart attack, and Tyler plans to bring peace to the ailing man.

GUEST CAST: John Glover (Mr. Luthor); Reynaldo Rosales (Tyler Randall); Jason Connery (Dominic Senatori); Sheila Moore (Mrs. Sykes); Tiffany Knight, Brian Drummond, Patrick Keating, Ralph Alderman, Dale Wilson.

18. "Drone" Written by: Michael Greene and Philip Leven. Directed by: Michael Katleman. Airdate: April 30, 2002.

A student running for class president is attacked by killer bees, and Peter convinces Clark to seek the office. Meanwhile, a sexy reporter tries to seduce Lex into giving her an interview. Another candidate for class president, an unpopular girl, has the ability to make bees do her bidding. After disposing of another candidate, Felice, the bee girl goes after Clark and nearly kills Mrs. Kent.

GUEST CAST: Hiro Kanawaga (Principal Kwan); Marguerite Moreau, Shonda Farr, Chelan Simmons, Simon Wong.

19. "Crush" Written by: Philip Levens, Alfred Gough, Miles Millar. Directed by: James Marshall. Airdate: May 7, 2002.

A young artist named Justin has lost his ability to draw because of a hit-and-run accident, and develops murderous psychic powers. Frustrated with Clark's romantic indecision, Chloe goes out with Justin, unaware of the danger he poses. Meanwhile, the nurse that cared for Lex during his mother's terminal illness visits Smallville seeking forgiveness for leaving the family nine years earlier. When Justin learns that Principal Kwan may have been the hit-and-run driver that injured him, he attacks, and Clark must stop him.

GUEST CAST: John Glover (Mr. Luthor); Adam Brody (Justin Gaines); Hiro Kanagawa (Principal Kwan); Donna Bullock (Pamela Jenkins); James Purcell, Kevan Ohtsui, Anaya Farrell, Catherine Barroll, Serge Houde.

20. "Obscura" Written by: Michael Green, Mark Verheiden. Story by: Greg Walker. Directed by: Terrence O'Hara. Airdate: May 14, 2002.

After being injured in a gas pipe explosion, Lana develops psychic powers just in time to experience a vision of Chloe being abducted from the hospital parking lot by a masked assailant. While Clark worries about the missing Chloe (now his girlfriend), Lex investigates the meteor shower that brought Clark to Earth. Clark rescues Chloe, and the masked murderer turns his attentions to Lana, who is seeing through his eyes. Meanwhile, Lex finds a piece of alien alloy in the field where Clark's spaceship crashed all those years ago.

GUEST CAST: Robert Wisden (Mr. Sullivan); Joe Morton (Dr. Hamilton); Tom O'Brien, Darrin Klimek, Aaron Douglas.

21. "Tempest" Written by: Alfred Gough and Miles Millar. Story by: Philip Levens. Directed by: Greg Beeman. Airdate: May 21, 2002.

A twister barrels into town, turning Smallville upside down. After saying goodbye to Whitney, off to join the marines, Lana is run off the road by the twister. At the Kent farm, Jonathan grapples with nosy reporter Roger Nixon in the basement, even as the tornado touches down. At the Luthor Estate, Lex and Lionel are also imperiled. Clark leaves a despondent Chloe at the dance to save Lana.

GUEST CAST: John Glover (Lionel Luthor); Tom O'Brien (Nixon); Robert Wisden (Mr. Sullivan).

SEASON TWO (2002-2003)

22. "Vortex" Written by: Philip Levens. Story by: Alfred Gough and Miles Millar. Directed by: Greg Beeman.

Tornadoes have struck Smallville, and Clark rescues Lana from the twisters. Meanwhile, nosy reporter Roger Nixon and Mr. Kent are trapped in a crypt together, and at the Luthor estate, Lex's dad is badly injured. A spot of meteor rocks and a motor home lined with lead prevent Clark from locating and rescuing his father. Lex shoots Nixon when the reporter attempts to kill Mr. Kent, ending the threat to Clark's secret. Meanwhile, the tornado has carried away Clark's spaceship.

GUEST CAST: Tom O'Brien (Roger Nixon); Rekha Sharma, Julian Christopher, Jerry Wasserman, Mitchell Kosterman.

23. "Heat" Written by: Mark Verheiden. Directed by: James Marshall. Airdate: October 1, 2002.

Everybody returns to Smallville High in September, and Lex's new fiancée, Desiree Atkins, is also Clark's substitute biology teacher. But there's more to this woman than meets the eye. She exudes a powerful pheromone that affects Lex and spurs the development of Clark's newest power: heat vision. Atkins tries to seduce Clark, but he is immune, so she seduces Jonathan Kent and orders him to kill Lex so she will inherit his wealth.

GUEST CAST: Krista Allen (Desiree Atkins); Shawn Reis, Mitchell Kosterman.

24. "Duplicity" Written by: Todd Slavkin and Darren Swimmer. Directed by: Steve Miner. Airdate: October 8, 2002.

Peter stumbles upon a car accident in a cornfield, and then discovers Clark's lost spaceship close by. He asks Clark to help him move the ship to his tool shed, unaware that the deranged Dr. Hamilton, terminally ill from exposure to the meteorites, is also desperately looking for the alien artifact. Clark tells Pete the truth about the spaceship and his own extraterrestrial origin, and Pete is upset — not because of the truth, but because Clark didn't trust him enough to tell him sooner. Later, while Lex deals with his blind father, Hamilton kidnaps Pete and tries to get the boy to reveal the secrets of the spaceship.

GUEST CAST: Joe Morton (Dr. Steven Hamilton); Sarah-Jane Redmond (Aunt Nell); Andrew Jackson, Michael Kopsa.

25. "Red" Written by: Jeph Loeb. Directed by: Jeff Woolnough. Airdate: October 15, 2002.

Clark buys an expensive class ring that has a red meteor rock doubling as the ruby, only to find that the stone is altering his personality. Clark's parents write off his odd behavior as teenage rebellion as he makes advances towards Lana and goes on a spending spree with the Kents' credit card. The red meteor rocks (red kryptonite) even causes Clark to alienate his friends at school and he plans to leave Smallville permanently, using his powers to make it big. The rock also causes Clark to expose a relocated member of the witness protection program

and his trouble-making daughter, Jessie, both of whom are being hunted by a corrupt U.S. marshal.

GUEST CAST: Sara Downing (Jessie Brooks); Michael Tomlinson (Mr. Brooks); Garwin Sanford.

26. "Nocturne" Written by: Brian Peterson and Kelly Souder. Directed by: Rick Wallace. Airdate: October 22, 2002.

Lana receives love poems from a secret admirer, and Clark becomes jealous. The poet is Byron Moore, a lonely boy held captive in his dark basement by his father. Lana and Clark try to help Byron but are shocked to learn that the boy was reported dead eight years ago. The truth is more complicated: Byron transforms into a super-powered monster by daylight because of a special drug therapy once administered by a company called Metron. The beast within Byron, a challenge to Clark's strength, goes after Lionel Luthor, the man who shut down all hope of finding an antidote to his condition, and nearly kills Martha Kent, who has taken a job working for the blind elder Luthor.

GUEST CAST: Sean Faris (Byron Moore); Gwynyth Walsh (Mrs. Moore); Richard Moll (Mr. Moore); Mitchell Kosterman.

27. "Redux" Written by: Russel Friend and Garrett Lerner. Directed by: Chris Long. Airdate: October 29, 2002.

Smallville's swim champ ages suddenly, dying during swimming practice. Meanwhile, the new high school principal, Mr. Reynolds, takes out his dislike of Lex Luthor on Clark. At the Kent farm, Jonathan is angry when Martha summons her estranged father to help save the struggling farm. At school, a cheerleader named Chrissie continues to suck the life out of more high school boys.

GUEST CAST: Maggie Lawson (Kristin "Chrissie" Parker); George Coe (Grandpa); Richard Gant (Mr. Reynolds); Sarah-Jane Redmond (Nell); Jesse Hutch, Fulvio Cecere, Neil Grayston.

28. "Lineage" Written by Kenneth Biller. Story by: Alfred Gough and Miles Millar. Directed by: Greg Beeman. Airdate: November 5, 2002.

A woman named Rachel Dunlevy arrives in town claiming to be Clark's biological mother, and promptly sets out to insinuate herself into his life. Furthermore, she claims to be the ex-mistress of Lionel Luthor, and that Clark is Lex's half-brother! Meanwhile, Lana traces her own lineage, hoping to reconnect with a man, Henry Small, that she suspects may be her biological father. Dunlevy abducts Lex to make his dad reveal the truth she wants to hear.

GUEST CAST: Patrick Cassidy (Henry Small); Blair Brown (Rachel Dunlevy); Mitchell Kosterman, Malkolm Albuquerque, Angela Moore, Matthew Nunn, Shelly Schiavoni.

29. "Ryan" Written by: Philip Levens. Directed by: Terrence O'Hara. Airdate: November 12, 2002.

The young psychic boy who knows Clark's secret, Ryan, is being held against his will at a scientific institute in Metropolis under the cruel care of the evil Dr. Garner. Meanwhile, Smallville's corrupt Mayor hits Lex up for funding, and Nell plans to move Lana to Metropolis to be with Nell and her new boyfriend, Dean. Clark races to Metropolis and breaks Ryan out of the lab, but their happy reunion is short-lived when it is revealed that Ryan has a terminal brain tumor.

GUEST CAST: Ryan Kelley (Ryan James); Martin Cummins (Dr. Garner); Sarah-Jane Redmond (Aunt Nell); William B. Davis (Mayor Tate); Mitchell Kosterman, Mark Gibson, Michael St. John Smythe.

NOTE: "Ryan" represents an interesting historical artifact for fans of the horror and science fiction genres on TV. It pits the regulars of *Smallville*, including Lex Luthor, against the villainous Cigarette Smoking Man (William B.

Davis) of *The X-Files*, the evil Ames White (Martin Cummins) of *Dark Angel*, and even *Millennium*'s femme-fatale and recurring *Smallville* guest, Sarah-Jane Redmond.

30. "Dichotomy" Written by: Mark Verheiden. Directed by: Craig Zisk. Airdate: November 19, 2002.

An enterprising sophomore, Ian Randall, wants to win the Lex Foundation scholarship at all costs, and goes to murderous lengths to get it. But smart Ian has a particularly devilish secret: he can split into two physical entities on occasion, like the time he wants to romance Lana and Chloe simultaneously. Meanwhile, Lex courts a doctor who is treating Jonathan Kent for a broken leg after an accident on the farm. While Clark tries to expose Ian, the boy and his double plot to toss Chloe and Lana off the Smallville dam for discovering his secret.

GUEST CAST: Jonathan Taylor Thomas (Ian Randall); Emmanuelle Vaugier (Dr. Bryce); Robert Wisden (Mr. Sullivan); Serge Houde, David Richmond-Peck.

31. "Skinwalker" Written by: Brian Peterson and Kelly Souders. Story by: Mark Warshaw. Directed by: Marita Grabiak. Airdate: November 26, 2002.

While mountain biking with Pete, Clark falls into a hidden Native American cave under a Luthor Corp. construction site and discovers cave paintings that foretell his arrival — a messiah's arrival. Clark grows close to Kyla, a young Indian woman sworn to preserve the ancient pictographs, and she learns his secret, thinking him the god Neman. But Kyla's tribe also has a history of lycanthropy, of "skin-walking," that could explain the strange murder of Lionel Luthor's construction foreman. When a wolf tries to kill Martha, also working for Lionel, Clark suspect that Kyla may know the truth about her tribe, and may be involved in murder.

GUEST CAST: Patrick Cassidy (Mr. Small); Tamara Feldman (Kyla); Gordon Tootoosis (Joseph Willowbrook); Mitchell Kosterman, Rob Morton, Michael Tiernan.

Supergirl

Kara, the Girl of Steel, landed on Earth in 1959 (in DC's *Adventure Comics*), shortly after the demise of *The Adventures of Superman* on television. Like her cousin, Kal-El, Supergirl hailed from the destroyed planet Krypton, donned a colorful yellow, blue and red suit (with a skirt), and possessed a variety of super powers, thanks to Earth's yellow sun. Kara, created by Otto Binder, also took up a secret human identity, that of Midwestern orphan Linda Lee, and soon began fighting crime from Midvale. She appeared in her own book, *The Daring New Adventures of Supergirl*, soon after her first appearance, which ended, ultimately, in her demise.[1]

Since then, Supergirl has been resurrected and killed off again, this time in the mid–1980s in the DC series *Crisis on Infinite Earths*, which attempted to put the baffling and contradictory DC timeline into a coherent new form. But, like all superheroes, Kara has never stayed dead for long. In 1984 the producers of the *Superman* film series, Ilya and Alexander Salkind, launched a big-budget adaptation of the comic heroine. This was a necessity if they wanted their successful (and profitable) movie line to continue after the poorly received *Superman III*, because Christopher Reeve had made the Sean Connery-esque promise that he would never play the Man of Steel again. When he was given a hand in the next film's story development, the actor relented and starred in *Superman IV: The Quest for Peace*; but for 1984, at least, a new leading character was required to continue the adventure.

Young Helen Slater (*The Secret of My Success* [1987], *City Slickers* [1991]) was cast as Kara/Linda Lee/Supergirl in the motion picture, directed by Jeannot Szwarc (*The*

Bug [1975], *Jaws II* [1979] and *Somewhere in Time* [1980]). "I wanted a girl who was sensitive, who had natural grace, intelligence and beauty — the kind of beauty that grows on you," he told interviewer Adam Pirani in *Starlog* magazine.[2] He found those qualities in the all–American, lovely Slater, an actress with twinkling eyes, a dancer's physique and an innocent charm.

Casting an unknown performer in the leading role had worked well with *Superman: The Movie*, in no small part because the supporting roles were filled by the impressive likes of Gene Hackman, Marlon Brando and Glenn Ford. *Supergirl* followed carefully in the same footsteps, casting Peter O'Toole as an Argo City resident named Zoltar, and Faye Dunaway as the film's nefarious villain, the witch named Selena. Just as Ned Beatty provided bumbling support to Hackman as Otis in *Superman: The Movie* and *Superman II*, comedienne Brenda Vaccaro played second fiddle to Dunaway in the distaff version.

Unfortunately, the big-budget ($50 million) *Supergirl* proved something of a bomb when released in 1984, and critics out-and-out hated the picture. An objective viewing nearly twenty years later reveals that Slater's performance, though naïve, is not lacking charm. Her first scene on Earth, a flying ballet near a wooded beach, is both whimsical and lyrical, a graceful dance that outdoes many of the flying scenes in the *Superman* film series. For once, the audience really feels the joy in such flight — the fun, the total freedom — and the resulting scene works as powerful wish fulfillment.

Other than those elements, however, the picture really was a botch job, teetering on camp for much of its running time. Considering the participation of the Salkinds, *Supergirl's* lack of internal consistency with the *Superman* pictures remains nothing short of startling. The production design is just one example. The Argo City interiors look cheap, oddly organic and made out of drapes of plastic sheeting. They do not at all resemble the elegant and otherwordly crystalline technology of Richard Donner's impressive Krypton from *Superman: The Movie.*

Furthermore, the script never establishes Linda Lee as a genuine hero, one to be admired. The set-up of the story, for example, involves the naïve girl causing a power unit, the Omegahedron, to become lost, thereby threatening the safety of her world and thousands of lives. This would be like Buffy accidentally misplacing a nuclear reactor and threatening everybody in Sunnydale.

Naturally, Kara heads to Earth to recover the im-

Kara (Helen Slater) is Kal-El's cousin and the Girl of Steel in *Supergirl* (1984).

portant item, which has landed in a plate of potato salad, but then is distracted by her new powers for the better part of the film's running time. She plays with her powers on a beach, signs up at a local girl's school, and falls in love with a lawn boy. The movie fails to establish any sense of urgency or danger whatsoever. Unseen from the prologue, those poor souls in Argo City just wait silently in invisible danger, seemingly forgotten by their champion.

In *Superman: The Movie,* the audience followed Clark Kent from boyhood to adolescence to adulthood, but Donner's exem-

plary film did not introduce the menace of Gene Hackman's Lex Luthor until late in the film, when such a villain was needed. *Supergirl* makes the fatal mistake of establishing a deadly threat in its first few minutes and then virtually ignoring it for the first hour as secret identities are forged, relationships commenced, and strategies plotted. The result is a genuine impatience with the movie when one should have felt swept away by the narrative instead.

Also, the 1984 *Supergirl* film, produced well before *Buffy the Vampire Slayer, Dark Angel, Witchblade* or any other contemporary female superhero effort, was very sexist in concept. Supergirl and Selena did not clash over stolen nuclear missiles, a deadly computer that could control the weather, or even world peace. What *did* they fight over? A man! They first engaged one another over the affections of Hart Bochner's dim Ethan, a hunky gardener. Two women could not possibly fight over more important things, right? It had to be the affection of a good-looking man? He was not even a smart or witty man, just a handsome one. That insulting plot point practically begged this superhero film not to be taken seriously.

The rest of the movie was not much better and meandered badly, with too many narrative contrivances. Supergirl and the Omegahedron just happened to land in a town where Lois Lane's sister lived and Selena was doing her villainous thing. (At least Clark moved from Smallville to Metropolis before encountering the evil Luthor.) And of all the landing sites on Earth, the Omnegahedron just happened to fall into the hands of an arch-criminal who understood what it could be made to do.

Another gaffe in logic: Supergirl fell through the trap floor in Selena's fortress, but chose not to fly, or even levitate to escape the trap. What's the use of super powers if you forget to use them in a crisis?

Bungled continuity? That's here too. In one early scene Lucy Lane told Linda Lee, "Sometimes, I can't figure you out," as if they've been best friends for years; but Linda had only been on the planet for a few days. Such gaffes stem from an inadequate screenplay by David Odell.

Despite the many and sundry problems dragging *Supergirl* to new super-lows, the Phantom Zone was well depicted on screen as a sooty, smoky wasteland. In the comics its denizens were supposed to be "formless forever" (i.e. phantoms), but the film's approach — a very inhospitable world — was probably more cinematic than non-corporeality. If only it looked more like real outdoor terrain rather than a carefully constructed interior set...

Since 1984 there have been no further adventures of *Supergirl*, at least not yet, but the film has been released in a longer, directors-cut DVD. The newer "international" version makes a bit more sense than the theatrical cut, but is still uncomfortably "girlish" and light-hearted in its approach, a condescending, cute little joke that might instead have made a powerful entry in a new super-franchise.

Supergirl (1984)
LIVE-ACTION FILM

"[It] ... has the impressive special effects and spectacle of the Christopher Reeve movies but verges lots closer to all-out camp than those films did. Fortunately, writer David Odell's dialogue has lots of spark and director Jeannot Szwarc never goes over the edge.... With her outrageous panache, Dunaway more than earns her top billing, but Slater has a naturalness and poise that suggests that she has a future beyond *Supergirl*."
　　—Kevin Thomas, *The Los Angeles Times*,
　　　　　　　　　　　November 21, 1984.

"The sets and special effects are as tacky as ever, while Jeannot Szwarc's direction is notable chiefly for his botching of the set piece of urban mayhem that Richard Lester would have realized with an elegant lightness of touch."
　　—Sheila Johnson, *Monthly Film Bulletin*,
　　　　　　　　　　　July 1984, page 213.

"Any way you slice it, it's super schlock."
　　—Rex Reed, *The New York Post*,
　　　　　　　　　　　November 21, 1984.

"This is one of those films that anyone feels almost compelled to like, and then feels a little sad that it's not a better film. It tries so hard to have the epic scope of the *Superman* films, complete with the all-star cast. And complain about her

wooden acting all you want, Helen Slater pulls off the part nicely. Like so many other superhero films, the fault can be found in the villain. Supergirl fighting a witch just isn't all that interesting. Which is too bad. There was a good film in here somewhere, but it was lost on delivery."
— William Latham, author of *Mary's Monster, Space: 1999 Resurrection.*

"Helen Slater's performance is quite good. Her exuberance when she discovers her powers, when she is seeing things on Earth for the first time, is wonderful. She portrays that beautifully, and is sincere and honest. The opening scene in which she flies over the park and dips her hand in the water is nothing short of beautiful, and Slater flew better than Christopher Reeve ever did. She was graceful and used a variety of poses. The Goldsmith score was powerful and yet had this beautiful lyricism. Where the movie fails is in its plot, when Supergirl becomes Linda Lee. Honestly, this movie does not hold up so well over time."
— Howard Margolin, host of *Destinies: The Voice of Science Fiction.*

CAST: Faye Dunaway (Selena); Helen Slater (Kara/Supergirl/Linda Lee); Hart Bochner (Ethan); Peter Cook (Nigel); Mia Farrow (Alura); Marc McClure (Jimmy Olsen); Maureen Teefy (Lucy Lane); Brenda Vaccaro (Bianca); Simon Ward (Zor-El); Peter O'Toole (Zoltar); David Healy (Mr. Danvers); Jennifer Landor (Muffy); Robyn Mandell (Myra).

CREW: Alexander Salkind Presents a Jeannot Szwarc Film, *Supergirl*. *Production Designer:* Richard MacDonald. *Director of Photography:* Alan Hume. *Film Editor:* Malcolm Cooke. *Special Visual Effects:* Derek Meddings. *Optical Visual Effects:* Roy Field. *Second Unit:* David Lane. *Casting:* Lynn Stalmaster, Toni Howard and Associates. *Music Conducted and Composed by:* Jerry Goldsmith. *Screenplay:* David Odell. *Executive Producer:* Ilya Salkind. *Produced by:* Timothy Burrell. *Directed by:* Jeannot Szwarc. *M.P.A.A Rating:* PG. *Running time:* 114 minutes.

In the sixth dimension, survivors of Krypton dwell in the inner-space realm called Argo City. Young Kara, cousin to Kal-El, visits the artist Zoltar, who has been using the city's power source, the Omegahedron, to create new elements of the city. He has even built a ship to carry him to Earth. While playing with the power source, Kara causes the city's outer wall to rip open, and the Omegahedron is lost in the void.

Using Zoltar's ship, Kara breaches the "warp" to outer space and arrives on Earth, where the power source has fallen into the hands of a grasping, maniacal witch named Selena and her cohorts.

Kara assumes the identity of teenage student Linda Lee in Midvale, a small American town, and searches for the Omegahedron, even as Selena gathers foot soldiers for world domination. Unfortunately, Selena and Kara both fall in love with a lawn boy, Ethan, and Selena concocts a love potion to seduce him. When Ethan escapes from her clutches, Selena uses the Argo City power unit to send a bulldozer to retrieve him, but Supergirl saves the day and rescues Ethan. Angry, Selena summons a dark force to kill Supergirl, but Kara beats it back with an electrified lamp.

Trying again, Selena banishes Supergirl to the Phantom Zone, even as she materializes a huge mountain fortress for herself. In the eternal prison of the Phantom Zone, Kara meets with Zoltar, who has banished himself there. She convinces him to help her find the way out through a dangerous rift. Selena sends fireballs to destroy Kara and Zoltar, summoning a demon storm. Zoltar is killed, but Kara survives and confronts Selena in her fortress.

Now Supergirl must not only save Ethan, but friends Jimmy Olsen and roommate Lucy Lane (sister of Lois). Selena summons a giant demon to kill Supergirl, but Supergirl saves the day and rescues everybody, including the denizens of Argo City.

Superman

According to acclaimed author and sometime media critic Harlan Ellison, the character Superman is the "twentieth century archetype of mankind at its finest." The Man of Steel represents "courage and humanity, steadfastness and decency, responsibility and ethics," and remains a walking, talking symbol of man's "universal longing for perfection, for wisdom and power in the service" of all humanity.[1]

Incredibly, this great hero, an inspiration that has lived longer than James Bond or the cast of *Star Trek* in this fickle American pop culture, was created by two unknown artists, Jerry Siegel and Joe Shuster, when they were little more than teens living in Ohio. These two young men attempted for many years to shepherd their trademark character, a man of great physical strength, endurance and prowess, into newspaper comic strips, but met with no good fortune until Superman first appeared in *Action Comics* #1 in the summer of 1938.

As the civilized world faced the possibility of a global war, with the Nazi threat escalating in Europe, the character Superman quickly and eternally came to represent all the great values of the American way, particularly truth, justice and peace through strength and determination.

Superman quickly became a comic book sensation with the advent of his own title in 1939, and by the time of the Japanese attack on Pearl Harbor, his book was selling over a million copies annually. In this era, the foundation of the long-lived (over 60 years) mythos was laid out. The child of another planet, Clark Kent was a mild-mannered reporter working for a Metropolitan newspaper who in his secret guise of Superman combatted mobsters, mad scientists and spies. He also was in love with a feisty lady reporter, Lois Lane.

Over the years, further details added layers to this mythos. Clark worked in Metropolis at the *Daily Planet*. His home planet was Krypton, and his father, Jor-El, had sent him to Earth in a small rocket. His hometown on Earth (where Clark's rocket crashed) was Smallville, Kansas. Jimmy Olsen and Perry White were associates at the newspaper — cub reporter/photographer and harsh, cantankerous editor, respectively.

And then came the villains, a bunch that would, over the years, come to rival the goons of Batman's Gotham City. There was the bald, mad genius Lex Luthor, freaky doppelganger Bizarro, the brilliant Brainiac, and Metallo, the man with the heart of kryptonite, to name but a few.

Over the years, the length and style of Superman's hair changed with the times. He has been married to Lois (1996) and even died for a time (in 1992), a gimmick employed to boost DC's sales. But always the character has remained a beacon for hope and equality and the better angels of our nature. Some analysts even suggest Superman's story is really nothing less than a Christ metaphor.

In the early 1940s one of the best representations of the Man of Steel arrived on movie screens. Artist Max Fleischer animated the character in a series of 17 shorts destined to air years before any feature-length movie adaptation. These shorts brilliantly captured the essence of the 1940s, the noir decade, as well as the human grace of Superman and his stylized world. This was the era of big cars, fedoras and deco gadgetry; and Superman, in his amazing red and blue costume, fit right in. Marvelous and compelling, these cartoons featured militant, inspiring theme music and well-told stories without the benefit (or weight) of much dialogue. So successful was this visual style that the Batman and Superman animated series of the 1990s effectively emulated it.

Also in the 1940s, a radio version of Superman was introduced to the world, replete with whooshing sound effects to express his amazing gift of flight, the dream of all mankind. The radio program ran for a decade, and Budd Collyer voiced the stalwart Man of Tomorrow.

The popular character first hit the silver screen in 1948 in the appropriately titled *Superman*. Producer Sam Katzman created a 15-part serial for Columbia Studios. Kirk Alyn played Superman, Noel Neill his love Lois Lane. The film inspired a sequel, *Atom Man vs. Superman* (1950), which saw Supes (Alyn again) duke it out with Lyle Talbot's villainous Lex Luthor. Directed by Spencer Gordon Bennett and produced by Katzman, this venture was another low-budget, black-and-white, multi-part serial for Columbia.

More than a decade after the character's birth in comic pages, the modern age of Superman commenced in 1951 with the third Superman feature. *Superman and the Mole Men*, directed by Lee Sholem, offered the world a new Superman — an imposing Iowa native named George Reeves (1914–1959) — when Kirk Alyn left the role, fearful of typecasting. A powerful man with great charisma and screen presence, Reeves (*Gone with the Wind* [1939], *Jungle Jim* [1948]) is still associated with the part of Superman today, decades after his unfortunate death. The 67-minute-long feature co-starred Phyllis Coates as Lois Lane and eventually led to the first Superman TV series. But even more than previous efforts, it was this film that showed the world the moral value of Superman.

Superman and the Mole People parted some with Superman comic tradition by taking reporters Kent and Lane out of Metropolis and into the American heartland, in particular a town out west called Silsby. There the reporters became involved in the mystery of two little mole men, creatures that lived in their own civilization beneath the Earth's surface. These beings found their way topside when a corporate oil drill cut deep into their terrain. Radioactive and therefore dangerous to humankind, the diminutive "aliens" had no idea that their presence was potentially fatal to townfolks. The humans of the town, led by the film's villain, Benson (Jeff Corey), reacted with prejudice and hatred towards the Mole Men and sought to destroy them.

A native of another world himself, Superman brokered a peace between the two distrustful species, and Clark alone saw the inherent dangers of the mob mentality. The film was about man's propensity to fear that which is different, and was something of a revelation in the conformist 1950s, the decade of Joseph McCarthy and the Red Scare.

"It's men like you that make it difficult for men to understand one another," Superman told Corey's Benson in the film, and a salient point was made. Bent on stopping hysteria and intolerance, Superman was a hero of great dignity and even objectivity. Strong, smart and steady, George Reeves portrayed the Kryptonian as an evolved man, a wise man — a *super* man. When the mob threatened to lynch him and his other-human wards, he importantly reminded the hysterics that they were acting like "Nazi storm troopers" and that it was they, not the Mole Men, who invaded a new territory by burrowing into the Earth. This proved that, even as an adopted child of America, Superman had the ability to see matters objectively, doing what was best to preserve the ideals — not the prejudices — of the country.

In the twenty-first century, the production values of the *Mole Men* movie seem pretty primitive. The title characters are midgets in black outfits wearing rubber skull caps and pointed hairy eyebrows. Their powerful laser weapon, perhaps the film's most traditional threat, resembles an old-fashioned vacuum cleaner.

Even the flying effects are basic. When

Yesterday's Man of Steel: Superman (George Reeves) and Lois Lane (Phyllis Coates) stand ready for action in *Superman and the Mole People* (1951).

Superman takes off, a wire pulley system lifts him up; while animated drawings double for his most daring airborne feats (like the rescue of a Mole Man falling from a dam). Regardless of these limitations, the film moves along at a splendid pace, features a dramatic and didactic theme, and offers more sense of character and scope than the recent *X-Men* production. Bigotry isn't just background noise here, or motivation for some super-villain, but a real and deadly threat that Superman must reject and overcome.

The success of these Superman films lead naturally to the creation of a TV series, which first aired in the fall of 1952, and was produced from July 1952 to November 1957. Sponsored by Kellogg's, the series, known as *The Adventures of Superman*, lasted 103 episodes, and starred George Reeves (in a padded super-suit), Jack Larson (as Jimmy Olsen), John Hamilton (as Perry White) and featured two very different Lois Lanes. Phyllis Coates played a more abrasive character in the first season and was ultimately replaced by the friendlier Noel Neill for the remaining seasons.

On a budget of barely $15,000 per episode, the syndicated series shot four episodes every ten days, with the actors receiving reportedly around $200 per episode.[2] Robert Maxwell produced the first season, which had a hard, adult edge to it and was decried in some corners as too violent. Whitney Ellsworth replaced Maxwell, who went on to produce *Lassie*, for the follow-up seasons of the syndicated program, and the show developed a softer, sillier, more fantastical format.

Special effects genius Thol Simonson developed Superman's trademark flying special effects, which included invisible wires, a springboard for Reeves to launch from, and a glass table for use in matte projection. German art director Ernest Fegte "gave a stark, Kafkaesque look" to the standing, threadbare Pathé Studio sets, and painted backdrops often doubled as real locales.[3] Furniture props appeared scarce and were often reused, and the cast wore the same clothes every week. When a Superman was required to confront a double of himself, there was no split-screen work, merely inadequate stunt-doubling.

Superman the TV series commenced with a wonderful offer of joy and exploration: "Come with us now on a far journey … a journey that takes us millions of miles from Earth." From that wonderful science fiction premise, the pilot film, "Superman on Earth," showed us the governing council of Krypton as the distant planet began to experience strange and disturbing phenomena. One scientist, Jor-El, inhabiting a laboratory filled with 1950s-era gauges, rockets and other so-called "future" technologies, sent his only son, Kal-El, off the planet shortly before it was destroyed, launching the craft on an acceleration ramp that resembled a roller coaster.

Once on Earth, Kal El grew strong in the care of the Kents, Midwestern farmers; and when he was ready to become Superman, his mother sewed a striking uniform out of the blankets he had been bundled in during his transgalactic flight from Krypton. One of the series' most interesting and unique installments, the pilot set the no-nonsense tone and breakneck pace of the remainder of the TV venture.

In the first season of *Superman*, produced by Maxwell, Superman fought some really nasty gangsters, and the series felt like an action adventure with a twist — superheroics. "Crime Wave" was one such extraordinary show, with exploding trucks, blazing gunfire and the strong intervention of "the First Citizen of Metropolis," the Man of Steel. The episode encapsulated so much action, in fact, that it resorted to the montage technique. Superman went after the city's twelve worst "public enemies," and the episode depicted him flying in the clouds while *Daily Planet* headlines touted his victories (with action sequences between police and crooks intercut with his one-man war against organized crime). As he took down "the Crusher," "Big Ed" and "Mr. Big," however, one could not help but notice that Superman seemed to apprehend criminals without any evidence but hearsay. This is, perhaps, the natural result of the superhero genre: The law sometimes stands in the way of "real justice" and superheroes like Kal-El offer easy answers to sometimes complex questions. One of the unspoken joys of the Superman mythos is that this hero can swoop down from the sky, cut through red tape, and stop the criminal element cold.

In the Ellsworth seasons of Superman, the fantasy elements were emphasized over mob warfare. Superman and the staff at the *Daily Planet* traveled to the prehistoric era via a time machine in "Through the Time Barrier." "The Wedding of Superman" was a fantasy on the part of Lois Lane as she imagined, correctly, that Clark was Superman and then set out to marry him. Unfortunately, her dream was spoiled, and she went on secretly longing for the Man of Steel.

Other episodes, such as "The Face and the Voice" and "Jimmy the Kid," featured dastardly doubles of the *dramatis personae* as they threatened the cast, a gimmick that cut back on guest star costs. The now-classic "Panic in the Sky" matched Superman against a meteor, and saw the hero lose his memory for a time as the giant space rock threatened Earth. This story is so important to the mythos now that it has been redone on both *Superboy* and *Lois and Clark*.

Amnesia, the main focus of the episode, is one of the most durable clichés in the superhero film and TV genre. Other episodes were innocent evocations of wish fulfillment, the desire of the audience to participate in the grand adventure. In "All That Glitters," Lois and Jimmy imagined they had super powers and could fly, a dream we all shared.

All of these thirty-minute stories were good, wholesome, rudimentary fun. Watching the series today, one remembers that television was considered the dirty cousin of film in the 1950s, and this show exemplifies that belief. It seems to have been filmed on a wing and a prayer, and yet it is thoroughly enjoyable (not unlike *Dark Shadows* or *Doctor Who*). Sure, Inspector Henderson (Robert Shayne) is a bit of a dope, and Jimmy Olsen comes off as an idiot man-child. Sure, the production could never afford any reporters or newspaper employees, besides Perry White's secretary, Ethel, and often depended heavily on stock footage. But special effects and money do not necessarily a superhero make, as big-budget productions like *RoboCop 3*, *Crow: The Salvation* and others have proven so dramatically.

On the other hand, the performances were delightful; and merely by lasting for five seasons (the last two in washed-out, primitive color), *The Adventures of Superman* laid the foundation for superheroes on television. If not an artful show, it was enormously entertaining.

In 1957, however, George Reeves, after directing a few episodes of the series, grew fatigued with the role, gained some weight, and began to fear typecasting. Production on the show shut down when Reeves abandoned the role; while producer Ellsworth hoped he could recapture the magic of the series with *The Adventures of Superboy* and *Superpup*, two pilots that never went to series. Then, in 1959, at the age of 45, George Reeves died. Newspapers blared the tragic

headline "SUPERMAN KILL SELF," but many in the industry believe to this day that his mysterious death was no suicide. His death also begat the "Superman curse," the belief that all actors playing the Man of Steel suffer bad luck.

The Adventures of Superman remains a landmark series in television history. As Los Angeles County Mayor Mike Antonovich declared during *The Adventures of Superman* Week in July of 2001:

> The series sparked the imagination of millions of children around the world and developed characters with integrity and a sense of compassion. It promoted understanding and tolerance among different people and championed truth and justice in our lives and promoted moral values.[4]

This author could not agree more with those sentiments. In preparation for this book, hundreds of hours of superhero movies and television were viewed, and few hours proved more enjoyable than those spent with this early and important series. *The Adventures of Superman* has no pretense, posturing, or narrative absurdities. It is straight-faced, simple fun that fills its audience with a sense of delight and joy. If only other series would emulate that formula, rather than delving into facile psychology about schizophrenic, angst-ridden brooders.

Sadly, the same amount of fun was not to be gleaned out of a viewing of *It's a Bird! It's a Plane! It's Superman!* a Cine World TV movie that aired in 1975. Based on the musical by David Newman and Robert Benton, and produced on Broadway in the 1960s during the heyday of ABC's campy *Batman*, this was a truly disastrous rendition of the Man of Steel's "origin" story. For those who have not seen it, one must imagine a combination of the 1960s *Batman* TV series with a Broadway musical of *Grease*. Yes, it is *that* bad.

It's a Bird... is a low-budget production, which means that the backgrounds are all cheap-looking, comic-strip, 1930s-style paintings behind props, and the settings are sparse. The songs are headache inducing, with lyrics like, "He flew my asthmatic son to Albuquerque," in "We Need Him"; and none of the cast (including Lesley Ann Warren, Loretta Swit and David Wayne) seem particularly capable while singing or dancing.

David Wilson portrayed Superman, but looked frail and uncertain in the pajama-like costume, his cape frequently appearing to be hanging crookedly from his neck. Worse, the program's idea of comedy was to have the unfortunate actors say their lines directly to the camera and mug shamelessly. "Superman will destroy *himself*," Dr. Sedgwick declares at one point. "You mean, Superman will destroy *himself*?" Max Mencken, a nasty columnist for the *Daily Planet* repeats. "Yes, Superman will destroy *himself*," Dr. Sedgwick affirms. Repetition is supposed to equal comedy, but in this case the final equation offered only boredom. It was all too horrible for words, this trashing of a real American icon.

Unbelievably, the same camp approach that sunk *It's a Bird! It's a Plane! It's Superman!* also appeared destined to dominate the planned feature film of Superman that was being produced as early as 1975. Lesley Ann Warren even auditioned for the part of Lois Lane in the anticipated movie, a tangible tie to the Broadway production and TV event. Fortunately, producers Ilya and Alexander Salkind made a brilliant decision in hiring director Richard Donner to helm the film when Guy Hamilton had to drop out because of tax issues. Donner's goal was to make a more respectful (and respectable) film version of the Man of Steel's beginnings. He explained to *Fantastic Films* how the script began to evolve from satire to serious fairy tale:

> Mario Puzo had written a brilliant screenplay, as far as the creation of the characters. Then Robert Benton and David and Leslie Newman came in, under the auspices of Guy Hamilton and the Salkinds.... The screenplay turned out to be a real parody in the *Batman* mode, and I couldn't see going that way.[5]

He brought in Tom Mankewicz to write a more dramatic, realistic, and reverent version of the heroic myth. Shooting in England at Pinewood Studios, Donner also had the opportunity and foresight to bring in the best special effects men in the industry to make the film believable from a visual standpoint. Matte artist Les Bowie, special effects genius Colin Chilvers, production designer John Barry and miniature builder Derek Meddings were among the talents assuring that the new *Superman* could compete in the age of *Star Wars* and *Close Encounters of the Third Kind*.

While Dennys Coop worked tirelessly to develop the technology for Superman's flight (a real hurdle before the age of C.G.I.), Donner went about shooting the film, which saw Marlon Brando star as Jor-El, Superman's father. Gene Hackman provided support as the film's villain, a comical but not ridiculous Lex Luthor. Margot Kidder (*Sisters* [1973], *The Amityville Horror* [1979]) played Lois Lane, and a young unknown inherited the double role of Clark Kent and Superman, Christopher Reeve.

Reeve immediately impressed not only Donner, but everybody in the cast and crew with his charming, vulnerable and yet strong interpretation of the last son of Krypton. It was he, not the special effects, Donner insisted, that made Superman's flying capabilities so believable:

> He knows what it is to fly, he feels it — his movements, his expressions, his instincts — the flying is as beautiful as it is because Christopher brought it to life.[6]

Despite a perfect lead actor and a director with an approach bound to please comic book fans, the set of *Superman: The Movie* was not without incident. The Mario Puzo script reportedly stretched some 300 pages long, which meant the film would have been six hours in length if released as one movie.

Also, Richard Donner fell behind during principal production, in no small part because of the extremely difficult technical nature of many of the film's more complicated shots, and executives at Warner Brothers, as well as the Salkinds, began to grow nervous about his stewardship. Richard Lester, the director of *A Hard Day's Night*, joined the production ranks to "assist" Donner, but was allegedly there (at least according to some sources) to replace him immediately should Donner misstep.

Finally, since so much money was being spent on the production, it was decided that the script would be split into two movies, *Superman* and *Superman II*; but with costs spiraling out of control, not all of the sequel footage was shot with the first film.

When *Superman: The Movie* premiered in 1978, accompanied by the ad line "You'll Believe a Man Can Fly," few people could quibble with any decision Donner had made. The $50 million production was an unqualified blockbuster, and Christopher Reeve became a star.[7] More to the point, at least for fans of the superhero character, Superman was treated with great respect and artistry.

Although over a quarter-century has elapsed since the release of Donner's remarkable motion picture, the film's relative age makes little difference. A production of extraordinary heart, great special effects and soaring characterizations, *Superman: The Movie* remains the greatest superhero movie made to date.

More than any other version of the Man of Steel legend, whether the 1950s TV show or the 1970s musical, Donner's film captured the mythic, almost religious nature of the Superman story. To wit: Jor-El, a wise, god-like representative of a distant, highly advanced planet, sends his only son (Jesus Christ?) to Earth to live among hu-manity. The fact that Krypton is almost totally and immaculately white (without dirt, grays, or other discolorations) harks back to the notion of the planet as some kind of utopian afterlife or Heaven. That the Kryptonians wear reflective, glowing uniforms (and in many cases even showcase white manes of hair), further develops the Heaven metaphor.

But the Christ/Heaven analogy goes further. Immediately before sending away the child messiah, Jor-El and his angelic people have proven themselves victorious in a war against an insurrectionist named Zod (representing Lucifer). Before being vanquished to a Hell-like domain (the Phantom Zone), this villain threatens to some day return to battle Jor-El and his heirs, an Armageddon that is highlighted more explicitly in *Superman II*.

Once on Earth, the alien Kal-El is adopted by kindly parents (the Kents), regular "humans" (like Mary's devoted husband, Joseph) that are at a loss to explain his miraculous arrival — not quite an immaculate conception, but close enough for viewers to get the point.

Then, of course, a grown Superman becomes nothing less than mankind's savior as he performs miracles (rescuing Air Force One, averting an earthquake, and so forth). That Superman is gentle, loving, kind and powerful also harks back to the stories regarding Jesus.

But lest *Superman: The Movie* sound like a religious epic, Donner also understood when to have some fun — *and* when it is time to pluck the heartstrings. After the majestic, beautifully orchestrated opening on Krypton, the film changes tonally and visually as it moves to Smallville, Kansas. At this point, the picture emerges as a lyrical, Norman Rockwell–like glimpse of American Midwestern life in the simpler 1950s. Geoffrey Unsworth's stately camera artfully captures many remarkable natural vistas, focusing on sprawling wheat fields, traditional farmhouses and those wide-open American skies of blue. This sequence of the film reeks of Americana, and provides the slow, quiet moments that most superhero films eschew in favor of action, violence, and vengeance.

From Smallville, *Superman: The Movie* launches into the more standard superhero stuff that people expected: the clash with Lex Luthor, and Superman performing feats of heroism in Metropolis while keeping his secret identity from plucky reporter Lois Lane. This final third of the film could have been the least interesting part of *Superman: The Movie*, had the casting not been so remarkable. Christopher Reeve *is* Superman, just as George Reeves was Superman to the generation before, and the actor effortlessly captures the Man of Steel's curiosity, purity, gentleness, and confidence in a way that never seems hokey or campy. This is a visitor who is amused and puzzled by mankind, but also reverent of the species' accomplishments. He can be strong and idealistic and sincere without seeming hopelessly square, and this fine characterization is no doubt the ultimate appeal of *Superman: The Movie*.

Unlike Tim Burton's *Batman*—in all, a solid adaptation of the Dark Knight mythos—there is little schizophrenia or angst associated with the first Superman movie. The crises in the film are more genuinely human, touching, and less melodramatic. Over the course of the movie, Clark loses two fathers (Jor-El and Jonathan Kent), searches for the purpose of his life in the Fortress of Solitude, falls in love with a flawed human being and embraces his adopted world. He isn't "darkly" obsessed with the death of his parents, nor motivated by ugly emotions like "revenge." He is not a kinky, rubber-suited vigilante who depends on gadgets, such as souped-up cars and utility belts.

Instead, he is an outsider of great strength and power who sees humanity for what it is and judges our species valuable, even good, despite its frailties. Admittedly, that description may sound corny to a generation weaned on the X-Men or Batman, but the Superman mythos touches a much deeper nerve. Even after twenty years, this film has a raw power and honest emotionality that so many superhero productions lack. It isn't afraid to wear its heart on its sleeve, and there isn't an ounce of cynicism in the mix.

Despite amazing work on *Superman: The Movie*, Donner was replaced by the Salkinds when it came time to finish shooting *Superman II*, and Richard Lester completed the film as its director in March of 1980.[8] Despite Donner's absence, Lester did very good work on the sequel, so impressive in fact, that many judged it as good as, if not better than, the original. The story involved Zod (Terence Stamp) and two compatriots (a vampy Sarah Douglas as Ursa and Jack O'Halloran as the hulking Non) as they escaped from the Phantom Zone and wrought havoc on Earth.

This entry in the film franchise might have been better titled *The Last Temptation of Superman* because the religious overtones continued. In the complex, witty screenplay, the Man of Steel was forced to choose between a life of mortality and human love with Lois, and one of super heroic duty, in which he perpetually "saves" humanity from all threats. Again the Christ metaphor was almost palpable. With Superman writhing in pain while losing his powers in a flash of light in his Fortress of Solitude, it was not hard to imagine Christ on the cross. The romantic angle was also very well played, and even if the sequel lacked the utter majesty of Donner's exemplary work, it featured some spectacular action scenes that have yet to be surpassed in superhero cinema. A mid-air encounter between Superman and his Phantom Zone nemeses remains a special effects showstopper, an urban battle that defies gravity and evokes a genuine sense of awe.

Beware of stand-up comedians bearing gifts. Gus Gorman (Richard Pryor) presents Superman (Christopher Reeve) with a chunk of deadly kryptonite in *Superman III* (1983).

With two such fine entries in its film series, one might have thought it would be clear skies for Superman in the years following the 1981 blockbuster *Superman II*. But, sadly, the high level of quality was not sustainable. All good things must come to an end, one supposes, and *Superman III*, again directed by Lester, proved a major disappointment.

The third movie in the *Superman* film franchise was scuttled by a number of problems, not the least of which was that appealing Margot Kidder returned as Lois Lane only in a glorified cameo, replaced by lovely Annette O'Toole (*Smallville*) as Clark's new small-town love interest, Lana Lang. That Lois was so suddenly "out" was a major blow to continuity and the reality of the characters, especially after Clark's agonizing decisions regarding her in *Superman II*. But worse than this problem, the script featured a character named Gus Gorman, a scheming con man played by overexposed comedian Richard Pryor.

In *Superman III*, Pryor gave a comedic performance that seemed wildly out of place in Christopher Reeve's serious-minded Metropolis. Who wanted to watch madcap, slapstick antics when they could be watching the all-powerful Man of Steel duke it out with super-villains and save the world? Because of this focus on Pryor's character, the film felt distinctly small potatoes after the Earth-shattering events of the previous pictures.

Also, Robert Vaughn (as tycoon Ross Webster) proved an ineffective villain, a poor man's Lex Luthor without that character's legendary background or sense of grandiose pomposity. Unlike the first two *Superman* movies, *Superman III* seemed a fairly cynical and campy entertainment.

Still, it had a few high points. The best sequence in the film involved Superman's exposure to a dangerous new variant of kryptonite invented by Pryor's Gorman. The Man of Steel thus became the Man of Vice, transformed into a whoring, drinking menace to society in a scene that was not only funny and surprising, but important to the character.

Ultimately, Clark Kent and Superman split into two, and battled each other to see which identity was really dominant. Despite all of the Bruce Wayne posturing about his double identity in the various *Batman* movies, it remains this sequence, in an inferior *Superman* movie, that best expresses the notion that superheroes are often men divided against themselves.

The second highlight of *Superman III* was Superman's battle with Gus Gorman and Ross Webster's supercomputer, a special effects showcase and brief reminder of the glory days of previous efforts. Yet even this satisfactory climax was undercut somewhat by jokey references to video games and other forced attempts at humor.

Superman IV: The Quest for Peace came along in 1987 and featured a story by series star Christopher Reeve. Many fans had high hopes that the fourth film would repair the damage to the character caused by the third, but, surprisingly, *The Quest for Peace* was a low-budget, slapdash effort, released not by the Salkinds but by Golan and Globus's now defunct Cannon films. Today the movie's problems have only worsened, as it looks like a relic of the Cold War era. Worried about escalating tensions between the United States and the Soviet Union, Superman resolves to interfere in mankind's affairs and rid the world of all nuclear weapons. His plan backfires, however, when Lex Luthor creates a "radioactive" super clone of Superman/Lex called Nuclear Man (Mark Pillow).

Superman IV, directed by Sidney Furie, had some 45 minutes deleted from its running time when theatrically released, leaving the film feeling sparse and poorly conceived. One interesting subplot that ended up the cutting room floor was an AIDS allegory, with a white-haired, wasting-away Clark rendered "sick" and alone by his exposure to the deadly Nuclear Man. Only the barest remnants of this subplot remain, and it is resolved with a *deus ex machina* conclusion (Clark's decision to revitalize himself with a Kryptonian power cell that he just coincidentally found in his long unused spaceship).

The most interesting aspects of the fourth film came in an early sequence unrelated to the plot. Clark returned to the family farm in Smallville, attempting to sell it if an appropriate buyer could be found. This was an elegiac, moody beginning for a movie that is, for the most part, very choppy. There is discussion of time's passage and a mention of Jonathan Kent, and one

The muscular Nuclear Man (Mark Pillow) wants to kill Superman in *Superman IV: The Quest for Peace* (1987).

realizes that Christopher Reeve has been playing this part for almost a decade. It is nostalgic and works to the film's favor, as does Superman's stirring speech to the assembled delegates of the United Nations.

Alas, after the first twenty-five minutes or so, the movie speeds to its conclusion with little rhyme or reason, becoming a poorly photographed battle that takes Superman from Italy to China and back to Metropolis.

Even without much narrative meat, what really undermines *Superman IV* is neither the pedestrian direction nor the silly plot, but its lousy special effects. In some sequences the wires suspending Christopher Reeve above a soundstage are visible, thus destroying the illusion that a man can fly. Blue screen work also tends to come undone via visible matte lines. And, oddly, at one point Superman develops the ability to rebuild the Great Wall of China with X-ray vision! Also deeply disturbing is the fact that the backdrop meant to represent outer space behind the lunar surface is quite obviously made of hanging fabric. For that matter, there are no stars visible in any moon-set shots. Superman is a character that requires grandeur and a big budget. *Superman IV*'s meager resources made the Man of Steel seem laughable and inconsequential.

On a thematic note, the message of *Superman IV*—that peace is not Superman's to give to the world but one that must be earned by mankind as a whole—is fine and worthy, but it does not seem to reflect any sense of reality. A better story would have seen many of the world's nations, including the United States, rejecting Superman's plan to clean up the planet. Think about this Superman disarmament plan realistically. How would the American president—*any* American president—react if he were notified by Superman that America needed to be divested of its weapons of mass destruction, its tactical advantage in this world? Dealing with that reality would have made for a smarter movie. Lex Luthor and Nuclear Man are easy criminal villains: psychotic and maniacal. How much more interesting would it have been if Superman had to fight against the military might and establishments of the United States (or the Soviet Union) to make disarmament a reality?

Even if the final two entries in the film series proved less than stellar, Reeve's understanding of the central characters bolstered all four *Superman* films. Frankly, his very presence provided some much needed and very welcome consistency between uneven film entries. One feels sorry for the generation that grew up with the *Batman* movies because Michael Keaton left after two films, followed by Val Kilmer, then George Clooney and now, apparently, Christian Bale. This revolving door of lead actors makes it difficult to identify with Batman. There is no opportunity to get to know the man's personality, and one can't escape the notion that the Dark Knight can be represented by anybody who happens to fit the musclebound suit. Christopher Reeve's continued presence assured that this notion was never true of Superman.

Perhaps more importantly, the *Batman* films—some of which are quite good—do not seem to be very happy films. There is no joy in anything about them. Batman is always brooding about his terrible past or facing sick (and sickening) criminals that society has either abandoned (like DeVito's Penguin) or perverted (like Michelle Pfeiffer's Catwoman). The *Superman* series, even aged from the 1980s, is different—and gloriously so. Like the *Star Wars* films, the *Superman* movies of the 1970s and 1980s feel pure and innocent. There isn't a shred of dysfunction to be found in these movies; and in today's world of angst-riddled, gloom-and-doom superheroes (*The Crow, The Shadow, Spawn, Daredevil*), that is a relief.

In the early 1990s the Salkinds resumed control of the Superman franchise by developing a syndicated *Superboy* TV series that ran for four seasons. When it proved successful financially, Warner Brothers quickly jumped on the Man of Steel bandwagon and began preparing a new Superman TV series that would take a very different approach than previous ventures, focusing on comedy and romance at the expense of high-flying adventure and crime fighting. The new title, *Lois and Clark: The New Adventures of Superman*, revealed the shift in tone. Superheroics were to come second, the primary romantic relationship first. "Is that kryptonite in your pocket, or are you happy to see me?" Lois Lane asked scandalously in one episode of the new program, and that kind of zinger set the tone for Superman in the 1990s, the age of Clinton.

Lois Lane (Teri Hatcher) and Superman (Dean Cain), the romantic couple from ABC's *Lois and Clark: The New Adventures of Superman.*

Why did such a change come about? As always, one can look back to the comic book source material for an answer. The 1990s saw a shift in tone and change in history regarding Superman in the comic book pages (thanks to writer/artist John Byrne). Suddenly, there was no more Superboy in the continuity, and Superman himself changed dramatically, perhaps for the first time in his storied history. No longer was Superman the "real" person, with Clark Kent — the secret identity — simply being the face Kal-El put on to deflect suspicion. Instead, that psychological dynamic flip-flopped, and Clark became "the real guy," the main character, while Superman was the "act." *Lois and Clark: The New Adventures*

of Superman emulated that change, and also took a very light approach to the material (not necessarily camp, just light).

The handsome and extremely buff Dean Cain signed on to play Clark Kent and his performance in *Lois and Clark* was an interesting and substantial, if not inspired, one. He brought humanity and compassion to the Superman character, seeming much more the "sensitive guy" than either George Reeves or Christopher Reeve. Oddly, Cain also chose not to really differentiate between Clark and the Man of Steel, except by his hairstyle. In his hands, both characters were somewhat interchangeable, and that may have been a mistake.

Sexy, sharp-tongued Teri Hatcher became Lois Lane in the new program. Interestingly, this updating of Lois proved very successful, and she emerged as a very 1990s kind of girl. In fact, the career-minded, ambitious, driven, lonely, emotionally-inept Lane not only seemed true to the heritage of the character (who was always rather feisty), but pointed the way towards series like *Ally McBeal*, which also focused intently on the 1990s career female and her lifestyle. Hatcher nailed the role, even if she lacked the softer side of a Margot Kidder or Noel Neill.

Cast as a villain was the charismatic John Shea (*Mutant X*). He portrayed a yuppie version of Lex Luthor, one that was a corporate raider, a playboy, and a scoundrel through-and-through. Eschewing tradition, John Shea's Luthor sported a full head of curly hair, not the chrome-dome audiences had come to expect. Today, Shea's performance has been eclipsed by Michael Rosenbaum's fine portrayal of the character on *Smallville*, but in the 1990s, when *Lois and Clark* aired, Shea was probably the best version of Luthor yet dramatized.

Others in the cast during the first year of *Lois and Clark* included Lane Smith as the irascible Perry White, in this incarnation an Elvis fan mired in a troubled marriage. Tracy Scoggins played a sexy, tarty gossip columnist named Kat who had an eye for men (especially Clark) and proved to be a nice romantic foil for Lois Lane, who was meant to seem unglamorous, despite Hatcher's beauty. Clark's parents from Smallville (K. Callan and Eddie Jones) also took part in the series, nudging their diffident boy towards the girl of his dreams and forming a support net for the Man of Steel. Even good old Jimmy Olsen was around (in the person of actor Michael Landes) — a little less on the up-and-up than innocent Jack Larson on *The Adventures of Superman*, a bit more of a schemer.

Developed for TV by Deborah Joy Levine, *Lois and Clark: The New Adventures*

of Superman premiered in the fall of 1993. Scheduled by ABC on Sunday nights at 8:00 P.M., *Lois and Clark* competed for audience attention against the successful *Murder She Wrote* and the new Steven Spielberg–produced underwater venture *Sea Quest DSV*. The new Superman series was not an immediate ratings victor in this combat, but it scored with the critics, who liked the romantic banter, and did well enough with audiences to merit a sophomore season. Particularly notable in the first season was an involving, multi-episode story arc that witnessed Luthor's attempts to woo Lois Lane and destroy the *Daily Planet*. Also in the first season, Clark's mother sewed a variety of Superman-style costumes for her superhero son, all in a humorous musical montage set to the song "I'm Holding Out for a Hero." Perhaps more importantly for the character of Kal-El, Clark came to learn his Kryptonian heritage in first-season episodes such as "Strange Visitor" and "The Green, Green Glow of Home," the latter concerning kryptonite.

Some dramatic changes were in the offing for the sophomore season. Michael Landes was considered too old for the part of Jimmy Olsen and consequently replaced by the younger, more impish Justin Whalen. Scoggins' Kat was dropped from the series and Lex was seen only as a guest star. The second season climbed in the ratings and began to develop the romance between Lois and Clark more explicitly. The final episode of the season, a cliffhanger, involved Clark's marriage proposal to Lois Lane. Audience numbers swelled and ratings skyrocketed.

In season three, Lois not only agreed to marry Clark, but actually learned of his secret identity as Superman. This was a problem, as Lois did not like to compete for her man's attention. The season kept holding out the promise of a wedding, but then began piling up increasingly absurd obstacles to prevent the union. As the wedding day for Lois and Clark finally came, Lois was secretly spirited away by a returned-to-life Lex Luthor and replaced at the altar by a frog-eating clone! Meanwhile, Lois developed amnesia, believing she was a low-class torch singer named Wanda Detroit, and the relationship with Clark was literally back to square one. Ratings remained high, but many felt that *Lois and Clark: The New Adventures of Superman* had jumped the shark, pulling ridiculous gimmicks once too often.

As if to rectify the error in judgment, the fourth season of *Lois and Clark* featured the real marriage of Lane and Kent in a weak episode entitled "Swear to God, We're Not Kidding This Time," featuring guest star David Doyle as a kindly guardian angel. Otherwise, it was business as before, and the ratings started to plummet. In 1996 the season began losing significant ground to CBS's *Touched by an Angel* and NBC's comedy *Third Rock from the Sun.* The series dropped from 25th place in the Nielsen ratings in its third year to the mid–50s in its fourth season. "Last year we were the victors and this year we're not, but there's been no talk of moving time slots," producer Brad Buckner assured worried fans in 1996, many of them fearing that Superman was about to crash land.[9]

Fans were buoyed by that news and by the fact that ABC had already committed to air *Lois and Clark* for a fifth season, but then word came that the decision had been reversed.[10] With ratings sliding, the series was cancelled after only four seasons. The last episode of the final season, "The Family Hour," brought the arrival of a baby into newlywed Clark and Lois's lives, but fans were never to know how it got there or to whom the baby actually belonged (since Clark and Lois were genetically incompatible).

Looking back at *Lois and Clark* today, one sees a remarkably enjoyable series. Cain and Hatcher made for excellent sparring partners and shared genuine romantic chemistry. The series was not, however, a serious superhero show, focusing instead on romance and celebrity villains, most of them lacking real menace.

Inhabiting the *Lois and Clark* rogue's gallery were Harry Anderson's Fat Head Mensa, a villain who used 98.6 percent of his brain, and Tempus, a time-traveling sociopath with a hatred of Superman. Tempus was played with scenery-chewing glee by Lane Davies and appeared in "Tempus Anyone?" "Soul Mates," "Tempus Fugitive," "Meet John Doe," and others. Cult star Bruce Campbell (*Evil Dead*) did a stint on the show as Billy Church, the leader of an international crime ring called Inter Gang, and Jonathan Frakes and his wife, Genie Francis, appeared as Amber and Tim Lake in "Don't Tug on Superman's Cape." Their story concerned rich collectors determined to add Superman to their collection.

Before the series had finished, Robert Culp, Bronson Pinchot, Cindy Williams, Shelley Long, Roger Daltrey, Sherman Hemsley, Isabel Sanford, Delta Burke, Antonio Sabato, Jr., William Devane, Emma Samms and even Drew Carey and Kathy Kinney had materialized to play comedic threats to the happiness of Kent and Lane. These actors all seemed to have fun, but none played a character who was a match for Superman, and that was the one glaring flaw of the series. After the first-season Lex Luthor story arc, not even one really tense story materialized, making the typical viewing of *Lois and Clark* a mild and amusing experience rather than an exciting one.

Still, *Lois and Clark* offered some interesting observations about the character of Superman and certainly delved deeper into his feelings than had *The Adventures of Superman.* In particular, Clark came to realize that he could not be Superman and have anything approaching a normal social life. When you can detect a crisis in every direction, all over the planet, which calls do you respond to and in what order? "Ultra

Woman," a story that saw Lois endowed with Clark's super powers, answered that question, and made Superman's plight almost tangible. At other times during the series, Lois became exasperated with Clark because he had to choose others over her. One wonders how their marriage would have developed given time...

Lois and Clark remains a cheesy show with tacky costumes, hokey villains and silly plots; but, in all fairness, it owns up to these flaws and attempts to twist them into strengths. The creators of this series realized it could only be taken half-seriously and therefore cleverly played with the conventions of the Superman myth (such as the absurdity that Lois would not recognize Clark as Superman because he wears glasses). In these moments of self-reflexive humor, *Lois and Clark* lived up to the glory of some of its predecessors, but Superman's finest hour probably remains Christopher Reeve's portrayal of the character in *Superman: The Movie* and *Superman II*.

As one might expect of a superhero who has appeared in four movies and two TV series, Superman has also been a regular player in the world of TV cartoons. Sixteen adventures of the Man of Steel were dramatized from 1966 to 1967 on the CBS series *The New Adventures of Superman*, created by Filmation. These same sixteen adventures were then re-aired over the years, under names such as *The Superman/Aquaman Hour* and *The Batman/Superman Hour*. *The Super Friends*, the 1970s dramatization of the JLA, also featured the Man of Steel as one of the core members.

In 1996 the team that created the very popular *Batman: The Animated Series* took their shot at the Superman mythos. *Superman: The Animated Series* premiered on the WB in September of '96, featuring the voices of Tim Daly (as Superman) and Dana Delaney (Lois Lane). Following the tradition set by the *Batman* series, a slew of celebrities gave voice to the villains. Malcolm McDowell was Corben/Metallo, Michael Ironside was Darkseid, Clancy Brown played a scheming Lex Luthor and Lori Petty voiced the character named Live Wire. The series never attained the same level of widespread, mainstream success as *Batman: The Animated Series*, perhaps because Superman's world was less dark, and Metropolis a little less distinctive than Gotham. The series folded after two seasons, but nonetheless produced some fascinating adventures.

In "The Way of All Flesh," Superman contended with Metallo, a man with a heart made of kryptonite. Corben hated Superman, but behind the scenes Luthor was manipulating events, and the episode was really an in-depth character study of Metallo/Corben, a pitiful man deprived of all human feelings. Numb, never able to feel pleasure or pain, Corben, unlike some villains, had a reason to embrace evil, and his tale of alienation proved particularly interesting.

Another unique story, called "Live Wire," pitted Superman against a shock jock who hated him. Leslie Willis (Lori Petty) had an axe to grind against the Man of Steel because "everything's so darn easy for him." She thought Supes was just a glorified con man, a fellow who could do anything and took advantage of that. Of course, in true comic book fashion, Willis was destined to become a super-villain, electrocuted during a concert appearance at Metropolis Park. Once "evil," Willis had the opportunity to understand and identify with Superman and his plight, but, like so many people, proved herself a hypocrite.

What made this particular episode of *Superman: The Animated Series* so special was some of the visual techniques deployed by the artists. As Willis droned on the radio about how useless Superman was, the episode cut dramatically to the hero's exploits as he saved a falling construction worker from plunging to his death and kept a tumbling winch from crushing a baby.

Ironic crosscutting and counterpoint — how often does one find that level of ingenuity in a cartoon?

Superman: The Animated Series folded before the end of the twentieth century, but that was not to be the end of the Man of Steel. In the year 2002, word came from Hollywood following the success of Sam Raimi's *Spider-Man* that Kal-El's origin story was going to be told in feature film format one more time. This time, *Alias* creator J.J. Abrams was writing the screenplay, and the story of Clark Kent had been "re-imagined" to fit the times. *Ain't It Cool News* reported the unfortunate news, describing a series of bizarre updates that seemed totally untrue to the character's legend. Lex Luthor was going to be an alien. Krypton was *not* going to explode. Jimmy Olsen was going to be a homosexual. And, oddly, all the fight sequences were to resemble the popular 1999 movie *The Matrix*.

Online fans protested this strange new world of Superman, one unfaithful to seventy years of comic book lore, and J.J. Abrams was quick to respond to criticism, arguing that the script he had written was an early draft. Reportedly, some of the more egregious discontinuities have been taken out of the mix in an effort to appease the fan base. Even with the protests, the new *Superman* film was racing towards production as this book approached completion. Director Brett Ratner (*Red Dragon* [2002]) had reportedly secured the services of Anthony Hopkins as Jor-El. Then, as this book was proofed, word came that Ratner and Hopkins had both departed the project.

Only time will tell if this new version of a re-imagined Superman becomes reality or crash lands in development hell.

Superman and the Mole-Men (1951)
LIVE–ACTION FILM

CAST: George Reeves (Clark Kent/Superman); Phyllis Coates (Lois Lane); Jeff Corey (Luke Benson); Stanley Andrews, Ray Walker, Hal K. Dawson, Phil Warren, Frank Reicher, Beverly Washburn.

CREW: *Original Screenplay:* Richard Fielding. *Based on a Copyrighted Feature Appearing in: Action Comics* and *Superman* Magazines. *Assistant Director:* Arthur Hammond. *Cameraman:* Clark Ramsey. *Script Clerk:* Mary Chaffee. *Sound Engineer:* Harry Smith. *Dialogue Editor:* Steve Carr. *Property Master:* George Bahr. *Wardrobe:* Izzy Berne. *Make-up:* Harry Thomas. *Art Director:* Ernst Fegte. *Film Editor:* Al Joseph. *Sound Cutter:* Bud Hayes. *Music:* Darrell Calker. *Special Effects:* Ray Mercer. *Produced by:* Barney A. Sarecky. *Directed by:* Lee Sholem. *Running time:* 67 minutes.

Clark Kent and Lois Lane travel to the small western town of Silsby to write a feature on the world's deepest oil well, only to learn that the Havenfirst Experimental Well has been closed down. Before being sealed, the well stretched some 32,000 feet into the Earth, six miles — much deeper than man has ever drilled.

On the reporters' first night in town, two diminutive creatures, mole people, climb out of the well to investigate the drilling site. Later, Lois and Clark find a man dead on the premises, seemingly the victim of a heart attack; but Lois spots the curious creatures and frightens them with her screams. Clark sends for the police, and the death of the watchman is ruled a heart attack. But one oilman, Carrington, tells Clark a wild story: when the drill reached 30,000 feet on June 26 he discovered samples of radium. At 32,600 feet, the drill went through the last solid layer of rock and hit a hollow chamber, where evidence of life was discovered. Now, whatever lives down below has a path straight up to the surface!

Soon, another Silsby resident spots the creatures, who seem to be leaving a swath of radiation in their path. Panic grips the town, and the citizenry gathers in a mob to hunt them down. When a little girl is frightened by the mole men, the mob turns ugly and Clark intervenes, this time as Krypton's last son, Superman! He blocks the mob, but a local thug, Luke Benson, is bent on killing the creatures.

One of the thugs shoots down a mole man on the dam, but Superman lifts the injured creature away before his radioactive body can contaminate Silsby's water. Luke Benson and a pack of dogs chase down the other mole man, tracking him to a cabin in the woods. They burn it down. But the scared mole man escapes and returns down the well to the center of the Earth. Mean-while, Clark assists Dr. Reed in saving the wounded mole man. The mob marches on the hospital to finish off the injured being, but Superman blocks their path and disarms the mob.

Elsewhere, three mole men, with their own destructive weapon, journey to the surface to free their comrade. Superman confronts them at the hospital, planning to return their friend to them. But Luke intervenes again. When the mole men blast Luke with their weapon, Superman steps in and deflects the rays. Ashamed of his behavior, Benson watches Superman escort the mole men home.

Not long after the Silsby incident, the mole men blow up the drill and casing at the well site so they will never again encounter mankind.

The Adventures of Superman (1952–58)
LIVE-ACTION SERIES

"Reeves gave the TV characters the same kind of visual appeal that Jerome Siegel and Joe Shuster had achieved with their original comic strip superhero. Handsome, humble and intelligent, the actor almost magically transformed into Superman…"

— David Smith, *Starlog #9*: "Vintage Video: The Golden Decade of SF Viewing." October 1977, page 54.

"You shoot him six times, and he stands and takes it. Then you throw the gun and he ducks. That's an image that's hard to forget, but it defines the George Reeves era of Superman. Everyone loved this show. There's no denying its special appeal. I was personally roped into seeing *Gone with the Wind* when I was seven because I was told Superman was in it, which he was, for about thirty seconds, and then I sat there disappointed for the rest of the film! *Superman and the Mole Men* is probably the finest moment of the George Reeves era (who knew vacuum cleaners could be so deadly?). From a Superman lore perspective, the show is weak, but it didn't really matter. The characters were brought to life compellingly, and, ultimately, that's what gives this show its special strength."

— William Latham, author of *Space: 1999 Resurrection* and *Mary's Monster*.

CAST: George Reeves (Clark Kent/Superman); Jack Larson (Jimmy Olsen); John Hamilton (Perry White); Robert Shayne (Inspector Henderson). FIRST SEASON: Phyllis Coates (Lois Lane). SECOND SEASON to SIXTH SEASON: Noel Neill (Lois Lane).

CREW: Based on the Copyrighted Feature Appearing in *Action Comics* and *Superman Magazine*. *Produced by:* Robert J. Maxwell, Bernard Luber. *Story Editor:* Mort Weisinger. *Associate Producer:* Barney A Sarecky. *Assistant Director:* Nate Barragar. *Cameraman:* William Whitley. *Directors of Photography (various episodes):* Joe Birac, Harold Stine. *Sound Engineer:* Harry Smith. *Art Directors:* Ralph Berger, Lou Croxton. *Wardrobe:* Izzy Berne. *Casting Director:* Harold Chiles. *Props:* George Bahr. *Special Effects:* Danny Hayes. *Dialogue Director:* Steve Carr. *Make-up:* Gus Norin, Harry Thomas. *Sound Editor:* Barton Hayes. *Film Editors (various episodes):* Harry Gerstad, Al Joseph, Sam Waxman. *Special Effects:* Thol Simonson. *Photograph Effects:* Jack R. Glass.

NOTE: No airdates have been included in the guide below, as there are some notable variations in the syndicated schedule from city to city, making pinpointing a definitive airdate (even down to weeks) impossible.

SEASON ONE (1952-1953)

1. "Superman on Earth" Written by: Richard Fielding. Directed by: Thomas Carr.

On the distant and highly advanced world of Krypton, the governing council listens to a report from the planet's lead scientist, Jor-El, about the imminent destruction of the planet when its irregular orbit carries it too close to Krypton's green sun. The council ignores Jor-El's prediction, leaving the scientist and his wife Lara to send away their only son to Earth in a tiny rocketship. The boy survives the destruction of Krypton and is adopted on Earth by Smallville residents Eben and Sara Kent, who raise him as their own. The young boy, now named Clark, leaves Smallville after the death of his father some 25 years later and goes to Metropolis to work as a reporter for the *Daily Planet*. Secretly, Clark is also Superman, protector of truth, justice and the American way.

GUEST CAST: Robert Rockwell (Jor-El); Ross Elliott, Herbert Rawlinson, Stuart Randall, Aline Towne, Francis Mary, Dani Nolan.

2. "The Haunted Lighthouse" Written by: Eugene Solow. Directed by: Thomas Carr.

On a remote island, Jimmy Olsen visits his aunt Louisa, only to learn that smugglers are using a nearby lighthouse — reputed to be haunted — as their new base of operations. When crooks imperil Jimmy, it's Superman to the rescue.

GUEST CAST: Jimmy Ogg, William Challee, Maude Prickett, Allene Roberts, Sarah Padden, Steve Carr.

3. "The Case of the Talkative Dummy" Written by: Dennis Cooper and Lee Backman. Directed by: Thomas Carr.

A villainous ventriloquist is using his skills and his dummy to transmit the coordinates for armored cars, which are then held up. Jimmy stumbles onto the scheme and is promptly locked in an air-tight safe, with his oxygen running out...

GUEST CAST: Tris Coffin, Syd Saylor, Pierre Watkin, Philip Pine, Robert Kent.

4. "The Mystery of the Broken Statues" Written by: William C. Joyce. Directed by: Thomas Carr.

Two crooks go in search of a set of keys that will grant them access to a secret fortune. Lois learns that the keys are hidden inside plaster statues (which are being systematically destroyed all over Metropolis), but the knowledge could prove fatal.

GUEST CAST: Tris Coffin, Michael Vallen, Maurice Cass, Phillip Pine, Joey Ray, Wayde Crosby, Steve Carr.

5. "The Monkey Mystery" Written by: Ben Peter Freeman and Doris Gilbert. Directed by: Thomas Carr.

The Cold War heats up in Metropolis when an atomic formula developed by a communist scientist falls into the wrong hands. An organ grinder's monkey becomes Superman's ally in finding the vital formula.

GUEST CAST: Allene Roberts, Michael Vallon, Harry Lewis, William Challee, Steve Carr.

6. "A Night of Terror" Written by: Ben Peter Freeman. Directed by: Lee Sholem.

While on a trip to Canada, Lois is captured and held captive by the notorious gangster Baby Face Stevens. Jimmy attempts a rescue, but is captured in turn, leaving Superman to come to the rescue once again.

GUEST CAST: Frank Richards, John Kellog, Ann Doran, Almira Sessions, Joel Friedkin, Steve Carr, Richard Benedict.

7. "The Birthday Letter" Written by: Dennis Cooper. Directed by: Lee Sholem.

A crippled young girl's greatest wish is to meet Superman, but when she inadvertently intercepts important information about a crime, foreign counterfeiters use this desire against her. They arrange for a "fake" Superman to capture her, leaving the real Superman to set matters straight and make a birthday wish come true.

GUEST CAST: Isa Ashdown, John Doucette, Virginia Carroll, Paul Marion, Maurice Marsac, Nan Boardman, Jack Daly.

8. "The Mind Machine" Written by: Dennis Cooper and Lee Backman. Directed by: Thomas Carr.

Mr. Cranek, the Kingpin of Crime, is about to go to jail for a very long time unless he can silence the testimony of the witnesses in his trial. To this end, he uses a terrible "hypnotic" machine that wipes out human brains.

GUEST CAST: Dan Seymour (Cranek); Ben Weldon, Griff Barnett, James Seay, Steve Carr, Harry Hayden, M. Frank Orth, Lester Dorr.

9. "Rescue" Written by: Monroe Manning. Directed by: Thomas Carr.

While attempting to rescue a prospector in an old mine, Lois becomes trapped herself. As the air runs out, and death looks inevitable, it's Superman to the rescue.

GUEST CAST: Houseley Stevenson, Fred E. Sherman, Ray Bennet, Edmund Cuff.

10. "The Secret of Superman" Written by: Wells Root. Directed by: Thomas Carr.

Dr. Ort wants to know Superman's secret identity, and captures Jimmy and Lois to find out the truth. When Clark becomes involved in the kidnapping, he pretends to have amnesia so as not to reveal the Man of Steel's secret.

GUEST CAST: Peter Brocco (Dr. Ort); Larry Blake, Helen Wallace, Joel Friedkin, Steve Carr.

11. "No Holds Barred" Written by: Peter Dixon. Directed by: Lee Sholem.

A dangerous professional boxer is using a deadly grip that permanently cripples his opponents. Lois recruits a college wrestler to

get to the bottom of the deadly crime, but it is Superman who ends up saving the day.

GUEST CAST: Malcolm Mealey, Richard Reeves, Richard Elliott, Herbert Vigran, Tot Renaldo, Henry Kelky.

12. "The Deserted Village" Written by: Dick Hamilton and Ben Peter Freeman. Directed by: Thomas Carr.

Lois comes across a mystery in her hometown: the few remaining people there are being terrorized by a sinister sea serpent. In fact, the monster is a ruse to hide a deadly secret — a rare element that could be used in a hydrogen bomb!

GUEST CAST: Maude Prickett, Fred E. Sherman, Edmund Cobb, Malcolm Mealey.

13. "The Stolen Costume" Written by: Ben Peter Freeman. Directed by: Lee Sholem.

A thief breaks into Clark's apartment and finds his Superman costume. Before long, another more powerful crook is extorting Clark, threatening to expose his secret identity, and Clark must use a chilling trick to keep the criminals on ice until he can clear the matter up.

GUEST CAST: Norman Budd, Frank Jenks, Dan Seymour, Veda Ann Borg, Bob Williams.

14. "Treasure of the Incas" Written by Howard Green. Directed by: Thomas Carr.

The *Daily Planet* reporters head to South America to investigate a Peruvian work of art, but when they get there, they find that a secret cave holds a treasure. And danger too, since desperate criminals are after the wealth for themselves.

GUEST CAST: Leonard Penn, Martin Garralaga, Hal Gerard, Juan Rivero, Steve Carr.

15. "Double Trouble" Written by: Eugene Solow. Directed by: Thomas Carr.

Dangerous radioactive material is stolen from a U.S. military base in western

Europe, and an old evil from World War II threatens to rear its ugly head. When Superman attempts to retrieve the radioactive core, he is confronted by a set of deadly identical twins.

GUEST CAST: Howard Chamberlin, Selmer Jackson, Rudolph Anders, Jimmy Dodd, Steve Carr.

16. "Mystery in Wax" Written by: Ben Peter Freeman. Directed by: Lee Sholem.

A strange sculptress, Madame Selena, predicts the suicides of many Metropolis citizens at her "suicide wing" in the gallery, including that of *Daily Planet* editor Perry White! When Perry vanishes, Lois investigates Selena and finds need of Superman's services one more time.

GUEST CAST: Myra McKinney, Lester Sharpe, Steve Carr.

17. "The Runaway Robot" Written by: Dick Hamilton. Directed by: Thomas Carr.

A highly advanced robot promises great achievements in science, but the machine is soon stolen by criminals. When the powerful robot is used to commit crimes, Superman faces an opponent unlike any before.

GUEST CAST: Dan Seymour, John Harmon, Russell Johnson, Robert Easton, Herman Cantor.

18. "Drums of Death" Written by: Dick Hamilton. Directed by: Lee Sholem.

Clark, Lois and Jimmy investigate voodoo in Haiti while searching for Perry White's missing sister. Before long they find trouble when a dangerous criminal organization is discovered to be using the cult as a cover. The person behind the criminal organization turns out to be a surprise.

GUEST CAST: Harry Corden, Leonard Mudie, Milton Wood, Mabel Albertson, George Hamilton.

19. "The Evil Three" Written by: Ben Peter Freeman. Directed by: Thomas Carr.

A fishing trip to Louisiana becomes an excursion into terror for Perry and Jimmy, who are terrorized by a trio of strange psychotics who seem to be hiding a terrible secret. Jimmy and Perry seek sanctuary in an old hotel, but it's up to Superman to save the day.

GUEST CAST: Rhys Williams, Jonathan Hale, Cecil Elliot.

20. "Riddle of the Chinese Jade" Written by: Richard Fielding. Directed by: Thomas Carr.

In the Chinatown district of the city of Metropolis a young man plots to steal a priceless jade heirloom that belongs to his future wife's family. Superman intervenes to stop the theft, and Lois finds herself in danger.

GUEST CAST: Victor Sen Yung, James Craven, Gloria Saunders, Paul Burns.

21. "The Human Bomb" Written by: Richard Fielding. Directed by: Lee Sholem.

Crooks kidnap Lois and threaten to blow her to smithereens if the Man of Steel should interfere in their plans to rob a Metropolis museum. Superman must find a way to save Lois and stop the crime at the same time.

GUEST CAST: Trevor Bardette, Dennis Moore, Marshall Reed, Lou Lubin.

22. "Czar of the Underworld" Written by: Eugene Solow. Directed by: Tommy Carr.

Inspector Henderson and Clark Kent are invited to consult on the set of a new film being produced in Hollywood, a film about organized crime. Unfortunately, a real gangster is behind the production and wants it halted at all costs, but he hasn't reckoned on Superman's insistence that "the show must go on."

GUEST CAST: Paul Fix, John Maxwell, Anthony Caruso, Roy Gordon, Steve Carr.

23. "The Ghost Wolf" Written by: Dick Hamilton. Directed by: Lee Sholem.

In the woods of Canada, lumber workers fear a deadly werewolf is stalking them, and Lois, Clark and Jimmy investigate. Worse, a forest fire threatens everybody, making Superman's intervention imperative.

GUEST CAST: Stanley Andrews, Jane Adams, Lou Krugman, Harold Goodwin.

24 & 25. "The Unknown People Part I & II" Written by: Richard Fielding. Directed by Lee Sholem.

Lois and Clark investigate a mystery in Silsby, where the deepest oil well in history has also proven to be an exit for two very curious under-dwellers, or mole people. When the people of the town insist on murdering the innocent (but radioactive) creatures, Superman steps in to put an end to the unreasoning prejudice.

GUEST CAST: Jeff Corey (Luke Benson); Walter Reed; Stanley Andrews; Billy Curtis (Mole Man); Jerry Marvin, Tony Baris, Florence Lake, Ed Hinton, J. Ferrell MacDonald, Paul Burns, Steve Carr, Irene Martin, Ray Walker, Adrienne Marden.

NOTE: This two-part episode is the feature film *Superman and the Mole Men* split into two halves.

26. "Crime Wave" Written by: Ben Peter Freeman. Directed by: Thomas Carr.

A wave of violent crime has struck Metropolis and the city responds to the racketeers and thugs by enlisting Metropolis' "first citizen," Superman! But when Superman declares war on crime and sets his x-ray sights on twelve public enemies, the gangsters answer the challenge with open warfare in the streets. When Superman aims for the biggest crime king of all, Mr. Big, the nefarious, hidden crook concocts a scheme to kill the superhero.

GUEST CAST: John Eldridge, Phil Van Zandt, Al Eben, Joe Mell, Barbara Fuller, Bobby Barber.

SEASON TWO (1953-54)

27. "Five Minutes to Doom" Written by: Monroe Manning. Directed by: Thomas Carr.

An innocent man will be executed for a crime he didn't commit unless Superman can help. He must use his super speed to send word from the governor to the executioner, or a man will die.

GUEST CAST: Dabbs Greer, Sam Flint, Lois Hall, John Kellogg, Lewis Russell.

28. "The Big Squeeze" Written by: David Chantler. Directed by: Thomas Carr.

An ex-con looking to clean up his act enlists Superman's help when a former partner tries to blackmail him.

GUEST CAST: Hugh Beaumont, John Kellogg, Aline Towne, Harry Cheshire, Ted Ryan.

29. "The Man Who Could Read Minds" Written by: Roy Hamilton. Directed by: Thomas Carr.

A very successful burglar is on a crime spree in Metropolis, and Lois and Jimmy decide to pursue the enigma. They are helped by a swami, who claims he has the ability to read minds.

GUEST CAST: Lawrence Dobkin, Richard Karland, Tom Bernard.

30. "Jet Ace" Written by: David Chantler. Directed by: Thomas Carr.

A jet pilot, a hero in the States, becomes the subject of great interest in a foreign land where his skills would come in handy. The pilot is captured and interrogated, at least until Superman takes on the case.

GUEST CAST: Lane Bradford, Selmer Jackson, Richard Reeves, Jim Hayward, Larry J. Blake, Ric Roman.

31. "Shot in the Dark" Written by: David Chantler. Directed by: George Blair.

A young photographer inadvertently photographs Superman as he resumes his identity as mild-mannered Clark Kent. Worse, the photograph falls into the hands of a notorious criminal thought dead, and he has plans to expose the secret of Superman.

GUEST CAST: Billy Gray, Verde Marsh, John Eldredge, Frank Richards, Alan Lee.

32. "The Defeat of Superman" Written by: Jackson Gillis. Directed by: Thomas Carr.

Superman has his first encounter with kryptonite, the only substance that can harm the Man of Steel. Thugs capture Lois and Jimmy and plan to expose Superman to radioactive material, meteors from his destroyed home world.

GUEST CAST: Maurice Cass, Peter Mamkos, Nestor Paiva, Sid Tomack.

33. "Superman in Exile" Written by: Jackson Gillis. Directed by: Thomas Carr.

Superman is contaminated by gamma rays, meaning humans cannot survive close contact with the Man of Steel. Superman leaves Metropolis, beginning a self-imposed banishment until the effects of the gamma rays wear off, but his absence proves an opportunity too good to be true for a daring jewel thief.

GUEST CAST: Leon Askin, Joe Forte, Phil Van Zandt, John Harmon, Robert S. Carson, Greg Barton, Don Dillaway.

34. "A Ghost for Scotland Yard" Written by: Jackson Gillis. Directed by: Thomas Carr.

Clark and Jimmy are assigned to a story in London, England: the tale of an illusionist who can arise from death. It's all a ruse, however, and Jimmy ends up in mortal danger again; fortunately, Superman is nearby.

GUEST CAST: Leonard Mudie, Colin Campbell, Norma Varden, Clyde Cook.

35. "The Dog Who Knew Superman" Written by: David Chantler. Directed by: Thomas Carr.

A crook's dog gets his paws on a glove that belongs to Superman's secret identity, Clark Kent. Now the dog just has to sniff out the Man of Steel's secret and a hero will be exposed.

GUEST CAST: Billy Nelson, Ben Weldon, Lester Dorr, Donna Drake, John Daly.

36. "The Face and the Voice" Written by: Jackson Gillis. Directed by: George Blair.

A thug named Boulder has plastic surgery and voice lessons to heighten his physical resemblance to Superman, and is soon robbing stores all over Metropolis as the hero from Krypton. Wearing a bulletproof vest under his costume, Boulder robs a jewelry store, confusing the public and even Clark himself about Superman's odd behavior. When the Metropolis bank is robbed of two million dollars in gold bullion, it's time for the two Supermen to meet face-to-face.

GUEST CAST: Carleton Young, Percy Helton, George Chandler, William Newell, Nolan Leary.

37. "The Man in the Lead Mask" Written by: Leroy H. Zehren and Roy Hamilton. Directed by: George Blair.

A man with the ability to change his face and fingerprints vexes the crew at the *Daily Planet* and Metropolis' finest. But even as crooks take advantage of the situation, Superman arrives to set things right.

GUEST CAST: Frank Scannell, John Crawford, Louis Jean Heydt, Paul Bryar, John Merton, Lynn Thomas, Sam Belter.

38. "Panic in the Sky" Written by: Jackson Gillis. Directed by: Thomas Carr.

A giant meteor is on a collision course with Earth and will kill millions when it strikes. Superman flies into space to smash the asteroid, but on impact is hurtled back home, where he loses his memory and wanders about as an amnesiac. With the asteroid still approaching the planet, Superman must recover his memory in time to deflect the deadly space rock.

GUEST CAST: Jonathan Hale (Professor Roberts); Jane Frazee, Clark Howat, Thomas More.

39. "The Machine That Could Plot Crimes" Written by: Jackson Gillis. Directed by: Thomas Carr.

Dr. Quinn has invented a computer that can do virtually anything. Unfortunately, criminals manipulate the machine so they can plot the perfect crime ... and learn the secret identity of Superman.

GUEST CAST: Billy Nelson, Sherry Moreland, Stan Jarman, Ben Walden, Sam Balter, Russell Custer, Sterling Holloway.

40. "Jungle Devil" Written by: Peter L. Dixon. Directed by: Thomas Carr.

Superman comes to the rescue of a jungle expedition. Unfortunately, the expedition has mishandled a primitive icon, losing a jewel in the eye of the statue, and the result is a very angry tribe.

GUEST CAST: Doris Singleton, Damian O'Flynn, James Seay, Leon Lontoc, Steve Calvert, Henry Escalante.

41. "My Friend Superman" Written by: David Chantler. Directed by: Thomas Carr.

A restaurant owner has a special way of avoiding the "protection" costs of local gangsters: he just claims he's a good personal friend of the Man of Steel. Unfortunately, this assertion, not at all true, lands the fella in hot water.

GUEST CAST: Tito Vivolvo, Yvette Dugay, Paul Burke, Terry Frost, Joseph Vitale, Ralph Sanford.

42. "The Clown Who Cried" Written by: David Chantler. Directed by: George Blair.

A clown imposter plans to rob a special charity event. When the real clown shows up, Superman must determine which clown is which.

GUEST CAST: Mickey Sampson, Peter Brocco, Harry Mendoza, George Douglas, Charles Williams, Richard Crockett, William Wayne.

43. "The Boy Who Hated Superman" Written by: David Chantler. Directed by: George Blair.

One of Clark's investigations leads to the arrest of a common criminal. The thug's young nephew holds a grudge and plans to play out his revenge against Jimmy Olsen.

GUEST CAST: Roy Barcroft, Leonard Penn, Tyler McDuff, Charles Meredith, Richard Reeves.

44. "Semi-Private Eye" Written by: David Chantler. Directed by: George Blair.

Suspecting a link between Clark Kent and Superman, Lois hires a private eye to follow her colleague. Unfortunately, Lois and her new friend get into trouble with criminals, and Jimmy tries to help them. When he lands in hot water too, it's up to Superman to rescue the gang again.

GUEST CAST: Elisa Cook, Jr. (Homer); Paul Fix (Fingers); Richard Benedict (Cappy); Alfred Linder, Douglas Henderson.

45. "Perry White's Scoop" Written by: Roy Hamilton. Directed by: George Blair.

Old Perry White decides it is time to put on his reporter's hat again after many years as an editor. He investigates a counterfeiting scheme while attempting to solve the mystery of a corpse garbed in scuba gear.

GUEST CAST: Steve Pendelton, Jan Arvan, Robert J. Wilke, Bibs Borman, Tom Monroe.

46. "Beware the Wrecker" Written by: Royal Cole. Directed by: George Blair.

One of Metropolis's most celebrated citizens may have a secret identity to rival Superman's, that of a slippery crook getting away with one crime after another. And, not surprisingly, he's in it for the insurance money.

GUEST CAST: William Forrest, Pierre Watkin, Tom Powers, Denver Pyle, Renny McEvoy.

47. "The Golden Vulture" Written by: Jackson Gillis. Directed by: Thomas Carr.

Lois and Jimmy follow a message in a bottle to a psychotic sea captain. Superman rushes to the rescue, but is he a match for the strange pirate?

GUEST CAST: Peter Whitney (McBain); Vic Perrin (Scurvy); Murray Alper, Wes Hudman, Saul M. Gross, Dan Turner, William Vincent.

48. "Jimmy Olsen, Boy Editor" Written by: David Chantler. Directed by: Thomas Carr.

Acting as the *Daily Planet*'s "editor for the day," Jimmy plans to snag a mobster with a false story. It works out fine, except that the criminal shows up to make sure that Olsen's got his facts straight.

GUEST CAST: Herb Vigran, Keith Richards, Dick Rich, Anthony Hughes, Jack Pepper, Ronald Hargrove.

49. "Lady in Black" Written by: Jackson Gillis. Directed by: Thomas Carr.

Jimmy is fooled by criminals into believing that a house is haunted. In actuality, the thugs are hoping to keep the reporter away because the house is close to a gallery they plan to rob.

GUEST CAST: Frank Ferguson (Mr. Frank); Virginia Christian (Mrs. Frank); John Doucette (Scarface); Rudolph Anders, Frank Marlowe.

50. "Star of Fate" Written by: Roy Hamilton. Directed by: Thomas Carr.

A strange jewel, the Star of Fate, is poisonous to those who come in contact with it, and Lois is infected by the cursed object. Superman must race to Egypt and the Great Pyramids to find an age-old cure, or Lane will die.

GUEST CAST: Lawrence Ryle, Jeanne Dean, Arthur Space, Paul Burns, Ted Hecht.

51. "The Whistling Bird" Written by: David Chantler. Directed by: Thomas Carr.

The irascible and hapless Professor Quinn becomes involved in another problem. This time, he's invented a new explosive, but only his pet bird, a parrot, seems to know the precise formula that desperately interests a group of criminals.

GUEST CAST: Otto Waldis, Marshall Reed, Allene Roberts, Toni Carroll, Sterlin Holloway, Joseph Vitale.

52. "Around the World with Superman" Written by: Jackson Gillis. Directed by: Thomas Carr.

A blind girl wins a special gift: a trip around the world with Superman. She gets an even greater gift from the Man of Steel: restored vision.

GUEST CAST: Kay Morley (Elaine); Patrick Aherne, Raymond Greenleaf, Judy Nugent, Ann Carson, Max Wagner, James Brown.

SEASON THREE (1955)

53. "Through the Time Barrier" Written by: David Chantler. Directed by: Harry Gerstad.

Turk Jackson, the ruler of a gangster empire for twenty years, turns himself in, under the custody of Clark Kent, but his surrender goes awry when Professor Quinn transports Turk, Jimmy, Clark, Perry and Lois back in time to the year 50,000 BC with his newly invented time machine. Unfortunately, the scientist has neglected the reverse process and needs a special radioactive metal (found only in meteors) to return the group to the present. And Turk wants to stay in the past to construct a new criminal empire.

GUEST CAST: Jim Hyland, Florence Lake, Ed Hinton, Sterling Holloway.

54. "The Talking Clue" Written by: David Chantler. Directed by: Harry Gerstad.

Inspector Henderson's son gets into trouble over a tape recorder. It seems he's recorded the sound of a certain safe being opened, and criminals think it would be very helpful. Now Superman must save the Henderson boy.

GUEST CAST: Billy Nelson, Richard Shakleton, Brick Sullivan, Julian Upton.

55. "The Lucky Cat" Written by: Jackson Gillis. Directed by: Harry Gerstad.

A society opposed to superstition is unlucky when targeted by criminals. But Superman is the group's good luck charm.

GUEST CAST: Harry Tyler, Ted Stanhope, Carl Harbord, John Phillips, Charlie Watts.

56. "Superman Week" Written by: Jackson Gillis. Directed by: Harry Gerstad.

Superman is honored when Metropolis devotes a week to celebrating his exploits and good character. At least a few others have a different honor in mind for Superman: a block of the deadly substance kryptonite.

GUEST CAST: Herb Vigran, Tamar Cooper, Jack George, Paul Burke, Buddy Mason.

57. "Great Caesar's Ghost" Written by: Jackson Gillis. Directed by: Harry Gerstad.

Perry White has been known to utter the phrase "Great Caesar's Ghost" from time to time, but he never meant it as an invocation. It seems that the crusty editor, now planning to testify in an important trial is being haunted by the ghost of the Roman

general. But is Perry going crazy or just plain losing his credibility?

GUEST CAST: Trevor Bardette, Jim Hayward, Olaf Hytten.

58. "Test of a Warrior" Written by: Leroy H. Zehren. Directed by: George Blair.

An older American Indian still hopes to prove his character by passing his tribe's greatest and most dangerous rite of passage. Jimmy tries to help him, but it is Superman who comes to the rescue.

GUEST CAST: Ralph Moody, Francis McDonald, George Lewis, Lane Bradford.

59. "Olsen's Millions" Written by: David Chantler. Directed by: George Blair.

Jimmy is richly rewarded by a kindly old lady when Superman rescues her cat from accidental confinement in her vault. Now a millionaire, the young Olsen becomes the target of criminals who see an opportunity.

GUEST CAST: Elizabeth Patterson (Miss Peabody); George Stone (Big George); Richard Reeves, Leonard Carey.

60. "Clark Kent, Outlaw" Written by: Leroy H. Zehren. Directed by: George Blair.

Has Clark Kent gone bad? It certainly looks that way when the straight-laced reporter joins a criminal gang (using Superman's incredible powers as a safecracker), but there is more to the plot than meets the eye, a fact which an in-the-know Perry White accidentally lets slip.

GUEST CAST: John Doucette (Foster); Sid Tomack (Curtis); George Eldredge, Lyn Thomas, Tris Coffin.

61. "The Magic Necklace" Written by: Jackson Gillis. Directed by: George Blair.

An archaeologist claims that he has discovered a mystical jewel necklace that renders its wearer invulnerable. Of course, a necklace of invulnerability would be just the thing for a crook hoping to defeat Superman, and that's just what a certain thug desires. Unfortunately, the archaeologist isn't exactly on the up-and-up about his discovery.

GUEST CAST: Leonard Mudie, Frank Jenks, John Harmon, Paul Fierro, Lawrence Ryle, Ted Hecht, Jake Morrell.

62. "The Bully of Dry Gulch" Written by: David Chantler. Directed by: George Blair.

Lois and Jimmy make a stopover in a small town out west, only to discover it is run by a very nasty bully. The overbearing fellow has Jimmy thrown in jail and then decides that Lois is to his liking.

GUEST CAST: Raymond Hatton (Sagebrush); Myron Healey (Gunner); Eddie Baker (Bartender).

63. "Flight to the North" Written by: David Chantler. Directed by: George Blair.

A strange and simple fellow accepts an invitation meant for Superman — to fly a certain item (a dessert) to Alaska. Unfortunately, there is danger in the invitation, and the real Superman must intervene.

GUEST CAST: Chuck Conners, Ben Welden, Richard Garland, Ralph Sanford, Marjorie Owens, George Chandler.

64. "The Seven Souvenirs" Written by: Jackson Gillis. Directed by: George Blair.

Professor Pepperwinkle becomes embroiled in a plot involving a criminal, Superman, and a pair of deadly knives. The crook believes that Superman's powerful x-ray vision will transform the daggers into a valuable substance — pure radium.

GUEST CAST: Arthur Space, Rick Vallin, Steve Calvert, Louise Lewis, Jack O'Shea.

65. "King for a Day" Written by: Dwight Babcock. Directed by: George Blair.

Jimmy Olsen gets into trouble again. This time he agrees to take the place of an endangered ruler (whom he resembles). While Jimmy becomes the target of assassins, the real ruler plots to stop those who would oppose him.

GUEST CAST: Peter Mamakos, Leon Askin, Phil Van Zandt, Jan Arvan, Carolyn Scott.

SEASON FOUR (1956)

66. "Joey" Written by: David Chantler. Directed by: Harry Gerstad.

The *Daily Planet* has purchased a horse and hopes for it to gallop to victory in an upcoming race. While the former owner of the horse, a kindly young girl, works with the animal, Superman works to expose corruption at the track.

GUEST CAST: Janine Perreau, Mauritz Hugo, Tom London, Billy Nelson.

67. "The Unlucky Number" Written by: David Chantler. Directed by: Harry Gerstad.

Clark foils the plan of criminals who had rigged a contest. Giving the money to a kindly old lady, Clark soon learns that the criminals feel double-crossed out of their ill-gotten gains.

GUEST CAST: Elizabeth Patterson, Henry Blair, Russell Conklin, Jack Littlefield, Alan Reynolds, Tony De Mario, Alfred Linder.

68. "The Big Freeze" Written by: David Chantler. Directed by: Harry Gerstad.

An ambitious politician knows he has no chance of winning an upcoming election, since Superman will be policing the event. To stop the Man of Steel's interference, the politician plans to put him on ice, literally, locking him in a freezer and keeping the hero in permanent cold storage.

GUEST CAST: Richard Reeves, George E. Stone, John Phillips, Eddie Baker.

69. "Peril by Sea" Written by: David Chantler. Directed by: Harry Gerstad.

Criminals learn that Perry White has apparently developed a formula to extract uranium from ordinary seawater. When Jimmy runs a story about the chief's exciting new discovery, he inadvertently endangers his friend.

GUEST CAST: Claude Akins, Julian Upton, Ed Penny.

70. "Topsy Turvy" Written by: David Chantler. Directed by: Harry Gerstad.

Another problem with Professor Pepperwinkle: his latest invention (a strange mirror) has been stolen by thugs.

GUEST CAST: Ben Welden, Mickey Knox, Charles Williams.

71. "Jimmy the Kid" Written by: Leroy H. Zehren. Directed by: Phil Ford.

Clark has been working on a story that will bring down the gangster Gridley, but the crook has an ace up his sleeve: an exact physical double of Jimmy Olsen named Kid Collins! Meanwhile, Superman has to put out a forest fire in the North Ridge Area, as the replacement Jimmy makes mistakes with Lois and Perry. The fake Olsen breaks into Clark's apartment and finds Kent's Superman uniform!

GUEST CAST: Rick Vallin, Damian O'Flynn, Diana Darrin, Steve Conte, Florence Ravenel.

72. "The Girl Who Hired Superman" Written by: David Chantler. Directed by: Phil Ford.

A reluctant Superman agrees to entertain at a party for a wealthy and Metropolis prominent citizen. But things take a strange turn when Superman is asked to become involved in smuggling!

GUEST CAST: Gloria Talbott, Maurice Marsac, George Khoury, Lyn Guild, John Eldredge.

73. "The Wedding of Superman" Written by: Jackson Gillis. Directed by: Phil Ford.

Swamped by letters for an advice column she has temporarily taken over, Lois dreams of being married to her true love, Superman. In her dream, Lois shatters a crime syndicate, accepts Superman's marriage proposal, asks the Chief to give her away on her big day and — causing an interesting problem — asks Clark to be the best man. Meanwhile, in the dream, public defender Faraday is a criminal boss who plots to disrupt the blessed day with a time bomb in the wedding cake.

GUEST CAST: Milton Frome, Julie Bennet, Doyle Brooks, John Cliff, Nolan Leary, Dolores Fuller.

74. "Dagger Island" Written by: Robert Leslie Bellem. Directed by: Phil Ford.

It's intrigue and murder on a desert island when the heirs to a fortune find that the owner of their intended wealth is still alive — and murderous. Jimmy and Lois are endangered, naturally, and it's Superman to the rescue again.

GUEST CAST: Myron Healey (Paul); Dean Cromer (Micky); Raymond Hatton, Ray Montgomery.

75. "Blackmail" Written by: Oliver Drake and David Chantler. Directed by: Harry Gerstad.

Inspector Henderson is unexpectedly arrested with stolen money on his person, a frame job by thugs working toward a different goal: the destruction of Superman with a new weapon.

GUEST CAST: Herb Vigran (Arnold); Sid Tomack (Eddie); George Chandler (Bates); Selmer Jackson.

76. "The Deadly Rock" Written by: Jackson Gillis. Directed by: Harry Gerstad.

Kryptonite goes on the open market,

and a criminal hoping to destroy Superman bids on it. Meanwhile, an F.B.I. agent and friend of Clark reacts to kryptonite as though he were Superman...

GUEST CAST: Robert Lowery (Gary); Lyn Thomas, Steve Geray, Robert Foulk, Ric Roman, Vincent Perry, Sid Melton.

77. "The Phantom Ring" Written by: David Chantler. Directed by: Phil Ford.

There's a new threat in Metropolis: a gang of criminals who can render themselves invisible while carrying special coins. Clark hopes to infiltrate the gang, but his ruse is discovered and he is thrown from a plane in mid-air.

GUEST CAST: Paul Burke, Peter Brocco, Lane Bradford, Ed Hinton, Henry Rowland.

78. "The Jolly Roger" Written by: David Chantler. Directed by: Phil Ford.

A small island in the Pacific is home to a cult of modern-day pirates, but the group is endangered by Navy plans to bomb the island. Superman must save Lois and Jimmy when they are taken hostage by the pirates, and the bombs start dropping.

GUEST CAST: Leonard Mudie, Myron Healy, Patrick Aherne, Jean Lewis, Pierre Watkin, Eric Snowden, Dean Cromer, Ray Montgomery.

SEASON FIVE (1957)

79. "Peril in Paris" Written by: David Chantler. Directed by: George Blair.

On a visit to Paris, Superman and Jimmy become involved with a defector harboring a secret motive. As a result, Superman finds that he has been used by a jewel thief and must set matters straight.

GUEST CAST: Lilyan Chauvin (Anna); Peter Mamakos (Gregor); Albert Carrier (Lamont); Charles La Torre, Franz Roehn.

80. "Tin Hero" Written by: Wilton Schiller. Directed by: George Blair.

An unlikely local hero, a nerdy banker, foils a robbery and receives his fifteen minutes of fame. Meanwhile, crooks plan to exploit the fellow, and Jimmy gets caught in the middle.

GUEST CAST: Carl Ritcher, Sam Finn, Frank Richards, Paula Houston, Jack Lomas.

81. "The Town That Wasn't" Written by: Wilton Schiller. Directed by: Harry Gerstad.

Jimmy gets stopped for speeding in a small town and must pay a ticket. Actually, the town, the ticket and the authorities are all part of a strange criminal plot, one intended to separate people from their hard-earned money. Superman and Lois intend to stop the fake town from filling its "quota."

GUEST CAST: Frank Connor, Charles Gray, Richard Elliott, Terry Frost.

82. "The Tomb of Zaharan" Written by: David Chantler. Directed by: George Blair.

Lois and Jimmy get into trouble again when foreign dignitaries believe the beautiful Ms. Lane is the ruler of their country reborn. According to legend, she must be sacrificed.

GUEST CAST: George Khoury, Jack Kruschen, Ted Hecht, Gabriel Mooradian, Jack Reitzen.

83. "The Man Who Made Dreams Come True" Written by: David Chantler. Directed by: George Blair.

A con man claiming he can make the wishes of others come true snares a gullible ruler of a foreign country. Can Superman cure the King's reliance on superstition and save his throne from the flim flam artist?

GUEST CAST: Cyril Delevanti (King Leo); Keith Richards, John Banner, Sandy Harrison, Hal Hoover, Laurie Mitchell, Nancy Boyd.

84. "Disappearing Lois" Written by: David and Peggy Chantler. Directed by: Harry Gerstad.

Hoping to one-up Clark, Lois stages her own disappearance to waylay her reporter friend. Then, with Jimmy in tow, she rushes to an exclusive and dangerous interview with a criminal kingpin.

GUEST CAST: Milton Frome, Ben Welden, Andrew Branham, Yvonne White.

85. "Money to Burn" Written by: David Chantler. Directed by: Harry Gerstad.

Burning buildings, firemen, and surreptitious crooks are the ingredients in an investigation of insurance fraud by Perry White. But where there's smoke, there's not just fire, there's Superman!

GUEST CAST: Mauritz Hugo, Dale Van Sickel, Richard Emory.

86. "Close Shave" Written by: Benjamin B. Crocker. Directed by: Harry Gerstad.

Jimmy's barber is actually a hypnotist/mesmerist of sorts, and his latest project is the rehabilitation of a gangster customer. But neither the gangster nor his gang appreciates being manipulated, and Jimmy and the barber find themselves facing a close shave.

GUEST CAST: Rick Vallin, Richard Benedict, Jack Littlefield, Missy Russell, John Ferry, Harry Fleer.

87. "The Phony Alibi" Written by: Peggy Chantler. Directed by: George Blair.

Professor Pepperwinkle has invented a matter materializer/dematerializer that can deconstruct people and transport them across vast distances. Criminals want the device to help them escape crime scenes, and Lois and Jimmy end up trapped in a frozen wasteland when they test it.

GUEST CAST: John Cliff, Frank Kreig, Harry Arnie, William Challee.

88. "The Prince Albert Coat" Written by: David Chantler. Directed by: Harry Gerstad.

Superman is kept busy while helping a lad recover his grandfather's missing life's savings, money that is hidden in a coat the boy discarded.

GUEST CAST: Raymond Hatton (Jackson); Stephen Wooton (Bobby); Daniel White, Ken Christy, Phil Arnold, Jack Finch, Frank Fenton.

89. "The Stolen Elephant" Written by: David Chantler. Directed by: Harry Gerstad.

A missing circus elephant ends up in the care of a boy who desperately wants a pet for his birthday. Clark must save the animal from a group of thieves who believe the elephant has something of value.

GUEST CAST: Gregory Moffett, Thomas Jackson, Eve McVeih, Gregg Martell, Stanford Jolley.

90. "Mr. Zero" Written by: Peggy Chantler. Directed by: Harry Gerstad.

Superman must go head to head with a powerful Martian citizen, Mr. Zero, who possesses abilities that rival his own. Unfortunately, criminals capture Mr. Zero and plot to use his powers for their own financial gain.

GUEST CAST: Billy Curtis (Mr. Zero); Herb Vigran, George Barrows, Leon Alton, George Spotts.

91. "Whatever Goes Up" Written by: Witlon Schiller. Directed by: Harry Gerstad.

Has Jimmy made a scientific breakthrough, developing an anti-gravity elixir? Some criminals think so, and go after the boy reporter and his "formula."

GUEST CAST: Tris Coffin, Milton Frome.

SEASON SIX (1958)

92. "The Last Knight" Written by: David Chantler. Directed by: Thomas Carr.

Lois and Jimmy are kidnapped while investigating a society of knights, and Superman must rescue them.

GUEST CAST: Marshall Bradford (Sir Arthur); Paul Power (Gawaine); Andrew Branham, Pierre Watkin, Jason Johnson.

93. "The Magic Secret" Written by: Robert Leslie Bellem and Whitney Ellsworth. Directed by: Phil Ford.

A villainous mobster plans to kill Superman with his new kryptonite gun. Lois and Jimmy are the bait.

GUEST CAST: Freeman Lusk, George Selk, Jack Reynolds, Buddy Lewis, Kenneth Alton.

94. "Divide and Conquer" Written by: Robert Leslie Bellem and Whitney Ellsworth. Directed by: Phil Ford.

Superman becomes embroiled in foreign politics when he saves a top leader from death. But the interference carries a price: Superman is incarcerated and, because of his values of law and order is unwilling to break out. Superman devises a unique method, splitting himself into two beings, to work as the Man of Steel and still stay in prison.

GUEST CAST: Donald Lawton, Everett Glass, Jack Reitsen, Jack Littlefield.

95. "The Mysterious Cube" Written by: Robert Leslie Bellem and Whitney Ellsworth. Directed by: George Blair.

A wanted criminal finds a unique place to hide: an apparently invulnerable cube of concrete. Superman devises a way to make the criminal leave his sanctuary and face justice before the statute of limitations on his crime ends.

GUEST CAST: Everett Glass, Ben Welden, Keith Richards, Paul Barton, Bruce Wendell.

96. "The Atomic Captive" Written by: Robert Leslie Bellem and Whitney Ellsworth. Directed by: George Blair.

Lois and Jimmy go hunting for a foreign atomic scientist seeking sanctuary in the U.S., unaware that he is emitting a dangerous level of radiation. With spies on their heels, Lois and Jimmy search for a man — a search that could end with their deaths!

GUEST CAST: Elaine Riley, Jan Arvan, Walter Reed, George Khoury.

97. "The Superman Silver Mine" Written by: Peggy Chantler. Directed by: George Blair.

A nasty imposter has usurped the rightful ownership of a Texas silver mine. Superman gets involved in the case, hoping to smoke out the double and restore the mine to its legal owner.

GUEST CAST: Dabbs Greer, Charles Maxwell.

98. "The Big Forget" Written by: David Chantler. Directed by: George Blair.

Criminals are using a memory altering device after they commit crimes, causing witnesses to their nefarious acts to forget all about them. Superman gets in on the action, and ultimately must use the "forgetting" gas to preserve his secret identity.

GUEST CAST: Herb Vigran, Billy Nelson.

99. "The Gentle Monster" Written by: David Chantler. Directed by: Howard Brotherton.

Professor Pepperwinkle builds a robot with a serious drawback: it is powered by a chunk of kryptonite, and is therefore deadly to Superman.

GUEST CAST: Ben Welden, Orville Sherman.

100. "Superman's Wife" Written by: Robert Leslie Bellem and Whitney Ellsworth. Directed by: Lew Landers.

Is Superman a married man? Actually, no. A police woman has gone undercover as his bride to help stop a nefarious criminal gang. And Lois isn't happy about it, either.

GUEST CAST: Joi Lansing, John Eldridge, Harry Arnie, Wayne Heffley.

101. "Three in One" Written by: Wilton Schiller and Whitney Ellsworth. Directed by: Lew Landers.

Superman becomes a suspect in a string of crimes seemingly accomplished by people with super powers. In reality, three rejects from the carnival are behind the crime spree.

GUEST CAST: Sid Tomack, Rick Vallin, Craig Duncan.

102. "The Brainy Burro" Written by: Wilton Schiller and Whitney Ellsworth. Directed by: Lew Landers.

Are criminals making asses out of the local constabulary in Mexico by using a telepathic donkey in their crimes? Superman flies south of the border to ferret out the truth about a most unusual mule.

GUEST CAST: Mark Cavell, Ken Mayer, Sid Cassell.

103. "The Perils of Superman" Written by: Robert Leslie Bellem and Whitney Ellsworth. Directed by: George Reeves.

A man wearing a metal mask plots revenge against Superman for sending his criminal cohorts to jail. His plan: to get at Superman through his friends. His advantage: there are a dozen identical villains on the loose all over Metropolis. The villain captures Clark and threatens to drop him into acid, while letting him know that Perry is in a sawmill sliding towards a fatal buzz saw. Meanwhile, Lois is tied to railroad tracks and Jimmy is trapped in a runaway car.

GUEST CAST: Michael Fox, Steve Mitchell, Yvonne White.

104. "All That Glitters" Written by: Robert Leslie Bellem. Directed by: George Reeves.

Professor Pepperwinkle has devised a method to produce gold from scrap elements like iron, but Clark, Perry White, the U.S. Secretary of the Treasury and the President of the World Bank urge him not to use the invention lest the global economy be ruined. Two thugs hold up the professor and order him to produce tons of gold for them, but when Jimmy and Lois investigate, another of Pepperwinkle's inventions come to light: a kryptonite pill that grants ordinary mortals the powers of Superman! After ingesting the pill, Lois and Jimmy get a chance to fly ... or do they?

GUEST CAST: Len Hendry, Jack Littlefield, Richard Elliott, Paul Cavanaugh, George Eldredge.

The New Adventures of Superman (1967-1968); a.k.a. The Superman/Aquaman Hour, The Superman/Batman Hour

VOICE TALENTS: Bud Collyer (Superman/Clark Kent); Joan Alexander (Lois Lane).

CREW: A Filmation Production. *Produced by:* Lou Scheimer and Norm Prescott. *Series Director:* Hal Sutherland. *Series Writers:* Robert Haney and Dennis Marks.

It's a Bird, It's a Plane, It's Superman! (1975)
LIVE-ACTION TV MOVIE MUSICAL

CAST: Kenneth Mars (Max Mencken); Lesley Warren (Lois Lane); Loretta Swit (Sydney Carlton); David Wayne (Dr. Abner Sedgwick); David Wilson (Clark Kent/Superman); Malachi Throne (King Big Boss); Al Molinaro (Thug); Phil Leeds (Thug); Harvey Lembeck (Thug); Allen Ludden (Perry White); George Chandler (Mr. Kent); Irene Tedrow (Mrs. Kent); Lou

Wills, Jr., Danny Goldman, Geoffrey Horne, Stuart Getz, Michael Lembeck.

CREW: Cineworld Corporation Presents *It's a Bird, It's a Plane, It's Superman! Directed by:* Jack Regas. *Music and Lyrics:* Charles Strouse, Lee Adams. *Adapted for TV by:* Romeo Muller. *Based on the Libretto by:* David Newman and Robert Benton. *Originally Produced on Broadway by:* Harold Prince, in association with Ruth Mitchell. *Music Coordinator:* Al Mello. *Costumes:* Bill Beleyv. *Art Director:* Ken Johnson. *Music Arranged and Conducted by:* Fred Werner. *Choreographed by:* Alex Plasschaert. *Associate Producer:* Elliott F. Alexander. *Produced by:* Norman Twain. *Production Assistant:* Wendy Charles. A Norman Twain Production. *Running time:* 90 minutes (approx.).

NOTE: This musical features several sections or chapters (eleven, actually). The titles are: *Chapter One: Who He Is and How He Came to Be*; *Chapter Two: Merchant of Doom*; *Chapter Three: Superman Makes It*; *Chapter Four: Sedgwick's Revenge*; *Chapter Five: The Net Tightens*; *Chapter Six: Clark Kent Finds Happiness*; *Chapter Seven: Oh Clark, Have You Been There All Along?*; *Chapter Eight: Superman—Trapped!*; *Chapter Nine: Get Lost Superman*; *Chapter Ten: Curtains for Superman* and finally, *Chapter Eleven: Superman Triumphant*.

In Metropolis, the great hero from Krypton, Superman, is beset by enemies on all sides, including the Mob, *Daily Planet* columnist Max Mencken, and the villainous Dr. Sedgwick, who is bitter because he has never won a Nobel Prize. As ace reporter Clark Kent, Superman attracts less attention. In fact, the beautiful Lois Lane does not even know he exists — she's too busy lusting after the Man of Steel.

Superman flies to M.I.T. (the Metropolis Institute of Technology) to stop Dr. Sedgwick's death ray. When Sedgwick fails to kill Supe, the mad doctor teams up with Mencken and the Mob. His new plan is to make Superman destroy himself! Unaware of this insidious plot, Clark Kent finds romance with Sydney, Max's assistant. She gives him the confidence to romance Lois, but that confidence quickly dissipates. Superman goes to M.I.T. to accept an award — a laundry building is named after him — but while he's there City Hall explodes. Now Max Mencken (who planted the bomb) wants to know: Where was Superman?! Metropolis turns against the hero, and, worse, Dr. Sedgwick and Max Mencken have discovered his secret identity. Sedgwick tries to psychoanalyze Clark, diffusing the rest of his confidence. But when Lois is captured and wired to TNT by Mencken and Sedgwick, Superman finds the confidence he needs to fight back.

Superman rescues Lois and defeats the villains. When the TNT explodes, it causes amnesia in Sedgwick and Mencken, and they forget Superman's secret identity and become contributing members of society.

Superman: The Movie (1978)
LIVE-ACTION FILM

"...the classic example of a near-perfect super heroic movie.... Reeve made you believe that his nebbish Clark Kent *couldn't* be the larger-than-life Superman..."
— Marc Bernadin. *Science Fiction Explorer #9*: "Uncut Gems." October 1995, page 8.

"*Superman: The Movie is* probably the greatest superhero movie of all time. More importantly, it's two films. Unfortunately, the first film is better than the second. From the first time we hear John Williams' epic score, one of his finest, we know we're in for something special. The scenes on Krypton work amazingly well, and were eye-popping in the 1970s. Clark Kent's childhood is handled with great pathos and a real sense of the American Midwest. The Fortress of Solitude scenes are absolutely amazing. Then we have Superman's first appearance in Metropolis, particularly his rescue of Lois Lane, which works amazingly well and may be the finest moment ever in a superhero film. Then the movie slips a bit. While the characters are fun, the special effects top notch, the music outstanding, the second half of the film just doesn't live up to the first half. There's something that's just not satisfying about it — probably this has much to do with the famous scene of Superman turning back the Earth in order to save Lois. Something just didn't gel, it was too easy a solution, and, unfortunately, makes one wonder why he doesn't do this all the time. Still, this is an absolutely amazing film, filled with good humor, an epic storyline, great characters, wonderful music — you name it, this film had it."

— William Latham, author of *Space: 1999 Resurrection* and *Mary's Monster*.

CAST: Marlon Brando (Jor-El); Gene Hackman (Lex Luthor); Christopher Reeve (Clark Kent/Superman); Ned Beatty (Otis); Jackie Cooper (Perry White); Glenn Ford (Jonathan Kent); Margot Kidder (Lois Lane); Jack O'Halloran (General Non); Valerie Perrine (Miss Tessmacher); Terence Stamp (General Zod); Susannah York (Lara); Jeff East (Young Clark); Marc McClure (Jimmy Olsen); Sarah Douglas (Ursa); Trevor Howard, Phyllis Thaxter, Harry Andrews.

CREW: Warner Brothers and Alexander Salkind Present a Richard Donner Film. *Executive Producer:* Ilya Salkind. *Produced by:* Pierre Spengler. *Directed by:* Richard Donner. *Production Design:* John Barry. *Photographed by:* Geoffrey Unsworth. *Editor:* Stuart Baird. *Music:* John Williams. *Superman Created by:* Jerry Siegel and Joe Shuster. *Story by:* Mario Puzo. *Screenplay:* Mario Puzo, David Newman, Leslie Newman, Robert Benton. *Creative Consultant:* Tom Mankiewicz. *Associate Producer:* Charles F. Greenlaw. *M.P.A.A. Rating:* PG. *Running time:* 154 minutes.

On the distant planet Krypton, a council of elders hears a legal case prosecuted by the great scientist Jor-El against three nefarious criminals, General Zod, Ursa and Non. The trio is found guilty of insurrection and assigned a terrible fate: eternal imprisonment in the dimension of dread known as the Phantom Zone.

Later, Jor-El pleads for a hearing regarding another, more important case. He believes that Krypton will destroy itself when it shifts orbit, and recommends an immediate evacuation of the planet. The council decides against Jor-El, and the scientist and his wife, Lara, send their only son, Kal-El, away to the distant planet called Earth. Kal-El's rocket escapes just as Krypton explodes.

Some years later, the Kryptonian spaceship crashes in Smallville, Kansas. A young Kal-El is adopted by kindly farmers, the Kents. Renamed Clark Kent, Kal-El's alien metabolism grants him remarkable powers, including x-ray vision, super speed and strength, and even the incredible ability to fly. Unfortunately, these abilities also make Clark an outsider, and he is unable to reveal his special gifts to the world. This secret is particularly hard to keep in adolescence, when Clark falls in love with cheerleader Lana Lang.

When Jonathan Kent, Clark's adopted father, passes away, Kal-El understands it is time to seek the truth of his own origin. He heads north with a green crystalline power cell from his spaceship, and it creates for him a palace, his fortress of solitude.

There Clark studies for many years, learning about his native people, his biological parents, and the Kryptonian edict that he should not interfere in human affairs. Now a grown man, Clark Kent dons a special uniform and cape, becoming a new hero called Superman.

Clark begins life in the city of Metropolis, working as a reporter for the *Daily Planet*. He teams up with acerbic but beautiful reporter Lois Lane, a woman who has eyes only for the incredible Superman. Unfortunately, some denizens of Metropolis are less pleasant than Lois or friend Jimmy Olsen. Lex Luthor, a master criminal, dwells in opulence in a cavern beneath Grand Central Station and plans the crime of the century. He plots to redirect two nuclear missiles to the San Andreas fault, hoping to knock sunny California right into the ocean, leaving Lex's worthless desert property the new west coast beachfront.

Superman intervenes to stop Luthor, but Lex learns of a substance fatal to Superman, a rock from Krypton called kryptonite. As Superman is sidelined by the green glowing kryptonite, Lex launches his plan, plunging the west coast of the United States into chaos. When Lois Lane's life is jeopardized and Clark is unable to save mil- lions of innocent people, he must contemplate violating Krypton's law of non-interference, and changing the very history of the planet Earth.

Superman II (1981)
LIVE-ACTION FILM

"*Superman II* is a marvelous toy. It's funny, it's full of tricks, and it manages to be royally entertaining, which is all it really aims for.... Mr. Reeve is so perfectly suited to the Superman role that he gives the film a warmth and energy it might not otherwise have."
— Janet Maslin, *The New York Times:* "Clark Kent Vamped," June 19, 1981, page C8.

"I was disappointed in the film, finding it, ultimately, less than super. It didn't deliver for me at the critical moments."
— Howard Zimmerman, *Starlog* #51: "Last-word," September 1981, page 66.

"*Superman II*, when it was first released, seemed to knock the first film right off its pedestal. This is probably the most satisfying superhero film of them all, but it has a darkness beneath it. Richard Donner's footage was reshot, and Richard Lester added a little more levity to the proceedings, which over the years has hurt the film. The strength of this film ultimately comes from Mario Puzo and Tom Mankiewicz—these two Superman films, as a written epic, work wonderfully well together. John Williams not returning to do the music removes some of its luster, as does the unfortunate substitution of Susannah York for Marlon Brando—what a film this could have been without these substitutions. One would hope someday that the Richard Donner version of the film might be restored. Terence Stamp as Zod is right up there with Ricardo Montalban in *Star Trek II: The Wrath of Khan* and Alan Rickman in *Die Hard* in the most beloved villains department. If this film were made today, the somewhat cheesy fight scenes between Supes and the other Kryptonians would no doubt work much better, but this is still a good film."
— William Latham, author of *Mary's Monster* and *Space: 1999 Resurrection*.

CAST: Gene Hackman (Lex Luthor); Christopher Reeve (Clark Kent/Superman); Ned Beatty (Otis); Jackie Cooper (Perry White); Sarah Douglas (Ursa); Margot Kidder (Lois Lane); Jack O'Halloran (Non); Valerie Perrine (Eve Teschmacher); Susannah York (Lara); Clifton James (Sheriff); E.G. Marshall (President of the United States); Marc McClure (Jimmy Olsen); Terence Stamp (General Zod); John Hollis (Kryptonian Elder).

CREW: An Alexander and Ilya Salkind Production, *Superman II. Photographed by:* Geoffrey Unsworth. *Director of Photography:* Bob Paynter. *Director of Miniature Effects and Additional Flying Sequences:* Derek Meddings. *Production Design:* John Barry and Peter Murton. *Film Editor:* John Victor-Smith. *Director of Special Effects:* Colin Chilvers. *Supervisor of Visual and Optical Effects:* Roy Field. *Director of Photography, Miniature Unit:* Paul Wilson. *Special Effects Director, Flying Unit:* Zoran Perisic. *Director of Photography, Flying Unit:* Denys Coop. *Production Executives:* Geoffrey Helman and Robert Simmonds. *Second Unit Directors:* David Tomblin and Robert Lynn. *Casting:* Lynn Stalmaster. *Assistant Director:* Dusty Symonds. *Costumes:* Yvonne Blake, Susan Yelland. *Music:* Ken Thorne. *From Original Material Composed by:* John Williams. *Superman Created by:* Jerry Siegel and Joe Shuster. *Creative Consultant:* Tom Mankiewicz. *Story:* Mario Puzo. *Screenplay by:* Mario Puzo, David and Leslie Newman. *Executive Producer:* Ilya Salkind. *Producer:* Pierre Spengler. *Directed by:* Richard Lester. *M.P.A.A. Rating:* PG. *Running time:* 127 minutes.

Pursuing a story in Paris, Lois Lane becomes involved in a terrorist scheme to blow up the Eiffel Tower. Superman flies to her rescue and sends the bomb (in an elevator) hurtling into deep space. Unfortunately, this act of bravery has dramatic repercussions. Far out in space, the detonation destroys the Kryptonian prison known as the Phantom

Zone and releases three insurrectionist criminals, General Zod, Ursa and the hulking Non.

Back on Earth, Clark Kent and Lois Lane work together on a story to expose a corrupt honeymoon hideaway at Niagara Falls, but Lois is more interested in proving that Clark is actually Superman, a charge vehemently denied by Clark. After a harrowing day in which Lois nearly drowns near the falls, Clark makes a mistake and reveals his identity to Lois. With so much to talk about, Clark and Lois begin a romantic relationship.

Meanwhile, trouble is brewing in two spots. First, master criminal Lex Luthor has escaped from prison; and, secondly, the Kryptonian criminals begin a reign of terror, destroying an astronaut crew on the moon and ravaging a small town in Texas. Superman flies Lois to his Fortress of Solitude and decides to give up his powers to know mortal love. He is unaware that even as he makes this fateful decision, the Kryptonian criminals are forcing the surrender of the United States. Lex Luthor, hoping to ingratiate himself with Zod and the others, plots to reveal important information about Superman in exchange for the rulership of Australia.

Human and without powers, Clark realizes the world needs Superman more than ever, and attempts to get his powers back. But will he be successful? And if so, can he defeat the super-powered criminals threatening Earth and still have a relationship with Lois Lane?

Superman III (1983)
LIVE-ACTION FILM

"The director, Richard Lester, sets the tone in the opening sequence, with a series of throwaway sight gags. And the mood stays light much of the way, except for a bout with kryptonite and a heavily symbolic scene wherein Superman literally wrestles with his "secret identity"—an intrusion on the fun of the movie, although it gives Reeve a chance to do some real acting for a change."
—David Sterritt, *The Christian Science Monitor*, July 14, 1983, page 17.

"It's Lester at the top of the physical sight-gag form he has semaphored so deliciously since his early Beatles movies. But that sublime innocence and invention now has a slight edge of nastiness, which, considering the audience for this film, is unsettling."
— Sheila Benson, *The Los Angeles Times*, June 17, 1983, page 1.

"*Superman III* is a disaster, and suffers from some of the same weaknesses as *Supergirl*—if the villain doesn't work, neither does the film. Margot Kidder's absence from most of the film is painful. Richard Pryor's inclusion is equally painful. This film is one of the most disappointing follow-ups to a worthy film in recent memory."

—William Latham, author of *Space: 1999 Resurrection, Mary's Monster*.

"...[T]he worst of the Superman visualizations. The first 20 minutes of *Superman III* hit an all-time low for heroic action."
—Dennis Dooley and Gary Engle, editors. *Superman at Fifty: The Persistence of a Legend*. Octavia Books, 1987, page 75.

CAST: Christopher Reeve (Clark Kent/Superman); Richard Pryor (Gus Gorman); Jackie Cooper (Perry White); Marc McClure (Jimmy Olsen); Annette O'Toole (Lana Lang); Annie Ross (Vera); Pamela Stephenson (Lorelei); Robert Vaughn (Ross Webster); Margot Kidder (Lois Lane); Gavin O'Herlihy (Brad); Paul Kaethler (Ricky).

CREW: An Alexander and Ilya Salkind Production, *Superman III*. *Production Executive:* Pauline Corteleno. *Director of Photography:* Robert Paynter. *Production Design:* Peter Murton. *Director of Special Effects and Miniatures:* Colin Chilvers. *Supervisor of Optical and Visual Effects:* Roy Field. *Flying and Second Unit Direction:* David Lane. *First Assistant Director:* Dusty Symonds. *Casting:* Debbie McWilliams, Mike

Fenton, Jane Feinberg. *Costume Design:* Evangeline Harrison. *Film Editor:* John Victor Smith. *Music:* Ken Thorne. *Based on Material Composed by:* John Williams. *Associate Producer:* Robert Simmonds. *Screenplay by:* David and Leslie Newman. *Executive Producer:* Ilya Salkind. *Producer:* Pierre Spengler. *Original Songs:* Giorgio Moroder. *Directed by:* Richard Lester. *M.P.A.A. Rating:* PG. *Running time:* 125 minutes.

With Lois Lane leaving the country on vacation, Clark Kent returns to his hometown of Smallville for a high school class reunion. There he befriends an old flame, lovely Lana Lang, and her young son. While Clark plays family man and finds time, as Superman, to douse a chemical plant fire, evil begins to brew in Metropolis. An unemployed con man, Gus Gorman, learns that he has a facility with computers and goes to work for tycoon Ross Webster. When Webster finds the computer genius embezzling money from his corporation, he realizes that Gorman is nothing less than a genius and puts him to work on his tyrannical plans to control the world economy.

Standing in Webster's way, naturally, is Superman. But Webster has a plot to stop the Man of Steel. Gus creates a deadly variant of kryptonite and exposes Superman to it. Superman very quickly loses his superluster, becoming a whoring, drinking "normal guy." Superman eventually overcomes this deficit, dueling with his id in the process. Once recovered, Superman finds he has lost valuable time. Ross Webster's supercomputer, a sentient thing, is ready to go "live" in a cavern. Superman must face down the deadly machine, which is fully capable of defending itself. With Gorman's help, Superman fights to stop Webster and the computer.

Superman IV: The Quest for Peace (1987)
LIVE–ACTION FILM

"*Superman IV* is an embarrassment."
— Michael Scheinfeld, *Films in Review*, October 1987, page 494.

"The story ... suffers from a fatal lack of narrative structure, degenerating into a series of virtually disconnected sketches."
— Anne Billson, *Monthly Film Bulletin*, September 1987, page 283.

"If it weren't so cheap, it wouldn't be such a bad movie, except that in one scene Superman basically rapes Lois Lane. He kisses her to erase the kiss he gave her in *Superman II*, just so he can tell her his problems. He scared the shit out of her by throwing her off of a building and then catching her and making her remember their mutual past. Then he asks her guidance on his problem and kisses her to erase her memory again. I'm sorry, but that is taking advantage of her. That's a symbolic rape as far as I'm concerned. Don't even get me started on Superman's 'brick' vision that he uses to repair the Great Wall of China..."
— Howard Margolin, host of *Destinies: The Voice of Science Fiction.*

"*Superman IV*'s heart was in the right place. The music was better than it had been in the previous film, Margot Kidder was back, there was an attempt to at least honor some of the legacy of the first two films, and even Gene Hackman was back as Luthor (but couldn't someone have explained to him that it's "nuclear" not "nukuler?"). This was an excessively preachy film, unfortunately, and while it was better than *Superman III*, it's unfortunate that this film came out in the condition it did — supposedly, significant edits prior to release changed the tone of the film, and one wonders what it was supposed to have been."
— William Latham, author of *Mary's Monster* and *Space: 1999 Resurrection.*

CAST: Christopher Reeve (Clark Kent/Superman); Gene Hackman (Lex Luthor); Jackie Cooper (Perry White); Marc McClure (Jimmy Olsen); Jon Cryer (Linny Luthor); Sam Wanamaker (David Warfield); Mark Pillow (Nuclear Man); Mariel Hemingway (Lacy Warfield); Margot Kidder (Lois Lane); Damian McLawhorn (Jeremy); William Hootkins (Harry Howler); Jim Broadbent (Jean Pierre DuBois); Robert Beatty (United States President).

CREW: Warner Brothers Presents a Cannon Group Inc., Golan-Globus Production of a Sidney J. Furie Film, *Superman IV: The Quest for Peace. Superman Motion Picture Series Initiated by:* Alexander Salkind. *Superman Created by:* Jerry Siegel and Joe Shuster. *Costume Designer:* John Bloomfield. *Visual Effects Supervision:* Harrison Ellenshaw. *Film Editor:* John Shirley. *Director of Photography:* Ernest Day. *Producer:* John Graysmark. *Music:* John Williams. *Music Adapted and Conducted by:* Alexander Courage. *Superman Appearing in Comic Books Published by:* DC Comics, Inc. *Executive Producer:* Michael J. Kagan. *Associate Producer:* Graham Easton. *Story:* Christopher Reeve, Lawrence Konner, Mark Rosenthal. *Screenplay:* Lawrence Konner, Mark Rosenthal. *Produced by:* Menahen Golan and Yoram Globus. *Directed by:* Sidney J. Furie. *M.P.A.A. Rating:* PG. *Running time:* 87 minutes.

After rescuing a cosmonaut hurled into space by a collision with space debris, the Man of Steel returns to Earth and his boyhood home of Smallville. As Clark Kent, he retrieves a Kryptonian power module with special properties, but which can be used only once.

Elsewhere, master criminal Lex Luthor escapes from a chain gang with the help of his idiot nephew, Linny Luthor, the "Dutch elm disease" of the Luthor "family tree." His only concern is destroying Superman.

Back in Metropolis, Superman rescues Lois Lane from a runaway subway train and then reports to the *Daily Planet* offices, only to learn that tabloid tycoon David Warfield has purchased the paper and made his lovely daughter, Lacy, an editorial assistant. At the same time, a failed international summit pushes the United States and the Soviet Union into stepping up the number of nuclear warheads in their respective arsenals. One little boy, Jeremy, writes a letter to Superman and asks the strange visitor from another world to rectify the situation for the sake of the planet.

While Superman contemplates his duty and responsibility in the situation (consulting a databank of Elders in his Fortress of Solitude and even his once-love, Lois Lane), Lex plots mischief. He steals one strand of Superman's hair at the Metropolis Museum Superman exhibit and uses it to build a mutant clone of the Man of Steel, one energized by nuclear power and completely loyal to Luthor.

Superman speaks before the assembled countries at the United Nations and announces he will act on Jeremy's request. He resolves to rid the world of nuclear weapons, gathering them up and hurling them into the sun with a giant net. Hoping to re-ignite the arms race, Luthor releases his creation, Nuclear Man, onto Metropolis and the world. But even the criminal genius cannot control this beast, one that draws his power from the sun.

Superman and Nuclear Man clash over the streets of Metropolis and around the world. Nuclear Man defaces the Great Wall of China and tries to destroy the Statue of Liberty, only to be stopped by the Man of Steel. But when Nuclear Man scratches Superman on the neck, the Kryptonian is badly injured by his exposure to radioactivity.

Clark wastes away, alone in his apartment, dying of exposure. His hair whitened, he uses the power module to revive himself and finally defeat Luthor's man-made terror.

Lois and Clark: The New Adventures of Superman (1993–1997)
LIVE-ACTION SERIES

"...[O]ne of the best things — smart and poignant — you can watch on the Tube. It's wonderful ensemble acting, and even when the individual episodes are dumb — there's a sense of high fun that even on the Tube can't be faked.... There may be better series on TV. I doubt very much if there is one more quirkily relevant to the state of the union."

—Frank McConnell, *Commonwealth:* "Superpersons: *Lois and Clark,*" June 17, 1994, pages 22–23.

"…One of the smarter decisions made in hatching this show is that *Lois & Clark* doesn't follow every detail of the Superman myth…. This has freed the series creator, Deborah Joy Levine … to make Clark a sympathetic yuppie surrounded by a city crawling with yuppies of lesser sympathy, including the dazzling hard-edged reporter Lois Lane (Teri Hatcher)…. [T]his comic book show is the smartest, most human hour of programming that Sunday night now has to offer."
— Ken Tucker, *Entertainment Weekly:* "Flying Right," September 24, 1993, pages 76–77.

"…[V]ery '90s in its hip facetiousness…. There's so much good-humored verve in *Lois and Clark* that it's a shame to admit that *SeaQuest,* with its New Age earnestness, is a more inviting place to spend early Sunday evenings. Take away the levitation effects from *Lois and Clark* and you've got a strained knock-off of *Moonlighting.*"
— Richard Zoglin, *Time,* October 11, 1993, page 82.

CAST: Dean Cain (Clark Kent/Superman); Teri Hatcher (Lois Lane); Lane Smith (Perry White); K. Callan (Mrs. Kent); Eddie Jones (Jonathan Kent). SEASON ONE: Michael Landes (Jimmy Olsen); Elizabeth Barondes (Lucy Lane); Tracy Scoggins (Kat); John Shea (Lex Luthor). SEASONS TWO to FOUR: Justin Whalen (Jimmy Olsen).

CREW: Warner Brothers Television Presents *Lois and Clark: The New Adventures of Superman. Co-Producers:* Philip J. Sgriccia, Jim Michaels. *Producers:* Thania St. John, Mel Efros. *Supervising Producer:* Bryce Zabel. *Co-Executive Producer:* Deborah Joy Levine. *Executive Producer:* David Jacobs. *Associate Producer:* Chris Long. *Executive Consultant:* Robert Butler. *Executive Story Editor:* Dan Levine. *Director of Photography:* Jim Bagdonas. *Production Designer:* Jim Pohl. *Film Editors (various episodes):* David Ekstrom, M. Edward Salier, Randy Wiles. *Music:* Jay Gruska. *Unit Production Manager:* Christopher Seitz. *First Assistant Director:* Neil Ahern. *Second Assistant Director:* Cynthia Stefenoni. *Executive in Charge of Casting:* Barbara Miller. *Casting:* Ellie Kanner. Based on the DC Comics. *Property Master:* Cheri Paul. *Costumers:* Judith Brewer Curtis, Darryl Levine. *Make-up:* Joyce Westmore. *Hairstylist:* Larry Waggoner. *Visual Effects Supervisor:* John Scheele. *Special Effects Coordinator:* Steve Purcell. *Sound Mixer:* Kenn Michael Fuller. *Re-Recording Mixers:* Vern Poore, Joe Charella, Dan Hiland. *Music Supervisor:* Gregory Sill. *Music Editor:* Lisa A. Arpino. *Supervising Sound Editor:* Michael E. Lawse. A Roundelay Production/December 3rd Productions, in association with Warner Brothers TV, a Time Warner Company.

SEASON ONE (1993-1994)

1. "Pilot" (two hours) Written by: Deborah Joy Levine. Directed by Robert Butler. Airdate: September 12, 1993.

Young Clark Kent of Smallville, Kansas, moves to the great city of Metropolis to pursue a job as a reporter at the city's foremost newspaper, the *Daily Planet*. But Clark is no ordinary journalist; he was adopted as a child by a kindly Kansas couple under unusual circumstances in 1966, and he possesses amazing super powers, including the ability to fly. After impressing *Planet* editor Perry White, Clark teams up with the beautiful and feisty investigative reporter Lois Lane on his first case: the sabotage of a space shuttle assigned to add an important module to the Prometheus Space Station. Even as Clark Kent assumes the disguise of a hero dubbed Superman to use his powers, the richest man in Metropolis, Lex Luthor, plots to sabotage the next shuttle mission so that he will have the opportunity to see his space station built in lieu of Prometheus.

GUEST CAST: Kenneth Tigar; Kim Johnston Ulrich (Dr. Baines); Mel Winkler; Gloria Le Roy (Beatrice); Shaun Tour (Asabi); Jean Montanti (Newspaper Worker); Gregory Millar (Homeless Man); Kamal Dawson (Carmen Alvarado); Robert Rothwell (Security Guard); Lee Weaver (Supervisor); Yolanda Gaskins (TV Announcer); Marco Hernandez (Worker); Georgy Paull (Elderly Woman); Adrian Ricard (Older Woman); Maggie Blye (Mrs. Platt); Linsey Beykowitz (Amy Platt); Persis Khambatta (Chairperson); Clyde Kusatsu (Public Affairs Officer); Mimi Maynard (Launch Commander); Gerry Black (Head Colonist); Jim Wise (Man #1); Greg Collins (Man #2); Sean Moran (Man #3); David Fury (Cop); Anne Wyndham (Reporter #2);

Christopher Dorga (Man with Binoculars); Timi Prulheire (Soap Opera Actress); Scott McCray (Soap Opera Actor); Jerry Hauck (Reporter #1); Mark Frazer (Young Technician).

2. "Strange Visitor from Another Planet" Written by: Bryce Zabel. Directed by: Randall Zisk. Airdate: September 26, 1993.

Officials of the U.S. government raid the *Daily Planet* offices in search of information about Superman, and force Lois and Clark to undergo polygraph tests on their knowledge of the strange visitor from another world. After finessing the test, Clark goes into hiding at Kat's place to avoid authorities. But soon Clark and Lois are back in action when they learn that the investigation is being led by Jason Trask, a rogue agent for "Bureau 39" who is fascinated by UFOs. While investigating Trask's office, Clark learns that there was indeed a flying saucer crash in Smallville in 1966, and that his parents found a baby in a spaceship.

GUEST CAST: Joseph Campanella (George Thompson); Terence Knox (Jason Trask); Tom Dugan (Soldier #1); Jeff Austin (Soldier #2); David St. James (Polygraph Technician); Randall Boffman (Government Agent); Alex Wexo (SWAT Leader); Steven E. Einsparr (Young Jonathan); George Murdock.

3. "Neverending Battle" Written by: Dan Levine. Directed by: Gene Reynolds. Airdate: October 3, 1993.

At Perry White's urging, the reporters of the *Daily Planet* scurry to learn more about the new hero of Metropolis, Superman! Meanwhile, Clark finds an apartment he likes, and Lex Luthor plots to test the limits of Superman's powers and abilities. When Superman saves a woman from a high fall, Lois steals Clark's story. Though ashamed of her behavior, she refuses to apologize. Superman confronts Lex Luthor about the dangerous tests he has prepared for the superhero and the criminal suggests that more innocent people will die so long as Superman remains in Metropolis.

GUEST CAST: Elizabeth Barondes; Larry Linville (Grover Cleveland); Roy Brocksmith (Apartment Manager); Miguel A. Nunez, Jr. (Woody); Tony Jay; Brent Jennings; Mary Crosby (Monique); Lou Cutell (Maurice); Ritch Brinkley (Stan); Shaun Toub (Asabi); Wil Albert (Businessman); Yolanda Gaskins (Linda Montoya); Rosa Li (Japanese Woman #1); Saemi Nakamura (Japanese Woman #2); Louis Pellegrino Rapport (Grandmother).

4. "I'm Looking Through You" Written by: Deborah Joy Levine. Directed by: Mark Sobel. Airdate: October 10, 1993.

An invisible man is being "seen" all over Metropolis, taking from the rich and giving to the poor. The invisible man's much-harried wife comes to Lois and Clark for help before long, because he's "disappeared." Upon investigating, the reporters learn that two invisible men may be terrorizing the city. The bad invisible man, wearing a special suit, arranges a break-out at Metropolis penitentiary to build an invisible army.

GUEST CAST: Leslie Jordan; Jack Carter; Patricka Darbo; Jim Beaver; Thomas Ryan; Miguel Sandoval (Eduardo Friez); Shaun Toub (Asabi); Yolanda Gaskins (Linda Montoya); Francine York (Mistress of Ceremonies); Leslie Rivers (Deputy Mayor); Cliff Medaugh (Old Man); Nancy Locke (First Woman); Teresa Jones (Debutante); Bob McCracken (Invisible Man); Estelle La Vine (Matronly Woman).

5. "Requiem for a Super Hero" Written by: Robert Killebrew. Directed by: Randall Zisk. Airdate: October 17, 1993.

At the behest of Perry, Lois and Clark officially become partners to investigate the upcoming "ultimate street fighting championship" being held in Metropolis. Unbeknownst to the reporters, Lex Luthor is behind the scenes manipulating the event, which is supposed to culminate in a boxing match featuring Superman. Lois calls on her estranged father, sports doctor Sam Lane, to learn about a plot that has led to a murder, a plot concerning boxers with robotic arms!

GUEST CAST: Dennis Arndt; Matt Roe; Joe Sabatino; John La Motta (Allie Dinello); Dave Sebastian Williams (Ringmaster); Jean Speegle Howard (Elderly Woman).

6. "I've Got a Crush on You" Written by: Thania St. John. Directed by: Gene Reynolds. Airdate: October 24, 1993.

To investigate the West River fires, Lois goes undercover at a club belonging to a gang of crooks called the Metros, pretending to be a torch song singer. Meanwhile, Lex Luthor plans to develop the West River area to build Lex Harbor. While the villainous arsonists, "the Toasters," continue to burn up the landscape, a new female leader rises among the Metros, and Clark, posing as a bartender at the club, gets close to her.

GUEST CAST: Jessica Tuck (Toni Taylor); Michael Milhoan; Johnny Williams; Audrey Landers (Toots); Alexander Enberg (Toaster #1); David DeLuise (Toaster #2); Shashawnee Hall (Bartender); Gregg Daniel (Newscaster); Tom Simmons (Reporter #1); Piper Perry (Girl #1).

7. "Smart Kids" Written by: Dan Levine. Directed by: Robert Singer. Airdate: October 31, 1993.

Four children from Metropolis's Beckworth School disappear after ingesting a top-secret intelligence-enhancing chemical created by Lex Luthor's associate, Dr. Carlton. The children team up to create mischief: maxing out Luthor's credit cards, tying up Lois in silly string, and learning that Clark Kent is actually Superman. Jimmy discovers that the synthetic serum that made the children smart will also render them comatose if not discontinued.

GUEST CAST: Michael Cavanaugh (Dr. Alfred Carlton); Courtney Peldon; Scott McAfee; Jonathan Hernandez; Emily Ann Lloyd (Inez); Sheila Rosenthal (Karen); Margot Rose (Mrs. Powell); Ralph P. Martin (Cabbie); Bergen Williams (Helga).

8. "The Green, Green Glow of Home" Written by: Bryce Zabel. Directed by: Les Landau. Airdate: November 14, 1993.

The U.S. military investigates Smallville, Clark's hometown, and discovers a green alien rock. This rock, kryptonite, is the only thing that can hurt Superman, it being a fragment of matter from his solar system. A deranged military officer, hoping to gain an advantage over Superman, plans to use the substance.

GUEST CAST: Terence Knox, Joleen Lutz, Jerry Hardin, Sharon Thomas, Thomas O'Brien.

9. "The Man of Steel Bars" Written by: Paris Qualles. Directed by: Robert Butler. Airdate: November 21, 1993.

Superman becomes the scapegoat of Metropolis when a heat wave incapacitates the city. Facing the hostility of the populace, Clark starts to ponder the notion of retiring Superman. But when the real threat emerges, only the Man of Steel can rescue the city.

GUEST CAST: Sonny Bono, Richard Fancy, Rosalind Cash, Tony Jay, Elaine Kagan.

10. "Pheromone, My Lovely" Written by: Deborah Joy Levine. Directed by: Bill D'Elia. Airdate: November 28, 1993.

Though Lex Luthor has cut off her funding for lack of results, the beautiful scientist Miranda has developed a perfume that causes its wearer to lose all inhibitions. She tests the new scent on the staff of the *Daily Planet* as it is publicizing another new perfume called Exclusive. Under the influence, the workaholic Lois makes an aggressive and seductive play for Clark. Meanwhile, Miranda wants a relationship with Lex and sprays him with the perfume, Revenge, but this only steers him towards Lois Lane.

GUEST CAST: Morgan Fairchild (Miranda); Tony Jay (Nigel); Courtney Taylor (April); Sophia Santi (Rehalia); Jeff Austin (Phil); Conrad Goode (Hans).

NOTE: This is the episode in which Luthor realizes he is in love with Lois Lane.

11. "Honeymoon in Metropolis" Written by: Dan Levine. Directed by: James A. Contner. Airdate: December 12, 1993.

Lois checks into a honeymoon suite to relax, only to become embroiled in an organized crime investigation involving a congressman and a secretive company called Apocalypse. Clark joins Lois in the suite—to her dismay—and they masquerade as newlyweds. They learn that an international arms dealer, Roarke, is trying to get a new weapons system approved by Congress.

GUEST CAST: Charles R. Frank (Harrington); Charles Cyphers (Roarke); Richard Libertini (Sore Throat); Fred Stoller (Phil); Andrea Stein (Ingeborg).

NOTE: This episode recycles an idea found in *Superman II* (1981)—Lois and Clark together as newlyweds in a romantic honeymoon suite.

12. "All Shook Up" Written by: Bryce Zabel. Story by: Jackson Gillis. Directed by: Felix Enriquez Alcala. Airdate: January 2, 1994.

A solar eclipse heralds the approach of Nightfall, a massive asteroid on a collision course with Earth. Superman is the world's only hope, and must fly a million miles into space to stop the asteroid before it strikes. After blasting the space rock to pieces, Superman is hurled back to Earth as an amnesiac. When a remaining three mile chunk of Nightfall continues on its course towards Metropolis, it becomes imperative that Clark regain his memory so he can complete his mission within the next 55 hours.

GUEST CAST: Richard Belzer (Inspector Henderson); J.A. Preston; Richard Roat; David Sage; Matt Clark; Jennifer Lewis; Suanne Spoke (Dr. Jerri McCorkle); Rick Fitts (Frank Madison); Shaun Toub (Asabi); Lee Magnuson (Ground Controller); Eric Laneuville (Vendor).

NOTE: This is a remake of the *Adventures of Superman* episode entitled "Panic in the Sky."

13. "Witness" Written by: Bradley Moore. Directed by: Mel Damski. Airdate: January 9, 1994.

Lois interviews a famous and enigmatic scientist, Vincent Winninger, and is present in his office—but hidden—when he is unexpectedly assassinated. The secret hit man, working for Barbara Trevino—the new head of a rain forest consortium—learns that Lois witnessed the crime and makes the reporter his next target. The assassin, a master of disguise, is able to alter his appearance. After Mr. Make-up is finally caught, Lois must still nab Trevino before she can exploit the rain forest.

GUEST CAST: Elliott Gould (Dr. Vincent Winninger); Richard Belzer (Inspector Henderson); Claudette Nevins (Barbara Trevino); Charlie Dell; Brian George; William Mesnick; Phil Mickelson; Julie Araskog (Reporter); Hal Sparks (Skateboarder); Roz Witt (Teacher); Bradley Pierce (Kid #1); Ahmad Stone (Kid #2); Megan Parlen (Girl #1).

14. "Illusions of Grandeur" Written by: Thania St. John. Directed by: Michael Watkins. Airdate: January 23, 1994.

Lois and Clark investigate the kidnapping of seven wealthy children—all returned safely, but with no memory of their captors. When a poor boy named Nicky is mistaken for the son of a wealthy Metropolis developer and kidnapped for a five million dollar ransom, his mother seeks help from the reporters. Nicky's trail leads to the world of magic, where Superman is hypnotized into helping the kidnappers. Lois's dislike of magic is magnified when she is "volunteered" to participate in a potentially fatal sword box trick.

GUEST CAST: Ben Vereen; Marietta De Prima; Eve Plumb (Rose); Jarrett Lennon; Stephen Burleigh; Penn Jillette (Romick); Adrienne Hampton (Mrs. Moskal); Christopher Miranda (Chris); Whitney Young (Little Girl); Vince Brocato (Florist).

15. "The Ides of Metropolis" Written by: Deborah Joy Levine. Directed by: Philip J. Sgriccia. Airdate: February 6, 1994.

Clark's dad is convinced that Martha is

having an illicit affair with a young artist and comes to Metropolis to stay with Clark. Meanwhile, Lois helps a man on trial for murder to establish his innocence after he escapes from custody. Lois and Clark harbor the fugitive, who points the finger at Lex Com, the employer of the dead man, as the culprit. Worse, there's a deadly computer virus out there — the Ides of Metropolis — coming to life even as the crime nears solution.

GUEST CAST: Todd Susman (Eugene); Melanie Mayron; Paul Gleason; Jennifer Savidge; Tony Jay; Richard Gant; Myrna Niles (Miss Bird); Yolanda Gaskins (Newscaster); Ben Bolock (Ben the Bailiff); Debbie Korkonis (Aerobics Trainer); Richard F. Whiten (Bodybuilder); Lee Mathis (Work Technician).

16. "Foundling" Written by: Dan Levine. Directed by: Bill D'Elia. Airdate: February 20, 1994.

Clark's apartment is robbed by a juvenile delinquent named Jack, and a Kryptonian artifact, a globe, is among the items stolen. Jack sells the globe on the black market to Lex Luthor! The problem is that the globe periodically transmits images of Jor-El and Lara, Clark's Kryptonian parents, and Luthor is learning much about his sworn enemy. As Clark attempts to retrieve his property, the globe dramatizes the destruction of Krypton and Superman's long journey as an infant to a distant world called Earth.

GUEST CAST: David Warner (Jor-El); Chris Demetral (Jack); Richard Belzer (Inspector Henderson); Robert Costanzo (Louie); Tony Jay (Nigel); Brandon Bluhm (Denny); Eliza Roberts (Lara).

17. "The Rival" Written by: Tony Blake and Paul Jackson. Directed by: Michael Watkins. Airdate: February 27, 1994.

The *Metropolis Star* and its ace reporter, Linda King, keep scooping the *Daily Planet*. The publisher is Preston Carpenter, a flamboyant millionaire who fancies himself a modern Charles Foster Kane. Soon Clark learns that Preston doesn't just report the news (like a series of hotel fires in Metropolis) — he causes them! Clark resigns from the *Daily Planet* to work for the *Metropolis Star*, a ruse to expose the truth about Preston, but one that makes a jealous Lois spitting mad.

GUEST CAST: Dean Stockwell (Preston Carpenter); Nancy Everhard (Linda King); Bo Jackson (Himself); Kevin Cooney (Secretary Wallace); Mike Sabatino (J. Harvey Stark); Dana Chelette (Fire Chief).

18. "Vatman" Written by: H.B. Cobb and Deborah Joy Levine. Story by: H.B. Cobb. Directed by: Randall Zisk. Airdate: March 13, 1994.

An exact, but child-like, physical duplicate of Superman appears in Metropolis after saving a plane in France, and this strange "child" of Lex Luthor swears that the real Superman is his enemy. Indoctrinated by Lex to hate his double, the false Superman also develops a lust for Lois. The double, in actuality a clone produced from a strand of Superman's hair donated at a charity auction, learns that Clark Kent is Superman. When Lex discovers that his clone is imperfect and doomed to die, he plans for a battle royale between the Men of Steel, unaware that the two men are rapidly coming to see one another as brothers.

GUEST CAST: Michael McKean; Ira Heiden (Messenger); Sam Rubin (Newscaster); Wil Albert (Delacroix); John McMahon (Cop); Cynthia Ettinger (Tour Guide).

19. "Fly Hard" Written by: Thania St. John. Directed by: Philip J. Sgriccia. Airdate: March 27, 1994.

A team of terrorists with a dirty nuclear device seize the *Daily Planet* building on a dreary Saturday night as Jimmy, Jack and Perry are doing their spring cleaning. Also in the office are Clark, doing his taxes, and Lois and Lex, out together on their first date. Held hostage, the group tries to figure out how to escape, and Luthor is shot and injured during an escape attempt. Perry realizes the terrorists may be robbers hunting for the treasure of a prohibition era gangster named Dragonetti, rumored still to be hidden in the building.

GUEST CAST: Chris Demetral (Jack); Robert Beltran (Fuentes); Macon McCalman; Alexandra Hedison; Cole Stevens (Schumak); Anthony Leonard (Blackman); Don Fohmel (George).

20. "Barbarians at the Planet" Written by: Dan Levine, Deborah Joy Levine. Directed by: James R. Bagdonas. Airdate: May 1, 1994.

Lex Luthor proposes to Lois, even as he plans to purchase kryptonite with which to kill Superman. At the same time, the *Daily Planet* experiences a financial crisis and is threatened with a shutdown until Luthor steps up to "save" it. Secretly, it's all part of Luthor's plan to separate Lois from her friends, thus making her vulnerable to his proposal. Luthor replaces Perry with a snot-nosed kid, transfers Jimmy and Jack to the printing plant, and then blows up the *Daily Planet* with a bomb (hidden in Jack's Superman lunch pail). With no *Daily Planet* edition going out for the first time in over 200 years, Lex offers Lois a job at his TV news network (LNN), and Lois, realizing she can never be with Superman, accepts Luthor's proposal.

GUEST CAST: Chris Demetral (Jack); Patrick Kilpatrick; Castullo Guerra; Beverly Johnson; Alex Nevil (Chip); Darby Hinton (Firechief); Barbara Beck (Sandra Ellis).

21. "The House of Luthor" Written by: Deborah Joy Levine and Dan Levine. Directed by: Alan J. Levi. Airdate: May 8, 1994.

The *Daily Planet* has been destroyed, its staff laid off, and Lois is scheduled to marry Lex Luthor. While Lois contemplates her new life, Jimmy, Jack, Perry and Clark search for a reputed gang lord called "the Boss," the man known to have framed Jack for destroying the *Planet.* But Luthor — the Boss himself— traps Superman in a kryptonite cage on the eve of the wedding, even as Lois begins to have second thoughts. Thanks to the investigation of the *Planet* team, the police come to arrest Luthor during the ceremony, even as Superman escapes, and Luthor finally meets his grim fate.

GUEST CAST: Chris Demetral (Jack); Richard Belzer (Inspector Henderson); Beverly Johnson; James Earl Jones (Franklin Stern); Phyllis Coates (Ellen Lane); Richard Stahl (Archbishop); J. Madison Johnston (Guard).

SEASON TWO (1994-1995)

22. "Madame Ex" Written by: Tony Blake and Paul Jackson. Directed by: Randall Zisk. Airdate: September 18, 1994.

Arianna Carlin, Lex Luthor's mysterious ex-wife, plots revenge against Lois Lane, while hostility towards Superman grows in Metropolis. Carlin murders a doctor at Luthor's business and then is hired as the *Daily Planet*'s new psychiatrist. She uses a surgically altered woman, who now resembles Lois, to spout anti–Superman rhetoric before news cameras, and manipulates the city's denizens with subliminal messages. Meanwhile, a female doctor works to resuscitate Lex Luthor.

GUEST CAST: Emma Samms (Arianna Carlin); Earl Boen (Dr. Heller); Thomas Ryan; Jack Kruschen; Barry Livingston; Julie Araskog (Sandy Martin); Tony DiBenedittio (News Stand Operator); John Wheeler (Shop Owner); Juan Garcia (Homeless Guy); Joe Ochman (Male Staffer); Bradley Weissman (Male Demonstrator); Traylor Hall (Secretary); Jessica Hecht (Female Staffer).

23. "Wall of Sound" Written by: John McNamara. Directed by: Alan J. Levi. Airdate: September 25, 1994.

A new criminal in Metropolis deploys a special "sound wave" weapon to incapacitate the patrons and staff at banks. The man manipulating the "thought-altering" machine is none other than Lenny Stokes, an unsuccessful rock star with a weak spot for brunettes. When his weapon fells Superman, sending the Man of Steel into retreat, Stokes imposes a sound tax on Metropolis, demanding 50 percent of all the money in the city's banks. Lois infiltrates Stokes' rock club as a "groupie."

GUEST CAST: Michael Des Barres (Lenny Stoke); Scott Colomby; Cory Everson (Amazon Woman #1); Barry Cutler (Wino #1); Richard Balm (Dr. Green); Morgan Hunter (Waiter); Pamela Roberts (Mayor Sharpe); Richard Gross (Wino #1); Erika Andersch (Amazon Woman #2).

24. "The Source" Written by Tony Blake and Paul Jackson. Directed by: John T. Kretchmer. Airdate: October 2, 1994.

The head of research at Viologic Electronics reveals to Lois that a Ferris wheel accident was the result of defective mechanical switches made by his company. Meanwhile, the Kents are in town and Mr. Kent is depressed about the sudden death of a dear friend. When Lois's top secret source changes his story at a press conference, and Lois is nearly drowned in the bay by goons working for Viologic, Superman investigates. Then Viologic files a $20 million defamation suit against the *Daily Planet* and Lois, and she is suspended from active duty, even as Thorpe, the CEO of Viologic, plans a deadly accident for the city's new subway.

GUEST CAST: Peter Scolari (Stuart Hofferman); Tim Grimm; Barry Livingston; Jeffrey Joseph; Patrick Pankhurst; Anndi McAfee (Vanessa); B.J. Jefferson (Secretary); William Schallert (Al); Jon Van Ness (Wick); Bernard Kuby (Daily Planet Guard); Stan Sellers (Security Guard); Marla Frees (Diane); Nick La Tour (Ferris Wheel Operator); Jim Maniaci (Man); John C. Anders (Police Officer); Fort Atkinson (Governor Winston).

25. "The Prankster" Written by: Grant Rosenberg. Directed by: James Hayman. Airdate: October 9, 1994.

A secret admirer sends Lois increasingly bizarre and dangerous gifts of affection. Behind the scheme is a criminal mastermind called the Prankster, an international arms dealer Lois helped send to prison five years earlier. Now the Prankster is back and plans to detonate a massive bomb under a science lab as an indication of his "explosive" love for Lois Lane. But all is not as it seems, as Superman finds out the hard way.

GUEST CAST: Bronson Pinchot (Kyle Griffin/the Prankster); Rick Overton (Victor); Harold Gould; Leonard Termo; John Fleck; J.D. Cullum; Maria Frees (Diane); Charles Emmett (Plant Manager); Kristin Bower (Mrs. Loomis); Ossie Mair (Store Owner).

26. "Church of Metropolis" Written by: John McNamara. Directed by: Robert Singer. Airdate: October 23, 1994.

An international criminal organization called Intergang, run by a Metropolis "do-gooder" named Bill Church, is setting fires to the properties in the city's South Side to lower the value of the real estate. Superman is warned not to interfere in Intergang's operations, or his close friends will be killed. Even as Superman tangles with a pesky district attorney who doesn't like him, Clark must fend off her advances. To help stop Intergang, Superman goes undercover as a street cop, and Lois sets up a courtroom sting for Intergang's head lawyer, the slippery Martin Snell.

GUEST CAST: Dick Miller (Michael Lane); Bruce Weitz (Martin Snell); Peter Boyle (Bill Church); Farrah Forke (District Attorney Mayson Drake); Steven Gilborn; Michael Holden; Dwayne L. Barnes (Baby Rage); Phillip Bergeron (French Operative); James Kiriyama-Lenn (Tech One).

27. "Operation Blackout" Written by: Kate Boutilier. Directed by: Michael Watkins. Airdate: October 30, 1994.

Lois and Clark investigate the possibility of a military plot to control a satellite that could wipe out the power in all of Metropolis.

GUEST CAST: J.T. Walsh, Melora Hardin, Tom Hatten, Gary Bolton.

28. "That Old Gang of Mine" Written by: Gene Miller and Karen Kavner. Directed by: Lorraine Senna Ferrara. Airdate: November 13, 1994.

Two crooks claiming to be Bonnie and Clyde hold up Perry White and Jimmy Olsen as they prepare to exhibit a classic car to celebrate the *Daily Planet*'s long publishing history. Before long, John Dillinger is in Metropolis too, and robs a bank. It turns out a weak scientist has resurrected these and other crooks (including Al Capone), in hopes of curing their antisocial behavior, but they have other plans. One of the out-of-date thugs shoots Clark — and Perry, Jimmy and Lois all mourn his death, unaware that he survived.

GUEST CAST: William Devane (Al Capone); John Pleshette, Joseph Gian, Amy Hathaway, Ray Abruzzo, Robert Clohessy, Sal Viscuso.

29. "A Bolt from the Blue" Written by: Kathy McCormick. Directed by: Philip J. Sgriccia. Airdate: November 20, 1994.

Superman sees his powers lost in an accident, traded to a money-hungry opportunist. Meanwhile, Lex Luthor's personal physician also wants Superman's powers for herself.

GUEST CAST: Cindy Williams, Leslie Jordan, Denise Crosby.

30. "Season's Greedings" Written by: Dean Cain. Directed by: Randall Zisk. Airdate: December 4, 1994.

Lois is cynical about Christmas and the holiday season, much to the sentimental Clark's dismay. Unfortunately, a villainous toymaker feels even worse about Christmas than Lois and unleashes a dangerous, greed-inducing toy called "the atomic space rat" on Metropolis. Before long the toys have the adults, including Lois, acting like children.

GUEST CAST: Isabel Sanford (Ms. Duffy); Sherman Hemsley (The Toymaker); Denise Richards (Angela); Dick Van Patten, Dom Irrera, Sandee Van Dyke, Doug Llewelyn, Jon Menick.

31. "Metallo" Written by: Tony Blake and Paul Jackson. Story by: James Crocker. Directed by: James R. Bagdonas. Airdate: January 1, 1995.

Agents of Lex Corp. transform a man into Metallo, a deadly cyborg with a kryptonite heart, creating a new danger to the Man of Steel.

GUEST CAST: Scott Valentine, John Rubinstein, Marla Frees, Doug Toby, Wallace Crowder.

32. "Chi of Steel" Written by: Hilary Bader. Directed by: James Hayman. Airdate: January 8, 1995.

A ninja warrior breaks into the vault of Perry's financial advisor, Harlan, and steals White's life savings. Lois and Clark look into the robbery, searching Harlan's office at his restrictive men's club. The trail leads to Chinatown, an Oriental cult, and Son Kwan Industries. It turns out that Harlan is importing cheap slave labor from China and planning to send a deadly karate master with unusual abilities to kill Superman.

GUEST CAST: Brian Doyle-Murray (Harlan); Yuji Okumoto; James Hong; Leile Lee Olsen; Steve Eastin; Dona Lee (Tong Gang Leader); Michael Yama (Chinese Father); Michael Leopard (Cop).

33. "The Eyes Have It" Written by: Kathy McCormick. Story by: Kathy McCormick and Grant Rosenberg. Directed by: Bill D'Elia. Airdate: January 22, 1995.

A nefarious doctor blinds Superman to further his criminal aims, snaring Lois in a murder investigation.

GUEST CAST: Farrah Fork, Gerrit Graham, Billy Mayo, Brian Reddy.

34. "The Phoenix" Written by: Tony Blake and Paul Jackson. Directed by: Philip J. Sgriccia. Airdate: February 12, 1995.

Clark works up the courage to ask Lois out on a date even as Lex Luthor comes out of a coma. Bent on revenge, a newly bald Lex plans to get his hands on kryptonite so as to destroy Superman. Even with his fortune lost (squandered by his lawyer, Sheldon Bender), Lex sets out to win Lois's heart anew — at any cost. Luthor captures Lois, but a shocking doublecross leads to the second undoing of Lex Luthor.

GUEST CAST: John Shea (Lex Luthor); Denise Crosby (Gretchen Kelly); Tony Jay (Nigel St. John); Barry Livingston; Sal Viscuso; Christian Clemenson (Rollie Vale); Randy Crowder (Bomb Squad Leader).

NOTE: This is the first and only episode in which Lex Luthor (Shea) appears in the guise familiar to comic book fans: hairless and chrome-domed.

35. "Top Copy" Written by: John McNamara. Directed by: Randall Zisk. Airdate: February 19, 1995.

A ratings-hungry news reporter, Diana Stride, tags Superman so as to follow him and unmask his private life on her trashy series, *Top Copy*. Diana also happens to be a hit woman for Intergang, and she's been given a new assignment: to terminate her ex-partner, who is currently planning to turn state's evidence. Superman vows to protect the witness, and Diana seeks kryptonite to kill him, planting a kryptonite kiss on his lips. Diana learns that Clark Kent is Superman and plans to broadcast that fact, necessitating a seeming impossibility: Clark and Superman must appear in the same place at the same time.

GUEST CAST: Raquel Welch (Diana Stride); Robert Culp (Head of Intergang); Farrah Forke (Mayson Drake); Wayne Pere, Tom Virtue.

36. "Return of the Prankster" Written by: Grant Rosenberg. Directed by: Philip J. Sgriccia. Airdate: February 26, 1995.

The villainous Prankster escapes from jail, angry that Lois put him away. The Prankster plots to immobilize Metropolis with a freeze ray and eventually kidnap the President of the United States.

GUEST CAST: Bronson Pinchot, Rick Overton, Cliff De Young, Sal Viscuso.

37. "Lucky Leon" Written by: Chris Ruppenthal. Directed by: Jim Pohl. Airdate: March 12, 1995.

While Intergang plots another heist, this one exploiting Superman, Lois and Clark plan their first date, a considerable and perhaps risky step forward in their romantic relationship.

GUEST CAST: Farrah Forke (Mayson); Mark Rolston, Robert Culp, John Kapelos.

38. "Resurrection" Written by: Gene Miller and Karen Kavner. Directed by: Joseph L. Scanlon. Airdate: March 19, 1995.

Mayson Drake is murdered, and Clark and Lois investigate. They uncover a weird scientific plot involving a substance that can simulate death, a drug that criminals intend to use to get some of their compatriots out of jail.

GUEST CAST: Dennis Lipscomb, Curtis Armstrong, Oliver Muirhead, Douglas Fisher.

39. "'Tempus Fugitive" Written by: Jack Weinstein, Lee Hutson. Directed by: James Bagdonas. Airdate: March 26, 1995.

H.G. Wells appears in the *Daily Planet* offices claiming that he has time traveled from the utopian world of the 22nd century and needs Superman's help. A criminal mastermind from the peaceful future, Tempus, has arrived with Wells and gone on a crime spree. Tempus is unhappy with a future of perfect peace, one forged by Superman and his wife, Lois Lane, and so travels back to Smallville in 1966 to kill the Man of Steel as a helpless infant. Building his own time machine, Clark takes Lois to the past to stop Tempus. By a strange twist of temporal mechanics, heroes and villains meet in 1866 before the dangerous rendezvous a hundred years later.

GUEST CAST: Terry Kiser (H.G. Wells); Lane Davies (Tempus); Robert Costanzo; Don Swayze; Joshua Devane; Adam Grupper (Man in Alley).

40. "Target: Jimmy Olsen" Written by: Tony Blake and Paul Jackson. Directed by: David S. Jackson. Airdate: April 2, 1995.

Jimmy uncovers evidence that as a youth he was programmed to become a *Manchurian Candidate*–style assassin.

GUEST CAST: Jim Pirri, Claire Yarlett, Meredith Scott Lynn, Charles Napier, Michelle Phillips.

41. "Individual Responsibility" Written by: Chris Ruppenthal. Directed by: Alan J. Levi. Airdate: April 16, 1995.

Billy Church, the new leader of Intergang, kidnaps Perry White in hopes of making him sell the *Daily Planet* to the corrupt organization. At the same time, Superman goes to visit a therapist. He's been exposed to red kryptonite, which makes him apathetic to his work. With Perry missing and Superman depressed, Lois investigates the crime and leaves the paper to a very nervous Jimmy Olsen.

GUEST CAST: Bruce Campbell (Billy Church); Barbara Bosson (Dr. Friskin); Ira Heiden (Delivery Guy); Bryan Clark (Older Guy); Jeri Gaile (Receptionist); Charles Dougherty (Karl); Myrna Niles (Older Woman); Kevin Fry (Guard #1); Christopher Michael (Guard #2); Kelly Christian (Shlomo).

42. "Whine, Whine, Whine" Written by: Kathy McCormick and John McNamara. Directed by: Michael Watkins. Airdate: May 14, 1995.

Dealing with legal woes (from a rescue gone wrong), Clark gets hit with a double whammy. Lois breaks up with him, tired of his "disappearing" act whenever their conversation turns to deep matters (and, in fact, Superman is needed elsewhere).

GUEST CAST: Jim Pirri, Barbara Bosson, Jason Carter, Sal Viscuso, Kay Lenz, Martin Mull, Ben Stein, Frank Gorshin, Adam West, Bruce Campbell, Joyce Meadows.

43. "And the Answer Is..." Written by: Tony Blake and Paul Jackson. Directed by: Alan J. Levi. Airdate: May 21, 1995.

The diary of the time traveler Tempus, trapped in the late 1800s, falls into the hands of an extortionist who uses it to expose Clark as Superman. Working with Nigel, Luthor's former right hand man, Jason T. Masic wants Superman to steal diamonds from his dead father's shop, now in the hands of a sibling. Worse, Lois is tired of Clark making excuses in their relationship, causing Clark to seriously consider revealing his identity. To ensure Superman's loyalty, Jason and Jay kidnap Clark's parents and lock them in a lead-lined chamber. After saving them, Clark proposes to Lois.

GUEST CAST: Maurice Godin (Jason T. Masic); Tony Jay (Nigel); Michael Leopard (Cop); Lamont Johnson (Marvin); Rick La Fond (Man #1); Timothy TC Camilleri (Maxwell).

SEASON THREE (1995-1996)

44. "We Have a Lot to Talk About" Written by: John McNamara. Directed by: Philip J. Sgriccia. Airdate: September 17, 1995.

After Clark proposes, Lois reveals that she knows his secret, that he is Superman. Worse, she's angry that he's lied to her for years about his identity. Meanwhile, Bill Church, the leader of Intergang, organizes a new personal police force to defend the innocent people of Metropolis. Church has indeed reformed (thanks to a marriage to his sexy nurse), but his villainous son has not, and is looking to take over the family business — with the help of a deadly time bomb.

GUEST CAST: Bruce Campbell (Billy Church); Peter Boyle (Bill Church, Sr.); Jessica Collins (Mindy); Sal Viscuso; Mark Goodman

(Grant Burton); David Sederholm (Man in Black); David Weisenberg (Timid Man); Michael Francis Clarke (Cop); Maurice Woods (Runner); Timothy Camilleri (Staffer).

45. "Ordinary People" Written by: Eugenie Ross Leming and Brad Buckner. Directed by: Michael Watkins. Airdate: September 24, 1995.

The evil Spencer Spencer wants Lois Lane dead for an exposé she wrote about his publishing empire. Also, the millionaire is searching for a new body so he can escape from his mechanical wheelchair, and is convinced that Superman's body should be his. Meanwhile, Lois is having trouble sharing her new beau — Superman — with the world. Clark and Lois go on vacation together to a remote island to work out their problems, but it's all a trick by Spencer to steal Superman's body.

GUEST CAST: Carlos Lacamara; David Leisure (Spencer Spencer); Vincent Guastaferro (Belzer); Peter Kent (Klavel); Greta Blackburn (Heidi); Ben McCain (TV Newscaster); John Allsopp (Patient).

46. "Contact" Written by: Chris Ruppenthal. Directed by: Daniel Attias. Airdate: October 1, 1995.

Lois is abducted by aliens, a fact proven by her new neighbor, the eccentric psychic named Star. Others have been abducted too and brainwashed to cooperate in what turns out to be a very earthly conspiracy involving a millionaire named Fences and stolen computer technology. Lois was abducted by Fences to provide a distraction for the meddling Superman, and she keeps getting herself into mortal danger, including a fall from a helicopter in flight.

GUEST CAST: Olivia Brown (Star); Patrick Laborteaux; Larry Hankin; Rochelle Swanson (Simone); Robby Robinson (Thief #1).

47. "When Irish Eyes Are Killing" Written by: Grant Rosenberg. Directed by: Winrich Kolbe. Airdate: October 15, 1995.

Clark is worried that his relationship with Lois is putting her in constant danger. His fears prove well founded when an auction attended by Lois, Perry and Jimmy is gassed by thieves who steal the jeweled scepter of Claudius. An old Irish friend of Lois's, Patrick Sullivan, may be involved in the crime (*and* other thefts of rare items). He's hoping to rejoin two valuable emeralds called "the Eyes of Ireland" that, when connected, will grant him the ancient power of the druids.

GUEST CAST: Julian Stone (Patrick Sullivan); Ilana Levine; Sheelagh Cullen; Olivia Brown (Star); Tom Todoroff (Shamus/Robber); J. Patrick McCormack (Mr. Carthy); Annie Gagen (Woman); Kelly Christian (Richie).

48. "Just Say Noah" Written by: Brad Buckner and Eugenie Ross Leming. Directed by: David S. Jackson. Airdate: October 22, 1995.

Lois's neighbors disappear after a disembodied voice and a burning bush lures them away from their apartment. Lane investigates, and the trail leads to Larry Smiley, a cult leader who espouses "equal opportunity lovingness" and "harmonicity." Lois and Clark, who are having relationship problems, go undercover as squabbling partners to one of Smiley's retreats. Smiley kidnaps Perry White, a graduate of his program, to become a part of his new dawn: a colony of couples who have succeeded in his program and have been chosen to survive after the next great flood.

GUEST CAST: Mac Davis (Larry Smiley); Olivia Brown (Star); Brian R. Richardson (Jeremy); Nancy Cassara (Michelle Sitkowitz); Rob La Belle (Arnod Sitkowitz); Michael C. Mahon (Brian); Erin Donovan (Betty); Jennifer Hope (Kathy); Marte Le Sloute (Cassandra Smiley); Tony Carlin (Peter Henson); Sharon Thomas (Nun).

49. "Don't Tug on Superman's Cape" Written by: David Simkins. Directed by: Steven Dubin. Airdate: November 5, 1995.

A rich, eccentric couple, Tim and

Amber Lake, break Bad Brains Johnson out of prison to help them acquire kryptonite. They rob Star Labs after killing Bad Brains and then pin the crime on him. Next, they set a trap for Lois using Bad Brain's electronic shock "whammy" device. Though believed dead, Lois actually is being held captive by the Lakes—at least until they can hunt and mount the ultimate prize: Superman!

GUEST CAST: Genie Francis (Amber Lake); Jonathan Frakes (Tim Lake); Michael Harris (Bad Brains Johnson); Kenneth Kimmins (Dr. Klein); Joe Ochman (Staffer); Holly Schroeder (Police Woman).

NOTE: This episode features stars Hatcher and Cain in a number of TV and movie parodies, including *I Love Lucy* and *Dragnet*. Ironically, there is a James Bond satire in which Hatcher (as Lois Lane) complains that the women in Bond films have no significant part in the plot, being something akin to "hood ornaments." Less than two years later, Hatcher starred as the Bond girl in *Tomorrow Never Dies* (1997).

50. "Ultra Woman" Written by: Gene O'Neill, Noreen Tobin. Directed by: Mike Vejar. Airdate: November 12, 1995.

Two scheming crooks, the Newtrich sisters, shoot Superman with a red kryptonite laser beam that transfers all of his remarkable powers to Lois, whom Superman was cloaking while targeted. Until the situation can be reversed, Lois uses her new super powers as a masked crusader called "Ultra Woman." Before long, the Newtrich Sisters, Lucille and Nell, plot to transfer Lois's newfound powers to themselves. When the twins capture Clark, it's up to Lois to save the day.

GUEST CAST: Shelley Long (Lucille Newtrich); Mary Gross (Cornelia "Nell" Newtrich); Kenneth Kimmins; Lawrence A. Mandley (Husband); Evie Peck (Woman); Thomas Rosales (Thug); Hal Harris (Driver).

51. "Chip Off the Old Clark" Written by: Michael Jamin and Sivert Glarum.

Directed by: Michael Watkins. Airdate: November 19, 1995.

A woman named Lee Anne claims that Superman is the father of her child. But Clark has other troubles to deal with, including a criminal who has stolen a deadly missile.

GUEST CAST: Dave Coulier (The Real Anonymous); Zale Kessler (Grandpa); Ernestine Mercer (Elderly Woman); Eric Saiet (Hacker); Kristine Konrad (Rebel Leader); Big Daddy Wayne (Secret Service Agent).

52. "Super Mann" Written by: Chris Ruppenthal. Directed by: James R. Bagdonas. Airdate: November 26, 1995.

Three Nazi agitators awake from suspended animation in Metropolis and team up with a wealthy neo–Nazi named Black, actually a U.S. Senator, in hopes of raising a Fourth Reich. Two years later, the Nazis are living as celebrities and planning to banish Superman to smooth their plans for world domination. The Nazis, part of the NSBA—the National Society for a Better America—expose Superman to a dirty bomb, rendering him radioactive for 30,000 years.

GUEST CAST: Sean Kanan; Paul Kersey; Sandra Hess (Lisa Rockford); Kenneth Kimmins; Linden Chiles (Senator Truman Black); Sean Whalen (Skip); Jack Stuaffer (Vos); Mary Jacobsen (Karen); Tom Hines (Ned); Jack Owen (TV Anchorman); Douglas Stark (William Stockdale); Robert Crow (Sportscaster); Gregg Tomzi (Reporter).

53. "Virtually Destroyed" Written by: Dean Cain. Story by: Dean Cain and Sean Brennan. Directed by: Jim Charleston. Airdate: December 10, 1995.

Lois and Clark become trapped in the virtual reality world created by a Lex Corp. employee who believes that Lois, as Luthor's almost-bride, possesses important information that could give him access to the Luthor fortune. Unfortunately, Clark has no powers in the computer-generated world, and cannot stop the villain from pressing his case or threatening Lois.

GUEST CAST: Andrew Mark Berman, Thomas Bailey, Andrew Bryniarski.

54. "Home Is Where the Hurt Is" Written by: Eugenie Ross Leming and Brad Buckner. Directed by: Goeffret Nottage. Airdate: December 17, 1995.

Is Intergang resurrecting itself? That seems like a possibility, especially when the heir to the gang gets her hand on a disease that could kill Superman. Meanwhile, Clark's parents have invited Lois's bickering, separated folks to spend Christmas with them, and problems abound.

GUEST CAST: Robert Carradine, Beverly Garland, Harve Presnell, Ben McCain.

55. "Never on Sunday" Written by: Grant Rosenberg. Directed by: Michael Lange. Airdate: January 7, 1996.

An angry nemesis from Clark's youth threatens the reporter with voodoo powers.

GUEST CAST: Cress Williams, Beverly Garland, Carol Lawrence, Olivia Brown, John Mueller.

56. "The Dad Who Came In from the Cold" Written by: David Simkins. Directed by: Alan J. Levi. Airdate: January 14, 1996.

Lois and Clark have been working on a series of articles about an espionage ring. They are unaware that Jimmy's father, long out of his life, is involved in the spying. When he shows up to right things with his son, Lois and Clark fear there is more going on than a personal rapprochement.

GUEST CAST: Ben Slack, Una Damon, James Read, Bud Collins.

57. "Tempus, Anyone?" Written by: John McNamara. Directed by: Winrich Kolbe. Airdate: January 21, 1996.

Tempus kidnaps Lois and transports her to an alternate dimension where Charlton Heston is president. There she meets an aged H.G. Wells and learns that Perry is running for mayor against Tempus, Clark is engaged to high school sweetheart Lana Lang, and there is no Superman! Worse, the Kents died when Clark was seven. After saving Lois from a dangerous fall off a high ledge, Clark works with her to make himself over into Superman. Unfortunately, this is just what Tempus had planned, and he intends to expose Superman as an alien during a televised debate.

GUEST CAST: Hamilton Camp (H.G. Wells); Emily Procter (Lana Lang); Lane Davies (Tempus); Lee Arenberg (Major Domo); Eric Stuart (Rookie Cop); Chuck Butto (Spy); Lee Spencer (Bank Guard); Elizabeth Maynard (Woman).

58. "I Now Pronounce You..." Written by: Chris Ruppenthal. Directed by: Jim Pohl. Airdate: February 11, 1996.

Strange frog-eating clones threaten not only the President of the United States, but the marriage of Lois Lane and Clark Kent. At the last minute, Lois is replaced by a juvenile clone, and Clark marries the wrong woman without knowing it.

GUEST CAST: Fred Willard (The President); Beverly Garland (Mrs. Lane); Tony Curtis; Harve Presnell (Mr. Lane); Wesley Mann, Oliver Muirhead.

59. "Double Jeopardy" Written by: Brad Buckner and Eugenie Ross-Leming. Directed by: Chris Long. Airdate: February 18, 1996.

Clark has unknowingly married the frog-eating clone of Lois Lane, while his real love is in the hands of an old enemy: Lex Luthor. The clone shuns Clark on their wedding night and cancels the honeymoon trip to Hawaii, spurring Clark's suspicions. While Lex plots to steal away to the Alps with the real Lane, the clone Lois learns the truth of Superman's secret identity. Trying to escape from Luthor, the real Lois is hit on the head and develops amnesia, taking on the fictional identity of a down-on-her-luck torch singer, Wanda Detroit.

GUEST CAST: Billy Dean, Troy Evans; John Shea (Lex Luthor); Paul Linke (Church Deacon); Ron Porterfield (Passenger).

60. "Seconds" Written by: John McNamara. Story by: Corey Miller and Philip W. Chung. Directed by: Alan J. Levi. Airdate: February 25, 1996.

Lex has stolen an amnesiac Lois away, convincing her that Clark is her enemy, and then declares war on Superman. The Lois clone offers to help Clark if he releases her from incarceration at Star Labs. Meanwhile, Luthor plans to exchange bodies with a fast-growing clone to avoid the authorities. The Lois clone spills the beans to Luthor that Superman is Clark Kent, and Luthor plans to have his "Wanda"—Lois herself—murder the Man of Steel.

GUEST CAST: Kenneth Kimmins (Dr. Klein); John Shea (Lex Luthor); Shaun Toub (Asabi); Andrew Shaifer (Leonard the Lab Assistant); Joseph Chapman (Bank Vice President); Mark Daniel Cade (Doctor).

61. "Forget Me Not" Written by: Grant Rosenberg. Directed by: James Bagdonas. Airdate: March 10, 1996.

Lois still hasn't recovered her memory; she recalls nothing of her relationship with Clark. She convalesces in a neuroscience clinic, but something is amiss there. While Clark investigates a murder, Dr. Mendenhall starts an unusual "treatment" on Lois, modifying her behavior to make her Perry White's assassin.

GUEST CAST: Larry Poindexter (Dr. Dieter); Charles Ciofi (Dr. Mendenhall); Audrie Neenan (Nurse Reilly); Julie Cobb (Sally Reynolds); Patrick Cranshaw (Homer Blackstork); Lillian Adams (Agnes Moskowitz); Vasili Bogazianos (Detective McCloskey); Steve Kehela (Robber); Michael Lee Gogin (Shifty Looking Man).

62. "Oedipus Wrecks" Written by: David Simkins. Directed by: Ken Michael Fuller. Airdate: March 24, 1996.

Lois still has no memory of her life with Clark; and, worse, her psychiatrist is manipulating her, hoping to convince her that Clark is evil and that she is in love with him instead. Clark investigates the psychiatrist, uncovering a dark past and a suspicious future.

GUEST CAST: Kenneth Kimmins (Dr. Klein); Daniel Roebuck, Renee Taylor, Larry Poindexter.

63. "It's a Small World After All" Written by: Teri Hatcher and Pat Hatzell. Story by: Teri Hatcher. Directed by: Philip J. Sgriccia. Airdate: April 28, 1996.

Lois's high school class reunion leads to trouble for the feisty reporter and Clark when reports of missing persons begin to surface. Is an old classmate really a crazed mad inventor, one who intends to destroy—or at least shrink—Superman?

GUEST CAST: Kenneth Kimmins (Dr. Klein); Steve Young.

64. "Through a Glass, Darkly" Written by: Chris Ruppenthal. Directed by: Chris Long. Airdate: May 5, 1996.

the newly christened United Nations Space Station, with one hundred scientists aboard, mysteriously plunges into the atmosphere until rescued by Superman. Dr. Klein at Star Labs helps backtrack the source of the fault, and its origin is Metropolis! Soon there's a second test of Superman's powers, this one involving a hidden time bomb. Superman passes the test, and then another, before learning that a *Daily Planet* intern named Sarah and her black-garbed companion, Ching, are behind the problems. And they have a secret.

GUEST CAST: Justine Bateman (Sarah/Zara); Jon Tenney (Ching); Kenneth Kimmins (Dr. Klein); Joyce Guy.

65. "Big Girls Don't Fly" Written by Eugenie Ross-Lemming and Brad Buckner. Directed by: Philip J. Sgriccia. Airdate: May 12, 1996.

Clark learns that a thousand Kryptonians survived the planet's destruction and founded a colony on a barren, distant world. Now their leader, Lady Zara, wants Clark — Lord Kal El — to wed her and thereby prevent a civil war. But her enemy, vicious Lord Nor, sends a shape-shifting assassin called Tez to kill Clark. After defeating the menace by turning Tez's power against him, Clark says his farewells to Lois and Earth and prepares to make the long trip to New Krypton.

GUEST CAST: Justine Bateman (Lady Zara); Roger Daltrey (Tez); Jon Tenney (Lt. Ching); Rosie Lee Hooks (Mrs. Cutler); Francois Girodan (Jor El); Shanna Moakler (Pretty Girl).

SEASON FOUR (1996–1997)

66. "Lord of the Flys" Written by: Brad Buckner and Eugenie Ross Leming. Directed by: Philip J. Sgriccia. Airdate: September 22, 1996.

Clark meets the New Kryptonians aboard the mother ship and weds Zara in a ceremony of union. While he's away from Earth, however, Lord Nor sends an advance party of super-powered soldiers to conquer Smallville. He captures the Kents and the city — in a bubble force field, prompting Clark's return to Earth. Lois, acting as Kal El's concubine, and Clark infiltrate Smallville to learn more about Nor, but Nor very quickly discovers their ruse and threatens to execute the Kents.

GUEST CAST: Justine Bateman (Lady Zara); Simon Templeman; Mark Kelly; Mark Lindsay Chapman; J.G. Hertzler (Trey); Richard Grove (General); Eric Allan Kramer; Dan Hildebrand; Leeza Gibbons (Herself); Rick Scarry (Rebel Worker); James Dumont (Ralph); Mark Kretzman (Lt. Small); Tom Poster (Cop).

67. "Battleground Earth" Written by: Eugenie Ross Leming and Brad Buckner.

Directed by: Philip J. Sgriccia. Airdate: September 29, 1996.

The Council of Elders convenes a tribunal to decide the disposition of Kal-El, whom Lord Nor has accused of high treason. Nor also claims Clark planned a sham marriage to Zara to rob him of the New Kryptonian throne. Clark is found guilty and sentenced to have his molecules scattered across the galaxy. But Clark is saved from annihilation and given a last chance to fight Nor because of a technicality in old Kryptonian law which allows two nobles to duel over their differences.

GUEST CAST: Justine Batemen (Lady Zara); Simon Templeman; Mark Kelly; Mark-Lindsay Chapman (Rann); J.G. Hertzler (Trey); Richard Grove (Colonel Cash); Eric Allan Kramer; Dan Hildebrand; Julian Barnes (Messenger).

68. "Swear to God, This Time We're Not Kidding" Written by: John McNamara. Directed by: Michael Lange. Airdate: October 6, 1996.

Myrtle Beech, the so-called "Wedding Destroyer," breaks out of prison and vows to destroy the long-delayed wedding of Lois Lane and Clark Kent. A guardian angel named Mike chooses to intervene to help the wedding day go off without a hitch. After a few false starts, and a confrontation at the altar with Myrtle, the nuptials finally occur at sunset, on a hill, at an undisclosed location, with Mike officiating, and Jimmy and Perry in attendance.

GUEST CAST: Charles Fleischer (Voyle); Delta Burke (Myrtle Beech); David Doyle (Mike); Harve Presnell; Ray Buktenica; Leann Hunley; Billy "Sly Williams (Lamont); Jerry Giles (Head Paramedic); David Lewman (Messenger).

69. "Soul Mates" Written by: Brad Kern. Directed by: Richard Friedman. Airdate: October 13, 1996

H.G. Wells interrupts Lois and Clark's honeymoon with news that an age old curse has been placed upon their souls, and that every time in history that they consummate their love, it ends badly. Lois, Clark and H.G. Wells travel back into antiquity to stop the curse at its source, where they learn that Clark — despite his alien origin — is a Robin Hood–like figure called "the Fox," Lois is a maiden, Perry is a friar, and Tempus is an evil, greedy baron bent on marrying Lane. Clark fears he must die to save his future relationship with Lois, but she realizes she must marry Tempus willingly — causing a devastating change in the time continuum.

GUEST CAST: Lane Davies (Tempus); Clive Revill (Sorcerer); Terry Kiser (H.G. Wells); Nick Meaney (Soldier #1); Tim O'Hare (Soldier #2).

70. "Brutal Youth" Written by: Tim Minear. Directed by: David Grossman. Airdate: October 20, 1996.

Lois and Clark return from their honeymoon to confront a mystery at the *Daily Planet*: A friend of Jimmy's, a young man, has died of old age. At the same time, an old crook, Conner Schenks, escapes from prison with the help of a scientist who has been experimenting with age. The scientist uses Jimmy as a donor, sucking away his youth and vitality to give to the thief in exchange for the secret location of decades-old loot. Meanwhile, Lois fears growing old, knowing that Superman will never age.

GUEST CAST: Caroline McWilliams (Dr. Vida Dudson); Kenneth Kimmins (Dr. Klein); John D'Aquino (Conner Schenks, Young); Jack Larson (Old Jimmy Olsen); Sandy Ward (Old Conner Schenk); Don Keefer (Old Benny Borkland); Randl Ask (Mister Larry); Lynn Tufeld (Bank Teller); Steven Rodriguez (Guard); Barbara Pilavin (Ancient Lois).

71. "The People vs. Lois Lane" Written by: Grant Rosenberg. Directed by: Robert Ginty. Airdate: October 27, 1996.

Lois is arrested for murder and prosecuted by a politically ambitious district attorney running for governor. But she's ac-tually been set up by Jefferson Cole, a vengeful professor obsessed with ruining her life. As Superman, Clark arranges for Lois to be released to investigate the murder she's been accused of committing, but Lois is returned to jail when a videotape and a murderous hologram generated by a hallucination device seem to prove her guilt. Testimony from Perry (another hologram) seals Lane's fate, and she is found guilty of murder in the first degree.

GUEST CAST: Alan Rachins (Jefferson Cole); Granville Van Dusen; Maryedith Burrell; David Kriegel; Kim Tavares; Julie Payne; Jim Jansen; Jasmine Guy (Angela Winters); Marianne Muellerleile (Matron); Peter Spellos (Elroy Sykes); Norman Large (Detective); Eric Fleeks (Bailiff); Brad Heller (Reporter); Anthony Ernbeck (Bobby).

72. "Dead Lois Walking" Written by: Brad Buckner and Eugenie Ross Leming. Directed by: Chris Long. Airdate: November 10, 1996.

Thanks to a hologram's devastating testimony, Lois is found guilty of murder and sentenced to die. Superman breaks her out of the slammer even as Cole attempts to get even with Dr. Klein at Star Labs for firing him. Cole then plans to unleash a deadly kryptonite hybrid on Metropolis. The villainous Cole gets his hands on the dangerous substance (thanks to a hologram of Superman) and kidnaps the freed Lois to give her a front row seat to the destruction of the city.

GUEST CAST: Alan Rachins (Jefferson Cole); Granville Van Dusen; David Kriegel; Kim Tavares; Kenneth Kimmins (Dr. Klein); Michael Krawic (Dr. Bains); Christopher Titus (State Trooper); Ken Thorley (Lou).

73. "Bob and Carol and Lois and Clark" Written by: Brian Nelson. Directed by: Oz Scott. Airdate: November 17, 1996.

Lois and Clark go out with another couple, Bob and Carol, unaware that Bob is hiding a secret identity as the costumed super-villain Deathstroke. He and Carol are actually after the subject of Lois's latest interview: the reclusive millionaire Grant Gendell. Before long, it's a battle between Deathstroke and Superman, and Superman barely survives — his blood chemistry is dangerously altered by Deathstroke's "magnetic" powers.

GUEST CAST: Antonio Sabato, Jr. (Bob Stanford); Kenneth Mars (Gendell); Kenneth Kimmins (Dr. Klein); Sydney Walsh; Steve Hytner; Rif Hutton; Beiny Lynn George (Aurora); Darryl Kunitomi (Dr. Kobayashi).

74. "Ghosts" Written by: Michael Gleason. Directed by: Robert Ginty. Airdate: November 24, 1996.

A petty criminal named Herbie tries to obtain ownership of a row of brownstones in an exclusive Metropolis neighborhood by scaring the owners with ghosts. Lois and Clark are the next targets of Herbie's scheme, but the small-time con man actually summons the real ghost of a dead housewife, Katie Banks! First she possesses Lois and Clark's kitchen, and then — seeing Clark's love for Lois — the lonely ghost possesses Lois Lane!

GUEST CAST: Drew Carey (Herbie); Richard Zavaglia (Mink); Kathy Kinney (Katie Banks); Lee Benton; Jean Speegle Howard (Bertha Emory).

75. "Stop the Presses" Written by: Brad Kern. Directed by: Peter Ellis. Airdate: December 8, 1996.

Lois becomes editor-in-chief of the *Daily Planet* when Perry moves upstairs to a corporate position. Meanwhile, a criminal named Press, along with his hacker brother, plots to kill Superman by draining his enormous energy reserves. Meanwhile, Lois is hell on wheels as editor, causing friction with Clark on the job. The Press brothers spring their trap on Superman with a quantum disrupter, a nuclear warhead and a dark silo where Superman is cut off from the sun, the source of his power.

GUEST CAST: Charles Esten (Eric Press); Jeff Juday; Ramond O'Keefe; James Dumont (Ralph); Bailni Turpin (Carly); Nicholas Shaffer (Technician); Tanika Ray (Researcher); Nichole Robinson (Reporter #1); James Martin, Jr. (Reporter #2); Krisinda Cain (Darlene).

76. "Twas the Night Before Myxmas" Written by: Tim Minear. Directed by: Michael Vejar. Airdate: December 15, 1996.

That devious dwarf from another dimension, Mr. Mxyzpltlk, returns to Metropolis with a new plot to stir up trouble. He wants to spoil Christmas Eve and rob the city's populace of the Christmas spirit. Can Superman play Santa Claus to a whole city in the nick of time?

GUEST CAST: Howie Mandel (Mr. Mxyzpltlk); Beverly Garland (Mrs. Lane); Harve Presnell (Mr. Lane); Keene Curtis, James Dumont, Ben McCain.

77. "Lethal Weapon" Written by: Grant Rosenberg. Directed by James Charleston. Airdate: January 5, 1997.

The former child program star Mr. Gadget uses a high-intensity, low-frequency sound wave weapon to threaten Metropolis. Meanwhile, Perry's ex-con son, Jerry, comes to town to visit and reconcile with his father, though he is secretly using red kryptonite against an unsuspecting Superman. When Jerry and Gadget team up, all of Metropolis could be leveled, with the red kryptonite making Clark's super powers go out of control. Worried about a superhero without super control, the mayor of Metropolis grounds Superman just when he is needed most.

GUEST CAST: Tom Wilson; Nancy Dussault (Mayor); Andre Nemec (Jerry White); Kenneth Kimmins (Dr. Klein); John Spencer (Mr. Gadget); Stephen Pocock (Thug).

78. "Sex, Lies and Videotape" Written by: Andrew Dettman, Daniel Truly. Story by: Dan Wilcox. Directed by: Philip J. Sgriccia. Airdate: January 19, 1997.

While Superman brokers peace between warring nuclear powers, a tabloid editor, Mr. Good, learns that Lois Lane may be cheating on her husband, Clark Kent — with Superman! A nosy reporter, Samantha, pursues the story and photographs Lois and the Man of Steel in an embrace at a romantic getaway. The story breaks all over Metropolis, threatening the peace talks and ruining the reputations of Lois and Superman. Clark realizes he must show the world that Superman and Clark Kent are one in the same, but would that just humanize Superman further, destroying his power as a role model?

GUEST CAST: Jack Wagner (Mr. Good); Julie Brown (Samantha); Tony Amendola (Kasparov); Alan Charof; Archie Hahn; Ben McCain (Brock Thompson); Scott Leva (Thug); Charles C. Stevenson, Jr. (Priest); Nina Blackwood (Jean Sally); Irene Olga Lopez (Mrs. Lopez); Robert Garrove (Boy Scout).

79. "Meet John Doe" Written by: Tim Minear. Directed by: Jim Pohl. Airdate: March 2, 1997.

With the aid of 25th century "sublimator" technology, Tempus manipulates the vote for the presidency as a mystery candidate called "John Doe." Once elected, Doe uses the American bureaucracy (including the IRS, the FAA and INS) to hassle the Man of Steel. Then, after attempting to make Lois kill herself, Tempus traps Superman in a time corridor, sending him into oblivion and undoing the future utopia in which Tempus was born.

GUEST CAST: Lane Davies (Tempus); Fred Willard (President Garner); William Christopher (Andros); Victor Raidler-Wexler; Robert Arce; Richard Cody (Rudolph); Robert Gallo (Guard); Dennis Fimple (Homeless Man); Ben McCain (Anchor).

80. "Lois and Clarks" Written by: Eugenie Ross Leming and Brad Buckner. Directed by: Chris Long. Airdate: March 9, 1997.

Superman has been cast through a time window, while John Doe (actually Tempus) assumes the presidency of the United States. H.G. Wells retrieves Clark Kent from an alternate dimension to help defeat Tempus, but his presence only disturbs Lois, who is mourning the loss of her husband. Tempus plans a global nuclear war, while Lois and Wells try to determine the exact nanosecond Clark was transported outside of time so they can use Wells' time machine to rescue him.

GUEST CAST: Lane Davies (Tempus); Fred Willard (President Garner); Hamilton Camp (H.G. Wells); Rick Dean (Dragon); Ben McCain (Anchor); John Kendall (Rustie).

81. "A.k.a. Superman" Written by: Jeffrey Vlaming. Directed by: Robert Ginty. Airdate: March 16, 1997.

A bored but beautiful worker at Diticom has applied science and mathematics to the search for Superman's secret identity, and the results of her study point to ... Jimmy Olsen! Meanwhile, a corrupt industrialist, Garrett Gray, plans a strategic missile defense program and kills a NASA astronaut who intends to interfere with the destructive plan. While all this is going on, Lois complains that Superman is spending too much time attending charity functions.

GUEST CAST: Kristanna Loken (Penny); Vito D'Ambrosio; Michael Paul Chan; Michole White; Dwight Schultz (Garrett Gray); Granville Ames (Steve McBride).

82. "Faster Than a Speeding Vixen" Written by: Brad Kern. Directed by: Neal Ahern. Airdate: April 12, 1997.

The *Daily Planet* has a new owner, Australian tycoon Lesley Luckabee, at the very same time that Metropolis acquires a new superhero: the incredibly fast and gorgeous Vixen. With all this going on, Lois and Clark investigate the disappearances of several important CEOs. While Superman and Vixen clash over superhero etiquette, a deformed criminal named Mr. Smith works in secret from below the city to manipulate events. Superman faces off against Vixen, who turns out to be a robot, and Lois and Clark wonder who built her.

GUEST CAST: Patrick Cassidy; Keith Brunsmann; Peter Vogt; Lori Feltrick (Vixen).

83. "Shadow of a Doubt" Written by: Grant Rosenberg. Directed by: Philip J. Sgriccia. Airdate: April 19, 1997.

Lesley Luckabee may actually be the son of Lex Luthor, and he sets out to see that all those involved in the creation of the super-robot Vixen are murdered before they can reveal his involvement. Luckabee is working in tandem with the deformed Mr. Smith and a shadowy assassin to resurrect Lex Corp. Perhaps more significantly, Luckabee seems bound and determined to split up Lois and Clark by making it look like he and Lois are having an affair.

GUEST CAST: Patrick Cassidy; Keith Brunsmann; Matt Roe; Kenneth Kimmins (Dr. Klein); John Shea (Voice of Lex Luthor); Leonard Kelly-Young (Detective).

84. "Voice from the Past" Written by: John McNamara. Directed by: David Grossman. Airdate: April 26, 1997.

Luckabee and the grotesque Mr. Smith learn from a recording left behind by Lex Luthor that Clark Kent is Superman. Luckabee hopes to use this information to make Superman a slave to the revived Lex Corp., but Mr. Smith has more devious, personal plans. He is in love with Lois Lane; and, actually, he is Lex Luthor, Jr., not Luckabee! Using a special bomb device, Smith forces Lois to leave Clark and end their marriage.

GUEST CAST: Patrick Cassidy; Keith Brunsmann; Kenneth Kimmins (Dr. Klein); Stacy Rekeyser (Carolyn); Terence Matthews (Cop).

85. "I've Got You Under My Skin" Written by: Tim Minear. Directed by: Eugenie-Ross Leming. Airdate: May 31, 1997.

A small-time criminal named Woody Samms is committing robberies all over Metropolis by switching bodies with a monkey. But to get the price off his head, Woody wants to switch bodies with a local mob boss. To do that, he needs to switch bodies with Clark, who is due to interview the criminal. But Woody gets more than he bargained for when he realizes he has switched bodies with the Man of Steel. Meanwhile, Clark must convince a skeptical Lois that he is her husband, even though he's inside a different body.

GUEST CAST: Tim Thomerson (Woody Samms); Shaun Toub (Asabi); Howard George; Stacy Keanan (Berky Samms); Joe Maruzzo (Mug); Frank Novak (Beat Cop); Dorian Gregory (SWAT Commander).

86. "Toy Story" Written by: Brad Kern. Directed by: Jim Pohl. Airdate: June 7, 1997.

Someone in Metropolis is kidnapping children, a crime that bothers Lois more than usual because she and Clark have been debating becoming parents themselves. The kids have been abducted by Dr. Kripsley, a scientist who has been working on a matter transporter called a "re-integrator." When Kripsley learns that Klein has been assigned to produce such a device (based on his own plans), he sends toys to abduct the good doctor too. Then the evil Kripsley sends a toy duck — an explosive — to keep Lois and Clark off the case.

GUEST CAST: Grant Shoud; Stacey Travis; Jeffey Byron; Irene Olga Lopez; Kenneth Kimmins (Dr. Klein); Mary Frann (Alice); Susan Isaacs (Nanny); Jillian Berard (Brittany Turner); Myles Jeffrey (Ryan); Ben McCain (Anchorman); Brian McLaughlin (Joey); Laurie Stevens (Woman).

87. "The Family Hour" Written by: Brad Buckner and Eugenie Ross Leming. Directed by: Robert Ginty. Airdate: June 14, 1997.

The evil, giant-brained Dr. Fat Head

Mensa leaves prison, armed with amazing psychic and telekinetic powers. When Lois and Clark learn they can't have children, they consult with Lois's dad, Dr. Sam Lane, in the process revealing Clark's secret identity. Mensa learns the secret of Superman from Lane and plots to blackmail the Man of Steel. Then, mysteriously, a baby shows up in Lois and Clark's apartment.

GUEST CAST: Beverly Garland (Mrs. Lane); Harvey Presnell (Mr. Lane); Harry Anderson (Dr. Fat Head Mensa); Brian George; Jane Morris; Rick Lawless; Michael E. Bauer (Guard); Eric Fleeks (Lieutenant); Denise Ryan-Sherman (Female Cop).

Superman: *The Animated Series* (1996–1998)
ANIMATED SERIES

VOICE TALENTS: Tim Daly (Superman/ Clark Kent); Dana Delaney (Lois Lane); George Dzundza (Perry White); David Kaufman (Jimmy Olsen); Mike Farrell (Jonathan Kent).

CREW: *Produced by:* Alan Burnett, Paul Dini, Glen Murakami, Bruce Timm. *Associate Producer:* Haven Alexander. *Production Manager:* Shaun McLaughlin. *Series Story Editors:* Stan Berkowitz, Alan Burnett, Paul Dini, Rich Fogel. *Series Writers:* Hilary J. Bader, Stan Berkowitz, Alan Burnett, Paul Dini, Rich Fogel, Robert

Goodman. *Series Directors:* Curt Geda, Butch Lukic, Dan Riba. *Theme Music:* Shirley Walker. *Voice Director:* Andrea Romano. Based on DC Comics Characters. *Superman Created by:* Jerry Siegel and Joe Shuster. *Character Design:* Shane Clines, Steve Jones, Dexter Smith, Tommy Tejeda, Glen Murakami, Bruce Timm. *Storyboards:* David Bullock, Butch Lukic, Lee Weeks. *Music Editor:* Diane Griffen. *Animation Services:* Koko Enterprises, Dong Yang Animation Company.

Swamp Thing

Created by writer Len Wein and artist Berni Wrightson, the character known as Swamp Thing began his life in the DC comic book *House of Secrets* in 1971 before moving to his own comic book in 1972. In essence, the tale of Swamp Thing was a familiar one to horror fans, a literate combination of both the Frankenstein and Dr. Jekyll and Mr. Hyde mythos. In this case, a scientist with good intentions (Alex Olsen originally, then Alec Holland) experimented with a bio-regenerative plant compound that could help battle starvation throughout the civilized world. Unfortunately, a disaster in the laboratory killed his wife, Linda, and sent a badly wounded Alec into the waters of a nearby swamp.

When the scientist emerged from the muck, he had become genetically re-structured, thanks to his compound, as a sen-

tient plant creature, one sworn to defend the swamp and local wild life. It was an ecology story, and Swamp Thing was an environmental superhero, the vegetable matter that understood why vegetables matter. In at least one sense, Swamp Thing was a voice for the disenfranchised, arguing the cause of those elements of the world (in this case, plants) that could not voice their own viewpoints to mankind. Swamp Thing used his enhanced strength, incredible healing powers, and symbiosis with living plants to further his cause.

Over the years, more elements of Swamp Thing's universe solidified. His enemy, Dr. Arcane, became the primary villain, and Abigail, Arcane's niece, emerged as the traditional damsel in distress. When writer Alan Moore and others came into the picture in the 1980s, the legend underwent a drastic rewrite, and readers learned that Swamp Thing was not Alec Holland at all, but a sentient plant that had absorbed Alec's memories when he fell into the swamp. Over the years, Swamp Thing's adventures took on new meaning and provocative issues. The comic book was cancelled in June of 1989 because one of the comic writers wanted Swampy to meet Jesus Christ.[1]

A dark superhero, one isolated from mankind and even, in a sense, his own humanity, Swamp Thing was in many ways the forerunner of the dark superhero that came to populate comics and cinemas in the late 1980s and early 1990s. Like Todd McFarlane's Spawn, Swampy (as fans knew him) was an outsider, marked by his "ugliness" and always apart from humanity. Like James O'Barr's the Crow, Swamp Thing was "born" after his natural death. That he was angst-ridden and violent helped him fit into the mold of the Dark Knight, RoboCop and others. Amazingly, Swamp Thing came to the movies almost seven years before the "dark trend" took hold in Hollywood comic adaptations, and he arrived in theaters mostly intact.

In 1981, director Wes Craven (*Last House on the Left* [1972], *The Hills Have Eyes* [1977], *A Nightmare on Elm Street* [1984], *Scream* [1996]), a horror icon, took the reins of a feature film adaptation of Swamp Thing. Michael Uslan and Ben Melnicker produced the movie, and later brought Tim Burton's *Batman* to the silver screen. The film was budgeted at $2.5 million, a paltry sum, even for the time, and principal photography occurred near Charleston, South Carolina, at Cypress Gardens and Magnolia Plantation. Louis Jourdan (*Octopussy* [1983]) was retained to play the sardonic villain, Arcane, and Ray Wise played Dr. Alec Holland before his accident.

Dick Durock donned the uncomfortable and heavy plant-suit that represented Swamp Thing, but the real star of the film was pin-up queen Adrienne Barbeau (*The Fog* [1980], *Escape from New York* [1981], *Carnival* [2003]), who played government agent Alice Cable. In the movie, Linda Holland became Alec's sister so that Swamp Thing might find romance with the lovely Barbeau.

Swamp Thing was a relatively faithful adaptation of the comic, though woefully low budget. The movie premiered in the summer of 1982 without fanfare and quickly disappeared from theaters. However, the burgeoning video market gave *Swamp Thing* a second life, and the film became a huge rental champ during its life in this new secondary market. The movie found favor with audiences and some critics (including Roger Ebert) because of its perfectly entertaining old-fashioned comic book style. Barbeau snapped off one-liners like a Howard Hawks heroine, and Louis Jourdan, in the style of the best Bond villains, quoted Friedrich Nietzsche and chewed the scenery. Swamp Thing himself came off as a likeable personality in the film, expressing love and even mourning the loss of his humanity.

Perhaps more importantly, director Craven nicely expressed the environmental aspects of the Swamp Thing mythos by forging a link between the natural landscape and the *dramatis personae* of his comic-based screenplay. Arcane, an exploiter, misunderstood the true nature of adaptability in his quest for invincibility. He brought a fully equipped boat into the swamp and expected it to serve his purpose (to destroy Swampy). But despite Arcane's boats, land vehicles and guns, Swamp Thing defeated the villain because he was born of the swamp. The suave Arcane misused the landscape, forcing alligators and snakes to do his bidding, even conducting a sort of scorched-earth policy by destroying Holland's laboratory and destroying all evidence of his tampering. Swamp Thing, the living and breathing extension of the land, had his revenge for this misuse of the environment. *Swamp Thing* was thus more than a film about a guy with super powers, but a revenge of nature film. Nature does not strike back with flood, tornado, volcano, hurricane or earthquake, but with a humanoid champion: Swamp Thing!

Some comic book fans may not appreciate Craven's somewhat clichéd approach to making the film resemble the page of the *Swamp Thing* comic, what with his wipe-like transitions and green "ooze" dripping down the screen, sometime blossoming into cartoon explosions. But these touches remind audiences of the source material, even in a basic way, and that is probably a good thing. If taken as anything other than a superhero or comic-inspired film, *Swamp Thing* runs the risk of appearing silly. Its science is suspect, its characters based on literary antecedents (Dr. Jekyll and Frankenstein), and its budget too low to really amaze viewers with fantastic action sequences. The visual flair gives the low budget film an extra, dynamic punch, and often that is enough to carry it over slow pacing and silly moments.

Seven years later, the heroic Swamp Thing returned in a much less artistically satisfying sequel, also produced by Uslan and Melniker. In 1989, Jim Wynorski directed *Return of the Swamp Thing*, another low budget entry, this one filmed in Savannah, Georgia.[2] Starring Louis Jourdan as Arcane and Heather Locklear as Abigail (now Arcane's stepdaughter), the film premiered in theaters and, like its predecessor, was shunned by audiences. Critics took note of the movie primarily for its campy tone (shades of the 1960s *Batman*) and the sex scene between Abigail and Swampy (Durock again, in a lighter plant suit), which pushed the envelope regarding animal and vegetable interaction. When Swampy feared that he and Abigail could not be together because of species differences, Locklear's character answered gamely, "It's okay ... I'm a vegetarian."

The humorous, PG–style approach of *Return of the Swamp Thing* was likely an at-tempt to bring the character into the popular mainstream, but it was sadly lacking in quality. It also eschewed the Phantom of the Opera/Frankenstein/Jekyll & Hyde approach of the comics and first film, leaving Sam Raimi's *Darkman* to pick up that mantel in 1990.

Despite a lackluster second chapter, plans went ahead to expand the Swamp Thing franchise. A line of Swamp Thing toys heralded the arrival of a five-part *Swamp Thing* animated series that aired on Fox in 1991. The thirty-minute series brought some aspects of the comic book back (including the Un-Men, Arcane's mutant minions), but was otherwise a further watering down of the Len Wein concept.

In the summer of 1990 the USA Network, a basic cable station in the United States, launched *Swamp Thing: The TV Series*, a half-hour program starring Dick Durock as the hero he made famous in movies. At the time, the USA Network was looking to attract bigger audiences with "brand name" series, programs that harkened back to popular network shows or even movie franchises. To wit, they had picked up *Airwolf* (1984–1987) for an additional season after CBS cancelled it, and even resurrected NBC's re-do of *Alfred Hitchcock Presents* (1985–1990), HBO's *The Hitchhiker* (1983–1991) and *The Ray Bradbury Theater* (1985–1992). *Swamp Thing* was another show that possessed wide name identification and could bring in the viewers.

Set in Louisiana, Swamp Thing's TV incarnation focused heavily on the character of Dr. Anton Arcane (Mark Lindsay Chapman), the character responsible for the destruction of Holland's laboratory and his transformation into the plant creature. In the TV series, Arcane was not seeking his own immortality, but wanted Holland's bio-regenerative formula so as to revive his dear wife, frozen in suspended animation. Swamp Thing (whose origin was not seen in the series) was still in mourning over the death of Linda (his wife again, not his sister), and befriended a family living in the swamp: the Kipps. Tressa (Carrell Myers), Jim Kipp (Jesse Zeigler) and later Will Kipp (Scott Garrison), were often endangered by Arcane, his mutants, or his plans to capture Swamp Thing.

Swamp Thing: The TV Series was produced under the banner of Uslan and Melnicker, and developed for TV by none other than Joseph Stefano (*The Outer Limits* [1962–64]). Later, talents such as Tom Greene (*Tales of the Gold Monkey* [1982-83] contributed fine stories, even though the writers were hamstrung by the half-hour length of the episodes, which made many of the shows seem simultaneously breakneck and scattershot. The show ran for several seasons, and was heavily rerun on the USA Network's sister station, the Sci-Fi Channel, in the early 1990s.

Animal, mineral or vegetable? Dick Durock is the Swamp Thing in a still from USA Network's *Swamp Thing: The TV Series.*

Swamp Thing (1982)
LIVE-ACTION FILM

"Craven adapted the DC Comics character with care and consideration.... Craven knew that most modern comic books were more sophisticated and poetic. *Swamp Thing* is enthralling…"
  —Richard Meyers, *The Great Science Fiction Films*, Citadel Press, 1983, page 240.

"An off-the-wall, eccentric, peculiar movie fueled by the demented obsessions of its makers.... With *Swamp Thing*, [Craven] betrays a certain gentleness and poetry…"
  —Roger Ebert, *Roger Ebert's Movie Home Companion*, 1993 Edition, Andrews and McMeel, 1993, page 640.

"…[It is] just plain silly."
  — Douglas Menville and R. Reginald, *Futurevisions: The New Golden Age of the Science Fiction Film*, Newcastle Publishing Company, 1985, page 133.

"A shoddy camp effort."
  — Carrie Rickey, *Village Voice*, August 1, 1982, page 48.

"Producers could spend millions and not replicate the flavor — the mediocre camerawork, the poor sound and color, the wooden performances.... *Swamp Thing* is about as scary as a chef's salad."
  — Alex Keneas, *Newsday*, July 30, 1982.

"If you've never read the comics, the *Swamp Thing* films are kind of fun. They're over the top superhero/monster action films, and they work on that level. Nothing special. The comics, unfortunately, represent a rich tapestry of novel storytelling, and pull elaborate switches on readers as to the true nature of Swamp Thing himself. The films barely scratched the surface, which is unfortunate, but taken on their own, they're basically harmless."
  — William Latham, author of *Mary's Monster, Space: 1999 Resurrection.*

CAST: Louis Jourdan (Dr. Arcane); Adrienne Barbeau (Alice Cable); Ray Wise (Dr. Alec Holland); David Hess (Ferret); Nicholas Worth (Bruno); Don Knight (Ritter); Al Ruban (Charlie); Dick Durock (Swamp Thing); Ben Bates

(Arcane Monster); Nanette Brown (Dr. Linda Holland); Reggie Bates (Jude); Mimi Meyers (Arcane's Secretary); Karen Price (Arcane's Messenger); Bill Erickson (Young Agent).

CREW: An Embassy Pictures Release, *Swamp Thing*. *Music:* Harry Manfredini. *Film Editor:* Richard Bracken. *Art Direction:* David Nichols, Robb Wilson King. *Director of Photography:* Robin Goodwin. *Executive in Charge of Production:* Al Ruban. *Based Upon Characters Appearing in Magazines Published by DC Comics. Written and directed by:* Wes Craven. *Producers:* Benjamin Melniker, Michael E. Uslan. Filmed on location in Charleston, South Carolina. *M.P.A.A. Rating:* PG. *Running time:* 91 minutes.

A beautiful and tough special government agent, Alice Cable, investigates the death of another agent in a fog-ridden swamp near the top-secret research facility run by the charismatic Dr. Alec Holland. In this small research compound, Holland has been working on a secret project involving plants. Alec and Cable become attracted to one another as they work together, unaware that an evil genius named Dr. Arcane is plotting a deadly strike. As Holland works on his project — to combine animal and vegetable matter and build a heartier stock of plant for the 21st century — the evil Arcane strikes. He threatens to kill Holland's sister, Linda, unless Holland turns over all materials, including a secret formula, related to his work. Despite Holland's compliance, Arcane kills Linda, and Holland is hurt in an accident. After being contaminated by the formula, he catches fire and runs out into the swamp.

Arcane has captured Cable and stolen Holland's formula, but now he must contend with Swamp Thing, a half-man/half-vegetable being, actually the mutated Holland. Defending the swamp and humanity, Holland strikes fear into the hearts of Arcane's men, foiling the evil genius' plans at every opportunity and exacting a mad vengeance. Unable to become human again, Swamp Thing becomes a permanent denizen of the swamp, despite his love for Cable. With the formula in his hands, Arcane plots to imbibe the material himself, creating a new and monstrous nemesis for the man in the swamp.

Return of the Swamp Thing (1989)
LIVE-ACTION FILM

"…[E]nough to drive you back to the comic book stand. Or even the swamp."
— Michael Wilmington, *The Los Angeles Times*, May 12, 1989, page 7.

"Only with those with the IQ of a plant are really going to love this little shop of horrors."
— Jami Bernard, *The New York Post*, May 12, 1989, page 27.

"It's pretty silly, but not much fun."
— Elliott Stein, *The Village Voice*, May 16, 1989, page 73.

CAST: Louis Jourdan (Dr. Arcane); Heather Locklear (Abby Arcane); Sarah Douglas (Dr. Zurrell); Dick Durock (Swamp Things); Joey Sagal (Gunn); Chris Doyle (Leech Man).

CREW: A Millimeter Films release of a Lightyear Entertainment Production, *Return of the Swamp Thing*. *Executive Producers:* Tom Kuhn and Charles Mitchell. *Producers:* Ben Melniker and Michael Uslan. *Directed by:* Jim Wynorsky. *Screenplay:* Derek Spencer and Grant Morris. *Director of Photography:* Zoran Hochstatter. *Film Editor:* Leslie Rosenthal. *Production Design:* Robb Wilson King. *Swamp Thing Created by:* Len Wein and Berni Wrightson. *Music:* Chuck Cirino. *M.P.A.A. Rating:* PG-13. *Running time:* 87 minutes.

The evil Dr. Arcane continues his strange experiments to prolong his life and discover the secret of immortality. His beautiful stepdaughter, Abby, is just another exploitable resource as far as he is concerned, and he plans to use her in his experiments. Preventing that eventuality is the protector of the swamp, the man-vegetable hero called Swamp Thing. While Arcane's thugs set out to destroy Swamp Thing, the former human being rescues Abigail and even begins a romantic relationship with her.

Swamp Thing: The TV Series (1990–1993)
LIVE-ACTION SERIES

"The grotesque half-plant, half-human comic-book hero slogs through the bayou once more in this low-rent thriller-chiller series."
— David Hiltbrand, *People Weekly:* "Swamp Thing," September 10, 1990, page 9.

CAST: Dick Durock (Swamp Thing); Mark Lindsay Chapman (Dr. Arcane); Carrell Myers (Tressa); SEASON ONE: Jesse Zeigler (Jim); SEASON TWO: Kari Wuhrer (Abigail); William Whitehead (Dr. Holister). SECOND AND THIRD SEASONS: Kevin Quigley (Graham).

CREW: *Swamp Thing Created by:* Len Wein and Berni Wrightson. *Developed for Television by:* Joe Stefano. *Producer:* Boris Malden. *Executive Producers:* Michael E. Uslan, Benjamin Melniker, Andy Heward, Tom Greene, Tom Blomquist. *Story Editors:* Judith and Sandra Berg. *Casting:* Melvin Johnson. *Film Editors:* Michael T. Elias and Greg Honick. *Directors of Photography (various episodes):* Joseph Mangine, Geoff Schaff. *Production Designer:* Orvis Rigsby. *Production Manager:* Charles Ziarko. *Special Effects/Make-up:* Jim Beinke. *Swamp Thing Appliances Manufactured by:* Alterian Studios. *Swamp Thing Bodysuit Designed by:* Carl Fullerton and Neal Martz. BBK Productions, in Association with Batfilm Productions.

SEASON ONE (1990-1991)

1. **"The Emerald Heart"** Written by: Joseph Stefano. Directed by: Fritz Kiersch. Airdate: July 27, 1990.

2. **"The Living Image"** Written by: David Braff, Judith and Sandra Berg. Story by: Joe Stefano. Directed by: John McPherson. Airdate: September 7, 1990.

3. **"The Death of Dr. Arcane"** Written by: Judith and Sandra Berg. Story by: Joe Stefano. Directed by: John McPherson. Airdate: September 14, 1990.

4. **"The Legend of the Swamp Maiden"** Written by: Lorenzo Domenico. Directed by: Yuri Sivo. Airdate: September 21, 1990.

5. **"Spirit of the Swamp"** Written by: Judith and Sandra Berg. Story by: Michael Reaves. Directed by: Yuri Sivo. Airdate: September 28, 1990.

6. **"Blood Wind"** Written by: Marc Scott Zicree. Directed by: Walter Von Huene. Airdate: October 5, 1990.

7. **"Grotesquery"** Written by: Michele Barinholtz. Directed by: David S. Jackson. Airdate: October 12, 1990.

8. **"Natural Enemy"** Written by: Robert Goethals. Directed by: Tony Dow. Airdate: October 19, 1990.

9. **"Treasure"** Written by: Jon Ezrine. Directed by: Tony Dow. Airdate: October 26, 1990.

10. **"New Acquaintance"** Written by: Lawrence DeTillo, Wade Johnson and Daniel Kennedy. Directed by: David S. Jackson. Airdate: November 2, 1990.

11. **"Falco"** Written by: Joe Stefano. Directed by: Fritz Kiersch. Airdate: November 9, 1990.

12. **"From Beyond the Grave"** Written by: Wade Johnson and Daniel Kennedy. Directed by: Tony Dow. Airdate: November 16, 1990.

13. **"The Shipment"** Written by: Judith and Sandra Berg. Story by: Joe Stefano.

Directed by: Walter Von Huene. Airdate: November 23, 1990.

14. "Birth Marks" Written by: Tom Greene. Directed by: Walter Von Huene. Airdate: February 1, 1991.

15. "Dark Side of the Mirror" Written by: William Whitehead. Directed by: Bruce Seth Green. Airdate: February 8, 1991.

16. "Silent Screams" Written by: Judith and Sandra Berg. Directed by: Walter Von Huene. Airdate: February 15, 1991.

17. "Walk a Mile in My Shoots" Written by: Jonathan Torp. Directed by: Bruce Seth Green. Airdate: February 22, 1991.

18. "The Watchers" Written by: Tom Greene and William Whitehead. Directed by: Lyndon Chubbock. Airdate: March 1, 1991.

19. "The Hunt" Written by: Wade Johnson and Daniel Kennedy. Directed by: Bruce Seth Green. Airdate: March 8, 1991.

20. "Touch of Death" Written by: Tom Greene and William Whitehead. Directed by: Walter Von Huene. Airdate: March 15, 1991.

21. "Tremors of the Heart" Written by: Wade Johnson and Daniel Kennedy. Directed by: Mitchell Bock. Airdate: March 22, 1991.

22. "The Prometheus Parabola" Written by: Tom Greene and William Whitehead. Directed by: Walter Von Huene. Airdate: April 5, 1991.

SEASON TWO (1992)

23. "Night of the Dying" Written by: Tom Blomquist. Directed by: Steve Beers. Airdate: January 3, 1992.

24. "Love Lost" Written by: Tom Blomquist. Directed by: David S. Jackson. Airdate: January 10, 1992.

25. "Mist Demeanor" Written by: Steven L. Sears. Directed by: David S. Jackson. Airdate: January 17, 1992.

26. "A Nightmare on Jackson Street" Written by: Jeff Myrow. Directed by: Walter Von Huene. Airdate: January 24, 1992.

27. "Better Angels" Written by: Babs Greyhosky. Directed by: David S. Jackson. Airdate: January 31, 1992.

28. "Children of the Fool" Written by: Fred Golan. Directed by: David S. Jackson. Airdate: February 7, 1992.

29. "A Jury of His Fears" Written by: Tom Blomquist. Directed by: Walter Von Huene. Airdate: February 14, 1992.

30. "Poisonous" Written by: Jeff Myrow. Directed by: Walter Von Huene. Airdate: February 21, 1992.

31. "Smoke and Mirrors" Written by: Tom Blomquist. Directed by: Steve Beers. Airdate: February 28, 1992.

32. "This Old House of Mayan" Written by: Steven L. Sears. Directed by: Walter Von Huene. Airdate: March 6, 1992.

33. "Sonata" Written by: Babs Greyhosky. Directed by: Chuck Bowman. Airdate: March 20, 1992.

SEASON THREE (1992-1993)

34. "Dead and Married" Written by: Steven L. Sears. Directed by: Steve Beers. Airdate: July 10, 1992.

35. "Powers of Darkness" Written by: W. Reed Morgan. Directed by: Chuck Bowman. Airdate: July 17, 1992.

36. "Special Request" Written by: Terry Nelson. Directed by: John McPherson. Airdate: July 24, 1992.

37. "What Goes Around Comes Around" Written by: Jim Byrnes. Directed by: Chuck Bowman. Airdate: July 31, 1992.

38. "Fear Itself" Written by: Brenda Lilly. Directed by: John McPherson. Airdate: August 7, 1992.

39. "Changes" Written by: Steven L. Sears and Jeff Myrow. Directed by: John McPherson. Airdate: August 14, 1992.

40. "Destiny" Written by: Jim Byrnes. Directed by: Tom DeSimone. Airdate: August 21, 1992.

41. "Tatania" Written by: Randy Holland. Directed by: John McPherson. Airdate: August 28, 1992.

42. "Mirador's Brain" Written by: Bruce Lansbury. Directed by: Tom DeSimone. Airdate: September 11, 1992.

43. "Lesser of Two Evils" Written by: Steven L. Sears and Tom Blomquist. Directed by: Walter Von Huene. Airdate: September 19, 1992.

44. "Revelations" Written by: Tom Blomquist and Steven L. Sears. Directed by: Chuck Bowman. Airdate: September 26, 1992.

45. "Easy Prey" Written by: Jim Byrnes. Directed by: Steve Beers. Airdate: October 3, 1992.

46. "The Handyman" Written by: Terry D. Nelson. Directed by: Andrew Stevens. Airdate: October 10, 1992.

47. "Future Tense" Written by: Terry D. Nelson. Directed by: Steve Beers. Airdate: October 17, 1992.

48. "Hide in the Night" Written by Steven L. Sears. Directed by: Andrew Stevens. Airdate: October 24, 1992.

49. "Pay Day" Written and directed by: Tom Blomquist. Airdate: October 31, 1992.

50. "The Return of La Roche" Written by: Babs Greyhosky. Directed by: Andrew Stevens. Airdate: November 7, 1992.

51. "Rites of Passage" Written by: John Lansing. Directed by: Chuck Bowman. Airdate: November 14, 1992.

52. "Never Alone" Written by: Fred Golan. Directed by: Walter Von Huene. Airdate: November 21, 1992.

53. "A Most Bitter Pill' Written and directed by: Tom Blomquist. Airdate: December 5, 1992.

54. "The Curse" Written by: Jeff Myrow. Directed by: Chuck Bowman. Airdate: December 12, 1992.

55. "Judgment Day" Written by: W. Reed Morgan. Directed by: Chuck Bowman. Airdate: December 19, 1992.

56. "Eye of the Storm" Written by: Brenda Lilly. Directed by: Chuck Bowman. Airdate: January 9, 1993.

57. **"Vendetta"** Written by: W. Reed Morgan. Directed by: Steven Beers. Airdate: January 16, 1993.

58. **"The Hurting"** Written by: Tom Blomquist. Directed by: Chuck Bowman. Airdate: January 23, 1993.

59. **"The Burning Times"** Written by: Katharyn Michaelian Powers. Directed by: Mitchell Bock. Airdate: January 30, 1993.

60. **"The Specter of Death"** Written by: Tom Blomquist. Directed by: Tony Dow. Airdate: February 6, 1993.

61. **"Cross-Fired"** Written by: John Lansing and Bruce Cervi. Directed by: Chuck Bowman. Airdate: February 13, 1993.

62. **"Patient Zero"** Written by: Judith and Sandra Berg. Directed by: Walter Von Huene. Airdate: February 20, 1993.

63. **"The Chains of Forever"** Written by Randy Holland. Directed by: Mitchell Bock. Airdate: February 27, 1993.

64. **"In the Beginning"** Written by: Terry D. Nelson. Directed by: Mitchell Bock. Airdate: March 6, 1993.

65. **"Brotherly Love"** Written by: Jim Byrnes. Directed by: Walter Von Huene. Airdate: March 13, 1993.

66. **"An Eye for an Eye"** Written by: Jeff Myrow. Directed by: Tom De Simone. Airdate: March 20, 1993.

67. **"Yo Ho Ho"** Written by: David Kemper. Directed by: Walter Von Huene. Airdate: March 27, 1993.

68. **"Heart of Stone"** Written by: Alan Jay Gluckman. Directed by: Mitchell Bock. Airdate: April 3, 1993.

69. **"Romancing Arcane"** Written by: Jeff Myrow. Directed by: Tony Dow. Airdate: April 10, 1993.

70. **"Swamp of Dreams"** Written by: Rand Holland. Directed by: John McPherson. Airdate: April 17, 1993.

71. **"Heart of the Mantis"** Written by: Steven L. Sears. Directed by: Walter Von Huene. Airdate: April 24, 1993.

72. **"That's a Wrap"** Written by: Tom Blomquist and Jeff Myrow. Story by: Steven L. Sears. Directed by: Walter Von Huene. Airdate: May 1, 1993.

Swamp Thing (1991)
ANIMATED SERIES

VOICE TALENTS: Len Carlson (Dr. Alec Holland/Swamp Thing); Paulina Gillis (Abby Arcane); Don Franks (Dr. Arcane); Harvey Atkins (Tomahawk).

CREDITS: A DIC/Batfilm Production. From Fox Television.

The Tick

The "mysterious blue avenger" known as the Tick was born in comic book form in the summer of 1988, written and drawn by creator Ben Edlund, later a writer on Joss Whedon's *Firefly* (2002–). The comic book followed the strange adventures of a bizarre blue giant, a costumed, would-be superhero with great bravado but not many smarts.

One day, the Tick (a character that featured few, if any, tick-like qualities) left his home in the insane asylum to fight crime in the realm known only as "the City." There he clashed with the real protector of the city, a hero by the name of the Caped Wonder. As the first twelve issues of *The Tick* comic progressed, the verbose hero tried to get a job at a major metropolitan newspaper (as a crossword puzzle editor). He even acquired a devoted sidekick in the form of the slightly pudgy Arthur, an accountant who wore a second-hand white flying moth suit and was considerably more intelligent than the Tick.

In the comics, the Tick's bizarre battle cry was "SPOON!" and the comic proved a cult sensation. Like the 1960s *Batman* TV series, *The Tick* was a parody of the ethos that defined various generations of *Superman*, *Batman* and *Spider-Man* comics.

In the mid–1990s, the Tick traveled to TV in cartoon form on the Fox Network. A faithful adaptation of the comic with Edlund as a writer and co-producer, the animated series ran for three seasons (from 1994 to 1996) and produced some three-dozen episodes before being shunted over to Comedy Central for two years of reruns. On the animated show, the Tick was given voice by Townsend Coleman, a veteran of *Teenage Mutant Ninja Turtles* and *Inspector Gadget*. Arthur was voiced by Rob Paulsen and, later, Micky Dolenz.

Like the comic, the animated series (with each episode lasting a half-hour) included a bevy of ridiculous superheroes, such as Bi-Polar Bear, Captain Lemming and Captain Decency. The villains were even funnier: Brainchild, Lavamen, Mr. Mental, the Mother of Invention, Mr. Smarty Pants and Dinosaur Neil.

It was not long before the cult popularity of the cartoon led to plans for a live-action version of *The Tick*. Fox shepherded the show to TV, recruiting comic book creator Ben Edlund once more, this time with Hollywood director Barry Sonnenfield (*The Addams Family* [1991], *The Wild, Wild West* [1999]) executive producing and directing the pilot. Patrick Warburton, of *Seinfeld* fame, was well cast as the pompous but good-hearted hero, and the actor noted it was "fun to do these odd characters."[1] He was also quick to note that, unlike with most superhero adaptations, producers on *The Tick* were attempting to stay faithful to what Edlund had wrought:

> We're not reinventing the Tick, but now that we're working in a three-dimensional realm, we've got to start exploring and taking some chances. I know how possessive ... Tick fans are of the character, and they're going to want to be very protective of him. But Ben Edlund is on board, so I'm sure we're not going to deviate far from the core essence of the Tick."[2]

That edict established, the TV series created some new and very interesting characters to inhabit the Tick's world, including Liz Vassey's Captain Liberty. The gorgeous Captain (who wore a Statue of Liberty–like tiara and was armed with a torch) was similar in concept to the comic book's heroic American Maid, but far more neurotic. Vassey wore an eye-catching get-up, exposing a great deal of cleavage (in a star-shaped "window" over her torso), so much so that Vassey noted on one occasion that she had "to lift men's chins up so they look me in the eye. I look like Super Whore."[3]

Another interesting character was Batmanuel, played by Nestor Carbonell, a Batman knock-off whose license plate read "batlove." Batmanuel was always seen talking to his agent on a cell phone and trying to get superhero groupies to go to bed with him.

The show made only one small change in the Tick's origin. In the pilot episode of the series, it was established that he had been hanging out at a bus stop (rather than a sanitarium) before arriving in the city to fight crime.

The primary setting of the half-hour *Tick* TV show was the Lonely Panda, a 1950s-style diner, and it was there, in their regular booth, that the Tick, Arthur (David Burke), Captain Liberty and Batmanuel hashed out the news of the week, debating matters important to superheroes. Unlike the cartoon series, or even the comic book, the live-action series was fairly static, and not much crime fighting was featured. Instead, the show was envisioned more as a sitcom along the lines of *Seinfeld*, with four characters experiencing odd situations. That said, the series was unremittingly funny.

Not surprisingly, the Fox Network, the same network that had cancelled Chris Carter's *Harsh Realm* after three episodes, had no idea what to do with such an odd series, a program that followed the "after hours" lives of bizarre superheroes. They held the series back for half a season, then another entire season until frustrated fans wondered if the show would ever premiere.

Finally, in the fall of 2001, *The Tick* premiered on Thursday nights at 8:30 on Fox, competing against NBC's murderous "Must See TV" lineup (including *Friends*). This funny, unconventional comedy thus bowed post–September 11, 2001, a time when all the major newspapers and media outlets were openly declaring that irony, the bread and butter of *The Tick*, was dead. Still, series producer Larry Charles hoped people could get into the bizarre world:

> If the show is perceived as merely a superhero parody show, I don't think it's going to work on a weekly basis. I think what's great about the comic book, and what was great about the cartoon also, is the characters and the interaction of the characters, and creating a world that you believe is real — a world in which the characters being superheroes is almost secondary consideration."[4]

He was right, in a sense. Though *The Tick* was clearly and openly a parody, it was also something much deeper and more valuable. The creators of the series had imagined an interesting conceit to spread across the stories. Even during its seven-episode run (eight episodes were produced), *The Tick* re-invented the world of superheroes, noting that the "life" of such characters was equivalent to an alternate "lifestyle choice."

"Lifestyle choice," a keyword for homosexuality, was even mentioned in one episode ("Arthur, Interrupted"). Superheroes, like gay men and women, were not quite understood by some regular folk, and even, in some cases, faced discrimination. "Is this *that* kind of place?" Arthur's shocked mother asked in "Arthur, Interrupted," acting as if the Lonely Panda diner, the gang's hangout, was a gay bar. Arthur attempted to hide the truth of his "lifestyle choice" from his family, but Captain Liberty was prompt to report that villains (and presumably family) could "smell a closeted superhero a mile away."

Another episode, notably titled "Couples," artfully and humorously compared the Tick-Arthur partnership to that of another superhero couple, the most-likely gay the Fiery Blaze (Ron Perlman) and his sidekick, Friendly Flamer, who operated out of a an HQ called the Fiery Station and wore little red hot pants. "Flamer," of course, has long been a derogatory term for flamboyant gay men. There was even a support group for sidekicks (called "Sidekicks Unite") featured in the same episode.

Further episodes of *The Tick* discussed discrimination at some length, but veiled the conversation in side-slapping humor. The Tick and Arthur were invited to join a club called the Hall of Heroes, which kept women, including Captain Liberty, out. The racist/sexist organization even came with its own hazing, a butt paddling ritual that the Tick found a "bit heiny-centric" for his taste.

The Tick series was thematically consistent, equating the superheroes with other outsiders, the disenfranchised peoples of America. But the show was perhaps most valuable for its unusual hero, an incredibly dense creature who understood nothing but basic black and white, good and evil. The Tick had to confront the finality of death when his superhero idol (ironically named the Immortal) died in the sack with Captain Liberty (in "The Funeral"). He learned about sex in "Arthur Needs Space," but didn't really get that idea, either. Still, the Tick was incredibly verbose and grandiose in explaining how he had learned a lesson each week. Regarding his choice to become a superhero, he noted that destiny had called him, and that even now he feels "her warm moist hand" at the small of his back, "pushing ... pushing." In another episode ("The License") he noted that "the stink of justice you can't shower off."

If the live-action version of *The Tick* had any weaknesses at all, it was a serious lack of crime fighting on the show, so it seemed more of a sitcom than an action-adventure. Though the villain in the pilot, a robotic Russian assassin (called Red Scare) programmed to kill Jimmy Carter, was quite a menace, the other villains of the series did not live up to the heritage of the comic book or the cartoon series. Some episodes did not feature any villains at all. Still, it was a shame that Fox had no faith in the series and cancelled it after airing only seven episodes. Fans who caught the show remember it as one of the funniest ever made in the "comedy" superhero mode.

The Tick (1994–1996)
ANIMATED SERIES

VOICE TALENTS: Townsend Coleman (The Tick); Micky Dolenz (Arthur); Rob Paulsen, Pat Fraley, Cam Clarke, Jim Cummings, Roger Rose, Dorian Harewood, Kay Lenz, Dan Castalanetta, Phil Proctor.

CREW: *Created by:* Ben Edlund. *Based on the Comic Book and Characters Created by:* Ben Edlund. *Executive Producers:* Joe Bacal, Tom Griffin, C.J. Kettler. *Producer:* Art Vitello. *Co-Producer:* Ben Edlund. *Supervising Writers:* Ben Edlund, Richard Liebmann-Smith. *Music and Title Song:* Doug Katsaros. *Voice Direction:* Art Vitello. From Sunbow Productions.

The Tick (2001)
LIVE-ACTION SERIES

"Based on Ben Edlund's cult comic, this is exactly the kind of highly ironic, hero-puncturing entertainment that is supposedly a no-no now. Except that it's also creative, appealing and spray-milk-out-your-nose funny.... Warburton is the first *Seinfeld* actor to find a truly original lead role."
— James Poniewozik. *Time Magazine:* "Super, Human Strength: In an Unconventional Kind of Wartime, Will Audiences Warm to Unconventional Superheroes?" October 22, 2001, page 77.

CAST: Patrick Warburton (The Tick); David Burke (The Moth/Arthur); Liz Vassey (Captain Liberty); Nestor Carbonell (Batmanuel).

CREW: *Created by:* Ben Edlund. *Film Editors (various episodes):* Steven Sprung, Steven Weisburg. *Production Design:* Bo Welch. *Directors of Photography (various episodes):* Greg Gardiner, Paul Maibum. *Producers:* Flody Suarez, Graham Place. *Executive Producers:* Ben Edlund, Barry Sonnenfeld, Barry Josephson. *Associate Producer:* Joe Deoliveira. *Unit Production Manager:* Gabriela Vazquez. *First Assistant Director:* Aldric Porter. *Second Assistant Director:* David Hyman. *Casting:* Ronna Kress. *Music:* Steve Bartek, Ian Dye. *Costume Designer:* Colleen Atwood. *Art Director:* Tom Duffield. *Set Decorator:*

Cheryl Carasik. *Key Make-up:* Debbie Zoller. *Key Hair:* Linda Arnold. *Property Master:* Doug Harlocker. *Sound Mixer:* Steve Bowerman. *Gaffer:* Chris Morley. *Key Grip:* Les Percy. *Script Supervisor:* Wendy Dallas. *Location Manager:* Robbie Goldstein. *Production Coordinator:* Kathy McHugh. *Transportation Coordinator:* Dave Roblin. *Special Effects Coordinator:* Joe Ramsey. *Visual Effects Supervisor:* Bill Powloski. *Visual Effects Producer:* Matt Gore. *Casting Associate:* Stacie Goodman. *Supervising Sound Editor:* Kerri Wilson. *Re-recording Mixers:* Bobby Mackston, Deb Adair. *Music Supervisor:* Billy Gotleib. *Post Production Services:* Moden VideoFilm. *Visual Effects:* Velocity Visuals. *Lab Services:* Deluxe.

1. "The Tick" Written by: Ben Edlund. Directed by: Barry Sonnenfeld. Airdate: November 8, 2001.

A strange blue avenger known as the Tick leaves his home base, the bus station, after vanquishing an uncooperative coffee machine, then heads to the City to fight crime. Meanwhile an accountant named Arthur quits his boring job to become a superhero called "the Moth." He and the Tick join up to stop Russian terrorists possessing 1979's greatest Soviet weapon: a robot monster called the Red Scare. The Tick and Moth team up with Batmanuel and Captain Liberty to save Jimmy Carter from the robot assassin, which is armed with a sickle and hammer.

GUEST CAST: William Newman (The Cape); Carrick O'Quinn (Red Scare); Brad Maynard (Jimmy Carter); Lisa Lu (Bartender); Jeff Doucette (Bus Driver); T.J. Callahan (Station Manager); Ray Xifo (Mr. Ferret); Adam Drechler (Salesman); Billy Peck (Octogenarian); Ahmed Stoner (Teenage Employee); Doug Motel (Comrade #1); Derek Mears (Comrade #2); Brian Turn (Comrade #3).

2. "The Funeral" Written by: Christopher McCulloch. Directed by: Andrew Tsao. Airdate: November 15, 2001.

The illustrious and popular superhero called the Immortal visits town on a publicity tour, but dies "in the saddle" with Captain Liberty in her bedroom. Batmanuel helps Liberty out by disguising himself as the Immortal during his book tour, but that leaves the Tick and Arthur to return the corpse of the superhero to his own hotel room so as not to destroy his memory. Later, the Tick delivers a moving eulogy for their fallen comrade, imploring mourners to "squeeze the milk of life into your dirty glass while it is still warm."

GUEST CAST: Sam McMurray (The Immortal); Meadow Sisto (Clarissa); Richard Penn (Five-Star General); T.J. Thyne (Kevin); Darin Cooper (General's Aide); Maury Ginsberg (Cop 2); Casey McDonald (Paralegal); Charley Rossman (Cop 1).

3. "Couples" Written by: Russ Venokur. Directed by: Danny Leiner. Airdate: December 5, 2001.

The Tick is impressed by the "immaculate" banter of the Fiery Blaze and his sidekick, Friendly Fire, but Arthur isn't sure the unequal partnership is worth emulating. Meanwhile, Captain Liberty realizes she is without sidekick, and thus lonely, so she buys a dog. When Friendly Fire leaves the Fiery Blaze, the Tick and Arthur have a new and not entirely welcome houseguest.

GUEST CAST: Ron Perlman (The Fiery Blaze).

4. "The License" Written by: Larry Charles. Directed by: Craig Zisk. Airdate: December 6, 2001.

The Tick needs a license to work in the City as a superhero, but can't remember any of his personal background information. While Arthur and the Tick search for his history, Captain Liberty dates a regular guy she meets at the dry cleaners. At the police station, a woman claiming to be the Tick's wife takes him home, and finally he decides on the name for his license: I.P. Dailey.

GUEST CAST: Larry Poindexter (Man); Kari Coleman (Woman); Yvette Freeman (Thelma); Mari Morrow (Medusa); Iobal Theba (Dry Cleaner); David Figlioli (Mugger); Teddy Lane, Jr. (Desk Sergeant); Charley Rossman (Cop #1).

5. "Arthur Needs Space" Written by: David Sacks. Directed by: Bo Welch. Airdate: December 13, 2001.

Captain Liberty is worried because nude pictures of her are about to be published in a magazine called *Peek-a-Boom*, and Arthur plans to date a crush from high school, Stacy Waxman. The Tick becomes jealous and confused about Arthur's relationship with Stacy, and Batmanuel and Liberty are forced to explain sex to the befuddled hero in blue.

GUEST CAST: Missi Pyle (Stacy Waxman); John Dennis Johnston (General Thomas); Simon Harvey (Liberty's Lawyer); Stephen Hood (Hustler); Cici Lau (Asian Woman); Chuck Sloan (Prosecutor); James Wellington (Worker).

6. "The Big Leaguer" Written by: Lon Diamond. Directed by: Bo Welch. Airdate: January 11, 2002.

The Tick and Arthur are invited to join the all-white, all-male Justice League, and Captain Liberty sues because she's never been invited. The Lodge sends the Tick and Arthur to convince Liberty to drop her suit.

GUEST CAST: Jonathan Penner (The Champion); Robert K. Mailhouse (Sonic Boom); Jack Armstrong (Captain Comet).

7. "The Tick vs. Justice" Written by: Ben Edlund and Larry Charles. Directed by: Mel Damski. Airdate: January 17, 2002.

Captain Liberty, Batmanuel, Arthur and the Tick haul the arch-villain Destroyo into court, then recount on the stand events leading up to his capture. When the Tick is thrown in jail for contempt of court, Destroyo's henchmen close in on Arthur, the last witness in the case.

GUEST CAST: Lori Alan (District Attorney); Joe Babile (Guard); Ping Wu (Bailiff); James Knudsen (Judget).

8. "Arthur, Interrupted" Written by: Richard Liebmann-Smith. Directed by: Dean Parison. Airdate: January 24, 2002.

Arthur hasn't told his family about his "lifestyle choice" to be a superhero. His Mom and sister have a hard time accepting his decision, stage an intervention, and commit him to the custody of the deranged Francis Peacock, a superhero deprogrammer with dreams of being a superhero himself.

GUEST CAST: Dave Foley (Francis Peacock); Beth Howland (Bea); Lisa Frederickson (Dot); William Newman (Cape); Cyd Strittmatter (Receptionist).

NOTE: Dave Foley's character in this episode (Francis Peacock) dances around his office to the theme song from ABC's *The Greatest American Hero*.

Unbreakable

Like a bolt of lightning, the remarkable and atmospheric feature film *Unbreakable* appeared out of the blue in the fall of 2000, with most comic book fans caught totally unaware that it was actually a superhero film, and one of the best ever made. The $65 million feature came from the acclaimed director of *The Sixth Sense* (1999) and, later, *Signs* (2002), M. Night Shyamalan. Surprisingly, the film was a highly personal meditation on the cultural meaning of superheroes and the impact of "powers" on a so-called normal man, in this case, David Dunn (Bruce Willis). As Shyamalan told the press of his radical deconstruction of the genre:

I was trying to show how powers could affect an ordinary person, but in a way that my parents, who aren't into comic books, wouldn't be embarrassed by. My version is in the milieu of the real world.[1]

Indeed, among its other triumphs, *Unbreakable* may just be the most plausible "superhero" film ever made, pinpointing believable motivations and reasons behind super powers, costumes, and even the duality of "good" and "evil" within humanity. But primarily, the film concerns the evolving relationship between two characters at "opposite ends of the spectrum," David Dunn, who has never been sick, and Elijah (Samuel L. Jackson), who suffers from a debilitating condition that makes his bones crack at the slightest stress or pressure. These characters are reflections of one another, mirror images — not just physically, but, as the shocking climax of the film reveals, morally as well.

What remains so interesting about *Unbreakable* is the manner in which Shyamalan hints at the true nature of his well-drawn characters. David Dunn is not just a common man after all, the audience learns, but a sort of "benched" superhero. His wife does not approve of violence, and so David has shelved the physical side of his personality, a side necessary for him to actively express "who he really is."

The audience knows David is special, not just because of his incredible strength, psychic flashes and finely tuned morality, but especially because of his alliterative name. David Dunn. Just like Peter Parker, Bruce Banner, Lana Lang, Lois Lane. Even Lex Luthor. Viewers and comic fans have become conditioned to expect the alliteration in superhero names, and David Dunn's name slips in right under the radar on the first viewing of the film.

Elijah, or "Mr. Glass" (as kids call him because of his physical ailment), is a supervillain, the audience learns, straight from the horse's mouth. A bad guy "general" is always known by the "slightly disproportionate size" of his head, thus marking his

evil, overdeveloped intelligence. Look at Samuel L. Jackson in the film. He is shown to be frail physically, incredibly thin, but with an oversized, awkward hairstyle, one that makes his head seem abnormally large. The evidence of Elijah's character is before the audience's eyes the entire time, and yet it is also missed on a first viewing.

But how can superheroes exist in a thoroughly realistic world? Shyamalan has devised the answer in a dramatic way. First, he wisely reaches for historical precedents. Elijah has studied the "form of comics" and believes it is humankind's last link to "an ancient way of passing on history," i.e. pictographs. Sure, comics are jazzed up, commercial versions of history, but these stories, told in pictures, are but "an exaggeration of the truth," a historical truth, he suggests. And what is that truth? That mankind, through the generations, has a protector walking among the people, someone destined to guard it from disaster, chaos and evil. Such a guardian is, in other words, a superhero, and in this case that fellow is David Dunn.

It is a startling conclusion Elijah makes about David, but one made wholly believable within the context of the film. What impulse makes firemen brave roaring flames to rescue trapped people? Why do some folk reveal enormous strength in times of stress, to save a child pinned beneath the wheels of an automobile, for instance? How do some people survive being struck by lightning, or falls of great distances, when others are immediately killed? In real life, the answer to those questions is not known, but in *Unbreakable* these anomalies are signs of the existence of a guardian. The superhero walks with us every day, but he (or she) just may not know it.

In fact, it is by setting up extraordinary situations, such as a train wreck, a hotel fire, or a plane crash, that Elijah exposes David — as well as his own dark identity as a super-villain. "There is a sole survivor, and he is miraculously unharmed," the newscasters report. That is the very trigger Elijah has been waiting for, the news that allows him to see himself in the context of "having purpose."

In keeping with the realistic tenor of the movie, David's "super" powers are not over the top or hard to believe. He has a strong immune system, protecting him from disease, great (but not unbelievable) strength, and psychic flashes of people that have committed crimes. This latter ability, a paranormal one, is not out of the realm of possibility at all, or so it is believed. *Psychometry*, a term coined by an American neurologist in 1849, is the ability to discern knowledge of persons or events simply by touching an object. In this case, David is merely connecting with a human being and seeing what acts they have committed. Certainly, this is a bit far-fetched, but there have been notable real-life psychometrists in the past hundred years (such as Peter Hurkos), so it is not so unbelievable that the realistic mood of the film is disrupted.

Perhaps more interestingly, Shyamalan captures the essence of established superhero mythos visually by garbing David, in his first "heroic" adventure, in a hood and poncho. This is not a "costume," not a colorful uniform with a giant S on it, but it has the same effect. He wears the poncho simply because it is raining outside. Yet the poncho resembles a cape, his hood a mask. It is another perfect real-life metaphor for comic book images. A protector appears out of darkness, his identity obscured by a mask, his cape flapping in the wind...

And, just as Superman fears kryptonite, David Dunn bears a notable weakness in *Unbreakable*. In this case, it is not an allergic reaction to a meteor from an alien world, but rather a psychological phobia. Because of a childhood incident in a pool, he possesses an overwhelming fear of water. This fear is so deep-seated that, at least momentarily, it immobilizes him. Again Shya-

malan has found and dramatized a real life metaphor for kryptonite, one that is very easy to relate to. Everybody has a weakness, even superheroes, even these "guardians."

Visually, *Unbreakable* depicts the difference between David Dunn and Elijah with stark color contrasts. David's world is all olive-green. His poncho and the interior of his house (particularly the kitchen) are depicted in shades of muted green. By contrast, Elijah's world and costuming is all flamboyant purple, a result, no doubt, of the fact that his first comic book (given to him by his mother when he was a child) was wrapped in a purple package. It's not just good versus evil, but green versus purple, reminding viewers of the contrasts between the two men. Again, this is a facet of superhero comics. The Joker is known for his green hair. The Penguin wears black. The Green Goblin is, well, green. Daredevil wears red. Superhero comics are color coded so that audiences remember which side is which. *Unbreakable* is the same way.

Many knowledgeable comic book fans have complained that *Unbreakable*'s opening card, the one that lays out the statistics about comic book sales, frames and other data, is inaccurate. While that may be true, this is nonetheless a film that understands the concept of superheroes, and examines that concept in the most human, fascinating terms yet put to film. Perhaps *Unbreakable* is most valuable to the genre because it demonstrates how people can act differently while attempting to learn of/ fulfill their destinies. Elijah murders people to learn his, orchestrating disasters and becoming a super-villain.

David studiously avoids his destiny, fearing it will destroy his personal relationships. But this only results in him drowning in sorrow and depression, as he lacks purpose. When David learns that he is a protector, a hero, and acts on that information, that sadness lifts. Perhaps we are all defined by the ways we struggle to find our destiny. We all need purpose — for good or evil — to get through this life.

Unbreakable is a thoughtful film that was praised by some and disdained by others; but few superhero films are as intelligent, well dramatized and beautifully performed. In a genre populated by the likes of *Captain America* (1989), *Batman and Robin* (1997), and other disappointments, *Unbreakable* is a high-water mark. Simply put, it reveals to us the reasons why superheroes are so resonant to so many people.

Unbreakable (2000)
LIVE-ACTION FILM

"About a man who learns that he may or may not be a superhero, the film is a brilliant mix of comic books and reality. It deconstructs the cultural reflections the comics make of society, something many other films have tried and failed to achieve."
—Douglas Pratt, *Denver Business Journal*, August 17, 2001, page 32A.

"Brilliantly acted by Bruce Willis and Samuel L. Jackson, *Unbreakable* is perhaps too esoteric and brainy for mainstream tastes. But more than any other film this year, it reminds us of the essential magic of cinema: to take us to a bold and dizzying journey into the great pop unknown."
— Christopher Kelly, *Fort Worth Star-Telegram*, December 28, 2000.

"...[It] bases much of its structure and symbolism on the ideals of comic book heroism, and comic fans are most likely the ones to gleefully reexamine the calculated clues leading to the movie's head-spinning ending.... [T]his is a rather peculiar movie, and the director's sheer daring and deft imagination is a pleasure to behold."
— Annabelle Villanueva, *Cinescape*, Volume 7, #4: "I See Strong People," May/June 2001, page 69.

"M. Night Shyamalan's *Unbreakable* is every bit as much a comic-book movie as *X-Men*, though it works much harder to ground itself in reality — and ultimately proves to be less satisfying."
— Bill Radford, *The Gazette*, December 7, 2000.

"By recycling Willis's performance and the mood of *The Sixth Sense*, *Unbreakable* is unable to escape its shadow."
— Shanda Deziel, *Macleans:* "In Search of a Superhero," November 27, 2000, page 89.

CAST: Bruce Willis (David Dunn); Samuel L. Jackson (Elijah Price/"Mr. Glass"); Robin Wright Penn (Audrey Dunn); Spencer Treat Clark (Joseph Dunn); Charlayne Woodard (Elijah's Mother); Eamonn Walker (Dr. Mathison); Leslie Stefanson (Kelly); Johnny Hiram Johnson (Elijah, Age 13); Michaelia Carroll (Babysitter); Bostin Christopher (Comic Book Clerk); Elizabeth Lawrence (School Nurse); David Duffield (David Dunn, Age 20); Laure Regan (Audrey, Age 20); Chance Kelly (Orange Suite Man); Michael Kelly (ER Doctor).

CREW: Touchstone and Blinding Edge Pictures Presents a Barry Mendel Production of an M. Night Shyamalan Film, *Unbreakable*. *Casting:* Douglas Aibel. *Costume Design:* Joanna Johnston. *Music:* James Newton Howard. *Film Editor:* Dylan Tichenor. *Production Design:* Larry Fulton. *Director of Photography:* Eduardo Serra. *Executive Producers:* Gary Barber, Roger Birnbaum. *Producers:* Barry Mendel, Sam Mercer. *Written, Produced and Directed by:* M. Night Shyamalan. *Unit Production Manager:* Sam Mercer. *First Assistant Director:* John Rusk. *Second Assistant Director:* Scott Robertson. *Production Supervisor:* Lynn Andrews. *Script Supervisor:* Dianne Dreyer. *Art Director:* Steve Arnold. *Original Comic Book Art/Illustrations:* Derek Thompson, Brian O'Connell. *M.P.A.A. Rating:* PG-13. *Running time:* 107 minutes.

A campus security guard, David Dunn, is the only survivor of a train wreck that kills 131 passengers. He survives without a single scratch or one broken bone, an odd fact that raises the interest of an unusual fellow named Elijah Price, a comic book aficionado and art gallery owner. Unlike David, Elijah has had numerous injuries throughout his life and suffers from a rare bone deficiency called *osteogenesis imperfecta*. Elijah believes that comic books are a form of history, and that people like David may be protectors, guardians, or even—in comic book terminology—superheroes.

David is reluctant to accept Elijah's postulate and instead tries to mend fences with his family, including his wife Audrey and young son Joseph. David has been suffering from a deep depression of late, and Elijah believes he knows why. He thinks David is "meant" to be saving people. David starts to believe Elijah and learns (through a weight room exercise) that he is incredibly strong, able to bench-press over 350 pounds. He also learns that as a kid he nearly drowned in a school pool, causing Elijah to suggest that water may be Dunn's own "kryptonite," or weakness.

David tests his powers one night, rescuing two girls from a psychotic maniac who has taken over their house and killed their parents. After navigating a dangerous swimming pool, Dunn defeats his first nemesis. He wants to thank Elijah for all his help in identifying his status as a hero, but is shocked to learn that Elijah has a special role to play in his life too. He is the force behind the train wreck that killed so many people, and believes he has discovered his destiny too: as a monstrous, "general"-type villain.

Witchblade

Voluptuous, sexy and forever donning high heels, Sara "Pez" Pezzini starred in Top Cow Comic's top-selling *Witchblade* title beginning in 1997, though the character appeared as early as 1995. Big-breasted and scantily clad, Pezzini worked as a New York City detective who was, in fact, "the Chosen One," the new—and sometimes reluctant—bearer of an ancient mystical weapon known as the Witchblade. Teaming with her cop partners, Sara fought criminals with the magical gauntlet, as well as opposing the terrible plans of Kenneth Irons, a business tycoon with supernatural ties to pure evil. Assisted by the mysterious Ian Nottingham, a powerful warrior/assassin with designs on the beautiful Sara, Irons ran Vorschlag Industries and was a constant thorn in Sara's side.

Though *JFK* (1991) filmmaker Oliver Stone originally planned to bring the *Witchblade* property to the world of cable television,[1] it was producer Dan Halsted and Marc Silvestri who shepherded the transition. Silvestri was the man who had formed Top Cow in 1992 and overseen Sara's remarkable ascension in the comic marketplace. In fact, Pezzini (and her Witchblade) became the top selling female comic character in the late '90s.

The beautiful Yancy Butler, star of the TV series *Brooklyn South* and the Wesley Snipes movie *Drop Zone*, was cast as Sara in the TV movie that aired in August of 2000 on the WB and launched the Witchblade series a year later. Fans of the comic were in for a shock, however. Sara, a buxom fantasy figure in the comics, was brought down to reality for the production, as Butler noted:

> Personally, I would find it quite hard to run down the streets of New York in a metal bra and stiletto heels.... So I am wearing jeans and sensible shoes and boots and definitely a cross form bra, so it's quite normal. But in the comic, she's in this metal-clawed bra and it's just out of control.[2]

That established, the TV version of *Witchblade* was not at all disrespectful to the source material. Instead, it merely sought for a more realistic, less obviously sexist approach to the lead character. Butler had thoughts about this as well:

> It's not this kind of fluff, *Barb Wire* thing. It's this real woman who has a real job,

Partners against crime: Cop Jake McCarty (David Chokachi) and Witchblade wielder Sara Pezzini (Yancy Butler) strike a pose on the set of the TNT series *Witchblade.* Notice the mystical bracelet on Sara's right hand.

who is very scared and very vulnerable and at the same time she's kind of sexy and can kick ass.... It's unlike anything I've ever seen.[3]

The series, set to run in the summer of 2001 on the basic cable station TNT, was also designed, according to the network's general manager Steve Kooning, as "pure summer fun."[4] Cast alongside the lovely, athletic Butler was a group of actors that, in many cases, looked like dead ringers for their comic counterparts. David Chokachi played Detective Jake McCarty, Sara's hunky but sometimes dim-witted partner. Not unlike Sara, Jake had a secret of his own: he was actually a secret agent for the Federal Government. Will Yun Lee portrayed Sara's deceased partner, Danny, a

specter that was literally Pezzini's "spirit guide." John Hensley joined the cast midway through the first season as the young Gabriel Bowman, the proprietor of a collectible shop called Talismania. Like Danny, Bowman understood something of the Witchblade's nature and was able to guide Sara in her quest.

Representing villainy was Anthony Cistaro as the deliciously evil Irons, and Eric Etebari as Nottingham. Oddly, one other character appeared in every episode: a strange man/woman played by the mysterious "Lazar." This actor/actress had no dialogue, but appeared in at least one background shot of every episode, signaling some as-yet-unknown facet of the Witchblade story.

In its first season on the air, *Witchblade* moved at warp speed. Sara, "the Chosen One," inherited the Witchblade on November 11, 2000, while chasing a crime lord's goon, and very soon learned much about the device, which appeared as a bracelet when not used in combat.

In keeping with the context of the era — the Dawn of the Woman in the superhero genre — the series revealed that only females could wear the gauntlet because they were "closer to nature," and more elemental than men. Women could also understand pain better and give life to others. A World War II spy (a dead ringer for Sara named Elizabeth Bronte), Joan of Arc, and an Irish warrior princess ("Sacrifice") were all known to be former wielders of the weapon.

The gauntlet granted Sarah great powers, including telekinesis, precognition and telepathy, but there was a price to be paid. Sara had to undergo a trial of worthiness, a "periculum" in which she and the blade became entangled in perfect symbiosis. It was also established throughout the series that the blade had a "violent, unpredictable mind of its own" ("Static"), and that, interestingly, it enhanced the feelings of pleasure derived from sex and violence ("Ubique").

In the first season, Sara learned about the powers of the Witchblade and her own role in the universal battle between good and evil. In doing so, she fought a group of bizarre villains, including the Devil himself (Roger Daltrey) in "Legion," and a super soldier named Moebius in "Parallax," a member of an elite squad called the Black Dragons that had "reptilian" brains so as to allow them to have greater feelings of aggression.

Then there was a Medusa-like woman and former wielder of the Witchblade, Dominique, who appeared in "Conundrum," and murderous, psychotic twins in "Diplopia." These folks were basically villains of the week, but what made *Witchblade* unique and compelling to watch was the presence of villains involved in a long-term story arc. Kenneth Irons and Nottingham represented one branch of omnipresent evil, perhaps the most dangerous. But Sara also investigated her own boss, Dante (Nestor Serrano), a member of a cabal called "the White Bulls." These corrupt cops had killed Sara's father, and wanted to kill Pezzini at all costs, fearing she would expose them.

The final episode of the first season brought all of these conflicts to the surface — showcasing Sara vs. the White Bulls, and Sara vs. Irons — and added a few surprise revelations. In the final moments of the series, confronted with the deaths of those around her (including Jake), Sara used the powers of the Witchblade to rewrite time, taking the series back to its beginnings on November 11, 2000, the day she inherited the weapon.

Filled with involving stories and good acting, *Witchblade* was a real treat for superhero fans. With its washed out, fluorescent "urban blight" look and juicy camerawork (including fast-motion and slow-motion photography, and arty transitions), the series was a visual feast. Strobe lights, action filmed in silhouette, and grand chase scenes brought a real feature-film punch to the proceedings. TNT's gamble with a top-notch quality production paid off. The first two episodes rated as number one among all basic cable shows, and drew in nearly 2.2 million viewers, a 60 percent rating increase over TNT's ratings in that slot the previous year.[5] Amazingly, the entire first season improved on the early ratings, and *Witchblade* averaged a 64 percent increase over ratings in that slot the previous year.[6] Accordingly, TNT very quickly renewed the series, contracting for 13 new episodes to air in the summer of 2002.

After so much success, however, *Witchblade* unexpectedly began to falter creatively. As the second season was planned, the producers apparently decided that the series needed to be more accessible to mainstream viewers. At the close of the first season, Sara had used the Witchblade to alter reality, going back in time to the day she inherited the mystical weapon. The producers decided to use this opportunity as a more mainstream reintroduction to the concept, presumably to lure more viewers.

This time around, Sara's partner Danny did not die, and lived to partner again with Sara throughout the season. Gabriel was introduced earlier in the continuity, along with his shop, Talismania. There was no periculum test. And this second time through the Witchblade universe, Sara did not avenge the death of her father and bring down the White Bulls.

Interestingly, in the "re-done" second season, Sara successfully eliminated Irons in the last hour of a two-hour presentation that began the season. This paved the way for thirteen episodes in which the presumably dead millionaire tried repeatedly to resurrect himself, going so far as to possess Ian Nottingham and even have his soul downloaded to a web site called Cyber Faust. Overall, the season seemed both different and the same simultaneously, making it "a bit like *Ground Hog Day*" (a film in which Bill Murray kept waking up to find it was the same day), at least according to producer Ralph Hemecker.[7]

The problem with this approach, perhaps, was that in-the-know viewers could not understand why certain events that occurred in the time-line the first time around did not follow during the second go-round. And the fact that Danny survived his conflict with the crooks in the first episode meant not only that Sara was deprived of an otherworldly authority, but that her partner, Jake McCarty, was suddenly of much less importance, with Sara and Jake's relationship receiving short shrift. Still, Sara's doomed lover Conchobar — a poet, folk singer and brawler — did make a return, if brief, appearance.

Witchblade's second season also appeared to boast a substantially lower budget, as it featured almost no major action scenes to compete with the rousing adventure of the first year. Sara used the Witchblade much less, and the series accentuated the more hackneyed "cop" elements of the show rather than focusing on the important history and legacy of the mystical gauntlet. There were some interesting stories, to be sure, and the battle between Irons (using the Longines Lance, the spear that pierced the chest of Jesus Christ on the Cross) and Sara's Witchblade was pretty fascinating.

Otherwise, the series trotted out such clichés as the evil doppelganger ("Palindrome"), the Hellish web site ("Ubique"), and even underground fight clubs. One story was a retelling of the Little Red Riding Hood tale, with guest Eric Roberts playing a villain named "Lupo."

When the press announced that production had unexpectedly shut down on the set of *Witchblade*, that was the beginning of the end for the series. Star Yancy Butler had to depart the series to check into a rehab clinic for an "alcohol related" problem.[8] Though the series resumed shooting a month later with star Butler back on the job, rumors in the industry circulated that the show might be recast with a new Witchblade wielder, or, worse, face cancellation outright. Despite continued strong ratings, such speculation was correct. TNT dumped *Witchblade*, its executives noting only that they wished to try something new and fresh in *Witchblade*'s spot come summer of 2003.

Devoted fans of the program have since lodged complaints about the cancellation, hoping to wrangle a renewal for the show. New York's "toughest cop," Sara Pezzini, was never to see her grand journey to mythic heroine finished. Worse, the premature end of *Witchblade*, along with *Birds of Prey* in the winter of 2002, indicated to some that the "Dawn of the Woman" era in the superhero genre had entered its twilight, leaving only Buffy, in her seventh and final season, to carry the torch.

Witchblade (2000–2002)
LIVE-ACTION SERIES

"…[A]s a stylized supernatural action thriller it does fill a void left by the deprogramming of *La Femme Nikita* and the grisly demise of *Xena: Warrior Princess*…. As Sara, Butler glowers, wisecracks and lays waste with aplomb, but unlike Buffy, she's pretty much stranded in a poorly cast ensemble of glum Euro-trash overseers and generic precinct buddies…. While not quite cutting edge, *Witchblade* is more often sharp than dull."

— Matt Roush, *TV Guide:*
"Glove Story," July 28, 2001.

"A raucous concoction filled with action, loud music and loads of visual effects. Paradoxically, it's also dull — a gigantically overblown cliché that tries to substitute an ever-shaky camera and fast paced editing in place of character and story. All premise and no payoff..."
— Steven Oxman, *Variety*, August 21, 2000.

"While *Witchblade*'s effects are a treat to the eyes, the shadowy tone and *The Matrix*–like stop motion action sequences can also overload the senses.... What isn't overloaded is the character development. Although the visuals are enough to get viewers to take a first look, the character development wasn't quite strong enough to get this reviewer to come back for more."
— Michael Demenchuk, *Multichannel News: "Witchblade* More Sorcery Than Substance," June 11, 2001, page 128.

CAST: Yancy Butler (Sara Magdalene "Pez" Pezzini); David Chokachi (Det. Jake McCarty); Anthony Cistaro (Kenneth Irons); Will Yun Lee (Danny); Eric Etebari (Ian Nottingham). SEASON TWO: John Hensley (Gabriel Bowman).

CREW: *Executive Producers:* Dan Halsted, Marc Silvestri. *Co-Executive Producer:* J.D. Zeik. *Producers:* Brad Foxhoven, David Wohl. *Consulting Producer:* Richard C. Okie. *Produced by:* Vikki Williams. *Based on the Comic Books Created by:* Top Cow Productions, Inc. *Director of Photography:* David Moxness. *Production Designer:* Franco De Coris. *Associate Producer:* Connie McKinnon. *Editor (various episodes):* Mike Lee, Gordon McClellan. *Costume Designer:* Lisa Martin. *Consultant:* Michael Turner. *Unit Production Manager:* Michael Wray. *First Assistant Director:* Raymond Elias. *Second Assistant Director:* Aren Kazazian.

1. "Witchblade" (aired as TV movie, 2 hrs.) Written by: J.D. Zeik. Directed by: Ralph Hemecker. Airdate: August 27, 2000.

On November 11, 2000, New York Detective Sara Pezzini and her partner Danny try to bring down Gallo, the underworld mastermind who killed Pezzini's friend Maria, and perhaps her adopted father too. Sara pursues Gallo's assassin to a museum, resulting in a deadly gunfight. During the battle, a strange glove stored in a display case bonds to Sara's arm, becoming a deadly weapon known as the Witchblade. Sara survives the battle, and the Witchblade transforms into a bracelet that brings her visions of women throughout recorded history — and even hallucinations of medieval knights in armor. Upset that his best hitman is dead, Gallo orders a hit against Sara and her partner.

GUEST CAST: Kenneth Welsh (Joe Siri); Conrad Dunn (Gallo); Jodi Racicot, Hal Eisen, Jim Codrington, Tony Munch, Katherine Trowell, Whitney Westwood, Phil Hay, Tyson McAuley, Noah Danby, Lazar.

2. "Parallax" Written by: Ralph Hemecker. Story by: Ralph Hemecker and Richard C. Okie. Directed by: Ralph Hemecker. Airdate: June 12, 2001.

Sara goes before a board of inquiry regarding the massacre at the Rialto Theater and locks horns with her belligerent new captain, Bruno Dante. Meanwhile, Ian Nottingham clashes with a powerful black assassin named Moebius who was once part of a specially trained military unit called "the Black Dragons." At the same time, Sara's retiring superior, Joe, brings her a box of personal items, including a bullet decorated with a bull that belonged to her late, adoptive father. Before long, Sara is hunting down Moebius when she learns that he is a product of Kenneth Iron's Vorschlag Industries — the result of an experiment involving psychotropic drugs that enhance a soldier's feelings of aggression and paranoia.

GUEST CAST: Nestor Serrano (Captain Bruno Dante); Peter Mensah (Moebius); Kenneth Welsh (Joe); Kathryn Winslow (Vicki); Jean Moon, Marni Thompson, Sandra Jackson, Robert Lee, Junior Williams, Lazar.

3. "Conundrum" Written by: Edithe Swenson. Story by: Ralph Hemecker and Richard C. Okie. Directed by: Neill Fearnley. Airdate: June 19, 2001.

"Pez" and Jake investigate the murder of a model whose body was seemingly digested by a snake and then regurgitated. The trail leads to a fashion photographer,

Dominique, a one-time wielder of the Witchblade. Sara and Jack protect one of Dominique's models, who they fear may be the next victim of the snake, but a 1940s photograph in the girl's apartment triggers a memory of another lifetime. Meanwhile, Dominique sets a trap for the blood heir to the Witchblade.

GUEST CAST: Laila Robins (Dominique Boucher); Malin Ackerman (Karen Bronte); Kathryn Winslow (Vickie); Will Corno (Jonathan Sandsman); Quancita Hamilton, Martin Samuel, Lazar, Malcolm Xerats.

4. "Diplopia" Written by: David Michaelson. Story by: Ralph Hemecker and Richard C. Okie. Directed by: Vern Gillum. Airdate: June 26, 2001.

The brutal murder of a man in the gay community leads Sara and Jake to a gay club called Badlands and an artist named Isaac Sullivan, whose murderous twin may be the perpetrator of the crime. Meanwhile, Sara continues to probe the history of the Witchblade, with the help of the incarcerated and a rapidly aging Dominique, who wants to stop Kenneth Irons out of revenge. Delving deeper into the murder, Sara questions an imprisoned doctor who has created a genetically perfect offspring, but needs a "brood mare," Sara, to continue creating his line of homicidal men — who all look like Isaac Sullivan.

GUEST CAST: John Hensley (Gabriel Bowman); Laila Robins (Dominique); Anthony Lemke (Isaac Sullivan); Rory Feore, Peter Crockett, Johnnie Chase, Shaun Austin-Olsen, Meleka Schiro, Lazar.

5. "Sacrifice" Written by: Richard C. Okie. Story by: Ralph Hemecker and Richard C. Okie. Directed by: David S. Jackson. Airdate: July 3, 2001.

A ritualistic killing draws Sara into an investigation of a local rock band whose logo matches the cryptic scrawl on the wall of the crime scene. Oddly, the murder has something to do with the ancient story of King Concobar and his warrior lover Kath-

ryn, who possessed the Witchblade. The killer is committing ritual sacrifices to summon Kathryn to defend her kingdom. But Sara is Kathryn, and the rock band's leader seems to be the reincarnation of Concobar.

GUEST CAST: Nestor Serrano (Captain Dante); John Hensley (Gabriel Bowman); Kim De Lury (Concobar); Paulino Nunes, Jean Moon, Martin Thompson, Robert Lee, Junior Williams, Lazar.

6. "Legion" Written by: Richard C. Okie. Story by: Ralph Hemecker and Richard C. Okie. Directed by: Neill Fearnley. Airdate: July 10, 2001.

Monsignor Bellamy, NYC's foremost expert on exorcism, is murdered in church, and a troubled young schizophrenic named Eddie Nolan is apprehended as the prime suspect. Sara doesn't believe Eddie is guilty, nor that he is possessed by demons, Bellamy's belief. Sara investigates Bellamy's life and finds that he kept a journal for many years, but she can't find any pages from World War II and his alleged interaction with the Witchblade. Then Sara must face Father Del Toro, a lawyer/priest who may be a demon — or even the Devil.

GUEST CAST: Roger Daltrey (Father Del Toro); Kim De Lury (Concobar); Nestor Serrano (Captain Dante); Paul Robbins, Neill Fearnley, Lazar.

7. "Maelstrom" Written by: Richard C. Okie. Story by: Ralph Hemecker and Richard C. Okie. Directed by: James Whitmore, Jr. Airdate: July 17, 2001.

Concobar, Sara's boyfriend, is kidnapped by Irish terrorists who wish to trade him for his revolutionary brother, Edward. Sara is forced to surrender the Witchblade and raise two million dollars to free Concobar. She asks Irons for the money, but he rejects her. In the final battle against the terrorists, she must go up against the Witchblade and its new wielder, and face the loss of Concobar.

GUEST CAST: Kim de Lury (Concobar)

8. "Periculum" Written by: Roderick Taylor and Bruce A. Taylor. Story by: Ralph Hemecker and Richard C. Okie. Directed by: Neill Fearnley. Airdate: July 24, 2001.

Despondent over the death of her lover Concobar, Sara retreats to her apartment for four days, even as Jake, Irons and Nottingham grow concerned over her state of mind. During the middle of one lonely night, the Witchblade coils around Sara's body like a snake and traps her in bed. Sara is visited in a dream-state by Joan of Arc, who tells her that she is to undergo the "Periculum"—a test of worthiness to wear the Witchblade— a trial of fire, of life and death. While Sara is tested by visits from Kathryn the warrior princess and Elizabeth Bronte, former owners of the Witchblade, Jake is invited by Bruno Dante to join a cadre of above-the-law police officers called "the White Bulls."

GUEST CAST: Nestor Serrano (Captain Bruno Dante); John Hensley (Gabriel); Lazar.

9. "Thanatopsis" Written by: Richard C. Okie. Story by: Ralph Hemecker. Directed by: James Whitmore, Jr. Airdate: July 31, 2001.

Sara and Jake's investigation of an arms dealer is squashed by an assassination and the involvement of a crooked cop working for Dante. Sara learns that a conspiracy is afoot, one involving Irons and the Witchblade.

GUEST CAST: Kathryn Winslow (Vicki); John Hensley (Gabriel); Nestor Serrano (Captain Bruno Dante); Bill McDonald, Lazar.

10. "Apprehension" Written by: Richard C. Okie. Story by: Ralph Hemecker and Richard C. Okie. Directed by: Robert Lee. Airdate: August 7, 2001.

Sara becomes more suspicious and paranoid as her awareness of a wide-ranging conspiracy against her grows. A mysterious package sent to Sara causes her to ask questions about the loyalties of those around her. Could Jake be in league with Dante and the White Bulls?

GUEST CAST: John Hensley (Gabriel); Nestor Serrano (Captain Bruno Dante); Kenneth Welsh (Joe); Bill McDonald, Eden Roundtree, Lazar.

11. "Convergence" Written by: Ralph Hemecker and Richard C. Okie. Story by: Ralph Hemecker. Directed by: James Whitmore, Jr. Airdate: August 14, 2001.

Irons is dying, aging rapidly without the rejuvenating potion that can restore his youth and vigor. Meanwhile, Sara's enemies surround her and she is forced to go on the run from the corrupt police. Jake offers a helping hand, but he has a secret he must first reveal.

GUEST CAST: John Hensley (Gabriel); Nester Serrano (Captain Bruno Dante); Eden Roundtree, Keir Dullea, Lazar.

12. "Transcendence" Written by: Ralph Hemecker. Story by: Ralph Hemecker and Richard C. Okie. Directed by: David S. Jackson. Airdate: August 21, 2001.

It's all come down to this—Sara and Jake's final gambit to take down the corrupt Bruno Dante and his cadre of crooked cops, the White Bulls. Sara is successful in this venture, but other evil forces are gathering against her, sparking a deadly confrontation with the devious Kenneth Irons. Before the day is over, friends and enemies alike will fall in battle, and Sara Pezzini will make a choice that alters the very fabric of reality and even her fate with the mystical talisman, the Witchblade.

GUEST CAST: John Hensley (Gabriel); Nestor Serrano (Captain Dante); Bill McDonald, Lazar.

SEASON TWO (2002)

13. "Emergence" and **"Destiny"** (two hour movie) Written by: Ralph Hemecker, Jorge Zamacona and William MacDonald. Story by: Jorge Zamacona, William J. Macdonald. Directed by: Joe Chappelle and David Carson. Airdate: June 16, 2002.

Time has reversed itself, and an unawares Sara Pezzini finds herself back on the day she first encountered the mystical weapon called the Witchblade. Again the weapon finds her and becomes her property, but time diverges when her partner, Danny, survives a confrontation with mob boss Gallo. Together, Sara and Danny investigate the murder of an Internet sex company co-owner. The trail leads back to Christina Wells, a woman secretly in league with Kenneth Irons to steal the Witchblade. After Christina attempts to bury Danny alive, Sara confronts and destroys her new opponent. Undeterred, Irons brings into play the Witchblade's opposite, a weapon called "the Longines Lance," which was used to stab Christ on the cross. When Irons learns of a plot to unseat him at Vorschlag Industries, he uses the lance to kill two board members. Meanwhile, Sara learns more about the lance and the Witchblade from talisman expert Gabriel Bowman. In the battle of the Witchblade versus the Longines Lance, Sara wins, killing Kenneth Irons.

GUEST CAST: Kathryn Winslow (Vicki); Mariki Dominczyk, Conrad Dunn.

14. "Agape" Written by: Larry and Paul Barber. Directed by: Paul Holahan. Airdate: June 17, 2002.

A narcotics detective, Dean, asks Jake to work a drug case with him while Sara and Danny continue to search for the man who killed Dean's partner, Torres. At the same time, Sara investigates the death of a young man at a rave, an apparent victim of erotic asphyxia. She learns of a new psychotropic drug called "Bob" that is hitting the streets, making people crazy, even murderous. Elsewhere, Dean sets Jake up for several murder raps during a drug bust. Sara tries to clear Jake's name while fitting together the pieces of the puzzle, including the death of Torres, and the dangerous new drug.

GUEST CAST: Kathryn Winslow (Vicki); Robert John Burke (Dean); Lazar.

15. "Consectatio" Written by: Richard C. Okie. Directed by: Neill Fearnley. Airdate: June 24, 2002.

Possessed by the dark heart of Kenneth Irons, Ian Nottingham pays two million dollars to genetically engineered bounty hunters called "Black Dragons" for the murder of Sara Pezzini. The mercenaries, led by the powerful Hector Moebius, arrange a hit on Pezzini in Central Park, but fail. Sara soon learns that the events in her life are mirroring those of the mythical wood nymph Saran and her would-be lover Gilgamesh. When Nottingham shakes free of Irons' evil influence, he fights Sara's assassins himself.

GUEST CAST: Peter Mensah (Hector Moebius); Kathryn Winslow (Vicki); Bobby Johnson, Lazar.

16. "Static" Written by: Larry and Paul Barber. Directed by: Neill Fearnley. Airdate: July 1, 2002.

A woman dressed as a hotel bellhop kills a popular rock star by pushing him out of a window on a luggage cart. As Sara investigates the murder, she becomes increasingly disturbed because the Witchblade is showing violent, unpredictable behavior of its own, even granting her the powers of precognition and telekinesis. When the rock star's girlfriend is driven to suicide, Sara is warned to be on her "guard" in pursuing the case. The trail of dead bodies leads to Anna Granger, a schizophrenic clinical psychiatrist with a history of treating and causing would-be suicides.

GUEST CAST: Tamara Gorski (Dr. Anna Granger); Kathryn Winslow (Vicki); Lazar.

17. "Nailed" Written by: Richard C. Okie. Directed by: Rick Rosenthal. Airdate: July 8, 2002.

A cunning sex offender and serial killer named Carl Dalack is released from prison on a technicality: Danny entered his apartment and gathered incriminating evidence without a search warrant. Blaming himself for the death of the killer's last victim, and the psycho's release back into the populace, Danny follows Dalack with a vengeance. But the villain throws Danny a curve and pursues his rebellious young niece, Miji. Soon it's a race against time to save the girl, as Sara starts to decipher the telepathic capabilities of the Witchblade.

GUEST CAST: Currie Graham (Carl Dalack); Kathryn Winslow (Vicki); Nestor Serrano (Captain Bruno Dante); Lazar.

18. "Heirophant" Written by: Jorge Zamacona. Directed by: James Whitmore, Jr., and Neill Fearnley. Airdate: July 15, 2002.

Sara investigates the ritualistic murder of Father Horton, and the corpse of Kenneth Irons comes to Pezzini in a vision, offering clues about the culprit, whom he claims is "death" itself. Skin samples from the unusual killer, found under the victim's fingernails, reveal that he is "undead"— unable to be killed and constantly regenerating. Meanwhile, Sara is attracted to a mysterious stranger named Daniel, in actuality the guard of Pontius Pilate, who was cursed by Jesus to walk the Earth until the Messiah's return. Only the Witchblade can kill Daniel and end his life, and he wants Sara, who has fallen in love with him, to put him out of his misery.

GUEST CAST: Jeffrey Donovan (Daniel German); Kathryn Winslow (Vicki); Lazar.

19. "Lagrimas" Written by: Roderick and Bruce Taylor. Directed by: Paul Holahan. Airdate: July 22, 2002.

A new crime boss in town, called "V", is putting the fear of God into gangster Gallo and murdering all criminal leaders who defy his bid to control the city. "V" leaves behind tarot cards at each crime scene, so Pez visits Madame Sesostris, a for-

tune-teller, and learns that there is something amiss with her "hierophant," her father figure. This unusual information earns credence when the fingerprints of Sara's dead father turn up on the cards. Sara grows convinced that her dead father is actually "V," and with Danny's help decides to dig up his grave; but this time she faces a terribly dark nemesis that, not surprisingly, is in league with the spirit of Irons.

GUEST CAST: James Acheson; Conrad Dunn; Kathryn Winslow (Vicki); Roger Daltrey (Madame Sesostris); Lazar, Arnold Tynnock.

20. "Veritas" Written by: Jorge Zamacona. Directed by: Paul Abascal. Airdate: August 5, 2002.

Danny and McCarty investigate a murder case that leads back to Gabriel Bowman and Talismania. Meanwhile, Sara meets the ghost of JFK in a dream, and Nottingham finds a photo album linking Irons to Eisenhower, J. Edgar Hoover, Hitler and LBJ. An FBI agent warns Sara that a cabal of assassins, responsible for coups all over the world, killed Danny's and McCarty's murder victim, Tickner. Did Tickner die while taking some film to Gabriel, film of the Kennedy assassination?

GUEST CAST: Victor Slezak; Kathryn Winslow (Vicki); Jeff Seymour, John Bourgeois, Dean Hagopian, Sam Moses, Patrick Garrow, Lazar.

21. "Parabolic" Written by: Jennifer Beck and Ralph Hemecker. Directed by: Anghel Decca. Airdate: August 12, 2002.

Sara investigates a series of hate crimes in the city, only to learn that a vigilante is actually killing the killers. After the vigilante strikes a second time, killing a gay-basher and foiling the plans of an international criminal called Lupo, Sara attempts to infiltrate a hate gang rally but is "made" on the way in and rescued by the vigilante: a young girl. The child, the model for Little Red Riding Hood, is on a mission to stop

Lupo's (the big bad wolf) hate mongering and avenge the long-ago death of her parents.

GUEST CAST: Alexis Dzienza (Vola); Kathryn Winslow (Vicki); Eric Roberts (Lupo); Lazar.

22. "Palindrome" Written by: Roderick and Bruce A. Taylor. Directed by: Paul Holahan. Airdate: August 19, 2002.

Danny and Jake infiltrate an underground fight club called the Spartacus Ring to find a murderer. Meanwhile, the spirit of Kenneth Irons warns Nottingham that there is another Witchblade wielder, one eerily similar to Sara in appearance. One of the combatants in the fight club turns out to be Concobar, Sara's lover from an alternate reality and a man who died because of their love affair. But Jake has to fight Concobar in the ring, and Nottingham recruits Sara's double — an alternate bloodline — to wield the Witchblade.

GUEST CAST: Kim De Lury (Concobar); Kathryn Winslow (Vicki); Joe Marsh Garland, Lazar.

23. "Ubique" Written by: Richard C. Okie and Ralph Hemecker. Directed by: Bradford May. Airdate: August 26, 2002

Pezzini dreams of her defeat at the hands of a new Witchblade wielder, Lucretia Borgia. When she awakens, Sara learns that the Witchblade is missing and people are committing murder all over the nation. The cause of the insanity seems to be a web site called Cyberfaust.net, run by none other than Kenneth Irons. Sara learns that Irons has downloaded his evil essence into all those people who have visited his web site, including innocent Gabriel; and now Sara must confront Borgia for possession of the Witchblade.

GUEST CAST: Kate Levering (Lucretia Borgia); Kim De Lury (Concobar); Kathryn Winslow (Vicki); Fulvio Cecere; Grace Slick (The Witchblade Voice); Lazar.

Wonder Woman

Wonder Woman, that star-spangled siren of justice, was created by an unusual fellow named William Moulton Marston, using the pen name Charles Moulton. Marston, a Harvard-trained psychologist with a law degree and Ph.D, believed that women could bring peace to the world and rule men through "allure."[1] He also believed that this was the natural order and development of humankind, since women were wiser, less war-like and nobler than males of the species. Hence the scholar created the famous Amazonian superhero, the female archetype for all such characters, injecting into the Wonder Woman mythos elements of bondage and sadomasochism (such as a golden lasso that could make men tell the truth).

Despite kinky flourishes, Wonder Woman became a role model to a generation of women because, according to Juanita Coulson in her essay *Of (Super) Human Bondage*, until that time, "women in comic books had either been spear carriers for the superheroes, or that abomination, 'girlfriends.'"[2]

Wonder Woman, drawn by H.G. Peters, first appeared in the pages of *All Star Comics* late in 1941, just as the Japanese attack on Pearl Harbor commenced. Later, the staunch Nazi fighter moved to *Sensation Comics*, and then transitioned to her own line at DC, where she has remained for over fifty years. As one might expect, a prime appeal of the Wonder Woman comic series was indeed the character's physical allure. The Amazonian was statuesque, large breasted, and garbed in a tight suit that displayed her fine form to sexy effect.

In some ways, the Wonder Woman

mythos was a reflection, or flipping, of the Superman legend. Wonder Woman hailed from a distant land — not Krypton, but Paradise Island. In addition to her innocence and love of justice, she possessed great strength and powers that made her supernormal. Adopted by America, she even had a kind of dense male love interest in the blond military man Steve Trevor, and nobody could detect that she had a secret identity (Diana Prince).

Trevor, like Lois Lane in the Man of Steel universe, pined endlessly for Wonder Woman, clueless that the same woman was under his nose all along. Like Marvel's Captain America, however, Wonder Woman was probably most famous for her tangles with Nazis, at least in the first few decades of her generations-spanning career.

It was only a matter of time before film and TV producers realized that a Wonder Woman production could be a major success. In the 1960s, producer William Dozier, who had been responsible for the camp take on *Batman*, forged a half-hour pilot film, but it never aired. This version of the myth featured Wonder Woman as a powerless, hapless, dateless, plain-looking mortal (living with her nagging mother, no less) who only *believed* she was a real superhero. Fortunately, this unfaithful concept never made it to series. Dozier moved on to the short-lived but well regarded *The Green Hornet*, a faithful adaptation of another superhero legend, instead.

Then, in the early 1970s, while Wonder Woman was appearing as one of the charter members of the Justice League of America on the Saturday morning animated series *The Super Friends*, a different set of talents gave a live-action TV series a spin at ABC. This time the pilot film, *Wonder Woman*, starred *That's Incredible* (1980–1984) co-host Cathy Lee Crosby as a modern-day (1970s) Wonder Woman. Steve Trevor appeared in this now-forgotten version too, played by Kaz Garas. Wonder Woman fought a mad genius (Ricardo Montalban as Abner Smith) in the two-hour TV movie. Written by John D.F. Black and directed by Vincent McEveety, the film, like Dozier's effort, ditched much of the original source material. Gone from the mythos was Wonder Woman's amazing outfit, and instead the blond Crosby wore a blue miniskirted suit. Ratings were lukewarm for the telefilm, which aired in March of 1974.

Conversely, ratings skyrocketed when a lovely, statuesque woman named Lynda Carter assumed the title of Wonder Woman in the cumbersomely named *The New Original Wonder Woman*, another two-hour movie that aired in November of 1975. Something of an Amazon herself, the very tall and startlingly beautiful Carter, with blazing eyes and jet-black hair, wore the original skimpy Wonder Woman costume of the comics in all of its sexy glory. Carter was an amazing sight to behold, and every red-blooded American male promptly fell in love with her. Garbed in a red crown (which could become a boomerang, in episodes such as "The Deadly Toys"), blue bikini shorts, a red and gold brassiere and high-heeled red boots, Lynda Carter's Wonder Woman was almost immediately a pop sensation on posters, in magazines, in toy merchandising and on the tube.

Sometimes, Carter also donned a blue cape (in episodes such as "The Man Who Could Not Die"), but, most importantly, Carter brought the necessary quality of believability to the role. Athletic, charming and with a twinkle in her eye, she handily competed with the other network super woman of the time, Lindsay Wagner's *Bionic Woman*.

"People want to get back to old-fashioned feelings," Carter noted of the character that made her a household name. "There's a strong romantic element in the show along with the fantasy-type characters.... Doesn't every girl still want to be a princess and every boy a hero?"[3]

The two hour *Wonder Woman* movie carefully (if cheaply) recounted Wonder Woman's origin on Paradise Island, as she came to care for and protect young Steve Trevor, an American Air Force pilot fighting the Nazis during World War II. Wonder Woman went to work with Trevor, played by dark-haired Lyle Waggoner (unlike the blond of the comics), as his glasses-bedecked secretary, Diana Prince, and a legend was born.

Like her comic book counterpart, TV's Diana Prince possessed an arsenal of unusual crime-fighting weaponry, including a lasso that made men tell the truth and whose use was always accompanied by weird sound effects. She also had bulletproof gold bracelets made of "feminum," and, on rare occasions, even an invisible plane to transport her into and out of danger.

The Diana Prince/Wonder Woman transformation was accomplished in an interesting visual manner. Diana would ditch her glasses and spin around in a circle with arms outstretched, and white light would expand outward from her spinning form. When the light receded, the heroine would be fully dressed as Wonder Woman.

ABC aired two further two-hour movies that year, and in 1976 the hour-long *Wonder Woman* became a regular primetime series, airing on Saturday nights at 8:00 against *The Jeffersons* on CBS and *Emergency* on NBC. The first season retained the 1940s setting of the original comic, and Wonder Woman even picked up a Boy Wonder–like sidekick in the person of young actress Debra Winger as "Wonder Girl," a character introduced in the episode "The Feminum Mystique."

The villains on the series were, predictably, Nazis. Third Reich spies challenged Wonder Woman in "Wonder Woman Meets Baroness Von Gunther," while a twisted Nazi Wonder Woman vied for supremacy with Diana Prince in "Fausta: The Nazi Wonder Woman." And in one truly preposterous installment, the lovely Carter was forced to go head-to-head with a Nazi gorilla ("Wonder Woman vs. Gargantua").

After one season fighting the Germans, *Wonder Woman* hit a snag. ABC cancelled the series due to faltering ratings. Very quickly, CBS scooped up the still-promising show and totally re-vamped it for a second season. In the new version, it was now 1977, and Diana Prince, eternally young, had long since returned to Paradise Island. But history mysteriously repeated itself, and Steve Trevor's son (played by Lyle Waggoner again) ended up on the island in need of Wonder Woman's assistance. Realizing her services were still required in the world, Diana returned to the United States in the era of Watergate, Vietnam, the E.R.A. and inflation, and resurrected Wonder Woman.

This time around, Diana was a government agent at the I.A.D.C. (the Inter Agency Defense Command), and she worked in Washington, D.C. She often received information from a computer named I.R.A.C., the only "individual" that knew Diana Prince and Wonder Woman were actually one in the same. Among the other office denizens was Rover, a little robot version of I.R.A.C. that looked like a mechanical golden chicken. Ed Begley, Jr., played a recurring character named Harold Farnum, a curious college kid who was in love with Diana and always getting into trouble, Jimmy Olsen–style.

The new and revised version of *Wonder Woman* lasted for two seasons on CBS, and, in response to concerns that the 1940s episodes had been "boring," featured a wackier brand of villains. The Skrill, aliens that could hide inside human bodies, were featured in one episode, the two-parter entitled "Mind Stealers from Outer Space." The Skrill also had an alien servant called "the Sardaur," a helmeted heavy-breather (like *Star Wars*' popular villain Darth Vader, but costumed as the alien seen in the *Logan's Run* TV series episode "The Collector").

Fighting for your rights in her satin tights. An inspiring shot of *Wonder Woman* (Lynda Carter).

Other villains included evil mimes ("Diana's Disappearing Act"), a gender-bending assassin ("Death in Disguise), a nefarious statue maker (Roddy McDowall in "The Fine Art of Crime") and a nasty toy-maker (Frank Gorshin in "The Deadly Toys"). Ever trendy, the makers of the *Wonder Woman* series noted the growing *Star Trek* sub-culture and set one episode at a science fiction convention ("Spaced Out").

CBS aired the reissued *Wonder Woman* on Friday nights at 8:00, landing it in direct competition with sitcom hit *Chico and the Man* on NBC and *Donny and Marie* on ABC. When the series again failed to live up to ratings expectations, it was briefly moved to Tuesday nights, but this time the competition was the ABC killer combo of *Happy Days* and *Laverne and Shirley*. By September 1979, the series was cancelled.

Most people that remember *Wonder Woman* today have a pretty good impression of it. Lynda Carter was a beautiful lead, and the series was not overtly childish and satirical (like *Batman*), boring (like *The Amazing Spider-Man*), or particularly realistic (like Kenneth Johnson's *The Incredible Hulk*). Still, the individual stories were not very memorable, and watching *Wonder Woman* in the twenty-first century, one is amazed at how cheap the show appears. In the aforementioned "Mind Stealers from Outer Space," for instance, Wonder Woman was supposed to address the United Nations with an alien friend, Andros, about the invasion of aliens called the Skrill. The U.N. lectern was depicted as a single wood desk against a plain, paneled wall. That footage was then intercut with what looked like decades-old footage of the real United Nations general assembly.

In the same episode, the Skrill invasion of Earth was notably limited in scope. "The Skrill have taken over an abandoned building downtown," Trevor exclaimed worriedly, but it hardly sounded as though the merciless aliens had won prime real estate. This episode was also rather funny because Andros the alien paraded all around Washington, D.C., while wearing his spacey Nehru jacket and silver boots. One might think the powers that be in the country's capitol might have seen to it that he be dressed less conspicuously.

The continuing and inappropriate use of stock footage was also a major stumbling block on *Wonder Woman*. The episode "Death in Disguise" provides one notable example. Working against time, Wonder Woman had to race across Washington, D.C., and scale the I.A.D.C. Building in an emergency. Every week prior to this episode, that edifice had been depicted as a massive, modern looking white Federal structure not that very different from the F.B.I. Building or even the Pentagon. For this one episode, however, the giant, normally ivory-colored I.A.D.C. headquarters became a little brick three-story construct instead, so an expensive stunt would not have to be staged. Instead, old footage from another episode was trotted out. This "cheating" was blatantly obvious, even to children.

Cheesy and very 1970s, *Wonder Woman* was nonetheless a fun TV series, and one that today is remembered with great affection. For many years now, a new *Wonder Woman* film has been in development, with various notable actresses reportedly signed for the lead role, including Julia Roberts and Sandra Bullock. As of this writing in 2002, Sandra Bullock had reportedly dropped out of contention, and producers were seeking a new Amazon to carry the *Wonder Woman* torch into the 21st century.

In 2001-2002, Wonder Woman could be seen on the Cartoon Network's *Justice League of America*, but she was a more impulsive, younger version of the heroine than the stolid, dependable Lynda Carter incarnation of the 1970s.

Wonder Woman (1975–79)
LIVE-ACTION SERIES

"The 1940s-era episodes are enjoyable and very faithful to how the characters were written in the comics. Those shows are infinitely watchable and capture the spirit of a comic book character better than any superhero TV show ever did. The 1970s episodes don't have the same charm; *Wonder Woman* became another secret agent show. And I don't know why they did it, but I don't think it served the series to relegate Steve Trevor to secondary status. Lyle Waggoner was too old to play the character. In the pilot of the 1970s episodes it is explained that he is the son of the original Steve Trevor. Well, you have to assume he was born after Wonder Woman went back to Paradise Island in 1945 and that would make him 31 or 32 years old at the most, but Waggoner was already going gray by the end of the second season. It looked like had the show continued another season it would have had a completely new supporting cast."

— Howard Margolin, host of *Destinies: The Voice of Science Fiction.*

"Lynda Carter's series worked almost solely based on her ability to fill that costume so nicely. For a brief period, she seemed a cultural icon, and all this for a show that many people watched only in snippets — you had to stop and watch (if you had a remote control) when she was in all of her regalia."

— William Latham, author of *Mary's Monster* and *Space: 1999 Resurrection.*

CAST: Lynda Carter (Diana Prince/Wonder Woman); Lyle Waggoner (Major Steve Trevor).

CREW: *Executive Producer:* Douglas S. Cramer. *Produced by:* Charles B. Fitzimons. *Based on Characters Created by:* Charle Moulton. *Developed for TV by:* Stanley Ralph Ross. *Supervising Producer:* Bruce Lansbury. *Associate Producer:* John Gaynor. *Executive Story Consultant:* Brian McKay. *Story Editor:* Anne Collins. *Director of Photography:* Robert Hoffman. *Art Director:* Stephen M. Berger. *Music:* Artie Kane. *Costume Designer:* Donfeld. *Casting:* Shelly Ellison. *Unit Production Manager:* William Derwin. *First Assistant Director:* Ed Ledding. *Second Assistant Director:* Kelly A. Manners. *Stunt Coordinator:* Ron Stein. *Assistant to Executive Producer:* Hudson Hickman. *Film Editors (various episodes):* Richard L. Ven Enger, Stanley Wohlberg. *Music Editor:* Jay Alfred Smith. *Sound Effects:* Al Gavigga. *Sound:* Richard Ragusa. *Set Decorator:* Sal Blydenburgh. *Special Effects:* Robert L. Peterson. *Make-up:* Edward Tormes. *Hairstylist:* Cheri Ruff. *Song "Wonder Woman" Music:* Charles Fox; *Lyrics:* Norman Gimbel. Filmed at Burbank Studios, Burbank, CA.

1. "The New Original Wonder Woman" (aired as TV movie) Written by: Stanley Ralph Ross. Directed by: Leonard Horn. Airdate: November 7, 1975.

The beautiful female warriors of Paradise Island live in peace, serenity and isolation in their uncharted utopia, at least until Nazi fighters shoot down American flyer Steve Trevor over the Atlantic and he crashes on the island. The American is tended to by one of the island's most athletic and curious denizens, Princess Diana. When it comes time to return Trevor to the outside world, Diana competes and wins the privilege of being the one to escort him. All memory of the island is wiped from Trevor's mind, and Diana, armed with a number of Paradise Island gadgets (including a golden belt, bulletproof bracelets and a magic lasso), takes a job as Trevor's assistant. All the while, she secretly helps fight the war against Hitler as the beautiful superhero Wonder Woman. Her first case involves espionage and an attempt by Nazis to steal a powerful new bomb.

GUEST CAST: Red Buttons (Norman); Kenneth Mars (Colonel Von Blasko); Stella Stevens (Marsha); Eric Braden (Captain Drangle); Fanny Flag (Doctor); Henry Gibson (Nicholas); Severn Darden, Ian Wolfe.

2. "Wonder Woman Meets Baroness Von Gunther" (aired as TV movie) Written by: Margaret Armen. Directed by: Barry Crane. Airdate: April 21, 1976.

Diana and Trevor are shocked when a war hero is accused of being a Nazi sympathizer. They soon realize that there is more to this case than meets the eye, and Wonder Woman must clash with Baroness Von Gunther, a fascist spy bent on destroying America and its heroes.

GUEST CAST: Christine Belford (Baroness Von Gunther); Bradford Dillman (Arthur); Ed Griffith, Edmund Gilbert.

3. "Fausta: the Nazi Wonder Woman" (aired as TV movie) Written by:

Bruce Shelly and David Ketchum. Directed by: Barry Crane. Airdate: April 28, 1976.

In hopes of neutralizing Wonder Woman, the Nazis create their own super-powered female fighter, the villainous Fausta. Fausta and Wonder Woman clash, and an apparently victorious Fausta defeats Diana and then captures her for further study in the Fatherland.

GUEST CAST: Lynda-Day George (Fausta); Christopher George (Rojak); Bo Brundin (Kesselman).

SEASON ONE (1976-77)

4. "Beauty on Parade" Written by: Richard Kinon. Directed by: Alan Crosland. Airdate: October 13, 1976.

The Nazis are up to no good again, using a wholesome beauty pageant as a front to sabotage American military installations. Of course, Wonder Woman fits in beautifully at just such a pageant, and investigates the case of espionage.

GUEST CAST: Anne Francis (Lola); Dick Van Patten (Jack); Bobby Van (Burns); Jennifer Shaw, Christa Helm, William Lanteau.

5. "The Feminum Mystique" (two hours) Written by: Jimmy Sangster. Story by: Barbara Avedon and Barbara Corday. Directed by: Herb Wallerstein. Airdates: November 6 and 8, 1976.

The Nazis apprehend Drusilla, Wonder Woman's sister from Paradise Island. Drusilla has taken on the identity of Wonder Girl, Diana's partner in crime fighting. Wonder Woman must work fast to save her, as the Nazis are working hard to determine how to duplicate the bullet-proof qualities of the Paradise bracelets, made of the unusual substance "feminum."

GUEST CAST: John Saxon (Professor Radell); Charles Frank (Knight); Pamela Susan Shoop (Magda); Erica Hagen (Delma); Curt Lowens (General Ulrich); Paul Shenar.

6. "Wonder Woman vs. Gargantua" Written by: Dave Ketchum and Tony DiMarco. Directed by: Charles Rondeau. Airdate: December 18, 1976.

Wonder Woman faces her strangest opponent yet: a massive gorilla trained specifically to assassinate her and apprehend a Nazi defector. Before long, it's a case of beauty versus the beast.

GUEST CAST: Robert Loggia (Eichler); Gretchen Corbett (Erica); John Hillerman (Conrad); Tom Reese, Mickey Morton.

7. "The Pluto File" Written by: Herb Berman. Directed by: Herb Wallerstein. Airdate: December 25, 1976.

Diana faces two problems. The first: a thief has stolen an important and classified document that explains how artificial earthquakes can be generated. The second: the thief himself is a carrier of the deadly bubonic plague!

GUEST CAST: Robert Reed (Fallon); Hayden Roarke (Professor Warren); Kenneth Tigar (Barnes); Albert Stratton, Jason Johnson.

8. "Last of the Two Dollar Bills" Written by: Paul Dubov, Gwen Bagni and Jimmy Sangster. Directed by: Stuart Margolin. Airdate: January 8, 1977.

A Nazi agent in the United States unleashes the Third Reich's latest dastardly scheme. He floods the market with fake two-dollar bills from counterfeit plates in hopes of destabilizing the economy. It's Wonder Woman to the rescue.

GUEST CAST: James Olson (Wooten); Barbara Anderson (Maggie); Richard O'Brien, John Howard, Dean Harens, Victor Argo.

9. "Judgment from Outer Space" (**Parts I & II**) Written by: Stephen Kandel. Directed by: Alan Crosland. Airdates: January 15 and 17, 1977.

A benevolent alien named Andros arrives on Earth to offer a warning and possible judgment. Mankind must stop his warring ways or face annihilation and destruction in his quest to conquer outer space. Unfortunately, Andros' message of unity and brotherly love is also an ultimatum; but this is of no importance to the Nazis, who kidnap the alien and take him to Germany for further study. Wonder Woman must risk her life to free Andros and preserve the future of mankind.

GUEST CAST: Tim O'Connor (Andros); Scott Hylands (Paul); Vic Perrin (Goral); Hank Brandt; Christopher Cary; Patrick Skelton; Film Fomicola; Christine Schnmidmter (Lisa).

NOTE: If the plot of this episode sounds familiar, it might be because Andros and his message of peace seem reminiscent of Klaatu and his similar message from the classic film *The Day the Earth Stood Still* (1951).

10. "Formula 407" Written by: Elroy Schwartz. Directed by: Herb Wallerstein. Airdate: January 22, 1977.

In Buenos Aires, Steve Trevor and Diana Prince face off against Nazi agents who have stolen the formula that turns ordinary rubber into an indestructible substance. If Hitler gets his hands on it, the balance of the war will tip his way.

GUEST CAST: Nehemiah Persoff (Professor Marino); Marisa Pavan, John Devlin, Charles Macaulay, Maria Grimm.

11. "The Bushwhackers" Written by: Skip Webster. Directed by: Stuart Margolin. Airdate: January 29, 1977.

Nazi cattle rustlers? Could it be? Wonder Woman travels to Texas to help a rancher in his battle against the Nazi scum.

GUEST CAST: Roy Rogers (Hadley); Henry Darrow (Lampkin); Lance Kerwin (Jeff); Tony George (Emmett); Justin Randi, Kevin Wong, Rita Gomez.

12. "Wonder Woman in Hollywood" Written by: Jimmy Sangster. Directed by: Stuart Margolin. Airdate: February 16, 1977.

In an effort to support the war, Hollywood plans to produce a film about the real-life exploits of heroic American soldiers in the struggle against the Axis Powers. Unfortunately, the Nazis have no intention of letting the show go on, and spies plot to kidnap the heroes before they are ready for their close-ups. But the show isn't over until Wonder Woman intervenes.

GUEST CAST: Harris Yulin (Mark); Robert Hays (Ames); Christopher Norris, Charles Cyphers, Alan Bergmann.

SEASON TWO (1977-78)

13. "The Return of Wonder Woman" (two hours) Written by: Stephen Kandel. Directed by: Alan Crosland. Airdate: September 16, 1977.

The 1940s and the war against fascism are long over, and Princess Diana, having returned to Paradise Island many years ago, is stunned when a plane carrying Steve Trevor arrives at her island home in the mid–1970s. To her shock, it is not actually Steve Trevor at all, but his grown son, now a top government official working for the Inter-Agency Defense Command. Understanding that a terrorist group plans to blow up a power plant in Central America, Diana determines it is time to resurrect Wonder Woman. She resumes her identity as Diana Prince and fights at Trevor Jr.'s side to stop evil.

GUEST CAST: Fritz Weaver (Dr. Solano); Jessica Walter (Gloria); Beatrice Straight (Queen); Russ Marin, Dave Knapp, Brooke Bundy.

14. "Anschluss '77" Written by: Dallas L. Barness and Frank K. Telford. Directed by: Alan Crosland. Airdate: September 23, 1977.

It is a case of déjà vu all over again when Diana Prince and Steve Trevor find themselves battling Nazis. This time, a Nazi scientist in hiding in South America plans to create a clone of his fuehrer, Adolf Hitler, and begin the Fourth Reich!

GUEST CAST: Mel Ferrer (Fritz); Julio Medina, Leon Charles, Barry Dennen, Peter Nyberg.

15. "The Man Who Could Move the World" Written by: Judy Burns. Directed by: Robert Kelljan. Airdate: September 30, 1977.

Another powerful villain from Wonder Woman's past arrives to hassle the IADC. This time it is a telekinetic Japanese soldier who has sworn vengeance against the Paradise Island heroine for opposing the Japanese cause in the 1940s.

GUEST CAST: Yuki Shimoda, J. Kenneth Campbell, Lew Ayres, James Long, Peter Kwong.

16. "The Bermuda Triangle Crisis" Written by: Calvin Clements, Jr. Directed by: Seymour Robbie. Airdate: October 7, 1977.

A plane disappears in the Bermuda Triangle, and Diana suspects sabotage. While she and Steve pose as a married couple to investigate a nearby resort island, she learns of a plot concerning nuclear terror, and becomes fearful that Paradise Island could be in jeopardy.

GUEST CAST: Charles Cioffi, Larry Golden.

17. "Knockout" Written by: Mark Rodgers. Directed by: Seymour Robbie. Airdate: October 14, 1977.

One of our agents is missing: Steve Trevor disappears without a trace on a mission; and with virtually no clues to go on, Wonder Woman must locate him.

GUEST CAST: Ted Shackleford (Pete); Jayne Kennedy, Frank Marth, Arch Johnson, Abraham Alvarez, Frank Parker.

18. "The Pied Piper" Written by: Dave Ketchum and Tony DiMarco. Directed by: Alan Crosland. Airdate: October 21, 1977.

A villainous rock musician named Rule has developed a method by which to control the minds of female fans. He is using music as a cover for this nefarious scheme of hypnotizing his audience members. Diana learns of the dastardly plot and sets out to stop Rule, but she, too, might be susceptible to the criminal's musical call.

GUEST CAST: Eve Plumb (Helena); Martin Mull (Rule); Bob Hastings, Denny Miller, Sandy Charles.

19. "The Queen and the Thief" Written by: Bruce Shelly. Directed by: Jack Arnold. Airdate: October 28, 1977.

Diana and Steve go undercover in a foreign kingdom to stop an international jewel thief. The matter is of special importance because the thief, a roguish scoundrel, has previously posed as an IADC agent.

GUEST CAST: Juliet Mills (Queen Kathryn); David Hedison (Evan); John Colicos (Orrick).

20. "I Do, I Do" Written by: Brian McKay and Richard Carr. Directed by: Herb Wallerstein. Airdate: November 11, 1977.

At a health spa, the wives of government officials are being hypnotized into revealing State secrets. Wonder Woman goes undercover to stop the espionage.

GUEST CAST: Celeste Holm (Dolly); John Getz, Simon Scott, Kent Smith, Henry Darrow, Steve Eastin.

21. "The Man Who Made Volcanos" Written by: Dan Ullman and Wilton Denmark. Directed by: Alan Crosland. Airdate: November 18, 1977.

A mad scientist has made a startling discovery: he can artificially create volcanoes, threatening geological stability across the world. Now Dr. Chapman has the means to make the world population listen to him, and he threatens global disaster if his demands are not met.

GUEST CAST: Roddy McDowall (Dr. Chapman); Roger Davis (Corbin); Richard Narita, Iren Tsu, Ray Young.

22. "Mind Stealers from Outer Space" (Parts I and II) Written by: Stephan Kandel. Directed by: Alan Crosland. Airdates: December 2 and 9, 1977.

Aliens from outside our solar system have landed on Earth and infiltrated the bodies of unsuspecting Earthlings. The Skrill, alien criminals whom Wonder Woman's extraterrestrial friend, Andros, calls a "deadly plague," are trafficking in stolen Earth minds! The Skrill discover Wonder Woman's secret identity and set out to capture her as Diana Prince, with the help of a terrifying space monster called the Sardaur. Diana escapes from the Sardaur with the help of Andros. When the Skrill occupy an abandoned building in downtown Washington, D.C., Andros rushes there to confront his enemy and is nearly killed when the Skrill collapse the building. Wonder Woman rescues Andros, even as the Skrill plan to capture a prominent senator and other valuable Earth minds. If Wonder Woman and Andros can't stop the Skrill within 48 hours, Andros' people will step in to rid the planet of the alien infestation, a procedure that could drive millions of humans insane.

GUEST CAST: Dack Rambo (Andros); Pamela Mason (Carla Burgess); Vincent Van Patten (Johnny); Earl Boen (Chaka); Barbara O. Jones (Sell); Allan Migicovsky (Dr. Rand); Curt Lowens (Nordling); Rege Cordic (Professor Eidleman); Lana Marie Henricks (Karen); Lorie Ann Henricks (Kim); Walt Davis (Security Guard); Phyllis Flax (Woman Delegate); Eric Mason (Senator Wainright); Dee Dee Young (Zambezia Delegate); Kristin Larkin (Debbie).

23. "The Deadly Toys" Story by: Carey Wilbur. Written by: Anne Collins. Directed by: Dick Moder. Airdate: December 30, 1977.

Diana is brought in to investigate the situation when a scientist on the secretive Project X-Y-Z is replaced by an identical android. Prince learns that strange toys are being utilized by some sinister force to go after the remaining two scientists on the weapons project. After a second scientist, named Prescott, is replaced by a humanoid robot, Diana traces toys found on the scene back to a shop in Georgetown and its eccentric owner, Hoffman. Realizing she is onto his plan, Hoffman sends a flying model airplane—*one that drops bombs!*—after Diana, hoping she will not uncover his plan to build an android duplicate of Wonder Woman.

GUEST CAST: Frank Gorshin (Orlich Hoffman); James A. Watson (Dr. Prescott); Jame Rubinstein (Major Dexter);

24. "Light-Fingered Lady" Written by: Bruce Shelly. Directed by: Alan Crosland. Airdate: January 6, 1978.

A $50 million booty is too much to resist for a legendary thief, but Wonder Woman is on the case (gone undercover as a fellow crook) to see that he doesn't get his hands on it.

GUEST CAST: Greg Morris (Anton); Christopher Stone (Ryan); Gary Crosby (Grease); Bubba Smith (Rojak); Saundra Sharp (Eve).

25. "Screaming Javelin" Written by: Brian McKay. Directed by: Michael Caffey. Airdate: January 20, 1978.

A delusional man who fancies himself the absolute ruler of a fictitious country believes that fame, fortune and, most importantly, respect, will be his if his imaginary homeland has a great showing at the Olympic Games. To that end, he begins kidnapping athletes from around the world to represent a country that doesn't even exist. Wonder Woman intervenes.

GUEST CAST: Henry Gibson, E.J. Peaker, Robert Sampson, Rick Springfield, Vaughn Armstrong.

26. "Diana's Disappearing Act" Written by: S.S. Schweitzer. Directed by: Michael Caffey. Airdate: February 3, 1978.

Cogliostro, an evil magician who has

learned the secret of transforming base metals into gold, orders Diana Prince kidnapped when a photograph by one of his underlings reveals that she has a special pendant in her possession. Cogliostro's evil associate, Morgana Le Fay, abducts Diana at a banquet for the Emir of Quiana, but Diana transforms into Wonder Woman and escapes from a crate on a moving truck. Meanwhile, evil mimes steal the pendant from the laboratory of Dr. Hutchins, a Nobel-Prize–winning scientist assigned to study the jewelry. Wonder Woman learns that the Emir and Cogliostro are working together on a deal involving cheap gold, a deal that could threaten world economies.

GUEST CAST: Dick Gautier (Maestro Cogliostro); Ed Begley, Jr. (Harold); J.A. Preston (Jazreel); Allen Williams (Dr. Hutchins); Aharon Ipale (The Emir); Brenda Benet (Morgana Le Fay); Saundra Sharp (Eve); George Skaff (Shopkeeper); Maurice Shebanee (Ambassador); James Mark Wilson (Magician #1); Don W. Brockhaus (Magician #2); Peter De Paula (Mime #1); Kathlyn (Mime #2).

27. "Death in Disguise" Written by: Tom Sawyer. Directed by: Alan Crosland. Airdate: February 10, 1978.

After evading an attempted assassination on horseback, Diana sets out to protect a sexist billionaire named Carlo Indrezzano from the villainous underworld figure Woodward Nightingale. Woodward has hired a cross-dressing assassin, Starker, to kill the womanizing Indrezzano, but Wonder Woman keeps getting in the way. As Diana soon learns, however, the real plot does not involve Indrezzano, but an effort to destroy the IADC's computer, IRAC, which could expose Woodward's client, a man named Marius. Now Wonder Woman must race forty-seven miles in four minutes to prevent a time bomb from destroying the vociferous computer.

GUEST CAST: Joel Fabiani (Nightingale); Jennifer Darling (Violet Louise Tree); Lee Bergere (Marius); Charles Pierce (Starker); George

Chakiris (Carlo Indrezzano); Art Batanides (Krug); Christopher Cary (Beamer); Saundra Sharp (Eve); Carol Worthington (Major Finley); Katharine Charles (Corporal); Jack Kissell (Plotkin); Maurice Marsac (Maitre d').

28. "IRAC Is Missing" Written by: Anne Collins. Directed by: Alexander Singer. Airdate: February 17, 1978.

The world-famous Ever Right Computer Company suffers a terrible loss when the main computer's central memory bank is drained and then assimilated by a secret saboteur. Trevor and Diana realize IRAC may be in line for similar treatment, and the worried computer module suggests putting Wonder Woman on the case. A lead at the Potomac Power Company goes south for the superheroine when the hot-tempered genius William Havitol arranges a diversionary crisis for her to handle. A disguised Havitol then steals into the IADC headquarters and makes off with IRAC, leaving Wonder Woman to find and stop the madman before he can assume control of the United States by manipulating IRAC and orbiting communication satellites.

GUEST CAST: Ross Martin (William Havitol); Lee Paul (Dirk); W.T. Zracha (Dick); Tina Lenert (Cori); Lloyd McLinn (Guard); Mathia Reitz (Technician); Jim Veres (Sgt. Dobson); Cletus Young (Official); Colin Hamilton (Director).

29. "Flight to Oblivion" Written by: Patrick Matthews. Directed by: Alan Crosland. Airdate: March 3, 1978.

A former NATO officer uses his potent power of hypnosis to crash Air Force missions, and Wonder Woman goes undercover in the military to stop him.

GUEST CAST: Alan Fudge, Corinne Michaels, Michael Shannon, Mitch Vogel.

30. "Séance of Terror" Written by: Bruce Shelly. Directed by: Dick Moder. Airdate: March 10, 1978.

An innocent young man is being manipulated for his psychic powers, to evil purposes. To wit, he has begun to affect the delegates at a long-awaited peace conference. Wonder Woman must win the trust of the boy and stop him before real harm is done to the international community and prospects of world peace.

GUEST CAST: Todd Lookinland, Rick Jason, John Fujioka, Adam Ageli, Hanna Hertelendy.

31. "The Man Who Wouldn't Tell" Written by: Anne Collins. Directed by: Alan Crosland. Airdate: March 31, 1978.

A hapless night janitor, Alan Ackroyd, has inadvertently discovered the secret formula to a powerful new explosive. With dueling corporations hoping to learn Alan's secret, Diana Prince is assigned by IADC to protect the scatterbrained young man, but finding the on-the-run student is no piece of cake. Alan is captured by the villainous Rudolph Furst, a competitor with Hopewell Enterprises for the formula, and is pressured to recreate the accident that resulted in his explosive discovery of days earlier. Furst captures Meg, Alan's true love, to force compliance, but Furst has made a fatal error in capturing Diana Prince as well!

GUEST CAST: Gary Burghoff (Alan Ackroyd); Jane Actman (Meg); Philip Michael Thomas (Rudolph Furst); Michael Cole (Ted); Millie Slavin (B.W.); Saundra Sharp (Eve); Tony Brubacker (Tom).

32. "The Girl from Ilandia" Written by: Anne Collins. Directed by: Dick Moder. Airdate: April 7, 1978.

A strange girl from another reality, the world of Ilandia, appears on Earth, alone and adrift in the ocean on a small life raft. Because she has special abilities, the girl almost immediately becomes a target of opportunistic criminals, at least until Wonder Woman arrives to defend her new friend.

GUEST CAST: Julie Ann Haddock (Tina); Harry Guardino (Penrose); Allen Arbus (Bleaker); Fred Lerner (Davis).

33. "The Murderous Missile" Written by: Dick Nelson. Directed by: Dick Moder. Airdate: April 21, 1978.

The U.S. is testing a brand new type of missile (controlled by mental abilities), and Wonder Woman is needed at the launch. She is detained, however, in a small western town, for mysterious purposes.

GUEST CAST: Warren Stevens (Sheriff Beal); James Liusi (George); Steve Inwood, Mark Withers, Lucille Benson, Hal England.

SEASON THREE (1978-79)

34. "One of Our Teen Idols Is Missing" Written by: Anne Collins. Directed by: Seymour Robbie. Airdate: September 22, 1978.

Kincaid, a much beloved teen star, is kidnapped and, in a strange twist, replaced by his twin brother. Diana must find out the reasons for the switch and save the real teen idol.

GUEST CAST: Leif Garrett (Kincaid); Dawn Lyn, Michael Lerner, Albert Paulsen, Michael Baseleon.

35. "Hot Wheels" Written by: Dennis Landa. Directed by: Dick Moder. Airdate: September 29, 1978.

A roll of microfilm containing information of national importance has been hidden in the hood ornament of a Rolls Royce. Unfortunately, the car is stolen, and Wonder Woman must break a car theft ring in order to get the important film back to its rightful owners.

GUEST CAST: Peter Brown (Bolt); Lance Le Gault (Fiske); John Durren (Alf); Marc Rose (Slim).

36. "The Deadly Sting" Written by: Dick Nelson. Directed by: Alan Crosland. Airdate: October 6, 1978.

A professor's mind-control device is being used on football teams in a racket to manipulate the winners of games. Diana must stop the illicit mind control and find out who is behind it.

GUEST CAST: Harvey Jason (Brubaker); Ron Ely (Bill); Scott Marlowe, Danny Drayton, Marvin Miller, Deacon Jones, Gil Stratton.

37. "The Fine Art of Crime" Written by: Anne Collins. Directed by: Dick Moder. Airdate: October 13, 1978.

Diana's pal Harold Farnum drags her to an exhibition by the flamboyant artist Henry Roberts, a world-famous maker of extraordinarily life-like statues. At the show, someone slips a note into Diana's car, tipping her off to a series of thefts. As it turns out, Henry is sending in his thugs, masquerading as high-priced statues, to steal jewelry and other valuables from rich art patrons. When Harold investigates the "living" statues for a term paper, he's kidnapped by Roberts and utilized in a trap set for the IADC and Wonder Woman.

GUEST CAST: Roddy McDowall (Henry Roberts); Ed Begley, Jr. (Harold Farnum); Joe E. Tata (Joe); Michael McGuire (Lloyd Moreaux); Patti MacLeod (Mrs. Ellsworth); Gavin MacLeod (Mr. Ellsworth); Joe Maross (Shubert); George Caldwell (Heavy #1); Mitchel Young-Evans (Berkeley Student).

38. "Disco Devil" Written by: Alan Brennert. Directed by: Leslie H. Martinson. Airdate: October 20, 1978.

At a disco, a diabolical psychic reads the minds of government officials to mentally steal national secrets. Wonder Woman discos her way into the operation to expose the plot.

GUEST CAST: Paul Sands (Franklin); Wolfman Jack (Infrared); Russell Johnson, Ellen Weston.

39. "Formicida" Written by: Kathryn Michaelian Powers. Directed by: Alan Crosland. Airdate: November 3, 1978.

A new super-villain is born. Formicida is a scientist with a love for insects and a hatred of pesticides. Striking a blow for bugs

everywhere, Formicida develops super strength and challenges Wonder Woman for species supremacy.

GUEST CAST: Lorene Yarnell (Formicida); Robert Shields (Doug); Robert Alda (Harcourt).

40. "Time Bomb" Written by: Kathleen Barnes and David Wise. Directed by: Seymour Robbie. Airdate: November 10, 1978.

A visitor from the future realizes a fortune could be made in the past — Wonder Woman's present — and uses knowledge of events yet to occur to make that happen. When another visitor from the future — who knows such opportunism cannot be allowed — follows the first, it becomes a battle of the time travelers, with Diana caught in the middle.

GUEST CAST: Joan Van Ark (Cassandra); Ted Shackleford (Adam); Allan Miller (Dan); Fred Wayne.

NOTE: Notice that the time traveler's name is Cassandra. In classical mythology Cassandra was a seer who nobody would believe. Here Cassandra knows the future and hopes to exploit it, but, like the mythological figure, is also less-than-successful in her efforts.

41. "Skateboard Whiz" Written by: Alan Brennert. Directed by: Leslie H. Martinson. Airdate: November 24, 1978.

A skateboarding champ with a photographic memory could be Wonder Woman's only hope in her efforts to bring down a mob leader. But will the teenage girl help bring the villain to justice?

GUEST CAST: Eric Braeden (Donaldson); Ron Masak, Art Metrano, John Reilly, James Ray.

42. "The Deadly Dolphin" Written by: Jackson Gillis. Directed by: Sigmund Neufeld. Airdate: December 1, 1978.

An innocent dolphin is trained and manipulated by a land baron who straps explosives to the mammal's back and orders it to sink an oil rig. The ensuing natural disaster — a spill of epic proportions — would devastate coastal property values, leaving the land baron a rich man. But can Wonder Woman stop the deadly dolphin in time?

GUEST CAST: Penelope Windust (Stubbs); Nicholas Coster (Lockhart); Albert Popwell, Brian Tochi (Darrel).

43. "Stolen Faces" Written by: Richard Carr. Directed by: Leslie H. Martinson. Airdate: December 15, 1978.

An unknown enemy is duplicating various important figures, including Wonder Woman and Steve Trevor. Wonder Woman trails her doppelganger back to the source and uncovers a criminal plot.

GUEST CAST: Kenneth Tigar (Austin); Joseph Maher (Percy); Diana Lander, John O'Connell.

44. "Pot o' Gold" Written by: Michael McGreevy. Directed by: Alan Crosland. Airdate: December 22, 1978.

Wonder Woman has the luck of the Irish while helping a man (a leprechaun?) recover his pot of missing gold.

GUEST CAST: Dick O'Neill, Brian Davies, Arthur Batanides.

45. "Gault's Brain" Written by: Arthur Weingarten. Story by: John Gaynor. Directed by: Gordon Hessler. Airdate: December 29, 1978.

A dying tycoon and megalomaniac has had his brain preserved. Now he wants to transplant it into a younger, perfect body.

GUEST CAST: John Carradine (Gault); Lloyd Levine (Stryker); Kathy Sheriff (Tara); Peter Mark Richman (Crippin); Erick Stern (Turk).

46. "Going, Going, Gone" Written by: Patrick Matthews. Directed by: Alan Crosland. Airdate: January 12, 1979.

Diana Prince must prevent nuclear hardware from being auctioned on the black market. Posing as a criminal, Diana investigates, but finds that it is a job for Wonder Woman.

GUEST CAST: Hari Rhodes (Como); Bo Brundin (Zukov); Mako (Brown); Charlie Brill (Smith); Marc Lawrence (Jones).

47. "Spaced Out" Written by: Bill Taylor. Directed by: Ivan Dixon. Airdate: January 26, 1979.

A science fiction convention (replete with guest Robby the Robot) causes trouble for Wonder Woman when she learns that a classified stolen item, a laser crystal, may be hidden among the trinkets there.

GUEST CAST: Rene Auberjonois (Kimbal); Paul Smith (Rohan); Bob Short (Robby the Robot).

48. "The Starships Are Coming" Written by: Glen Olson and Rod Baker. Directed by: Alan Crosland. Airdate: February 2, 1979.

An alien abduction has been reported, and news outlets claim that an invasion is imminent. Can Wonder Woman ferret out the truth about an extraterrestrial invasion and save the Earth?

GUEST CAST: Andrew Duggan (Steele); Jeffry Byron (Wilson); Tim O'Connor (Elliott); Sheryl Lee Ralph (Bobbie); Frank Whiteman.

49. "Amazing Hot Wax" Written by: Alan Brennert. Directed by: Ray Austin. Airdate: February 16, 1979.

Diana pretends to be an up-and-coming singer cutting a new album in order to expose corruption in the recording industry.

GUEST CAST: Kate Woodville (Adele); Bob Hoy (Mary); Sarah Purcell (Barbie); Martin Speer (Billy); Rick Springfield (Anton); Judge Reinhold (Jeff).

50. "The Richest Man in the World" Written by: Jackson Gillis. Directed by: Don McDougall. Airdate: February 19, 1979.

A billionaire has disappeared without a trace. Making matters worse, he has apparently taken with him the secret to a top-secret missile-scrambling device. Wonder Woman and Trevor must find the missing man, and fast!

GUEST CAST: Jeremy Slate (Marshall); Roger Perry (Dunfeld); Barry Miller (Barney); Marilyn Mason (Lucy).

51. "A Date with Doomsday" Written by: Dennis Landa and Roland Stark. Directed by: Curtis Harrington. Airdate: March 10, 1979.

A tube containing a deadly virus has disappeared, and Diana thinks it might have something to do with a dating service company.

GUEST CAST: Donnelly Rhodes, Carol Vogel, Arthur Mallett, Michael Holt.

52. "The Girl with the Gift for Disaster" Written by: Alan Brennert. Directed by: Alan Crosland. Airdate: March 17, 1979.

A girl named Bonnie Murphy, who seems to be a magnet for destructive accidents, becomes embroiled with two small-time thieves and their big-time employer, William Mayfield. Bonnie's strange "gift" may be the result of electrochemical brain impulses that bring out the "more remote" possibilities of a given situation; in other words, she's a jinx! When white-collar crook Mayfield decides to use the unlucky girl as a diversionary weapon during his illegal operations, she ends up at IADC in the company of a perplexed and suspicious Diana Prince. Very soon, Diana knows something is wrong with the extraordinary young woman and must stop her random acts of unintentional destruction before Mayfield can steal the Declaration of Independence and other important United States documents.

GUEST CAST: Jane Actman (Bonnie Murphy); Ina Balin (Dr. Koren); Dick Butkus (Neil); Charles Haid (Bob Baker); Raymond St. Jacques

(William Mayfield); James Sloyan (Mark Reuben); Renee Brown (Joan); Dulcie Jordan (Receptionist); Tom Kratochvil (Voice of IRAC).

53. "The Boy Who Knew Her Secret" (two hours) Written by: Anne Collins. Directed by: Leslie H. Martinson. Airdates: May 28 and 29, 1979.

It's an invasion of alien body snatchers! Tiny metal pyramids are appearing all over America; when humans touch them, their minds become trapped inside. Wonder Woman teams with a teenager to stop the invasion, only to learn that the pyramids are not evil, but are simply searching for an alien shape shifter, a criminal!

GUEST CAST: Clark Brandon (Skip); Michael Shannon (Cameron); John Milford (Keller); Lenora May (Rose); Tegan West (Pearson); Joyce Greenwood.

54. "The Man Who Could Not Die" Written by: Anne Collins. Directed by: John Newland. Airdate: August 28, 1979.

Diana is transferred to an IADC field office in Los Angeles, and her first assignment involves Tobias, a super chimpanzee engineered to be invincible by one Dr. Akers. The scientist reports that a former partner, Joseph Reichman, wishes to take over the world with an army of similarly invulnerable human super-soldiers. Unfortunately, Reichman has already made one man invulnerable, a former football star-turned-computer science professor named Kandel. Kandel helps Wonder Woman track down the deranged scientist, using his own super powers in conjunction with hers.

GUEST CAST: John Durren (Dale Hawthorn); Robert Sampson (Dr. Akers); Bob Seagren (Bret Cassidy); John Aprea (Dupris); Hal Frederick (The Professor); Brian Davies (Joseph Reichman); James Bond, III (T. Burton Phipps, III); Sherry Miles (Admissions Clerk); Douglas Broyles (Mover).

55. "Phantom of the Roller Coaster" (two hours) Written by: Anne Collins. Directed by: John Newland. Airdates: September 4 and 11, 1979.

An amusement park may be the headquarters for a dastardly spy ring. But it is definitely the stomping grounds of a phantom, a strange man who haunts the grounds. Wonder Woman must deal with the spies and learn the truth of the phantom of the roller coaster.

GUEST CAST: Joseph Sirola (Finch); Jared Martin (Gurney); Ike Eisenmann (Randy); Marc Alaimo (Pearce); Jocelyn Summers (Patrick); Jessica Rains, Judith Christopher.

X-Men

The most popular superhero team of all time, the X-Men commenced their comic book life in the year 1963. The team of mutants was thus born in a turbulent decade that saw the assassination of President John F. Kennedy, the start of the Vietnam War, and America embroiled in a Civil Rights Movement as controversial as it was widespread. Stan Lee and Jack Kirby created the X-Men as a response to the tumult they saw going on around them, wanting to make the idea of tolerance and diversity accessible to the young. Like all good superhero books, X-Men comics featured a strong and valuable moral subtext, in this case one regarding discrimination and bigotry.

In the beginning, the X-Men comic was the story of one unusual man and his dream. Bound to his wheelchair, the bald and rather severe Professor Xavier (or Professor X) was a powerful telepath. He had been harnessing his mental abilities since puberty (the onset of "mutantcy," according to the comic — a nice metaphor for the physical changes undergone during adolescence). Because he felt isolated as a young man, because mutants needed guidance to make the transition to adulthood, he formed a school, the Xavier Institute. This campus was, in fact, an academy of sorts where people that were "different" (read: mutants) could learn to control their powers responsibly and become valuable, contributing members of society.

Beneath the school, Xavier operated an underground headquarters replete with labs and an array of devices. More importantly, he led a brigade of his most gifted and powerful mutants, dubbed X-Men. Wearing yellow jumpsuits, this team would fight injustice and evil in the world, despite the discrimination they faced as a new kind of racial minority. Back in the 1960s, the original team consisted of Xavier, Cyclops (who, despite his name, actually had both eyes intact and could shoot dangerous laser beams from them), Iceman, the Beast and lovely Jean Grey, another powerful psychic.

In 1975 the X-Men received an upgrade, and it was at that time that their ranks swelled, adding memorable characters including Colossus, Banshee, Storm (who had the helpful ability to stir up the weather), and, best of all, Wolverine, an anger-prone mystery man with an "adamantium" metal skeleton and retractable claws. Though Wolverine looked half beast himself, with thick sideburns and a mane of wolfman-like hair, his attitude and strength very quickly made him the most popular X-Man.

Over the years, the X-Men occasionally appeared as guests in Marvel franchise cartoon series on TV (such as 1982's *Spider-Man and His Amazing Friends*), but the stalwart team didn't receive its own series until 1992. *X-Men: The Animated Series* ran on the Fox network Saturday mornings for five seasons, racking up some 76 episodes. The program earned amazing ratings, often besting all other network competition, and

Mutants in yellow spandex: A team shot from *X-Men: The Animated Series* (1992) showing traditional X-Men gear rather than the now ubiquitous black spandex of the feature films.

went into syndication in 1998 on UPN before a triumphant return to reruns on Fox Kids in the year 2000. This series featured Xavier, Jubilee, Storm, Gambit, Jean Grey and Wolverine as they fought Marvel's incredible array of X-Men villains, including the dastardly Magneto, Mr. Sinister, Apocalypse and others.

In 2000, X-Men fever swept America as a live-action, big-budget feature film was produced, and the X-Men returned to TV in a second animated series, *X-Men: Evolution*. This second series was sort of an "X-Men: the Next Generation," as Jean Grey, Xavier, Storm, Wolverine and the like were joined by many younger characters, such as Rogue (who could absorb other mutants' abilities), Spyke, Shadowcat, and Nightcrawler. *X-Men: Evolution* was even more popular than its predecessor, and some of the stories proved quite intriguing. Aired under the WB Networks' Kids banner, this series pitted the X-Men against shapeshifter Mystique, the beastly Sabertooth, the long-tongued Toad, the obese Blob, Quicksilver and Avalanche, among others.

One two-part episode, "The Cauldron," written by Simon Furman and directed by Gary Graham, involved Magneto's brutal "survival of the fittest" contest, as he arranged for a series of one-on-one combats between Xavier's mutants and his own. The winners would then be whisked off to a secret asteroid in space where they would carry the legacy of the future.

This grand battle was interesting not only because comic book fans always love such match-ups, placing odds on which mutant could defeat which, but because it coupled this big story with a more personal one. The "B" story was about the reunion of Cyclops with his brother Alex, who was tempted by Magneto's offer to join his "master race." It was a complex and involving story, especially for a half-hour-long animated series.

Other episodes were equally impressive. The mysterious origin of Wolverine was recounted (via flashbacks) in "Grim Reminder," and once more the well-structured teleplay (by writer Len Unley) featured a more personal, "slice-of-life" look at life at the Xavier School (via a new student writing home to his family).

Thoughtfully written, if crudely animated, *X-Men: Evolution* has already been on the air for two years, generating 24 episodes by the end of the second season. The third season was commencing as of this writing.

Though both animated series were well-received by fans, it was no doubt the 2000 *X-Men* feature film that first brought mass recognition to Marvel's nearly forty-year-old superhero team. At a cost of $75 million, the 20th Century–Fox film was a major event, directed by young Bryan Singer (*The Usual Suspects* [1995], *Apt Pupil* [1998]). To nobody's surprise, the A-budgeted picture boasted a remarkable cast. Patrick Stewart, *Star Trek: The Next Generation*'s Captain Picard, was a perfect Professor Xavier — temperate, honorable and wise.

He was joined by 2002 Academy Award winner Halle Berry as Storm, 1994 Academy Award winner Anna Paquin as Rogue, Ian McKellen (*Lord of the Rings* [2001]) as Magneto, Famke Jansen (*Goldeneye* [1995]) as Jean Grey, Bruce Davison (*Willard* [1971]) as Senator Kelly and James Marsden as Cyclops. But the actor that stole the show was no doubt Hugh Jackman as the loner Wolverine. After *X-Men*, Jackman became a bonafide star, headlining in *Swordfish* (again with Berry) and romantic comedies such as *Someone Like You* and *Kate and Leopold* (both 2001).

Singer's film adaptation began with a dark prologue in Nazi Germany as a young Jewish boy in 1944 Poland watched the mistreatment of his people at the hands of Hitler's soldiers. This boy, discriminated against and despised, grew up to become

Polar opposites: Professor Xavier (Patrick Stewart) faces off against his arch-nemesis, Magneto (Ian McKellen), during the final moments of *X-Men* (2000).

Magneto, a vengeful villain with the power to control metal, and, more to the point, a point of view about the real qualities of human nature.

This disturbing prologue was lensed in a rainy, gray, washed-out look, and the stylish opener kept the promise Singer had made, to remain faithful to the spirit of X-Men comics. Already, in its very first frames, the film took the subject material seriously and adhered to the theme of bigotry so prominent in Stan Lee's comic books.

In fact, many important symbols of Americana, and therefore its 200-year legacy of immigration and integration, appeared in *X-Men*, paying homage to the social underpinnings of Marvel's long-running series. Ellis Island, the Statue of Liberty and even a McCarthy-like senator all played prominent roles, reminding Americans of their place in human history, and of their achievements and failures in Civil Rights.

On these grounds, *The X-Men* was a flawless film, and Singer did a marvelous job dealing with the moral aspects of the story while drawing good performances from the actors. Even when Singer was deliberately unfaithful to the core concepts of the franchise (replacing the yellow X-Men jumpers with black ones), there were good reasons to do so. His film is one that was carefully crafted and respectful.

For many fans of the franchise, that was enough, and *X-Men* became a blockbuster with general audiences and a triumph for the fans. Many heralded the movie as the best comic-to-silver-screen adaptation yet, but that was hyperbole. While unfailingly good at handling the thematic elements of his screenplay, Singer failed — on a rather grand level — to endow *X-Men* with the cinematic scope it needed to become an epic, and a benchmark of the superhero genre. Much of the film was shot blandly, in close-ups and two shots, making the movie resemble an overblown TV series rather than the cinematic event it should have been. In addition, the action scenes proved terribly confusing and badly arranged. From a visual standpoint, the final battle atop the Statue of Liberty was almost a complete botch. Character perspectives, special effects backgrounds and inadequate CGI work all contributed to a weak finale that undercut the film's strong thematic elements. (A similar Statue of Liberty battle — and one set in the daytime, to boot — had been better realized in *Remo Williams: The Adventure Begins*, some fifteen years earlier.)

And, though shot with a sense of gravitas, some aspects of the *X-Men* film simply failed to come across. The comic relief one-liners (particularly Storm's query of Toad on the Statue of Liberty regarding what happens when lightning strikes a toad) were unbelievably bad. Hugh Jackman came off very well, appearing both dramatic and very funny, but most of the rest of the cast, particular Marsden, Jansen and Berry, were underutilized (admittedly a risk in any superhero "team" effort).

X2: X-Men United was released the first weekend of May 2003, the same weekend that Sam Raimi's *Spider-Man* had conquered a year earlier. As fans had hoped, Singer's respect for the popular comic-book material came through even more strongly in the sequel, and the resulting film revealed that the director had learned to have fun with the franchise and enliven the action sequences. The story was splashed across a wider canvas, with rousing battle scenes high in the sky, inside the Oval Office, in middle America and an underground fortress manned by the bad guys.

Halle Berry's Storm was more substantial the second time around, after the actress's Academy Award win in *Monster's Ball*, and Jackman's Wolverine was again a bad-ass action hero and a treat for fans. The film opened with a spectacular shoot-out in the White House as a mutant called Night-

Crawler (Alan Cumming) ambushed the president of the United States, and then introduced a delightful détente between good mutants (led by Patrick Stewart's Xavier) and bad ones (led by McKellen's Magneto) as they tried to figure out exactly who was behind the attack. As it turned out, there was only one bad apple pulling Nightcrawler's strings, and not surprisingly, that bad apple was a human being! General Stryker (Brian Cox) wanted to foster humanity's hatred for mutants and build a cerebro-style device to ferret the mutants out, wherever they might be in the world. Complicating matters, Stryker was a man with the key to Wolverine's past.

The *X-Men* sequel employed a new metaphor, comparing the mutants and their coming-of-age experience not to World War II and the Holocaust this time, but to a sort-of homosexual "coming out," with young Mutants forced to reveal to their family that they are "different" from others. Shawn Ashmore's Bobby/Iceman faced his family's disapproval and shock that he could be "one of those" people, and the film made a solid point while playing lightly (and inoffensively) with the idea. "Have you ever tried not being a mutant?" a desperate mother asked pointedly.

Also, considering the post–2001 environment in the United States, it was hard not to view *X2* as a parable of racial stereotyping and the profiling of Muslims who people feared might be terrorists. The mutants were derided by the government as "traitors" to the country. The U.S.A. of *X-Men 2* didn't have a privacy lacerating Patriot Act, but it did attempt to revive the Mutant Registration Act so prominent in the first franchise film, another law restricting the rights of a feared minority.

Fast-paced, exciting, good-humored and surprisingly relevant, *X2: X-Men United* even paused for a moment of pathos as one of the mutants sacrificed herself, Mr. Spock style, to save the team. A sure-footed and high-flying effort, the film met with real success at the box office and by late summer of 2003 had already outgrossed its predecessor, assuring an *X3* down the road.

X-Men: The Animated Series (1992–1997)
ANIMATED SERIES

VOICE TALENTS: Norm Spencer (Scott Summers/Cyclops); Cedric Smith (Professor Xavier); Cal Dodd (Logan/Wolverine); Alison Sealy-Smith (Storm); Chris Potter (Gambit); Catherine Disher (Jean Grey); Lenore Zann (Rogue); Alyson Court (Jubilee).

CREW: A Marvel Films/Saban Entertainment/Graz Entertainment Production. *Animation:* Akom.

X-Men (2000)
LIVE-ACTION FILM

"While it's clear Singer is neither a natural action director nor a visual craftsman—*X-Men* lacks both the baroque beauty of Tim Burton's *Batman* or the gee-whiz giddiness of Richard Donner's *Superman*—he's committed to imbuing his mutants with emotions using a restrained, sober tone that defies genre formulas.... [A] fun adaptation that overcomes its flaws..."
—Annabelle Villanueva, *Cinescape*, Volume 6, Number 8: "X-Appeal." November/December 2000, pages 72–73.

"This one [action movie] has a noisy climactic tussle inside the Statue of Liberty. Mightn't a few feds be guarding the premises? Again, no. It's a mistake for a fantasy film in the realistic mode to be deficient in both magic and plausibility.... A muted film ends on a minor chord."
—Richard Corliss, *Time:* "Where's the Wow Factor? Dour and Draggy, This Live-Action Film of the Marvel Comics Superheroes Series Is Less Than Marvelous." July 24, 2000, page 65l.

"When the film version isn't assaulting you with gizmos, it's an awkward, depersonalized piece of hackwork, and a rather earthbound one at that. This is a movie that was shot in Toronto and looks it. As directed by Bryan Singer, it has a diffuse, stop-and-go rhythm that makes it hard to tell where dystopian ominousness leaves off and sluggish amateurishness begins."
—Owen Gleiberman, *Entertainment Weekly:* "Un 'X'-ceptional: The Sci-Fi Fantasy X-Men Has Dazzling Effects That Overpower the Movie's Team of Mutant Superheroes." July 21, 2000, page 50.

"*The X-Men* represents the challenge in making superhero films in the present day and age—particularly moody superhero films. The film is almost weighed down by its own seriousness, which is in keeping with the comic, to the point where it never gets the viewer's blood boiling. The mutants in this film and in the comic are portrayed as victims, and therein lies the rub. Can a hero be portrayed as a victim? Is Batman portrayed as a victim, even though he is? The X-Men represent a team of very powerful mutants who don't really like each other all that much. It's fascinating to think of how the character of Wolverine has taken over the franchise—the X-Men were a fairly happy-go-lucky bunch in their earliest incarnations in the comics, but now, they're very, very serious. Spider-Man is a refreshing counterpoint, with his incessant wisecracking, but judging a franchise like this on only one film may be unfair—establishing the backstory, particularly a complex back story, eats up a lot of screen time. The next film will hopefully show us what the franchise can do without the restraints or need to establish the reality. That said, Patrick Stewart was born to play Professor Xavier."
—William Latham, author of *Mary's Monster, Space: 1999 Resurrection.*

"Look, I'm a purist, I prefer costumes on my superheroes. I'm not of the commonly held belief that every character must look like he or she walked out of *The Matrix* or *Blade*. But as far as the characterizations in *The X-Men* go, they were pretty close to the comics. Hugh Jackman was great, and overall it was a very good translation. But I thought Halle Berry was terrible as Storm. Just very flat."

— Howard Margolin, host of *Destinies: The Voice of Science Fiction.*

CAST: Patrick Stewart (Professor Charles Xavier); Ian McKellen (Magneto); Hugh Jackman (Logan/Wolverine); Anna Paquin (Rogue/Marie); James Marsden (Cyclops); Halle Berry (Storm); Famke Jansen (Jean Grey); Ray Parks (Toad); Bruce Davison (Senator Kelly); Rebecca Romijn Stamos (Mystique); Tyler Mane (Sabretooth).

CREW: 20th Century–Fox and Marvel Entertainment Group Presents *X-Men. Directed by:* Bryan Singer. *Screenplay by:* David Hayter. *Story by:* Tom De Santo and Bryan Singer. *Produced by:* Lauren Schuler Donner and Ralph Winter. *Executive Producers:* Avi Arad, Stan Lee. *Executive Producers:* Richard Donner, Tom De Santo. *Director of Photography:* Newton Thomas Sigel. *Production Designer:* John Myhre. *Edited by:* Steven Rosenblum, Kevin Stitt, John Wright. *Co-Producers:* Joel Simon, William S. Rodman. *Visual Effects Supervisor:* Michael Fink. *Special Make-up Design:* Gordon Smith. *Music:* Michael Kamen. *Costume Designer:* Louise Mingenbach. *Casting:* Roger Mussenden. *First Assistant Director:* Lee Cleary. *Stunt Coordinators:* Gary Jensen, Rick Forsayeth. *Associate Producers:* Karen Feige, Scott Nimerfrod. *Art Directors:* Tamara Deverell, Paul Denham Austerberry. *Set Decorator:* James Edward Ferrell. *Set Designers:* Gordon White, Thomas Carnegie. *Production Coordinator:* Janine Anderton. *Costume Consultant:* Bob Ringwood. *Chief Make-up:* Anne Brodie. *Special Effects Consultant:* Colin Chilvers. *Special Make-up Effects:* FX Smith, Inc. *Visual Effects Director of Photography:* David Stump. *Special Visual Effect and Digital Animation:* Digital Domain. *Visual Effects and Animation:* Cinesite. *Visual Effects:* Hammerhead Inc., Pop Film and Animation, Inc. *M.P.A.A. Rating:* PG-13. *Running time:* 120 minutes.

In the not-too-distant future, a powerful mutant girl flees her home, terrified of her strange powers, even as the U.S. Senate debates Senator Kelly's discriminatory Mutant Registration Law. At the hearing, a wise mutant, wheelchair-bound Professor Charles Xavier, attempts to convince a cynical friend, concentration camp survivor Eric, that humans won't threaten the mutant populace. But hate-mongering Senator Kelly undercuts the point.

Meanwhile, the runaway girl, Rogue, befriends a pugilistic mutant, Wolverine, in Canada. Wolverine can sprout blades and metal out of his body, but he has no memory of how he acquired this ability. Confronted on a snowy road by one of Eric's agents of evil (Sabretooth), Wolverine and Rogue are defended by two of Xavier's students, X-Men Storm and Cyclops. They learn that Eric, actually a supervillain called Magneto, has secret plans for either Wolverine or Rogue, who can absorb the powers of other mutants.

Magneto kidnaps Senator Kelly and replaces the conservative politician with a doppelganger, actually a shapeshifting mutant called Mystique. Then Magneto uses a powerful new weapon to turn Kelly into a mutant himself.

At Xavier's school, Wolverine gets to know the inner circle of X-Men, making a play for the lovely and telepathic Jean Grey, who is romantically involved with the laser-eyed Cyclops. As relationships develop, Mystique infiltrates the school and convinces Rogue to leave Xavier's care because her power to steal the abilities of other mutants is dangerous. When the X-Men realize Rogue has left, Xavier uses a mind-enhancing device called Cerebro to telepathically locate her. He finds her at a train station and deploys his students to retrieve her. Unfortunately, Sabretooth and the evil Toad are already there, making trouble for Cyclops, Wolverine and Storm, a beautiful African-American with the ability to harness meteorological forces. In the end, Rogue is captured by Magneto.

Senator Kelly, now a mutant, arrives at the school and laboratory of the X-Men, and Xavier telepathically learns of the machine that mutates humans. He discovers that the machine draws power from Magneto at great physical cost and pain, and that his "friend" wants Rogue because she can use her power to harness his strength, use the machine, and then die powering it.

Meanwhile, Kelly doesn't survive his transition into a mutant, and Xavier is injured when Mystique sabotages Cerebro. That leaves the other X-Men to fly to Ellis Island and save a gathering of World Leaders from Magneto's plan to turn them into mutants.

A battle royale commences on Liberty Island, with the X-Men victorious. Magneto is captured, rogue is rescued, and Xavier healed. Wolverine, still mystified by his origins, sets out in search of his true nature.

X-Men: Evolution (2000–)
ANIMATED SERIES

VOICE TALENTS: Meghan Black, Richard Cox, Neil Denis, Michael Dobson, Michael Donovan, Noel Fisher, Christopher Gray, Matt Hill, Christopher Judge, David Kaye, Scott McNeill, Kirby Morrow, Maggie Blue O'Hara, Brad Swaik, Venus Tenzo, Colleen Wheeler, Kirsten Williamson.

CREW: *Executive Producers:* Rick Ungar, John Bush, Avi Arad, John Hyde, Stan Lee. *Producer:* Boyd Kirkland. *Story Editors:* Greg Johnson, Bob Forward. *Animation Producer:* Mike Wolf. *Animation Executive Producers:* John Bush, John Hyde. *Original Music:* William Anderson. *Characters Designed by:* Steven E. Gordon. *Assistant Character Design:* Kimberly Bowles. *Background Supervisor:* Ted Blackman. *Background Design:* Christian Lignan, Alan M.W. Simmons, George W. Stokes. *Storyboard Artists:* Rick Farley, Garay Graham. From Marvel Studios and Film Roman Productions.

X2: X-Men United (2003)
LIVE-ACTION FILM

"*X2: X-Men United* is a substantial improvement over *X-Men* in many ways, especially in visual and special effects departments. Director Bryan Singer returns to lord it over a comic-book universe that dazzles."
— Jami Bernard, *The New York Daily News:* "Same claws, but better FX, Wolverine & Co's sequel turns up the power a notch." May 2003, page 1 of 2, www.dailynews.com

"As eye-filling as it is, it's hard not to feel that the film suffers from sequel-itis: the bloom is off the rose, the magic is roughly the same as before…. Still, on a purely visceral level, the movie is a doozy."
— William Arnold, *The Seattle Post-Intelligencer:* "Exhilarating *X2* is sure to leave fans united." May 2, 2002, page 1 of 2, *www.seattlepi.com*

"*X2* can boast of a more polished script, vastly improved special effects, lengthier battle sequences and a longer running time … that gives more players more time to strut their stuff. But I can't claim that it's a better movie than the first flick, which among other attributes, displayed a sense of wonder that's been replaced here by a business-as-usual attitude emblematic of many big budget affairs."
— Matt Brunson, *Creative Loafing* (Charlotte): "The X-Philes: Exciting Sequel Rewards Faithful Fans." May 7, 2003, page 1 of 1. *www.creativeloafing.com*

CAST: Patrick Stewart (Professor Charles Xavier); Ian McKellen (Magneto); Hugh Jackman (Logan/Wolverine); Anna Paquin (Rogue/Marie); James Marsden (Cyclops); Halle Berry (Storm); Famke Jansen (Jane Grey); Bruce Davison (Senator Kelly); Rebecca Romijn Stamos (Mystique); Brian Cox (General Stryker); Alan Cumming (Night Crawler); Aaron Stanford (Pyro); Shawn Ashmore (Bobby/Iceman); Cotter Smith (U.S. President).

CREW: 20th Century–Fox and Marvel Entertainment Group presents *X-Men. Directed by:* Bryan Singer. *Produced by:* Lauren Schuler Donner and Ralph Winter. *Executive Producers:* Avi Arad, Stan Lee, Tom De Santo, Bryan Singer *Director of Photography:* Newton Thomas Sigel. *Film Editors:* Elliott Graham, John Ottman. *Music:* John Ottman. *Casting:* Coreen Mayrs, Roger Mussender. *Story by:* Zak Penn, David

Hayter, Bryan Singer. *Screenplay by:* Michael Daugherty, Dan Harris, David Hayter. *Co-producers:* Ross Fanger, Kevin Feige. *M.P.A.A. Rating:* PG-13. *Running time:* 135 minutes.

A mutant assault on the president of the United States in the White House is the only excuse that a hateful and paranoid General Stryker requires to launch a raid against Xavier's school. While Storm and Jean Grey are out of town investigating the Oval Office attack, a military team strikes the school and begins rounding up the innocent mutant students. At the same time, Cyclops and Professor Xavier are abducted by Stryker's forces as they visit the imprisoned Magneto. Back at the school, an angry Wolverine rescues a few mutant kids, getting many of them to safety. With Rogue, Iceman and Pyro in tow, Wolverine heads off to find Jean and Storm and find out what is happening.

As Jean Grey's telepathic powers grow, the X-Men catch up with one another and soon make unlikely allies in Magneto and Mystique, who realize that Stryker must be stopped, lest all mutants in the world be destroyed. Stryker has a daring plan. Using his own son, a mutant who can project fantasies, Stryker hopes to steal the secret of Cerebro from Professor Xavier's mind. If he is successful, the new Cerebro could be utilized to pinpoint and then telepathically murder all mutants in an instant! The X-Men and their former enemies head north, to Xavier's top secret underground installation, to prevent this terrible reality from coming to pass. Cyclops has been brainwashed to hate his former allies, and a new foe waits to greet Wolverine.

Unfortunately, one of the X-Men will not survive the final confrontation.

Part III
Conclusion

Superheroes will remain a staple of America's popular culture for years to come, especially with the success of *Spider-Man*, *Daredevil*, and so many other adaptations already in the pipeline. The question is not if superheroes will continue to thrive on our movie and TV screens, but in what ways.

Of all superhero productions, few have successfully gone beyond fan expectations or Hollywood misconceptions about the genre, but one must wonder, will that continue to be the case? The success of *Buffy the Vampire Slayer* on TV suggests that some serious action, a little situationally appropriate humor, and a few self-referential rips at the conventions of the genre combine to make a workable formula. Either intentionally or not, *Spider-Man* and *Smallville* mimic that approach, respecting their source material but including little in-jokes for in-the-know fans to relish.

One thing is certain: the days of camp are over. That approach was purged in the overcompensating fire of the Dark Age, and future superhero productions will be liberated by the fact that they no longer have so much to prove, such high hurdles to jump.

On the other hand, fans have become more vocal about their likes and dislikes, courtesy of Internet posting boards. Fan response to *Batman and Robin* (1997) mothballed the Dark Knight's movie franchise

for six years and counting. Likewise, bad Internet word of mouth, most of it unjustified, photon-torpedoed the most recent *Star Trek* film, *Nemesis* (2002). Is it possible that this new level of online nitpicking will set the superhero genre back again, downing unfaithful "re-imaginations" like the proposed J.J. Abrams *Superman* re-do? Will purists, so intent on keeping the faith, actually scare off Hollywood producers from adapting comic books and superhero properties?

That is one possible future, no doubt, and at this point in the history of the genre there is a dawning realization that it is the newer, less storied heroes — those from *Buffy*, *Blade* and the like — that may succeed. Why? Simply because these icons need not contend with the heavy weight of seventy years of beloved back story, and therefore possess fewer targets for fans to attack.

This encyclopedia began with the notion that superheroes are uniquely American and modern creations, though based on old human truths and myths. As America marches into the unknown future, so will our heroes reflect the next steps of the journey. The immigrant that makes good (Superman), the injured orphan out for revenge (Batman), the Civil Rights crusaders (the X-Men), and the little girl with the strength and fortitude of a dozen men (Buffy) may all lose their value to this nation as older contexts pass into the mists of history. What new American stories and trends will spur the heroes and adventures of tomorrow, and what will they look like?

Tune in tomorrow to find out. Same bat time. Same bat channel.

Appendix A

CONVENTIONS AND CLICHÉS OF SUPERHERO FILMS AND LIVE-ACTION TELEVISION

Some of the best stories ever told, based on myth, bear repeating. Others don't. By its very nature, the superhero genre is thoroughly repetitive, dealing with the creation and development of a being who becomes "super" and stops evil forces. Listed below are some of the most common clichés or conventions of the genre. To be included, the cliché or convention had to appear in at least three different productions (television or film). These examples are not necessarily the only conventions, but certainly some of the most common.

Amnesia

Superheroes carry the great burden of responsibility, and sometimes they desperately yearn to escape their duties, even for a moment. Well, in the ever-popular amnesia story that is precisely what happens. Destiny, duty and memory are all forgotten, and heroes must rediscover their true nature. Sometimes that's a bittersweet thing — rediscovering that the weight of the world is on your shoulders. Amnesia may also afflict both sidekicks and supervillains.

The Adventures of Superman: "Panic in the Sky"
The Adventures of Superman: "The Secret of Superman"
The Adventures of Superman: "The Big Forget"
Man from Atlantis: "Man from Atlantis"
The Incredible Hulk: "Of Guilt, Models and Murder"
The Incredible Hulk: "Mystery Man"
Superman II
The Adventures of Superboy: "Superboy ... Lost"
Lois and Clark: "All Shook Up"
Buffy the Vampire Slayer: "Halloween"
Buffy the Vampire Slayer: "Tabula Rosa"
Angel: "Spin the Bottle"
Mutant X: "Presumed Guilty"

The Biker/Motorcycle Gang

Motorcycle-riding gangs have been the favorite villains of televised superheroes for twenty years. Leatherclad, bearded, traveling in packs, they form a potent menace for our heroes.

The Greatest American Hero: "Hog Wild"   *Automan:* "Renegade Run"
The Incredible Hulk: "Long Run Home"   *Birds of Prey:* "Primal Scream"

Bounty Hunters

Sometimes even the most competent arch-nemesis can't seem to get the job done, so he/she puts a price on the hero's head and hires a mercenary to off those pesky superheroes.

The Incredible Hulk: "Bring Me the Head of the Hulk"   *Birds of Prey:* "Slick"
Buffy the Vampire Slayer: "Homecoming"   *Daredevil*

Bugs and Bugmeisters

The men and women who control creepy-crawly bugs often decide to pit these critters against superheroes.

Wonder Woman: "Formicida"   *Smallville:* "Metamorphosis"
Now and Again: "The Bugmeister"   *Smallville:* "Drone"

The Carnival/Circus:
Something Wicked This Way Comes

Although ostensibly a place of fun and happiness, the carnival, at least in superhero productions, is a place of spies, criminals and danger.

The Six Million Dollar Man: "Carnival of Spies"
The Man from Atlantis: "Deadly Carnival"
The Incredible Hulk: "Sideshow"
The Greatest American Hero: "Just Another Three Ring Circus"
The Adventures of Superboy: "Carnival"
The Crow: Stairway to Heaven: "Voices"

Chinatown

In this cliché, the hero must visit the Asian portion of town, usually Little China or Chinatown, to help exploited residents there.

The Green Hornet: "The Preying Mantis"   *Manimal:* "Breath of the Dragon"
The Incredible Hulk: "East Winds"   *Dark Angel:* "Radar Love"
The Incredible Hulk: "Another Path"

Deep Freeze

A trope of the genre, "freeze rays" (or other manifestations of "extreme cold") are often deployed by cold-hearted villains.

The Adventures of Superman: "The Big Freeze"
Batman: "Instant Freeze"
Batman: "Green Ice"
Misfits of Science: "Deep Freeze"

Buffy the Vampire Slayer: "Smashed"
Smallville: "Cool"
Batman and Robin

Dr. Jekyll, I Presume?

The gent on the surface; the beast within. Since superhero stories often deal with the duality of human nature, the schizophrenic Jekyll/Hyde dynamic frequently appears in superhero productions.

Man from Atlantis: "C.W. Hyde"
The Incredible Hulk: series premise
Buffy the Vampire Slayer: "Beauty and the Beasts"
Smallville: "Nocturne"

Mutant X: "Double Vision"
Mutant X: "Altered Ego"
Spider-Man (2002)
Birds of Prey: "Split"

The Dogged Reporter

Superheroes get no rest, especially from pesky reporters who seem bound and determined to expose their secret identities.

Lois Lane (*The Adventures of Superman, Superman: The Movie, Superman II, Superman III, Superman IV: The Quest for Peace, Lois and Clark: The New Adventures of Superman*)
Mike Axford (*The Green Hornet*)
Knox (*Batman*)
Chloe (*Smallville*)
Urich (*Daredevil*)

Double Vision: Doppelgangers, Imposters and Evil Twins

Villainous doubles and twins are constantly showing up in superhero productions to pester and often frame stalwart superheroes. Sometimes side-kicks get "doubled" too.

The Adventures of Superman: "Double Trouble"
The Adventures of Superman: "The Face and the Voice"
The Adventures of Superman: "Jimmy the Kid"
The Adventures of Superman: "Divide and Conquer"
The Green Hornet: "Corpse of the Year"
The Six Million Dollar Man: "Look Alike"
The Bionic Woman: "Deadly Ringer"
The Gemini Man: "Sam Casey, Sam Casey"
Wonder Woman: "Stolen Faces"

ElectraWoman and DynaGirl: "Spider Lady"
The Incredible Hulk: "Broken Image"
Superman III
Buffy the Vampire Slayer: "Doppelgangland"
Dark Angel: "Pollo Loco"
Smallville: "X-Ray"
Smallville: "Dichotomy"
Witchblade: "Diplopia"
Witchblade: "Palindrome"

Electric Bugaloo

The Power to harness electricity is not one to be taken lightly, and many heroes and villains in the history of superhero productions have been able to zap people with lightning and other manifestations of electric power.

Man from Atlantis: "Hawk of Mu"
The Greatest American Hero: "The Shock Will Kill You"
Misfits of Science: series character Johnny B.
M.A.N.T.I.S.: "Switches"
Mutant X: series character Brennan Mulwray
Angel: recurring character, Gwen Raiden

Enronitis, the Corporate Crooks

We all know that corporate America is corrupt. Superhero television shows and films knew it first. When will we learn?

Automan: "*Unreasonable Facsimile*"
RoboCop
RoboCop 2
RoboCop 3

RoboCop: The Television Series
Now and Again: "The Insurance Man Always Rings Twice"
RoboCop: Prime Directives

Evil Rockers/Rock Music/Rock Concerts

In line with the thinking that rock music lyrics are evil, superhero programs have often presented villainous musicians, malicious music and other music-related issues (notably, trouble at concerts).

Wonder Woman: "The Pied Piper"
ElectraWoman and DynaGirl: "Glitter Rock"
The Incredible Hulk: "Metamorphosis"
Automan: "Murder MTV"
Black Scorpion: "Face the Music"

The Adventures of Superboy:
  "Bringing Down the House"
The Adventures of Superboy: "Superstar"
Lois and Clark: "Wall of Sound"

Exposed! (or Almost Exposed...)

Despite their best efforts, superheroes often find their secret identities discovered by the bad guys, or even by reporters.

The Adventures of Superman: "The Stolen Costume"
The Adventures of Superman: "Shot in the Dark"
The Adventures of Superman: "The Dog Who Knew Superman"
The Adventures of Superman: "Semi-Private Eye"
The Six Million Dollar Man: "The Peeping Blonde"
The Amazing Spider-Man: "The Deadly Dust"
The Incredible Hulk: "Proof Positive"
The Incredible Hulk: "Deathmask"
M.A.N.T.I.S.: "To Prey in Darkness"
Black Scorpion: "Blinded by the Light"

Fight Club

In a multitude of superhero productions, characters are abducted and forced to fight opponents in an underground fight club, a modern-day gladiatorial ring.

M.A.N.T.I.S.: "Gloves Off"   *Witchblade:* "Palindrome"   *Angel:* "The Ring"

Fire!

Arsonists, psychic fire starters and spontaneous combustion have all challenged superheroes throughout the history of the genre.

Captain Nice: "Is Big Town Burning?"
The Green Hornet: "The Hornet and the Firefly"
The Incredible Hulk: "Wild Fire"
The Greatest American Hero: "Fire, Man"
M.A.N.T.I.S.: "Fire in the Heart"

Now and Again: "Fire and Ice"
Now and Again: "Disco Inferno"
Nightman: "Burning Love"
Black Scorpion: "Love Burns"
Black Scorpion: "Fire and Brimstone"
Mutant X: "Crimes of the New Century"

Gargoyle Pose

It's an iconic shot. A shorthand to coolness. Your favorite superhero stands proudly in costume, physique incredible, looking out over his/her city, against the gothic urban jungle of skyscrapers. (Disclaimer: not all of these examples of the "gargoyle pose" include actual gargoyles.)

Batman (1989)
Batman Returns (1992)
Black Scorpion (1995)
Black Scorpion 2: After Shocks (1996)
Spawn (1997)

Dark Angel (2000–2002)
Spider-Man (2002)
Birds of Prey (2002-2003)
Daredevil (2003)

Greedy Land Developers

Land is our most valuable resource, and crooks are always out to exploit it. Until superheroes come to the rescue.

Superman: The Movie   *The Adventures of Superboy:* "Troubled Waters"
Wonder Woman: "The Deadly Dolphin"   *The Adventures of Superboy:*
The Incredible Hulk: "Triangle"   "The Invisible People"

Heroes on Wheels

Intrinsically a genre about mankind overcoming obstacles and disabilities, superhero films and television shows offer a handful of wheelchair-bound heroes and sidekicks, limited by their paralysis but not their heroism.

Dr. Miles Hawkins (*M.A.N.T.I.S.*)   Logan Cale (*Dark Angel*)
Sparks (*Steel*)   Barbara Gordon/Oracle (*Birds of Prey*)

Hooray for Hollywood

In this cliché, a superhero travels to Tinsel Town and becomes enmeshed in the production of a movie.

The Adventures of Superman: "Czar of the Underworld"
Wonder Woman: "Wonder Woman in Hollywood"
Automan: "Murder Take One"
The Adventures of Superboy: "Hollywood"

Horse Sense

The horse once played a crucial role in westerns, the predecessors of the superhero genre. Now horses have a habit of showing up in superhero adventures, perhaps as a link to the past, or perhaps because the noble creatures still peak our interest even in the twenty-first century.

The Adventures of Superman: "Joey"   *The Incredible Hulk:* "Rainbow's End"
Batman: "Horse of Another Color"   *Manimal:* "High Stakes"
Shazam: "Thou Shall Not Kill"

I Demand a Recount: A Mayoral Election

All politics are local. There is always a spoiler running for mayor in superhero film and TV, either a super-villain or a superhero. Sometimes the Supreme Court chooses the winner.

Batman: "Hizzoner the Penguin"   *Nightman:* "The People's Choice"
Batman Returns   *Black Scorpion:* "Face the Music"
Lois & Clark: "Tempus, Anyone?"

I Made You? You Made Me!

This is the cliché in which superhero and super-villain learn that they are each responsible for making the other one what they are. Joker killed Batman's parents, thus creating the Dark Knight. The Dark Knight let Jack Napier fall into a vat of toxic chemicals, thus making Joker.

Batman (1989)   *The Flash* (1990)   *The Crow* (1994)   *Daredevil* (2003)

Invisibility

Now you see 'em, now you don't. Invisible heroes and villains have become a mainstay of superhero productions over the decades.

The Greatest American Hero:
  "Here's Looking at You Kid"
The Flash: "Sight Unseen"
Lois & Clark: "I'm Looking Through You"

Buffy the Vampire Slayer: "Invisible Girl"
Buffy the Vampire Slayer: "Gone"
Smallville: "Shimmer"
Mutant X: "Whiter Shade of Pale"

Justice Is Blind, and So Am I...

Sightless characters that witness crimes, fight evil, or have enhanced senses form a unique corner of superherodom.

The Incredible Hulk: "Blind Rage"   *Angel:* "Blind Date"   *Daredevil* (premise)

Lost Powers

What's the worst thing that could happen to a proud superhero? Waking up one morning and learning that his/her superheroic powers have gone with the wind ...

Superman II
Lois and Clark: "Ultra Woman"
Crow: City of Angels

Buffy the Vampire Slayer: "Helpless"
Smallville: "Leech"

Misfits, Mutants and Meta-Humans

In the 1990s and early 2000s, mutants, misfits, and meta-humans populated superhero productions. Trust a few. Fear the rest.

Misfits of Science: series premise
The Adventures of Superboy: "Mutant"
Generation X: television movie premise
Dark Angel: series premise

X-Men: movie premise
Mutant X: series premise
Smallville: series premise
Birds of Prey: series premise

Murdered Parents

Vengeance must be wrought so cool action scenes can occur. And what is the most common cause of vengeance in the genre: the murder of a superhero's mom or dad, or both.

Batman   *Birds of Prey* (Huntress/Catwoman)   *Black Scorpion*
Daredevil   *The Phantom*

The Newlywed Game

Another reliable cliché, in which a superhero and his intended (usually the damsel in distress) investigate some kind of "scam" by posing as a newly married couple.

The Adventures of Superman: "Superman's Wife"   *Superman II*
The Six Million Dollar Man: *Lois and Clark:*
   "Target: Steve Austin"   "Honeymoon in Metropolis"

No Reservations (the Native American Story)

When they aren't visiting Chinatown, superheroes find themselves involved with Indian burial grounds, vision quests, or other aspects of Native American mythology.

The Adventures of Superman: "Test of a Warrior"
The Six Million Dollar Man: "To Catch the Eagle"
The Adventures of Superboy: "The Birdman of the Swamps"
Buffy the Vampire Slayer: "Pangs"
The Crow: Stairway to Heaven: "Before I Wake"
Smallville: "Skinwalker"

Obituary for a Superhero

The headline blares the terrible, unbelievable news: Superman is dead! But we know better, don't we?

The Adventures of Superboy: "Obituary for a Superhero"
The Death of the Incredible Hulk
Buffy the Vampire Slayer: "The Gift"
The Tick: "The Funeral"

The One and Only? (the Superhero Predecessor)

The cliché in which a superhero learns that before he/she came along, there was another, one that has inevitably been killed in battle or gone rogue.

The Greatest American Hero: *Buffy the Vampire Slayer:* "Restless"
   "Don't Mess with Him"   *Now and Again:* "I Am the Greatest"
The Incredible Hulk: "Kindred Spirits"   *The Incredible Hulk:* "The First"

Origin of a Superhero

Probably the most commonly told superhero story: how it all started, how a person came to be a superhero.

The Adventures of Superman: "Superman on Earth"
Wonder Woman: "Wonder Woman"
The Six Million Dollar Man: "The Six Million Dollar Man"
The Bionic Woman: "The Bionic Woman"
The Incredible Hulk: "The Incredible Hulk"
The Greatest American Hero: "The Greatest American Hero"
Buffy the Vampire Slayer: "Fool for Love" (origin of Spike)
The Crow: Stairway to Heaven: "The Soul Can't Rest"

Now and Again: "Origins"
Sheena: "Buried Secrets"
Smallville: "Smallville"

Red Kryptonite

What evil plan or object could make our beloved superheroes act out of character?

The Adventures of Superboy: "Super Menace"   *Smallville:* "Red"
Lois and Clark: "Individual Responsibility"

Road Trip

In this convention, superheroes and their sidekicks band together and hit the roads of America, usually squabbling while in such close quarters.

The Six Million Dollar Man: "Cross Country   *The Incredible Hulk:* "Fast Lane"
   Kidnap"   *Buffy the Vampire Slayer:* "Spiral"
The Greatest American Hero: "The Hit Car"

Run, Forrest, Run!!!! (Running for Your Life)

In this cliché, a superhero has no choice but to flee the city, sometimes from an enemy, sometimes from the law.

The Green Hornet: "Bad Bet on a 459-Silent"   *The Gemini Man:* "Run, Sam, Run"
The Six Million Dollar Man: "Run, Steve, Run"   *M.A.N.T.I.S.:* "Thou Shall Not Kill"
The Six Million Dollar Man: *Now and Again:* "The Eggman Cometh"
   "Steve Austin, Fugitive"   *The Bionic Woman:* "On the Run"

Send in the Clones

Superheroes seem constantly to be running into defective clones, creatures with the heroes' DNA but usually not their dedication to justice.

M.A.N.T.I.S.: "Progenitor"   *Lois and Clark:* "Seconds"
The Flash: "Twin Streaks"   *Dark Angel:* "She Ain't Heavy"
Lois and Clark: "Vatman"   *Black Scorpion:* "Zodiac Attack Part 2"

Shape-shifters

The technology of morphing has resulted in a whole new class of villains and heroes, those who can shape-shift into any creature on Earth.

Manimal: series premise   *Sheena:* series premise
RoboCop: "Faces of Eve"   *Smallville:* "X-Ray"
Lois and Clark: "Big Girls Don't Fly"   *Smallville:* "Skinwalker"
Nightman: "Face to Face"   *Birds of Prey:* "Slick"
X-Men: character, Mystique

Tech Support

In superhero productions these days there always seems to be a sidekick who sits in front of a laptop computer and provides important information to the hero. He/she often wears a headset or searches the Net at an appropriate moment, providing just the information necessary to defeat a villain.

Sparky (*Steel*)   Raleigh (*Nightman*)   Logan (*Dark Angel*)
Willow (*Buffy the Vampire Slayer*) Oracle (*Birds of Prey*)   Chloe (*Smallville*)

Technical Knockout: The Big Boxing Match

There's always some terrible crook out there who wants a good, talented athlete to throw the big game (or boxing match) and take a fall. The superhero, of course, is there to help.

The Adventures of Superman: "No Holds Barred"
Batman: "Ring Around the Riddler"
The Gemini Man: "Eight — Nine — Ten — You're Dead"
The Incredible Hulk: "The Final Round"
The Adventures of Superboy: "The Fixer"
Lois and Clark: "Requiem for a Superhero"
Now and Again: "I Am the Greatest"
Daredevil

Time Travel

Superheroes have a propensity to move back and forward through time, encountering villains and friends from the past and future.

The Adventures of Superman: "Through the Time Barrier"
The Six Million Dollar Man: "Just a Matter of Time"
Wonder Woman: Time Bomb"
Man from Atlantis: "Shoot Out at Land's End"
ElectraWoman and DynaGirl: "The Sorcerer"
M.A.N.T.I.S.: "The Eyes Beyond"
Lois and Clark: "Tempus Fugitive"
Mutant X: "Time Squared"

The Trial

The cliché in which a superhero, superhero sidekick, or villain must stand trial, universally for a crime they didn't commit.

The Trial of the Incredible Hulk
The Flash: "Trial of the Trickster"
Lois and Clark: "The People vs. Lois Lane"
The Crow: Stairway to Heaven: "The People vs. Eric Draven"
The Tick: "Tick vs. Justice"

Undercover Hero

This week our stalwart hero must go undercover as a (fill in the blank) to stop a deadly criminal! This cliché would fill a small volume, so only *some* examples appear below.

The Six Million Dollar Man: "Target in the Sky" (lumberjack)
The Six Million Dollar Man: "The Blue Flash" (longshoreman)
The Six Million Dollar Man: "Bionic Badge" (cop)
The Six Million Dollar Man: "The Thunderbird Connection" (pilot)
The Six Million Dollar Man: "The Infiltrators" (boxer)
The Six Million Dollar Man: "Rollback" (roller derby participant)
The Six Million Dollar Man: "Walk a Deadly Wing" (air show wing walker)
The Bionic Woman: "Bionic Beauty" (beauty pageant contestant)
The Bionic Woman: "Fly Jaime" (stewardess)
The Bionic Woman: "The Ghosthunter" (nanny)
The Bionic Woman: "In This Corner, Jaime Sommers" (wrestler)
The Bionic Woman: "Sister, Jaime" (nun)
The Bionic Woman: "Jaime's Shield" (cop)
The Gemini Man: "Suspect Your Local Police" (cop)
Wonder Woman: "Beauty on Parade" (beauty pageant contestant)
Wonder Woman: "Hot Wax" (recording artist)

Vampires

Vampires really get around, starring not just in horror shows, but menacing superheroes in film and television. Call it fresh blood.

The Adventures of Superboy: "Young Dracula"
The Adventures of Superboy: "Run, Dracula, Run"
Buffy the Vampire Slayer: series premise
Angel: series premise

Nightman: "Constant Craving"
Mutant X: "The Lazarus Syndrome"
Blade and *Blade 2*

Visiting Dignitaries

The stock plot for a superhero TV program involves a visiting emissary from a foreign country (usually the Middle East) targeted for assassination or embroiled in a crime.

Batman: "A Riddle a Day Keeps the Riddler Away"
Batman: "The Joker Trumps an Ace"
Captain Nice: "How Sheik Can You Get?"
Green Hornet: "Trouble for Prince Charming"
The Amazing Spider-Man: "Escort to Danger"
M.A.N.T.I.S.: "Cease Fire"

The Wild Children

They were raised in the wild, sometimes by animals, and now they must reintegrate into society.

The Six Million Dollar Man: "The Wolf Boy"   *Sheena:* "The Feral King"
Manimal: "Female of the Species"

Your Show or Mine? (the Crossover)

What's better than one superhero? Why two, of course. In this cliché, one superhero with his/her own series visits another superhero with their own program.

Batman: "A Piece of the Action" (*The Green Hornet*)
The Six Million Dollar Man: "Return of the Bionic Woman" (*The Bionic Woman*)
The Six Million Dollar Man: "Welcome Home Jaime" (*The Bionic Woman*)
The Bionic Woman: "A Thing of the Past" (*The Six Million Dollar Man*)
The Bionic Woman: "Return of Big Foot" (*The Six Million Dollar Man*)
Isis: "The Funny Girl" (*Shazam!*)
Isis: "Now You See It" (*Shazam!*)
Buffy the Vampire Slayer: "Pangs" (*Angel*)
Nightman: "Manimal" (*Manimal*)
Angel: "In the Dark" (*Buffy the Vampire Slayer*)
Angel: "I Will Remember You" (*Buffy the Vampire Slayer*)
Angel: "Five by Five" (*Buffy the Vampire Slayer*)
Angel: "Sanctuary" (*Buffy the Vampire Slayer*)

The Youth Stealer/Sucker/Succubus

In which some nasty-spirited ghoul, scientist steals the youth and vigor of the good guys.

The Adventures of Superboy: "Metamorphosis"   *Angel:* "Carpe Noctem"
Lois and Clark: "Brutal Youth"   *Smallville:* "Redux"
The Crow: Stairway to Heaven: "A Gathering Storm"

Appendix B
INCARNATIONS

Just as many actors have interpreted the role of Hamlet over the years, so have many thespians taken their shot at portraying famous superheroes, villains and sidekicks. Included below is a list of different actors and actresses who took on a "super challenge" in live-action television and motion pictures.

Superman/Clark Kent (as an adult)
George Reeves (*The Adventures of Superman*)
David Wilson (*It's a Bird, It's a Plane, It's Superman!*)
Christopher Reeve (*Superman: The Movie, Superman II, Superman III, Superman IV: The Quest for Peace*)
Ron Ely (*Superboy*)
Dean Cain (*Lois and Clark: The New Adventures of Superman*)

Lois Lane
Phyllis Coates (*Superman vs. the Mole Men, The Adventures of Superman*)
Noel Neill (*The Adventures of Superman*)
Lesley Ann Warren (*It's a Bird! It's a Plane! It's Superman!*)
Margot Kidder (*Superman: The Movie, Superman II, Superman III, Superman IV: The Quest for Peace*)
Teri Hatcher (*Lois and Clark: The New Adventures of Superman*)

Perry White
John Hamilton (*The Adventures of Superman*)
Allen Ludden (*It's a Bird! It's a Plane! It's Superman!*)
Jackie Cooper (*Superman: The Movie, Superman II, Superman III, Superman IV: The Quest for Peace*)
Lane Smith (*Lois and Clark: The New Adventures of Superman*)
Michael McKean (*Smallville*)

Jimmy Olsen
Jack Larson (*The Adventures of Superman*)
Marc McClure (*Superman: The Movie, Superman II, Superman III, Supergirl, Superman IV: The Quest for Peace*)
Michael Landes (*Lois and Clark: The New Adventures of Superman*)
Justin Whalen (*Lois and Clark: The New Adventures of Superman*)

Lex Luthor
Gene Hackman (*Superman: The Movie, Superman II, Superman IV:
The Quest for Peace*)
Scott Wells (*The Adventures of Superboy*)
Sherman Howard (*The Adventures of Superboy*)
John Shea (*Lois and Clark: The New Adventures of Superman*)
Michael Rosenbaum (*Smallville*)

Superboy/Young Clark Kent
Jeff East (*Superman: The Movie*)
John Haymes Newton *(The Adventures of Superboy)*
Gerard Christopher (*The Adventures of Superboy*)
Tom Welling (*Smallville*)

Lana Lang
Annette O'Toole (*Superman III*)
Stacy Haiduk (*The Adventures of Superboy*)
Emily Procter (*Lois & Clark*)
Kristin Kreuk (*Smallville*)

Jonathan and Martha Kent
Stuart Whitman and Salome Jens (*The Adventures of Superboy*)
Eddie Jones and K. Callan (*Lois and Clark: The New Adventures of Superman*)
Jonathan Schneider and Annette O'Toole (*Smallville*)

Batman
Adam West (*Batman, Batman: The Movie, Legend of the Superheroes*)
Michael Keaton (*Batman, Batman Returns)*
Val Kilmer (*Batman Forever*)
George Clooney (*Batman and Robin*)
Christian Bale (future *Batman?*)

Catwoman
Julie Newmar (*Batman*)
Lee Meriwether (*Batman: The Movie*)
Eartha Kitt (*Batman*)
Michelle Pfeiffer (*Batman Returns*)

Riddler
Frank Gorshin (*Batman, Batman: The Movie, Legend of the Superheroes*)
John Astin (*Batman*)
Jim Carrey (*Batman Forever*)

Joker
Cesar Romero (*Batman, Batman: The Movie*)
Jack Nicholson (*Batman*)
Mark Hamill (*Birds of Prey*)

Penguin
Burgess Meredith (*Batman, Batman: The Movie*)
Danny DeVito (*Batman Returns*)

Mr. Freeze
George Sanders (*Batman*)
Otto Preminger (*Batman*)
Eli Wallach (*Batman*)
Arnold Schwarzenneger (*Batman and Robin*)

Batgirl
Yvonne Craig (*Batman*)
Alicia Silverstone (*Batman and Robin*)
Dina Meyer (*Birds of Prey*)

Commissioner Gordon
Neil Hamilton (*Batman, Batman: The Movie*)
Pat Hingle (*Batman, Batman Returns, Batman Forever, Batman and Robin*)

Alfred Penniworth
Alan Napier (*Batman, Batman: The Movie*)
Michael Gough (*Batman, Batman Returns, Batman Forever, Batman and Robin*)
Ian Abercrombie (*Birds of Prey*)
Michael Caine (future *Batman?*)

Robin
Burt Ward (*Batman, Batman the Movie, Legend of the Superheroes*)
Chris O'Donnell (*Batman Forever, Batman and Robin*)

Peter Parker/Spider-Man
Danny Segren (*The Electric Company: The Adventures of Spidey*)
Nicholas Hammond (*The Amazing Spider-Man*)
Tobey Maguire (*Spider-Man, The Amazing Spider-Man*)

Black Scorpion
Joan Severance (*Black Scorpion, Black Scorpion II: Aftershocks*)
Michelle Lintel (*Black Scorpion*)

Captain America
Reb Brown (*Captain America, Captain America II: Death Too Soon*)
Matt Salinger (*Captain America*)

The Crow
Brandon Lee (*The Crow*)
Vincent Perez (*Crow 2: City of Angels)*
Eric Mabius (*Crow: The Salvation*)
Mark Dacascos (*Crow: The Stairway to Heaven*)

Darkman
  Liam Neeson (*Darkman*)
  Arnold Vosloo (*Darkman II: Return of Durant, Darkman III: Die Darkman Die*)

RoboCop/Murphy
  Peter Weller (*RoboCop, RoboCop 2*)
  Robert Burke (*RoboCop 3*)
  Richard Eden (*RoboCop: The Series*)
  Page Fletcher (*RoboCop: Prime Directives*)

Daredevil
  Rex Smith (*Trial of the Incredible Hulk*)
  Ben Affleck (*Daredevil*)

Dr. Banner/The Incredible Hulk
  Bill Bixby (*The Incredible Hulk*)
  Eric Bana (*The Hulk*)

Appendix C

MEMORABLE SUPERHERO AD-LINES

The "tags" used to advertise superhero films are often very creative and catchy, successfully sticking in the memory. More often than not, ad-lines in this genre consist of brief, bold and heroic declarations, like the granddaddy of the list, from *Superman: The Movie:* "You'll Believe a Man Can Fly." Sometimes an ad-line is *too* brief, like *The Phantom*'s "Slam Evil!" leaving potential viewers unsure of what to make of the film.

Below is a brief chronological sampling of some superhero movie ad-lines that have decorated movie house posters over the decades. But keep in mind that the best advertising for a superhero film is not verbal at all. For instance, Tim Burton's *Batman* was heralded successfully by a poster featuring the famous bat crest on the Caped Crusader's costume. The famous Superman "S" emblem has adorned DVD covers and film posters for generations, providing instant recognition. Indeed, it is often the case that advertising lines are needed most for the less familiar superheroes (like *The Crow*, *Blade*, and *Spawn*).

"You'll Believe a Man Can Fly"—*Superman: The Movie* (1978)
"Soar to Hilarious Heights!"—*Condorman* (1981)
"The Future of Law Enforcement."—*RoboCop* (1987)
"They destroyed everything he had, everything he was. Now, crime has a new enemy, and justice has a new face."—*Darkman* (1990)
"From Zero to Hero!"—*The Mask* (1994)
"In a world without justice, one man was chosen to protect the innocent."—*The Crow* (1994).
"Who knows what Evil Lurks in the Hearts of Men?"—*The Shadow* (1994)
"Slam Evil!"—*The Phantom* (1996)
"Born in Darkness. Sworn to Justice."—*Spawn* (1997)
"Heroes Don't Come Any Bigger"—*Steel* (1997)
"Against an Army of immortals, one man must draw first blood."—*Blade* (1998)
"The power of an immortal. The soul of a human. The heart of a hero."—*Blade* (1998)
"For Vengeance. For Justice. For Love."—*The Crow: Salvation* (1999)
"Are you unbreakable?—*Unbreakable* (2000)
"Trust a Few; Fear the Rest."—*X-Men* (2000)
"Justice is blind."—*Daredevil* (2003)
"Don't Make Him Angry."—*The Incredible Hulk* (2003)

Appendix D

THE BEST, WORST AND MOST INFLUENTIAL PRODUCTIONS

Rating the best superhero films and television series from 1951 through 2003 is not an easy task. Actually, some superhero productions, while not of particularly high quality, are enormously influential in the genre, whether for box office clout (*X-Men*), stylistic conceits (the *Batman* television series) or audience fall-out (*Batman and Robin*). In some manner this influence should be taken into account when compiling a list such as this one, so in addition to offering this author's choices for the best and worst the superhero genre has to offer, lists for "most influential" productions have been included as well. No doubt some fans will want to quibble with the selections below — that's what fans do; but each of the ten best in the film and television categories took the notions, philosophies, look and theme of the superhero genre to new heights.

In film, *Superman: The Movie* proved that the sky is the limit when a director takes his subject matter seriously and marries that sincere approach to innovative special effects and an affecting central performance, in this case from Christopher Reeve. *Darkman* and *Spider-Man* bear that distinctive Sam Raimi charm: popping visualizations, knowing humor and knowledge of film history. *Unbreakable* imagines what a superhero might look and feel like in the real world, rather than in a blown-up comic book. *Batman Returns*, *Superman 2*, and *Blade 2* all prove that sequels need not be inferior retreads of past glories, but rather innovative and fresh second chapters.

In the worst adaptation category, who can forget that *Batman and Robin* and *Superman IV* scuttled their respective film franchises? *Captain America*, *RoboCop 3* and *Condorman* are merely inferior pictures, badly drawn, written and acted. In the "most influential category," it would be hard to deny that Burton's *Batman*, Raimi's *Spider-Man*, Singer's *X-Men* and Donner's *Superman: The Movie* all inaugurated booms in superhero film production. As for 1997's *Batman and Robin*, it single-handedly put the brakes on the "Dark Age" movement.

On television, Joss Whedon's *Buffy the Vampire Slayer* and Glenn Gordon Caron's *Now and Again* proved that superhero programs fly high when they focus on characterization rather than super-villains. Both shows were touching, tragic, and very human, highlighting the difficulties of growing up (*Buffy*) and marriage (*Now and Again*). *The Greatest American Hero* was a pioneer in the same arena, recognizing that humor and humanity had to be part of the heroic equation on television. Alas, the worst television series were not hard to pinpoint; there have been some real stinkers, and few viewers who have suffered through *Black Scorpion* or *Nightman* would care to repeat the experience.

Interestingly, the most influential superhero television series are not necessarily the best, nor the worst. The *Batman* program of the 1960s brought tongue-in-cheek, camp humor to the masses and influenced generations of producers and journalists, all of whom seem to believe that superheroes shouldn't be taken seriously; while *The Adventures of Superman*, an early superhero program, proved influential simply because it lasted so long and covered all the basic story ideas, from amnesia to the loss of super powers.

Among the better influential series, *The Incredible Hulk* demonstrated that shows about superheroes could work on television in as realistic a fashion as a kitchen sink–type drama. *Buffy* not only inspired its own spin-off, *Angel*, but a slew of adolescent superhero programs, including *Smallville* and *Birds of Prey*.

The Ten Best Superhero Movies
1. *Superman: The Movie* (1978) (dir: Richard Donner)
2. *Darkman* (1990) (dir: Sam Raimi)
3. *Spider-Man* (2002) (dir: Sam Raimi)
4. *Unbreakable* (2000) (dir: M. Night Shyamalan)
5. *RoboCop* (1987) (dir: Paul Verhoeven)
6. *Superman 2* (1981) (dir: Richard Lester)
7. *Batman Returns* (1992) (dir: Tim Burton)
8. *Blade 2* (2002) (dir: Guillermo Del Toro)
9. *Blade* (1998) (dir: Stephen Norrington)
10. *Batman* (1989) (dir: Tim Burton)

The Five Most Influential Superhero Movies
1. *Batman* (1989) (dir: Tim Burton)
2. *Spider-Man* (2002) (dir: Sam Raimi)
3. *X-Men* (2000) (dir: Bryan Singer)
4. *Superman: The Movie* (1978) (dir: Richard Donner)
5. *Batman and Robin* (1997) (dir: Joel Schumacher)

The Five Worst Superhero Movies
1. *Batman and Robin* (1997) (dir: Joel Schumacher)
2. *Captain America* (1989) (dir: Albert Pyun)
3. *Condorman* (1981) (dir: Charles Jarrott)
4. *Superman IV: The Quest for Peace* (1987) (dir: Sidney Furie)
5. *RoboCop 3* (1993) (dir: Fred Dekker); Runner up: *The Hullk* (2003) (dir: Ang Lee)

The Five Best Superhero Television Series
1. *Buffy the Vampire Slayer* (1997–2003)
2. *Now and Again* (1999–2000)
3. *The Greatest American Hero* (1981–1983)
4. *The Tick* (2001)
5. *The Incredible Hulk* (1977–1981)

The Five Most Influential Superhero Television Series
1. *Batman* (1966–68)
2. *The Adventures of Superman* (1952–1958)

3.   *Buffy the Vampire Slayer* (1997–2003)
4.   *The Incredible Hulk* (1981)
5.   *The Greatest American Hero* (1981–1983)

The Five Worst Superhero Television Series
1.   *Black Scorpion* (1999–2000)
2.   *Nightman* (1997–1999)
3.   *Birds of Prey* (2002–2003)
4.   *Manimal* (1983)
5.   *Mutant X* (2000–)

NOTES

Introduction

1. Kevin Smith. *TV Guide:* "A Superman for All Seasons." December 8, 2001, page 24.

2. Stephen Humphries. *The Christian Science Monitor:* "Stuck on Superheroes: *Spider-Man* Opens Today. Why Do Fantastic Heroes from Comic Books Remain So Popular?" May 3, 2002, page 13.

3. David Bloom. *Variety:* "Warner's Superheroes Suit Up for Toy Wars." July 15, 2002, volume 387, page 7.

4. Barbara Kollmeyer. *The Daily News/New York Knight Ridder/Tribune News:* "Comic Publishers, Studios Enjoy Popularity of Superheroes." August 26, 2002, page 1 of 3.

5. James Inverne. *Time International:* "Hero Worship: Armed with Colossal Budgets and Fancy Special Effects, Hollywood Is Bringing Old Comic Book Characters to the Big Screen. Get Ready for the Summer of the Superheroes." April 15, 2002, p. 60.

6. Andrew Arnold, Benjamin Nugen, Heather Won Tesoriero. *Time Magazine:* "Superhero Nation: The New Sensitive Incarnation of the Webbed Wonder Reminds Us How America Likes Its Superheroes: Human." May 20, 2002.

7. John Kenneth Muir. *An Askew View: The Films of Kevin Smith.* Applause Theatre and Cinema Books, 2002, page 142.

8. Philip Kerr. *New Statesman:* "Day of the Arachnid: Philip Kerr Watches a New Superhero Dangle Against an Old Skyline." June 3, 2001, page 45.

A History of Superheroes

1. James Poniewozik. *Time* magazine: "Superhero Nation." May 20, 2002, page 77.

2. Phil Hardy, Editor. *The Film Encyclopedia: Science Fiction.* William and Morrow Company, Inc., 1984, page 106.

3. R. Lee Sullivan. *Forbes:* "Batman in a Bustier." April 8, 1996, page 37.

4. Trina Robbins. *The Great Women Super Heroes.* Kitchen Sink Press, 1996, page 114.

5. Melanie McFarland. *Knight-Ridder/Tribune News Service:* "New Crop of Post-Modern Superheroes Toss the Spandex, Go for Grit." January 28, 2002, page K6604.

6. Tom Russo. *Entertainment Weekly:* "Monster Ink: New Deals, More Superheroes — Spider-Man Isn't the Only Comic-Book Creation Going to Hollywood." May 10, 2002, page 38.

The Amazing Spider-Man

1. Stephen Lynch. *Knight-Ridder/Tribune News Service:* "A New Spin on Superheroes — Spider-Man Changed Comics." April 29, 2002, pK1631.

2. Samantha Miller. *People Weekly:* "Web Master: Tobey Maguire, Hollywood's Go-To Sensitive Young Guy, Pumps Up His Pecs, Delts and Career with Spider-Man." May 20, 2002 v57, i19, page 67.

3. Galina Espinoz, Jason Lynch, Sophronia Scott. *People Weekly:* "How to Get Super Fit: Spider-Man Tobey Maguire Went from Soft to Solid in Six Months. Could You?" May 27, 2002, v57, i20, page 82.

Angel

1. Annabelle Villanueva and Cindy Pearlman. *Cinescape:* "Angel." September/October 1999, p. 53.

2. Ken Tucker. *Entertainment Weekly:* "Dynamic Duo: Though They Don't Wear Fancy Costumes, the Young Men of Smallville and Angel are Fitting Superheroes." November 2, 2001, page 58.

Automan

1. Michael Stein. *Fantastic Films*, Volume 7, #3: "Automan." May 1984, page 49.

Batman

1. Mike Benton. *The Illustrated History of Superhero Comics of the Golden Age.* Taylor Publishing Company, 1992, page 69.

2. Annabelle Villanueva. *Cinescape*, Volume 5, #8: "Picture This." November/December 1999, page 80.

3. John Skow. *The Saturday Evening Post:* "Has TV GASP! Gone Batty?" May 7, 1966, page 93.

4. Steve Swires. *Starlog* #75: "Lorenzo Semple, Jr. The Screenwriter Fans Love to Hate. Part Two." October 1983, page 46.

5. *Time Magazine.* January 28, 1966, page 61.

6. John Skow. *The Saturday Evening Post:* "Has TV GASP! Gone Batty?" May 1966, pages 95–96.

7. Troy Patterson. *Entertainment Weekly:* "Hero Worship: TV's Hippest Superheroes Signed Off 31 Years Ago." March 12, 1999, page 80.

8. Adam West. *Back to the Batcave.* Berkley Publishing Group, 1994, Pages 103–104.

9. Doug Nye. *Knight Ridder-Tribune News Service:* "Holy DVD! West Turns on the Bat Signal for '66 Batman." August 7, 2001, page K2602.

10. Mike Lacy. *Knight-Ridder/Tribune News Service:* "Batman Gets a New Life on TV Land." April 22, 2002, page K7197.

11. John Consoli, Marc Berman, Megan Larson, Jeremy Murphy. *Media Week:* "Sweeps Take Us Back to the Future: Holy Nielsens, Batman! Welcome to the Age of Comfort Food TV." December 3, 2001, page 4.

12. Robbie Fraser. *TV Guide:* Holy Déjà vu! TV's Favorite Dynamic Duo Reunite for One More Caped Crusade." March 8–14, 2003, page 5.

13. Howard T. Brody. *Starlog* #51: "Batman: The Movie Update." October 1981, page 21.

14. Marc Bernadin. *Entertainment Weekly:* "A Knight to Remember: After 15 Years Away, Comic Book Visionary Frank Miller Returns to His Grim Gotham City Roots for The Dark Knight Strikes Again, a Three-Part Sequel to the Graphic Novel That Changed the Face of Batman." December 7, 2001, page 46.

15. Richard Reynolds. *Superheroes: A Modern Mythology.* University of Mississippi Press, 1992, page 100.

16. Richard Reynolds. *Superheroes: A Modern Mythology.* University of Mississippi Press, 1992, page 100.

17. Bill Radford. *Knight-Ridder/Tribune News Service:* "Batman Fans Eager for Return of the Dark Knight." December 6, 2001, page K6144.

18. Alan Jones. *Cinefantastique*, Volume 22, #2: "Batman II." 1992, pages 12, 62.

19. Steve Daly. *Entertainment Weekly:* "Batlash." July 31, 1992, page 34.

20. Bronwen Hruska and Frank Spotnitz. *Entertainment Weekly:* "Batman 3." October 1, 1993, pages 6 and 7.

21. Dave Karger. *Entertainment Weekly:* "Big Chill." July 11, 1997, page 7.

22. Sharon Waxman. *The Washington Post:* "George Clooney, Uncowled." September 28, 1997, page G04.

The Bionic Woman

1. *Time Magazine.* April 26, 1976, page 85.

2. Mark Schwed. *TV Guide:* "Hollywood Grapevine." December 21–27, 2002, page 13.

Birds of Prey

1. R.D. Heldenfels. *Knight-Ridder/Tribune News Service:* "3 Birds of Prey Swoop Down on Crime with the Aid of Ex-Soap Star." July 24, 2002, page K2319.

2. Ken Tucker. *Entertainment Weekly:* "Let Us Prey." September 13, 2002, page 70.

3. Rick Porter. *Zap2it News:* "Angel on the Move for the WB." November 25, 2002, page 1 of 1. *http://www.tv.zap2it.com/news/*

4. A.J. Frutkin. *MEDIAWEEK:* "Birds Exec Questions WB; Producer Robbins Says Network Had "Buyers Remorse" from the Start." December 2, 2002, page 6.

Black Scorpion

1. *Business Wire:* "Beware the Scorpion's Sting! Sci-Fi Channel Acquires the Exclusive Rights to the *Black Scorpion* Series." July 11, 2000, page 1 of 3.

2. Len P. Feldman. *Personal Training:* "*Black Scorpion:* Catch the Bug." January 2001. Page 1 of 2.

3. Len. P. Feldman. *Personal Training:* "Black Scorpion: Catch the Bug." January 2001. Page 2 of 2. *http://physicalenchancemant.com/trainer/black_scorpion.htm*

4. Paula Bernstein. *Variety:* "*Scorpion* Entices Vet TV Thesps." July 17, 2000, page 1 of 1.

5. Bridget Freer. *FHM Magazine:* "The Girls of Sci-Fi." July/August 2001, page 199.

6. *Video Business:* "Black Scorpion Returns." August 20, 2001, page 11.

Buffy the Vampire Slayer

1. Barbara Lippert. *New York:* "Hey There, Warrior Girl." December 15, 1997, pages 24–25.

2. Anthony C. Ferrante. *Cinescape* #53. October, 2001, page 48.

Captain America

1. *Business Week:* "Another Battle for Captain America." May 8, 2000, page 14.

2. *Stan Lee Presents Captain America.* Pocket Books and Marvel Comics Groups, a Cadence International Company, 1979, page 1.

Condorman

1. Michael Smith. *Starlog* 44: "Condorman — or — 'It's a Birdman, It's a Comic Strip, It's a Movie!'" March 1981, pp. 40–41.

The Crow

1. *The Crow Fan Club:* "About James O'Barr." *www.crowfanclub.com/about.asp.*
2. Gregory Cerio. *People Weekly:* "Truly Ravenous: as The Crow Sequel Flies, so Does Vincent Perez." September 23, 1996, page 99.
3. Gregg Spring. *Electronic Media:* The Crow Will Soar Into Syndication in 1998. November 17, 1997, page 10.

Daredevil

1. Shawna Malcom. *TV Guide:* "The Daredevil Inside." February 8–14, 2003, page 18.

Dark Angel

1. James Poniewozik. *Time Magazine:* "2020 Vision." October 2, 2000.
2. Teresa Blythe. *Sojourners:* "*Dark Angel.*" March 2001, page 61.
3. *The Christian Science Monitor:* "*Dark Angel* Kicks Off Season with New Angle." September 28, 2001, page 16.
4. Honor Brodie. *In Style:* "Jessica Alba of *Dark Angel.*" September 1, 2001, page 458.
5. *Entertainment Weekly:* "The Terminatrix." March 16, 2001, page 26.
6. R.D. Heldenfels. *Tribune News Service:* "Producer Tells of New Plans for *Dark Angel.*" July 20, 2001, page 2 of 4.
7. Shawna Malcom. *TV Guide:* "Angel Hearts." October 20, 2001, page 22.
8. *TV Guide.* September 8, 2001, page 50.
9. *Publishers Weekly:* "Century Fox's Recently Cancelled *Dark Angel.*" August 26, 2002, page 26.

Darkman

1. Kyle Counts. *Starlog* #162, "Black Heart." January 1991, page 68.
2. Stanley Wiater. *Dark Visions: Conversations with Masters of the Horror Film.* Avon Books, 1993, page 139.

Dr. Strange

1. Richard Meyers. *Starlog* #17: "Doctor Strange Comes to Television. Master of the Mystic Media Arts." October 1978, page 65.

ElectraWoman and DynaGirl

1. Hal Erickson. *Sid and Marty Krofft: A Critical Study of Saturday Morning TV, 1966–1993.* McFarland and Company, Inc., Publishers, 1993, p. 179.
2. David Martindale. *Pufnstuff and Other Stuff: The Weird and Wonderful World of Sid and Marty Krofft.* Renaissance books, 1998, page 206.

The Fantastic Four

1. Ted Sennett. *The Art of Hanna-Barbera: Fifty Years of Creativity.* Viking Studio Books, 1989, page 263.
2. Steve Biodrowski. *Cinefantastique,* Volume 24, Number 3 of 4: "Made for a Fantastic $4 Million: Fantastic Four." October 1993, page 8.
3. Steve Daly. *Entertainment Weekly:* "The Fantastic Forsaken." September 30, 1994, page 14.

Generation X

1. *TV Guide.* Feb. 17–23, 1996, page 145.

The Greatest American Hero

1. *The Wall Street Journal:* "New ABC-TV Hero Faces Powerful Foes Before His Premiere." March 17, 1981, page 20.
2. *The Wall Street Journal:* "Greatest Hero Defeats Superman in Federal Court: Judge Declines to Block Debut of ABC's Comedy Series Despite Copyright Claim." March 19, 1981, page 41.
3. James H. Burns. *Starlog* #53: "Juanita Bartlett Part 1: The View from the Top." December 1981, Page 34.
4. Don McGregor. *Starlog* #55: "Robert Culp Part 2: Building a Career in the Hollywood Jungle." February 1982, page 64.
5. *Starlog* #52: "News Briefs." November 1981, page 16.
6. *Starlog* #109: "Media Log: Another Greatest American Hero?" August 1986, page 8.
7. John Dempsey. *Daily Variety:* "Cannell Back in Series Fold." June 20, 2002, page 3.
8. http://www.scifiwire, May 20, 2002.

The Green Hornet

1. *Newsweek:* "Hornet's Nest," July 18, 1966, page 96.

The Incredible Hulk

1. Milo George, Editor. *The Comics Journal Library, Volume 1: Jack Kirby.* Fantagraphic Books. May 2002, page 39.
2. Jon Abbott. *SFX* #18. November 1996, p. 76.
3. Richard Meyers. *Starlog* #12: "Superheroes on TV." March 1978, page 73.

Isis

1. Alan Morton. *The Complete Directory to Science Fiction, Fantasy and Horror Television Series: A Comprehensive Guide to the First 50 Years, 1946–1996*. Other World Press, 1997, page 684.

The Justice League of America

1. Ron Goulart. *The Comic Book Reader's Companion*. Harper Perennial, 1993, Page 96.
2. Eric J. Moreels. *Cinescape* #53, October 2001, page 57.
3. Rich Sands. *TV Guide:* "And Justice for All." November 17, 2001, page 36, (article pages 33–37).
4. Paul Karon. *Variety:* "Fewer Toons Hit Primetime Spot; Cartoon Network Plans Two New Superhero Animated Shows." August 6, 2001, page 35.

The League of Extraordinary Gentlemen

1. Tom Russo. *Entertainment Weekly:* "Gentleman's Club: The Literary Superheroes of *The League of Extraordinary Gentlemen* Return to the Comics — and Take on the Big Screen." July 26, 2002, page 16.

The Man from Atlantis

1. David Houston, *Starlog #9:* "Patrick Duffy: TV's Man from Atlantis." October 1977, page 28.
2. Edward Gross, *Starlog #131:* "Michael O'Herlihy, Storyteller of Tomorrow & Yesterday." June 1988, page 72.

M.A.N.T.I.S.

1. *Entertainment Weekly:* "New Shows." September 16, 1994, page 70.
2. *Jet:* "M.A.N.T.I.S. and Murder She Wrote Are Most Expensive Black, White Primetime Programs to Produce." December 19, 1994, page 60.
3. Steve Coe. *Broadcasting and Cable:* "Fox Shuffles Three Nights." February 13, 1995, page 19.

The Meteor Man

1. Rene Rodriguez. *Knight-Ridder/Tribune News Service:* "Meteor Man Robert Townsend Isn't a Shooting Star." August 10, 1993, page 0810K8074.
2. Lester Sloan. *American Visions:* "Robert Townsend: Role Model and Regular Guy." February-March 1993, page 46.
3. Christopher Vaughn. *Entertainment Weekly:* "Homemade Heroes." January 28, 1994, page 72.
4. *Jet:* "Robert Townsend's *The Meteor Man* Uses Cast of Stars to Battle Drugs, Violence and Gangs." August 9, 1993, page 58.

Misfits of Science

1. Marc Weinberg. *Starlog #101:* "Kevin Peter Hall: Tall Tale." December 1985, page 32.
2. Marc Shapiro. *Starlog #124:* "Maiden to Master & Misfits." November 1987, page 53.

Mutant X

1. Joe Schlosser. *Broadcasting & Cable:* "Mutant X." January 8, 2001, page 50.
2. Chris Pursell. *Electronic Media:* "Stars Turned into Mutants; Shea to Head Cast of Tribune Drama." June 4, 2001, page 3.
3. *TV Guide:* "The Insider: X-Factions." July 28 — August 3, 2001, page 3.
4. Daniel Frankel. *Media Week:* "*Mutant X's* Muted Launch." October 1, 2001, page 10
5. Janet Shprintz. *Daily Variety:* "Court Restores Fox Claim in *Mutant-X* Series Suit." January 16, 2002, page 7.

Mystery Men

1. Jeff Jenson. *Entertainment Weekly:* "Funny Men: Batman's Grounded and Superman's Nowhere. With a High Price and a Hip Cast, Can Mystery Men Save the Day?" August 6, 1999, page 18.

Nightman

1. Cynthia Littleton. *Broadcasting & Cable:* "Action Breaks Out of Formulas: New Offering Are Mix of Sci-Fi, Action, Adventure, Mystery and More." January 13, 1997, page 41.

Now and Again

1. Kristen Baldwin. *Entertainment Weekly:* "Now and Again: Close Encounters." November 26, 1999, page 2 of 3. *http://www.ew.com/ew/report/0,6115,271848-7/15091/0-00.html*
2. Craig Seymour. *Entertainment Weekly:* "Now and Again: Close Call." April 21, 2000, page 1 of 3. *http://www.ew.com/ew/report/0,6115,85146-3/15091/0-00.html.*

Plastic Man

1. Jeff Lenburg. *The Encyclopedia of Animated Cartoons*, Second Edition. Facts on File, Inc., 1999, pages 484–485.

RoboCop

1. C.V. Drake. *Cinefantastique*, Volume 17, #1: "RoboCop." January 1987, page 13.
2. Ed Niderost. *Starlog #122:* "War, Remembrance, and RoboCop." September 1987, page 36.

3. Bill Warren. *Starlog #128:* "I, RoboCop." March 1988, page 25.

4. Judy Gerstal. *Knight-Ridder/Tribune News Service:* "Costume Contains More Steel and a Different Actor, Besides." November 4, 1993, page 1104K6209.

5. Mike Freeman. *Broadcasting and Cable:* "RoboCop Formula: Humor, Humanity, Hormones." January 24, 1994, page 67.

6. Michael Freeman. *Media Week:* "With 29 of the 30 Nielsen..." March 28, 1994, page 16.

The Rocketeer

1. Marc Shapiro. *Starlog #166:* "The Rocketeer." May 1991, page 48–49.

2. Harry and Michael Medved. *The Golden Turkey Awards.* A Perigee Book, 1980, pages 75–76.

Silver Surfer

1. Susan Adamo. *Starlog #12:* "Log Entries: Silver Surfer to Silver Screen." February 1980, page 12.

The Six Million Dollar Man

1. Jonathan Etter. *Filmfax #88:* "*Forbidden Planet*'s Richard Anderson: How Gary Cooper Got Him Into the Movies." February/March 2002, page 62.

2. William Rabkin, *Starlog #111:* "Martin Caidin: Better Living Through Science Fiction." October 1986, page 65.

Spawn

1. Carolyn Giardina. *Shoot Magazine.* August 8, 1997, page 7.

2. *Jet:* "Cover Story: Buffed, Bold and Bad: Hollywood's Black Action Heroes." July 29, 2002, page 62.

Steel

1. Chuck Arnold. *People:* "Mr. Nice Guy." September 8, 1997, page 140.

Superboy

1. Deeny Kaplan. *Back Stage:* "Orlando Studio Wars: "Superboy" Flies from Disney MGM to Universal." July 14, 1989, page 1.

2. Eric J. Moreels. *Cinescape #53:* "Smallville." October 2001, page 45.

3. Chelsea J. Carter. *Iwon.news.com:* "Iwon News: "New Superman Story Takes Teen Twist." October 16, 2001.

4. *Variety.* October 22, 2001, page 8.

5. Hal Hinson. *The New York Times:* "Girls, Villains and X-ray Vision; in the Hit Show *Smallville,* the Teenage Clark Kent Experiences a Sort of Super Puberty in His Journey to Not Only Survive High School, but Become a True American Hero." March 25, 2002, page 18.

Supergirl

1. Mike Gold. *Fantastic Films #43:* "The Girl of Steel." January 1985, page 42.

2. Adam Pirani. *Starlog #90:* "Jeannot Szwarc — Filming the Fantasy of *Supergirl.*" January 1985, page 37.

Superman

1. Ennis Dooley and Gary Engle. *Superman at Fifty: The Persistence of a Legend.* Octavia Books, 1987, page 12.

2. Gary Gerani. *Fantastic Television.* Harmony Books, 1977, page 16.

3. Paul Mandell. *Starlog #76:* "TV's Superman Remembered, Part 2." November 1983, page 61.

4. "*Superman* Television Series to Be Honored by Los Angeles County." Tuesday, July 3, 2001. http://antonovich.co.la.ca.us/pressrel/070301-superman.htm. Page 1 of 2.

5. James Delson and Patricia Morrisroe. *Fantastic Films,* Volume 2, Number 2: "*Superman: The Movie.* An Exclusive *Fantastic Films* Interview with Director Richard Donner." June 1979, pages 11–12 (pages 8–17).

6. Richard Meyers. *Starlog #20:* "*Superman: The Movie.*" March 1979, page 46 (pages 40–46; 74).

7. Kent Dorfman. *Starlog #19:* "*Superman* Ready for Takeoff." February 1979, page 58 (pages 58–59).

8. Robert Greenberger. *Starlog #46:* "*Superman II:* The Adventure Continues." May 1981, page 32 (pages 31–33; 63).

9. Chris Nashawatay. *Entertainment Weekly:* "Crash Landing." October 18, 1996, page 8.

10. Eric Schumuckler. *MEDIAWEEK.* October 21, 1996, page 16.

Swamp Thing

1. *Time Magazine:* "Swamp Thing's Quagmire." June 10, 1989, page 47.

2. Dan Scapperotti. *Cinefantastique,* Volume 16, #4: "The Return of Swamp Thing." May 1989, page 16.

The Tick

1. Annabelle Villanueva. *Cinescape:* "Faces of the Future." March/April, 2001, page 22.

2. Annabelle Villanueva. *Cinescape:* "A Bug's Life." March/April 2001, page 74–75.

3. Mark Schwed. *TV Guide:* "Hollywood Grapevine." October 8, 2001, page 6.

4. Michael Tunison. *Cinescape:* "The Tick." October 2001, page 43.

Unbreakable

1. James M. Pethokoukis. *U.S. News and World Report:* "Breaking the Comic-Book Mold." December 18, 2000, page 69.

Witchblade

1. Paula Bernstein, *Variety:* "*Witchblade* Swings Without Stone." February 14, 2000, page 33.

2. Terri Roberts. *Ross Reports Television and Film:* "A New Blade Runner with an Old Twist: TNT's *Witchblade* Returns for a Second Season and Becomes TV's Latest Comic Book to Small Screen Success Story." July–August, 2002, page 3 of 5.

3. Steven English. *TV DATA:* "TNT Cuts Closer to Reality in Original Series *Witchblade.*" June 10–16, 2001, page 3.

4. *TV Guide:* "Blade Runner." July 21–27, 2001, page 9.

5. *Broadcasting and Cable:* "*Witchblade* Scores a 2.7 Rating." June 18, 2001, page 11.

6. *Multichannel News:* "TNT to Bring Back *Witchblade.*" August 27, 2001, page 2.

7. Bill Radford. *Knight-Ridder/Tribune News Service:* "*Witchblade* Series Gets a New Beginning." June 13, 2002, page K4558.

8. *Broadcasting and Cable:* "Turner Network Television Star Enters Rehabilitation Clinic." May 27, 2002, page 17.

Wonder Woman

1. Nick Gillespie. *Reason:* "William Marston's Secret Identity: The Strange Private Life of *Wonder Woman's* Creator." May 2001, page 52.

2. Richard A. Lupoff, Maggie Thompson, Editors. *The Comic-Book Book.* Krause Publications. 1998, page 231.

3. Ed Naha and Sam Maronie. *Starlog #9:* "Lynda Carter: TV's Only Amazon Princess Gets a New Life." October 1977, page 37.

BIBLIOGRAPHY

Books

Benton, Mike. *The Illustrated History of Superhero Comics of the Golden Age*. Taylor Publishing Company, 1992.

Brooks, Tim, and Earle Marsh. *The Complete Directory to Prime Time Network TV Shows, 1946–Present (Third Edition)*. Ballantine Books, 1985.

Brosnan, John. *Future Tense: The Cinema of Science Fiction*. St. Martin's Press, 1978.

Brown, Les. *The Encyclopedia of TV (Third Edition)*. Gale Research Inc., 1992.

Cotta Vaz, Mark. *Tales of the Dark Knight—Batman's First Fifty Years: 1939–1989*. Ballantine Books, 1989.

Dooley, Dennis, and Gary Engle. *Superman at 50: The Persistence of a Legend*. Octavia Books, 1987.

Erickson, Hal. *Sid and Marty Krofft: A Critical Study of Saturday Morning TV, 1966–1993*. McFarland, 1993.

George, Milo, editor. *The Comics Journal Library, Volume 1: Jack Kirby*. Fantagraphic Books, May 2002.

Gerani, Gary, and Paul Schulman. *Fantastic Television*. Harmony Books, 1977.

Gianakos, Larry James. *Television Drama Series Programming—A Comprehensive Chronicle 1975–1980*. The Scarecrow Press, 1991.

Goulart, Ron. *Comic Book Culture: An Illustrated History*. Collectors Press, 2000.

_____. *The Comic Book Reader's Companion*. Harper Perennial, 1993.

Hofstede, David. *Hollywood and the Comics*. Zenne-3, 1991.

Javna, John. *The Best of Science Fiction TV*. Harmony Books, 1987.

Kinnard, Roy. *The Comics Come Alive: A Guide to Comic-Strip Characters in Live-Action Productions*. The Scarecrow Press, 1991.

Kisseloff, Jeff. *The Box—An Oral History of Television, 1920–1961*. Viking Books, 1995.

Lenburg, Jeff. *The Encyclopedia of Animated Cartoons (Second Edition)*. Facts on File, Inc., 1999.

Lupoff, Richard A., and Maggie Thompson, Editors. *The Comic-Book Book*. Krause Publications, 1998.

Martindale, David. *Pufnstuff and Other Stuff: The Weird and Wonderful World of Sid and Marty Krofft*. Renaissance Books, 1998.

Medved, Harry, and Michael Medved. *The Golden Turkey Awards*. A Perigee Book, 1980.

Morton, Alan. *The Complete Directory to Science Fiction, Fantasy and Horror Television Series: A Comprehensive Guide to the First 50 Years, 1946–1996*. Other World Press, 1997.

Muir, John Kenneth. *An Askew View: The Films of Kevin Smith*. Applause Theatre and Cinema Books, 2002.

_____. *Terror Television*. McFarland, 2001.

_____. *Wes Craven: The Art of Horror*. McFarland, 1998.

Robbins, Trina. *The Great Women Superheroes*. Kitchen Sink Press, 1996.

Rovin, Jeff. *The Encyclopedia of Super Villains*. Facts on File Publications, 1987.

_____. *A Pictorial History of Science Fiction Films*. Citadel Press, 1975.

Sennett, Ted. *The Art of Hanna-Barbera: Fifty Years of Creativity*. Viking Studios Books, 1989.

Stanley, John. *Creature Features Movie Guide Strikes Again*. Creatures at Large Press, 1994.

Terrace, Vincent. *Fifty Years of Television: A Guide to Series and Pilots, 1937–1988*. Cornwall, 1991.

West, Adam. *Back to the Batcave*. Berkley Books, 1994.

Articles

The Advocate: "The Original Amazon (Cartoonist Phil Jimenez and Publishing Wonder Woman Comic Books)." November 21, 2000, page 24.

Arnold, Andrew and Ed Gabel. *Time*: "Holy Multi-Media! Six, Count 'em, Six Superheroes Make the Leap from Comic-Book Pages to the Big Screen." May 20, 2002, pages 76+.

Baldwin, Kristen. *Entertainment Weekly:* "Close Encounters." November 26, 1999, pages 1 to 3. *http://www.ew.com/ew/report0,6115,271848-7/15091//0-00.html*

Bloom, David. *Variety:* "Warners Superheroes Suit Up for Toy Wars (Caped Commerce)." July 15, 2002, page 7.

Blythe, Teresa. *Sojourners:* "Dark Angel." March 2001, page 61.

Brodie, Honor. *In Style:* "Jessica Alba of *Dark Angel.*" September 1, 2001, page 459.

Brown, Scott. *Entertainment Weekly:* "Inside-Man: Meet Avi Arad, the Marvel Studios Exec Overseeing the Big-Screen Invasion of Spidey and Other Superheroes." July 12, 2002, pages 28+.

Burns, James H. *Starlog #53:* "Juanita Bartlett Part 1: The View from the Top." December 1981, pages 33–34.

Business Week: "Another Battle for Captain America." May 8, 2000, page 14.

Butler, Robert W.. *Knight-Ridder/Tribune News Service:* "Mystery Men." August 3, 1999, page K6509.

Cerio, Gregory. *People Weekly:* "Truly raven-ous; as *The Crow* Sequel Flies, So Does Vincent Perez." September 2, 1996, pages 99–100.

Cheshire, Godfrey. *Variety:* "Mystery Men." August 2, 1999, page 32.

Coe, Steven. *Broadcasting and Cable:* "Fox Shuffles Three Nights; *Get Smart, M.A.N.T.I.S., Model's Inc* and *House of Buggin'* are Bugging Out to Make Room for New Shows." February 13, 1995, page 19.

Consoli, John, Marc Berman, Megan Larson and Jeremy Murphy. *MEDIAWEEK:* "Sweeps Take Us Back to the Future: Holy Nielsens, Batman! Welcome to the Age of 'Comfort Food' TV." December 3, 2001, pages 4–5.

Cook, Stephanie. *The Christian Science Monitor:* "*The Greatest American Hero.*" August 26, 1999, page 23.

Corliss, Richard. *Time:* "The Hero in the Mirror: In the Hip, Funny *Mystery Men*, Saving the World Is Less Important Than Finding Yourself." August 9, 1999, page 66.

Counts, Kyle. *Starlog:* "Black Heart." January 1991, pages 66–68.

Daly, Steve. *Entertainment Weekly:* "The Fantastic Forsaken." September 30, 1994, pages 14–15.

Demenchuk, Michael. *Multichannel News:* "*Witchblade* More Sorcery Than Substance." June 11, 2001, page 128.

Dempsey, John. *Daily Variety:* "Cannell Back in Series Fold." June 20, 2001, pages 3–5.

Dougherty, Margot. *People Weekly:* "Green with Indignation, Lou Ferrigno Is Back in Bulk as the Incredible Hulk." May 16, 1988, pages 63–65.

Drake, C.V. *Cinefantastique,* Volume 17, #1: "RoboCop." January 1987, pages 13; 53.

Elder, Robert K.. *Knight-Ridder/Tribune News Service:* "Superheroes Go Hollywood as Marvel Stages a Comeback." July 14, 2000, page K2174.

Frankel, Daniel. *MEDIAWEEK:* "*Mutant X's* Muted Launch." October 1, 2001, page 10.

Freeman, Michael. *MEDIAWEEK:* "With 29 of 30 Nielson … (RoboCop: The Series Posts Strong Ratings Share). March 28, 1994, page 16.

Freeman, Mike. *Broadcasting and Cable:* "*RoboCop* Formula: Humor, Humanity, Hormones." January 24, 1994, pages 67–68.

Fries, Laura. *Daily Variety:* "Birds of Prey." October 8, 2002, page 7.

Frisch, Gary. *Video Business:* "No Mystery Here." January 17, 2000, page 16.

Gerstal, Judy. *Knight-Ridder/Tribune News Service:* "Costume Contains More Steel and a Different Actor, Besides." November 4, 1993, p. 1104K6209.

Gillespie, Nick. *Reason:* "William Marston's Secret Identity: The Strange Private Life of Wonder Woman's Creator." May 2001, pages 52–53.

Gleiberman, Owen. *Entertainment Weekly:* "Un 'X'-ceptional: The Sci-Fi Fantasy *X-Men* Has Dazzling Effects That Overpower the Movie's Team of Mutant Superheroes." July 21, 2001, page 50+.

Gold, Mike. *Fantastic Films #43:* "The Girl of Steel." January 1985, pages 40–42.

Goodale, Gloria. *The Christian Science Monitor:* "*Dark Angel* Kicks Off Season with New Angle." September 28, 2001, page 16.

Gray, Ellen. *Knight Ridder/Tribune News Service:* "WB's Estrogen Level Gets a Boost with *Birds of Prey.*" October 8, 2002, page K0233.

Gross, Edward. *Starlog #131:* "Michael O'Herlihy, Storyteller of Tomorrow & Yesterday." June 1988, pages 62, 63, 72.

Guider, Elizabeth. *Variety:* "*RoboCop* to Patrol Air Again." November 15, 1999, page 35.

Heldenfels, R.D. *Knight-Ridder/Tribune News Service:* "Producer Tells of New Plans for *Dark Angel.*" July 20, 2001, page K3712.

_____. *Knight-Ridder/Tribune News Service:* "3 *Birds of Prey* Swoop Down on Crime, with the Aid of Ex-Soap Star." July 24, 2002, page K2319.

Hensley, Dennis. *The Advocate:* Original Valarie: Valarie Rae Miller, Who Plays Saucy Lesbian Ass-Kicker Original Cindy on *Dark Angel*, Talks Up Her Film *All About the Benjamins* and explains '*the Glitter Moment.*" March 19, 2002, pages 50–52.

Hiltbrand, David. *TV Guide:* "Star of the Show: From Superman to Seven Dwarfs, Kreuk's Got the Classics Covered." March 16–22, 2002, page 10.

Hinson, Hal. *New York Times Upfront:* "Girls, Villains and X-Ray Vision: In the Hit Show *Smallville*, the Teenage Clark Kent Experiences a Sort of Super Puberty in His Journey Not Only to Survive High School, but Become a True American Hero." March 25, 2002, pages 18–19.

Houston, David. *Starlog #9:* "Patrick Duffy: TV's Man from Atlantis." October 1977, pages 24–28.

Hulse, Ed. *Video Business:* "*Black Scorpion* Returns." August 20, 2001, page 11.

Inverne, James. *Time International:* "Hero Worship: Armed with Colossal Budgets and Fancy Special Effects, Hollywood Is Bringing Old Comic Book Characters to the Big Screen. Get Ready for the Summer of the Superheroes." April 15, 2002, page 60.

Jarvis, Jeff. *People Weekly:* "*Once a Hero.*" October 19, 1987, page 15.

Jensen, Jeff. *Entertainment Weekly:* "Shows of Strength: Giving the Superman Saga a Well-Needed Kick in the Tights, *Smallville* Leads the Way as Five Formula Busting New Series Come to the Rescue of the Fall TV season." November 23, 2001, pages 26+.

Jet: "Buffed Bold & Bad: Hollywood's Black Action Heroes." July 29, 2002, pages 58–62.

Jet: "*M.A.N.T.I.S.* and *Murder She Wrote* Are Most Expensive Black and White Prime-Time Programs to Produce." December 19, 1994, pages 60–62.

Jet: "Robert Townsend's *The Meteor Man* Uses Cast of Stars to Battle Drugs, Violence and Gangs." August 9, 1993, pages 58–62.

Jet: "Robin Givens: Uses Beauty and Brains in *Blankman* Comedy to Create Superhero." August 15, 1994, pages 58–62.

Karon, Paul. *Variety:* "Fewer Toons Hit Primetime Sot (Cartoon Network Plans Two New Superhero Animated Shows)." August 6, 2001, page 35.

Kenny, Glenn. *Entertainment Weekly:* "*The Meteor Man.*" February 4, 1994, page 58.

Kollmeyer, Barbara. *Knight-Ridder/Tribune Business News:* "Comic Publishers, Studios Enjoy Popularity of Superheroes." August 26, 2002, page ITEM0-2238025.

Lacy, Mike. *Knight-Ridder/Tribune News Service:* "*Batman* Gets New Life on TV Land." April 22, 2002, page K7197.

Logan, Michael. *TV Guide:* "X-Factions." July 28–August 3, 2001, page 3.

Lovece, Frank. *Entertainment Weekly:* "*Captain America.*" July 31, 1992, page 74.

Lynch, Stephen. *Knight-Ridder/Tribune News Service:* "A New Spin on Superheroes; Spider-Man Changed Comic Books." April 29, 2002, p. K1631.

Mabe, Chancey. *Knight-Ridder/Tribune News Service:* "*Witchblade* Forges Its Heavy Metal Heroine Anew." June 13, 2002, page K4684.

Malcom, Shawna. *TV Guide:* "The Daredevil Inside." February 8–14, 2003, pages 14–20.

_____. *TV Guide:* "Is *Dark Angel* Heaven-Bound?" March 16–22, 2002, page 10.

Martinez, Jose A. *TV Guide:* "About to Launch: A Preview of TV's Hottest Upcoming Sci-Fi Programming." July 5, 1997, page 33.

McGregor, Don. *Starlog #55:* "Robert Culp Part 2: Building a Career in the Hollywood Jungle." February 1982, pages 45–48; 64.

Meyers, Richard. *Starlog #12:* "Superheroes on TV." March 1978, pages 72–75.

_____. *Starlog #17:* "Doctor Strange Comes to Television. Master of the Mystic Media Arts." October 1978, pages 64 – 65.

Naha, Ed, and Sam Maronie. *Starlog #9:* "Lynda Carter: TV's Only Amazon Princess Gets a New Life." October 1977, pages 35–38.

Nesselson, Lisa. *Variety:* "*The Crow: Salvation.*" June 26, 2000, page 22.

Niderost, Ed. *Starlog #122:* "War, Remembrance, and RoboCop." September 1987, pages 36–39.

Nollinger, Mark. *TV Guide:* "Make Room for Mutants." February 17, 1996, pages 36–39.

Nye, Doug. *Knight-Ridder/Tribune News Service:* "Holy DVD! West Turns on the Bat Signal for '66 *Batman* Movie." August 7, 2001, page K2602.

Pearlman, Cindy. *Entertainment Weekly:* "Holy Casting! (Actors Michael Keaton and Christopher Reeve Both Say Their Days of Playing Superheroes Are Behind Them." January 13, 1995, page 10.

Pirani, Adam. *Starlog #90:* "Jeannot Szwarc — Filming the Fantasy of *Supergirl.*" January 1985, pages 37–41.

Poniewozik, James. *Time:* "*Birds of Prey.*" October 14, 2002, page 86.

_____. *Time:* "Super Human Strength: In an Unconventional Kind of Wartime, Will Audiences Warm to Unconventional Superheroes?" October 22, 2001, page 77.

_____. *Time:* "Superhero Nation: The New, Sensitive Incarnation of the Webbed Wonder Reminds Us How America Likes Its Superheroes: Human." May 20, 2002, pages 77+.

Prideaux, Tom. *Life:* "The Whole Country Goes Supermad." March 11, 1966, page 22.

Publishers Weekly: "Century Fox's Recently Canceled *Dark Angel.*" August 26, 2002, page 26.

Radford, Bill. *Knight-Ridder/Tribune News Service:* "Marvel Introducing Second Generation of Superheroes." July 30, 1998, page 730K5433.

_____. *Knight-Ridder/Tribune News Service:* "*Witchblade* Series Gets a New Beginning." June 13, 2002, page K4558.

Rafferty, Brian M. *Entertainment Weekly:* "Dynamic Duel: Holy Franchise! Can *Batman vs.*

Superman leap tall box office hurdles in a single bound?" July 26, 2002, page 6.

Roberts, Terri. *Ross Reports Television & Film:* "A New Blade Runner–with an Old Twist: TNT's *Witchblade* Returns for a Second Season and Becomes TV's Latest Comic Book to Small Screen Success Story." July–August 2002, pages 5–10.

Russo, Tom. *Entertainment Weekly:* "Monster Ink: New Deals, More Superheroes, Spider-Man Isn't the Only Comic-Book Creations Going Hollywood." May 10, 2002, page 38.

Sands, Rich. *TV Guide:* "And Justice for All." November 17, 2001, pages 34–37.

Schlosser, Joe. *Broadcasting and Cable:* "Mutant X." January 8, 2001, page 50.

Schwarzbaum, Lisa. *Entertainment Weekly:* "Heroes, Extra Cheese: Absurd Crime Fighters Swoop in from the Sidelines in *Mystery Men,* a Superhero Satire That Doesn't Try to Mask Its Silliness." August 6, 1999, page 39.

Seymour, Craig. *Entertainment Weekly:* "Close Call." April 21, 2000, pages 1–3.

Shapiro, Marc. *Starlog #166:* "The Rocketeer," May 1991, pages 47–51; 75.

Sherman, Joseph. *The Writer:* "Creating Superheroes in Science Fiction and Fantasy." July 1995, pages 13–16.

Shprintz, Janet. *Daily Variety:* "Court Restores Fox Claim in *Mutant X* Series Suit." January 16, 2002, pages 7–8.

Sloan, Lester. *American Visions:* "Robert Townsend: Role Model and Regular Guy." February–March, 1993, pages 46–48.

Smith, Kevin. *TV Guide:* "A Superman for All Seasons." December 8, 2001, page 24.

Smith, Paul. *Computer Weekly:* "*Mystery Men* DVD." June 29, 2000, page 65.

Spelling, Ian. *The Houston Chronicle:* "For *Now and Again* TV Series Is Close Call." May 12, 2000, pages 1 to 3. *www.sundance.hisspeed.com/naa/magazines/online/houston.html.*

Spring, Greg. *Electronic Media:* "*The Crow* Will Soar Into Syndication in 1998." November 17, 1997, pages 10–11.

Stein, Michael. *Fantastic Films Volume 7, #3:* "Automan." May 1984, pages 48–49.

Stewart, Michael. *Entertainment Weekly:* "Zeroes to Heroes: The Motley Crew of *Mystery Men* May Save the Day but Other Comical Caped Crusaders Don't Fly as High." January 14, 2000, page 80.

Sullivan, R. Lee. *Forbes:* "Batman in a Bustier." April 8, 1996, page 37.

Tucker, Ken. *Entertainment Weekly:* "Dynamic Duo: Though They Don't Wear Fancy Costumes, the Young Men of *Smallville* and *Angel* are Fitting Superheroes." November 2, 2001, p. 58+.

_____. *Entertainment Weekly:* "*Wonder Women:* The Dynamic Dames of Both *Alias* and *Birds of Prey* Deliver the Action, but Only One Packs an Emotional Punch." October 25, 2002, page 62+.

Vaughn, Christopher. *Entertainment Weekly:* "Homemade Heroes." January 28, 1994, page 72.

Vincent, Mal. *Knight-Ridder/Tribune News Service:* "Paul Reubens Vents His Spleen in *Mystery Men.*" August 3, 1999, page K6544.

The Wall Street Journal: "Greatest Hero Defeats Superman in Federal Court." March 19, 1981, page 41.

The Wall Street Journal: "New ABC-TV Hero Faces Powerful Foes Before His Premiere." March 17, 1981, page 20.

Warren, Bill. *Starlog #128:* "I, RoboCop." March 1988, pages 23–26 ; 64.

Washburn, Mark. *Knight-Ridder/Tribune News Service:* "*Birds of Prey* Premiering Wednesday on WB." October 8, 2002, page K0093.

Weinberg, Marc. *Starlog #101:* "Kevin Peter Hall: Tall Tale." December 1985, pages 32–33.

Whalen, John M. *The Washington Post:* "*Green Hornet* Generating a New Buzz; DVD Film Provides a Platform for the Short-Lived TV Series and Its Stars." January 21, 2001, page G8.

Internet

"All About the *Wonder Woman* TV Show"

The Big Cartoon Database

"*Black Scorpion* Episode Guide"

Dark Angel TV.com

The Episode Archive: The Man from Atlantis

Len P. Feldman. Personal Training: "*Black Scorpion:* Catch the Bug."

Garn's Episode Guides for Sci-Fi, Fantasy and Animation

Steven Lance. *TV Then:* "Faster Than a Speeding Bullet." April 1998.

Andy Mangels. *Mania Magazine's Andy Mangel's Hollywood Heroes:* "New *Nightman* Episodes." January 22, 1999, page 1 of 2.

Howard Margolin. *Destinies: The Voice of Science Fiction:* "Climbing the Walls for Different Reasons: An Interview with Burt Ward." November 25, 1989, pages 1–6.

Misfits of Science Episode Guide

John Kenneth Muir. *Deep Outside Science Fiction, Fantasy and Horror:* "You'll Still Believe a Man Can Fly: The *Superman* Film Collection Lands on DVD at last."

Nightman: the Official Site

"*Nightman*'s Creator, Steve Englehart"

Now and Again Episode Guide

Sci Fi Wire: A News Service of the Sci Fi Channel: "Disney Preps *Greatest American Hero.*" May 20, 2002.

Sci Fi Wire: A News Service of the Sci Fi Channel: "Hulk to Start Shooting." March 10, 2002.

Sci Fi Wire: A News Service of the Sci Fi Channel: "Snipes Prowls on Black Panther." March 12, 2002.

"Superman Television Series to Be Honored by Los Angeles County." Tuesday, July 3, 2001.

Swamp Thing: An Episode Guide

TV Land Shows: The Adventures of Superman

INDEX

Numbers in *italics* refer to photographs.